Modern Women
Playwrights of Europe

Modern Women Playwrights of Europe

Edited by

Alan P. Barr

New York   Oxford

OXFORD UNIVERSITY PRESS

2001

Oxford University Press

Oxford   New York
Athens   Auckland   Bangkok   Bogotá   Buenos Aires   Calcutta
Cape Town   Chennai   Dar es Salaam   Delhi   Florence   Hong Kong   Istanbul
Karachi   Kuala Lumpur   Madrid   Melbourne   Mexico City   Mumbai
Nairobi   Paris   São Paulo   Shanghai   Singapore   Taipei   Tokyo   Toronto   Warsaw

and associated companies in
Berlin   Ibadan

Published by Oxford University Press, Inc.,
198 Madison Avenue, New York, New York 10016
http://www.oup-usa.org

Oxford is a registered trademark of Oxford University Press

Library of Congress Cataloging-in-Publication Data

Modern women playwrights of Europe / edited by Alan P. Barr.
    p. cm.
  ISBN 0-19-513536-9 (alk. paper)
    1. European drama—Women authors. 2. European drama—20th century. I. Barr, Alan P.
1938–
PN6119.8 .M65 2000
808.82'0082'094—dc21   99-086027

Printing (last digit):   9   8   7   6   5   4   3   2   1

Printed in the United States of America
on acid-free paper

For Eli, Leah, and Zinta
the next generation of theater enthusiasts

CONTENTS

ACKNOWLEDGMENTS

Appreciations and acknowledgments always risk inviting the perfunctory and rhetorical. Such, I sincerely hope, will not be the suspicion here.

Second only to the delight in exploring and reading a world of wonderful literature, has been the joy of working with so many generous and forthcoming scholars and artists. For me, this evolved into a singular, richly collaborative enterprise.

The genuine give and take and profound helpfulness that I encountered from the onset was an unanticipated and magnificent revelation. After I had read what I could about the drama of each country and its women dramatists, I sought out scholars in the field, explaining my project and asking, as specifically as I could, for guidance, responses, and suggestions. For obvious linguistic and geographical reasons, I was inevitably dependent upon them—for plays that I had never heard of, for informed judgments, for the location of unpublished translations, for the whereabouts of authors and translators. Almost universally, people—women, men, established, new to the profession, American, European—were overwhelmingly free with their help. I remember very early phone calls with Halina Filipowicz and Patricia O'Connor. Both were then and have continued to be unstinting in their encouragement and assistance. Pirkko Koski, of the University of Helsinki, has been far more patient than I deserved with her suggestive corrections. Hanne Wilhelm Hansen, of Nordiska Strakosch Teaterførlaget, personifies what I have learned to recognize as the Scandinavian spirit of inquiry: how many more plays and brochures may I please send you? Anneli Kurki, of the Finnish Theatre Information Center, echoed this spirit. Katrin Sieg, Phyllis Zatlin, and Judy Miller, in correspondence and phone conversations, offered ideas and information with similar generosity.

Many of the playwrights themselves proved to be extraordinarily accessible, responsive, and helpful. It was a particular delight to interact with Gerlind Reinshagen, Elfriede Jelinek, Daniela Fischerová, and Hrafnhildur Hagalín Gudmundsdóttir.

To the scholars who were kind enough to critique and correct my introductions, I owe whatever balance, accuracy, and caution they have: to people like Michael Heim, David Willinger, Verne Moberg, Katrin Sieg, Neil Bermel, Janet Garton, Rory McTurk, Rhoda Kaufman, Susanne Lindskog, Mary Russell, and Wendy Wall.

From my first contact, I have been superbly fortunate in having Tony English as my editor at Oxford. He could not have been quicker in his responses, more straightforward, open, and reasonable: a pleasure to work with. I am also thankful to John Bauco for the courteous and efficient manner in which he has guided the manuscript through publication. My debt to Rose Kirk for her meticulous proofing is best characterized by awe.

I am grateful to Indiana University Northwest, not only for the sabbatical that propelled this collection forward, but for its clear, loud, and affectionate support.

Closer to the hearth, I am immeasurably indebted to my son Josh for keeping me online (e-mail and the Internet as a life support is more than a metaphor) and to my son Dan for showing me that he could maintain the plaster and paint every bit as well as I. To Daina I owe the impeccable, instantaneous translations of occasionally turgid German business correspondence and to Mara an expert reading of the introductions en masse.

Most of all, to Dace I can only hint at my gratitude for her readings, corrections, and on-going, enthusiastic support. If every drama shelf does not teem with *Modern Women Play-wrights of Europe*, it will not be for lack of her trumpetings.

TRANSLATORS

Barbara Bray was born in London, England, and graduated with honors in English from Cambridge University. After lecturing in Egypt, she became BBC radio drama script editor. Since the 1960s, she has lived and worked in Paris as a freelance writer, critic, and translator. She is well known for her translations of works by Marguerite Duras, including the award-winning translation of *The Lover*. Ms. Bray has collaborated with Harold Pinter and Joseph Losey on the film adaption of Proust's *A la recherche du temps perdu*. She is the president and *metteur en scène* of "Dear Conjunction," a bilingual professional theater company based in Paris.

Frank Caucci is Chair of the Department of Modern Languages at Indiana University Northwest. With a D. E. A. in modern French literature and a Ph.D. in comparative literature from the Sorbonne, he has worked extensively in Francophone literature and Canadian studies. He has divided his scholarly efforts between criticism and translation. His books include: *Les voix d'eros; la poésie amoureuse de Paul Eluard et de Pablo Neruda* and translations of the poetry of Pier Giorgio Di Cicco (*Les amours difficiles*) and Mary Di Michele (*Pain et chocolat*). Many of his recent articles have been about Canadian, particularly Quebecoise, literature.

Stratos Constantinidis is an associate professor in the Theater Department at Ohio State University. He is a specialist in performance theory and criticism and in modern Greek drama. He has written *Theatre Under Deconstruction* and numerous articles for such journals as *Comparative Drama, Journal of Modern Greek Studies, Code/Codikas, Ars Semiotica, New Theatre Quarterly, Journal of Dramatic Theory and Criticism, Poetics Today,* and *World Literature Today*. He has edited *Classical Drama in Modern Performance* and special issues of the *Journal of Modern Greek Studies* on modern Greek drama and on Greek film. He has translated into both English and Greek, and is currently working on a new translation of Aeschylus's *Prometheus Bound*.

Victor Contoski received his Ph.D. in American Literature. He is professor of English at the University of Kansas. He has published short fiction and several collections of his own poetry, as well as translations of such contemporary Polish poets as Rosewicz, Grochowiak, Harasymowicz, and Sliwonik. His most recent volume of poems is *Homecoming* (New Rivers, 2000).

Wieslawa Contoski, who died in 1998, had degrees in ancient and Middle-Eastern languages and in international law from Jagellonian University in Cracow. She received many awards for her photography and her collages. A book of her collages will be published shortly by Western Hills.

Véronique Firkušný-Callegari grew up trilingual, in Czech, English, and French. A graduate of Barnard College, she has worked on a number of translations from Czech. She lives in New York City with her husband and two children.

Brian FitzGibbon is an Irish playwright and screenwriter based in Iceland. His most recent play, *The Papar,* was produced by the Abbey Theatre at the Peacock in Dublin, in July 1997, and subsequently adapted into a short film called *Stranded.* He is currently writing a screenplay for Icelandic film director Fridrik Thor Fridriksson.

Janet Garton received her Ph.D. from Cambridge in modern and medieval languages. She is a reader in Scandinavian Studies at the University of East Anglia, Norwich. She has written several books on Scandinavian literature, including *Jens Bjørneboe: Prophet Without Honor* (1985) and *Norwegian Women's Writing: 1850–1990* (1993), and translated, among others, the work of Paal-Helge Haugen, Bjørg Vik, Cecilie Løveid, and Knut Faldbakken. She is president of the International Association of Scandinavian Studies, editor of the journal *Scandinavaca,* and a director of Norvik Press.

Robert T. Jones is a music critic and editor who has written for many publications, including *Time, The New York Times, Opera News, Time & Life Books, Reader's Digest,* and the *Buenos Aires Herald.* As editor, he has worked with Philip Glass (*Opera on the Beach,* Faber and Faber, 1988), and has a special interest in Czech music and literature. His English edition of Rudolf Tesnohlidek's novel *The Cunning Little Vixen,* made from translations by Maritza Morgan and Tatiana Firkušný and with pictures by Maurice Sendak, was published by Farrar Straus in 1985. With Tatiana Firkušný, he has also completed a new English translation of Capek's *From the Life of the Insects.* He lives in South Carolina and writes an arts column for the *Charleston Post and Courier.*

Herbert Lomas has received Guinness, Arvon, and Cholmondely awards for his poetry. His most recent books have been *Selected Poems* (Sinclair-Stevenson, 1995) and *A Useless Passion* (London Magazine Editions, 1999). His *Contemporary Finnish Poetry* (Bloodaxe, 1991) won the English Poetry Society's biennial translation award; it has reached the status of a classic and made him a Knight First class, Order of the White Rose of Finland. He has available a one-hour radio adaptation of *Burnt Orange.* Mr. Lomas lives in Suffolk, England.

Malene S. Madsen, though Danish by birth, has lived most of her life in the United Kingdom. After gaining a first-class B.A. honors degree at the University of East Anglia in Norwich, she worked as a translation manager before becoming a full-time freelance translator. Although she specializes in commercial translations, she has done some literary work, including this translation of Saalbach's *Morning and Evening.*

Tinch Minter has been a prolific translator of German (and other) drama, concentrating recently on such new women playwrights as Elfriede Jelinek, Gundi Ellert, Kerstin Specht, Elfriede Müller, Edi Shukriu, and Lina Wertmüller. In 1988 she began a fruitful collaboration translating for Annie Castledine, who directed *Sunday's Children* at Derby. In 1990 her work on Marieluise Fleisser's Ingolstadt plays won her the first Empty Space Award. She wrote *Fairplay* and is currently working on an original play about Brecht and Fleisser. In 1997, she produced the film *No Chair for Donna* and cowrote and directed *Off the Buses* at Cambridge Drama Center. She lives in Cambridge and gives workshops at various universities.

Tony Mitchell is a senior lecturer in Writing, Performance, and Cultural Studies at the University of Technology, Sydney. He is the author of *Dario Fo: People's Court Jester, File on Dario Fo, High Art in a Foreign Tongue: Adelaide Ristori's 1875 Australian Tour,* and *Popular Music and Local Identity: Rock, Pop and Rap in Europe and Oceania.* His translations of plays by Dario Fo and Dacia Maraini have been performed in Australia, New Zealand, Papua New Guinea, and South Africa.

Verne Moberg is a Swedish American translator and teacher of Scandinavian literature who lives in New York City. Her translation of Kristina Lugn's play *Aunt Blossom* was awarded the Inger Sjöberg Prize by the American-Scandinavian Foundation in 1997. She was the coproducer of the Nordic Theater Festival at Barnard College in 1995, which featured Lugn's *Aunt Blossom* and *The Old Girls at Lake Garda,* as well as works by Hrafnhildur Hagalín, Eeva-Liisa Manner, and Bjørg Vik. Dr. Moberg is a Lecturer in Scandinavian languages at Columbia University, where she has taught Swedish language and Scandinavian literature courses since 1988. She is currently at work on a book of English translations of plays by Lugn.

Stephen Mulrine teaches art history at the Glasgow School of Art, and has written extensively for radio and television. A poet and playwright, he began translating from Russian in the late 1980s (mainly drama), and his published and produced work now ranges from translations of Gogol, Ostrovsky, Turgenev, and Chekhov to the contemporary plays of Gelman and Petrushevskaya. His adaptations include Yerofeev's cult 1960s novel *Moscow Stations,* Bulgakov's *Heart of a Dog,* and Leskov's *Lady Macbeth of Mtsensk.* Works in progress include Gorky's *Lower Depths* and *Children of the Sun,* and a second collection of plays by Ostrovsky.

Patricia W. O'Connor is Charles Phelps Taft Professor of Romance Languages and Literatures at the University of Cincinnati; she is also a Corresponding Member of the Royal Spanish Academy. In 1982 she received the Rieveschl Award for Scholarly Work and in 1990 was named Distinguished Research Professor. From 1975 to 1992, she was editor of *Estreno.* She has a special interest in play translation and has published in English plays by Antonio Buero Vallejo, Jaime Salom, Charles Muñiz, Antonio Gala, Miguel Mihura, Eduardo Quiles, Manuel Martínez Mediero, Juan Antonio Castro, Concha Romero, and Lidia Falcon. Of particular interest among her fourteen books are *Plays of the New Democratic Spain* (1992), *Dramaturgas españolas de hoy* (1997), and *Mujeres sobre mujeres/One-Act Spanish Plays by Women about Women* (1998).

Anthony Vivis was for years a dramaturg with the Royal Shakespeare Company and a script editor and producer for the BBC. He has had more than sixty translations (some done collaboratively) performed or read, including plays by Georg Büchner, Reinshagen, Fassbinder, Goethe, Schiller, Hauptmann, and Karl Kraus. His translations have been published by Methuen, Bloomsbury, and Cambridge University Press. He has also translated poetry and written articles or reviews for *Times Literary Supplement, Gambit, The Listener, Theater Heute,* and *The Independent.* He is translator-in-residence at the British Centre for Literary Translation, at the University of East Anglia, where he lectures part-time.

Barbara Wright studied music in Paris and London and worked briefly as an accompaniest. A contributor to *Times Literary Supplement* since 1965, she has also worked as a reporter for a local London newspaper and as a critic for the *Arts Review,* London, for twenty years. Her first translation was Alfred Jarry's *Ubu Roi* and her second Raymond Queneau's *Exercises for Style.* She has since translated ten other books by Queneau and numerous works by other twentieth-century French writers, such as Robert Pinget, Nathalie Sarraute, Michel Tournier, Tristan Tzara, Alain Robbe-Grillet, Fernando Arrabal, Marguerite Duras, Jean Dubillard, Eugéne Ionesco, and Jean Genet. She has received the Scott Montcrief translation prize three times and is Officier de l'Ordre des Arts et des Lettres. In 1997 her translation of Nathalie Sarraute's *Here (Ici)* won the French-American Translation Prize. She lives in London.

Modern Women
Playwrights of Europe

Introduction

This volume is the fortuitous offspring of frustration begat upon inequity. After years of teaching modern Continental drama and lamenting the dearth of plays by women available in print in English, I thought it time to replenish that gap. No comprehensive anthology of modern European plays includes a single play by a woman. Women authors have begun to appear in world collections, in national volumes, and of course in single-authored and single-play issues, but not in a text suitable for the study of Continental drama. I knew wonderful female-authored plays existed; I had often enough scurried to find copies I could use to supplement my syllabus. Thus the genesis of *Modern Women Playwrights of Europe.*

My defense of this project against what some might object to as the ghettoizing of literature by women (Nathalie Sarraute's objection, for example, and why she does not appear here) is simple enough—more pragmatic than philosophical. These plays deserve to be known, and it seems unlikely that existing anthologies will be reassembled to reflect what is really "out there." I envision this as a source of twentieth-century plays supplementary or parallel to the collections now in print. I recognize the problematic nature of a women's anthology; it seemed the alternative was no women's anthology.

Using the familiar criteria—the ones that presumably determine the contents of anthologies of drama by men—dramatic structure, depth and deftness of characterization, thematic texturing, linguistic richness, and overall cohesion and effectiveness, I systematically searched the literary histories and bibliographies of each country in Europe, as best I could, looking for first-rate plays by women of this century. (I excluded England and Ireland, where the problems of availability and inclusion are not so apparent.) Some of these traditional criteria may be under scrutiny and disputed by contemporary theorists, but that seems properly an undertaking subsequent to including women's writing within the recognized canon.

Though I used national divisions as a way of locating playwrights, in fact the only substantial criterion that I imposed on each play I read (or asked or read about) was that of quality. I did not seek or prefer plays of any particular mode or style or social or political agenda. I had to feel that each play included was genuinely among the finest modern dramatic literature. One qualification of this is that my biases have been toward literary drama. This excludes agit-prop, improvisational, and performance theater, areas where feminist theater has often been very successful. From every other perspective, the seventeen plays in this book are randomly selected and potentially interesting for what, as a group, they reveal.

1

Probably the most striking reality that emerged was how much more difficult it was for women to succeed as playwrights than as poets or novelists. This was as true in countries that had produced the most remarkable women dramatists as it was in those where I could find none of note. What Melissa Smith writes in respect to Russia pertains throughout:

> [D]ramaturgy is mostly a one-party system that seldom selects women. While there has been no dearth of women writing plays, their legacy is scant. The designation of "playwright" is provisional, for playwriting tends to be a phase in a woman's career rather than an area of her major emphasis, even among the most prolific female writers for the stage. This is not an exclusively Russian phenomenon. The phrase "and also wrote plays" is a common bibliographical appendage. ("Waiting in the Wings," cited in Petrushevskaya bibliography, p. 433)

My own foraging certainly confirms this observation. To a far greater extent than male authors, female playwrights are also novelists and/or poets. Granted, we recognize in the author of *Hamlet* and *Lear* a maker of sonnets, and Strindberg and Chekhov also wrote fiction, but Sophocles, Molière, Calderón, O'Neill, Shaw, and Arthur Miller, who are clearly playwrights (despite occasional meanderings into other genres), represent the more usual case.

Women have long been dedicated poets (Sappho) or novelists (Lady Murasaki), but a career as a playwright has proven to be a more hazardous and less likely undertaking (Aphra Behn is striking for her rarity as well as for her genius and success). With women dramatists, whether they be as known and established as Nathalie Sarraute, Marguerite Duras, Suzanne Lilar, or Eeva-Liisa Manner, or as current as Gerlind Reinshagen, Ludmila Petrushevskaya, Elfriede Jelinek, Dacia Maraini, Bjørg Vik, Astrid Saalbach, or Kristina Lugn, the practice seems to be to divide their literary creativity between or even among genres. The greater difficulty that women have had succeeding as playwrights, which parallels their experiences as film or theater directors, very likely derives from the public nature of the art. Writing and getting a play performed require experience in the theater. They also require large blocks of time and financial support. A successful production depends upon a great deal of cooperation, from people as various as bankers, actors, stagehands, and even reviewers. Directors and even playwrights are in positions of control over other people. All of these factors have been barriers for women. Virginia Woolf's demand for "a room of one's own" and five hundred pounds income remains instructive. The story of her imaginary Judy Shakespeare makes clear how the social and public nature of drama discourages female authors. It is not rhetorical or eccentric when Jelinek finds the notions of woman as artist and of woman as wife and mother incompatible.

Closely related to this difficulty is an extraordinary criticism women artists have sometimes encountered. Because of traditional and long-standing ideals of "femininity," Daniela Fischerová and Jelinek in particular have been chastised for their cold, emotionless intellectuality, for not writing as *women* should write. Fischerová chafes—quite appropriately—that no man writing as she does would be so criticized. Many, including these two women, but also Petrushevskaya and

Maraini, have been rebuked for writing provocative, unpleasant ("unfeminine") dramas. Intellect, cynicism, nastiness, or querulousness remain unequally valued in men and women artists, which echoes the tremor that some of these same figures (Jelinek, Lugn, and Paloma Pedrero, for example) occasion when they treat sex, lust, and desire forthrightly.

An introduction to a moderately large collection of dramas by women is an obvious place to abstract differences: are they different from plays by men? When I began this research, I anticipated, given the stratifications and inequalities that still exist in the usual positions of men and women, that it would be improbable for a woman to write unaware or independent of her situation as a woman. To clarify: by contrast, a white, heterosexual male writing in our society can quite easily write untrammeled by his status; his surroundings and encounters less insistently remind him of what he is (and its limitations). As an artist, he does not write from what the Existentialists identified as the position of "the Other." A woman who wants to be an artist or have a career is still *statistically* more likely to have to think about juggling competing and diverse roles than a man would. At least that was what I expected to be apparent in these plays. I am no longer so convinced that a woman cannot write unself-conscious of her gendered position. Even as designedly feminist a play as Kalliroi Siganou-Parren's *The New Woman* arguably does not necessarily convey a woman's sensibility so much as it does an egalitarian one. More obviously, I would be hard-pressed to argue that in *A Trip to Venice* Vik and even Ana Diosdado in *Yours for the Asking* could not escape their awareness of being women.

A significant strain of feminist theoreticians (including Teresa de Lauretis, Elin Diamond, Catherine Belsey, Sue-Ellen Case, and Jill Dolan) variously critique Realism and its generic "illusionism" as instruments perpetuating existing patriarchies. Realism, as a convention at the heart of modern literature, invites many responses and critiques beside the feminist one (and Marxist, if we think of Brecht). But looking at the strategies of the basically feminist writers in this volume suggests that their responses to Realism are mixed and the dismissal of it by no means universal. Usually, the attitudes are varied, incorporating realistic conventions alongside surrealist or poststructuralist ones. The spread of styles, in fact, is what one would expect in any random modern anthology.

What does emerge as a difference is the frequently despairing attitude toward family life and domesticity, its hopelessness. Women writers, not surprisingly, show little interest in stories of war, political intrigue, and traditional heroism (those bastions of male experience) and a great deal of interest in relationships, familiality, and personal communication. It is striking how many of these plays are essentially bleak in their outlook, from the realist attack upon bourgeois hypocrisies of Gabriela Zapolska to the psychological, surrealist exposés of Manner, Lugn, and Hrafnhildur Hagalín Gudmundsdóttir, to the almost polemical assaults of Jelinek, Petrushevskaya, and Maraini. Each dramatization is distinct, but none finds the prospects of family life and nurturing very satisfying, reaffirming, or even tolerable. In the lone instance where mothering is portrayed positively, *The New Woman*, it presupposes first discarding the husband/father. By contrast, Zapolska, Jelinek, Lugn, Petrushevskaya, and Reinshagen are all skeptical if not out-right negative about the idea of maternal devotion. Duras seems alternately ap-palled and overwhelmed by it.

The greater discomfort that sociological and psychological surveys report women have in marriage than men is reflected in the plays. Frequently, as in Par-ren's *New Woman,* lies and deceit characterize family life, and, as in *Music Lessons, Aunt Blossom, Yours for the Asking,* and *Lauren's Call,* the setting is a claustrophobic space. We sense the traplike images and the urgent desire to escape.

Another discernible motif is cross-dressing. Cross-dressing is as old as theater itself. Men, of course, played the women's roles in Periclean Athens as they did in Elizabethan England. This, especially in such romantic comedies as Shakespeare's *Twelfth Night,* proved to be imagistically and thematically suggestive. Although there were certainly admonitions about the dangers of cross-dressing in the Re-naissance, of how it might rile the natural order, it was, however, not until the philosophical and political discussions of gender so central to feminist theory, that transvestitism became so resonant a theatrical trope. Simone Benmussa and Pe-drero obviously make it the central image in their discussions of gender; but oth-ers like Lugn and Hagalín also make significant if less prominent use of it. Cos-tumes, because they allow us to put on or take off identities and personalities, are apt vehicles for investigating the extent to which gender, as distinguished from sex, is socially constructed and malleable.

Two other observations worth mentioning surfaced while writing the intro-ductions. At first, I found disconcerting the space that male authors like Strindberg and Ibsen occupied in my comments. My attitude, however, shifted. Not only were they unavoidable reference points, but frequent comparisons to them and to such others as Chekhov, O'Neill, Pinter, Miller, Beckett, and Ionesco—which came so naturally—indicated the real and useful comparability of these women play-wrights to the more familiar pantheon.

The second observation is a reflection more on the history of the women's movement than on women's drama. Parren's Lela, in 1897 Constantinople, envies Russian women as having "some education and refinement." Her (or our) Russian (or Polish) contemporary might look across with similar envy to the lives of French and German women, who might, in turn, cast a wistful eye at the imagined suf-fragette or liberated Yankee woman. This in a world where American women con-tinue to protest social, financial, and political disparities.

This collection is not only an attempt to disseminate the literature written by women; it is also necessarily a venture in comparative literature. English has be-come so powerful and dominant a language, in culture as well as in commerce and science (and tourism), that it becomes a formidable task for foreign literatures to assault our citadels and markets. Conversely, we risk being lulled by the wealth of literature available in English into a narrow, cultural insularity if efforts of transla-tion are not made. For many of the translators in this volume, making foreign lit-eratures available to the anglophone world has become a crusade. Verne Moberg and Frank Caucci have spoken to me of it. Stratos Constantinidis has written about it. It obviously inspires the work of Janet Garton and Pat O'Connor. Others have simply made it their profession.

In the individual introductions to the plays, I have tried to provide some comments about the national milieu of the author, some about her, and some commentary about the play itself. I made no attempt to standardize or "boilerplate" them. Rather, their content and emphases reflect the secondary literature that is available. That the format of an introduction does not smoothly accommodate notes and scholarly documentation should not obscure my indebtedness to the scholars who have written about the various modern dramas. The bibliographies in English are for the use of those who want to look further and also to make this indebtedness clear. There is, inevitably, something amiss and much missing in each of the introductions. I can only hope that the ensemble offers a useful and reasonable preface to modern European drama by women.

My principal apology is for the extraordinary plays I overlooked or misjudged. Grasping at a continent's literature is a humbling experience. It puts into sharp, if bewildering, focus the contentious issue of canonicity.

The order of the plays in the table of contents is primarily chronological. I have bent that a couple of times, to keep plays from the same countries next to each other. This led to further bendings, where I tended to place a later play by a dramatist of an earlier generation before an earlier play by a younger writer. Because translated titles can be so variable and even capricious, I have provided in parentheses the original titles of any works that would not be immediately familiar or obviously translatable so that they can be more easily pursued and researched.

Gabriela Zapolska (1857–1921)

In 1795 Poland was partitioned out of existence as a nation, its territory divided among neighboring states. Not until 1918 was the country reconstituted. Polish culture and the language, of course, persisted, but as ethnic rather than national entities. Theater and theater people looked toward Berlin, St. Petersburg, Paris, and Moscow, as well as toward Warsaw and Cracow. The comedies of Wojciech Boguslawski (1757–1829), the "father of Polish drama," and a repertoire of romantic drama played in the nineteenth century. But the strong, cohesive tradition of Polish drama and a national theater, with a corps of dramatists and directors, only emerged in stages in the second half of the twentieth century.

Gabriela Zapolska was one of the extraordinary Polish literary figures who lived during this politically complicated and uncertain period. An actress, theater manager, dramatist, novelist, and journalist, she belonged to the heady artistic and intellectual, bohemian world that surfaced in European cities in the last quarter of the nineteenth century. Her mother was a ballerina and her father belonged to the lower Polish nobility. She was briefly married to a Petersburg grenadier and spent much of her life in the theater circles of Warsaw, Lvov, Cracow, and Paris—first determined to succeed as an actress and then as a writer.

Her first play, *Wild Strawberries* (*Poziomki*, 1880), and her early fictions—*Malaszka* (1883), *Kaska Kariatyda* (1885), and *The Human Menagerie* (*Ludzka menazeria*, 1893)—established Zapolska as part of the same socially conscious, realist—even naturalistic—tradition as Zola and Shaw. Her unwavering attacks on the hollow pieties and iniquities of bourgeois society, the sensual directness of her writing, her outspokenness and lack of inhibition, and her "scandalous" behavior (a liaison with a theater mentor, Marian Gawalewicz, and an out-of-wedlock child) resulted in a career marked by notoriety.

In 1900 Zapolska abandoned the idea of acting, devoting herself to writing. She married her second husband, Stanislaw Janowski, a painter, the next year. In 1906 she wrote her most successful play, *The Morality of Mrs. Dulski* (*Moralność pani Dulskiej*), which quickly became a classic in the Polish dramatic repertoire. She and Janowski founded the very successful Gabriela Zapolska Theater the following year, touring in provincial Poland through 1908.

Of the many plays, novels, and journalistic pieces that Zapolska wrote in her prolific career—many of which were seen as "potboilers" or "pulp"—*Mrs. Dulski* stands out as her enduring achievement—though *Foursome* (*Ich czworo*, 1907), *Skiz* (1909), and *Miss Maliczewska* (1910) remain popular in the Polish dramatic reper-

Gabriela Zapolska, no date. (Photographer unknown.)

toire. In it the bitter and caustic view she often conveyed is contained within an effective dramatic framework highlighted by a poignant undercurrent of comedy
(she described the play as an "obscurantist tragifarce").

The *Morality of Mrs. Dulski* belongs to the social-protest literature that irritated
the conservative sentiments of turn-of-the-century Europe. But, like the best of that
critical literature, it is no dry and dated polemic; it has a spirit and sparkle, artistry
and energy that make it universally pertinent and enduring. She creates her figures
and devises their situations with satiric wit and aplomb.

From the initial stage directions, specifying solid furniture, gilded frames, and
artificial palms, to Zbyszko's recognizing himself as a congenital philistine who
cannot escape his skin, the scathing exposure of bourgeois mores is determined
and consistent. Mrs. Dulski's assured view, that "A secure living is the *base* of life.
And as for a husband, you can train him," employs the conventions of bourgeois
realism to savage the inadequacy and hypocrisy of bourgeois life. The imagery of

imprisonment, with Mrs. Dulski as landlady/gatekeeper (and ultimately as inmate), elaborates this attack.

Mrs. Dulski's compartmentalized morals (she can rent to whores, but not greet them; she can accept immorality if it is hidden indoors, but evicts a tenant who creates a scandal by trying to escape her abusive husband) reflect the divided lives and roles of her family world. Her daughters, Mela, who is struck by the sadness of it all, and Hesia, are incomplete, almost complementary figures. Her son's divided motives and sensibilities are irreconcilable.

Poland was not especially welcoming to its early women dramatists, but writing in an often helter-skelter and uneven way, Zapolska bequeathed a remarkable social comedy to the beginnings of Polish drama by women. Perhaps only the plays that Stanislawa Przybyszewska wrote in the late 1920s about the French Revolution—*Thermidor, Danton's Case,* and *Ninety-Three*—and possibly Maria Jasnorzewska-Pawlikowska's antitotalitarian satire, *A Weird Woman* (*Baba-Dziwo,* 1938), and Anna Bojarska's *The Polish Lesson* (1988) can stand alongside it—and these lack the universality of *Mrs. Dulski.* Like some of Shaw's early works, Zapolska's drama benefits from the tradition of the well-made play, in pacing and structure, without seeming mechanical or lifeless. It flirts with the manner of comedy, while, like Molière's plays, exulting in its chastening effects.

SELECTED BIBLIOGRAPHY IN ENGLISH

Ariel, Katriel Ben. "Universal Value of the Plays of Gabriela Zapolska." *Etudes slaves et est-européennes* 19 (1979), 75–85.
Czerwinski, Edward J. *Contemporary Polish Theatre.* New York: Greenwood, 1988.
Drozdowski, Bohdan, ed. *Twentieth Century Polish Theatre.* London: John Calder, 1979.
Goscilo, Helena. "Gabriela Zapolska." *Russian and Polish Women's Fiction.* Knoxville: University of Tennessee Press, 1985.
Milosz, Czeslaw. *History of Polish Literature.* Berkeley: University of California Press, 1983.

THE MORALITY OF MRS. DULSKI
Gabriela Zapolska

Translated by Wieslawa and Victor Contoski

CHARACTERS

MRS. DULSKI

MR. DULSKI

ZBYSZKO DULSKI   their son

HESIA   their daughter

MELA   their daughter

MRS. JULIASIEWICZ née DULSKI

A TENANT (FEMALE)

HANKA   a servant

MRS. TADRACH   a washerwoman

ACT I

The stage shows a living room in a bourgeois house, tapestry on the walls, solid furniture. In gilded frames on the walls are art reproductions and God knows what else. There are horns of plenty, artificial palm trees, and an embroidered landscape framed under glass, as well as a beautiful old mahogany glass case and a small screen in French Empire style, a lamp with a blotting paper shade, and few small tables with photographs. The window blinds are closed. It is dark. When the curtain rises a clock in the dining room strikes six. During the first few scenes the stage grows brighter and brighter and becomes entirely lit when the blinds are raised.

Scene I

For a while the stage is empty. The noise of shuffling slippers can be heard. MRS. DULSKI, *carelessly dressed, enters from the left, the main bedroom, curlers in her hair, and some strands of hair hanging down in back. She is dressed in a white bodice that is not very clean and a short wool petticoat with a tear at the stomach.* MRS. DULSKI *walks in muttering, a candle in her hand. She puts the candle on the table, and then goes into the kitchen.*

MRS. DULSKI: Cook! Hanka! Get up! [*A murmur in the kitchen.*] What? There's still time? Princesses! No royal blood in me, but I'm up already. Quiet, cook. Don't argue! Go make a fire in the stove. Hanka! Come and make a fire in the living room. [*She goes toward the door on the right.*] Hesia! Mela! Get up! Go over your lessons, practice your scales. Hurry up, don't rot in bed! [*For a while she walks around the stage muttering. She goes to the first door on the right, looks into the room, wrings her hands, then enters the room with the candle still in her hand.*]

Scene II

HANKA *is barefoot, her skirt scarcely tied on. She has on a shirt and a bodice thrown over her shoulders. She carries pitchwood and coal. She squats down at the stove, starts the fire, sniffs and sighs.* MRS. DULSKI *enters, angry.*

MRS. DULSKI: Is that how you make a fire? Is that how you make a fire? Good God! Cows, that's what you're good for—cows! Not civilized stoves. Why are you wasting so much pitchwood! Wait. Get out of the way. You're good for nothing. I'll show you. [MRS. DULSKI *squats down and makes a fire in the stove herself.*] Go and wake up the young ladies, and if they won't get up, pull off their quilts. [HANKA *goes to the young ladies' room.* MRS. DULSKI *makes the fire. As she blows on it, a bright flame lights up her fat, bloated face.* HANKA *returns.*] What about the girls? Are they getting up?
HANKA: I pulled off the covers. Miss Hesia kicked me in the stomach.
MRS. DULSKI: Big deal. You'll be all right.

[*A moment of silence.*]

HANKA: Please, ma'am . . .
MRS. DULSKI: Do you see how to make a fire in the stove?
HANKA: Please, ma'am . . .
MRS. DULSKI: I have to think about everything. I'll be in my grave soon because of you.
HANKA: [*Kissing* MRS. DULSKI*'s hand.*] Please, ma'am . . . I want to tell you that I will be leaving the first of next month.
MRS. DULSKI: What? How?
HANKA: [*Softer.*] I'm going to leave.
MRS. DULSKI: Don't you dare. I paid for you at the agency. You have to stay on. Leaving— that's a fine idea!
HANKA: I'll get somebody for my place.
MRS. DULSKI: Just look at her! How sassy. Her head is turned already. Oh, just see how the city has changed her. Maybe you'd like to be a qualified maid?
HANKA: Please, ma'am . . . it's on account of the young master.
MRS. DULSKI: Huh?
HANKA: Yeah . . . I don't want to because . . .
MRS. DULSKI: Again?
HANKA: All the time. It's either this or that. And after all, I . . .
MRS. DULSKI: [*Not looking at her.*] Well, all right. I'll tell him.
HANKA: Please, ma'am, it won't work. After all, you told me more than once or twice already that you talked to . . .
MRS. DULSKI: But now it will help.
HANKA: Because the priest said I should leave.
MRS. DULSKI: Do you work for the priest or me?
HANKA: But I have to obey the priest.

MRS. DULSKI: Go and get some milk and rolls.

HANKA: I'm going, ma'am. [*She goes out.*]

MRS. DULSKI: [*Going toward the door of the main bedroom.*] Felician! Felician! Get up! You'll be late to the office! [*She goes to the door of her daughters' bedroom.*] Hesia! Mela! You'll be late for school.

HESIA: [*Offstage.*] Mama, it's so cold. Can I have some warm water?

MRS. DULSKI: And what else? Harden yourselves. Felician! Are you getting up? Do you know that your clown of a son hasn't come home yet! What? Nothing to say? Naturally. A tolerant father. Like father like son. But if there are bills, I won't pay them.

HANKA: [*Opening the kitchen door.*] Missus, the caretaker came to ask about the registration cards of those people who just moved in.

MRS. DULSKI: I'm coming! Hesia! Mela! Felician! What a sleepy family. Up! Up! If it weren't for me, we'd be beggars. [*She enters the kitchen.*] Caretaker, why did you leave the new broom outside? It's been raining. [*She closes the door. Her voice dies away.*]

Scene III

HESIA, MELA. HESIA *and* MELA *hurry out of their room. They wear the same short skirts and fustian bodices. Their hair is loose. They run to the stove and squat down.*

HESIA: Come on! Come on!

MELA: Is she here?

HESIA: No. Listen how she's chewing out the caretaker. Ah, it's nice to get warm.

MELA: Well, don't push. I want . . .

HESIA: Wait, I'll fix it. And now, give me your comb. I'll do your hair.

MELA: Leave me alone. If she sees us, there'll be a fuss.

HESIA: So what? I'm not afraid.

MELA: But I am. It's so unpleasant when somebody's screaming.

HESIA: That's because you're sentimental. You take after our father. You're a mouse.

MELA: How do you know what father is like? After all, father doesn't say anything.

HESIA: Oh, I know. Besides, you've got his nose.

MELA: That's strange.

HESIA: [*Doing* MELA's *hair.*] What is?

MELA: That a child resembles its father or mother. How come?

HESIA: Oh, I know. I know.

MELA: [*Timidly.*] You know? Tell me.

HESIA: I'm no fool. I won't tell you, but I know.

MELA: Who told you?

HESIA: Cook.

MELA: Oh, when?

HESIA: Yesterday when mama went to the theatre and didn't take us because it was a naughty play. I went to the kitchen, and there Ann told me. Oh, Mela, Mela! [*She rolls on the carpet laughing.*]

MELA: Hesia, I think that's a sin.

HESIA: What?

MELA: To talk with the cook about such things.

HESIA: But it's true. It's really true.

MELA: If mother knew . . .

HESIA: So what? She'd scream—she's always screaming.

MELA: [*After a while.*] Won't you tell me?

HESIA: No. I don't want to have you on my conscience. Don't scandalize the innocent. [*They are silent for a while.* HESIA *gets up and tiptoes to* ZBYSZKO'S *bedroom, looks in, and returns to the stove.* MELA *follows her halfway. Then both sit down,* HESIA *in the armchair, and* MELA *braids her hair.*] Okay, now make me a country girl with a black braid.

MELA: Then don't squirm.

HESIA: You know that Zbyszko went out on a spree.

MELA: He's not here?

HESIA: No. I'll tell you something, but swear you won't tell it to anybody. Bend down. Zbyszko chases Hanka.

MELA: What for?

HESIA: Oh, you. There's no point in talking to you about it. Well, tell me, is it possible to talk to you?

MELA: Yes, but you say he chases her.

HESIA: Well he does, or makes advances, or loves her, or . . .

MELA: Oh, Hesia, Zbyszko?

HESIA: Well, didn't you see "Halka"? Don't you know how it happens? The young master and "the unfortunate Halka who comes and can't be stopped. . . ." [*She laughs heartily.*]

MELA: But that's on the stage. Besides, it happened in times when they wore split-sleeve coats. But Zbyszko . . . O, Hesia!

[HANKA *enters. She kneels down before the stove.*]

HESIA: Hanka! I'll ask her. You'll see if I'm lying.

MELA: [*Fearfully.*] Hesia, don't ask her, I beg you.

HESIA: Why not? It's okay. Besides, mama's not listening.

MELA: HESIA, I'm ashamed somehow in front of Hanka.

[*Silence.*]

HESIA: [*Softly.*] Well, then I won't ask her, but yesterday I saw him pinching her here and there.

MELA: And you say he's in love with her.

HESIA: That's right.

MELA: But if he were in love with her, he wouldn't be pinching her.

HESIA: You know what? You should be kept under glass. Brother!

MELA: Why under glass, Hesia?

HESIA: Because of your stupidity! [*Silence. Then suddenly.*] Oh, wouldn't I like to know where Zbyszko goes at night!

MELA: [*Naively.*] Perhaps to the park for a walk. It's so nice out now.

HESIA: You're stupid. [*Suddenly to* HANKA.] Hanka? Don't you know where gentlemen usually go at night?

HANKA: Me?

HESIA: Well, the same place as Zbyszko. They stay up until morning almost every day.

HANKA: Yeah. Got to go someplace.

HESIA: I asked him. He said on a spree, and the cook laughed too and said that it was to cabarets. O God! When will I finally really find out something? When I'm a grown-up! Then there won't be any secrets from me!

MELA: But I prefer it this way.

HESIA: What?

MELA: Not to know about anything. It's nice somehow. I prefer not to know anything.

HESIA: Blockhead!

Scene IV

The same persons, also MRS. DULSKI, *who comes on the scene like a hurricane.*

MRS. DULSKI: Why here? What's this? Get dressed. Hanka, clean the house. Mela, practice the piano! Felician! [*She bursts into the main bedroom.*]

HESIA: [*To* MELA.] Stay here a while. The wind has already died down. Felician!

MELA: Hesia!

HESIA: What? Our mother! Ach, superstitions.

MELA: [*Shocked.*] Hesia, look. Hanka is laughing.

HESIA: So what? Let her laugh. Can't I have my own opinion? [*To* HANKA.] Why are you laughing, you idiot? Clean the house! Or wait. Have you even been in a cabaret?

HANKA: Hee hee! What on earth you say, miss? I even don't know where.

HESIA: Because you're stupid. Cook was there when she was young. She says that gentlemen sit there, drink liquor, and have a good time. Cook told me there are pretty young girls there and . . .

MELA: Be quiet, Hesia. Mama might hear you.

[HANKA *leaves.*]

HESIA: Go on! Go on! It's not because of mama, but because you don't want to find out.

MELA: I told you, I prefer not to know.

HESIA: A while ago you asked about it yourself.

MELA: About what?

HESIA: About those . . . children.

MELA: That's different.

HESIA: Why?

MELA: Because that about children is interesting, and this . . . it's ugly.

HESIA: Oh no. It's even more interesting.

MELA: Maybe, but I feel sad after.

HESIA: Oh, here he comes from his spree.

Scene V

HESIA, MELA, ZBYSZKO. ZBYSZKO'S *collar is raised, his face crumpled. He is shivering with cold.* ZBYSZKO *is young and already unbearable, though at times some flash appears in his eyes.*

HESIA: Where were you? Where were you?

ZBYSZKO: [*Shoving her away with his cane.*] Go away!

HESIA: Where were you? Did you go on a spree? Tell me, tell me. I won't tell mama anything.

ZBYSZKO: Go away!

HESIA: You speak so politely. You won't tell, but I know. You were at a cabaret. You drank liquor. There were pretty girls. Yes, you smell so nice of cigars. Ooh, ooh, how I like it!

ZBYSZKO: I'm telling you, go away.

MELA: Hesia, leave him alone.

HESIA: So this is how you treat me? Wait, I'll grow up too, I'll go on a spree too. I'll go to cabarets and drink liquor. I'll go to cabarets just like you, just like you! [*She jumps on one leg in front of him.*]

ZBYSZKO: Nice education! Very promising.

HESIA: And now, to teach you politeness in the family circle . . . [*She calls.*] Mama! Zbyszko's home!

ZBYSZKO: Quiet!

MRS. DULSKI: [*Bursting in like a bomb.*] Are you here?

ZBYSZKO: Yes, and I'm already gone. I'm going to take a nap before going to the office.

MRS. DULSKI: No, you'll stay here. I've got something to say to you.

ZBYSZKO: Ah, I can't stand up.

MRS. DULSKI: [*Rudely.*] I believe you. [*To her daughters.*] Go and get dressed, please. Mela, practice your scales.

MELA: It's too late.

MRS. DULSKI: There's enough time for five-finger exercises. Hesia tore her galoshes again.

ZBYSZKO: Isn't there any black coffee?

MRS. DULSKI: No, there isn't, dear sir. Hesia respects nothing. You'll never be a proper lady.

[*The girls hurry out of the room.*]

ZBYSZKO: Isn't there any coffee in this place?

MRS. DULSKI: Where have you been?

ZBYSZKO: Huh?

MRS. DULSKI: Where have you been till now?

ZBYSZKO: If I told you, ma, you'd really jump.

MRS. DULSKI: Oh!

ZBYSZKO: So it's best not to ask.

MRS. DULSKI: I am your mother.

ZBYSZKO: That's why you shouldn't ask.

MRS. DULSKI: I have to know how you waste your time and health.

ZBYSZKO: Do you see what I have under my nose, ma? A moustache, not milk, so . . .

MRS. DULSKI: [*Wringing her hands.*] How you look!

ZBYSZKO: Huh?

MRS. DULSKI: You're green.

ZBYSZKO: It's a fashionable color. You ordered the balconies and windows to be painted green too.

MRS. DULSKI: What girl will take you if you look like this?

ZBYSZKO: They take even worse. Isn't there any coffee in this place?

MRS. DULSKI: Don't speak to me like that. You still think you are in the company of loose women.

ZBYSZKO: It's as good company as any other. Besides, ma, why do you make a fuss about loose women? It isn't as if there weren't any in our building. You yourself rented the first-floor apartment to one.

MRS. DULSKI: But I do not greet her.

ZBYSZKO: But you take her rent money without objection.

MRS. DULSKI: I'm sorry, but I do not take *such* money for myself.

ZBYSZKO: And what do you do with it?

MRS. DULSKI: [*Majestically.*] I pay taxes with it.

ZBYSZKO: Ha! Well, I'm going to bed.

MRS. DULSKI: Are you going to stop playing around?

ZBYSZKO: *Jamais*!

MRS. DULSKI: I will not pay your debts.

ZBYSZKO: Uh . . . We'll talk about that later.

MRS. DULSKI: Zbyszko! Zbyszko! For this I nursed you with my own milk—for you to drag our decent and respected name through cabarets and taverns!

ZBYSZKO: You should have fed me with Nestle's Baby Milk. I've heard it's excellent. [MRS. DULSKI, *depressed, sits at the table.* ZBYSZKO *approaches her, sits on the table, and speaks to her familiarly.*] Ah, don't worry, Mrs. Dulski. What do you want, ma—that I stay home with you? Nobody comes here. We live all by ourselves.

MRS. DULSKI: These are difficult times. There's no money for parties.

ZBYSZKO: Huh! Man is a sociable animal. From time to time he needs to exchange thoughts. Oh, you see, ma, *thought* is a big word. Though we get rid of it here, it crops up over there.

MRS. DULSKI: But I don't have time to think.

ZBYSZKO: Exactly, exactly. So I clear out because our home is really a cemetery. And a cemetery for what? For thought, free, broad thought.

MRS. DULSKI: And so you go to coffee shops, to . . .

ZBYSZKO: Yes, yes! To . . . What can you know, ma, about the roads human thought takes, even the thought of such a Philistine as myself?

MRS. DULSKI: You're stupid. You and your father—one soul. Every day he's in the candy shop, and you—God knows.

Scene VI

MRS. DULSKI, MR. DULSKI, ZBYSZKO. MR. DULSKI, *a mummified official, enters dressed very neatly for going out. He is cleaning his hat.*

MRS. DULSKI: Well, at last.

[MR. DULSKI *adjusts his collar in front of the mirror.*]

ZBYSZKO: Good morning, father.

[MR. DULSKI *greets his son with a gesture.*]

MRS. DULSKI: [*To her husband.*] You get your salary today?

[MR. DULSKI *nods.*]

MRS. DULSKI: But be careful not to lose it. What are you waiting for? Ah, a cigar. Zbyszko, give your father a cigar from above the stove.

[ZBYSZKO *gets father a cigar.* MR. DULSKI *lights it.*]

MRS. DULSKI: And do you know what time your little son came home? [MR. DULSKI *shrugs his shoulders to show his indifference and leaves through the center door.*] One can go mad with that man.

ZBYSZKO: That's the way you made him.

MRS. DULSKI: No, this is too much.

ZBYSZKO: Good night. I'm going to take a nap.

MRS. DULSKI: And the office?

ZBYSZKO: [*Yawning.*] It won't run away.

MRS. DULSKI: [*Stopping him.*] Zbyszko, promise me that you'll reform.

ZBYSZKO: Never. I prefer to take the civil service exam. [*He goes to his room.*]

Scene VII

MRS. DULSKI, HANKA, *later* ZBYSZKO.

MRS. DULSKI: Dust the piano. Fix the stove. Is cook ready to go to town?

HANKA: Yes, ma'am.

[MRS. DULSKI *goes to the kitchen.* HANKA *is busy cleaning for a while.* ZBYSZKO *sticks his head out the door.*]

ZBYSZKO: Hanka? Are you alone?

HANKA: Lemme alone, sir.

ZBYSZKO: What's wrong? [HANKA *is silent.*] Come here. Show me your mug. Why are you angry? [HANKA *is still silent. She cleans more and more energetically. One can see she has an inner struggle.*] How ugly you are when you're mad!

HANKA: [*Suddenly.*] Those ladies you come back from are prettier.

ZBYSZKO: Ah, that's the matter! That's what's bothering you!

HANKA: Nothing's bothering me, only I don't want you teasing me.

ZBYSZKO: If you'll be nicer to me, I'll stay at home.

HANKA: I don't need that. You can go to them ladies.

ZBYSZKO: That's not true. You want me.

HANKA: Go away, sir. The missus may come in.

ZBYSZKO: But oh . . . kiss your master's hand. You made him angry.

HANKA: [*Laughing.*] Nothing doing! [*She hits his hand.*]

ZBYSZKO: O you rascal . . . [*He wants to embrace her.* MELA *enters, utters a soft cry, then blushing, her eyes down, she goes to the piano.* HANKA *flees.* MELA *sits down at the piano and plays five finger exercises. She plays alone for a while, then gets up, goes to* ZBYSZKO'S *room, and knocks on the door.*]

MELA: Zbyszko!

ZBYSZKO: [*Sticking his head out. He is partly undressed.*] What?

MELA: [*Mysteriously.*] Don't be afraid. I won't tell mama anything.

ZBYSZKO: You're really crazy.

MELA: But it's not your fault anyway.

ZBYSZKO: What?

MELA: [*Bashfully.*] Well . . . Hanka and you . . . if you both . . .

ZBYSZKO: Ah foo! To speak about such things! You should be ashamed. Your panties still show under your dress and you're already so depraved.

MELA: Me? But Zbyszko, I just think differently. I . . .

ZBYSZKO: Leave me alone. [*He withdraws.*]

[MELA *stands for a while deep in thought; then goes to the piano and begins to play. At this moment,* HESIA, *dressed in a coat and hat, bursts into the room. In her hand she has the same coat and hat for* MELA. *She carries books tied up with leather strings and throws them on the floor.*]

Scene VIII

MELA, HESIA, MRS. DULSKI, HANKA.

HESIA: Get dressed, Ophelia! Hurry up! The boys are already on their way to school.

MELA: [*Getting up and putting on her coat and hat.*] Hesia, you won't ogle that tall student.

HESIA: I'll do what I like.

MELA: I'm ashamed of you.

HESIA: Be ashamed! And try to say something about it to mama, and I'll tell her right away that you sigh at night instead of sleep. Mama will be more angry about that than the student.

MELA: I doubt it.

HESIA: But I don't. Mama knows me, that I know how far to go and that I won't forget myself.

MELA: What do you mean by that?

HESIA: I know exactly what I'm saying, you lily of our native fields!

MRS. DULSKI: Hanka! Come and take the girls to school.

HANKA: [*In the kitchen.*] I'm coming.

MRS. DULSKI: Do you have your umbrella? Walk straight, don't look around. Remember, modesty is a girl's treasure. [*To* HESIA.] Don't hunch your back.

[HANKA *enters with a shawl on her head.*]

HESIA: [*Throwing her books at her.*] Take them, you bumpkin. Good-bye, mama.

[*The girls leave with* HANKA. MRS. DULSKI *walks around, dusts, sighs. Then the bell rings in the hall.* MRS. DULSKI *cautiously goes to open the door. When she sees the tenant, she draws back and lets her in.*]

Scene IX

<small>MRS. DULSKI, TENANT</small> (*female*).

<small>MRS. DULSKI</small>: I'm sorry I'm not dressed yet. Please come in. I'll be right back.

<small>TENANT</small>: I'll only be a moment. Please don't bother.

<small>MRS. DULSKI</small>: Yes, yes, I'll just put something on. [*She runs into her room.*]

[*The* <small>TENANT</small> *walks in slowly. She is very pale and sad. Obviously she has undergone a serious illness and has serious moral problems. She sits down in the nearest chair and looks down at the floor, motionless. After a while* <small>MRS. DULSKI</small> *comes in dressed in a rich fustian dressing gown.*]

<small>MRS. DULSKI</small>: Please sit on the sofa.

<small>TENANT</small>: Thank you. I have only a few words to say. I received your letter . . . [*She breaks off. Silence.*]

<small>MRS. DULSKI</small>: Did you leave the hospital for good?

<small>TENANT</small>: Yes. The day before yesterday; my mother brought me home.

<small>MRS. DULSKI</small>: I see that you are well.

<small>TENANT</small>: [*With a sad smile.*] Oh, far from it.

<small>MRS. DULSKI</small>: Well, in your own little home you will get well soon. For a woman there is nothing like home, I always say.

<small>TENANT</small>: Yes, if one has a home.

<small>MRS. DULSKI</small>: But you have a husband, a position.

<small>TENANT</small>: Yes, but . . . [*Silence. With effort.*] Please, is it really necessary for me to move out the first of the month?

<small>MRS. DULSKI</small>: I really need your apartment for my relatives.

<small>TENANT</small>: I would prefer to stay. It will be difficult to find something in the winter time.

<small>MRS. DULSKI</small>: Oh, it's impossible. I say it's impossible.

<small>TENANT</small>: But, with no disrespect, I know you ordered a "for rent" sign put up on the apartment, so your relatives are not moving in.

<small>MRS. DULSKI</small>: [*Compressing her lips.*] Please don't force me to be unpleasant.

<small>TENANT</small>: What do you have against me?

<small>MRS. DULSKI</small>: O dear lady, this is too much! You created a scandal by taking poison!

<small>TENANT</small>: So that is the matter!

<small>MRS. DULSKI</small>: What else? Your husband—you, you paid me rent regularly. You don't have children or dogs. The only thing I had against you was that dusting the carpets outside in the morning. And you and your husband could live here still, but then . . . when I think about it, I blush. An ambulance in front of my house! An ambulance! Like in front of a tavern where people fight.

<small>TENANT</small>: But Mrs. Dulski, an accident can happen anywhere.

<small>MRS. DULSKI</small>: In a decent house, accidents don't happen. Have you ever seen an ambulance in front of a count's house? No! And after that, the publicity in the newspapers! The name Dulski, my name and my daughters', was mentioned three times in this scandal.

<small>TENANT</small>: But Mrs. Dulski, you surely know the reasons.

<small>MRS. DULSKI</small>: It's really nothing. Your husband and that girl. That's your business.

<small>TENANT</small>: But it was my maid. It was hideous. I couldn't take it. As soon as I was convinced . . .

<small>MRS. DULSKI</small>: You ate matches. Such a trivial poison! People laughed. And to think how it ended. A complete comedy. If you had died, well . . .

<small>TENANT</small>: I'm sorry I didn't.

<small>MRS. DULSKI</small>: I don't say it in that sense, except that death is always something . . . but as it was . . . well . . . as I said, people laughed. One day I took a streetcar. We were

just passing my building, because the stop is a little farther, and two gentlemen pointed to my house and said, "Look, this is the house where that jealous wife tried to commit suicide." And they started laughing. I thought I was going to die in the streetcar on the spot.

TENANT: [*Humbly.*] I am very sorry for all this unpleasantness.

MRS. DULSKI: Oh, my dear, publicity is publicity.

TENANT: I was very sick because of it all. Besides, I didn't know what I was doing. At that time I was like crazy . . . [*She cries silently.*]

MRS. DULSKI: Of course. Every suicide must be crazy and lose his morality and faith in the presence of God. It is cowardice. That's right, cowardice . . . And besides that, to destroy your own soul. It's good that they bury suicides separately. They shouldn't crowd in among decent people. To kill yourself! And for whom? For a man. And no man, my dear, is worth eternal damnation.

TENANT: Mrs. Dulski, it was not a man, but my husband.

MRS. DULSKI: Eh!

TENANT: I couldn't take it any more under my own roof.

MRS. DULSKI: It's better under one's own than somebody else's. Less publicity. Nobody knows.

TENANT: But I know.

MRS. DULSKI: My dear, the reason we have four walls and a ceiling is to wash our own dirt so nobody will know about it. To drag that dirt around is neither moral nor decent. I have always lived in such a way that nobody could say I caused a scandal. A woman should go through life silently and quietly. That's the way it is and nothing can be done about it.

TENANT: Nevertheless, if Mr. Dulski forgot himself with a servant . . .

MRS. DULSKI: Felician? That's impossible. You don't know him. And besides . . . it's your problem. I have to guard myself and my family from publicity. You may try again to commit such a sin, because this kind of madness, they say, comes back. Therefore . . .

TENANT: [*Getting up.*] I see. I'll move out. But I would like to tell you that to force me to look for another place now is not good, not decent. I am still so weak.

MRS. DULSKI: [*Getting up, offended.*] You won't teach *me* about honesty. I know what honesty is. I come from a decent, established family and I don't cause any publicity.

TENANT: [*Controlling herself.*] I don't doubt it. Yet, you needn't worry. I won't take poison again. It requires a great courage, in spite of your calling it cowardice. And later one suffers a great deal. I don't have the strength for it any more, and I wouldn't be able to go through such suffering again. Besides, I'm leaving my husband. That is the best guarantee I won't be jealous any more. [*She smiles sadly.*]

MRS. DULSKI: Are you leaving your husband? That's very bad. It's more publicity and nobody will take your side. For this reason alone I couldn't rent you an apartment any longer in my house. A woman alone—it's not . . . it . . . well, you understand.

TENANT: [*Ironically.*] Yes, I understand. However, that woman from the first floor who comes back at night . . .

MRS. DULSKI: [*With dignity.*] She is a person who lives by her own means and behaves very modestly indeed. She hasn't yet brought an ambulance in front of my house.

TENANT: [*Ironically.*] Only carriages and cars.

MRS. DULSKI: They always stop a few houses away. And besides, it seems to me I have no obligation to explain my decisions to you.

TENANT: Certainly. That would get us too far afield. Good-bye.

MRS. DULSKI: And please do not discourage people who come to see the apartment.

TENANT: [*Leaving.*] I'll tell them that it is damp, because it really is.

MRS. DULSKI: There is a court for that, my dear.

TENANT: My conscience tells me to do so. Good-bye.

[MRS. JULIASIEWICZ *appears in the doorway*.]

MRS. DULSKI: [*Upset*.] Niece! Did you hear that? You'll be a witness. She says that . . .
TENANT: Good-bye, Mrs. Dulski. [*She leaves*.]

Scene X

MRS. DULSKI, MRS. JULIASIEWICZ.

MRS. DULSKI: [*Angry*.] This . . . this . . . such a thing, this . . .
MRS. JULIASIEWICZ: Calm down, aunt.
MRS. DULSKI: If things go on like this, I'll have to go to Carlsbad this summer and drink mineral water.
MRS. JULIASIEWICZ: I'll go with you.
MRS. DULSKI: No thanks.
MRS. JULIASIEWICZ: What caused it? I think that was the tenant from the main floor, the one who tried to commit suicide.
MRS. DULSKI: Yes, yes. She's the one. She's already left the hospital. Scandal! Of course, after such a thing I cannot keep her in my building any longer. You yourself were a witness. When they took her out to the ambulance, she was almost naked. Monstrous! I cancelled her lease on the apartment.
MRS. JULIASIEWICZ: You did? That's rather fortunate. Our rent just went up. We can take her apartment.
MRS. DULSKI: That's not necessary.
MRS. JULIASIEWICZ: But aunt, you could do this for us, for relatives.
MRS. DULSKI: Times are too hard for such luxuries.
MRS. JULIASIEWICZ: I see. You think we won't pay.
MRS. DULSKI: I think nothing. Only I know you spend more than you can afford.
MRS. JULIASIEWICZ: So . . . so . . .
MRS. DULSKI: You go to the theater. [*Rudely*.] And to the most popular plays.
MRS. JULIASIEWICZ: After all, you can't expect . . .
MRS. DULSKI: You subscribe to periodicals.
MRS. JULIASIEWICZ: I beg your pardon, aunt, but . . .
MRS. DULSKI: I always borrow them and that's enough. If somebody won't lend them, well, the world won't collapse because I don't read that printed junk. And you invite guests for supper . . .
MRS. JULIASIEWICZ: We have to.
MRS. DULSKI: Well, if you have to, don't complain that you don't have enough money.
MRS. JULIASIEWICZ: We can't live like . . .
MRS. DULSKI: [*Ironically*.] Like we do? You'll sing a different song when you're old. I and Felician, we have different principles in this matter.
MRS. JULIASIEWICZ: My husband is not very good at saving money, neither am I.
MRS. DULSKI: If that's the way you are, you should have married that druggist from Bobrka. I encouraged you.
MRS. JULIASIEWICZ: But he died a year ago of tuberculosis.
MRS. DULSKI: Exactly. You'd have the house and you'd be a widow.
MRS. JULIASIEWICZ: Oh!
MRS. DULSKI: There is no need to *oh!* A secure living is the *base* of life. And as for a husband, you can train him. Take away his salary when he brings it home. Give him some change every day for a cup of coffee, and buy cigars for him yourself and dry them up on the stove. Otherwise, such a man can ruin you.

Scene XI

ZBYSZKO, MRS. DULSKI, MRS. JULIASIEWICZ.

ZBYSZKO: Such a racket. A person can't sleep.

MRS. DULSKI: So much the better. You can go to the office.

ZYBSZKO: Huh! [*To* MRS. JULIASIEWICZ, *with whom he shares a common jargon.*] And how are you, old lady?

MRS. JULIASIEWICZ: And how are you, buster?

ZBYSZKO: [*Looking into the mirror, then toward* MRS. JULIASIEWICZ.] Am I very green?

MRS. JULIASIEWICZ: What's it to you? Going to propose to somebody today?

ZBYSZKO: What the . . . Only the old man, you know who, the councillor, is going to look at me again with his rotten eye. And there'll be heaps of work, just heaps . . .

MRS. DULSKI: Behind in your work! Behind!

ZBYSZKO: It's not me that's behind, but the people who come to see me. [*He leans against the stove, warming himself.*]

MRS. DULSKI: [*Taking off her dressing gown and remaining in skirt and bodice.*] You will forgive me, my dear, but I'm going to dust, and I have to save my gown.

MRS. JULIASIEWICZ: But of course. Make yourself at home, aunt.

[MRS. DULSKI *dusts and casts furious looks at* ZBYSZKO.]

ZBYSZKO: So mama really threw out that one who tried to commit suicide?

MRS. DULSKI: What's that to you?

ZBYSZKO: Yes, I heard only a bit of it. I was edified by mama's pettiness. Besides, she seems to me very nice, that woman.

MRS. DULSKI: I believe you entirely. Scandal-maker.

ZBYSZKO: She did it out of love for her husband. That's your style. Matrimonial love.

MRS. DULSKI: Uhuh, it's true—for her husband. I don't believe in such love. Her silks rustle under her dress.

ZBYSZKO: That doesn't prove anything.

MRS. DULSKI: It proves she is not a decent woman. For her own husband, my dear, a woman does not need to dress herself up underneath. And those who rustle are . . .

ZBYSZKO: [*To* MRS. JULIASIEWICZ.] Sit still. You rustle too. And anyway, as far as that one from the main floor is concerned, I can vouch for her honesty.

MRS. DULSKI: How do you know that?

ZBYSZKO: [*Indifferently.*] Because I tried and I got snubbed.

MRS. DULSKI: At least you could leave the tenants alone. Step aside. How long are you going to stand here by the stove? [*Passionately.*] When I look at you, sometimes I find it hard to believe that you are my child.

ZBYSZKO: Well, if mama has her doubts . . .

MRS. DULSKI: [*To* MRS. JULIASIEWICZ.] I'm telling you, don't ever have children.

MRS. JULIASIEWICZ: Oh, we're not trying to.

MRS. DULSKI: [*To* ZBYSZKO.] No, you are a monster, not my son.

ZBYSZKO: But I am, mama! Unfortunately I am! And that's my whole tragedy. [*He goes to the piano and begins to play with some skill.*]

MRS. DULSKI: Did you hear that? He said "unfortunately"!

ZBYSZKO: I expected that. To be a Dulski is a catastrophe.

MRS. JULIASIEWICZ: Really, Zbyszko, you are going too far.

ZBYSZKO: Leave me alone.

MRS. DULSKI: [*To* MRS. JULIASIEWICZ.] No morals, no principles . . .

ZBYSZKO: No theoretical cover like mama has.

MRS. DULSKI: You'll end up joining the socialists.

ZBYSZKO: [*Closing the piano.*] I'm too stupid for that.

MRS. JULIASIEWICZ: [*Laughing.*] To become a socialist you don't have to take an exam.

ZBYSZKO: Yes, you do. And a very difficult one.

MRS. JULIASIEWICZ: From whom?

ZBYSZKO: From your own conscience and soul, my sweet angel.

MRS. DULSKI: To be a socialist, first of all, a person doesn't need to have God in his heart.

ZBYSZKO: It's a . . . It's a long time since we mentioned God in this house.

Scene XII

The same persons, HANKA.

HANKA: [*From the kitchen.*] Missus, if you please, here's the umbrella.

MRS. DULSKI: Leave it there. Then go and clean the hall. Did cook come back?

HANKA: [*Returning from the hall, she goes into the kitchen.*] Yes, she's here.

MRS. DULSKI: Excuse me a minute. [*She runs to the kitchen.*]

MRS. JULIASIEWICZ: [*To* ZBYSZKO.] Really, she is right. You could settle down a bit. You look like death warmed over.

ZBYSZKO: You're not bad yourself.

MRS. JULIASIEWICZ: Me? I didn't go out yesterday.

ZBYSZKO: Which means that I went out for my spree, and you had yours at home.

MRS. JULIASIEWICZ: [*Laughing.*] You are unbearable.

ZBYSZKO: Sometimes. [HANKA *passes through the room carrying a dustpan and broom.* ZBYSZKO *looks at her.*]

MRS. JULIASIEWICZ: [*To* ZBYSZKO.] Why are you looking at Hanka like that?

ZBYSZKO: Because I like her.

MRS. JULIASIEWICZ: A servant?

ZBYSZKO: So what? Isn't she a woman? I assure you, she's very much . . .

MRS. JULIASIEWICZ: Do you know something about that already?

ZBYSZKO: None of your business.

MRS. JULIASIEWICZ: I thought your taste was more refined.

ZBYSZKO: You're stupid with those Philistine esthetics of yours. And besides, I'm like a pianist. If he sees a piano, he must immediately play something.

MRS. JULIASIEWICZ: Yes, but a piano won't . . .

ZBYSZKO: My dear, every woman is a piano—only you have to know how to play. Ah, how sleepy I am.

MRS. JULIASIEWICZ: Why do you tramp through those taverns?

ZBYSZKO: Where am I supposed to tramp? I have to go somewhere.

MRS. JULIASIEWICZ: In your place, I'd try to make an acquaintance, a steady woman. There are so many married women who . . . oh, I'll tell you.

ZBYSZKO: Thank you. I have enough Philistinism at home and in myself.

MRS. JULIASIEWICZ: Why do you think you're a Philistine?

ZBYSZKO: Because I was born that way, my angel! Because already in my mother's womb I was a Philistine, and even if I tore my skin off, I would still have underneath in my soul a whole layer of Philistinism and nothing could root it out. Something, a new, different person, fights with that basic one. But I know that it's only a matter of time until the family Philistinism will take me by the hair, that the time will come when I'll be Felician collecting rent. I'll be . . . Dulski, grand-Dulski, super-Dulski, and I'll give life to Dulskis, entire legions of Dulskis. I'll have a silver wedding anniversary and a solid tombstone far from the suicides. And I won't look green any more, but I'll be puffed up with fat and puffed up with theories, and I'll talk a lot about God . . . [*He breaks off, goes to the piano and plays nervously.*]

MRS. JULIASIEWICZ: [*Approaching him from behind.*] You can free yourself from Philistinism.

ZBYSZKO: Not true. You think you're liberated because you have a bit of polish on the outside, but you're only imitation mahogany like your Secession style furniture and your dyed hair. It's a brand, Mrs. Councillor's wife, a brand.

MRS. JULIASIEWICZ: [*Joining him with one hand in playing the piano.*] Have you studied the piano?

ZBYSZKO: Me? I don't know a single note. It's something inside me that plays . . . something inside me that rattles. But all of it will be killed off in due time. Huh! Hello there . . . [*He embraces her.*] You know, you're not bad, not bad at all.

MRS. JULIASIEWICZ: [*Laughing.*] Oh, leave me alone.

ZBYSZKO: [*Laughing.*] Exercises, my dear, exercises.

[HANKA *passes through the room and casts a gloomy glance at both of them. She goes on to the kitchen.*]

MRS. JULIASIEWICZ: [*Taking a close look at* HANKA.] You know, that's interesting.

ZBYSZKO: What is?

MRS. JULIASIEWICZ: That girl. If you saw how she looked at us . . . In your shoes . . .

ZBYSZKO: Me, too, when I have time.

MRS. JULIASIEWICZ: You don't understand me. I'd keep away from her, far away.

ZBYSZKO: Huh!

MRS. JULIASIEWICZ: She's jealous. She'll make trouble.

ZBYSZKO: That would be just great.

Scene XIII

The same persons. MRS. DULSKI.

MRS. DULSKI: [*To* ZBYSZKO.] Are you still here? Aren't you ashamed? Your father works, I work, your sisters . . .

ZBYSZKO: [*Going to the hall and taking his coat and hat, coming back and putting them on.*] Dear mama, whether one works or not, everything comes to the same end.

MRS. DULSKI: That's not true. We are people who work, and loafers are . . .

ZBYSZKO: And yet we and you, in the same way . . .

MRS. DULSKI: What? What?

ZBYSZKO: . . . kick the bucket. Bye-bye. [*To* MRS. JULIASIEWICZ.] Bye-bye, doll. [*Leaves.*]

Scene XIV

MRS. DULSKI, MRS. JULIASIEWICZ, HANKA.

MRS. DULSKI: Terrible things, terrible. You hear what he said! The worst of it is that he is so intelligent, so talented! If he only wanted to, he could have a career. But he doesn't want to, he doesn't want to. We'll have lunch now. He doesn't want to, I say. Only no and no. He only goes on one spree after another. As soon as he picks up his salary, he disappears. And think how it looks! Nothing but cabarets and skirts. [HANKA *comes in carrying a tray with vodka, cheese, and snacks.*] Help yourself, my dear.

MRS. JULIASIEWICZ: Thank you. [*They sit down and start eating.*] He is irritated somehow, unhappy.

MRS. DULSKI: [*Angrily.*] Does he himself know what he wants? He should thank God that he's handsome and healthy. Here's to you. [*She raises her glass of vodka and drinks.*] Hanka, go and clean the young master's room. [HANKA *leaves.*]

MRS. JULIASIEWICZ: [*Looking after* HANKA.] Are you satisfied with Hanka?

MRS. DULSKI: She's all right.

MRS. JULIASIEWICZ: [*Softly.*] Send her away, aunt.

MRS. DULSKI: Why?

MRS. JULIASIEWICZ: I noticed something.

MRS. DULSKI: She steals?

MRS. JULIASIEWICZ: No, worse.

MRS. DULSKI: What?

MRS. JULIASIEWICZ: I think Zbyszko has his eye on her.

MRS. DULSKI: [*Unwillingly.*] Oh, that.

MRS. JULIASIEWICZ: I know what I'm saying. Send her away, aunt, while there's still time.

MRS. DULSKI: My dear, that's just the way things look to you. And besides . . . [*Looking away.*] in view of what's going on, if . . . well, you understand. Where there's smoke, there's fire.

MRS. JULIASIEWICZ: Ah.

MRS. DULSKI: In a word . . . that . . . you know?

MRS. JULIASIEWICZ: It's better at home?

MRS. DULSKI: I don't say that, but . . .

MRS. JULIASIEWICZ: You know, aunt, you may be right. [*A moment of silence.* HANKA *passes through and disappears into the kitchen. Both women look at her.*] But you have to admit men have peculiar taste.

MRS. DULSKI: Oh, never mind. Just so he won't take to the streets and lose his health. You have to be a mother to understand the pain of watching your own child go downhill.

MRS. JULIASIEWICZ: I see. But just so afterwards she won't . . .

MRS. DULSKI: That woman? No problem. She'll be satisfied. That kind are without decency and faith. Let me show you the hat I had remodeled. [*She goes into the hall and comes back with a hat of violets and white feathers, puts it on her head. She is dressed in a fustian bodice and an underskirt. Everything together makes a very strange effect.*] How do I look?

MRS. JULIASIEWICZ: Entirely . . . entirely . . .

MRS. DULSKI: [*In the hall.*] I have to economize. I'm having an old one remodeled.

MRS. JULIASIEWICZ: Well on you, aunt, everything looks good. Are you raising the rent this year?

MRS. DULSKI: I should hope so. I must. Everybody raises it. I'll show you the renters' list.

MRS. JULIASIEWICZ: Hmm . . . hmm.

MRS. DULSKI: [*She takes a paper out of the drawer and leans against the table. Both of them study the paper with interest.*] The apartments in the basement I'll raise twenty. I'll put a mangle in the hall.

MRS. JULIASIEWICZ: It's narrow. They'll knock their teeth out.

MRS. DULSKI: Makes no difference to me. I never go there. Both parts of the main floor I'll raise five. The first floor, that little kitten ten . . .

MRS. JULIASIEWICZ: For that kitten? Too little. I'd raise it at least twenty.

MRS. DULSKI: Do you think so?

MRS. JULIASIEWICZ: [*Laughing.*] Of course. She has money. It comes easily to her. Let her pay.

MRS. DULSKI: [*Brightening.*] Let her pay.

MRS. JULIASIEWICZ: [*Laughing.*] Let her pay!

MRS. DULSKI: So twenty for her, the councillor ten. On the second floor . . . [*Both of them doggedly bend over the table reading the list. The curtain goes down slowly.*]

ACT II

The same scenery as in the previous act. It is slowly getting dark. Violet-gray shadows come through the frosted windowpanes. On stage MR. DULSKI *in a dressing gown, a watch in his hand, walks up and down like an animal in a cage. He closes his eyes and walks like a wooden puppet. Finally he stops. Immediately the door of the main bedroom opens, and* MRS. DULSKI *appears wearing a full girdle and a skirt.*

Scene I

MR. DULSKI, MRS. DULSKI, HESIA.

MRS. DULSKI: Felician! Felician!

[MR. DULSKI *wakes up and looks at her.*]

MRS. DULSKI: Walk! Why don't you walk? It's not even two kilometers. I'm counting. [MR. DULSKI *shows her his watch.*] Don't bother me with your watch! I have the best watch in my head. All right, don't walk! Don't walk! I'll tell the doctor. I purposely make you walk in the room as far as the Higher Castle and not on the street, so I can watch that you don't cheat. And you—but that's your business. [*She disappears behind the door.* MR. DULSKI *begins again to walk automatically.* HESIA *comes into the room in a light blue dress, shoes, and blue stockings. She kisses her father on the hand.*]

HESIA: Are you walking to the Higher Castle, father? [MR. DULSKI *nods.*] And how far do you have to go yet? [*He holds up five fingers.*] Five hundred? [*He nods.*] Then you're about on Teatynska Street? [*He mumbles.*] Yes! Yes! But walk faster because they are demolishing the tunnel. [MR. DULSKI *looks at her severely and shrugs his shoulders.* HESIA *jumps up on the sofa and looks at herself in the mirror.* MR. DULSKI *goes to her and drags her down from the sofa.*]

HESIA: Mama doesn't see. [*She runs to the door of the girls' bedroom.*] Mela, Mela!

MRS. DULSKI: [*Offstage.*] Hesia, is Mela dressed?

HESIA: She's still monkeying around. [MR. DULSKI *stops and mutters something.*] You don't understand, father? Well, she's getting dolled up. In your time they didn't use such an expression? So what? They use it now.

MRS. DULSKI: [*Sticking her head out. She is fully dressed in her Sunday best.*] Felician! Stop walking. You are already at the Higher Castle. Tomorrow you will walk up to Kaiserwald. [*She disappears.*]

HESIA: [*Goes to the window, blows on the frosted pane, and sings.*] How thick the frost!

[MR. DULSKI *looks around and quietly goes to the stove, stands on a chair, and steals a cigar. At this very moment,* HESIA *turns around and sees him.* MR. DULSKI *hems and haws, goes to the hall, puts on his coat, approaches* MRS. DULSKI's *door, and knocks.* MRS. DULSKI *puts her head out.*]

MRS. DULSKI: To the coffee house already? Well, here's your twenty cents. From now on I'll give you twenty cents every day. Weekly, nothing—not a cent. You lose everything right away with those pals of yours. And come back for supper! [*She disappears.* MR. DULSKI *stands a while in front of the mirror, then finally leaves.* HESIA *runs immediately to the stove, climbs on the chair, and steals a cigar.*]

Scene II

HESIA, MELA. MELA *enters dressed the same as* HESIA. *She is pale and sick. She stops at the door shocked, then runs to* HESIA, *who sticks her tongue out at her and runs to the sofa.*

MELA: Hesia! Show me. What did you take?

HESIA: Ha . . . cigars. Big deal!

MELA: Did you steal?

HESIA: Oh, a moment ago father stole too. If a distinguished landlord can do it, why can't I?

MELA: What do you need them for?

HESIA: What for? I will smoke them.

MELA: Oh. When?

HESIA: At the school party. And then I'll go . . .

MELA: Where?

HESIA: To the Baltic, the seashore. No wait—I'll give a cigar to our cook's lover. I tell you I saw him. He's an orderly. Do you understand? An orderly to a lieutenant, very, very . . .

MELA: How can you look at such people!

HESIA: Why not? Why not? Why are you so pale?

MELA: I have a headache.

HESIA: Maybe you pinched a cigar, too?

MELA: Oh, no! I feel so weak all the time. I only want to sleep.

HESIA: You'd better dance with me. I always forget which leg to start with, dearie, and that teacher will make me feel embarrassed again. Here we go . . . My shoe came untied. Hanka! Hanka! [HANKA *enters. She is pale and changed.*]

Scene III

HESIA, HANKA, MELA.

HESIA: Tie my shoe. What's the matter? Are you sick, too? See how she looks. Mela.

HANKA: It only seems so to you, miss.

HESIA: But you can hardly walk. Now you can go. [HANKA *leaves.* HESIA *shakes her head.*]

MELA: It's nothing strange. I know why she changed so.

HESIA: You know? Tell me!

MELA: Nothing, Hesia. It's her secret. I'm not allowed to say anything—at least not up to a certain time.

HESIA: As you wish. What kind of secrets can *she* have? Come, come, give me your hand. How do these chassés go? [*She whistles.*]

MELA: Hesia, don't whistle!

HESIA: Aha! The earth is trembling, eh? And now a waltz, my precious . . . [*She embraces* MELA. *They waltz.*]

MELA: Why do you hold me so close?

HESIA: [*Dancing.*] Because I am a man.

MELA: But I can't breathe.

HESIA: Exactly. And if I'm a woman, then . . . this. [*She puts her hand on* MELA'S *and assumes the woman's role.*] Languidly! Languidly! And then, into the eyes . . . into the eyes. I always do that.

MELA: You?

HESIA: Yes, me. I tell you students blush like beets.

MELA: Let me go.

HESIA: What's the matter with you?

MELA: I don't know, but . . .

HESIA: Well, go and play quietly, so mama doesn't come. I can't get the tempo. [*She pushes* MELA *to the piano.*] A waltz. [MELA *plays quietly.* HESIA *wants to dance, does a pas, laughs, and starts a cake walk.*] Mela, cake-walk! [MELA *quietly plays a cake walk.* HESIA *dances wildly.* ZBYSZKO *enters.*]

Scene IV

The same persons, ZBYSZKO.

ZBYSZKO: And what is that?

HESIA: [*Dancing.*] Cake walk! Cake walk! Cake walk! How about it? Bad? Material in me for a cabaret singer?

ZBYSZKO: Not only for one but two.

HESIA: [*Triumphantly.*] What about it?

ZBYSZKO: Where did you learn that?

HESIA: Ignania taught me. You know, Ignania Olbrzycka. Her brother always sits in cabarets, so he taught her, and she taught me.

ZBYSZKO: [*Ironically.*] I thought your cook taught it to you.

HESIA: Cook?

ZBYSZKO: After all, she fills in the gaps in your education.

HESIA: Why, no! No, so help me God.

ZBYSZKO: [*Passionately.*] How you lie! Huh! Everybody lies here. But at least leave God out of it.

HESIA: Are you angry again? I thought your disposition had improved. Come on, Mela, a bit more. Tell me, Zbyszko, how am I doing, your highness? Okay? [*She dances.*]

ZBYSZKO: Not like that. Bend a bit more.

HESIA: How? How? [*They both dance.*] That's good, that's nice—like flying through the air.

Scene V

The same persons, MRS. DULSKI.

MRS. DULSKI: [*Bursting into the room.*] What's going on here? What kind of ballet is this?

ZBYSZKO: I'm filling the gaps in my sister's education.

MRS. DULSKI: Hesia! How can you? What? [*To* ZBYSZKO.] With you it's always some national crisis. Either you walk like a wild pig, or you do something crazy and bring the girls into it.

ZBYSZKO: All right, all right. That's enough! Where are you tramping off to in such a parade?

MRS. DULSKI: First of all, we're not tramping.

ZBYSZKO: Your legs, don't they tramp?

MRS. DULSKI: It's not decent; one does not speak about legs.

ZBYSZKO: And is it decent to dress girls like ballerinas? And such transparent material!

MRS. DULSKI: They're children. They can dress that way.

ZBYSZKO: Some children! They're girls to the tips of their toes.

MRS. DULSKI: All the girls from good homes go to dancing lessons dressed like that.

ZBYSZKO: Let them practice, let them practice.

MRS. DULSKI: For what? For what?

ZBYSZKO: When you grow up, you'll dress for a ball with your top bare. Now, as a naive child, it's your bottom.

MRS. DULSKI: Zbyszko! Silence! How dare you? [*To* MELA.] Why are you so pale?

ZBYSZKO: What's strange about that? She's cold.

[*It is getting dark.*]

MELA: I have a headache, mama. I don't want to go.

MRS. DULSKI: Show me your tongue. White. You ate something again. [*She puts her hand on* MELA's *forehead.*] A fever. Well, with you it's . . . Maybe something hurts?

MELA: It hurts me here.

MRS. DULSKI: Your left shoulder? Put a plaster on it. There's one over there already used by your father. And take off your clothes.

ZBYSZKO: Take off what? She's already undressed. She should put on her clothes.

MRS. DULSKI: Hesia, your coat! Gloves!

ZBYSZKO: Are you going for a walk? With her like that? They may arrest you yet.

MRS. DULSKI: Good heavens! I can't take any more! And don't light the lamps yet. [*To* ZBYSZKO.] Are you going out?

ZBYSZKO: No.

MRS. DULSKI: Then look after the stove. We'll be back in an hour. Mela, go and change your clothes. [HESIA *and* MRS. DULSKI *leave.* MELA *goes to her room.*]

Scene VI

ZBYSZKO *alone, later* HANKA. ZBYSZKO *stands motionless for a while. Then he stretches his hands in front of him with a lazy, bored movement. He comes back to the stove, opens the stove door with his foot, pushes the armchair closer to the stove, sits down and stays there quietly with a cigarette glued to his lips, his hand hanging down. A red light is on him. He is tired and sad. The door opens quietly.* HANKA *slips into the room. She sees him, approaches him, kneels down, and with dog-like humbleness delicately kisses his hand. He strokes her head mechanically, not looking at her.*

ZBYSZKO: Well, it's all right, all right.

HANKA: Sir, I . . .

ZBYSZKO: What? What do you want?

HANKA: I'm going . . . where you told me.

ZBYSZKO: Ah, yes. Go, go. And don't be afraid. Only speak out boldly and clearly, tell what happened and how. [HANKA *kneels motionless wrapped in her shawl.*] Well, what are you waiting for?

HANKA: I don't know. It's . . . a . . . um . . .

ZBYSZKO: Oh don't hesitate. Go. They'll come back.

HANKA: I'll go. [*She leaves slowly. There is the sound of her closing the door heavily.*]

Scene VII

ZYBSZKO *and* MELA *in a tiny bodice, her head wrapped up. She approaches* ZBYSZKO *quietly and sits down on the small stool opposite him.*

MELA: [*Bashfully.*] Zbyszko!

ZBYSZKO: Didn't you go to bed?

MELA: I can't. I feel even worse. Am I disturbing you?

ZBYSZKO: No. Of all our family you're the most bearable. Maybe it's because you're sick that there's something nicer in you, something different from the others.

MELA: Something different? And you think it's because I'm sick?

ZBYSZKO: Yes. You don't have much vital strength, so you don't go through life elbowing your way but you steal up, you know?

MELA: Yes. I also think I step out of others' way, that any moment somebody will push me, that . . .

ZBYSZKO: It's bad. Miss Dulski should get ahead that way, you know. Somebody pushes you, you push him. That should be our principle. As much room as possible. *Für die obere zehn tausend Millionen Koltunen!*

MELA: [*Looking at him for a while.*] Zbyszko, why do you dislike us all so?

ZBYSZKO: "Dislike" isn't strong enough. I hate you all, myself included.

MELA: You hate yourself, too. I on the other hand . . . Let me talk with you a bit, will you? At dusk I would give everything for a good, easy, quiet conversation with someone. Only it's impossible in our house. Here it's like a sawmill. Mama says that she works. But you can work with your mind too, right, Zybszko? [*She slips down on the floor in front of him, so that the light from the stove shines on them both. They are sad and depressed.*]

ZBYSZKO: Keep talking, keep talking.

MELA: You hate yourself, and I pity myself. Horrible. Nothing bad happens to me. I have father, mother, you, and Hesia. I go to school. I am not crippled. They take care of me, give me iron, massage me with water. I study everything. And yet, yet, Zbyszko, it seems to me that something is wrong with me, that somebody locks me up, that there's pressure on my throat, that . . . I can't describe it to you, but . . .

ZBYSZKO: It's bad, Mela, that you feel this way. Bad. It's best to get rid of these feelings. Soon you'll grow up, marry well, and smash the world with your elbows.

MELA: No. I'll go to a convent.

ZBYSZKO: Rubbish! The inner layer will come out. You'll be like mama.

MELA: But father doesn't go around elbowing people out of the way.

ZBYSZKO: Father chose a more convenient road. Mama elbows through the world for him, and he follows her.

MELA: [*After a while.*] All of it is somehow very sad.

ZBYSZKO: It would make a horse cry.

MELA: You always laugh at everything.

ZBYSZKO: Gallows humor.

[*A moment of silence.*]

MELA: [*Bashfully.*] Zbyszko!

ZBYSZKO: What now?

MELA: I wanted to tell you something . . . but . . . you won't be angry, will you? It's with the best intention. Because . . . when . . . I saw . . .

ZBYSZKO: What?

MELA: [*Quieter.*] You and Hanka. You shouted at me so awfully, and I just . . .

ZBYSZKO: Why do you talk about it?

MELA: Because I feel sorry for you and Hanka. I think about both of you all the time. I even pray for you. You both must be very unhappy.

ZBYSZKO: We? Why?

MELA: Oh yes. She's just a servant and you're an official in the Ministry of Finance. And you're in love with each other. It's very sad. Mama will be very much against it.

ZBYSZKO: Against it?

MELA: Why, getting married.

ZBYSZKO: Are you crazy? I and Hanka?

MELA: What does it matter that she's supposed to be of the lower class. Zygmunt August and Barbara . . .

ZBYSZKO: You are even more stupid than I thought.

MELA: Please don't abuse me. I'll be on your side. I'll teach Hanka to talk like other people do and eat with a fork, and I'll teach her everything I know until she's like us. I'll help you.

ZBYSZKO: You're a curiosity.

MELA: Only there is something that worries me very much. I don't know whether I should tell you this . . .

ZBYSZKO: Well, stammer it out.

MELA: Only don't tell Hanka. Give me your word. You see, Hanka has a fiancé at her village. Yes, it's true. But don't worry. She doesn't love him . . . He's a customs guard. I found a post card from him to Hanka. There was beautiful writing on it: "Miss Hanka, Madam! By dove I send this card to your feet and I ask why you write to me so rarely."

That's what it said. Oh! "By dove"—that's nice. But on this card there wasn't any dove but only a little pink pig and four piggies, but he wrote it from the bottom of his heart. And he must love her. Except that she writes him back, and it's not good from her side, because he writes on that card . . .

ZBYSZKO: I ask you one thing. Don't poke your nose into this business. You have a headache. Go and lie down.

MELA: But I meant well.

ZBYSZKO: I know.

MELA: [*Getting up bashfully.*] And you're not angry?

ZBYSZKO: No. Come and kiss me.

MELA: [*Kissing him.*] Then you don't hate me?

ZBYSZKO: [*Stroking her head.*] No, not now.

MELA: Thank you. It's so nice when someone speaks gently. Thank you, Zbyszko.

[*She leaves quietly for her room.* ZBYSZKO *gets up, goes to the window from which a street light shines. He leans his forehead against the windowpane and remains there.*] HANKA *enters, her face stained with tears. She is wrapped in a shawl. She approaches* ZBYSZKO *and speaks softly.*]

Scene VIII

ZBYSZKO, HANKA.

HANKA: Sir . . .

ZBYSZKO: What now? What now?

HANKA: It's like I said. [*She chokes with silent sobs.*]

ZBYSZKO: That's just great! What a break! [*He starts walking around the room.* HANKA *remains at the window in the light, looking tragic in her black shawl.*]

HANKA: What am I to do now?

ZBYSZKO: Go back home.

HANKA: Why? So my father can beat me? I won't go.

ZBYSZKO: Besides, don't blubber. There's still plenty of time. Something may still happen.

HANKA: But fortune tellers always got the worst for people like me. The worst always happens to me. Just what I needed. O God! God! All I got left to do is drown myself.

ZBYSZKO: That would be a great help.

HANKA: Death helps everything.

ZBYSZKO: Stupid, that's what you are.

HANKA: But . . . [*She cries.*]

ZBYSZKO: Stop it! Don't cry or I'll get angry.

HANKA: [*She covers herself with her shawl and tries to suppress the sobs. There is a long period of silence.*] Sir, what am I to do now?

ZBYSZKO: [*He looks at her for a while, then goes to his room.*] Such luck! Such rotten luck!

[HANKA *bursts into spasmatic sobs and nestles close to the wall.* MELA *tip toes out of her room.*]

Scene IX

MELA, HANKA. MELA *goes up to* HANKA *and stops in front of her. She is embarrassed.*

MELA: Hanka, I heard. Zbyszko was angry with you about something, wasn't he?

HANKA: No.

MELA: But I heard. I'm afraid it's because of me. Probably because of that fiancé you have in your village. But why did you hide it? Only now you have to stop writing to him. Why do you look at me in such a way? I know everything. [HANKA *looks at* MELA *ter-*

rified.] Well, everything that concerns you and Zbyszko, you know. [HANKA *covers her face with the shawl.*] And you needn't be afraid. I'll be on your side. And I'll win father over to your side too. Everything will change, and when the wedding is set . . .

HANKA: What are you saying, miss? Who would marry me now?

MELA: What do you mean—who?

HANKA: Well, who would take somebody else's child?

MELA: [*Surprised.*] Somebody else's child? What are you talking about, Hanka? Are you a widow already, that you have a child? And you haven't told this to ZBYSZKO . . .

HANKA: [*After a pause.*] What are you talking, miss, that you know everything!

MELA: Why, you and Zbyszko. It won't be a suitable marriage, but that can't be helped. [HANKA *is silent. She bites her shawl and looks at the floor.*] Why don't you say something, Hanka? Why do you keep on crying? After all, I only want to help. Don't cry! It will all get better somehow.

HANKA: [*Crying violently.*] Nothing will get better. I'm cursed. Bad luck . . . Oh, why was I born?

MELA: My God! Don't cry, Hanka.

HANKA: I wish I had broken my legs before I came to this house!

MELA: Hanka! Don't cry. My heart will break. [*She bends over* HANKA.]

HANKA: Let me go, miss.

Scene X

MELA, HANKA, MRS. JULIASIEWICZ.

MRS. JULIASIEWICZ: Is anybody home? The door to the kitchen is open. [*She notices* MELA *and* HANKA.] What are you doing in the dark? [HANKA *runs away.*] What have you to do with the servant, Mela?

MELA: [*Excitedly.*] I don't have anything to do with her, only this is something entirely different. Hanka is very unhappy, and I am consoling her.

MRS. JULIASIEWICZ: Better to light the lamp. [MELA *lights the lamp.*] And why is Hanka so unhappy?

MELA: Oh, it's a horrible story.

MRS. JULIASIEWICZ: Tell me, Mela.

MELA: I can't, auntie. I just can't. But it's horrible. It may end up just awful.

MRS. JULIASIEWICZ: The best thing is to tell me. Maybe I can do something.

MELA: It's true. You're so smart, auntie. You can manage mama the best.

[*They sit at the table under the lamp.*]

MRS. JULIASIEWICZ: And why is mama going to have something to do with it?

MELA: Why not? She'll be the main one. [*After a pause.*] I'll tell you everything, auntie, like in confession. But, auntie, if you betray me, that I was the one who . . . then I just don't know. Auntie! Auntie! Something bad happened here. Zbyszko fell in love with Hanka.

MRS. JULIASIEWICZ: [*Bursting out laughing.*] That's all?

MELA: Auntie, don't laugh, auntie. God knows how it will turn out because mama won't agree to marriage. You'll see, auntie.

MRS. JULIASIEWICZ: First of all, where did you learn this?

MELA: I saw them, by accident—I swear it! I closed my eyes as soon as I could.

MRS. JULIASIEWICZ: It would have been better if you closed them before. What did you see?

MELA: Auntie, they have to get married. They're already kissing each other!

MRS. JULIASIEWICZ: [*Laughing.*] Well, if they're already kissing each other . . .

MELA: Yes, yes. Since I saw it, I can't sleep any more. Each time I remember it, something shakes me in such a strange way. And I feel like crying, and I feel sad and nice too. But that's me. But mama will surely curse Zbyszko.

MRS. JULIASIEWICZ: Don't worry, my darling. Mama won't curse Zbyszko.

MELA: If only that was all there was to it, but there are many more complications. There is the customs guard in the village and besides . . . I don't know exactly . . . there is somebody else's child.

MRS. JULIASIEWICZ: Somebody else's child?

MELA: Well, yes. Hanka said so.

MRS. JULIASIEWICZ: [*Interested.*] Come on, what did she say?

MELA: I was telling her, "You will get married," I supposed with Zbyszko, I kept thinking. And she didn't cry but wailed and screamed, "Who would take me now with somebody else's child!"

MRS. JULIASIEWICZ: She said so?

MELA: Auntie, I don't lie. Only I can't put it all together. Do you understand it?

MRS. JULIASIEWICZ: I understand. I understand.

MELA: [*Leaning against the table.*] Explain it to me, auntie dear.

MRS. JULIASIEWICZ: No, miss. I won't explain it to you. Only remember, Mela—keep your tongue behind your teeth. Not a word to anybody about it. Not a word. And don't peep at them any more. If you happen to see something, close your eyes.

MELA: And will you take care of it, auntie?

MRS. JULIASIEWICZ: Maybe.

MELA: My good auntie. They may run away or kill themselves. Such a thing happened in Kiev. Quiet! It's Zbyszko.

Scene XI

The same persons, ZBYSZKO. ZBYSZKO *is dressed to go out.*

MRS. JULIASIEWICZ: How are you? Are you going out?

ZBYSZKO: Yes.

MRS. JULIASIEWICZ: Are you going to let off steam again?

ZBYSZKO: Again. That's right.

MRS. JULIASIEWICZ: You've stayed at home more lately.

ZBYSZKO: Obviously I've had enough of it.

MRS. JULIASIEWICZ: A shame. You look better. You put on some weight.

MELA: Zbyszko, everyone will be back soon. We'll have tea.

ZBYSZKO: Don't wait for me.

MELA: Mama will be angry again.

ZBYSZKO: Leave me alone.

MRS. JULIASIEWICZ: You could be more polite.

ZBYSZKO: What for?

MRS. JULIASIEWICZ: Even with me you behave so . . .

ZBYSZKO: My dear, one time you want to be treated rough, you almost ask for it. Another time you want to be treated with respect. Make up your mind—matron or coquette.

MRS. JULIASIEWICZ: [*Angry.*] It's best for me not to talk with such a brute.

ZBYSZKO: That's right. And stop putting so much make-up on your face, because you look like a house repainted to receive Caesar. Adieu.

MRS. JULIASIEWICZ: Yes! And watch out that you're not sorry for your brutality.

ZBYSZKO: I'm never sorry for anything! [*He leaves.*]

MELA: He's angry again. Just like before. And he and Hanka quarreled so. Yes, they did. Oh, mama is coming through the kitchen.

Scene XII

MRS. DULSKI, HESIA, MRS. JULIASIEWICZ, MELA, *later* MR. DULSKI.

MRS. DULSKI: [*To* MRS. JULIASIEWICZ.] How do you do? I'm completely upset.

MRS. JULIASIEWICZ: What happened?

MRS. DULSKI: In the streetcar. Another quarrel. When Hesia sits down, she looks like a child less than a meter tall. So I told her to sit up . . .

HESIA: Oh, mama please . . .

MRS. DULSKI: She stretches herself up out of spite, and right after that we have a scene with the conductor with everybody watching.

MRS. JULIASIEWICZ: All because of a cent or two.

MRS. DULSKI: The man who doesn't respect a penny is worthless. Hanka, set the table! We'll have tea here now, because the stove in the dining room gets worse and worse.

MRS. JULIASIEWICZ: Why don't you repair it?

MRS. DULSKI: You think I'm a fool? I won't live here next year anyhow; I'll just rent it to somebody. Then the tenant will repair the stove for me. I'm going to change into a dressing gown. Hesia, go change your clothes. Mela, serve tea. [*She leaves.* HANKA *sets the table with* MRS. JULIASIEWICZ *observing her.*]

HESIA: Today's lesson was awful. You didn't miss a thing. Only schoolboys, [*She runs out.*]

MRS. JULIASIEWICZ: Hanka, why are you so thin?

HANKA: I have a toothache.

MRS. JULIASIEWICZ: Toothache?

[MRS. DULSKI *enters.*]

MRS. DULSKI: [In her dressing gown.] Hurry up. Samovar, rolls . . . Will you have tea with us?

MRS. JULIASIEWICZ: Certainly.

[MELA *enters. She carries a book and a basket with sewing. A little later.* HESIA *comes in with books and notebooks. They sit down.* MRS. DULSKI *and* MRS. JULIASIEWICZ *sit at the front side of the table.*]

MRS. DULSKI: I'm happy that I'm at home now. For a woman there is nothing like home, I always say. Call Zbyszko.

MELA: Zbyszko went out.

MRS. DULSKI: Went out?

MELA: But he'll probably be right back.

MRS. JULIASIEWICZ: And you said he reformed.

MRS. DULSKI: He did. He realized that there is nothing like home and family. Something must have turned up.

MRS. JULIASIEWICZ: Nothing at all. He said he's sick of this house and the family.

MRS. DULSKI: He did?

MRS. JULIASIEWICZ: Yes, just now, though he didn't say it so clearly. What he was sick of I don't know. But he went.

HESIA: He'll go on another spree.

MRS. DULSKI: That's none of your business. I just can't cope with that boy. I pamper him so just to keep him home.

MRS. JULIASIEWICZ: [*Significantly.*] Ah, excuse me, but maybe this pampering does just the opposite.

MRS. DULSKI: I don't understand. After all, where can he feel better than in the family circle?

MRS. JULIASIEWICZ: Hm!

MRS. DULSKI: [*To* MELA.] Are you making faces at your aunt?

MRS. JULIASIEWICZ: At me? You're imagining things. And as for the family circle . . .

MRS. DULSKI: What can you know about it? You're always running off somewhere. And I'll tell you this, they're beginning to talk about you.

MRS. JULIASIEWICZ: They talk about everybody.

MRS. DULSKI: They say what you want them to.

MRS. JULIASIEWICZ: For instance?

MRS. DULSKI: That you are a coquette.

MRS. JULIASIEWICZ: Eh!

MRS. DULSKI: It's your own fault. Why doesn't anybody say that about me?

MRS. JULIASIEWICZ: [*Irritated.*] Aunt, could you please stop lecturing me in front of the girls?

MRS. DULSKI: They're children, so they don't understand. And besides, let them hear. It will be a lesson for them in the future. It will show where frivolity and popularity may lead them.

[MR. DULSKI *comes in. He greets* MRS. JULIASIEWICZ *with a wave of his hand. He takes a newspaper out of his pocket, sits at the table, and begins to read.*]

MRS. JULIASIEWICZ: [*More irritated.*] Really, aunt, you have a peculiar view of hospitality.

MRS. DULSKI: My dear, I above all have moral principles, and I keep them in mind whether here at home or . . .

MRS. JULIASIEWICZ: Does that mean my life is not moral?

MRS. DULSKI: From the outside. People always see you on the street.

MRS. JULIASIEWICZ: I can't walk on the roofs.

MRS. DULSKI: You dyed your hair red. Where did you see a decent woman with red hair?

MRS. JULIASIEWICZ: Well, that's too much.

MRS. DULSKI: Yesterday, for instance, Mrs. Krezel said . . .

MRS. JULIASIEWICZ: [*Getting up.*] Oh, that's enough already. Really, aunt, you persist in upsetting me. I don't poke my nose into your business, but maybe more things than one could be said.

MRS. DULSKI: Be my guest, be my guest. My conscience is clean and I am not afraid of the light of day.

MRS. JULIASIEWICZ: Well, it's better not to come around here in the light of day. Somebody might see more things than one. And furthermore, don't provoke me, aunt, because really . . .

MRS. DULSKI: [*Provokingly.*] Go ahead. Be my guest. Please don't be bashful on my account.

MRS. JULIASIEWICZ: I am thinking of the children.

MRS. DULSKI: Hesia, Mela, please leave the room! Felician, you too. [HESIA *and* MELA *leave.* MR. DULSKI *takes the newspaper and goes into the bedroom.*] Now, if you please, we are alone. What do you have to say?

MRS. JULIASIEWICZ: Really, aunt, you should learn about it. And I'll tell you this, too—if you go looking for dirt in my house, you should first clean your own.

MRS. DULSKI: Nothing dirty takes place in my home. And at least my house is not bandied about on the street.

MRS. JULIASIEWICZ: It will be, it will be. In due time it will be bandied plenty.

MRS. DULSKI: What do you mean?

MRS. JULIASIEWICZ: I'll explain it all when you invite me for the baptism.

MRS. DULSKI: My dear, that's a tasteless joke. Felician and I stopped that silly thinking long ago.

MRS. JULIASIEWICZ: I'm not saying you'll be the mother, but the grandmother.

MRS. DULSKI: What? How?

MRS. JULIASIEWICZ: Zbyszko arranged it.

MRS. DULSKI: Zbyszko? Zbyszko?

MRS. JULIASIEWICZ: And . . . Hanka.

MRS. DULSKI: God in heaven! What? How? You lie, you lie. You want to kill me! Good Lord! It's not enough that they took my caretaker, but now they think up something like this.

MRS. JULIASIEWICZ: Me lie? The best thing is to ask Hanka yourself.

MRS. DULSKI: Scandal! Hanka! Hanka! Come here this instant!

MRS. JULIASIEWICZ: I'd rather not listen. I'm going to the girls. And when you make sure that I didn't lie, you can ask my pardon.

MRS. DULSKI: Tomorrow morning. Hanka! Hanka!

[MRS. JULIASIEWICZ *leaves quickly.* HANKA *bursts into the room carrying laundry.*]

Scene XIII

MRS. DULSKI, HANKA.

HANKA: You called for me, missus? I'm going to mangle.

MRS. DULSKI: Hanka, answer me as you would a priest. Is it true that you . . . that you are . . . that . . . [HANKA *withdraws toward the wall and stays there motionless, eyes open wide.* MRS. DULSKI *opposite watches her fiercely.*] Answer me!

HANKA: [*With effort.*] Yes, missus.

MRS. DULSKI: Maybe you're lying? Maybe you want something.

HANKA: I don't lie.

MRS. DULSKI: As you want a priest when you die?

HANKA: As I want a priest when I die. [*A long silence.* HANKA *stands motionless leaning against the wall. Big, heavy tears run down her face.*]

MRS. DULSKI: [*After a while.*] I'll give you back your registration book. I'll pay you up to the first of next month, and you get out of here.

HANKA: I want to go away right now.

MRS. DULSKI: [*Regaining control of herself.*] That will be better. Pack your things. Put down the laundry. I cannot keep girls who do not care for their good reputation. You'll get out right away. I'm going for your registration book.

[*She goes to the bedroom.* HANKA *stands motionless for a time. Finally she wipes her face and goes toward the kitchen.* MRS. JULIASIEWICZ *comes out of the girls' room.*]

Scene XIV

MRS. JULIASIEWICZ, HANKA, *later* MELA, ZBYSZKO.

MRS. JULIASIEWICZ: Hanka!

HANKA: What?

MRS. JULIASIEWICZ: What happened?

HANKA: [*Bursting into tears.*] The missus is getting rid of me.

MRS. JULIASIEWICZ: Go and see Zbyszko.

HANKA: Aw . . . what for? But let them pay for my wrong. [*She runs into the kitchen.*]

MELA: Auntie, auntie! What happened? What happened? I'm so frightened!

MRS. JULIASIEWICZ: Go to your room and stay there.

MELA: My God, Auntie! Please don't leave them.

[MRS. JULIASIEWICZ *pushes her into the girls' room.* ZBYSZKO *enters.*]

ZBYSZKO: [*To* MRS. JULIASIEWICZ.] You here? That's strange. Your officer is waiting for you over there in front of the entrance.

MRS. JULIASIEWICZ: And what business is that of yours? You'd better watch out here, or you'll get what you deserve.

ZBYSZKO: What kind of tone is that?

MRS. JULIASIEWICZ: You'll change your tone. You'll sing a different song soon. Your doings with Hanka are out in the open.

ZBYSZKO: Oh, Goddamn!

MRS. JULIASIEWICZ: Go ahead, curse! That's a big help. Your mother is getting rid of Hanka. I'm curious what your seducer's honor will have you do for your victim. [*She laughs ironically.*]

ZBYSZKO: [*Grabbing his hat.*] You viper!

MRS. JULIASIEWICZ: I knew it. Hat in hand and bye-bye. The best solution.

ZBYSZKO: Shut up! Don't make me mad.

Scene XV

MRS. DULSKI, MRS. JULIASIEWICZ, ZBYSZKO.

MRS. DULSKI: [*Registration book in hand.*] Hanka! Ah, you're here! Don't leave. I have a bone to pick with you.

ZBYSZKO: Yes, yes. I already know what's going on. And mama, you'd show more tact if you didn't talk about it.

MRS. DULSKI: Tact? Tact? You dare speak of tact? You, who caused such a scandal under your own family roof? When it spreads to the street, we'll probably have to sell the house and move to Brzuchowice or Zamarstynow.

ZBYSZKO: It's my business.

MRS. DULSKI: You are shameless! To let things go to such a point that just anybody could throw this in my face.

MRS. JULIASIEWICZ: Oh pardon me. Just *anybody*—is that supposed to be me? That's too much. And my own aunt says so. And do you know, aunt, that I need to say only a couple of words to change that beautiful story.

MRS. DULSKI: Whatever you say will be a lie. Nobody will believe somebody like you.

MRS. JULIASIEWICZ: I am what I am, but I never did what has been done in this house. [*To* ZBYSZKO.] You should know that your mother knew about Hanka from the very beginning.

MRS. DULSKI: It's not true.

MRS. JULIASIEWICZ: Aha! It's not true? You covered your eyes and peeked through your fingers. Only now, when a big scandal hangs over everything, you jump at Zbyszko, at Hanka.

ZBYSZKO: Oh, that's a beautiful story. Why should she do that?

MRS. JULIASIEWICZ: So you would stay home.

ZBYSZKO: Aha! I understand!

MRS. DULSKI: She lies.

ZBYSZKO: She is telling the truth. It looks very much like your kind of morality.

MRS. DULSKI: [*Hitting the table with her fist.*] She lies!

MRS. JULIASIEWICZ: [*Doing the same.*] I don't lie!

ZBYSZKO: [*Doing the same.*] She is telling the truth! I feel it! I know it! This is the thing that crawls around here, so dirty, so horrid. Everything is fine as long as it doesn't come out. But who sows the wind reaps the whirlwind! [*He runs to the kitchen.*] Hanka! [MELA *and* HESIA *appear in the doorway.*]

MRS. DULSKI: Zbyszko!

ZBYSZKO: And do you want to know what I am going to do, mama? Do you want to know? I'm going to marry Hanka!

MRS. DULSKI: Good God! I'll drop in my tracks.

MELA: Mama! Forgive them! Give them your blessing!

MRS. DULSKI: Shut up!

ZBYSZKO: [*Dragging* HANKA *into the room.*] Hanka! Get rid of these rags! You're going to stay here for good.

HANKA: But the missus fired me.

ZBYSZKO: You'll stay. I'm going to marry you.

HANKA: Good Lord!

MRS. DULSKI: I won't let you.

ZBYSZKO: It won't work, mama.

MRS. JULIASIEWICZ: Zbyszko! You're out of your mind!

[MR. DULSKI *comes in and looks at them surprised.*]

MRS. DULSKI: Felician! Look! See what kind of daughter-in-law your son is giving us! [MR. DULSKI, *interested, goes up to them.*] Come on, get a move on, you father. Curse him or something. Maybe he'll recover his senses.

ZBYSZKO: It's no good. I'll do it. For once let such horror drown in its own filth.

MRS. DULSKI: For God's sake! If somebody asks me what home my daughter-in-law is from . . .

ZBYSZKO: Then say she's not from any home but a hut. That will be the worst punishment. Hanka, kneel down and ask her blessing.

HANKA: Missus, I only . . .

MRS. DULSKI: Get out! Felician, say something!

MR. DULSKI: Go to hell, all of you! [*He goes to the bedroom.*]

MRS. DULSKI: [*Falling down on the sofa.*] I can't take it. I tell you, I can't take it.

ZBYSZKO: Sit down, Hanka, right here next to mama. That's your place now. [*He forces* HANKA *onto the sofa.*]

MRS. JULIASIEWICZ: Zbyszko!

[*The bell rings.* HANKA *jumps up to open the door.*]

ZBYSZKO: Sit down! Don't move.

HANKA: I only want to open the door.

HESIA: Somebody is coming.

ZBYSZKO: [*Forcing* HANKA *back onto the sofa. He starts out, stops in the door, and says.*] Cook, open the door and say that both MRS. DULSKIs are ready to receive guests!

[*The curtain goes down.*]

ACT III

The stage shows the same room. It is morning. The blinds are up, letting in the gray light of a winter day. On a small stool at the cold stove HANKA *sits asleep, a black shawl on her head. When the curtain rises, the noise of the wind beating against the windows can be heard. A moment of silence. The only voice is* HANKA'S. *She breathes heavily and from time to time moans, "O God." The door opens.* MELA *comes in silently. She is dressed in a white, fustian skirt with a shirt and a fustian bodice thrown over her shoulders. Her hair is loose. She carries a roll and a cup of coffee. She hesitates for a moment, then rushes to the door of her parents' bedroom, listens, comes back, leans over* HANKA, *and delicately and carefully wakes her up.*

Scene I

MELA, HANKA, *later* HESIA.

MELA: Andzia, Andzia, wake up.

HANKA: Ha? What?

MELA: Wake up, my poor Andzia.

HANKA: Ah, it's the young lady. I'll do it right away . . . milk . . . [*She rubs her eyes.*]

MELA: No, no. You won't go for milk any more. The cook has already brought it in. I took care of breakfast.

HANKA: And the missus?

MELA: Mama feels weak. She is lying down. Have some coffee. Drink it. And eat the roll.

HANKA: [*Regaining her memory.*] Ah . . . yeah, yeah. I forgot. Now I remember. [*She starts to cry.*] O God! O dear God!

MELA: Why are you crying? Everything is all right now. The worst is over. Mama already knows everything. She doesn't want to permit it, but she must. Now you and Zbyszko only have to be firm and overcome everything with your love. Mama herself will be moved.

HANKA: I'll go make fires in the stoves.

MELA: No, no. Let them alone. It's better for you not to do things any more. Because if you start being a servant again, it will be still worse. Sit down here quietly and wait for what will come.

HANKA: And the laundry ain't been mangled.

MELA: Don't bother with that. A chamber maid will come now, and she'll do all of it for you. Now you are Zbyszko's fiancée, so you can't go to the mangle or make fires in the stoves. Please drink your coffee.

HANKA: Thank you, miss. I can't. After what happened yesterday I'm so . . . [*She blows her nose.*] O God!

MELA: [*Squatting down in front of her.*] My Andzia, I know it is unpleasant, but it can't be helped. You'll see that you will be very happy with Zbyszko yet. Dress differently. I'll rub lotion on your hands. I'll teach you to write nicely. You won't do anything.

HANKA: Eh! Them that don't work rots.

MELA: Well, you will have other things to do. Besides, I'll always be with you and near you. I won't marry anybody because I'm not healthy, and mama says, for marriage a person has to have the health of a horse. And I also wanted to tell you about the child that you mentioned and that I don't understand—if you were already married and are afraid because men aren't supposed to be very eager to marry widows who have children, you needn't be afraid. I'll take care of the child and bring it up. And whatever mama gives me as a trousseau or dowry, I'll give away to the child. I decided that last night. I wanted to go to a convent because it must be silent there and nice behind those walls when the bell rings on a May morning. But a person can also have silence in the outside world. And I'd rather sacrifice myself for you. Well, eat the roll. Eat it. And because of this, you must be very good to me and address me as "my dear, good, beloved Mela." Come on, repeat it.

HANKA: What are you saying, miss? What are you saying?

MELA: Call me Mela and I'll call you Andzia.

HANKA: But I'm Hanka.

MELA: No, as Zbyszko's wife you're Andzia.

HESIA: [*She bursts into the room in one stocking, jumping on one leg.*] Great . . . it's almost nine. Silence at home. No school? Great!

MELA: Be quiet. Mama is sick.

HESIA: Today the whole house is sick. Nobody goes to work but daddy, of course. [*To* HANKA.] What now, *belle soeur!* Ah . . . hee hee . . . Hi, scarecrow!

MELA: Hesia, how can you?

HESIA: Do you take this seriously? It's a complete comedy. Chaos, nothing more. Wow, it's cold here. No fire in the stove. That's what they mean by a family crisis. [*Suddenly she sits next to* HANKA.] Tell me, did you make the first move toward Zbyszko or did he start it?

HANKA: That the young lady ain't afraid of God . . .

HESIA: Oh, you already learned to take God's name in vain. You're not even a member of the family yet. Hee hee! Can you imagine, you clod, that Zbyszko will really marry you? [HANKA *cries.*]

MELA: Hesia, don't hurt her.

HESIA: No, no. I even promise to be your bridesmaid and lead the blushing bride to the altar. Look, Mela, how my legs have grown since yesterday.

MELA: You'll catch cold.

Scene II

The same persons, MRS. DULSKI. *She is pale, in her dressing gown, her head bandaged.*

MRS. DULSKI: What's going on? Why are you here? Not in school?

HESIA: There's nobody to take us.

HANKA: I'll go with you.

MRS. DULSKI: You? Take the young ladies? Come, come. Go get dressed, both of you.

HESIA: But school isn't important today, mama.

MRS. DULSKI: Of course. Everything's like that. And it's because of . . . [MELA *kisses her mother's hand.*] What do you want?

MELA: Mama dear, forgive them! Don't be angry! All her life she'll . . .

MRS. DULSKI: Please don't get involved in this. [MELA *goes to her room with her head down.* MRS. DULSKI *speaks to* HANKA] You go to the small room where we keep the laundry. Sit there and don't move till I call you. Not a word with the cook or anybody, understand? Your godmother, that Mrs. Tadrach who did our laundry twice, does she still live on St. Joseph Street?

HANKA: Yes, ma'am.

MRS. DULSKI: All right, now go. [HANKA *goes to the main bedroom. To* HESIA.] Did you send that message to your aunt?

HESIA: I did. And I also told the caretaker to ask auntie to come here right away because mama wanted her to. [MRS. DULSKI *sits down, worried.*] Mama, do you want me to do the dusting? [MRS. DULSKI *makes a gesture of indifference. A period of silence.*] Mama, will Zbyszko really marry that thing?

MRS. DULSKI: Leave me alone!

HESIA: I thought it would be impossible too, even if only for us. Would anybody decent want to marry me or Mela?

MRS. DULSKI: Leave me alone!

HESIA: After all, Mela is less important because she wants to be a spinster anyhow, but me . . .

MRS. DULSKI: I'm telling you to leave me alone or else.

HESIA: Only I don't understand, mama, how come you didn't see it? I knew it a long time ago. I . . .

Scene III

MRS. DULSKI, HESIA, ZBYSZKO. ZBYSZKO *is dressed to go outside. He paces up and down the room.*

ZBYSZKO: Where is Hanka? [*Silence.*] I'm asking, where is Hanka?

HESIA: The Bride of Lammermoor is doing the dishes.

ZBYSZKO: Please don't use her for any more kitchen work. Where did Hanka sleep today?

HESIA: On the stool by the side of the stove, very decently indeed.

ZBYSZKO: We ought to take better care of her. [*Silence.*] Because . . . if . . . well, anyhow, I'm going out. I'll be back soon. I have to set things in order.

HESIA: [*Laughing.*] Put a canopy bed in the sitting room.

ZBYSZKO: Shut up!

HESIA: I don't want to. I don't want to. Cake walk! Cake walk! [*She does a few steps.*] Hanka, the sweet bride, the girl with the face like a raspberry . . .

ZBYSZKO: Aw, go . . . [*He leaves quickly.*]

HESIA: Horrible! I've never seen anything like that as long as I live. [*She listens.*] The care-taker is in the kitchen. I'll find out. Only you know, mama, I doubt if auntie will come because yesterday she was pretty angry.

MRS. DULSKI: Go on, go on. [HESIA *goes out.* MRS. DULSKI *fixes the bandage on her head. She hears the carpets being dusted, listens, jumps up, runs to the window, opens it and shouts in an entirely different voice.*] No dusting carpets, no dusting in the back yard. It's not allowed.

HESIA: Auntie said she'll be here right away.

MRS. DULSKI: Now go and get dressed.

HESIA: And later maybe a walk outside, right?

MRS. DULSKI: What's gotten into you? Such a scandal on our hands, and she thinks about a walk.

HESIA: Well, all right, all right. I'm going! [*She runs to her room.*]

Scene IV

MRS. DULSKI, MRS. JULIASIEWICZ. MRS. JULIASIEWICZ *is in a morning coat. She speaks with dignity.*

MRS. JULIASIEWICZ: Did you wish to see me?

MRS. DULSKI: Yes.

MRS. JULIASIEWICZ: Strictly speaking, I shouldn't have come here after such an insult, but in an emergency, a person should forgive. What do you want?

MRS. DULSKI: [*Bursting out.*] Have pity! Help me! Save me from this situation. Such a mar-riage for Zbyszko is certain ruin. How could I look other people in the face?

MRS. JULIASIEWICZ: My dear aunt, this is your own brew. I told you to let Hanka go.

MRS. DULSKI: But when I explained why I kept her, you yourself agreed that it was better. I did it, after all, for his own good. I couldn't stand to see how he behaved. People often do it. I wasn't the first nor the last.

MRS. JULIASIEWICZ: Yes, certainly.

MRS. DULSKI: Advise me! Help me! You're clever as a thief. You'll think of something. First of all, take that woman, that Hanka, to your place. I can't get rid of her, because she'll speak of us around town. At your place you can keep an eye on her so she won't go shooting off her mouth.

MRS. JULIASIEWICZ: Oh no, not that. No thanks for such a piece of furniture. With such people you never know how the wind blows. But we certainly ought to do something, because it's very unpleasant for us, too. My husband couldn't even eat supper when he learned of it. Does she have a family?

MRS. DULSKI: Here she has only her godmother, that washer-woman.

MRS. JULIASIEWICZ: We have to get her here.

MRS. DULSKI: I sent the cook for her.

MRS. JULIASIEWICZ: Maybe something about Hanka will come out. Maybe she fooled around in her village. If Zbyszko learns of that . . . though if you ask me, Zbyszko did it all just to spite you.

MRS. DULSKI: To spite me? His mother? That's the thanks you get for bearing children. I took such good care of him, took him to Rabka when he graduated. It was me I suppose . . . well, I steered him to the Ministry of Finance. And now, and now . . . [*She weeps.*]

MRS. JULIASIEWICZ: Calm yourself, aunt. That won't help at all. We have to do some-thing. What does she say?

MRS. DULSKI: What can she say? Nothing.

MRS. JULIASIEWICZ: We're still in luck that she's so stupid; otherwise she could get stubborn. Give her some vodka and bread and butter.

MRS. DULSKI: What?

MRS. JULIASIEWICZ: I know very well what I'm saying. You catch flies with honey, not vinegar.

Scene V

MRS. DULSKI, MRS. JULIASIEWICZ, MRS. TADRACH

MRS. TADRACH: Praised be Jesus Christ.

MRS. DULSKI: Oh, it's you. [*To* MRS. JULIASIEWICZ.] It's the washer-woman.

MRS. TADRACH: Good day, madam. And what is it to be, another big wash?

MRS. JULIASIEWICZ: Let me handle this, aunt. [*To* MRS. TADRACH.] No, my dear woman, we called you for quite a different reason.

MRS. TADRACH: I'm at your service.

MRS. JULIASIEWICZ: It's about Hanka.

MRS. TADRACH: Ah . . .

MRS. JULIASIEWICZ: Look, this is what happened. Hanka has a chance to get an excellent husband.

MRS. DULSKI: What are you . . . ?

MRS. JULIASIEWICZ: Wait, aunt—an excellent husband. And because he is an honest craftsman, my aunt's foster child, we want to know first of all, is she a decent girl? Because in such a small town all kinds of things go on, as you know. Mrs. Tadrach.

MRS. TADRACH: Yes, yes, that's true. Yes, missus. I suppose . . . you got a right to know.

MRS. JULIASIEWICZ: Exactly. Now about Hanka, how did she behave herself at home? Just tell us the truth under oath, like in confession, because this is a serious matter.

MRS. TADRACH: I suppose. About Hanka? Ah, missus, that girl was like glass—not a scratch on her.

MRS. JULIASIEWICZ: Could you swear to it?

MRS. TADRACH: Before the Holy Sacrament. I could swear for her like for myself.

MRS. JULIASIEWICZ: Well, but what about that customs guard?

MRS. TADRACH: That's different. He's engaged to her. But as for that one, oho!—only there was no money, I suppose, for setting up a household, so it's going slow. But it's all honest and honorable. The priest himself could tell you.

MRS. JULIASIEWICZ: And here, in the city?

MRS. TADRACH: Ah, here. You ladies probably know because, I suppose, the girl is here in your care.

[*A moment of silence.*]

MRS. JULIASIEWICZ: Perhaps you'd like some vodka, Mrs. Tadrach?

MRS. TADRACH: Thank you so much, missus. I promised to stay away from vodka. [*She laughs.*]

MRS. JULIASIEWICZ: [*Also laughing.*] And from liqueur too?

MRS. TADRACH: Well, I suppose . . .

MRS. JULIASIEWICZ: [*To* MRS. DULSKI.] Anielka, give us something sweet. [MRS. DULSKI *leaves.*] Mrs. Tadrach, do you think that Hanka can marry this other man with a clean conscience?

MRS. TADRACH: Missus, if he likes her, he won't be particular. Only society people have such ideas. And besides, how do I know?

[MRS. DULSKI *comes back with a glass of liqueur and puts it in front of* MRS. TADRACH.]

MRS. JULIASIEWICZ: Drink it up!

MRS. TADRACH: Thank you so much, thank you so much. [*She drinks.*] Hee hee hee.
MRS. JULIASIEWICZ: Is it good?
MRS. TADRACH: So good I'm wobbly.
MRS. JULIASIEWICZ: So . . .

Scene VI

The same persons, ZBYSZKO.

MRS. TADRACH: Good day to you, sir, good day.
ZBYSZKO: Wait a minute. Wasn't it you who once took my suit to the tailor's?
MRS. TADRACH: That's me, sir. After the last wash.
ZBYSZKO: Are you a relative to Hanka's?
MRS. TADRACH: Her godmother.
ZBYSZKO: Oh, how convenient. I would like to inform you that I am going to marry Hanka.
MRS. TADRACH: Sir, you are making fun of me!
ZBYSZKO: I am going to get married. [*He looks at* MRS. DULSKI.] I am going to get married and very fast. I went to find out about the formalities. Where was Hanka baptized? We need her birth certificate at once. Do you understand? Come over tomorrow and everything will be settled. [*He goes to his room.*]
MRS. TADRACH: In the name of the Father and the Son . . . Maybe the young master is crazy or very sensitive about his honor.
MRS. JULIASIEWICZ: What do you mean by that?
MRS. TADRACH: Well, missus, I'm not blind. After all, I see how things are. It was enough to see how bad Hanka looks. And she cried all the time and dropped by my place. I kept telling her, "Don't cry. The master is a gentleman. He had good parents. He'll provide for you." But to marry her . . .
MRS. DULSKI: Do you really think I will consent to this marriage! Such an honest thing. If the young master wants it, he must be inspired by God not to wrong an orphan. Her decency was her only dowry, and today nobody will take her because she can't cover her shame with wealth, and you can pull the wool over people's eyes only with money.
MRS. JULIASIEWICZ: Yes, you're right, with money. One more glass? Anielcia!
MRS. DULSKI: I don't have any more.
MRS. JULIASIEWICZ: [*Leading* MRS. DULSKI *aside.*] Aunt, maybe we could offer money.
MRS. DULSKI: Good Lord, to think only of money.
MRS. JULIASIEWICZ: It can't be helped.
MRS. DULSKI: You'd better talk with Zbyszko once more, my dear. Maybe he'll listen to you. God help us—to pay her! If he says that he doesn't want to get married, then everything will be settled. Talk to him.
MRS. JULIASIEWICZ: All right, but you know it will be difficult. [*To* MRS. TADRACH.] So you say that money . . .
MRS. TADRACH: It's basic, missus. That's the way the world is now. One Judas sells another for money. Oh, the times! No feed for cattle, no human decency.
MRS. JULIASIEWICZ: You're right. I must discuss this matter further with Mrs. Dulski.
MRS. TADRACH: About Hanka? What is to discuss? The young folks want each other. You won't be tough, missus. After all, even nobility sometimes marry somebody lower class. And besides, Hanka is not just anybody. She may be a bricklayer's daughter, but she's from a settled family.
MRS. DULSKI: Go to the dining room, Mrs. Tadrach, and wait there till we call you.
MRS. TADRACH: Good day to you, missus. I'm going, placing myself in the hands of Jesus. Good day. Please don't be hard, dear mother-in-law. [*She leaves.*]

Scene VII

MRS. DULSKI, MRS. JULIASIEWICZ, MELA.

MRS. DULSKI: Did you hear that? Mother-in-law! Look how fast she becomes familiar. I feel sick. It's too much.

MRS. JULIASIEWICZ: I'll talk with Zbyszko. Go to your room, aunt, please.

MRS. DULSKI: Help me. Do everything possible. Tell him that it will kill his parents, that he'll be disinherited, that he won't ever get a cent, that . . .

MRS. JULIASIEWICZ: All right, all right, I know. Just leave me here alone.

MRS. DULSKI: I'm going, I'm going. Do everything you can, my dear. I feel faint. [*She leaves.*]

MELA: [*In the door.*] Psst, psst, auntie!

MRS. JULIASIEWICZ: And what do you want?

MELA: What about mama? Does she agree?

MRS. JULIASIEWICZ: Mela, please go to your room and stay there!

MELA: Ah God, God! What's going to happen? [*She disappears.*]

Scene VIII

MRS. JULIASIEWICZ, ZBYSZKO. *She hesitates, then goes to the door of* ZBYSZKO*'s room.*

MRS. JULIASIEWICZ: Zbyszko! Come here a moment.

ZBYSZKO: What for?

MRS. JULIASIEWICZ: Just come here. I can hardly go into your room. I'm too old for that, and too young, too.

ZBYSZKO: [*In the door.*] Just what do you want?

MRS. JULIASIEWICZ: First of all, don't look at me like an enemy, because I'm not your enemy in spite of the way you treat me. And besides, I have the impression that you'll be glad to talk with somebody who has common sense and sees your behavior in perspective. Come here, don't pout. After all, it won't hurt to talk about things.

ZBYSZKO: [*Entering the room.*] If it's about Hanka, then there is no discussion. Everything is set, and that's final.

MRS. JULIASIEWICZ: Naturally. And don't imagine that I'm against your project. Just the opposite. Since you want to "right, the wrong," I'm only trying to support you. Your mother wanted me to take your fiancée to my place, but . . .

ZBYSZKO: Well?

MRS. JULIASIEWICZ: I refused.

ZBYSZKO: Why?

MRS. JULIASIEWICZ: I have a husband and *c'est le premier pas qui coûte.* Where there's no sense of morality as with that girl, one can never be sure about anything.

ZBYSZKO: Is that all you have to say?

MRS. JULIASIEWICZ: No, wait. Something has to be done with Hanka. She won't work in another house. Put her in a boarding house—Oh, God, no!—such a decayed and debauched milieu, such instincts before the wedding day! Perhaps a school, but I doubt if they'd take her, and besides . . .

ZBYSZKO: You're just making fun of her.

MRS. JULIASIEWICZ: I doubt if your mother can keep her for long in the storage room. So what are you going to do? [ZBYSZKO *walks silently around the room. She looks at him.*] And of course any contact with the outside world is out of the question.

ZBYSZKO: I don't care about the outside world.

MRS. JULIASIEWICZ: You're right. I don't either. But we live in constant contact with others.

ZBYSZKO: I spit on contact!

MRS. JULIASIEWICZ: Naturally. Only you have to be the whole world to each other. I don't know her. She must have a high native intelligence. [ZBYSZKO *is silent.*] You will develop it, so there are no moral problems, only material ones.

ZBYSZKO: I don't care about them.

MRS. JULIASIEWICZ: Easy enough to say. But your salary is sixty zloties a month. And besides that, you have a lot of debts. A lawsuit hangs over your head. Can three people live on that? It's poverty. Hanka won't earn anything, unless she's going to be a servant to herself, and even then . . . And you, accustomed to spending your own money and others' too . . .

ZBYSZKO: [*Sitting down in the armchair.*] It's going to be like I said.

MRS. JULIASIEWICZ: Yes, but the main thing is money. And think—what are you going to live on? You can do some extra work evenings. My husband will give you some things to copy at home. But even that . . .

ZBYSZKO: Leave me alone!

MRS. JULIASIEWICZ: Let's be logical. An apartment, one bedroom and small kitchen costs twenty-five to thirty zloties. For food you need at least a gulden, and that's on the poverty level. But if you're in love . . . So there's your entire salary. And what about the rest?

ZBYSZKO: I'll borrow money.

MRS. JULIASIEWICZ: Your mother will announce she's not responsible, and nobody will give you a cent. And your parents may live thirty years yet. You'll be a poor man a long time, a very long time, but . . .

ZBYSZKO: Leave me alone!

MRS. JULIASIEWICZ: Dear God! If one could really just say, "Leave me alone!" But life jumps at your neck like a hydra and strangles you. [*She goes to him and sits on the arm of the armchair.*] Zbyszko! Look at me. You regret what you've done.

ZBYSZKO: Let me go!

MRS. JULIASIEWICZ: I won't. This is something more serious than making your mother mad.

ZBYSZKO: It was not to make her mad. I wanted just once to destroy whatever it is that's black, the soul of evil within these walls. I wanted just once to fight that elusive substance and . . .

MRS. JULIASIEWICZ: So you started fighting. You struggled, showed your fangs, and now you have to give up.

ZBYSZKO: I don't have to. I won't.

MRS. JULIASIEWICZ: Do you have enough strength to continue the fight? [ZBYSZKO *is silent.*] Aha, aha! You don't even answer. You're already completely exhausted. This one fight defeated you, and a whole lifetime . . .

ZBYSZKO: O you, you!

MRS. JULIASIEWICZ: What about me? My aunt said I'm clever as a thief. She's right. I accept life and steal the best parts of it. That's the smartest thing to do. Fight? Don Quixote! It's ridiculous. Besides, as you said yourself, we all kick the bucket sooner or later.

ZBYSZKO: You know how to awake the Philistine in me.

MRS. JULIASIEWICZ: It was never asleep even for a moment. Don't fight it. You know that's no good. Besides, what do you want from your mother? She loves you, she gave you life.

ZBYSZKO: Ha ha! I didn't ask for it.

MRS. JULIASIEWICZ: That's a cliché. She brought you up by her morals as best she could.

ZBYSZKO: As best she could! It's frightening to listen to you.

MRS. JULIASIEWICZ: By her morals? Everything she did was for love of you. And now she's weeping, Zbyszko, weeping.

ZBYSZKO: Huh.

MRS. JULIASIEWICZ: Don't say, "Huh." She is your mother. [ZBYSZKO *dejected, sits on the armchair. She goes to him.*] Well, what are you going to do about it, Zbyszko? [*He is silent.*] Come on, come on.

ZBYSZKO: There's still time.

MRS. JULIASIEWICZ: Oh no. Such things must be done at once, right away. You'll see that you'll feel better yourself when you finish this.

ZBYSZKO: [*Quietly.*] But how?

MRS. JULIASIEWICZ: We'll find a way.

ZBYSZKO: There'll be a scandal.

MRS. JULIASIEWICZ: You see? And you were saying you don't care about the world. [*A moment of silence.*] So you won't get married? [*He is silent.*] And you will ask your mother's forgiveness?

ZBYSZKO: What for?

MRS. JULIASIEWICZ: Do it. You offended her very deeply. She's sick, she feels miserable. [*She goes to the door.*] You can come in now.

ZBYSZKO: But no harm will come to her because of it?

MRS. JULIASIEWICZ: Relax. I'll take care of everything. Come in.

Scene IX

ZBYSZKO, MRS. DULSKI, MRS. JULIASIEWICZ.

MRS. JULIASIEWICZ: Aunt, Zbyszko takes back what he said. He has returned to his senses and asks your forgiveness.

[MRS. DULSKI *weeps.*]

ZBYSZKO: [*He goes up to her, kisses her hand, and speaks to her quietly.*] Forgive me, mama . . . oh Goddamn, goddamn!

MRS. DULSKI: [*To* MRS. JULIASIEWICZ] You see, he's cursing again.

MRS. JULIASIEWICZ: It's nothing. It doesn't matter.

ZBYSZKO: [*Bursting out.*] It does! It does! It matters!

MRS. JULIASIEWICZ: Do you take back what you said?

ZBYSZKO: Yes, yes. I'll be just like I was. Oh, you can be proud of me. [*With a nervous outburst.*] I'll be such a scoundrel! Such a scoundrel!

MRS. JULIASIEWICZ: Until you get married. You'll marry well, a good girl from a decent family.

ZBYSZKO: Until I marry well with a dowry, a house, a devil. [*He runs to his room.*]

MRS. DULSKI: God! O God!

MRS. JULIASIEWICZ: Let him blow off steam. The main thing is done. Now we have to work on her. Are you giving me *carte blanche?*

MRS. DULSKI: I don't understand.

MRS. JULIASIEWICZ: [*Going to the door.*] Mrs. Tadrach!

Scene X

The same persons, MRS. TADRACH.

MRS. TADRACH: Good day. Here I am.

MRS. JULIASIEWICZ: My dear Mrs. Tadrach, some changes have taken place. The young master does not want to marry Hanka.

MRS. TADRACH: How so? He announced it himself.

MRS. JULIASIEWICZ: But he changed his mind.

MRS. TADRACH: Well, I suppose, *mir nichts, dir nichts?*

MRS. DULSKI: With my blessing.

MRS. TADRACH: Big words. But this is wrong for Hanka. I'm her godmother. I won't let her get hurt.

MRS. JULIASIEWICZ: Nobody wants to hurt her. You are a very decent woman, Mrs. Tadrach, and perhaps you could give a little something to Hanka as compensation.

MRS. DULSKI: [*Quietly.*] Don't go too far.

[MRS. TADRACH *is silent.*]

MRS. JULIASIEWICZ: Well, a little something, maybe . . .

MRS. TADRACH: If you please, missus, Holy Matrimony and money are two different things.

MRS. JULIASIEWICZ: Yes, of course, though money is good too. Any other mother would get rid of the girl without even a good word. But here we are concerned and want to add a little something. So, my dear Mrs. Tadrach, you have to admit that there aren't many people who would do this.

MRS. TADRACH: I always said this is a good house. But wrong is wrong.

MRS. JULIASIEWICZ: Oh, you yourself said that money covers everything. If Hanka has a bit saved, nobody will ask about the other.

MRS. TADRACH: Maybe.

MRS. JULIASIEWICZ: What do you think?

MRS. TADRACH: Missus, this is Hanka 's matter. I need to talk to her.

MRS. JULIASIEWICZ: Naturally. We'll send her here right away. Let's go, aunt.

MRS. TADRACH: Good day to you, ladies.

[MRS. DULSKI *leaves.*]

MRS. JULIASIEWICZ: And use your common sense. My aunt does this out of the kindness of her heart, not because she has to. Do you understand?

MRS. TADRACH: I suppose.

[HANKA *enters,* MRS. JULIASIEWICZ *leaves.*]

Scene XI

MRS. TADRACH, HANKA.

MRS. TADRACH: [*Looking around.*] Come here! Come on.

HANKA: How are you?

MRS. TADRACH: This is a fine state of affairs!

HANKA: So you know about it, huh?

MRS. TADRACH: Yes. He wanted to marry you.

HANKA: Ah.

MRS. TADRACH: And now he doesn't.

HANKA: That's his problem. What's with the marriage? Is it my idea or what? They kick me around since yesterday. Thought it's a big deal for me.

MRS. TADRACH: It's honorable, anyhow.

HANKA: Eh.

MRS. TADRACH: You'd be a lady with an apartment house.

HANKA: Eh.

MRS. TADRACH: It would be better than your customs man. He's something, I suppose, but not much.

HANKA: That's my business. But nobody wouldn't kick me around. Everybody got his own honor.

MRS. TADRACH: So you don't insist the master marry you?

HANKA: I told you—I should care about *him*? Let it be my fault.

MRS. TADRACH: They won't hurt you. They want to give you a little something.

HANKA: [*Weeping.*] Leave me alone, godmother, leave me alone.

MRS. TADRACH: You're dumb, dumb. You're young, and you don't know the world. When you get money you'll be strong. Why you crying? Marriage is out. Now the thing is for them to do right by you.

HANKA: [*Crying.*] Leave me alone, godmother.

MRS. TADRACH: They're not doing you no favors. I'll talk for you. I won't let them harm you.

HANKA: [*Irritated.*] Godmother, leave me alone!

Scene XII

The same persons, MRS. DULSKI, MRS. JULIASIEWICZ.

MRS. JULIASIEWICZ: And what now? Did you talk it over? We don't have much time. It's late. Time to go downtown.

MRS. TADRACH: [*In a different tone.*] Please, missus, it's like this. Hanka says the young master himself promised to marry her.

MRS. JULIASIEWICZ: He was joking. Hanka doesn't think he was serious.

MRS. TADRACH: There were witnesses, ma'am.

MRS. DULSKI: Who?

MRS. TADRACH: You, missus.

MRS. DULSKI: Impertinence!

MRS. JULIASIEWICZ: Just a minute. Marriage is out of the question. I repeat, the master was only joking. Hanka knew very well what she was doing.

MRS. TADRACH: I'm responsible for her like for myself.

MRS. JULIASIEWICZ: And out of kindness my aunt wants to do something. You should be grateful. At least I think so.

MRS. DULSKI: Don't go too far.

MRS. JULIASIEWICZ: Well, some twenty crowns . . .

HANKA: [*Suddenly coming to the table and standing impudently between them.*] I'll talk for myself.

MRS. TADRACH: Hanka, wait. I . . .

HANKA: Godmother, keep out of this. If they want to pay for my harm, let them pay!

MRS. DULSKI: Look how insolent she's grown.

HANKA: Okay. Pay me, pay me! And if no, let's get out. They'll pay later anyhow. There are courts and child support and I can swear . . .

MRS. DULSKI: Good God! That's all I need!

MRS. JULIASIEWICZ: My girl, wouldn't your conscience bother you?

HANKA: Oh, did they do me with conscience what they done? If they didn't have no conscience, let 'em pay now!

MRS. TADRACH: Hanka, don't shout.

HANKA: Godmother, keep out of this! I can take care of myself. And Jagusia Wajda, didn't she win child support in court? Remember? If somebody don't have a conscience for me, I got none for them.

MRS. DULSKI: [*To* MRS. JULIASIEWICZ.] Help me. Give her what she wants, only don't let this scandal get out.

MRS. JULIASIEWICZ: How much do you want?

HANKA: A thousand crowns.

MRS. DULSKI: What?

HANKA: A thousand crowns.

[*A moment of silence. The women look at each other.*]

MRS. JULIASIEWICZ: [*Softly.*] Give it to her, aunt. Otherwise there'll be a scandal.

MRS. DULSKI: O dear God! [*To* HANKA.] What do you want, my skin?

HANKA: And didn't I lose my virtue here in this house? I wanted out. Come, godmother!

MRS. DULSKI: Wait . . . But you have to sign a paper that you have no complaint against us and everything is settled.

HANKA: [*Gloomily.*] I'll sign it.

MRS. DULSKI: And you won't ever bother us?

HANKA: Me, never. But what the kid does when it grows up, that's its business and God's.

MRS. DULSKI: I'll be dead then. Come. [*They go to the bedroom.*]

Scene XIII

MRS. JULIASIEWICZ, MELA.

MELA: Auntie?

MRS. JULIASIEWICZ: What?

MELA: Auntie, what's going on? Hesia is listening all the time at the door, and she laughs so. What's going on?

MRS. JULIASIEWICZ: Nothing. Everything is fine.

MELA: Thank God!

[MRS. JULIASIEWICZ *goes to the bedroom. After a while* HANKA, MRS. TADRACH, *and* MRS. DULSKI *come out.*]

Scene XIV

HANKA, MRS. TADRACH, MRS. DULSKI, MRS. JULIASIEWICZ, *later* ZBYSZKO, HESIA, *and* MELA.

MRS. DULSKI: And now take your things and get out! I don't want you here one more minute.

MRS. TADRACH: We're leaving, missus. Good day.

HANKA: Come, godmother. How come so polite? [*They leave.*]

MRS. DULSKI: Ah! [*She falls down on the sofa.*] God! What a day! I hardly lived through it. Horrible—what I had to go through. A thousand crowns!

MRS. JULIASIEWICZ: But you saw that the knife was at your throat.

MRS. DULSKI: Yes, yes.

MRS. JULIASIEWICZ: Good-bye. I'm going home. I've gotten a migraine out of all this. But maybe now, aunt, you could rent us that apartment.

MRS. DULSKI: Never. My home is quiet, my dear. Besides, you might not pay me, and I have to get back what they took.

MRS. JULIASIEWICZ: You'll never learn.

MRS. DULSKI: [*Proudly.*] And what am I supposed to learn? And from whom? Thanks be to God that I know myself what is proper. [MRS. JULIASIEWICZ *shrugs her shoulders and leaves.* MRS. DULSKI *runs to* ZBYSZKO'S *door.*] Zbyszko! To the Office! [*To the girls.*] Hesia, the dusting . . . Mela, exercises! [*To the bedroom.*] Felician, to the office! [HESIA *runs in.*] Hurry, Mela! [MELA *enters.*] Open the piano. Well, now we can start to live right again. [*She hurries to the kitchen. Inside the hall* MRS. TADRACH *and* HANKA *can be seen carrying out* HANKA'S *trunk.*]

MELA: [*Running toward them.*] Andzia! Andzia! Where are you going? Are you leaving for good?

HANKA: Good day to you, miss. You're the only decent person here. I wish you good luck, and for the others . . . [*she makes a threatening gesture.*].

MELA: [*Running to* ZBYSZKO's *door.*] Zbyszko! Hanka is moving out! He locked himself in. Zbyszko!

HESIA: Mela! Have you gone mad?

[*The door closes with a heavy bang.*]

MELA: Mama's getting rid of her, Zbyszko! She's already out. [*She runs to the window.*] I can't see her. Oh, she's walking, carrying her trunk. Where is she going? Such snow! Now she's disappeared around the corner. O God! [*She cries.*]

HESIA: [*Laughing.*] I know, I know! I heard everything. What's this? Something shiny . . . a piece of paper . . . [*She crawls under the piano.*]

MELA: [*Standing before the window and leaning on the frame.*] Where did she go? She was crying.

HESIA: [*Rolling on the floor laughing.*] I know! I know!

MELA: Hesia, don't laugh. Something bad happened here. Like somebody being killed. Hesia, she may even drown herself!

HESIA: [*Rolling on the floor.*] She won't drown herself! She took a thousand crowns and will marry that customs man of hers!

MELA: [*With a kind of tragic despair.*] Be quiet, Hesia! Be quiet. Don't laugh, Hesia!

HESIA: [*Still rolling on the floor.*] She took a thousand crowns and will marry her customs man.

[*The curtain goes down.*]

Kalliroi Siganou-Parren (1859–1940)

Modern Greece, as a nation-state, dates from the 1820s, when it gained independence from the Ottoman Turks. In the nineteenth century, the country was drawn, ambivalently, into a game of catch-up—with the West and with its own ancient, seminal place in the Western tradition. In the half century following independence, an increasingly large segment of the upper and better-educated social strata sought to imitate the "advanced" European nations. This included the desire to import Western dramatic models. Militating against efforts to energize, in this birthplace of drama, a professional theater, were the tensions between the more Western-focused elites and those who were often suspicious of the West.

Modern Greece was being built on the competing interests of Western imperialism and Greek nationalism; and the contradictions inherent in this polarity extended to the theater. The class and cultural antagonisms that came into play were economic, political, social, and religious. The monied classes patronized Italian and other European touring companies, and the hoi polloi preferred folk entertainments. Eventually, the resolution of these conflicts was that Greek drama gravitated toward a Western style of literary theater.

During the decades when modern Greece was reshaping itself, it experienced, like the rest of Europe, the insistence of the "woman question" and the nascent women's movement. As a former province of the Ottoman Empire, Greece was not a country congenial to feminism and to women's independence and empowerment. Among urban and upper-class rural Greeks, domesticity was generally accepted as the role of women. There have been few declared or overt feminists, even among the women dramatists. Still, for Greeks the women's movement was an issue that mingled importantly in the forging of a national identity.

Kalliroi Siganou-Parren is all the more remarkable in this context. Born into a middle-class family and well educated, she became the leading and most outspoken turn-of-the-century Greek feminist. After teaching and administering a school in Adrianopole, Parren established herself in journalism. She married a French journalist, Ioannis Parren, in 1880, and in 1887 began publishing *The Ladies Newspaper* (*Efimeris ton kyrion*), a very successful and widely distributed weekly that was an important voice in the campaign for women's rights. Parren was a very effective and articulate public figure, working with European and American feminist organizations and representing Greek women at international conferences. Highly sophisticated, she was also at the center of Athenian intellectual and cultural circles, hosting her own literary salon.

Kalliroi Siganou-Parren, no date. (Courtesy of the Theater Museum, Athens.)

Parren wrote fiction, plays, drama, and literary criticism. In her writing, she described the double role of women writers: to free themselves from the image of servility and to champion the equality and liberty of the New Woman. Her fictional trilogy, *The Books of the Dawn* (*Ta Vivlia tis Avyis,* 1900–02), exposes the tension between this political platform and the surrounding Mediterranean cultures.

It is useful to see Parren's *The New Woman* (*I Nea Yineka,* 1907) in the context of the movement or idea of that name. She quickly and forcefully picked up on this important current in British and European social history. The New (or Advanced) Woman was identified with the comedies and social criticisms of George Bernard Shaw, who had acted as the English publicist for Henrik Ibsen. Shaw presented her in such figures as Vivie Warren, Candida, Lady Cicely Waynefleet, and even Major Barbara. His strong women figures may have been idealizations, but the phenomenon he propelled was very real. For one thing, it provoked real anger, and for another it coexisted with a spate of less-known "New Woman" plays—more realistic and less glib and glamorous than his. Among these plays, with their educated, assertive, and financially self-supporting or independent-minded female protagonists, Parren's play and her lead character, Mary Myrtou, stand very tall.

The issue in *The New Woman* is straightforward. The lies, hypocrisy, match-making and dowry customs, and obsession with money are challenged by the in-dependent, artistic spirit of Mary. What makes Parren's drama effective are the de-tails. It is not simply that lies abound, but that they dramatically and ironically recur (think of the parallel references to wives' lying about bills). Money, as Mrs. Memusselov claims, may (or may not) make the man, but it clearly undoes him. Even the subjects of Mary's paintings tellingly contribute to the texture of the play. She gleans insight from the Circassian Woman and financial success from the Gypsy Girl—implying not only the need to transcend the narrow class borders of Greek society, but also an essential international sisterhood. Within the conven-tions of the play's realism, the furnishings of Mrs. Memusselov's house and of Mary's lodgings pointedly contrast them.

What to contemporary sensibilities, living almost a century after Parren wrote, are likely to remain troublesome in her play are the nationalist fervor and the cult of motherhood. Despite Parren's (and Mary's) principled quest for freedom and self-fulfilment, the ethos of the time was inescapable. Even she, ardent feminist as Parren was, embraced the infectious spirit of Greek nationalism. Pregnant and fi-nancially precarious, Mary could reject her weak and hypocritical husband, Costas—demanding freedom and honesty. But eighteen years later she preens her-self on having devoted her life to her son, Paul. Parren is unequivocal in present-ing us with the strength of what Simone de Beauvoir, for one, could describe (and reject) as the myth of maternalism. What her creation, Mary, does affirm is the be-lief common among Greeks that women would play a crucial role as mothers and teachers in transmitting their language and customs, thus helping to regenerate the nation.

SELECTED BIBLIOGRAPHY IN ENGLISH

Anastasopoulou, Maria. "Feminist Awareness and Greek Women Writers at the Turn of the Century: The Case of Kallirroe Parren and Alexandra Papadopoulou." *Greek Society in the Making: 1863–1913.* Ed. Philip Carabott. Brookfield, Vt.: Ashgate, 1997. Pp. 161–75.

————. "Feminist Discourse and Literary Representation in Turn-of-the-Century Greece: Kallirrhoë Siganou-Parren's *The Books of the Dawn.*" *Journal of Modern Greek Studies* 15 (1997), 1–25.

Constantinidis, Stratos E. "Greek Drama and Multiculturalism: Is it Drama? Is it Modern? Is it Greek? A Prolonged Prologue." *Journal of Modern Greek Studies* 14 (1996), 1–30.

————. "Greek Theater: An Annotated Bibliography of Plays Translated and Essays Writ-ten from 1824–1994." *Journal of Modern Greek Studies* 14 (1996), 123–76.

Fitzsimmons, Linda, and Viv Gardner, eds. *New Woman Plays.* London: Methuen, 1991.

Myrsiades, Linda Suny. "The Struggle for Greek Theater in Post-Independence Greece." *Journal of Hellenic Diaspora* 17 (1980), 33–52.

Patsalidis, Savas. "Greek Women Dramatists: The Road to Emancipation." *Journal of Modern Greek Studies* 14 (1996), 85–102.

THE NEW WOMAN

A Drama in Four Acts

Kalliroi Siganou-Parren

Translated by Stratos E. Constantinidis

CHARACTERS

GEORGIE MEMUSSELOV

KATINGO MEMUSSELOV   his wife

COSTAS   their son

OLGINA   their daughter

LELA   their daugther

EMMA   their daughter

MARY MYRTOU   wife of Costas

HELEN   cousin and former flame of Costas

DORA   cousin and friend of Mary

PAUL MYRTOS   son of Mary

ANNA   maid of Mary

IRENE   maid of the Memusselovs

A BELL BOY

A GYPSY GIRL

A JOURNALIST

The story takes place in Constantinople (Istanbul) in the early fall of 1897, and, in the last act, in Athens in the late spring of 1916.

Act One: Mrs. Katingo Memusselov's boudoir

Act Two: Mary Myrtou's studio

Act Three: Mrs. Katingo Memusselov's drawing room

Act Four: Mary Myrtou's hotel suite

The play was first produced in the Theatre of Constitution Square in Athens, Greece, in 1907. It was published by Par. Leonis, at 16 Pericles Street in Athens in 1908.

ACT ONE

Scene One

The set represents a boudoir which is furnished with some luxury. One of the doors leads to the master bedroom. Enter MRS. MEMUSSELOV *and her three daughters wearing ballroom dresses, while the maid lights the lamps.* MRS. MEMUSSELOV *is no more than forty five years old, in a low-cut decolletage. She plops herself in an armchair, exhausted.*

MRS. MEMUSSELOV: Whew! I'm roasting. Ballroom dancing is nice, but in the winter, not in this hot weather. And on top of that we had to walk home!

EMMA: It's only two steps from here to Mrs. Kalila's house, Mama. [*She takes off her cape and headband, and joins her sisters in front of the mirror. She nudges* LELA *aside and takes her place.*] Let me take a look. I'm a mess. My God! My hair! My dress, too! It's all wrinkled.

OLGINA: If you had danced less, you wouldn't be so disheveled. You brought the roof down, especially with the Russian officer.

EMMA: Oh, but he was so handsome! And what a dancer! [*She walks away from the mirror, while her sisters step in front of it again and look at themselves.*] He held me, he whirled me around, and I felt as if my feet barely touched the ground. I was flying like this [*Spreads her arms like wings.*] It seemed to me that I had wings on my feet.

LELA: [*Sits on a chair and kicks off one of her dancing shoes.*] Whew! It's too tight. I, for one, was not flying with these shoes. Where were *you* flying?

EMMA: I was in heaven.

OLGINA: [*Brushes out her hair.*] It looked more like lovers' lane to me.

MRS. MEMUSSELOV: Nonsense, Olgina, nonsense. Emma is still a child.

EMMA: A child! You're stuck on the thought that I'm still a child. I'm more than twenty years old. It was about time that you decided to take me with you to the ball and to let me lengthen my dresses a bit! [*To* OLGINA.] Stand still and I'll fix your hair like Kate's.

OLGINA: They took you along because it was your friend's birthday.

LELA: And the ball was sort of like a coming out party. Poor Emma! How long you'll have to wait before it is decided that you can properly come out to society. You'll remain the eternal baby to the families in the city who have daughters older than you they want to marry off.

MRS. MEMUSSELOV: Nonsense!

LELA: Our aunt in Petrograd introduced me to society when I was sixteen years old.

MRS. MEMUSSELOV: [*Teasing her.*] So there they now consider you one of the old maids. "Oh dear, I remember Lela," they'd say. "She's been at the balls for ten years now." [*Counts on her fingers.*] Ten, and she was probably twenty, so she's a full thirty years old." This is what the tongue waggers would say.

LELA: Mother, you think that in Petrograd people live by the gossip from Constantinople; and that they care to spend their time wondering how old one girl is or what another girl did or said.

OLGINA: Sure, there they concern themselves only with politics! There women become nihilists.

LELA: There women become good people, refined, liberated. They read and write, they study and work.

EMMA: Sure, that's why you mock us when we read.

LELA: But what you're reading is not educational; moreover it's also ruining your minds.

[*Father's voice is heard calling* MRS. MEMUSSELOV *from downstairs: "Katingo! Katingo!"*]

MRS. MEMUSSELOV: [*Stands up.*] Right away, Georgie dear! I'm coming! I'm coming!

[*Exit* MRS. MEMUSSELOV *in a hurry.*]

LELA: It must be that he needs her help to get undressed.

EMMA: Shame on you for making fun of our father.

LELA: What are you talking about? It hurts me. I feel sorry for you. I'm not making fun of him. What kind of a life is this for our mother and all of you in this house I wonder?

[*Shouts are heard.*]

OLGINA: [*Stops brushing out her hair and runs to the door that leads downstairs.*] Shhh! He's yelling. Too bad, it'll be a rough night! He asked for his bottle.

EMMA: [*Also approaches the door. The sound of a breaking glass is heard.*] He smashed the glass, too. It's a good thing he didn't break anything else.

LELA: Like someone's head! Surely this wouldn't have been the first time!

OLGINA: Stop it! Things have calmed down. Mother told him that his kitten broke the bottle.

EMMA: Mother did well this time.

LELA: It's frightening. This cat, our little kitten, is higher in our father's affections than his wife.

OLGINA: You're always so judgmental and critical. Dad loves his cat because he can't help it.

Scene Two

The same. Enter MRS. MEMUSSELOV.

MRS. MEMUSSELOV: I got off easy. It was about the bottle. If you only knew what I said.

OLGINA: We heard it, Mother. We would have said the same.

MRS. MEMUSSELOV: [*Glances at the clock.*] Oh, dear, it's four A.M. and Costas hasn't returned yet. I can't believe that he didn't show up at Kalila's ball, not even for the sake of appearances.

OLGINA: Especially when he was away for so many months.

EMMA: Do you know that his new flame, the artist who started painting grandma's portrait last March, was also away all summer?

OLGINA: [*To* EMMA.] Look, would you get done with styling my hair? Well, Costas' new flame, Mme Marie, the "Master" as he calls her, spent her summer in the heart of the fertile crescent in Asia, doing paintings of old churches.

MRS. MEMUSSELOV: [*Stands up.*] What! Who told you that? In the heart of the fertile crescent? But that's where Costas also spent his summer.

LELA: Why can't you leave people alone for a change. That's no way to spend your time! Not only are you spying on the women of Constantinople, but also on women from out of town.

MRS. MEMUSSELOV: Not so! This is an important matter! Costas liked this young woman. He followed her around like someone madly in love with her.

LELA: [*Reclines on the sofa.*] I don't blame him. Mary Myrtou is wonderful! She's an outstanding, remarkable woman!

MRS. MEMUSSELOV: Say these things to your brother, and he'll lose his head. [*Sits down.*]

EMMA: What does she care about the misfortune that awaits us if Costas is truly in love!

LELA: [*Stands up.*] This love would be his salvation. In the first place, with a woman like this who is intelligent, refined, energetic, industrious, he would likewise change his lifestyle. He would feel the need to work, to become something better than a dandy! In the second place, he would save himself from the ill-fated matchmaking that you've arranged for him.

MRS. MEMUSSELOV: Listen here, Lela. You've gone overboard this time. Just because I let you say every silly thought that comes into your head and every bit of nonsense that you've learned at school up there in Petrograd, you think that you are in a position to judge things better than me.

LELA: But, Mother!

MRS. MEMUSSELOV: Don't you "but mother" me! I know what must be done and what mustn't. What I want will be done! [*Stands up angrily.*] Costas must marry Mrs. Petrov even if it's the end of the world.

LELA: But what if Costas doesn't want her?

MRS. MEMUSSELOV: I want her, and that's enough. Even if he were married, not just in love, I would still make him marry Mrs. Petrov. His marriage to Mrs. Petrov must take place. It must, it must, it must.

LELA: What if he is truly in love with the other woman?

MRS. MEMUSSELOV: He'll fall out of it.

OLGINA: Oh, he falls out of love easily. So far, he's fallen in and out of love with all of my friends. Do you remember how he felt about Helen? He would have died for her, he would have left home, he would have killed her fiancé.

EMMA: He's still in love with Helen. When he saw her downstairs the day before yesterday, he turned white like a sheet. I tell you he's still in love with her.

LELA: [*To her mother.*] Why didn't you let him marry her since he loved her so? Helen is young, beautiful, full of life, open hearted. And she has money.

MRS. MEMUSSELOV: She has only very recently inherited that money. And what's more, she is also a flirt. She has a past. But never mind! I would never have imagined that her uncle would leave all of his estate to her.

EMMA: If she wasn't already engaged, there might have been hope for Costas.

MRS. MEMUSSELOV: Oh, her engagement doesn't mean anything.

LELA: What! It doesn't mean anything? You're not thinking of breaking her engagement to this other man now that she is an heiress?

MRS. MEMUSSELOV: From what little I've heard she'll break it herself. She was only going to marry him for his money. And let me tell you, if Costas insists that he doesn't want Petrov, let him marry Helen.

LELA: If he's still in love with Helen, and if his love for Mary—

MRS. MEMUSSELOV: His love for this other woman is just a fling. It couldn't be anything else than a fling. How can Costas in his right mind fall in love with this kind of woman?

EMMA: Don't worry, she hasn't given him time to cultivate such feelings. She runs from palace to palace and from harem to harem. She works tirelessly. She's not the marrying kind. She's against marriage and for women's liberation. She's a suffragette [*She laughs sarcastically.*]

LELA: Nonsense! Why a suffragette? Because she works? Because she faces life on her own? Because she's her own creation? Because she's a person and not a doll? In Russia, all those women who have had some education and refinement, are like this. Not to mention the American women.

MRS. MEMUSSELOV: But Costas is neither Russian nor American. Besides, this kind of woman doesn't fall in love easily. In fact, I think she's heartless.

LELA: [*Stands up and puts her face in front of her mother's.*] In other words, she has a different kind of heart capable of great feelings and ready to sacrifice itself for beautiful ideals.

[*The sound of a horse and carriage is heard.*]

MRS. MEMUSSELOV: [*Jumps out of her chair and runs to the window.*] Be quiet! A carriage has stopped in front of our house. It must be Costas. [*Steps are heard coming upstairs.* LELA *runs to the door and opens it.*]

Scene Three

The same. Enter COSTAS. *He is wearing a black tuxedo with a rose in his lapel.*

LELA: Welcome, you bad boy. Now you're in for it! You're going to be scolded! [*She curtseys to him.*] Do you like my ballroom dress?

OLGINA: [*To* COSTAS.] It's a fine thing you did. Poor Kate was waiting for you to come so she could sing to us.

LELA: In this case, you did a fine thing for not coming.

COSTAS: [*Goes to his mother.*] You don't look like you had much fun, Mother. I see that you're angry.

MRS. MEMUSSELOV: [*Sighs.*] And rightly so. I can't believe that you promised to come and you lied to us. Bad, bad manners, my child! Your father was beside himself with anger again.

LELA: But father is always beside himself.

MRS. MEMUSSELOV: Shhh! He may hear you, for God's sake! [*She opens the door to the master bedroom and peeks in. She closes the door.*] He hasn't come upstairs yet. [*Back to her topic.*] That's right! Beside himself! This time with good reason.

COSTAS: But Mother, it was impossible for me to come. I was invited to a wedding. And I thought the reception would be over sooner.

[*His sisters run to him and surround him excited. All three speak almost at the same time.*]

OLGINA: Whose wedding?

LELA: Tell us!

EMMA: Do we know the couple?

LELA: [*Puts her hand on his shoulder and withdraws it quickly.*] Oh dear, your jacket is wet!

COSTAS: Yes, it rained at one o'clock.

MRS. MEMUSSELOV: [*Worried, feels his clothes.*] You're soaking wet, my child!

COSTAS: Don't worry, Mother, there is no danger of catching a cold in this hot weather.

MRS. MEMUSSELOV: Yes, but your tuxedo might be stained. Take it off so I can brush it for you. If you leave it like this, it'll be full of spots by tomorrow morning. [*Aside.*] Maybe I can find out where he was.

OLGINA: Well, what about the wedding? You didn't tell us.

[*Father's voice is heard calling to his family from upstairs: "Tell me, will you stay up all night in there, don't you intend to go to bed tonight? Have you lost all consideration?"*]

MRS. MEMUSSELOV: [*In a soft voice.*] He was downstairs earlier. Maybe he heard what we said! [*In a louder voice.*] Right away, Georgie dear! [*To the girls.*] Quickly. Enough chattering. You won't be able to get up tomorrow morning. [*The girls pick up their things.*]

OLGINA: [*To* COSTAS.] Phooey! What does he care when we go to bed. Our father is a tyrant. During the ball, as soon as the fun started, he was following us around, sometimes mama and sometimes us. [*She imitates her father's voice.*] "Hey, you have danced enough already! Let's go! It's late. Quit dancing."

LELA: He did that so he wouldn't get out of the habit of nagging.

EMMA: How horrible! Our father must never have been young.

[*Exeunt* OLGINA, LELA, *and* EMMA.]

Scene Four

The same.

MRS. MEMUSSELOV: Come on, take it off. The dampness will make you sick.

COSTAS: [*Removes his jacket and hands it to her. While she is laying it on the sofa,* COSTAS *puts on a cardigan that he takes from the armoire.*] You'd better hurry up with it. He'll start yelling again.

MRS. MEMUSSELOV: Never mind, Costas, he came upstairs to his bedroom. He'll be snoring in five minutes. [*Dries off the tuxedo with her handkerchief.*] This must have been a shoddy wedding! The guests must have returned on foot from the church. That's why you ended up in this mess.

COSTAS: [*Sits down and lights a cigarette.*] Why bother now, Mama?

MRS. MEMUSSELOV: Why bother? Even Mrs. Petrov was at Kalila's house and you, instead of showing up, you attended a shoddy wedding who knows where.

COSTAS: [*Ironically.*] Don't worry! The scion of our noble family did not come into any contact with the commoners! Our coat of arms remains intact.

MRS. MEMUSSELOV: Spare me from your irony, Costas, my child. Don't be sore because I don't want you to associate with shoddy people. You know that the gossips have started talking again, this time about your new acquaintances, and your love affair! And your father is beside himself with anger.

COSTAS: People talk about my love affair and my father is beside himself with anger. Answer this question for me: When haven't people spoken about other people's affairs, and when hasn't father been beside himself? Didn't people talk when I frequented Mrs. Dederis' house? They did, but father was twirling the edges of his mustache and was saying, "Bravo to Costas! Mrs. Dederis is some piece." Can it be that you all became virtuous overnight?

MRS. MEMUSSELOV: But Mrs. Dederis was harmless, my child. She was a married woman, one of our circle, and well known for her affairs.

COSTAS: Ah, yes, of course, in the case of Mrs. Dederis, I was following your principles: flirt, have fun, and create a little scandal. I was getting practice in love making. I was training my heart to live a lie. I was shielding myself against love. Your scheme to have me marry a rich bride wasn't endangered by Mrs. Dederis. In this case, I was a man, so you said, and men can do whatever they want.

MRS. MEMUSSELOV: [*Approaches him.*] But my child, my son, don't you know money is everything today? Aren't you worried that we're drowning in debt? that you have three sisters? that Olgina is already an old maid? that if you don't marry Princess Petrov, Olgina doesn't stand a chance of marrying Themos? How else will your father be able to find the 4,000 pounds sterling that he promised to pay Themos for Olgina's dowry?

COSTAS: [*Stands up exasperated, facing his mother.*] Well, you may break off my engagement and your daughter's right now because I won't become the husband of your princess. Do you understand? Never ever!

MRS. MEMUSSELOV: But, Costas, my child, all of us will be relieved with this marriage. We'll pay off the mortgage for our house at Halki, you'll have capital to invest in your father's water utility company. You *know* it's a goldmine!

COSTAS: [*Pacing back and forth while talking to his mother.*] Whew! It's hot and humid in here! [*Opens the window.*] In this heat, any talk about an arranged marriage to Petrov is more than enough to drive one crazy.

MRS. MEMUSSELOV: But yet, see how everybody waits on her hand and foot, and how they try to get in with her at banquets and tea parties. "The princess was one of my guests! The princess was also there!" She may be a bit ugly, and yet she's always surrounded by our high society, the entire aristocracy from Embassy Row.[1]

COSTAS: Well of course, why wouldn't they? She belongs to every clique.

MRS. MEMUSSELOV: But my child!

COSTAS: Child or not, let's face it. She is the ring leader of a bunch of gamblers. She gambles all night long. She smokes like a train stack. And neat cigars from Havana, too.

MRS. MEMUSSELOV: Have you seen the golden cigar box, the one that's decorated with rubies and pearls? It's a masterpiece of art and riches.

COSTAS: And a gift from the last Grand Duke for being his mistress! What *noblesse*, Mother! And my marriage to her will once again gild our family's coat of arms with her Midas[2] touch! Right?

MRS. MEMUSSELOV: You know what, Costas, you're insufferable. To be smeared by our enemies is unavoidable! But to hear you repeat what they're saying and to degrade the nobility of our family, which is the only thing left to us, is something I can't stand.

COSTAS: I assure you, Mama, that only the day before yesterday I learned about the base roots of our family tree. Mrs. Dederis sent me a message with her tiny friend to prove to me that I'm shoddy, and that's why I jilt the ladies with pedigree and I prefer shoddy women. I think she titled it "Birds of a Feather." Would you like me to recite it to you? I've memorized it you know: My great grandfather, my father's grandfather, was a street vendor of mussels. In other words, he was selling mussels on Embassy Row. My grandfather, my father's father, was a supplier of mussels, fish, and other seafood at wholesale to the palace. He was the favorite of the Sultan's procurator-general around the time he changed his name. Instead of the French "de," he added the prefix "me" and the ending "ov" to make it sound more Russian, and it became Memusselov. My father, George Memusselov, was heir to a great fortune, and became a landowner and a banker, but he has also been such a spendthrift and so unorganized that today he needs to revive the delicate companies of his "noble" ancestors with the princely gold of Mrs. Petrov.

MRS. MEMUSSELOV: [*Walks frantically towards him trying to interrupt him, without success. In the end, she puts her hands on the table and leans her head over it.*] Shame on you for repeating these things! Do you hear me? Shame on you! [*Takes his tuxedo and drapes it on an armchair.*]

COSTAS: [*Takes off his vest and throws it on a chair.*] What for? It's the truth.

MRS. MEMUSSELOV: [*Picks up his vest and folds it.*] Be quiet! You've upset me again. Go, it's late. [*She takes the watch out of the watch pocket of his vest and she checks the time with the clock in the boudoir; then she goes to set it on the table. She observes a wedding ring hanging from the chain like a breloque. Worried.*] What's this?

---

[1] Embassy Row is a substitute translation of the Greek word "Stavrodromi" ("Crossroads"). It is a suburb of Constantinople which the Turks renamed Beyoğlu. The Greeks called it "Crossroads" because its main avenue intersected with all the major streets of the area, and "Pera" (Πέραν, "beyond") because it lay on the other side of the channel of the Golden Horn. Later it expanded on the other side of the medieval walls of Galatas where rich foreign merchants and ambassadors built their sumptuous mansions. It was the quarter in which most of the Europeans and Christian minorities (Greeks and Armenians) resided. It retained its cosmopolitan, polyglot flavor up until 1923.

[2] Costas plays with words. The pronunciation (not the spelling) of the adjective *midika* (μηδικά) which describes the coat of arms, has three different meanings: (a) "of Media" (της Μηδίας), meaning "of the rich land," i.e., the land NW of Iran; (b) "of Midas" (του Μίδα), meaning "of the rich King Midas of Phrygia," i.e., the greedy king whose touch turned everything into gold according to the Dionysian cycle of legends dramatized in the Athenian satyr plays; and (c) "of midas" (του μυδά) meaning "of the mussel man," i.e., of Costas's grandfather who acquired his wealth through the trade of mussels.

COSTAS: [*Dashes over to take the ring from her, but she clasps it in the palm of her hand.*] So be it! Look at it if you want to. Figure it out.

MRS. MEMUSSELOV: [*Approaches the lamp light, examines the wedding ring, and reads aloud in a trembling voice.*] "MARY MYRTOU, July 8, 1897." [*Her knees grow weak and she drops, instead of sitting down, on the sofa. Shocked and with a look of agony in her face and gestures, she holds out the wedding ring to her son.*] What's the meaning of this?

COSTAS: [*Sits down. Distressed and speaking in a voice that is hardly audible.*] This is my wedding ring. The betrothal of my wife!

MRS. MEMUSSELOV: [*Like a mad woman.*] Of your wife! What did you say? Your—? So, you are married. [*Stands up, holds her head in her hands and walks back and forth.*] This isn't possible! It can't be! Tell me it's a lie. My God, I'm losing my mind.

COSTAS: Mother! Please, don't take it so hard.

MRS. MEMUSSELOV: You're my child. You're my hope. You've married a woman who works for a living. She snatched you, made you lose your mind, blinded you. She made you stop thinking, stop worrying about anyone, even about your own mother. Oh, my child. My Costas! What a disaster!

COSTAS: It's not a disaster, Mother. Mary is a good woman, intelligent, refined, perfect. She is the only one who can help me with my life, to save me from my bad habits, to make me a good person. When you get to know her better, you'll love her, too. She's not at all like other women.

MRS. MEMUSSELOV: [*Ticked.*] Sure, other women are not as cosmopolitan and know-it-all as she is. They don't know how to beguile and snatch men.

COSTAS: [*Stands up, displeased.*] Mother, don't forget that I love her, and she's my wife!

MRS. MEMUSSELOV: How terrible of you to raise her up to our position; in fact, to think that she is better than us. She's a thief, she stole our happiness.

COSTAS: [*Angry and almost threatening.*] That's enough! Not another word. Do you hear me, Mother? I won't have it. I'm a man, and I did what I wanted.

MRS. MEMUSSELOV: And look where it got you. You, a man? I can't believe it.

COSTAS: Up until now, you thought that I was man enough for all the things I did, and that men do whatever they want. Isn't this your golden rule? Didn't you sing lullabies to me when I was a child and didn't you bring me up as a young man with this tune? How many times have you told me, "Have a good time, my son, you're a man! Only be careful not to get involved with anyone."

MRS. MEMUSSELOV: [*Sits down. More calmly.*] Whatever I said, I said it for your own good. Every mother wants the best for her child. And if you were still listening to me, you wouldn't have done this craziness.

COSTAS: Instead, I would have married a princess with big money.

MRS. MEMUSSELOV: Nowadays, it's money that makes the man. You surely won't change the world.

COSTAS: How can I? What am I worthy of doing the way you brought me up? Do I have any strength of character? Don't you see that I chose to get married secretly; that I lied to my wife that you approved of our marriage; that I didn't dare to defy the expectations that other people and you and my father have of me. You want me to shoulder the deceit of two generations which is now tied to the strings of a golden purse lined with millions!

MRS. MEMUSSELOV: [*Is crying while her son is speaking. Her sobs become more frequent.*] Be quiet! Be quiet! When I think about what you've done, and what will become of us now, I'm going crazy. [*She springs to her feet grasping her chest.*] My God! I don't feel well. I'm choking. I'm dying! [*She falls to the floor as if she had fainted.*]

COSTAS: [*Is terrified and is feeling guilty.*] My God! Mother! Easy now. I'll get you a glass of water. I'll call for help.

[*Exit* COSTAS *running.*]

MRS. MEMUSSELOV: [*Springs back to her feet.*] No, she won't have her way. I'll stop her before she ruins my family! If she only knew what's coming to her.

[*Curtain.*]

ACT TWO

Scene One

The studio of an artist, furnished with great eccentricity but also in disorder. Statuettes, plaster castings, and paintings are standing on the shelves and the tables. Some paintings are mounted, some are on the furniture, and others are leaning against the walls and all over the place. In the middle of the studio stands an easel with a painting that is barely started. Enter COSTAS *wearing a sport jacket and a soft hat.*

COSTAS: [*Looks right and left.*] How come she's not here? Mary! Mary! [*He wanders around the room.*] It seems she didn't expect me this early. She is probably working across the street. [*Approaches the table.*] Ahuh, a letter. [*Examines it.*] She's writing to her girlfriend. I wonder what her secrets are. [*Lies down on the sofa, unfolds the letter, and reads aloud.*] "Dear friend, you've been complaining that I haven't written to you for several months now. You're right. But listen, I was traveling in the heart of the Middle East, in a wilderness of unimaginable beauty. That's where I've been all this time. And there I found the rare bird of happiness quite unexpectedly in the presence of a young and handsome man who became my husband." [*To himself.*] How flattering a thought! [*Reads on, mumbling.*] "Our love began last spring, but then it started to scare me, so I left Constantinople." [*To himself.*] Her escape brought us together. [*Reads on very softly to himself; stops reading and exclaims.*] This is beautiful! She expresses herself so poignantly. [*He reads on softly to himself, and then he speaks up.*] ". . . because freedom, love, and truth are the foundations of happiness. And what strong foundations they are, my dear." [COSTAS *sets the letter aside, stands up and strolls around.*] Yes, they were strong foundations only as long as we lived down there as strangers among other strangers. But now, what a living hell our marriage has become! I have to lie to her and to my parents. My mother became ill for three days when she found out about my marriage. And here I am telling Mary that my mother is enthusiastic about it. [*Paces, looking unhappy.*] Freedom and love! These are only words. I see now that my life is enslaved. True happiness was what I had the way I lived before. [*Stops, looking pensive.*] I feel that I was not made for great truths and lofty ideals! For great parties, yes! And for romances and revelries. [*Paces, looking pensive.*] I think mother was right. This marriage was a foolish thing to do. [*Stops, looking unhappy.*] Helen was like me, she saw and experienced life the way I do. Why did I go and marry Mary when I was madly in love with Helen, my one true love? It was my weak character! As mother aptly put it, I mistook my admiration of Mary for love. It was her self-respect and her resistance, that's right, her resistance that made me take this big step. [*He sits down.*]

Scene Two

The same. Enter MARY. *She is wearing a white dress, a big straw hat, and is holding a bouquet of white roses close to her chest.*

MARY: Ah, there you are. Good morning, my baby! [*Kisses him. She removes her hat while she is talking.*] I thought that you'd be late again like you were yesterday, so I went to work on the portrait of the Circassian woman. [*Sits next to him.*] What's the matter with you, my love? You look unhappy. [*She pulls out a rose and puts it in the button hole of his lapel, asking again.*] What's the matter with you?

COSTAS: [*In low spirits.*] Nothing is the matter. [*Changing the subject.*] So, you're making progress with your Circassian woman?

MARY: Oh, yes! [*Sighs.*] I'm making progress. However, I regret that I went there this morning. I'm totally upset! I'm worried!

COSTAS: Why?

MARY: Because of the things that she told me. They were entirely new to me. I would never have expected so much philosophizing, so much psychological analysis from a Turkish woman, a woman caged in a harem.

COSTAS: Turkish women are refined nowadays, they read. In fact, I think there are also Turkish women who are authors.

MARY: [*Stands up, puts on her apron, picks up a large photograph, stands in front of the easel, and she begins to paint, while she is talking.*] I must work on this painting because the Gypsy Girl may leave town any day now.

COSTAS: [*Is lying on the sofa, smoking.*] Well, what did the beautiful Circassian woman tell you?

MARY: Strange things. For instance, that she's pleased with her life; that Turkish women live locked in a cage, but they are tended to like little birds with sweets and music; unlike the rest of us who build our own nests in the open air only to be ruined by other birds. You can't imagine what an impression her words made on me!

COSTAS: Nonsense. Your Turkish woman must have read all of that somewhere, in some book written on purpose for these unhappy creatures in the harems.

MARY: But she also told me words of wisdom about life in a harem!

COSTAS: What! She spoke to you in praise of polygamy? [*Teasing her.*] Mary, are you perhaps jealous of her? Huh? [*He laughs.*] Go on, tell me.

MARY: [*Quits painting and comes to sit opposite him.*] Do you want me to tell you exactly what she said to me?

COSTAS: [*Sits up.*] Of course I want you to! I'm dying to hear her defense of the wonderful institution of having many wives.

MARY: She said that their men do God's will because they are ordered by their law and their religion. In our case, however, because our law and religion forbid polygamy, our men secretly have mistresses whom they love more than their wives. Then, to persuade me further, she said: "Under our law, all girls get married, all of them fulfill their purpose in nature, all of them have children, all of them have their own wealth—the dowry which they received from their husband—and all of them have someone to love."

COSTAS: To tell you the truth, Mary, I agree with her. Your Turkish woman is absolutely right. Well, of course Turkish men and Turkish women are happier than us. Imagine what a wonderful thing it is to have a harem, to know that so many women love you.

MARY: [*Draws very near to him with a frightened look.*] So, you find this lifestyle appealing? You would like to spread your love among many women?

COSTAS: What I mean is that just as you found her words to be wise, so do I.

MARY: But the wisdom of their law is not that it gives men many women, but that it provides for the future of their race. It eliminates illegitimate children, unhappy spinsters, and life without love, and without joy. Do you know what it means to spend your life desolate and alone like so many unhappy girls who don't have a dowry in order to get married? And like so many children who are illegitimate and spend all their lives dishonored and in shame without ever knowing who their father is or their mother. These are the things the Turkish woman told me, and I admit that they made me feel sad. Her conversation with me today, particularly the allegory about our homes being ruined by other women, sounded like a bad omen to me; like a prophesy. [*She stands up, sets the palette down, and sits down in a chair.*] I was seized with fear as if some threat endangered my happiness.

COSTAS: Happy people are like this. They always find something to worry about.

MARY: But I'm no longer truly happy.

COSTAS: What?

MARY: Costas, I'm afraid you don't love me as much as you did before. Your love has lessened, has faded since we've come back. And may I tell you this? During the first month that we were there, you were crazy about me. You were so much in love that your obsession made me unhappy, almost hurt me. Then, the more I grew to love you, the colder you became. Now, since we've returned home, my God, how frightened I've become! [*She cries.*]

COSTAS: [*Hugs her.*] Mary! My love!

MARY: You don't love me like you did before.

COSTAS: You don't believe that. Otherwise, you wouldn't have written to your girlfriend that we are so happy together.

MARY: [*Stands up and looks at her unfolded letter on the table.*] What! You've read this letter?

COSTAS: Yes! I thought that I could.

MARY: No! I have never ever asked to read *your* letters.

COSTAS: But it's different for me, my dear. The golden age of equality hasn't arrived yet. We men must know what goes on in your tiny heads.

MARY: [*Ironically.*] Then mustn't we know what goes on in your fat heads? [*Points at his head.*] Have you forgotten that, after all, our happiness, our love rests on the foundation of my freedom and your freedom?

COSTAS: These freedoms cannot co-exist in marriage.

MARY: Yes, they can when Cupid opens his wings and love prevails.

COSTAS: No they can't when we live in a society which is oblivious to all these new theories. Different ideas and different customs were kneaded into us from the time we were born.

MARY: But Costas, you had promised me down there—

COSTAS: [*Interrupting her.*] Down there, as you said, I was crazy.

MARY: And now you've come to your senses?

COSTAS: What I mean is that now with every step I stumble over some difficulty, and I find that all those dreams of ours can only remain dreams. [*Stands up and paces around.*] Now, my dear, reality, the way of the world with its countless demands raises impregnable fortresses before your beautiful principles. For every step forward that we would like to take, someone else must be knocked down.

MARY: You mean that someone else will be trampled on by some principle; we'll give in and submit to falsehoods and superstitions. And so, when we drop all my ideas and my principles like dead bodies before your fortress—isn't that what you called these Elysian Fields of hypocrisy?—then we'll enter wearing a mask, any mask, to play the part we are given.

COSTAS: [*Laughing.*] Ah! *Les femmes savantes!* The suffragettes!

MARY: You knew who I was before you married me. You chased me all the way down there because, as you used to say, my love was beautiful, grand, and different from the love of other women. And you gave me your word that Mary Myrtou will always be free.

COSTAS: But if I hadn't consented to what you wanted, our marriage wouldn't have taken place.

MARY: You'd rather marry a little woman with no ideas in her head other than how to decorate it with flowers and feathers. [*She stands up and goes to a painting of a beautiful girl.*] You know, these tiny heads and these delicate, tiny hands often, quite often, conquer great men, great cities, great races.

COSTAS: Maybe so, maybe so. However, I think you're exaggerating.

MARY: [*Points at her self-portrait.*] Now, this head here, on the other hand, isn't one of those that you like any more, but she has eagle eyes.

COSTAS: [*Goes to stand behind her and he looks at the portrait.*]—eyes which see beautifully—

MARY: —Deep into the future, the distant future where humanity is bigger and better, and love reigns supreme and provides access to happiness and joy.

COSTAS: [*Gives her a hug.*] My beautiful dreamer.

[*A knock is heard at the door.*]

MARY: Come in.

Scene Three

The same. Enter ANNA.

MARY: What is it, Anna?

ANNA: [*She signals with her hand that she needs to talk to* MARY *in private.*] Ma'am, one moment if you please.

MARY: You can tell me, Anna. What is it?

ANNA: Ma'am, I can't say it. Come here, please.

MARY: [*Approaches* ANNA *at the door.* ANNA *whispers in her ear.* MARY *bursts into laughter. To* COSTAS.] Imagine what the secret was! They brought my dress from the dressmaker's.

ANNA: [*Peeved.*] I said that they brought the bill along with the dress.

MARY: Oh, so the bill was the secret! [*Laughs.*]

ANNA: I thought that in this house, like the other homes, I shouldn't mention any bills in front of the master. Everywhere else I've worked up until now, these were my orders. In fact, at one time, a couple nearly ended up getting divorced over a bill.

COSTAS: No kidding.

ANNA: Yes, Sir. You know Mrs. Mina, the wife of Mr. Radis.

COSTAS: Yes, so?

ANNA: Mr. Radis did not want to pay his wife's bills. I was the new maid at their house and I didn't know. Heaven protect me, I brought in the bill from the merchant as I'm bringing this bill to you now. My Lord and Savior, all Hell broke loose! My goodness, it almost came down to a divorce!

MARY: It's okay, Anna. You may go now. [*Exit* ANNA. MARY *turns to* COSTAS.] What do you think of what you've just heard?

COSTAS: [*Shrugs his shoulders.*] What should I think? It's a true scene from everyday life. I've heard about such scenes.

MARY: These scenes belong to a life filled with falsehoods and to this kind of life you've urged me to sacrifice my principles. Can you imagine what happens to love in families where they almost get divorced over a bill?

COSTAS: But women are costly to keep. They've become a luxury item.

MARY: That's because they don't work. If you let them work, they would learn to appreciate the value of money and would help their husbands. Any husband who is tormented and torments his wife about expenses, would also feel ashamed if his wife was working as I do.

COSTAS: Not every woman has a talent.

MARY: Every woman has some unknown talent which helps create happiness. But men smother it, destroy it.

COSTAS: You're a wonderful advocate and defender of women.

MARY: No, Costas, I'm neither an advocate nor a defender. I'm just an artist who observes, an analyzer who reads deep into women's souls. And it hurts me to see so many hidden treasures lost.

COSTAS: [*Approaches her with admiration.*] You know, Mary, you'd make a wonderful lawyer, or a great apostle.

MARY: All of us women should be both.

COSTAS: [*Glances at his watch.*] What a pity! I don't have time to listen to more of your beautiful speeches. I must go now. But I forgot to tell you. I haven't told you the good news. My mother will be here in a little while, and I must go down to Skoutari[3] to pick her up.

MARY: [*Joyfully.*] Shame on you! Your mother is coming, and all this time you let me chatter even though the place is a mess. [*She springs to her feet and begins to straighten things up.*] So, she's all better now? You know, Costas, I had this silly suspicion that you were lying to me. I was afraid that your mother did not approve of our marriage, that she didn't hold to the ideas you were telling me about when we were in Baghdad.

COSTAS: Mary, my mother never says no. She has never said no to my father in her entire life. And now she doesn't say no to me either.

MARY: I admire her.

COSTAS: Well, I'm off. *Au revoir.* [*Kisses her.*]

Scene Four

The same. Enter DORA.

COSTAS: Good morning, Dora, and *au revoir.*

DORA: *Au revoir.*

MARY: Dora, good news, my mother-in-law is coming! Ring for Anna right away. We must tidy up the place. I'll see Costas out.

[*Exit* COSTAS *and* MARY.]

DORA: [*Alone.*] The mother-in-law is coming. Bad news! [*Begins to tidy up the studio.*] It's impossible to tidy up this place. It's a maze! My God! The City[4] woman, the uniquely fussy housewife with her lorgnette [*Imitates the way* MRS. MEMUSSELOV *holds her glasses up to her eyes.*] is arriving to check out every corner in the house, to find everything in a mess, and to spread her poison everywhere. [*She rings the bell. Enter* ANNA.] Anna! Is the rest of the house orderly, clean, and tidied up?

ANNA: Yes, Mrs. Dora.

DORA: I don't mean just the way we like it, but the way the City women expect to find things. The master's mother is on her way here. The mother-in-law, Anna! Do you understand?

ANNA: [*Alarmed.*] Oh, ma'am! Then we must also scrub the floors. Her ladyship, Mrs. Katingo, will go and check out even the laundry room. [*They get down to cleaning the studio.*]

---

[3]Constantinople is divided into European and Asian sections by the Bosporous Straight. Skoutari (Uscudar in Turkish) is a suburb of Constantinople on the Asiatic shore. It occupies the site of the harbor of ancient Chrysopolis (meaning "City of Gold"). Costas implies that he will pick up his mother at the ferry station (the "iskele") beside the square known as the Square of the Falconers or Iskele Meydani. It takes a ferry about half-an-hour to reach Skoutari from the Galatas Bridge. Iskele Meydani was the rallying place for the Sacred Caravan (Surre-i-Humayun) that departed for Mecca and Medina each year. It was also the beginning of the camel caravan route to Bagdad and the East until the construction of the railway at Haydar Pasha in 1900. The play does not specify the location of Mary's residence, or how she and Costas traveled to Baghdad.

[4]The Greeks referred to Constantinople (Κωνσταντινούπολις i.e., "the City of Constantine") as The City (Η Πόλις). A City woman ("Politissa" in Greek) is a Constantinopolite. The Turkish Post Office changed the name of the city into Istanbul in 1930. Istanbul is a distortion of the Greek phrase "In the City" ("Eis ten polin," i.e., "Is-tan-bul") which was adopted by the Arabs in the thirteenth century when they came in contact with Byzantine Greeks.

Scene Five

The same. Enter MARY *with an armful of greenery and flowers.*

MARY: We must sprinkle beauty and joy in here! [*She arranges the flowers.* DORA *helps her with the flowers.*]

DORA: What for? To celebrate the arrival of your mother-in-law, *the* Mrs. Memusselov? How naive you are!

MARY: How naughty *you* are!

DORA: Okay, okay. Ask Anna who knows her.

MARY: [*To* ANNA.] I don't want to hear any shoddy gossip! Listen, Dora. I don't want you to tell me anything bad about Costas' mother. She is a saint. Just imagine, in all her life, she has never said no about anything either to her husband or to her son.

DORA: That's because both her husband and her son always do whatever she wants.

MARY: Clearly, Dora, you can't stomach my mother-in-law. Leave the flowers alone. You don't know how to arrange them nicely. [*To* ANNA.] We will serve tea to the master's mother.

ANNA: Very well, ma'am.

MARY: Everything everywhere must be arranged beautifully.

DORA: That won't do. We must use expensive silverware! What will catch her eye is the silver, gold, diamonds. Only these will impress her. [*To* MARY.] Hurry. Go put on all your rings and chains! [*To* ANNA.] Go borrow the fine china from the Circassian woman across the street.

[*Exit* ANNA.]

MARY: You're being naughty, Dora.

DORA: And you're being artsy-fartsy.

MARY: Dust my Magdalene over there. Uncover that portrait, too. These are my very own riches.

DORA: [*Laughs.*] You expect to impress her with these? I can't imagine her ladyship Katingo being able to appreciate your paintings. [*Laughs and continues to tidy up the studio.*]

[*Enter* ANNA *carrying a wide basket full of silverware and sets it down. She helps* DORA *to pull a serving table, and they put out the tea set.*]

DORA: Bravo, Anna, bravo! You even brought the gold plates from the Circassian woman.

MARY: The gold plates must be returned immediately.

DORA: The gold plates will stay because happiness here can only be had with gold plates. [*She makes another effort to tidy things up and gives up.*] It's impossible for anyone to put things in order in this place.

MARY: Don't bother anymore, Dora. This is my studio. My mother-in-law should see it the way I like it, and should see me the way I truly am everyday. This mess is beautiful. You go take care of the rest of the house. First, the dining room. Then go up in the turret to straighten up.

DORA: All right, but I would rather that this lady didn't show up.

[*Exit* DORA. *The sound of a horse and carriage is heard.*]

ANNA: [*Looks out the window.*] Ma'am, they're here!

[*Exit* ANNA.]

Scene Six

The same. Enter COSTAS *and* MRS. MEMUSSELOV.

MARY: [*Hastens to the door.*] Welcome! [MARY *and* MRS. MEMUSSELOV *embrace.*] How nice of you to come. Now my happiness is complete. [*Kisses* MRS. MEMUSSELOV's *hand.*

MRS. MEMUSSELOV *sits down on the sofa.* MARY *pulls up a foot stool and sits in front of her.* COSTAS *leans on the wood frame of the sofa.*]

MRS. MEMUSSELOV: I pray that you will always be happy! [*She looks around the room.*] And what a beautiful place you have!

COSTAS: Do you like it, Mama? Didn't I tell you that this place is a true paradise?

MRS. MEMUSSELOV: [*With a bitter-sweet expression.*] It should look even better than paradise to you, especially now.

MARY: [*Picks up the bowl of bonbons and offers them to* MRS. MEMUSSELOV.] Will you have a piece of candy before tea is ready?

MRS. MEMUSSELOV: [*Takes a piece of candy. She then opens her jacket and takes out a bracelet box from her inside pocket.*] I have a little present for you since I had the misfortune and the great sorrow not to be present at your wedding. [*She sighs.*]

MARY: It took place so far away, you know.

MRS. MEMUSSELOV: Yes, down there in Baghdad.

MARY: It is a very nice place. It was Costas' idea that we should get married there. I couldn't even imagine that he would come to find me down there! Actually, I left Constantinople in order to avoid him. One day, when I was painting an isolated Byzantine country chapel, I saw him standing in front of me! And he said to me: "What a nice chapel for the wedding of two lovebirds like us." At first, I didn't accept his proposal. But he was so persistent!

MRS. MEMUSSELOV: [*To* COSTAS *who sits next to her and hugs her.*] So, it was your idea to get married down there.

COSTAS: Yes, Mama. [*Kisses her and strokes her.*] How beautiful you are! Look at us, Mary, don't we look like siblings?

MRS. MEMUSSELOV: [*Slaps him affectionately in the face.*] You rascal! [*To* MARY.] Well, go on!

MARY: Well, we got married that same evening when the sun spread deep red veils across the western sky. What a beautiful evening it was! Right, Costas? Lovely, absolutely lovely! What a pity you couldn't be there.

MRS. MEMUSSELOV: [*Aside.*] I'm going to explode!

MARY: Thousands of birds were singing around us. The flowers, which were languishing and intoxicated like us by the golden glow of the sun, anointed the evening breeze and adorned the isolated Byzantine country chapel with unimaginable beauty.

MRS. MEMUSSELOV: You were alone, like two urchins as if you didn't have any parents!

MARY: We had our love which was grand and so gigantic that, to us, it looked like the entire world. There was also a mother present.

MRS. MEMUSSELOV: What? Your mother was invited? [*To* COSTAS.] You didn't tell me that.

MARY: No. It was the mother of God, a beautiful medieval icon of the Virgin Mary, wearing the crown of a Byzantine empress. She was looking sweetly down at us from inside her rusty frame.

MRS. MEMUSSELOV: Who performed the marriage?

MARY: A priest who hardly knew how to read blessed our marriage. I wove our wedding wreaths with ivy and pure white wildflowers from the valley. [*Opens the box and takes out the bracelet.*]

MRS. MEMUSSELOV: [*To* COSTAS.] How beautifully she speaks! [*Pats* COSTAS *on the head.*] It's no wonder this child lost his head. [*To* MARY.] Well now, what's done is done.

MARY: And you've forgiven us. This bracelet is a token of your love. What a fine bracelet! How I love this stone. It looks as if it were alive, it seems to be aware of us, it appears to respond to us. [*Kisses* MRS. MEMUSSELOV's *hand. To* COSTAS.] What shall I give your mother in return? [*Stands up and picks up a painting of the Parthenon from a table, and offers it to* MRS. MEMUSSELOV.] This is the most valuable gem of the world. It is the temple of my religion, the religion of beauty.

[MARY *goes to get a statuette of Hermes.*]

MRS. MEMUSSELOV: [*To* COSTAS.] What religion is she talking about?

COSTAS: Mother, Mary is an artist. She worships all beautiful things.

MRS. MEMUSSELOV: [*Aside.*] I see! She has a rotten mind!

MARY: [*To* MRS. MEMUSSELOV.] Would you accept this Hermes as well?

MRS. MEMUSSELOV: [*Aside.*] Thank God she didn't give me any of those nudes to take to my girls!

MARY: [*Comes to her with the statue of Hermes.*] Would you like to take off your hat and freshen up a little? [MRS. MEMUSSELOV *stands up and removes her hat.*] Would you like to walk around in the garden or to see the house before tea is ready?

MRS. MEMUSSELOV: If you don't mind I'll have tea first. I was so upset at noon that I haven't eaten anything.

MARY: I'll get it right away. [*Hastens to the serving table and draws the drape aside.*] Costas, give me a hand. Tell Anna, and bring in something with you from the kitchen. [*Exit* COSTAS.] Since you're hungry, we'll prepare a little *goute* for you. We have cold poultry and caviar. If you will excuse me, I'll go see to it. I'll leave you by yourself for a moment.

[*Exit* MARY.]

MRS. MEMUSSELOV: Oh, my God! I'm going to explode. I can't restrain myself any longer. [*She approaches some of the paintings.*] These are the things she worships. What a charlatan! With this and this she made him go crazy over her. We'll see how long her religion will help her.

[*Enter* COSTAS *with two dishes in his hands.*] •

COSTAS: Mother, I always find here the most exquisite and rare delicacies. We will eat extremely well. I'm also hungry with all the excitement today. [*Sets the dishes on the table and sits near his mother.*] Isn't it true, Mama, that your mind is at peace now that you have met Mary? Well? Tell me that you're no longer in despair; that you will stop at last repeating what you've been telling me for the past three days. You almost convinced me that I'm ruined; that I made a big mistake. Wasn't I right that Mary is wonderful and different from other women?

[*Enter* MARY *and* ANNA *carrying several dishes, nuts, and wines on trays.* ANNA *sets the table right away.*]

MARY: I'm sorry that it took us so long. [*Pours tea in the tea-cups.*] Come sit at the table.

[MRS. MEMUSSELOV *and* COSTAS *approach.*]

MRS. MEMUSSELOV: What wealth! What luxury! [*To* MARY.] You knew how to catch this gourmet. Of course everyone knows, the fastest way to a man's heart is through his stomach.

MARY: [*Hands* MRS. MEMUSSELOV *a cup of tea and she prepares tartine with caviar.*] Don't you think that this could also be said about women? I haven't changed anything about the way I live my life. I assure you.

MRS. MEMUSSELOV: So, you always live with such luxury? Then you must have great expenses.

MARY: [*Offers her a tartine and a glass of wine.*] But there are two of us, and we'll both work and we will each have an income.

MRS. MEMUSSELOV: [*Ironically.*] What? You will continue working even now that you're Mrs. Memusselov? In this case, your marriage cannot be made known in this city. Work is not part of the customs for the members of our class and circle.

MARY: We will make it so. Right, Costas?

MRS. MEMUSSELOV: Why work when you don't need to?

MARY: There are so many unfortunate people who need help. So many poor people whom I would like to help.

MRS. MEMUSSELOV: Who will take care of your house?

MARY: Oh, the house. There are so many domestic servants for each house these days that there is nothing else for the mistress to do but to oversee things. Besides, I'll work when I have time to spare. It'll be the best kind of fun. Don't you have anything fun to do?

MRS. MEMUSSELOV: Yes, but certainly not as a means to earn money.

COSTAS: Of course you do, Mother. What about when you're playing cards?

MRS. MEMUSSELOV: Gambling is not work. It's something that excites my interest.

MARY: Do you think that when I stand in front of a blank canvas and I begin to give life to my thoughts and dress them up with lines, light, and colors that my work doesn't interest me? I get excited when I feel that I'm creative, when I put on the canvas the best things in my life, my soul, and my imagination. This kind of work is uplifting, ennobling. It is power, honor, and joy. Costas and I will open this good path together.

MRS. MEMUSSELOV: [*Extremely ironic.*] So, Costas Memusselov will allow his wife to work.

MARY: Allow? Your word is loaded. This word doesn't exist in the dictionary of love. "Allow" is a servile word. We understand each other only with words of love. What's more, we agreed on these matters before we got married. Even if Costas were a millionaire, I would never have given up my work. It's a matter of honor!

MRS. MEMUSSELOV: In our class, a woman's honor and joy is caring for the household of her husband.

MARY: Our household will be a nest that we'll build together. In any misfortune, the two of us will stand together armed, strong, prepared to wrestle and win. In our nest, there will only be songs of joy. Never any nagging or crying.

MRS. MEMUSSELOV: What optimism! [*With malice.*] You have a beautiful personality, Mary, and too much imagination. [*Checks her watch.*] Costas, my child, you must call me a carriage.

MARY: [*Stands up surprised.*] Must you leave so soon?

MRS. MEMUSSELOV: His father doesn't know that I've come here. He wouldn't approve. Men don't take things the way we do, you know. [MARY *looks at* COSTAS.] In fact, Georgie is a bit upset with you because you've left his mother's portrait unfinished for so many months now.

COSTAS: [*Stands up.*] I'll go get us a carriage. You two settle the issue of the portrait.

MRS. MEMUSSELOV: Don't be long. [*Exit* COSTAS.] Yes, well, this portrait was the reason—

MARY: —that I met Costas, and my happiness.

MRS. MEMUSSELOV: [*Aside.*] And I met my unhappiness!

MARY: I'll finish her portrait. I'll make her look very beautiful. But how can I come to work at your house now. Costas lied to me. He told me that, like you, his father approved of our marriage. I can't come to your house now. This bothers me terribly, you know. Costas' lie is inexcusable. I won't go to your house to participate in a farce.

MRS. MEMUSSELOV: I have an idea! Come by the house tomorrow morning at nine. You'll hardly see us and we'll hardly see you. Georgie will be gone. And we'll leave you alone to work on grandma's portrait. Neither will Costas know about it because he'll go home with me now to tend to some business, and he'll have to stay at home tonight. Georgie and I will take a friend of ours to the ship. She's going to Alexandria. Costas, the girls, and their cousin Helen will go shopping. You will start up again where you left off with the portrait. And in this way, I will find an occasion to talk with Georgie, mention your name, and smooth things over.

MARY: Well then, all right. I'll come if I can be all alone with my model.

[*A horse and carriage are heard outside.*]

MRS. MEMUSSELOV: [*Stands up and puts on her hat.*] You'll be left alone for two whole hours.

[*Enter* COSTAS.]

COSTAS: Are you ready, Mother?

MRS. MEMUSSELOV: [*To* MARY.] Well, it's settled. [*Embraces* MARY.] Goodbye, Mary.

MARY: Goodbye. Goodbye, Costas.

COSTAS: Goodbye.

[*Exeunt* MRS. MEMUSSELOV *and* COSTAS.]

MARY: [*Throws herself in a chair.*] I don't understand anything! My mother-in-law is a strange woman. It seems as if she says one thing and she means another. [*Looks at the stone on the bracelet.*] What a beautiful opal! What a wonderful stone with so many different colors! Perhaps that's why it has such a bad reputation! The stone of bad luck, the stone of misfortune. [*She looks pensive.*] Did my mother-in-law know this when she gave it to me? A promise of misfortune. [*A knock is heard at the door.*] Come in.

[*Enter* ANNA.]

ANNA: Ma'am, your model, the Gypsy girl, is here. She's asking if you'll work on her portrait today.

MARY: Yes, let her come in. We must finish it.

Scene Seven

The same. Enter a GYPSY GIRL *wearing a red satin dress, a headband with gold coins, a necklace with gold coins, and has a tambourine in her hand.*

GYPSY GIRL: Good health and happiness to you, my lady.

MARY: Welcome. You know, I'm tired today, and I'm short of time. I can't work a lot.

GYPSY GIRL: My lady, you must finish it because we're leaving town tomorrow.

MARY: [*Places the* GYPSY GIRL *in position and begins to paint.*] Where are you going?

GYPSY GIRL: Where God wills. My lady, one doesn't ask where the birds go when the north wind begins to blow and the first rains come.

MARY: [*Aside.*] What beautiful words she uses, and how colorfully she talks. [*To the* GYPSY GIRL.] Tell me, what country is your homeland?

GYPSY GIRL: Anywhere there is open land with flowers and light; anywhere there is a sky sprinkled with stars, that's where my homeland is.

MARY: What a nice homeland—except you spend your entire lives on the road. Don't you ever get tired of this homeless life? [*She helps the* GYPSY GIRL *restore her pose and continues to paint.*]

GYPSY GIRL: Tired? Why get tired? We live off mother earth and she smiles back at us with her flowers; and we talk to the stars which shed light into our souls.

MARY: You talk to the stars?

GYPSY GIRL: Oh sure! If we didn't talk with them, how could we tell the girls' fortunes and how could we make any potions to fix broken hearts? [*She notices the bracelet on* MARY's *wrist. She breaks out of her pose, alarmed.*] My lady, what enemy of yours gave you this bracelet? This stone is jinxed with bad luck. [*Looks around her for signs of inspiration. The fluttering of a bird and the howling of a dog are heard outside. She points to something outside the window and says to* MARY.] Did you hear that? Your dog is lamenting the loss of your happiness. This bird crowing at your doorstep is the cursed bird of sorrow. [*Grabs* MARY's *hand.*] My lady, take off this bracelet. This stone brings disasters and misfortunes. Take off this jinxed bracelet!

[*Curtain.*]

ACT THREE

Scene One

The Memusselov family is gathered in the drawing room. The three girls are all dressed up and ready to go shopping. OLGINA *puts her hat on,* EMMA *puts one of her gloves on, and* LELA *is sitting at the desk writing a shopping list.*

OLGINA: Father hasn't come downstairs yet. Oh, I forgot. He stayed behind with mama to take Mrs. Vili to the ship.

EMMA: Do you know that mama is expecting MARY [*Draws out the next three words with an ironic tone.*] the "Mistress Artist," this morning? She'll be here any minute now.

OLGINA: [*Also ironically.*] Fortunately, we're going shopping, otherwise I would have been very upset if I had to stay here with our "distinguished" guest.

LELA: [*Puts down her pen.*] You'll always be blockheads and conceited.

EMMA: [*To* LELA.] You be quiet!

OLGINA: [*To* LELA.] You should go back to writing your list. Put down what we have to buy and where we have to buy it.

Scene Two

The same. Enter MRS. IRENE *with a bottle of wine and a box of rusk.*

MRS. IRENE: Here's the old wine that was delivered for the master. [*Sets the bottle and the box on a table.*] Listen, girls, see that you have a smile on your face when the master comes downstairs because he's already a pack of nerves. You know, grandma complained again that she didn't sleep well last night.

[*Exit* MRS. IRENE.]

LELA: [*Stops writing the shopping list for her sisters, and jumps up from her chair.*] Well! And then they wonder why I can't stomach any of this. Grandma, a ninety-year-old woman, should not complain that she feels sick in the morning because that will upset father! "Don't talk, father will get angry! Don't laugh, father will be irritated!" Don't tell him this, don't do that. Hide things here, keep secrets over there, we are always lying.

[*Enter* MRS. IRENE *with a package of lace, and hands it to* OLGINA.]

MRS. IRENE: The vendor delivered it just now with this bill. He said that your mother picked it out.

OLGINA: [*Reads the bill.*] Ten feet, five pounds sterling.

EMMA: [*Opens the package and unrolls the lace.*] Oh, how beautiful! It's for mother's black silk dress.

OLGINA: [*Looks at it.*] When I get married, I will only put real lace like this on my dresses.

LELA: Of course, that's why you need Princess Petrov's millions for your dowry.

[EMMA *puts the lace on her dress and shows off. Father's voice is heard as he is coming downstairs.*]

OLGINA: Father is coming! [*Takes the bill and hides it in her pocket.*]

[EMMA *pulls the lace that gets tangled around her feet, while* OLGINA *pretends that she is straightening up the buffet.*]

Scene Three

The same. Enter GEORGIE *dressed to go out in his day suit.*

GEORGIE: [*Sees the lace.*] What's this? Another new purchase again? [*Angrily.*] You'll eat up what's left of my fortune with these rags you're buying!

OLGINA: [*In a hurry.*] But father, this lace was delivered by the Armenian. He sells his merchandise at very low prices. We got it for one pound, and it's really worth five pounds sterling. In any case, we'll buy it only if mother wants it. If she doesn't want it—

[*Enter* MRS. MEMUSSSELOV *holding her hat. She looks worried when she sees the lace in her husband's hands, and she pretends that she knows nothing about it.*]

MRS. MEMUSSELOV: What's this?

OLGINA: [*Takes the lace from her father's hands and shows it to her.*] Mama, the Armenian brought it. He'll stop by later to see if you want it.

MRS. MEMUSSELOV: Oh no! Another expense! I don't need any more lace.

OLGINA: It's for your new dress, Mama. You know, the Armenian has offered it to us for only one pound.

GEORGIE: [*To* MRS. MEMUSSELOV.] And the children say that it's worth five.

MRS. MEMUSSELOV: [*Looks at the lace, pretending that she sees it for the first time.*] Even six or eight pounds. [*Turns to her husband and she straightens his necktie.*] Let me fix it for you. There! You must look handsome for Mrs. Vili even on the last day.

GEORGIE: [*Examining the lace.*] Maybe he sells at very low prices because he's selling us stolen goods.

MRS. MEMUSSELOV: Of course not, Georgie dear. The lace must belong to a Turkish woman. As I've told you before, some Turkish women can buy on credit at the shops. Their husbands won't let them have cash because they throw it away gambling. So, what do you think they do? They buy merchandise on credit from the shops and they resell it for whatever price they can get in order to have petty cash.

LELA: [*Aside.*] My God! What a lie!

GEORGIE: And the winner in all this is you, Lady Katingo! You dress yourself in fine clothes at rock bottom prices. [*To* LELA.] Leloutsia, see how well your mother manages! You must tell your aunt about this—that here in Constantinople, our women can dress beautifully even on a shoestring budget. You see, we've lost all our money, thousands of pounds sterling, and we must make do in any way we can.

MRS. MEMUSSELOV: [*Pours* GEORGIE *a glass of wine and* EMMA *offers him some rusk.*] You look rather pale, Georgie. Have a sip and dip your rusk toast in your wine. [OLGINA *hastens to fetch him a napkin.* MRS. MEMUSSELOV *looks at her watch.*] Mrs. Myrtou will arrive any time now. You know her, the artist from Athens. When she returned from her trip, she notified me that she'll come to finish grandma's portrait. I'll stay behind for a moment to take care of her. If we take care of her, she'll do it for free. Go ahead, and I'll catch up with you in ten minutes.

[*Exit* GEORGIE.]

EMMA: What a relief that he's gone!

OLGINA: Did he leave us any money?

MRS. MEMUSSELOV: You will buy on credit, and we'll pay it off little by little. [*A knock is heard at the door.*] She's here. It must be her.

[MRS. MEMUSSELOV *hastens and opens the door herself.*]

Scene Four

Enter MARY *with her art box.*

MRS. MEMUSSELOV: Good morning.

MARY: Good morning. [*To the girls.*] Good morning, ladies.

LELA: You've forgotten about us.

MARY: I haven't forgotten you. [*Looks unhappy.*] I was away. I wasn't here. I'll work hard to make it up to you. One or two more sittings and we'll be done.

MRS. MEMUSSELOV: Please sit down. Will you have a glass of water?

MARY: No, thank you. I won't have anything. We must not waste any time.

LELA: We won't delay you, nor will we have the pleasure to keep you company. Unfortunately, we have a commitment to show up at the dressmaker's, and then we'll go shopping.

MARY: Well then, each of us to her task. [*To* MRS. MEMUSSELOV.] Where will I be working?

MRS. MEMUSSELOV: Here in the next room. [*Opens the door to the adjacent room.*] This is where you worked last time. We have everything ready. Come in.

[*Exeunt* MRS. MEMUSSELOV, MARY, LELA, *and* EMMA *into the next room.*]

OLGINA: [*At the door.*] I'll close the door just in case the light from this room bothers you. [*Closes the door. Puts on her other glove, and looks for* LELA'*s shopping list.*] Where did she put the shopping list?

Scene Five

Enter HELEN *wearing a morning dress. She looks very elegant and smart to the point of affectation.*

HELEN: Good morning, Olgina. Are you ready? I'm not late, am I?

OLGINA: What do you mean? You've come half an hour early. Now you'll have to wait for us here because first we have to go to the dressmaker's for a fitting.

HELEN: But your mother wrote to me first thing in the morning, asking me to be here at nine o'clock sharp.

OLGINA: Unless you want to come with us to the dressmaker's and share your fine taste with us.

HELEN: [*Removes her gloves.*] Thanks, but I don't feel like going to the dressmaker's. Where is Costas?

OLGINA: He's out. He'll come to pick us up at the dressmaker's at half past nine.

HELEN: Will he stop here first to pick me up?

OLGINA: Yes.

HELEN: Then, I'll wait. I have to write a letter. I'll mail it at the post office on my way downtown. Where do you keep the stationary?

OLGINA: You'll find anything you need over there. [*She points to the desk.*] Well, *au revoir.*

[*Exit* OLGINA.]

HELEN: *Au revoir.* [*Sits down at the desk, opens a drawer, takes out a piece of stationary, and begins writing. She finishes her letter, reads it, and puts in an envelope.*]

Scene Six

Enter COSTAS. *He stops short when he sees* HELEN.

COSTAS: What! Are you alone? Mama and the girls haven't come downstairs yet?

HELEN: You didn't even say good morning to me! Poor Costas, how you've changed!

Whenever you found me alone in the past, you were crazy with excitement. But now that I actually have lot's of news to share with you—

COSTAS: I thought that you'd rather share your news with someone else now; and that we don't have anything more to say to each other.

HELEN: [*Stands up and approaches him.*] Oh? Is that what you think? You're wrong, my friend. People who've been together for as long as we have—[*Takes him by the arm.*] Come on in. Or, are you afraid to be alone with me?

COSTAS: [*Pushes her gently away.*] Yes, I'm afraid of you. You're a dangerous woman.

HELEN: Are you afraid for your virtue? My God, how the times have changed! In the past, I was the one who was afraid to stay alone with you.

COSTAS: I've no intention of taking away the rights of another man.

HELEN: How virtuous you've become! What an honorable child! [*She quickly goes behind him, nudges him into the room, shuts and locks the door.*]

COSTAS: What are you doing? They may come downstairs and find us locked in here.

HELEN: Don't be afraid. They've all gone out. Your mama and my uncle are taking Mrs. Vili to the ship. The girls are on their way to the dressmaker's. They'll be waiting there for you and me to go shopping with them. So, we're alone.

COSTAS: It makes no difference to me! [*Goes straight for the door.*]

HELEN: [*Stands in front of the door with her arms open.*] I won't let you go past me. We've met here by chance, but I intended to see you anyway.

COSTAS: [*Stands and crosses his arms.*] Perhaps your multi-talented suitor lost his money in the stock exchange, and also lost your love along with it.

HELEN: [*Approaches him so closely that her face is almost touching his face. Passionately.*] No, my love. I have money of my own now. Didn't you hear the great news? I'm the sole heir to twenty thousand pounds sterling, and I'm waiting for one word from you, one nod to send my rich suitor back where he came from.

COSTAS: [*Sarcastic.*] No kidding. What a costly sacrifice!

HELEN: Don't be naughty! I'm not making any sacrifice. You know that I have always loved you madly, and I would have always remained in love with you, no matter how many times I was married. But we were both poor. How could we have survived? Your mother made it clear to me. "Helen dear, this marriage cannot and will not take place!"

COSTAS: And now? [*Sits down.*]

HELEN: Now, with twenty thousand pounds sterling there isn't any fear that we'll starve to death or that we'll nag our love to death. If we give five thousand pounds sterling as a gift to your parents to marry off Olgina, your mother will allow us to get—

COSTAS: [*Interrupts her.*] This has all come too late. I advise you to brace your heart, assuming you have one, to forget about me, and to return to your Andrew's lap of gold. I'm no longer—

HELEN: [*Interrupts him.*] I know, you have other lovers. The Athenian woman is your latest victim. In fact, the gossips say that your trip to Asia took place in her company.

COSTAS: Damn it! You're very well informed.

HELEN: [*Sits down.*] Better than you think. All this time, my heart and my mind were with you.

COSTAS: [*Stands up.*] Tiens! Tiens! How complex a mind and a heart a woman like you has. So when you were offering your lips to this other man, your heart was flying back to me.

HELEN: [*Charges at him, takes his head in her two hands, and kisses him.*] Never has he ever seen me like this in front of him. I've never felt with him what I feel with you. My love, my obsession, my passion for you has never been put out, nor will it ever. Remember, Costas, remember how happy we were; how you would say that no other woman will ever make you happy. Costas, my love, I'm yours and you're mine.

COSTAS: No, I'm not yours. No, it's too late now. All women love the same way. But not all women know how to lie like you do. Now I can no longer believe your eyes. Your eyes are clever and insincere.

HELEN: [*Sad, on the verge of tears.*] You are naughty, Costas. You are unfair and heartless. It's not my fault the way things happened. Your mother found this suitor, she urged me, she threatened me, and she pushed me into his arms. Oh, if only you knew how I fought back, how I resisted all this, how many tears I shed. But what else could I do? I was besieged by my entire family. In order to save myself and preserve our love, I even ended up going to Andrew and telling him that I don't love him. Do you know what he said to me? "I love you," he said, "I like you and that's enough. You'll come to love me in time." What else could I do? But now that I have money, oh, now I can really be yours, Costas.

COSTAS: It's too late now, Helen. [*Paces, looking unhappy.*] I don't belong to myself any more.

HELEN: [*Puts her arms around his neck and looks him in the eye.*] You belong to me. Look at me! Look into my eyes. What other woman could look at you this way? What other woman could love you the way I do?

COSTAS: [*As if mesmerized, he embraces and he kisses her.*] None, you enchantress! None, you charmer! Only you! Yes, I know. We're made for each other. We are chained together by our passion for each other, our past revelries, and the intoxication of our love. Our souls are sealed together by a common desire, a common thirst, something that I've tried for a year now to smother with a new love, a noble love, and I failed!

HELEN: [*Is happy and caresses him.*] So, you're mine again! Always mine! What joy!

COSTAS: [*Pulls her close to him and they sit reconciled.*] How much I wanted you and how much I suffered when I thought of you with that other man! What didn't I try to do to forget you. I lost myself in the biggest revelries. I gambled with my entire life. I sacrificed my future, my ambitions.

HELEN: So what did you actually do?

COSTAS: No matter what I did, I'm still yours! Your name would come to my lips when I was talking to this other woman.

HELEN: What has happened to your love for this other woman now?

COSTAS: Oh, my love for her has now turned into a love of duty. That's why it didn't last any longer than a beautiful dream. She was the drug that I was taking to help me forget you, and now it has begun to wear me down.

[*A sound of footsteps is heard behind the door which leads to the adjacent room.*]

HELEN: [Jumps up.] Someone is coming. [*Unlocks the door leading to the hallway.*] I don't want them to find us together. I must go now.

[*Exit* HELEN.]

Scene Seven

The door leading to the adjacent room opens. Enter MARY *looking pale with glassy eyes.*

COSTAS: [*Surprised out of his wits.*] Mary! What are you doing here? When did you arrive? How did you happen to be in there? [*He approaches her.*]

MARY: Your mother put me there. Don't touch me. You horrify me. I've heard everything. [*Collapses in a chair and begins crying.*]

COSTAS: [*Pulls a chair over and sits next to her.*] Mary, forgive me. She was an old flame. I confessed to you about this wild adventure of mine. [*Tries to embrace her.*] Forgive me, Mary.

MARY: [*Avoids him by standing up and walking away from him.*] Don't touch me! You horrify me! Your hands are still warm from holding her. Your lips are still afire from kissing her. [*Angry.*] Don't you touch me! You horrify me! Go away!

COSTAS: She seduced me, Mary. Listen to me.

MARY: [*Angry.*] I don't want to listen to anything.

COSTAS: So, have you never ever loved me?

MARY: How dare you talk to me about my love when at this very moment you are still intoxicated with the words of this other woman; her form is still reflected in your eyes; and her vows still echo in your ears. How horrible! [*Stares at him with something frightening in her look.*] You were preparing an entire lifetime for me to be chained to such dishonest acts! And you would come to give me the cold kisses of a dead heart, and caresses that would hurt me, and glances that would denigrate my love!

COSTAS: Mary, don't get excited!

MARY: And later, when your pity would have turned to contempt and hatred, you would become vulgar and rude to me, and you would kill every bit of beauty in my spirit, and you would destroy any sign of nobility in my suffering soul.

COSTAS: Mary, you're getting all flustered by your own thoughts. They make you lose your mind. They make you despair. If you loved me, you wouldn't have judged me so harshly. My mother has received my father's mistress even in her own house.

MARY: You mother is a slave and your father is an Oriental tyrant. And slaves give birth to men of weak character, and cowards, and liars, and traitors! But I don't want my child to spread around him disaster and despair, I don't.

COSTAS: Calm down, Mary.

MARY: [*Goes to the door.*] I'm leaving you. I will at least save my child!

COSTAS: [*Runs after her.*] Mary, where will you go?

MARY: [*In a desperate voice.*] Any place where women are treated like people, not like objects of pleasure; any place where love is not denigrated and is not betrayed as it is here.

[*Exit* MARY.]

[*Curtain.*]

ACT FOUR

Scene One

A hotel suite richly furnished and decorated with flowers, laurels and trophies. MARY *has white hair and she is dressed beautifully in a very expensive black dress. She is reading the newspapers. Her son is eighteen years old. He sits, writing a letter.*

MARY: Listen to this, Paul. [*Reads aloud.*] "The athlete who was the surprise of the Olympics at the Stadium, who broke all records and ranks first among the Olympic champions is a Greek this time, the young Myrtos. Handsome like a statue, he brings to mind the young men of ancient times whose good looks were immortalized by the chisel of the great sculptors."

PAUL: [*Interrupts her.*] Oh, mother, the Greek journalists are exaggerating.

MARY: [*Gives him a hug.*] Whatever they say, my child, they can add nothing to my pride and glory. I'm the happy mother of an Olympic champion.

PAUL: [*Hugs her back.*] The glory is entirely yours, Mama, and so is the honor; my wreaths, too. [*Takes two laurel wreaths and sets them at her feet.*] And all these flowers and gifts, I lay them down as a tribute to your tenderness and affection!

MARY: My child, I only did my duty.

PAUL: Only your duty? Which martyr and which heroine ever lived the way you lived, and did what you did, to save her child? From a sickly, degenerate, almost malformed child with a sluggish and bad character you helped me become what I am today. Mama, do you remember when you took me to the exercise room of the orthopedic clinic what the trainer doctor told you? "Ma'am, your child will never become a complete man, a strong man, because he has the seeds of a degenerative disease in his blood."

MARY: I don't want to remember any past troubles today.

PAUL: The more I remember them the more I admire you. [*He stretches his arms out in front of him.*] These hands with these muscles, and this chest with this rib cage killed all the seeds of the degenerative disease even those that must have been in the wise head of my trainer.

MARY: That poor man! How much he loved Greece! I remember that he always said things that would encourage you and inspire you, like "Don't ever forget that you're a Greek, and you have an obligation to become handsome."

PAUL: I was ugly back then, nearly a hunchback.

MARY: Forget all of this now. We should remember only the beautiful and pleasant things in life.

PAUL: But I would have an ungrateful memory and a cruel heart if I stopped remembering your hard work, the sacrifice of your entire youth, your self-denial, and all of your other sorrows which you did not tell me about but I guessed. Remember the little house on Division Street where you had painted all the walls with your favorite places in Athens and Constantinople? You taught me to love this homeland as much as my other homeland. When I was a little boy you told me so many beautiful stories taken from the real history of Greece, but also from your own painful experiences.

MARY: [*In tears.*] I remember! Yes, I remember! My dear child! My good child! You're a great consolation to me.

PAUL: Your entire life was a tireless, endless life of work and struggle and courage. And finally recognition came when your painting, *The Gypsy Girl,* won a prize. Good luck smiled on you, and money began to pour in from all directions in great quantities. Kate told me about all of your sacrifices. She told me about the happiness that you turned down so that I would remain your exclusive and only love.

MARY: Kate? But what does Kate know?

PAUL: She knows what her father told her the day she informed him that she and I are in love. "Well, my child," said her father, "it is fated for you to have the distinguished Mrs. Myrtou as your mother. It has been ten years since I proposed to her that she become my wife and your mother. She refused even though she wasn't rich back then. 'I can't divide my love between my child and someone else,' Mrs. Myrtou said to me, 'All of my love belongs to my child'."

MARY: Good old Mr. Derby, what a great heart he has. What he didn't tell his daughter is that he had proposed to me to adopt you and to share his millions with you and Kate.

[*The telephone rings.* PAUL *answers it.*]

PAUL: Hello? [*Listens.*] The reporter of what newspaper? [*Listens.*] Yes, he may come in. [*Hangs up.*]

MARY: Another interview? And you accepted of course?

PAUL: Yes, because I know that you would be displeased if I didn't. You have a soft spot in your heart for all the people here. It seems to me that I would cause you great sorrow if I refused to see even the lowest of the low in this country.

MARY: [*Laughs.*] You're right. Here it seems to me even the stones have beautiful souls.

PAUL: Some stones, yes, I agree. For instance, those that support the Parthenon. But please no more sentimental exaggerations.

MARY: You're right. You don't know what it means to feel homesick for the land where I was born and grew up, where I dreamed about the first joy of my life and experienced my first sorrow and cried for the first time. You can't understand my thirst for hearing people speak my language, for being with people who feel the same way I feel, who live by the same ideals, who share the same sorrows! I can't explain to you what it meant for me to live like an exile away from home for twenty years, no matter how poor my home was, and to lose my family one by one without any hope of ever seeing them again.

PAUL: [*Wipes a tear.*] My mother, my good mother!

MARY: [*Moved even more.*] Yes! Even when I hear the "lowest of the low" chatting in the streets, they seem to me as if they are filling the air around me with harmonious music!

[*A knock is heard at the door.*]

PAUL: Come in.

Scene Two

The same. Enter a JOURNALIST.

MARY: Come in, Sir. [*Shows him to a chair.*]

JOURNALIST: Thank you. [*Hands out his business card.*]

MARY: That's not necessary, Sir, All of you have written such beautiful things about my Paul that you're no longer strangers to us. Our appreciation and gratitude bring us closer to you.

JOURNALIST: Madam, it is we who have cause to be grateful to your son because he moved us so much.

PAUL: Gratitude is a heavy thing unless we share it with those who most deserve it in the first place. Therefore, enough has been written about Paul Myrtos, Sir. The champion, the real winner of the Olympics, is my mother, Mrs. Myrtou! [*Points at the wreaths.*] I was transferring my trophies to her right before you arrived.

JOURNALIST: [*Aside.*] This will be a first class story for the front page! [*To* PAUL.] Thank you for giving me an opportunity to present a beautiful portrait of an exemplary mother to our Greek women.

MARY: [*Embarrassed.*] Paul! [*To the* JOURNALIST.] Please, don't listen to him.

JOURNALIST: May I have a photograph of the lady? [*To* MARY.] Oh, I absolutely must publish your photo.

MARY: I don't have any.

PAUL: Wait, I do! I'll fetch you one right away.

MARY: [*Follows him.*] Paul, my child, please! [*Exit* PAUL. *She returns to the* JOURNALIST.] Sir, please, limit your story to just the Olympic champion. Don't mix the women with the wrestlers in the arena. It is premature, at least here. Don't forget that the ancient Athenians didn't even allow women to enter into the Stadium.

JOURNALIST: [*Changes the subject.*] How do you like the Stadium, madam? What was your first impression when you saw it?

MARY: It was like a white apparition in a blue dream. A huge beautiful baptismal bowl that survived the ravages of time for so many centuries so that the Greek race could be baptized in the holy light today.

JOURNALIST: Am I to assume that the wrestling arenas in America are much inferior? Is there anything comparable to the Stadium in that great land?

MARY: The Stadium is incomparable, Sir, because it is the immortal seat of Greece. Our motherland from good old times has preserved it deep inside her. Today it can once again embrace its new children who are stronger and healthier and crown them like heroes.

JOURNALIST: What a wonderful thought! [*Makes a note in his notebook.*]

[*Enter* PAUL *holding a photograph in his hand.*]

MARY: [*Objecting politely.*] Paul, my child, please.

PAUL: Come, Sir, my mother's modesty will prevent us from talking about her. If you'd like, come to my room.

JOURNALIST: [*Bowing to* MARY.] Goodbye, Madam. And thank you.

MARY: Sir, don't believe what this naughty boy will tell you.

[*Exeunt the* JOURNALIST *and* PAUL. *A knock is heard at the door.*]

MARY: Another one. My God! I'm worn out by all these emotions. Come in.

[*Enter a* BELL BOY.]

BELL BOY: Madam a gentleman would like to see you. He has tried to see you many times before. He says that it is an absolutely urgent need that you see him today.

MARY: No doubt, he is another journalist again. Show him in. [*Exit the* BELL BOY.] These poor journalists, they write with such feeling about my Paul. [*A knock is heard at the door.*] Come in.

Scene Three

The same. Enter COSTAS *with a grey beard and in a grey suit.*

MARY: Come in. Your name? [*Recognizes him.*] Oh, my God!

COSTAS: Costas Memusselov.

[MARY *is shaken up and todders to a chair.*]

COSTAS: It's me, Mary. Most guilty and most unhappy.

MARY: Unhappy?

COSTAS: Very much so, Mary. I'm one of life's wrecks who lived through the ten days of the Olympic Games like a man in Hell. During the celebration of the beauty of youth and the dazzling glory of athletics in the white glow of the Stadium, I realized how miserable my entire life has been, how I destroyed our happiness with my own hands, causing pain and despair.

MARY: But who told you we would be here?

COSTAS: My heart, Mary, my heart because I always preserved a small, pure, and beautiful place in it where I hid whatever memories of goodness and nobility were left to me. The only moments of true joy that I felt during these past twenty years of my dishonest and depraved life were those that reminded me of our past happiness. The little letters of my child that arrived once every year told me that a great heart, an outstanding mother was wrestling with life abroad and was victorious. Heartless as I was, I would have forgotten my own child if you didn't remind me of him and didn't make me love him through his photographs. All these things built a special place in my soul made of bright rays of tenderness and fatherly love. During the folly of my dishonest life and the exhaustion of the horrible orgies and the disgust, this place always gave me hope for a life that would look like a resurrection.

MARY: This hope was snuffed out and lost forever by that frightful scandal. My child knew up until then that he had an unfortunate father. But when that frightful scandal snuffed out my dream for a happy new dawn, and my own hopes were also lost, I told my child that his father was dead.

COSTAS: [*Looks down guiltily.*] Yes, it was a horrible scandal! By then I had become a raging beast who drank, gambled, and forged signatures and counterfeited money, and would stop at nothing because he saw all around him an abyss, a darkness, and Hell. [*He wipes away a tear.*] Oh, Mary, why did you go away and leave me all alone? You could have saved me if you had stayed with me.

MARY: I went away to save my child; to save myself from becoming like the women you had around you. Lies beget more lies and dishonesty is the death of the soul. I needed to save my soul and I saved it. During my grieving and tears over the past twenty years, I maintained a mother's love that was beautiful, immaculate, and pure like a clean and clear mirror where my child could look at himself without embarrassment and without sorrow. Children must be happy and full of laughter throughout their childhood. The sorrow of misfortune should not cloud their beautiful souls. Neither should the shame of their father or their mother wound them.

COSTAS: I sensed that you heard about the scandal. I felt that I lost my right to be called a father. So, I stopped writing to you and my child since that unfortunate day. Only on rare occasions was I able to find out how you were doing from a friend of mine in America. Just a few days before the Olympics, my friend sent me a telegram telling me that my son and the other athletes had left the United States heading for the Olympics in Athens.

MARY: Who is this friend of yours? Mr. Derby perhaps?

COSTAS: Perhaps. Very recently, I grew sick and tired of living the way I had lived. People who live like me, see every door and every avenue to salvation closing before them. Everywhere I passed, I left ruins behind me. Wherever I stepped, poisoned thorns sprung up and wounded me and my family. When I received the news, it seemed to me as if night turned into day. It seemed to me as if my last hope for a good life, like the life we lived together during the first days of our marriage, was shining in my soul. I didn't waste any time. I left for Athens immediately. I arrived here on the first day of the games. Right away, without a moment to spare, I ran to the Stadium.

MARY: You were there! Then you saw our Paul's triumph! Isn't he really handsome and strong?

COSTAS: Oh, Mary, no matter what I say, it can't be compared to what I went through in the last ten days. I recognized our child immediately from the very first moment that he appeared in the arena, but I didn't dare to look at him in the eye, nor could I go and shake his hand like a perfect stranger. My heart which had been dead to every joy and every emotion, was revived and fluttered and grew so much that it seemed to me, how can I say it, as if it had reconciled itself with the whole world. [*Is moved to tears, and his voice breaks.*]

MARY: [*Is also moved to tears, and approaches him.*] My poor friend! What torture!

COSTAS: Each time Paul won a victory, each time our flag was raised on the pole—only then I understood the beauty of our flag there in the Stadium—and our son's name resounded in glory amidst the cheers of all that crowd applauding with wild enthusiasm, great emotion, and sacred joy, oh, Mary, it seemed to me that my soul, too, was growing big and tall up there next to the blue symbol of a proud moment, and it became pure and beautiful and young and born again and re-baptized in the joy, the victory, and the triumph of my child. And Mary, yesterday, each branch from the wild olive tree of Althaea,[5] each wreath, like these here, was for me a symbol of your grandeur but also of my humiliation and shame.

MARY: What grandeur? I did what any mother would have done in my place.

COSTAS: No, Mary, take a look at me. What did my mother do for me? Look at my shame and my loneliness and my despair. My mother, the gentlewoman of Constantinople, as she called herself, gave me her cold beauty, and the soul of her degenerate race, and a mind corrupted by lies. Let my mother look at me now! May she be damned!

MARY: [*Crying.*] No, please don't, poor man! It wasn't her fault. She became what she was brought up to be by dishonest prejudice, the chains of slavery, the old ideas, the blindness of the mind, and the flattering of foolish people.

COSTAS: You, on the other hand, Mary, raised a child to become a hero, a champion of the

---

[5]Althaea (Ἀλθαία or Ἀλταία) was daughter of Thestios, King of Pleuronae. When she was pregnant with Meleagros, she swallowed the young shoot of an olive tree. When she gave birth to her son Meleagros, she also gave birth to the young shoot. On the seventh day from his birth, the Fates prophesied that Meleagros will die when the shoot was burned (Apoll. A, 8, 2). Indeed, when Meleagros later killed his mother's brothers, Althaea caused her son's death by burning the shoot (Schol. Tzetzes in Lycophr. 492), and hanged herself. Phrynichos dramatized Althaea's story in his drama Πλερωνιαι: "κρυερόν γὰρ οὐκ ἤλυξεν μόρον, ὠκεῖα δὲ νιν φλὸξ κατεδαίσατο, δαλοῦ περθομένου ματρὸς ὑπ' αἰνᾶς κακομηχάνου" (Pausanias I, 31, 4).

best and most honest life, a fine young man who is happy, brave, and wise. With your own two hands, you, a woman, you the great champion of life, you nourished him with all kinds of wealth and all kinds of treasures. You see, I know what you've accomplished! You've also made Paul rich with your work, your art, your skillful hands. And now the two of you are happy. You are the worthy mother of a worthy son! Oh, Mary, why didn't you feel sorry for me, why didn't you love me as much. Why did the mother in you kill the woman in the depths of your beautiful soul?

MARY: I was young, too. I had dreams, and a proud soul. My love for you was so beautiful that it could only be nourished by lofty ideals and truths. I realized that if I didn't leave you immediately, I would gradually feel contempt for you, I would feel both hatred and revulsion for you. I left because I was not born to hate those whom I once loved. You see, I no longer wanted my husband who was my first and last love.

COSTAS: Mary dear, does this mean that I can still hope?

MARY: This was my dream which I kept alive for many years. I imagined a happy day like this, and I was waiting for it to come with great joy. I thought of coming back to you when you least expected me, as a mother proud for our son who is good, honest, industrious, and as a wife who stayed faithful to the first and only love of her life. Rich as I am today, I could have taken you far away to renew our love which would be strengthened by the sorrow of our separation. We would both forget all of our past troubles through the worship of our child.

COSTAS: Well, Mary, why didn't you?

MARY: Oh, my God! If only that disastrous, shameful scandal hadn't happened! But right now Paul is merciless and implacable on any issue of honor. If this child learns that you are his father, he will also inevitably learn about the latest scandal in your life. And, Costas, I don't want your child to judge you and to condemn you. He mustn't.

COSTAS: Oh, that is my misfortune!

MARY: No, he mustn't know what I know or that I've forgiven you. He is young, happy, unchallenged by life, and for this reason, he has an unbending character.

COSTAS: Then every consolation and every hope is lost to me.

MARY: My God, I don't know what to say or do. Be brave, Costas, for the sake of his happiness. Our child is the hope and the joy of the future. We went through life on a bad, dark, rotten path. We are the past. His life is floating in the light. Our life is drowning in a pitch dark abyss. And our wrecked souls mustn't cloud, no, they mustn't shade our son's happiness. Costas, the bonds that unite children with their father and mother must be woven out of beautiful and fragrant flowers. Otherwise, they become like the chains of convicts that wound them and hurt them and discourage them throughout their lives.

COSTAS: You're right, Mary. I must go. There is no place for me here without destroying his happiness. Damned souls like myself have no place in Paradise. I'm condemned. [*He turns to leave, feeling very distraught.* MARY *stands up, makes a desperate move, and gives him her hand. He turns around grabs it and kisses it frantically. Then he hastens to the door. The door opens. Enter* PAUL. COSTAS, *on his way out, embraces* PAUL *and kisses him.*] I congratulate you, son. You've honored your motherland.

[*Exit* COSTAS. MARY *takes a step forward as if she wants to call* COSTAS *back.*]

PAUL: [*Surprised.*] Who was that man, mother? He hugged me with so much passion!

MARY: [*Suppressing a sob.*] An unfortunate man, Paul. He had a son like you, and he lost him.

[*Curtain.*]

Suzanne Lilar (1901–92)

From the time it became an independent nation in 1830, Belgium has struggled with its divided cultural and linguistic heritage. The majority Flemish, Dutch-speaking population has, until recent decades, been largely controlled by the Walloon, French-speaking minority. This division is manifest in the theater, where it is compounded by the relatively small size of the available audience. The country's drama has tended to be engulfed by neighboring countries, most notably France. Because of both economic and cultural forces, the place for native writers in the Belgian theater has always been problematic. French has generally been considered the more prestigious language—again until recently, and Paris the choice theatrical destination.

Modern Belgian theater can be said to begin with the publication of Maurice Maeterlinck's *The Princess Maleine* in 1889 in Paris. Like Maeterlinck, Michel de Ghelderode, the other internationally prominent Belgian dramatist of the first half of the twentieth century, wrote in French and saw most of his plays open in Paris. Belgian theaters have often been reluctant to risk introducing a new Belgian play, preferring to wait until after it has returned (from Paris) as part of the accepted international repertoire—a pattern that for the last twenty years has drawn the ire of Brussels and Antwerp critics. And yet Belgium has contributed and continues to contribute impressively to modern drama, with a vibrant avant-garde as well as the more mainstream modernist plays of Maeterlinck and Ghelderode. Since the seventies, Liliane Wouters, Michèle Fabien, and Lucienne Stassaert have been contributing significantly to the library of female-authored plays.

Suzanne Lilar, as a successful playwright, novelist, and critic, exemplifies the international artist hailing from a small country, one that shares a language with a large neighbor. She may insist that the "Belgian theater is a Flemish theater" (whether written in French or Dutch), and that she is completely Flemish, but her masterpiece, *Le Burlador* (1946), premiered at the Théâtre Saint-Georges in Paris. French-language plays, including the three she wrote, seemed inexorably to be a Parisian offshoot. Lilar, as a lawyer and the wife of a minister of justice (Albert Lilar), was prominent in Belgian society and letters. She wrote ten books, ranging from dramas, to memoir, to social analysis. The central theme that animates her writing, one that she elaborates in her treatise *Aspects of Love* (*Le Couple*, 1963), is that of erotic love. Written in the wake of Simone de Beauvoir's *Second Sex* and of Jean Paul Sartre's writings, her "history" traces from as far back as Plato's *Symposium* the "divinizing," "sacralizing" power of love—especially as embodied in the

Suzanne Lilar, late 1980s. (Courtesy of Marie Fredericq-Lilar.)

"conjugal" couple, whether regular or irregular. For her, "the *érotique* is either sacred or nothing," and it is, she argues, very much in the interests of women to restore this power and dignity to love. And she is clear that the love to which she refers, *l'amour fou,* is unreasonable, daimonic, sublime.

Lilar sees her championing of love as an advance for women and as an attempt to reconcile the body and the erotic with Christianity, which has mistakenly been hostile to Eros. She sees herself as a feminist insofar as she recognizes and declaims against the injurious position in which traditional morality and politics have put marriage. This same advocacy, with its focus on the couple and its component of self-effacement and even masochism, along with her belief in an "eternal feminine," would be difficult for contemporary feminists to endorse. Though she wrote of the Existentialism of Sartre and de Beauvoir, she does not seem to find the philosophical freedom and individualism of *The Second Sex* compelling.

It is not surprising that Lilar's preeminent literary achievement is a neoromantic reworking, this time from the perspective of a female writer, of the Don Juan legend. The protagonist is no longer El Burlador, the trickster seducer, but the engulfing spirit of love. Gone are the villainy and cruelty and gone is the punishing statue of Tirso de Molina (Lilar's primary source), of Molière, of Mozart, and of Pushkin. In their stead is an enraptured Don Juan, or rather, as the author would have it, an enraptured couple. Lilar has taken this centerpiece from the library of misogynistic libertinism and transformed it into a dramatic essay on love triumphant.

Lilar takes this legendary seducer, who lives "on the edge," challenging the laws of society and religion, and makes of him an avatar of the divinity of Eros. The play is a celebration of the union of the carnal and the sacred, of an archetypal couple. Such earthly cares as jealousy, punishment, and death lose consequence. From the way Don Juan touches Isabel's hair in the dark to his assertion that they are "angels," the play trumpets the salvational power of love. This perspective is Lilar's challenge—and her contribution to the legend. The animating eroticism leads to a wondrous serenity—the very opposite of damnation. Whether she achieves her goal of combining carnality and fidelity in an acceptable, convincing way is an open question. But once the solidity of the ground has been disturbed and the safe ordinariness, as represented by Octavio, is dismissed (because he is opaque and obscures the horizon), nothing less than this erotic-angelic love will do. Don Juan's hedonism, his rule of pleasure, overwhelms. His features are in every convent prayer book; the primal sin, adapting the spirit of Existentialism, is not to have lived.

SELECTED BIBLIOGRAPHY IN ENGLISH

Lilar, Suzanne. *Aspects of Love in Western Society.* Trans. Jonathan Griffin. London: Thames and Hudson, 1965.

———. *The Belgian Theater since 1890.* Trans. Jan-Albert Goris. New York: Belgian Government Information Center, 1962.

Quaghebeur, Marc. "Introduction." *Gambit* 11 (1986), 9–24.

Willinger, David, ed. *An Anthology of Contemporary Belgian Plays: 1970–1982.* Troy, New York: Whitston Publishing, 1984.

———, ed. *Theatrical Gestures from the Belgian Avant-Garde.* New York: New York Literary Forum, 1987.

EL BURLADOR

Suzanne Lilar

Translated by Frank Caucci

CHARACTERS

THE DUCHESS ISABEL

DON JUAN TENORIO

DON PEDRO TENORIO   Spanish ambassador

THE KING OF NAPLES

DUKE OCTAVIO   Isabel's fiancé

DOÑA JACINTA   Isabel's nurse

ROSALINE   Isabel's sister

DOÑA MARIANA DE MENDOZA

DOÑA FRANCISCA DE GUEVARA

DOÑA MERCEDES DE VILLAFRANCA

ANA DE ULLOA

RIPIO   Duke Octavio's attendant

FERNANDO

THE CAPTAIN OF THE GUARDS

MAIDS, VALETS, GUARDS

THE GARDENER'S VOICE

The action is set in Naples and Seville, in the past.

ACT ONE

A hall of the King's Palace in Naples. It is night, almost completely dark.

ISABEL: Follow me, and don't make a sound. The King is asleep in his room at the end of this hallway. Wait. Just another moment. I can't decide to let you go. It's absurd, as if you were never coming back. Promise me you'll return.

DON JUAN: I promise.

ISABEL: Octavio, tonight was the first time I've ever loved you. Do you know when it all began? When you slipped into my room, I didn't love you yet. It's when you touched my hair. I could feel your hand softly on my head. I felt like a bird trapped in a cage, trying in vain to escape.

DON JUAN: Why did you think that? So you wanted to escape me then. Isabel, please tell me I didn't do anything against your will. Tell me again that what you did was for love alone, that I truly conquered you, and not possessed you by force.

ISABEL: Men! How can you think about nursing your pride at a moment like this? Octavio, no matter how old I get, I'll never forget the weight of your silence when you approached me. I felt your sweet cruelty gather over me. For the first time, I tasted the delight of letting go, and becoming your victim.

DON JUAN: How proud, even in your humility. What about your desire, Isabel?

ISABEL: My desire waited for each of your caresses. What are you making me say? I'd be blushing with shame if we hadn't gone beyond that. It's only tonight that I was born. Everything's new, and strong, as on the first morning of creation. You smell good, my love. Do you know that your hair smells like incense? And your lips, like raspberry. How could I never have noticed? It's so obvious.

DON JUAN: Fool. My sweet fool. I don't recognize you any more. In just one night you've blossomed like a rose that opens before the dawn, and surprises the morning gardener.

ISABEL: You too, Octavio, aren't the same any more. First of all, your voice is deeper. It's much more solemn. And your caresses are both softer and more expert. Octavio . . .

DON JUAN: Stop calling me by that name.

ISABEL: Why?

DON JUAN: Let's just say I don't like it. It's a name you'd use for an innocent, little boy.

ISABEL: But you've always been an innocent, little boy.

DON JUAN: And . . . what about tonight?

ISABEL: Perhaps not . . .

DON JUAN: Then find me a name for tonight only.

ISABEL: What name?

DON JUAN: Well . . . I don't know. One that suits me. Let's see . . . Juan, maybe?

ISABEL: How peculiar! Juan . . .

DON JUAN: What are you thinking about?

ISABEL: About Don Juan, the Spanish ambassador's nephew.

DON JUAN: Don't you like him?

ISABEL: You don't expect me to like that seducer of nuns, wives, and fiancées, do you? El Burlador! What a glorious title! Tricking women can't be too difficult when you see how fast they are at letting themselves be duped. Except for me, they all blush with pleasure when he speaks to them.

DON JUAN: Just the same, it's you he's looking for. Are you sure you didn't provoke him with your charm?

ISABEL: Me! I don't think I've looked at him twice since his arrival at the Palace.

DON JUAN: That's just it. Ignoring Don Juan is to him the height of coquetry.

ISABEL: Oh, you bore me! I don't like him, I tell you.

DON JUAN: Do you find him ugly?

ISABEL: Well . . . first of all, I don't like that face with the eyes and beak of a bird of prey, nor the arrogance of those lips so well shaped you can't help but notice them. They're indecent. Did you see that look in his eyes? One moment it covets and dominates, and the next it becomes sweet and sly like the expression on a cat. And that slivering manner of his. That man's a scoundrel.

DON JUAN: For a man you've looked at only twice, you didn't perceive him poorly. Don't mind me. The day is dawning. I must leave, if you don't want your maids to see me.

ISABEL: Do you want me to light the way?

DON JUAN: No! . . . or rather yes, but in a minute. Tell me, Isabel, are you happy?

ISABEL: I think I'm happy. I feel so light, so very light, as though my feet were suspended above the earth. And the ground, isn't it strange, the ground feels like it doesn't have its usual consistency. It's changing under my very feet, rising like dough under the fists of a kneader. Is this happiness?

DON JUAN: Maybe. I don't know. It's the first time this has happened to me.

ISABEL: Do you feel the same way? Does the earth feel like it's coming alive under your feet?

DON JUAN: No. To me, it's like walking on clouds.

ISABEL: That sounds like heaven, Oct . . .

DON JUAN: Shhh . . . Isabel . . . is the man you love your lover or your betrothed?

ISABEL: Just yesterday, I could have forgotten you. But nothing could now break this bond between us.

DON JUAN: [*Sighing.*] Go now, my heart, get a light and gaze at the face of the man you love.

ISABEL: Wait . . . , I don't dare any more. Your voice has changed suddenly . . . I've lost my peace of mind . . . A bad thought must have gone through you, Octavio, like a bat across your path. Something is wrong. Tell me. I no longer recognize my happiness.

DON JUAN: [*Lighting a torch.*] Do you want to see the face of your happiness? Look.

ISABEL: [*Dumbfounded.*] I must be mad. This isn't possible. Where is Octavio? Could it have been you, just now? [DON JUAN *nods.*] It was you, the whole time? Ah! [*Angrily.*] You, Don Juan!

DON JUAN: Yes, Don Juan, imploring your forgiveness, Madam. He is guilty only of having loved you too much.

ISABEL: I beg you, keep quiet.

DON JUAN: It's true I love you. I haven't deceived you at all. Ever since I arrived in Naples, I've lived only for you. Alas, having been warned about me, your virtue was obstinately set upon ignoring me. You repelled even the most innocent kindness I showed you. You pushed aside my attention when I offered my arm to you. Such steadfast hate toward me only increased my love. I wanted insanely to convince you that what you abhorred wasn't Don Juan so much as his nasty reputation. [*A momentary silence.*] I beg you, Madam, forgive me. I didn't want to take advantage of you. I only wanted you to listen to me. I only wanted to approach you as I really am, not as they've described me. If I took Duke Octavio's place, please concede in all fairness, that I owe him nothing. I only wanted from you what I myself could conquer . . .

ISABEL: So you even go so far as to brag about the goodness you've found in me. Coward. I can well see you attack women without so much as showing your face. I thought you had more pride.

DON JUAN: I've put myself in the position of accepting the worst insults from you.

ISABEL: Who between us dares speak of insults? How could I listen to you, even stand to hear you? Go, or I'll denounce you. If you value your life, Don Juan, be quick to leave before my screams gather a crowd around us.

DON JUAN: I don't value my life, Isabel, and I will not run away. But I beg you to lower your voice. You must not be discovered with a man in the middle of the night.

ISABEL: How kind of you to concern yourself with my honor when you've just stripped it away forever. What do I care about rumors and shame now? [*Her voice breaks.*] What I can't bear is how you've hurt me. You tricked me.

DON JUAN: Only your pride is hurt.

ISABEL: And even so, my pride belongs to me alone. Did you have the right to harm it?

DON JUAN: By deluding yourself about the man you held in your arms, you suffered only a common fate. What woman claims to know the man in her arms? What woman in love doesn't project on the man she loves the fires of her imagination? You're happier than the others because you were deceived less. You didn't love a mirage; it is not a mirage but a real man who adores you, who kneels before you, and begs you to command him. Isabel, is your hand shielding your heart? You don't want me to see it beat like a crazed bee hitting the windows of a closed room. My wild one! You don't want me to know that you're trembling with love when you think you're trembling with anger. [*A certainty in his voice.*] You love me, Isabel!

ISABEL: Love you! I'd rather have my heart ripped from my bosom. Don't touch me! Go away. Leave me, I tell you.

DON JUAN: Will you be quiet. I heard a door open. Someone's coming! Hurry, go back to your room. Do I have to carry you? Have you lost your mind?

[*It is too late.* DON PEDRO TENORIO *enters carrying a torch, as* ISABEL *and* DON JUAN *move away from each other.*]

DON PEDRO: [*Approaching* DON JUAN *and recognizing him.*] Why, Count, are you the one making this commotion? What's going on? No doubt another woman?

ISABEL: [*Walking out of the shadow.*] Indeed, your Excellency.

DON PEDRO: Madam, you here! I didn't realize . . .

DON JUAN: Uncle, I'm guilty of having kept the Duchess. I wanted her to explain why she said unpleasant things about me . . .

DON PEDRO: At this hour of the night?

ISABEL: That would be too easy.

DON JUAN: You're condemning yourself, Madam!

ISABEL: I want your crime punished. Excellency, your nephew sneaked into my room. He used the darkness as a cover, and pretended to be my fiancé, Duke Octavio. He took advantage of me.

DON PEDRO: Is this possible, Count? This newest imposture is the last straw. Have you lost all reason as well as all decency? I deplore, Madam, that fate has chosen a Tenorio to offend you so grievously. [*To* DON JUAN.] My son, you have a peculiar way of acknowledging my indulgence. It wasn't enough to have outraged public opinion by betraying a Spanish lady. You start over with a woman whose virtue would have assured a gentleman's respect, if her high rank hadn't sufficed. You abandon yourself to your profligate ways in the King's Palace, two steps from his own bed! Is this your way of thanking me for having welcomed you to Naples while you wait for the scandals of your exploits in Seville to die down? [*Aside, to* DON JUAN.] You must be mad! A woman of such rank! Keep your school pranks for the maidservants! Isabel, a Lucretia, the most virtuous widow of the Court! You are completely mad. [*To* ISABEL.] Madam, I know my nephew will repair the wrong he has done you to the extent you so desire.

ISABEL: I want no reparation other than the punishment reserved for the culprit under the King's justice.

DON PEDRO: Alas, I fear that very punishment will surprise you by its severity. You know the King's harshness in dealing with such offences. Ever since an unfortunate inclination toward envy has poisoned his heart, he resents lovers, pursues them, and hunts them down. You witnessed this disposition, Don Juan, when he greeted you so coldly. Only my personal credit has kept you at the Palace. I fear your folly will serve the

King's hostility toward you as well as his desire to redress the easy morals of his Court, and that he will punish you pitilessly as an example.

DON JUAN: I am ready to die, uncle.

ISABEL: Die! You must be joking. There's no question of dying, is there, Excellency? That isn't the punishment you were thinking of, is it?

DON PEDRO: But, Madam, I don't see any other. The condition under which the offense was committed further aggravates the crime by attacking the King's honor. The very person of the Monarch has every reason to be offended. What's more, your royal title of Lady-in-waiting to the Queen assures you special protection. Lastly, Don Juan, you are a Spaniard, a foreigner in this Court where you are a guest. [*Pause.*] Before complaining to the King, Madam, you may wish to consider the effects of your words. Measure the consequences for yourself, and the sorrow they will surely inflict on Duke Octavio.

DON JUAN: I beg you, uncle, do not attempt to dissuade the Duchess. She has made up her mind.

ISABEL: I will reconsider this matter. Go back to your rooms, Don Juan. Tomorrow, I will let you know . . .

DON PEDRO: Listen! It's the King, Madam. Do you hear? [*The sound of a walking cane and of limping. To* DON JUAN.] Run, jump from the balcony. There is no guard on this side.

DON JUAN: No. I'm staying.

ISABEL: Then hurry into my room.

DON JUAN: No.

ISABEL: For the love of me, Don Juan.

DON JUAN: So then . . . [*He goes into her room* . . . THE KING *enters.*]

THE KING: Is it you, Don Pedro, whom I hear speaking in this manner? I've been trying to sleep, in vain. [*Noticing* ISABEL, *who has remained to the side.*] You, Madam? What is going on? Were you involved in this dispute?

ISABEL: We were discussing . . .

DON PEDRO: Sire . . .

THE KING: Come, Don Pedro, explain yourself.

DON PEDRO: Sire, only the Duchess may release me from a secret I stumbled on unwittingly.

THE KING: Well, Madam, I expect no less of your courtesy. You must agree it is quite natural to be curious about the goings-on in my Palace, at this hour of the night. [*A moment's silence.*] Whose voice did I hear before yours, Don Pedro? Another man was here. Who was he? [*To* ISABEL.] You don't want to answer? Very well. I will have all the rooms searched. Don Pedro Tenorio, would you call my guard.

ISABEL: It's no use, Excellency. I will tell you everything. A man that sneaked into my bedroom tried to take advantage of me, Sire.

THE KING: Who is this man?

[ISABEL *remains silent.*]

THE KING: I insist on knowing.

ISABEL: [*Her voice a whisper.*] Duke Octavio.

THE KING: The Duke! That's impossible. And where is he now?

ISABEL: He jumped from the balcony and is probably in his rooms by now.

THE KING: Very well. Don Pedro Tenorio, please see to the Duke's arrest, and take him secretly to me.

ISABEL: Sire . . .

THE KING: Please, Madam! [DON PEDRO *exits.*] Until now, I believed virtue to be desirable. I see I will have to revise that opinion. [*Silence.*] Beauty is a risky power, Madam, and one day you will have to account for it before a judge more powerful than I.

ISABEL: Sire, I am sorry for having provoked this disturbance. My imprudence must have pushed the Duke to extremes . . .

THE KING: Never mind the Duke. This is about you. About you and the illusion I was under . . . I thought it was possible to cherish certain women unselfishly. You know I nurtured friendship for you. What you didn't know is that this friendship was the last of my concessions. It was my last defense against a barrenness that leaves me parched. All of the emotions revolving around beauty, grace, and innocent pleasures that remained in the most austere man, everything that softened his rigor, I vowed to you. On the arid path I have chosen, I thought I could reserve for myself this drink of fresh water. But God does not want me to have this, and I am grateful to Him for showing me the light. The tenderness a loving woman fills us with, the disposition of being happy about everything so long as she is present, these rhythms we imagine to be pure carry a terrible name: lewdness.

ISABEL: Oh! What sorrow, Sire, to discover the strength of your friendship at the moment it turns from me. May I at the very least count on that sentiment to ask you to be indulgent toward the Duke?

THE KING: Rest assured. I do not wish to magnify the scandal by inflicting on Duke Octavio a punishment too severe. Besides, seeing him would be unbearable. I will urge him to retire for a few weeks to his domain in Mantua, where I should like to see you join him soon to marry him.

ISABEL: How can I thank you, Sire! I would like to be able to speak freely to you. I have always imagined you as living on a mountaintop where the air is too sparse for the common mortal. But it seemed at times that I might be able to reach you there for a brief instant. Tonight, I see even more clearly that steep cliff at the top of which you stand. Alas, I have lost all means of getting there.

THE KING: Believe me, Madam, it's all for the best. I know a little about the soul. Yours has an earthly vocation. It's in the world that it will realize its longing for the absolute. [*Silence.*] Good night, Madam. You must be tired. I advise you to retire to your apartments, and go to bed. I too, will retire.

ISABEL: Good night, Sire.

[THE KING *departs.* ISABEL *makes a movement toward her door, hesitates, turns away, and goes to the window. Footsteps may be heard.* DON PEDRO TENORIO *is with* DUKE OCTAVIO.]

OCTAVLO: [*Backstage.*] I do not wish to explain myself until I have spoken to the Duchess Isabel.

DON PEDRO: She's right here.

OCTAVIO: Ah, Isabel. Do grant me a few moments of your time.

DON PEDRO: I'll wait for you in the library. [*He exits.*]

OCTAVIO: My dear, excuse me for appearing so disheveled before you. DON PEDRO dragged me out of bed with some ridiculous story. I grabbed whatever clothing I could find. Look at how I'm dressed. I was in a hurry to see you. What happened? Tell me. Were you in any danger? Tell me you have nothing to do with this mad accusation. Answer me . . . Come now, Isabel, say something. It can't be true that a man sneaked into your room and was seen running away, can it?

ISABEL: Yes, it is true.

OCTAVIO: But who dared say that the man was Duke Octavio?

ISABEL: I did.

OCTAVIO: But that's absurd. I dare hardly imagine your reasons for saying such a thing. Who was this man? A thief? But in that case, you wouldn't have thought of sparing him. Why protect a man behind my name, a man who attempted to take what you refused him? Unless he was so unworthy of you that you prefer the shame of accusing an innocent man to the shame of exposing him? Could it have been a valet, perhaps, paying me the dubious honor of preceding me in your bed?

ISABEL: Your mind is failing you, Octavio.

OCTAVIO: I can only hope you are right. Oh, if only I were struck mad, delirious, or caught in some enormous farce! Anything seems more real to me, Isabel, than to find you mixed up in this unpleasant joke. Come, now, Isabel. Explain yourself. I don't know what to think anymore. This is not a dream. Last night you left me, the way you do every night. You pressed your arm against mine as we walked to the terrace. Your eyes were so clear that no shadow could obscure them. The other man was waiting for you all the while. What monstrous self-control in your actions, what coldness, what concerted wickedness.

ISABEL: Please, Octavio, stop judging me before you hear what I have to say. Everything you are stating is true, my arm pressed against yours, the words I uttered, all of it is true. Don't deny everything that's happened between us up to this day. Rather, take solace in it. Don't be afraid that it's all slipping away under your feet. It's good and real. But it belongs in the past. It's no longer possible now.

OCTAVIO: But why?

ISABEL: It's true I spent the night with an unknown man, and that I wanted to spare him by denouncing you instead. I had no other way of protecting him. For reasons I can't divulge, he was running risks far greater than those to which you find yourself exposed. In a few days, I will convince the King of your innocence.

OCTAVIO: So that's it, then. It's all true. You have no idea how much faith you have just destroyed. Everything I once thought as set, now wavers. I built my world around you. Nothing was more certain to me than our resemblance. I looked at myself in you as in a mirror. You, so transparent . . . How can your image suddenly tarnish and shatter? Everything seems hopeless now. How can I continue to believe in anything . . . And what should I think of women now, when the soul of the strongest of them could not honorably withstand such base temptation?

ISABEL: I was sure you would see something base in my conduct, and that people would pounce on my virtuous reputation, if only to condemn me from a higher position. You're mistaken, Octavio, nothing base happened here tonight. My actions have never felt more defensible. I have never felt so in tune, nor resonated as well. Don't speak to me of baseness when I feel happy, like a little girl who has done a good deed.

OCTAVIO: It's folly to give up in an hour the unity of an entire lifetime!

ISABEL: What you call folly strikes instead as a perfect boldness! Yes, I give up all I've thought till now; everything I thought I was sure of, vanishes before this truth that springs from me like the dawn.

OCTAVIO: And so you renounce even our friendship. I won't dare mention love, even though you've said enough about it. Your love! It was always expressed on your lips.

ISABEL: The taste of love so easily resembles the features of a particular man. I thought I loved you, that I had chosen you. I should have known that there is for each of us a person we aren't even free to choose. Destiny chooses that person for us. The minute he puts his hand on you, you try to free yourself, you shudder, you flap your wings. But you are powerless. It's as though you belonged to him from the beginning of time. You recognize him from the start. You have more in common with him than with your parents; he is closer to you than relatives. You speak a language with him that comes from a forgotten childhood. Your gestures echo his own, with marvelous ease, and his person seems so natural, so predestined, that when you touch his skin, his hair, you feel the kind of pleasure that you sense when you return home after a long absence.

OCTAVIO: You hurt me, Isabel.

ISABEL: I beg your pardon. You don't deserve that. Perhaps you really do love me.

OCTAVIO: Perhaps? To the point of trying to understand you. Everything you say should revolt me, but it doesn't. I pity you. You look like such a little girl. I'm sure you're going to be hurt.

ISABEL: Maybe. I know I could have been happy with you. You are one of those strong men, as sturdy as the great oaks women like to lean against. I would have lived a secure life in your shadow. At times, though, I would have dreamed about escaping from that protective shadow to live the life of a nomad.

OCTAVIO: You seemed so perfectly adapted to the life you had chosen. Never once have you intimated the slightest dissonance.

ISABEL: I did feel it.

OCTAVIO: I don't believe you.

ISABEL: I never saw you come to me without striving to compensate in my imagination for that—forgive me, Octavio—for that something unpleasant in your form.

OCTAVIO: What are you reproaching me? I'm neither bowlegged, nor a cripple.

ISABEL: There's little that I reproach you. A certain opaqueness, a way of obscuring my horizon. Since I can't see through you, I should like to see you encroach less on space.

OCTAVIO: You're not serious. If I understand you well, you are reproaching me for not being transparent.

ISABEL: More or less. But I am being serious. Some men seem to glide on water, or move across a meadow without trampling the grass. You try with all your senses to assure yourself of their presence. You want them to scratch you, to leave their bite marks on you to be sure they're really there. You would want them to say your name aloud, to bellow it so as to let you know they're not a shadow from your dreams, but that they really do have you.

OCTAVIO: I don't see how it's less irritating to have to deal with a ghost.

ISABEL: Oh, it's not the same! When you are annoyed about not being able to reach someone, you are quite ready to follow him. It's an irritation that becomes an obsession. It's a hunger, a thirst. But something borne out of an excessive presence, so easily produces satiation and lassitude.

OCTAVIO: You're being harsh, Isabel. What man could possibly have undone you in one night? If I understand you well, you didn't know him before.

ISABEL: Hardly. Perhaps I already loved him without knowing it.

OCTAVIO: I'll find him. I'll track him with my hatred.

ISABEL: You would malign me, too.

OCTAVIO: Don't ask too much of me. It's one thing to suffer for the King the consequences of something I didn't do. I accept covering for your behavior out of a weakness I can't forgive myself but that I can't help feeling, either. However, I refuse to spare a man cowardly enough to let another suffer the punishment he himself deserves.

ISABEL: He doesn't know. I saved him without his knowledge of it. Go now to the King, Octavio. Your tardiness can only irritate him.

OCTAVIO: Fine. I'd better stop listening to you. Everything you say is hurtful to me. Farewell, Isabel. How strange: you're the one sending me away, and yet I'm left feeling that I'm abandoning you. My poor girl, I feel as though I'm sending you to a world where you'll be torn to shreds. Precious one. I reproach myself for not having been better able to keep you. [*He caresses her.*] Your long hair . . . I remember the day you allowed me to untie it. I recognize the scent. I thought all of this was mine, without ever having tried to conquer it. No man will ever love you as I do.

ISABEL: I fear you may be right.

OCTAVIO: You will suffer.

ISABEL: I'm brave.

OCTAVIO: [*Stepping away from her.*] Yes, I can see that. Nothing will change your mind. Good-bye. If you need help, don't be ashamed to call me back.

ISABEL: Forgive me, Octavio.

[*He exits.* ISABEL *remains dreamy for a long while. A door may be heard opening, followed by some footsteps in the hallway.* DON PEDRO *enters.*]

DON PEDRO: Madam, the Duke is entering the King's chambers. It would be wise to warn Don Juan.

ISABEL: I'll do that. I would ask you to keep the Duke's arrest a secret, and to see to it that Don Juan leave Naples today.

DON PEDRO: Of course, Madam.

ISABEL: Call him, please. Thank you. [*He leaves and returns again with* DON JUAN.]

DON PEDRO: [*Aside, to* DON JUAN.] She didn't do badly. Yet another one you've put your hands on. What blood the Tenorios have in their veins! [*He exits.*]

DON JUAN: It's about time. I couldn't stand it any longer. I was miserable at the thought of all the problems I've caused you. Twenty times I wanted to leap out of that room.

ISABEL: You would have ruined everything.

DON JUAN: What happened? Didn't I recognize Duke Octavio's voice? How did you tell him?

ISABEL: Don't worry about that. I succeeded in assuaging his suspicions as well as the King's. I told them the perpetrator was a stranger. You are free.

DON JUAN: [*Shows* ISABEL *a charming demeanor, natural and youthful. He kisses her hands.*] I'm so grateful to you, Isabel! How can I express my meekness, my recognition?

ISABEL: With your departure.

DON JUAN: Leave now, just as I learn that you love me? Couldn't you choose a torture less cruel to test me?

ISABEL: The slightest sign of my love for you would uncover you and be fatal to you.

DON JUAN: The love you have for me! How sweet to hear you admit it for the first time. Tell me that you love me, Isabel. You told the Duke just now, but not me.

ISABEL: Yes, I love you . . . Go now.

DON JUAN: Listen. I'll do what you wish, but let me abandon myself to you for a few moments. Don't deprive me of this happiness. I don't know whether I prefer my triumph or my defeat, knowing you love me, or that I love you. But why are you sad, my angel? Don't I fill your heart as you fill mine?

ISABEL: I'm not sad, I'm thoughtful.

DON JUAN: What are you thinking about?

ISABEL: About everything I'm giving up.

DON JUAN: And I, about all that we'll discover together. I know your presence will make everything sharper.

ISABEL: Haven't you gained from me everything you wanted?

DON JUAN: You're mad. Do you actually think I would leave like a thief after tonight? Do you believe I could pick up my life from where I left off? Would you be capable of it?

ISABEL: I've already given up everything. I'm distancing myself from everything I loved. From Octavio, from my little sister, Rosaline. I see their faces fade and disappear like the shoreline from a ship taking me away.

DON JUAN: Were you happy, Isabel?

ISABEL: In small things. I loved having a well-ordered soul, like a linen chest with its neat piles of clothes. I loved my dog, roses, the sound of raindrops.

DON JUAN: But why would you lose these pleasures?

ISABEL: They would no longer be the same. They would bear a different expression. I wouldn't caress my dog any more without sighing. I think my heart would explode, as do roses, in a sudden burst of petals. And when I'd hear the sound of warm, falling rain, with the scent of jasmine, I would wonder if the approaching gallop of a horse were that of my cherished love, all washed by the rain of the stormy night like a proud iris, heavy with dew.

DON JUAN: How I love your voice tonight, Isabel. Let me look at you against the dawn. I've hardly been able to until now. Let me take possession of this face. I have never seen eyes as clear.

ISABEL: And yet how many eyes must be buried in this heart; as many as there are violets in a meadow.

DON JUAN: I remember only yours.

ISABEL: I'm learning to know you with my hands. Yours is the kind of face that is possessed only with the hands that caress it, as if it were cast in bronze or sculpted in marble. I didn't know you had a mark on your forehead, above your right brow.

DON JUAN: Nor did I know that scar on your wrist.

ISABEL: Tell me what it is.

DON JUAN: You go first.

ISABEL: Mine is just a small thing. A dog bit me when I was a little girl. I plunged an iron rod in the embers and I purified the wound with the red, hot iron just like the peasant women do where I'm from.

DON JUAN: Tough little girl! And they talk about Spanish fierceness. Are you always as cruel to yourself?

ISABEL: So much so that it's exasperating. People are tempted to hurt me to see how long I can refrain from screaming. You, too, will try one day.

DON JUAN: I so badly want not to make you suffer.

ISABEL: Your turn now, tell me where you got the scar on your forehead.

DON JUAN: From a stone my older brother threw at me when I was ten.

ISABEL: Were you fighting?

DON JUAN: I was running after him. He was afraid.

ISABEL: Why was he afraid of you?

DON JUAN: He really hurt me. I once captured and tamed an owl. I found it crucified one day, but still alive. It was staring at me. Oh, Isabel, what a stare! I won't say it was a human look. No look I had seen from a human till that day could compare.

ISABEL: Have you seen such a look since?

DON JUAN: Perhaps. Some women look at you so, as if they were saying "you're crucifying me but I forgive you."

ISABEL: What did you do with the owl?

DON JUAN: I killed it savagely in a rage that was unjustly turned against it. I wanted to finish it as quickly as possible so as not to bear any longer the reproach in its eyes. But the pity I tried to contain made me awkward.

ISABEL: And what do you do with the women, Juan?

DON JUAN: [*Harshly.*] The same . . . Are you afraid?

ISABEL: No, not at all. I have a trust in you that nothing justifies. No one has ever duped me the way you did tonight. And yet I feel secure with you.

DON JUAN: You are.

ISABEL: But what is trust to someone that we know is capable of lying and deceiving?

DON JUAN: It's an animal trust. It goes much more deeply than words and promises. It can withstand lies.

ISABEL: Tell me, Juan, do all women trust you?

DON JUAN: I feel embarrassed by such a question.

ISABEL: I see. You have some delicate scruples.

DON JUAN: You're nasty!

ISABEL: I intended it that way. Your turn will come soon enough. You haven't answered me. Do women trust you?

DON JUAN: They generally start that way.

ISABEL: And when do they start calling you El Burlador?

DON JUAN: Don't distress me with that ridiculous name I don't even deserve. I deceive so poorly . . . I never said "I love you" without believing in it, at least momentarily. But as soon as I stopped loving, I'd feel ill at ease to pretend I was still in love. Whenever a circumstance or a pique of jealousy refueled for a few hours the fervor I had spent, how quickly I would express my love to the woman who thought I had forgotten her. Alas, my gestures of sincerity were construed as cleverness and coquetry.

ISABEL: It's what people call the innocence of the tiger.

DON JUAN: I wonder why I'm telling you all this. I trust you, too, without understanding why. It's a trust that comes from far.

ISABEL: I have the feeling I recognize you rather than discover you for the first time. Tonight, it felt like you took me by the hand and led me to a garden of my childhood, where I might have strolled with my eyes shut. It felt like I could hear the squeaking of the little wooden door that takes you back so many years; like I could recognize every meander along the path, the precise point along the way where the smell of the marigolds welcomes you, like a friend that couldn't bear waiting for you, and so comes to meet you . . .

DON JUAN: How you look at me!

ISABEL: I'm looking at the man I love . . .

DON JUAN: Are you getting used to me?

ISABEL: Hardly. For a long time I imagined that I would love a tall, blond boy, as fresh and golden as bread coming out of the oven. Perhaps an Englishman, or a Saxon. I accepted Octavio because he resembled that dream to some extent. And here I am now, in love with this somber, beautiful face. I could see for me an easy and peaceful life, a kind of daily happiness far from Court intrigues, with a house to govern, and children all around me like ears of corn. I realize I'll have to give all of that up. It's as though I were sucked up by something powerful.

DON JUAN: By happiness, Isabel.

ISABEL: If it were only happiness, it would be easy to give it all up. No, it's the need of a certain rigor in life.

DON JUAN: There's moodiness in your words. You're upset with me for having troubled you.

ISABEL: I was used to wanting my life. Now I must learn to accept it. But it's such a relief to know that it's useless to fight, that there's nothing to prepare for it. Yesterday, I thought I hated you. I thought I hated your nose, your mouth, your forehead, your whole demeanor. Surely, my heart was fighting what had been victorious over it, and would so completely subjugate it. I was irritated that it already belonged to you. I should have been wary about that passionate attention I paid you. I was familiar with the lively and graceful way you ride your horse, with the insolence of your manners, and the nonchalance of the furtive caresses you're always paying women that you seem to alight like the lightest of birds.

DON JUAN: I like you, too, Isabel. I offer you this word as a kernel of love. I like myself in your company. Loving could just be a beautiful lie, a trick played by the soul; but liking oneself reveals the truth of our flesh and blood, the only truth we can't help.

ISABEL: And yet, Juan, I want you to tell me that you love me also.

DON JUAN: Yes, dear fool, I love you. Never has a woman cast such a spell on me. You're the only one. Nothing remains of the memory of other loves, of other women.

ISABEL: How many loves, how many women did you really love?

DON JUAN: I don't know any more. None. I realize it wasn't love. There are certain faces you do not mistaken. The face of love is one of them. I never felt myself free of all attachment. I never felt I was living a full life. This dissatisfaction, this constant search, this same, constant flight, was not in vain since it led to this unimaginable repose. Don Juan is happy, Isabel. He seizes and touches the paradise he's longed for behind the bars of his cage. You lifted the malediction that weighed on me.

ISABEL: I hope so! [*Pause.*] Juan, you must leave now. They've already announced matins. Soon the Palace will be filled with chambermaids, and the valets will be taking the hounds out. You must get back to Don Pedro's chambers before their arrival.

DON JUAN: How do I see you again?

ISABEL: What are you going to do?

DON JUAN: Flee to Spain with you.

ISABEL: With me . . . what folly! Why burden yourself with a woman?

DON JUAN: All right. I'll leave by myself. But promise you'll join me.

ISABEL: I can join you within two months. But will you still be waiting for me then?

DON JUAN: I'd wait for you all my life if need be. I won't have any other care but to prepare for your arrival. I'll give you the life you want, Isabel. Do you want me to marry you?

ISABEL: [*Pause.*] No, I don't think I would like that.

DON JUAN: Why not?

ISABEL: I'm afraid of putting the slightest halter around your neck. You're not a domesticated animal.

DON JUAN: How do you know? Domesticated animals were once wild.

ISABEL: I think I prefer wild animals.

DON JUAN: We'll see.

ISABEL: You must leave now, Juan. The verger is already opening the doors. Embrace me. Harder. Again. You will take care of yourself, won't you? Don't be imprudent. Promise me you won't fight a duel.

DON JUAN: [*Laughing.*] I'll try not to.

ISABEL: My God, I don't even know where to find you. You're leaving and I know nothing about you.

DON JUAN: [*Departing.*] I'll wait for you in Valencia. We'll travel together to Seville.

ISABEL: Farewell, my love.

DON JUAN: Farewell.

[*He exits.* SERVANTS *and* GUARDS *enter.* ISABEL *is about to retire when she notices her little sister,* ROSALINE, *with* DOÑA JACINTA.]

ISABEL: Why, is that you, Rosaline? Up already?

DOÑA JACINTA: Rosaline wanted to come along for the service of the Holy Virgin. Tito was serving Mass for the first time.

ISABEL: Is that so! Good morning, my little one. [*She kisses* ROSALINE.]

ROSALINE: Good morning, Isabel. Guess what happened to me?

ISABEL: I don't know. Tell me.

ROSALINE: Well I dreamt that we were leaving to go very far on a big ship with Doña Jacinta.

ISABEL: Why, that's amazing because we truly are taking a long trip.

ROSALINE: We are? Is it true?

ISABEL: We certainly are. Listen. [*She takes the child on her knees and gestures* JACINTA *to leave.*] Would you like to cross the sea?

ROSALINE: Yes!

ISABEL: Wouldn't you be afraid?

ROSALINE: Yes, but it doesn't matter. I'd like that. Do you think we'd see any pirates?

ISABEL: I don't think so. But we'll go on a beautiful ship that will sail the waves and go as straight as an arrow, to an unknown city. Isn't it awesome to cross a whole sea for a big wish! . . .

ROSALINE: What's the name of the city?

ISABEL: Valencia. There's a big pier, a crowd on the pier, and in the crowd, there are eyes looking hard for someone. And then, there's the moment when the eyes meet . . .

ROSALINE: And what comes after the city?

ISABEL: After that, there's the countryside, green at first, with orange groves, and then dry, as fierce as flowing lava. Then comes the monotonous sway of the carriage, and the horses' hooves on the cobblestones, and the inns with their rooms of virgin wood that still smells like trees, and the coarse linen sheets where you can sleep so deeply . . .

[*The curtain falls as* ISABEL *talks to the listening child.*]

ACT II

An antechamber at Seville's Alcazar, next to the music room. As the curtain rises, DOÑA MARIANA DE MENDOZA *is spying through the open window on some people in the Palace gardens. As* DOÑA FRANCISCA DE GUEVARA *enters,* DOÑA MARIANA *turns from the window and pretends to be busy.*

DOÑA FRANCISCA: Don't bother, Mariana. You can't fool me. [*A momentary silence.*] What do you expect? It's a bad patch to cross. You've had better moments, though, haven't you? So why complain? . . . You're just a child. Still young enough to be playing dolls, and you imagine you're in pain. Twenty, you have twenty years ahead of you, you hear, to learn to suffer.

MARIANA: But you can't understand, Doña Francisca.

DOÑA FRANCISCA: Naturally, I'm an old nag, and you invented love. [*She goes to the window.*] Is it Mercedes that's worrying you? You're wrong. Don Juan isn't her lover. He only got a few kisses out of her, a few caresses. Bold ones, but surely furtive.

MARIANA: That's precisely what irritates me. For months, she's held onto him thanks to that bait she is always dangling before him.

DOÑA FRANCISCA: You're wrong. She's holding his attention, but in the meantime, she doesn't possess him. The day she gives in, and they always give in to Don Juan, the whole system of precautions will crumble in an instant. The brief moment of her joys will consume that of her victory. A man's desire must be given time to mature. You mustn't arouse it too quickly, nor let it swell too much. Believe me, Mariana. In love, one of the best chances a woman has, is to know when to give in. Too early, she surprises; too late, she disappoints. In both cases, the desire cools.

MARIANA: I think it's dishonest to hold a man's interest by coquetry. It amounts to cheating other women. Among friends, it's not a loyal game.

DOÑA FRANCISCA: I stopped believing in loyalty among women a long time ago. Our friendships are always more or less the friendships of harems. They turn in the wind like the weathervane on the cathedral spire.

MARIANA: Look at them play ball. Did you hear him laugh?

DOÑA FRANCISCA: Why don't you join them.

MARIANA: No. I don't feel like it.

DOÑA FRANCISCA: You're wrong, I tell you. He doesn't like you to be sad when he's happy.

MARIANA: He's a terrible egotist, isn't he?

DOÑA FRANCISCA: Of course not, he's just very sensitive. Look how happy he is right now. He's surrounded by charming women who only think about pleasing him. Look how he picks up a handkerchief with his left hand, and adjusts someone's hair with his right. He enjoys his grace and his skill. He plays hard, he laughs, and has fun like a child. Not quite like a child. Something betrays him. Is it something too insistent in his gaze, or too relaxed in his walk? He's watchful and vigilant. His playfulness is like a tiger's game. Those women are his prey. He never forgets it.

MARIANA: Why does he please women? He's not even handsome.

DOÑA FRANCISCA: Not handsome? Of course he doesn't have the childlike freshness, nor the brutal energy that fascinates the young. He makes me think of the overpowering things I hated as a child, the wines, the aromatic pears, the spices, whose taste I learned to enjoy when I grew older. Look at that face burdened by bitterness, cruelty, and sweetness. How bland handsome faces will appear to the one whose lips remember that taste . . . Have you been in love with him for a long time, Mariana?

MARIANA: Oh! No. Only since his return from Naples. I saw him for the first time at the theater, where I had gone secretly. He was shamelessly inspecting the women's gallery, pretending to be looking for someone.

DOÑA FRANCISCA: It's simple; he was looking for a woman.

MARIANA: Our eyes met for a long time. He stared at me very seriously, as if to say he wasn't joking. Then, suddenly, he smiled at me. He smiled so sweetly that I felt I had to do something. I sent the little vendor over to ask him if he wanted to offer me oranges. He bought twelve and had him tell me that he would be happy to put before my feet anything else I might want. After the theater . . .

DOÑA FRANCISCA: He was waiting for you at the door. He invited you to a restaurant at Las Delicias. The same night, you gave him all that he asked.

MARIANA: That's it. How did you know?

DOÑA FRANCISCA: Oh! Nothing is more monotonous than the rites leading up to the act of love. But at times Don Juan's ingenuity makes a mess of everything: he runs off with women, and even has their duennas carried away. He hides behind a mask, takes his mistresses to mysterious palaces where they wake up next to fountains and roses. At other times, he indulges in the easiest ways. I suppose the night you met him, he felt somewhat tired.

MARIANA: Oh! I assure you he didn't give me that impression.

DOÑA FRANCISCA: [*Dreamily.*] He didn't? Besides him, Mariana, haven't you ever had a lover?

MARIANA: Oh! I haven't had time for that. The very day my husband died, my tutor sent me back to the convent. I left it as Lady-in-waiting to the Queen, two days before I met Don Juan.

DOÑA FRANCISCA: I see you didn't waste any time. And . . . did you see him again often?

MARIANA: Three or four times. But for the last few days he said he was very busy. If it's not hunting, he's engaged with private audiences. Tell me truthfully, Doña Francisca, should I fear a break-up?

DOÑA FRANCISCA: Don Juan doesn't break up; he releases. He's so clever at weakening the bonds he creates, you never catch him at it. Once you've been that man's mistress, you're never certain of not becoming so again.

MARIANA: That makes me feel better.

DOÑA FRANCISCA: Don't even think of it. A nice separation is not unhealthy. You reimmerse yourself; you wipe the slate clean, and you're ready to start again. As for him, he leaves you a little hope, like a thorn in your heart. Try going back to that splinter paralyzing your every impulse. [*Pause.*] But you're young. As a matter of fact, why do you love him?

MARIANA: I don't know. Perhaps because he's the first, or almost. The Marquis was sixty. And, also, he's as sweet as a girl.

DOÑA FRANCISCA: Oh, yes, he does purr; he offers a velvet paw!

MARIANA: And you always wonder what he's thinking about . . .

DOÑA FRANCISCA: You're a child. How old are you?

MARIANA: Eighteen.

DOÑA FRANCISCA: The Holy Virgin grants you the grace of sending you Don Juan as your first lover, and you find this to be a natural thing. Do you know what self-control is, Mariana? I'll give you a comparison. You've been to the corrida. You've heard people talk about the matador. He is the star of all Spain. So there he is, advancing. From the very first movement, you know who he is. You know you can be sure of him. You can quietly abandon yourself to his game in all confidence. You're in his hand like a bird in its nest. Then, oh wondrous art, you forget about the power of art. He is so unaware of himself that he makes everything look effortless. He gives way to a power of invention which makes light of physical difficulties, and appears to unravel in a world devoid of gravity. Do you believe that in the course of your life you will abandon yourself to many men with the knowledge that they won't make one false move, that they'll dance on the tightrope of love with the grace and the lightness of a funambulist? A lover, Mariana, cannot be found more than once in a lifetime, and most women never find one. Their only consolation is men. Perhaps you'll discover, one day, that most men love the way they eat; because they enjoy it, or even because they're hungry. It's like the bestial and voracious look a dog gives the bone you're holding out to him. You might then think: the only one who treated love the way one approaches the altar was that libertine, that debauched man, Don Juan Tenorio.

MARIANA: You know quite a lot about him, Doña Francisca.

DOÑA FRANCISCA: More than you, perhaps. Don't stare at me as though you had never seen me. You'd think I was your grandmother! Stupid little goose! Look, they're coming back. Don't tell him about our conversation. You know how he hates his legend. He suffers from it. He surrounds his adventures with the greatest discretion.

MARIANA: Then where does he get his fame?

DOÑA FRANCISCA: From women, only from women. They feel so glorious about having been pursued by him that they practically proclaim their good fortune with a trumpet.

MARIANA: Why isn't the Duchess Isabel among them? Have you noticed she doesn't join in the fun? What is she doing in Seville, then, if she's not joining in the pleasure?

DOÑA FRANCISCA: Who knows? Will you accompany me to the concert?

MARIANA: I'll meet you there.

DOÑA FRANCISCA: In that case, I'll be leaving you.

[*She exits.* DON JUAN *and* MERCEDES *enter pursuing each other. Not noticing* MARIANA, *they exchange the following dialogue in the foreground.*]

DON JUAN: You did it on purpose.

MERCEDES: Not at all. It was just by chance.

DON JUAN: So you were afraid of being alone with me!

MERCEDES: Your conceit is misleading you.

DON JUAN: Your eyes have never gleamed as vividly.

MERCEDES: You know it's a great pleasure to say no to you.

DON JUAN: Naughty girl. You're like a child. You're much nicer when you sleep.

MERCEDES: What do you mean?

DON JUAN: Nothing more than what I'm saying.

MERCEDES: Does that mean you have a memory, Count? That's a nasty defect for a professional lover.

DON JUAN: My dear, memories fail me to a point you can't imagine. It's quite simple. I don't remember anything except the few months I had a wet nurse.

MERCEDES: I'm relieved. At least they have nothing to do with memories of love.

DON JUAN: What would you know?

MERCEDES: Tell me. We'll see.

DON JUAN: I don't know if I should. It'll shock you. You're such a prude.

MERCEDES: Impudent!

DON JUAN: Do you remember having suckled?

MERCEDES: You're joking.

DON JUAN: Not in the least . . . I remember a kind of globe of happiness.

MERCEDES: You're exaggerating. Everything for you is about sex.

DON JUAN: And for you, nothing is about sex. You are one of those women who embrace love only when it is emasculated. You have to skirt around it, hide it like a magician pulling a pigeon through his sleeve.

MERCEDES: Oh! This time you're going too far.

DON JUAN: Not at all. You love hearing the truth about you. You find a kind of voluptuousness in it which you don't want to pursue through more natural ways.

MERCEDES: You're getting bitter, Count. This is no longer in jest, it's a quarrel.

DON JUAN: Then grant me permission to put an end to it. I won't see you alone again unless you promise me what I ask.

MERCEDES: Too bad. I was starting to enjoy myself quite a bit with you. Perhaps I was even going to love you.

DON JUAN: I'm not stopping you.

MERCEDES: Tell me, if I let you go ahead with your turn, the pigeon through your sleeve, would it be . . . how shall I say . . . an isolated show, or would you accept the regular title of magician?

DON JUAN: That would depend on you.

MERCEDES: To have to listen to this!

DON JUAN: Then is it yes?

MERCEDES: Maybe. I'll give you my answer after the concert. Do you love me, at least?

DON JUAN: [*With amiable persuasion, nothing more.*] Do I love you! [*He kisses her.*]

[MARIANA, *who has been giving signs of distress for the last few instants, is about to get away. In her haste, she drops the book she was carrying. She stops, confused.* DON JUAN *and* MERCEDES *turn around and see her.* DON JUAN *is a little annoyed.* MERCEDES *is quite insolent.*]

MERCEDES: I knew you to be more expert at the convent, Mariana. On the other hand, you always eavesdropped behind doors.

MARIANA: And you were already so affected in the parlor.

DON JUAN: Doña Mariana de Mendoza, do us the honor of joining us at the concert.

MARIANA: But . . .

[*Little* ROSALINE *runs in and goes straight to* DON JUAN.]

DON JUAN: [*To the two women.*] Do excuse me for a moment.

MERCEDES: We'll go on ahead. Come, Mariana. Let's leave him to his private meeting. Eight years old. We can leave them alone. [*They exit.*]

ROSALINE: [*To* DON JUAN, *in a hushed voice.*], Are you sure there's no one here? Isabel sent me to get you.

DON JUAN: Is she coming here?

ROSALINE: Yes. Can I wait for her with you?

DON JUAN: Of course.

ROSALINE: Why were those two making fun at me? What's so funny about being eight?

DON JUAN: I don't think so. Eight is a very nice age.

ROSALINE: Would you still like to be eight?

DON JUAN: Maybe.

ROSALINE: What's that red ribbon doing on your shoulder? Is it to say you're being good?

DON JUAN: More or less.

ROSALINE: What did you do to get it?

DON JUAN: Not very much.

ROSALINE: Who gave it to you? Tell me.

DON JUAN: The King did. He said to me: I hereby name you Knight of the Banda. In exchange for this ribbon, you must promise never to lie, never to be vainglorious, to serve the ladies, and to fight bravely against the Moors.

ROSALINE: I'm supposed to be a good girl. They only told you to promise to be good. That's much easier.

DON JUAN: What you say there is sadly true.

ROSALINE: So did you fight against the Moors?

DON JUAN: A little.

ROSALINE: You cut their heads off. Oh, I'd love to see that!

DON JUAN: Would you really?

ROSALINE: I don't like being a little girl. I'd like to fight later on, like boys do.

DON JUAN: Is that what you dream about when you play with your dolls?

ROSALINE: I don't like dolls. When I get them, I poke holes into them. I push my fingers in their eyes and I make a hole in their tummies. After that, I let the sawdust run through my fingers just like this, from one hand to the other, like sand.

DON JUAN: Don't you pretend you're fighting someone?

ROSALINE: Oh, no. I'm all alone. I play with the geranium leaves, too. I have fun cutting them in small pieces so that they'll smell stronger.

DON JUAN: It's funny, for me it's just the opposite. I love playing with dolls.

ROSALINE: You still play with dolls at your age!

DON JUAN: I sure do.

ROSALINE: I really like talking to you.

DON JUAN: Why's that?

ROSALINE: You take me seriously. But I'm still thinking about your promise. Fighting the Moors must be fun, but it must be really hard never to lie.

DON JUAN: Oh, you can't imagine how complicated that is.

ROSALINE: So how do you manage it?

DON JUAN: I'll tell you when you're a big girl.

ROSALINE: That's too bad. It would be really useful for me now.

[ISABEL *enters.*]

ISABEL: I hope I haven't made you wait too long? [ROSALINE *exits.*] This room is the only cool one in this wing of the Palace.

DON JUAN: Do you miss Naples, Isabel, and the sea breeze?

ISABEL: I assure you. I don't. I love the afternoon indolence where you drift away to another world.

DON JUAN: And I, the moment when I slip into your room. I find you crushed by the heat, on your bed, like a fully bloomed carnation whose fragrance the sun has multiplied tenfold. Why didn't you let me join you today? I love those pearls of perspiration that are like dew on your forehead. You are all moist here, in the hollow of your elbows and all the way down your arms. Tender little thrush.

ISABEL: You know me better than I know myself. Do all women resemble each other, Juan?

DON JUAN: To a certain extent, yes, my sweet one.

ISABEL: The knowledge you have of women sometimes feels monstrous to me. At times, I fancy you less infallible. I would like you capable of a mistake, of making a less precise gesture, a less effective one, a caress that would miss its object of desire. Next to you, I feel naked all over again.

DON JUAN: Why didn't you want to receive me this afternoon?

ISABEL: I want you to come tonight and stay until dawn. I love the promise of an entire night before me, deep and soft like an eternity.

DON JUAN: How many such nights have we already had, Isabel? Twenty?

ISABEL: No, twelve! How poorly you remember. [*The music has begun in the adjoining room.*] I remember them all: the night in Naples, the one in Valencia, the nights at the inn, and our four nights in Seville. And the night we quarreled after I surprised you kissing the chambermaid.

DON JUAN: I wasn't kissing her.

ISABEL: Be quiet. You'll get angry again. How is it that the anger of a man you love can go to your head like the headiest of wines?

DON JUAN: Do you remember the night we were so chaste? We talked until morning.

ISABEL: Our kisses were as light as sighs. Our hearts were beating the same rhythm against each other.

DON JUAN: What rest! What illusion I held about attaining at last something absolute!

ISABEL: And then the night your caresses seemed so base at first, so vile. You made me feel the voluptuousness of humiliating myself before the thing I love most in the world. What a delight to escape one's own pride.

DON JUAN: But that's still pride, Isabel.

ISABEL: You think so? . . . And the last one, the night you made me go through all of the ages of love, one after the other. I remember seeing us, you and me, like a strange and monstruous flower of flesh. It felt as if we were going back to the very heart of creation, to a fabulous world where forms wait to follow their human destination, still confounded in common matter. [*They daydream for an instant while listening to the concert.*] Wouldn't you rather listen to the music from the hall?

DON JUAN: You can hear it quite well from here.

ISABEL: But all of your admirers are there.

DON JUAN: Why do you call them my admirers?

ISABEL: They're all there: Mercedes, Doña Francisca, the French ambassador's wife, right up to the young Mariana who spies on you through the cracks in the doorjambs, and all the others.

DON JUAN: Jealous?

ISABEL: Yes.

DON JUAN: There's no reason to be, I assure you. What I feel for you is so deep, so serious. And what I feel for the others is so light, like down floating on the surface of my heart. All that's necessary is a little breeze to remove it, a caress.

ISABEL: You look like an innocent little boy. I like it when you put your head on my knees, like a cat that sticks out and pushes its little round head into you to nest it better in the curve of your body. Tell me, what can you possibly tell these women to make them revolve around you this way?

DON JUAN: Only very harmless things.

ISABEL: I was watching you play on the lawn just now. As soon as you appeared, the game shifted to your person, and organized itself according to your whims. You saw the intertwining and muddle of intrigues around you. Each woman had her eyes fixed on your face. She awaited a favor from you, a sign, a glance. And you let none of them down. You shared yourself; you distributed yourself. You seemed to obey the rules of a mysterious equity.

DON JUAN: My darling madwoman, you alone see me this way, like a stool pigeon women throw themselves on. Your love for me gets the better of your imagination.

ISABEL: At times I get the impression you've already conquered all of them. The carnal familiarity between them and you betrays you. I, who dreamed of lofty and tough romances, have chosen the easiest of lovers, the lover of all women.

DON JUAN: There's only bitterness in your words! I should think that watching female desire converge on your lover, you would feel a certain pride.

ISABEL: It remains to be seen what floats on the surface. I think it's bitterness.

DON JUAN: You're glum today.

ISABEL: There you go! To you, everything's a matter of mood. I shouldn't have followed you here. You were different before you arrived in Seville.

DON JUAN: I obviously have to pretend here. You yourself asked me to do so.

ISABEL: That was when we loved each other the same way. We were so immersed in our enchantment that people turned around to see it reflected on our faces. Love opened up a path for us. We advanced like a royal couple among our people.

DON JUAN: You're unfair. I still love you the same way. If I appear to be different, it's because I'm bothered by some news I must share with you.

ISABEL: What is it?

DON JUAN: The King has put it in his mind to marry me off.

ISABEL: You! But to whom?

DON JUAN: To the daughter of Commander de Ulloa. The King was so delighted with the results of his mission in Lisbon that he conferred all kinds of distinctions on him, and promised to marry off his daughter to me.

ISABEL: And . . . did you accept?

DON JUAN: Not at all. No one even asked my opinion. But King Pedro's fantasies resemble orders. I'll need all my subtlety to discourage him from this plan.

ISABEL: Is she pretty?

DON JUAN: That's what they say. I'll know in a few moments.

ISABEL: So you're going to see her?

DON JUAN: I'm supposed to meet her right here after the concert.

ISABEL: You aren't going to do that. If I beg you . . .

DON JUAN: I don't see how I can refrain without insulting the young woman. Since she's without doubt innocent about this project, she doesn't deserve such an insult.

ISABEL: Oh, I already sense that you're taken by her. A woman you don't know! What leaven for your desires! Juan, I don't want you to meet that woman.

DON JUAN: But I have to, Isabel.

ISABEL: Listen to me. You know the faith I have in omens. It's the sixteenth day of the month. You know this is a disastrous date for me. I don't want you to meet this young woman today. It's not a wish; it's an order.

DON JUAN: Fine, then. I'll obey you.

ISABEL: Don't make that awful face. Are you angry with me?

DON JUAN: Yes.

ISABEL: This is the first time I've used my power over you.

DON JUAN: I don't recommend you do it again.

ISABEL: When you're cross it makes you look unattractive.

DON JUAN: It's boredom. Nothing makes me uglier than being bored.

ISABEL: Are you bored with me?

DON JUAN: Yes, for the last few moments.

ISABEL: You're like a child. As soon as I go against your caprices, you get headstrong. Must I give in to each of your whims?

DON JUAN: You don't have to resist my desires. I was barely interested in that interview with the young Ulloa. You embroil it with obstacles, and you excite my desire. Now I'm longing to meet her.

ISABEL: I hate you! I hate you for the talent you've acquired to make me suffer. Everything that comes from you, your voice, your words, your gestures, is associated with that mysterious power to hurt me. Your nearness is often more painful to me than your absence. If I didn't see you for three days last week, it wasn't because I was sick. I was hiding from you to avoid suffering.

DON JUAN: Isabel . . .

ISABEL: What else can I do about it, since you've become the dispenser of my joys and sorrows? Yes, this is how much I love you. I've reduced my universe to your person.

DON JUAN: You frighten me!

ISABEL: I know. You don't like being forced to such heights. You're averse to their rigors. You live for love, and you have yet to explore its apex. You've never known the desire to isolate a person in your possession more exclusively each day, have you Juan? Otherwise you wouldn't be amazed at my attempts to screen you from others.

DON JUAN: If I've ever been able to imagine it for a woman, Isabel, it was for you. For the first time, I think I can actually be faithful. I think a slight effort would suffice.

ISABEL: If it's possible, then do so my love. I beg you. And go ahead and meet the young Ulloa after the concert. I trust you.

DON JUAN: I don't want to. I don't feel like seeing her. I was irritated . . . Will you wait for me tonight?

ISABEL: Yes . . . [DOÑA JACINTA *comes in running.*]

DOÑA JACINTA: My Lady!

ISABEL: What is it, Jacinta? You're all excited again. All day long you wander about like a soul in Purgatory.

DOÑA JACINTA: I have to, Madam. Who would tell you the news from the Court, the rumors circulating about you? You live with your head buried in the clouds. Someone has to worry about you.

DON JUAN: Don't get carried away, Doña Jacinta. The Duchess enjoys teasing you a little. Tell me what brings you here.

DOÑA JACINTA: Duke Octavio has just arrived at the Palace. At this very moment, the King is receiving him.

ISABEL: I can't believe he's followed me to this place.

DON JUAN: Why not? From my standpoint, I would find it quite improper for him not to be coherent about his feelings.

[FERNANDO *enters.*]

FERNANDO: Duke Octavio wishes to confer with Duchess Isabel. He will not be long.

DON JUAN: There he is!

ISABEL: Don't stay here.

DON JUAN: Why would I run away?

ISABEL: It would be better not to irritate him. Go listen to the music. I will join you shortly.

DON JUAN: Very well. I leave you to that faithful lover. Oh! This man is entitled to your gratitude! [*He exits, followed by* FERNANDO. DOÑA JACINTA *sighs deeply.*]

ISABEL: You're sighing, Jacinta dear. You don't like being here. [*Pause.*] Are you pouting? Do you long for your daily life, your bed, your kitchen? Aren't you ashamed? Oh! You would never believe a pirate raped your mother. You'd swear you had milk in your veins instead of blood. Look at me. The man I have offended most in this world has come to ask me to explain my actions. Do I look frightened?

DOÑA JACINTA: You're taking it in stride. Unlike you, I don't have a handsome suitor throwing powder in my eyes.

ISABEL: So you recognize he's handsome. That's the first time. Confess you wouldn't have been able to resist him, nurse, no more than any other woman.

DOÑA JACINTA: You don't know what you're saying! [OCTAVIO *enters.*]

OCTAVIO: Isabel! [JACINTA *exits.*]

ISABEL: Dear Octavio! What a pleasure to see you again!

OCTAVIO: You'll always surprise me. Pleasure is surely the last feeling I would have expected from you.

ISABEL: Why?

OCTAVIO: What do you think I've come to Seville for?

ISABEL: I have no idea.

OCTAVIO: I tortured myself with impatience on that ship that dragged on like a little skiff and couldn't orient itself towards a favorable wind. Nothing separates me from that vengeance my eyes followed over the sea, like a star. All the while your own gaze might have been fixed on your love. I hate Don Juan, Isabel, as much as you love him.

ISABEL: But what do you imagine you'll do?

OCTAVIO: It seems beyond imaginable.

ISABEL: Doesn't it? It's absurd.

OCTAVIO: Don't try to fool me.

ISABEL: Come now . . . what if I told you Don Juan is finally going to settle down. He is engaged . . . to the daughter of the Commander of Ulloa.

OCTAVIO: Listen to me, Isabel. All of that is futile. I forced Don Pedro Tenorio to tell me the truth. Alas, I have no doubts remaining. I know you love Don Juan.

ISABEL: Even so. What would you accomplish by pursuing him? I was once fond of you, but I'll hate you. Yes, I love Don Juan and I'll love him till my final breath. His image will be the last to leave my eyes. Even when I am chilled by death, his memory will warm my blood and let it flow to my heart one last time.

OCTAVIO: Unfortunate woman. He'll abandon you long before that.

ISABEL: What does it matter? Will that prevent me from loving him? I feel so distant from such petty reasoning. What does that bartering mentality have to do with love? Something in return for something else; is that how you see love? You don't know what it is to accept a person's weaknesses, his vices, and betrayals. Don Juan may be unfaithful, I know, but I like his way of being unfaithful. He's sly; I love slyness. You cannot conceive that one could love this way, can you Octavio?

OCTAVIO: Yes, since this is how I love you.

ISABEL: Poor man! Then you must understand me.

OCTAVIO: No. I can't accept that you love such a man. It's a jarring error on the part of your whole being. You think you know him. You imagine him chasing ideals. On the contrary. He's a man who is happy with anyone, the chambermaids he fondles, the country girls he seduces . . .

ISABEL: You think you can wound him with your base words? What does the class of the woman he desires matter to Don Juan? Love itself provides the condition. A worldly duchess may not be worthy of tying her chambermaid's boots.

OCTAVIO: I recognize there your obsession with equality. I know you've fallen prey to the spirit of the times.

ISABEL: That has nothing to do with it.

OCTAVIO: But, Isabel, you can't excuse that man's crimes. He's killed countless husbands and fiancés.

ISABEL: Yes, but in true combat!

OCTAVIO: What about the incestuous love he nurtured for his sister Lucretia; and the kidnapping of his young sister-in-law, a child of fourteen snatched from her husband the very night of their wedding . . .

ISABEL: And so smitten by her kidnapper that she couldn't rest until she succeeded in getting her unconsummated marriage annulled. I grant you, Octavio, the man lives at the margins of divine and human laws. His rule is his own pleasure. Have you met many truly strong men who did otherwise? You're surrounded by little despots who think they can govern because of their tyranny. You accept their will because they claim their authority from what you call serious matters, public concerns, the good of the state. When you grant them the desire to appropriate material well-being, could you not also grant to others the desire to dominate the soul?

OCTAVIO: My word, you speak of that debauched man as if he were an apostle!

ISABEL: You speak of him as if he were a villain. I know, there are men so absolutely hermetic to others that they ask "What could women possibly find in them?" But the women know. When they hear about such men, they simply sigh. As for Juan, he is the only one who doesn't disappoint their love. Loving Juan is like attaching oneself to a prey that's always in flight. How can you not understand, Octavio, that this mobility and this elusiveness are the very elements which exasperate their desire to fix a man? For Don Juan love has such a desperate quality. And such a bitter and wild vitality. The man one is never sure of, who must be reconquered every day, with whom it is necessary to reestablish the game of love from the beginning, every time, with its ruses and pretenses . . . Such a man sows life wherever he goes. He bestows it with the same generosity as nature. Yet you would have limits placed on him. You would tie him to a web of obligations designed for the common man.

OCTAVIO: We no longer speak the same language, Isabel. Stop singing me the praises of that man. You hurt me needlessly.

ISABEL: What are you going to do, Octavio? Provoke him to a duel? It's absurd. It'll be the death of you.

OCTAVIO: Perhaps. But before that I'll have made his crimes public. I'm going to the King to tell him about the conduct of his favorite courtier.

ISABEL: If you do such a cowardly thing, I'll never see you again.

OCTAVIO: I don't care about seeing you again since I'll always imagine that man at your side from now on.

ISABEL: But I'm telling you he will marry Ana de ulloa.

OCTAVIO: I would have to have proof of it.

ISABEL: What if the engagement were made public?

OCTAVIO: Would the marriage matter anyway? It wouldn't change the way you feel about me.

ISABEL: How do you know? Why put this new obstacle between you and me? Why provoke my resentment by pursuing Don Juan with your hate . . .

[*Several people come in from the concert room, among them are* MERCEDES *and* MARIANA, *followed by* DON JUAN.]

OCTAVIO: If you allowed me the hope of taking you back to Naples and if I had the proof of Don Juan's marriage, perhaps I would wait.

ISABEL: Then wait, Octavio! And don't act without asking me first.

OCTAVIO: Very well.

ISABEL: Thank you. [*He exits.*]

MARIANA: [*Addressing* MERCEDES.] The Duchess Isabel has a visitor.

MERCEDES: It must be bad news. Look how she sighs.

MARIANA: We all have problems. I'm not about to pity her.

DON JUAN: What are you talking about, dear souls? [*Perceiving* ISABEL, *he bids farewell to the two ladies who retire after curtseying to the Duchess.*]

ISABEL: [*Who had been looking for* DON JUAN.] Juan, you must talk to the young Ulloa.

DON JUAN: Again! I don't understand you. I've hardly given in to you, and you've changed your mind again. I don't like whims.

ISABEL: It's not a whim. It's about saving you. Octavio has come to Seville to seek revenge.

DON JUAN: And so? Do you think I'm incapable of defending myself?

ISABEL: But, Juan, he'll denounce you to the King.

DON JUAN: Never mind, I don't want to hear any more talk about your meeting.

ISABEL: Fine.

[*She exits. With the exception of* DON JUAN, *all of the characters go into the music room.* ANA DE ULLOA *enters, dropping her handkerchief as she passes in front of* DON JUAN.]

DON JUAN: [*Picking up the handkerchief.*] What a ravishing handkerchief!

ANA: And what a silly compliment.

DON JUAN: What silliness would one not commit for the pleasure of knowing such a pretty person?

ANA: That depends on you, Count.

DON JUAN: I might have missed so charming an opportunity. Please allow me at once to make amends . . .

ANA: All of a sudden you're in quite a hurry, Don Juan.

DON JUAN: Where do you know me from?

ANA: Who wouldn't recognize the proud forehead and nose of a Caesar? Your features are well known in the convent. If you look closely enough you'll find a replica in each prayer book.

DON JUAN: But how would my picture end up there?

ANA: Oh, a friend or other who spent some time at the Court and knows how to draw a little comes back with such a trophy, if not with more direct and special confidences.

DON JUAN: Your story is very interesting to me. And what is the effect of this glory?

ANA: It's easy. The day of the procession of the Virgin, when you walked through the streets with the Knights of the Banda, the entire convent was spying on you behind a curtain perforated with holes in order to see you go by.

DON JUAN: I didn't know such pretty eyes were watching me.

ANA: Not mine, Count, I wasn't among them.

DON JUAN: Why not? I'm very pained to hear you say it.

ANA: It's that I wasn't in a hurry to see you. I was right since here you are before me, for my eyes only and, my word, perfectly accessible. So here he is, this Don Juan, this eighth wonder of the world. Despite what they say about meeting something famous for the first time, be it a man or mountain, you're always astonished that it's not more imposing than it is.

DON JUAN: Are you making fun of me, Doña . . . ?

ANA: Ana de Ulloa.

DON JUAN: I thought so.

ANA: Now that we know each other, confess that you weren't in a great hurry to meet me.

DON JUAN: I was delayed.

ANA: Isn't it you who bragged that there's never an obstacle to your desires?

DON JUAN: There won't be any more, when it comes to seeing you.

ANA: I recognize there your honeyed words. But let's talk seriously now. The delays preventing you from meeting me lead me to suppose that, like me, you find absurd the proposal to marry us.

DON JUAN: But I hadn't made up my mind about that. You're further along than I. And may I know why you think it's absurd to marry me?

ANA: Well, first of all . . . I can understand taking Don Juan as a lover, but surely not as a husband.

DON JUAN: I can see that God's daughters have inculcated in you some fine principles.

ANA: Second, because I have already planned my marriage.

DON JUAN: I can see I'm dealing with a very determined young woman. And may I know whom you have chosen?

ANA: My cousin, the Marquis de la Mota.

DON JUAN: Manoel de la Mota? He's twenty. How old are you?

ANA: Fifteen. It's time to think about settling down.

DON JUAN: And what about romance? [*The music has started again in the adjoining room.*] The long stares exchanged with one another, the stolen kisses behind the duenna's back . . .

ANA: The notes and letters smuggled in the parlor . . .

DON JUAN: The scented handkerchief a young man presses against his lips, the lock of hair he requests. Show me, where did you cut it?

ANA: He didn't ask me for one.

DON JUAN: And the dream you continue each night, unrealized for too long. That trembling, that fever taking hold of you the day love swooped down on you, like an eagle.

The surprise of that encounter in the palace halls, one night. The embrace that threw you into each other's arms, and whose burning you will never forget . . .

ANA: Oh! We're no longer as gallant.

DON JUAN: Yes, I see, sorcery doesn't interest you. So what are you passionate about? Let me guess. Your little face seems as hard as a medal. Oh, you're not sentimental, I see. Let's look for the fault in this beautiful armor. Give me your hand.

ANA: Naturally, you're also a diviner, an astrologist, and perhaps even a cabalist.

DON JUAN: Why not? [*He looks into her hand.*] A child could read it for you. It's as clear as a map. Women often embarrass me. They offer me their hand with a dying mien and say: so tell me what you see there. Nine times out of ten, there's only an indistinct scribble; the very image of the confusion they're macerating in. In general, destiny is interested in few people. You can see it right away in the palm of the hand. One wouldn't dare say it's uninterested in you.

ANA: What do you see?

DON JUAN: Look at these two beautiful lines representing Mars and Saturn. It's your will opposing fate. Just before meeting Saturn, the Martian line hesitates, it gets tangled up, it branches out.

ANA: Meaning?

DON JUAN: That an event midway between your twelfth and twentieth year will change the direction of your life, which will henceforth blindly obey fate. Kronos rules this hand.

ANA: Show me yours. This strong line circling your thumb is the lifeline, isn't it?

DON JUAN: Yes.

ANA: How strange. It disappears abruptly like a stream that vanishes into the earth. What does that mean?

DON JUAN: The meaning is clear.

ANA: At what age?

DON JUAN: The intersection between the lifeline and a diagonal line through the middle of Mount Apollo: forty.

ANA: And how old are you?

DON JUAN: Forty.

ANA: So aren't you afraid?

DON JUAN: No one says you have to believe in omens.

ANA: Well I believe in dreams. Last night I had a horrifying dream. I saw my father stabbed to death by a stranger. It happened in the study of an alchemist that we had gone to visit. The alchemist had the King's face.

DON JUAN: And the stranger?

ANA: He was dressed in black from head to toe, but he possessed a marvelous, diabolical beauty. That is, I only guessed he was beautiful since I could hardly distinguish his face. It's quite strange in a dream with details so precise that the colors still linger in my mind.

DON JUAN: What colors were there?

ANA: A red as brilliant as a ruby. There were several such spots. There was one in the egg that was cooking in the alchemist's retorts. There was also a large spot on the floor, my father's blood. But there was still more of that same red. I remember the stranger had one on his shoulder. [*She automatically looks at the ribbon on* DON JUAN's *shoulder.*] Oh!

DON JUAN: Well let's chase away those phantoms. So what does this Manoel have that you like so much?

ANA: Stop caressing my hand. I don't dislike him, and I do what I like with him.

DON JUAN: You'd do as much with any man.

ANA: Do you think so?

DON JUAN: You haven't realized the extent of your power yet. Look at its effect on me. Look at me, Ana.

ANA: I don't like looking at you. Your gaze is a petrifying one. I can't bear it. You force me to lower my eyes.

DON JUAN: Don't speak any more, Ana. You remind me of a face I was in love with as a child.

ANA: How strange, whenever you talk about being young, you get the eyes of a child. A while ago, they were the eyes of a falcon in search of its prey. But how could I be suspicious of your eyes now? What kind of little boy were you?

DON JUAN: A sad little boy. Even then I desperately loved the things that exasperate desire: the sea, the sky, souls. Believe me, Ana, souls are what I loved particularly. It's yours I love tonight, its harshness, its transparency. I recognize my penchant, my old desire for extremes. But you don't like me to speak to you this way. This little hand I'm squeezing is pulling away; this celestial nose and this mouth scoff at me. They seem to say that Don Juan is just an old man.

ANA: Oh . . .

DON JUAN: And there's a scintillating curiosity in your eyes of simulated softness. It seems to wonder how far you can lead him. Very far, my child. Would you like to try? How far can you carry your cruelty? There'd be a twofold and delicious curiosity in it for you: love and power. Too bad then, you'll satisfy it with the Marquis de la Mota. Personally, I prefer to protect myself against your claws. I risk getting hurt too deeply. Pity, though, to waste so much beauty . . .

ANA: Why wasted?

DON JUAN: I would have liked to see you deliver your first attacks on another partner. An adversary that knows how to keep his part of the bargain is so important for acquiring an aptitude. The Marquis is nice, but he's very young. He doesn't know women and he's mainly involved with hunting. I prefer a slightly older man whose sufficient experience would have prepared him for an assured fidelity as well as for love.

ANA: What about marriage?

DON JUAN: But we were talking about love, not marriage. The beginnings of love are so delicate and fragile. You must avoid complicating it with the slightest bond. You must leave it its nonchalance, its charming spontaneity. Nothing falsifies a woman's mind more than the confusion between love and marriage that they claim is imposed on her.

ANA: And so?

DON JUAN: Think about loving first. You don't know anything about men. Why not accept a few innocent honors?

ANA: Maybe . . .

DON JUAN: Has anyone ever serenaded you?

ANA: No.

DON JUAN: Can I come and do so tomorrow evening?

ANA: I'd like that.

DON JUAN: Can I come up and stay with you for a few minutes? I'd like to see the room you sleep in, your little bed, your medals and relics. Do you wear a scapular?

ANA: Yes.

DON JUAN: Would you allow me to kiss it?

[*She pulls it from her corsage, and hands it to him.*]

ANA: Off with you now, someone's coming. [ISABEL *enters.*]

DON JUAN: See you tomorrow.

ANA: On second thought, come tonight. My father's away. It'll be easier for me to let you in.

DON JUAN: It's that tonight . . .

ANA: Yet another obstacle?

DON JUAN: Well, then, I'll come. You're delicious.

[He leaves her and goes to ISABEL.]

DON JUAN: [*Addressing* ISABEL.] You see, I can't say no to anything you ask. I've given into your whims. That was the young Ulloa I was talking to.

ISABEL: Oh? Well . . . she's nice . . .

DON JUAN: Somewhat trivial. My God, she's just a girl.

ISABEL: You must announce your engagement to her. Octavio is threatening you. I'll talk to you about it later tonight.

DON JUAN: I almost forgot. I won't be able to come to you tonight.

ISABEL: Oh?

DON JUAN: A family matter is calling me to Lebrija. I'll be back tomorrow. [*Pause.*] Aren't you going to say anything, Isabel?

ISABEL: What do you want me to say? God keep you, Juan.

ACT III

ISABEL's *room at the Alcazar, Seville.*

DON JUAN: Never have I longed to see you again as much as I do now. I changed horses three times. I was an hour ahead of the King's messenger. As I reached the outskirts of Seville, I was so afraid you had fled that I felt chilled. Finally, here you are. I'm holding you, you're part of my breath.

ISABEL: You're trembling, Juan. What's wrong?

DON JUAN: I don't know. I'm afraid of losing you. I came to you today with the anguish and impatience of our first encounter. You should have seen me press my steed. At Montilla, where I changed horses, there was a delightful young girl sitting in a coach by the roadside. She looked at me engagingly. I pretended not to notice her. I made myself look ridiculous to please you. Are you happy?

ISABEL: Very. I don't even recognize you any more.

DON JUAN: I wanted to be here before night.

ISABEL: That was reckless. Ever since Octavio started watching you, I don't like you to come to me before nightfall. If he should ever discover us, he would seek immediate revenge.

DON JUAN: I love it just now, when the darkness slowly creeps into the room. Keep me here with you, would you? And talk to me. Enchant me with your words. Let them fall one by one, at first spaced like the early drops announcing the rain. And then trap me in their web. Surrender to your incantations, dear sorceress.

ISABEL: Oh, if I were only a sorceress! I would keep all of the women from you.

DON JUAN: But there aren't any more women. There's only you. Don't you see that I finally love you as much as you love me? Smile at me. I'm terribly happy. You're not as happy as I am this evening. Why?

ISABEL: Octavio came. He's irritated by the new delays on your marriage. He insists they are excuses.

DON JUAN: It seems to me the Commander's murder and his daughter's mourning can hardly be called excuses.

ISABEL: He wants to take me away. He claims I only have wrong reasons for staying in Seville.

DON JUAN: Stop tormenting yourself. Have I lost the power to sweep you off the ground and transport you to another world? Nothing matters, Isabel, but the enchantment that possesses us. I must admit that every time I come to you, it's with the anguish of finding us cold and shameful, no longer charmed. But each time everything begins afresh.

ISABEL: And yet I've seen you tormented.

DON JUAN: When was that?

ISABEL: The night you came to me with your clothes torn and soiled, like an alley cat after a night of prowling. It was the night of Saint James.

DON JUAN: I don't think so. It was well before that. Wasn't the night of Saint James when the Commander was killed?

ISABEL: I think so.

DON JUAN: Don't you realize how dangerous your association is, my dear? Why do you think it was the night of Saint James?

ISABEL: I don't remember. I may be mistaken. Don't worry about it.

DON JUAN: I'm not worried.

ISABEL: Forgive me, Juan. It's for you I feel tormented. If someone attacked you, who would defend you? How is it you haven't a single friend? Men hate you. They avoid you as if you were cursed.

DON JUAN: I still have children, women, animals. That's not such a bad trade-off. Look at me. Let me chase those phantoms away. What can fate do to a love such as ours?

ISABEL: Don't say that word, Juan. It brings bad luck.

DON JUAN: I only said it to avoid upsetting you. Do you know what I was thinking? What can God Himself do to lovers like us?

ISABEL: Be quiet, Juan, that's blasphemous!

DON JUAN: Look at me. [*Pause.*] Are you still afraid of something?

ISABEL: No. When you gaze at me, it's as if I'm drinking from your lips. It's the sacrament of communion. I feel your life flowing through me. I feel myself becoming you. Do you know what words I feel like saying?

DON JUAN: No.

ISABEL: The ones from the Lord's Prayer: My Lord, Thy will be done.

[*Someone knocks at the door.*]

DON JUAN: Someone's knocking.

[ISABEL *goes to the door. It's* DOÑA JACINTA.]

ISABEL: I thought I had forbidden you . . .

DOÑA JACINTA: It's Doña Ana, Madam. She found out that Don Juan was here. She wants to talk to him. She says it's important.

DON JUAN: Did you tell her I was here?

DOÑA JACINTA: No. She then requested to speak to Duchess Isabel.

DON JUAN: What could she want from me? I should find out.

ISABEL: No, no. She must not know you're here with me. Go into the closet, and don't come out before I call you.

DON JUAN: All right, then. [*He exits.* ANA DE ULLOA *enters.*]

ANA: Duchess Isabel? [ISABEL *nods.*]

ISABEL: Please sit down.

ANA: Don Juan is here! Isn't he?

ISABEL: I thought you had already received an answer to that question. Don't forget that if I receive you, *Señora*, it's because you asked to see me.

ANA: Don't try to intimidate me with your Italian tactics. Don Juan is here.

ISABEL: Since you take on that tone, I must say I deplore your Spanish arrogance. What do you want, Señora?

ANA: I want to know what Don Juan is doing here!

ISABEL: By what right do you ask me this question?

ANA: Don Juan is my fiancé, Madam.

ISABEL: I have indeed heard rumors about the marriage. It seems the date is quite close.

ANA: No, that you haven't heard. It's not close at all. Don Juan is cunning. I know perfectly well he's hiding here and that he's cowardly waiting until I have my word with you.

ISABEL: Please, Señora. You abuse the indulgence of your youth. If Don Juan were hiding here, it would be on my orders. A woman may exercise other rights on a man than those of a fiancée.

ANA: I can imagine the kind of rights you might have over him. When a woman hides Don Juan in her chamber, everyone knows what that means. If Don Juan is your lover, you should know he is mine, too.

ISABEL: Oh?

ANA: Perhaps you knew? [*Pause.*] No, you didn't know. Too bad. It's your turn to know. As for me, this is the second betrayal of Don Juan I've learned about today.

ISABEL: There's yet another?

ANA: Yes, a decidedly base betrayal with one of my chambermaids. I see you don't know very well the kind of man Don Juan is.

ISABEL: Oh, I have an inkling.

ANA: No, you don't know him. I'll tell you how he seduced me, his vows, his promises, the fidelity he told me would last a lifetime and which he tired of after three weeks. But all of that doesn't matter; neither does that girl he most likely told the same lies to. After all, she's tired of pursuing him, and she's now letting her hatred explode by accusing him . . .

ISABEL: What is she accusing him of?

ANA: It doesn't matter if you know that, too. Don Juan killed my father, Madam.

ISABEL: I was sure of it!

ANA: Really? And that's all such a confession inspires in you? You think it's natural? You're ready to absolve Don Juan of this crime that must strike you as quite insignificant.

ISABEL: But, Señora, may I ask you a question? Why did you want to see Don Juan? Was it to express your rebuke?

ANA: I wanted to warn him against a danger.

ISABEL: A danger? [*Pause.*] So you love him?

ANA: I don't know. I often hate him . . . He took my honor, killed my father. I have a right to dispose of him if I wish. Whatever you may think, Madam, he will marry me.

ISABEL: He is capable of it.

ANA: Oh! I know you're deaf to this marriage. I know the power you have over him. Even with me, he can't help mixing your name in his words. Though he has traveled so much, I only ever hear him speak of one trip, Naples; and if he calls my dog Jacinta, it's doubtlessly because that's the name of your maid.

ISABEL: [*Smiling.*] These are quite innocent coincidences.

ANA: What is less of a coincidence, is your way of holding him. You're still beautiful, but that's not what attaches him to you. I, too, am beautiful, and I'm fifteen years younger. If he stays with you, it's that you hold on to him with your charm, and through a complicity that my innocence can scarcely depict.

ISABEL: Your innocence seems capable enough to imagine these things. You have a way, Señora, of throwing your youth in my face. No, it's not experience that captivates Don Juan. He overflows with it; and always has enough left over for two. He has a will for discovering new callings. That tells you how fond he is of innocence, too. No, if there is between us a complicity that cannot exist between him and you, it's made of a rarer quality. Don Juan is forty, Señora. That's the time a man like him needs more than ever to try his power on young girls. But it's also the time he is hurt by the insolence of their youth. Their sparkle, their freshness, reminds him that he's getting older. It's cruel for such a man to wake up next to a young, tireless body, and next to a face unmarked by time. I do not humiliate him.

ANA: I admire your patience. I knew just how complacently you accepted his worst vices.

ISABEL: I imagine you content yourself by accepting only those that don't make you suffer.

ANA: What insolence! It is cowardice, Madam, to accept a man who betrays you. It is you who overestimate the pleasure he gives you, if you pay that kind of price. What are you expecting? That he'll keep you? He will leave you like he left all the others.

ISABEL: Why would you want me to theorize about that?

ANA: Aren't you sure of him then?

ISABEL: I'm sure of something, but I don't know what. It's not his fidelity, nor even his love, although I'm certain of it. It's like a conviction. It came to me at the same time as his first lies, and his first deceit.

ANA: There's something disarming about you. Oh, you haven't quite managed to touch me. I don't like you. But you have a way of discouraging those who wish you harm. There is such a power of persistence in you.

ISABEL: I call that love.

ANA: I understand that on the point of getting old, he would want such a safe harbor. Getting old! May God grant him the time.

ISABEL: What do you mean?

ANA: By now the King must have been informed of his crime.

ISABEL: Why didn't you say so? Here we are reveling in our quarrel, while his life is in danger. We must act, Señora! Who took it upon himself to uphold the accusation?

ANA: Manoel de la Mota.

ISABEL: There's no proof, is there?

ANA: Yes. A belt buckle was found at the site of the murder.

ISABEL: How did it get into his hands? Hurry, Señora, tell me. Time is short.

ANA: My father surprised Don Juan as he was leaving my room one night. My father followed him into the street, and Don Juan killed him in self-defense. No one would have suspected him if he hadn't lost the buckle my maid picked up. The girl is crazy about him. At first, she spoke to no one about what she had found. But since Don Juan's rejection of her, she ran over to Manoel's in a moment a fury and told him that I had received Don Juan several times at night, and that he had murdered my father. The Marquis immediately left for Seville, like a madman. He must be with the King even as we speak.

ISABEL: How did you learn all of this?

ANA: The same girl. As soon as she denounced him, she was horrified by what she had done. She threw herself at my feet, in tears, and confessed.

ISABEL: What do you think the King will do? Don Juan only defended himself. It wasn't murder.

ANA: Such distinctions hardly bear any weight on King Pedro's decisions. I know how moody the King can be. In one hour Don Juan will pay for the favors the King has showered upon him over a lifetime.

ISABEL: We must do something to save him. First of all, we must call him . . .

ANA: I can only see one possible defense against that girl's statement. The statement of another woman with whom Don Juan would have spent the night . . . your own statement.

ISABEL: I understand, Señora.

ANA: In exchange for my help, however, you must promise me that you will leave Seville, alone, this very night.

ISABEL: How do you expect me to leave tonight?

ANA: The post to Tarragona departs tomorrow morning at five. Take it.

ISABEL: And what will happen if I refuse?

ANA: I think you know what will happen.

ISABEL: Very well . . . Jacinta, call the Count.

ANA: Do I have your word of honor?

ISABEL: Yes . . . How did Juan ever manage to conquer a heart so devoid of weakness?

ANA: But I don't love Don Juan. I only want him. [DON JUAN *enters.*]

DON JUAN: Good evening, Ana. What urgent news do you have for me that you should follow me even to the Duchess'? [*Pause.*] What did she tell you, Isabel? Something that might have upset you? You seem sad. Look at me. It's as though a veil has come over your eyes.

ANA: You forget yourself strangely in front of your fiancée, Juan.

DON JUAN: What have I said to hurt you? What did you say to her? Isabel, what convent babble did this little fool tell you? [*Pause.*] What stillness! I can tell instantly that you're plotting against me. Women . . . always torturing each other! Fools! Must your jealousy poison even the sweetest bonds? [*Pause.*] What do you want from me? I'm waiting. Kill me with your grievances. Indulge in your hunger for explanation. Well, go on. You, Isabel, answer me if you don't want me to lose my patience. What did she tell you about her and me?

ISABEL: Oh, as far as that's concerned, nothing of consequence. There's one thing that matters, Juan. At this very moment, the Marquis de la Mota is accusing you before the King of having murdered the Commander.

DON JUAN: Oh! And on what grounds is he accusing me?

ANA: On Marcella's testimony, and on the belt buckle she found.

DON JUAN: Oh, how uncalled-for!

ANA: Above all, it's rife with consequence.

ISABEL: What will you do, Juan?

DON JUAN: What do you want me to do? This isn't the first time God has set up His machinery against me. I've always pulled through at the last moment by skillful maneuver.

ISABEL: You're irreverent, Juan. You will pay for that.

DON JUAN: Everything has to be paid for. We've known it from the beginning of time. There's only one thing that can't be made up for, and that is not to have lived.

ISABEL: But if we found a way to save you . . .

DON JUAN: Tell me.

ANA: One testimony may be weighed against another.

ISABEL: I could remember that I spent the night of Saint James with you.

DON JUAN: And what would you do about Octavio's fury?

ANA: But why would you expect him to know?

DON JUAN: Everything is eventually found out at this Court. The King's anger would turn against Isabel. No, I cannot accept such an offer . . . [DOÑA JACINTA *enters.*]

DOÑA JACINTA: Madam, Ripio has come to warn you of an imminent danger to you.

ISABEL: Let him come in. [*To* ANA.] Ripio is Duke Octavio's attendant.

DOÑA JACINTA: [*Pushing* RIPIO *forward.*] Go ahead. Speak to her yourself. Don't be afraid to tell her. She might believe you. She won't even listen to me.

RIPIO: May it please the Duchess to question me. I'll answer.

ISABEL: What do you know, Ripio?

RIPIO: Duke Octavio surprised Don Juan.

ISABEL: How so? Where?

RIPIO: He saw him sneaking into your room.

ISABEL: When was that?

RIPIO: Tonight. If I may give the Duchess a piece of my advice . . .

ISABEL: By all means.

RIPIO: Beware. The Duke is furious. He immediately sent me to request an audience with the King.

DON JUAN: Did the King receive Duke Octavio?

RIPIO: He has just called for him.

ISABEL: Thank you, Ripio. You may go.

[*He exits, as does* DOÑA JACINTA.]

ANA: This is excellent.

DON JUAN: And how! Now I feel completely beset. I really have the impression that the elements are conspiring against me.

ANA: It's quite the contrary. Octavio's testimony will fortunately confirm that of the Duchess. From murderer to simple libertine, you become once again El Burlador. It's a title that has never been disputed. At most, it will only warrant you a reprimand. You will have to leave Seville for a few weeks. All of Castille will open its arms to you.

ISABEL: Juan, since Octavio and the King are abreast of my actions, why do you refuse my testimony?

DON JUAN: Perhaps . . .

ANA: Once again, you will escape God's machinations. All we need is a slight distortion of the truth made by this innocent hand.

ISABEL: The King won't delay in calling you. Whatever you do, don't bungle it.

ANA: Try not to contradict each other. Agree on the exact time you entered her room the night of Saint James'. Let's say it was dusk. It's your hour, Juan. The hour that neither hurts the eyes nor the soul. Right, Juan? You have several fine variations on that theme.

DON JUAN: Peace, Ana! You stand there like a weasel, licking the blood that oozes from Isabel's throat. Just be aware that words and gestures are the same. Only love is unique.

ANA: Oh what a gratifying invention! I dare you to put a name on your unique love. Is it Isabel? Then I defy you to say so. Answer, Juan, which one of us do you prefer? But I'm not distraught. You'll never choose between two women. If you chose one, it would be while fondling the other furtively to restore the balance.

DON JUAN: Ana, you are provoking me!

ANA: Go on, I dare you to say that you prefer her to me. To me, your little whore.

ISABEL: Get out, both of you!

DON JUAN: Listen, Isabel, listen so that you may never forget the sound of my words. In the name of Christ, I swear . . .

ISABEL: Be quiet, Juan.

ANA: Liar! Have you forgotten your word that even the most sacred oath cannot bind you?

DON JUAN: In the name of Christ . . .

ANA: You're lying, you're lying to humiliate me. Do you want me to bow to the ground before you, like the others?

DON JUAN: Ana, you are crying . . .

ANA: From anger. You think I love you. If you only knew how tired I am of being glued to you. I know what you're thinking. Only yesterday, I wanted to see you, that I showed you my desire for your presence. So what? Don't you know that? That need of the other, over and over again and, at the same time, that revulsion and saturation of the soul. I will prove to you that I don't love you. You can go to the Devil! I won't lie to save you!

ISABEL: Stop tearing each other apart. Nothing good can come of it. Tomorrow other words will come to your lips. I will leave, Ana. Don't forget you are obligated by my promise.

DON JUAN: Your words are a blessing, Ana. You reminded me just in time of my honor. Women have often served my desires, never my cowardice. In what kind of plot were you going to embroil me? That's what I get for being nonchalant with women. I was almost going to let myself be indebted to you. You would not have failed to use it against me.

ANA: What little generosity you grant me.

ISABEL: Don't be so proud, Juan. Ana did not intend to hurt you.

ANA: There you are brooding over every word. You know I'm spirited.

ISABEL: Don't be obstinate, Juan.

DON JUAN: Don't insist.

ANA: Help me save him, Isabel. I won't impose any conditions on you.

ISABEL: Juan, do keep quiet. You owe us that much respect.

ANA: Your silence, Juan. Grant us your silence.

DON JUAN: That would only serve the King's wrath against you.

ANA: It wouldn't!

DON JUAN: It's useless. You know I don't easily change my mind about a position I've taken. Look at Isabel. She knows me. I hesitated until your bitter words hastened my decision.

ANA: But they were words of love, Juan.

DON JUAN: I took them as such, but that doesn't change their meaning.

ANA: Are you angry with me?

DON JUAN: No, my child, I'm not angry with you. I love you when your pride suddenly ebbs like the fallen wind. You are like a stilled sky at night, after a stormy day. [*He kisses her.*]

ANA: Oh, Juan, I do want to save you. I have an idea. I'll run to the King's confessor. I'll try to sway him. Farewell, Isabel. [*She exits.*]

DON JUAN: What now?

ISABEL: And now . . . poor Ana. Mind you when I say poor Ana, I mean poor Isabel. [*Pause.*] Aren't you going to say anything, Juan?

DON JUAN: What can I say? Poor Isabel, your feet on the ground once again. Let me bury my head in your lap so I won't see my broken image in your eyes. Don't say a word. I fear what you are about to say. Hold your tongue for an instant. Put your hand on me. What is still possible between Don Juan and you?

ISABEL: Everything, Juan.

DON JUAN: Everything? What about your love that ennobled me? I have lied so much. Tell me then, are you not displeased?

ISABEL: How can I explain? You always surprise me, even if you always act as I imagined you would, albeit a little better. Your reality is always bolder, more artful and more glamorous than the image I had formed of you. I love you, Juan. It's awful to say, but I'm proud of all that you do.

DON JUAN: So are you not distressed?

ISABEL: What can it matter?

DON JUAN: I reproach myself about all of that, just the same.

ISABEL: About what? Ana, Marcella? It's nothing, it doesn't matter. If I could, I would bring every woman to you. Now it's your turn to explain. Everything today has conspired to bring me down, yet I feel unbelievably happy. Never before have I felt a happiness so towering and intense.

DON JUAN: Neither have I, Isabel. Alas! I fear God may have given us a reprieve before the ordeal.

ISABEL: For a long time, Juan, I wanted to be the only one to lay claim on you. But you always eluded me. Now that I've given up isolating you, that I know you're everywhere open to others, and that I've accepted not limiting you, I gain a kind of possession of you that no one can take away, not even you. I am finally complying with Don Juan's destiny.

DON JUAN: And you would want me to evade it?

ISABEL: What do you mean by that?

DON JUAN: That there are moments when destiny clearly awaits us. I have never tried to evade these warnings. [*Pause.*] I truly admire God's ingenuity. Octavio, Ana, the Commander, Marcella, Manoel are but the threads that have been used to weave the rope that will hang me.

ISABEL: I don't understand you. You mean you're so defenseless before your fate that you haven't thought of a way to escape it?

DON JUAN: I haven't.

ISABEL: I wouldn't call that honor. It's obstinacy.

DON JUAN: At best it's nonchalance.

ISABEL: What would change your mind?

DON JUAN: Nothing. Besides, time has run out.

[*Sound of marching guards and of weapons drawing near.* CAPTAIN *and* GUARDS *enter.*]

CAPTAIN: Count Juan Tenorio?

DON JUAN: I am he.

CAPTAIN: The King has ordered me to arrest and disarm you.

DON JUAN: How can I be disarmed without even being accused? Where are you taking me?

CAPTAIN: To the King. [*He orders his men.*] Disarm him.

DON JUAN: Wait. Isabel, I'm sorry you had to witness this scene . . .

[OCTAVIO *enters, followed by* JACINTA.]

OCTAVIO: Are you sorry that I'm a witness, too?

ISABEL: Octavio! How shameless can you be? Why have you come here? To watch me suffer?

OCTAVIO: I must speak with you.

ISABEL: Be quick.

OCTAVIO: No. I shall wait for this man to leave.

[ISABEL *bolts.*]

DON JUAN: Listen to him, Isabel . . . [*He whispers.*] Let me teach you this last pleasure of restraining your passions. Don't be afraid. I'll see you again.

CAPTAIN: Your sword, my Lord.

ISABEL: Jacinta, help the Count.

DON JUAN: My coat, Jacinta.

JACINTA: Here it is, my Lord.

[*They take him away.* JACINTA *leaves.*]

ISABEL: Now, speak.

OCTAVIO: I learned today the extent to which you've deceived me. I saw Don Juan enter your chambers. I thought my fury would find some relief in denouncing your lover's crimes to the King. Alas! As soon as I discerned my vengeance, I realized the pain it would cause you. I am very unhappy, Isabel.

ISABEL: I don't know whether you even see what you've done, Octavio. You have condemned the man I love. Are you expecting me to console you now?

OCTAVIO: That depends on you, Isabel. Don Juan has been convicted of murder. He has lost favor. He's no longer of any use to you now, Isabel. His sentence is only a matter of time.

ISABEL: Did the King tell you that?

OCTAVIO: Yes.

ISABEL: [*Pause.*] Death?

OCTAVIO: Without doubt.

ISABEL: I see. Go now, Octavio. Please leave me.

OCTAVIO: No. I can't leave you now. I'm your only friend.

ISABEL: That's a mockery.

OCTAVIO: We must leave, Isabel. I found a ship for Naples. Call Jacinta.

ISABEL: Are you mad?

OCTAVIO: Oh, don't make any mistakes about my intentions. I'm not trying to win you back. The outrage you committed against me divides us. But you are alone here, and I have a duty to take you back to safety . . .

ISABEL: Did you imagine I would abandon Don Juan when everything is against him?

OCTAVIO: As you speak time is passing. Every moment . . .

ISABEL: Time? . . . You're right. Time matters. You must leave, Octavio. Leave me. I'm going to pray.

OCTAVIO: Pray for an atheist?

ISABEL: There are rebels that God loves.

OCTAVIO: I don't understand you.

ISABEL: I do understand you, Octavio. But I can't forgive you. I pity you. It's the only weakness I still have for you.

OCTAVIO: Thank you for this last insult. The only thing I owe you is my disdain. I will finally be free to hate you.

ISABEL: Good. You should know, Octavio, that I have never loved you. Not a single moment.

OCTAVIO: Be happy then. I hate you, Isabel. Farewell. You'll never see me again. [*He leaves.*]

ISABEL: Jacinta! Wait at the door. I don't want to see anyone but Don Juan. Call me if he comes back.

[*She exits.* DOÑA JACINTA *goes to the window and starts a conversation with the gardener, who is tending the grounds.*]

JACINTA: Good evening, Pepe.

PEPE: Good evening, Señora.

JACINTA: The pomegranates are doing well this year.

PEPE: Oh, in Seville the orchards do well. It's not like the rocky soil in Estremadura.

JACINTA: Is that where you come from?

PEPE: No, I'm a Berruguete, from Triana.

JACINTA: You're working quite late.

PEPE: All day long, the architects are in the way. I wait for the evening to work.

JACINTA: There's no arguing that your King is a great builder.

PEPE: Indeed!

JACINTA: What do you think about all these changes? The patios they replaced were charming.

PEPE: Whatever the King does, he does well.

JACINTA: Everything?

PEPE: Yes!

JACINTA: Why, then, do they say he's cruel?

PEPE: I have no idea.

JACINTA: You're not very talkative.

PEPE: What do you expect, Señora? In the Berruguete family all the males are gardeners of the King, from father to son. The King protects and feeds us. A bird sings wherever it is fed.

JACINTA: Did you see Don Juan come back?

PEPE: Not yet.

JACINTA: It's been a bad day for him. Do you think they'll keep him?

PEPE: If they do, he won't be trampling on my basil to climb up to his sweetheart, anymore. At least I'll have that.

JACINTA: You're a bad man, unkind!

PEPE: There he is!

JACINTA: My God, yes. Holy Mary, how many men are guarding him? Twelve! Could they be that afraid of him? After all, he's only one man.

[*A few moments later,* DON JUAN *enters. He is alone.*]

JACINTA: Well, my Lord?

DON JUAN: I've been sentenced to the fortress of Lebrija. Does Lebrija mean anything to you? Poor innocent one. It means that in the next few hours some vexatious thing will happen to me. In other words, it means death . . .

JACINTA: My Lord!

DON JUAN: What irony. Lebrija is where the Commander is buried. The King does not lack a sense of humor! God knows what the imagination of men will make of it.

JACINTA: My Lord, what about the Duchess? She loves you . . .

DON JUAN: I know, I can assure you I'm thinking about that. Jacinta, you must not weep over the fate of lovers that God has separated before the end of their love. All love is mortal, and every beautiful thing is destined to die.

JACINTA: My Lord, how will I tell her?

DON JUAN: Go with her. Go home across the sea. Take good care of her the way you did when she had scarlet fever, at thirteen. Above all, do not leave her alone at night. You know how sad she gets when night falls. Don't let her stay out after the sun sets. She catches cold.

JACINTA: Very well, my Lord.

DON JUAN: Jacinta, one day, when she learns of it, tell her that I died with her name on my lips.

JACINTA: Yes, my lord.

DON JUAN: Now tell her I'm waiting.

[JACINTA *exits.* ISABEL *enters.*]

ISABEL: There you are! Well, what has the King decided? Will you answer me? Speak.

DON JUAN: He is sending me away to a fortress for some time.

ISABEL: Oh! What a relief. For a moment, I imagined the worst. The expression on your face was so grave. Why weren't you answering me?

DON JUAN: I saw you come to me so pale in your white dress. It was as if I was looking at you for the very first time. You know how one gets used to the sight of a loved one. Their features become blurred like those of an image one has looked at for a very long time. Is it because your lip trembles that I notice the slight hollow casting a soft shadow on your cheek?

ISABEL: Tell me what happened, Juan. What did the King say? Where is he sending you?

DON JUAN: To Lebrija.

ISABEL: Did they give you back your arms?

DON JUAN: Only to take them away more easily. The Knights of the Banda have the solemn privilege of stripping me of my arms. At this moment they are being called to arms. After that, I will return before the King.

ISABEL: How did you get here?

DON JUAN: The Commander of the Guard is a poor devil I saved from the hands of the police one day. He allowed me to be at your side for a few moments. Don't you hear them? They're right under your windows. Poor men. They're uneasy about taking responsibility for me. You said once, Isabel, that I didn't have friends. Yet they surrounded me like a pack of faithful dogs. On the other hand, the King's secretary could hardly conceal his joy. His pleasure at seeing the favorite fall in disgrace literally left him speechless.

ISABEL: You can flee, Juan. We can get you out of the Palace. We can disguise you and hide you until tomorrow.

DON JUAN: Would you want me to betray the man who placed his confidence in Don Juan and who received his word? Listen to me, Isabel. I'm in the middle of two equally cruel ordeals. I have just left the King. I've been his confidant and his playmate for the past fifteen years. Do you think I was able to see in him the slightest sign resembling, not friendship, but justice? I only saw him determined and in a hurry to execute an imprudent man who dared create a scandal. In a few moments, I will appear before my peers. I can imagine the revenge their envy will seek under the guise of honor. Before I go, there remains one respite for me: these few instants I am spending with you. I still have this sweetness to compensate for my bitterness. I think so poorly of men. Only you can absolve them in my eyes. Speak to me before I go.

ISABEL: I don't know what to say to you. My only desire is to touch you, to make sure you are still within my reach.

DON JUAN: You must talk to me, about anything. About the bird you can hear singing, about the evening calm that augurs beautiful weather for the days to come, and of which you will take advantage to return to Naples.

ISABEL: But from there I'll be helpless to do anything for you.

DON JUAN: You mustn't do anything for some time if you don't want to hurt me. Don't debate every one of my wishes. I'm no longer in a position to protect you. I want you to leave this Court as of tomorrow. Promise me.

ISABEL: I'll obey you, Juan. Will you come to me?

DON JUAN: My thoughts will always be with you.

ISABEL: You worry me. You seem so resigned to your fate. How calm you are.

DON JUAN: It's only my way of showing courage. If I didn't see you again, Isabel, how long would it take you to forget me?

ISABEL: You are cruel. Even if my mind lost its memory, my body would still remember yours. It would remember the exact proportions of your frame. At night my arms would close around your specter. I would only have to open them to welcome you to bed and, so as not to disturb you, I wouldn't have to retreat an inch on account of having made room for you so well. I'm sure of it. Do you remember, Juan, that one day I recognized you by your height?

DON JUAN: The day we played blind man's bluff?

ISABEL: The moment I put my hand on your shoulder, I felt overcome by such well-being, such freedom. I didn't yet know I had recognized you, that I was already blossoming upon recognizing the shape of your embrace.

DON JUAN: That was the day I broke your heavy necklace. I can see you so well, so straight, a little startled, with that doe-like air you kept from your childhood. I've loved you, Isabel.

ISABEL: Why are you talking in the past tense? Other days will come, and even other women . . .

DON JUAN: Not any more now. My weariness will find its rest. I would like you to remember the calm that has come over me.

ISABEL: I have never seen such tranquillity in your features. Perhaps after making love to me.

DON JUAN: What are you thinking about?

ISABEL: I was thinking that ever since I've known you, Juan, my spectacle has been your face. I have loved looking at you. I have loved lingering over the moisture in your eyes, over those small, dark beaches furrowed by premature lines, like the sand that retains the imprint of the sea. I returned to those small beaches over and over again. They were my oases.

DON JUAN: I loved your determination to look at me when I took you.

ISABEL: Sometimes I resisted my own pleasure in order to observe better yours. Leaning over you, I watched the tide come. How you seemed far from pleasure. What words can describe the anticipation of that bliss, which your brow seemed to contemplate with eyes closed, beyond life itself?

DON JUAN: At times you would shout, "Look at me."

ISABEL: No sooner was I reborn than I would look at you again to surprise in your features the last reflection of that inner light that had illuminated you like translucent matter. But even by then you abandoned your waiting gesture to take on that majesty you get after making love. You no longer belonged in this world. You were a figure lying still on its tomb. All you needed to transform you into a glorious corpse was to stop the beating of that restless heart.

DON JUAN: I loved your face, too, Isabel. It was like a transparent dawn.

ISABEL: But you loved every face, my love.

DON JUAN: I truly loved yours with a special tenderness. I was used to it, familiar with it, but it's true I loved many others. I loved the faces of children playing in alleys, of little girls who came away with baskets that were too heavy, and the faces of many animals, and of all dogs.

ISABEL: And what about women's faces, Juan, have you anything to say about them?

DON JUAN: It's true. I loved seeing them distraught. No one had yet come to say the magic formula that would awaken them from sleep. They looked as though they were stuck in matter. It was such a temptation to bestow life on them, to show them their own face, their own gaze, their own mouth.

ISABEL: So you would tell them the words that were needed.

DON JUAN: Very few words. Or else very innocent ones. For instance, "It's odd how your geraniums flower more than those of the haberdasher's wife"; or, "Does your gate always creak so, or only at night?" You see how harmless it all was. But after these words, I wanted to say others. Their faces sought more direct words, more precise, more insistent ones. They requested love, and when they received it, there was an increasingly more intense radiance, from one step to the next. It was that ephemeral but most radiant beauty, that richness avariciously accumulated during years of vigilance that suddenly erupted. It's very tempting, Isabel, to instill life into inert matter.

ISABEL: I know, you've always liked doing God's work. But didn't you ever think that you would one day cover those faces with tears?

DON JUAN: Lovers hardly think about the end of love. Does a healthy man worry about death? The faces enjoy their season of happiness. Then comes winter, and we warm our hands over the embers, and our hearts, with the memories of the good times.

ISABEL: Are six months of summer a long time, Juan?

DON JUAN: Very long, my dear, but I feel like our beautiful season never ended.

ISABEL: Did you keep your women a long time?

DON JUAN: A month, a night, sometimes a few hours.

ISABEL: Is it because they disappointed you?

DON JUAN: Not even that. Women have never disappointed me. It was more like a book whose pages turned all by themselves.

ISABEL: Did they hold a grudge against you?

DON JUAN: Not for long. As for me, I always kept a warm, tender feeling for all those who gave themselves to me.

ISABEL: Juan, imagine for an instant that you abandoned me the night you left my bed, in Naples, do you know that I would never have regretted it? I would have continued to drink from it for the rest of my days, as from a fountain of youth.

DON JUAN: How strange, it seems you have said the last word. I realize now I counted on you to justify me. Ever since I've known you, Isabel, I have seen myself reflected in you. I have gazed at myself in your limpid pool; you have taught me who Don Juan is.

ISABEL: Look at me, my love. I can't bear the thought that your eyes will know the darkness. It's as if they buried you alive and threw fistfuls of earth at you. Look at me again. I have never seen your two eyes the same. One was always smiling while the other was sad, and everything that came from you was at once sweet and bitter. As though, in you, joy and sadness came from a mingled source.

DON JUAN: Let me touch you again, for the last time. Soon, those men will come. Promise me you won't cry.

ISABEL: Won't there be anyone to accompany you? Must you go on all alone from now on?

DON JUAN: Alone with my love, Isabel, just as you will be alone with yours. Impatient for the men to leave me so that I may quietly cherish your love. Tonight the flavor of your lips will still be on mine. But tomorrow there will only remain between you and me the most tenuous and obstinate of bonds: our love.

ISABEL: Juan, I will always be faithful to you.

DON JUAN: I believe you, but that will perhaps be in the arms of another.

ISABEL: I'm sure it won't.

DON JUAN: Why not? You will perhaps look for me in other men. Never be ashamed of yourself. Don't forget you and I can allow us anything. We would never get dirty.

ISABEL: Truly?

DON JUAN: I'm happy to see that smile through your tears. Do you know why?

ISABEL: No.

[*The* CAPTAIN *enters.*]

CAPTAIN: My Lord, the King is waiting . . .

DON JUAN: Because we are . . . I'm coming Fernando . . . angels. [*He disappears.*]

ISABEL: [*As she moves to the window, she changes her mind and then calls.*] Jacinta!

[JACINTA *enters.*]

ISABEL: Come here.

JACINTA: Yes, my Lady.

ISABEL: Look through the window and tell me if they have put him in chains.

JACINTA: No, my Lady.

ISABEL: What is he doing?

JACINTA: He is walking very straight. He is going on ahead with the Captain. The soldiers follow. He is turning around. He waved to the gardener's daughter. They're going to disappear behind the chapel. He's stopping, he's leaning over, and he's picking a rose. [*Pause.*] They have disappeared.

ISABEL: Jacinta, prepare the coffers. We're leaving tomorrow.

[*Curtain.*]

Eeva-Liisa Manner (1921–95)

Finland was relatively late in developing its own national theater. As an officially bilingual country, its artistic and financial resources were divided between its Swedish- and Finnish-speaking populations, with the higher status initially often falling to the Swedish. Not until the 1860s did a native drama really begin, with the advent of Aleksis Kivi and the Finnish Swedish Josef Julius Weckspell. Even after the Finns established themselves as among the most receptive and avid of playgoers, the division between Finnish and Swedish productions persisted, played out in competing troupes. Both language theaters were subject to the occasional and varying influences of such neighboring cultures as Swedish, Russian, and German.

What is even more striking about Finnish drama than the curious happenstances of language and geography, is the singular prominence of women. Of the five most likely dramatists to come to mind, Kivi, Minna Canth, Eeva-Liisa Manner, Hella Wuolijoki, and Maria Jotuni, four are women. One could speculate or quip about the high toll of being surrounded by Ibsen and Strindberg and even Chekhov and Brecht, but the strength and place of women in Finnish drama are remarkable.

Eeva-Liisa Manner further stands apart in this group for her literary achievements. A lyricist in everything she wrote, and known principally for her poetry, Manner's contribution to Finnish and European drama is formidable. The lyricism of her writings embraces the delicate, almost evanescent quality of her poetry, the charged, subjective descriptions in her prose, and the imagistic, surreal elements of her drama. She is perhaps the major modernist force in Finnish literature, and manages to make her lyrical expression very much a part of her modernist texture. Her Orphic inclinations do not, however, render her unresponsive to the very real social and psychological issues of mundane existence, as occurs in the tradition of the High Moderns.

Born to Helsinki parents in the publishing trade, Manner, though very much an internationalist in her poetry, prose, drama, and translations, inclined toward solitude. She often divided her year between Tempere in Finland and Spain. Her first acclaimed success was with her volume of poems, *This Journey* (*Tämä matka*, 1956). Her major dramas were *Eros and Psyche* (in verse, 1959), *New Year's Night* (*Uuden vuoden yö*, 1965), *Snow in May* (*Toukokuun lumi*, 1966), and, in 1968, *Burnt Orange* (*Poltettu oranssi*).

As a modernist drama, *Burnt Orange* examines the tangled subject of the bourgeois family's struggle to contain its eighteen-year-old daughter through the

Eeva-Liisa Manner, no date. (Photographer: Tammi.)

agency of a psychoanalyst. Cannily advancing Manner's sardonic view of domestic relations, love, and the awkward needs to dream and articulate is a web of allusions: to Yeats (the ironic, "A terrible beauty is born"), an Ionesco-like stocking that just grows, a title and concerns that recall Eliot's "Burnt Norton," and a conflagration that may wink at Max Frisch's *Firebugs*. She has the modernist urge to allude and the familiar disillusionment with life as repressive and psychically debilitating—but all delivered under her own very distinct, surrealist stamp.

Manner creates, in the figure of Dr. Fromm, someone who is both a parody of psychoanalysis, psychobabble, and transference theory and an appealing character who can't easily be dismissed. Marina's glossolalia, his Double Dutch talk, and their babble are simultaneously absurd, reflections of individual isolation, and avenues of communication. What is a nonsense poem to the imperviously philistine Mrs. Klein may be Marina's ultimate attempt at lyric self-expression. This is a play where any love dare not speak its name, or, if spoken, is necessarily—it would seem—rejected, a world that may not be very intelligible but is marked by suffering. As the doctor, who began by lamenting, "I'm so used to dealing with the insane, I've gotten into the habit of saying what I think," tells Marina, "You'll not find a world to suit your temperament anywhere. . . . Life's equally hopeless everywhere." The passions of love, gardens, dreams, and the visions of horses and burnt orange are part of life's ephemera.

SELECTED BIBLIOGRAPHY IN ENGLISH

Ahokas, Jaakko A. "Eeva-Liisa Manner: Dropping from Reality into Life." *Books Abroad* 47 (1973), 60–65.

Niemi, Irmeli. "Modern Women Playwrights in Finland." *World Literature Today* 54 (1980), 54–58.

Sala, Kaarina. "Eeva-Liisa Manner: A Literary Portrait." *Snow in May: An Anthology of Finnish Writing: 1945–1972.* Eds. Richard Daenhauer and Philip Binham. Rutherford: Fairleigh Dickinson UP, 1978. Pp. 58–59.

Tiusanen, Timo. "Introduction to 20th Century Drama in Finland." *20th Century Drama in Scandinavia.* Proceedings of the 12th Study Conference of the International Association for Scandinavian Studies, 1978. Eds. John Wrede et al. Helsinki: University of Helsinki, 1979. Pp. 19–25.

Tuohimaa, Sinikka. "Language of Silence: A Feminist Analysis of Eeva-Liisa Manner's Play, *Burnt Orange.*" Proceedings from ISI Conference in Imatra, 1991. *Center and Periphery in Representations and Institutions.* Eds. Eero Tarasti et al. Imatra: International Semiotics Institute, 1992. Pp. 323–31.

BURNT ORANGE

A Ballad in Three Acts
Concerning the Snares of the Word and the Blood

Eeva-Liisa Manner

Translated by Herbert Lomas

CHARACTERS

DR. FROMM	an imperial-bearded middle-aged gentleman
ERNEST KLEIN	a leather-manufacturer: a moustached, slightly shabby old man
AMANDA KLEIN	his wife, youthful, forceful, angular
MARINA KLEIN	their daughter, slender, withdrawn, evasive
NURSE-RECEPTIONIST	open, direct, of the earth

The scene is a small town in the decade before World War I.

ACT ONE

Scene One

The DOCTOR's *surgery, white walls. Up L. a desk with an antiquated telephone. L. behind the desk a wall painted yellowish. R. an empty white wall-surface. Up R. a backless black leather sofa, with a small table by it. The receptionist ushers in a large woman, overdressed in an early century fashion that makes her look vain and slightly vulgar.*

DOCTOR: Do sit down. [*He consults his notes; she does not sit but props her umbrella against the sofa.*] Your name's Klein. I think? Is it Mrs. or Miss?

MRS. KLEIN: It'd better be a Mrs. I've got twelve children. Or I did have.

DOCTOR: Ah, housewife. Well, it's clear you haven't been sitting round twiddling your thumbs.

MRS. KLEIN: Or with my legs crossed either. And I'm no housewife either. I'm the wife of a Counsellor—Ernest Klein, in fact, the leather manufacturer.

DOCTOR: [*Miffed by the lady's intransigence.*] Hm. I can't quite see how I'm expected to know who every leathertanner . . .

MRS. KLEIN: I beg your pardon, Doctor?

DOCTOR: I was about to say . . . I don't see how . . . But don't take offense. I've got so used to coping with the insane, I've dropped into the habit of saying what I think.

MRS. KLEIN: Oh, so is that the way you deal with the insane?

DOCTOR: Well, they always say what they think, you see, to me—except for the catatonic, who don't say a word. But the others—it's sheer information. In that sense the world of the mad's a big advance on the normal world. In the normal world people say nice things and think nasty ones. They hatch out intrigues, nurture lies, get up to dirty little tricks, think one thing, say another. The world of the mad's a bit more hygienic.

MRS. KLEIN: Ah . . . So are you sort of recommending it?

DOCTOR: Er, well . . . You're not sick, then?

MRS. KLEIN: Certainly not! It's my daughter. She's with me now.

DOCTOR: Ah, I see!

MRS. KLEIN: Quite. She's in the waiting room.

DOCTOR: Yes indeed. Lots of desperately healthy people bring their daughters here. Hm. What was it you said? Twelve of them, was it?

MRS. KLEIN: No. Not in the waiting room. But yes, this is the one: more of a trial and tribulation than the other eleven put together. Sometimes I think those eleven got the full supply of brains, and there wasn't a spoonful left for this one, the last. Weak in the head she is.

DOCTOR: Well, yes. Late children can sometimes be a bit on the weak side. What about the others. Are they all right?

MRS. KLEIN: Both twins died, still very small. The others are married, out in the world. The only one still at home is this one.

DOCTOR: Right. So tell me about her.

MRS. KLEIN: Goodness gracious, she's such a worry, for us, the Counsellor and me. Sees people walking around without heads—men, that is. According to her, men go around completely headless. How d'you explain that?

DOCTOR: Hm. Can't say off the cuff. But it could be hysterical blindness.

MRS. KLEIN: And what's that—hysterical blindness?

DOCTOR: Blindness caused by the mind—as opposed to by the brain.

MRS. KLEIN: [*Hesitating.*] I see. And then she speaks a completely daft language—the sort children muck about with, little kiddies. "Boop boop dittom dottom wottom poo." Now and then she speaks like anybody else, but then she's off on one of these fits: speaking with tongues.

DOCTOR: Hm. Is yours a religious household then?

MRS. KLEIN: Not particularly—just normal. Church wedding, confirmation, children christened, funerals—the usual thing: absolutely normal.

DOCTOR: And your daughter's got no religious conflicts?

MRS. KLEIN: Not that I know of. Why should she?

DOCTOR: Because religious indoctrination is one thing that can cause mental and linguistic confusion. What about school? Did they drum religious ideology in her there?

MRS. KLEIN: What was that? . . . ideology?

DOCTOR: I mean, was there a lot of stress on Jesus?

MRS. KLEIN: No more than the usual, I suppose. The regular stuff, like we used to get, singing: "We Thy call have disobeyed, /Into paths of sin have strayed"—but whether she took the hymns literally I've no idea—though, of course, she does, in general, take everything very literally.

DOCTOR: How do you mean—very literally?

MRS. KLEIN: I mean she's got no nous. Till she was sixteen she was just ordinary. Oh, aloof and tense, you know, but all right in the head. Now she's completely in her own world, does everything like a big stupid doll. It's so aggravating: that kind of numb, clockwork obedience. If I tell her to wash up, she washes up all day, the same dishes, over and over again. First she can't start, then she can't stop. I tell her, "Crack the eggs carefully, but not too carefully. Don't be soft about it." So she goes and gets the hammer and gives them a great biff. When that idiotic gabbling gets on my nerves and I tell her to shut up, she's goes dumb, completely dumb, shuts up for a week. Though, in fact, she's a lot easier to put up with when she is tongue-tied than when she's gabbling that weird gabble. In my opinion she's going downhill all the time. Before, she was amenable enough, doing whatever you told her, though there was something aggravating about the way she did it. Now she's really up in arms, making a long-drawn-out business of everything, and gabbling away.

DOCTOR: Yes, that sort of language may indeed be a kind of syntactical revolt. Can you give me an example—imitate her speech a bit?

MRS. KLEIN: You ought to ask a hen to do it! "Awk. Gok. Hu pik cuck cum." What do you make of that, Doctor? She opens her mouth, and it's like opening the henhouse door.

DOCTOR: Well, it doesn't have to be all that dangerous, you know. As a child I spoke Double Dutch myself. We had a real little gang, and we used to try and outdo each other in the lanes—talking so the grown-ups wouldn't understand us. There was no system in it: just sounds and rhythm. Let me think, now. . . . Gongola fo fum mago bangibonk yoga . . . Those who spoke it best were the most gifted verbally: [*Getting enthusiastic.*] garafongula lendum effula sendum birojereboa titcher fo fum . . . gosh, it's coming back . . . congogurgledick amazonia . . . and we had a devil of a good time . . . [*Suddenly vexed at himself for letting himself go in the presence of a client, he changes his tone to an acid dryness.*] Surely, madam, yourself, you must have played games when you were a child?

MRS. KLEIN: Oh me? You must think I'm a half-wit, Doctor? Of course I played games, but that's not the point with my daughter: she's not playing games. What's mad about it is, she's in deadly earnest. When she comes out with this stuff, she means something with it. You can see it in her face. What is it? What does it mean?

DOCTOR: It may not mean more than this: perhaps she just wants to hide her real self from you.

MRS. KLEIN: Ah! She wants to keep even her name a secret. They sent her home from school because she went on claiming her name was Nielk Aniram.

DOCTOR: Nielk Aniram? But that's Marina Klein spelt backwards! Mirror-language. Many schizophrenics are inclined to that.

MRS. KLEIN: To what?

DOCTOR: Mirror language. Their brain switches a word or a whole sentence round, as a mirror does. America—Acirema. When I was a young Kandidat—a houseman, you know—in a large German hospital, doing my specialist training, a schizophrenic patient used to greet me on my rounds every morning. He'd say "Tadidnak rehgat netug." He repeated it week after week—Tadidnak rehgat netug—and it completely foxed me, till suddenly I hit on it: It was "Guten Tag, Herr Kandidat!" said backwards: a mirror image: "Good morning, Houseman." His brain was concocting a left-hand reading of a conventional greeting.

MRS. KLEIN: [*Carried away by the* DOCTOR's *story.*] Good morning, Doctor. Rotcod gninrom doog!

DOCTOR: [*Drily.*] You're quick off the mark with it! You've got a talent for this schizophrenic language!

MRS. KLEIN: Sknaht!

DOCTOR: Lla ta ton!

MRS. KLEIN: [*Enthusiasm declining.*] Yes, you could easily run on like that. But it's not pretty: for something beautiful, you ought to try pig Latin.

DOCTOR: Pig Latin? So what's that?

MRS. KLEIN: Difficult to explain, it's what we used as children.

DOCTOR: No need to explain, just speak it. What's "Good morning, Doctor" in pig Latin?

MRS. KLEIN: Gomadened mormamadening, Docmadenedtor.

DOCTOR: Goodness gracious, pretty long-drawn-out!

MRS. KLEIN: Goomadenedess gracmadenedous, whamadened amadened . . .

DOCTOR: [*More formally.*] But let's get back to your daughter.

MRS. KLEIN: [*Taking a sheet of paper out of her handbag.*] This is a sample of how she writes.

DOCTOR: [*Takes the sheet and reads it slowly aloud.*]

To the Field Marshal of the Salvation Army:

Dear God, forgive me
for I'm a tangled hair
Dear God, give my locks a tug
for I don't comb my hair
Beloved Jesus saviour
save thyself from the cross
and for us, don't give a toss
I'm a Salvation Army Lieutenant
and can save myself myself.

Hm. Hair-raising poem all right. Or, well . . . is it more than the woolly thoughts of a tanner's daughter? But what's that "Salvation Army Lieutenant"? What's she getting at there. Is she—

MRS. KLEIN: No, of course not. It's just a nonsense poem. When she was at school, there were bits of poems lying around all over the place.

DOCTOR: What sort? Just as gloomy?

MRS. KLEIN: Can't remember. I burnt the whole lot.

DOCTOR: [*Reproachfully.*] So why haven't you burnt this one too?

MRS. KLEIN: I decided to keep it when these mad symptoms started growing. I decided I'd better let you see it, Doctor, and ask . . . well, what it means?

DOCTOR: That I can't say. Might be the deadly truth—might be nothing at all. Schizophrenics are unpredictable. Some write a stiff, stilted language, others fire off thunderous phrases. They fire them off as if they'd a gun in their mouth. A third sort—and your daughter could be one of these—they write from the bottom of their heart: personal statements, inscribed in blood, as it were. But, mechanical or inflated, the writing's packed with human suffering, even if you can't find much sense in it. And sometimes the bombast can bring you up sharp: there is sense there. And there may be sense here too [*Raises the paper.*]: "Save thyself from the cross . . . I can save myself myself." Could be, her religious feelings have been wounded. Maybe she finds the idea of salvation hurtful—can't accept the idea that someone else might expiate her sins. And, by the way, that scapegoat concept is a thoroughly pagan notion, sheer primitive salvation-magic. In fact, it revolts me too, always has.

MRS. KLEIN: [*Cuttingly.*] Doctor, you do seem to be able to unearth an awful lot of deep thought out of hocus-pocus.

DOCTOR: Sometimes a melancholy mind may be a deep mind, a split mind a complex mind.

MRS. KLEIN: Nowadays there's less sense in what she says than in that scribble. It's worse: babble bubble gubble scrubble—

DOCTOR: [*Continuing matter-of-factly.*] Double double toil and trouble. Yes, madam, when the psyche regresses to more primitive modes—goes back to the infantile or, let's say, the savage state—it starts forming words like a child or savage would. Look, how did language develop? It didn't just spring up: language as we know it began with the grouping and connecting of words. People that are severely ill, or disturbed in their development, can lack this capacity to group and connect: often they fall back on monosyllables or disyllables—more like cries than words. And each little individual sound may well be associated with some particular image in their mind. A primitive expression has got into the savage's blood: "wie in Schnabel gewachsen"—they say what comes into their gob. But sometimes, too, there's no longer any corresponding notion in the psyche: the speech-motor's just turning over, turning over: adelante biolente enten tenten limpu lempu amemora lalzipempu. It's glossolalia, in fact—speaking with tongues, as with the pentecostals: everything's coming down from the heavenly father. This, however, is a fascinating topic, and I forecast that, before long, as the human mind becomes more and more mechanized and impoverished, we'll see a worldwide glossolalian literature. We've already got a book industry. Soon we'll have an alphabet industry. We could give it a name: gibberism.

MRS. KLEIN: This is all gibberism to me now.

DOCTOR: Well, no use offering any further explanations then. Was eine Frau nicht von sich selbst ver-steht, das kann man nicht für sie er-klaren. [*The hyphens point to the* DOCTOR's *fragmenting speech.*]

MRS. KLEIN: Doctor, now you're going on like my daughter!

DOCTOR: That was German. All I said was: what a woman doesn't understand on her own, it's no use explaining.

MRS. KLEIN: Well, I wish you'd at least explain one thing to me: what is schizophrenia, Doctor?

DOCTOR: Ah, a big subject, that. Not something to be summed up in two minutes. And when did I say this was schizophrenia? Hebephrenia is more probably it—

MRS. KLEIN: [*Getting impatient.*] Well, hebephrenia then? What's that?

DOCTOR: [*Also getting impatient.*] What is it, what is it. You keep throwing questions at me, continually, like a catechism. And then, when I explain, you're still not satisfied.

MRS. KLEIN: Yes, because you always give such difficult explanations.

DOCTOR: [*Evasively.*] Hebephrenia is a form of schizophrenia, a split mind in youth. Children who are intelligent and original may, after puberty, start turning rigid and apathetic. Life you see's a sort of combustion, a burning up, and hebephrenia's a too rapid burning-out. The psyche—or the body—can, in a way, burn itself to a frazzle. [*Gets an idea, takes out a matchbox and demonstrates.*] It's just as if, instead of lighting matches individually, so they'd be useful, you set the whole box alight at one go. [*He puts the matchbox into the table's large brass ashtray and ignites the matchheads: the whole box goes off explosively and burns out in a moment.*]

MRS. KLEIN: Good heavens! What in heaven was that!

DOCTOR: Hebephrenia.

MRS. KLEIN: A flare-up like that?

DOCTOR: Yes, a ballistic flare-up, following on a too-early blunting of the intelligence and the feelings.

MRS. KLEIN: Good Lord. Is it any wonder then we've been so upset, the Counsellor and me.

DOCTOR: Are we still dealing with gibberism?

MRS. KLEIN: Well, you could say so. [*Hastily.*] And indeed I've got to be off now. The Counsellor'll be waiting—and the roast. We're having roast goose today.

DOCTOR: So, good-bye then. And ask your daughter to come in and see me.

[MRS. KLEIN *gives a little nod and leaves.*]

DOCTOR: [*After the door has closed.*] Roast goose!

Scene Two

After a short interval the RECEPTIONIST *opens the door and ushers* MARINA KLEIN *into the surgery. Exit the* RECEPTIONIST. MARINA *immediately goes to the end of the room and presses herself against the white wall. The white surface makes her look very isolated in her ascetic black dress. The* DOCTOR, *who now appears to be headless—an impression produced by the lighting and the yellowish background—half-turns towards her.*

DOCTOR: Well, Miss . . . tell me . . .

> [*He stops, disturbed by the girl's rigidity. Silence.*]

DOCTOR: Don't be afraid. Tell me what's worrying you.

> [*No response.*]

DOCTOR: I heard from your mother that you see everyone as headless. Is it everyone? Or just men? Do you see me without a head?

> [*No response.*]

DOCTOR: Your mother also said you speak your own homemade language. Why? Can't speak any other? Or is it that you don't want to?

> [*No response.*]

DOCTOR: I expect what you're feeling is: They don't understand me anyway, so it's all the same to me what I say?

> [*No response.*]

DOCTOR: [*He sighs.*] What if I spoke your language? Bi di fa gi da do ga? Mama nam do re mi why?

MARINA: [*Mechanically and timidly.*] Mi kri.

> [*As soon as contact is established, the* DOCTOR's *head reappears.*]

DOCTOR: Ah yes. You do trust me, don't you? Do you trust me?

> [*No response.*]

DOCTOR: Higami hogami?

MARINA: [*Responding mechanically now, but as timorously as if she'd like to vanish into the wall.*] Hogami.

DOCTOR: Bigami digami. Gramme decagramme decadent centimetre [*To himself.*] Now I'm going wrong . . . [*Concentrating.*] Mele kalimaka.

MARINA: Hauoli.

DOCTOR: Makahiki hou. As you see, we're getting on quite nicely now, together. Your language is, indeed, extremely . . . difficult, and perhaps you'll forgive me if from time to time I get it a little wrong. I did speak it myself, as a child, but it doesn't come back all that easily . . . so you'll bear with me, then, won't you . . . But it's a bit difficult to find the proper things to say, spontaneously, you know, if I have to think it all out . . . ah . . . rabatsi filu rabatsi fefo escola granimui slaavibuffo garafang . . .

MARINA: Gang gongola.

DOCTOR: Halleluja. Hell's bells . . . But I'm trying my best. Spektakel. Takel sakel. Demiurgi.

MARINA: Gurki.

DOCTOR: Well, look, we're getting on fine. Do sit down, please. Try that sofa over there, and settle yourself comfortably. Bitte setzen Sie sich. [*To himself.*] Wrong again! But no: maybe she will take to a foreign language, all consonants. Probably only allergic to her mother tongue—her mother's tongue!

> [*She seats herself cautiously on the sofa, by the small table.*]

DOCTOR: Now, if I ask you politely, will you do something for me? Write something about yourself? Any language you like—just to please me? You'll do that, won't you? Tell me a little story, say—short as you like, or long as you like. Joyful or sad, it can be what you like, so long as it's true, and about yourself. Zaragui ragatsi? I've got some paper here, and a pen [*Holding them out; she comes and takes them.*]. Pluma zuma. Just let it all come out, let it flow . . . as if you were combing your hair in your thoughts. Gadji beri bimba tankredi glandridi dideroid.

[*She sits calmly down again by the table, pen in hand.*]

DOCTOR: Good, now write. Berimba bimbana zimzala gadjama.

MARINA: [*Compliantly.*] Gadji. [*Writes.*]

DOCTOR: Ah. Anodi katodi. Asphaltflplaster rattaplasma. So what am I going to do in the meantime? There's that new anthropological encyclopedia, I could scan that. [*He jingles a bell loudly; enter the* RECEPTIONIST.] You know that encyclopedia, the new one, would you let me have it, please!

[*Exit the* RECEPTIONIST *and enter a moment later carrying a huge volume. She sets it on the* DOCTOR's *table and exits. In what follows, while the* DOCTOR *is reading and soliloquizing, surrealistic and schizophrenic paintings, such as Dali's Soft Constructions, are projected onto the white wall-surface. The* DOCTOR *leafs through the fat volume, reads:*]

DOCTOR: "Schizophrenic patients may write meaningless poems, very uncommunicative as regards content, but formally very disciplined and outwardly resembling children's language or Latin." She won't, let's hope, [*Glancing at the girl*] resort to any New Latin . . . With luck, motor coordination will do it: set a longing going for ordinary letter-connections . . . Ah, now, Miss Klein, you've finished your piece. Splendid.

[MARINA *rises timidly and takes the pen and sheets of paper over to the* DOCTOR, *returns to her sofa, and sits rigidly and motionless while he is reading.*]

DOCTOR: [*Disappointed.*] A poem. And abracadabra. Damn it! Miss Klein, you won't mind, will you, taking a rest on the sofa, full-length, while I'm reading this?

[MARINA *obeys mechanically.*]

DOCTOR [*Reads.*]

Mentus nudros nuachtus magna
Monotos tondros tandras tecta
Dion akton dol dolar.
Vilon silont, dinonnemal.
Ilpo valpi avan toles
Leron tonte avant tarant
Isson sensum essim selta
Ardientum idontum delta.

Hm. Hellish long too. A tiny puffa-train: it toils along miles and miles, carrying coal, and then, when it gets there, the coal's no good. No, I'm wrong: she's writing exactly what she thinks. But the Lord knows what it is she is thinking. [*The projections stop. He regards the girl.*] She's gone to sleep. [*Looks at his watch.*] Been asleep a few minutes already. Hm. Boring poem. Those trotting trochees'd be enough to send me off too. I do hope she turns out a bit more communicative when she wakes up. They do sometimes. [*Whispering.*] Miss Klein—

[*She sits up—rigid as a string-puppet—and opens her eyes wide like a doll.*]

DOCTOR: Have you been dreaming?

MARINA: [*Absently, astonished.*] Yes.

DOCTOR: Can you tell it to me?

MARINA: [*Still hovering between sleep and waking but nevertheless much more alert than before; speech hesitant but, following her own private logic, quite matter-of-fact; her dream-images are very real to her.*] I was hoping to get across the frontier, into Russia, but I didn't know where the frontier was. For ages I was wandering in a dark wood. Then suddenly I was there: in the customs hall. There was a customs officer. He asked me if I'd anything to declare. No, I said. But he was really stubborn, and he asked me again: Had I really nothing to declare? I said the only thing I had was this little handbag . . . about the size of a hymn book . . . [*Squeezes her small bag with both hands.*] So he took it from me, and out of it he pulled a mattress, a complete mattress, huge, and I was astounded. "What is it?" he asked. I couldn't say a word, and so he took me by the hand. And he led me down to a lake shore. The lake, it was sort of a long and narrow gulf. And then I realized. It marked the frontier. He lowered the mattress into the water, and suddenly it was a boat. I stepped in, and then I crossed over the border, ever so easily.

DOCTOR: Well. Let's have a look, then, shall we, together, at that dream of yours? As for me, I'm a customs officer too, and I'm going to help you across the frontier. Into a great unknown country. Which is an unknown part of yourself. Of your soul. Let's say this is the frontier—it's the gulf of a lake. [*The* DOCTOR *illustrates his discourse with various objects: he first puts a pencil case in the middle of the table.*] First I start insisting. I want to know what goods you have to declare. And just as insistently you claim you have none. You're taking no baggage on that journey of yours, into your soul. Then, lo and behold, I pull a mattress out of your handbag. [*He picks up a small rectangular rubber.*] That huge erotic piece of luggage—it fits into your handbag, even though your handbag's as small as . . . a hymn book. [*He shows her the rubber.*] You're not pleased. By no means. For you don't want to admit it—even to yourself. I lead you to the shore. I'm going to help you across the frontier. And suddenly your mattress, it's a boat, a boat that'll hold you up. [*He inserts the rubber into the empty pencil case.*] So. Now listen, confide in me, and this journey—this journey in your soul—it'll be a success. And I'll be able to help you across the frontier. That's right, isn't it, so far?

[MARINA *nods silently.*]

DOCTOR: All these things are symbols—symbols in the soul. Archaic images you dream up. And they look two ways. You know, that customs officer: he's not just me: he's you: he's the anonymous guardian of your soul. When you confide in me you're confiding in yourself too; and that puts things properly—in their true light, in the right perspective. It'll be a burden off you. This isn't just a sexy mattress we're dealing with: it's a boat too; and a boat's not just something to cross a frontier with. It's—[*With a sudden, swift, imperiousness.*]—What? What is it really? Answer!

MARINA: I don't know.

DOCTOR: I'm the customs man. I can only help you through if you tell me.

[MARINA *opens her handbag and, slowly and demonstratively, takes out a handkerchief.*]

MARINA: I don't know. All I have is this handkerchief.

DOCTOR: But all I want to do is help you!

MARINA: I don't know. I don't know. [*In a panic.*] I don't KNOW. I don't know I don't know. [*Grinding on hysterically.*] Idon'tknow Idon'tknowIdon'tknow.

DOCTOR: Don't get upset, dear girl. [*To himself.*] Not much use going on now. [*Rises: gently touches her shoulder.*] Your mother's outside, waiting. There'll be another time. And we can carry on then.

[*Accompanies her to the door. Darkness.*]

[*End of Act One.*]

ACT TWO

Scene One

MARINA *at home, in* MR. KLEIN'*s living room. The wallpaper is dark violet, almost black, with widely spaced gold or silver stripes. The chairs, of which there are many round the oval table, are ceremonious and unnaturally high-backed. Some ornate, outstandingly ugly detail from the age of the bustle. A lot of leather everywhere, and the smell of leather. Hanging high, close to the ceiling, are some oval pictures: old-fashioned family portraits; at a normal height, framed in the same style, is an oval mirror. Marina paces slowly back and forth in the room, as if restraining her lack of restraint. Her motions are at once helpless and violent: some sudden or exaggerated movements reveal an intense inner conflict between impulse and inhibition. Her mien alternates between dignity, even pride, and collapse: occasionally the girl doggedly controls herself, but when emotion overwhelms her, the outburst is violent, and bizarre: she goes, for instance, to the mirror, studies her reflection carefully and long, then covers her face with her hands and turns abruptly away. She picks things up, thrusts them away, and each time unconsciously wipes her hand on her sides. She then circles the table and, in a thin high-pitched voice, sings a song with childish words and a totally contrary tune, mature, yearning, elegiac, or even a sad hymn-tune perhaps.*

MARINA:

> I went to sea in a sieve, I did,
> in a sieve I went to sea,
> I took my scarf and I raised a sail,
> I raised my scarf to catch the gale,
> it was a flag and a mascot, but it didn't avail
> when I sailed away to sea.

> I never arrived at my journey's end,
> for my cat was sick and longed for land,
> and he'd been in charge of the ship, you see.
> In his captain's cap he decided to flee
> and he abandoned ship for the deep blue sea
> and swam like mad for the strand.

If only I could have drowned that time, when I jumped! My hands seemed to be suddenly growing wings in the water and keeping me afloat. The wings were stopping me . . . the wings are stopping me. I was flying, and down there, down below, it was the Lake of Tears. And then that man pulled me out and into the boat, and his kisses gave me a body. Oh God, what shall I do? My body wants one thing, and my soul something else . . . my body stops me . . . or what is it stops me?

[*Spreading her arms and moving them as if to fly, she flits round the table.*]

MARINA: Who split my body from my soul? But before that happened I wasn't human, I was a spirit.

[*Goes to the mirror and breathes on it, clouding it over. She questions her image in anguish.*]

MARINA: Body? Or soul?

[*Enter* MR. *and* MRS. KLEIN. *The father's face is partially concealed by massive eyebrows and a large moustache.*]

MRS. KLEIN: [*To her husband.*] Talking to herself again, you see—and in perfectly ordinary language.

MR. KLEIN: Marina . . .

MRS. KLEIN: Repeat to me what you just said to the mirror.

MARINA: Sokobano sokokabano bir olibör.

MR. KLEIN: Oh, my daughter.

MARINA: Mangula kili bulala.

MRS. KLEIN: Dear child, whatever have we done to you. Why are you like this? Why are you getting at us?

[MARINA *creeps under the table.*]

MRS. KLEIN: [*Quietly to her husband.*] Seven visits to the DOCTOR, and she's still just as mad as before.

MR. KLEIN: What did the Doctor say last time?

MRS. KLEIN: Oh he said, you can't put seventeen years' damage right in seven weeks. Seventeen years' damage! Just as if he was blaming us!

MR. KLEIN: Well, why not. We produced her. Didn't we?

MRS. KLEIN: Not for seventeen years! We've not been producing her for seventeen years, have we?

MR. KLEIN: In a way. Especially you.

MRS. KLEIN: Especially me! Naturally. It's me who's at fault! I'm guilty! But maybe she made herself! Even when she was tiny she was a case. So much as touch her, and she was off screaming. As if I was going to eat her. That's how much she hated me.

MR. KLEIN: Perhaps she thought you wanted to swallow her.

MRS. KLEIN: Wanted to swallow her? What on earth do you mean by that?

[MARINA *emerges from under the table and rushes out of the room; she flings the door shut after her. The lights dim a little.*]

MR. KLEIN: Well, you're a bit overpowering in a way, you know, as a person. And you're hidebound as well: always at action stations. I don't know how to put it—but when you come into the room, even the lights seem to go dim. Haven't you noticed it yourself?

[MR. KLEIN *adjusts the wick on the oil lamp dangling from the ceiling, and it gets brighter.*]

MRS. KLEIN: [*Whispering intensely.*] It's she who makes the lights go dim! Marina! Sometimes I think even things get uneasy when she's there.

MR. KLEIN: Who knows? But supposing things make her uneasy too. Look around. Quite a few ugly looking items here, you know. Just look. Though what we can do God knows. All inherited! Handed down. God, how dreary it is, this inheritance business! Ugliness, so much ugliness they leave you.

MRS. KLEIN: There you go. More than a bit peculiar yourself. Here am I, in a real agony, and what's your response? Philosophizing! It's too much! That child, she's awful! Yesterday, I was listening at the door, there she was: walking round and round the room, talking to herself.

MR. KLEIN: And saying what?

MRS. KLEIN: "It's terribly dangerous. Anything can happen. We're all in it, in the danger. The whole world." Going on like that.

MR. KLEIN: She's a Cassandra.

MRS. KLEIN: What?

MR. KLEIN: I mean, do you think she could know something? There are people like that: those who know and can't bear what they know. Perhaps she's right: the whole world really is in danger. Take the arms race: all piling up arms like mad, for war. Him with the moustache [*Twists his moustache.*] . . . Kaiser Wilhelm! Mad for war, and soon it'll be France as well, mad for it too; and then it'll be England. And after that, all the little states nearby. You'll see, they'll all start coming into it, some because they're under threat, and some just to get in on the act . . . And then we'll have it: world war.

MRS. KLEIN: You don't say. But what's that got to do with this? We were talking about our daughter, weren't we, not war?

MR. KLEIN: This is war, our private war. She takes after you.

MRS. KLEIN: Oh, after me! Does she? Well naturally, according to you. And why not after you, just as well?

MR. KLEIN: Remember? How hysterical you were—when you were young? . . . before we got married?

MRS. KLEIN: No. No, I don't.

MR. KLEIN: What about the honeymoon? Have you forgotten? Austria, with that family we knew? They bedded us in the library, remember?

MRS. KLEIN: No I don't: not in all that detail. And what's that got to do with it? Old stuff, dead and gone.

MR. KLEIN: The old stuff's the new stuff: it's here again: the girl's a new edition . . . of you. Damn it, I couldn't even get a kiss out of you. Whenever I tried, there were you shouting, "I'm suffocating, I'm suffocating!"

MRS. KLEIN: Well, what about it? Licking's never really been much up my street.

MR. KLEIN: Anyway, you were always on the point of suffocating. No air, you said. Always beefing. Finally, I got so fed up I said "Break the window, then: I'll pay."

MRS. KLEIN: Well, yes. I never did like close rooms.

MR. KLEIN: And you did break the glass. With your shoe. And that calmed you down, and we got to sleep.

MRS. KLEIN: Well, then, that just shows you.

MR. KLEIN: Only, in the morning, we realized: it wasn't the window you'd broken. It was the glass in the bookcase. You'd smashed that. So what do you call it? Explain that away: what else was it but hysteria?

MRS. KLEIN: How can you be bothered bringing all that up? All that old stuff! Old as the hills. And is it a wonder, people getting nervous on their wedding night? Otherwise, I've always been as sensible as they come. Marina, now: she's a mental deficient.

MR. KLEIN: How can you say that! She's not stupid, even if she is mad. On the contrary: she's extremely intelligent; and it shows, too, when she's willing to speak. You're not seeing things properly: there's intelligence, and there's making sense! She's intelligent, but she's not making sense.

MRS. KLEIN: Intelligent, you call her? Well, take cooking. I try to teach her the very simplest things, and what does she do? An egg, for instance. It's a complete farce: the poor child can't even crack an egg. First she does it so mushily, everything's all over the stove. Then, when I say, give it a good crack, hard, she panics, gets a determined look, grabs a hammer and smashes the egg.

MR. KLEIN: She's trying to be thorough. That's not particularly crazy, just rather—well, bizarre. She's been far worse than this.

MARINA: [*Enters, now much more relaxed than before. She is cradling a kitten and is wearing a man's large fur hat, with the ear flaps up. She sings.*]

I never arrived at my journey's end,
for my cat was sick and longed for land,
and he'd been in charge of the ship, you see.
In his captain's cap he decided to flee
and he abandoned ship for the deep blue sea
and swam like mad for the strand.

[*Adds brightly.*] When the cat gets better, everything'll be all right again. [*Exits.*]

MR. KLEIN: That's symbolic: she's so fond of symbols. For her, animals aren't animals: they're always something else. They represent something.

MRS. KLEIN: Sheer poppycock! Daft that is, looking for a meaning in everything.

MR. KLEIN: The Doctor does it. He's always looking for a meaning in everything.

MRS. KLEIN: And where that's got us you can see. Tripe and onions she comes out with, and sings it to a hymn tune. A loony girl singing a loony song.

MR. KLEIN: Yes. Well. No doubt she is rather mad. And yet, sometimes, I can't help thinking, in spite of everything, she's—what? The only wise person in the house.

MRS. KLEIN: The only wise person in the house! What's that supposed to mean? You're a riddle yourself, like your loony daughter. You're the one she takes after.

MR. KLEIN: No. Maybe I have brought something out. What I mean is: her raving's a kind of wisdom—because there's something more that she knows. Yes, sometimes I do feel that way myself. I do too—know, I mean. I get this feeling. It comes all over me, really oppressive. It weighs me down. As if the whole world were on my shoulders, on my chest. It's like that suffocating feeling of yours—only more so, more overwhelming: a tremendous feeling of grief—grief about everything, oppression, depression. Amanda, it's not my grief alone. It's the grief of everything, the whole of creation—the dark times we're heading for.

[*Darkness.*]

Scene Two

The same room a few days later. The DOCTOR *has been invited to the* KLEINS' *home. He walks around the living room alone, taking it in with his hands behind his back, and talking to himself.*

DOCTOR: God, it's gloomy here . . . archetypically ugly. And up there, those family portraits. Almost on the ceiling, staring down. Like . . . like what? The Elders round the Judgment Seat! But I expect they think it's all . . . [*Shrugs shoulders.*] the perfection of taste.

[MARINA *pushes the door ajar and slips shyly in.*]

DOCTOR: I'm here because your parents invited me here . . . They want us to have our usual session, but here. So: shall we sit ourselves down then? . . . How about here by the table?

[*They sit opposite each other.*]

DOCTOR: You've already let me into quite a lot about yourself. But here, at home, your parents say, you're still as . . . you know, closed in on yourself. With me, of course, you're matter-of-fact. Totally.

MARINA: Yes, but they humor me, you know—treat me like a mad girl. You were friendly: you treated me like an ordinary person.

DOCTOR: [*Looking round.*] I can't think this environment does a lot for you. Can't make you feel much at home, can it? Hm. So what do you do with your spare time?

MARINA: Me?

DOCTOR: Yes.

MARINA: Oh, I don't know . . . Sometimes I water the flowers.

DOCTOR: You don't read books?

MARINA: Books are boring. Unless . . .

DOCTOR: Unless?

MARINA: It'd be nice to find some . . . well, fairy tales about water lilies.

DOCTOR: Water lilies? And nothing else?

MARINA: [*After a pause.*] Reference books . . .

DOCTOR: Reference books? What sort? About water lilies?

MARINA: Oh no, not at all. No one knows about water lilies—their real secrets. [*Whispering.*] Water lilies have golden hearts.

DOCTOR: Ah? So reference books about what then?

MARINA: About how to cast tin soldiers.

DOCTOR: Hm. Very original. Is that the lot? Water lilies and tin—are those the only things that interest you? Tin . . . That's for fortune-telling. New Year's Eve, you melt the tin, throw it in a bucket of cold water—and the shape tells you what your future's going to be.

MARINA: Yes . . . and then there are parades.

DOCTOR: Parades? Why parades?

MARINA: Oh, I don't know. They're . . . they're beautiful. Parades are very orderly.

DOCTOR: No doubt. And order makes you secure. doesn't it? [*To himself.*] Great disorder in oneself, and one loves order, yes. [*To* MARINA.] What else do you like.

MARINA: Circuses. They took me to the circus once. There was a trained dog. She was dressed as a person. She wore a crinoline and a hat. She was waiting for her fiancé. And there was a man, all covered with makeup, and he blew on a trumpet. And the dog danced.

DOCTOR: You like music? Trumpet-playing?

[MARINA *nods enthusiastically.*]

DOCTOR: There's only one problem about trumpet-playing: it's not turned on all the time— there to hear whenever you like. But books—they're always to hand. Don't you even read novels?

MARINA: I can't. He always gets in between.

DOCTOR: In between? Where in between?

MARINA: Between me and the page.

DOCTOR: And who's he?

MARINA: Mikael.

DOCTOR: Mikael? And who's Mikael?

MARINA: Oh just a . . . stranger.

DOCTOR: [*Trying a throw.*] And you love him?

[*She nods languidly.*]

DOCTOR: How long have you been in love? Has it been a long time? From . . . childhood perhaps.

MARINA: [*Shakes her head.*] No. As a child, all I loved was machines.

DOCTOR: Machines?

MARINA: Yes I'd hug the heating-stove, and the mangle. And the whisk. With the whisk, I used to . . . [*Whispers.*] whisper my secrets to it.

DOCTOR: And then Mikael came?

[MARINA *nods, lowers her eyes, and simultaneously moves to another chair. The* DOCTOR *also moves, so that he is again sitting opposite her. They make these moves throughout the whole subsequent session, sometimes faster, sometimes slower, and thus get round the whole table.*]

DOCTOR: You were . . . how old then?

MARINA: Sixteen. [*Moves again.*]

DOCTOR: [*Also moves.*] And he is . . . married?

MARINA: [*Moves.*] Naturally. All the good-looking men are.

DOCTOR: And something happened?

MARINA: Mikael . . . [*Moves.*] came to our summer cottage, alone.

DOCTOR: [*Moves.*] Mikael was alone, and you too were alone?

MARINA: [*Nods.*] Father and mother were away in town.

DOCTOR: Why?

MARINA: [*Absently.*] The town's in great danger. We're all in great danger.

DOCTOR: I mean, why did he come—alone, when you were alone? Was it on purpose? De- liberately?

[MARINA *does not reply, moves to the next chair.*]

DOCTOR: [*Moves.*] What did he want from you?

MARINA: [*Moves.*] He wanted us . . . to go rowing.

DOCTOR: [*Moves.*] So you did. You went rowing with him, didn't you?

MARINA: Yes. On the lake.

DOCTOR: And on the lake he told you how much he loved you?

MARINA: [*Whispering.*] Yes, and . . .

DOCTOR: And what did you do?

MARINA: I . . . [*Moves.*] I jumped.

DOCTOR: [*Astonished.*] Into the lake?

MARINA: Yes.

DOCTOR: And what happened then?

MARINA: He pulled me out.

DOCTOR: He rescued you?

MARINA: [*Repeats.*] He pulled me out.

DOCTOR: And then?

MARINA: He . . . [*Moves.*] kissed me.

DOCTOR: [*Moves.*] Right there, in the boat?

MARINA: [*Moves.*] Yes and—

DOCTOR: [*Moves.*] And?

MARINA: He carried me to the cottage and—[*Moves.*]

DOCTOR: [*Moves.*] Please go on.

MARINA: Put me into bed and—[*Moves.*]

[*The* DOCTOR *nods and moves too.*]

MARINA: And undressed me, and then—[*Moves.*]

DOCTOR: [*Moves.*] And then?

MARINA: [*She covers her face.*] It was the moment . . . the moment of truth.

[*The moving stops. The truth has come out, and* MARINA *does not need to escape any more.*]

DOCTOR: You didn't resist?

MARINA: [*Nods affirmatively.*] I said it was a sin.

DOCTOR: And what did he say?

MARINA: He said—that sin was the salt of life.

DOCTOR: And then?

MARINA: And then. No . . . well . . . That's about it. The end.

DOCTOR: I mean, what did he say then?

MARINA: That wolves don't whistle . . . I had to keep quiet.

DOCTOR: Oh did he?

MARINA: Yes.

DOCTOR: Did you meet often?

MARINA: No. I only saw him once after that. It was in the street.

DOCTOR: And he was without a head?

[*She nods.*]

DOCTOR: Symbolically, then, you, so to speak, beheaded him. Why?

MARINA: If people were really modest, they'd hide . . . their faces. They'd not hide . . . [*Hides her face.*] . . . that thing.

DOCTOR: Why so?

MARINA: There's nothing special about that thing. But the face—that's where all the nasty words, and the nasty looks, come from.

DOCTOR: And so that's why he's got no head now?

MARINA: Yes.

DOCTOR: And yet you see him everywhere, you say, even on the pages of a book?

[MARINA *nods earnestly.*]

DOCTOR: Yes, that's how it always is. When we really want something, very badly, we see it everywhere. Stop wanting, and you'll get peace.

MARINA: [*Repeats woodenly.*] Stop wanting . . . stop wanting . . .

DOCTOR: All the disappointments and delusions come from wanting. As long as we go on wanting, we're caught—even reading a book. We're caught in those snares: the snares of the word and the blood.

MARINA: [*Lowers her head onto the table and rests it between her arms, repeating.*] The snares. The snares of the word and the blood.

[*She sobs almost inaudibly. The* DOCTOR *gets quietly up from the table and moves towards the door. As he goes, he says, mysteriously—translating and distorting Rochester.*]

DOCTOR: Poetry's a snare too. Plenty of room, in the asylum; there's plenty of room there. Watch out! Your poems: they'll grieve you but divert us . . . the psychopathological muses.

[*Exits. The scene dims. Darkness.*]

Scene Three

The DOCTOR*'s surgery a few weeks later. A great step forward has occurred—a portent, however, of a new crisis approaching.* MARINA*—in contrast to the previous scenes, where she was ascetically dressed—is wearing a long tight-fitting dress of glowing "burnt-orange" silk.*

MARINA: My father and my mother, they hate me, both of them, especially my mother.

DOCTOR: Surely not. Why should they hate you?

MARINA: Because I'm mad you see.

DOCTOR: You're not mad, merely unhappy. And—yes "different." In the old days people wanted to be different, original, now all they want is: to be normal. That's a kind of madness too—or stupidity. [*The* DOCTOR *deliberately speaks at length and in a manner alien to the girl's mental atmosphere, in order to get her to withdraw into herself.*] And where does it come from—all this newfangled banality, this ineptitude? From education—shallow superficial education, that's it, Procrustes' bed as a training for the mind. First elementary school, then the papers, and now the wireless—this wretched little crystal set. You watch. Some day it'll expand, you'll see. They'll give it a picture. They'll send out images—flying through the air—to be captured in little receivers: a talking picture-box. The images'll come tumbling out like cigarettes—at a mental level suitable for the under-tens. And then it'll be on tap, like the water supply: a handy universal source of stupidity. Everyone, or nearly everyone, will be made to want anything that needs selling: lipstick, aspirins, enemas, rotgut, ratgut, wars to end wars. But there I go: running on. You see, what I'm doing is trying to get you to talk. What I want is for you to talk: to tell me still more about yourself. Miss Klein, you've already let me into what happened in the boat—and afterwards. But it doesn't go far enough. You know, a thing like that doesn't make a healthy girl go crack. Everyone comes a bit of a cropper sometime. I'm not asking you to think. Don't think too much—just ramble on. Say whatever comes into your head. Go on like I was just now. Let it rip.

MARINA: [*During the* DOCTOR*'s discourse she has withdrawn into herself and speaks dreamily at first, and then more freely and briskly.*] The neighbor's garden: that's what comes back. June, yes June it was. The maples and the blackthorns were green, so lush, and we were playing at hide-and-seek—in the bushes: Alan and I. I was eight, Alan was ten, or eleven. I rather liked him. Suddenly my mother was there: she was dragging me out of the bush, driving Alan away. She was bending over me and pushing her face right up to mine. She was wearing that little hat, and a veil. It made her head flat, like a snake's. She was red as a peony. And without a word she hit me hard, so hard. It knocked me out of my wits. I couldn't say a word. And when I did finally manage to get something out, it was a shout. I was shouting. I shouted I hadn't done anything. But then she was dragging me off. She took me to the garden basin and shoved my head under the tap. She sprayed water all over my head. She was shrieking: "Now! Admit it! What were you doing in the bushes with that boy? Or do you want another dose?" I was suffocating. And I was such a coward. I confessed—I confessed to anything she wanted: anything to get her to stop. Though actually I hadn't done a thing, not a single thing. When she let me go, I was almost fainting. And I knew then: she hated me and wanted to kill me.

DOCTOR: I see. And did she leave you alone after that—after her water—treatment?

MARINA: Yes, she did. And I kept out of her sight in any way I could. I was scared stiff of her, and at the same time I despised her. I felt destroyed, you see—crushed and finished.

DOCTOR: And the boy? What about him? Alan, did you say?

MARINA: Yes, Alan. I never really played with Alan any more: I always said no to everything.

DOCTOR: You still went round to see him, though?

MARINA: I did, but it had all changed, somehow. Everything was different. The garden was such a quiet place now: I can't think of a quieter place than a garden in summer. I heard the gravel rasp, but it was as though my ears were miles away, high up above the ground. A dog barked in the distance—and it was like a barking in a dream. Everything had got muffled, as if it was under a sort of glass dome.

DOCTOR: [*Nods.*] You know what you're describing, don't you: shock, estrangement, withdrawal. The origin of autism.

[*While speaking* MARINA *has let down her hair and dropped her luxuriant red locks over her shoulders. She is hiding her face with her hair, as if she would like to screen herself behind it.*]

MARINA: Does that mean I'm mad?

DOCTOR: No. [*A little wearily.*] And even if you were . . . A person has a right to be what they are. Remember your rights! There are always people ready to pass judgement. They won't even let others be mad. Human rights . . .

MARINA: What do I care about human rights? Father's always going on about rights—and duties as well. A person has a duty: it's to go to work in the morning. If he does that, he has a right: the right to eat dinner in the evening. He can smoke his pipe in peace, and read his paper. Dad's so careful and methodical. It's in everything. But he's resigned, that's what it is really, and he's grudging with it. It's as if he didn't really believe in his own rules, just obeyed them. I'm not after rights and duties. [*Whispering.*] I want to love.

DOCTOR: But often a person doesn't have the right to love, either . . . at least, not to love just whoever she wants. Hm. Who is it that you'd like . . . to love?

MARINA: [*After a long silence, humbly.*] You.

DOCTOR: Pardon me. Now that is mad!

MARINA: You yourself said I'd the right to be mad.

DOCTOR: Yes. Indeed. That's your particular burden. Hm. All rights bring their own burdens. Believe me, I'm removing another burden from you when I say: you don't have the right to love me—any more than I have the right to love you. Or . . . well, there are many sorts of love. What exactly do you have in mind when you say you love me?

MARINA: I don't know, I just think about you . . . every moment of the day and night. I long for you. As I go along the street, I'm hoping I'll bump into you, and at the same time I'm afraid I will. I pass your house in the evening, and I can see a light on there, and I feel good. I think: he's there. Then I go home, and I think about your house, all the evening. Or rather, I don't actually think about it: I see it in front of me. I see it very clearly, right from its stone foundations to the cowl on your chimney-pot. The outlets on the drainpipes, they're shaped like dragons, and there's a metal frill round the eaves. The railing on the outside steps, it's worn, and it smells like an old woman's hand. No one ever looks out of the windows. Inside it's mysterious and quiet. Nevertheless each stone, each cleft in the stone, even, of that house is a joy to me. But I don't always see it . . .

DOCTOR: And then?

MARINA: Nothing. Those are the boring, dreary days: as if it was always Monday. I sit in my room and long for Friday, for it to be Friday . . . the day I get to be with you, here. But even the Fridays aren't always good: sometimes you're distant, cold, and then . . .

DOCTOR: And then?

MARINA: It's as if something were falling apart, as if the wind were sinking wells in my yard. And I sit there alone, and my room's full of bad thoughts—not my thoughts: thoughts coming from Evil. And I sit there waiting for the roof to fall in on me.

DOCTOR: Hm. The room doesn't seem to suit you very well. Why? Your mother said you'd got a darling little room, with white furniture . . .

MARINA: Father bought that when I was fifteen. No one adores it but father. Maybe it is lovely . . . but it goes with unbearable memories . . . years, weeks, days, long-drawn-out hours. Utter dreariness.

DOCTOR: When a person's got all she might need, and even more, including what she doesn't need, it does feel dreary. It's not like that for everyone, you know. No room of their own, no home even . . . have you ever given a thought to that?

MARINA: [*Not listening.*] But sometimes everything glows red. The sofa's red, the cat on the sofa's red. [*Pause.*] The room glows . . . like a lantern. [*Painfully.*] Some day it'll catch fire.

DOCTOR: But you're fantasizing.

MARINA: Yes. I know. But knowing doesn't change anything. My body fantasizes, and I can't control it. Sometimes I think: when the room catches fire I'll have less pain.

DOCTOR: Why do you think that way?

MARINA: I don't know. That's how it is. [*Pause.*] And a terrible beauty was born—

DOCTOR: What did you say?

MARINA: Nothing. Something from a poem.

DOCTOR: So you do read poems then?

MARINA: No, I just came across it somehow.

DOCTOR: But if you did try to read? Or at least try to think about something else? What do you do for preference?

MARINA: Nothing. I wait for the day to end.

DOCTOR: A life like that's unbearable; no one could bear it. Maybe, waiting for the day to end, you could find a little something to do? And think a bit?

MARINA: I've brought my handiwork along. Knitting. [*She takes out of her bag an unnaturally long, shapeless stocking.*] But it's no help. You can't think about a stocking.

DOCTOR: [*Pityingly.*] I do see you've not given much thought to your stocking.

MARINA: No, because I was giving all my thought to you.

DOCTOR: [*He peers at and turns the stocking-foot.*] There's several feet of horrible sock there. Why don't you unravel it?

MARINA: Because I don't want to. From the length of the stocking, I can reckon how many metres you've been with me.

DOCTOR: [*Drops the stocking.*] Listen, that's just a bee in your bonnet.

MARINA: I can't help it . . . [*Whispering intensely.*] if I love you.

DOCTOR: Rubbish! You could just as easily have fallen for someone else.

MARINA: [*Calmly and earnestly.*] But I haven't fallen for someone else.

DOCTOR: That's the madness of the heart. You'd better get over it.

MARINA: I don't want to get over it.

DOCTOR: Get in touch with some people. Mix with them. The town's full of young men keen to get married, and you . . . you must be rich.

MARINA: How can you speak like that?

DOCTOR: Because you force me to. And I only mean well.

MARINA: It hurts me, when you speak like that. How can you do it? How can you mean well and do harm?

DOCTOR: Sometimes well-meant advice does feel cruel; but it has to be given nevertheless. In these parts, there are lots of good-looking good young men—

MARINA: They're not good! Not good at all! They're conceited, stupid, hard. [*Whispering.*] You're the only good one.

DOCTOR: You're mistaken, Miss Klein. You ought to trust people more.

MARINA: I've trusted people quite too much.

DOCTOR: Well. You're obstinate. Remember, I was only trying to help you.

MARINA: You weren't! You were trying to deceive me! But I know better! This is a small, miserly, cold town. And the people here are all alike. But perhaps you think this town's wholesome, like fresh bread! I'll tell you what it is: it's a rat-infested rubbish heap.

DOCTOR: Rat-infested?

MARINA: Rats! Rats! Sewer rats! Why should I love them? The idea's hopeless!

DOCTOR: [*Wearily.*] Perhaps it is hopeless, but not specially here. Don't get to thinking that life, somewhere else, in another town, or in another house—in this house—is any sweeter or better. You'll not find a world to suit your temperament, anywhere. I'm not deceiving you any more now. Life's the same, equally hopeless everywhere.

[*A short silence.*]

MARINA: [*Sadly.*] I could die of dreariness. Sometimes a day drags on like a century.

DOCTOR: One doesn't die of dreariness. One just gets worn down. Yes, and ugly. [*Wearily, brusquely.*] And as for rats, don't you yourself have even one tiny vice?

MARINA: Yes, one.

DOCTOR: Oh? And what is it?

MARINA: I despise virtue.

DOCTOR: Virtue, ah. As the Chinese sage Lao Tsu said "Virtue is light as a hair; and the heavens work silently, and without odour!" Is that what you despise?

MARINA: No, that's Lao Tsu's virtue, and heaven's virtue. You won't find either of those virtues in this place. And why should I despise what doesn't exist? What I despise is bourgeois virtue.

DOCTOR: Ah! Many jaded bourgeois daughters despise what they've been taught, and particularly the manners. There's nothing specially personal about that. It's your class you ought to despise.

MARINA: Are the other classes any better then?

DOCTOR: No. The peasants are greedy, stupid and treacherous. The educated are stuck-up, hidebound and stereotyped, often to the point of idiocy—

MARINA: You too?

DOCTOR: Me? [*Gives a soft laugh.*] I'm a radical. [*Slightly amused.*] Me, I'm a genius. But—

MARINA: [*Matter-of-factly.*] So why should I despise my class then?

DOCTOR: [*Quickly.*] One shouldn't adhere to a class that wrongs others.

MARINA: The bourgeoisie?

DOCTOR: Yes. They live off other people's work.

MARINA: Is that my fault? I didn't choose my class personally. I didn't make my father, he made me. I'd be glad if That One—[*She raises a lock of hair to her lips, imitating her moustached father.*]—weren't my father.

DOCTOR: Make an effort. Do some work and pull yourself up out of this miserable class of market operators.

MARINA: [*Earnestly, appealingly.*] Work, what work should I do? I can't do anything, I've not been taught anything. I only know. [*Hesitates.*]

DOCTOR: Yes?

MARINA: One means of getting out of my social class.

DOCTOR: [*Curiously, slightly patronizingly.*] And what may that be?

MARINA: [*Simply.*] For you to marry me.

DOCTOR: [*Morally indignant.*] Make that sort of proposition to a young man, if you like, but not to me!

MARINA: Oh. Forgive me. [*Blushing and going pale.*] I've hurt you. [*Calmly*] But I love you.

DOCTOR: [*Very deliberately.*] If you have erotic love in mind, then you'd better know that it—

MARINA: It?

DOCTOR: Is war.

MARINA: I didn't know. Or no, yes I did know, but I didn't remember. [*Whispering.*] I could die of shame.

DOCTOR: One doesn't die of shame. Faints, at the most.

MARINA: [*Raising her head.*] I've no intention of fainting. I'm in control of myself.

[*A cold light comes into her face and remains there for the rest of the scene.*]

DOCTOR: [*Drily, slightly embarrassed.*] Good. Very good.

MARINA: [*Palely stiffening.*] Everything's going round and round in my head.

DOCTOR: [*Speaking calmingly.*] Relax. Lean back. Let your thoughts calm down. Be completely peaceful.

[*During all of the following exchange both* MARINA *and the* DOCTOR *speak calmly, without affect. Even when the girl accuses the* DOCTOR, *she is calm, and her style is more mechanical than accusatory. Emotions burst out only at the end of the scene, during the test.*]

MARINA: [*Almost whispering.*] Why are you hypnotizing me? You yourself want me to love you.

DOCTOR: [*Still calmingly.*] Dear Miss Klein, I don't want anything. And I'm not hypnotizing you either—I've never gone in for hypnotism. What do you mean by . . . "hypnosis"?

MARINA: You press on my head.

DOCTOR: Press on your head? How? When?

MARINA: At night and . . . when it hurts.

DOCTOR: That's another bee in your bonnet, Miss Klein.

MARINA: If it is, you put it there.

DOCTOR: Really.

MARINA: Really. I can't prove it, but I know it. When the hypnotism starts, I hear voices.

DOCTOR: Voices, what voices?

MARINA: Your voices. You hypnotise me and say: Jung-Frau-hau. . . . Many times.

DOCTOR: Hm. Really. Did you do German at school?

MARINA: No.

DOCTOR: Do they speak German at home?

MARINA: Father does sometimes.

DOCTOR: With your mother?

MARINA: No, mother doesn't know anything. With visitors.

DOCTOR: What you just said—Jung-Frau-hau—was half German, half bark. Why should I hypnotize you in German?

MARINA: That I don't know. No one but you can know that.

DOCTOR: Really.

MARINA: But of course I can guess.

DOCTOR: Really?

MARINA: So I won't understand. And because you want to impose on me.

DOCTOR: Why should I want to impose on you?

MARINA: To have complete power over me.

DOCTOR: Why should I want that?

MARINA: That I don't know. But everyone wants it: Father. Mother. The teacher . . . when I was at school. [*Hesitantly.*] Mikael. Everyone.

DOCTOR: I'm not your father, or your mother, or your teacher. I want to help you.

MARINA: That's what they all say. They think they want to help, but really they want something else. Power.

DOCTOR: I see. But I don't. That's another bee in your bonnet. There's nothing more unlovely, or more of a strain, than power.

MARINA: But still, they all want it. First they want love, and when they don't get love, they want respect, and when they don't get respect, they want power, and when they don't get power, they want . . .

DOCTOR: What then?

MARINA: Anything whatever. Money, things.

DOCTOR: That was very logical. You've intelligence, though not sense. You're not really sensible.

MARINA: Probably not, because you hypnotize me.

DOCTOR: By pressing on your head?

MARINA: Yes, and with the voices.

DOCTOR: Jung-Frau-hau?

MARINA: Yes. And Zung Sau Tau. Hung Mau Poi. Giiga, de Roi.

DOCTOR: Now you're on to Chinese.

MARINA: I'm just saying what you say.

DOCTOR: I see. I'm afraid I'm going to have to resort to cardiazol.

MARINA: Yet another magic word. What's that?

DOCTOR: [*Sighs.*] Oatmeal gruel. I'm going to put you on a course of oatmeal gruel.

MARINA: You're lying. First you wheedle me, then you threaten me, and finally you lie to me.

DOCTOR: I'm far from threatening you in any way. I want, with all my power, to help you.

MARINA: So you say. Always contradictory. When I say I love you, and you're good, and you're the only one who is good, you disagree, and you say you're not good and I can't love you. When I say you're threatening me and you're bad, you again disagree, and again everything's contradictory. Everything's going round.

DOCTOR: I'm not good and not bad. In general, I'm not so mysterious as you think. I just listen, that's all. I don't practice witchcraft.

MARINA: You practice deceit. You pretend, like all the rest. You promise to heal the soul, though you don't believe in the soul.

DOCTOR: It may be what we call the soul doesn't exist. The soul is a medium. We're affected, though, by things that don't exist.

MARINA: [*On the alert.*] Are you telling me I . . . I've lost my way in a love that doesn't exist?

DOCTOR: Your mind has a philosophical turn, and I was, in fact, speaking more philosophically, more generally; but you could bring it down to that.

MARINA: That I'm lost? In a love that doesn't exist?

DOCTOR: Yes. Put it how you wish.

MARINA: Now it's you withdrawing from the game.

DOCTOR: There's no game here. I'm merely sorting out your muddles.

MARINA: [*Coldly.*] What are you sorting out?

DOCTOR: I'm sorting out your . . . your tangled threads, your worries.

MARINA: [*Calmly.*] I don't have any worries. I have sorrows.

DOCTOR: Well those then.

MARINA: You're sorting nothing out. You just go on hinting . . . And . . . hypnotizing.

DOCTOR: [*Wearily.*] I see. Well. But don't I ever speak clearly and, so you can understand, when this . . . hm . . . hypnotizing is going on?

MARINA: Yes, you do.

DOCTOR: Ah? And then?

MARINA: And then I have to do what the voices tell me to. I have to go for a walk, though I don't want to. I have to fling a plate at the wall. I have to go to the well and drop money in, and wish, though I don't want to. And—

DOCTOR: Wish—what for?

MARINA: [*She does not reply to the question but carries on from where she was.*] And when I'm cooking I have to say obscene things and smash eggs with the hammer, though I don't want to.

DOCTOR: Symbolical activities.

MARINA: What did you say, Doctor?

DOCTOR: I said, actions that point to something else.

MARINA: All that happens is just a symbol.

DOCTOR: Where did you pick that up from? Where?

MARINA: . . . of something greater.

DOCTOR: What?

MARINA: All that happens is just a symbol of something greater.

DOCTOR: That's a very interesting observation. [*Muttering to himself.*] Out of the mouths of babes and the mad . . .

MARINA: Mother once said the mad come from bottles.

DOCTOR: Oh?

MARINA: Yes. Mother's always pretty crude in how she puts things. But in fact that was symbolic.

DOCTOR: A symbol? That the mad come out of bottles?

MARINA: What she was hinting at was father's drinking.

DOCTOR: Your father drinks, then?

MARINA: Has been blind drunk sometimes. But nowadays he only does it on the sly. He used to be boozer, though, and mother . . .

DOCTOR: What, your mother drank too?

MARINA: No, but mother used to say . . . [*Feeling shame on her mother's behalf.*] "Those children of ours were begotten by drink."

DOCTOR: Hm. I think your mother was overstating it. If drunkenness begot madmen, the whole country'd be . . . well, due for the bin.

MARINA: Perhaps it is.

DOCTOR: [*Sighs.*] Yes, may well be. Can't say . . . I haven't examined the whole country. But I've done plenty of random spot-checks, and they can always . . . make you think.

MARINA: Yes. And they're always so sharp, your thoughts . . . So piercing. It makes my head ache.

DOCTOR: It's only your own thoughts can give you headaches.

MARINA: You miss the point. When you think about me, it's so piercing, it hurts my head.

DOCTOR: Truth to tell. I think about you very rarely.

MARINA: If that's the truth, it's even more hurtful.

DOCTOR: There we are again. It hurts if I think about you, it hurts when I don't.

MARINA: But you touch me, thinking or not.

DOCTOR: Touch you?

MARINA: You press on my head and won't let me sleep.

DOCTOR: Round and round we go, in a circle. How did you put it: "Everything's going round." Our talk's no use if you won't come out of your little circle.

MARINA: What circle?

DOCTOR: Of fantasy. What you're calling hypnosis or . . . love.

MARINA: Out of that? Out of the circle of love? I don't want to come out of that. And that's no one else's business—not even yours.

DOCTOR: [*Wearily.*] In that case, I can't help you. In that case, you might just as well close yourself up in your room and water the flowers. Play patience, or stare at the wallpaper. Or knit away at that horrible sock.

MARINA: [*Clouding.*] Close myself up in my room. Water the flowers. Knit the sock . . . I watered the flowers today. At ten past three.

DOCTOR: Why at ten past three exactly? Is it important for the timing to be so precise?

MARINA: No. But I know it was ten past three, because, as I began watering, it was five past, and then I saw the hearse, and the funeral horses: two of them, brown and black, coming up the street. The wheels rumbled on the cobbles, and the horses ambled along, oh so slowly, meditating, and they had masks on.

DOCTOR: Masks?

MARINA: Yes, black masks, as always here.

DOCTOR: Oh, you mean blinkers, to keep the flies away.

MARINA: No: these were funeral horses, and wearing masks. It was ten past three as they passed out of sight, and I went back to my watering. It was like a painting, or a motion picture, and it left me thinking: "Slow horses draw the dead. Slow horses draw the dead."

DOCTOR: Why were you so involved with the time?

MARINA: I can't feel evening any longer, or morning. So I have to keep checking with the clock. Time has stopped, there's no time any more, and I can't feel any more.

DOCTOR: What can't you feel?

MARINA: Anything . . . ordinary feelings—pleasure, being tired, feeling concern. When those horses were pulling that body, I didn't feel a thing—though I knew it was an omen. All I thought was: there's a body in there now. Or two. For don't they have a separate horse for each dead body?

DOCTOR: How do you mean?

MARINA: Oh, I don't know, I was just thinking: What does a horse stand for?

DOCTOR: A horse stands for a horse of course.

MARINA: But in the highest sense? And in a dream?

DOCTOR: An Arabian dream-book says: "Das Pferd—o du Weiser—ist eine Frau, und beide sind das Eigentum des Mannes." A horse—O wise one—is a woman, and both are the property of the man.

MARINA: But in my dream?

DOCTOR: It could be various things. A horse can represent wandering, or it can be a symbol of change, of death . . . but generally a horse is the self, yourself.

MARINA: No it isn't. A horse is an angel.

DOCTOR: Hm. Perhaps it could be that too. A guardian angel . . . thus the soul. When the soul is integrated, it protects a person.

MARINA: My angel's dead.

DOCTOR: What did you say?

MARINA: My angel died last night. That's why I'm wearing this lovely orange dress today.

DOCTOR: In memory of the angel?

MARINA: Yes, or the horse. In my dream it was red. It's name was Burnt Orange.

DOCTOR: Ah. So that's why you've let loose all those colors which you were holding in? Protective coloring. You love protective coloring.

MARINA: I don't know what protective coloring is.

DOCTOR: Just now, that is your protective coloring. But your dream, please tell me your dream.

MARINA: There was a beautiful reddish-brown horse—it was still a colt really. It came to my lap, and I warmed it, for it was frozen stiff: its back legs were so stiff, they were almost like paralyzed. And then suddenly, it revived: it was completely alive again, and it ran away from me, and galloped up and down in my room. Its red mane was flowing. And then, in a flash, it was out through the window, its mane flaming. And it crashed down onto the pavement. It was all smashed, and, oh, I could hear it weeping.

DOCTOR: [*Sadly, after a longish pause.*] Yes, the angel has died. [*Pause.*] You know, I can't help you any more. [*Pause.*] I'm sorry, but I can't help you, and I've no wish to arouse any false illusions in you: that would be a sort of betrayal. [*He starts walking up and down in the room.*] Look, in trying to help you, I'm in fact trying to help myself. For every time I abandon a patient, I feel as if I've lost the game. Just for that reason, I'm going to test you once more . . . though, quite frankly, I admit it, now it feels more like a hopeless party-game to me. [*He goes back to his desk, opens a drawer and takes out a series of enlarged pictures. The following test is a free imitation of Szond's test and is to be thought of as the* DOC-TOR's *own invention.*] What I have here is a group of pictures. I'll put them up on the wall.

[*He begins to hang them. Most are of well-known personalities with very powerful or otherwise special facial traits: they include a straggly haired Schopenhauer, and a walrus-moustached Nietzsche. Hence, the* DOCTOR's *test-pictures are enlarged portraits of historical personages known to have had morbid traits. The end-picture on the wall is of a human-looking ape or ram.*]

DOCTOR: Now, this is what you have to do. Tell me something: whom do you like best, and whom you like least out of all these faces. Please.

[MARINA *regards the pictures with reserve and doesn't reply.*]

DOCTOR: Well, Miss Klein. Whom do you like most?

MARINA: None of them! Not a single one of them! They're all horrible! [*She goes towards the pictures and points to each one separately, suddenly beginning to diagnose them.*] That one's [*Pointing to Voltaire.*] godless, cynical and ugly! That one's [*Pointing to Rousseau.*] good-looking but a swindler and a thief! [*Pointing to E. T. A. Hoffmann.*] Drunken sot! [*Point-ing to Schopenhauer.*] Groucher! [*Pointing to Ibsen.*] Pewit! [*Pointing to Danton.*] Blood-hound! That one's . . . [*Pointing with feeling to Nietzsche.*] father. [*Whispers.*] A stupid little dog.

DOCTOR: Is he the one you like best?

MARINA: No! None of them, I don't want to like any of them! They're all revolting! Why are you torturing me? Photographs of mad people! Why are you probing into me? Go and probe into yourself!

[*She rushes out of the room and slams the door hard to behind her.*]

DOCTOR: [*He stands glumly in the middle of the room.*] Failed again. Superb test of mine, no use at all. Well, pioneers must be humble. [*He wipes his glasses in embarrassment.*] Hm. She's so full of affects. The same thing, practically every time: the session ends in a scene. Well, perhaps that's better than being drab. Maybe it was a good thing too—her going off like that: I mightn't have got her out at all otherwise. [*He pulls a watch out of his waistcoat pocket.*] Damn! Soon be eleven. [*He opens the window, looks out.*] Night, deep, and black. Scent of mignonette from the garden . . . It's as if there were no unhappi-ness in the world. There's her house, almost opposite. [*Lowering his voice.*] And there she goes . . . taking her load of pain with her . . . into the loneliness of the night.

[*Eleven clear strokes come from a clocktower nearby. Soon the chimes are joined by another clocktower, then a third one further off. The series of strokes persists, and thins out until the last clangour trembles and fades.*]

There it is: a light now, in one of those windows. The curtain's being drawn. She must be home now—back in her room, so full of . . . how did she put it? Sighs? Long hours? Utter dreariness? A mad girl, and I can't help her. How did it go in pig Latin? Adama irlga, nda antca elpha erha. Sad but true.

[*End of Act Two.*]

[*Interval.*]

ACT THREE

Scene One

MARINA's *room. Extremely pale wallpaper, simple white furniture. Up C. a delicate oval table with a chair or two round it and a bowl of flowers on it. Down C. a wardrobe whose mirror has been removed, leaving a large space in the door, and with no back. The effect of a mirror is, however, produced by a bowl of flowers at the back of the wardrobe, an apparent mirror-image of the one on the table. This effect is needed for the end of the scene when the* DOCTOR *disappears "into the mirror."*

MARINA *is sitting knitting her stocking, which now extends across the whole room, and staring unseeingly in front of her. Her expression is of someone asleep: not dreaming but empty. She is wearing a pale airy blouse and a grey taffeta skirt.*

Shortly music begins to be heard in the distance: traditional jazz—Louis Armstrong, "High Society." The girl wakes up and runs to the window.

MARINA: Music!

[*She opens the window, and the music flows in. The girl nods an accompaniment to it. She then takes a large pen off the table and blows on it as if she were taking part in the session. The scene that follows is to be thought of as* MARINA's *hallucination, or wish-fulfillment dream. The double door into the room opens silently and is lit up extremely brightly. Into the room steps the* DOCTOR, *wearing morning clothes, a tight-fitting bell-shaped jacket and striped trousers. He has a bowler in one hand and a folded umbrella in the other. He approaches the girl and gives her shoulder a friendly touch.*]

DOCTOR: My daughter. My sister. My bride.
MARINA: Now you'll always be with me, forever, won't you?
DOCTOR: Forever.
MARINA: You'll never leave me, abandon me, ever?
DOCTOR: Never. I'll never abandon you, ever.
MARINA: I can hear a trumpet—it's playing in the park.
DOCTOR: Let's go. Let's go to the park and take a walk.
MARINA: Whither thou goest I go too.

[*They walk arm in arm round the table, slowly and dignifiedly. Ragged shadows suggesting trees in leaf are projected onto the pale wall. Now the music changes: "Bach's Prelude and Fugue No. 1 in C major" from* The Well-Tempered Clavier.]

MARINA: What a lovely morning!
DOCTOR: The morning's a woman. It's you—
MARINA: No, I'm evening.
DOCTOR: Together, we'll walk through the parks—
MARINA: —Through the songs—
DOCTOR: —With the leaves coming out—
MARINA: —With the leaves falling—
DOCTOR: The rains'll pass over us—[*Opens his umbrella.*]
MARINA: The birds'll doze in the shelter of the trees—
DOCTOR: We'll hear music traveling across the water—
MARINA: My boat's empty. Dear heart—
DOCTOR: Dear heart. Sister.

[*They stop.* MARINA *presses her head against the* DOCTOR's *chest. The* DOCTOR *caresses her lightly.*]

DOCTOR: Tell me, what are you feeling now?
MARINA: That you're speaking to my hair.
DOCTOR: And now?

MARINA: That you're smiling at my hair.

[*Silence.*]

MARINA: [*Sadly.*] Oh dear, it's all too much: I simply can't watch over the world, and over this house, all the time.

DOCTOR: You don't need to. [*He closes his umbrella and leans it against the table.*]

MARINA: But, if I don't, it'll all collapse in ruins.

DOCTOR: Not now.

[*They begin walking again.*]

DOCTOR: Not anymore, not after this.

MARINA: [*She begins repeating mechanically like an echo.*] After this. After this.

DOCTOR: I'll be keeping watch for you. After this, your heart can never be completely dark.

MARINA: Completely dark.

[*There is a whispered repetition of the echo.*] "Dark. Dark."

[MARINA *turns slowly, twisting her whole body round. The music dims.*]

DOCTOR: Don't turn! Don't look behind you!

[*The girl separates herself from the* DOCTOR *and will-lessly turns round.*]

DOCTOR: Why did you turn? I told you not to look back!

[MARINA *walks, unhearing, like a sleepwalker in the opposite direction. As the fugue fades the* DOCTOR *steps silently through "the mirror" and creeps away. The hallucinations continue.* MARINA *leans apathetically and motionlessly on the table. Enter her father, shrunken, shabby, moustache dropping. He approaches* MARINA.]

MR. KLEIN: [*Dejectedly and unsympathetically.*] Daughter, what's the matter with you?

MARINA: I've lost hope.

MR. KLEIN: Ah, that's the saddest sentence in the world, isn't it? I've lost hope. It's the name of your sickness, I think, isn't it? It's your own name: "I've-lost-hope."

[*Enter a bird-masked* MRS. KLEIN, *wearing a large blue bird's head and carrying a handbag decorated with feathers, and a fan resembling a peacock's tail. She grabs a chair and raises it in the air as if to strike* MARINA, *but simultaneously notices the crazy stocking and changes her mind. She picks the knitting off the floor and pulls it on the chair-leg as far as she can. Even so the stocking stretches almost to the forestage.* MRS. KLEIN *gives a horrible bird-laugh. Noticing the umbrella, she thrusts its curved handle into her husband's collar and drags him out of the room.* MR. KLEIN *trots after her, putting up no active resistance.* MARINA *watches all this stiffly, with no change of expression. Projection slowly turns the room red; it turns still redder and then gradually goes dark.*]

Scene Two

The DOCTOR's *surgery. The* DOCTOR *is sitting at his desk in an ordinary informal suit of the day, and writing. The silence and arrested expectation are protracted to the point of unbearableness. Suddenly a fire-alarm bell is heard from the street. The* DOCTOR *goes to the window and opens it. The noise increases: it is as if the whole town were being called out. Gradually the ringing dies away; then a rumbling of wheels is heard from the street.*

DOCTOR: [*Looking out of the window and listening for a while.*] Well, she's done it now.

RECEPTIONIST: [*Coming into the room.*] There's a fire! That was the fire brigade racketing by. It's at the Kleins'! Two fire-engines—loaded with men.

DOCTOR: [*Still looking out.*] They've got it early, I think. I can't see any flames, no smoke even.

RECEPTIONIST: Thank the Lord.

[*The* DOCTOR *closes the window but remains standing by it. The* RECEPTIONIST *goes on.*]

RECEPTIONIST: We've had our share of disasters this week. Couple of days ago it was the apprentice at the chemist's: drank lysol. Fiancé had deserted her. Not dead, I hear, but terrible burns inside. Heard while I was getting the milk.

DOCTOR: Lysol, hm. You'd think a chemist'd find something a bit more congenial than lysol, apprentice or not. But get them on that tack, and they don't choose their poison, the poison chooses them.

RECEPTIONIST: Sometimes, these days, I think the whole town's gone round the bend. That Klein girl. What was up with her? So different at different times!

DOCTOR: Up? Tedium.

RECEPTIONIST: Tedium, funny name for a disease.

DOCTOR: It is, though. Probably the chemist's apprentice has it as well—losing her wits for love. [*Taps on the window.*] Oh yes, I remember now: she's a tall thin girl, isn't she?—the anxious type: can't take it in that disasters occur without fail in their own good time. Has to rush out and fix one up, seek destruction for herself. Twenty years she goes on being quietly docile, compliant, does what she's told. Then after that it happens: head over heels in love. She's bewitched. She loses interest in everything but that. She's no will of her own. She's given her heart to this fellow—stubbornly, no one knows why— and now he's the whole world to her. He may be good, bad, rich, poor, bright or a bumpkin, it makes no difference. But let him cheat on her, and she's in still more of a frenzy. Now she's all yearning. She goes to pieces. She'll do anything, anything at all, to hang onto her beloved—to seal their union. [*He goes over to the desk.*] No point in telling her he's beneath her, a waste of time: the wretch gets his value from his wretchedness. His crudity's his trump card. Weird, preposterous, but true. Inferior people—mediocrities—get glamour from the pain they give: and that's exactly why they do it. [*The telephone rings. The* DOCTOR *replies curtly:*] Yes. Yes, I did hear. Right. Of course. Just bring her round. Don't mention it. [*To the* RECEPTIONIST.] That was KLEIN, of course. They're bringing her here. You know what it's all about, don't you? What's behind it all? Dreaming. It's dreams that keep the globe bowling round. Dreams—they create geniuses, lunatics and lovers, and dreams can knock a young girl completely sideways.

RECEPTIONIST: Oh yes, I know about dreams. They come from . . . Hm, you know . . . the peritoneum.

DOCTOR: Well, no one's ever accused you of beating about the bush.

RECEPTIONIST: Beating about the bush? So why should I? It's all very well for you, sir, in your job, being a doctor, looking into dreams, and all that. But I've got to do the cleaning up. No time to beat about the bush.

DOCTOR: All very well, my job, eh? What's so very well about it? A baker has a better time of it. He at least can get the bread to rise. But how to get these dreamers to rise? These . . . ? You go mad yourself, consorting with the mad . . . Sometimes it seems as if all the lunatics in the world were wanting to come to me. And, you know who are the worst? Those that are sane. One lunatic comes to you and says: "Doctor, I'm depressed, clinically depressed. I need a prescription for Johnny Walker." The next comes and says "I'm neurasthenic: I need a prescription for a shot of laudanum." They know it all, in advance, and they roll up with their diagnoses, prognoses and prescriptions at the ready.

RECEPTIONIST: Well, that Klein girl didn't. She didn't hoick along her diagnosis, did she?

DOCTOR: What she did bring was a horrible sock—yards and yards of filthy knitting. It was a combined distress signal and diagnosis.

RECEPTIONIST: Her father's an old sock, if you ask me. You know what they say: he's so short, the bags under his eyes are his scrotum.

DOCTOR: [*Dissatisfiedly.*] Well, look at the mother. I can't stand either of them, but the mother takes the biscuit. Her manic eyes, and the father's vacant ones—they give me the heeby-jeebies. The girl got it right about her mother. She won't admit to reading poetry, but quotes things half-awake . . . "Mother's a warship," she said, "in full sail, with all her flags and streamers flying."

RECEPTIONIST: Ten warships, more like.

DOCTOR: You could say that. Amanda's her name, but she's an Armada. Ten shiploads of unemployed energy. I loathe women like that: gun at the cock always, though no enemy's in sight. Her husband's no match for her. Klein's about as wide-awake as a baby-minder at midnight. If only it were the other way! He should be the horse-power, she the one giving way. A set-up like theirs is deadly: incubator for unstable, dithering kids. Year after year goes by, the father holding himself in: then one fine day, he's look-ing for his collar-stud, he flies into a rage, and he has a heart attack. He's dead. The mother, though, she doesn't hold anything in: all her upsets come flying out. And they all go into the child. But the child, no: the child can't get upset. Every little childish ges-ture gets sat on, as soon as it shows itself. Just think, what the girl told me: as a child she loved machines. She used to hug the heating-stove instead of her mother.

RECEPTIONIST: Do you have to go all that way back—to the stove—to find the cause?

DOCTOR: You do. It's always a good thing to look for a cause where there is one, not where there isn't. There's a colleague of mine in London, for instance: very famous surgeon, Doctor Lane. When people are depressed he cuts their colon out. "All the filth collects in there," he says. Nutty as a chestnut himself, they say, but so far he's not let anyone near his colon.

RECEPTIONIST: [*Laughing.*] I expect he thinks no one else can do it as well as he can.

DOCTOR: Perhaps. Anyway, it's better to look for the cause in the dustbins and constricted colons of childhood. But that's what gets me down: causality—the causes of every-thing. Everything has to go back, back to the past, to childhood, and even beyond that. That's what makes this work such a problem: nothing's definitely what it seems: it's something else, rather . . . You're always turning the clock back, going widdershins: the clock hands always lie. Nothing's simple, everything's complicated . . . and therefore impossible. How much simpler life'd be if we believed in demons! Then we could drive them out into the swine.

RECEPTIONIST: Very scientific, that!

DOCTOR: If only you knew. How the word scientific's overvalued. In actual fact, we know nothing about anything. Half of what we call science is stereotyped, prejudiced stuff. Take the telephone. [*Indicating the old-fashioned table telephone.*] When they first demon-strated the telephone at the French Academy of Sciences, a certain distinguished pro-fessor, an extremely eminent scientist, declared it was a fraud: someone was ventrilo-quizing.

[*The doorbell rings violently, as if the bellpull were being wrenched off. The* DOCTOR *picks the telephone receiver up mechanically, but the* RECEPTIONIST *speaks.*]

RECEPTIONIST: It wasn't the telephone. Someone's ventriloquizing.

[*She flies to open the door. The* DOCTOR *gets up and puts on his white coat. The* RECEPTION-IST *ushers in* MR. *and* MRS. KLEIN, *who bring in their daughter, her hair tousled and her face sooty.*]

MRS. KLEIN: Now you've got to put her away! This is it. She's been trying to burn us alive!

[*The* DOCTOR *goes to receive them and tries to grip* MARINA *by the shoulder, but she wriggles free and bangs her head on the wall.*]

DOCTOR: [*Returns to sit as his desk.*] I was only trying to help.

MARINA: I don't need help. I've not asked for help. I'm all right.

DOCTOR: But your mother has asked for it.

MARINA: Help her then.

MRS. KLEIN: Put her away! We can't keep her in the house a single day. I can't stand it! Not a single moment more with her.

MARINA: [*She suddenly loses her Maenad pride, grasps the* DOCTOR's *actuality and appeals with anguish.*] Take me! Take me!

DOCTOR: That I'll certainly do, but not into my department, I'm afraid. You can't be admitted. I'm in the men's wing, you see. [*As he replies, the* DOCTOR *sits head bent, drawing mechanically.*]

MARINA: Put me in the men's wing then! Dress me as a man, take me as your wife!

DOCTOR: I can't do that. If I took to wife everyone seeking my protection, I'd have been locked up for polygamy ages ago.

MARINA: [*Dropping on her knees in front of the* DOCTOR, *embracing his legs, and whispering intensely.*] Take me! Take me!

[MRS. KLEIN *goes to the girl and gives her a sharp blow. The girl seems to feel no pain at all.*]

DOCTOR: [*Rising and raising the girl from the floor.*] That is not permitted! Don't you dare to hit her.

MRS. KLEIN: [*Angrily.*] She didn't feel anything anyway.

[*During this incident the* RECEPTIONIST *has taken the girl's handbag and been emptying it, putting the knitting on the* DOCTOR's *desk, with the balls of wool and knitting needles.*]

DOCTOR: This is not the first time you've struck her. If she didn't feel anything just now, that's shock. Do you think, just because feeling's gone at this moment, it's dead for ever? Pains keep coming back. They do keep coming back till all feeling's burnt out. Yes, that can happen. And then there's nothing, nothing but cinders and ash, coldness, emptiness.

MRS. KLEIN: God in heaven, tell me what's the matter with her! What's made her like that?

DOCTOR: What's the use of names—labels? [*Deliberately employing outlandish and obscure words.*] Hyperophrenia . . . athymia . . . morosis . . . or maybe a mixture of all three . . . [*Shrugging his shoulders.*] How should I know myself? And if I did know . . . names are no help to anyone except the Doctor. And, about your daughter, I've no certainties.

MRS. KLEIN: Because I think she's got persecution mania.

DOCTOR: So why are you asking me, if you know better yourself?

MRS. KLEIN: What I want to know is: is persecution mania catching?

DOCTOR: Yes, in a way. To some extent. But don't worry. You are safe. You're quite different from your daughter. Traits that, in your hands, are weapons [*He picks up a bunch of knitting needles and sets them on end.*] have turned into acute sensibilities in your daughter: organs of feeling pointing inwards [*He points the needles at himself.*] The children of monsters are also monsters—but usually monstrous to themselves.

MRS. KLEIN: Ah!

[*She raises herself to her full height. Her skirt swishes threateningly, the black silk vine leaves in her hat sway. The girl, who during the exchange has been rigid and withdrawn, senses her mother's aggressiveness and becomes disturbed again. The* DOCTOR *signs to the* RECEPTIONIST, *who comes over to him; the doctor whispers something to her. The* RECEPTIONIST *goes to the door and opens it. Enter two helmeted, uniformed policemen, who take hold of the struggling girl and silently take her out.*]

DOCTOR: [*To the* RECEPTIONIST.] Go along with them. To Ward Four. There's room there. Then come back. I'll give you the other details later.

[*The incident proceeds quickly and quietly. The* DOCTOR *continues his doodling.*]

MRS. KLEIN: Was that really necessary—taking her off by main force, with the police?

DOCTOR: It was. That's the procedure. To ensure a proper report in the records. For she did try to commit arson. And besides, after dealing with you so long, that girl'll soon be a match for a couple of policemen. [*Doodles.*]

[MRS. KLEIN *rears her head arrogantly but says nothing.*]

MR. KLEIN: [*Looking over his shoulder and pointing to the* DOCTOR'*s drawing.*] The doctor's drawing flowers.

DOCTOR: [*Pushing the sheet away.*] I was intended for a botanist, and not . . . and not . . .

MR. KLEIN: [*Helping.*] A psychiatrist. Doctor, you hurt my wife just now.

DOCTOR: But I stick to what I said anyway. You wanted to know why your daughter was sick, and I told you: because she couldn't endure the family dressage—all that going round and round with the whip. She told me she liked the circus—the circus: that cruel world of clever tricks. She identifies with maltreated animals. Well, at least she hasn't learned to cycle round on a little wobbly wheel. She's not like so many others, trained animals, tricked out in finery and little jingle bells. Your daughter's no little bear or dog: she has some mind, some understanding, and therefore she's in revolt. But the protests of young women are weak and confused. Ultimately, the rebellion always turns inwards, against themselves. The truth, however, is this: she hasn't adapted: she hasn't adapted to this world of din and jingle bells.

MRS. KLEIN: [*In distress.*] Hasn't adapted. And you make us guilty of that?

DOCTOR: No. What would be the use? I merely state. Besides, the world's a mess of unpredictable things. A fragile girl—usually so docile and compliant—turns into a pyromaniac . . . The body's no mirror of the soul.

MR. KLEIN: [*Slowly.*] I've never needed to want anything . . . Everything always came to me, ready-made: the factory, my job, the home. There was my wife, though, Amanda: she was the only thing I ever wanted . . . once upon a time, that is, when I was young. Well . . . Now I don't believe in the freedom of the will. I have none. My wife does the wanting for me.

MRS. KLEIN: [*Quickly, cuttingly.*] Do you still write poems, Doctor?

DOCTOR: No, not for twenty years. It ended with a dream: I was washing my house with mercury sublimate—and ever since then I've been sterile.

MRS. KLEIN: Flowers, dreams, poems. After all, Doctor, you're a dreamer!

DOCTOR: "Gentlemen, dream!" . . . So my professor, Professor Justus Liebig, the discoverer of artificial fertilizers, said, in a lecture. He was training a bunch of us—up-and-coming scientists. He wanted us to develop a critical perspective, and he said, "Gentlemen, dream!"

MR. KLEIN: Yes, I can get that, I can understand that very well. Even in a leather factory you need dreams . . . everything from a tanning barrel to a stretching rack has been dreamt up by someone . . . No big industrial complex could get started without a dream, an idea. And a dream's what holds everything together.

DOCTOR: Nevertheless, dreaming doesn't always hold things together. Your daughter . . .

MRS. KLEIN: [*Now already more amenable.*] But, Doctor, couldn't you, after all, take her . . . as your private patient . . . she's so clearly attached to you.

DOCTOR: In the asylum I have no private patients. I only have private patients at my surgery . . . But this case has gone too far now. It wouldn't be any use . . . I could of course try analyzing her: in Austria they're curing people by talking—or rather, by getting the patients to talk. But for that you need years, decades maybe, and the cost: it'd be very expensive . . . Setting fire to houses is a cheaper therapy . . .

MRS. KLEIN: As for that, expense is no object. Couldn't you even try?

DOCTOR: I did try, and I didn't succeed. There was one great obstacle: the girl herself. All those feelings—feelings fixated on her mother, her father, her uncle, her teacher, her nurse, and even her wet nurse perhaps—were transferred onto me. It was a great shock for her when I didn't behave like . . . some darling man. Instead I was some wretched authority . . . like those old authoritarian darlings that'd done her in . . . You saw yourself: she's in love . . . she almost proposed to me. Nor was it the first time. So what can I do? Marriage with her is out of the question. Psychological means are no use any more. Nothing but injections will do now. And for that, my colleague in the asylum will be the best.

MRS. KLEIN: But that means tearing her away from us! I beg you, I pray you . . .

DOCTOR: It's no use praying to me: I'm not God. And, besides, in my opinion she ought to have been torn away from you long ago!

MRS. KLEIN: [*A little hysterically.*] But, in the asylum, so I've heard, the doctors do terrible things. Treatments. Treatments with ice-water . . . holding their heads underwater while they say grace . . . disciplining them, whipping them, whirling them round on a wheel, knocking them unconscious . . .

DOCTOR: Oh yes, and we roast them on a spit too.

[MRS. KLEIN *opens her mouth gaping wide and begins to shout, shouts like a fire siren, until the doctor grabs a ball of wool from the desk and pushes it into her mouth. The voice breaks off as if cut.*]

DOCTOR: Well. Now you can put that in your mouth and chew it . . . while we say grace.

[MRS. KLEIN *recovers her senses, takes the wool out of her mouth and hurls it on the floor.*]

MRS. KLEIN: How dare you . . . Phoo . . . Any sacrifice I'd have made, any, and you . . . you . . .

DOCTOR: You've already sacrificed your daughter. There'll be no dividends on sacrificing anything more.

MRS. KLEIN: [*Furiously tossing the garden in her hat.*] And you . . . after all this . . . you start abusing us . . . You've been insulting us the whole evening. I'll complain. I'll put in a serious complaint to the chief medical officer at the asylum!

DOCTOR: Please do. I myself am the chief medical officer at the asylum.

MRS. KLEIN: What brazen impudence! Gangula fofo . . . lanima skabba! Come along, Ernest. We've been swindled here! [*She takes her husband by the arm and tows him after her.*] I'll never set foot in this place again!

[*She exits in full sail and slams the door after her.*]

DOCTOR: [*Left alone.*] Let's hope so! Dreadful woman . . . An ogress. It's no wonder the girl hugged machines as a child: heating-stoves, mangles . . . Hm. Such a pretty and serious girl. And she set fire to her home. I understand it, I understand it! It's a protest against the foul institution she had to call home. The mother a sort of cactus, the father a sort of dog . . . a little spaniel, sniffing at the cactus . . . But rich as the devil. Leather he produces . . . straps, saddles, boots, glue—straps, saddles, boots, glue . . . And, as for himself, he's very much glued in his old woman's leather saddle. Got a proper old war-horse under him . . . Though, in the end, how do I know? How do I know who's riding whose neck. Last night I had another dream: that I was riding my wife . . . Then the roles reversed, and my wife was riding me . . . and then it was the other way round again . . . and so it'll go, till the earth convulses underneath us, and death knocks down the lot, horses, riders, both. Why, as a boy, couldn't I stay put in the saddle? . . . I didn't want to, that's why. Didn't want to learn those skills—those skills everyone's put to learning. Somehow I knew it was a symbol: for the life we've got's a great military academy. We're all riding our own horse, riding our own soul, riding it into the ground. That girl, she sent her horse flying out of the window . . . or how was it? . . . No, the horse went mad, jumped, its mane burning. "Burnt Orange." And now the burning's happened.

RECEPTIONIST: [*Enter, dressed for outdoors.*] A poor do that. Awful. In the ward she went completely crackers—completely off her rocker. We tried to feed her, and she screamed as if we were killing her: poured the soup under the bed. In the end they had to give her a dose of morphine. But, after all, it seems, Doctor, she was in love with you . . . How do you account for that?

DOCTOR: Because she didn't have anyone else.

RECEPTIONIST: There's a letter here for you.

DOCTOR: [*Taking it and reading the envelope.*] The Honourable Director Form. [*Opens it.*] She's inked a black surround on the paper.

RECEPTIONIST: Yes, first she asked if we had some mourning paper, as she was going to write a mourning letter. But when we didn't have any, she inked in the black surround herself.

DOCTOR: [*Reads aloud.*]

As dead leaves drop from a tree
souls drop into eternity.
So long it is since I heard
about my life from Mikael.
Instant love
your beard was so warm.
But the water's made of flowers.
Brook, flow back home.

[*Disturbed, the* DOCTOR *rubs his beard.*] Hm. Indeed.

RECEPTIONIST: I scolded her. I said she shouldn't be writing all this rubbish to the doctor: he's too busy for that. But she said "It's not me writing: it's the writing nerve, writing in me."

DOCTOR: No point in scolding if they're mentally ill. In a way she's right: it's automatic, whether it's talk or writing she's turning out. A patient of mine, every now and then, used to go off into terrible roaring fits—so bad I had to cover my ears. He had an explanation for them. They were "miraculous apparitions of bellowing." These poems are miraculous apparitions of writing. But those two lines are beautiful:

As dead leaves drop from a tree
souls drop into eternity.

You could imagine they were from some mystic's pen. In madness there's also a great deal of beauty.

RECEPTIONIST: As for beauty, I'd rather watch the sun setting than someone's brain setting.

DOCTOR: As you like. [*Quotes.*] "Schoenberg Scotus Schoenberg Tenriffa Sulaco Venafro Region of Mount Olympus."

RECEPTIONIST: What's all that?

DOCTOR: That was Hölderlin, a late poem by Hölderlin. And it goes on: "Jacca to Imperial Bacchus. Genua Larissa Syria." . . . Well, so how's the patient getting on now?

RECEPTIONIST: Who? Hölderlin?

DOCTOR: No. Miss Klein.

RECEPTIONIST: The injection did calm her, at least for tonight. I was able to talk with her a bit . . . though it was all airy fairy, up in the clouds. When I went and asked "How are you getting on, Miss Klein?" she said "I'm not Miss Klein, I'm Burnt Orange." When I said "You're not called Miss Klein, then?" she said "Marina Klein died in a fire a long time ago." I asked her how old she was, and she said "Not very old at all, I'm 28." "Then you've aged ten years in a day?" I said. She nodded seriously and said "Yes, perhaps. From sorrow." Then, getting a bit crafty, I said "If you're someone else, are there perhaps two of you—and what will your father and mother say about that?" She said "No, I'm alone, I've always been alone: I don't have a father and mother, and never have had." "Really?" I asked: "then what about Miss Klein's parents?" What she said about her mother I can't repeat. All she knew about Mr. Klein, she said, was that he produced leather stockings. When I asked her again if she wasn't the daughter of the Kleins, she said she wasn't anyone's daughter, and she had no memories, no past, only a present. She is Orange, born in Apokoinu. She'd been wrongfully brought here, and physical and metaphysical experiments were being carried out on her.

DOCTOR: Yes, that line of thinking's very common. But that she has no memories I don't really believe. She's spinning a yarn. I think why she started the fire was specifically to awaken memories. Nothing resuscitates memories like flames and smells. Well, please go on.

RECEPTIONIST: Then I asked where this place called Apokoinu was, and she said it was a leather town in the Far East—and she said proudly that when she gets married, ten master leather-workers'll be making shoes for her there from ten ox-hides. "Oh," I said, perhaps a bit more sharply than I should: "Oh, so you're going to dance away ten oxen at your wedding." That made her change again, and she said very sadly and earnestly: "Yes, all the animals die for us." And, like an idiot, I said: "Well, we're all under the same law of death, aren't we?" And I asked her what she thought about death, not in general, you know, but applying to herself.

DOCTOR: Well, and what did she say to that?

RECEPTIONIST: She thought a long time before she answered. Then she said: "Most people die; perhaps I shall too." Then I asked her what she thought of the other women who were with her in the room, and she said they'd lost their reason, at least most of them had. They'd been wronged for so long, they'd lost their reason. So I said, if she insisted they'd all been wronged, hadn't she best turn to God for redress. "Do you pray?" I asked. "I pray as I was taught," she said; "but there's no meaning in it, because the angel's died." I couldn't fathom what she was getting at, so I asked her again if she prayed, and she said again: "No, since he's dead."

DOCTOR: The angel means a horse she saw in a dream. She identifies herself powerfully with that horse.

RECEPTIONIST: Yes, now I remember: she also said: "We've all been higher beings once." "What kind of beings?" I asked. "Horses," she said. Then she turned in on herself, withdrew, and I couldn't get another word out of her.

DOCTOR: Yes, withdrew into her horse-soul. It's a sad case. Nothing much I can do for her now—just some cardiazol shocks.

RECEPTIONIST: Gosh. But they're dreadful, those: agonizing pains.

DOCTOR: [*Wearily.*] Do you think those thoughts of hers, and those feelings, aren't agonizing pains?

RECEPTIONIST: Well, no doubt the doctor knows best. [*Pause.*] I'm not so sure myself, though. [*She is about to go but adds.*] So that girl only got worse here, then—went stark raving mad?

DOCTOR: [*Shocked, resisting.*] The illness merely regressed to another . . . I mean . . . it went underground, to escape my scrutiny . . . [*With sudden contrition he continues more frankly and thoughtfully.*] I can try to probe ever lower, deeper, down to the root, find the root; but then I lose my conspectus on the whole. And the truth's not in the root: it's in the whole. That's why, in these things, we so often go wrong.

RECEPTIONIST: I see.

DOCTOR: Look: in a person, the softest and profoundest thing is the skin: it responds to everything. Science's big mistake is to split that delicate envelope and dissect the whole into separate bits. We know ever more and more about less and less. That's where science is going these days.

RECEPTIONIST: I think I know what it is, Doctor. You're feeling very dissatisfied with yourself.

DOCTOR: It may be so. [*More to himself than to the nurse.*] So many times I've regretted changing when I was young . . . Other people's thinking, it seemed to me, was leading nowhere, while I, myself, was making new discoveries—all the time. I threw myself in the grass, full length, and . . .

RECEPTIONIST: [*A little scornfully.*] And you saw the whole?

DOCTOR: No. I saw the grass. I understood trees. The water could speak at will. The world was close, in order, orderly. Now I've lost it. Then, I was a sort of combined botanist and artist. And I was happy. An artist, you see—he takes no more than a piece of skin or a flower from it all. And invariably he finds something. Psychologists—we lose exactly what we're looking for.

RECEPTIONIST: Mmmm. But artists are a flighty lot.

DOCTOR: Let them be; they see. We psychologists are moles. I wish I could put it properly, in a medieval way. I'd say: psychology's the Devil. Psychology's ruined the psyche, damned the soul.

RECEPTIONIST: [*Gruffly.*] What then? Maybe the girl'll recover without it. Give her some cardiazol.

DOCTOR: [*Dejectedly.*] Yes. So what. Cardiazol.

[*The* RECEPTIONIST *nods and exists.*]

DOCTOR: [*Flicks through his papers, speaks to himself.*] Take me! she begged—take me! Not in hints, not obscurely, but in agony, openly—as if her heart were crying out for a man, her constricted woman's heart. She hugged my legs, as she'd hugged that stove as a child . . . Could I still have got somewhere with psychology? Not all of them go mad by themselves: some are made mad. What if, fundamentally, she's a thoroughly healthy and ordinary girl?

[*He remains thinking, pen poised, while the following episode, the* DOCTOR's *fantasy, is shown concretely to the audience. The traditional-jazz piece, "High Society," heard during the girl's fantasy love-scene earlier, returns, and after a moment the girl dances onstage in her glowing dress, completely healthy, joyful, free. She laughs gaily, turns in front of the* DOCTOR *and disappears, exiting from where she entered. Everything in this "apparition" is flickeringly fast, the movements, and also the duration. Then the* DOCTOR *rises, throwing his pen on the desk.*]

DOCTOR: Sheer fantasy, the whole thing, impossible.

RECEPTIONIST: [*Enter once more, now dressed as a nurse.*] The Counsellor's wife left her umbrella in the hall.

DOCTOR: Take it to her, for God's sake, or she'll be back. Quick!

RECEPTIONIST: [*Looking at her dangling nurse's watch.*] She's hardly likely to come now: it's four in the morning.

DOCTOR: Really? But anyway, to be on the safe side. You never know. If she wants to come, it'll give her a pretext.

RECEPTIONIST: She must be fast asleep by now.

DOCTOR: Do take it, please. Leave it on the steps, or, damn it, anywhere. Please. I beg you— no, I order you.

[*She exits. He goes slowly to the window, opens it.*]

DOCTOR: And again it's morning, but so dark. And the flowers smell so lovely: some late variety . . . So there are scents here, in this leafy town . . . in every other house a garden, in every other one a well . . . how sweet. But, to the spirit, how inimical, how murky. It's as if the whole town were a sketch of perdition.

There she goes, that faithful soul, carrying the lady's umbrella. As if it were an oar . . . as if she were rowing through this scented dark . . . delicately as a gondolier. [*He whistles a fragment of a waltz.*] The Kleins' house is in darkness too . . . and the girl. She's now in another, a locked house, where all the doors lead inwards . . . A tidy closeted hell, behind seven locks, and seven more locks . . .

Cold it is now, the sky's so deep up there . . . [*The thin irregular creaking of a flock of geese comes, resembling the creaking of an unoiled cartwheel.*] What's all that creaking? Ah, wild geese, on the move . . . very high, very far up . . . Unless it's Auriga, the imaginary Charioteer, hurling on his way past the weary earth?

[*The scene darkens, and the creaking becomes ear-splitting, until it fades abruptly. Finally Paderevski's music, from, for example, his "Anaklasis."*]

[*End of Act Three.*]

[*Curtain.*]

Marguerite Duras (1914–96)

Modern French drama is famously rich and diverse. Beginning perhaps with the notorious opening of Alfred Jarry's *King Ubu* on December 11, 1896, it quickly exploded in a dozen different directions. Guillaume Apollinaire's exhilarating, avant-garde *The Breasts of Tiresias* (1917), Jean Cocteau's playfully surrealist dramas, and Tristan Tzara's Dadaist pieces were among the exciting experimental happenings that followed. They, in turn, anticipated the metaphysical plays of Sartre and Camus, the frothy comedies of Jean Giraudoux and Jean Anouilh, the absurdist plays of Eugène Ionesco and Samuel Beckett, and the rebelliousness of Jean Genet.

France also has a tradition of women writers equal to any culture's—beginning with Marie de France and Christine de Pisan in the Middle Ages and including Marguerite de Navarre and the Marquise de Lafayette in the Renaissance. But women—except onstage—were not a significant presence in the theater in France until recently. Modern feminism, so important and articulate a part of French literary and philosophical culture, came surprisingly late to France—and remains a charged notion. Women got the vote only in 1945.

Although Simone de Beauvoir had important precursors as far back as Olympe de Gouges and the women's clubs of the early Revolutionary period, her encyclopedic *Second Sex* (1949) is one of the monuments in the literature of feminism. Since its publication, French feminism, like French drama, has branched in a variety of directions. In the theater, women now occupy with men the top places as playwrights and directors in Paris. And sharing the pinnacle of French letters is Marguerite Duras.

Born in French Indochina, of parents who were economically marginal school teachers, Duras's childhood provided her with enough impressions to suffuse her sixty-three works of fiction, twenty films, and two dozen theatrical pieces. The exact biographical details remain obscure—and relatively unimportant—compared with the use (and reuse) to which she eloquently, passionately put them. The story of her widowed mother's battle to wall the sea out and protect her farmlands from flooding is the core of her first successful novel, *The Sea Wall* (*Un Barrage contre le Pacifique*, 1950). It reappears in shifting forms in her writings, most obviously in *Eden Cinema* (1977), where the barrier is also cultural. What Duras called her "Creole" status, being culturally "privileged," but economically distressed and exploited, growing up speaking both French and Vietnamese and moving off to Paris at about seventeen, but never feeling a part of French culture, provided the thematic content for her art.

Marguerite Duras, no date. (Courtesy of Editions Gallimard Photo Archives.)

As one of France's—and Europe's—leading twentieth-century writers, Duras has pursued a recognizable set of themes. She has routinely challenged the established notions of genres, impatient with their arbitrariness and untenability. In adapting and transplanting the same thematically related incidents, she has not simply teased at the tensions that exist, for example, between fiction and drama. Her deepest literary impulses are to explore the subjects of desire, love, loss, memory, time, observation, and reflection, subjects that are for her interconnected. Incidents become gateways to these explorations and evocations. For Duras, the place of the narrator and narration is central, effectively connecting all of her work, from interviews and memoirs to feature and documentary films to novels and dramas. Voices, which become her controlling focus, are often separated from the bodies we see onstage. They often speak from a different time period. The screenplay that brought her international acclaim and that is probably still her best known work, *Hiroshima, Mon Amour* (1959), exemplifies this—with its obsessive concern with love and desire, its insistence upon the inescapability of memory, and its reliance upon lyrical, emotive voice-overs. *The Lover (L'Amant),* for which Duras won France's most pretigious literary award, the Prix Goncourt, in 1984, exhibits the same concerns. Often Duras's narrations slip between first and third person, compounding the merging of past and present.

Duras turns away from the plots and actions and even the distinct characters of traditional drama. She relies on the theatrical potential of fantasy-like figures and voices, mined from her own experiences and reimagined. They reappear in different guises, always emphasizing her themes rather than individuated stories and existences. The seawall is a metaphor for the barriers that constrain us, barriers that separate people, simultaneously intensifying and deflecting desire. It also suggests divisions within individuals. Part of the glory of desire and sex is their attempt to merge two bodies; it is also part of their pain and frustration. To Duras, this dilemma is heightened in incest, where the closest, most desired body is the most taboo.

The title of *Eden Cinema* derives from a movie house near Saigon where Duras claims her mother accompanied silent films on the piano. The play's situation refers to her mother's attempt to use all of her savings to establish a rice plantation. The corrupt colonial administration sold her land that was worthless, and she went mad trying to wall the sea out. At the same time, the young Marguerite was encountering her Chinese lover and her intense feelings for both her brother and her mother. Out of this skeleton of past events, the mother's mad conflict with the sea and the daughter's impulsive desires, the play unfolds its figure of haunted loves, pained memories, and loss—climaxing in the image of the mother's dead body. The French homonyms (both feminine), *la mère* and *la mer* (mother and sea), reverberate across the stark world of the minimalist stage setting—a lit rectangle surrounded by space, with a great deal of offstage narration addressed at the essentially silent mother. Like Mr. Jo's brilliant but flawed diamond, the land, Suzanne, everything has a price, and nothing can ultimately be bought. In her tortured love for her children and the land, the mother knew nothing about "the fundamental injustice that reigns over the world's poor" nor how implacable were the tides of the Pacific. But the great sea's name is not without suggestiveness, as the tears of anger yield at the end to a relative calm or numbness—and we recall that the whole tale has been related after the fact. Desire, including Suzanne 's for her brother Joseph, followed by loss and separation, is the fundamental situation for Duras.

SELECTED BIBLIOGRAPHY IN ENGLISH

Gross, Janice Berkowitz. "Writing Across Purposes: The Theatre of Marguerite Duras and Nathalie Sarraute." *Modern Drama* 32 (1989), 39–47.

Harvey, Robert and Hélène Volat. *Marguerite Duras: A Bio-Bibliography.* Westport, Conn.: Greenwood, 1997.

Knapp, Bettina L., ed. *Critical Essays on Marguerite Duras.* New York: G. K. Hall, 1998.

Lydon, Mary. "*L'Eden Cinéma:* Aging and the Imagination in Marguerite Duras." *Memory and Desire: Aging—Literature—Psychoanalysis.* Eds. Kathleen Woodward and Murray M. Schwartz. Bloomington, Ind.: Indiana University Press, 1986. Pp. 154–67.

Miller, Judith Graves. "Contemporary Women's Voices in French Theatre." *Modern Drama* 32 (1989), 5–23.

Schuster, Marilyn R. *Marguerite Duras Revisited.* New York: Twayne, 1993.

Silva, Eurìdice Silva. "The Voice Beyond, Beyond the Voice: Ecriture et Théâtre in Marguerite Duras's *L'Eden Cinéma.*" *Romance Notes* 34 (1993), 3–12.

EDEN CINEMA

Marguerite Duras

Translated by Barbara Bray

CHARACTERS

THE MOTHER

SUZANNE

JOSEPH

MR. JO

THE CORPORAL

PART ONE

The stage is a large empty space surrounding another, rectangular, space. The rectangular space represents a bungalow, furnished with chairs and tables of a Colonial type. Very ordinary, very worn, very poverty-stricken furniture.

The empty space around the bungalow is the plain of Kam, in Upper Cambodia, between Siam and the sea.

Behind the bungalow there should be an area of light, representing the road used by hunters, which runs alongside the mountains of Siam.

It is a simple, large, decor, allowing the actors to move around freely and easily.

The MOTHER, SUZANNE, JOSEPH *and the* CORPORAL *come on, in front of the rectangular space.*

The MOTHER *sits on a low chair and the others group themselves around her. They all freeze and remain immobile, facing the audience, for perhaps thirty seconds while music is played.*

Then they talk of the MOTHER, *her past, her life. Of the love she inspired.*

The MOTHER *remains motionless in her chair expressionless, as if turned to stone, distant, separate—as is the stage—from her own story.*

The others touch her, stroke her arms, kiss her hands. She remains passive: what she represents in the play goes far beyond what she is and far beyond her own responsibility.

Everything that can be said in the play is said by SUZANNE *and* JOSEPH. *The* MOTHER—*the subject of the story—never speaks directly about herself.*

[*Music.*]

JOSEPH: Our mother was born in the North of France, between the mining country and the sea. She was born and raised in the endless plains of Northern Europe. More than a hundred years ago now.

[*Music.*]

SUZANNE: It's the year 1924. The purchase of the concession swallowed up every penny our mother had put in the savings bank in Saigon over ten years.

JOSEPH: The concession was a big one; four hundred acres, on the Western plain of Cambodia, beside the Elephant mountains, close to Siam.

SUZANNE: The first year the mother built the bungalow. And started to farm half of the land.

THE MOTHER: [*Speaking mechanically, as if unaware that she's speaking.*] The July tides come up over the plain and drown the harvest.

SUZANNE: [*As if reading.*] Half her savings were left. [*Pause.*] She started again.

THE MOTHER: [*Idem.*] The July tides come up over the plain again and drown the harvest.

[*Music.*]

SUZANNE: The Mother faces the facts: Her concession was unworkable. She had bought four hundred acres of salt marsh. She had thrown her savings into the waters of the Pacific.

[*Music.*]

[SUZANNE *and* JOSEPH *look at the* MOTHER, *so that their backs are to us and only the* MOTHER *is facing us. They put their arm around her as if she was suffering. The* MOTHER, *still far away, listens to the strange story being told by her children. Her own story.*]

JOSEPH: [*Lovingly, sweetly.*] She didn't know. Didn't know anything.

THE MOTHER: It's true, I knew nothing.

SUZANNE: She emerged from the darkness of the Eden Cinema not knowing anything. Not knowing anything about the great vampire of colonialism. About the fundamental injustice that reigns over the world's poor.

[*Music.*]

JOSEPH: [*With great tenderness.*] She found out too late.

SUZANNE: [*Smiling.*] She never found out.

THE MOTHER: [*Smiling.*] No, I never did.

JOSEPH: [*Reciting flatly, as if reading out some unintelligible decree.*] To get a fertile concession, then, in French Indochina, you had to pay twice.

[*Pause.*]

Once, openly, to the Colonial Authorities. . . . And then again, under the counter, to the officials of the Land Commission.

[*Silence.*]

THE MOTHER: Nothing would grow in the plain. The plain didn't exist. It was part of the Pacific. It was salt water; a plain of salt water.

[*Pause.*]

You couldn't tell where the Pacific began, or where the plain ended, between the sea and the sky. It was sold. And it was bought.

[*Music.*]

JOSEPH: The whites who stayed on in the plain made a living by smuggling opium and Pernod. Some were dead. Others had been repatriated. She, she knew nothing about all that.

THE MOTHER: No, I knew nothing about all that.

SUZANNE: So the Mother had nothing left. Nothing but her widow's pension and her teacher's pension from the Colonial Service.

[*They turn to the* MOTHER.]

So, what did she do?

[*They smile at the* MOTHER: *she looks at them and waits for a reply.*]

JOSEPH: As she couldn't move men, she attacked the tides of the Pacific.

[*Loud music, very loud.*]

[*Silent, rapturous laughter from the two children. (What remains to be told is above all the story of the mother's folly. The injustice of which she was the victim is taken for granted.)*]

[*The laughter stops. Close attention is paid to the terrible story.*]

SUZANNE: She mortgages her bungalow. She sells her furniture. And then, she builds sea-walls to hold back the tides of the Pacific Ocean.

[*Music at some length.*]

JOSEPH: The sea-walls consisted of piled-up sand and wood. They should have held out for a century. She was sure they would. Her method was the best.

[*Music.*]

SUZANNE: The peasants were just as hopeful as she was. The children dying of hunger, the harvests burned by salt, no, that couldn't go on for ever. They believed her.

[*Music.*]

The children would die no longer. There would be no more hunger. No more cholera.

[*Music.*]

JOSEPH: The work began in the dry season. It took three months. The Mother went out with the peasants at dawn and came back at nightfall.

[*Music at some length, full and strong like hope itself. Then fading away.*]

THE MOTHER: [*Idem.*] Then with the high tides the sea came up and attacked the plain. The sea-walls weren't strong enough. In one night they were swept away.

[*The* MOTHER *has been listening to her own voice, trying to remember.*]

JOSEPH: Many of the peasants went away, on junks, to other parts of the Pacific.

SUZANNE: The rest remained in the plain. So the children went on dying. No one blamed the Mother for having hoped.

[*Music.*]

[SUZANNE *closes her eyes.*]

The children went back to the mud of the rice fields, to the land of the wild mountain mangoes.

[*They get up. Remain standing. The* MOTHER *gets up too—as if obeying: remains standing near her children.*]

[*Music.*]

It is the year 1931. I'm sixteen. Joseph is nineteen. We still have the Corporal. He's deaf. We've stopped paying his wages. He stays. He loves the Mother very much.

JOSEPH: The place is called Prey-Nop. The name's on the Ordinance Survey maps. Prey-Nop. A village of forty huts. Eighty kilometers from Kampot, the last white outpost between there and Siam. Kampot.

[*Music.*]

SUZANNE: The sea is not so far. Thirty kilometers away from the gulf of Siam. There are islands; and on the islands fishing villages. The forest skirts the sea and the road. It has overflowed onto the islands. It is full of danger. It looms up in front of the bungalow every evening, in front of Joseph, my little brother, who hunts tigers. Our mother is afraid.

[*Music.*]

JOSEPH: It's there that we were young. There that the Mother lived her greatest hope. There she died.

[*Music. Silence.*]

[*They all get up. The* MOTHER *and the children, and the* CORPORAL. *Slowly, in time with the music, they separate and walk towards the rectangular space.*]

[*The children go in one direction. The* CORPORAL *in another. The* MOTHER *remains alone in front of the rectangular space. The music is fading all the while. She waits motionless for the sound effects to emerge: the noises of night and the plain.*]

[*Then, children's cries, laughter, dogs barking, drums. The crack of a whip. And* JOSEPH *shouting through the noises of the plain. Then the rectangular space lights up with a white light and the* MOTHER *is released and goes into the light, alone, adult. She walks to and fro and then leans against one of the posts supporting the bungalow. She looks towards where the horse should be. From the other direction come* SUZANNE *and the* CORPORAL *who also stop and look towards where the horse should be.*]

SUZANNE'S VOICE: It was a week since we'd bought the horse and cart, and Joseph had been using it to drive the peasants from Prey-Nop to Réam and back.

[SUZANNE, *from a distance, turns towards the* MOTHER.]

I remember her that evening: she is wearing her red silk dress, worn threadbare over the breasts. When she washes it she goes to bed and sleeps till it is dry. She is barefoot. She looks at the horse. She starts to cry. [*Pause.*] She weeps.

JOSEPH: The horse didn't move. I dragged it over the rice field. It tried to eat, then gave up. They'd lied to us about its age. The sun was sinking. I knew the Mother was watching the horse.

SUZANNE'S VOICE: She was already very ill. She couldn't speak now without screaming. Sometimes she'd go into a coma that lasted several hours. Out of fury, the doctor said. Since the sea-walls collapsed.

JOSEPH: I too see the Mother.

[*Pause.*]

She is going to get a blanket and a rice cake and give them to the horse.

[*We see what is being described enacted: the* MOTHER *goes out with the blanket and the rice.*]

[*Silence.*]

JOSEPH: She shouts that the horse is dying. That it's spent its life dragging great logs from the forest to the plain. She says it's like her. It wants to die. It's dead.

[*The* MOTHER *drops the blanket and the rice. Stands still. Then crosses the rectangular space, sits down in a wicker chair, looks out.* SUZANNE *reappears near the bungalow. Looks at the* MOTHER. *Then her attention wanders, she sits down on the ground, idle. Music.* JOSEPH *comes up to her.*]

SUZANNE'S VOICE: Night falls quickly. It always frightens me. Before dark, we bathe in the river, Joseph and I. Joseph makes me go into the water.

[*Pause.*]

I'm frightened. The river comes down from the mountain. In the rainy season drowned animals come down with the current, birds, musk-rats, deer. Once, a tiger.

[*Pause.*]

Joseph plays with the children of Prey-Nop. He sits them on his shoulders and swims. In the distance the Mother shouts.

[*We hear other cries as well as the* MOTHER's. *Then they all die away.*]

JOSEPH: She wears herself out shouting.
Then she doesn't shout so much.
Then she doesn't shout at all.

SUZANNE'S VOICE: Then the sun goes down behind the mountains. The peasants light fires to keep off the tigers. The children go into the huts.

[*Pause.*]

I remember it: the smell of fire rising up out of all the plain. It's everywhere. Under the sky, the road, white, with dust. On the mountainside, the green squares of Chinese pepper-trees. Above them the haze from the fires. The jungle. And then the sky.

[*Music.*]

SUZANNE: Already we were thinking of leaving the Mother. Of leaving the plain.

[*Sounds from the plain.*]

JOSEPH: Leaving the sea breeze, the smell of the islands, the sour smell of fish pickling in brine, the smell of the marshes, the smell of the fires.

[*Distant drums: sounds of the plain.*]

SUZANNE: Already we'd begun to think it would be better if she died.

[JOSEPH *and* SUZANNE, *as children, come back.*]

[*Silence.*]

[*No music.*]

[*Only the noises of the plain. The light fades.*]

[*A multitude of children's shouts and laughter.*]

[SUZANNE *and* JOSEPH *go into the bungalow.*]

[*Disappear inside.*]

[*Reappear.* SUZANNE *comes from the veranda.*]

[*She starts up a gramophone.*]

[JOSEPH *comes back with a gun. Sits down and cleans it. Tests an acetylene lamp, his bunting lamp.* SUZANNE *watches him. Looks out on to the plain. The record she's put on is the play's theme-song: the waltz from the Eden Cinema—as if their lives still revolved around it.*]

[*The* MOTHER *comes and goes.*]

[*Lays the table: two plates, the children's.*]

[*Brings the steaming food to the table. The children look at it with disgust. The* MOTHER *looks at the children. The* CORPORAL *comes in with hot rice, puts it on the table: then sits in a corner and looks at the* MOTHER.]

[*Nobody eats.*]

Then Joseph suggested we all go to Réam to cheer ourselves after the death of the horse.

[*Slowly they get ready to go to Réam.*]

[*The* MOTHER *does her hair up in a bun.*]

[SUZANNE, JOSEPH *and the* MOTHER *put shoes on.*]

[*The* CORPORAL *goes out and comes back with a watering-can.*]

[*Music throughout these preparations.*]

SUZANNE'S VOICE: Réam was the port at the end of the road, used by coastal traffic taking pickled fish and pepper to Bangkok. On their return voyage the boats smuggled in Pernod and opium.

JOSEPH: There was a sort of Bar at Réam. There was dancing there in the evenings. And sometimes there were sailors on shore leave, Merchant Navy officers, and white prostitutes who went back and forth between Siam and Indochina.

[*Distant music.*]

[*They go out, one after the other, through the back of the house.*]

[*Music increasingly insistent.*]

[*The light fades after they leave the bungalow. The bungalow is left in darkness.*]

[*Then the music fades as a mauve light fades up the front of the stage.*]

[*And they reappear.*]

[*The four of them together, walking round the stage as a whole in time to the waltz. They smile. They walk together, or, if preferred, they dance as they walk towards Réam, all equally young and full of excitement.*]

[*Violent music.*]

[*They have fallen out of step. They dance, move apart, come together, freely, in different patterns. The* MOTHER *and the* CORPORAL *are in time with one another. They turn off, disappear, come back. All of them are deeply childlike. The most obvious thing about them is their pleasure. As they walk,* SUZANNE'S *voice speaks.*]

SUZANNE'S VOICE: Ah! The road between Réam and the sea. How beautiful it seemed to me.

[*Pause.*]

It had been built by prisoners. Chained together. But how beautiful it seemed to me. It was the road by which we'd leave the Mother. By which we'd go away, Joseph and I. A hunter would stop and take us away with him. A day. A day would come. Every day I sat by the side of the road. Watching them go by. A day would come. He'd be young. Joseph's age. A hunter.

[*Loud music without any words. Then it softens.*]

I can see it all: the hunter stops in front of the bungalow. A burst tyre. And Joseph helps him to change it. I can see her, too, the woman with the hunter: she's a platinum blonde, she smokes Player's 555, she is very made-up, very white. She is for Joseph. I take her and give her to Joseph. How I loved him, my quiet, wild little brother.

When he was fourteen, he went hunting panthers by the estuary, in broad sunlight. I remember, the Mother saying he would be the death of her. He came back at night, with the dead panther in the prow of his boat. I started crying. He said the next time he'd take me with him.

[*Music.*]

Together we'll leave the Mother. Together we'll leave her behind. On the plain, alone with her madness.

[*Music.*]

Without warning, while she's having her afternoon nap. She wakes up. She calls us. There's no one left to answer, no children left in the plain. She cooks the meal. There's no one left to eat it. The plain is empty. The Mother will be punished. For having loved us.

[*Silence. Then music. Then the music gradually fades. They all stand still, their backs to the audience, waiting outside the unlit Bar (which is, of course, the same rectangular area as the bungalow). Then they go in. SUZANNE's voice goes on in the dark.*]

That evening, there was a big black car in the yard outside the Bar in Réam. Inside it, waiting, sat a uniformed chauffeur.

[*Music.*]

[*The bar lights up.*]

[*Electric lighting: naked bulbs, a reddish, gloomy light. When the bar is fully lit the characters are already seated, motionless, frozen in the loud music and light. A powerful image. In the centre of the acting area is MR. JO, dressed in white with a diamond ring on his finger and very strongly lit. The others are in shadow, looking at him. Except for SUZANNE. MR. JO looks at her.*]

Mr. Jo was rich.

Mr. Jo's father had bought up the Red Lands plantations in North Cambodia during the rubber crisis, ten years before. Now he was re-selling them at exorbitant prices to foreign companies. The sole heir of this immense fortune was there that evening in Réam.

[*Music.*]

The diamond on his left hand was enormous.

[*Pause.*]

His suit was made of Chinese silk—tailored in Paris. The car was magnificent. He was alone. A millionaire. And he was looking at me.

[*Pause. Music. Scene without words: The MOTHER catches MR. JO looking at her daughter. She starts looking at her too. And the daughter is smiling at the heir to the Northern Plantations. Silently, the CORPORAL comes in and crouches on the floor. The MOTHER and the CORPORAL look at SUZANNE smiling at the son of the owner of the plantations. Not JOSEPH. JOSEPH looks down at the floor.*]

[*Champagne is served at the tables.*]

[*Loud music, then it fades.*]

I knew the Mother was frightened of dying while we were still so young. I understood my mother's glance. I smiled at the planter from the North.

[*Pause.*]

It was my first prostitution.

[*Silence. Music, but soft. (The music must never interfere with the spoken words.)*]

[*MR. JO rises and bows to the MOTHER.*]

[*The MOTHER makes as if to get up.*]

THE MOTHER: [*Very softly.*] But, of course . . . Please do . . .

[*MR. JO goes over and asks SUZANNE to dance.*]

[*They dance.*]

[*The MOTHER watches. Not JOSEPH. Perhaps JOSEPH is looking out at the harbour to avoid looking at SUZANNE. A slow conversation starts up between MR. JO and SUZANNE.*]

MR. JO: [*In a soft, distinguished voice.*] Do you live round here?

SUZANNE: Yes.

[*Pause.*]

Is that your car in the yard?

MR. JO: Yes.

[*Pause.*]

Would you do me the honour of introducing me to your mother?

SUZANNE: Yes.

[*Pause.*]

What make is it?

MR. JO: A Morris Léon Bollée. [*Pause.*] My favourite make. [*Pause.*] Are you keen on cars, then?

SUZANNE: Yes. [*Pause.*] What horse-power is it?

MR. JO: Twenty-four I think.

SUZANNE: [*Pause.*] How much does a car like that cost?

MR. JO: [*Hesitant.*] About fifty-thousand piastres, I think.

[SUZANNE *stops dancing for a few seconds and looks at* MR. JO.]

SUZANNE: That's incredible.

MR. JO: [*Surprised.*] It's because it's a special model.

[*No reply from* SUZANNE *who becomes pensive.*]

[JOSEPH *stops looking out at the barbour. He looks at his sister. They look at each other. The* MOTHER *sees them. She's as if dazzled by* MR. JO *and disturbed by the look between* JOSEPH *and* SUZANNE.]

MR. JO: I'm here to supervise the loading of a cargo of latex . . .

[*No reply from* SUZANNE.]

A pretty girl like you must get bored here on this plain . . . You're so young.

[*No answer from* SUZANNE.]

[*Loud music. They dance without speaking for a while.*]

[MR. JO *is a good dancer.* SUZANNE *is preoccupied.*]

[*The dance ends. The music starts up again at once.*]

[MR. JO *and* SUZANNE *go over to the* MOTHER*'s table.*]

[*The* MOTHER *rises to greet* MR. JO.]

[JOSEPH *remains seated.* MR. JO *sits down. Then* SUZANNE.]

[*So they are all seated. There's champagne on the table, in front of them. They talk.* SUZANNE *speaks first.*]

SUZANNE: [*To* JOSEPH *in a rush.*] He's got a Morris Léon Bollée.

MR. JO: I've got a sports car that I like better.

SUZANNE: Twenty-four horse-power.

JOSEPH: How many litres to the hundred kilometers?

SUZANNE: How many?

MR. JO: Seventeen. In traffic, twenty.

JOSEPH: Does it hold the road well?

MR. JO: Yes. It does eighty like a bird. In the other one I can do a hundred easily.

SUZANNE: It's worth fifty-thousand piastres.

THE MOTHER: [*Thinking she's misheard.*] What?

MR. JO: [*In the same even tone.*] What kind do you have?

[*They look at each other without answering.*]

THE MOTHER: [*Pause.*] Our's a Citroën.

MR. JO: Yes, you get more mileage out of a Citroën. And with a road like that . . .

[JOSEPH *and* SUZANNE *burst out laughing.*]

JOSEPH: A hundred kilometers for twenty-four litres: that's what ours does.

MR. JO: Really?

JOSEPH: Instead of twelve . . . But then the carburettor's full of holes.

[*The* MOTHER *catches the children's laughter.*]

SUZANNE: If that was all it'd be nothing . . . if it was only the carburettor . . . But there's the radiator too . . .

[*Another outburst of laughter.*]

[MR. JO *smiles, disconcerted.*]

JOSEPH: It's a record . . . Fifty litres to the hundred kilometers.

THE MOTHER: [*Repeats.*] Fifty litres to the hundred kilometers.

JOSEPH: [*Taking up* SUZANNE'*s joke.*] If that was all it wouldn't be so bad . . . If it was only the carburettor and the radiator . . .

[*They all wait. Then an uncontrollable outburst of laughter.*]

But there are the tyres . . . guess what our tyres are filled with . . .

[*Climax of laughter.*]

Banana leaves . . . We stuff them with banana leaves.

[MR. JO *waits for the laughter to subside.*]

MR. JO: It's certainly original . . . It's a scream, as they say in Paris.

[*No one pays any attention to him. They go on.*]

JOSEPH: When we start out on a trip, we tie the Corporal onto the mudguard with a watering-can . . .

[*The three of them start laughing again.*]

SUZANNE: And put a hunting lamp on the front. Because as for our lights . . . Well, they haven't worked for ten years . . .

[*A pause in the laughter. Then they start up again.*]

JOSEPH: And if it was only that . . . If it was only the car . . . But there were the sea-walls too . . . The sea-walls . . .

[*He can't talk any more he's laughing so much.*]

[*Shrieks of laughter from the* MOTHER *and* SUZANNE.]

The story of our sea-walls . . . It's enough to make you die laughing . . .

[*Laughter. More laughter.* MR. JO *is stupefied.*]

We thought we could do it. Yes . . . We wanted [*Pause.*] We wanted to hold back the Pacific.

MR. JO: And why would you want to hold back the Pacific? [*Pause as he remembers something.*] Oh! yes . . . yes, I heard about it . . . The sea-walls. [*Pause.*] You were unlucky . . . A rotten piece of land . . .

JOSEPH: Yes . . . That's it . . . [*He points to the* MOTHER.] She didn't know.

THE MOTHER: [*As if apologising.*] I didn't know.

SUZANNE: She didn't know anything. Not a thing.

JOSEPH: She wanted to hold back the Pacific . . . She thought she could.

SUZANNE: She still thinks she can.

JOSEPH: It's true. Look at her. She still thinks it can be done.

[*They look at the* MOTHER. *The* MOTHER *looks somewhere else. Remains silent.*]

SUZANNE: [*Dreamily.*] She must be a bit mad. [*Pause.*] We must all be a bit mad.

JOSEPH: [*Pointing to the* MOTHER.] *She* is. She's quite mad.

[*Suddenly the* MOTHER *looks frightened.* JOSEPH *goes on looking at her, then bursts out laughing again.* SUZANNE *does the same. And then the* MOTHER *too. The three of them are laughing at her, at her madness. The children repeat.*]

JOSEPH AND SUZANNE: . . . quite mad . . . quite mad . . . [*They go on saying this.*]

[*The laughter stops. The music begins again, softly. The lights start to dim.* MR. JO *looks at* SUZANNE. JOSEPH *and* SUZANNE *are silent. Music.* MR. JO *offers* JOSEPH *a cigar.* JOSEPH *smokes it. The* MOTHER *is silent and half asleep.*]

MR. JO: Can I see you again?

SUZANNE: We live in the bungalow on the left of the Kampot road. At kilometre 184.

[*End of this scene.*]

[*The lights grow very dim inside the bar.*]

[*They all fall silent.* SUZANNE'S *story continues.*]

SUZANNE'S VOICE: And so we got into the habit of letting Mr. Jo drive us into Réam. We liked riding in his car. [*Pause.*] It went on for a month. It cost us nothing. We drank champagne every night. We used to come home late. Our mother used to go to sleep in the Morris Léon Bollée on the way home. It was my first affair. It was just as much Joseph's and my mother's affair really.

[*Pause.*]

[*The light changes as* SUZANNE *speaks, the exterior becoming brightly lit, while the Bar-space grows dark.* SUZANNE *takes up her story again.*]

He used to come in the afternoon, long before it was time to go to Réam.

[*Pause.*]

We used to stay in the bungalow, he and I.

[*The bungalow lights up. Strong light matching sunlight outside.*]

[MR. JO *and* SUZANNE *are sitting there alone.*]

[*Again, the only difference between the bar and the bungalow resides in the lighting.*]

[*The same wicker chairs, the same table, the same view (of the mountain).*]

[*Slowly the* MOTHER *and the* CORPORAL *cross the empty space behind the bungalow.*]

[*The* CORPORAL *is carrying gardening tools.* THE MOTHER *wears a straw hat. They vanish.*]

They're weeding round the banana trees. I don't know what Joseph is doing.

[SUZANNE *gets up and goes to the gramophone.*]

[*Silence.*]

[*She winds up the gramophone. Puts on a record.*]

[*Music. The Eden Cinema Waltz.*]

Mr. Jo had no choice. Either he never saw me alone, ever; or else he married me. The Mother had said: marriage or nothing. She was full of hope. Sometimes I went to sleep. Then I'd wake up, and find Mr. Jo just where he'd been before, always under the Mother's eye.

[*Pause.*]

Joseph had said so too: marriage or nothing.

[*Music. The next scene is between the actors.*]

MR. JO: That's a very old gramophone.

SUZANNE: It's Joseph's. My mother bought it for him when she was at the Eden Cinema.

[*She turns towards the audience but without changing her position.*]

You've already given me a blue dress, a compact, some nail varnish and lipstick, some expensive soap and beauty creams.

MR. JO: It's a very old model. I know something about gramophones. I've got an electric one at home. I brought it back from Paris.

SUZANNE: Your electric gramophone's all right when there's electricity. There isn't any here.

MR. JO: There are battery operated just as good as electric ones.

SUZANNE: Oh!

[*Silence and music.*]

MR. JO: Suzanne . . . My little Suzanne . . . It's agony . . . Being so near to you and yet so far . . .

[SUZANNE *starts unfastening her dress.*]

[*Music.* SUZANNE *stops undressing.*]

[SUZANNE *goes on undressing.*]

[MR. JO *gets up, comes over to her, then stops.*]

[*In the distance, in the doorway, we see the* MOTHER, *who stops and looks.*]

[MR. JO *goes outside.* SUZANNE *remains alone for a while.*]

[*She looks suddenly exhausted, gloomy. She does up her dress. In the distance is the* MOTHER, *motionless.*]

[MR. JO *comes back; he is followed by the* CORPORAL *carrying a huge parcel. They both go right round the bungalow, first on the roadside, then on the side where the audience is.*]

[*Then* JOSEPH *arrives.*]

[JOSEPH *and the* MOTHER *look at each other.*]

[*The* CORPORAL *puts the package on the table.*]

[*Everyone stands still and silent around the package.*]

SUZANNE'S VOICE: Nothing new had come to the plain for six years.

MR. JO: It's a gramophone. I'm like that. I keep my word. I hope you'll get to know me.

[MR. JO *goes over to the gramophone and starts to untie the strings.*]

[SUZANNE *signs to him to stop.*]

SUZANNE: We must wait for them.

[*The* CORPORAL *has squatted down inside the room; he's waiting too.*]

[MR. JO *looks outside, sees the* MOTHER *and* JOSEPH *standing, watching, and sits down. Then slowly* SUZANNE *turns towards the* MOTHER *and* JOSEPH *and gives them a long, loving smile.*]

SUZANNE'S VOICE: The gramophone was the price of MR. JO being allowed to look at me. I was giving it to Joseph, my brother, my little, since-dead, brother. How I loved him. Mr. Jo stood there crying.

MR. JO: I love you so much. I don't know what's happening to me. I've never felt like this before about anyone.

SUZANNE: Don't say anything to *them*.

[*Pause.*]

[JOSEPH *and the* MOTHER *enter the room.*]

When they ask what it is, I'll tell them.

MR. JO: I mean nothing to you, less than nothing.

[*The* MOTHER *and* JOSEPH *walk around the package as if it wasn't there. The* MOTHER *sits down.* JOSEPH *goes out of the bungalow to have a shower. The* CORPORAL *waits outside the bungalow, now, facing the audience.*]

[*The* MOTHER *talks about the* CORPORAL *to avoid talking about the package.*]

THE MOTHER: He's getting deafer and deafer.

MR. JO: I could never make out why you ever hired a deaf man. It's not as if labour was scarce around here.

[*The* MOTHER *doesn't answer.*]

[*She sits down.*]

[*Distant music. The package is still on the table.*]

[*Enormous. Invisible.*]

THE MOTHER: [*To* MR. JO.] You can stay to dinner if you'd like.

MR. JO: [*Startled.*] Thank you very much, there's nothing I'd like better . . .

SUZANNE: There's nothing to eat; always the same old wader-birds (Heron), they smell of fish and make you want to throw up. There's never anything else.

THE MOTHER: It's very nourishing.

MR. JO: You don't know me, I have very simple tastes.

[*We hear the sound of running water.*]

[JOSEPH *having a shower.*]

[*The* CORPORAL *has been gone for some time. He comes back with a dish of steaming rice. Puts it on the table beside the dish of wader-bird.*]

[JOSEPH *comes out of the shower. Into the room.*]

[*Sees the dishes.*]

[*Everyone is motionless around the package.*]

[*At last* SUZANNE *speaks.*]

SUZANNE: It's a gramophone.

JOSEPH: We've got a gramophone already.

MR. JO: This is more up to date.

[SUZANNE *opens the package.*]

[*The gramophone emerges. She shows it to* JOSEPH, *who winds it up. And, in front of* MR. JO, *questions* SUZANNE.]

JOSEPH: Did you ask him for it?

SUZANNE: No.

JOSEPH: Why did he give it to you?

SUZANNE: [*Looking at* MR. JO.] I don't know.

SUZANNE: [*To* MR. JO.] Why did you give it to me?

[MR. JO *starts to cry, and doesn't answer.*]

[JOSEPH *puts on a record we already know: the Eden Cinema Waltz.*]

[*The old theme emerges more clear, more perfect.*]

[MR. JO *is still crying.*]

[*And the miracle happens.*]

[JOSEPH *and* SUZANNE *dance together.*]

[*The mother watches them, enchanted.*]

[*The* CORPORAL *watches them too.*]

[*The dance becomes like something inherited by them both: they dance together like one body.*]

[*Night falls.*]

SUZANNE'S VOICE: For us it was the most beautiful thing we'd ever heard. That music. The Eden Cinema Waltz. Everything became clear: When we went away, we'd be singing that tune.

[*They dance.*]

THE MOTHER: [*To* MR. JO.] At least I've got two beautiful children. Look at them. They're very alike I think.

[*They go on dancing.*]

SUZANNE'S VOICE: That tune was the song of her death. Born of our longing for fabulous cities. Born of our impatience. Of our ingratitude. Of my love for my brother. The mother watched us. She was suddenly old. We were dancing on her dead body.

[*Music. And the dance goes on.*]

THE MOTHER: [*To* MR. JO.] If I were you, I'd marry her. Look at her.

MR. JO: She's so young . . . It's terrible. My feelings for her are so strong.

THE MOTHER: [*Gently.*] I believe you. I believe it.

[*Pause.*]

I suppose it's your father who's against it?

MR. JO: [*Prevaricating.*] It takes more than a fortnight to decide about getting married.

THE MOTHER: [*Still gentle.*] Yes. In certain cases.

[*Pause.*]

I'm going to die, you see. So I need to have my mind at rest about what's going to become of my little girl.

[*The bungalow slowly darkens, while the stage outside—the area representing the road, etc.—grows lighter.*]

[*The characters leave the stage in the darkness.*]

[*The scene changes with the music and the light.*]

[*Distant shouts.*]

[*We discover* MR. JO *and* SUZANNE *sitting outside the bungalow.*]

[*She is wearing a blue dress.*]

[*She is inexpertly made-up. She is doing her nails.*]

[MR. JO *is watching. The* MOTHER *is inside the bungalow.*]

[*She paces to and fro and looks—towards the audience—at* SUZANNE *and* MR. JO.]

[*Then she goes towards the transparency at the back, where the road is supposed to be.*]

[*There the* CORPORAL *is laying plants in the ground.*]

SUZANNE: You've damaged the bridge. You should leave the car on the road.

[*Stricken silence from* MR. JO.]

She won't let us stay in the bungalow any more. We have to stay outside.

[*Music.*]

What kind of car shall I have when we're married?

MR. JO: If we did get married. I think I'd be terribly unhappy. I can't think what to do to make you love me.

SUZANNE: [*Taking up where she left off.*] What kind of car?

MR. JO: A white Lancia. I've already told you . . .

SUZANNE: And Joseph?

MR. JO: I don't know that I'll give Joseph a car . . . I can't promise.

[SUZANNE *is silent.* MR. JO's *frightened.*]

[*Music throughout.*]

It depends on you, as you well know. On how you treat me.

SUZANNE: [*Gently.*] You could give my mother a car, it would be the same thing: he could drive it.

MR. JO: [*In despair.*] But there's never been any question of giving your mother a car. I'm not as rich as you seem to think.

SUZANNE: [*Very calm.*] If Joseph doesn't get a car, you can keep all your Lancias and marry whomever you please.

[MR. JO *turns to* SUZANNE.]

MR. JO: [*Imploring.*] You know quite well Joseph will get his car. You're turning me into someone horrible.

[MR. JO *takes* SUZANNE's *hand in his and kisses it.*]

[JOSEPH *has appeared behind the transparency. He's helping the* CORPORAL *mend the bridge.*]

[*The* MOTHER *joins them.*]

[SUZANNE *looks down at the ground.*]

SUZANNE'S VOICE: The day before he had promised me a diamond ring if I'd go with him on a trip to the city. He told me that the diamond was at his place and that he was waiting for me to make up my mind before he brought it.

[SUZANNE *leans her head on her arm while we hear her voice.*]

I asked how much it was worth: he didn't say exactly, but he did say it was worth more than the cost of the bungalow.

[*Music. Silence.*]

I tried to work out how to get the diamond, how to get it out here on the plain, how to get it to my mother.

[*Music or silence.*]

[MR. JO *looks at* SUZANNE.]

[*The* MOTHER *watches both of them.*]

MR. JO: You're so lovely. [*Pause.*] And so desirable.

SUZANNE: I'll be lovelier when I'm older.

MR. JO: When I've taken you away from here you'll leave me: I'm sure of it.

[MR. JO *looks crushed beneath the weight of his desire.*]

SUZANNE'S VOICE: He'd said he was staying on out here to supervise, overseeing the loading of the latex at Réam. But I knew he was trying to get the better of his father.

[*Music.*]

He'd said: "Three days. Three days in the city. I won't touch you. We'll go to the cinema."

[*Music.*]

[JOSEPH *roams round the couple. Crosses the front of the stage, goes out in the direction of the* MOTHER. *The* MOTHER *comes back towards the house, enters it and sits down.*]

[*She wipes her forehead.*]

[JOSEPH *and* SUZANNE *observe her.*]

We were always afraid she'd die. Always. Every minute. One diamond worth the whole bungalow.

[SUZANNE *leaves* MR. JO, *goes into the bungalow and towards the* MOTHER. *She lifts her mother's feet onto a stool. Then goes out and comes back with a glass of water and some pills. The* MOTHER *is passive. Takes the pills. Drinks the water. Distant sound of running water:* JOSEPH *having a shower.* MR. JO *moves forward and, with the audience, looks at the* MOTHER *and* SUZANNE *and their silent, fierce relationship.* SUZANNE *goes out again, comes back with a damp cloth which she puts on the* MOTHER'S *forehead. Then she crouches beside the chair and starts fanning the* MOTHER. *The* MOTHER *starts to drowse, lulled by the regular movement. Quieter now, the* MOTHER *looks like a child.* SUZANNE *doesn't flinch. They speak to each other plainly, roughly.*]

THE MOTHER: Have you spoken to him about it?
SUZANNE: I speak to him about it all the time.

[*Pause.*]

It's his father. He wants his son to marry someone rich.
THE MOTHER: Oh!
SUZANNE: I don't think he's even mentioned me to his father yet.

[*Pause.*]

But he'd gladly just go off with me.
THE MOTHER: What do you mean?

[*Then she understands without being told.*]

No.

[*Pause. She pulls herself together.*]

And what do you want?
SUZANNE: [*Pause.*] Me? I want to stay with Joseph.

[*The* MOTHER *considers, muttering to herself.*]

THE MOTHER: Joseph . . . Always Joseph.

[*Pause.*]

How old are you now? I forget.
SUZANNE: Sixteen.
THE MOTHER: [*Groans.*] Sixteen . . . My god . . . My god.

[*Silence.*]

[JOSEPH *comes in. It looks as if he's been listening.*]

[*Silence. Then the* MOTHER *speaks.*]

He's not going to marry her.
JOSEPH: Then, he'd better not come back any more.

[*Silence or music.*]

[JOSEPH *goes out.*]

SUZANNE'S VOICE: I didn't mention the diamond. I was afraid of what she'd say. Just to hear what it was worth would have been enough to kill her.

[*Silence.*]

[*The* MOTHER *falls asleep.*]

[SUZANNE *goes back to the strip of land in front of the bungalow. Which lights up. With a white light. It's still early. The sun hasn't reached the mountain.* SUZANNE *sits down by* MR. JO *and looks around her. In the distance, inside the bungalow, the* MOTHER *is sleeping: the sleeping* MOTHER *is at the centre of everything.*]

So it's all finished with Mr. Jo. I've already forgotten him. Children are still singing, riding on the buffaloes by the river. I can see them. Hear them. Hear their shrill little voices. There's no wind: the air's scorching hot.

[*Sound of children singing in the distance, in Cambodian.*]

They were everywhere. Perched up in trees. Squatting by the creeks in the estuary. Alive. Dead. And as well as the children there were the stray dogs and the madmen of the plain. The children used to play with them.

[SUZANNE *looks at* MR. JO *who is sweltering in the heat.*]

SUZANNE: She doesn't want me to see you any more. It's all over.

[*Sounds of children. Evening noises.*]

MR. JO: I can't accept that. I can't.

[*Silence.*]

[SUZANNE *sings the song we heard on the gramophone.*]

MR. JO: I love you, Suzanne.
SUZANNE: She doesn't want to wait.

[*Pause.*]

She knows your father's against me.

[*She starts to sing again.*]

MR. JO: She's terrible.

[*Pause.*]

Terrible, your mother.
SUZANNE: Yes.

[*Pause.*]

She's mad.

[*Pause.*]

If we'd got married she'd have asked you for money to rebuild the sea-walls. So you see . . . She imagines them twice as big as before and built of concrete. So you see . . .

[*Pause.*]

She'd have asked you to pay for having Joseph 's teeth seen to. His teeth are in a very bad state. So you see . . .

[SUZANNE *laughs.*]

MR. JO: I can't . . . I can't accept it . . .
SUZANNE: What?
MR. JO: Losing you . . .

[SUZANNE *laughs.*]

SUZANNE: So when do we get married?
MR. JO: [*Prevaricating.*] I've told you: when you prove that you love me.
SUZANNE: [*Laughing.*] You mean when I've agreed to go on that trip. Three days with you, in Saigon.

[*She laughs.* MR. JO *doesn't answer.*]

SUZANNE: It's not true.

[*Pause.*]

If we got married your father would disinherit you.

[SUZANNE *sings the gramophone tune.*]

[JOSEPH *goes by. She half gets up and watches him disappear.*]

SUZANNE: I'm going for a swim with Joseph. We won't be coming to Réam with you any more.

[*Pause.*]

Joseph agrees with her.

[*She gets up and goes.*]

MR. JO: [*Without moving.*] I've brought them.

[SUZANNE *halts.*]

[*Stands there, her back still turned.*]

SUZANNE: What?

MR. JO: The diamonds.

[*Pause.*]

You could just see which one you like best.

[*Pause.*]

You never know.

[*She turns round slowly. He takes out a little tissue-paper package from his pocket: unfolds it. Three smaller packages fall out.* SUZANNE *comes over and looks at the rings held out in an open hand adorned with its own enormous diamond.*]

MR. JO: They belonged to my mother. She was crazy about them . . .

[SUZANNE *looks at the rings and points to one of them.*]

SUZANNE: How much is that one worth?

MR. JO: About twenty-thousand piastres: I don't know exactly.

[*Silence. Then music.*]

[*In the distance the* MOTHER *wakes.*]

[*She stands up and disappears inside the bungalow.*]

SUZANNE'S VOICE: I was familiar with figures. How much my mother owed, the price of an evening's work at the Eden Cinema, the price of a piano lesson or a French lesson, what I didn't know yet was the price of money. Suddenly, I felt immensely tired, exhausted, I remember: the plain suddenly looked strange. Everything had gone dark.

[SUZANNE *sits down, then lies down and looks at the diamond on her finger, closes her eyes.*]

[*Silence. Music.*]

[MR. JO *leans towards* SUZANNE.]

MR. JO: My little Suzanne. . . . My treasure.

[SUZANNE *opens her eyes and looks at him.*]

MR. JO: Is that the one you like best?

SUZANNE: It's the one that's worth most.

MR. JO: That's all you think about.

SUZANNE: Yes.

MR. JO: You'll never love me . . .

[*Pause.*]

SUZANNE: Even if I did love you, we'd sell it.

MR. JO: It's hopeless.

[*Music.*]

[JOSEPH *goes by in the distance.*]

SUZANNE'S VOICE: Joseph went by, on his way to the river. I called out to him. He stopped. He didn't see the diamond in my hand.

[*We see what is being described enacted. We don't hear the call.* JOSEPH *comes over to* SUZANNE. *Silently, she holds out her hand, shows him the diamond.* JOSEPH *shows no surprise.* SUZANNE *waits, still holding out her hand. Waits. No reaction from* JOSEPH. *Then she speaks.*]

SUZANNE: It's a diamond.
JOSEPH: What?
SUZANNE: It's worth twenty thousand piastres.

[JOSEPH *smiles, as if at a childish joke.*]

JOSEPH: Twenty thousand piastres.

[*He stops smiling and looks at* MR. JO.]

[*A long pause.*]

[MR. JO *lowers his eyes.*]

SUZANNE: He'll give it to me if I go with him.
JOSEPH: Where to?
SUZANNE: The city.

[JOSEPH *looks at* SUZANNE.]

JOSEPH: For ever?
SUZANNE: For three days.
MR. JO: [*Cries out.*] Suzanne hasn't understood. . . . She hasn't understood. . . . It's my only chance.

[JOSEPH *is silent. Then looks at the bungalow, as if making a calculation. He looks at* MR. JO *He looks at* SUZANNE, *and is silent. Then, suddenly, far off, the* MOTHER's *voice, shouting. At first, we can't understand what she's saying. Then she comes into the visible part of the bungalow followed by the* CORPORAL. *It's the* CORPORAL *she was and still is talking to: to the* CORPORAL, *who can't hear a word. That's why she's shouting. She sits down at a table and starts to write, building her sea-walls all over again. The* CORPORAL *sits at her feet, listening to words he can't hear. But what the* MOTHER *says is quite precise, even if barely audible, even to the audience.*]

THE MOTHER: What we should do is dig deeper. . . . get down past the mud. . . . and on to the clay. . . . [*Pause.*] Reinforce the banks all along the river and on the other side of the bungalow . . . but above all get the props down deep, at least a metre deep . . . try to reach the clay, get past the mud . . . it all depends on that . . . and every so often, lay down concrete foundations . . . You can buy half price cement at Réam. That's not the problem . . . the problem is to dig through the mud and reach . . . reach the bottom of the marsh, the clay . . . that's what was missing the first time . . . concrete . . . remember the millions of crabs that got through the sea-walls . . . then the tide came through . . . [*Pause.*] We mustn't delude ourselves about the first year, there'll still be some salt left . . . We'll have to wait till all the soil's been washed right through, right down to the clay . . . It'll take at least three years if you ask me . . . etc. etc.

[*This all goes on at the same time as the scene between* JOSEPH, SUZANNE *and* MR. JO. *None of these three pays any attention to the* MOTHER *and the* CORPORAL. JOSEPH *goes off without a word.* SUZANNE *takes the ring off her finger and holds it out to* MR. JO *who takes it, and puts it in his pocket. Then stands there, crushed.*]

MR. JO: Now you've wrecked everything.

SUZANNE: I don't want to go with you. I still feel the same about it.

[MR. JO *cries.*]

I'd have told him sooner or later about the diamond. I couldn't have helped it.

[*Silence. Still, in the background, we can hear the loud confused mutterings of the* MOTHER *about the new sea-walls.* JOSEPH *goes by, not looking at* SUZANNE.]

I don't think you should bother to come back.

MR. JO: It's terrible . . . terrible . . . Why would you have to tell him?

SUZANNE: You shouldn't have shown it to me. You can't understand.

[MR. JO *cries. She is silent.*]

MR. JO: It's terrible . . . I can't Suzanne, I can't give you up . . . I can't.

[*Silence.*]

SUZANNE'S VOICE: I wanted to go into the forest with Joseph. It was the best moment, in the cool of the evening freshness, to go to the villages on the mountain. Mr. Jo looked as if he was suffering torments.

[*Silence.*]

I called Joseph. I told him it would be a good idea to go to the mountain tonight. He came. I stood up. It was then, I think, that Mr. Jo cried out. He said he'd give me the diamond anyway.

[JOSEPH *and* SUZANNE *freeze. The* MOTHER *suddenly stops talking.*]

[*Silence. No further sound. Then* MR. JO *goes over to* SUZANNE.]

[*He gives* SUZANNE *the ring.*]

[*Everyone watches: the* MOTHER, JOSEPH, *the* CORPORAL.]

[*And suddenly* SUZANNE *runs towards the bungalow. Reaches it.*]

[*She holds out the ring to the* MOTHER.]

[*The* MOTHER *holds out her hand. The bungalow goes dark.*]

[*The rest of this scene takes place in the darkened bungalow.*]

[*Lights only outside. We don't see* SUZANNE *speaking.*]

She took the ring and looked at it. Then she asked me how much it was worth. I said twenty thousand piastres and that he'd given it to me. She seemed not to take it in. I repeated what I'd said. That it was worth twenty thousand piastres and he'd given it to me. Suddenly I could scarcely recognise her. She went into her room and shut the door. I knew she'd gone to hide the ring. She always hid everything: quinine, tinned food, tobacco. In crevices in the wall, in her mattress. She hid things on herself too, tied round her body under her clothes.

[*Music.*]

[*The bungalow lights up. And now it's night outside. There are three, the three of them, in a different time sequence from the narration:* SUZANNE *and* JOSEPH *are eating. Not the* MOTHER. *Silence. Then, again,* SUZANNE *describes what happened—which we have not seen.*]

Then she came back from hiding the ring, she threw herself on me and beat me. She was shouting. Joseph came in. At first he let her beat me, and then he took her in his arms and kissed her.

[*Music.*]

She wept. We all wept. Together. All three of us.

[*Music.*]

And then we all laughed.

[*The following scene is between the actors. Direct dialogue, but disjointed, as the telling of the story has been: it's the scene which must have followed the beating, the tears, the laughter.*]

THE MOTHER: What did you say to him?

SUZANNE: I explained it all. A ring is nothing to him.

JOSEPH: You mustn't worry about her any more. It's all over.

SUZANNE: You mustn't worry about Joseph any more, either.

THE MOTHER: I probably worry too much. You're right.

[*Pause.*]

Just look at the way she handled Mr. Jo! But you're right. I can't stop worrying: ever.

[*She shouts.*]

But it's not just the rich who have things: if we want it, we can be rich too.

[*The children repeat the* MOTHER'*s last sentence.*]

SUZANNE: The mother fell asleep while we were having dinner. As he was putting her to bed, Joseph saw Mr. Jo's ring in a string round her neck.

[*Music.*]

[*Dinner. The* MOTHER *falls asleep.*]

[*The light fades again.*]

While she was sleeping, we went to the village on the mountain to buy some chickens. To eat on the way, Joseph said. Because the next morning we were leaving for Saigon, to sell Mr Jo's diamond.

[*End of the First Part.*]

PART TWO

In the front of the stage, in a yellow light, the MOTHER *sits on a red sofa—in extremely bad taste— with brightly coloured pink and green cushions and two fair-ground dolls. She wears a straw hat, black shoes, much-mended cotton stockings and her dark red dress. She's holding a big, bulging hand- bag.* SUZANNE *sits next to her, "made-up like a tart," in a blue dress, also with a straw hat and a handbag. They are sitting side by side as if on a train.*

On a small table behind them is a notice: "For Sale. Magnificent Diamond." Once more there is a silence before anyone speaks, while the background noises are established: city noises—shouts of market traders, bicycles, squeaking of streetcars, car horns, the click-clack of mah-jong games, clogs on cobbles, etc.

SUZANNE: The Central Hotel looked out on the Mekong River on one side, and on the other, on the tramway between Cholen and Saigon. The hotel was run by Carmen, Mademoiselle Marthe's daughter. Mademoiselle Marthe had worked in a brothel in Saigon harbour. She'd bought the hotel for her daughter.

Both Mademoiselle Marthe and Carmen were very fond of the Mother. For years they'd let her stay in the hotel for nothing. Now, again, Carmen had tried to help her. She'd tried to sell the diamond to the guests staying in the hotel. But none of them would buy it. So, the Mother decided to sell the diamond herself.

The first dealer she takes it to offers her ten thousand piastres.

He says it's got a serious flaw, what's known in the trade as a "toad." It halves it's value. The mother doesn't believe it. She wants twenty thousand piastres. She goes to another dealer. Then to a third, then to a fourth. They all point out the toad. The mother persists. She still wants twenty thousand piastres. The less they offer the more she wants her twenty thousand. Twenty thousand piastres is what the new sea-wall will cost, the one she wants to build before she dies. She's offered eleven thousand piastres.

Six thousand. Eight thousand. She refuses. This goes on for a week. She goes out every morning. She comes back every evening when it gets dark. First she goes to the white dealers. Then to the others. The Indians. And finally to the Chinese in Cholen. For a week Joseph and I wait for her to come out of the dealers' shops. Then, one evening, Joseph doesn't come back to the hotel. He's gone off in the Citroën. The Mother doesn't pay much attention to Joseph 's disappearance. She's obsessed with the diamond. She's already beginning to identify Mr. Jo with the "toad" in the heart of the diamond.

[*Silence.*]

[SUZANNE *smiles at the* MOTHER. *The* MOTHER *looks at her. This interruption of their stillness must be performed in silence. It's as if the* MOTHER *were trying to remember something.*]

THE MOTHER: "I ought to have been suspicious of that toad right from the beginning. Right from the moment I met him in the bar at Réam."

[*The* MOTHER *smiles.*]

SUZANNE'S VOICE: And then, one evening, she gets it into her head that she must find Mr. Jo.

[*Music.*]

She tells me *she'll* find Mr. Jo in the city, and then she'll bring him to me. I promise the mother to ask him for the two other diamonds he showed me out on the plain. The mother waits for Mr. Jo outside cinemas. Looks for him in cafés, outside luxury shops, in hotel lobbies. She never finds him.

[*Pause.*]

[SUZANNE *gets up and moves away from the* MOTHER.]

[*The* MOTHER *remains alone.*]

[SUZANNE *looks at her. The* MOTHER *doesn't move.*]

[*It should be a terrible moment.*]

SUZANNE: So what did she do, my mother? She tried to sell me instead of the diamond. Yes, my mother wanted to sell me instead of the diamond. She asked Carmen to find a man who would take me far away, for ever. The mother wants to be alone.

[*The* MOTHER *slowly turns and looks at* SUZANNE. *A shattering look, denying nothing, excusing nothing.*]

[*Pause.*]

She doesn't want children any more.

[*Music.* SUZANNE *buries her face in her hands.*]

[*The* MOTHER *turns away. They are cut off from one another.*]

Carmen makes me sleep in her room. She doesn't want me to sleep with my mother any longer. She is frightened for me.

[*Music.*]

Carmen tells me I must forget the Mother: says we should free ourselves of our love for her. That any kind of marriage would be better: "Any man'll do," she says. "You can take up with somebody else after a couple of months." But I must leave my mother. She's crazy.

[*Music.*]

[SUZANNE *changes her position; goes and stands behind the* MOTHER.]

[*All of* SUZANNE'S *movements should produce a sense of great violence.*]

She's a monster of destruction. The things she can make people believe! The things she made the peasants on the plain believe! She ruined their peace. And now she wants to start all over again. Sell her children and start again. She wants to overcome the force of the winds, the force of the tides. To be stronger than the Pacific. She still imagines roads over the waters of the Pacific. And fields of rice.

[SUZANNE *moves away from the* MOTHER.]

[*The* MOTHER *senses this movement; she looks as if she's sorry for having been so outrageous.*]

[*Music.*]

[SUZANNE *moves again. Turns away from the* MOTHER.]

[*The* MOTHER *lowers her eyes.*]

SUZANNE'S VOICE: Carmen does my hair. Dresses me up. Gives me some money. She tells me to go into the city. And forget. I take Carmen's clothes, and her money. I go to the fashionable part of the town.

[SUZANNE *stands motionless, facing the audience.*]

It is five o'clock in the afternoon. The whites are feeling refreshed after the siesta. They've taken their evening shower. They're dressed in white. White linen. They're off to the tennis courts. I'm looking for Joseph, my little brother.

[*She walks to the music of the waltz, while the* MOTHER *watches with the elemental smile that means "my child."*]

The sun has already set. The sprinklers are going along the Boulevard Catinat. It's hot: soon the monsoon will descend on Indochina. I'm lost. My dress pains me, my whore's dress. My face pains me too. And my heart. I'm ugly. The whole city knows it. It's laughing at me. I'm pursued by laughter. By stares. I have no mother any more. No brother. I'm going to die of shame. That old bitch, my mother, where is she now? Chasing around somewhere in the city. Without me.

[*Pause.*]

It'll be Joseph who kills her. He's started already. My brother: where is he? Lost somewhere in the city. The liar. Lost amid all the vulgarity, among all these ordinary people I'm looking for him, to kill him.

[*Music. Loud at first, then softer.*]

I go back to the Eden Cinema. The piano's still there. The lid's shut. I weep.

[*Music. Softer still.* SUZANNE *looks at the* MOTHER. *The* MOTHER *looks at her.* SUZANNE *goes over to her, sits down beside her.*]

Tonight, I want to sleep with her, my mother, in her room. She's started to wait for Joseph. She's losing hope about selling the diamond. All hope. She speaks.

[SUZANNE *leans towards the* MOTHER. *Embraces her.*]

[*Silence.*]

THE MOTHER: [*Quietly.*] Carmen's found someone.

[*Pause.*]

He's called Barner. He travels for a factory in Calcutta.

[*Pause.*]

It's a good job.

[*Pause.*]

He'd give thirty thousand piastres.

[*Pause.*]

You'd go away for ever.

[SUZANNE *doesn't answer.*]

[*The* MOTHER *goes on absently.*]

Perhaps JOSEPH's dead. Why shouldn't he be . . . ? He could have been run over by a tram . . .

SUZANNE: [*Quietly.*] No.

THE MOTHER: [*Indifferent.*] Oh. [*Pause.*] You think he'll come back?

SUZANNE: Yes.

[*Silence. Music.*]

THE MOTHER: He's called Barner. He's English.

[*Pause.*]

He's forty.

[*Pause.*]

His mother's still alive.

[*Pause.*]

He works for a big cotton manufacturer in Manchester. In England. He wants to get married. He's been talking about it for years.

[*Pause.*]

Carmen offered him the diamond. He almost bought it. [*Pause.*] He'd have liked to buy it for his mother.

[*Pause.*]

And then he couldn't make up his mind. But he'd buy it for his wife.

[*Pause.*]

Which would make . . . thirty thousand piastres plus twenty thousand piastres: fifty thousand piastres.

[*Silence.* SUZANNE *doesn't move.*]

[*The* MOTHER *has been speaking mechanically, without energy, without conviction.*]

THE MOTHER: [*Lifeless.*] You know, if JOSEPH doesn't come back, it would be safer.

[*Silence.*]

[*Then the* MOTHER *starts stroking her child's hair, very gently, as if thinking of something else.* SUZANNE *huddles to her mother's body.*]

Well?

SUZANNE: I'd prefer a hunter.

THE MOTHER: [*With a distant smile.*] Why a hunter? Why is it always a hunter?

[*Silence.*]

[*No answer from* SUZANNE.]

[*The* MOTHER *goes on talking, without waiting for* SUZANNE *to reply.*]

THE MOTHER: A hunter. You can always find a hunter.

[*Pause.*]

Well . . . Yes . . .

[*Pause.*]

I'll tell him you don't want to leave me. That's what I'll tell him.

SUZANNE: Yes.

[*Silence.*]

[SUZANNE *lifts her head and looks at the* MOTHER. SUZANNE *speaks roughly. The* MOTHER *is distant, dim, listless. Does she believe* SUZANNE's *lies? Impossible to guess.*]

SUZANNE: Joseph will come back.

THE MOTHER: Oh.

SUZANNE: I saw him. In the Boulevard Catinat. He told me he'd be back.

[*Pause.*]

He met a woman at the cinema.

THE MOTHER: Oh . . . So he'll be going away.

SUZANNE: [*Pause.*] No . . . He'll come back. I saw Mr. Jo, too.

THE MOTHER: Oh.

SUZANNE: I spoke to him about the diamonds.

[*Pause.*]

THE MOTHER: Oh . . . He wouldn't discuss it?

SUZANNE: No.

THE MOTHER: And what about marrying you?

SUZANNE: Nothing. Still the same.

THE MOTHER: [*Pause.*] Is it his father?

SUZANNE: [*Pause.*] I think so. [*Pause.*] They don't want to have anything to do with us.

[*Pause.*]

THE MOTHER: Oh well . . . I see their point . . .

SUZANNE: [*Pause.*] Yes.

[*Music.*]

[*They're silent.*]

[*The* MOTHER *seems to be thinking. Closes her eyes.*]

[*Half-closes them.*]

THE MOTHER: [*Reflectively.*] I've already forgotten what Mr. Jo looks like.

[*Pause.*]

SUZANNE: Don't think about him.

[*Music.*]

THE MOTHER: What have you been doing?

SUZANNE: I went to the Eden Cinema.

[*Pause.*]

The piano's still there.

[*Pause.*]

Not used any more.

[*The* MOTHER *wanders off into her memories of the Eden Cinema.*]

THE MOTHER: [*Pause.*] There was a time when I thought of buying it.

[*Pause.*]

I didn't say anything about it.

[*Pause.*]

So that you could go on with your music . . .

[*Pause.*]

You were quite good at it. Weren't you?

SUZANNE: I don't know.

THE MOTHER: But you see . . .

[*Silence.*]

[*The* MOTHER *sits rigid, upright.*]

[*The light dims.* SUZANNE *puts her arms around her* MOTHER.]

[*The* MOTHER *just sits there.*]

[*Blackout.*]

SUZANNE'S VOICE: That evening, I slept clinging to her body. To my mother's body. It was as if she'd already forgotten me. But her smell was there. The smell of the plain.

[*Music. A child's sobs*—SUZANNE'*s sobs—in the darkness.*]

Then, the next morning, Joseph came back.

[*Loud music. Long silence.*]

[*Then light on part of the stage.*]

[SUZANNE *and the* MOTHER *straighten up as if they've just heard a noise. They wait. Facing the audience.* JOSEPH *appears in the light. He doesn't look at them, doesn't look at anything. They don't turn round.* JOSEPH *goes up to them. They wait. Everyone motionless. Then.*]

He said he'd come to fetch us. To go back to the plain.

[JOSEPH *turns away.* SUZANNE *looks at* JOSEPH.]

He's got thinner. He's smoking American cigarettes. He looks as if he hasn't slept for several nights. Sometimes, at Prey-Nop, when he came home from hunting, he used to look like that. Through his anger at having to take us back, I can see that Joseph is marvellously happy. And that he's finished with us and with the plain. He goes up to (our) mother and says he's sold the diamond for the price she wanted: twenty thousand piastres. His voice is gentle, almost unrecognisable.

[JOSEPH *silently puts the twenty thousand piastres on the table, not looking at the* MOTHER. *The* MOTHER *keeps her back turned, doesn't look around. She seems to be listening.*]

[*It's* SUZANNE *who picks up the money and gives it to the* MOTHER. *The* MOTHER *takes the money, looks at it, and puts it in her handbag.*]

[*Everyone is motionless as* SUZANNE *looks at her brother.*]

I think: if I die, he'll look at me. I don't die.

[JOSEPH *looks at* SUZANNE. *They look at each other.*]

[*The* MOTHER *is isolated.*]

[*They stop looking at each other. At anything. They wait. Standing up, motionless. As if all three of them were lost.*]

[*That part of the stage gradually darkens, and at the same time, the bungalow-space lights up very slowly and we find ourselves back there again. While this lighting change is taking place, they all go off in the direction opposite to the one* JOSEPH *came in by.*]

[*Music.*]

Our mother talked the whole way back. About the new sea-walls she had to build before she died. About a new method of building them. By digging down to the bottom of the marsh. The trouble was the salt. She'd invented the new method lying awake at night. By the time we reached the last white outpost before the Réam road, it was six o'clock in the evening.

[*The light changes.*]

Joseph got some gas. When he paid, he pulled a bunch of ten piastre notes out of his pocket. The mother saw it. She didn't talk any more. JOSEPH sat down on the running-board of the Citroën: he ran his fingers through his hair like someone just waking up. He wasn't alone. He was with her, the woman he'd met at the Eden Cinema. From now on, wherever he went he'd be with her. We could already see the Elephant mountains, its trees, gradually being swallowed up by the dark. Joseph looked at the forest. He wouldn't be going hunting there any more. He stretched himself, slowly, and at length. Then he said he was hungry. Those were the first words he'd spoken since we left Saigon.

The mother had some sandwiches that Carmen had made up for the journey. We ate them. While we were eating them she quietened down at last. I think she'd been frightened, our mother, of not even having to cook for us any more. Of not having even that much left.

JOSEPH: When she woke up, it must have been about two in the morning. The car was going along, quite smoothly. She got the blanket out from under the seat. She said she was cold.

SUZANNE: It was then that JOSEPH suddenly remembered. [*Pause.*] He felt in his pockets and held something out to the mother. In the palm of his hand.

[*The* CORPORAL *enters. Rearranges furniture: brings in tea service.*]

I saw it too. In the palm of his hand lay Mr. Jo's diamond. The mother gave a cry.

[*Music.*]

Joseph said Carmen had given him the diamond to sell the day before. And he'd sold it. And then he'd been given it back. There was no point in trying to understand. The mother took the diamond. Reluctantly. She put it away in her handbag.

[*Pause.*]

Then she started to cry again.

[*The* CORPORAL *has gone into the bungalow. He brings in steaming hot tea.*]

We didn't ask her why she was crying. We knew. She'd hoped this time would have been the last. That after this trip to the city there'd be nothing more to do, no trying to sell again, no more money to be got. The thought of the twenty thousand piastres that could be got from selling the diamond again appalled her.

[*Music.*]

[*The* MOTHER *goes into the bungalow.*]

[*The* CORPORAL *brings her hot tea. They drink it: the* CORPORAL *and the* MOTHER.]

Far away, towards Siam, the sun was rising. Towards the Pacific it was still dark.

[*The light increases gradually.*]

[*Deep silence.*]

[*No music.*]

It was in the days that followed, just before Joseph left, that our mother wrote her last letter to the Land Commission in Kampot.

[*In the silence the* MOTHER *straightens up and starts to read out (or recite) the letter. The* CORPORAL *listens. The* MOTHER, *too, listens to her own letter. While she reads, neither* JOSEPH *nor* SUZANNE *is visible.*]

THE MOTHER: Prey-Nop. 24th March 1931.

Gentlemen, I am writing to you once again to tell you this: No one will come here, after me. If you ever manage to evict me, and come to show the concession to some new tenant, a hundred peasants will crowd around and say to the new tenant: "Dip your finger into the mud of the rice fields and taste it. Do you think rice can grow in salt? You'll be the fifth tenant of this concession. The others are all dead or ruined."

I know how powerful you are, and that by virtue of the power invested in you by the Government of the Colony, the whole plain is in your hands. I know too that all my knowledge of your wickedness, and the wickedness of your colleagues, of those who preceded you is useless if I alone possess it. This is something it took me a long time to learn. But now I know. And so there are already hundreds of others in the plain who know what you're like.

[*Pause.*]

This is a long letter. I can't sleep any more, since my misfortunes, since the sea-walls were swept away. I hesitated a long time before writing this letter to you. But now it seems to me that I was wrong not to have written it before.

To make you take an interest in me, I have to talk to you about yourselves. Only about how wicked you are, perhaps—but anyway about yourselves. And if you read this letter, I am sure you will read all future letters, if only to find out how much I have progressed in the knowledge of your wickedness. I've talked to all the people who came to build the sea-walls, and I never tire of telling them what you're like.

[*Pause.*]

I've talked to my children too. I always told myself I'd tell them when they were older, so as not to spoil their childhood. Now they know.

A lot of children die here. The only workable land in the plain is full of the bodies of dead children. So I—so that at last their deaths may serve some purpose, you never know—I tell the people what you're like. It's a long time now since I first started turning these things over in my mind at night. It's been so long that all this misery has served no purpose that I'm beginning to hope a time will come when it will be of some use. And that when my children go away forever, young as they are, they'll know about the consequences of your wickedness: perhaps, that will be something to be going on with.

[*Pause.*]

Where is the money I earned, the money I saved sou by sou to buy this concession? The money I brought you one morning, seven years ago? That morning, I gave you everything I possess, everything. It was as if I had offered up my own body as a sacrifice, so that out of my ashes a whole future of happiness for my children might spring. And you took that money. You took it quite matter-of-factly and I went away happy. It was the most glorious moment in my life. It still amazes me. I can see you now: you knew you'd just sold me land riddled with salt. You knew I was throwing everything I had into the Pacific. And you just smiled politely. How can men be like you and still look like ordinary people? How can people steal from the poor and grow rich on their hunger without their wickedness being visible? Without it killing you too?

You have been my obsession, for the last seven years. Soon I'll be left alone on this impossible land and this is what I'll do. I'll see that all the officials of the Land Commission in Kampot are killed. Every one. How better could I fill the emptiness of my life? And so I say to the peasants: when you kill them, don't any of you admit it. Or else all of you admit it. If a thousand of you are guilty, they can't do anything.

I repeat, for the last time, we must have something to live for. And if it is not the hope, however vague, of new sea-walls, it will have to be the hope of corpses, even if they are only the loathsome corpses of the officials of the Kampot Land Commission.

[*Music.*]

SUZANNE'S VOICE: This letter never reached the officials of the Kampot Land Commission. It was found near the Mother's body after her death, together with a final demand for the rent. Mr. Jo's diamond was still on a string around her neck.

[*The bungalow becomes completely lit.*]

[*Silence. It is day. The* MOTHER *sleeps.*]

[*As if her own story had rocked her to sleep.*]

[*The* CORPORAL *lowers a blind to shade the* MOTHER's *sleeping body.*]

[*Her body is no longer visible: it has become a dark shadow in the white light.*]

[*Silence.*]

For a week after we got back Joseph stayed in bed. He only got up in the evening to eat. Then he'd sit on the veranda looking at the mountain, at the forest. We knew he'd soon be leaving. One afternoon, during the siesta, he called me. Said he wanted to tell me what had happened. So that I'd remember afterwards, when he was gone. And later on, too. And also because he was afraid he might forget it himself, later on, when he had forgotten this particular love affair. We went and sat by the river, in the shade of the bridge, away from her, our mother.

[*Music.*]

[*The bungalow is lit round the outside, but the black shadow of the* MOTHER's *body is still visible.*]

[JOSEPH *and* SUZANNE *come to the river separately.*]

[*She sits or lies down some distance away from him.*]

I listened to Joseph's story. But he was talking to himself. He didn't see me.

JOSEPH: It happened at the Eden Cinema. One evening. She arrived late. I didn't notice her at first. There was a man with her. I think I saw him first. Suddenly I heard very heavy breathing, right next to me. It was him. She saw me looking at him and turned towards me. She smiled. She said: "It's always like this." I said: "Always?" She said: "Yes, always." I asked her who he was. She laughed. She said he was her husband. She took out a packet of cigarettes from her bag, Players 555. She asked for a light. I gave her one.

[*Pause.*]

I saw her hands. Her eyes. She was looking at me. Her hand was very slim and supple. [*Pause.*] It felt almost as if the bones were broken. We didn't talk any more. I don't know how long it went on. The lights were going up. I let go of her hand. But it sought mine again. I thought I'd leave. But I couldn't. I said to myself, she must be used to picking men like this in cinemas. The lights went up. Her hand was withdrawn. I didn't dare look at her. She, yes, she dared—she looked at me. The man had suddenly woken up. I thought he was rather good looking. She pointed me out to him. She said: "He's a hunter from Réam." We'd left the cinema. I was just behind her. They went up to an eight-cylinder Delage. The man turned round, said to me: "Are you coming?" I said: "Yes."

[*Music. The Eden Cinema Waltz.*]

We stopped at a night-club. "We'll have a whisky," said the man. It was then I understood. When he had that whisky. We left that club. Went on to another one near the port. Had more to drink. And so it went on. And on. Suddenly, it was morning. I asked myself what I was doing there, with those people. It was six o'clock in the morning. The man had fallen asleep with his head on the table. She leaned towards me, stretching over him. We kissed. I felt as if I'd died. I'm rather hazy about what happened next. I remember there were gardens round the night-club, waterfalls, swimming pools. Everything was . . . very light . . . and empty . . . emptied . . . I drove the Delage. We went to a hotel. We stayed there for a week. Once she asked me to tell her about my life. I told her about the diamond. She told me to fetch it. Said she'd buy it. When I got back to the Central Hotel I found it in my pocket, together with the money.

[JOSEPH *has stopped talking.*]

[JOSEPH *and* SUZANNE *remain as they are.*]

[*They look at the bungalow.*]

[*The* CORPORAL *pulls up the blind and the shadow over the* MOTHER *vanishes.*]

[*Then the* CORPORAL *comes and goes with hot rice and hot tea. No one else moves.*]

SUZANNE'S VOICE: The Mother was waiting for Joseph to leave. She didn't want to cook for us any more. It was the Corporal who bought the rice bread, who cooked wader-bird stew. The mother didn't speak any more. She just sat in a chair, facing the Pacific. With her back to the road. She never looked at us once during all that time. She didn't try to sell the diamond again. One day she asked me to sell Mr. Jo's gramophone. I put it in a bag and gave it to the driver of the Réam bus to give to Agosti, a planter in Réam. Another time I took Mr. Jo's presents, the blue dress, the compact, the nail polish, and threw them in the river. That meant there was nothing left to sell. I remember those days: like a long-drawn-out deathbed. The sun. The drought. It gave everyone a fever. The waiting lasted a month.

[*Music.*]

Then one evening . . . It was eight o'clock . . .

[*Headlights appear suddenly, flooding the stage, the bungalow. They are all three of them there: and the* CORPORAL, *too, sitting by the* MOTHER. *All are transfixed by the light.*]

No one heard the car coming, not even Joseph. She must have been there some time, waiting on the other side of the bridge, before she decided to sound her horn. Then she sounded the horn.

[*Music.*]

[JOSEPH *gets up and goes over to the* MOTHER.]

[*The* MOTHER, *still turned towards the Pacific, lies back in her chair. Careful, suddenly. She's very pale.*]

[*It's almost as if she hadn't heard. For the first time since they got back from the city.* JOSEPH *looks at the* MOTHER.]

JOSEPH: I'll be back.
THE MOTHER: Yes.

[*Music.*]

JOSEPH: I'll be back in a few days.
THE MOTHER: Yes.

[*Music.*]

JOSEPH: [*Insists.*] I'll come back. We'll sell up everything. I'll take you both away.
THE MOTHER: Yes.

[*Music.*]

[*The* MOTHER *doesn't move.*]

[*Suddenly, a huge light inside the bungalow.*]

[SUZANNE *looks.*]

JOSEPH: I'm leaving everything here. Even my guns.

[*Pause.*]

[*The* MOTHER *doesn't answer.*]

[*He turns towards* SUZANNE.]

Tell her I'll be back.
SUZANNE: He'll be back.
JOSEPH: A week from now.
SUZANNE: [*Repeats.*] He'll be back a week from now.

[*The* MOTHER *doesn't speak. She shuts her eyes.*]

[*No one moves.*]

[JOSEPH *crouches by the* MOTHER *and looks at her all over but doesn't touch her.*]

[*Then he looks at* SUZANNE.]

[*The headlights sweep over the forest, over the road, over the sleeping village, then over the* MOTHER, SUZANNE *and* JOSEPH.]

[*The car has been turned round and is now facing towards the city.*]

[JOSEPH *looks at the road. Looks again at the* MOTHER, *gets up, goes off.*]

[*The headlights recede. Disappear.*]

[*Music.*]

[*The* CORPORAL *comes in with hot rice—just as he always does. But this time he stays. The* MOTHER *speaks.*]

THE MOTHER: Go and eat.

SUZANNE: [*Crying out in rage.*] No.

THE MOTHER: Very well. He'll leave her. He'll leave everyone and everything.

SUZANNE: [*Still shouting.*] Be quiet!

THE MOTHER: The longest he'll ever have stayed anywhere will be here on the plain.

[*Pause.*]

I'll be quiet now.

[*Music.*]

[*The* CORPORAL *helps the* MOTHER *to undress. Takes her into the next room.*]

[SUZANNE *remains for a moment crouched on the floor of the room, her face almost touching the ground.*]

[*Then she goes out.*]

[*The bungalow darkens.*]

[*Music. The Eden Cinema Waltz.*]

[*Day breaks.*]

[*Sunlight.*]

[SUZANNE *comes towards the audience.*]

[*Sits down. Talks to us.*]

[*Music.*]

SUZANNE: Three weeks went by in which nothing happened. The Mother slept. I spent all day by the road waiting for hunters. Every three hours I went in to look after my mother. She'd had an attack the day after Joseph left. The doctor came from Réam: heart trouble.

[*Music.*]

Then one evening Agosti came. He'd heard there was a girl all on her own at Prey-Nop. So he came. I took him in to see my mother. He told her he had started a pineapple farm. They sold well, he used artificial fertilisers. In three years' time he'd be able to leave the plain. My mother said Agosti's land was healthy but in her concession anything like that was impossible, because of the salt. Then she fell silent.

[*Music.*]

I went into the forest with Agosti. It was cool under the trees, after all those fields of pineapple. Cool and dark.

[*Long pause.*]

He took out his handkerchief and wiped the blood from my dress and from me. Night fell there in the forest.

[*Distant music.*]

That night, for the first time, I slept in Joseph's room. It was just as he'd left it. With his guns, some empty cartridges, a pack of cigarettes. The bed was unmade. If Joseph had been there I'd have told him what had happened with Agosti. But he wasn't here any more. I remember that night. The forest and the Pacific all round the house. The sound of the wind. Beating against the mountainside. Sweeping over where I lay.

[*Silence.*]

Agosti came back the next day. He asked me if I'd marry him. I said no. Said I'd rather go away with Joseph when he came back.

[*Distant music.*]

[SUZANNE *walks slowly across the stage.*]

[*Then she stops and sits down facing the audience, while the bungalow darkens, goes quite dark.*]

And then a letter came from Joseph. He said he was all right. That we could write to him at the Central Hotel.

[*Music. Death theme.*]

And then the Mother died. One afternoon. I was in the forest with Agosti. She'd told me to go out with him. The Corporal was there to look after her. When I came back she couldn't breathe. Gasps and groans issued from her body, and moans addressed to her children.

[*Silence.*]

Agosti went back to Réam to phone the Central Hotel.

[*Music. Death theme.*]

By evening my mother had stopped moaning. Her face grew strange. First it looked weary. Then extremely happy. And then she wanted to talk again: one last time.

[SUZANNE *hides her face in her hands.*]

I told her I was there, I spoke my name, and said I was her child. She didn't seem to take it in. Didn't seem to remember. It can't have been to us, to her children, that she wanted to speak one last time, but to someone beyond us, to others. Who knows? To many, many others perhaps, to whole nations, to the world. Before she died a smile flickered over her lips and over her closed eyes. Then vanished. By the time Agosti got back, my mother's heart had stopped.

[*Music.*]

[*The* MOTHER *is still there, sitting in the bungalow, while her death is being described.*]

[*The* CORPORAL *helps her to lie down on the camp bed he has set out on the stage. So the* MOTHER *lends herself, while still alive, to the enactment of her dying.*]

[*And now it's over.*]

[*The* MOTHER *is lying down, "dead," before the audience, her eyes open.*]

SUZANNE'S VOICE: As often happens in the evening, a strange breeze from the Pacific came up and blew over the plain, over the Mother's body, and was lost in the forest. Everything went dark. Night had fallen very suddenly, as it does in those parts. The forest had turned blue. Joseph came just after nightfall. He went in to our mother. We both stood looking at her for a long time.

[*Sound of a very strong wind. Of waves.*]

[*And then everything goes dark.*]

[JOSEPH *arrives at the same time as the darkness.*]

[*He goes slowly over to the* MOTHER.]

[SUZANNE *doesn't move.*]

[JOSEPH *bends down, touches the* MOTHER *and lays his face against her.*]

[*He straightens up and looks at her.*]

SUZANNE: His eyes were full of dull, mauve shadows. His mouth . . . His hands. His northern peasant's hands. His hands . . .

[*Noises around the bungalow. Peasants arriving.*]

The peasants came up from the plain and gathered around the bungalow.

[*Music.*]

On the road, in a car, the woman from the Eden Cinema waited for Joseph.

[*The whole stage is motionless.*]

[JOSEPH *leaves the* MOTHER, *comes and faces the audience.*]

[*Silence. Then he speaks.*]

JOSEPH: The house is open to you all from now on. Come in. Take everything. I leave you my guns. Do what you like with them.

[*Pause.*]

You can go in and see her if you like: the children as well.

SUZANNE'S VOICE: One of the peasants asked me if we were going away for good. Joseph looked at me, he said yes.

[*Pause.*]

[*Music.*]

[*Pause.*]

JOSEPH: We'll take her body far away. She was not of your race. Even though she loved you, even though her hope was your hope and she mourned the children of the plain, she was not of your race. She was always a stranger in your country.

[*Pause.*]

All of us were always strangers in your country. She'll be buried in the French Cemetery in Saigon.

[*Everyone goes out except the* CORPORAL *who remains squatting beside the* MOTHER.]

[*Children's laughter. Distant drums.*]

[*Music.*]

[*The End.*]

Simone Benmussa (b. 1938)

Born in Tunisia of Jewish-French parents, Simone Benmussa went to Paris in 1955 to study at the Sorbonne—and there became thoroughly immersed in the frothy world of Parisian theater. She has, since the late fifties, participated in almost every aspect of theater, from ushering and tidying up to writing and directing. With a book on Eugène Ionesco (1966), numerous published articles, and twenty years (1958–78) as a founder and editor of the theatrical journal *Cahiers Renaud-Barrault*, she has formidable credentials as a critic. Beyond that, she has written a novel, *Le Prince répète le Prince* (1984), translated Edward Bond's play *Lear* from English into French (1975), and directed a film about Nathalie Sarraute.

There is a tradition, exemplified by Ariane Mnouchkine and her Théâtre du Soleil, of ensemble work, of a director's controlling and shaping every aspect of the dramatic material, including the troupe. It is a tradition that is particularly evident in France and among women, and one to which Benmussa very much belongs. Her first production (the lines between authorship and directing blur) occurred by chance in 1976. She was asked to adapt quickly for the stage at the Petit Orsay Hélène Cixous's novel, *Portrait of the Sun*—itself derived from Freud's 1905 report on Dora, "Fragment of an Analysis of a Case of Hysteria." The play, *Portrait of Dora*, was a wonderful success, in France and abroad, and established for Benmussa a theatrical mode that she obviously found congenial.

She is fascinated by the boundaries between the genres of fiction and drama and between narration and theatrics. Every major theatrical presentation of hers consciously develops in this manner. Like *Dora*, her next play, *The Singular Life of Albert Nobbs* (*La vie singulière d'Albert Nobbs*, 1977), derives from a fictional source, George Moore's 1927 short story, "Albert Nobbs." And just as Cixous had worked from an earlier, "nonfictional" source, Freud's case study, so, too, was Moore's tale inspired by an 1860s Dublin newspaper report. Two years later, in 1979, Benmussa used Henry James's story "Private Life" as the source for her play *Appearances*.

Drama takes its special character from conflict. For Benmussa an important form this can take is the tension between the genres of fiction and drama and between narrative—an element most immediately associated with fiction—and staging or spectacle. As she makes clear in her preface to *Dora*, Benmussa enjoys working with a text that is not theatrical, that comes ill-adjusted and ill-fitting to the theater. Adjusting this fit seems to provide her, as playwright and dramaturge, with a freedom and flexibility she cherishes. In each of these plays, she clearly delights in transforming the original author into a narrating character or voice.

Simone Benmussa, ca. 1980. (Photographer: Jerry Bauer.)

As Benmussa dramatizes the strains between different forms, different perspectives, and different pasts and the present, she exercises complete dramatic control. Her adaptations are thorough. They do not simply transfer a told tale to the stage for viewing; in adapting a story she radically reconceives it, often daringly opposing, for example, the offstage narrative voice of the parent medium to the visuals of its offspring. She is fastidious and explicit, as a playwright-director, about the details of scenes, placement, props, lighting, materials, and, of course, costumes.

Fiction often relates its narrative through an authorial voice; drama, by contrast, tells its story visually: we see it unfold. In *The Singular Life of Albert Nobbs*, Benmussa capitalizes on this difference. The controlling male voice of the offstage character George Moore surrounds and pervades the action on stage, ironically at odds with it. This tension, originally of genres and points of view, readily becomes thematic, as Benmussa shifts Moore's original concern with the loneliness of the human condition (with a special nod to women) to an indictment of the realities of gender and the untenable position women are in, left lonely, bereft of real companionship and love.

That all of the men are disembodied voices offstage and the women variously costumed and active onstage inevitably directs our interest and sympathies toward the women. With Albert increasingly isolated in her chair, perched on the landing, as people pass and the hotel door swings, the audience recognizes that the destructive, stifling antagonism is not so much between individuals as it is between this unfortunate miscreant and the world that has denied her any legitimate name and identity, that has made her a perhapser. In this play, with its stories within stories, Albert, as a bastard, belongs to a story without a beginning. She and her sisters have been existing on the margin from time immemorial.

The illusory tension between Victorian Ireland and the contemporary world of the audience minimally masks the real tension that exists between sex (including the much-discussed love and kisses) and the constructed, restrictive genders of society. The costumes, which Benmussa stresses are crucial and precise, amplify this struggle—as does the exaggerated importance of the money over which Albert obsesses. Marriage is a risky, unsatisfying arrangement because gender is much like a theatrical role that women corset-up for and assume, within a coercive, male-oriented economy.

SELECTED BIBLIOGRAPHY IN ENGLISH

Ammen, Sharon. "Transforming George Moore: Simone Benmussa's Adaptive Art in *The Singular Life of Albert Nobbs*." *Text and Performance Quarterly* 11 (1991), 306–12.

Benmussa, Simone. "Introduction." *Benmussa Directs*. London: John Calder, 1979. Pp. 9–26.

Case, Sue-Ellen. "Gender as Play: Simone Benmussa's *The Singular Life of Albert Nobbs*." *Women and Performance: A Journal of Feminist Theory* 1 (1984), 21–24.

Cohn, Ruby. "Benmussa's Planes." *Theater* 13 (1981–82), 51–54.

Diamond, Elin. "Benmussa's Adaptations: Unauthorized Texts from Elsewhere." *Feminine Focus: The New Women Playwrights*. Ed. Enoch Brater. New York: Oxford University Press, 1989. Pp. 64–78.

——— . "Refusing the Romanticism of Identity: Narrative Interventions in Churchill, Benmussa, Duras." *Theatre Journal* 37 (1985), 273–86.

Elam, Harry J., Jr. "Visual Representation in *The Singular Life of Albert Nobbs*." *Text and Performance Quarterly* 11 (1991), 313–18.

THE SINGULAR LIFE OF ALBERT NOBBS

Simone Benmussa

Adapted for the stage from George Moore's short story "Albert Nobbs"
and translated from the French by Barbara Wright.

CHARACTERS

ALBERT NOBBS

HELEN DAWES

HUBERT PAGE

MRS. BAKER

KITTY MACCAN

FIRST CHAMBERMAID

SECOND CHAMBERMAID

GEORGE MOORE'S VOICE

ALEC'S VOICE

JOE MACKLINS' VOICE

OTHER VOICES

Prologue

The house lights go out.

GEORGE MOORE'S VOICE: Good morning, Alec.

ALEC'S VOICE: Good morning, your honour.

GEORGE MOORE'S VOICE: And what story are you going to tell me today, Alec? Will it be as strange as the one about the hermit? Upon my word, there is nothing like the bank of a river for storytelling.

ALEC'S VOICE: 'Tis true that they seem to come swirling up from the river bed.

GEORGE MOORE'S VOICE: The old storytellers of Mayo, your ancestors, always looked for inspiration in running water.

ALEC'S VOICE: But it is your turn today, your honour.

GEORGE MOORE'S VOICE: So it is . . . Well then, I shall tell you a true story.

[*This takes place in the 1860s, in Ireland.*]

[*The voice of a drunken old Irishman can be heard in the distance, singing "The Boys of the Column." It fades away as* GEORGE MOORE *begins his story.*]

[*Two chambermaids, dressed identically in black dresses and long white aprons, gently pull back the curtains, just as they would draw bedroom curtains in the morning. They reveal the interior of a hotel: Morrison's Hotel. In the half light it is just possible to make out: on one side, in the void, a swing door leading to the kitchen; its upper part is glass, its lower part wood. On the other side, equally isolated, a revolving, wood and glass door such as are to be found in old hotels: this is the front door. The two doors will later revolve or swing of their own accord, the one opening on to the world of the kitchen, the other on to that of the clients, as if ghostly visitors or maids, fairies or voices, were passing through them.*]

GEORGE MOORE'S VOICE: When we went up to Dublin in the sixties, Alec, we always put up at Morrison's, a big family hotel. I can still see Morrison's: the front door opening into a short passage, with some half-dozen steps leading up into the house, the glass doors of the coffee-room showing through the dimness, and in front of the visitor a big staircase running up to the second landing. I remember long passages on the second landing, and half-way down these passages was the well. I don't know if it's right to speak of the well of a staircase, but I used to think of it as a well. A very big building was Morrison's Hotel, with passages running hither and thither, and little flights of stairs in all kinds of odd corners. I remember the pair of windows, their lace curtains and their rep curtains; I can remember myself looking through the pane, interested in the coal carts going by, the bell hitched on to the horse's collar jangling all the way down the street, the coalman himself sitting with his legs hanging over the shafts, looking up at the windows to see if he could spy out an order.

[*After the maids have attached the curtains to their loops they walk backstage, each keeping to her own side. When they get to the doors they stop, and look at each other through the glass. The doors swing gently, though no one has touched them.*]

[*The decor and the characters can just be made out on the dimly-lit stage.*]

[*A backcloth: the different doors of the rooms on the upper floors, and the characters.* These are guests, maids, menservants, etc., painted in trompe l'oeil, some going into the rooms, others carrying trays, maids leaning over the banisters looking down at the floor below, shoes waiting to be cleaned outside the closed doors. Some doors and windows can be opened to let the light through. In the middle of the staircase, half way up, sitting on a chair but only just visible, a real character, a waiter, his napkin over his shoulder, as if he were an integral part of the centre of this backcloth, one of its painted characters. This is* ALBERT NOBBS.]

[*The other characters are:* MRS. BAKER, *at her table, bending over her account book, and* HUBERT PAGE, *a house-painter, standing on a ladder.*]

[*A child is looking out of one of the windows backstage, he has his back turned, he shuts the window, goes downstairs, crosses the stage and exits.*]

[*The lights come up.*]

[*The two "ghost-maids" are blinded by the light and disappear, as if the brightness has dissolved them into thin air.*]

[*The hotel comes to life.*]

[*The doors swing and revolve, carrying on a dialogue with each other.*]

GEORGE MOORE'S VOICE: I'm telling you these things, Alec, for the pleasure of looking back and nothing else. I can see the sitting-room—and the waiter that used to attend on us, I can see him too. And to this day I can recall the frights he gave me when he came

---

*These characters are taken from English paintings of the Victorian era.

behind me, awaking me from my dream of a coalman's life. I used to be afraid to open the sitting-room door, for I'd be sure to find him waiting on the landing, his napkin thrown over his shoulder. I think I was afraid he'd pick me up and kiss me. And yet all the guests liked Albert Nobbs. And the proprietress liked him, as well she might, for he was the most dependable servant in the hotel: no running round to public-houses and coming back with the smell of whisky and tobacco upon him; no rank pipe in his pocket; and above all, no playing the fool with the maid-servants. Holidays he never asked for. A strange life his was, and mysterious.

[ALBERT NOBBS *gets up from his chair and goes over to an open window next to the one where the child had been. He leans out, just as the child had, and then comes down.* MRS. BAKER *goes over to another window downstage, stays there a moment, leaning out like the child and* ALBERT NOBBS. HUBERT PAGE *comes down from his ladder and goes to put it and his brushes away. He reappears and passes* ALBERT NOBBS. *They gaze at each other.*]

[MRS. BAKER *is standing in front of* ALBERT NOBBS, *looking amazed.* HUBERT PAGE *stops and glances from one to the other, surprised, smiling, embarrassed.* MRS. BAKER *is both perplexed and displeased. It is as if they are frozen in their conversation—a conversation that has not yet taken place.*]

ALEC'S VOICE: Why mysterious?

GEORGE MOORE'S VOICE: Because when he died, we learnt that Albert was a woman.

ALEC'S VOICE: A woman?

GEORGE MOORE'S VOICE: Yes, a woman, and Hubert Page too.

ALEC'S VOICE: I don't understand, your honour.

GEORGE MOORE'S VOICE: You soon will. His willingness to oblige was so notorious that Mrs. Baker, the proprietress of Morrison's Hotel at the time, could hardly believe she was listening to him when he began to stumble from one excuse to another for not sharing his bed with Hubert Page. You see, Alec, it was Punchestown week, and beds are as scarce in Dublin that week as diamonds are on the slopes of Croagh Patrick.

ALEC'S VOICE: But your honour—you still haven't told me who Page was.

GEORGE MOORE'S VOICE: I'm just coming to him, Alec. Hubert Page was a house-painter, well known and well liked by Mrs. Baker. He came over every season, and so pleasant were his manners that one forgot the smell of his paint.

A CHAMBERMAID'S VOICE: Good morning, Mr. Page, what a pleasure to see you back at the hotel!

GEORGE MOORE'S VOICE: He went about his work with a sort of lolling, idle gait that attracted and pleased the eye.

MRS. BAKER: I suppose you fully understand that Page is leaving for Belfast by the morning train, and has come over here to ask us for a bed, there not being one at the hotel in which he is working, nor in all Dublin.

GEORGE MOORE'S VOICE: Albert Nobbs understood well enough, but he began to mumble something about being a very light sleeper.

MRS. BAKER: Now, what are you trying to say?

GEORGE MOORE'S VOICE: He complained that his mattress was full of lumps.

MRS. BAKER: Your mattress full of lumps! Why, your mattress was repicked and buttoned six months ago. What kind of story are you telling me?

GEORGE MOORE'S VOICE: That he had never slept with anybody before, and that Mr. Page would get a better stretch on one of the sofas in the coffee-room.

MRS. BAKER: A better stretch on the sofa in the coffee-room? I don't understand you, not a little bit.

GEORGE MOORE'S VOICE: Page, for his part, said that the night was a fine one, that he would keep himself warm with a sharp walk, and that his train started early.

MRS. BAKER: You'll do nothing of the kind, Page!

GEORGE MOORE'S VOICE: Seeing that Mrs. Baker was now very angry, Albert thought it time to give in. You'll do nothing of the kind, Mr. Page, he repeated.

MRS. BAKER: I should think not indeed!

GEORGE MOORE'S VOICE: But I'm a light sleeper, he said again.

MRS. BAKER: We've heard that before, Albert! [*Going out.*] No inconvenience whatever, Page.

[ALBERT NOBBS *goes over to a panel on which a sideboard and a pile of plates are painted in trompe l'oeil. She opens it. On the other side, her bedroom is painted. She pulls out a folding bed and sets it up, helped by* HUBERT PAGE. HUBERT *is so dog-tired that he tumbles into bed, and a moment after is asleep.* ALBERT *stands listening, not yet undressed, her loosened tie dangling. When his heavy breathing tells* ALBERT *that* HUBERT *is sound asleep she approaches the bed stealthily. Relieved, she gets into bed, though she hasn't dared to undress completely. They sleep for a moment.*]

The Flea

Suddenly ALBERT NOBBS *awakes with a start. A flea has bitten her, and out goes her leg. She is afraid that this lively movement has awoken* HUBERT PAGE, *but* HUBERT *only turns over in the bed to sleep more soundly.* ALBERT *sits down cautiously on the bed, is reassured at seeing that* PAGE *is still asleep, and sets herself to the task of catching the flea. She lowers her shirt until one of her shoulders is naked. With her back to the audience, she starts scratching herself.*

This scene must be played with the greatest modesty and austerity, to enhance its innocence.

HUBERT PAGE: Why, you're a woman!

ALBERT NOBBS: You won't tell on me and ruin a poor man, will you, Mr. Page? That is all I ask of you, and on my knees I beg it.

HUBERT PAGE: Get up from your knees. And tell me how long you have been playing this part?

ALBERT NOBBS: Ever since I was a girl. You won't tell upon me, will you, Mr. Page. You wouldn't prevent a poor woman from getting her living?

HUBERT PAGE: Not likely; but I'd like to hear how it all came about . . .

ALBERT NOBBS: How I went out as a youth to get my living?

HUBERT PAGE: Yes, tell me the story; for though I was very sleepy just now, the sleep has left my eyes and I'd like to hear it. But before you begin, tell me what you were doing, wriggling about like that.

ALBERT NOBBS: It was a flea. I suffer terribly from fleas, and you must have brought some in with you, Mr. Page. I shall be covered in blotches in the morning.

HUBERT PAGE: I'm sorry for that. But tell me how long ago it was that you became a man? Before you came to Dublin, of course?

ALBERT NOBBS: Oh yes, long before . . .

HUBERT PAGE: Tell me . . .

ALBERT NOBBS: It is very cold.

HUBERT PAGE: . . . Come, tell me.

Albert Nobbs' Tale

ALBERT NOBBS: You know I'm not Irish, Mr. Page. My parents may have been, for all I know. The only one who knew who they were was my old nurse, and she never told me.

HUBERT PAGE: She never told you?

ALBERT NOBBS: No, she never told me, though I often asked her, saying no good would come of holding it back from me. She might have told me before she died, but she died suddenly.

HUBERT PAGE: Without telling you who you were!

ALBERT NOBBS: Yes.

HUBERT PAGE: You'd better begin at the beginning.

ALBERT NOBBS: The story seems to me to be without a beginning; anyway I don't know the beginning. I was a bastard. My old nurse hinted more than once that my people were grand folk, and I know she had a big allowance from them for my education. When they died the allowance was no longer paid, and my nurse and myself had to go out to work. There was no time for picking and choosing. We hadn't what would keep us until the end of the month in the house . . . The first job that came our way was looking after chambers in the Temple. We had three gentlemen to look after, so there was eighteen shillings a week between my old nurse and myself; the omnibus fares had to come out of these wages, and to save sixpence a day we went to live in Temple Lane. [*Pause.*] My old nurse didn't mind the lane; she had been a working woman all her life, but with me it was different. I got my education at a convent school, you know, and the change was so great from the convent that I often thought I would sooner die than continue to live like the animals, indecently, and life without decency is hardly bearable, so I thought. I've been through a great deal since in different hotels, and have become used to hard work. [*Pause.*] And then my nurse's brother lost his post.

HUBERT PAGE: What did he do?

ALBERT NOBBS: He'd been a bandmaster, a bugler, or something to do with music in the country. He came to stay with us. My old nurse was obliged to give him sixpence a day, and the drop from eighteen shillings to fourteen and sixpence is a big one. My nurse worried about the food, but it was the rough men I worried about; the bandsman wouldn't leave me alone, and many's the time I've waited until the staircase was clear, afraid that if I met him or another that I'd be caught hold of and held and pulled about. I might have been tempted if one of them had been less rough than the rest, and if I hadn't known I was a bastard; it was that, I think, that kept me straight more than anything else, for I had just begun to feel what a great misfortune it is for a poor girl to find herself in the family way; no greater misfortune can befall anyone in this world, but it would have been worse in my case, for I should only be bringing another bastard into the world.

HUBERT PAGE: But the gentlemen you worked for—were they at least pleasant?

ALBERT NOBBS: They were barristers, pleasant and considerate men they all were—yes, pleasant to work for. One of them was called Mr. Congreve. He had chambers in Temple Gardens overlooking the river, and it was a pleasure to us to keep his pretty things clean, never breaking one of them. Looking back I can see that I must have loved Mr. Congreve very dearly. [*Pause.*] I can see him now as plainly as if he were before me— very thin and elegant, with long white hands. I used to know all his suits, as well I might, for it was my job to look after them, to brush them; and I used to spend a great deal more time than was needed taking out spots with benzine, arranging his neckties—he had fifty or sixty, all kinds—and seven or eight greatcoats. A real toff—my word, he was that, but not one of those haughty ones too proud to give one a nod. He always smiled and nodded if we met under the clock, he on his way to the library and I returning to Temple Lane. I used to look round after him saying: He's got on the striped trousers and the embroidered waistcoat.

HUBERT PAGE: Was there no woman in Mr. Congreve's life?

ALBERT NOBBS: That was just it: I never found a hairpin in his bed. But one day, when I took him his letters, I said to myself: Why, this one's from a woman. Nice, that's in France, I said to myself. And thought no more of the matter until another letter arrived from Nice. Now what can she be writing to him about, I wondered. Then a third letter arrived, and a box full of flowers. I can still see it. So overcome was I as I picked them up out of the box that a sudden faintness came over me, and my old nurse said: What is the matter with thee? Of course I never thought that Mr. Congreve would look at me and I don't know that I wanted him to, but I didn't want another woman about the place. I told myself that these rooms would be mine no longer. Of course they never were mine, but you know what I mean. A week later he said to me: There's a lady coming to luncheon here, a French lady, and I remember the piercing that the words caused me, I can feel them here still. [ALBERT *puts her hand to her heart.*] [*Pause.*] Well, I had to serve the luncheon. [*Pause.*] I'm sure no one ever suffered more than I did in those days. I don't think I ever hoped he'd fall in love with me. It wasn't as bad as that. It was the hopelessness of it that set the tears streaming down my cheeks. Mr. Congreve's kindness seemed to hurt me more than anything. If only he'd spared me his kind words, and not spoken about the extra money he was going to give me for my attendance on his lady, I shouldn't have felt so much that they had lain side by side in the bed that I was making. I said to myself: I can't put up with it any longer. I began to think how I might make away with myself. I don't know if you know London, Hubert?

HUBERT PAGE: Of course I do, I'm a Londoner. I only come here to work every year.

ALBERT NOBBS: Then if you know the Temple, you know that the windows of Temple Gardens overlook the Thames. I often used to stand at those windows watching the big brown river flowing through its bridges, thinking all the while of the sea into which it went, and that I must plunge into the river and be carried away down to the sea, or be picked up before I got there. I could only think about making an end to my trouble and of the Frenchwoman. I'm sure if I hadn't met Bessie Lawrence I should have done away with myself.

HUBERT PAGE: Bessie Lawrence?

ALBERT NOBBS: She was the woman who used to look after the chambers under Mr. Congreve's. We stopped to talk outside the gateway by King's Bench Walk—if you know the Temple, you know where I mean.

[*Simultaneously.*]

BESSIE'S VOICE: There is a big dinner at the Freemason's Tavern tonight, and they're short of waiters. If it wasn't for my hips and bosom I'd very soon be into a suit of evening clothes and getting ten shillings for the job. If only I had a figure like yours.	ALBERT NOBBS: Bessie kept on talking . . . but I wasn't listening . . . only catching a word here and there . . . not waking up from my dream how to make away with myself . . .

ALBERT NOBBS: My figure!—No one had ever spoken about my figure before—what had my figure got to do with it?

BESSIE'S VOICE: You haven't been listening to me.

[*Almost at the same time, but just slightly out of phase.*]

ALBERT NOBBS [*To* HUBERT.] You haven't been listening to me, she said. I only missed the last few words.

BESSIE'S VOICE: Just missed the last few words . . . . ? You didn't hear me telling you that there is a big dinner at the Freemason's Tavern tonight, and they're short of waiters.

ALBERT NOBBS: But what has that got to do with my figure?

BESSIE'S VOICE: Didn't I say that if it wasn't for my hips and bosom I'd very soon be into a suit of evening clothes and getting ten shillings for the job.

ALBERT NOBBS: But what has that got to do with my figure?

BESSIE'S VOICE: Your figure is just the one for a waiter's.

ALBERT NOBBS: Oh, I'd never thought of that. Mr. Congreve had given me a bundle of old clothes to sell. A suit of evening clothes was in it. You see, Mr. Congreve and myself were about the same height and build. The trousers will just want a bit of shortening, I said to myself, and I set to work; and at six o'clock I was in them and down at the

Freemason's Tavern answering questions, saying that I had been accustomed to wait-ing at table. I was taken on, and it was a mess that I made of it, getting in everybody's way; but my awkwardness was taken in good part and I received the ten shillings, which was good money for the sort of work I did that night.

But what stood to me was not so much the ten shillings that I earned as the bit I had learned. It was only a bit, not much bigger than a threepenny bit, but I had worked round a table at a big dinner. The food I'd had, and the excitement of the dinner, the guests, the lights, the talk, stood to me, and things seemed clearer than they had ever seemed before.

Another job came along, and another and another. Each of them jobs was worth ten shillings to me, to say nothing of the learning of the trade; and having the making of a waiter in me, it didn't take more than about three months for me to be as quick and as smart and as watchful as the best of them, and without them qualities no one will suc-ceed in waiting. I have worked round the tables in the biggest places in London and all over England in all the big towns, in Manchester, in Liverpool, and Birmingham. It was seven years ago that I came here, and here it would seem that I've come to be looked on as a fixture, for the Bakers are good people to work for and I may as well be here as else-where.

HUBERT PAGE: Seven years working in Morrison's Hotel, and on the second floor?

ALBERT NOBBS: Yes, the second floor is the best in the hotel; the money is better than in the coffee-room, and that is why the Bakers have put me there. They've often said they don't know what they'd do without me.

HUBERT PAGE: Seven years, the same work up the stairs and down the stairs, banging into the kitchen and out again.

ALBERT NOBBS: There's more variety in the work than you think, Hubert. Every family is different, and so you're always learning.

HUBERT PAGE: Seven years! Neither man nor woman, just a perhapser.

[HUBERT PAGE *had spoken these words more to himself than to* ALBERT NOBBS, *but feeling he had expressed himself incautiously he raised his eyes and read on* ALBERT's *face that the words had gone home, and that this outcast from both sexes felt her loneliness perhaps more keenly than before.*]

ALBERT NOBBS: Neither man nor woman; yet nobody ever would have suspected me till the day of my death if it hadn't been for that flea that you brought in with you.

HUBERT PAGE: But what harm did the flea do you?

ALBERT NOBBS: I'm bitten all over.

HUBERT PAGE: Never mind the bites; we wouldn't have had this talk if it hadn't been for the flea, and I shouldn't have heard your story.

[ALBERT NOBBS *tries to keep her tears back, but they are soon running quickly down her cheeks.*]

ALBERT NOBBS: I thought nobody would ever hear it, and I thought I should never cry again.

It's all much sadder than I thought it was, and if I'd known how sad it was I shouldn't have been able to live through it. But I've jostled along somehow, always merry and bright, with never anyone to speak to, not really to speak to, only to ask for plates and dishes, for knives and forks and such like, tablecloths and napkins . . . It might have been better if I had taken the plunge.

[*She calms down.*]

But why am I thinking these things? It's you that has set me thinking, Hubert.

HUBERT PAGE: I'm sorry if . . .

ALBERT NOBBS: Oh, it's no use being sorry, and I'm a great silly to cry like this. I thought that regrets had passed away with the petticoats. But you've awakened the woman in me. You've brought it all up again. But I mustn't let on like this; it's very foolish of an old perhapser like me, neither man nor woman. But I can't help it. You understand . . . the loneliness . . .

[*She begins to sob again.* HUBERT PAGE *waits until the paroxysm is over.*]

HUBERT PAGE: Lonely, yes, I suppose it is lonely.

ALBERT NOBBS: You're very good, Mr. Page, and I'm sure you'll keep my secret, though indeed I don't care very much whether you do or not.

HUBERT PAGE: Now, don't let on like that again. I'm sure it's lonely for you to live without man or without woman, thinking like a man and feeling like a woman.

ALBERT NOBBS: You seem to know all about it, Hubert. I hadn't thought of it like that before myself. You're quite right. I suppose I was wrong to put off my petticoats and step into those trousers.

HUBERT PAGE: I wouldn't go so far as to say that.

ALBERT NOBBS: Why do you say that, Hubert?

HUBERT PAGE: Well, because I was thinking that you might marry.

ALBERT NOBBS: But I was never a success as a girl. Men didn't look at me then, so I'm sure they wouldn't now I'm a middle-aged woman. Marriage! Whom should I marry? No, there's no marriage for me in the world; I must go on being a man. But you won't tell on me? You've promised, Hubert.

HUBERT PAGE: Of course I won't tell, but I don't see why you shouldn't marry.

ALBERT NOBBS: What do you mean, Hubert? You aren't putting a joke upon me, are you? If you are, it's very unkind.

HUBERT PAGE: A joke upon you? Not at all. I didn't mean that you should marry a man, but you might marry a girl.

ALBERT NOBBS: Marry a girl? . . . a girl?

HUBERT PAGE: Well, anyway, that's what I've done.

ALBERT NOBBS: But you're a young man, and a very handsome young man too. Any girl would like to have you, and I dare say they were all after you before you met the right girl.

HUBERT PAGE: Listen to me, Albert. [*Pause.*] I'm not a man.

ALBERT NOBBS: Ah! Now I know for certain you're putting a joke upon me.

HUBERT PAGE: No, I'm not a man, I'm a woman.

[*They look at each other. The sincerity in* ALBERT NOBBS' *gaze gives* HUBERT PAGE *the courage to continue.*]

My husband was a house-painter. After the birth of my second child, he changed towards me altogether. He drank, he beat me, he left me without money for food, and sold up the home twice. At last I decided to have another cut at it, and catching sight of my husband's working clothes one day I said to myself: He's often made me put these on and go out and help him with his job; why shouldn't I put them on for myself and go away for good? It broke my heart to leave the children, but I couldn't remain with him.

ALBERT NOBBS: But the other marriage?

HUBERT PAGE: It was lonely going home to an empty room; I was as lonely as you, and one day, meeting a girl as lonely as myself, I said: Come along, and we arranged to live together, each paying our share. She had her work and I had mine, and between us we made a fair living; and this I can say with truth, that we haven't known an unhappy hour since we married. People began to talk, so we had to move. I'd like you to see our home. I always return to my home after a job is finished with a light heart and leave it with a heavy one.

ALBERT NOBBS: But I don't understand.

HUBERT PAGE: What don't you understand? It's very simple.

ALBERT NOBBS: I can't think now of what I was going to ask you . . .

HUBERT PAGE: You're falling asleep, and I'm doing the same. It must be three o'clock in the morning and I've to catch the five o'clock train.

ALBERT NOBBS: But you'll tell me later . . .

HUBERT PAGE: Yes, go to sleep now. I'll tell you later.

[ALBERT NOBBS *remains sitting on the bed, motionless.*]

[HUBERT PAGE *gets up, looks through the windows at the dawn rising and steals away very quietly, while* ALBERT *lies down and falls asleep.*]

[*It is morning.* HUBERT PAGE *has gone.* ALBERT NOBBS *is alone in her bed.*]

ALBERT NOBBS: His train started from Amiens Street at . . . I must have slept heavily for him—for her not to have awakened me, or she must have stolen away very quietly. But I mustn't fall into the habit of sheing him. Lord amassy, what time is it?

[*She looks at the time, and jumps out of bed. Folds it. Dresses . . .*]

An hour late . . . Such a thing never happened to me before. And the hotel as full as it can hold. Why didn't they send for me? Lord, if the missis knew everything! But I've overslept myself a full hour. The greater haste the less speed.

[ALBERT NOBBS *puts her bed away and, still dressing, runs out on to her landing. The swing door comes into operation. Bedroom bells can be heard, and the voices of maids and cooks.* ALBERT *gets into her apron, laces her shoes, buttons her waistcoat, puts on her jacket, etc. . . .*]

ALBERT NOBBS: We're late today, and the house full of visitors.

A VOICE: 54 has just rung, Albert.

MRS. BAKER: How is it that 54 isn't turned out? Has 35 rung his bell?

ALBERT NOBBS: Not yet, Mrs. Baker.

A COOK'S VOICE: 22 and 12 want their breakfasts.

ANOTHER COOK'S VOICE: Fried or boiled egg for 22?

[ALBERT NOBBS *is surrounded by all these voices. She stops, and seems to be thinking, dreaming. It isn't clear whether the voices are her real, everyday noises, or those she heard during the night, or the result of her fatigue . . .*]

A VOICE: Sitting up half the night talking to Mr. Page, and then rounding on us.

[*She is tying her tie.*]

ALBERT NOBBS: Half the night talking! Where is Mr. Page? I didn't hear him go away; he may have missed his train for aught I know. But do you be getting on with your work, and let me be getting on with mine.

ANOTHER VOICE: You're very cross this morning, Albert.

THE HEAD PORTER'S VOICE: Well, Mr. Nobbs, how did you find your bed-fellow?

ALBERT NOBBS: Oh, he was all right, but I'm not used to bed-fellows, and he brought a flea with him, and it kept me awake. When I did fall asleep, I slept so heavily that I was an hour late. I hope he caught his train.

[ALBERT NOBBS *goes up to her landing and takes her seat in the passage, her napkin over her shoulder. She asks herself, anxiously.*]

ALBERT NOBBS: But what is all this pother about bed-fellows?

[*Enter* MRS. BAKER. *She sits down at her work table.*]

[*The hotel has calmed down. The light in the windows changes; the morning sun turns into that of the late afternoon. It is as if time is standing still at the beginning of the evening.* ALBERT speaks *in a monologue with three voices: her inner voice and that of* GEORGE MOORE *coming from somewhere quite different. A soft light, with occasional patches of semi-darkness.*]

Albert's Dream

ALBERT NOBBS: Page hasn't said anything, no she's said nothing, for we are both in the same boat, and to tell on me would be to tell on herself. [*Pause.*] She's woman right enough. But the cheek of it, to marry an innocent girl! Did she let the girl into the secret, or leave her to find it out when . . . The girl might have called in the police!

GEORGE MOORE'S VOICE: This was a question one might ponder on. She wouldn't have had the cheek to wed her, Albert said to herself, without warning her that things might not turn out as she fancied.

ALBERT NOBBS: Mayhap she didn't tell her before they wedded, and mayhap she did.

[MRS. BAKER *passes, on her way to the bedrooms on the first floor.*]

MRS. BAKER: Were you speaking to me, Albert?

ALBERT NOBBS: [*Starting up from her chair guiltily, as if woken out of a dream.*] No no, Mrs. Baker, I didn't say anything.

MRS. BAKER: Did you sleep well last night then, Albert?

ALBERT: Yes thank you, Mrs. Baker, I only just awoke from time to time . . .

[*She goes and sits down. At* MRS. BAKER'S *next order she jumps up again like a puppet.*]

MRS. BAKER: Don't forget 35's tea.

[MRS. BAKER *disappears behind a door.* ALBERT NOBBS *goes back to her reverie. She walks up and down slowly, keeping time with her thoughts.*]

ALBERT NOBBS: Right away, Mrs. Baker.

[ALBERT NOBBS *comes down from her landing, walks slowly over to the kitchen to fetch a tea tray, and comes back. She is so lost in her thoughts that she has forgotten where she was supposed to take the tray, and goes back to the kitchen with it.*]

ALBERT NOBBS: But Hubert did say that she had lived with a girl first, and wedded her to put a stop to people's scandal. Of course they could hardly live together except as man and wife. She always returned home with a light heart and never left it without a heavy one.

So it would seem that this marriage was as successful as any, and a great deal more than most.

[*The light changes. It is evening. The gas lamps come on. The backcloth seems to come to life. A guest, whom we don't see, comes downstairs. She passes by, and goes out of the hotel through the revolving door, which rotates of its own accord. The very real* MRS. BAKER *follows the guest.*]

THE GUEST'S VOICE: Have a good evening, Albert; we're off to the theatre.

ALBERT NOBBS: Have a good evening, Mrs. Lavery. I'm sure it will be an interesting play.

MRS. BAKER: Albert, I'm going out; I'm leaving you in charge of the hotel.

ALBERT NOBBS: Have no fear, Mrs. Baker.

[ALBERT NOBBS *goes back to her reverie, and automatically makes her way up to her chair again.*]

Hubert married.
Of course it wasn't a real marriage, it couldn't be that.
But a very happy one it would seem. [*Pause.*]
For after all I've worked hard . . . Five-and-twenty years . . . a mere drifting from one hotel to another, without friends.

[*A chambermaid,* ALBERT NOBBS' *double, her feminine counterpart, appears behind* AL-BERT—*follows her, helps her and accompanies her in her reverie.* ALBERT *goes and picks up a pair of shoes left outside a door and returns to her chair. Her feminine double hands her the duster and brush.*]

ALBERT NOBBS: But what if Hubert was putting a joke upon me? [*Pause.*] I didn't ask her what her home might be like. I should have asked if she had a clock and vases on the chimney-piece.

[*Voice of a maid calling from the end of the passage.*]

VOICE: Albert!

ALBERT NOBBS: Coming.

THE VOICE: 54 wants his bottle of mineral water.

[ALBERT NOBBS *stands up, puts down the shoes, goes into the kitchen and comes back with a bottle of mineral water on a tray. She takes it through one of the doors and comes and sits down again in her place. During this time the fairy-chambermaid, her double, has been cleaning the shoes, and when* ALBERT *picks them up they are already beautifully polished.*]

ALBERT NOBBS: It seems to me that Hubert said that her wife was a milliner. She may not have spoken the word milliner; but if she hadn't, it is strange that the word should keep on coming up in my mind. There is no reason why the wife shouldn't be a milliner, and if that is so it is as likely as not that they own a house in some quiet, insignificant street, letting the dining-room, back room and kitchen to a widow or to a pair of widows. The drawing-room would be the workroom and showroom.

GEORGE MOORE'S VOICE: On second thoughts it seemed to Albert that if the business were millinery it might be that Mrs. Page would prefer the ground floor for her show-room.

ALBERT NOBBS: Or rather, they would have kept the whole of the ground floor and only let the rooms above. No, that would have meant that the widows would have had to go through their part of the house. That's always annoying. No lodgers at all. [*Pause.*]

[*Her feminine double imitates every movement she makes. It is as if they are superimposed on each other.*]

On further thoughts, not a milliner but a seamstress. . . . A small dressmaker's business in a quiet street would be in keeping with all Hubert said about her home.

I'm not sure, however, that if I found a girl willing to share her life with me it would be a seamstress's business I would be on the look-out for. . . . I rather think that a sweet shop, newspapers and tobacco, would be my choice.

Why shouldn't I make a fresh start? Hubert had no difficulties.

ALBERT NOBBS' VOICE: She said:

ALBERT NOBBS: I can recall her very words.

ALBERT NOBBS VOICE: I didn't mean you should marry a man, but a girl.

ALBERT NOBBS: I've saved—oh! how I've tried to save, for I don't wish to end my days in the workhouse. . . . Upwards of five hundred pounds, which is enough to purchase a little business. . . .

GEORGE MOORE'S VOICE: If it took her two years to find a partner and a business, she would have at least seventy or eighty pounds more, which would be a great help, for it would be a mistake to put one's money into a falling business.

ALBERT NOBBS: If I found a partner, I'd have to do like Hubert, for marriage would put a stop to all tittle-tattle. I would be able to keep my place at Morrison's Hotel, or perhaps leave Morrison's and rely on jobs with my connections; it would be a case of picking and choosing the best: ten and sixpence a night, nothing under.

ALBERT NOBBS' VOICE: I could make a round: Belfast, Liverpool, Manchester, Bradford . . . and after a month's absence, a couple of months maybe, I would return home, my heart anticipating a welcome—a real welcome, for though I would continue to be a man to the world, I would be a woman to the dear one at home.

[*She goes and puts the shoes down outside a bedroom door. Her double remains standing behind her chair.*]

ALBERT NOBBS: With a real partner, one whose heart is in the business, we might make as much as two hundred pounds a year—four pounds a week! And with four pounds a week our home would be as pretty and happy as any in the city of Dublin.

GEORGE MOORE'S VOICE: Two rooms and a kitchen were what she foresaw. The furniture began to creep into her imagination little by little. A large sofa by the fireplace covered with a chintz!

ALBERT NOBBS: But chintz dirties quickly in the city.

GEORGE MOORE'S VOICE: A dark velvet sofa might be more suitable.

ALBERT NOBBS: It will cost a great deal of money, five or six pounds; and at that rate fifty pounds won't go very far, for we must have a fine mattress; and if we are going to do things in that style, the home will cost us something like eighty pounds.

GEORGE MOORE'S VOICE: With luck, these eighty pounds could be earned within the next two years at Morrison's Hotel.

ALBERT NOBBS: The people in 34 are leaving tomorrow; they are always good for half a sovereign . . . tomorrow's half-sovereign must be put aside as a beginning of a sum of money for the purchase of a clock to stand on a marble chimney-piece or a mahogany chiffonier.

The Concert

Enter MRS. BAKER, *coming from the kitchen, followed by the* SECOND CHAMBERMAID. *The* FIRST CHAMBERMAID *comes down the stairs, fetches two chairs and puts them down with their backs to the audience.* MRS. BAKER *and the* FIRST CHAMBERMAID *sit down on them, ready for the concert. The* FIRST CHAMBERMAID's *movements are rapid and unreal.* ALBERT NOBBS *is about to go upstairs.*

MRS. BAKER: What can Albert be dreaming of? Albert, you took the drinks to 5 yesterday, but you forgot the cigars.

[ALBERT NOBBS *turns round like a sleep-walker and goes upstairs.*]

ALBERT NOBBS' VOICE: A shop with two counters, one for cigars, tobacco, pipes and matches, and the other for all kinds of sweets.

MRS. BAKER: [*Continuing a conversation with* THE CHAMBERMAID.] Morton asked her whether she loved him as much as she had loved Ralph. That was quite different. He was very good to me, she said. Do you think I won't be good to you? said Morton. If you loved me, you wouldn't kiss me like that—just a little peck. I don't know how to kiss any other way, she replied. This is the first time we have walked out together. I have never been out so late with a man. You can't love me, you only met me yesterday. But I am going to love you. Let me kiss you, that's the only way, he said. I would like a man to love me before he kissed me. Then you will never be loved, for it is by way of the lips that love enters into the blood, and so on and so forth—she was twisting him round her little finger.

THE CHAMBERMAID: She was leading him on.

[ALBERT NOBBS *comes down with two suitcases, following an invisible* GUEST.]

THE GUEST'S VOICE: I'm sorry to disturb you, Mrs. Baker, but I'm leaving now, the carriage is at the door.

MRS. BAKER: [*To the gentleman, whom we still cannot see.*] Goodbye, Mr. Ruttledge. What a pity you will not be at the concert. We shall see you next season, I hope.

THE GUEST'S VOICE: No doubt about that, Mrs. Baker.

[*He laughs rather stupidly.* MRS. BAKER *does the same, and waves goodbye to him. The revolving door rotates of its own accord as the invisible* GUEST *passes through it.*]

MRS. BAKER: Goodbye, have a good journey!
THE GUEST'S VOICE: Goodbye, and thank you.

[*During this exchange of courtesies,* ALBERT*'s thoughts are far away. She puts the luggage into the carriage automatically. She comes back and we see her in the doorway, holding out her hand, coming to life and bowing when she is given her tip. The carriage can be heard leaving.*]

ALBERT NOBBS' VOICE: A sovereign! That's good for a pair of pretty candlesticks and a round mirror.

[*Meanwhile, the* FIRST CHAMBERMAID *has brought in an easel, and then a picture which she places on the easel, in front of* MRS. BAKER. *The picture shows a lady singing, and another accompanying her at the piano. This is the concert.*]

MRS. BAKER: Oh, I was forgetting: are you there, Albert?

[ALBERT *comes back.*]

Mrs. Swift left me a crown for you.
ALBERT NOBBS: Thank you, Madam.
GEORGE MOORE'S VOICE: This unexpected crown set her pondering on the colour of the curtains in their sitting-room.

[*The concert begins. During this scene,* GEORGE MOORE*'s and* ALBERT NOBBS' *voices are heard. Music: the Irish song: "I Once Loved a Boy."*]

GEORGE MOORE'S VOICE: Albert became suddenly conscious that a change had come into her life: the show was the same, but behind the show a new life was springing up, a strangely personal life. She wasn't as good a servant as heretofore. She knew it. Certain absences of mind, that was all.

[*The lights in the hotel go down.*]

ALBERT NOBBS: A widow with a child of three or four, a boy the son of a dead man. No, a woman who had been deserted before the birth of her child. I should be the father in everybody's eyes, except the mother's of course. [*Pause.*] A babe that would come into the world some three or four months after our marriage, a little girl. What matter whether she calls me father or mother? They are but mere words that the lips speak, but love is in the heart, and only love matters. [*Pause.*]

Some revivalist meetings are soon going to be held in Dublin.
Many of our girls attend them, and an unlucky girl will be in luck's way if we should run across one another.

[*The concert ends.*]

MRS. BAKER: Now whatever can Albert be brooding?

[*Voices of maidservants, chambermaids, floor waiters and cooks. The swing door swings of its own accord; the hotel is at its busiest.* MRS. BAKER *goes into the kitchens. The* FIRST CHAMBERMAID *removes the concert: the easel and picture. The* SECOND CHAMBERMAID *puts away the chairs.*]

CHAMBERMAIDS' VOICES: [*Whispered.*]—Brooding a love-story?
—Not likely.
—A marriage with some girl outside? He isn't over-partial to any of us.
—Have you noticed that he is eager to avail himself of every excuse to absent himself from duty in the hotel?
—I have seen him in the smaller streets looking up at the houses.
—They say he has saved a good deal of money, and some of his savings are in house property.

—What would you say if Albert was going to be married, and was looking out for a house for his wife?

—He's been seen talking with Annie Watts.

[*These voices are mainly coming from the kitchen and are very audible every time the swing door opens.*]

MRS. BAKER: Quiet, please! Less talk and more work!

[*The hotel calms down. The lights dim. Three chambermaids sing "The Butcher's Boy."*]

ALBERT NOBBS: Annie Watts? No, not she. After all, she is not in the family way, and her heart is not in her work. That isn't the sort for a shop. Whereas Dorothy Keyes is a glutton for work, but I couldn't abide that tall, angular woman with a neck like a swan's. And her manner is abrupt. While Alice's small, neat figure and quick intelligence mark her out for the job . . . But alas! Alice is hot-tempered. We should quarrel.

[*She picks up her napkin, which had slipped from her knee to the floor, and puts it back on her shoulder.*]

What about the maids on the floor above? Mary O'Brien would make an attractive shopwoman . . . she has a certain stateliness of figure and also of gait. Ah! But she's a Papist. And the experience of Irish Protestants show that Papists and Protestants don't mix.

A CHAMBERMAID'S VOICE: Is that the new one?

[*This remark vaguely interrupts* ALBERT NOBBS's *musing.*]

ALBERT NOBBS: There's that lazy girl Annie Watts, on the look-out for an excuse to chatter the time away instead of being about her work.

[ALBERT NOBBS *goes over towards the kitchens and holds the swing door open. She speaks to* ANNIE WATTS, *who cannot be seen.*]

ANNIE WATTS' VOICE: Helen Dawes has arrived, Mr. Albert—the new kitchen-maid.

ALBERT NOBBS: Ah!

ANNIE WATTS' VOICE: She must be here.

[*She almost bumps into a girl coming through the swing doors:* HELEN DAWES.]

The Meeting with Helen Dawes

ANNIE WATTS' VOICE: She is not at all what I had imagined.

ALBERT NOBBS: So you're the new one—Helen Dawes?

HELEN DAWES: I am indeed, sir.

[HELEN DAWES *doesn't move.* ALBERT NOBBS *walks away then half turns back, looking at Helen over her shoulder. The lights dim a little. They are quite a distance from each other, and remain motionless during the following speeches.*]

ALEC'S VOICE: She has white, even teeth, your honour.

GEORGE MOORE'S VOICE: Yes, but unfortunately they were protruding, giving her the appearance of a rabbit. [*Pause.*] Her eyes seemed to be dark brown, round eyes that dilated and flashed wonderfully while she talked.

[*The lights come up again.* ALBERT NOBBS *and* HELEN DAWES *move. The swing door comes to life.* HELEN *is about to go through it and* ALBERT *is about to go upstairs. She stops, as if a thought has just struck her and as if she were changing her mind. She is standing in* HELEN's *way.*]

ALBERT NOBBS: I shall be off duty at three today, and if you are not engaged . . .

HELEN DAWES: I am off duty at three.

ALBERT NOBBS: Are you engaged?

HELEN DAWES: Well, the truth is . . . I was to have walked out with Joe Mackins. I can't give you a promise until I have asked him.

[ALBERT NOBBS *goes upstairs and disappears into the wings.*]

[HELEN DAWES *is alone on stage, talking to* JOE MACKLINS *in the wings.*]

JOE'S VOICE: He wants to walk out with you?

HELEN DAWES: He's harmless in himself, and with a very good smell of money rising out of his pockets. You seldom have a train fare upon you.

JOE'S VOICE: Why, he has never been known to walk out with man, woman or child before. Well, that's a good one! I'd like to know what he's after, but I'm not jealous; you can go with him, there's no harm in Albert. Poke him up and see what he's after, and take him into a sweetshop and bring back a box of chocolates.

HELEN DAWES: Do you like chocolates?

JOE'S VOICE: Where are you going to meet him?

HELEN DAWES: At the corner.

[*She goes over to one of the windows.*]

[*He is there already.*]

JOE'S VOICE: Then be off.

HELEN DAWES: You wouldn't like me to keep him waiting?

JOE'S VOICE: Oh, dear no, not for Joe, not for Joseph, if he knows it. [JOE *lilts the song.*]

HELEN DAWES: You won't peach upon me to the others, will you?

The Walk in the Street

There are three shop signs in the street: A confectioner's, a jeweller's and a draper's. ALBERT NOBBS *is sitting waiting on a bench.*

[HELEN DAWES *joins him.*]

HELEN DAWES: Were you afraid I wasn't coming?

ALBERT NOBBS: [*Very shyly.*] Not very.

[HELEN DAWES *pouts slightly. This seems a stupid answer to her. Silence. They sit down on the bench. An embarrassed pause.* HELEN DAWES *looks round her and stands up. She reads the shop sign: O'Toole, Confectioner.*]

ALBERT NOBBS: Do you like chocolates?

HELEN DAWES: Something under the tooth will help the time away.

ALBERT NOBBS' VOICE: A shilling or one and sixpence will see me through it.

[*They are looking in the window of the confectioner's shop.*]

HELEN DAWES: Might I have one of those large, pictured boxes?

ALBERT NOBBS: Yes . . . I'm afraid they'll cost a lot.

[HELEN DAWES *shrugs her shoulders disdainfully.* ALBERT NOBBS *hastens to add.*]

ALBERT NOBBS: Oh, I'll buy you two, Helen. One to pass the time with and another to take home.

HELEN DAWES: I love chocolates. Of course you will say, Albert, that they make you fat. But I don't mind; if you had to go without . . .

ALBERT NOBBS' VOICE: Three and sixpence! How dreadful!

HELEN DAWES: Joe likes chocolates too, but he prefers cigars. That's natural for a man, isn't it?

ALBERT NOBBS' VOICE: Yes, but she has expensive tastes. If every walk is to cost me three and sixpence . . .

GEORGE MOORE'S VOICE: In fact, there wouldn't be a lot left for the home in six months' time. And Albert fell to calculating how much it would cost her if they were to walk out once a week.

ALBERT NOBBS' VOICE: Three fours are twelve and four sixpences are two shillings, fourteen shillings a month, twice that is twenty-eight; twenty-eight shillings a month if Helen wants two boxes a week. At that rate I'd be spending sixteen pounds sixteen shillings a year.

[*In the meantime* HELEN DAWES *has wandered off and is gazing into the shop windows. They come to the jeweller's.*]

ALBERT NOBB'S VOICE: Lord amassy! But perhaps Helen won't want two boxes of chocolates every time we go out together.

[ALBERT NOBBS *suddenly realizes that* HELEN DAWES *is looking in the jeweller's window, and tries to avert her attention.*]

ALBERT NOBBS: Look, Helen—that cyclist only just managed to escape a tram car. He gave a sudden wriggle.

[HELEN DAWES *comes over, happily.*]

GEORGE MOORE'S VOICE: But Albert was always unlucky.

HELEN DAWES: Oh! I've been wishing this long while for a bicycle, Albert!

[*She goes back to the jeweller's.*]

What pretty bangles!

GEORGE MOORE'S VOICE: For a moment Albert's heart seemed to stand still.

[ALBERT NOBBS *tries once again to lead her away from the shop windows.*]

ALBERT NOBBS: Come, Helen, I want to show you the north side of the city.

HELEN DAWES: I have little taste for the meaner parts, and I wonder what you can find to interest you in those streets.

ALBERT NOBBS: They're so pleasant! And there are all those small newspaper and tobacco shops. Their daily takings are very good. You might take as much as four pounds a week, two hundred pounds a year! And if you add on the sweets . . . That would be even better. They would make a very pretty home, with a parlour . . .

[HELEN DAWES *arrives at the draper's shop.*]

HELEN DAWES: I would like a pair of six-button gloves. If I had a silk kerchief and some new stockings and shoes, I would wear them next Thursday, if you invited me to walk with you, Albert.

[*They walk off.*]

[HELEN DAWES *immediately returns to her conversation with* JOE. *She is making a show of doing some housework, but most of the time she stops at the swing door to talk to* JOE.]

HELEN DAWES: Until I remembered suddenly that he had invested his savings in house property. Did you know that, Joe? Could those be his houses? All his own? Who knows? I reckon that he is a richer man than anybody believes him to be, but he is a mean one. The idea of his thinking twice about a box of chocolates! I'll show him, I said to myself, and it seemed to me that the time had come to speak of bangles. For three pounds I could have a pretty one, I told him, and I even said: one that it will be a real pleasure to wear; it will always remind me of you.

JOE'S VOICE: How did he take that?

HELEN DAWES: He coughed up. And I felt that I had "got him."

JOE'S VOICE: So he parted easily. But I say, old girl, since he's coughing up so easily you might bring me something back; a briar-wood pipe and a pound or two of tobacco, that's the least you might obtain for me.

HELEN DAWES: To get those I would have to ask Albert for money.

JOE'S VOICE: And why shouldn't you? It's the first quid that's hard to get; every time after it's like shelling peas.

HELEN DAWES: Do you think he's that far gone on me?

JOE'S VOICE: Well, don't you? Why should he give you these things if he wasn't? [*Pause.*] What do you think of him?

HELEN DAWES: It's hard to say. I have walked out with many a man before but never with one like Albert Nobbs.

JOE'S VOICE: In what way is he different?

HELEN DAWES: There's a sort of slackness about him.

JOE'S VOICE: [*Amused.*] You mean he doesn't pull you about?

HELEN DAWES: There's something of that in it, but that isn't the whole of it. I've been out before with men that didn't pull me about, but he seems to have something on his mind, and half the time he's thinking.

JOE'S VOICE: Well, what does that matter, so long as there is coin in his pockets?

HELEN DAWES: I don't like it. I don't want to go out any more with Albert. I'm tired of the job.

JOE'S VOICE: Next time you go out with him, work him up a bit and see what he is made of; just see if there's a sting in him or if he is no better than a capon.

HELEN DAWES: A capon? And what is a capon?

JOE'S VOICE: A capon is a cut fowl. He may be like one.

HELEN DAWES: You think that, do you? I shall get the truth of the matter. It does seem odd that he should be willing to buy me presents and not want to kiss me. In fact, it is more than odd. I might as well go out with my mother. It may be as you say. Or is it a blind? . . . some other girl that he . . .

I'm beginning to feel ugly towards him. He must know that I'm partial to you.

[MRS. BAKER *comes from the kitchens, followed by* HELEN DAWES, *who has taken a pile of plates from the sideboard.* ALBERT NOBBS *comes downstairs with a pile of sheets. During the following speeches they look at each other over* MRS. BAKER, *who doesn't understand a thing, and exits.* HELEN DAWES *stays for a moment, legs apart, in front of the wing door, and then goes out.* ALBERT NOBBS *goes upstairs, puts her sheets down outside one of the doors in the backcloth, then comes down again slowly for the rest of the scene.*]

HELEN DAWES: It really is a bit much.

ALBERT NOBBS' VOICE: I know that Helen is carrying on with Joe Mackins. I even suspect that some of the money I have given her has gone to purchase pipes and tobacco for him.

GEORGE MOORE'S VOICE: A certain shrewdness is not incompatible with innocence.

HELEN DAWES: Good morning, Mrs. Baker.

MRS. BAKER: Yesterday, Helen, you went off duty before you'd dried the glasses.

HELEN DAWES: I did, Mrs. Baker? I'm sorry, Mrs. Baker.

ALBERT NOBBS' VOICE: It's better for her to have her fling before than after marriage.

HELEN DAWES: I can't see what he is after.

[*Both voices can be heard simultaneously.*]

ALBERT NOBBS' VOICE: She might hanker for children. I feel that I would like a child as well as another. But if Joe Mackins was the father, I foresee trouble.

HELEN DAWES: In any case, I've had enough; I prefer Joe.

[ALBERT NOBBS *goes up to her favourite place on the chair in the middle of the staircase. The lights dim.*]

ALBERT NOBBS: I would prefer another father. [*Pause.*] Almost any other. [*Pause.*] Of course, there would be the expense of the lying-in. [*Pause.*] But how should I tell Helen? Blurt it out?—I've something to tell you, Helen. I'm not a man, but a woman like your-self. [*Pause.*] No, that wouldn't do. How did Hubert manage? If I had only asked her I should have been spared all this trouble. [*Pause.*] But she has a violent temper. [*Pause.*]

Though after her first outburst she might quieten down, when she began to see that it might be very much to her advantage to accept the situation. [*Pause.*] But if she were to cut up rough and do me an injury! She might call the neighbours in, or the policeman, who'd take us both to the station. I'd have to return to Liverpool or to Manchester.

GEORGE MOORE'S VOICE: Her thoughts wandered on to the morning boat.

ALEC'S VOICE: One of the advantages of Dublin, your honour, is that one can get out of it as easily as any other city.

ALBERT NOBBS' VOICE: On the other hand, if I take the straight course, Helen might promise not to tell but she might break her promise. What a hue and cry! Life in Morrison's Hotel would be unendurable. [*Pause.*] If it hadn't been for that flea I wouldn't be in this mess.

ALEC'S VOICE: It was a different sort of girl altogether that she would have needed.

GEORGE MOORE'S VOICE: But she liked Helen, with her way of standing on a doorstep, her legs a little apart, jawing a tradesman, and she'd stand up to Mrs. Baker and to the chef himself. She liked the way Helen's eyes lighted up when a thought came into her mind; her cheery laugh warmed Albert's heart as nothing else did. Before she met Helen she often feared her heart was growing cold.

ALBERT NOBBS' VOICE: I might try the world over and not find one that would run the shop I have in mind as well as Helen.

The Break

Enter HELEN DAWES, *coming downstairs.*

HELEN DAWES: Are you dreaming, Albert, or are you dozing?

ALBERT NOBBS: I was thinking . . .

HELEN DAWES: If we went out together this evening we might go for a walk on the banks of the Dodder.

ALBERT NOBBS: Oh, I should like that.

[ALBERT NOBBS *hurries up the stairs, removes her apron and takes her jacket from a peg.* HELEN DAWES *sends her apron flying and snatches up a little cape. All these movements must be rapid. Both of them pass through the revolving door as if caught up in the movement of a top, and then immediately re-enter. They have come back from their walk: they have quarrelled, and are furious. During the next scene the two chambermaids are always in the place where* ALBERT NOBBS *ought to be, facing* HELEN DAWES. HELEN DAWES *is thus encircled by two women* ALBERTS *and one man* ALBERT. *As for* ALBERT NOBBS *herself, she is encircled by three Helens. By this mirror game and by "trompe-l'oeil," refusal and incomprehension are shown.*]

ALBERT NOBBS: I beseech you not to cast me off. If I've been stupid today it's because I'm tired of the work in the hotel. I shall be different when we get to Lisdoonvarna: we both want a change of air; there's nothing like the salt water and the cliffs of Clare to put new spirits into a man. You will be different and I'll be different; everything will be different.

[HELEN DAWES *shakes her head.*]

Don't say no, Helen; don't say no. I've looked forward to this week in Lisdoonvarna. I have already engaged the lodgings, we shall have to pay for them, and there's the new suit of clothes that have just come back from the tailor's. I've looked forward to wearing it, walking with you in the strand, the waves crashing up into the cliffs, with green fields among them, I've been told! We shall see the ships passing and wonder whither they are going. I've bought three neck-ties and some new shirts, and what good will these be to me if you'll not come to Lisdoonvarna with me?

HELEN DAWES: Oh, don't talk to me about Lisdoonvarna. I'm not going to Lisdoonvarna with you.

ALBERT NOBBS: But what is to become of the hat I have ordered for you? The hat with the big feather in it; and I've bought stockings and shoes for you. Tell me, what shall I do with these, and with the gloves? Oh, the waste of money and the heart-breaking! What shall I do with the hat?

HELEN DAWES: You can leave the hat with me.

ALBERT NOBBS: And the stockings?

HELEN DAWES: Yes, you can leave the stockings.

ALBERT NOBBS: And the shoes?

HELEN DAWES: Yes, you can leave the shoes too.

ALBERT NOBBS: Yet you won't go to Lisdoonvarna with me?

HELEN DAWES: No, I'll not go to Lisdoonvarna with you.

ALBERT NOBBS: But you'll take the presents?

HELEN DAWES: It was to please you I said I would take them, because I thought it would be some satisfaction to you to know that they wouldn't be wasted.

ALBERT NOBBS: Not wasted? You'll wear them when you go out with Joe Mackins.

HELEN DAWES: Oh well, keep your presents.

ALBERT NOBBS: We cannot part like this! Let us talk things over and do nothing foolish. You see, I had set my heart on driving on an outside car to the Broadstone with you, and catching a train, and the train going into lovely country, arriving at a place we had never seen, with cliffs, and the sunset behind the cliffs . . .

HELEN DAWES: You've told all that before. I'm not going to Lisdoonvarna with you. And if that is all you had to say to me . . .

ALBERT NOBBS: But there's much more, Helen. I haven't told you about the shop yet.

HELEN DAWES: Yes, you have told me all there is to tell about the shop; you've been talking about that shop for the last three months.

ALBERT NOBBS: But Helen, it was only yesterday that I got a letter saying that they had had another offer for the shop, and that they could give me only till Monday morning to close with them; if the lease isn't signed by then we've lost the shop.

HELEN DAWES: But what makes you think that the shop will be a success? Many shops promise well in the beginning and fade away till they don't get a customer a day.

ALBERT NOBBS: Our shop won't be like that, I know it won't. We shall be able to make a great success of that shop, and people will be coming to see us, and they will be having tea with us in the parlour, and they'll envy us, saying that never have two people had such luck as we have had. And our wedding will be . . .

HELEN DAWES: Will be what?

ALBERT NOBBS: A great wonder.

HELEN DAWES: A great wonder indeed. But I'm not going to wed you, Albert Nobbs.

[ALBERT NOBBS *goes back to the bench. A simultaneous scene.*]

JOE'S VOICE: What happened on the walk?

HELEN DAWES: Phew! I've broken with Albert. It was in the hope that the river's bank might tempt him into a confidence that I suggested that we might spend the evening by the Dodder.

ALBERT NOBBS: The river's bank might tempt me into a confidence.

HELEN DAWES: But he said nothing. He seemed to be afraid.

ALBERT NOBBS: The silence round us . . . the river flowing over its muddy bottom without ripple or eddy . . . I felt as if I were choking.

JOE'S VOICE: And did he not speak on the way there?

HELEN DAWES: Not a word.

JOE'S VOICE: But tell me—what happened?

HELEN DAWES: There is nothing to tell. . . . It was all very simple . . . you'll see.

[HELEN DAWES *gets dressed again and goes and sits down beside* ALBERT NOBBS *for the following flashback.*]

The Banks of the Dodder

HELEN DAWES: What are you thinking of?

ALBERT NOBBS: [*Startled.*] Of you, dear; and how pleasant it is to be sitting with you.

[*The sound of laughter, and of people passing.*]

A LAD'S VOICE: I'll see if you have any lace on your drawers.

A LASS'S VOICE: You shan't.

HELEN DAWES: There's a pair that's enjoying themselves.

GEORGE MOORE'S VOICE: She looked upon this remark as fortunate, and hoped it would give ALBERT the courage to pursue his courtship. Albert, too, looked upon the remark as fortunate.

ALBERT NOBBS: [*With an effort.*] Is there lace on all women's drawers?

GEORGE MOORE'S VOICE: She hoped that this question might lead her into a confession of her sex. But the words: "It's so long since I've worn any" died on her lips, and instead of speaking them . . .

ALBERT NOBBS: What a pity the Dodder isn't nearer Morrison's.

HELEN DAWES: Where would you have it? Flowing down Sackville Street into the Liffey? We should be lying there as thick as herrings, without room to move, and we should be unable to speak to each other without being overheard.

ALBERT NOBBS: [*Frightened.*] I dare say you are right. But we have to be back at eleven o'clock, and it takes an hour to get there.

HELEN DAWES: [*Sharply.*] We can go back now if you like.

ALBERT NOBBS: I'm sorry, I didn't mean that. [*Pause.*] Morrison's after all, is a good hotel for servants. Is the Dodder pretty all the way down to the sea?

HELEN DAWES: There are woods as far as Dartry—the Dartry Dye Works, don't you know them? But I don't think there are any very pretty spots. You know Ring's End, don't you?

ALBERT NOBBS: No.

HELEN DAWES: Some Sundays ago I saw a large three-masted vessel by the quays.

ALBERT NOBBS: You were there with Joe Mackins, weren't you?

HELEN DAWES: Well, what if I was?

ALBERT NOBBS: Only this; that I don't think it is usual for a girl to keep company with two chaps, and I thought . . .

HELEN DAWES: Now, what did you think?

ALBERT NOBBS: That you didn't care for me well enough for . . .

HELEN DAWES: For what? You know we've been going out for three months, and it doesn't seem natural to keep talking always, never wanting to put your arm round a girl's waist.

ALBERT NOBBS: I suppose Joe isn't like me, then?

[HELEN DAWES *gives a scornful little laugh.*]

ALBERT NOBBS: But, isn't the time for kissing when one is wedded?

HELEN DAWES: This is the first time you've said anything about marriage.

ALBERT NOBBS: But I thought there had always been an understanding between us, and it's only now I can tell you what I have to offer.

GEORGE MOORE'S VOICE: The words were well chosen.

HELEN DAWES: Tell me about it.

ALBERT NOBBS: Well, the shop, you know, could bring in a good income. We might make as much as four pounds a week—two hundred pounds a year! We could make a little more, especially if I now and then got jobs in hotels or even, why not, in private houses. I have enough connections. We would have a very pretty home. I foresee a pair of candlesticks, or perhaps you don't like . . . a round mirror . . .

HELEN DAWES: [*Bored.*] All you say about the shop is right enough, but it isn't a very great compliment to a girl.

ALBERT NOBBS: What? To ask her to marry?

HELEN DAWES: Well, no, not if you haven't kissed her first.

ALBERT NOBBS: [*Whispering.*] Don't speak so loud, I'm sure that couple heard what you said, for they went away laughing.

HELEN DAWES: I don't care whether they laughed or cried. You don't want to kiss me, do you? And I don't want to marry a man who isn't in love with me.

ALBERT NOBBS: But I do want to kiss you.

[ALBERT NOBBS *leans over and kisses* HELEN DAWES *on both cheeks.*]

Now you can't say I haven't kissed you, can you?

HELEN DAWES: You don't call that kissing, do you?

ALBERT NOBBS: But how do you wish me to kiss you, Helen?

HELEN DAWES: Well, you are an innocent! People kiss on the lips!

ALBERT NOBBS: I'm not used to that.

HELEN DAWES: Because you're not in love.

ALBERT NOBBS: Not in love? I loved my old nurse very much, but I never wished to kiss her like that.

HELEN DAWES: So you put me in the same class with your old nurse! Well, after that! . . . Come [*Taking pity upon* ALBERT NOBBS *for a moment.*]—are you or are you not in love with me?

ALBERT NOBBS: I love you deeply, Helen.

HELEN DAWES: You love me? The men who have walked out with me were in love with me.

ALBERT NOBBS: In love? I'm sure I love you.

HELEN DAWES: I like men to be in love with me.

ALBERT NOBBS: But that's like the animals, Helen.

HELEN DAWES: Whatever put that nonsense in your head? I've had enough. I'm going home.

ALBERT NOBBS: You're angry with me, Helen?

HELEN DAWES: Angry? No, I'm not angry with you. You're a fool of a man, that's all.

ALBERT NOBBS: But if you think me a fool of a man, why have we been keeping company for the last three months? You didn't always think me a fool of a man, did you?

HELEN DAWES: Yes, I did.

ALBERT NOBBS: Then what reason did you have for choosing my company?

HELEN DAWES: Oh, you bother me, asking reasons for everything.

ALBERT NOBBS: But why did you make me love you?

HELEN DAWES: Well, if I did, what of it? And as for walking out with you, you won't have to complain of that any more.

ALBERT NOBBS: You don't mean, Helen, that we are never going to walk out again?

HELEN DAWES: Yes, I do.

ALBERT NOBBS: You mean that for the future you'll be walking out with Joe Mackins?

HELEN DAWES: That's my business.

ALBERT NOBBS: I beseech you to change your mind.

[HELEN DAWES *walks off, and comes back to* JOE.]

HELEN DAWES: [*To* JOE.] His old nurse! Just imagine, Joe Mackins! "That's like the animals . . ." Let him keep his shop. . . . There! that's what happened!

[*She takes off her hat, goes and fetches her apron, puts it on as she passes through the swing doors, and disappears.*]

The Meeting with the Prostitute

ALBERT NOBBS *is in the street. Enter a prostitute, continuing a conversation with one of her colleagues, whom we cannot see.*

KITTY MACCAN: It was almost a love dream.

ALBERT NOBBS' VOICE: They at least are women. Whereas I am only a perhapser . . .

ALBERT NOBBS: If I speak to her, she'll expect me to . . . [*Pause.*] Almost a love dream? What are you two women talking about?

KITTY MACCAN: My friend here was telling me of a dream she had last night.

ALBERT NOBBS: A dream? And what was her dream about?

KITTY MACCAN: She was telling me that she was better than a love dream; now do you think she is, sir?

ALBERT NOBBS: What is your name?

KITTY MACCAN: Kitty MacCan.

ALBERT NOBBS: It's odd we've never met before.

KITTY MACCAN: We're not often this way.

ALBERT NOBBS: And where do you walk usually—of an evening?

KITTY MACCAN: In Grafton Street, or down by College Green; sometimes we cross the river.

ALBERT NOBBS: To walk in Sackville Street . . . That must be difficult for you . . .

KITTY MACCAN: I hope you are not one of them that think that we should wash clothes in a nunnery for nothing?

ALBERT NOBBS: I'm a waiter in Morrison's Hotel.

KITTY MACCAN: Is the money good in your hotel? I've heard that you get as much as half-a-crown for carrying up a cup of tea. I—when I was but a girl, it was not cups of tea they asked of me for less than that. But you are not interested in my story . . . [*Pause.*] The river is pretty all the way down to the sea. There are woods as far as Dartry. [*Pause.*] Do you know Ring's End?

ALBERT NOBBS: No.

KITTY MACCAN: Nor do I. [*Pause.*] There are big boats, three-masters, so they say . . . the waves breaking against the cliffs—the green meadows atop the cliffs—so they say! . . . Large vessels with every stitch of canvas spread. [*Pause.*] You wonder where they are going! [*Pause.*] Do you know Connemara, sir?

ALBERT NOBBS: No.

KITTY MACCAN: They say it is a very pretty place, with fishing boats, and tall cliffs, too, full of seagulls. When you are up upon them you can see the sun sinking into the sea. . . . [*Pause.*] Are you very unhappy?

ALBERT NOBBS: It doesn't matter about me.

KITTY MACCAN: Perhaps I can help you out of your sorrow, if only for a little while. Things do not always go so well for me, you know. . . . I have only three and six pence left out of the last money I received, and my rent will be due tomorrow. I daren't return home without a gentleman, my landlady will be at me, and the best time of the night is going by. . . . You're a waiter, aren't you? I've forgotten which hotel you said.

[ALBERT NOBBS *doesn't answer.*]

I'm afraid I'm taking you out of your way.

ALBERT NOBBS: No, you aren't; all ways are the same to me.

KITTY MACCAN: Well, they aren't to me. I must get some money tonight.

ALBERT NOBBS: I'll give you some money.

KITTY MACCAN: But you won't come home with me?

[*They stand facing each other, not moving, while* GEORGE MOORE'S VOICE *is heard.*]

GEORGE MOORE'S VOICE: But if they were to go home together her sex would be discovered. Though what did it matter if it were discovered? Albert asked herself, and the temptation came again to go home with this woman, to lie in her arms and tell the story that had been locked up so many years. They could both have a good cry together, and what matter would it be to the woman as long as she got the money she desired? She didn't want a man; it was money she was after, money that meant bread and board to her. She seems a kind, nice girl, Albert said to herself.

[KITTY MACCAN *suddenly sees one of her friends.*]

KITTY MACCAN: Oh, there is James. Excuse me.

[*She runs over and calls to him, then returns.*]

KITTY MACCAN: I'm sorry, but I've just met an old friend. Another evening, perhaps.

[ALBERT NOBBS *puts her hand in her pocket, wanting to pay the woman with some silver for her company, but she has already gone.*]

ALBERT NOBBS: I have let all my chances go by me. . . . Is it better to be casual, as these girls are, or to have a husband that you cannot get rid of? This is an idle question.

[ALBERT NOBBS *goes back to the hotel.* MRS. BAKER *is at her table.* ALBERT NOBBS *takes off her overcoat and puts on her apron. She is sad, depressed, tired.*]

MRS. BAKER: [*After looking at her indicator board.*] It's 34, Albert.

[ALBERT NOBBS *goes up to 34 and comes down very quickly, passing in front of* MRS. BAKER.]

MRS. BAKER: What was it?

ALBERT NOBBS: It was for the kitchen, Mrs. Baker.

[ALBERT NOBBS *is ready to dash into the kitchen.*]

MRS. BAKER: Leave it, Albert; you can go upstairs.

[ALBERT NOBBS *walks off, disappointed.*]

MRS. BAKER: [*Calling.*] Helen Dawes, for 34.

[HELEN DAWES *comes out.* ALBERT NOBBS *waits for her at the bottom of the stairs. They pass each other.*]

ALBERT NOBBS: Are you going to pass me by without speaking again, Helen?

HELEN DAWES: We talked enough last night. There's nothing more to say.

[HELEN DAWES *goes up, and into 34.* ALBERT NOBBS *goes and sits on his chair.* HELEN DAWES *comes down again and exits. Through the swing door* JOE *can be heard guffawing, and talking.*]

JOE'S VOICE: I loved my old nurse, but I never thought of kissing her like that.

[*Sound of plates falling with a great clatter.*]

MRS. BAKER: What has come over you, Joe Mackins? I shall keep that back out of your wages.

ALBERT NOBBS: That is well deserved!

[ALBERT NOBBS *is alone on stage in her usual place, her napkin over her shoulder. The lights go down and the maids' voices are heard like a flight of birds. The two ghost-chambermaids can be seen between the doors.*]

CHAMBERMAIDS' VOICES: Well, Albert! You cannot get a word out of him today.
        —"I loved my old nurse" [*Giggling.*]
        —Be quiet.
        —Be quiet, Kathy.
        —After all, he loves the girl, there's nothing to laugh about.

—That Helen! Why should she have kept company with Albert if she didn't mean to wed him?

—Look at him; there is no more colour in his face than is in my duster.

—I poured out a glass of wine for him that was left over, but he put it away.

—And the shop he was offering her—that was no small thing.

—A newspaper and tobacco shop, that can hardly fail to prosper, especially with the sweets. . . . Helen will live to regret her cruelty.

—I would rather say treachery.

—Alice is right; Helen's face is full of treachery.

[*All these voices must follow each other very quickly, or rather all talk at once, like the hubbub of a recreation ground heard over the background of the music of an Irish reel.*]

GEORGE MOORE'S VOICE: And they dispersed in different directions, flicking their dusters.

[*From now on,* ALBERT NOBBS *spends almost all her time on her chair on the landing.*]

GEORGE MOORE'S VOICE: Almost any one of the women in the hotel would have married Albert out of pity for her. But there was no heart in Albert for another adventure, nor any thought in her for anything but her work.

ALBERT NOBBS: I shall never see Lisdoonvarna, nor the shop with the two counters, one for the tobacco, cigarettes and matches, and the other for the sweets. It only existed in my mind—a thought, a dream.

GEORGE MOORE'S VOICE: Yet it had possessed her completely; the parlour behind the shop that she had furnished and refurnished, hanging a round mirror above the mantelpiece, papering the walls with a pretty colourful paper. . . . With curtains about the windows, two armchairs on either side of the hearth, one in green and one in red velvet, for herself and Helen. . . . There had never been anything in her life but a few dreams, and henceforth there would be not even dreams. . . . She had been unlucky from her birth; she was a bastard . . .

[ALBERT NOBBS *nods her head; this last sentence incites her to speak.*]

ALBERT NOBBS: My old nurse and I had to go out charring. Mr. Congreve had a French mistress, and if it hadn't been for Bessie Lawrence I might have thrown myself in the Thames, but I shall never throw myself into this Dublin river. Perhaps because it is not my own river. If one wishes to drown oneself it had better be in one's own country. But what is the difference? For a perhapser like myself, all countries are the same. [*Pause.*]

GEORGE MOORE'S VOICE: Only to Hubert Page could she confide the misfortune that had befallen her.

[ALBERT NOBBS *listens to* GEORGE MOORE'S VOICE, *and still seems to be answering it.*]

ALBERT NOBBS: Now with Hubert, the three of us might set up together. A happy family we might make. Two women in men's clothes and one in petticoats. But if Hubert were willing his wife might not be. Though she might be dead, and Hubert on the look-out for another helpmate.

GEORGE MOORE'S VOICE: And from the moment that she foresaw herself as Hubert 's future wife her life began to expand itself more eagerly than ever in watching for tips. As the months went by, and the years, she remembered, with increasing bitterness, that she had wasted nearly twenty pounds on Helen, that cruel, heartless girl. She took to counting her money in her room at night. The half-crowns were folded up in brown-paper packets, the half-sovereigns in blue, the rare sovereigns were in pink paper, and all these little packets were hidden away in different corners. . . . A sense of almost happiness awoke in her the day she discovered herself to be again as rich as she was before she met Helen. Richer by twenty-five pounds twelve and sixpence. Her eyes roved over the garret floor in search of a plank that might be lifted.

ALBERT NOBBS: Hubert . . . A wandering fellow like him might easily run out of money and return to Morrison's Hotel to borrow from me. If he came back he might threaten to publish my secret if I didn't give him money to keep quiet. No . . . that is an ugly thought. . . . But even so . . .

GEORGE MOORE'S VOICE: As time went on, a dread of Hubert took possession of her.

[MRS. BAKER *enters, looks at a part of the wall and says to herself.*]

MRS. BAKER: That could do with a good spring clean.

[*She notices* ALBERT NOBBS.]

Ah, you are there, Albert. . . . By the way, I cannot think what has become of Hubert Page; we've not had news of him for a long time. Have you heard from him, Albert?

ALBERT NOBBS: Why should you think, ma'am, that I hear from him?

MRS. BAKER: [*Displeased with* ALBERT's *tone.*] I only asked.

[*They are speaking with their backs turned to one another.*]

ALBERT NOBBS: [*Mumbling as he goes out.*] A wandering fellow . . .

[*They go out, each on her own side.* ALBERT NOBBS *picks up a pair of shoes and starts cleaning them with tired, mechanical movements. The lights go down. Death merely halts her movements and freezes her sulky expression on her face.*]

Albert's Death

GEORGE MOORE'S VOICE: Albert remained at Morrison's Hotel till she died.

ALEC'S VOICE: An easy death I hope it was, your honour, for if any poor creature deserved an easy one it was Albert herself.

GEORGE MOORE'S VOICE: You, mean, Alec, that the disappointed man suffers less at parting with this world than the happy one? Maybe you're right.

ALEC'S VOICE: That is as it may be, your honour.

GEORGE MOORE'S VOICE: Albert woke one morning hardly able to breathe. When the maidservant came to make the bed she ran off again to fetch a cup of tea. It was plain that Albert could not eat or drink, and it was almost plain that she was dying, but the maid-servant did not like to alarm the hotel and contented herself with saying: He'd better see the doctor tomorrow. She was up betimes in the morning, and on going to Albert 's room she found the waiter asleep, breathing heavily. An hour later, Albert was dead. [*Pause.*] Which did not seem natural, but when the doctor came down with his report that Albert was a woman, this put all thought of the cause of death out of everybody's mind. Never before or since was Morrison's Hotel agog as it was that morning. The men giggled over their glasses, and the women pondered over their cups of tea; the men questioned the women, and the women questioned the men.

Hubert's Return

A pretty spring light floods the stage, coming through all the doors and windows, but leaving some patches of soft shadow.

Enter HUBERT PAGE, *with his paint pots and brushes.*

HUBERT PAGE: Is anyone there?

[*He goes over to the swing doors and leaves his equipment in the middle of them. He goes into the kitchen. During the whole of this sequence the doors swing gently and the conversation in the kitchen can be heard.* ALBERT NOBBS, *dead, is in her usual place, on the chair half-way up the staircase. As if she were pinned on to the backcloth, with her napkin over her shoulder, sitting facing the audience, her legs a little apart, holding on her knees, with one hand, the pair of shoes she was polishing.* . . . . *In this soft spring light, the door swings as if wafted on the breeze of the voices.*]

HUBERT PAGE: Good morning, all!

VOICES: —Good morning, Hubert!

   —Why, it's Hubert Page!

HUBERT PAGE: How is Albert Nobbs?

DIFFERENT VOICES: Albert Nobbs! Don't you know?

HUBERT PAGE: How should I know? I've only just come back to Dublin. What is there to know?

VOICES: Don't you ever read the papers?

HUBERT PAGE: Read the papers?

VOICE: Then you haven't heard that Albert Nobbs is dead?

HUBERT PAGE: No, I haven't heard of it. I'm sorry for him, but after all, men die; there's nothing wonderful in that, is there?

VOICE: No, but if you had read the papers you'd have learnt that Albert wasn't a man at all, he was a woman.

HUBERT PAGE: Albert Nobbs a woman!

DIFFERENT VOICES: [*At the same time.*]—So you never heard?

   —She courted Helen.

   —A real broken heart.

   —Helen preferred Joe Mackins.

HUBERT PAGE: If you all speak together, I shall never understand it. Albert Nobbs a woman!

A SCULLION'S VOICE: The biggest deception in the whole world.

HUBERT PAGE: So Helen went away with Joe Mackins?

VOICE: Yes, and they don't seem to get on over well together.

VOICE: And the hundreds of pounds that Albert left behind.

VOICE: Nearly a hundred in ready money.

VOICE: Much more! Rolled up in paper.

VOICE: A great scoop it was for the Government.

VOICE: I think that the real reason at the start was that she would be getting better wages as a man than as a woman.

DIFFERENT VOICES: [*Rather low.*] Everyone knows that.

VOICE: Now I come to think of it, Mr. Page, it's you that should be knowing better than anybody else what Albert 's sex was like. Didn't you sleep with her once?

HUBERT PAGE: Oh! I fell asleep the moment my head was on the pillow. If you remember rightly, I was that tired Mrs. Baker hadn't the heart to turn me out of the hotel. I'd been working ten, twelve, fourteen hours that day. When Albert took me up to his room I fell asleep right away, and I left in the morning before he was awake. A woman, I just can't believe it. How ever did she manage to play such a part for so long?

[MRS. BAKER *enters during this speech and is delighted to discover* HUBERT PAGE's *paint pots and brushes.*]

MRS. BAKER: Mr. Page! Come over here, do.

HUBERT PAGE: Good morning, Mrs. Baker.

MRS. BAKER: Good morning, Hubert. Have they told you the news?

HUBERT PAGE: It is quite extraordinary, Mrs. Baker. It is also very sad that poor Albert is dead.

MRS. BAKER: Yes, we all liked him well. Are you going to stay the night here, Hubert?

HUBERT PAGE: If I may, Mrs. Baker. I have nowhere else to stay.

[HUBERT PAGE *puts his paints and brushes away in a corner while* MRS. BAKER, *still talking, opens the door of* ALBERT NOBBS' *cubby-hole.*]

MRS. BAKER: There's Albert's bed.

[*She pulls out the bed and unfolds it.* HUBERT PAGE *helps her. She goes and fetches some sheets, puts them on the bed, etc., etc., while she goes on talking.*]

MRS. BAKER: Yes, it's an incredible story. I was only the other day telling a friend of mine such an amazing story about a woman that my friend thought it couldn't be true, it must be made up. Well that's just it, I told her, it is made up. I've just read it. But this one is even more amazing, and yet it's true. [*Pause.*] Towards the end I was beginning to observe him. He used to mumble things in a disrespectful tone; he had developed a fault which I didn't like, a way of hanging round the visitor as he was preparing to leave the hotel that almost amounted to persecution. Worse than that, a rumour had reached me that Albert's service was measured according to the tip he expected to receive. I didn't believe it, but if it had been true I would not have hesitated to have him out of the hotel in spite of the many years he had spent with us. Another thing: Albert was liked, but not by everybody. You know the little red-headed boy on the second floor, little George Moore, well, he told me—I took him for a walk out to Bray—he told me that he was afraid of Albert. He even confided to me that Albert had tried to pick him up and kiss him one day when he was quite simply looking out of the window at the coal cart going by. Couldn't he see the child didn't like him? Ah well! . . . we cannot keep sentiment out of our business, Mr. Baker and I, and we were very fond of Albert. He remained at Morrison's Hotel until he died. I will leave you, Hubert. Sleep well. There will be plenty of work tomorrow. I still have a few accounts to see to.

HUBERT PAGE: Goodnight, Mrs. Baker. I'll see you in the morning. Thank you, Mrs. Baker.

MRS. BAKER: You're welcome.

[MRS. BAKER *goes to her table, opens her account book and stays immersed in it until the end of the play, going over and over her accounts, ruling lines, writing. Her movements are very orderly; she turns the pages of her account book, and thus lets the time pass.* HUBERT PAGE *sits down on the bed.* ALBERT NOBBS *is still at her place on her chair. It is evening.*]

HUBERT PAGE: I wonder what Annie Watts was thinking of just now when she stood looking into my eyes; does she suspect me? [*Pause.*] What a piece of bad luck that I shouldn't have found Albert alive. It was for her that I returned to Dublin. Now that my wife is dead, Albert and I might have set up together. One of us would have had to give up her job to attend to the shop. . . . I would have preferred it to be me, for I'm tired of going up all those ladders. [*Pause.*] I wonder what is going to be the end of my life. My husband . . . he might now be a different man from the one I left behind. Fifteen years makes a great difference in all of us. . . . And the children, what will they be like now? Lily was five when I left home. She's a young woman now. Agnes was only two. She is now seventeen, still a girl. . . . Lily's looking round, thinking of young men, and the other won't be delaying much longer. . . . Young women are much more wide-awake than they used to be in the old days. [*Pause.*] Their father could have looked after them till now, but now they are thinking of young men he won't be able to cope with them, and maybe he's wanting me too. . . . It's odd how easy it is to forget ill-usage, and remember only the good times. . . . The house must be there still. . . . I recall it all: the pictures on the wall, the chairs I sat in, the coverlets on the beds, everything. But how would I return home? Pack up my things and go dressed as a man to the house? No, they wouldn't understand. I must put on woman's clothes again. [*Pause.*] But what story would I tell them?

ALEC'S VOICE: But sure; 'twas an easy story to tell.

GEORGE MOORE'S VOICE: Really? Well then, Alec, what story should she have told them?

ALEC'S VOICE: In these parts, a woman who left her husband and returned to him after fifteen years would say she was taken away by the little people whilst wandering in a wood.

GEORGE MOORE'S VOICE: Do you think she'd be believed?

ALEC'S VOICE: Why shouldn't she, your honour? A woman that marries another woman, and lives happily with her, isn't a natural woman; there must be something of the fay in her.

[*The lights on the stage dim. It is just possible to make out* MRS. BAKER, *at her table,* ALBERT NOBBS, *in her place half-way up the stairs, with the shoes to be cleaned on one knee and the napkin over her shoulder, and* HUBERT PAGE, *dreaming, sitting on the bed. The two chambermaids pull the curtains, just as they would pull curtains over a window, and a woman's voice sings, in the Gaelic:*]

"Roisin dubh"

Ana Diosdado (b. 1938)

Before the Spanish Civil War (1936–39), women were minimally present as playwrights in Spain. The most accomplished female dramatist of the early twentieth century, Maria Martinez Serra, chose to publish under the name of her husband, Gregorio. During the intensely conservative Franco dictatorship (1939–75), only one woman managed to penetrate the guild of male playwrights and to survive as their recognized peer: Ana Diosdado.

Born into a theatrical family, Diosdado began her career on stage at four, in Buenos Aires, where she lived until her family returned to Madrid in 1950. By the time *Teatro español* concluded its chronicling of Spanish dramatists in 1973, she was the only woman to appear in it. Although she continues to act—both onstage and in her own television series—and is a successful novelist, from 1970 on, when Diosdado wrote *Forget the Drums* (*Olivada los tambores*), it is as a playwright that she has been best known. Beginning both her life and her career in times when it was politically very difficult to straddle safely the line between independent assertion and trite conformity, Diosdado learned this balancing act astutely in her formative years as an artist. Without either compromising her integrity or offending the authorities, she was remarkably successful with the Madrid theater audiences.

From the onset, Diosdado has, as a woman dramatist, resisted equally being labeled a feminist and staging the expected endorsements of domestic felicities and what we might now lump together as "family values." Rather than accepting the image of women as subservient, happily nurturing, and self-sacrificing, she began by showing, cautiously within the parameters of the censorship, feistier, more questioning and resilient female figures. Although her later plays, *The Eighties Are Ours* (*Los ochenta son nuestros*, 1988) and especially *The Silver Path* (*Camino de plata*, 1988), tend to be more conservatively skeptical about the possibility or even the wisdom of undoing established roles and customs, Diosdado throughout recognizes the strain that pervades a society whose mores and attitudes are proving problematical—as has so apparently been the case in Spain since the death of Franco.

Diosdado's most compelling and most performed play is *Yours for the Asking* (*Usted también podrá disfrutar de ella*), which won the highly respected Fasternath prize of the Real Academia de la Lengua, when it appeared in 1973. Always an extraordinarily attentive and skillful scenarist, she is superb in how she constructs this play. Diosdado tells her story out of chronological sequence, with five spots of time or scenes, set in six different places, all located on the same stage simultaneously. She manages to use the same prop—a phone, a door—to shift from one time

Ana Diosdado, ca. 1980 (Photographer: Simon Lopez.)

and place to another; levels of the stage suggest distinct locations and facilitate the transitions. The many movements back and forth in time and space occur smoothly, coherently, and support a suspenseful narrative. Not only does she accomplish these shifts in a dramatically cogent and effective way, she makes them tellingly comment on the action. Her technique allows her a variety of dramatic irony that is almost cinematic, as she jumps and cuts from "shot" to "shot." The present becomes intelligible as the past unfolds and is brought into focus.

The prolog is an ad for SHE, a new perfume, which immediately anticipates the play's criticism of cosmetics, the pharmaceutical industry, and consumerism. The use of doors, phones, and especially the centrally placed stalled elevator constitute an imagistic tour de force rendering of the painful feelings of isolation so common in modern commercial society. Diosdado's characters are stuck within themselves and with others. It would be fantastic to escape to an island, a magic spaceship as Susi imagines; but, as Juan chafes to her, he can't stay; he just has to get off—back presumably into the tabloid world of sham, corruption, guilt, and truncated relationships. There's no escape from the Agent's comment: "It's all image. . . . Advertising is seduction, baby. What you have to do is seduce the buyer, the man in the street." Or, if there is the possibility of escape, it's likely to be through the Coroner's office—a figure who wanders across the play early and whose intermittent presence hovers until he brings the final curtain down. But despite the surrounding consumerism and shallowness, Diosdado seems far more respectful of Susi's ultimate strength to survive than she is of Juan's conviction that it's all hopeless, that nothing can be done.

SELECTED BIBLIOGRAPHY IN ENGLISH

Anderson, Farris. "From Protest to Resignation." *Estreno* 2 (1976), 29–32.

O'Connor, Patricia W. "Spain's 'Other' Post-War Dramatists: The Women." *Letras Peninsular* 1 (1988), 97–107.

——— . "Women Playwrights in Contemporary Spain and the Male-Dominated Canon." *Signs* 15 (1990), 377–90.

Zatlin, Phyllis. "Ana Diosdado and the Contemporary Spanish Theater." *Estreno* 10 (1984), 37–40.

——— . "Traditional Roles in the Theatre of Ana Diosdado." *Mid-Hudson Language Studies* 10 (1987), 71–77.

YOURS FOR THE ASKING

Ana Diosdado

Translated by Patricia W. O'Connor

CHARACTERS

SUSI

JUAN

CELIA

MANNY

THE "MAN IN THE STREET" (Martinez, Coroner, Neighbor,
Super, Agent, all played by the
same actor)

*Projected on the closed curtain is a huge billboard advertisement of a nude young woman being show-
ered with rose petals. Splashed across the image is the product slogan:*

SHE is . . . yours for the asking

*The curtain opens slowly on a movie screen showing a TV commercial featuring the young woman
of the billboard. She runs nude in slow motion on a bed of roses toward the camera. The background
music can be by Bach, Corelli, Albinoni—any classical composer except Mozart. The image, softly
diffused at first, becomes sharper as the young woman approaches the camera. When very close, she
gazes upward in ecstasy as the shower of rose petals continues.*

AD VOICE-OVER: SHE is . . . yours for the asking. SHE . . . can make life wonderful,
happy, full of promise . . . Come with us, and you will see. Come with us, and
SHE . . . will fill your life with fragrance. SHE is . . . yours for the asking . . .

[*With the announcer's final words, an image is superimposed on the screen.*]

SHE
a fragrance by York

The screen disappears, and the lights come up slowly as the action begins. The props and other staging elements should be kept to an absolute minimum; everything that can be suggested should be eliminated. Only words and attitudes are specified. The characters move in undefined places and times, and occasionally there is simultaneous action in different areas. The stage will be a space in which anything can happen.

[JUAN, *thirty-eight years old, enters carrying a tape recorder. Looking tired and defeated, he goes over to the table and puts down the recorder. He picks up the telephone as though suddenly wanting to make a call but changes his mind. Finally, he sits down at a typewriter, puts a sheet of paper in the carriage, lights a cigarette and begins to type.*]

[*The telephone rings.* JUAN *grabs the phone expectantly.*]

JUAN: Yes? [*He sighs, disappointed but resigned, when he recognizes the caller's voice.*] Oh, hello. What's up? . . . Sure, I just got in . . . With her, with the girl . . . [*Speaking louder.*] I said with the girl! . . . Yes, until today, until just now. [*Looking at his watch.*] Well, until half an hour ago, the time it took me to get here . . . Yes, mostly talking . . . Talking, I said! Why don't you put the phone on your other ear? . . . Yes, we spent the week talking . . . Sure I interviewed her. I was just beginning to write the article . . . [*Getting impatient.*] Of course I started to work as soon as I got in. I'm the model employee, wouldn't you say? . . . Yes, it's going to be wonderful. All your little housewives are going to swoon with ecstasy in the beauty parlors . . . Beauty parlors, I said! Isn't that where they read us? . . . No, that's not optimism; it's more like disgust. I just can't take it anymore . . . Can't take it, I said! . . . Yes, tons of pictures . . . No, Manny took them. Julio had a photo session with a countess . . . Yes, lots of bare leg and all the closeups you could ask for. You're going to love it . . . I said Thursday, didn't I? That means it'll be on your desk in a few hours. Look, I'm in no mood to talk right now. See you later.

[*He hangs up. Only then does he realize that there is someone else in the room, observing him.* CELIA, *in her pajamas, looks as though she has just gotten out of bed. Twenty-five or thirty years old and pretty, she treats* JUAN *affectionately, but with a hint of maternal over-protection. His tone suggests that he is distracted and thinking about something else.*]

JUAN: What are you doing here?
CELIA: I live here, remember?
JUAN: What I meant was: what are you doing up at this hour?
CELIA: [*Smiling as she looks at him.*] Just taking in the view . . .
JUAN: You've seen it plenty of times before.
CELIA: You're right, and it's looking all parched and wilted at the moment. But I like it anyway.
JUAN: How nice.
CELIA: You're welcome.
JUAN: That doesn't follow.
CELIA: What doesn't?
JUAN: I said "How nice," not "Thank you."
CELIA: [*Noticing something strange.*] Are you all right?
JUAN: Yes.
CELIA: You don't look it. And it's four in the morning. Aren't you going to get some sleep?
JUAN: I can't. I have to write a wonderful article about this wonderful young model.
CELIA: Right now?

JUAN: Martinez wants the copy on his desk by nine.

CELIA: [*Remembering.*] Yes, he's been trying to reach you all week. He starts calling in the morning and keeps at it.

[CELIA *pauses for a moment to see if he will say something else, but he is absorbed in his papers. As* CELIA *observes him, she catches something imperceptible to anyone else. Friends and lovers,* CELIA *and* JUAN *know each other well. Their jokes, ironies and even their reproaches are simply different expressions of the bond common to people who live and work together. The principal difference between them is that* CELIA *is strong and* JUAN *is weak.*]

CELIA: [*Attacking, but in a good-natured way.*] How about some coffee?

JUAN: How about your going back to bed?

CELIA: How about your letting me plan my own schedule?

JUAN: And how about your not treating me like a child?

CELIA: Why don't you just tell me if you want some coffee?

JUAN: Why don't you come out with it?

CELIA: Out with what?

JUAN: What's on your mind.

CELIA: I was wondering if you'd like some coffee.

JUAN: [*Giving in.*] Okay, pour me some. [*Finally looking up at her.*] Celia, what does a person do who just can't take it anymore?

CELIA: [*Keeping an even tone after a barely perceptible pause.*] He probably shoots himself.

JUAN: [*With the same tone.*] That would be hard. He doesn't have a gun.

CELIA: Then he slits his wrists.

JUAN: Ugh! Disgusting!

CELIA: And messy.

JUAN: That too.

CELIA: How about an overdose of pills?

JUAN: Too risky. They usually revive you.

CELIA: What more could you ask for? You make the effort, but you don't die . . . Was it that bad?

JUAN: Was what that bad?

CELIA: That "wonderful young model."

JUAN: I don't know why you call her that "wonderful young model" or use that tone of voice.

CELIA: I was just repeating what you said a minute ago.

JUAN: I'm a real idiot.

CELIA: Can I ask you a personal question?

JUAN: [*Suddenly interested in the machine in front of him.*] I'd rather have a cup of coffee.

CELIA: [*Smiling.*] Yes, sir.

[*She exits briefly. After studying the page in front of him,* JUAN *starts writing again.* CELIA *interrupts him as she puts down the coffee utensils. She looks at him playfully.*]

CELIA: Can I now?

JUAN: Can you what?

CELIA: Can I ask you that personal question?

JUAN: I was doing the interview. Now I'm trying to write the article, if you'll let me. Is that what you wanted to know?

CELIA: What do you mean: "doing" the interview?

JUAN: [*Ironically.*] More or less what I always mean: ask questions, take notes. You know.

CELIA: For a week straight, without any breaks?

JUAN: That's right.

CELIA: This must be the best article you've ever written.

JUAN: Don't you believe it. I don't even know how to start.

CELIA: [*Smiling.*] Easy, just start this one like you start the others: "So-and-So lives in a luxurious apartment on such-and-such a street. She opens her door to us cordially, dressed simply in . . ."

JUAN: Thanks.

CELIA: What for?

JUAN: This isn't the first time you've made me feel like a fool, but today, I really needed it.

CELIA: [*Not wanting to take him seriously.*] Oh-h-h-h dear! You didn't come home all set to be charming. [*She turns to leave.*] But come to think of it, have you ever tried to charm anyone?

JUAN: [*Attempting to match her irony.*] Way down deep, I'm a charmer. It's just down pretty deep.

[CELIA *exits, and* JUAN *crosses out what he has written, dragging on his cigarette in deep thought as he gazes intently at the page in front of him. Meanwhile, the lights go up on the space that will become* SUSI's *apartment. Standing behind the door, loaded with photographic equipment, is* MANNY. *As soon as* SUSI *opens the door, the flashbulbs on* MANNY's *camera begin to pop. Surprised,* SUSI *smiles.* MANNY, *about twenty-six years old, has a lot of personality. He is aware of his charm and does not hesitate to use it.* SUSI, *the girl in the billboard and TV ads, is about twenty. Although less beautiful than in the pictures, she is more appealing.*]

MANNY: Hi! I'm Manny Gomez from *Woman Talk* magazine.

SUSI: Yes, I figured.

MANNY: Sorry to have kept you waiting. What happened was . . .

SUSI: [*Interrupting him.*] No problem. Come on in.

MANNY: First we have to get a guy out of the elevator.

SUSI: What guy?

MANNY: Gomez. The one who's going to ask all those dumb questions. He's stuck in the elevator.

SUSI: In the elevator?

MANNY: In the elevator.

SUSI: Then how did you get out?

MANNY: I didn't have to. I just got here, so I had to walk up. It looks like he's been in there quite a while.

SUSI: Poor thing! He must have claustrophobia by now.

MANNY: [*Laughing.*] I wouldn't be surprised. I could hear him kicking the door. He's not yelling yet, but it's probably because he's too embarrassed.

SUSI: [*Decisively.*] I'll call the super.

MANNY: Don't bother. There's no one down there.

SUSI: Oh, he lives in another building. But I have his telephone number somewhere.

[SUSI *goes for a small address book and looks up the number.*]

MANNY: If he doesn't live here, who did I call from the street?

SUSI: You rang the ground-floor apartment, and it's empty.

MANNY: That's a coincidence.

SUSI: Not really. A lot of these apartments are empty, and in the summer, there's nobody around. [*Referring to* JUAN.] Tell that guy to be patient. We're going to get him out soon.

MANNY: [*Putting down his photographic equipment.*] I'm off.

SUSI: What floor did he get stuck on?

MANNY: Between this one and the one below. You didn't hear anything?

[MANNY *exits.* SUSI *goes toward the telephone—the same one that* JUAN *used, if possible— and dials a number. The scene shifts back to* JUAN *and* CELIA. *The latter has a coffee pot in her hand and the same playful expression on her face.*]

CELIA: About not being able to take it anymore: am I included in that "it," by any chance?

JUAN: [*Wearily.*] Will you let me work, Celia, please?

CELIA: I just want to know if I'm included or not.

JUAN: [*Resigning himself.*] In what?

CELIA: [*Pouring coffee into* JUAN's *cup.*] In what you said about not being able to take it anymore.

JUAN: When did I say that?

CELIA: Just now, on the telephone.

JUAN: I was talking to Martinez about work. Why would I be talking about you?

CELIA: I don't know. But were you?

JUAN: Was I what?

CELIA: Feeling like you can't take *me* anymore?

JUAN: At four in the morning, you decide to ask esoteric questions?

CELIA: [*Beginning to laugh.*] I decide *what*, you say?

[SUSI, *impatient, hangs up, re-dials and waits.*]

JUAN: No, you're not what I can't take anymore.

CELIA: Well, that's consoling . . . But I'd appreciate something a bit more positive, a certain . . . How shall I put it? . . . A certain recognition of my role . . . my help, at least. [*Still in a joking manner, and as though suddenly remembering something.*] Six years! Really, that's a long time. Do you think we should give some thought to ending it all?

JUAN: [*Looking at her steadily and emphasizing the importance of his reply.*] Yes, I do.

[*At that moment,* SUSI, *tired of waiting for a response, hangs up and leaves quickly through the apartment door, slamming it behind her. She stops a moment in front of the elevator, straining to hear something. Between* CELIA *and* JUAN, *there is a pause.* CELIA *looks at* JUAN *without reacting, and* JUAN *continues to look her in the eye very steadily.*]

CELIA: I think you're serious.

JUAN: I *am* serious, Celia.

CELIA: [*Attempting to pass it off.*] Well, gee . . . I guess I should have gone back to bed. [*She goes toward the door.*]

JUAN: Wait . . .

CELIA: Forget it. This has been coming on for some time now, hasn't it? I'd rather you didn't say anything else . . . But just tell me one thing: what made you come to this decision? Was it the "wonderful young model"? [JUAN *looks at her a few moments as though not knowing what to respond. Finally, he nods affirmatively.*] Congratulations. And good luck with the article. [JUAN *stands up and makes a gesture to stop her.*]

JUAN: Celia . . .

CELIA: Get back to work.

[CELIA *exits.* JUAN *seems immobilized, as though not knowing what to do. Then, nervously, he turns again to his typewriter, tears out the page, rips it to pieces and tosses it away. He gets up brusquely, just to be doing something and then lights another cigarette. At the stairway landing,* MANNY *appears.*]

MANNY: [*To* SUSI.] What's new?

SUSI: Nothing. There's no answer. I don't know what to do.

MANNY: I know what we can do: eat.

SUSI: [*Pointing toward the elevator.*] And what about that poor guy down there?

MANNY: Maybe we can find some way to give him a glass of water. That'll make him feel better while we wait.

SUSI: But the super won't be back till tonight.

MANNY: You got a better idea?

SUSI: No. Want something to drink?

MANNY: Whacha got?

SUSI: Beer, soda, things like that.

MANNY: Anything else?

SUSI: Whisky?

MANNY: Good stuff?

SUSI: Not bad.

MANNY: Okay. I'll have some. And the "sandwiched" too.

SUSI: [*Frowning.*] I don't know if I have anything to eat.

MANNY: I was making a bad joke about JUAN, the poor guy that got "sandwiched" in the elevator. Get it?

SUSI: [*Making an effort to laugh at what* MANNY *has said.*] I'll be back in a minute.

> [SUSI *goes to the door of her apartment and finds it closed.* JUAN *puts out the cigarette he has just lit and goes toward the door through which* CELIA *has just exited. He knocks gently and waits.*]

JUAN: Celia . . .

MANNY: [*Toward the elevator.*] Food is on the way, buddy. Hang in there.

SUSI: Now you did it. You closed the door.

MANNY: [*Alarmed.*] What?

SUSI: I don't have my keys.

MANNY: Doesn't one of the neighbors have a set?

SUSI: The super does. [MANNY *is about to utter a strong oath when* SUSI *puts her hand over his mouth.*] Don't say it. [MANNY *knocks on the wall of the elevator.*]

MANNY: Juan . . .

> [JUAN *also knocks on the wall as a third character, the middle-aged, serious and intelligent-looking* CORONER, *crosses the stage. Immersed in some papers in his hand, he knocks on a non-existent third door.*]

CORONER: Nurse . . .

JUAN: Celia . . .

MANNY: Hey, Juan, did you die down there?

CORONER: Nurse . . .

JUAN: Celia, don't be silly. Open the door. I have to talk to you . . .

CORONER: [*Speaking toward the audience, as though someone had opened the imaginary door.*] Is that man I told you about out there? . . . Well, have him come in to see me as soon as he gets here. [*He goes over to a corner of the stage, puts on his glasses and carefully examines some papers.*]

JUAN: Celia, please. I need to talk to someone. Listen . . .

MANNY: If you've died, let us know, so we can leave.

JUAN: [*Giving a hostile bang on the door.*] And there's one for you too, buddy. [*He returns energetically to the typewriter and puts another sheet of paper into the carriage.*]

MANNY: [*To* SUSI.] He knows you're here.

SUSI: He does?

MANNY: Sure, if he hadn't known, he would have said something a lot stronger . . . Hey, ya' know, you speak perfect Spanish, no accent at all.

SUSI: Thanks. You do, too.

MANNY: Yeah, but I'm Spanish.

SUSI: So am I.

MANNY: I thought you were from the United States!

SUSI: Well, I'm from Toledo, as in Spain.

MANNY: But all the papers say . . .

SUSI: The papers say a lot of crazy things . . .

MANNY: [*Laughing.*] Hey, just a minute. The press is like a mother to me!

SUSI: Well, now you know: you're a son of a . . .

MANNY: [*Putting his hand over her mouth as she had done to him.*] Don't say it!

SUSI: You know what we should do?

MANNY: What?

SUSI: [*Pointing to the elevator door.*] We should try to get that little wheel back on the track. I think that's the problem.

MANNY: [*After glancing at the possibility proposed by* SUSI.] I have a better idea.

SUSI: What's that?

MANNY: [*Pointing to the elevator.*] Let's put him out of his misery. What do you say we cut the cables?

SUSI: Oh, please!

MANNY: [*Decisively.*] Oh, well, I guess I'd rather die cracking my head open heroically than doing something ridiculous, like I do every day. But this jerk doesn't deserve it. [*He has crawled into a precarious position between the elevator shaft and the wall.*] Now, what was I supposed to do in here?

SUSI: That little wheel . . .

MANNY: Can I ask you a question?

SUSI: That's what you came for, isn't it?

MANNY: No, that's not my job. I came to take pictures.

SUSI: Well, what did you want to ask me?

MANNY: Why you turned down all those other interviews and then agreed to one with a magazine like ours?

SUSI: [*Hesitating a moment, then evading the question.*] What do you mean, a magazine "like yours"?

MANNY: I mean it's a lousy publication. But then maybe you never read it.

SUSI: I took this interview, because I liked what your friend said on the telephone.

MANNY: First of all, he's not my friend. But tell me what he said, anyway.

SUSI: Oh, something like: "I'm not interested in hearing what you have to say, and you're not interested in talking to me . . . But these people at the magazine want me to interview you, and since that's how I make a living, if you're willing, you'll be doing me a huge favor."

MANNY: I'll bet he didn't say that stuff about it being a huge favor.

SUSI: Well, it was something like that.

MANNY: Maybe. But he's a real cynic. So you took the bait, huh?

SUSI: I didn't take any bait. I just told him to come over. Why aren't you two friends?

MANNY: For the same reason that some people don't have red hair or can't carry a tune.

SUSI: And what reason might that be?

MANNY: It's just not in the cards. It's as simple as that.

SUSI: Did you fix the wheel?

MANNY: I broke it.

SUSI: Oh, no!

MANNY: [*Jumping to the floor.*] I'm going to get some liquid refreshment. You have a place to buy something around here, don't you?

SUSI: On the corner.

MANNY: You see? God is merciful. What do you want me to bring you?

SUSI: Anything, just as long as it's cold.

MANNY: I'll be right back.

[MANNY *exits. At the same time,* JUAN *pauses in front of his work, wondering how to proceed.* SUSI, *alone now, sits down on the floor, close to the elevator. The only separation between* JUAN *and* SUSI *is the difference in levels.*]

SUSI: [*Loudly.*] Hey, if you want to talk to somebody, we can talk about anything you want. Or, if you don't want to talk, I'll be quiet, but I'm here, you know? I mean . . . you're not alone.

[JUAN *turns in the direction of* SUSI's *voice.*]

JUAN: Hi. You're Susi, aren't you? Susi Roman.

SUSI: Yes.

JUAN: Ah . . . beautiful.

SUSI: What's beautiful? My name? Actually, it's Asuncion Gomez Roman. Your name is Gomez too, isn't it?

JUAN: Yes.

SUSI: But they don't call you that, do they?

JUAN: No, you're right. People usually call me by my other last name: Villar.

SUSI: Of course.

JUAN: Yes.

SUSI: Your friend went to get something to drink.

JUAN: He's not my friend, remember?

SUSI: You could hear us?

JUAN: I'm hearing you now.

SUSI: Well, I'm talking real loud.

JUAN: Well, don't. There's no need to.

SUSI: Oh, all right. Are you okay?

JUAN: I have good moments and bad.

SUSI: What?

JUAN: I mean, it depends on the time. Summer, for example, is good. I like the sun. How about you? Are you okay?

SUSI: I'm fine. But I was asking about your nerves. How are they holding up?

JUAN: What nerves?

SUSI: Your friend said . . .

JUAN: [*Interrupting her, amused.*] He's not my friend.

SUSI: Okay, your enemy.

JUAN: He's not my enemy, either.

SUSI: Well, that guy who means nothing to you and who said you were about to kick the door down.

JUAN: I was kicking the door so someone would know I was in here. Now I'm not doing it anymore.

SUSI: Strange.

JUAN: What's strange?

SUSI: Nothing's changed. You're just as trapped and alone as you were before.

JUAN: So?

SUSI: Nothing. It's just different when you're not alone.

JUAN: [*Continuing to make light of the situation.*] Right. Especially when that someone is out there rather than in here with me. That could be worse.

SUSI: But don't you feel like you'll never get out of there?

JUAN: What are you trying to do? Cheer me up?

SUSI: Oh, don't pay any attention to me . . . But it is awful, isn't it?

JUAN: What's awful?

SUSI: That feeling.

JUAN: Have you ever been stuck in an elevator?

SUSI: No. Not in an elevator . . .

JUAN: Where, then?

SUSI: I don't know exactly.

JUAN: What?

SUSI: I only know that I'm as trapped as you are.

[JUAN *senses what she's getting at and adopts a cynical attitude.*]

JUAN: Oh, sure.

SUSI: What does that mean?

JUAN: I have to warn you about something.

SUSI: About what?

JUAN: The recorder isn't on yet. Even if I had it on, I doubt that at this distance it would pick up what you're saying.

SUSI: I don't know what that has to do with anything.

JUAN: It means that you can save the philosophizing. We'll do the interview later.

SUSI: Some nice person you turned out to be! Maybe that other guy was right about you . . . that, uh, not-so-good friend of yours. What's his name?

JUAN: The pretty boy? You're gonna laugh.

SUSI: Why would I laugh?

JUAN: Because he has such a common label: Gomez. That's his name.

SUSI: Well, that makes three of us, then. What's his first name?

JUAN: Manuel, but everyone calls him Manny. But I don't like to play the cynic.

SUSI: You don't?

JUAN: No. Because I really *am* one.

SUSI: And how is it working out for you?

JUAN: I'm not setting the world on fire, but I get along. It was my cynicism that got me the interview with you.

SUSI: Wrong. That wasn't what did it.

JUAN: No? What was it, then?

SUSI: Fear.

JUAN: Fear?

SUSI: Fear. I was scared to death. I needed to talk to someone

JUAN: Okay, tell me about it.

SUSI: [*Getting back at him.*] I thought you didn't have the recorder on. [JUAN *smiles, starting to like* SUSI.]

JUAN: I have a great memory. Anyway, we're talking off the cuff now, aren't we? What are you afraid of?

SUSI: It's hard to explain.

JUAN: I'm sure . . .

SUSI: [*After a brief pause.*] Where do you get . . . ? [SUSI *suddenly stops, as though listening.*] Wait a minute! I think there's someone in the apartment downstairs . . . I heard another noise. Maybe whoever's there can give us a hand.

JUAN: A noise? You want to go see?

SUSI: What?

JUAN: You want to check it out?

SUSI: [*Unconvinced.*] Well . . .

JUAN: It's probably Gomez.

SUSI: No, it's in the apartment downstairs, inside. I'm going down there. I'll be right back.

[*She leaves, as though acting on impulse. As* SUSI *disappears, the* CORONER *stands up to greet someone.* MANNY, *serious, crestfallen, nervous, crosses the stage to meet him.*]

CORONER: I appreciate your stopping by. I asked you to come in, because I had some questions. The other day, you were very upset, but perhaps today [*Pause.*]

MANNY: [*Interrupting him excitedly.*] I know what happened is all my fault. I accept the blame, and . . .

CORONER: [*Also interrupting.*] No one is accusing you of anything.

MANNY: What does that have to do with anything? What's important is that I feel responsible, and I *am* responsible. And so are you. Haven't you ever thought that . . . ?

CORONER: Calm down, please. This is not an official visit. My only duty is to take care of the body, to perform an autopsy, and in due time, make my statement to the judge. You don't even have to talk to me if you don't want to.

MANNY: Ask whatever you want.

CORONER: Thank you. You see, as a coroner, I constantly deal with accidents, murders, suicides and physical attacks of all kinds. I am familiar with violence and death. They don't faze me anymore.

MANNY: You're lucky.

CORONER: You think so?

MANNY: I don't know.

CORONER: What I'm trying to tell you is that for me, this isn't just another case. There are circumstances associated with this one that intrigue me. The article by Gomez Villar was especially interesting. I read it several times. It's really . . . well, mind boggling, don't you think? [*The expression "mind boggling" amuses* MANNY.]

MANNY: Mind boggling? On the contrary: I find it absolutely logical and reasonable; even revealing.

CORONER: It's just that I had never encountered such a negative and hopeless vision of the world we live in as the one in that article. Do you share his point of view?

MANNY: In general, I do, but I don't agree with his conclusions.

CORONER: H-m-m-m. The article is very well written, very well written.

MANNY: That's the least important thing about it.

CORONER: Using what happened to that girl to make his point was brilliant.

MANNY: [*Shocked.*] You think that's brilliant?

CORONER: Yes, I do. I'll be frank with you. I don't usually read that kind of publication. I don't know anything about the world that made this girl an idol, but I recall that I felt an aversion toward her as a person. I really didn't like her. If I'd had some contact with her, I probably would have reacted in a hostile way. I wouldn't have known why, and I wouldn't even have stopped to ask myself why. We ponder these cases of conscience only when the situation becomes serious or spectacular, hardly ever in our daily lives. According to Villar, that's how they manipulate us.

MANNY: Don't you think you're exaggerating?

CORONER: No. I don't think so. That's why I found the article so compelling. [*Softening his attitude,* MANNY *is not so hostile now.*] For that reason and because of some really chilling words. The title, for example: "There Is No Place on Earth." There's not the least glimmer of hope in all those pages. Was that really the writer's attitude, or did the case of SUSI ROMAN impress him so deeply?

MANNY: He always talked like that. SUSI just convinced him more than ever that he was right, so he decided to make an example of her, just like you said.

CORONER: What kind of relationship did they have?

MANNY: [*Evasively.*] I don't know what you mean.

CORONER: I mean, to stay in the house with someone for a week to get an interview . . . Is that how you people usually operate?

MANNY: In the kind of work we do, not really, but . . .

CORONER: [*Interrupting him.*] Then, how do you explain . . . ?

MANNY: I don't know if I can explain it! Why does everything have to be explained, anyway? At the moment, it seemed perfectly logical. No, no, "logical" isn't the word. [*He laughs, because "logical" seems as out of place as "mind boggling."*] Logical! It just seemed the thing to do. We just couldn't leave the girl by herself. Anyway . . . [*He stops, realizing that he can't explain what happened.*]

CORONER: Go ahead. Anyway . . . ?

MANNY: We went to her house thinking it would be the same old thing: an interview like all the others. But we found something much more important there. JUAN wanted to do a kind of eye-witness report: a "you-are-there" story, like staying with someone in a cave for three months or crossing the ocean in a sailboat with somebody, or . . .

[*The telephone rings. If possible, it should be the same one that* JUAN *and* SUSI *have used before. The* CORONER *goes over to answer it.*]

CORONER: [*To* MANNY.] Excuse me a minute. Hello. Yes, speaking . . . Oh, yes, yes. Just a minute. I'm going to take this call on another line. [*He puts down the telephone.*] It's a call from the lab about the tissue samples. Would you mind waiting a minute?

MANNY: No, go ahead.

CORONER: Thank you.

[*The* CORONER *exits. After a few seconds,* MANNY *stands up, walks over to the* CORONER's *papers and begins to leaf through them.* JUAN *has continued to write during the exchange between* MANNY *and the* CORONER. *As the latter exits,* CELIA, *dressed in street clothes, enters with a folder under her arm.* MANNY's *expression changes completely when he sees her. He puts the papers down and smiles. He is the old* MANNY *again.*]

CELIA: Hi, there. Is the slave driver in the other room?

MANNY: Are you talking about Juan or the boss?

CELIA: I'm talking about both of them. I'm bringing in the translations so the boss'll toss me a crumb.

[*She goes over to* JUAN *and kisses him in an absent-minded, routine way as she peeks over his shoulder to see what he's writing.* JUAN, *uncomfortable, tries to keep her from seeing anything.*]

CELIA: I didn't expect to see you around the office. I have some gum if you want it.

JUAN: No, thanks. It takes away my appetite.

CELIA: That's good. Then we'll save money. By the way, did you get your check?

JUAN: Yes.

CELIA: What's that you're writing?

JUAN: Something that is going to catapult me to fame: captions.

CELIA: Important ones?

JUAN: You have no idea! Miss So-and-So makes her debut.

[MARTINEZ *enters. About fifty, nondescript, and full of nervous energy, he wears garters around his shirt sleeves and on his head the transparent green visor of the old-time newspaperman. The same actor who plays the* CORONER *performs this role as well.* CELIA *stares at him, amused by his attire.*]

MARTINEZ: [*Speaking toward the audience.*] Medina! Get down here right away about that photo layout! Hi, Celia.

[CELIA *makes a gesture of greeting.*]

MARTINEZ: Come on! What's happened to the feature of the week? It's not here yet. [*Before leaving, he turns around as though remembering something.*] Hey, Juan! You've got to get an interview with that girl in the big cancer stink. Take Julio with you.

[MANNY *looks up, interested.*]

MARTINEZ: That girl in the ad, you know. There's the phone number. [*He drops a piece of paper on the desk.*] Her name is something or other Roman [*Pronouncing "Row-man," accenting the first syllable, as in English.*] and she's a dancer. They want something about her in the next issue.

JUAN: Her name is Román [*Accenting the second syllable, as in Spanish.*] not Roman. And she's not really a dancer. She does a number in a go-go club.

MARTINEZ: Whatever. Just do the interview, and get a bunch of pictures.

JUAN: [*Feigning indifference.*] Have somebody else do it.

MARTINEZ: What?

JUAN: Send someone else. I've had it with the starlets and the athletes and the singers and all those people who say the same things all the time.

MARTINEZ: Could it be because you always ask the same questions?

JUAN: [*Exploding.*] I ask the same questions because all you people care about is filling up pages! Let me do an article my own way and you'll see some interesting stuff. I assure you it's out there.

MARTINEZ: Tell that to the guys in the front office. Don't bug me about it. Anyway, all magazines have a special audience and function. [CELIA *and* MANNY *laugh.*] What's so funny?

JUAN: The function of this one must be to incite the morbid curiosity of a handful of housewives who have nothing better to think about, so that some detergent or canned tomato-sauce company can pay our salaries. All the readers of this rag want to know is who So-and-So is going to bed with. In order to tell them that, I have to talk about So-and-So's "fiancé." Just let me do some "man-in-the-street" interviews—talk to your average citizen—and if people are willing to talk, you'll see some real questions. Assign me an investigative report on banking, or on why there are so many robberies, or why buildings are bombed, or why fewer and fewer students go to college, or so many other things! People should at least know we're talking about this country and not some place on Mars!

MARTINEZ: Look, tell that to the guys in the front office, like I said, okay? If this magazine isn't worthy of your talent, get a job with some publication like *Vogue.* They must be desperate for your services.

CELIA: Gee, your journalistic ideal is *Vogue?*

MANNY: [*Attempting to defuse the tension.*] Whatever would we do without that illustrious publication, Bwana? Who would insult us morning and night? Who would tell us that what we write is garbage, huh? Who would inspire us to keep on wallowing in the mire? We need them, Bwana!

MARTINEZ: Don't give me all that stuff about what we do here. I've had it with you idealists! It's okay to have your head in the clouds at twenty, but at thirty, it's time for your feet to start touching ground.

JUAN: [*Calmer and more resigned now.*] And to start kissing up, too, right?

MARTINEZ: [*Giving up.*] Look, Villar, don't get me started. I have work to do. [*He starts to leave, but* JUAN *stops him wearily.*]

JUAN: Martinez . . . We can't talk about advertising, right? Because how would this magazine ever survive without its advertisers?

MARTINEZ: So?

CELIA: [*Joking sarcastically.*] And since we have no honor, let's at least protect our behinds, huh?

MANNY: [*Imitating her tone.*] Which means that if we mess with them, they just may get mad or something.

MARTINEZ: But why would you want to write about them anyway? [*To* JUAN.] Do an interview with the girl, and leave the advertisers alone.

JUAN: [*With studied patience.*] Let's see if I got this straight: I'm going to interview this chick who has never done anything special other than get caught up in a publicity scandal involving the poisoning of three children, a lawsuit against a laboratory, and the closing down of an advertising agency. So, let's see: what do you want me to ask her? About her vacation plans? Or should we talk about her parents, or what?

MARTINEZ: Look. Can I give you some advice? Don't make me any hotter under the collar than I already am. Just do what you're told, and don't make waves. And go interview that girl, for Pete's sake! Who wouldn't jump at the chance? They say she's refused to talk to the press! This is your golden opportunity to prove you're a first-rate journalist! [*He exits.*]

MANNY: That's great, isn't it? In addition to playing the fool, they want us to suffer in the bargain. [*He exits behind* MARTINEZ.] Bye, Celia, my fair beauty. Hey! Bwana! Don't you want to see my pictures?

CELIA: What role is Martinez trying to play, anyway?

JUAN: It's his newspaperman routine. He must have seen some old movie, and it got to him.

CELIA: Aren't we going out to celebrate your getting paid?

JUAN: Just a minute. I have to call that girl.

CELIA: [*Unpleasantly surprised.*] But didn't you say that . . . ?

JUAN: [*Dialing a number he has on a piece of paper.*] She'll probably tell me to get lost, but at least they can't say I didn't try . . . Hello . . . Susi Roman? . . . Oh, good. My name is Juan Gomez Villar, and I work at *Woman Talk* . . . Yes, yes, I know, and I understand, but . . . Look, sorry to have bothered you. I'm not really interested in what you have to say, and I'm sure you don't want to talk to me either, but the people here at the magazine want an interview, and since that's how I make a living, if you'll talk to me . . . What? . . . No, no, whenever you say. Soon, if it's all right with you, because they want the article for the next issue.

[MANNY *is about to leave, but he stops to listen, interested.*] Tomorrow? Whenever you say. . . . At five? Fine. Yes, we have your address. Thanks. See you tomorrow. [*He hangs up.*]

MANNY: She said yes?

JUAN: Yes, Pretty Boy.

MANNY: How about fixing it so I can go instead of Julio?

JUAN: Why?

MANNY: [*Ponderously.*] Haven't you seen her?

JUAN: Who hasn't?

MANNY: Aren't you impressed?

JUAN: Nope, not at all. She's not my type.

MANNY: Well, she sure is mine. I'm a man of simple tastes.

CELIA: Be prepared for a disappointment. Pictures can be very deceptive.

MANNY: Tell me about it! Sometimes I photograph gorgeous chicks who come out looking like real dogs in the pictures. [*To* JUAN.] We can say that Julio had a photo session with a countess. Around here, anyone with that kind of a title is sacred.

JUAN: And what will we tell Julio?

MANNY: We don't have to tell him anything. Let him find out. Anyway, what's it to him? He's too old to give a damn.

JUAN: [*Giving in.*] Oh, well . . .

MANNY: Tomorrow at five, where?

JUAN: [*Showing him the address on the paper that* MARTINEZ *gave him.*] There's the address. But don't be late, like you usually are.

MANNY: That's my very own mother talking! [*He exits.*]

CELIA: Congratulations.

JUAN: For what?

CELIA: You have just gotten an important interview and mothered an idiot, all in one day. What more could you ask?

JUAN: For you to leave me alone, to start with.

CELIA: Why did you make that call? [JUAN *sighs but does not respond.*] You get all hot and bothered with Martinez, and for what? To bow your head and go like a lamb to the slaughter?

JUAN: Celia, do we always have to go around and around about the same old things?

CELIA: It's just that for a moment, you made me believe. I actually thought you were going to stand up to the magazine, that you were going to tell them to shove it once and for all . . . But what really gets me is that you could have a much better job, but here you are, just getting more bitter by the day, and for that pittance they call a salary.

JUAN: So that's what's bothering you?

CELIA: Are you surprised?

JUAN: If I quit this job and become an important writer with a big salary, will you be happy?

CELIA: [*Hurt.*] You can forget the "big salary" part. It's not important.

JUAN: Okay, but without that, would you be happy?

CELIA: What are you getting at?

JUAN: At what you really want. What is it? To live better? Have your friends envy you, because . . . ?

CELIA: To start with, I'd like to see you more satisfied with your life.

JUAN: Then don't change my job. Change the country I live in.

CELIA: Oh, here we go again!

JUAN: If you don't like what I have to say, don't make me talk.

CELIA: What I'd really like is for you to *do* something. I've had it with all the talk. If this country is so important to you, why don't you *do* something about it yourself?

JUAN: I did! And I ended up in jail!

CELIA: I did it again! I always seem to set you up, don't I? All right, my poor dear martyr, put on your medals. But you're not in jail right now, are you?

JUAN: That's what you say! I feel like I'm still there . . . Celia, if I had faith in something or in someone, I'd keep on sticking my neck out, just like I did before. I'd keep on handing out pamphlets, writing between the lines, anything. But I can't fabricate faith out of nothing. Don't you get it?

CELIA: Well, it's certainly a comfortable attitude, very convenient.

JUAN: [*Understanding her game and smiling.*] After a few years of goading my self-esteem, you should know that I don't have any.

CELIA: Well, then, keep on writing captions and interviewing idiots. But don't expect the Nobel Prize.

JUAN: What makes you think everyone wants a prize?

CELIA: It was just a manner of speaking.

JUAN: A very significant one.

[MARTINEZ *enters again as hurriedly as before and leaves a big stack of papers on the desk.*]

MARTINEZ: [*He does not stop walking.*] Villar, don't be such a stubborn jackass, and call that number. In this business, we have to do lots of things that maybe we'd rather pass up. Life isn't always . . .

[JUAN *begins to chuckle, and* CELIA, *uncomfortable, looks away.*]

JUAN: I already called, Bwana. I did it already. And she said yes. Tomorrow, five o'clock, at her place.

MARTINEZ: [*Looking to* CELIA *for confirmation.*] Really?

JUAN: Really.

MARTINEZ: Then day after tomorrow, I want the interview on my desk so it can make the next issue.

VOICE: [*Interrupting from offstage.*] Hey, Bwana!

MARTINEZ: I'm coming! [*With his customary haste, he exits in the direction of the voice.*] I want pictures! And stop calling me Bwana! It's wearing a little thin. [*He exits.*]

[*There is a strained pause between* JUAN *and* CELIA. *Then he, in a conciliatory gesture, puts the papers in his desk drawer.*]

JUAN: The guy you live with is no hero, Toots, what can I tell you? But let's celebrate anyway.

[CELIA *sighs in resignation as she smiles at him.*]

CELIA: Just a minute. I have to hand this in. I'll be right back.

[*She leaves in the direction of* MARTINEZ's *exit. At the same time,* SUSI *returns. Very excited, she approaches the elevator.*]

SUSI: Gomez!

JUAN: What's up?

SUSI: It's the guy from downstairs. He's on his way. He's looking for a tool that will get you out of there. [*Very relieved.*] I don't think they recognized me.

JUAN: [*Surprised.*] What if they did?

SUSI: [*Taking no notice of his question.*] At first, they looked at me a little funny but didn't say anything. I mean, nothing special . . . They just talked normally . . . or at least I think so. They didn't seem to recognize me.

JUAN: [*Beginning to notice something strange.*] Hey, Susi . . .

[SUSI *interrupts him, as though alarmed.*]

SUSI: We're finally going to see each other. What do you think of that?

JUAN: [*Joking.*] To tell the truth, it bothers me a little.

SUSI: [*Forcing herself to follow up with some levity.*] Well, really, my face isn't all that tough to take . . . Yours is?

JUAN: It's not exactly that it's tough to take, Gomez.

SUSI: What kind of face do you have then?

JUAN: A pretty foolish one, probably.

SUSI: No, seriously.

JUAN: I don't know. I don't pay much attention to it. But it's probably a bitter face.

SUSI: And why is that?

JUAN: Because I'm a bitter person.

SUSI: Then maybe you don't have that kind of face at all. Bitter people usually just look sour. So-o-o . . .

JUAN: What?

SUSI: Do you have a sour puss?

JUAN: Could be.

SUSI: Well, you know something? Cross my heart: I've liked you from the first. [*She waits a minute to see if he says something.*] And what about me? What was your first reaction?

[JUAN *laughs.*]

JUAN: I don't know . . . I'd have to see you first.

SUSI: Gee! You've seen me in plenty of places! I was everywhere!

JUAN: Maybe, but it's not the same.

[SUSI, *liking what he said, smiles and repeats it.*]

SUSI: No. It's not the same. I bet you didn't like me. Tell the truth. Am I right? Did you ever buy any of . . . that stuff? Did you ever buy it?

JUAN: That perfume of yours? No. Why?

SUSI: [*Harshly.*] It's not *my* perfume.

JUAN: Well, I meant . . .

[*The* NEIGHBOR *enters with a lever in his hand. When she sees him,* SUSI *scrambles to her feet, as though guilty of something. She interrupts* JUAN.]

SUSI: Here's the neighbor now!

JUAN: Hallelujah!

NEIGHBOR: I'll bet he's happy someone's here. Let's see what we can do. [*To* SUSI.] So? Your husband been down there long?

SUSI: No, and he's not my husband. He's just a friend.

NEIGHBOR: Oh. Well, anyway, let's see if this works . . . [*He begins to work with the tool he has brought.*] I thought you were mighty young to be married. But since getting married young is "in" these days . . . Well, getting married or whatever . . .

JUAN: The world is going to the dogs . . .

NEIGHBOR: What's that you say?

SUSI: [*Frightened.*] Don't pay any attention to him.

[*The* NEIGHBOR *knows perfectly well who* SUSI *is and shows it. He wants to tell her but doesn't know how.* SUSI *is alarmed.*]

NEIGHBOR: [*Getting bolder.*] Excuse me, but don't I know you from somewhere?
SUSI: . . . Maybe.
NEIGHBOR: Could it be from TV?
SUSI: I guess, maybe . . .
NEIGHBOR: Do you work on TV?
JUAN: [*Spoiling the* NEIGHBOR's *game.*] She's the one in the perfume ad.
NEIGHBOR: [*As though suddenly remembering.*] That's it! You're that girl in the big cancer thing!
SUSI: [*Screaming.*] NO!

[*The* NEIGHBOR *stops abruptly, and* JUAN *beats on the wall several times.*]

JUAN: Susi . . .
SUSI: [*Anguished.*] I didn't even know what they were going to advertise.
NEIGHBOR: Sure.
SUSI: Don't you believe me?
NEIGHBOR: [*Becoming more and more uncomfortable.*] Why wouldn't I believe you?
JUAN: Susi . . .
SUSI: [*Sharply.*] What?
JUAN: What's the matter?
SUSI: Nothing.

[*The* NEIGHBOR *makes another attempt at repairing the elevator and tries to restore a normal tone.*]

NEIGHBOR: I think that this door . . .
SUSI: [*Forcing herself to be cordial again.*] Well, that little wheel up there is broken.
NEIGHBOR: Oh, boy. Yeah, we'd heard that you were in the neighborhood, but we never figured you'd be right here in the same building with us.
SUSI: [*Upset again.*] And that bothers you?
NEIGHBOR: [*Becoming impatient.*] Look, I'm sorry, but . . .
SUSI: You think I'm stupid? You think I don't know how people look at me? You and your wife. Both of you.
NEIGHBOR: But . . .
SUSI: What do you think? Does it offend you to have to pass me on the stairs? Or do I scare you, or what?
NEIGHBOR: Listen, I never did anything to you.
SUSI: Oh, no? What do you call looking at me like I have the plague?
NEIGHBOR: Wait a minute, I never . . .
SUSI: They paid me for those pictures. Tell that to your wife. Go on. Tell her and all her little friends who sent me insulting letters after they rushed right out to buy that junk, simply because of all the brainwashing on TV. Or were you the one who bought it?
JUAN: [*Alarmed.*] Susi!
SUSI: Oh, sure! I bet it was you! "Please, Miss, I'll have some of that naked babe over there. It isn't the smell that turns me on!" Is that the way it was?
NEIGHBOR: Wait a minute! I came up here to do you a favor, and now you're . . . Say, are you drunk or something?
JUAN: Hey, listen here!
NEIGHBOR: [*Preparing to take the ladder away.*] I've heard enough; a lot more than I wanted to. [*To* JUAN.] And who the hell are you anyway? Somebody else who goes around selling poison? [*To* SUSI.] Well, truth is, when people around here heard you had moved into the neighborhood, they weren't too happy.
JUAN: Get out of here! Leave her alone!

SUSI: Shut up! What business is it of yours anyway? What do you want? Some exclusive interview? You already have it! This gentlemen isn't in that kind of business, is he?

NEIGHBOR: You're nuts.

JUAN: Get out of here, or you won't recognize your face when I get through with you!

NEIGHBOR: Well! [*To* SUSI.] If you want some good advice, move to another neighborhood. Or better yet, go to another country. Because you have the kind of face that people remember. I'm telling you for your own good.

SUSI: I don't want any of your advice! I don't want any of it, any of it!

[*The* NEIGHBOR *disappears down the stairway as* SUSI *follows after him.*]

SUSI: Idiots! You're all like a bunch of sheep!

JUAN: Susi!

SUSI: Leave me alone.

JUAN: Susi!

SUSI: Oh, shut up!

[*Not knowing what to do,* JUAN *pretends to be upset, although he is really quite calm in his isolation.*]

JUAN: Susi! Please, I need you to help me.

SUSI: What's the matter?

JUAN: I'm starting to feel sick.

SUSI: What do you want me to do?

JUAN: I want you to get Gomez. Hurry!

SUSI: Who?

JUAN: The photographer, remember? The third Gomez.

SUSI: I can't.

JUAN: Please, Susi, hurry, get him! He's at the corner . . .

SUSI: Yes, but . . .

JUAN: Susi, there's no air in here. I can't breathe . . .

SUSI: Okay, okay. I'm going.

[*She runs toward the stairway but stops there as though suspicious, pausing a moment to look back toward the elevator. When* JUAN *thinks that she has gone, he lights a cigarette.* SUSI *slowly goes back close to* JUAN.]

SUSI: Hey . . .

JUAN: [*Startled.*] You still here?

SUSI: I'm okay now. You weren't really feeling sick, were you? You put on that little act for my benefit, didn't you?

JUAN: Why did you get so upset?

SUSI: You think I'm a little flaky.

JUAN: Are you okay now?

SUSI: Those people recognized me the minute I moved into the building, the wife, especially. Every time she saw me, she stared.

JUAN: So what?

SUSI: Now they're going to tell everyone that I live here!

JUAN: Will you please get Manny?

SUSI: No! He'll be back any minute now.

JUAN: Are you afraid to go to the corner alone?

SUSI: Yes. [*Tries to laugh as she dabs at tears.*]

JUAN: What did these people do to you, Susi?

SUSI: They really did a number on me, Gomez.

JUAN: [*Quietly.*] Well, you seem okay now.

SUSI: [*Calmer now and laughing as she remembers something.*] From in there, how did you plan to do anything to that guy's face?

JUAN: [*Laughing with her.*] I have no idea.

SUSI: Well, anyway, real punishment would be letting him keep the face he's got.

JUAN: Is he that ugly?

SUSI: Worse yet. He has the kind of face that you wouldn't look at twice. You'd pass him on the street and never notice.

JUAN: [*Amused.*] Oh! The famous "man in the street."

SUSI: Is that a common expression?

JUAN: The "man in the street"? Yes, you hear it a lot.

SUSI: Well, I hadn't heard it until recently. The first time was when that guy came to hire me for those darned commercials. "Advertising is seduction, baby! You have to seduce the man in the street. He's the buyer." That's what he told me.

JUAN: Did you understand what he was getting at?

SUSI: It was easy. He was the "man in the street." Ever since then, I've been noticing, and it's true: there is such a thing, or just one model, anyway. They all look alike, have the same way about them. I read somewhere that we're all turning into machines: you press a button and out pops a pack of cigarettes. Press another button, and you get a chain reaction. What's a chain reaction, anyway?

JUAN: [*Laughing.*] It's when one thing makes something else happen, and then that thing causes something else, and . . .

SUSI: [*Quite surprised.*] That's it! I'm a chain reaction.

JUAN: You are?

SUSI: First of all, because of the campaign. When they selected me as the "SHE" girl, they said I was going to be a kind of logo. Do you know what they were talking about?

JUAN: Yes.

SUSI: I don't mean just about me, but in general, in advertising.

JUAN: Yes, I do.

SUSI: [*Disappointed.*] Oh . . .

[*Being very careful to make no sound,* JUAN *turns on the tape recorder and positions the microphone close to* SUSI.]

JUAN: But maybe I didn't understand it as well as I thought . . .

SUSI: The people in the advertising agency turned in different proposals for the campaign, but the company didn't like any of them. And there were good ones, too. I saw them. But no, they weren't having any. So all of those creator people were in a dither.

JUAN: Creative.

SUSI: What?

JUAN: You mean "creative" people.

SUSI: Whatever . . . it's ugly any way you say it.

JUAN: What is?

SUSI: What those people do. Anyway, those "creative" people were stumped until one day I came in to model clothes for a show on young fashions. That's when they saw me and decided that instead of making a whole bunch of posters . . . Is posters the right word?

JUAN: [*Smiling.*] Posters is the right word.

SUSI: So instead of taking lots of different pictures with different models for posters and billboards, they decided to go with a single image for everything, even the packaging.

JUAN: [*Nodding.*] A logo.

SUSI: That's right.

JUAN: And did you know what they were planning?

SUSI: Well, sure.

JUAN: H-m-m-m . . . Tell me something, Susi. When they hired you to pose for those pictures, did you have any idea what was going to happen?

SUSI: [*Excited.*] You mean, did I know anything about what might happen to those children?

JUAN: Oh, no. You couldn't have known anything about that. I meant what all the publicity was going to do to your life.

SUSI: No. I thought of it as a few days' work. I took the job to earn some money. I didn't even think the agency would call me back for other things. But I know why they did, because I became the "in" model. I was just lucky, I guess . . . Well, maybe that's not the word. At first, anyway, at the time, it seemed like I was lucky.

JUAN: Did they pay you well?

SUSI: For the ad campaign? No, they paid me next to nothing. And then the laboratory put me under exclusive contract.

JUAN: You mean, the agency did that.

SUSI: No, the lab. They didn't want me to promote anything but their perfume. They said if I did, I would lose my identification with the product. Apparently a movie producer talked to them, or something like that, but I was already under contract to them. It came out in all the papers. Didn't you read about it?

JUAN: [*Bored hearing the same old story, he turns off the recorder.*] Yes, I guess I did.

SUSI: So the press started talking about me. I don't know why. I was on the cover of all the magazines. "Susi Roman, a rising star," they said, and other things like that. Then they began to say I was foreign, that I was a dancer, that I was involved with this one or that one. [JUAN *yawns and looks at his watch.*] They wanted me everywhere. Oh, people just went crazy over me . . . Until *that* happened.

JUAN: [*Interested again.*] Until *what* happened?

SUSI: You know.

JUAN: [*Turning on the recorder again.*] Tell me about it anyway.

SUSI: About the children?

JUAN: What children?

SUSI: The ones who died. Of cancer. Three of them.

JUAN: Is that what you think, too? It wasn't from cancer. They died from some kind of toxic reaction. I don't know who started that cancer rumor. It's probably because cancer gets so much press. It really makes an impression.

SUSI: Apparently *I* was what really made an impression. And I didn't have anything to do with it. You saw that guy who was just here.

JUAN: No, I can't say as I did see him, as a matter of fact. But I thought you were pretty defensive. You really provoked him.

SUSI: I guess that's some kind of chain reaction, too, huh? Maybe I did kind of provoke him, but did he or didn't he tell me to get out of the neighborhood?

JUAN: [*Conceding.*] He did.

SUSI: And that's nothing. You have no idea of the letters people have written me or the things they've said to me on the telephone. That's why I moved in the first place. They wouldn't even renew my lease. All for the same reason.

JUAN: Hey, couldn't you be exaggerating all this?

SUSI: You come out of there, and you'll see whether the bump on my head is an exaggeration.

JUAN: The what?

SUSI: The bump on my head, from someone who threw a rock at me.

JUAN: That can't be.

SUSI: Oh, yeah? Well, it is. When I was about to go into my apartment building—the one I used to live in—some kids started calling me names, and since I didn't just shut up and take it, a rock came flying at me out of nowhere. And then they began throwing rocks at my window until I moved away. And you know why I moved?

JUAN: Because they wouldn't renew your lease.

SUSI: No, I still had a month left. I moved because they killed my dog.

JUAN: They did what?

SUSI: They killed my dog. They poisoned him, and they left him in front of my door, just like in the movies. That was the day the papers published the story about the third dead child.

JUAN: But Susi, those children died because of an accident, some mistake in the laboratory. There are no guilty people here. The agency had already launched that massive ad campaign with their product, and they couldn't just stop everything in a day. And anyway, what did you have to do with any of that?

SUSI: The people associate me with the whole thing because my face *is* the product to them. I'm the logo, remember? "We're going to show them this girl until her image is indelibly stamped on their brains." That's what they said, and you see? They succeeded. People really associate me with the product. If they could burn me at the stake right now, like in the Dark Ages, they'd do it in a minute.

JUAN: You know, I can't say that I have a very exalted opinion of the human race, but there are a few good people out there. I'm surprised that . . .

SUSI: Sure there are. That man who just left is probably one of them. What's really scary is that good people do these awful things. Other people make them do it, you know? They let themselves be led. Someone starts it, and then it just keeps rolling. Haven't you ever noticed what happens when you're waiting for a red light to change?

JUAN: [*Smiling.*] What happens?

SUSI: You never noticed? It's funny. You're standing there with a group of people all waiting for the light to turn green, but while it's still red, you just take a step forward, and everybody starts to walk. Then they're surprised when all the horns start blowing. In my case, there must have been someone who saw me in an ad and said: "Let's do that girl in." And see what happened? A chain reaction.

JUAN: Susi, what you're telling me could make a very interesting story.

SUSI: For me, it *is* already interesting. It's the story of my life. Hey, you're not interviewing me now, are you?

JUAN: Why do you ask?

SUSI: Because if you are, there's something I want to tell you.

JUAN: What's that?

SUSI: You probably came to ask me if I have a boyfriend, if I wear miniskirts or if I like French films. But I think there are more important things to talk about.

JUAN: [*Interrupting her with his interest.*] Yes, absolutely. Go on.

SUSI: I don't know if I can explain it. Before you came, I knew exactly what I wanted to say, but I'm just not putting it into words very well.

JUAN: Keep trying.

SUSI: I think something started going wrong a long time ago. Something very important. I don't know what it was exactly, or when or where it all started. But I see it in everything. I'm just a small part of it, you know?

JUAN: Yes, I do.

SUSI: I'm just a tiny sample, not anything that makes news. After all, they didn't kill me. They just slammed doors in my face and left me without a job, without friends and with no desire to go on living. The result is the same as if they had sicked their dogs on me.

[*There is a strange noise, and* JUAN *leaps to his feet in alarm.*]

SUSI: What was that? Juan!

JUAN: I don't know. This thing moved.

SUSI: I'm going for your friend!

JUAN: [*Anguished.*] No! Wait!

SUSI: But . . . it can be dangerous.

JUAN: Please don't leave.

SUSI: I have to get help!

JUAN: The elevator could fall any minute!

SUSI: That's why I have to get help!

JUAN: Please, Susi, don't go!

SUSI: I'm here.

JUAN: [*Trying to calm himself, he attempts humor.*] Good God, if this thing falls now, won't it be absurd?

SUSI: It's not going to fall. Just don't move, and . . .

JUAN: That's the kind of death I have coming, I guess: sudden and stupid.

SUSI: Juan . . .

JUAN: I suspected it might be this way . . . an absurd death after an absurd life. I always thought: death can strike at any minute, and, so what? Just one less person, that's all. But what I hadn't counted on was dying in such a ridiculous way, you know? Susi!

SUSI: Yes, I'm here.

JUAN: Please don't leave.

SUSI: Don't worry. I'm not going anywhere.

JUAN: [*Nervous again.*] If this thing's going to fall, I wish it would get it over with! I'm sorry . . . Please talk to me, will you? Tell me something, anything.

SUSI: Now you understand why I told you to come when you called me?

JUAN: What?

SUSI: I was going through *then* what you're going through *now:* terrible fear and the feeling of being trapped, of having only one way out.

JUAN: What are you saying?

SUSI: That I wanted to tell my story before . . . so as not to be so alone, you know? So that someone out there would hear me. I wanted to pretend that what I went through would make a difference . . .

JUAN: Before what?

SUSI: Gomez, what do people do when they can't take it anymore?

JUAN: Are you serious?

SUSI: What do they do?

JUAN: Hey, you weren't really planning . . . ?

SUSI: I gave it a lot of thought. It may sound strange, but that solution was the only thing that kept me going. I kept saying to myself: "Whenever I want to, I can call a halt to this whole thing."

JUAN: You're talking crazy. You're just upset now . . .

[*Another noise from the elevator.*]

SUSI: Don't move! . . . Well, at least you forgot about the elevator for a few minutes.

JUAN: Yes . . .

SUSI: Be quiet!

JUAN: What's the matter?

SUSI: I hear noises downstairs. I think they're leaving. I'm not going anywhere, don't worry. I'm just going over to the stairwell to tell them something.

JUAN: Aren't you afraid of those people?

SUSI: [*Surprised.*] Not any more.

[SUSI *walks quickly toward the stairwell and exits as* CELIA *enters, dressed to go out.*]

CELIA: Did you finish it?

JUAN: Yes, just a minute ago.

CELIA: You must be dead tired.

JUAN: Yeah, really tired . . . but, Celia . . .

CELIA: [*Attempting to avoid a confrontation, she adopts a playful manner.*] Oh, please, please, no explanations, no explanations. Explanations horrify me. Just wish me luck. I wish you luck, too, and since our paths will doubtless cross from time to time, we'll keep right on wishing each other the best, don't you think? If you like, I'll take that to the office, and you can go to bed.

JUAN: Thanks.

[JUAN *takes the final page of what he was writing from the typewriter carriage. He places it on top of other papers on the desk and hands the stack to her.*]

CELIA: All this is an article?

JUAN: Yes.

CELIA: Gee! It looks more like a book than an interview . . . Mind if I read it?

JUAN: No, no. I was going to ask you to, anyway.

CELIA: There'a fresh pot of coffee in the kitchen . . . in case you want some.

JUAN: Thanks.

[JUAN *exits briefly as* CELIA *sits down and reads with increasing interest what* JUAN *has written.* JUAN *returns with the coffee pot.*]

CELIA: This is really good.

JUAN: You think so?

CELIA: Yes, I do. It's much too good for a tabloid. You could sell it to a better publication.

[JUAN *smiles a little bitterly.*]

JUAN: Finish it.

[CELIA *continues reading.* SUSI *and* MANNY *appear at the head of the stairs.*]

SUSI: Gomez! That noise downstairs was the other Gomez coming up.

JUAN: Whadaya know! I thought you weren't ever coming back.

MANNY: I was having a couple of beers.

JUAN: Oh, isn't that nice? Why didn't you take in a movie, too?

MANNY: A guy in the bar went out to look for the super, so I was waiting for him to come back.

JUAN: And did he ever find him?

MANNY: He's on his way up. Apparently getting you out is no big deal. [*Turning toward* SUSI, *as though recalling something.*] Hey, by the way: what did you do to that guy, anyway?

JUAN: Be quiet, Susi.

MANNY: [*Surprised.*] Why do you say that?

SUSI: What did he tell you?

JUAN: Shut up, Manny. It isn't important what an idiot like that says anyway.

MANNY: What's the matter with him?

SUSI: He's just upset in there. So what did he tell you?

JUAN: Nothing. He was nice, willing to help; sent one of his kids to look for the super, who was somewhere or other playing cards. So the guy invited me to have a couple of beers with him, that's about all.

SUSI: Until you told him who I was.

MANNY: Yeah.

SUSI: And then everything changed.

MANNY: I'll say! He even made me pay for the beers.

SUSI: He didn't say anything special?

MANNY: First you tell me what you did to him.

JUAN: Will you shut up, Manny?

MANNY: [*Not understanding.*] Okay. I won't say another word.

SUSI: Why not? Tell me. It could be funny. That guy and I argue all the time. I kid him, you know? Come on: what did he say?

JUAN: Shut up, Manny.

MANNY: What's going on around here?

[*The* SUPER *appears.*]

SUPER: [*In a foul mood.*] Okay, what's wrong with the elevator?

MANNY: Nothing. It's a wonderful elevator. It just doesn't work.

SUPER: If people would treat the equipment right . . .

SUSI: This elevator has never worked properly.

SUPER: You're the only one who ever uses it, so . . .

SUSI: I am *not* the only one who . . . !

SUPER: [*Interrupting her.*] Turn down the volume! People can hear you all over the neighborhood. [MANNY *looks at* SUSI, *amused, but she doesn't notice. The* SUPER *begins to work on the elevator call button.*] This is easy. All you have to do is press here. But you have to do it nice and easy, treat it right.

MANNY: So you lost the card game, huh?

SUPER: What?

SUSI: I need the keys to my apartment.

SUPER: What keys?

SUSI: Don't you have the spare set?

SUPER: I have the ones the owners gave me, but the building president told me . . .

SUSI: The owners gave me keys, too, and said that you had an extra set, just in case I ever needed them.

SUPER: What happened to yours? Lose 'em?

SUSI: I locked myself out.

SUPER: I won't *give* them to you, but if you come downstairs, I'll *lend* you my set.

SUSI: You started to tell me what the building president told you . . .

SUPER: Oh, nothing special. But if you want some good advice, start looking for another apartment. The owners in this building don't like renters. That's what the president told me.

SUSI: The one from the United States?

SUPER: Okay, it's fixed now. I'm going upstairs to check the cables, but I think they're all right.

SUSI: Have you noticed how everyone wants to give me some good advice?

MANNY: Everybody? Who?

SUSI: The "man in the street."

MANNY: In what street?

JUAN: Will you shut up?

MANNY: Take it easy in there, little buddy, take it easy. You're going to be out before you know it.

SUPER: [*Offstage.*] Come down here if you want your keys! And, you: stay up there a minute and press the button when I give you the word.

MANNY: Whatever you say. [SUSI *exits.*] Boy, he's something else!

[CELIA *puts down the papers she is reading and looks at* JUAN, *shocked.*]

JUAN: Did you read it all?

[*He is extremely calm and distant now, as though his mind were a million miles away. During this conversation, he will demonstrate an eerie serenity and pay more attention to the objects and minute details of his surroundings than to what* CELIA *has to say. He will put his papers away methodically, close his typewriter case carefully, position his tape recorder precisely, take off his watch and ring, etc.*]

CELIA: This didn't really happen, did it?

JUAN: Yes.

CELIA: It can't be.

JUAN: You forgot one of the ways, before. You mentioned shooting, slitting wrists, pills. But gas is really a lot easier. It's even cheaper. She's dead by now.

CELIA: You can't be serious.

JUAN: But I am.

CELIA: I don't understand. Why did she do it?

JUAN: She didn't want to live.

CELIA: But that's not a reason.

JUAN: And that's a strange conclusion.

CELIA: [*Standing up and going over to him.*] Juan, you would never help anyone commit suicide.

JUAN: Oh, yes I would. And I did. I helped her close all the windows. When I left, she was in bed, listening to her favorite music and breathing in gas. That was five hours ago.

CELIA: [*Decisively.*] Where does she live?

JUAN: Why do you want to know?

CELIA: Look, I don't know what happened during those days, but you weren't yourself when you came in here, and you still aren't. Somebody has to get her out of there before . . .

JUAN: It's too late now.

CELIA: How could you do such a thing?

JUAN: It was the only way out.

CELIA: Out of what?

JUAN: She was practically dead already. They had almost killed her.

CELIA: Who had?

JUAN: [*Smiling because what he is about to say strikes him as simplistic.*] People . . . The system.

CELIA: Don't talk nonsense! That's a cliché!

JUAN: You really think so?

CELIA: How can you be so calm, knowing that . . . ?

JUAN: Do you know how many people die every day? Do you know how many die for reasons that ought to be a real wake-up call to us all? But no, we keep on sleeping, eating, telling jokes . . .

CELIA: It's not the same!

JUAN: Of course it is! She at least took control.

CELIA: Give me her address, or I'm calling the police.

JUAN: I don't think you'll do that, but here it is.

[*He takes a piece of paper out of his pocket and hands it to her.* CELIA *rushes toward the door.*]

JUAN: Celia . . . In case you decide to call the police, don't forget about my article. I want it published.

[CELIA *looks at him briefly and leaves. At that moment,* SUSI *rejoins* MANNY, *who has been waiting for instructions from the* SUPER.]

SUPER: [*Offstage.*] Hit the button! [SUSI *rushes to push the button.*]

MANNY: Now don't panic when you see him, okay? He can be pretty scary, but he doesn't bite. I mean, not usually, anyway.

[*The different levels between* JUAN *and* SUSI *are now equalized.* MANNY *opens the nonexistent elevator door, dramatically humming a catchy presentation tune.* SUSI *and* JUAN, *now face to face, look at each other. From the side,* MARTINEZ *enters excitedly waving some papers.*]

MARTINEZ: [*Speaking toward the audience.*] Hold everything on the next issue! We gotta pull an article. I don't care which one or who wrote it. We're running Juan Villar's interview: cover story and lead article. And I want all the pictures he was in with the girl. Everything in full color!

JUAN: [*Smiling.*] Hi, Gomez.

SUSI: Hi, Gomez.

ACT II

SUSI's *apartment.* JUAN's *head is in* SUSI's *lap. With one arm over his eyes and a glass within reach, he seems very relaxed. On the record player, Mozart's Concerto No. 21.* SUSI *looks down at* JUAN, *affectionately touching his face and smiling as she suddenly remembers something. Taking a sandwich from a plate close by, she playfully offers it to* JUAN. *When he realizes what she is doing, he takes his arm down and looks at her for a long moment. He smiles and shakes his head to refuse the sandwich.*

SUSI: Aren't you hungry? If I were you, I'd eat. This is the last of our food.
JUAN: Manny will be back soon.
SUSI: Today?
JUAN: Yes.
SUSI: How do you know?
JUAN: Because he called a little while ago.

[SUSI *takes his glass and is about to get up. He stops her. They kiss.*]

JUAN: Where are you going?
SUSI: [*Standing up.*] Your glass is empty.
JUAN: It doesn't matter.
SUSI: Can't I get you something to drink?
JUAN: If you like.
SUSI: But do you want it or not?
JUAN: Well, okay . . .

[SUSI *pours some whisky into* JUAN's *glass and stands beside the record player as the music ends.*]

SUSI: Isn't that music beautiful?
JUAN: Yes.

[*The music stops.*]

SUSI: Shall I put it on again?

[JUAN *laughs softly, a bit condescendingly.*]

JUAN: You've already played it twice today.
SUSI: You want to hear something else? [*He shakes his head.*] Why don't you like it?
JUAN: I do like it. But it makes me want to laugh.

[SUSI *returns to* JUAN *and hands him the glass.*]

SUSI Want to laugh?
JUAN: [*Sitting up.*] Yes. Every time I hear it, I think about soap.
SUSI: [*Not understanding.*] Soap?
JUAN: The one they advertise with that music.
SUSI: This music? Oh, no! This is from a movie: "Elvira Madigan."
JUAN: [*Amused.*] You see?
SUSI: Do I see what?
JUAN: Susi, this isn't "Elvira Madigan." It's a Mozart Concerto.
SUSI: [*Showing him the record label.*] Look: "Theme from 'Elvira Madigan.'"

[JUAN *checks for himself.*]

JUAN: What thieves.
SUSI: Who?
JUAN: Well, to tell you the truth, I don't know who's to blame: them or us. But it's certainly

a sign of the times. We use classical music to sell soap, beautiful women to sell perfume, and Italian paintings to sell wigs. And we swallow whole everything they dish out. Oh, in small, expertly-packaged doses, of course. One of these days, we'll probably end up selling our own hair to buy a wig. What is this crazy world coming to?

[JUAN *seems bitterly amused by his surroundings, including his own words. He speaks ironically, but* susi *takes him seriously, listening adoringly. He realizes it, smiles, and playfully tweaks her nose.*]

JUAN: What are you looking at?

SUSI: I just like to hear you talk.

JUAN: Well, that's a new one for me.

SUSI: Oh, no, I bet that's not so.

JUAN: I don't know of anybody who thinks what I say is important.

SUSI: That's not true. Gomez just sits there with his mouth open when you talk.

JUAN: That's because Gomez is an idiot, and idiots always have their mouths hanging open.

SUSI: I like him!

JUAN: Really? Well, he likes you too.

SUSI: I don't mean that way.

JUAN: What way do you mean?

SUSI: I mean, I like the way he is. He's not dumb, and he's a good person.

JUAN: Yes, I guess you're right.

SUSI: Both of you say you're not friends. Why not?

JUAN: That's one of his little jokes. When I say he's my only friend, he always answers: "Me? I'm no friend of yours!" And he thinks it's funny. He has a weird sense of humor. [*They laugh.*]

SUSI: What about Celia? Doesn't she like to listen to you?

[JUAN *looks at her, surprised to hear her mention* CELIA. SUSI *eventually looks away.*]

SUSI: By the way, you never did call her back, did you?

JUAN: When did I call her?

SUSI: The first day. You called to let her know not to expect you: "Celia, I'm going to be away for a few days. I have some work to do. I'll call you later." But you never did.

JUAN: I haven't had anything to tell her.

SUSI: [*Surprised.*] Not anything?

JUAN: Not anything.

SUSI: [*Disappointed.*] Oh . . .

[*There is a pause. In order to be doing something,* susi *suddenly remembers her sandwich and goes back to it.* JUAN *stands up and playfully takes it away from her.*]

SUSI: Didn't you say you didn't want it?

JUAN: Well, now I do.

[*They kiss again, but soon* susi *draws away gently, unwilling to be distracted.*]

SUSI: I've been doing all the talking, and I'm thinking . . .

JUAN: [*Resigning himself and showing a sudden interest in the sandwich.*] What?

SUSI: That I don't know anything about you.

JUAN: I don't know anything about you, either.

SUSI: What do you mean, you don't know anything about me?

JUAN: You've only given me the facts: that you were born twenty-one years ago, that you have no family, because you don't like the one you have; that you don't have any friends, because the ones you had didn't stick by you; that . . .

SUSI: [*Interrupting him.*] But I don't know when you were born, or if you have a family, or who your friends are . . .

JUAN: But none of that's important.

SUSI: It isn't?

[JUAN, *taking* SUSI *by the hand, gets her to sit down beside him.*]

JUAN: No. The important things about people aren't the facts. It's who they are as people, what their human possibilities are. Take cities, for example. It's one thing to live in a city and something very different to memorize areas in a guidebook. Have you ever been to Paris?

SUSI: No.

JUAN: So what would you say about Paris?

SUSI: Well, I'd say that it has an Eiffel Tower, the Champs Elysées, a lot of artists . . . Have you ever been there?

JUAN: Oh, briefly.

SUSI: And what would you say?

JUAN: That I like to go there from time to time.

SUSI: What about London? Ever been there?

JUAN: Only a time or two.

SUSI: Well, I haven't been there even once, but I know about Big Ben, the changing of the guard, what they do in Hyde Park . . .

JUAN: [*Amused.*] What? What do they do in Hyde Park?

SUSI: Oh, people can make speeches about anything they want and sit in the sun in their undershirts. [JUAN *laughs.*] And if I had to say something about Rome, I'd say . . .

JUAN: [*Interrupting her.*] And what about Madrid? Would you say that we have great monuments to Greek gods but no springtime?

SUSI: No. I'd say that's where I met you.

[JUAN *is disconcerted for a moment but recovers and kisses her.*]

JUAN: [*Very tenderly.*] And what else?

SUSI: Well . . . I'd like to know something about your Madrid, the streets you like, why you like them, the places you go. Then I could tell you about my neighborhood, show you where I was born, the school I went to as a little girl, the park I played in . . .

JUAN: [*Interrupting her.*] And what would you say about me if they asked you?

SUSI: [*Immediately entering into the spirit of the game.*] What would they ask me?

JUAN: Let's see, Miss Roman: What is Juan Gomez Villar really like?

SUSI: O-o-o-h-h . . . that's hard to explain. He's very introverted, you know. He doesn't tell me anything. He doesn't like to talk about himself. And we've known each other a million years. Since the flood, at least, maybe even before.

[JUAN, *uncomfortable with the direction of the conversation, draws away from* SUSI *and gets up on some pretext.*]

JUAN: So you were in the Ark, were you, Miss Roman?

SUSI: Oh, no. Juan was in the Ark. In fact, the Ark belonged to him. I was in the water swimming alongside.

JUAN: [*Making a "tsk-tsk" sound with his tongue.*] My, my . . .

SUSI: Well, I wasn't exactly swimming. I was drowning.

JUAN: Uh huh. And did he toss you a rope from up there?

SUSI: No, he didn't have any rope to toss. But he did have two pigs, two hippopotamuses, two ostriches, two of everything.

JUAN: Everything except two ropes.

SUSI: Right.

JUAN: So what did he do, push you under?

SUSI: No. He jumped into the water with me.

JUAN: Oh, good grief!

SUSI: Why do you say that?

JUAN: Because he didn't know how to swim.

SUSI: He learned.

JUAN: He wasn't capable of learning anything, and least of all, how to swim in those waters.

[SUSI *goes up to him and puts her arms around his neck.*]

SUSI: Well, he *did* learn. He learned for me.

[JUAN *hesitates a few moments, then draws away from* SUSI *and continues the game as a defense mechanism.*]

JUAN: Now, Miss Roman, if you're going to lie, I don't want to hear another word.

SUSI: Well, you tell me how it was, then.

[JUAN *smiles and answers without looking at her, with a certain sadness in his voice.*]

JUAN: The Ark really wasn't his. He was just another one of the animals. He didn't even know where they were taking him or why.

[SUSI *doesn't completely understand what* JUAN *is saying, but she senses his purpose and reacts instinctively. She knows that she should not speak of anything concrete and that she must continue the game if she is to get what she wants.*]

SUSI: But I know why he was there! So that he could save me from the lions.

JUAN: [*Laughing.*] From what lions?

SUSI: How could you forget? It was awful! And so wonderful afterward. There I was in the arena, terrified, wanting them to open the door so the wild beasts could come out and end things once and for all. The people in the stands were screaming and insulting me. They scared me a lot more than the wild animals. Until you came along, that is. You jumped into the arena and took me away from all those terrible things. You killed the lions and rescued me while all those people kept yelling to sacrifice me.

[*When she says "until you came along,"* JUAN *begins to shake his head, slowly, without looking at her, but smiling in an affectionate, ironic way.*]

JUAN: I didn't jump into the arena. I was already in there with you. I was just another victim, tied to a post, like you. I couldn't do anything.

SUSI: People can always do something.

JUAN: No.

SUSI: Yes.

JUAN: Okay, go on. What else happened?

SUSI: I don't want to go on. You don't take me seriously. You're always changing the story.

JUAN: You can't imagine how seriously I'm taking you. It's just that you scare me.

SUSI: How do I scare you?

JUAN: It's your imagination. You have a dangerous tendency to embellish things.

SUSI: What's wrong with that?

JUAN: It's not real, Susi. What we don't know *can* hurt us.

SUSI: Since I met you, nothing can hurt me anymore.

JUAN: [*Returning quickly to the game.*] What if you were persecuted by the Inquisition?

SUSI: Me?

JUAN: It comes after everybody! Everywhere! It pops up when you least expect it!

SUSI: Well, it never bothered me!

JUAN: What do you mean? You told me about it yourself. People thought you were a witch. Three children died, and they blamed you.

SUSI: [*Suddenly sad.*] It's true . . . But at first, it was wonderful, you know? People believed in my magical powers and said that I had a special gift. The pilgrims came from miles around just to see me . . .

JUAN: And your image was on all the village walls.

SUSI: [*Laughing in delight at the analogy.*] Yes, that's right.

JUAN: [*Reproaching her.*] And you let them have their way, and you got involved in that
. . .

SUSI: [*Interrupting him.*] Because I enjoyed it! I liked being recognized everywhere. I enjoyed having people come up to me. I liked it when they clamored for me and threw flowers at my feet. I enjoyed being loved!

JUAN: They didn't really love you, Susi. One fine day, everything changed, and they began to throw rocks at you.

SUSI: [*Sad again.*] Yes . . . How can everything turn upside down so suddenly?

JUAN: Because the very people who adored you began calling you a witch.

SUSI: How could it be so easy for them to believe that?

JUAN: It's absolutely amazing how gullible people are.

SUSI: The only really awful thing in the world is to be rejected or hated. You know when I realized that? One day in the dentist's office . . . Don't laugh, now. This is the truth. He was drilling my tooth.

JUAN: And he hit a nerve.

SUSI: More than once. But that wasn't the important part. I've always been brave. Anyway, the dentist was real nice and told jokes to distract me. And I pretended to be a very good patient until . . . You're going to think I'm crazy.

JUAN: Try me.

SUSI: I don't know why, but I began to wonder if this person was really a dentist. What if he was doing this awful thing to me because he hated me, for the sheer pleasure of hurting me? And then I couldn't take it anymore. I pushed him away and jumped out of the chair. Then I began to scream. Poor man! I really scared him . . .

JUAN: Susi . . .

SUSI: What?

JUAN: I wish I were the kind of person you want me to be.

SUSI: I don't want you to be any special way.

JUAN: [*Smiling.*] You believe I'm capable of saving you from the Inquisition.

SUSI: Yes, because you did.

JUAN: No, I didn't.

SUSI: [*Returning to the game, very enthusiastically.*] Of course you did! Look, I was like in prison, desperate, not understanding why they . . .

JUAN: [*Nervous and interrupting very brusquely.*] But I wasn't anybody special! [*Softening his tone when he sees her alarm.*] I was just a poor guy who happened to be there . . . [*Trying to return to the game.*] I was your confessor. But I could only listen. I couldn't do anything for you. [*He sighs wearily and looks away.*] I'm a coward, Gomez. I'm such a coward that I don't even dare speak to you directly about what's on your mind.

SUSI: May I just contribute one cold and miserable fact to this conversation?

JUAN: [*Avoiding her gaze.*] What's that?

SUSI: I love you.

[JUAN *closes his eyes, deeply moved. He opens them immediately, looks at* SUSI *and holds her as tight as he can. They kiss again.*]

JUAN: [*Pulling away from* SUSI.] It has been beautiful, hasn't it?

SUSI: Has been? Are you leaving?

JUAN: Don't you want me to?

SUSI: [*Offended.*] Well, now I'm not so sure.

JUAN: Think it over.

SUSI: I can't.

JUAN: You don't know if you want me to stay or not?

SUSI: I don't know if you want to stay. Do you?

JUAN: [*Smiling.*] I don't know either.

SUSI: You see what I mean? But . . . What's wrong with us, Gomez?

JUAN: Maybe the spell is broken.

SUSI: Why is that?

JUAN: It was probably a trick all along.

SUSI: Sir! Why do you have to see tricks everywhere?

JUAN: Because they're there.

[SUSI, *really frightened now, and trying to play down the importance of* JUAN's *words, speaks to him maternally.*]

SUSI: You know what we have to do? Get out of here. We need to clean up, get dressed up, and go out . . .

JUAN: We can't, Susi.

SUSI: We can't go out?

JUAN: Not together.

SUSI: [*Serious again.*] Why not?

JUAN: [*Drawing her close to him again and speaking to her as though to a small child.*] Because we met on board a magical spaceship in an invented atmosphere outside the real world.

SUSI: And where's the ship taking us?

JUAN: Nowhere. We have to get off.

SUSI: I don't want to get off!

JUAN: Stories have to end at the right time, so they'll always seem beautiful.

SUSI: But . . .

JUAN: [*Pause.*] It had to happen sometime . . . I'm going to take a shower, get my things, and be off.

SUSI: [*Frightened.*] I don't want you to go!

JUAN: I don't want to go either, Susi . . . But that's the way it is. This is real life.

SUSI: You're going home to Celia?

JUAN: [*Shrugging his shoulders to indicate that it is of little consequence.*] Home to Celia . . .

[SUSI *stands looking at the door where* JUAN *has exited, understanding nothing. Her eyes begin to fill with tears. Offstage, the sound of the shower is heard.* SUSI, *crying softly, approaches the record player as though in a daze and puts on the Mozart Concerto. The music begins to change, almost imperceptibly at first, but eventually takes on a contemporary sound of violent rhythms. The lights dim around* SUSI *until only one spotlight illuminates her. She dances to the music as it becomes louder and louder. This spotlight changes into a mixture of psychedelic colors and flashing lights. The small space in which* SUSI *moves—the same space of the elevator—begins to rise, becoming the nightclub stage on which she now dances in a frenzy. From the side, the publicity* AGENT *enters. He goes up to her and from his position below tries to communicate through gestures as the music continues.*]

AGENT: Hello there!

[SUSI *continues dancing without paying any attention to him.*]

AGENT: Hi, honey! Hello! Don't you remember me? [SUSI *does not stop dancing, but she catches sight of him, recognizes him, and waves briefly.*] Will you be long?

[SUSI *indicates that she will be finished soon.*]

AGENT: I'll wait for you at the bar. I have good news!

[*He sits down before the imaginary bar and gestures to be served. A few seconds later, he begins to drink from one of the glasses used by* SUSI *or* JUAN. *The music becomes softer. The flashing lights have dimmed to become low, steady, and atmospheric, as in a night club.* SUSI—*but not the* SUSI *as we know her but as she was before the scandal—jumps down from the stage and joins him. She is the garden-variety superficial, fun-loving young woman who rarely has serious thoughts.*]

SUSI: [*Breathless.*] Hi.

AGENT: Hi. What'll you have?

SUSI: I don't know. I'm tired of drinking.

AGENT: How about a whisky? That's a harmless drink. What are you laughing about?

SUSI: I hear that a dozen times a day!

AGENT: Isn't it true?

SUSI: I don't know. It just seems funny.

AGENT: How do you stand it, spending so many hours here?

SUSI: It's no problem. This is how I get my exercise.

AGENT: What?

SUSI: I like it. I can't wait for the intermission to be over to start dancing again. I think that says it all.

AGENT: Why do you do it?

SUSI: You're really asking that question?

AGENT: Yes.

SUSI: [*As though the answer were obvious.*] Because I enjoy it.

AGENT: Really?

SUSI: Sure.

AGENT: Isn't it tiring?

SUSI: Look. Before I did this, I went door-to-door selling educational records and cookbooks. I've worked in an office, in a department store. I've worked in a gym and been a switchboard operator in a hotel. I can take a lot. So, tell me. Did I get the modeling job?

AGENT: What modeling job?

SUSI: Didn't you say you had good news for me?

AGENT: Yes.

SUSI: I went by the office and tried out as model for a fashion show.

AGENT: Oh, I don't know anything about that.

SUSI: [*Disappointed.*] Then what's the good news?

AGENT: How would you like to model for some product promotion?

SUSI: [*Not daring to believe him.*] Who? Me?

AGENT: That's more like it, eh? You'll have to do a couple of screen tests, but, oh, I think it's in the bag. You're just what this company wants. Of course, they'll have to take some nude photographs . . .

SUSI: [*Standing up.*] Forget it.

AGENT: [*Stopping her.*] Come on, let me tell you about it.

SUSI: No, thanks. I already know all about it.

AGENT: Wait a minute. It's not what you think.

SUSI: You're asking me to pose for pictures without my clothes on? In this country?

AGENT: But it won't look like you're really nude. There will be rose petals at the strategic points. You know what I mean?

SUSI: To advertise what?

AGENT: A perfume. It's the first product in a whole new line.

SUSI: Yeah, well, you can get somebody else. If you want, I'll introduce you to Nelly, that blond over there. She'd be great for perfume. She always looks like she just got out of the shower. Besides, she's very tall and very . . . everything you want. Come on.

AGENT: [*Stopping her again.*] But why don't you want to do it? Listen, you wouldn't really be nude. It'd be like . . .

SUSI: [*Interrupting him.*] Listen, that's not what bothers me. I'm no prude. It wouldn't faze me to dance stark naked right here. I wouldn't do it, though, because of all those ogling eyes in the crowd. As far as I'm concerned . . .

AGENT: Well, then? . . . I'm telling you this is a good deal! Come by the office tomorrow and you'll see it's for real. Don't you understand that this is a great opportunity?

SUSI: [*Vacillating.*] Really?

AGENT: Imagine! It'd be like starting at the top! It'll make you famous! The opportunity of a lifetime! Understand?

SUSI: [*Joking but inclined now to accept.*] To advertise perfume, huh?

AGENT: That'll just be the beginning! This will be your springboard to bigger and better things! You're practically in the movies!

SUSI: The movies?

AGENT: That's right! Can't you just see it? Posters, billboards, television commercials, all with your face! With your looks, you'll take the place by storm, you know what I'm saying? This is a real stroke of luck!

SUSI: It is?

AGENT: We've had problems with this particular promotion. The company has already rejected a bunch of our proposals. The day you came by the office, they turned down another one, but the head of the group—their group, I mean—said he'd take our logo idea if you'd be the model.

SUSI: They'd take your what?

AGENT: The logo: having just one symbol for everything, you know?

SUSI: Not really, but . . .

[*The* AGENT *launches into his spiel like a con artist. The youngest of the* MAN-IN-THE-STREET *characters, the* AGENT *wears sporty, modern clothes, is agile and always appears to be in a hurry.*]

AGENT: It means having just one picture for all the promotion and packaging. Force the image on the public until they think they can't live without the product. In the trade, we call it subliminal advertising. You make people do what you want, and they don't have a clue as to what's going on.

SUSI: [*Warming to the idea.*] Well . . .

AGENT: [*Continuing his pitch.*] This is the way everything works these days: publicity, advertising, promotion. What do you think people do in public relations, business or political campaigns? It's all image. What you see is much more important than what you hear, because you don't have to interpret or even think . . .

[SUSI *nods, attempting to say something.*]

AGENT: They give you everything already thought out. It's a lot more subtle than using words. Advertising is seduction, baby. What you have to do is seduce the buyer, the man in the street. You know what I mean?

SUSI: Yes, I think so . . .

AGENT: Can I give you some good advice? You gotta open that door when opportunity knocks. You gotta play to win, you gotta . . .

SUSI: Okay, okay, but spare me all that! What's the deal? I have to jump around somewhere else, right? Just tell me when, where and what time.

AGENT: [*Turning practical now, as though closing a deal.*] Then you'll do it.

SUSI: To get all the things you just talked about, I guess I'd jump into shark-infested waters.

AGENT: That's what I wanted to hear! In this world, you gotta be where the action is, be where the deals are cut! You understand what I mean?

SUSI: Look, I may not be too bright, but do you really have to ask me if I understand every time you open your mouth? Just tell me when I start.

AGENT: Tomorrow. Be at the office at ten o'clock.

[SUSI *nods in agreement before returning to the platform.*]

SUSI: And thanks for that harmless drink!

AGENT: See ya, babe. Good luck!

[*In a parting gesture, the* AGENT *raises his arms in a victory sign. From the platform and dancing now,* SUSI *duplicates his gesture. The* AGENT *exits. The platform begins a slow descent as the music reverts back to the Mozart Concerto. In the midst of this musical transformation, a note heard in isolation will sound like a machine grinding to a halt. The platform is still now, and* SUSI *beats on the walls—real and symbolic—that imprison her.*]

SUSI: No, no! Not now! Please God! Oh, how stupid of me! Not now! Please! Isn't anybody in the building? Help! Help! I'm here in the elevator! The elevator! [*Realizing that no one hears her, she collapses and begins to cry.*] Oh, please! Not now! Not now!

[*The Mozart Concerto starts again and continues its normal sound. The platform is completely down, and* SUSI *will hear the rest of the music with her eyes full of tears.* MANNY *enters loaded down with packages and a folder full of papers.*]

MANNY: Hello, there, my fair beauty. Here comes jolly old Saint Nick.

[SUSI, *startled, dries her tears furtively.* MANNY *notices and stares at her for a few seconds.*]

MANNY: Where's Gomez?
SUSI: He's taking a shower. [JUAN *enters.*] He *was* taking a shower.
MANNY: [*To* JUAN.] Hi. [*Joking.*] You two want me to go out and come back in a little while?
JUAN: [*In the same tone.*] Better yet, go out and don't come back.
MANNY: Uh huh, but leave the stuff here, right?
JUAN: You got it. And also leave some money, if you have any. We're completely broke.
MANNY: Right away! And since I'm already here, shall I shine your shoes, too, Boss?

[*Although* JUAN *tries to maintain the jocular tone, he continues to watch* SUSI *worriedly. She turns her back.* MANNY *finally decides to break the ice.*]

MANNY: You know, every time I leave you two alone, when I come back I get the feeling that about ten years have gone by.
SUSI: Did you really miss us that much?
MANNY: It's not that. It's the changes. You guys are passing through stages at the speed of light . . . The first day, I was only gone for an hour. When I left, you two didn't even know one another, and when I got back. Gee, if this one hadn't been caged up during that time, I don't know what would have happened.
JUAN: You wouldn't understand. You've never been through anything like this.
MANNY: Let's not get into that, because today I have come to amaze you. I have something here that is going to blow you away.
JUAN: Pipe tobacco.
MANNY: What do you mean, pipe tobacco? This is more like dynamite!

[MANNY *opens a folder full of papers and newspaper clippings.*]

JUAN: What does all this mean?
MANNY: It means that while you two were locked up in here rocking each other blissfully, I've been out working, which is what we came to do in the first place. [*Pauses to ask* JUAN *a question.*] Will you please tell me what's going on here?
SUSI: [*Turning to him suddenly with false animation.*] Shall I tell him, Gomez?
MANNY: Out with it.
SUSI: Do you know the story of "Sleeping Beauty"?
MANNY: [*A bit surprised.*] Yeah, I remember it a little . . .
SUSI: Did you know that's who I was?
MANNY: [*Entering into the game.*] What are you saying?
SUSI: Just what you're hearing. And do you know who the brave knight was who came to awaken me with a kiss on the lips?
MANNY: I'm afraid to guess.
SUSI: It's really quite a story, isn't it?
MANNY: A little sentimental for my taste. On the other hand, the one I brought here . . .
SUSI: [*Interrupting him.*] Sentimental? It's a love story that's harsh and cruel and unfair.
JUAN: [*Softly.*] Why do you say that?

SUSI: Because the story doesn't end when the books say it does. [*She is talking to* MANNY, *who has begun to take some of the clippings out of the folder.*] Do you know what happened when the Princess woke up?

MANNY: Maybe you'd better not tell me that part.

SUSI: She and the knight lived some wonderful days in the castle, without seeing anyone. Nobody bothered them . . .

MANNY: Thanks . . .

SUSI: Until one fine day the brave knight announced that he was leaving. He'd lost interest in the princess.

JUAN: Susi, I never said . . .

[MANNY *looks up, curious.*]

SUSI: He was only attracted to her because of some spell. She was just a passing fancy, another adventure.

JUAN: Will you listen to me?

SUSI: [*Ironic.*] Spare me the facts, will you. Let's just say they aren't important.

JUAN: He really wasn't a brave knight at all. He was just a poor . . .

SUSI: [*Interrupting him.*] A troubadour!

MANNY: I'm not bringing you two any more whisky.

SUSI: That's what he was! A troubadour! That's why he stayed with her: to write his ballad, because that's how he made his living, and his job was the only thing that mattered to him.

JUAN: Has it ever occurred to you . . . ?

SUSI: Don't say it! Just don't say anything.

[*There is a silence that* MANNY *breaks once again.*]

MANNY: Now can this fool, this lowly mortal say something? Here is the Susi Roman file, almost complete.

[JUAN *picks up his glass again and turns away, perturbed.* MANNY *continues talking to* SUSI, *who responds without enthusiasm.*]

MANNY: I wasn't able to cut out everything. They used more ink on you than on Rudolph Valentino, but these will do.

SUSI: Do I get a complete set as a souvenir?

MANNY: I have a surprise for you. And for you, too. Are you listening to me, Gomez?

[JUAN *gives a nod from his corner without looking at him.*]

MANNY: But first of all, I must confess something. When we came here, we were like two simple little reporters to do a simple little interview for our simple little housewives.

JUAN: They're not so simple.

MANNY: Anyway, what I mean is that I came here to do a job and take pictures of this cute young thing, but when I got here, I was inspired to do some serious work. All these days, I've been digging into the files and talking to people, and I've found a few really curious things. Look at this, for example: the cover picture and story about Susi Roman . . . "The surprising personality" . . . "An unusual attraction" . . . "A new star twinkles on our bleak horizon." All kinds of stuff. Look at this. And this other one is funny too: "Susi Roman is anxious to become a real Spaniard!" What else can she be, for God's sake? And check this about "The rapid rise of a young woman bent on success." And this other one: "Susi Roman, on the road to stardom." To sum it all up, they don't say much of anything: just a lot of insinuation, a lot of color and a lot of pictures. And, hey, here's another gem . . .

JUAN: [*Interrupting him.*] What are you getting at?

MANNY: What I'm getting at is that when all those stories were being written, all Susi Roman had done was model for some ad campaign . . .

JUAN: So?

MANNY: Where I come from, they call that blowing things out of proportion. And you know what kind of money goes into all that hot air? Millions. A heck of a lot more than what cologne brings in, no matter how much of it they sell. And especially considering how little was sold in this case.

SUSI: Well, they couldn't have known that.

MANNY: Apparently they sold so little simply because they produced very little. And they produced very little, because what they were promoting wasn't the perfume.

SUSI: What was it, then: me?

MANNY: No, sweetie. You were just a front. Think back: what else was in the ad, besides your picture?

SUSI: Nothing . . . Well, there was the slogan: "Yours for the asking."

MANNY: No, there was something else. It was in the movie and TV ads, too. There was something there that you seem to have forgotten.

SUSI: There wasn't anything else.

JUAN: The name of the laboratory.

MANNY: Exactly. And do you know what those famous three children died of?

JUAN: Some kind of toxic reaction.

MANNY: Yes, but not because of the perfume, Susi. That was just another smoke screen.

SUSI: Then, why did they die?

MANNY: Because of a polio vaccine produced by this same laboratory. But more than three children died. There were a lot more.

SUSI: What are you saying?

MANNY: First of all, companies don't advertise vaccines. They have to promote the product in other ways. Second, this company has been enormously successful, much more than average. They can't keep up with the demand. So they get careless and somebody blows it. Third: if a lab makes a mistake producing cologne and three children die, people get upset. They don't panic, though. But if they make a mistake with a vaccine and a lot of children die, what happens? To start with, families quit getting inoculations for their children, and that increases the possibility of illness. And the bad thing for the lab is that they don't make money. So what should they do? Fabricate a story to suit their purposes and then change the decoy—you in this case—since it has already taken the flak. Come over here, Susi. Take a look at this.

[SUSI *looks at him in horror and moves to where he is standing.*]

SUSI: At what?

MANNY: Your successor. A little tyke, this time, only six months old. Since he can't advertise cologne, he's promoting a lotion. But it's the same thing. Look at the slogan: "How wonderful to feel safe." You see what's going on here?

SUSI: Yes.

MANNY: What a coincidence: The ads with the baby came out in the newspapers first, almost always near an article that talked about the "unfortunate accident that caused the deaths of three innocent little children, etc. etc." Here's a typical one with a wonderful headline: "Shocking photographs turn a young woman into a symbol of shame." How do you like that? Somebody paid for this article. I have it on good authority. What do you think of that?

JUAN: This whole thing reminds me of the Loch Ness Monster.

SUSI: What's that?

JUAN: A monster who comes up in a lake somewhere in Scotland when the press has nothing else to talk about or can't talk about what there is to talk about.

SUSI: Is that what they did with me?

JUAN: That's what they do with everybody, Susi.

SUSI: You say that so calmly.

JUAN: How am I supposed to say it?

SUSI: Don't you realize that you're talking about my life, the only one I have, and that they don't have any right to do this to me? No right at all! [*Turning to* MANNY.] What's the monster's name, the one in that lake?

MANNY: Loch Ness.

SUSI: Well, they're not going to get away with this, Gomez. I'm not someone who just takes things lying down.

MANNY: Of course you're not.

JUAN: How did you find this out?

MANNY: I can't say I did, for sure.

JUAN: So where do we stand?

MANNY: Well, all I did was get the information and come to conclusions, but nobody has actually confirmed my suspicious, you know? To figure out that they're doing a number on you isn't so hard. That's something we more or less have gut feelings about. The problem is that you never really know for certain how they do it or why.

SUSI: I'm not like that. I'm going to find out.

JUAN: How, Susi?

SUSI: By doing whatever it takes. We have to try.

JUAN: Why?

SUSI: Is that a serious question?

MANNY: [*To* JUAN.] You drunk or what?

JUAN: I'm just asking what we have to gain by knowing.

SUSI: To start with, we won't stand around and let them walk all over us.

MANNY: We can find out why this lab is getting away with murder and who's behind it all.

JUAN: So we could do what?

SUSI: What do you mean? Don't you spend your life talking about how this country has gone to the dogs? So, this is your chance . . .

MANNY: Exactly! Why don't we start tinkering around to see if we can bring it around!

JUAN: Tinkering wouldn't do any good. What this country needs is radical change, a makeover, a transformation, top to bottom.

SUSI: So let's transform it!

JUAN: [*Smiling again.*] How in the world could we ever do that, Susi?

SUSI: I don't know how, but . . .

MANNY: [*Interrupting.*] I don't know how either. All I know is the news business, and when at last I have a great story . . . [*Suddenly remembering something.*] Hey, weren't you saying this just the other day? You said that SUSI was a good example of how the system uses the individual. You said that what people are really interested in is other people, real people, and that you could do a story on Susi that would bring in all that other stuff. Isn't that what you said? Well, come on. I'm bringing you meat for the grille— choice cut at that, I think. Or aren't you interested in investigative reporting anymore?

SUSI: Of course he is! Why do you suppose he's here? Show him the notes you've been making all these days. You don't want him to think you've been goofing off, do you? Give them to him. Go on. He can add those notes to his Susi Roman file. I found them last night and read them. I hope you don't mind.

JUAN: Why would I mind?

SUSI: Because researchers don't usually tell their guinea pigs about experiments they're performing on them.

MANNY: What did his notes say?

SUSI: Nothing spectacular. Notes usually aren't very specific. Just a sentence here, ideas to develop there. Isn't that right?

MANNY: Then why are you taking it that way?

SUSI: How should I take it? Don't you realize that he has done with me what everybody else has done? Don't you see how he has used me? Don't you see that he's just like everybody else?

MANNY: [*To* JUAN.] Come on. What did your notes say?

SUSI: [*Going toward the bedroom.*] I'll read them to you.

MANNY: Will you tell me what you wrote?

JUAN: [*Shrugging.*] Nothing.

[SUSI *returns with some papers in her hand.*]

SUSI: Listen . . . Well, not this one. It's from the start. It only has stupid things like my vital statistics: facts, as he says. [*Going through some of the papers.*] But this one, yes. When he wrote it, he'd been here three days, and he was able to spice up his writing. You do that for a good article, you know, to give it a little drama, so the guinea pig will cooperate and tell all. After all, can you think of a more comfortable place to talk than in bed?

JUAN: [*Softly and very calmly.*] You're mistaken, Susi.

SUSI: I am? [*Reading.*] "It's amazing how easy it is to destroy a human being. Generally it's enough to create a wall of hostility. But even stranger is how easy it is to revive the desire to live. A little of what they call love, and people are ready to go back for more abuse from others who smile and enjoy letting their fists fly. How easy it is to believe in others again and be deceived like a fool."

[JUAN *begins to laugh. The nervous tension that has been building in* SUSI *now explodes, and she rushes at him.*]

SUSI: Don't you dare laugh!

[MANNY *rushes to separate them.*]

MANNY: What the hell's gotten into you two?

SUSI: [*Crying again.*] That's the only complete sentence he wrote. Everything else is just words, phrases. "Commercially," for example, or "conditioned reflexes." I wonder what he meant by "conditioned reflexes."

JUAN: Will you give me those papers!

SUSI: Sure. They're yours.

[*She hands them to* JUAN *and he tears them up.*]

SUSI: What do you want me to do? Applaud?

JUAN: I want you to listen to me. The sentence that offended you so had nothing to do with you, Susi. I was talking about myself. And as far as the interview is concerned, don't worry. It's not something I can use for an article. What happened to you isn't dramatic enough for the average reader. They've seen children deformed by starvation or destroyed by bombs, and they don't even lose their appetite. The particular problem of just one young woman isn't going to bring in more readers.

MANNY: That's not what you thought the other day.

SUSI: And that's what he still thinks. It's just that they turned down his article. My name isn't news anymore. It's old hat. That's what they told you, didn't they? I'm "old hat." Don't you think that's funny?

MANNY: Who turned down what of yours?

SUSI: Probably a very important publication. In this world, everybody wants to win, didn't you know that? Win at any cost! But he wanted a lot of money for his work, so they turned him down. My manners aren't wonderful, Juan. When you were talking on the phone in the living room, I was listening in from the bedroom. Because I thought you were calling Celia. Isn't that silly? So go on: tell me you weren't using me.

MANNY: What's wrong with what he did? He's a writer, Susi.

SUSI: If your mother were dying, would you take pictures of her to sell to the press?

MANNY: If she was big news, sure.

SUSI: But you wouldn't kill her to get the pictures, would you?

JUAN: She's pretty sharp, Manny, and you always fall into people's traps. Would you mind leaving us alone for a few minutes.

MANNY: You better believe I mind! I have a better suggestion. My car is parked outside. I just filled it up with gas. How about a little fresh air and . . . ?

[JUAN *resumes his usual cynical, ironic posture.*]

JUAN: Fresh air, you say? It's completely polluted.

MANNY: Well, go out and have a little pollution. Just take my car and . . .

JUAN: Did you know that the car was the most deadly human invention of all time? Did you know that economic excess is what spurs its production? Did you know . . . ?

MANNY: So go out for a walk! Do me a favor, will you? Get out of here! Go on. You've been cooped up in here stewing and simmering in your own juices so long that you've just gone off the deep end. There's more to life than talking, talking, talking in here between four walls.

JUAN: That's the way they do scientific experiments, Gomez: in isolation, no contact with the outside world.

MANNY: It's more important to face that outside world, fight for important things, and you . . .

JUAN: [*Exploding and completely serious now.*] I wouldn't lift a finger for this shitty country! Who lifted a finger for me when I was arrested? And nobody has moved one since! Can't you see how things are? People are hypocrites. They're interested in you only if you can help *them*. What about all those guys who could have helped get me out of jail? They found it more comfortable to sit around *talking* about freedom over coffee! That's all they do, you know: talk! Look at them, all self-satisfied and preoccupied with their new cars and their fancy electronic gadgets. When three or four of us naive idealists try to do something for everybody, they look in the other direction!

SUSI: [*Interrupting him.*] Couldn't it be that what's really eating at you is that you weren't rewarded for all your trouble? Isn't it possible that you expected your jail adventure to get you a lot of attention and a better job? Maybe even a new car? Or how about some fancy electronic gadgets? Isn't it just possible that you . . . ?

JUAN: [*His pride completely wounded.*] What are you saying?

MANNY: [*Conciliatory as always and trying to break the tension.*] Hey, come on! Take my killer car, and go out for a little polluted air!

JUAN: You're right.

MANNY: Are you sick? Did you actually say I was right about something?

JUAN: You're right a lot more than I let on. I'm a jerk sometimes. Sorry.

MANNY: [*Smiling, he turns to* SUSI.] Go on, Susi. Get dressed and . . .

SUSI: Leave us alone, please . . .

MANNY: But . . .

[MANNY *looks at* JUAN, *as though seeking confirmation.*]

JUAN: [*Nodding.*] I'll see you tomorrow.

MANNY: You bet you're going to see me. As soon as that sun comes up, I'll be here. I'm leaving you all this stuff. Tomorrow we'll look at it together. Maybe there's nothing there we can use, but I want to look it over anyway, just in case. [*He starts to leave but stops a moment.*] Hey . . . Gomez. [*Both respond to their names, but he gestures to* JUAN.] You. You're right, we started out being friends, because you were in a position to help me professionally.

JUAN: Manny . . .

MANNY: But at least we started something, and we're friends, now, aren't we? So this world gave us that, anyway. See you tomorrow.

[*He exits.* JUAN *sighs, worried.*]

JUAN: I liked it better when he said he was no friend of mine.

SUSI: Why is that?

JUAN: When people feel they have to make a point of saying things, it's usually because there's some doubt.

SUSI: It's scary to hear you talk like that! Didn't anything ever work out right for you? Ever?

JUAN: Yes. Once. It was the only time I ever got stuck in an elevator . . . and when I got out . . .

[*Before he can finish the sentence,* SUSI *rushes into his arms.*]

SUSI: Don't you see? You'll *have* to take me with you!

JUAN: But don't you see that I have nowhere to take you? I'd do anything for you, but the only thing I know how to do is my work, and I tried selling it. And I mean sell in the worst sense of the word. You know, that publication I talked to on the telephone represents everything that I hate. Nevertheless, I called and offered myself. You know what happened. They rejected me. They don't consider me a good buy.

SUSI: But just because something isn't . . .

JUAN: The real failure wasn't the rejection, Gomez. It was having offered myself in the first place.

SUSI: I guess so. And I guess my real failure isn't your rejection but rather my dependence on you. Isn't that right? But thanks anyway.

JUAN: For what?

SUSI: For not being hypocritical . . . But, what have they done to you, Juan?

JUAN: [*He smiles, remembering her response to the same question.*] They did a real number on me, Gomez.

SUSI: And the funny thing in all this is that you love me. I know you love me.

JUAN: Yes, I do.

SUSI: Then . . . ? [*He stands motionless as he looks as her.*] No. There is nothing we can do. You're going to leave me here alone.

JUAN: [*Looking away.*] It's the only thing I can do. I'm just not up to starting over.

[SUSI *sobs quietly for a while. Then, as though coming to a decision, she speaks firmly.*]

SUSI: Yes. Yes you can. You didn't let them burn me at the stake.

JUAN: What are you saying?

SUSI: And when you found out that they were going to throw me to the lions, you killed me yourself.

JUAN: Listen, don't be . . .

SUSI: You didn't want to leave me swimming forever in that space around the empty Ark. That would be awful, much too cruel.

JUAN: Susi . . .

SUSI: So you helped me out of my misery, because you loved me, and because it was the only thing you could do for me.

JUAN: Will you please stop talking foolishness?

SUSI: Foolishenss? When you go out of that door, what will become of me? A week ago, when you found me, I was terrified . . . desperate, because I had no place to run. I didn't know what to do. But it was less awful then, because I didn't love you; because I wasn't losing you as well. But now, everything's different . . .

JUAN: Yes, now you're not afraid anymore. You'll fight back and . . .

SUSI: But you taught me that fighting back doesn't do any good!

JUAN: [*Emotional.*] No, Susi, I . . .

SUSI: You have proved to me that nothing does any good; that there is no way out, no hope . . .

JUAN: [*Shrugging his shoulders.*] But we have to live. There's no other way.

SUSI: I don't know how to say "there's no other way." And I don't want to learn either!

JUAN: Susi . . .

SUSI: I don't want to live without you. No, I don't want to.

JUAN: Don't say that. You're young.

SUSI: Is that a reason to live? I don't ever want to be like you! [JUAN *looks at her, shocked by what she has said.*] My love . . .

JUAN: No . . . You should never be like me.

SUSI: Juan . . .

JUAN: You're right, Susi.

SUSI: Then help me. Like you wanted to. Stories should end while they're still beautiful. It's simple. You'll close all the windows, and you'll turn on the gas. They say you don't feel a thing. You'll just leave me asleep, that's all. And then they'll want your interview. I'll be news again. They'll pay attention to you and read what you write. You can tell them all those important things, and some of your readers will understand. Some will even think . . . What you do will be worthwhile, even though most people have heads made of cement. Even though they don't want to learn anything, there will always be one . . . And you don't have to be afraid that this is going to be like everything else in your life. You won't have to worry that I'm going to disappoint you, or that after a while, I'll be different, or that I'll leave. You won't have to worry about where I am or who I'm with. You'll stop being afraid of my being so young . . .

JUAN: [*Amazed.*] Susi!

SUSI: You think I'm silly, Gomez?

[JUAN *holds her close in a kind of automatic desperation. They kiss.* MARTINEZ *enters from the side, dressed exactly as at the end of the first act.*]

MARTINEZ: [*Speaking toward the audience.*] Hold everything on the next issue! We gotta pull an article. I don't care which one or who wrote it. We're running Juan Villar's interview: cover story and lead article. And I want all the pictures he was in with the girl. Everything in full color!

[*He exits at the side.* SUSI *and* JUAN *separate.*]

SUSI: [*Beginning to get frightened.*] But do it right now! Juan! Right now!

[JUAN *begins to close windows as she watches a little apprehensively. Soon, she joins in the activity. She pulls the record player close to her and puts on the Mozart Concerto. Having made his decision now,* JUAN *waits for her at the bedroom door. They exit together as* MANNY *enters and begins to go through the papers, just as he was doing in the scene with the* CORONER. *The latter enters a few seconds later. The music stops as he speaks.*]

CORONER: Sorry. I didn't realize I was going to be so long.

MANNY: No problem. I was rereading this.

CORONER: Oh, yes. The article. When are they publishing it?

MANNY: They're not.

CORONER: [*Surprised.*] Why not?

MANNY: We're not allowed to say that people don't like the way the country is being run. We have to say everything's just hunky dory.

CORONER: I don't understand. He doesn't attack anybody in particular.

MANNY: No, but he attacks everything in general. Besides, you know that in this country, nobody commits suicide. What we have here are "accidents."

CORONER: Is that the reason the article was censored?

MANNY: It didn't get as far as the government office. It didn't have to. The magazine turned it down . . . well, the editor, I mean. The rest of us wanted it published.

CORONER: That's strange.

MANNY: What's strange?

CORONER: The very fact that it was turned down shows that he was onto something important. And he was right, too, don't you think?

MANNY: Of course he was right . . . in all but one thing.

CORONER: What's that?

MANNY: That there's nothing anybody can do.

CORONER: And what do you think we can do?

MANNY: I know we can't give up.

CORONER: I'm glad to hear you say that.

[MANNY *looks at the* CORONER *ironically.*]

MANNY: Can I ask you a question?

CORONER: Of course.

MANNY: Why did you tell me to come here?

CORONER: Well, you see . . . The official reason was the inquest. We have to determine if this was a suicide, and if it was, whether anyone else was involved. We need to know if a crime has been committed.

MANNY: [*Indignant.*] A crime? I'll say a crime has been committed! Just read that. It'll tell you who the guilty parties are! [*Indicating* JUAN's *article.*]

CORONER: I agree with you completely, so calm down. I was explaining my official reason, the pretext, we might say, of why I asked you to come. What I really wanted was to talk to you. I am very interested in what you think.

MANNY: [*Surprised.*] In what I think?

CORONER: Yes. I belong to a different generation, so I don't understand exactly what you mean by certain words, but I sense that they are not positive. Villar's generation had it rough. Maybe that's why I'm interested in knowing what people like you . . . or like that girl . . . think. Can I give you some advice? [MANNY *recognizes the question and smiles wryly.*] Don't let what he says influence you too much. There is always something positive in spite of everything.

MANNY: [*Painfully ironic.*] Can you be more specific?

CORONER: The very fact that you and I are talking about it. I'd like to know what you expect to do?

[MANNY *decides to put an end to the interview and walks toward the door.*]

MANNY: I'm going out to look for the Loch Ness Monster.

CORONER: [*Not understanding.*] What?

[MANNY *bids farewell to the* CORONER, *patting him on the shoulder, as he has already done in the course of the conversation.*]

MANNY: It's a long story. [*He exits.*]

[*For a few seconds, the* CORONER *stands looking pensively after* MANNY. *Finally, he goes back to his desk, sits down, puts on his glasses and begins to go through his papers again. In her apartment,* SUSI *staggers, dizzy and anguished. She opens the windows, breathes deeply and seems to wake up. As soon as she can, she goes to the telephone and dials three numbers.*]

SUSI: Please, Miss. Can you give me the number of a magazine called *Woman Talk?* No, I don't have the address . . . Not listed? . . . Oh, please, please, Miss . . . It's urgent . . . All I know is that it's across the street from a movie house. The Princess Theater, I think . . . Yes, that's the one! If you'll give me the address, I'll find it . . . Thank you so much.

[*She hangs up and rushes toward the bedroom, still unsteady on her feet. She returns immediately, hastily putting on the first clothes she can find before going out into the hall. She goes into the elevator and presses the button. The platform begins to descend but stops suddenly, as before, and, as before,* SUSI *begins to beat on the walls and cry out.*]

SUSI: No! No! Not now! . . . Good God, how could I have been so stupid, so stupid? . . . Not now. Please help me! Isn't there anyone in the building? The elevator! Please, not now! Not now!

[*SUSI curls up on the floor of the elevator and will remain motionless. The* CORONER *is preparing his report. He looks at his notes and begins to prepare the first few sentences, speaking into a microphone.*]

CORONER: Your Honor . . . ladies and gentlemen. We are here to consider the results of an investigation into a possible suicide. I will go into the circumstances and physical evidence that caused death, but I want to preface my report with some reference to the psychological motives involved here.

[*The* CORONER *switches off the recorder and continues working with his papers at the same time that* JUAN *enters, exactly as he was at the beginning of the first act. He will duplicate those attitudes, gestures and words. He sits down at the typewriter, puts paper in the carriage, lights a cigarette, etc. The telephone rings.* JUAN *grabs the phone expectantly.*]

JUAN: Yes? [*He sighs, disappointed but resigned, when he recognizes the caller's voice.*] Oh, hello. What's up? Sure, I just got in . . . With her, with the girl . . . [*Speaking louder.*] I said with the girl. Yes, until today, until just now. [*Looking at his watch.*] Well, until half an hour ago, the time it took me to get here . . . Yes, mostly talking . . . Talking, I said! Why don't you put the phone on your other ear?

[*The* CORONER *pushes the playback button on the recorder to hear what he has said. His words drown out what* JUAN *is saying on the telephone.*]

TAPE: Your Honor . . . ladies and gentlemen. We are here to consider the results of an investigation into a possible suicide. I will go into the circumstances and physical evidence that caused death, but I want to preface my report with some reference to the psychological motives involved here.

[*The* CORONER *turns on the machine again and continues recording.*]

CORONER: It's no mystery to any of us that suicide in this country is on the rise, and for a reason that affects us all: our inability to cope with stress. We are often unable to adjust to a difficult, often hostile environment that . . .

[*He turns off the recorder and continues working. Meanwhile, in* JUAN's *space,* CELIA *enters, dressed as we saw her at the end of the first act. She holds* JUAN's *article and stands as she did when she finished reading it in the first act. As the* CORONER *finishes recording,* JUAN, *no longer talking on the telephone, stands up. He is in exactly the same spot where he was when* CELIA *finished reading the article. The appearance of this scene must be identical to the scene of the first act.*]

JUAN: Did you read it all?

CELIA: This didn't really happen, did it?

JUAN: Yes.

CELIA: It can't be.

JUAN: You forgot one of the ways before. You mentioned shooting, slitting wrists, pills, but gas is really a lot easier. It's even cheaper. She's dead by now.

CELIA: You can't be serious.

JUAN: But I am.

CELIA: I don't understand anything. Why did she do it?

JUAN: She didn't want to live.

CELIA: But that's not a reason.

JUAN: That's a strange conclusion.

CELIA: [*Standing up and going over to him.*] Juan, you would never help anyone commit suicide.

JUAN: Oh, yes I would. And I did. I helped her close all the windows. When I left, she was in bed, listening to her favorite music and breathing in the gas. That was five hours ago.

CELIA: [*Decisively.*] Where does she live?

JUAN: Why do you want to know?

CELIA: Look. I don't know what's going on with you these days, but you were acting funny when you came in, and you're still not yourself. Somebody has to get her out of there before . . .

JUAN: It's too late.

CELIA: How could you do such a thing?

JUAN: It was the only way out.

CELIA: Out of what?

JUAN: She was practically dead already. They had killed her.

CELIA: Who had?

JUAN: [*Smiling because what he is about to say strikes him as simplistic.*] People . . . the system.

CELIA: Don't talk nonsense! Those are clichés!

JUAN: You really think so?

CELIA: How can you be so calm, knowing that? . . .

JUAN: How many people do you suppose die every day? Do you know how many die for reasons that ought to be a real wake-up call to us all? But no: we keep right on sleeping, eating, telling jokes . . .

CELIA: It's not the same!

JUAN: Of course it isn't. She at least took control.

CELIA: Give me her address, or I'm calling the police.

JUAN: I don't think you'll do that, but here's her address. [*He takes a piece of paper out of his pocket and hands it to her.* CELIA *runs toward the door.*] Celia . . . In case you decide to call the police, don't forget about my interview. I want it published.

[CELIA, *shocked, looks at him long and hard for a few seconds before she exits. Alone now,* JUAN *gives a tired sigh, as though finally at peace. He straightens up his desk and looks through his records until he finds the one he wants: Mozart's Concerto No. 21. He smiles and puts the record on the turntable. The music begins, very softly. He leaves the lighted cigarette in the ashtray and walks slowly toward the bedroom. He exits. For the few moments while the* CORONER *works and* SUSI *remains motionless on the elevator floor, the music plays. At the stairwell,* MANNY *appears. He pauses in surprise at the open door of* SUSI's *apartment. He goes in, calling out to her.*]

MANNY: Susi! . . . Susi! . . . Juan!

[*He goes into the bedroom but returns immediately and picks up the telephone to dial a number.* JUAN's *telephone rings, but no one answers.* MANNY *hangs up, rushes to the door of the apartment, goes out, closes the door behind him, and runs into* CELIA, *who has just come up the stairs.*]

MANNY: What are you doing here?

CELIA: [*Excited.*] Where is she?

MANNY: [*Misunderstanding* CELIA's *intentions.*] Hey, I never expected this of you. It's not like you at all.

CELIA: Let go of me!

MANNY: Listen, go back home. Juan will explain everything when . . .

CELIA: He's already told me everything! That poor girl tried to commit suicide last night.

MANNY: [*In disbelief.*] What are you talking about?

CELIA: [*Trying to get free of* MANNY.] Let me go in there, please!

[MANNY *leads her away from the apartment.*]

MANNY: Celia, people don't usually commit suicide if they threaten to do it. Where's Juan?

CELIA: [*Vacillating.*] At home. Sleeping peacefully after writing his "poem." That's what he usually does.

MANNY: Listen, Celia . . . Maybe I'm not the one to tell you this, but . . . it's serious: they've fallen in love. They love each other . . .

CELIA: You think I'd be here if it weren't for . . .

[*Hearing them,* SUSI *sits up.*]

SUSI: Who's there?

[MANNY *goes over to the elevator.*]

MANNY: Susi?

SUSI: Who's up there?

MANNY: It's Manny. I'll get you out of there right away.

SUSI: I've been here since last night. Hurry, please, hurry!

[MANNY *and* CELIA *look at each other.* CELIA *sighs with relief and smiles, a little embarrassed at the scene she has just made.*]

SUSI: Where is Juan?

MANNY: Well . . . [*He looks at* CELIA.] He'll be here any minute . . . It's just that . . .

SUSI: He won't come!

MANNY: Yes he will. He just told me . . .

SUSI: Did you see him?

[CELIA *makes a move to leave.*]

MANNY: No. But I know he's asleep. He was writing all night and he was very tired.

SUSI: But have you spoken to him yourself, in person?

[CELIA *pauses.*]

MANNY: Well, no, but . . .

CELIA: Why?

SUSI: Who's that with you?

MANNY: Nobody. Listen . . .

SUSI: Who is that?

MANNY: It's Celia. Susi, calm down. I'm going to try to open this. What did that guy say to do?

SUSI: What is she doing here?

MANNY: Nothing. It's just that . . . [*Giving up.*] I have absolutely no idea.

SUSI: Celia . . .

CELIA: [*Very composed.*] I came to tell you that Juan will be back soon. This time, to stay.

SUSI: But, didn't he tell you? . . . Didn't he really believe that I? . . .

CELIA: [*Interrupting her.*] Of course he didn't believe it, not for a minute.

SUSI: [*Immensely relieved.*] Oh, thank goodness.

CELIA: He told me that you . . . wanted to frighten him. He'll be here soon. [*To* MANNY.] I'm leaving.

SUSI: Oh, Gomez. Life is wonderful after all!

[*This sentence stops* CELIA *again, who looks toward the elevator in anguish.*]

MANNY: [*Struggling to make the elevator work.*] It is, isn't it? Hey, what was that about . . . ?

SUSI: If you knew what I've been through tonight! Hours and hours in this cage, kicking and screaming, and crying and calling out to Juan . . .

MANNY: Will you tell me what the super did the other day?

SUSI: Do you believe if you have enough faith, you can do anything?

MANNY: Anything but fix this damned elevator, sweetheart. But how . . . ?

SUSI: All we need is someone to fight for. If we have that, we can do anything. I feel strong now, like I could change the world! I'd change it for Juan! And I could even convince him that it's worthwhile, that it's not true that things are hopeless. It's not true that there's only one way out.

CELIA: [*Suddenly alarmed.*] Is that what he said?

SUSI: [*Surprised that she is still present.*] Celia?

[CELIA *bends over the elevator opening.*]

CELIA: What was it you were afraid of all night? What?

SUSI: Why? What's the matter?

CELIA: [*Pressing.*] What were you afraid of?

SUSI: That Juan might do the same thing after writing the article. This piece was very important to him. He said it would be the only decent thing he had ever written in his whole life, the only really honest article he would ever write.

[MANNY *stops what he was doing and comes over to* CELIA, *alarmed now, too.*]

MANNY: [*To* CELIA.] What are you thinking?

[*Frightened, she puts her hand over his mouth as she continues to listen to* SUSI.]

SUSI: [*Pause.*] I was out of my mind last night. I didn't know what I was doing or what I was saying. But as soon as I heard him close the door, I forgot about myself, and I was just afraid for him. It was awful. I suddenly realized that he isn't as strong as I am and that he's tired and can't fight anymore . . . So I ran out after him, but . . .

[MANNY *shakes* CELIA *violently, but she seems glued to the spot as though in a trance, her eyes filling with tears.*]

MANNY: What's the matter?

SUSI: What's the matter, Celia?

[CELIA *recovers and represses a scream.*]

CELIA: Let me go! She's right! Let me go!

MANNY: Didn't you say he was asleep when you left?

[CELIA *shakes her head and dashes down the stairs.*]

SUSI: Manny, what's going on up there?

MANNY: [*Rushing after* CELIA.] I'll be right back, Susi. I can't stay!

SUSI: Don't leave me here all alone!

MANNY: [*Disappearing at the stairwell.*] I'll be right back!

SUSI: Wait! Get me out of here!

MANNY: [*Offstage.*] I can't right now, Susi!

[SUSI *beats on the walls and cries out in desperation.*]

SUSI: Wait . . . Wait . . . Juan! [*She sinks to the floor, understanding that her efforts are futile.*] JUAN, wait for me, please, wait for me . . . Juan! Juan! Juan!

[*The lights of the entire stage go down slowly except for a single spotlight on the* CORONER.]

CORONER: [*Turning on the microphone and dictating very deliberately from his notes.*] Juan Gomez Villar, a thirty-eight-year-old male, was found dead in his apartment on the morning of September 2, 1973 . . .

[*Blackout.*]

Paloma Pedrero (b. 1957)

Born in Madrid, into the first generation of women playwrights unfettered by the legal and social censorship of the Franco dictatorship, Paloma Pedrero has emerged as one of the preeminent figures in contemporary Spanish theater. No longer subject to the pressure of the state, church, and military, she belongs to the democratic period's more confident and certainly less diffident women dramatists.

Like many of her sister artists, Pedrero has shown little interest in temporizing with the inherited patriarchal traditions, its subjects and views. She is far more drawn to the subtleties of relationships, emotional tensions, and issues of personal and social equity than questions of honor, heroism, or adventure.

As a dramatist, Pedrero concentrates her craft on couples or small groups, exquisitely unraveling the dynamics that both support and threaten their relationships. She is very precise and deft in the way she makes the sometimes pedestrian or odd theatrical gesture unexpectedly charged or significant. Subterfuge personalities, ambiguous responses, and psychological irregularities are front and center on her stage. The fluidity with which she can invoke and effectively elevate colloquial speech has become a hallmark of her dramaturgy.

Pedrero's first produced play, *Lauren's Call* (*La llamada de Lauren*, 1984), launched her career as a major new dramatist and has remained her most performed work. Initially, it was alternately heralded as innovative, sharp, and searing and vilified as vulgar, perverse, and shocking—particularly to men. These antipodal reactions usually occurred across generational divides; the play found little favor with the older, established community of critics and theater-goers.

In 1987, Pedrero won the prestigious Tirso de Molina Prize for *Winter's Happy Moon* (*Invierno de luna alegre*). Other successful plays that followed include: *The Voucher* (*Resuguardo personal*, 1988), *Color of August* (*El color de agosto*, 1989), *A Night Divided* (*La nocha divida*, 1989)—all published in English translation in a volume of her short plays, *Parting Gestures*—and *Lovesick* (*Locas de amar*, 1996).

In taking as her material cross-dressing, sexual difficulties and confusions, and Carnival, Pedrero is doing nothing that is unfamiliar. But in reclaiming sexually explicit material from the quasi-pornographic theater that flexed its newly found prowess after Franco died in 1975, she produces a shocking, provocative drama that is anything but titillating or trivially obscene. That it was a woman writer dealing with frustrations and dildos only compounded the shock. Carnival—the legendary holiday from propriety when anything goes as we prepare to bid the flesh farewell before Lent—becomes the setting against which the couple, Pedro and

Paloma Pedrero, no date. (Courtesy of Patricia O'Connor.)

Rosa, reexamine themselves, their covert feelings and identities, and the implications for their relationship. The carnavalesque revelations emotionally involve the audience as well, challenging it with seriously conceived, difficult suggestions.

We are, in quick succession, puzzled, reassured, and conflicted, as we watch Pedro put on cosmetics and women's clothing (a combination of Lauren Bacall's and Rosa's), discover it's carnival time, and then learn that the wig, lipstick, and lingerie are not simply play. Rather, the game, in the tradition of *homo ludens*, is not discountable as innocent frolic. Holiday time, the freedom to simulate transvestitism, and assuming the roles of Bacall and Humphrey Bogart all form the shoals of an identity crisis, specifically a crisis of sexual identity. Though the tone and dialogue could not be more different, *Lauren's Call* is similar in strategy to a Harold Pinter play: put two people in a room and watch what happens. It even closes in the open-ended, indeterminate fashion of, for example, *The Dumb Waiter* or *The Lover*.

It is the couple's third anniversary, an occasion Rosa remarks that will always occur at Carnival. Carnival is a time that invites people to imagine whom they might want to be; it is a fitting opportunity for them (and us) to see which clothes really suit us and what we really like. What's normal? When Pedro hands Rosa a dildo as part of the Bogart outfit and demands that she reverse roles, seduce, and even penetrate him, Rosa—who has been intrigued by the masquerade—balks and declares that such an act would be beyond normalcy. But "normal" is difficult, and we, like her, are left unsettled, as Pedro-Lauren struts out into the Carnival.

SELECTED BIBLIOGRAPHY IN ENGLISH

Lamartina-Lens, Iride. "An Insight to the Theatre of Paloma Pedrero." *Romance Languages Annual* 2 (1990), 465–68.

Leonard, Candyce. "Body, Sex, Woman: The Struggle for Autonomy in Paloma Pedrero's Theater." Eighteenth Louisiana Conference on Hispanic Literature, Tulane, 1997. *La Chispa '97: Selected Proceedings.* Ed. Claire Paolini. Pp. 245–54.

Macias, Irene. "The Uneasy Politicisation of Spanish Women Playwrights and their Theatre." *Forum for Modern Language Studies* 35 (1999), 286–95.

O'Connor, Patricia W. "Postmodern Tendencies in the Theater of Marisa Ares and Paloma Pedrero." *Letras Peninsulares* 4 (1991), 307–18.

——— . "Spain's 'Other' Post-War Dramatists: The Women." *Letras Peninsulares* 1 (1988), 97–107.

——— . "Women Playwrights in Contemporary Spain and the Male-Dominated Canon." *Signs* 15 (1990), 377–90.

Podol, Robert. "Sexuality and Marital Relationships in Paloma Pedrero's *La llamada de Lauren* and Maria Manuela Reina's *La cinta dorada.*" *Estreno* 17 (1991), 22–25.

Sullivan, Mary Lee. "The Theatrics of Transference in Federico Garcia Lorca's *La Casa de Bernarda Alba* and Paloma Pedrero's *La Llamada de Lauren.*" *Hispanic Journal* 16 (1995), 169–76.

Zatlin, Phyllis. "Paloma Pedrero and the Search for Identity." *Estreno* 16 (1990), 6–10.

LAUREN'S CALL

Paloma Pedrero

Translated by Patricia W. O'Connor

CHARACTERS

PEDRO

ROSA

Efficiency apartment; kitchenette visible stage rear and, adjacent to it, a door. Stage right: a table with four chairs and a shelf holding books and small decorative items. Stage left: a double bed flanked by nightstands. The closet door has a full-length mirror. Posters and a few pictures decorate the walls; plants in flowerpots fill empty spaces on the floor. The general decor is tasteful.

On a dressing table, a variety of make-up items: rouge, powder, eye pencils and assorted shades of eye shadow. On a chair, a long, brown, wavy wig. The radio broadcasts classical music in live concert.

PEDRO, wearing a bathrobe, emerges from the bathroom. He is about thirty and of youthful appearance. He approaches the closet, opens the door and takes out a woman's slinky black satin dress and black stockings. He pulls out a drawer and rummages around until he finds some sexy underwear. Without taking off his robe, he tries on the panties and evaluates the results in the mirror. He searches again in the drawer; this time, he pulls out a brassiere and struggles to put it on. He goes over to the table, picks up a large roll of cotton and begins to stuff his bra. When he is satisfied with the result, he examines himself in the mirror again as he carefully puts on the dress and stockings. From under the bed, he pulls a box with black high-heeled shoes and tries them on. He sits down at the dressing table and, with great care, begins to make himself up as a woman.

The transformation of PEDRO takes place before our eyes. He almost looks like a woman. As a finishing touch, he puts on the wig and turns toward the mirror to check the total effect. He turns off the radio and puts on an album of vintage movie music. Immediately we hear a song from To Have and Have Not, *as sung by Lauren Bacall. Little by little, timidly at first, PEDRO sings along. He gradually gets more into the spirit of the music and eventually sings and dances with abandon. At the high point of his performance, the front door opens and ROSA enters with a bouquet of flowers in her arms.*

ROSA: [*Startled.*] What the f . . . !

PEDRO: [*Taken aback.*] Hey, it's me! It's just me! Don't freak out! It's just me.

ROSA: [*Recovering her composure, she looks him up and down.*] Wow! Awesome! How'd you come up with this? Nobody will ever guess it's you! [*Laughing.*] I love it!

PEDRO: [*Playfully opening the slit in his skirt to reveal a stockinged leg.*] Do you know how to paint a beauty mark?

ROSA: [*Seeing the disarray on the dressing table.*] Holy shit! Look at all the mess you made with my makeup! And those are my new stockings! You're going to ruin them!

PEDRO: I've got your undies on too!

ROSA: [*Giving him a puzzled look.*] And where'd you get the shoes? You're going to kill yourself in those high heels.

PEDRO: What are you talking about? Watch this. [*He struts around, very sure of himself.*] Whaddaya' think? How'm I doin'?

ROSA: [*Surprised*] Hey, babe! You're something else! Everybody's going to be after you! I'll have to watch you like a hawk tonight. If you're really going out like that, I mean, which I doubt.

PEDRO: Yeah? Be honest. Do I look like a woman or a transvestite?

ROSA: Well, to tell you the truth, those broad shoulders do give you away, but if you say you're a swimmer and you specialize in the crawl. [*Short pause.*] If I were a man, I'd sure make a beeline for you. Look at those eyes! [*Observing him closely.*] You don't miss a trick, do you? Where'd you get all this stuff to wear?

PEDRO: I rented it. I went into this place and said to the clerk: "I want a dress for my wife; she's tall and a little on the muscular side." I wanted to surprise you.

ROSA: [*Remembering their special day.*] Hey, I almost forgot! Here; this is my surprise for you. Happy anniversary.

PEDRO: Thanks, honey. They're beautiful. [*He kisses her.*] Happy anniversary. [*He returns the flowers to her.*] Here, put them in some water.

[PEDRO *rushes to uncork a bottle of champagne as* ROSA's *back is turned.*]

ROSA: Champagne!

PEDRO: Something special for our special day! [*He hands* ROSA *a glass and pours the champagne.*]

ROSA: A toast to you, because in spite of being the hardest-to-get-along-with human being in this apartment, you are still my love. Here's to you.

PEDRO: And here's to you, too, because without you, I wouldn't be so hard to get along with; no, I wouldn't be. Therefore, to you.

[*They sip their champagne, and* PEDRO *pulls* ROSA *down on his lap.*]

PEDRO: How time flies! Three years, already!

ROSA: That's right. It's hard to believe.

PEDRO: Remember our honeymoon in the Canary Islands?

ROSA: How could I forget? It was Mardi Gras, just like now. Our anniversary will always be at Mardi Gras.

PEDRO: No, silly, only when it happens to fall on that date. [*He begins to hum a typical Mardi Gras song.*] We were really out of it on our honeymoon, weren't we? Remember how everybody was in costume, except us?

ROSA: Yes, all the men dressed up like women, and all the women in clown outfits, just like the one I brought home to wear today. Why didn't you tell me what you were planning? I could have picked out something a little more original.

PEDRO: My wig is falling off. Can you put some pins in it for me?

ROSA: Here. Sit down and let me fix it. [ROSA *begins to anchor the wig with hairpins.*] If you won't get mad, I'll tell you something.

PEDRO: What's that?

ROSA: Promise you won't get mad?

PEDRO: I don't know. Tell me, and we'll see.

ROSA: Well, your costume took me by surprise; I like it.

PEDRO: I really want to laugh and have fun tonight. Let's forget about the bills and all the things we need. I want to forget the students. I want to go to Mardi Gras like this with you.

ROSA: To tell you the truth, I never figured you for anything like this. You always claimed guys who dressed like that were fags.

PEDRO: What are you insinuating?

ROSA: [*Adding a little rouge.*] No, really. I like it. It's as though you had taken off that hideous businessman mask. I look at you and I see a whole new man.

PEDRO: Hey, if you like it so much, I can stay this way.

ROSA: [*Laughing.*] Oh, sure, great! [*She sits down and picks up the newspaper.*] Honey, fix dinner. I'm hungry.

PEDRO: But I'm not like that.

ROSA: Ahem, ahem. Pretty close.

PEDRO: [*Uncomfortable.*] No way.

ROSA: [*Getting up.*] Hey, don't get mad. I was just kidding. [*She goes toward the closet.*] I'll put on my costume so we can go out and celebrate.

PEDRO: [*Holding her back, mysteriously.*] I have a surprise for you, too.

ROSA: Really? What is it?

PEDRO: Turn around and close your eyes.

[ROSA, *intrigued, obeys.* PEDRO *takes a Humphry Bogart–style suit, hat and raincoat out of the closet.*]

PEDRO: Now you can open your eyes.

ROSA: Is that for me?

PEDRO: Yep.

ROSA: What is it?

PEDRO: [*Pointing to himself.*] Lauren Bacall and [*Pointing to* ROSA.] Humphrey Bogart.

ROSA: [*Laughing.*] Hey! That's right! We'll be the hit of the evening! When you want to be, you're wonderful. [*Picking up the outfit.*] I'm going to try it on and see how it fits.

PEDRO: No, let me dress you.

ROSA: You really want to?

PEDRO: Take your clothes off.

[PEDRO *picks up a stool and puts it in front of the mirror.* ROSA *undresses.*]

ROSA: Okay. Now what?

PEDRO: Sit down. [ROSA *sits in front of the mirror.*] How do you like your body?

ROSA: [*Looking at herself in the mirror.*] More important is how do you like it?

PEDRO: [*Helping her put on the pants.*] We'll see in a minute. Now a delicate operation. [*He picks up a long band of cloth.*] I'm going to tie this around you.

ROSA: What's that?

PEDRO: We've got to the hide your breasts. Did you ever see Humphrey Bogart with tits?

ROSA: No! I'm not going to wear that!

PEDRO: Why not?

ROSA: Because it'll hurt! Besides, we don't need it. With a big shirt, you won't notice a thing.

PEDRO: But there will be a hint of something there, and that's worse. Come on, let me put this on you.

ROSA: Oh, Pedro, no! I'll be uncomfortable! No!

PEDRO: [*Affectionately.*] If it bothers you too much, I'll take it off, okay?

ROSA: [*Raising her arm obediently.*] Oh, shit! What a perfectionist!

[As PEDRO *wraps the band around her, he flattens her breasts.*]

PEDRO: Breathe. [*He pulls the band tighter.*]

ROSA: Ouch!

PEDRO: What's the matter?

ROSA: Not so tight! You're squashing my boobs! I'll be permanently flat chested!

PEDRO: Oh, come on. Don't be a crybaby. You've got to look like a real man.

ROSA: That's impossible.

PEDRO: Nothing's impossible! [*He ties the ends of the band together.*] You're done.

ROSA: I feel mutilated.

PEDRO: Now for the shirt. [*He puts it on her.*] Let's see? Good. Now the jacket [*He puts it on her.*] and the bow tie.

ROSA: Aargh! You're choking me!

PEDRO: Stop griping! You're done.

ROSA: What about shoes?

PEDRO: [*Taking some of his own from the closet.*] Here. These will do.

ROSA: I'll be the tiny little man with the great big feet. [PEDRO *looks her up and down.*] Am I what you want now?

PEDRO: The hat. [*He puts it on her.*]

ROSA: What do you think?

PEDRO: Now sit down. I'm going to make you up.

ROSA: What do I need makeup for?

PEDRO: Be quiet. You'll see in a minute. First, the eyebrows. [*He makes very thick ones.*] Look this way. Sideburns; you need sideburns.

ROSA: Sideburns?

PEDRO: Hush. Wait till you see the hunk that's been hiding inside you all these years. [*He paints the sideburns.*]

ROSA: [*Laughing at her image in the mirror.*] Am I what you want now?

PEDRO: I don't know. Something's missing. You still look like a girl.

ROSA: So what else is new? [*She puts a cigarette in her mouth, Bogart style.*] How about now?

PEDRO: No, you're not there yet. Something's still missing. [*He brings out a press-on moustache.*] Put this on.

ROSA: Hey! Bogart didn't have a moustache!

PEDRO: So what? Other men do. [*Pressing on the moustache.*] This is much better. Now walk. [ROSA *walks.*] No! Not that way! Don't wiggle your hips!

ROSA: Like this?

PEDRO: Drop your shoulders. Relax. Pull in your ass; tuck it under. More! Look down at the floor! Act defeated!

ROSA: Hey! What's the deal here? You gonna enter me in some contest?

PEDRO: Clothes don't really make the man, hon.

ROSA: Yeah; the body language of the inner person, right?

PEDRO: You got it, and that's what you gotta change—the inner person.

ROSA: [*Attempting a masculine walk.*] The person within has got to show on the person without! [*She looks at herself in the mirror.*] Well, my person may be a little short, but it's not bad; not bad! At least, I'm interesting. [*She glances at him.*] Shall we go? [PEDRO *does not respond.*] Well, aren't we going out?

PEDRO: And now for the finishing touch. [*He brings out a gift-wrapped box with a large bow on top.*] Here.

ROSA: [*Excitedly.*] My present!

PEDRO: Open it.

ROSA: [*Looking at the box curiously and trying to guess what's inside.*] Is it a bottle of perfume?

PEDRO: [*Mysteriously.*] M-m-m, well . . .

ROSA: What is it?

PEDRO: Open it.

ROSA: [*She unwraps the package excitedly; then suddenly her smile freezes, and she abruptly thrusts the box back into* PEDRO*'s hands.*] That's sick. Where in the world did you get that thing?

[*It is a sex-shop dildo.*]

PEDRO: Aw, come on! Put it on!

ROSA: Don't be gross. It's not funny.

PEDRO: It's funny to me. Come on. Let's see what it looks like on you.

ROSA: [*Very serious.*] This is going too far. No, I'm not going to put that thing on. I never thought you could be so disgusting.

PEDRO: Oh, sweetheart, don't be like that. It's just a gag. I just wanted us to have some fun; I thought we could celebrate our third anniversary as though it were our wedding night, all costumed up for Mardi Gras.

[PEDRO *stops short when he sees that* ROSA *does not find his plan funny. He puts the dildo away, and there is a tense moment.* PEDRO *approaches* rosa *affectionately, but she rejects his advance.*]

ROSA: Pedro, are you glad we got married?

PEDRO: Of course. I want to spend many, many Mardi Gras with you.

ROSA: Are you sure?

PEDRO: Why are you asking me that right now?

ROSA: I don't know. For a long time, you've been so . . . [*Short pause.*] I have the feeling that you're keeping something from me; that we're drifting apart. I hadn't seen you so excited for a long time! What are you going to be like when you take off all that makeup? I don't know. Yesterday I was watching you while you slept, and you looked old. I'm sorry, Pedro, but it's true. You really looked old and sad. I think you're bored with me; I don't turn you on anymore. It's been two months since we . . .

PEDRO: [*Interrupting her.*] Rosa, please. Let's just drop it, all right? This is our anniversary. Let's go out, have a few drinks, dance and . . .

ROSA: You see? You never want us to talk. And today would be a good time for that. We can talk things over and do a kind of review of . . . it's been three years, Pedro, three years! [*Decisively.*] We have to talk. [*She pulls off the moustache.*]

PEDRO: [*Raising his voice.*] Don't take that off! [*He goes over to* ROSA *and gently presses the moustache back in place as he speaks.*] Please don't take off the moustache, okay? Even if you really were a guy, I'd try to seduce you.

ROSA: Well, go ahead and try. We haven't made love in so long.

PEDRO: [*Caressing her.*] *You* seduce *me*. Do it to me.

ROSA: You want me to?

PEDRO: Go ahead.

ROSA: I'm all out of practice. I don't know if . . .

PEDRO: Let's get it all back tonight. Seduce me.

ROSA: [*After a pause.*] All right, my fair damsel. I'm going to show you how to seduce a woman. Nothing wrong with a little refresher course every now and then. Can I offer you a drink, young lady?

PEDRO: [*Joining in the game.*] Yes, thank you.

ROSA: Whiskey, rum, gin?

PEDRO: [*Coyly.*] Yes, whiskey, please; on the rocks.

ROSA: [*Going over to a minibar and taking out some glasses.*] How about some music?

PEDRO: [*Very much into his role.*] Oh, whatever you like.

ROSA: [*After pouring two drinks, she selects* PEDRO's *favorite recording from the file and puts it on. With the music playing, she approaches* PEDRO *and hands him his glass*]. Here you are.

PEDRO: Thank you, Charles.

ROSA: [*Barely able to suppress a giggle.*] You're welcome [*Short pause.*] Muffie. [*Making an effort to be serious.*] So tell me something about yourself. I don't know anything about you, and I'm really interested. What do you do? Who do you live with? Things like that.

PEDRO: I'm a hairstylist. I work in a very exclusive salon, and I live with my mother. Actually, I wanted to be a high-fashion model, but the agencies told me I needed to slim down and that my breasts were too small.

ROSA: [*Ogling him.*] Well, it doesn't look that way to me.

PEDRO: No, it doesn't, does it?

ROSA: I think you're just right. You have beautiful eyes and a very sexy mouth. [*She comes close and tries to kiss him.*]

PEDRO: Oh, no; not yet; please.

ROSA: Pedro, sweetheart, it's eleven thirty, and if we don't hurry, we're not going to go anywhere.

PEDRO: [*Angrily.*] Either you do it right or we won't do it.

ROSA: Then don't be such a prude. We can't play around like this all night. [*Rubbing her lip.*] Besides, this thing itches.

PEDRO: You have a beautiful apartment. Do you live alone?

ROSA: For the moment, I do. Until a few months ago, I lived here with my wife. She was wonderful, and very imaginative. She did all the decorations. I'm not good at anything like that. Can you believe I even had to track down my own underwear after she left?

PEDRO: [*Laughing softly.*] You're funny.

ROSA: And you're sweet enough to eat [*She moves in boldly, but* PEDRO *holds her off.*]

PEDRO: What happened? Why did you two break up? I mean, if you don't mind my asking.

ROSA: Oh, I'm not sure. I guess I wasn't a very good husband. I'm a busy man, you know. Mornings, I work in an office, and afternoons, I teach. Then when I get home, I'm beat, and of course . . .

PEDRO: [*Cutting her off.*] If you're going to play like you're me, the game's over.

ROSA: Does seeing yourself like this make you uncomfortable?

PEDRO: Oh, please, Charles; don't be vulgar.

ROSA: Well, that's what happened. She . . .

PEDRO: Who?

ROSA: My wife. She was alone all the time. So one day, she packed her bags and she [*Short pause.*] died.

PEDRO: She died?

ROSA: Yes. Of a broken heart.

PEDRO: How sad.

ROSA: Now I'm a widower. But a merry widower.

PEDRO: Well, when I get married, it will be forever. I'll marry a strong, masculine man. And I'll have three children and a dog.

ROSA: [*Putting her arm around his shoulder and saying very pointedly.*] Three children? [*Touching his hair gently.*] You have lovely hair.

PEDRO: Well, I'm a hairstylist.

ROSA: You drive me crazy! [*She kisses him on the mouth and tries to put her hand down his dress, but* PEDRO *resists the advance.*] Gee, you're playing hard to get!

PEDRO: You're supposed to seduce me; put me in the mood.

ROSA: [*Angry.*] And just what does one have to do to put the lady in the mood?

PEDRO: I want you to be like Bogart. Don't you remember how he was?

ROSA: Well, no. I don't remember.

PEDRO: I want you to be rough and romantic, all at once, and I want you to be deep and mysterious. You're doing it all wrong.

ROSA: Well, gee. Look who's talking.

PEDRO: We're playing a game, and you're going to lose.

ROSA: And how does the loser act in a game like this? I don't know what to do.

PEDRO: All you have to do is watch them; they're all around you. Come on. Make me fall in love. Be Bogart, Bogart!

ROSA: Bogart. I should be Bogart.

PEDRO: Yes, that's what I want.

ROSA: [*Decisively.*] Okay; you asked for it. [*Beginning to swagger, she picks up a bottle of water.*]

Rum. [*She drinks ostentatiously; then flips down a cigarette disdainfully.*] We're on a desert island full of hungry beasts. A place that wouldn't change at all if I disappeared.

PEDRO: Oh, it wouldn't be the same.

ROSA: One of these days, I'll vanish. There will be no trace of who I was or of our lost love. Nothing. I'll take that final bit of me and plunge it into the ocean. I'll just sail off into the sunset, disappear out beyond the horizon.

PEDRO: I love poets.

ROSA: And I'll slay the monsters who approach my ship.

PEDRO: Oh, I like strong men.

ROSA: I'll sail the seas where pure mermaids play.

PEDRO: I love purity.

ROSA: Mermaids out there have no necklaces or polished nails, and when they rise up out of the water, they don't smell of cheap perfume but rather of salty seaweed.

PEDRO: I like that sea smell, too.

ROSA: Mermaids don't need music, or alcohol, or stupid words to make love. They need only my kisses.

PEDRO: Tell me about that rough sailor's kisses.

ROSA: They're fearless kisses, baby.

PEDRO: I want to be your mermaid. May I? [*When he reaches out to touch her,* ROSA *draws back.*]

ROSA: You want fearless kisses?

PEDRO: Kisses; yes, I want kisses. [*He tries to kiss her.* ROSA *draws away regally.* PEDRO *looks at her intently with great longing.*]

ROSA: All right, I'll take you with me. Let's celebrate our approaching voyage. [PEDRO *puts on the music.*] Shall we dance?

PEDRO: Oh, yes.

[*They begin to dance, their bodies touching.*]

ROSA: I love you, I love you.

[*She puts her arms around his neck and, touching him gently, kisses him.* PEDRO *submits to her advances.*]

ROSA: Take off your dress.

PEDRO: No, wait. Let's play a little longer.

ROSA: [*Kissing him on the neck.*] You smell like me. [*She takes off her shoes and begins to unzip the trouser.*]

PEDRO: No! Don't take anything off! Don't break the spell! I want to do it like this!

ROSA: But . . . [PEDRO *doesn't allow her to speak; he pulls her toward him and kisses her.*] Take this band off my chest. I can't breathe.

PEDRO: No. [ROSA *tries to speak, as* PEDRO *frantically silences her with his kisses and caresses.*] I want you, my love. I want you more now than I've ever wanted you. [ROSA *tries again to take her clothes off, but* PEDRO *won't let her.*] Rub my breasts.

ROSA: [*Putting her hand down the front of* PEDRO's *dress with great difficulty.*] I can't. Take that thing off.

[PEDRO *takes her hand and rubs it over his dress on top of the stuffed bra.*]

PEDRO: This is wonderful. You're such a romantic man.

ROSA: [*Showing signs of discomfort.*] Pedro, I can't do anything dressed like this. I'm burning up. My whole chest hurts. [*She struggles to take off the band.*]

PEDRO: [*Taking hold of her hands.*] No, no! Don't spoil everything.

ROSA: [*Out of breath.*] I can't. I can't do it this way!

PEDRO: Come on. Let's get on the bed. [PEDRO *practically drags her over to the bed. Then he pulls her down on top of him, squeezes her between his legs, and hands her the dildo.*] Fuck me with it.

ROSA: What?

PEDRO: [*Fairly shouting.*] Fuck me with it?

ROSA: Pedro!

PEDRO: [*Frantic.*] Don't call me Pedro! Come on, put it in me, please. Put it in!

ROSA: That does it! You've gone too far. [*She tries to get up, but* PEDRO *grabs her and pulls her back.*]

PEDRO: Don't leave me this way! I need you.

ROSA: [*Angrily snatching the wig off his head and jumping out of the bed.*] The game's over!

[ROSA *quickly takes off the suit.* PEDRO *looks at her sadly and a little confused.*]

PEDRO: Aren't we going to celebrate Mardi Gras in our costumes?

ROSA: You want more Mardi Gras? I know I've had enough for one day. [*She quickly cleans off her face.*]

PEDRO: But Rosa.

ROSA: Just shut up! You're acting like a real jerk! I don't understand you. I don't understand anything. I don't know what you want. You're going to drive me nuts; and I do mean nuts! [*She puts on her coat.*] I'm going out for a walk. I've got to think.

PEDRO: [*Grabbing her hand.*] Don't leave! I love you, I love you.

[ROSA *yanks her hand away, opens the door and exits.* PEDRO *stands motionless as he looks at the door. He reacts suddenly by pounding the wall as he speaks.*]

ROSA: No! No! No!

[*The front door then opens and* ROSA *enters again. Seeing how upset* PEDRO *is, she is frightened, goes over to the bed and sits down beside him.* PEDRO, *face down, does not dare to look at her. After a pause, she puts her hand on his shoulder.*]

ROSA: Tell me what's the matter. [PEDRO *does not respond.*] Tell me.

PEDRO: Nothing; nothing's the matter.

ROSA: Don't you want to tell me about it?

PEDRO: No, that's not it; it's not that I don't want to. It's that [*Short pause.*] Oh, I don't understand it myself.

ROSA: Tell me what you're feeling. Why did you do this?

PEDRO: Why did I do [*Short pause.*] what?

ROSA: You're actually asking me "what"? I'm talking about what happened here. You think what you did was [*Short pause.*] normal?

PEDRO: I don't know.

ROSA: You must know, and you've got to tell me. Do it for me. I feel awful, awful. If you don't care about me any more, just come right out and tell me. I'd rather you just said it in so many words. I can't stand this!

PEDRO: I love you, Rosa.

ROSA: But you really aren't attracted to me. You make me aware of it constantly. When I try to touch you at night, you pretend not to notice, but you just sort of push my hand away. And when I go to kiss you, you turn the other way. It seems like our only kisses are those little hello pecks on the cheek.

PEDRO: You know I come home bushed.

ROSA: So what! You've got to do something about this problem. [*After a moment.*] I don't even feel like a woman anymore. You make me feel ugly, unwanted.

PEDRO: Don't say that. You're wonderful, a dream come true.

ROSA: No; I'm a flesh-and-blood woman. I need to feel wanted; I'm a real person, and I need you to look at me differently, with desire. But, Jesus Christ, for that to happen, you've got to disguise me! You've got to hide who I really am to . . .

PEDRO: [*Interrupting her.*] It was just a game.

ROSA: That's not so! Just tell me. Are you in love with somebody else? Tell me.

PEDRO: I love you and only you. There is nobody else! Nobody!

ROSA: Then, what's the matter?

PEDRO: It's strange. I can't explain it.

ROSA: Try, please.

PEDRO: [*After a pause.*] When . . . When I was little, I could walk in high-heeled shoes better than my sister. She used to tell me that all the time.

ROSA: But, what's that got to do with anything?

PEDRO: Look. Just now, when I put on those shoes, I felt just like back then; that I know how to walk in heels. Isn't that crazy? [*He puts his hands to his head.*] Everything is up here, inside. You're in here too. It's like people are always looking for something. I have to be on guard all the time; I have to keep things in, and sometimes I feel like I'm going to explode.

ROSA: Keep what in?

PEDRO: Everything. Sometimes it's so hard to be normal. I mean, sometimes I have feelings; urges I can't even admit to myself.

ROSA: Things you can't admit? What kind of urges?

PEDRO: They aren't exactly concrete. It's as though what's expected of me contradicts what I am. I mean, sometimes it seems to go against my internal desire or logic.

ROSA: You mean what I expect from you?

PEDRO: It's not only what you expect. It's what everybody expects. Look, when I was little, all the boys on my street got together and tried to beat up the guys on the next street. I went along with them, but I was scared out of my mind. I was panicked.

ROSA: That's logical. I'm sure the other kids were scared too.

PEDRO: In order to hide my fear, I shouted and laughed louder than anybody else. I always had to be on the front line, facing the enemy gang. I dared them to throw rocks. It made me seem bigger, somehow. I wanted them to see me as fearless and tough! A real little bully!

ROSA: Little boys are like that.

PEDRO: Yes? Why? I felt so awful; so awful. After our fights, I went out to a vacant lot behind my house and sat there all alone, just looking at the stars.

ROSA: You've always been something of a loner. But that's all right. I like the way you are. You're a very private person, sort of like a stray cat. But that's not unusual. There are lots of people who don't like throwing rocks at people. I'm scared, Pedro. I saw you all excited just now, like I've never seen you before. You were in a frenzy; like you needed to destroy something.

PEDRO: One day, my father slapped me in the face, you know? I was playing make-believe; singing for my sister. I was all dressed up like some glamorous movie star of the past, like Marlene Dietrich or Marilyn Monroe. Anyway, we were having a great time. Then my father came in and smacked me. What really got to me was that he hit my sister too, and he said to her: "You're going to turn your brother into a damned queer."

ROSA: But we all dress up and pretend to be other people when we're kids. What little boy never put on his sister's clothes? No, I don't understand the problem.

PEDRO: From that day, I promised myself I'd be more masculine than anybody. I wasn't going to fail! Do you understand? I had to do what was expected of me. And I've spent my life doing things like that. And now, I don't know who I really am. I don't know myself. At my age, that's pretty scary, don't you think?

ROSA: You've always been a little . . . I don't know. But what you did today is [*Short pause.*] something else. It's a lot more serious.

PEDRO: Yes, today I didn't give you what you wanted, and you did just like my father— you gave me a slap in the face.

ROSA: A slap? I don't know what you mean.

PEDRO: I've had it with conforming! Can't you understand that? I'm fed up with everybody telling me what I have to do, when I have to do it, who I have to do it with and how I have to do it. Didn't you want me to tell you what was bothering me? Well, that's it. It bothers the hell out of me that I always have to prove to everybody that I can throw rocks.

ROSA: [*Raising her voice.*] I don't understand a thing! Stop talking in circles and come out with it. And take off that damn dress! I can't stand looking at it anymore!

PEDRO: Then why don't you just look at *me*?

ROSA: [*Without looking at him.*] I've seen enough of you. [*Shouting.*] I can't stand seeing you like that!

PEDRO: Wait. Just look at me. Look at me carefully. Look at me. Look at me!

ROSA: [*She turns around and looks at him angrily.*] What is it? What do you want?

PEDRO: I *like* dressing this way . . .

[*Not allowing* PEDRO *to finish,* ROSA *leaps at him and furiously rips the dress in an attempt to get it off; then she begins to hit* PEDRO.]

ROSA: Take that damned thing off! Take off all that shit! You look like a damn queer! Like some freaking faggot!

PEDRO: [*Taking her hands to calm her.*] Please! Calm down! I'll take it off, and the makeup too, if that's what you want.

[PEDRO *drops her hands and begins to undress quickly. Exhausted and emotionally drained,* ROSA *throws herself on the bed and puts a pillow over her head as* PEDRO *finishes removing his disguise.*]

PEDRO: I wanted you to help me, but you didn't even want to hear me out. You were the only person who could have understood. Or at least, that's what I thought. I always heard that love made people understand everything, but it's a lie. It's a fucking lie! I can't *look* at myself, and you don't want to see who I really am.

[*He begins to put on classic male attire—trousers and a white shirt. After removing quickly the last of the makeup, he sits at the desk and takes out some papers and books.* ROSA *turns over in bed and looks at him. On seeing him in his customary clothes, she gives a little start, as though she had just awakened from a dream. She sits up on the side of the bed pensively. She wants to say something, but doesn't know how to begin. She hesitates before speaking.*]

ROSA: Pedro . . . [PEDRO *makes no response.*] Pedro!

PEDRO: [*Without looking up from his work.*] Yes?

ROSA: I'm sorry, Pedro; I overreacted, and . . .

PEDRO: [*Interrupting her.*] No problem. Actually I was just spouting off a bunch of shit.

ROSA: No, not at all. I really want you to talk. I need for you to. And then finally, when you open up to me, I don't handle it very well. I'm the one who acted stupid. It's just that you scared me. I'm sorry.

PEDRO: No big deal.

ROSA: Oh, but it is. [*After a moment of silence.*] You . . . At heart, you're very sensitive. I noticed that right away the first time we met. There was something special about you; a different way of looking at me. Then, later . . .

PEDRO: [*Continues working as he interrupts her.*] Rosa, honey, drop it, will you? We should just forget what happened tonight.

ROSA: I can't forget it. I need to know the whole truth.

PEDRO: The truth is that we're together, right?

ROSA: Yes, but let's be honest, Pedro. Things aren't going very well.

PEDRO: Don't worry. It's not your fault. It's my problem, and I'll solve it. [*Looking at her affectionately.*] And how could you ever think of yourself as ugly?

ROSA: How are you going to solve the problem?

PEDRO: I need a vacation; I gotta get some rest.

ROSA: You think the whole problem is overwork?

PEDRO: Of course it is; you don't know what it's like, having to put up with the same idiots every day at the office, going over the same boring papers every day, hearing the same dumb conversations.

ROSA: And what about your childhood and what you told me?

PEDRO: Look, Rosa, when things aren't going well, our mind does funny things. We say things we shouldn't, and we blame the wrong people. In a nutshell, we sort of go off the deep end. [*Convincingly.*] There's really nothing wrong; I was just having a bad day, honest.

ROSA: And . . . And what you said about wanting to be a [*Short pause.*] that you like to dress up that way.

PEDRO: I'd like to be a lot of things I'm not, just like everybody. I'd like to be smarter. Hell, I'd like to be more popular, more important, have more money. I'd like to be a good person and be good looking, too, like you.

ROSA: And that part about wanting to be a woman?

PEDRO: No, you misunderstood. I was playing at finding new things, you know? It was like a game, getting caught up in new situations; pretending to be completely different; just anybody else.

ROSA: But I want you to be who you are. I don't want you to be a different person. [*Closing his books firmly.*] Give up the afternoon classes. I can get a job.

PEDRO: Don't be silly. We've already gone over that. I don't want you to.

ROSA: I've got to help you. You're working too hard.

PEDRO: You help me by just being here. I don't want you working at just any old job out there. I want you here, presiding as queen over our castle.

ROSA: You really want me to be your queen?

PEDRO: [*After a short pause, he looks at her lovingly.*] Yes, my only queen.

ROSA: Know something? When I was a little girl, I loved to play cowboys and Indians with the boys. You should have seen me screaming at my horse and galloping around firing a cap pistol. I was a real little tomboy!

PEDRO: I guess we're a couple of weirdos.

ROSA: What do you mean? The weirdos are the other guys! Those complacent jerks who drift through life just doing what they're told. I don't give a damn about what other people think.

PEDRO: You're beginning to sound like some wild-eyed revolutionary.

ROSA: Well, yeah. And why not? Sure I'm a wild-eyed revolutionary! And your father's a son-of-a-bitch!

PEDRO: Hey, you're really into this, aren't you?

ROSA: [*After a moment's reflection.*] Are you sure I'm the only one you want?

PEDRO: Of course, silly.

ROSA: [*Standing behind* PEDRO, *she touches him hesitantly.*]—Then, why don't we have a baby?

PEDRO: [*Pulling away from her.*] Because we can't. We can't give a baby the things we want it to have.

ROSA: Maybe a baby would bring us back together.

PEDRO: Oh, please. You always have to remind us of our problems.

ROSA: But I'm sure . . .

PEDRO: [*Getting up brusquely.*] All this excitement makes me hungry. What do we have around here to eat?

ROSA: [*Standing motionless.*] No doubt about it. The other you—the evil twin—is back. [*She laughs bitterly.*] How silly! The power of make-believe! Right?

PEDRO: [*Who returns eating an apple.*] What did you say?

ROSA: The power of make-believe! Don't you agree?

PEDRO: Yes. [*Offering her some of his apple.*] Want a bite?

[*Deep in thought,* ROSA *does not respond.* PEDRO *looks at her for a moment then goes back to work.*]

ROSA: [*Holding her head.*] I'm tired; really beat. I'm going to bed.

PEDRO: All right. I'm going to stay up a while longer and work. I can prepare my classes for Monday.

ROSA: Sure.

[ROSA *puts on a nightie and gets into bed. She turns off the bedside lamp, leaving the room in semidarkness.*]

PEDRO: Good night, my queen.

ROSA: Good night.

[*Alone now,* PEDRO *puts down the apple. Pause. He reads what he has written and suddenly crumples up the paper. He doesn't know what to do. At last, he makes a decision and closes the books. He glances at the makeup, the dress tossed on the floor, the stockings, the gloves. Then he begins quickly to gather up everything. He searches for the wig and, finding it behind the bed, very quietly picks it up as he looks at* ROSA, *who appears to be sleeping.*]

PEDRO: Rosa! Rosa! You awake?

[ROSA *does not respond.* PEDRO *goes toward the dressing table and puts on the wig and other parts of his costume. A tube of lipstick falls to the floor.* PEDRO *picks it up, takes off the top and swivels the base until a bright red shaft of color emerges. He turns toward the mirror and paints his lips timidly. At that moment,* ROSA *turns over. Startled,* PEDRO *wipes the lipstick off on his sleeve. Like someone caught in the act, he stands paralyzed, holding his breath as he looks at himself in the mirror and awaits what he considers the inevitable. Since* ROSA *makes no sound,* PEDRO *begins to breathe again. Then he makes a decision. Picking up a bag, he slowly, methodically, puts everything—wig, purse, shoes, etc.—into it. Bag in hand, he goes toward the door; he takes his raincoat off the hanger, puts on the coat and opens the door. At that moment, the bedside lamp goes on.*]

ROSA: Where are you going?

PEDRO: [*Petrified.*] I'm not sleepy, you know? So I thought I'd just go out for a walk; maybe lose myself in the crowds.

[ROSA *gets up and* PEDRO *leans on the door, feeling unable to do anything else.*]

ROSA: Wait! [*She goes over to the table where there is more light.*] Come here.

[PEDRO *goes toward her slowly.*]

ROSA: Your lipstick isn't on straight. [*She takes the lipstick and retouches his mouth very carefully. Then she looks at him.*] That's the way it ought to be.

[PEDRO *makes an effort to say something, but he can't.* ROSA *is very quiet.*]

ROSA: Just a minute! [*She goes over to the vase where she put the flowers and picks out a rose. She cuts the stem and, returning to* PEDRO, *places it carefully in the lapel of his coat. She steps back to observe him. Then she shakes her head. She removes the rose and hands it to him.*] Here. You should decide where you want to wear it. Happy Mardi Gras!

[PEDRO *returns the smile timidly and, without saying a word, leaves, closing the door behind him.* ROSA *stands looking at the door for a long moment. A strange chill comes over her and she starts to tremble. She looks around at the disorder of the empty room and appears to remember something. She picks up the Bogart suit and looks at it thoughtfully before taking the cigarettes out of the pocket. She walks slowly toward the record player and puts on the same music heard as she and* PEDRO *were making believe. Her gaze falls on Bogart's hat; she picks it up, puts it on and looks over at the bed where* PEDRO *had pretended to be someone else. She smiles; then laughs. She mimes a conversation and seems to say "no." Then she offers a cigarette and, in general, plays the seducer. Suddenly her smile freezes, and she hugs the pillow in a desperate attempt to keep from crying.*]

[*The lights go down slowly.*]

Dacia Maraini (b. 1936)

Few internationally known and successful writers have been so identified in their countries with the expression of feminist outrage as Dacia Maraini. She has been at the vanguard of Italian feminist political expression. Her sustained argument, in her numerous novels, plays, poems, essays, and interviews, is that the centuries of Italian history (church, state, and social) and the overbearing traditions of patriarchy, especially intense in her own youth in Sicily, have rendered women a commodity and made prostitution an apt image of their situation. Her own leftist-oriented family—which ran from fascist Italy to Japan, only to be interred there—fostered her awareness of the prevailing inegalitarianism.

Born in Florence to a father, Fosco Maraini, who was an ethnologist, and a mother, Topazia Alliata, who was a painter, she has spent much of her life sharing the outsider's perspective. When she moved from Sicily to Rome in the late fifties, she quickly became associated with a group of writers, artists, and critics, which included Alberto Moravia—who left his wife for her in 1962 and became her companion for eighteen years—Pier Paolo Pasolini, Bernardo Bertolucci, and Natalia Ginzburg. Maraini's art and politics have, from that time, favored communal participation. She was active in founding a series of theater groups: Compagnia Blu, La Compagnie del Porcospino, the Theater of Centocelle, and La Maddelene, a company composed entirely of women.

The Italian women's movement had developed from the comparatively cautious criticism of such turn-of-the-century women novelists as Sibilla Aleramo to those who wrote in the wake of the war and the defeat of fascism to the greater assertiveness of the present generation. Maraini's feminism similarly evolved in stages, as her awareness of the anomalous position of women sharpened. Theater, particularly when produced by a socially conscious group, is, for Maraini, the most appropriate avenue for social and political growth—hence her thirty plays tend to be more politically focused than her dozen novels or five volumes of poetry. After Pirandello, Italian theater seemed weak and inconsequential (something he recognized and satirized in his plays). Maraini, along with Natalia Ginzburg and Franca Rame, was instrumental in its contemporary rejuvenation.

In 1963, Maraini received the Prix Formentor for her second novel, *Age of Discontent* (*L'Eta del malessere*, 1962); in 1991, her novel *The Long Life of Marianna Ucria* (*La lunga vita di Marianna Ucria*, 1990) won Italy's Premio Campiello, and in 1999 she was awarded the Strega prize for her collection of stories, *The Dark* (*Buio*)—all prestigious honors. Throughout, she has been an important presence in Italian let-

Dacia Maraini, ca. 1993. (Photographer: Camille Maheux.)

ters and theater, consistently fascinated by people who live on the margins—most obviously, thieves and prostitutes. Often she will recast, almost reinventing, classic stories, as in *The Dreams of Clytemnestra (I sogni di Clitennestra,* 1981), where the royal couple are Tuscans and the focus is on sex and the power struggles it engenders, or in *Mary Stuart* (1980), where the struggle between the queens becomes a struggle over erotic self-assertion—an assertion that is literally decapitated by the ostensibly triumphant cousin, Elizabeth. Maraini's contemporary dramas even more firmly focus on the issue of sexual passion, especially for women.

In *Dialogue Between a Prostitute and Her Client (Dialogo di una prostituta col sua cliente,* 1978), Maraini provocatively stages her uncompromising view of women's status as prostitutes. Her belief that for historic reasons the observing eye has tended to be feminine is exploited effectively and comically throughout *Dialogue.* The play opens with the prostitute Manila demanding that her client remove his shirt and undress so that she can get a good look at him; it features a memorable disquisition by her on "the dick"—in all of its prized, deceptive, pompous absurdity, and is trenchantly punctuated by how appealing she intermittently finds the Client—with his nice eyes, nice mouth, and nice smile.

Manila has a degree in philosophy and literature, is obviously independent and sensual, and has made a calculated decision to be a prostitute. Nor is her argument a frivolous, exaggerated polemic. It just makes more sense than being a full-time whore (a wife), an office whore (a typist), or a shop whore (a clerk)—an argument that dramatically extends Mrs. Warren's defense of her profession in Shaw's "unpleasant" comedy. Prostitution is more honest and more independent; banding together with other working women, Manila can even reject the protection of a pimp.

Enriching Maraini's dynamics are the ways she invokes the image of the Client's beautiful but unapproachable fiancée ("a qualified shorthand typist") and his incestuous inklings toward his mother, which impede his sexuality. The play's agitprop addresses to the audience, reminiscent of Brecht, reinforce its disturbing challenge to existing sexual and power relations. The Client complains that Manila sees things from his (the Client's) perspective, which is weird to him and puts him off—perhaps the ultimate audacity in gender relations.

SELECTED BIBLIOGRAPHY IN ENGLISH

Amoia, Albe della Fazia. *Twentieth-century Italian Women Writers: The Feminine Experience.* Carbondale: Southern Illinois University Press, 1996.

Anderlini, Serena. "Prolegomena for a Feminist Dramaturgy of the Feminine." (interview) Trans. Tracy Barrett. *Diacritics* 58 (1984), 148–62.

Kaufman, Rhoda Helfman. "Introduction." Dacia Maraini, *Only Prostitutes Marry in May.* Montreal: Guernica, 1994. Pp. 9–29.

Lazzaro-Weis, Carol. "Dacia Maraini." *Italian Women Writers: A Bibliographical Sourcebook.* Ed. Rinaldina Russell. Westport, Conn: Greenwood, 1994. Pp. 217–25.

Mitchell, Tony. "'Scrittura femminile': Writing the Female in the Plays of Dacia Maraini." *Theatre Journal* 42 (1990), 332–49.

Pallotta, Augustus. "Dacia Maraini: From Alienation to Feminism." *World Literature Today* 58 (1984), 359–62.

Weinberg, Grazia Sumeli. "Dacia Maraini: Interview with an Italian Feminist." *Sojourner: The Women's Forum* 15 (1990), 21–23.

Wood, Sharon. "Women and Theater in Italy: Natalia Ginzburg, Franca Rame, and Dacia Maraini." *Romance Languages Annual* 5 (1993), 343–48.

DIALOGUE BETWEEN A PROSTITUTE
AND HER CLIENT

Dacia Maraini

Translated by Tony Mitchell

CHARACTERS

MANILA

CLIENT

MANILA: Well, are you going to take your clothes off?
CLIENT: What do you think I am, a woman?
MANILA: No, I can see you've got a dick.
CLIENT: And what the hell are you?
MANILA: I'm wearing a skirt, aren't I?
CLIENT: You're not one of those transvestites are you? Look, I don't go with guys.
MANILA: Don't be silly. I'm a woman.
CLIENT: Women don't behave like that.
MANILA: How do they behave?
CLIENT: I don't know . . . they flirt more—wiggle their ass—play up to you.
MANILA: I am not a dog. Take your clothes off.
CLIENT: Is this some sort of put-down?
MANILA: Take your shirt off so I can have a good look at you.
CLIENT: What's there to see?
MANILA: I want to see what your chest's like.
CLIENT: Sorry, but I'm the one who's doing the buying, not you.
MANILA: I realize you're the customer, but I'd like to have a look at what I'm getting. I'm a voyeur. Let me see your chest.
CLIENT: There's nothing special about my chest. I never went in for sports. My mother wanted me to row on a crew team, but I never got into it. Pellizetti reckons you can find more homosexuality in male team sports than in a bar full of screaming queens.
MANILA: Who's Pellizetti?
CLIENT: You've never heard of Pellizetti? No, of course not—you're just a pro.
MANILA: Why have you still got your clothes on?
CLIENT: What sort of woman are you?

MANILA: This isn't an interrogation. You're buying. I'm selling. It's strictly business.

CLIENT: Right. And the deal is I take and you get taken.

MANILA: Oh no, you don't. You're buying and I'm selling. That's all there is to it.

CLIENT: What are you selling?

MANILA: My cunt.

CLIENT: Don't say that word please.

MANILA: Why not? Does it disgust you?

CLIENT: Look, just don't say it when I'm around. It's gross. It shows a lack of respect for your own body.

MANILA: What's the matter? This is strictly business, right?

CLIENT: Sure, but if you don't keep up your end of the deal I'll get turned off. I'll lose my desire . . .

[*Pause.* MANILA *watches the* CLIENT. *He puts his handkerchief to his temples. He's got a headache.*]

CLIENT: Why don't you say something?

MANILA: So you don't just want my cunt, you want conversation too? I'm not a geisha girl.

CLIENT: I already asked you not to be gross.

MANILA: Is "cunt" gross?

CLIENT: Please don't say that word. I can't stand it.

MANILA: You can stand to buy it by the pound though.

CLIENT: Look, I'm paying . . . I'm paying a lot of money for this and I don't want to hear those words, ok?

MANILA: You're not paying that much. I'm selling you my body at a discount if you include use of the room, the bed, the sheets, the ashtray, the window, the toilet . . .

CLIENT: God, how mercenary. All you can think of is money. Haven't you got anything inside—any emotions? Don't you ever suffer, or cry? Haven't you got a soul?

MANILA: No.

CLIENT: Bloody hell. I can't get rid of this headache.

MANILA: How old are you?

CLIENT: Twenty-five. Why?

MANILA: You sound like you're about fifty.

CLIENT: I'm burnt out. I've been on the go non-stop for about a month.

MANILA: How come?

CLIENT: It's election time. How else do you think I got the money to come here?

MANILA: Who were you campaigning for?

CLIENT: Oh, just what I needed. Talking politics with a prostitute.

MANILA: Are you a liberal?

CLIENT: If you say another word about politics I'm going.

MANILA: It's like that, is it? Do you want some coffee?

CLIENT: No, I want to rest. Is it ok if I lie down?

[*She watches him lie down and smoke a cigarette. To audience.*]

MANILA: I look at him. Look all over him. Every bit of him, head to toe. I like looking at things. I always have. I look at something, then I look again, and then suddenly I fall right into what I'm looking at. It's dangerous—looking gives me a jolt, like cold water on my back. If I go on looking after a certain point I just throw myself right into whatever it is I'm looking at, and I'm not there anymore. I fall right to the bottom and sink. Then I start swimming, running, spreading out. I say to myself, I'm me, Manila, don't worry. But it's not me at all. I've turned into the thing I'm looking at. A dog for example. A dog crapping on the pavement; the turd won't come out of its ass. Its owner is pulling on the leash and nearly choking it, the idiot's ashamed of his dog being seen shitting against the corner shop. A soft yellow turd—must have a bad liver. Its owner probably hasn't got time to look after it properly—too lazy, sleeps in the mornings, and feeds the dog any old rubbish, so it gets sick. So here's this dog—or Manila who's become the dog—trapped with its hind leg stuck up in the air, its ass straining, head looking up at the man saying, "Hang on, master, can't you see I'm trying to shit?"

[*Pause. The* CLIENT *hasn't heard anything. He moves.*]

CLIENT: This silence is getting on my nerves. What are you doing? Are you asleep?

MANILA: No. You were asleep.

CLIENT: You're not a prostitute. I'm an expert. You're something else. A nut case, some sort of pervert, or an actress. You're just playing games. I don't know. Anyway you're not what I'm paying to fuck.

[*First interruption and debate with the audience.*]

MANILA: Shut up.

CLIENT:

[*Prompting her.*]

What the hell do you want . . .

MANILA: I know what my next line is. I was just thinking about the word "prostitute." What does being an "expert on prostitutes" mean?

[*To a man in the audience.*]

Are you an expert on prostitutes? Have you ever been to one? Would you say a prostitute behaves in a particular kind of way? If so, how?

[*The discussion goes on as long as the audience responds. Then the actors go back to the script.*]

CLIENT: You're not a prostitute. I'm an expert.

MANILA: What the hell do you want? And take off that shirt.

CLIENT: Anyone'd think you were buying and I was selling. You're starting to get on my nerves.

MANILA: Right. You say what you want and we'll do it.

CLIENT: Let's pretend I picked you up on a bus, and you're not sure if you should be unfaithful to your husband or not.

MANILA: That's no good. I haven't got a husband anyway.

CLIENT: You can pretend.

MANILA: So I have to be an actor now too?

CLIENT: It's got nothing to do with acting. Just do what I say.

MANILA: I don't do acting. I just sell cunt.

CLIENT: Would you stop saying that word? Goddamn prostitute. You're spoiling everything.

MANILA: You've got lovely green eyes. Or are they blue?

CLIENT: Really? You think so?

MANILA: You're a bit skinny though. Let's see your hands.

CLIENT: You're screwing it all up.

MANILA: Very nice. You obviously don't work with hands like these. You must work with your head. Is that why you've got a headache?

CLIENT: My work needs brains and brawn. And guts.

MANILA: Nice mouth too.

CLIENT: That's what they all say.

MANILA: Give us a smile . . . nice teeth too.

[*He smiles.*]

Smile again—you've got a nice smile. A bit moody, but nice. What's your name?

CLIENT: What's all this nice mouth stuff? Who's the customer here anyway?

MANILA: Bet you're pretty well-off, huh?

CLIENT: You don't make much out of a candy store.

MANILA: You're a shopkeeper?

CLIENT: My father is.

MANILA: And what do you do?

CLIENT: I'm a student. Business and Economics. Look, Manila. I'm not one of those macho types. If I was, I would have thrown you down on the bed by now, no messing around. I like to get to know people first. I like to have a good look at them and try to understand them. I like you to be you and me to be me. I don't get any kicks out of treating you like an animal. I believe in good manners. You might say I'm a bit of a gentleman.

MANILA: You're not a fascist, are you?

CLIENT: No, I'm not. I vote democrat. Why?

MANILA: I don't go with fascists.

CLIENT: Bit picky for a prostitute, aren't you?

MANILA: Mind your own fucking business. And take your shirt off.

CLIENT: I'm not taking anything off. God, my head. Have you got any aspirin?

MANILA: I'll have a look.

[*She finds some aspirin and holds the packet out to him.*]

CLIENT: Not like that.

MANILA: Like what?

CLIENT: In the palm of your hand. Like this. So I can pick it up with my tongue and taste your flesh. That's how my mother always does it. She always laughs when I lick her hand, and calls me her little puppy dog. Would you massage my feet, Manila?

[MANILA *takes his feet in her hands.*]

MANILA: Feet can talk. They can tell you a lot, feet. My grandmother used to say, always look at a man's feet. If they're too small, stay away from him. If they're too hot and clammy, stay away. If they're like two little corpses, stay away. But if they're ticklish and a bit smelly, hang on to them—they're friendly feet. Are you going to take off your shirt?

CLIENT: All right. There. What do you think?

MANILA: Not bad. A bit hairy. I don't like men with hairy chests. I always judge a man by his chest. If it's hairy, it means he's vain and hypocritical. Then I look at his hips. Then his ass. The last thing I look at is his dick. It's the least expressive part of a man. And the most false. If you really want to know something, dicks never tell you the truth. When they're hard, they stick out like they want to skewer you. But the minute you criticise them, they shrivel up in terror like pansies. But the shy, cute ones that are a bit clammy and give you the impression they're having a hard time staying up, are often the most cunning and devious ones. They never get tired, and they're likely to spurt seed into your belly when you least expect it and make you pregnant before you've got time to say "be careful." Then there are the moody dicks: long and thin, and smooth and warm. When you hold them in your hand they feel nice and sleek, but they're real creeps, and they're so full of themselves they'll only stand up for you if you flatter them. Then they go limp at the crucial moment and you spit them out coughing. Then there are pear-shaped dicks, thin on top and fat underneath. They're a pain in the ass—always arguing. The base says one thing and the superstructure says another, and between the two of them they can never manage to get anything together. The spare-part dicks look like they've swallowed a broom; they're always standing at attention like soldiers. They're hopeless—they go off to war, stick their bayonets into the enemy's body and then head back to the trenches for orders. They're the worst sort—stupid ignorant dickheads. They are a real drag. Then you've got the dicklets. They flit around without a care in the world, gossiping and snooping around. They usually stink of fish and chips, and worm their way into every nook and cranny, especially mouths and butts. They like to spread themselves around, and if you don't like it they bitch and moan and wriggle around like worms. Then there's the dick that sulks if you so much as say hello to it, and the touchy type with no sense of timing, that always hangs around when its not wanted. The childish dick wants mommy to stroke it all the time. The masochistic dick turns up its nose at you and won't keep still unless you give it a whack the minute you see it. So much for the two-faced dicks who never tell the truth.

[*Pause. The* CLIENT *wakes up.*]

CLIENT: What are you doing holding my feet?

MANILA: You said you wanted a massage.

CLIENT: I must have fallen asleep. How long have I been asleep?

MANILA: About half an hour.

CLIENT: Shit, what a waste of half an hour. We'll knock twenty dollars off the bill, eh?

MANILA: Fuck that. You might have been sleeping but I've been working.

CLIENT: On a dead man's feet?

MANILA: It's work as far as I'm concerned, feet or no feet. You pay for the use of the bed and the pillow too, you know.

CLIENT: You sound quite educated. Where do you come from?

MANILA: I've got a degree in literature and philosophy, for what it's worth.

CLIENT: Christ, this bloody headache! What's a university graduate doing in a place like this? If you don't mind my asking.

MANILA: What do you think?

CLIENT: Why aren't you teaching in some school somewhere, instead of going to bed with strangers?

MANILA: Mind your own business.

CLIENT: You're really turning me off, you know, Manila. It's getting me down.

MANILA: Well, I'll get you up again in a minute, so what are you complaining about?

CLIENT: How about taking some clothes off?

MANILA: Look, you're the good-looking one. I'm a bit shop-soiled, like most consumer products, so I don't feel like stripping.

CLIENT: All right. If that's the way you want it. Would you put your hand on my forehead? You know what my mother says when I've got a temperature? "Temperature, temperature sickness disease, Off you go home as fast as you please."

MANILA: I bet your mother works the register.

CLIENT: How did you know?

MANILA: And at noon she goes off to cook lunch and your sister takes over.

CLIENT: My girlfriend, actually.

MANILA: Why do you have to come see me if you've got a girlfriend? Do you sleep with her?

CLIENT: Of course I do. We're not living in the Victorian age.

MANILA: So?

CLIENT: So what?

MANILA: Why do you need me to screw you?

CLIENT: You sound just like my mother. Why do you have to go with those tarts? Spending good money you should be buying furniture for your house with!

MANILA: Don't you like your girlfriend?

CLIENT: She's beautiful. She's tall, slim, blonde, delicate—I'm almost afraid to touch her. She's a qualified shorthand typist—makes good money too. And she loves me. When she comes over to my place the first thing she asks me is what I want to eat. I can take my pick from the gourmet cookbook, so I always choose the most complicated dishes I can find and she cooks them for me. Have you ever tried truffle consommé?

MANILA: What's that?

CLIENT: Truffle consommé is frog's leg soup with milk, cream, peas, cinnamon, saffron, nutmeg, rolled oats and butter with grated truffles on top. My mother's really proud of her. They're always ganging up on me and spying on me. So I play tricks on them. I've got a right to be independent. And there are some things I can't do with her—she'd think they were dirty.

MANILA: For example?

CLIENT: Like holding my feet—she'd never do that.

MANILA: Are your feet dirty?

CLIENT: And my mother's always in the way. When I fuck her I feel like I'm fucking my mother.

MANILA: Do that again!

CLIENT: Do what again?

MANILA: That—raising your eyebrows. You've got lovely eyes.

CLIENT: Look deep into my eyes and you'll see a rose palpitating.

MANILA: Is that what your mother says?

CLIENT: Well it's true, isn't it?

MANILA: What are your girlfriend's eyes like?

CLIENT: Small and dark. She's small all over. Small teeth, small eyes—like a pig's, small hands like a monkey's, small feet like a mouse, small breasts like turnips. How can a woman go around without any breasts? Let me see your breasts, Manila.

MANILA: Leave my breasts alone.

CLIENT: I've got a thing about breasts. They really turn me on. I can't do a thing without them.

MANILA: What do you do with them? They're only breasts.

CLIENT: I cling to them, chew them, suck them. Breasts are everything.

MANILA: Well mine are full of milk.

CLIENT: Milk? My God. Full of milk? How come?

MANILA: Because I had a baby a few months ago, idiot.

CLIENT: Oh God, I'm getting a hard-on.

MANILA: At last. Take your pants off then.

CLIENT: You're wierd, you know. You keep seeing things from my point of view, and it really turns me off. You're not normal. You keep putting me off.

MANILA: What the hell do you care if I'm normal or not?

CLIENT: Have you really got milk?

MANILA: Yes. Why?

CLIENT: You've really blown the top off my head, you know. I've had this obsession ever since I was a little kid. I used to hide in the church when it was dark so I could be alone with the statue of Mary and hold on to her breasts and cry. I used to swallow my tears and pretend they were milk flowing and flowing, and then I'd end up coming in my pants like a little fool. Would you let me do it to you?

[*Interruption and discussion with audience.*]

MANILA: This business about the milk. I hear it quite often, and I find it offensive. Apart from the fact that it makes you into a surrogate mother, it means only one particular part of your body is the object of desire, not your whole body. I bet you . . .

[*To audience.*]

. . . have favorite parts of the female body too, like a butcher's shop. A shoulder of lamb, a chicken thigh . . . the female body is chopped up and idolized in pieces.

[*To a man in the audience.*]

Which part do you prefer? Breasts? Thighs?

[*Discussion with the audience. When it is over the* CLIENT *says his last line.*]

MANILA: What does your girlfriend think about you going to prostitutes?

CLIENT: I don't tell her about it. And don't call yourself that. Don't degrade yourself.

MANILA: What should I call myself?

CLIENT: I don't know—masseuse, escort, courtesan . . . You need a bit of fantasy in your life, why don't you use your imagination? I mean, here I am in a room with a person I don't even know, with everything to discover, a whole world to invent . . . Anything can happen. That's the way I see things—it's like an adventure.

MANILA: How much do you expect for the little bit you're paying me?

CLIENT: Why do you have to ruin everything?

MANILA: I don't think I could ever have an adventure with you.

CLIENT: Why not?

MANILA: Because you're as flat as an ironing board. You're a bore.

CLIENT: All you need is a bit of imagination . . . If I close my eyes I can imagine you're a virgin . . . a completely different sort of girl, who's lonely, who's never had a man before and won't let anyone touch her.

MANILA: You'd love to rape me, wouldn't you? I look at him. I look into the dirty dishwater of his heart. I look into those green eyes and desire creeps down my spine. A desire to get inside this student of business and economics, into his chest, his black eyelashes, his breath that smells of cigarette smoke. I almost become him.

CLIENT: You're a bit weird, aren't you Manila? A bit of a perv, eh?

MANILA: What the fuck are you talking about?

CLIENT: Don't be vulgar.

MANILA: Take off your underpants.

CLIENT: Fuck off, bitch! Who's the customer here, me or you?

MANILA: You're the one with the money, so you're the customer. But you're the only one who'll be getting any pleasure out of it, so you're really buying yourself through me.

CLIENT: You're not a prostitute. I don't know what you are, but you're not a prostitute. You're really turning me off.

MANILA: Shall we screw then?

CLIENT: No. Not like that. I need to relax. A bit of atmosphere. Would you turn on the radio?

[MANILA *turns on the radio. Music.*]

CLIENT: There. Music. Soft lights, and a warm female body. What more can you ask?

MANILA: Do you want to know how many I go through in a day?

CLIENT: Shut up—you're turning me off!

MANILA: Between three and five o'clock, two. Six to eight, five. Some of them only want fifteen minutes, so they don't have to pay as much. On Saturday afternoon I went through fifteen.

CLIENT: Christ, this damn headache! Turn that contraption off will you.

[MANILA *turns the radio off.*]

CLIENT: You ruined it. You really fucked it up. Haven't you got any sense of fantasy? To think I could come here every week for the next ten years.

MANILA: Who'd put up with you for ten years? Are you crazy?

CLIENT: Maybe not in August. I usually go to the beach with my family. But for the rest of the year. We could fix a price. Regular payments.

MANILA: You mean so much a month, like a salary?

CLIENT: My father has been going to the same prostitute for twenty-five years.

MANILA: What does your mother think about that?

CLIENT: What's my mother got to do with it? She only sleeps with my father out of duty. She doesn't even know what sex is. She's never had an orgasm in her life. She's had five kids and never had an orgasm.

MANILA: How do you know?

CLIENT: Once I came home and saw her sitting on the couch in her nightie talking on the phone. The radio was on—it was one of those FM talkradio programs and she was telling them everything. "I've never had an orgasm. My husband's a pig who just gets what he wants and then rolls over and goes to sleep. My son's a disgusting selfish faggot bastard. I've been scrubbing floors for fifty years and now I don't even know who I am." Guess what I did.

MANILA: You smashed the radio against the wall, slammed the door and ran out of the house?

CLIENT: I beat her up.

MANILA: You do look a bit like a Gestapo officer with your little blond beard and your snaky eyes.

CLIENT: What would you do? She was pouring out all her intimate secrets on the radio! I nearly strangled her.

MANILA: I bet you were sorry afterwards.

CLIENT: I felt bad when I saw her all bruised and crying. I said I was sorry, and gave her a hug and a kiss. She is my mother after all.

MANILA: Take off your underpants.

[*The* CLIENT *takes his underpants off.*]

MANILA: You've got a nice dick. A bit stupid though. It's not one of those dicks that realizes right away what it's supposed to do.

CLIENT: Are you insulting me now?

MANILA: Not you, just your dick.

CLIENT: We're one and the same person. It's gone down now.

MANILA: I'll soon get it up again. That's my job, isn't it?

[*To the audience.*]

I take this piece of limp and flabby meat in my hand. There's not a drop of blood in it—it's soft and floppy like a glove. I squeeze it and knead it and pull it and stroke it and make it dance, until the beast sticks its head up and then quick as a flash I get on top of it. He's angry: who said you could get on top? You're suffocating me! I say keep still and keep quiet or we'll be in big trouble. I've worked my ass off getting you hard, and I'm on top so I can push you out when I want to so I don't get pregnant. He shifts about a bit—he's not a bad swimmer. He moves about from side to side and it's quite pleasant. But the hideous, horrible thing about it is I'm falling into this sweaty body. I hang on to the sides with my fingers, but I can't stop it. I hardly notice I'm slipping into the slimy water and turning into him—timid, gurgling, thirsting for his mother's milk. I undo my blouse and give him my milk to drink and he, or rather I, comes like a fountain, a river, a cascade, a flood. I'm a lovestruck dick inside my mother's cunt and the milk I'm pouring down his thoat arouses me, churns me up and tugs at my breast until I become milk in my son's throat. I'm my son spitting his sweet seed into my belly which is his belly and I'm inside my mother and the son of the mother who is milk for my beloved maternal love.

[*Silence. He revives and puts his underpants back on. Then he looks in the miror.*]

CLIENT: Pity you're a prostitute. It doesn't suit you. Couldn't you find something better to do, like teaching or something . . . working in a school? Aren't you ashamed of being so educated and doing a shitty job like this?

MANILA:

[*Still stunned.*]

What?

CLIENT: A nice girl like you.

MANILA: Have you taken up preaching now?

CLIENT: In a few years no one'll want you anymore, you know. You'll be on the scrapheap, sinking lower and lower.

MANILA: What are you getting at?

CLIENT: You took something from me too, Manila. You got pleasure from me. You didn't think I noticed. Just because I didn't say anything doesn't mean I'm stupid. I noticed you were getting pleasure—so in a way our relationship's not just a financial agreement anymore.

MANILA: What exactly are you getting at? Let me get this straight. If it's not just a financial agreement anymore, what the fuck is it? A present? You think I should give your washed-out Nazi face a present?

CLIENT: You got it, Manila. I knew you were intelligent.

MANILA: Got what?

CLIENT: We're even. We're not from two opposite social classes, buying and selling. We're equal. We're both poor, and both exploited, aren't we?

MANILA: Sorry, hang on a minute, will you? Can you say that again? What the fuck are you trying to tell me?

CLIENT: I'm telling you I'm really crazy about your body Manila. You've got a really amazing body. I'm saying I really like making love with you, you've got incredible breasts, your milk's really sweet, and you like having sex with me because I'm young and good-looking and I've got a good body. We could start getting involved and maybe in the future . . .

MANILA: In other words, you're refusing to pay.

CLIENT: Why pay for something that involves giving yourself spontaneously? This is love, Manila. True love.

MANILA: Listen, snake-eyes. If this is your way of saying you're not going to pay me I'll stick a knife in your guts. Got it?

CLIENT: People don't like to use knives, or guns. We're rational, feeling people. Like Lenin said, discipline, work and study.

MANILA: I use knives when I have to.

CLIENT: You love me, Manila.

MANILA: I don't love you in the slightest. I couldn't give a shit about you.

CLIENT: You do, you know. I could be the man in your life. I could give you back the tenderness you've lost in this shitty profession. I could be a father to your child. What do you think?

MANILA: Get your money out.

CLIENT: You'll get your money, don't worry. Christ, I don't believe it. You haven't understood a thing I've said. It's not the money I'm talking about. It's our future.

MANILA: Your future, fuckwit.

CLIENT: No. Ours. How old are you? Thirty, thirty-five? It doesn't matter, I don't want to know. You could be eighteen as far as I'm concerned. We're two of a kind, Manila. We both like money, wealth, dreams and love.

MANILA: We're not at all alike, thank God. Speak for yourself.

CLIENT: There's something I want to confess to you. I want you to know everything about me, and show you how naked and vulnerable I am.

MANILA: I don't want to know. You're boring me to death with the bullshit you talk.

CLIENT: For years I was in love with a boy the same age as me, Steve. We went to school together, played football together, even slept in the same bed. Steve was always my best friend, but that was all there was to it. We used to pick up foreign girls together. We'd cruise the tourists in the square, take them down to the bridge and screw them stupid. I used to watch him while I was making it with my girl, otherwise I couldn't get it up. I'd shout at him: get into her, Steve, sock it to her, give her one for me! Fuck her ass off!

[*Third interruption and discussion with the audience.*]

MANILA: Stop it. You're getting too violent.

CLIENT: It's in the script. The lines are violent, so I say them violently.

MANILA: Well the script's too violent then. Those lines turn my stomach every time I hear you say them.

[*To the women in the audience.*]

Aren't you frightened by the violence in those lines? Lots of men talk to women like that. Has that ever happened to you?

[*To a woman in the audience.*]

What do you think it means when men see sex that way? Have you ever had any experiences like that?

[*When the discussion is over the houselights go down, and the stage lights go up. The client says his last line and* MANILA *continues with the text.*]

MANILA: You're a real fascist.

CLIENT: Bullshit. I'm a socialist. I'm in the democratic party. I used to be in the International Socialists, but I'm more moderate now. I'm still antiviolence though. And I'm all for this new morality—living together in peace and harmony and all that. Anyway, Steve had to do his military service, so all that business came to an end. I got myself a girlfriend, and got serious with her. Now I'm going to marry her.

MANILA: But you still come here to see me.

CLIENT: Marriage is one thing, sex is another. You know how long it is since I last made love with her? Five months. I'm scared I won't even be able to make it with her. I can with you though. Do you think I'm sick?

MANILA: I couldn't care less.

CLIENT: Look, I could marry you!

MANILA: So I could be a full-time whore? No thanks.

CLIENT: A man's offering you his freedom and you turn it down just like that!

MANILA: I don't want your freedom. You'd make me pay for it every single hour, day and night.

CLIENT: Why don't you get a job then? You could be a typist, like my girlfriend. Would you like me to help you look for something?

MANILA: So I can be a whore in an office? No thanks!

CLIENT: You could work as a store clerk.

MANILA: A shop whore? No thanks.

CLIENT: Why are you never satisfied? You make it sound like a prostitute's the only job a woman can do.

MANILA: You said it, snake-eyes. The only choice a woman's got is whether she prostitutes herself in public or private—on the street or at home. Right?

[*The* CLIENT *comes up to her and kisses her on the neck.*]

MANILA: He kisses me, the shit. He kisses me so tenderly my arms just flop. Watch it, Manila, this one's trying to pull a fast one on you. He'll take your breath away, and leave you high and dry and get it all for free. He knows I like his eyebrows, his eyes, his skin. If I look at him any longer I'll fall right into him, like the time I fell right into an old woman on the bus and couldn't get out . . . I could feel people looking at my wrinkles in disgust, but I was so lightheaded I thought my brain had flown away. My head was like a shrivelled nut full of black dust. I had a big green bag on my lap and every so often my withered fingers checked that the catch was fastened. I was chewing away like an old goat, and my watery eyes were looking out the window at the ugly and remote world outside. Under my arms I could feel my thighs pressing together but not touching. My heart was beating sluggishly and I couldn't care less about anybody else, all I wanted to do was eat a lovely cake I had in my green bag. That was why I kept checking the clasp of the bag, I was scared someone would steal the cake. I knew my life depended on that cake and nothing else mattered. Fucking old woman, I could have strangled her.

CLIENT: You know what I think, Manila? I think you're really quite respectable. I don't be-lieve you're just going to have a wash, get dressed and go back on the street to pick up more clients.

MANILA: I haven't felt a thing for eight months. What the hell's happening to me with this jerk?

[*To* CLIENT.]

You can lay off the flattery, you won't be getting any discount.

CLIENT: What are you talking about? I'm no cheapskate. I'll give you what I owe you, what we agreed on, don't worry. But you haven't got a pimp.

MANILA: I don't need a pimp. I've got a different kind of set-up, with my girlfriends.

CLIENT: What if I told you I'm strong and I do karate, I can beat anybody in a fight, but I like you and I swear to God I won't rip you off, and offered to look after you? I wouldn't cause any trouble, I'd do whatever you say, and all I'd take is a small per-centage. Maybe ten percent. What would you say?

MANILA: I'd say no.

CLIENT: Goddamn it, Manila, I'll leave that ghost of a girlfriend, I'll leave home, I'll leave the university. We could live together, go on a trip together to Paris, Madrid, South America. What do you say?

MANILA:

[*To audience.*]

What a sense of order there is inside this shitty mint-eyed bastard. Everything clean and tidy, all the furniture neatly arranged, soft carpet under your feet. His family sits on straight, hard-backed chairs: his mother with her mouth full of fish, his fiancée with see-though glass arms, his father with a lead ass. In the middle there's a big comfort-able armchair just for him, the favorite son. He's got a big bowl of golden coins on his lap, fresh from the mint. Everything is so neat and tidy inside. Everyone's smiling kindly and affectionately. Then they show me there's a place for me too, on top of a kind of altar. His father takes me up there and forces me to go down on all fours. Then he ties me up with cold, heavy gold cords, still smiling sweetly. Now I'm tied up tight to the wall and the floor. After a while two hands grab my bare breasts, squeeze them and pull them down towards the floor with a savage jerk. Under my belly there's a bucket the milk spurts into with a metallic noise. The pain takes my breath away.

CLIENT: Hey, Manila! What are you doing? Were you asleep? What sort of prostitute are you? You spend all your time day-dreaming, off in a world of your own!

MANILA: I wish I didn't need your body. Or any man's body.

CLIENT: You need me just like I need you. We should join forces, Manila, and make a deal. Its our destiny.

MANILA: No. Just pay up. I don't want to make any deals with you.

CLIENT: Don't you like me?

MANILA: Yes, I do like you. That's just the point. It's a trap. So pay up and get out.

CLIENT: If I pay you I'm finished with you, don't you realize? I want to start something. This could be the start of something new . . .

MANILA: Look, I've had enough. Give me my money!

CLIENT: How are you going to make me pay, darling? What'll you do if I refuse to pay? Call the cops? Pull a gun? Look at you—you're small, you've got no muscles, you're exhausted, you haven't even got a dick. What could you do about it? I'm going to go right out that door and leave you. *Ciào!* Just to show you you need a pimp. No one would dare treat you like this if I was looking after you. See?

MANILA: Don't be an asshole. Pay me what you owe me. Weren't you talking about the new morality before? Well you can start by keeping your end of the bargain.

CLIENT: Getting rid of prostitution is part of the new morality. A new society of peace and harmony! There, I'll give you half. You can have the rest next time. *Ciào, amóre!*

[MANILA *goes to the door and hollers.*]

MANILA: Anna! Carmela! Marina! He won't pay up! Quick, he's going!

[*Shouts and blows are heard, and sounds of protest. Then, a baby crying.* MANILA *goes and gets her baby and carries it in. She sits and sings to it.*]

Ninna nanna child of mine
Sleep tight don't worry about your future
I'll sew your lips together with string
So you won't be tempted to kiss anyone
You'll say your mother was a witch
You'll say your mother was a fairy godmother
I'll sew up your cunt with silken thread
So you won't be tempted to fuck anyone
You'll say your mother was a witch
You'll say your mother was a fairy godmother
Sleep my baby, eat and get fat
I'll sew up your eyes with verdigris
So you won't be tempted to look at anyone
You'll say your mother was a witch
You'll say your mother was a fairy godmother
When you grow up you'll live with other women
And you'll be a witch, a fairy godmother.

[*End.*]

Gerlind Reinshagen (b. 1926)

The theater has traditionally belonged to men—male producers, directors, playwrights, and often actors. In Germany this control has been a particularly difficult and interesting one for women to challenge. Male dominance, whether in the theater (which is government subsidized), in politics, or in the home, has, in Germany, been uniquely linked to the question of national identity and to the overwhelming stain of political brutality. Do the Teutonic heroes, be they Wotan or Wallenstein, imply a radically hierarchical and racist society? This struggle for power, by women or other disempowered groups, has, in fact, been played out in many dramas about authoritarianism, about the nation's history, and about the ambiguous relationship between land and home, including who is sovereign where—men or women.

For Gerlind Reinshagen, Germany's preeminent woman dramatist and a strong contributor to that nation's fiction and poetry, the issue of German national identity is entangled not only with authoritarianism and fascism, but also with feminism and the climate of domestic life. She rejects the historical separation of spheres, seeing the superficially distinct world of men and women, of public and private—whether Nazi or post-Nazi—as in fact reflecting and supporting each other. She does not see the family, the world of women, as separate and insulated from the public, political "outside" world.

Like Marieluise Fleisser in her Weimar-period Ingolstadt plays, Reinshagen, writing a generation later, after World War II, adapts the conventions of the German history plays to subvert them. If for Schiller in his *Wallenstein* trilogy and even for Wagner in his *Ring Cycle,* history or mythical history provided the constructive, positive artistic expression of German identity, for both Fleisser and Reinshagen history told the story of delusions, oppressions, and frustrations. Recently, scholars have become increasingly interested in domestic history. Reinshagen, as a playwright, shares this focus, not only in *Sunday's Children* (*Sonntagskinder,* 1977), but in *Ironheart* (*Eisenherz,* 1982), where the work world of women is scrutinized, and even in *The Life and Death of Marilyn Monroe* (*Leben und Tod der Marilyn Monroe,* 1971), where she examines the devastating price women pay for acceding to socially dictated images.

Perhaps it was no idle thrust that an early, classic salvo in the American women's movement of the sixties bore in its title "Kinder, Küche, Kirche." The German expression seemed particularly apt to Naomi Weinstein, the essayist, to describe how women had been enthralled, pedestalized, and effectively made pow-

Gerlind Reinshagen, ca. 1990 (Photographer: Isolde Ohlbaum.)

erless by the combined ideals of children, kitchen, and church. The ostensible up-side was of course that they were safe from worldly wear and taint, living pro-tected within their domesticities.

Reinshagen is impatient with so naive and politically retrograde a view. Dur-ing the Hitler years women were removed from the public sphere and power and urged into the nursery. It later became disturbingly easy to see them as having ex-isted outside of fascism and its politics. In Reinshagen's dramatization of history, especially these catastrophic years, the German family, the realm of women, pro-vided not an evasion of Nazism but a seedbed for it. In her montage of thirty-two scenes, divided into three parts ("Dream of Victory," "In the Thick of It," and "De-feat"), she exposes German home life from the beginning of the war in 1939 to de-feat six years later. For Elsie and her cohort, it exactly corresponds to their blighted adolescences. The center of the home, the living room, trenchantly echoes Hitler's infamous clamor for *Lebensraum.*

Within this women-home-centered world, the children constitute a micro-cosm. They are Sunday's Children, so "full of expectation, so beautiful within"—perhaps recalling Strindberg's student Arkenholtz in *The Ghost Sonata,* a Sunday Child who could see what others could not. This identification of the children with bright expectations and special sight is not entirely ironic, anticipating as it does the dismal ends awaiting them: enfeeblement and death. It is also poignant as a literal indication of what might have been: a free-spirited, imaginative Elsie who need not have been driven to distraction had the world been otherwise. Elsie and her Aunt Tilda suggest the possibilities of resisting the horrors of the Third Reich, but their gestures are pale and the risk awful.

Reinshagen sees fascism, whether public or domestic, as a political structure that demands a reaction. Her characters dramatize the complexities and nuances of responses, each contributing to the author's scathing attack on mindless, brutalizing tyranny, Nazi or other. She derides the faint hope at the ending of the war; Elsie's mother will marry Rodewald, but all around them are death and rubble. Reinshagen builds the Nazi fascination with death into her play—from the early appearance of Death's Head to the final carnage of youth—to emphasize the prevailing morbidity in both spheres and across generations. Frau Belius's *Mutterkreuz* (medal for German mothers) is a savage mockery. Children, including hers, are nurtured to die; to the extent that they imply a future, that future is blighted.

SELECTED BIBLIOGRAPHY IN ENGLISH

Case, Sue-Ellen, ed. *The Divided Home/Land: Contemporary German Women's Plays.* Ann Arbor: University of Michigan Press, 1992.

Czekay, Angelika. "German National Identity and the Female Subject: Gerlind Reinshagen's German Trilogy." *Other Germanies: Questioning Identity in Women's Literature and Art.* Eds. Karen Jankowsky and Carla Love. Albany: SUNY Press, 1997. Pp. 217–35.

Sieg, Katrin. *Exiles, Eccentrics, Activists: Women in Contemporary German Theater.* Ann Arbor: University of Michigan Press, 1994.

———. "The Representation of Fascism in Gerlind Reinshagen's *Sunday's Children*." *Theatre Studies* 36 (1991), 31–44.

SUNDAY'S CHILDREN
Gerlind Reinshagen

Translated by Tinch Minter and Anthony Vivis

More innocent! Children know far more, or so
It seems, than we adults . . .
—FRIEDRICH HÖLDERLIN

CHARACTERS

LUDWIG WOELLMER (Father)   a chemist (pharmacist)

THERESE WOELLMER (Mother)   his wife

ELSIE WOELLMER   their daughter, 14 years old

LONA   their maid, 18 years old

METZENTHIN   an apprentice in Woellmer's chemist's shop, 19
      years old

TILDA   Woellmer's sister-in-law

HEINRICH BELIUS   Infantry General

ANNA-SOPHIE BELIUS   his wife

INKA BELIUS   their daughter, 15 years old

RODEWALD   a headmaster

NOLLE (NORBERT)   his son, 16 years old

HERR OSWIN   Woellmer's bookkeeper

ALMUTH   his daughter, 15 years old

KONRADI   "the hero of Crete," student teacher

DEATH'S-HEAD   a lance-corporal in the tank corps

A PASSER-BY

A POLE (Non-speaking role)

[*The ages of the children given here are for 1939, the beginning of the war. By the end of the play they have aged accordingly.*]

BASIC SET

The cathedral square in a medium-size town in central Germany, with church towers, the Renaissance facade of Woellmer's chemist's shop, statue of Roland, John the Baptist Fountain, Mausoleum, and part of the wall. Consecutive scenes take place in different parts of the multiple set, and only the props are changed: a table with smoker's requisites on it, a stove, a sewing-machine, a grandfather clock, etc.

PART ONE
DREAMS OF VICTORY

Scene 1

By the stove. LONA *is stirring a pot.* TILDA *is sewing something on her machine.* METZENTHIN, *in a white overall, is sitting on the stove's metal surround, attempting to dissolve a substance in a conical flask over the flame.* ELSIE *is lying on the floor in front of the sewing-machine, colouring in a fashion magazine. She is singing:*

> My Bonnie lies over the ocean,
> My Bonnie lies over the sea
> My Bonnie lies over the ocean
> Oh, bring back my Bonnie to me!
> Bring back, bring back, oh bring back my Bonnie to me . . .

[She breaks off suddenly and, at the top of her voice, joins in with the soldiers' song, which has been audible off-stage for some time now, and whose rhythm she clearly finds overpowering.]

> Lore Lore Lore Lore Lore
> Give us lovely girls of seventeen and eighteen
> Lore Lore Lore Lore Lore . . .

[She breaks off again. The song dies away. Silence. ELSIE *stands up. We see that she is wearing the half-finished dress which* TILDA *is making for* ELSIE's *mother, as well as high-heeled shoes. She totters over to* TILDA.]*

ELSIE: Are fichus in nowadays?
TILDA: Yes, fichus are in.

*[*ELSIE *whistles in appreciation, pins on the fichu, totters across to* LONA, *and adopts an adult pose.]*

ELSIE: Chat me up, Lona. Go on, chat me up!
LONA: How?
ELSIE: The way they do: you're eighteen. You must know. *[Affectedly.]* The way men say things.
LONA: I've got to keep an eye on the sauce.
TILDA: *[Stands up to take the fichu from* ELSIE.]* I've still got to hem it. Let me have it.

*[*ELSIE *pulls off the fichu, throws it over the machine, totters over to* METZENTHIN *and nods graciously at him.]*

ELSIE: Hello, Karli—or rather Herr Metzenthin!—Well, fancy bumping into you! How are you? *[She puts on a hat.]* How long is it since we last met? Ten years? Twelve years?

*[*METZENTHIN *makes no response, just shakes his solution.* ELSIE *digs him in the ribs.]*

ELSIE: I'm your . . . old pal Elsie . . . the boss's daughter, from when you were a lad—ah—ah—when we were both young and lovely . . .

[METZENTHIN *taps his forehead with his finger.*]

ELSIE: Why are you gaping? Take me for a ghost? You haven't changed much. Grown a paunch, gone bald . . . I'd hardly know you, I'm sorry to say. Unlike my Lona . . . [*She puts her arms round* LONA's *waist.*] In another twelve years' time, you'll still look exactly the same—you'll *always* be beautiful! [*Back in a conversational tone.*] If you find me changed, Fräulein Lona, bear it in mind that I've had boys—whoops, children. [*She whistles for her imaginary children through two fingers.*] Franz-Eberhard, Inka, Karl-Hermann, come along! Left right, left right! Caps off! Hands out of pockets! Our youngest, little Max—you remember him, he starved on us. Dreadful, dreadful.

LONA: [*Shocked.*] What do you mean starved?

ELSIE: We had to bury him . . . in a tiny little coffin . . . with gold handles, oh doesn't time fly. The good old days. Don't you remember? The timber-market, the fish-market, that crooked house, old Spindleshanks, John the Baptist's Fountain, St. Martin's Church—but now . . . not a stone left standing!

METZENTHIN: What do you mean: not a stone left standing?

ELSIE: Because we've had a war in the meantime, people shout it from the roof-tops: War's round the corner, and in a war—not a stone is left standing . . . —we all know that. And on top of everything, turnips morning, noon and night! [ELSIE *shields her eyes with one hand, and looks out over the square.*] Agh, and lovely Roland's head's been knocked off!

METZENTHIN: Gossip! Gossip! There won't be a war.

ELSIE: The nation needs space to live, so our teacher says: Poland must become German.

METZENTHIN: [*Laughs.*] "The Führer offers peace with his own hand, but it is spurned."

ELSIE: And Frau Belius is already hoarding lentils!

METZENTHIN: Rubbish! Why do you think Chamberlain went to Munich? And everyone's grateful to be in work. [*Quotes.*] "Even you can travel now"! How can it happen, if nobody wants it?

ELSIE: Do you want a war, Aunty Tilda?

TILDA: One was enough for me.

ELSIE: Lona?

LONA: Oh God, all the men would disappear overnight!

ELSIE: Metzenthin! Look me in the eye!

METZENTHIN: They wouldn't want me anyway. You see, I've got a congenital defect. A war wouldn't do me any good.

ELSIE: [*Seeing the lame book-keeper hobbling in from the shop, she calls out.*] Someone I know wants a war! [*To* OSWIN.] Herr Oswin, you want a war, don't you?

OSWIN: [*Puts down his briefcase and taps* ELSIE *on the temple.*] What's bothering that little brain of yours? Head always in the clouds, in the clouds, in the clouds! Then—you come down to earth! Howls of anguish! You youngsters would fall to your deaths if it wasn't for others, quietly getting on with things, holding everything together. The centre's strong, I tell you! The majority don't want a war! All we need [*Grinning.*] is a lick of flame. To seek out decay. The slums, where the riff-raff live, the Commies, and those women with mirrors in front of their windows, it'll seek out the rotten elements! But no more than that. I'm a man of the centre, I like stability. [*Laughing.*] Twenty-two years on the same stool . . . I tell you: when the centre's strong, peace is guaranteed! [*Tries to slip his arm suggestively around* LONA's *middle.*] I'm right, aren't I, Fräulein Lona?

TILDA: Herr Oswin, you can't be serious for one moment. Keep your jokes to yourself.

METZENTHIN: Specially as they're pathetic!

OSWIN: We shall see, Herr Praktikant. [*Goes out.*]

METZENTHIN: [*To* ELSIE.] Only kids laugh at his jokes anyway.

ELSIE: I know! Are you frightened, Metzenthin? Do you think we can talk ourselves into it? I can make it happen? . . . War . . . by just talking?

METZENTHIN: I believe what my eyes tell me.

ELSIE: But you are frightened, aren't you? It's written all over your face, Metzenthin!

METZENTHIN: The only thing that would frighten me is going out of my mind. I'd be so frightened I'd panic.

TILDA: Your Uncle Bummi, Elsie, the Captain, the one who finished up in an institution, he always used to say . . .

METZENTHIN: But you can do something to prevent it, thank God. You can do something about that particular illness.

TILDA: "I'd rather be crazy." Uncle Bummi used to say, "than grown-up." He was an eternal child in every way. "Stand clear, all of you—it's catching!" he kept shouting . . . Then hanged himself in the barn.

LONA: Oh, God. Well, I've never had anything catching but measles.

METZENTHIN: It's almost the only illness you can do something about. If you have the will, that is.

TILDA: I think Bummi didn't have the will. [*To herself.*] He wanted to escape.

METZENTHIN: It takes common sense and willpower—willpower's important—and given you don't contract syphilis. [*He picks up his solution on his way out.*]

ELSIE: [*Stands in his way.*] What's syphilis, Metzenthin?

METZENTHIN: [*Trying to get past.*] Nothing. Nothing at all special . . .

ELSIE: Metzenthin! [*She stares at him.*]

METZENTHIN: A bit like a cold. Right, I must get on. [*He goes out quickly.*]

ELSIE: [*Following him.*] He's lying! And now he's gone red. He can't do anything properly! And all day long he's been hanging around in here. Instead of being in the dispensary. Why does he always sit in our kitchen? [*Abruptly changing; to herself.*] If I was nineteen, like him, I'd be able to tell proper lies. I'd be able to do everything. Everything—and more. [*Pause.*] I'm never frightened.

[LONA *looks hard at* ELSIE. *The machine rattles frenetically. The lights change.*]

Scene 2

At the table. FATHER *is staring in front of him with some newspapers on his knee.* MOTHER *is holding a cigarette as if she isn't used to smoking. Her parents take no notice of* ELSIE, *who is lounging about nearby. She seems preoccupied. But she perks up as soon as she becomes aware of irritation between her parents. She then follows their actions with great interest. The grandfather clock strikes 5.*

MOTHER: I thought you'd nodded off, Ludwig.

FATHER: [*Opening his eyes.*] I sometimes think whether we read the paper or not . . . it doesn't make a scrap of difference.

MOTHER: There are books, what about the books? I get them for you specially from old Bode. You start them, then leave them lying around.

FATHER: Don't get so het up. These family sagas . . . all the same. Bad ideas in bad taste. Let's play cards.

MOTHER: What about the other one, the one he recommended—the political one, issues for the nation?

FATHER: It's written by self-taught people, in a deplorable style. You're not expected to have read that.

MOTHER: But perhaps you ought to know about it.

FATHER: They call it literature . . .

MOTHER: . . . the most influential lines of thought . . . [*Quietly.*] And opposing views from abroad . . . They're painting frightening pictures in émigré papers . . . Downright apocalyptic, so Bode says . . . [*Quietly.*] He could get a copy.

FATHER: [*Also in a quiet voice.*] Take care what you say, Therese!

MOTHER: Only for information of course. We know how many lies are being told out there . . . Anyone with any sense knows that.

FATHER: But it would be round the whole town in no time . . . that mustn't happen. [*Yawns.*] I've been feeling so tired lately.

MOTHER: You look pale, Ludwig, you're working too hard . . . You must get more fresh air.

FATHER: The pharmacy runs itself. I do my daily round: the park, Petergate, the green at Buchardi . . . Like a donkey drawing water . . . my daily circuit . . .

[*Pause.*]

MOTHER: You stare into space and do nothing, Ludwig. Why do you do nothing . . . ?

FATHER: [*Smiling.*] Perhaps I'm ill.

MOTHER: You ought to give up smoking and drinking, then. And see Dr. Kittel. Like I'm always telling you. It's . . . not natural just sitting there, I think, not doing a thing.

FATHER: Sorry, I was only mentioning it.

MOTHER: I understand, Ludwig.

FATHER: No more than a mood, Therese, I'm just a bit touchy. Don't take any notice.

MOTHER: . . . I'm always the first to understand you: it's not as if I'm immune, the narrowness, it's so limiting here . . . but there is this to be said for it, Ludwig. You walk round this little town of ours and the people you bump into all knew your father, your grandfather, even your great-grandfather . . .

FATHER: [*Lost in thought, smiling.*] The other evening, as I was closing the shop, who should I see but Elsie and the apprentice sitting by the fountain like a couple of ghosts . . . Quiet as mice, all of a sudden . . . Like a little monument.

[ELSIE *looks up.*]

MOTHER: [*Uneasily.*] But Ludwig, we've always agreed, all the years we've been together we've agreed it's good for the child . . . playing out there on the wall, near the Gleimhaus . . . she'll obviously grow up here with a sense of history, knowing the names, Tilly . . . Wallenstein . . .

FATHER: And Albrecht the Bear, and Heinrich the Lion . . . these . . . mottos everywhere, on every house, it just goes on forever, it's not at all narrow, Therese, it strikes me as being quite the opposite, limitless, quite the opposite, endless . . . Take our Lona, she came to us, from God knows where, and in a couple of years she'll be off, and for these two years all she's had to be is a human being, a lovely human being, just that . . .

MOTHER: [*Anxiously reaches for* FATHER'*s hand.*] It's a good job I know you, Ludwig, you're talking like a child, suddenly like a child . . .

[ELSIE *looks up.*]

FATHER: Just imagine: being able to go, wherever you want . . . a new life in a different town . . . with no name, no family tree . . .

MOTHER: For goodness sake, Ludwig!

FATHER: [*Smiling.*] No family vault!

MOTHER: You've got it all out of proportion—it's not true, you must pull yourself together.

FATHER: Years ago, it used to make me . . . ecstatic, when I came back from university, here. I thought to myself, here there is proportion, and style . . . I stood at John the Baptist's Fountain, and Petergate, here you'll find peace . . . Nowadays, I sometimes think—as if I'm an old man, Therese—suddenly I can't help but think about that street, where I used to live, in Berlin, those cheap, ugly tenement blocks, the whole area cheap, ugly but . . . anonymous . . .

MOTHER: Don't say any more, Ludwig, please.

FATHER: I won't say another word. [*He looks at the newspaper.*] Lilian Harvey's got married. He's no more than a boy. Silly fool.

MOTHER: Why shouldn't she get married? And what makes you call her silly?

FATHER: Quite. What makes me call her silly?

MOTHER: [*In a monotone.*] Why do you say what makes you?

FATHER: Quite . . . I'm not sure myself now . . .

MOTHER: I can't understand why you *won't* understand, all of a sudden . . . You don't answer . . . haven't we always talked openly with each other, for seventeen years . . . always . . . always. . . . [*In desperation.*] Ludwig, why don't you speak to me?

[*She stares at* FATHER, *begins to sob, and then weeps uncontrollably.* ELSIE *watches the whole thing intently.* FATHER *goes over to* MOTHER *and strokes her tenderly.*]

FATHER: What's the matter? There's nothing to worry about. What have I said? What's upset you? Why are you in floods of tears all of a sudden . . . you've no reason to . . . [*Pause.*] And in any case, there might be a war.

MOTHER: [*Hopefully.*] Do you really think so?

[FATHER *says nothing.*]

MOTHER: We'd have other things to think about then . . .

FATHER: They certainly would in Berlin . . .

MOTHER: . . . It would relieve the tension! [*Taking fright.*] But you . . . Ludwig, you'd stay here with us, wouldn't you?

FATHER: In my profession I can't be called up.

[MOTHER *goes to the radio and puts on a slow waltz. The parents sway in time to the music, then they dance—formally and awkwardly, as they have been taught. At the same time* MOTHER *half-sings, half-says.*]

MOTHER: Let there be war, let's have a war, let the whole world go up in smoke . . . War, war, there's a war, and we're dancing because there's a war, because there's a war . . . [*Catching sight of* ELSIE, MOTHER *suddenly checks herself.*] That's the way it is, darling, that's the way it's got to be. Seventeen years, just look, your parents are still dancing after seventeen years, and after thirty years together we'll still . . . [*In a different voice.*] I've been wanting to say this, Elsie, you'll be spending more time at home in future, not messing about in the square any more . . . and don't see so much of that Metzenthin creature. Not because he's from the slums; there are some really decent families down there, really hard-working, it's just that . . . you're too old now for that. Now, child, go and do your homework.

[ELSIE *goes off, sulking. The grandfather clock strikes. The lights change.*]

Scene 3

LONA *by the window, knitting, and looking out every now and again.* ELSIE *sidles up to her, putting her hands over* LONA's *eyes.*

ELSIE: He's passing the window right now, you can't see him.

LONA: Too late, Elsie. He's just gone past.

ELSIE: He might suddenly turn round and come back!

LONA: That's not his style. He's walking round the square, like he always does. Save your-self the bother . . . Anyway, I'd sense it, a sort of magnetism, if he was heading this way . . .

ELSIE: Aha! He is coming back, staring at us through the window. Any second now it'll crack!

LONA: [*Pulls* ELSIE'*s hands away from her eyes.*] What? Honestly? [*Disappointed.*] Oh, it's only the General!

ELSIE: General Belius and his lady wife, Anna-Sophie. I call her "Maria-Theresa"! Tee-hee-hee. Father says he didn't invent gunpowder, but she invented childbirth.

LONA: I think he's got wonderful blue eyes.

ELSIE: [*Opening her history book.*] He looks a bit like General Moltke . . . don't you think?

LONA: [*Points outside, yelling.*] Almuth! Almuth in a fur collar! In midsummer!

ELSIE: I wonder, Lona, do the same people come back again and again, all those who've ever been . . . just differently dressed . . .

LONA: I've always thought she'd go loony again, that Almuth, and in midsummer!!

ELSIE: Indians say people come back again and again in all kinds of forms, what do you think, Lona? Are you listening? Lona, you've gone all red! [*She looks into the street.*] Ah, your big crush, Herbert Nickel! [*She goes on turning over pages. Then holds the book up in front of* LONA'*s nose.*] Bonaparte in miniature!

LONA: He can't be more than two centimetres shorter than me! And he's a Sergeant!

ELSIE: This one was a general at twenty-four. Beautiful! With his forehead and his curl . . . Like this! Your Nickel and him are like two peas in a pod. If we ignore the logo. Perhaps he'll be a Field Marshal one day!

LONA: I think so too, sometimes. [*Putting her arms round* ELSIE.] Oh, Elsie. It's getting so exciting. The whole town's bursting with soldiers. And more are enlisting every day. There's something about a man in uniform.

ELSIE: They're never dreary like civilians.

LONA: It isn't just their clothes, or the cut of them . . . soldiers, especially when they're young, are somehow [*Pause.*] like Sunday's children, so . . . full of expectation, so beautiful from within . . .

ELSIE: Now I'm going to show you the very best one of all! [*Pointing to a picture.*]

LONA: [*Reading.*] Carl von Clausewitz. Oh, him.

ELSIE: [*Pointing outside.*] No, him.

LONA: [*Comparing them.*] Clausewitz . . . he could be. [*Then, with conviction.*] No, it's more like . . . [*She thinks it over.*] your student teacher, isn't it . . . Konradi . . .

ELSIE: Doesn't he look good as a paratrooper . . .

LONA: I could fall for him too.

ELSIE: Half the school already has. You're wasting your time. [*Pause.*] Lona, I want to tell you something. A long time ago, when I was a child, I . . .

LONA: [*Laughs.*] When you were a child . . .

ELSIE: Whenever I thought about the future, and my one . . . special . . . I always used to think I'd walk right round the world for him, in my bare feet, or, if he rejected me, live in a cave, for years on end, with my son . . .

LONA: What son?

ELSIE: Or live in a forest, like Genoveva, drinking doe's milk.

LONA: It's just possible no-one would ask that of you?

ELSIE: Lona, would you walk right round the world, too?

LONA: Well, that would certainly be . . . quite a step, eh? [*Checking herself.*] Elsie, I'm sup-posed to keep an eye on you, you've got to stop daydreaming, do something useful, your mother says, because your nerves aren't all that strong. [*Gives* ELSIE *her knitting.*] Here, take this stocking, give me a hand with the knitting.

ELSIE: When I'm knitting I have to keep counting. When I have to keep counting, I can't talk. So I can't tell you who I think *you* are.

LONA: Oh, I'm only Lona. [*She puts on her silk stockings, checking the seams are straight with the help of a pocket mirror. Silence.*] Who, who do you think I really am?

ELSIE: [*Immediately stops knitting and leans backwards.*] Once upon a time there was a beautiful water sprite, called Undine. She looked a bit like you. And because she fell in love with the knight, Huldbrand, she was given a human soul, even though she was a water nymph.

LONA: Well? Did they get married?

ELSIE: Unhappily for Undine, her soul was better and more perfect than any human soul.

LONA: So it didn't come out right in the end?

ELSIE: It did, it did—he married her!

LONA: And then? Did it end unhappily?

ELSIE: I can't remember how it ends.

LONA: You always remember how stories end. It's sad, isn't it, and you don't want to tell me any more! [*Pause.*]

ELSIE: I've forgotten it. [*Silence.*] It was only made up, after all!

[*The lights change.*]

Scene 4

In the pharmacy, the cellar. METZENTHIN *pouring a liquid from a beaker through a funnel into a small bottle.* ELSIE *hands him another bottle.*

ELSIE: Metzenthin, will you fill this with cough mixture for me?

METZENTHIN: What will you pay?

ELSIE: You can't expect me to pay for what's ours, Metzenthin! You're always after something! You've already had heaps of old exercise-books, hair clips, and clumps of hair. What do you do with it all? What are you really after?

METZENTHIN: Write me a letter, Elsie.

[ELSIE *laughs uproariously.*]

METZENTHIN: They're all writing each other letters. All the women have been sitting writing, ever since things got going, over in Poland . . . Anyone who doesn't write might well regret it, once it's too late. [*Pause.*] When her man's pushing up daisies.

ELSIE: You'll never be pushing up daisies, because you've got a weak heart. Anyway, I see you every day.

METZENTHIN: That's why people ought to write to each other, that's exactly why they ought to write, so you can see they're serious.

ELSIE: Are you trying to tell me when Lona writes . . . till her fingers bleed . . . to her Herbert Nickel, she's lying?

METZENTHIN: I'd like a letter that's really written to me, and not to [*Pause.*] a fantasy figure.

ELSIE: So you're saying all that lot out there getting letters, all soldiers are fantasy figures?

[METZENTHIN *doesn't respond.*]

ELSIE: Metzenthin? Would you die for a letter?

[*Silence.*]

METZENTHIN: I'll have to sleep on it.

ELSIE: I can tell you, Metzenthin, I'll never write you the kind of letter you're thinking about, and I'll never wear silk stockings, never, as long as I live. [*Pause.*] And if I ever do write letters . . .

METZENTHIN: It'll only be to a "hero," eh? In a uniform covered with pips? [*Pause.*] Shall I tell you a story? You're always mad keen on stories. I'm the son of a "hero," Elsie. He was wounded at the eleventh hour in the last war. In the final round of gunfire you could say. He dragged himself around for another two years. His poor widow gave me a simple but respectable upbringing. It was all pretty grim. But *he* became more and more fantastic. Only in my head, though. That's why I don't care about all that, medals and status . . . I haven't got any status in this town, no family, like you. But believe me, I don't *want* any, it's only superficial, nothing but show, nobody can fool me . . . any more than I can fool myself. Perhaps it's a weakness. [*To himself.*] We all need to fantasise about ourselves . . . [*Pause.*]

ELSIE: [*Giving it some thought.*] I don't see what you've got against yourself.

METZENTHIN: I know, I know. People shouldn't be in conflict with themselves. But our paths will always cross, Elsie, wherever you are, whether or not you want it. [*Pause.*] Now you seem completely transparent. Sometimes I'm frightened you'll dissolve into thin air.

ELSIE: [*Takes the bottle of cough mixture from him.*] Yes. I might sometime this afternoon. You see, we're going to the cave, then along the subterranean passage. We're going to tunnel through to the slums. I'll look at the house where you were born. And if the whole lot collapses behind us, that'll be that.

METZENTHIN: And the whole world will go into deepest mourning . . . and beg forgiveness for the wrongs it's done you.

ELSIE: People say there are gold rings down there, buried by the Merovingians. You might find things a thousand years old. You'd see the earth from the inside. Metzenthin, how long do you think it takes to suffocate?

METZENTHIN: [*Grins.*] You're about to find out. If that's the way it is: good-bye forever!

[*He goes out.* ELSIE *stamps her foot. The lights change.*]

Scene 5

In the cave, lit by candles. Bunting and flags cover the walls. NOLLE, ALMUTH *and* INKA *are all sitting on the floor in uniform.* ELSIE *joins them. Then* METZENTHIN.

NOLLE: [*Reading from a letter.*] Konradi says: "That was the best ever blitzkrieg. Our infantry marched as no army has ever marched in the history of the world . . . our tanks always in the van. Tomorrow there's the victory parade in Warsaw! We're sitting here at the airfield waiting for another go. Some more fun, somewhere else."

ALMUTH: We'll never have any more fun, ever again. Nothing but a deathly hush. No more ceremonies in the School Hall; not even a special announcement.

INKA: Frenchies are turning tail. Tommies are in a blue funk.

[ELSIE *comes in.*]

NOLLE: We're thrusting forward on every Front. All law-abiding citizens want it to come to an-end, says Konradi, but they're wrong there. "Poland is only the foundation stone, the first step. Whoever wants to create a new order must think in broader concepts. We will fashion a new order, otherwise . . . Europe slips back into the Middle Ages, fearsome prospect!"

[*Silence as this sinks in.*]

ALMUTH: Konradi . . . is one of the people who understands . . . who's in the know . . .

ELSIE: What's he supposed to know?

[METZENTHIN *comes in.*]

ALMUTH: Some things have got to be secret . . . Things most people will never know. Only a tiny minority are in the know. People who matter. Natural leaders. I don't think they're ever frightened.

NOLLE: Rubbish. That's not true. The Langemarck volunteers are a thing of the past: cheering mindlessly as they marched into the line of fire. Everyone's frightened.

ALMUTH: I am every morning, when I wake up and it hits me that I've got to die. But it's only a moment, and it soon passes.

NOLLE: That's no cause for shame. What is shameful, is not overcoming that fear, turning into a coward because you're frightened. Or a traitor. Thinking only of yourself, not of the greater whole. Konradi says he gets frightened too. He's shit scared before every jump. [*Reads from the letter.*] "Then, my friends, once you're marching in line, keeping step with all your old mates, and you feel you're a part of the greater whole, your pathetic little fright disappears. It's a mystic experience." [*He looks across at* METZENTHIN.] I'd love to know: what's your apprentice up to, Elsie?

ELSIE: What's he supposed to be up to?

NOLLE: He's got such a funny laugh . . .

ELSIE: He's short-sighted.

NOLLE: As if he's not all there up top. Haven't any of you noticed, he's got a funny laugh?

[*They all laugh.*]

NOLLE: What are you laughing about? This is no place for mockery. Either clear off or treat the flag with proper respect. Salute the flag, go on, give the flag a full salute, right now.

METZENTHIN: What would happen if I spat on it, eh? Will the cave collapse? Will I be struck by lightning? Will I have a "mystic experience," complete with claps of thunder?

[*He is about to spit. That second* NOLLE *pulls out his sheath-knife and cuts* METZENTHIN's *hand.* NOLLE *grabs the hand so that the blood drips onto the flag.*]

NOLLE: Now the flag's sanctified by blood. I know it's only wood, cloth and blood. But from now on, you worm, whenever you look at a flag something will snap inside you, instantly, like a reflex. That's the mystic experience you'll have, there and then.

[*Silence.*]

Why doesn't anyone give him a handkerchief? Can't you see he's bleeding?

ALMUTH: [*Giggles in embarrassment.*] He's still laughing, that funny laugh.

NOLLE: What? I can't see anything. What's he laughing for?

[*Suddenly they all stop laughing.*]

NOLLE: I can't see any suggestion of laughter.

[*He throws a handkerchief onto* METZENTHIN's *shoulder, who shrugs it off and goes out. As if to himself.*]

Feeling frightened isn't the problem. The problem is: being able to harden yourself. To stop your hands shaking. Being able to make enemies, like all great men . . . Laying your head at your adversary's feet. Like Genghis Khan. With a smile on his face he put men, women and children to death. For the good of the cause. A true leader is always a judge as well. That's how far we've got to go, I tell you. That's how far I'm going to go.

[*The girls blow out the candles, and they all leave the cave.* INKA *throws her spikes over her shoulder.*]

INKA: Now it's dark at last. I'm off.

ELSIE: But the sports ground is closed.

INKA: There's a hole in the fence near the Holtemme. I get in there. I like training at this time of day. And on my own. People always say you run faster against a pace-setter. The pace-setter eggs you on. But I'm fastest when I'm alone at night. When I can't feel anyone near me, when I can't feel anything, least of all myself. Suddenly, everyone's left behind; it's as if I'm making my final spurt and they're yelling: Inka! Inka! But I don't hear a thing . . . I'm just left there, nothing but yelling . . . It's fantastic . . . [*Matter-of-factly.*] If my mother comes looking for me, you don't know a thing.

[*She goes.* NOLLE *watches her go.*]

NOLLE: That girl's wonderful! [*He leaves.*]

ALMUTH: Nolle wants her as his girlfriend. Everybody wants her as a girlfriend. She looks too muscular to me, but she, she's one of the certain people . . . She knows the secret and . . . so does Nolle. But those in the know, Elsie, always keep to themselves! Him and her . . . [*Bursting into tears.*] He never looks at me!

ELSIE: Oh, don't cry, Almuth! [*Pause.*] You know what I think, Almuth? We mustn't lose heart. We must believe in ourselves. We can all become like them . . . natural leaders, if we believe in ourselves. We have to work at it. For instance, go down into the slums at night, into the street where women with red-lights live, with syphilis. Do you know what syphilis is? I'll tell you later. It's dangerous down there. They don't let strangers in on their patch. Or . . . go to the Mausoleum right now . . . It's scary there and stinks of rotting bodies. They've already found two women done in there. If we can manage that . . .

[ALMUTH *looks at* ELSIE *in horror.*]

ALMUTH: You really are . . . so childish still! These ideas of yours . . . crazy! It's ever so dark. I must go home.

[*She runs off as if she's being chased by the Devil.* ELSIE *stays for a moment, lost in thought. Then, looking all round her in fright, she sets off slowly towards the mausoleum. She picks up a stick from the ground, suddenly jumps at a bush and belabours it with the stick, then takes a step back, goes up to it again, and peers into it gingerly: in the moonlight we now see* LONA, *naked to the waist, lying with* ELSIE'S FATHER. LONA *sits up, catches sight of* ELSIE, *smiles, in complete silence.* FATHER *doesn't notice anything. After a while,* ELSIE *turns away and goes slowly back to the house through the darkness. Once more we can make out the soldiers singing in the distance: "early in the morning when the cocks crow." The lights change.*]

Scene 6

At the table. A champagne cork pops. FATHER, MOTHER, GENERAL *and* FRAU BELIUS *and* HEADMASTER RODEWALD *drinking spring punch. The children*—INKA, NOLLE, ELSIE—*in the background, also with glasses.* ELSIE *fills a glass.*

FRAU BELIUS: I grant you the German army has lost its style.

FATHER: It's their morality, I maintain. They kicked Blomberg out because of his tart, and poor old Herr von Fritsch . . .

RODEWALD: You like your drink, Woellmer, no one could call you a killjoy. "Morality"— that sounds a bit odd coming from you.

MOTHER: It's so humid today. It's only the first of May.

FRAU BELIUS: But this punch of yours is excellent. [*She drinks.*]

MOTHER: Thanks to your woodruff . . .

FATHER: They finished off General von Fritsch with their slanderous gossip. Now his gentlemanly colleagues say nothing, or so we're told, attend his State funeral and say nothing . . . they're little General von Brauchitsches!

RODEWALD: All these allegations, not one of them holds water or would stand up in court, but I have to listen. Wherever I am, with friends or at work, I'm obliged to listen: as a teacher I'm obliged to listen to all kinds of things, unbelievable things, just because I'm a Headmaster! If they ever look inside my head one fine day . . . I wish I'd never heard a word, Woellmer!

[NOLLE *tunes out* RODEWALD *by putting his hands over his ears. The other two laugh.*]

FATHER: I'm only saying "so we're told," "so they say" . . .

RODEWALD: They say too much then!

MOTHER: That's what I always say!

FATHER: I only offer this as a topic for discussion: the way they chase after rank and medals in the German army . . . take the uniforms of the brigadier of the rifle corps, are they immoral or just lacking style?

RODEWALD: Everybody keeps finding fault, carping about something, and the top brass more than anyone—that's all we're good for.

FATHER: Doesn't that count, may I ask? A hard objective look at oneself? Honesty: that's our greatest virtue. Shouldn't we protect it?

RODEWALD: I ask you, do we have the right to carp, we of all people, whose heads are crammed so full we've no room left for thought?

MOTHER: [*Quickly to* FRAU BELIUS.] Do tell me, where do you find your woodruff?

FRAU BELIUS: We'd have brought you nothing but nettles, if Abromeit's buddy hadn't lent us a hand.

MOTHER: [*Raising her glass.*] Here's to Abromeit's buddy!

[*No one joins in her toast. The children come nearer, listening.*]

RODEWALD: For example, take me as an example, I'm not exceptional in any way, I'll be honest, without sparing anyone: I'm a very popular Headmaster, Fritz the Little they call me, I know their name for me, I've nothing against it, nicknames denote popularity. To a certain extent in certain respects, I live up to my name: I too am enlightened, love music, like to believe I have good taste, live a bachelor life with only my son for company, have a discriminating mind and gout. By the way—does anyone know why he has gout? That visible expression of his turmoil? It's really fascinating . . . Yes, I too, as you can see [*He shows his deformed hands.*] fight my baser instincts, I fulfil my duty and more, but even all this is not enough . . .

FATHER: What do you want to do, Herr Rodewald?

RODEWALD: I wear this badge on my lapel and say nothing, every Monday morning I raise the flag to the national anthem, give the German salute and say nothing, I see this and it doesn't agree with me, I bite my tongue and say nothing, but it's clear to me, it isn't enough.

FATHER: But surely there are some things, Herr Rodewald, to do with education and up-bringing, an attitude to life . . . you can't just turn your back on.

RODEWALD: There's a kind of energy, my dear chap, suddenly, after long years of hardship, economic incompetence, after years of national humiliation, an unprecedented popular movement, which we ought to support . . . I don't mind admitting that I admire this energy, that I'm struggling to get over my scepticism, just as *he* got over his friend Katte, my innermost feelings, [*In desperation.*] believe you me, ladies and gentlemen, this damnable obsession with style, Herr Woellmer, we're too bloody spineless!

FATHER: But, you must grant this, Rodewald, their trousers look dreadful. I'd have joined the mounted SA long ago, if I hadn't had to wear those trousers!

[*They burst out laughing.*]

RODEWALD: [*Starting to go.*] It's a waste of time arguing with aesthetes.

FATHER: Well, let's have another drink. The punch is superb. We put a '35 into it. You should only use the very best vintages . . .

RODEWALD: I won't listen to another word. I'm a Government employee.

FRAU BELIUS: [*Holding him back.*] You're only here as a friend, Herr Direktor. [*To* WOELLMER.] And as for you, you old defeatist, count yourself lucky we're all of the same mind here. I give you my word, we'll soon find our morality again once we've won the war, [*Simultaneously to her husband, and* WOELLMER.] and when we move West next week I bet the two of you will see Paris sooner than you think . . . Abromeit's buddy will take snaps of Compiègne for you, and what resounds to the world from there won't have the ring of style or morality.

RODEWALD: But it will have the ring of impact and power!

FRAU BELIUS: And we'll meet again when the wild strawberries are ripe.

MOTHER: What's our General's assessment of the situation?

FRAU BELIUS: My Heinrich says nothing, like Moltke before a battle, but here [*Pointing to her head.*] ideas bubble day and night, he thinks while I sleep, and believe me, the four children and I sleep like logs, my Inka, Carl-Eberhard and the two little ones, we sleep the sleep of the just . . . oh, I'm chattering again, chattering far too much, the words just tumble out. It's because I come from the Baltic, socially I'm the cannon and he [*Pointing to the* GENERAL.] rams home the shot! [*She catches sight of* NOLLE, ELSIE *and* INKA.] Pater peccavi, your son, Herr Rodewald, my Inka, Elsie . . . [*Quickly beginning to sing.*]

Marlborough, s'en va-t-en guerre,
Mironton, mironton,
Mirontaine . . .

Sing with me, children.

[*The children say nothing.*]

MOTHER: Come on Elsie, join in!

RODEWALD: [*To* NOLLE.] Go on, my boy, you've learned a lot of French . . .

[FRAU BELIUS *starts singing the Marlborough song again. All the adults join in. The children say nothing, and slink off in embarrassment.*]

FRAU BELIUS: What kind of children won't sing, refuse to join in . . . What's it all about . . .

[*The lights change.*]

Scene 7

By the stove. LONA *polishing the metal parts.* OSWIN *attempts to approach her.* ELSIE *comes in slowly.*

OSWIN: When you're not so busy, Fräulein Lona, sometime when you're not rushed off your feet, I'd be happy to walk round the Mausoleum with you.

[LONA *slaps him on the hand.*]

ELSIE: Who's going off to war, Lona?

LONA: Your father, Elsie.

[ELSIE *looks in disbelief.*]

OSWIN: Herr Pharmazist is off to the Siegfried Line. Any minute now. First Class. People have seen Herr Pharmazist going for frequent walks lately. Particularly in the vicinity of the District Military HQ.

LONA: Herr Woellmer is unwell, and needs plenty of fresh air.

OSWIN: He's often been sighted calling on the Major. He hands out the tickets to the Front. Herr Pharmazist is longing to see Paris.

ELSIE: He's indispensable, because he's in charge of medical supplies, so he can't be called up, Mother says.

OSWIN: When the war's over and he's sitting behind his carved desk again . . . "Those were the best years of my life," he'll say one day in the future.

LONA: You're going round and round in circles, I've got a headache.

ELSIE: What a whopper, she's never had a headache in her life.

OSWIN: [*As he goes out, to* ELSIE.] There you are, little Fräulein, you see how suddenly things change. Lie down, Fräulein Lona, and think comforting thoughts. You shouldn't treat a bad head as if it's a joke. [*He goes out. Silence.*]

ELSIE: Lona, can you imagine anyone enlisting, when he doesn't want to, for a cause . . . he doesn't hold with, volunteering, Lona, he doesn't have to . . . can you grasp that, Lona?

LONA: Well perhaps, Elsie.

ELSIE: Has father told you about it?

LONA: I'd never dare talk about it. It would be too intimate. Anyway it wouldn't be fair to your mother.

ELSIE: But even so you do know, Lona?

LONA: Well, I know what's going on here.

[*Pause.*]

ELSIE: I know about it too.

[*The lights change.*]

Scene 8

In the pharmacy. ELSIE *squatting on the floor, staring into space.* FATHER, *wearing a major's uniform, comes in.*

ELSIE: Isn't Mother going to the station with you?

FATHER: She's upstairs dolling herself up to go out.

ELSIE: [*Laughs.*] It's pitch dark already. [*Pause.*] I like walking through the town in the dark.

FATHER: [*Stroking her.*] Me too. You're a chip off the old block.

ELSIE: You look so handsome. And completely recovered. You ought to wear your uniform later on . . . when the war's over.

FATHER: Don't let's talk about that now. [*He gives* ELSIE *his wristwatch.*] Will you keep this watch for me?

ELSIE: Your gold one . . . ? [*Pause.*] Won't you be needing it?

FATHER: I've got another one. It's just as good.

ELSIE: I'll keep it for you till you come back.

FATHER: You must look after it for ever. [*Pause.* ELSIE *stares intently at him.*]

ELSIE: Can I . . . put it on?

FATHER: Yes. But don't let your mother see . . .

ELSIE: It would frighten her . . . [FATHER *smiles.* ELSIE *smiles.*] I'll go straight to Lona's room and put the light on and wave from there.

FATHER: It shines a long way. All the way down Seydlitz Street.

ELSIE: Today you look so . . . happy.

FATHER: Yes, because I'll be able to see you the whole length of the street.

[*For a moment they stand very close together. The lights change.*]

Scene 9

Towards evening, ELSIE *sitting, shivering with cold, by the fountain.* DEATH'S-HEAD *comes across the square. A lance-corporal with a tank regiment, his face is deeply scarred and badly disfigured by gunpowder. He is a terrifying sight. He stops in front of* ELSIE.

DEATH'S-HEAD: You live round here, I assume?

[ELSIE *nods.*]

DEATH'S-HEAD: I'm looking for someone. She's called Elsa Woellmer. She writes to me, she lives above the chemist's shop.

[ELSIE *stares at him and says nothing.*]

DEATH'S-HEAD: Would you go and fetch her for me?

[ELSIE *says nothing.*]

DEATH'S-HEAD: You can tell her her boyfriend's here. She's bound to come then.

[ELSIE *says nothing.*]

DEATH'S-HEAD: She'll come running with her hair streaming. [*Pause.*] My little stranger. Devil only knows how she got hold of my forces postal number. For the last six months we've been writing to each other every other day. [*He takes a bundle of letters out of his pocket.*] Here they are. [*He laughs.*] We're already quite intimate.

[ELSIE *says nothing.*]

DEATH'S-HEAD: I'm surprised she's not at her window. [*Pause.*] She wrote: I'll be waiting for you every evening this week. [*Pause.*] She's not there. [*Pause.*] If she's not there, something must have happened.

[ELSIE *shakes her head.*]

DEATH'S-HEAD: That means she can't come.

[ELSIE *shakes her head.*]

DEATH'S-HEAD: [*Crossly.*] Can't she, I'm asking you, or . . . won't she?

[ELSIE *shakes her head.* DEATH'S-HEAD *grabs her roughly by the shoulders.*]

DEATH'S-HEAD: Can't you talk? Say something! What you doing here? Someone posted you here? Like a sentry? Is it for your sister? Was she at her window, then saw me? What did she say? Was she all excited? Has she done herself up, lips, hair, eyebrows . . . is she all hot and bothered, or [*Pause.*] suddenly shivery, up there by her window, did she say: someone's coming across the square, stand outside the house and keep him away from me . . . [*Pause.*] Keep that Death's-Head well away from me!

[ELSIE *shakes her head.* DEATH'S-HEAD *in a fury.*]

DEATH'S-HEAD: You might say something! Was one look enough for her, at this bloke who'd risked his life for her . . . Because his face has been burnt, the poor sod can freeze to death outside her window . . .

[ELSIE *reaches for the soldier's hand and pulls him along with her; the next minute, they are both in the pharmacy. Leans against a carboy, tired.*]

DEATH'S-HEAD: Tell me the truth. [*Silence. He throws the bundle of letters onto the table.*] There you see, child, a little bundle, a destiny. I've dragged it around with me in my combat-pack. In the tank, in the turret, it was with me at Cambrai, at the battle of Montcornet. You don't understand yet. You're still too innocent for such a story! But I'll tell you anyway: As I said, at Cambrai. We were the spearhead for days on end. Reinforcements somewhere to our rear. During a lull in the fighting, I sit and write. By the side of the road I write. At night, on my knees. What do I get in return? Stupid stories. She writes to me about her aunt, an aunt with supernatural powers! About a subterranean cave! I want to give her the push. But destiny steps in. I get a face full of explosive.

I am done for. We own a men's outfitters. How do you serve clients without a face? I know I can't expect anything more from life. But then, child, it happens. She changes in a flash. Suddenly she can write letters. At death's door, she gives me courage. She says she loves me even without a face. Why does anyone need a face, she asks. There are so many jobs you can do in the dark. Photography, for instance, or conducting. In the orchestra-pit, she says, it's always dark. And I'm very talented . . . she can tell from my hand-writing, she says. Between you and me, little Fräulein, I'm not at all musical . . . But if she thinks I am, [*Laughing.*] . . . People can overcome all kinds of limitations. If she believes in my potential . . . [*Pause.*] You see, that's love . . . [*Pause.*]

I can say all this to you . . . speak to you almost like a father . . . because I'm experienced . . . I'm already twenty. [*He puts a hand over his eyes. Silence.*]

ELSIE: I wrote the letters, Hans.

DEATH'S-HEAD: [*Laughing.*] Come off it! You haven't got to carry the can for her. [*Crossly.*] I can't take any more. I can't take a joke any more . . . since my . . . accident. I'm not to be provoked . . . [*Suddenly pushing pen and paper into ELSIE's hand.*] Here! Start writing! I want to see your handwriting!

[*In a beautiful hand,* ELSIE *writes her name on the paper.* DEATH'S-HEAD *bursts out laughing.*]

DEATH'S-HEAD: What's this? Pulse racing? Like just now, out there . . . like every time . . . So you . . . really? Where did you pick it up? From Daddy's bookcase? Copied it straight from the poet? I've been writing to a child, almost a hundred times . . . wasting my nights, throwing away my feelings . . . on a kid! [*Laughing frenziedly. He suddenly stops and listens.*] She is here somewhere, isn't she? In her room? In her bed? She's got long blonde hair, hasn't she? She's already a full-grown woman. Only twenty-one, she says, but mature for her age. She's seen life. She's been through a lot. If it wasn't for her, I wouldn't be here now. She knows it all . . . [*He is suddenly struck by a ghastly suspicion.*] Tell me! What does she know? Who else has she been writing to? And how many have written back? Has she already been intimate with them all? Are there pictures over her bed? Has someone else come on leave? An officer, perhaps? Fat, well-fed? With a complete face? Has he been decorated for a battle wound? The Narvik clàsp? The close combat medal? Iron Cross, First Class? Is he [*Pointing upwards.*] there in her room, right now? [*He is seized by a mad fit of rage.*] Whatever you are, whore or child! [*He pulls her round to face him.*] No-one gets away from me scot-free! The Fatherland can't do this to us! I know my rights! [*He tries to rape* ELSIE, *then puts his hands round her throat and squeezes.*] Oh, oh, you half-starved cat, you're only fit to strangle, that's all you're good for, agh, that's . . . good, it's . . . [*He suddenly slides off* ELSIE, *who is lying motionless on the floor. Then gently takes her in his arms, and murmurs to her, half-asleep.*] My God, little Moggy. It's cold. Snuggle up so your warmth comes through. My first night of love in the Fatherland . . . If only I wasn't so tired, forty hours from down there to here . . . [*Sings.*] "For a single night of total bliss . . . " [*He tries to get up, but falls back.*] Give me a few minutes. [*Kissing* ELSIE's *hand and mumbling.*] Pay my respects to your Daddy and Mummy, give them my regards, off again in the morning, back home . . . Who knows, somewhere or other I might [*Pause.*] even I might . . . still find happiness . . . [*Falling asleep.*]

Scene 10

In the pharmacy. ELSIE *comes to, gets up in a dazed state.* LONA *appears and at first does not notice the soldier.*

LONA: Elsie! Where are you? We're on our own. They've gone out to the theatre . . . your mother, Fräulein Tilda. To the operetta. [*She sings.*] "My Lord Marquis . . ." You should go up to bed, Elsie. [*She notices the soldier.*] Oh, my God, Elsie.

[ELSIE *flings herself into* LONA's *arms and sobs.* LONA, *understanding what has happened, smooths* ELSIE's *clothes down, then strokes her hair and neck.*]

ELSIE: But I wasn't at all frightened, Lona. Well, hardly, Lona. And I never will . . .

[*Putting her head on* LONA's *shoulder. A long silence.* LONA *starts carefully observing the soldier in his sleep.* ELSIE *looks up.* LONA *points to his face.*]

LONA: There!

ELSIE: I know.

[*Silence.*]

LONA: As if he's laughing.

ELSIE: But he can't laugh any more, because of the scars.

LONA: I don't know.

ELSIE: It might be the pain.

LONA: Horrible!

ELSIE: As if he's already dead and buried.

[*Silence.*]

LONA: But now . . .

ELSIE: Now it looks different . . .

LONA: Getting calmer.

ELSIE: Like a thing . . . it's getting, a piece of wood or something.

LONA: Or a stone.

ELSIE: Funny. Now it doesn't look so awful. Now he hasn't got a care in the world. Lona, have you ever seen one with . . . such an expression?

[LONA *smiles.*]

LONA: Well, sometimes. [*Pause.*] Once in a while. [*She covers the soldier with his overcoat.*] He must have been really good-looking before.

[*The lights change.*]

Scene 11

The cathedral square. METZENTHIN *sitting on the base of Roland's statue. Early morning. The sun shining. He's playing "My Bonnie Lies Over the Ocean" on his mouth-organ, jazzing it up, which is against the law.* NOLLE *comes in wearing a uniform, carrying a collecting-box.*

NOLLE: What are you playing it like that for?

[METZENTHIN *goes on playing.*]

NOLLE: You learned that from your Mammy, I suppose? Sounds a bit odd, my dear MET-ZENTHIN. Got a really exotic beat to it. Where did you pick it up? You didn't make it up yourself? Heard it on certain broadcasts? Or was your Mummy a nigger?

[METZENTHIN *goes on playing.*]

NOLLE: You should join a military band. At least you'd be doing something useful. And you'd keep in time.

METZENTHIN: [*Stops abruptly.*] I'm doing something more useful than you all put together, working all hours in the dispensary, because our chemical industry is making nothing but gunpowder nowadays.

NOLLE: You work only to please yourself, always alone, without anyone else setting the standard. In a military band you'd know who you were playing for.

METZENTHIN: If you were crippled with colic and crying out for some of my powders, you wouldn't give a damn who set my standards; you'd be grateful to me, solitary or no.

NOLLE: It's a disgrace. I think the world of you. You're not what the others make you out to be.

METZENTHIN: [*Disturbed.*] What do the others make me out to be?

[NOLLE's *silence speaks volumes.* INKA *and* ALMUTH *arrive with collecting-boxes and tins decorated with brightly coloured butterflies, which they are trying to sell.*]

INKA: Badges! Badges! Buy one of my badges!

ALMUTH: [*Rattles her collecting-box.*] Hand over your Groschen!

INKA: Nobody gets past me without paying!

NOLLE: Do you believe in vibrations? [*He grabs* METZENTHIN *by the wrist.*] There's no mis-
taking it. You're no Commie, even though you come from the slums, and you're not a
Jew, I can tell at a glance. But your ideas are all askew, I know that for a fact. They're totally illogical. You're still having an inner struggle. [*Pause.*] Whatever they say in the
town, I have a high opinion of you. Get that into your thick head, pillroller.
METZENTHIN: Sometimes, on mornings like this, everything seems to fall into place; it
seems to me there's a climate of common sense seeping into everything. And I imagine
it ought to have some effect on people, [*Pause.*] so that *this* could work its way into people's minds, and then, I have the feeling . . .
ALMUTH: Oh, I agree, I agree . . .
INKA: When the morning sun shines on the cinder-track, and it smells so . . .
METZENTHIN: Then I'd like to believe everyone quite spontaneously . . . would start
being sensible, in what we might call an ideal way . . . like this house [*He points at the
pharmacy.*] This house is my ideal of beauty—so why be uncertain: can I possibly be the
last person, the only person . . . ? Then I think I want to have my own opinion about
the world, like everyone else, so that I have the courage of my convictions.

[*They say nothing, just listen. For a few moments the sun is so intensely brilliant that you could
almost pass out. Suddenly laughter, which is unnerving, because we can't tell whether it's a
scream or not.*]

NOLLE: Someone's gone crazy.
METZENTHIN: [*Jumps up and runs to the front door, listening.*] Elsie!
INKA: Something must have happened!
METZENTHIN: I had a premonition. We forgot to touch wood.
ALMUTH: It's always the same. Always, whenever I'm really happy, something happens.

[LONA *comes out of the house carrying milk-bottles.*]

METZENTHIN: [*To* LONA.] What's happened?
LONA: What do you mean, what's happened?
ALMUTH: Was it Elsie laughing?
INKA: Or screaming?
LONA: Oh, that. That's nothing to worry about. She got over-excited. She was just having a
dream.
INKA: What about?
LONA: She's always having dreams like that.
INKA: Tell us about them.
ALMUTH: [*Precociously.*] Dreams always have an inner truth.
LONA: The other night she dreamed she was starving. She got up and made for the larder.
There were three mothers blocking her way. They looked like her mother, her aunt, and
Inka's mother. But all much bigger. Pitch black clothes. They kept the door closed. Elsie
took a run at it to break it open. But an invisible force held her back. She tried to scream
but couldn't. Then she heard a voice saying: "That's not my daughter." Then she
screamed too. Even worse than today.
NOLLE: It sounds treacherous . . . a dream like that.
ALMUTH: It's all psychological.
NOLLE: It shows what enemy propaganda can do.
ALMUTH: Through the subconscious.
NOLLE: But everything's still available. More than enough.
LONA: Oh yes. You can still get milk, but it is skimmed.
MOTHER: [*Appearing with* ELSIE *at the window. Calls down to* LONA.] Are you going for the
post?
ELSIE: [*Calling out to her friends.*] You go on ahead. I'll come later. I'll soon catch you up.

MOTHER: Dreams, Elsie, it's because they're illogical, isn't it . . . what we can't make out frightens us. In the light of day it is all different: we can work out cause and effect . . . Look, the sun's out. It's going to be a lovely day. So drink your tea.

OSWIN: [*Rushes in.*] Paris has fallen! Quick! Turn the radio on!

[*Loud fanfares, signalling an announcement.*]

OSWIN: Listen, everybody! They've been announcing it all morning. Paris has been liberated. Without any resistance. Without a shot being fired. German soldiers are marching in. Paris: the Eiffel Tower, the Pantheon, the Folies Bergères!

[*Clicking his tongue.* INKA, ALMUTH, NOLLE *and a* PASSER-BY *throw their arms around each other and dance in the street.*]

OSWIN: Another example of German precision at work!

MOTHER: [*To* LONA.] So where is the post?

LONA: It still hasn't come.

MOTHER: Oh, I see, that explains it. All the trains are heading West, everything is going towards Paris, so how could any post come from there? Thank heavens, Elsie, it's almost over. We've won! Any moment now he'll be outside the door, we can't be sure when; it could be next week, or tomorrow, or . . . even today . . . Lona, we must get some flowers!

METZENTHIN: I'd hold on . . . just in case, if I was you . . . so you don't waste any money.

MOTHER: [*To* OSWIN.] He always has to have the last word! Even if something's as obvious as two times two equals four, he has to argue the toss! It's a nasty habit, I think.

OSWIN: It's about time the war was over. What's left in the Fatherland is only the rubbish. If it wasn't for this . . . [*Pointing to his shorter leg.*] I still can't take it in, we're in Paris! Today in Paris and tomorrow, who knows!

[*We now hear the England song on the radio: "Give me your hand, your white hand, farewell my sweetheart" etc.*]

Scene 12

INKA, ELSIE, ALMUTH *at the sewing machine with* TILDA, *who is swinging a pearl necklace over a photograph.*

ALMUTH: If it goes round and round, he's still alive.

INKA: But if it just goes to and fro, he isn't.

ELSIE: Has it always told the truth, Aunty Tilda?

TILDA: Every time. Everything has always come true. Once with our mother, your grandmother, Elsie, and then with little Charlotte, your first cousin, who died, and with lots and lots of others.

ELSIE: It's going round! It's going round!

ALMUTH: Thank God, it's going round!

TILDA: *So far* it's going round.

ALMUTH: I'll come back every week.

TILDA: Poor child. Are you sure your parents . . . approve?

ALMUTH: Why my parents?

TILDA: I mean, does he often come to your parents' house?

INKA: But she's never even met him!

TILDA: I don't understand.

ELSIE: She took him out of an illustrated magazine. He's got the Knight's Cross. She cut him out. Practically everyone in the class has got one.

INKA: But Almuth's is the most famous!

TILDA: [*Pushing aside the picture that* ALMUTH *gave her.*] I don't like all this. All these fantasies. And to cap it all, a complete stranger. In the last War when I was engaged—I refused to allow myself any fancy ideas. And a good thing, a good thing too! Then he was killed in action, Herr Doktor Struck, my fiancé—so I wasn't to blame.

INKA: I don't think there's any harm in it.

TILDA: It'll burn you, my darling, every unfulfilled desire, every dream you suppress, will burn you like fire.

ELSIE: People can tolerate so much.

TILDA: Nobody can tolerate everything. People numb themselves: swapping old pain for a new fancy idea, an even crazier image, and so on ad infinitum.

ELSIE: Like in films!

TILDA: Yes, that's right! Inside us there's a film running, getting more intense, wilder all the time . . . A dream no-one must know about. But dreams we repress . . . become night . . . [*Quietly.*] nightmares, yes. I've seen it all. People maintain I know nothing about life, they're wrong there. I know far more. More than my sister, Therese, more than any married couple . . . and everyone else out there, Elsie. I see them growing insatiable; I tell you, people are never satisfied. I know life . . . yes, and love, I know love too.

ELSIE: But how . . . Aunty Tilda?

TILDA: I think about things.

ELSIE: So you do have fancy ideas too?

TILDA: Yes, that's right. But based on scientific theories, that's what makes them different from these orgies of self-indulgence. So stop going on about these soldiers of yours.

ELSIE: [*Pushing* ALMUTH *and* INKA *aside.*] Stop going on about soldiers, only relatives from now on. [*Giving* TILDA *a photo.*]

TILDA: [*Thrilled.*] Oh, it's . . . yes, Ludwig, a very good likeness, your father! [*She starts swinging the necklace.*] It must have been taken that first Easter at Aunt Aldi's . . .

ELSIE: [*Warning her.*] Aunty Tilda!

TILDA: The time he made a snowman in the garden. Oh, Elsie, he's got such a wonderful smile!

ELSIE: Aunty Tilda, it's not going round!

TILDA: What? [*She stops swinging the necklace.*] What a poor photograph, so out of focus! You can hardly make him out.

ALMUTH: But my Captain was even more blurred . . .

[*Silence.*]

TILDA: Take a closer look. Can't you see it's going round? Father's alive. He's on his way home. [*She stops, taking* ELSIE's *hand, she swings the necklace over it.*] And now let's ask how many children you're going to have!

[*The lights change.*]

Scene 13

Open country in front of the mausoleum. ELSIE, INKA, *and* ALMUTH *pulling up turnips.* INKA *is a long way ahead of the other two.*

ALMUTH: [*Straightening up.*] Isn't it lunchtime yet?

ELSIE: We've got to finish this row. Inka's already done hers.

ALMUTH: She cheats. She just yanks the whole lot out. That's not the right way. The strongest plants have to stay. I can never make up my mind which should stay, that's why I'm behind. And my knees hurt. Don't yours hurt, Elsie?

[ELSIE *shows her knees.*]

ALMUTH: Oh no, you've gone right through them! I'm dying of thirst. [*She calls out.*] Hang on!

[*They all straighten up.*]

ELSIE: Suppose the siren goes.

INKA: It wouldn't worry us.

ALMUTH: They don't throw their bombs away on open country.

ELSIE: In Karlsruhe they've had lots of fun. Friends of Aunty Tilda's have been bombed out, their next-door neighbors buried alive, and their youngest son burnt to death on the street. All they found was a skeleton, tiny and black.

ALMUTH: But some they dug out of the cellars looked as if they were still alive. As if they were sleeping.

INKA: They'd just suffocated.

ELSIE: From the carbon monoxide.

ALMUTH: [*Quietly.*] Elsie, do you believe in Providence, as they're always telling us? Not God, Providence? Do you believe . . . Elsie?

ELSIE: Sometimes I do, sometimes I don't.

ALMUTH: They won't spot us here. [*Looking in fright up at the sky.*]

ELSIE: Unless they're flying very low.

INKA: If you lie flat in a furrow they'd only get you with a direct hit.

[INKA *and* ELSIE *lie flat among the turnips.* ALMUTH *has a drink. A Polish prisoner-of-war, with the letter "P" on his jacket, appears without a sound.* ALMUTH *shudders.*]

ALMUTH: God, I nearly jumped out of my skin. Come over here, so we're together! The way he stares.

[*Silence. The Pole and the girls stare at each other.*]

ALMUTH: Dangerous!

ELSIE: He might just be hungry.

[INKA *takes some bread out of her bread-bag, and hands it to* ELSIE.]

INKA: Here! Throw it to him. There's dripping on it. It makes me feel sick.

ELSIE: [*Holds the bread out to the Pole.*] He won't take it.

INKA: They stuff everything.

ALMUTH: And you mustn't talk to them. It's against the law.

ELSIE: I haven't said a thing.

ALMUTH: But you're giving him something. That's far worse. He really does look subhuman.

ELSIE: [*Tempting him as if he's a dog.*] Come on, Fido, come on!

ALMUTH: Stop that, Elsie, you mustn't have anything to do with them!

ELSIE: [*Going up to the Pole, who doesn't move, just stares at the bread.*] Tt-tt-tt, you're nothing but a poor dog. It's not illegal with dogs. He looks starving.

[INKA *suddenly snatches the bread and throws it away.*]

ALMUTH: What are you doing now?

INKA: I'm throwing it in the stream.

ALMUTH: It's all beyond me! Why didn't you throw it somewhere where he could find it later. Now he'll fly into a rage—and we're all alone here. If he murders us, no-one would see.

[*The Pole walks away, smiling at* INKA.]

ALMUTH: Now he's grinning at us. [*To* INKA.] How can he smile when you've behaved like that? Perfectly good bread! No, it's beyond me!

INKA: Who knows what he needs? Do you know, Elsie?

[*She pushes* ELSIE *over, who falls, taking* INKA *with her. They roll about on the ground together in high spirits.*]

INKA: Some know things, others don't! Eh, Elsielein, the two of us know everything! [*She gets up suddenly. After a pause.*] Saint Peter, I'd rather have a direct hit right now . . . here . . . in the open field, than just rot away back home at school!

[*End of Part One.*]

PART TWO
IN THE THICK OF IT

Scene 1

We see simultaneously TILDA *with* FRAU BELIUS *at the sewing-machine, and* LONA *with* AL-MUTH *at the stove.* ELSIE *looks more grown-up, but is back again in her favourite place, sitting on the floor between the two acting areas.*

FRAU BELIUS: [*To* TILDA, *who is working on a black veiled hat.*] You can turn your hand to absolutely anything, Fräulein Tilda! A really wonderful hat!

TILDA: What should we do with the voile? Have it draped or leave it in front of the face as a veil?

[*She tries it on* FRAU BELIUS *to see which looks better.*]

FRAU BELIUS: [*Behind the veil.*] This might look elegant. But they're only worn like this for one's husband, I think.

TILDA: Oh yes, forgive me, it's only your son.

FRAU BELIUS: Only my son, Fräulein Tilda, it's so easy to say it. Count yourself lucky you have no children. [*She gives her attention to the hat once more.*] You're right, of course! It might look a bit . . . de trop. As if one was distancing oneself from events. Quite inappropriate.

TILDA: We could twist it into a garland. What do you think of this? Or how about little tufts on either side?

FRAU BELIUS: Let's keep it plain and simple, Tilda. We're living in hard times. But no-one can afford to be distant. We've all just got to put a brave face on things until we're victorious. So let's settle for no veil, just tufts. Though it would look more becoming.

ALMUTH: [*To* LONA *who is making her up.*] Make my mouth a bit bigger, Lona, so it looks rounded. I want to look different for once.

LONA: But it would completely change your expression. It won't look natural if I round it out too much,

ALMUTH: Oh go on . . . make it as round as you can.

LONA: With such white powder, you'll look like a vamp.

ALMUTH: That's the whole idea! I'm sick of going round, so . . . so tired of the same old face, every day, always looking just like me . . . !

LONA: Who else could you look like?

ALMUTH: Like . . . the kind of woman a man might dream about, in the street, at night, in the underground shelter, somehow . . . more demonic . . . You must know what men like, Lona. [*Pause.*] Soldiers . . . it's not as if you don't know what they like.

LONA: Some one thing, some another. No-one could say you're ugly, Almuth. I really don't understand . . .

ALMUTH: When I meet him at the station tonight, when he looks at me for the last time . . . he's got to be . . . astounded, Lona, is that Oswin's daughter, he's got to ask, is that really Almuth, or . . . That's how he will remember me.

LONA: If only we could wave a magic wand.

FRAU BELIUS: These tufts at the side aren't bad. [*She finally lights the cigarette she's had to do without while trying on the hat.*] Yes, Fräulein Tilda, as I've always said, we have to pay the price and . . . say nothing. At night, when I can't sleep, I tell myself: You're so fortunate in still having three children! But the firstborn, Tilda, you don't know . . . can't possibly know what it means! The others, obviously, get their share of love too, one looked forward to having them, but when all's said and done, they just tumbled into the world, they just happened to one by accident, one only planned the firstborn, even before he came into the world . . . [*Pause.*] What are we going to do with this? [*She points to the décolletage of her black dress.*] Looks a little exposed, doesn't it? What was I trying to say . . . yes, the firstborn, is the very incarnation of one's thoughts.

LONA: Like it?

ALMUTH: How do I know what's good or bad! But you know. You're meant to be on more intimate terms with practically everyone in the town. It's quite natural, in a way, but a bit unusual. What is it about you? How do you do it?

LONA: Some of it's to do with my personality.

ALMUTH: Don't make me laugh!

FRAY BELIUS: [*Taking her Mutterkreuz out of her handbag, holding it up to her décolletage.* TILDA *with a hand-mirror in front of her.*] What do you think of this? I've never worn it, between you and me, it's so vulgar, but here with this dress, in my situation? [*To* ELSIE.] How do you like it with the Mùtterkreuz, Elsie?

ELSIE: Is Inka getting a new dress now as well?

FRAU BELIUS: [*Laughs.*] There you are, the children . . . are cheerful about it! So long ago Hölderlin knew it: children and old maids are, yes, that's it, immortal and always cheerful, Pater . . . Sorry! Of course Inka will have a new dress as well, one with a black-and-white pattern to wear on other occasions.

ALMUTH: [*Now also looking at herself in a hand-mirror.*] Call that done . . . is that all you're going to do?

LONA: [*Shrugs her shoulders.*] It looks fine to me.

ALMUTH: [*Holding the mirror at arm's length, she suddenly starts to wipe the make-up off her face, and screams.*] It's all pointless when you're ugly, and you're nothing else, with no personality or anything, no looks and don't come from "a good family" . . . I'm Oswin's daughter and nothing else . . . and today's the last day . . . [*She clings to* LONA.] Please help me, Lona, make him look at me, Nolle, when he leaves, please help me, help me . . .

[*She holds tightly on to* LONA, ELSIE, *who up to now had been fiddling with* FRAU BELIUS's *hat, and trying it on, runs across to* ALMUTH *and* LONA, *holding the veil, and stares at them both.*]

FRAU BELIUS: [*Calling after her.*] Elsie, for goodness sake! She's completely crumpled the veil.

[*The lights change.*]

Scene 2

At the mausoleum. KONRADI, *now a paratroop captain, on a bench.* ELSIE, METZENTHIN, ALMUTH *and* LONA *hiding behind a bush. Later,* INKA. *Martial music in the distance.*

ELSIE: He's sitting over there!

ALMUTH: But miles away.

ELSIE: As if he'd never come back home.

ALMUTH: He's still thinking about all *that*.

METZENTHIN: He's meant to have had malaria.

LONA: They say he leapt into the direct line of fire at Malame. My girlfriend knows someone that was there with him. Then he held the position for hours on end. He was the last survivor. It's a miracle he got out.

INKA: [*With a bunch of flowers.*] We've had a ride on a tank! The soldiers lifted us up! But I didn't throw my flowers, because Konradi wasn't in the parade.

LONA: Give them to him now.

INKA: I can't. [*To* ELSIE.] You go!

ELSIE: No, you!

LONA: It must look spontaneous.

INKA: I can't.

ELSIE: Lona, will you?

INKA: [*Standing there undecided, then suddenly.*] I'll go.

ELSIE: And I'll lie down in those bushes. [*To* ALMUTH *and* METZENTHIN *and* LONA.] You stay here. I'll soon let you know what I can hear.

[INKA *goes slowly forwards, with* ELSIE *behind her.*]

ALMUTH: [*Softly.*] She really is going.

ELSIE: [*Turning back to the others.*] He's noticed something now. She's stopped. He says she should come closer. [*Pause.*]

LONA: What's he saying?

ELSIE: Shh! I can't hear anything. He says . . . she should come, he says. But not from there. She should come from the other side. So he can see her against the sun. He says . . .

ALMUTH: What?

ELSIE: "You look as if you're radiating light, my girl," he says.

METZENTHIN: Bit odd, isn't it?

[ELSIE *hides near the bench.*]

LONA: Now she's sitting down next to him . . .

ALMUTH: They're talking . . .

LONA: They say, he never talks to anyone.

ALMUTH: None of them talk much, the ones who were in Crete.

LONA: But he, so my girl-friend says . . . he's meant to be really odd.

ALMUTH: But now . . . he's talking to Inka, can't you hear . . . ?

[ELSIE *comes running back, horrified.*]

ALMUTH: What's happened?

LONA: What's he saying?

ALMUTH: Why are you making such a face?

ELSIE: [*Repeating what we've just heard.*] "You look as if you're radiating light, my girl." [*Quickly, mechanically.*] Buddhists say: a human being is nothing but a bundle of light. Lovely idea—dissolving into light, when your time has come! Or exploding in mid-air . . ."

ALMUTH: What?

ELSIE: "If you'd been in Crete, my girl, you'd have seen people exploding in the skies. And flying corpses . . ."

ALMUTH: Stop, stop!

ELSIE: [*Quickly.*] "Flying corpses . . . that float down to earth, and split open. Lying there. Rotting. Turning into carrion . . ." [*She covers her ears.*]

LONA: [*Looking at* KONRADI *and* INKA.] He's stopped talking now.

ALMUTH: He's whispering.

LONA: He's covered his face with his hands . . . now! He's laying his head in my lap . . . Lord, what am I saying, I mean in Inka's lap.

ELSIE: He's swallowing in a funny way, as if he's crying.

ALMUTH: It can't be true!

METZENTHIN: Has he gone crazy?

ELSIE: Or maybe he's laughing. Now he's getting up. Shh! He's about to go.

[*They're all speechless.*]

ALMUTH: [*Calls out.*] Inka! Do wait, Inka! Why won't she talk to us?

LONA: Come on, leave her alone . . .

[*She goes with* ALMUTH. ELSIE *squats on the ground, staring after* KONRADI *and* INKA. METZENTHIN *crosses to her.*]

METZENTHIN: How can people say it was malaria? It's not malaria, Elsie . . .

ELSIE: Why is she following him, and why won't he look at her? He hasn't even turned round!

METZENTHIN: There must be something else wrong with him . . .

ELSIE: She's running after him . . . and he doesn't want her!

METZENTHIN: It's slowly dawning on me . . .

ELSIE: Lets him push her away . . . Metzenthin . . . look! . . . she's fallen over . . . she's got up again . . . and running after him . . . [*Indignantly.*] Metzenthin, hasn't she any pride?

METZENTHIN: [*Absent-mindedly.*] What did you say?

ELSIE: Do you really think he's gone crazy?

[*Metzenthin shakes his head.*]

ELSIE: But Inka . . . has she gone out of her mind, that she's so . . . I don't understand, Metzenthin, do you understand what it's all about?

METZENTHIN: [*Draws her closely to him.*] *This* is what it's all about, Elsie.

ELSIE: [*Still watching* KONRADI *and* INKA, *who are now walking side by side.*] Yes, but how can she . . . ?

METZENTHIN: [*Holds her tightly.* ELSIE *slowly forgets the other two and turns towards him.*] You're here . . .

[*They embrace. The lights change.*]

Scene 3

By the stove. LONA *is polishing the silver (!),* ELSIE *is lounging about.* MOTHER *comes in, carrying a dress.*

MOTHER: Lona, I came across this dress, as I was going through my wardrobe, something seems not quite right about it, the hem's come down, the sleeves are sweaty, and it's got a funny smell; how could it happen when it's been hanging in the wardrobe? Where were you last night, Lona, till the small hours; I heard the stairs creaking, even though you always come in in your stockinged feet, how was the dance? I don't begrudge anyone their bit of pleasure, I'm the last person to begrudge you anything, but now—now that there's no-one left in town but the decrepit and crippled, your boyfriend, Herbert Nickel, writes every week—he *still* writes, he's serving at Voronezh, laying his head on the line; to be perfectly frank, it's beyond me, I cannot understand what you can have been thinking of, my best dress—one of my best dresses—let's say: borrowing it . . . I'm saving it up to wear *after* the war, even if I don't give a hoot what I wear any more, even if my husband doesn't come back, but he *might* come back, some listed as missing have come back; I'm not harbouring any illusions, but I'm taking everything into account, people have to take account of all possibilities, and even the future, no-one knows what it holds. A hundred points on the clothing ration don't go far; these days you've got to have your wits about you, no-one can afford to dream any more, must think, Lona, think, just to survive. Common sense, that's what it's about, Lona . . . I would like an answer: what in Heaven's name were you thinking of?

LONA: I thought, no, I didn't think at all. Or rather . . . I've not thought about it till now . . .

MOTHER: [*Drops the dress into the dustbin.*] That's the end of that! [*She stalks out.*]

LONA: Yes, that's what I thought.

[ELSIE *rescues the dress from the dustbin, spreads it out on the floor and lovingly smooths it out. The lights change.*]

Scene 4

At the table. ELSIE *doing her homework, drawing bark from nature.* TILDA *is rummaging about in a small cupboard.*

ELSIE: [*Holding up her drawing.*] What do you think of this, Tilda?

TILDA: Since you ask, it should have more colour, yellow or red, so it's more eye-catching. It looks dull to me. But I don't know the first thing about it.

ELSIE: They're only nature studies. I feel like going out, to the square, for some fresh air.

TILDA: Whatever for? People never stop going out, going out; if your mother lets a day pass without going into town, she's in a bad mood, but nothing of any importance happens out there, all the important things happen at home. I know, I've always been at home, even as a young girl, I was always with my mother, and I was too serious. And after what happened to Doctor Struck . . .

ELSIE: Haven't you ever felt like going away?

TILDA: Shall I tell you a secret? What's meant to happen, will catch up with you wherever you are. It will even catch up with me. All we have to do is wait. I've been waiting for so many decades . . . it hasn't been so bad. After all, people have described it . . . the world, in pictures and books. [*As she searches in the little cupboard a bouquet of withered flowers falls out.*]

ELSIE: Withered and dried up, what a shame, Tilda!

TILDA: No, no, give them to me, my beautiful roses! I have to keep them safe forever. [*She gives* ELSIE *a quick look at a family tree.*] . . . For ever, you see, it's all laid out on the family-tree, what used to be, you don't have just an individual life, but lots; it all goes so far back, as they say; into the mists of time.

ELSIE: It looks good, just like a tree.

TILDA: Yes. Here are the roots, these are the ancestors we know about . . .

ELSIE: They've got lovely names: "Auf dem Westen," "Vom Goldenberg" . . .

TILDA: But here's the main branch; here's the first Woellmer we know about, in the time of Frederick the Second he moved East, and made a very good match: do you see: he married Petronella—a Polish countess [*Lowering her voice.*] with a dowry in money and enormous estates. Their son, a good-for-nothing gambler, lost the lot in a single night, playing cards, you can probably thank Slavic blood for that . . .

ELSIE: That was great-great-grandfather!

TILDA: [*Putting a finger on* ELSIE*'s mouth.*] We don't talk about him in this family. But his sons moved back West, and all made something of their lives! And so did their sons and grandsons; and ever since then we've gone from strength to strength, and this here, this little twig is you . . .

ELSIE: And you, Tilda?

TILDA: Oh . . . I'm a bit of dead wood. [*Wistful silence.*] Don't worry. So long as you continue the line, some time, my dear. Do you see, here's the space for your children.

ELSIE: But the name will die out with me.

TILDA: "Through our blood we are given eternal life," a professor wrote in *Das Reich* recently! If only I had children . . . One day you'll be more fortunate. You must just see to it that the man of your choice comes of good genetic stock, so nothing gets squandered . . . so to speak.

ELSIE: I'd love to know what Petronella looked like, or her son, the good-for-nothing.

TILDA: There are no pictures. They've got lost.

ELSIE: So if the family tree gets lost, everything will be forgotten, even the names.

[*A short pause.*]

TILDA: As if they'd never been.

ELSIE: Does it make you feel funny to think about it, too?

TILDA: It's not something to think about. [*Checks herself.*] And we shouldn't even try. We should let sleeping dogs lie! [*She gives* ELSIE *a quizzical look.*] Your're beginning to look a bit better since your mother's been keeping you at home. At least you've put on a bit of weight. Get on with it, and you'll soon be finished.

[*She goes out. At the same time* ELSIE *knocks on the floorboards three times with her pencil. Within seconds* METZENTHIN *appears.*]

ELSIE: Metzenthin, does this drawing look dull to you?

METZENTHIN: [*Sits down next to* ELSIE, *putting his arm round her shoulders. They look very intimate. He looks closely at the picture for some time.*] I've always thought you know something other people don't know. And always have. It's obvious. Give me the picture.

ELSIE: Who would want to hang bark up? [*Pause.*] Anyway, I've got to give it in to be marked.

METZENTHIN: I'll wait, then. [*He goes on standing by the table, indecisively pushing the bark to and fro.*] Why is this piece of bark riddled with holes?

ELSIE: [*Going on drawing.*] It's a feature.

METZENTHIN: And its edges burnt-looking? Where did you get it?

ELSIE: From Central Government. They're bullet holes, Konradi says. Poles are shot at night against the trees.

METZENTHIN: What Poles?

ELSIE: Konradi says: we should look very closely at the bark. To study its structure. He had it sent by some army mates. There are such lovely old trees in Poland. [*She stares fixedly at* METZENTHIN.]

METZENTHIN: As I've always suspected. It can't possibly be malaria. He's been shot in the head, Konradi.

ELSIE: [*Still staring at him.*] And he could supply the whole school. [*Pause.*] He's going to . . . show us some other things.

METZENTHIN: I'm prepared to believe a great deal. But these fairy stories . . . are just . . .

ELSIE: It's only a bit of bark, Metzenthin!

METZENTHIN: It would be . . . an outrage!

[*He examines the bark again. The lights change.*]

Scene 5

Outside the pharmacy. A winter morning. Headmaster RODEWALD *with a crutch and a three-pointed fur cap, near him a woman in a black veil.* ELSIE, *some way away, is crouching in front of the Roland statue, listening.*

RODEWALD: Your opinion is, I should make an exception? With the greatest respect, my dear madam, where would that lead me . . . I'd be obliged to make scores of exceptions, if I were to take everything into account, every decimated family, for instance, when there's scarcely a family that hasn't been decimated, the whole social order is in turmoil. Our sole criterion must continue to be performance . . . [*Prodding the snow with his stick, uncertainly.*] Though . . . people react to suffering in different ways, I do know, I do know . . . [*Pause.*] You tell me she's taken a turn for the worse recently, overeating, consuming colossal portions, at a time when everything has been cut back, the fat ration to 125 grams a week, here she is taking food out of other people's mouths, a little parasite, don't you think, a little leech on the nation. [*Shaking his head.*] Curious, such a phrase . . . how vital the language is, or rather: has once more become . . . A leech on the nation, is such a graphic phrase, it fascinates me as a philologist . . . "Fatherland awake!" they say, and we shouldn't sneer, because there's a kind of truth in that, for when language is awakened, language acts as a mirror of the nation's soul . . . Your respected husband, my dear . . . I held him in higher esteem than I can say, but did he not keep himself rather [*pause*] aloof, somewhat distanced from the universal upsurge . . . [*bowing*] though this in no way diminishes my compassion . . . I made my position clear to you at the time: we, who through our education and environment have become spineless, we must learn to be resolute again, not spineless, resolute . . . And I *shall* take resolute action, dear Frau Woellmer. I shall . . . [*In desperation.*] I *cannot* move your daughter up a class.

MOTHER: [*Suddenly whips the veil away from her face, aroused.*] My husband fell at Dijon, his identity disc wasn't found for eleven months, my eldest brother at Salonika, one cousin perished in the Atlantic . . .

RODEWALD: [*Taking her hand.*] Who could see less sense in it all than I do! My family has also had to pay the price, and a heavy one; if I were to list them all . . .

MOTHER: I haven't got round to all the others yet, second cousins, and an uncle . . . a grand total of six, Herr Rodewald, six men in the one family, Herr . . .

RODEWALD: It's . . . almost like an ancient Greek tragedy, a colossal, a fearful reckoning, in our family we can only claim [*He counts on his fingers.*] no, we can only claim four, but even that . . . a considerable sacrifice, though, naturally, without hesitation . . .

MOTHER: [*Beside herself.*] We have, in all truth, fertilized enemy lands, from Narvik to El Alamein, with our blood!

RODEWALD: You see, now you're employing the same imagery, the same graphic phrases . . . [*Kissing her hands, holding them till the end of the scene.*] I swore I'd never compromise again, but already, you see, my father always warned me: don't be so introspective, my boy, and here I am being introspective again, weighing things up, seeing both sides . . . [*Abruptly.*] Go home, the matter will be resolved. This is the last time, I'm afraid . . . that I swear to you!

Scene 6

MOTHER *in black,* TILDA, LONA, ELSIE, FRAU BELIUS *and* INKA *are sitting by the stove, shelling beechnuts.*

MOTHER: They give you a liter of oil now for two kilos of beechnuts, ready shelled.

FRAU BELIUS: Perhaps we should hand these over instead of making cakes with them.

MOTHER: A liter of oil is not to be sneezed at.

FRAU BELIUS: [*Smoking.*] But who's to say what it's made of? It might be castor oil or paraffin. If only they'd exchange them for cigarettes. Was that being seditious again? I didn't say a word.

ELSIE: I vote we bake a cake.

[*They all laugh.*]

FRAU BELIUS: What are you counting, Inka?

INKA: Six women. Soon there'll be only women left in the world.

ELSIE: But we'll survive!

[*They laugh.*]

LONA: We've survived this long.

FRAU BELIUS: Sometimes, I think, better than before. When we sit round the stove in the evening, the children and I . . .

LONA: If there was a knock right now and a man came in . . .

MOTHER: But none will!

FRAU BELIUS: Good thing too! We don't need them! We've got used to doing without them. [*Pointedly.*] Isn't that right, Fräulein Lona?

MOTHER: Please, please, Frau Belius.

FRAU BELIUS: *Pater peccavi* . . . all I meant was . . . I could cope alone.

TILDA: I couldn't

[*They all laugh.*]

TILDA: I can't manage without men.

[*They all laugh.*]

TILDA: Whenever there is a gentleman present, conversation immediately reaches a higher plane.

[*More laughter. A knock at the door.*]

FRAU BELIUS: Come in, unless you're a man!

[*They laugh.* ALMUTH *comes in.*]

FRAU BELIUS: Oh, thank God!

[*They laugh.* ALMUTH, *who is speechless with happiness, holds up her left hand showing an engagement ring. They all crowd round her.*]

LONA: An engagement ring!

FRAU BELIUS: My dear girl, you are totally transformed.

MOTHER: Really beautiful, all of a sudden!

INKA: Silver-plated tin, but all the same.

FRAU BELIUS: At long last a dress that fits you!

ELSIE: And a ring!

TILDA: The blushing bride!

MOTHER: Aren't you lucky, Almuth!

TILDA: It's young Nolle, isn't it? I can see him now, still a boy, leading his little troop through the streets. And now he's wounded! And a bridegroom!

INKA: Is he back from the field hospital?

MOTHER: When is the happy day?

FRAU BELIUS: You'll be well off. He'll have his army pay.

MOTHER: And you'll have your wages from the ration card office.

FRAU BELIUS: Oh, do look at her!

MOTHER: After all, it is the best thing that can happen to a woman.

FRAU BELIUS: It makes you understand why you're on this earth.

[TILDA *coughs.*]

ELSIE: Why didn't you bring him with you?

ALMUTH: [*In some embarrassment.*] He's outside, he wouldn't come in with me.

FRAU BELIUS: That really is silly. I'll go and get him!

[*Running out.* ALMUTH *tries to hold her back, but fails.* BELIUS *calling from outside.*]

FRAU BELIUS: Here's an end to this women's clique, at last!

MOTHER: [*Dashing around, rearranging chairs.*] Quick, make the place presentable!

LONA: Anybody got a comb?

INKA: Take off your aprons!

MOTHER: He mustn't think he's fallen among gypsies. And, Elsie, what do I tell you every day: pull your stockings up!

[*All pulling their dresses straight, smoothing their eyelashes with spit,* TILDA *surreptitiously putting on a necklace. Suddenly,* FRAU BELIUS *appears, pushing a wheelchair, with* NOLLE *in it, more dead than alive. He apparently has a spinal injury, for he is half-hanging over the arm-rest. He also shows the effects of strong painkillers; he is asleep. The seven women gather round him in shocked silence.*]

FRAU BELIUS: [*Finally pushing the wheelchair to* ALMUTH, *as if it was a pram.*] Why don't you take him? I really don't know . . .

ALMUTH: [*Pulling the cover up over him.*] He's fallen asleep. He often just drops off. He can be quite lively sometimes. But then the pain hits him again. Then I have to give him some more medicine. [*Pause.*] He was in the thick of it at Demjansk.

MOTHER: [*With embarrassment.*] I see.

TILDA: That's near Lake Ilmen, not far from Staraya Russa.

ALMUTH: No, it's a bit further right.

MOTHER: Yes, it was pretty bad. They fought for months on end; they had to hold their ground.

FRAU BELIUS: And when they did break out . . . they didn't even have time to bury their dead. They left the wounded where they lay. Why? Because the strategy was imbecilic, the relief forces were wrongly deployed, because those ignoramuses . . . oh no, we must say nothing! I can tell you this: if my husband had been in command, the outcome there would have been very different, much less loss of life; not these thousands upon thousands of . . . we must say nothing!

LONA: [*Pointing to* NOLLE.] What a blessing they didn't forget him.

MOTHER: Yes. [*Pause.*] He can count his blessings. And you're better off than a hundred thousand other women, ALMUTH.

TILDA: We must all be thankful.

[*Silence.* NOLLE *wakes up and starts muttering.* ALMUTH *counts drops into a glass, and is about to give it to him. He grabs it from her hand, it falls to the floor.* ALMUTH *immediately starts counting out more drops.*]

NOLLE: Can't you hurry up? [*He comes to looking around.*] The old pharmacy near the Cathedral, isn't it? Cozy, really cozy! [*He takes a tube of tablets out of his pocket and gives it to* MOTHER.] I want to buy more tablets like these. Please, if you wouldn't mind . . .

MOTHER: [*Looking at the label.*] I can't let you have any of these, Norbert. These strong drugs need a prescription. You must bring it with you. As soon as you do . . .

NOLLE: [*Furious because he's highly addicted.*] Is that how it is? What? Is the Fatherland corrupt? Does it abandon its boys at the Front? [*Knocking* FRAU BELIUS'*s cigarette out of her mouth with his crutch.*] The Fatherland is smoking. The Fatherland is profiteering, wallowing in excess. It'll have to change. I've still got eyes. And ears. I've very good hearing! I swear to you, we won't be stabbed in the back a second time. Gee up, girl, start pushing!

[ALMUTH *pushing him round in a circle at great speed.*]

NOLLE: We've still got backbone . . . even if it's shot to pieces!

[*Laughing.* ALMUTH *pushing him round in a circle, he collapses again, mutters, and falls asleep. She stops.*]

ALMUTH: [*Softly.*] Sometimes he doesn't know what he's saying. It's the drugs. But sometimes he understands everything perfectly. Then he screams and bursts into tears. And sometimes he sits for ages without moving a muscle, just thinking. Then he looks like one of the Stoics.

NOLLE: [*Jerking up.*] Gee up, girl, gee up!

[*The lights change.*]

Scene 7

Sunset at the mausoleum. METZENTHIN *walking behind* KONRADI, *who tries to avoid him, ostentatiously turning his back.*

METZENTHIN: Listen to me! Just a moment . . .

[*Pause.*]

KONRADI: [*Abruptly turning round.*] What?

METZENTHIN: [*Suddenly self-conscious.*] I'd like to know . . . yes, er . . . what the time is?

[*Pause.*]

KONRADI: [*Picks up a leaf from the ground, shows it to* METZENTHIN.] Extraordinary, isn't it?

METZENTHIN: What is?

KONRADI: The markings on this leaf . . .

METZENTHIN: There are more pressing problems.

KONRADI: I've been studying it all with my class, the formation of stones, leaves . . . bark . . .

METZENTHIN: I do wish you'd stand still for a moment!

KONRADI: What interests me right now, is the internal structure . . .

METZENTHIN: [*Blocking his path.*] Just listen to me!

KONRADI: [*Undeterred, putting his ear to a boulder.*] Quarries, for instance, anything underground . . .

METZENTHIN: The hero of Crete! He won't talk to ordinary mortals. We must not look him in the eye. He wants to be the voice speaking from the burning bush!

KONRADI: [*Stopping, gives* METZENTHIN *a stern look.*] You're the apprentice, aren't you? You have a scientific mind? I've something here that might interest you.

METZENTHIN: And I . . . I've been looking for you for ages. Waiting outside your house . . . every evening. There's something we need to talk over, I think . . . Now at last . . . we can discuss it . . . [*Shining his torch into* KONRADI's *face.*]

KONRADI: [*Kneeling on the ground.*] Would you mind lying down on the ground!

METZENTHIN: What?

KONRADI: Here! Put your ear to the ground.

METZENTHIN: My dear man!

KONRADI: You'll hear something to give you food for thought.

METZENTHIN: Devils in hell, I suppose!

KONRADI: We can't have any conversation, unless you do what I say.

METZENTHIN: [*Lying down on the ground with a contemptuous grin, listening. Silence. Suddenly jumping up.*] Whatever is it?

KONRADI: [*Laughs.*] Devils.

[*They stare at each other.* KONRADI *goes across to* METZENTHIN.]

KONRADI: Keep calm.

METZENTHIN: I am calm. Calm as a tree-stump, I tell you.

KONRADI: You're trembling from head to foot, my lad. All right, all right. Let's attempt to explain these phenomena, even if it doesn't help us much. [*Laughs.*] "There are more things in heaven and earth" . . . but you might find it amusing. It'll help us pass the time, if we do some exercises in logic. Listen carefully: Well . . . the war's entering its fourth year. It's common knowledge we're gradually running out of weapons. We must have more. For that we need factories. But where do we put them? If we build them above ground, they'll get flattened almost at once. That's common sense, isn't it? What do you think of tunnels, for instance. A system of underground tunnels?

METZENTHIN: How valid are your conclusions if your premises are only speculative?

KONRADI: It's obviously nothing more than speculation. Human beings have always had to speculate, for reassurance, or for fun. See that fence over there? Military installations, as we're all well aware. What connection is there between the thudding noise and the fence? Just for fun I tried to walk right round it. It's a huge site. There must be thousands of them down there.

METZENTHIN: There isn't anything wrong with your ears, I suppose? [*He covers his own ears.*] Or mine, for that matter? Thousands of them!

KONRADI: I've often asked myself the same question . . . who would you get to work down there, who could be banished underground? Certainly not our own manpower, the purest blood . . . It's not impossible . . . that inferior elements might be brought in, the impure, racial aliens, those who don't matter anymore. Does that strike you as a logical explanation, have I drawn the right conclusions?

METZENTHIN: How are you feeling? Are you better now? Your head, your nerves, everything in working order?

KONRADI: The big question? Is it my nerves? [*Hitting his head.*] My head? Has something . . . gone off the rails in there . . . Getting out of control? Trying to escape? Or is it coming from there? [*He points to the fence.*] Is there something behind that fence trying to get in here? [*Hits his head again.*] Have I discovered what all the rumours are about?

METZENTHIN: There's no end of them nowadays.

KONRADI: Even so, they say such installations do exist.

METZENTHIN: But under our very noses . . .

KONRADI: [*Laughs.*] You're right! Too close for comfort. It *can't* be true.

METZENTHIN: [*Decisively.*] No.

[*Pause.*]

KONRADI: Perhaps I have gone crazy . . .

[*Pause.*]

METZENTHIN: Then your pupils must be protected from you . . .

KONRADI: Yes, they might get infected . . .

[*Pause.*]

KONRADI: But do you know what I have discovered? Children never go crazy, they already are. Every single child, who is a real child, is a little fool . . . seeing visions, living in a dream world, believe me, I've been in this job long enough . . . like fools they see everything in its worst, most realistic light . . . I show them a section of barbed wire fencing . . .

METZENTHIN: You ought to be muzzled!

KONRADI: A little bit of bark, and immediately . . . they're on the alert, never taking their eyes off me, listening for every hidden meaning. They're following the scent . . . children always want to take these things to extremes . . .

METZENTHIN: Under lock and key . . . you and your pupils, that's where you should all be!

KONRADI: . . . they're after something, but haven't found it. *Can't* find it. They're in the thick of it, encircled. All round them the delusions of their elders, these . . . an avalanche of propaganda. They can't move any more, you understand, they can't follow the scent, can't play their games, can't make their plans . . . Do you know what's happening? They're drifting . . . I've been studying my pupils' destinies . . . drifting towards death like sleepwalkers. It's a gruesome spectacle, I can tell you!

METZENTHIN: Do you know what you are?

KONRADI: [*Miles away.*] Yes. Let them drift. Let them . . . die!

METZENTHIN: A sadist, a repulsive . . .

KONRADI: Before they become like everyone else, normal people, the living corpses . . . [*He laughs.*] Take no notice of me, I've had malaria. And my brain's been damaged. [*Quietly.*] But have you ever noticed how beautiful they are? And how ugly they become when they hide their dreams and repress their feelings? Only children know what death is, and suffering, animals . . . corruption . . . and experience compassion, love, fear, everything we despise nowadays, they feel with the utmost intensity, *want* to feel, they surrender themselves . . . That's what's different from the nightmare world their elders have forged. That's what makes a child's dreams totally moral. I ask myself how it all hangs together, beauty, feelings and dreams . . . I don't know the answer. I can only observe. Since my firsthand experience of . . . destruction I've been able to observe the beauty of children. And I love them . . . how do I say it . . . no, it can't be said. I love children more than I can tell you.

METZENTHIN: With the lust of a sex-offender.

KONRADI: You might well be right. It's the purest, most self-centered urge. One all teachers have, incidentally, if they're any good. [*Laughing.*] I have a new approach to teaching, my dear Metzenthin! I'm going to explore the adolescent mind—its moral universe. I'm going to invent a new teaching method. [*In some confusion, he kneels on the ground, rolling about in the leaves.*] I shall take them away from their mothers . . . make a new start here . . . where everything starts, and . . . ends . . . [*Laughs.*] I'll take them to the victims . . . lay their hands on the corpses, and let them respond through their dreams . . . "People must have their dreams," so said a great man—whose name we must not mention nowadays—that's where everything must start, every change, every new order—whatever the society, otherwise . . . nothing can thrive . . . [*Going right up to* METZENTHIN.] Do you think that time will ever . . . can you imagine it? [*Laughing, suddenly, as if it's nothing to do with him.*] There I go, flying off at a tangent. Take no notice of me. You see, I've had malaria. My brain doesn't work!

METZENTHIN: I'll put an end to this game of yours.

KONRADI: [*Looking at* METZENTHIN.] I doubt it! [*Laughs.*] You still see yourself as an individual!

METZENTHIN: And for me, the end justifies the means!

KONRADI: It's been nice talking to you. I can't say why. I don't often talk to adults. Do you know something? It has nothing whatever to do with age, incidentally. You're hardly more than a child yourself! [*Laughing, he swiftly turns round and disappears into the darkness.*]

METZENTHIN: [*Following him.*] There must be something . . . some other way . . . This only leads to death . . . Unless you can come up with an answer . . . [*Angrily.*] You wait and see! I mean what I say: *any* means are justified!

[*Lights change.*]

Scene 8

At the table. MOTHER, TILDA, LONA, GENERAL BELIUS *in uniform,* FRAU BELIUS, RODE-WALD, NOLLE *in his wheelchair,* ALMUTH *and* INKA *either standing around or sitting down, all with coffee cups.* ELSIE *and* METZENTHIN *a little to one side, on the floor. Later,* OSWIN.

MOTHER: I can't tell you how we've been looking forward to today . . . Seeing you once again, Herr Belius!

TILDA: And you're looking so well, my dear General. Tanned. In the best of health!

MOTHER: [*Shaking her head.*] But already showing the strain!

TILDA: As if just back from holiday!

MOTHER: Though one can detect signs of your exertions. [*To* OSWIN, *who approaches reverentially.*] Good evening, Herr Oswin, a very good evening to you. [*Abruptly.*] What can I do for you?

OSWIN: [*Handing her a bottle.*] Sloe gin, they've been steeped . . . in pure spirit . . . [*In a whisper.*] Don't tell a soul! I won't disturb you any longer . . .

MOTHER: [*Coolly.*] You must stop and have a cup of coffee with us! [*Calling out.*] Lona, a cup! [*To* GENERAL BELIUS.] It's been *the* talking-point for weeks, whenever one's met one's friends, or at night in the air-raid shelter, when will General Belius come home on leave . . . not that we've lost heart here in the Fatherland . . .

NOLLE: [*Wheeled in by* ALMUTH, *touching an imaginary cap.*] Herr General . . .

OSWIN: But we'd like more details . . .

TILDA: We'd love a straw to clutch at, a glimmer of hope.

MOTHER: It's not that we sit around complaining here in the Fatherland, it's just that all the . . .

TILDA: Our nerves are getting a little frayed . . .

MOTHER: No, no, Herr Belius, the Fatherland is resolute, and we're always kept well informed, we keep abreast of events; but once in a while, things happen so quickly, we pin on our little flags, and the Front's in a completely different place . . .

TILDA: They've already broken through!

MOTHER: [*Signalling furiously to* TILDA, *clapping her hand over her mouth.*] Broken out, she meant broken out, needless to say!

TILDA: It's time to set things to rights again . . .

MOTHER: Our Tilda's led such a sheltered life; at Kiev, we broke out and just look what progress we've made!

LONA: [*To* INKA.] So Konradi . . . I'm not at all surprised . . . When did he ask you?

INKA: Two months ago. On the last day of summer. The day before the swimming pool closed. I was lying on the high board, staring at the water. He was suddenly standing beside me, asking me if I'd go with him, on the first plane out . . . once the war's over. Yes, if I'd fly out with him . . .

LONA: You'd be happy to go on foot, I imagine . . .

MOTHER: [*Calling.*] Lona! What are these teaspoons doing here! I distinctly said "coffee spoons," even if we can only offer malt coffee . . . but this is intolerable. Kindly change the spoons!

NOLLE: [*Holding an exercise-book under his father's nose.*] Do you recognize this? Ever seen these sentences before?

RODEWALD: Exercises, as far as I can see . . .

NOLLE: Of course. In the Saxon genitive. Here's a good one: "Bright of eye, the soldier marches towards the thick of the battle" . . . [*Pause.*] All I can say is, if he was *my* student teacher, I wouldn't allow him to write such sentences.

RODEWALD: [*Shaking his head.*] Konradi is the best teacher on my staff. In my opinion he's a quite exceptional human being. There is nothing objectionable in that sentence. Who is this soldier? For all we know, he could be a Russky, or a Macaroni-eater . . .

FRAU BELIUS: Or even . . . a Napoleonic solider . . . ?

NOLLE: Napoléon never experienced the thick of a battle! Go on . . . What do we have here?

ALMUTH: [*Reading.*] "Cool of head, the nation demands total war." [*Pause.*]

RODEWALD: That's, well now . . . the way she read it . . . You could read it that way or, I suppose you could interpret it ironically? Nevertheless . . . [*Grinning.*] it depends on your tone of voice . . . One cannot lay down the law about tone of voice. [*Becoming uneasy.*] If there was anything . . . I'd be the last person to stand by him. But I'm sorry to say, we've no concrete evidence to hand, my dear Nolle! [*Holding up his crippled hand.*]

NOLLE: [*Taking some bark out of his pocket.*] No? None at all? Then what is this . . . [*Laughing, calls out.*] "Gee up!" [*And gets* ALMUTH *to push him over to* GENERAL BELIUS.]

OSWIN: [*To* GENERAL BELIUS.] I've heard we're rearming, in preparation for a counteroffensive?

NOLLE: [*To* GENERAL BELIUS.] Has that traitor Paulus finally been brought to justice? And Seydlitz-Kurzbach?

LONA: [*Timidly, to* GENERAL BELIUS.] I've been told all leave's been cancelled. Is it true?

MOTHER: Oh, do stop talking about things you don't understand!

NOLLE: That's enemy propaganda at its most blatant!

TILDA: Will there be peace this year? Please, tell us what we can expect, dear General Belius!

[*Smiling,* GENERAL BELIUS *looks out over the assembled faces as if they were the steppe.* FRAU BELIUS *hurries up to him.*]

FRAU BELIUS: I might have known, I can't leave him alone for a second, without a crowd forming around him, demanding he hold forth, which isn't his style, in fact he hates it like the plague . . . so I'll bring you up to date, act as his mouthpiece, well, where shall I start? How shall I put it . . . of course, we have sustained losses, it was a hard winter, a very hard winter, out there, just as it was for us, testing us all to the limits of our endurance. I'd take my oath on that in court, I'm not the sort to mince words, I call a spade a spade. I call a spade a spade because . . . [*Beating her breast.*] here, in my heart of hearts, my confidence remains unshaken, I see no cause for alarm, I'm convinced things are on the up-and-up. General Frost has been defeated, General Mud has yielded . . . piano, piano . . . the German retreat has been halted, our fallback position is as solid as a rock. Our General Staff is getting a second wind. Needless to say, we must *still* be vigilant, still need to work round the clock, do without sleep, for fear of surprise attack if nothing else, there's no such thing as behind the lines any more, the Front is everywhere. Partisans spring up all over the place, but we can reform our strategy, our strategy gets better by the day, I can tell you, we're applying the lessons we learnt last winter . . .

METZENTHIN: [*To* ELSIE.] Shouldn't we go and join them, listen to their tales of our glorious battles . . . put our fingers on "the pulse of history"? What do you, think, Elsie? Elsie, you're miles away. What are you thinking about?

ELSIE: I was just imagining . . . making up a story about you . . . I'd so love to know what you used to think when you were younger; and what you looked like, what I mean is, what kind of a person you were . . .

METZENTHIN: [*Suddenly getting up.*] Do you know what that means, Elsie?

ELSIE: What?

METZENTHIN: Asking someone questions like this, about their childhood, there's always a special reason . . . wanting to know *everything* about this other person, can only mean . . . Oh, Elsie. [*Laying his head in her lap.*] This is the *most wonderful* day of my life!

RODEWALD: [*To* MOTHER.] . . . whatever is humanly possible, my dear . . . madam . . . without a shadow of doubt, my school has no more faithful servant than yours truly, no-one exerts himself more in the cause of justice, and yet . . . [*Frightened.*] I'm surrounded . . . surrounded by suspicion, why does he look at me like that, as if he's a stranger . . . can you understand it . . . cold as . . . ice, my own son?

LONA: [*To* INKA.] Konradi . . . there's not a better man in the whole town. Whatever he does, he does wholeheartedly. Even when he's pretending to be crazy. If you hadn't had him, I would. [*She looks at* INKA.] You're looking so lovely today, Inka, so . . . beautiful, you're the only one who deserves him.

INKA: Lona, it's not my looks that make me deserve him!

LONA: No. Of course not . . . but on second thoughts, I don't know . . . yes, I think they do!

[*Going off, with their arms round each other.*]

FRAU BELIUS: [*Taking her leave.*] It's time we were gone! Frau Woellmer, Fräulein

Tilda . . . one must have enjoyment. We're arranging a little drawing-room concert, just family, gather ye rosebuds . . .

GENERAL BELIUS: [*Smiling absentmindedly.*] Carpe diem!

[*They both leave.*]

MOTHER: [*Watching them go, enraptured.*] The General . . . he's a symbol, no, Germany cannot be defeated!

[*The lights change.*]

Scene 9

OSWIN, *in SA uniform, on a chair at a desk.* METZENTHIN *standing in front of him.*

OSWIN: Herr Metzenthin filed a report. Now he comes to retract the report. Herr Metzenthin is suffering pangs of conscience! [*Laughing.*] But the avalanche is already rolling. What should we do about it? My advice is: let's not take ourselves so seriously! You're only a small cog, Metzenthin! I'm only a small cog, too, even though I'm sitting here at Regional Headquarters, as a deputy . . . How can you afford a conscience? Isn't that a bit presumptous of you? Isn't that bordering on arrogance? I'm warning you! If I've learned anything, it's this: a miss is as good as a mile. Let's take the Herr Pharmazist: a wealthy man, immaculate in his made-to-measure suits! Held in high esteem by the whole town. Suddenly he wants to see Paris. Why? It wasn't as if he had to. And now he's pushing up daisies. Herr Konradi wanted to go to heaven. He couldn't get his way. But he's still got his head in the clouds. He needs to be brought down a peg or two. [*Suddenly full of hate.*] I hate everyone who's presumptuous! But do you know what I've discovered? Things find their own level in the end. I'm a man of the center, as I've already suggested. It's a fortunate position to be in. I see what's going on beneath me, and above me. I have it all in perspective. And everywhere I see the edges fraying. Let's take this town of ours. Right at the bottom, in what you might call the eternal slime, where the proletariat, the antisocials live, it's all plain sailing. At the first sign of foment, they're disinfected. The layer above that is striving upwards. I'd like to maintain that the lower strata exist only on the say-so of the upper strata. Here, in turn, there are also tendencies towards presumption. But too high up, the air becomes thin. There they sit in their beautiful houses, the Woellmers, Beliuses, and Rodewalds, cozy and well-respected, and I don't begrudge them it. I never ask: why am I not in their shoes? And when they say: "Good morning" to me, with a suggestion of: "Good morning to you my man," in a tone you know only too well, I don't get upset, I don't suddenly run amok, I go on being the prankster I appear . . . because I know things will sort themselves out. Here, or there, the extremists and the hotheads disappear. Their positions become vacant; new blood must be found. It might be you and it might be me. Because we're next in line. The eternal balance must be maintained. My faith in justice is unshakable. And the Reichsführer SS shows the same faith when he refers to Wotan, our ancient hero. There is an eternal law, my dear Metzenthin, a divine mission, which a mere human, with delusions of grandeur, has no business to resist. And this regime understands that. Which gives us, the people of the center, the believers, the means to restore the balance . . . [*Again full of hatred.*] And I can tell you this: if, as a result of your report, they string up Herr Assessor Konradi from the nearest lamppost, I'll get a ringside view of every jerk; his pupils, whether his mouth twitches, every word he utters while choking to death; I'll want to have a complete picture of it, draw conclusions from it, observations of a more general nature, such as: which is more reprehensible, a murder committed out of passion or the daily [*Imitating.*] "good morning"; like a judge, I'll weigh up the evidence: is hanging the appropriate punishment or would some other method . . . slow strangulation for instance . . . [*Suddenly breaking off and grinning.*] Do you know what it will mean if you retract your report? [*Pause.*] Do you know you've identified yourself? [*Pause.*] Do you know you too could be . . . [*Pause.*] Are you sure you want to retract?

[METZENTHIN *looks at* OSWIN *without saying a word. Silence.* OSWIN *smiles cheerfully.*]

OSWIN: We don't want anyone playing the hero here! Your report was sent on a long time ago. I'll say nothing more about it. I've been playing another little joke, Herr Metzenthin! Didn't you once tell me my jokes were pathetic? What a tiresome thing memory is! A pathetic little joke to frighten my friend Metzenthin . . . incidentally . . . Herr Rodewald beat you to it . . . with similar revelations . . . or, to put it more courteously: questions, about his art classes. A man of high moral principles, Herr Rodewald . . . With plenty of common sense . . . You're not the only one, Herr Praktikant, several tributaries feed any denunciation . . . it forces its way through a thousand little sources, before it brings about a man's downfall . . . a rivulet, then a flood, a flood . . . what a wonderful image I've created. [*Grinning.*] You can go, Herr Metzenthin, and sleep soundly once more!

[*The lights change.*]

Scene 10

By the river Hollemme. Dusk. LONA, ELSIE, ALMUTH, NOLLE, *in his wheelchair,* OSWIN, MOTHER *on* RODEWALD's *arm, later,* TILDA. *They are all moving slowly, as if in a procession, towards the mausoleum; two lifeless shapes are lying under a blanket in front of it.*

LONA: There they are.
MOTHER: Dreadful.
ALMUTH: Both covered up, even their heads; you can't see a thing.
RODEWALD: I wouldn't want to.
LONA: I've heard they're in a terrible mess.
ALMUTH: It's always like that with a shot in the head.
ELSIE: Could they have done it to themselves?
LONA: No. I've heard they were shot. Trying to escape.
ALMUTH: That's not true. It's only hearsay.
ELSIE: I don't understand, why? We were playing rounders this morning; we were in the same team, and we won. Whenever Inka was in our team, we won. But now . . .
MOTHER: A guest worker, so I've heard, on the run . . .
LONA: But his neighbours saw the car they sent to collect Konradi. They say Inka was with him. The two of them escaped through the back door . . .
ALMUTH: I think it was a suicide pact.
LONA: They let them walk through the town undisturbed. But there were marksmen here among the bushes . . .
ALMUTH: I don't believe it. Even if Konradi did say more than he should, and even if Inka always was a bit stuck-up, they'd still never do that, just like that, without any trial. That's slander! Nolle, say something!

[NOLLE *says nothing.*]

MOTHER: I can't take it in.
RODEWALD: [*Quietly.*] It was beyond my power to protect him. It was common knowledge among his pupils. Parents came and pestered me . . .
MOTHER: Yes. He was a kind of . . . soul in torment . . .
LONA: [*Looks around.*] People are coming from all directions . . .
OSWIN: Except her mother.

RODEWALD: [*Quietly.*] I went to the Regional HQ myself. I tried to put in a good word for him with the authorities . . .

OSWIN: Frau Belius is sitting at her window, with her long cigarette-holder. "That is no daughter of mine," she says. That's the way to do it.

RODEWALD: This is one case when I'm glad of my infirmity . . . because I have kept my hands clean . . . [*Holding up his crippled hand.*]

TILDA: [*Comes running in.*] I've come . . . only for a moment . . . I've left the house . . .

OSWIN: The world's going from bad to worse! Fräulein Tilda, out in the street for the first time in twenty years!

TILDA: But you have to . . . somehow or other . . . pay your last respects . . . [*Giving* ELSIE *a bunch of withered flowers.*] Elsie, please take them this bouquet, will you! I've been saving it up. It was very precious to me, but now . . .

MOTHER: [*Taking the bouquet from* ELSIE, *she throws it away.*] Tilda! Have you taken leave of your senses? After all, they were traitors. I don't know what's to become of you!

[*The lights change.*]

Scene 11

By the stove. LONA *and* ELSIE *pricking gooseberries with knitting-needles, which the cookbook says is advisable to help the juice ooze out into the jars.* MOTHER *comes in and checks the berries.*

MOTHER: Each one must be pricked twice. Haven't I made that clear? *Twice!* You haven't even dented this one. Here, here, and there! [*She digs about in the berries.*] Haven't I shown you how to do it? [*She snatches* LONA's *needle, and demonstrates how to do it.*] Like this, like this, right through, so the fruit can absorb the syrup and swell up; but it's a waste of breath. I talk and nobody takes any notice, you sit around talking nonsense, living for the moment, I'm the only one who does any thinking. It's not the berries I care about, I can tell you, it's the principle: doing a job properly, *one* job properly, in the midst of all the sloppiness. All this slovenliness will be the death of me. It's like mildew, once it's got hold it goes on spreading, I can't . . . control it. I can't even protect Elsie any more from certain elements, who shall be nameless, certain people who hold nothing sacred. Herr Oswin has the gall to make advances to me—my bookkeeper!—rolls his eyes whenever he sees me;

[*Shaking* ELSIE, *who flees to* LONA, *and embraces her.*]

MOTHER: What's being said? What stories are being told here in the kitchen . . . why are the gooseberries in such disorder? Answer me this minute! [*She throws the gooseberies all over the kitchen.*]

LONA: [*Suddenly shrieking, she takes* ELSIE's *hand, which is bleeding, and, putting it to her mouth, licks the blood off.*] Elsie! She's pricked herself with the needle, twice in the same finger.

MOTHER: This is impossible! What can it all mean?

LONA: Blood everywhere.

MOTHER: It's the last straw . . . [*Snatching* ELSIE's *hand away.*] Oh God, what is going on? This is the sort of influence I was talking about. [*To* LONA.] Look at the way the girl's gaping, all forlorn. Those eyes. [*She weeps.*] No-one can be expected to know everything. It's deplorable, standards are slipping everywhere. To think my own flesh and blood does this to me.

[*The lights change.*]

[*End of Part Two.*]

PART THREE
DEFEAT

Scene 1

The pharmacy. The sewing machine. Table. Evening. TILDA *sewing,* ELSIE *reading, music on the radio: "And Down the Snowy Mountains . . ."*

TILDA: [*Bending over her work.*] Are you keeping yourself usefully occupied, Elsie?
ELSIE: Can't you see I'm reading.

[*Pause.*]

TILDA: [*Standing up to take a look at* ELSIE'*s book. She reads out.*] "Discipline and Liberty: the Life and Work of Heinrich von Kleist." Have you got to read this for school?
ELSIE: You know what they say, TILDA: *Non scholae sed vitae* . . . Parumpumpum.
TILDA: We're beginning to make it quite comfortable down here, aren't we?
ELSIE: Well . . . [*Pause.*] almost as comfortable as a nunnery.
TILDA: [*Changing the subject.*] I've been trying for years to make people understand real happiness is to be found at home. If people lived nice and comfortably in their . . . cells, concentrating on what really matters, no-one would feel the urge to go marching all over the place . . . Things would be different. Where has Therese got to? The siren went ages ago.
ELSIE: Nothing's going to happen. Nothing ever has happened.
TILDA: Apart from three bombs on the parade ground.
ELSIE: They were off target.
TILDA: How would you know?
ELSIE: [*Rather flustered, childlike.*] It was a young soldier. An English soldier. [*Pointing to the sky.*] up there. He pictured it all. The house going up in flames, perhaps. People screaming. Fire and smoke. But he knew he couldn't take any bombs home. So he dropped them outside, on open country.
TILDA: He must have sensed you lived here, my pet.
ELSIE: Aren't we pathetic, sitting underground every night . . . when nothing ever happens . . .
TILDA: People say the Front's already reached the Oder. It can't go on much longer.
ELSIE: But things could suddenly change.
TILDA: Once our miracle weapons are ready. The V3 and V4.
ELSIE: You can wipe out whole districts with those. [*Pause.*] I think I'm going to seed.
TILDA: [*Gives* ELSIE *a sharp look.*] I don't like the look of you, Elsie; you've put on weight recently. And you're always so pale.
ELSIE: Oh, I feel fine! [*She laughs.*] The refugees from Warthegau, the ones camped in the School Hall, are having a good time.
TILDA: What do you mean by good?
ELSIE: Living like gypsies. And riddled with fleas.
TILDA: Heaven help us!
ELSIE: [*Suddenly clinging to* TILDA.] Tilda, let's both pack a little case . . . So we can get away, Tilda, the two of us . . . let's go now, this minute . . . Do you know what would be wonderful? If everything collapsed around us, if everything collapsed so totally no-one could ever find us . . . and in the place we went to nobody knew us. It would have to be a long way off, and all new . . . let's go, Tilda, right now . . .
TILDA: Oh God, do shut up, Elsie . . .

[MOTHER *and* LONA *come in,* MOTHER *supporting* LONA.]

MOTHER: Here you are, Lona, sit down on the deck chair. Let me give you a hand. Why shouldn't I look after *you* this once? Everything's at sixes and sevens. All the rules we've ever lived by, all gone up in smoke.

TILDA: I must say, Therese: suddenly, there's something not quite right about the way you talk.

ELSIE: Isn't Metzenthin coming?

MOTHER: He can't be bothered coming down here anymore. And there's probably no point, anyway.

TILDA: I've noticed a change in him lately.

MOTHER: He's got above himself since he became the assistant.

TILDA: Though he's still in the dispensary at this hour!

ELSIE: When he always used to be so slapdash.

TILDA: Perhaps he's . . . pining.

MOTHER: It's a natural development. Everyone comes to their senses sooner or later.

ELSIE: [*Singing along with the radio music.*]
   And down the snowy mountains
   There flows a little stream . . .

   [*Newsflash: "Large formations of enemy bombers are approaching Central Germany." Then back to the song.*]

ELSIE:
   . . . And from it I have taken
   Many a cooling drink.
   I have not grown mature yet
   For I am still . . .

   [*The lights change.*]

Scene 2

Near the mausoleum. Night. NOLLE *in his wheelchair, hiding behind a bush.* METZENTHIN *comes along. The noise of airplanes.*

NOLLE: Halt! Hands up! Empty your pockets!

METZENTHIN: There aren't any briquettes in them.

NOLLE: Lucky for you. I tell you, things happen here, some nights, that aren't quite right, when the siren goes. You wouldn't believe it. Perfectly respectable men with sacks over their shoulders, and mothers with shopping-bags; they forget who they are for a little bag of coke. The most disgusting behavior imaginable! Anyone found stealing or looting will be beheaded. [*Pause.*] I get a really good view from here.

METZENTHIN: Are your eyes better?

NOLLE: [*Giggling.*] They think I can see them! Between you and me my sight's rapidly deteriorating. I've only got 15 percent vision now. But it's good enough to stand guard here. [*He takes a pill.*]

METZENTHIN: Aren't you cold?

NOLLE: Very.

METZENTHIN: You'll catch your death.

NOLLE: I'll stay as long as I can.

METZENTHIN: You don't think your life is . . . how shall I put it . . . worth living?

NOLLE: We live for as long as we are useful to the nation. That's a law of nature.

METZENTHIN: So you still enjoy life?

NOLLE: That's not the point. One does one's duty.

METZENTHIN: But the problem is . . . facing the consequences of your mistakes; admitting: "Yes, I was mistaken." Facing the consequences of continuing to . . . [*Pause.*] trail around in a futile way just because you've invested *so much* in it . . . Be honest, Nolle: haven't you ever considered blowing your brains out? [*Saying nothing,* NOLLE *grins, then pulls a pistol out from under his blanket, and plays with it.*]

METZENTHIN: Is the safety-catch off?

NOLLE: Always!

METZENTHIN: Christ! [*Pause.*] You know, I'd like to have seen more in my life. The town of Talamone, for instance.

NOLLE: Where's that?

METZENTHIN: Haven't a clue. Still, if things had worked out better . . . I'd have really liked to go there.

NOLLE: I'd have liked to live long enough for them to find out if there's life on other planets. Human life, I mean, yes, that's what I'd have liked . . . But what's the point of talking about it? [*Putting his pistol back.*] We're not in that position yet.

METZENTHIN: I'm in no position. Or any position. Whatever position I find myself in . . . [*Pause.*] I've committed no crime, Nolle! No-one's committed any crime. You'll only find great criminals in the theater . . . I haven't really committed any crime. [*Pause.*] But I do have one thing, Nolle . . . I have something like a . . . direction in life . . . everything I do now is guided by my sense of direction . . . If you study the lives of great historical figures, they all had an idea of what to expect from life, an image of their own life, and . . . even of their own death, perhaps. You've got to have a direction in life, otherwise . . . it won't be worth living.

NOLLE: I agree with you wholeheartedly.

METZENTHIN: I never thought I'd find anyone with the same conviction. Perhaps we should waste no time . . . put it into effect tonight?

NOLLE: [*Whistling through his teeth as the air-raid siren goes off.*] I'm going to be busy. [*Looking through his binoculars.*] If I'd ever taken a wrong turn in life I'd do it immediately . . . here and now. I wouldn't simply stagnate, I'd never be so stupid as not to notice I'd made a mistake. Incidentally, I'm told you're working actively for our cause?

METZENTHIN: Poor sod.

[*He goes out. The lights change.*]

Scene 3

Immediately afterwards METZENTHIN *appears on the cellar steps.* ELSIE *goes to meet him.*

METZENTHIN: Have you read that book I told you about?

ELSIE: *The Life of Kleist?*

METZENTHIN: Have you?

ELSIE: [*Flustered.*] Yes. Lovely. What I read was lovely.

METZENTHIN: It wasn't lovely. It was ghastly, abandoned by everybody . . . right up to his death . . .

ELSIE: I haven't got that far.

METZENTHIN: His death was different. Kleist's death was fantastic.

ELSIE: [*Now very confused.*] So . . . it was a quick death? A direct hit? Did they have bombs in those days?

METZENTHIN: [*Holding* ELSIE'*s hand tight.*] He shot himself . . . along with his fiancée.

ELSIE: In open country . . . among the turnips . . . Whoosh, then they exploded in mid-air! [*Giggles.*]

METZENTHIN: [*Looking at* ELSIE, *he lays his head against hers for a moment, then says quietly.*] Good night, my bonnie . . .

[*We then hear the tune* METZENTHIN *played under the statue of Roland one morning in Part One.* METZENTHIN *goes out quickly. The lights change.*]

Scene 4

The pharmacy. LONA *in the deck chair.* MOTHER *on a stool next to her.* TILDA *is sewing as if her life depended on it.* ELSIE *looks as if she is reading.*

MOTHER: Yes, you see, Lona—I went through it myself when I was your age. I suffered for months on end, and no amount of pills and potions helped at all; it was all emotional, you see. But no-one had the faintest idea at the time. Of course, there were psychologists by then, but most people knew nothing about them. And nowadays, people won't have anything to do with them, because the early ones were all Jews. But in those days an elderly doctor was a frequent visitor at our house, and he knew a great deal. He kept asking: "What is worrying the little lady? We must get to the roots of her anxiety," he said, "vinegar compresses won't do the trick." He was right, Lona, I was terribly frightened. But what of? We had everything you could wish for, we were secure from the day we were born, and I was so sheltered . . . This is how I came to understand it: I was completely innocent. In those days people were innocent for a long time . . . I still believed in my childhood dreams: one day I wanted to be a ballerina, the next a Red Cross nurse in the jungle. I wanted a life on the ocean wave, as the woman Captain of a ship and then there was romance . . . and Heaven knows what else; my imagination ran riot: such fancy ideas! But they are poison, Lona! They stop you moving with the times. Having common sense. Rooting out dreams and anything else that isn't sensible is a painful process. I only felt better once I completed it. I overcame my fright, and the symptoms gradually disappeared as well.

I don't really know what's troubling you, but I feel sure as soon as you find out where you belong and put an end to all this drifting hither and thither, with a family of your own, you'll have a place in society . . . They're making such a racket tonight, they must be flying very low . . . I think, once you start using your common sense as well, things will go better for you, Lona. Yes, there really is a lot to be said for psychology.

[*Loud aircraft noise.*]

MOTHER: Oh God, it's getting even worse out there. Can't you ever stop sewing, and you, Elsie, stop reading. Put your book away, for Heaven's sake . . . It's dreadful tonight, completely unnerving.

[*The lights change.*]

Scene 5

At the fountain. Night. METZENTHIN, *wandering about, meets* FRAU BELIUS, *who is pushing a loaded handcart, which is covered by a woollen blanket.*

FRAU BELIUS: Well, I'll be damned, I've had a funny feeling all day; what on earth are you still out here for?

METZENTHIN: I'm just stargazing.

FRAU BELIUS: Have you gone crazy, a young man like you? If I was hit on the head, because I'm older than you, I'd say "Amen," get used to the idea, and make the best of it.

METZENTHIN: [*Cautiously.*] Do you want to die, too?

FRAU BELIUS: I don't much care either way, Metzenthin. I've been so badly battered. But it's a funny thing, I think I could stand directly under the bombs and they'd keep out of my way.

METZENTHIN: Then stay here. I attract them. Perhaps we'll strike lucky.

FRAU BELIUS: What do you mean "we"? I wasn't talking about you. You young people shouldn't give in to such pessimistic ideas. [*Pause.*] Who knows, maybe I'll help myself on my way . . . one of these days . . . But now, you see, I must get on, I must get this little hoard of mine to a safe place. [*She lifts the cover off the handcart and reveals a small white coffin with gold handles.*] Beautiful workmanship, isn't it, with these little handles, look, a joiner out in the country; I managed to track him down . . . twelve kilometers away . . . out of town.

METZENTHIN: [*Flabbergasted.*] But why . . . why . . . gold handles, what has it got . . . [*Pause.*] gold handles for!

FRAU BELIUS: He just ran off, my youngest, just turned thirteen, Metzenthin, ran away from me to play war-games with a bazooka. Now he's laid out in the potato cellar. [*Bursting into tears.*] So you see, it's not easy for me to depart this life either, no matter how much I'd like to, I must still care for the others . . . I've still got to transfer them to new graves . . . one of these days. I don't suppose you've got a fag-end you can spare me?

[*It suddenly gets very bright . . . but still deathly quiet.*]

FRAU BELIUS: Dear Lord! Marker flares. Now we're in for it. Let's make ourselves scarce. [*Hurrying off.*]

METZENTHIN: [*Throwing himself on the ground. screams.*] Stay here! Don't run away! Please, wait a minute!

[*The lights change.*]

Scene 6

The pharmacy. Deathly silence. MOTHER, TILDA, LONA, *and* ELSIE *huddling up against the wall in fright.* ELSIE *singing softly.* TILDA *pressing a screen against her.*

MOTHER: Over here!

LONA: No, no, on the stairs!

ELSIE: [*Singing.*] If it snowed red roses and rained chilled wine . . .

MOTHER: It's about to start.

TILDA: Just wait . . .

ELSIE: [*Sings.*] . . . You still wouldn't come back, oh sweetheart mine . . .

MOTHER: We don't know if the roof timbers are on fire. That's their tactic: they drop high-explosive bombs, to expose the roof timbers. Then, the incendiary bombs on the rafters . . . it burns like tinder.

LONA: No, the other way round: first, it's set on fire, so that people will come to douse the flames . . .

ELSIE: Then the aerial mines, kerwhoosh; they don't give you time to say your "Our Father." [*Giggling.*]

MOTHER: Someone must go up and do fire-duty.

TILDA: It'll be noticed soon enough.

MOTHER: It'll be too late then.

LONA: Venske, the town surveyor, was down here once, and he said the only safe place in this house was the stairs.

MOTHER: What exactly were you up to in the cellar with Herr Venske?

[*Noise of aircraft, very quiet and unnerving.*]

MOTHER: My God, my God! Tilda, why on earth do you clutter the place up with all this stuff? We're far too cramped here as it is. And for pity's sake, stop singing, Elsie! Just concentrate.

ELSIE: There's a spider's web.

MOTHER: It makes me want to scream, the way you all just sit there, like stuffed dummies.

TILDA: [*As if she was in a trance.*] What will be, will be. You needn't get so agitated, Thesa, I never get agitated about anything these days. It's bound to happen. In times of wide-spread agitation, everything's in flux. It'll overhwelm you. Keys are turning in locks.

Doors are moving on their hinges and bursting open. And all the soldiers who were taken prisoner in the First World War, who laid low in Siberia, from the Urals, from the past, the prisoners from the forgotten villages, will all come back home, any minute now there'll be a knock, he'll be standing at the door . . . [*Rolling out a screen.*] I'll partition the room with this screen, because we never got married, Herr Doktor Struck and I . . . we haven't yet.

MOTHER: [*Horrified.*] Tilda! I suspected as much.

[*The room slowly filling with an eerie light.*]

MOTHER: Quick, give me your hands!

LONA: [*Begins to run up the stairs.*] I can't take any more, I'd rather be burned alive outside, than spend one minute more down here . . . in this trap.

MOTHER: Pull yourself together, Lona.

LONA: [*Wavering an instant.*] Right. Thanks for everything. Good-bye. I'm going. [*She rushes out.*]

ELSIE: [*Trying to go after her, screaming.*] Take me with you, Lona!

MOTHER: My child, my child, my child!

[*Blinding light as bright as day. Then suddenly, darkness.*]

Scene 7

At the fountain. Smoke and fire. ELSIE *trying to lift up* METZENTHIN, *who is sprawled there, lifeless. Everywhere is devastated. The Roland statue has lost its head.*

ELSIE: Lie quietly. It's all over now. It's only a bit hot still. Storm. All the fire. Like a storm in the desert. [*Putting a blank piece of paper in his lap.*] Look, the letter. It's gone already. "Dear Karli . . ." and now it's blown away. [*Trying to put his glasses back on his nose.*] Keep quiet, Karli.

PASSER-BY: [*Carrying household effects on his back.*] What do you mean, quiet? He stopped screaming a long time ago. He's been silent for hours. [*Shaking his head. Pause.*] Your house has burned down, Fräulein. Except for the cellar. That's still there. That lovely old house . . . gone!

[*The lights change.*]

[*Music is played softly: "And down the snowy mountains," or "My Bonnie . . . ," which crossfades into the next scene. It must follow straight onto the next scene as though nothing significant had happened in the interim.*]

Scene 8

In the cellar. The room has a new roof. A few optimistic details intimate that the war is over, and that life is beginning again. MOTHER *standing in the middle of the room in a tailored suit adapted from a man's suit.* FRAU BELIUS *putting a white hat on* MOTHER, *and fiddling with it.* ELSIE, *in a petticoat, shivering, pressed up against the wall.* TILDA *is fantastically dressed, with her hair loose, on a stool in the corner.*

MOTHER: It looks rather silly on me, this attempt at a veil; only suitable for a young bride.

FRAU BELIUS: Well, aren't we? A bride? And still on the young side.

MOTHER: [*Fiddling around with the hat.*] Perhaps one could make it a bit higher?

FRAU BELIUS: With tufts, perhaps? On one side? Your dear sister was always so good at those things.

MOTHER: That looks much better.

FRAU BELIUS: [*With a glance at* TILDA.] She hardly has anything to say these days. Isn't she sewing any more?

MOTHER: Not a stitch. [*Quietly.*] Do you know something? She just drifts about all over the place, nowadays . . . in spite of her thrombosis . . . sits outside, on some ruin or other, gossiping. I dread to think what types she mixes with.

FRAU BELIUS: [*Quietly.*] Perhaps she ought to be put away in a clinic?

MOTHER: And sometimes she stays out the whole night.

FRAU BELIUS: Where she can be properly looked after.

MOTHER: According to her, her mind's more lucid now than ever. And when my sister digs her heels in . . . you know what she's like.

FRAU BELIUS: Yes, I do. She was always a bit . . . How shall I put it: headstrong.

MOTHER: We're step-sisters, but we were brought up together. Every minute of my life I've had to look after her. She's never really grown up. And she's extremely timid. She's not had a hard time of it . . . in a home with everything provided.

FRAU BELIUS: I'd say it was an enviable position, mmh?

MOTHER: She has an easy enough time of it—you can be sure—and nowadays more than ever . . . she takes advantage of other people's kindness . . . But there isn't a family in the land that hasn't got its problems.

FRAU BELIUS: A sad day for your Herr Oswin. He really took a shine to the Frau Pharmazist. Even fancied his chances, didn't he?

MOTHER: Those days are over and done with now. Oh God, yes . . . in normal times, we'd be having quite a party today.

FRAU BELIUS: But they are not yet normal.

MOTHER: Do you think things will ever get back to normal?

FRAU BELIUS: Well, this once we're going to pretend they are! We'll wave a magic wand, Abracadabra! [*She takes two packets out of her pocket.*] And hey presto, there's . . . coffee . . . Abracadabra . . . and hey presto, tea! [*To* ELSIE.] And you'll undergo a transformation too, Elsie, in Inka's last new dress. [*She dabs her eyes.*] I mustn't think about it, she always loved wearing it, it'll be too big for you. We'll have to take it in. [*She looks at the clock.*] Oh God, is that the time already? They'll be here in a minute.

MOTHER: Do at least comb your hair, Elsie.

ELSIE: [*Turning round and smiling as if somewhere else.*] I want Lona to do my hair.

MOTHER: [*Embarrassed.*] That's enough of this nonsense! [*To* FRAU BELIUS.] She's nineteen, but still behaves like a real baby! Always talking about that girl . . .

ELSIE: Lona.

MOTHER: I can't understand it. She really was a thoroughly bad lot. Somehow had no roots. You know, I'd be prepared to bet the night we were bombed she ran off with the first bit of riffraff that came her way.

FRAU BELIUS: They would surely have found some sign of her. But nothing's ever come to light?

MOTHER: Not even a button.

MOTHER: [*Noticing* FATHER's *watch on* ELSIE's *wrist.*] Elsie, what's that?

ELSIE: [*Holds on to the watch.*] I'm going to give it to him when he comes back.

MOTHER: Oh my God . . . Ludwig's watch, Elsie, how did you come by that? Give it me, this instant . . .

[*A knock on the door.* FRAU BELIUS *throws a bathrobe over* ELSIE, *then opens the door.* RODEWALD *comes in, behind him,* OSWIN; *followed by* ALMUTH, *holding a bunch of flowers and pushing* NOLLE, *who is now blind.*]

FRAU BELIUS: The bridegroom, the bridegroom. And he's five minutes early! He can't wait! [*Imitating a clergyman.*] Do you, Herr Friedrich-Karl Rodewald, take Frau Anna Therese . . . and so on and so forth . . . [*Holding both their hands together.*] . . . to love and to honour till death do you part.

MOTHER: [*Laughing, takes the flowers from* ALMUTH, *while* RODEWALD *puts his arms round* MOTHER.] Oh, Almuth, flowers! I haven't had flowers for ages; I'd almost forgotten what they look like . . . I'm so grateful, Almuth, Herr Oswin. [*She presses both* AL-MUTH's *and* OSWIN's *hands; noticing the* GENERAL *coming in.*] Oh, now Herr Belius in person! [*Quietly.*] It's almost like a . . . miracle, so upright, Herr Belius, so . . . un-broken, you almost inspire new hope in one . . .

RODEWALD: And with good reason. Now at last we have both hands free to make a new start. [*Raising his crippled hands.*]

[*Laying her head on his shoulder,* MOTHER *weeps.*]

[FRAU BELIUS *presents the* GENERAL, *who stands smiling in the doorway, wearing a uniform which has been refashioned to look like a sort of national costume—complete with antler buttons.*]

FRAU BELIUS: Don't be despondent. He certainly isn't. Here he is, ladies and gentlemen, just as he's always been, in his old, proud posture . . . His health improved while he was in prison, he's even got rid of his neuralgia . . . Yes, dear friends, you can breathe again, everything's going to be all right, we're all having a new lease of life. This is our first celebration of peacetime.

RODEWALD: That's a wonderful word!

[*A long, emotionally charged silence follows.* ELSIE *looks closely at the* GENERAL, *and also smiles; but suddenly she no longer sees an ex-general in national costume but something horrifying, as frightening as a monster with absolutely no connection to its environment—the kind of phenomenon described in certain mental disorders. Grinning, she circles the* GENERAL, *and suddenly attacks him with her scissors.* MOTHER *and* ALMUTH *scream: "Elsie!" "Take the scissors from her!" and "Get hold of her!"* FRAU BELIUS *saves the situation by flinging* INKA's *dress over* ELSIE's *head.*]

FRAU BELIUS: [*Calming* ELSIE *down.*] There, there . . . Calm down, calm down. It's all right, child. Everything's all right . . .

[*Then* FRAU BELIUS *slowly does up all* ELSIE's *buttons at the back. During this treatment,* ELSIE *becomes calmer, and gradually adopts the same cheerful smile as all the others who have gathered here for the first celebration of peacetime.* MOTHER *gives her the bouquet of poppies.* ELSIE *clasps them to her.*]

FRAU BELIUS: Now, ladies and gentlemen, would you prefer coffee or tea?

[*The End.*]

Daniela Fischerová (b. 1948)

The history of the Czech theater in this century has been tumultuous and highly political. During the First Republic, from the end of World War I until the Munich Pact (1938), Czechoslovakia had a robust and internationally recognized national drama. Under the German occupation (1939–45) and under the Communist regime from 1948 until the midsixties, the Czech theater was severely controlled. The rejuvenation in the Prague Spring, culminating in 1968, witnessed a new artistic flourishing. With the imposition of censorship in September 1969, following the Soviet-led Warsaw Pact intrusion, the scene again became bleak, what has been called "the silenced theater." Playwrights were forced either to be constrained by the restrictions imposed and remain officially acceptable or to write from exile (Ivan Klíma, Pavel Kohout, and Milan Kundera). They could also choose to maintain their expressive integrity and risk imprisonment (Václav Havel) or circulate their typescript manuscripts (*samizdat*) underground, occasionally smuggling them out of the country for foreign publication. The only possible venue for dissident theater was in a private apartment, hence the origins of living room productions.

Daniela Fischerová was twenty when the tanks rolled into Prague. Havel, Klíma and Kohout were the acclaimed dramatists. She inherits their tone of dissidence and artistic strength, appreciating early the political dimensions and possibilities of theater. In a climate where the mass media and the public stages were rigidly controlled and censored, drama remained an important if risky avenue for political expression—one to which Czechs were sharply attuned. Fischerová clearly recognized this.

Her first play, *The Hour Between Dog and Wolf* (*Hodina mezi psem a vlkem*, 1979), was closed by the authorities after three performances, and though her works were not technically banned, she was among the prohibited authors. Eventually, *Dog and Wolf* and her subsequent plays, including *A Tale* (*Baj*, 1982)—based on the Pied Piper legend, *Princess T* (1986)—recalling the story of Turandot, and *Sudden Misfortune* (*Náhlé neštěstí*, 1993) secured for her a place among the first rank of Czech dramatists.

Fischerová is both an intellectual and a subversive author—explicitly mining historical and literary sources to subvert them for their contemporary social and political significance. She has often been criticized for her unfeminine lack of emotion, that is, for being too complex and intellectual, layering her plays with historical references and sociopolitical implications. Her response to this criticism is dismissive, that no man writing as she does would be attacked in this way.

Daniela Fischerová, ca. 1996. (Courtesy of photographer and author.)

Because her career as a dramatist was so precarious between 1979 and the Velvet Revolution of November 1989, she studied at the Film Academy (FAMU) and worked as a screenwriter. She also wrote children's books and short fiction. As a further financial safeguard, she trained as a psychotherapist.

The Hour Between Dog and Wolf overtly refers to the biography and poetry of François Villon (1431–63?), focusing on a few select events, recalled from the central situation of his trial in 1462. But in its selection of events and its postmodern scuttling of chronology and anachronistic props (cameras, tapes, and costumes), Fischerová reveals her interest to be elsewhere. On trial is not Villon, his age, nor his crimes (ruffianism, murder, and "sacred" robbery), but the social deviancy identified with his art.

Villon serves as the example of the unsquelchable artist straddling a divided world. Is he an artist or merely, as Philippe Sermoy asserts, a "compulsive troublemaker" who masks his "personal aberrations" with his artistic genius? Like the hours of the dog and the wolf, separated by the twilight during which the trial plays itself out, the extremes are not so black and white and distinct as they might seem. People come in different shades and dress and times, as we witness in almost filmic cut and montage style. The only characters, in fact, who remain stable are

Villon—as he faces the trial court composed of the state, the church, friends, lovers, family, and "the holy university of Paris"—and Angèle, "a romantic invention of Villon's biographers."

Ultimately, as the Bishop makes clear, it is Villon's poetry that is on trial. In a view disturbingly consonant with that of Plato in the last book of *The Republic,* his song threatens order. It also converges with the demand, as expressed by Régnier, for "total and unconditional freedom for Villon." This demand, which the Bishop rejects as delusory, crosses the centuries; Régnier closes the play requesting an appeal, in Prague, on March 23, 1979 (the day the play actually opened and the curtain line that provoked the censors to ban it).

Régnier's definition of *medieval,* where "the stronger eats the weaker, and between bites forces it to say 'bon appétit!'" perfectly, painfully describes the twentieth century. The oddly appearing tape recorders and cameras convey the reality of historical research; we comprehend the past (and, by extension, our own times) with the aid of intellectual and technological invention. *Vita brevis. Ars longus.*

SELECTED BIBLIOGRAPHY IN ENGLISH

Ambros, Veronika. "Daniela Fischerová's New Palimpsest Between 'Living in Truth' and 'The Battle for an Island of Trust.'" *Canadian Slavonic Papers/Revue Canadienne des Slavistes* 36 (1994), 363–76.

Bermel, Neil. "Introduction." Daniela Fischerová, *Fingers Pointing Somewhere Else.* New Haven, Conn.: Catbird Press, 1999.

Czerwinski, Edward J. "The Invasion: Effects on Theater and Drama in Eastern Europe." *The Soviet Invasion of Czechoslovakia: Its Effects on Eastern Europe.* Eds. E. J. Czerwinski and Jaroslaw Piekalkiewicz. New York: Prager, 1972. Pp. 191–210.

Day, Barbara, ed. "Introduction." *Czech Plays: Modern Czech Drama.* London: Nick Hern, 1994.

Fischerová, Daniela. "Interview." *Theatre, Czech and Slovak* 4 (1992), 16–20.

Goetz-Stankiewicz, Marketa. "Ethics at the Crossroads: The Czech 'Dissident Writer' as Dramatic Character." *Modern Drama* 27 (1984), 112–23.

———. *The Silenced Theatre: Czech Playwrights Without a Stage.* Toronto: University of Toronto Press, 1979.

Königsmark, Václav. "Wandering and Searching." *Theatre, Czech and Slovak.* 4 (1992), 4–9.

THE HOUR BETWEEN DOG AND WOLF
Daniela Fischerová

Translated by Véronique Firkušný-Callegari and Robert T. Jones

CHARACTERS

FRANÇOIS VILLON   the accused

THE BISHOP OF D'AUSSIGNY

RÉGNIER DE MONTIGNY   also called Wolf

PHILIPPE SERMOY   priest

FATHER VILLON   foster father of the accused

GUY TABARY   companion of the accused

MOUSTIER   bailiff

PICHART   bailiff

MOTHER OF THE ACCUSED

CATHERINE DE VAUSSELLES

ANGÈLE   harlot

JEANNETTE   harlot

MARGOT   known as Fat Margot, innkeeper

THE CHORUS

The specific selection of Villon's poems and the extent to which they are used in the play is up to the director. The only poems specified are:

"The Ballad of Dead Ladies," with its refrain, "But where are the snows of yesteryear."
"The Best Tongues Wag in Paris"
"Epitaph (Quatrain)"

Their length depends on the rhythm of the production and should be decided by the director. In the case of a choice between translations, the director should choose the most contemporary-sounding one.

ACT ONE

An empty courtroom: a raised half-circle of ten stools with places for the accused, the judge, the accuser, the defender. A gallery with the Chorus in it. A witness box and a bench for the accused. A cross.

The Chrous begins the prelude: a musical clattering of many voices, at first disorganized, then growing louder. Someone whistles, someone beats out a rhythm, and the melody gradually comes together until it is a wordless musical number accompanying the entire first scene.

The members of the cast gather unwillingly in the room. They are in period costumes, except for ANGÈLE, *the younger harlot, who is barefoot and dressed as an angel in a tunic with a wreath on her head. She doesn't look at anyone and, with the anxiousness of a diligent schoolgirl, is trying out dance steps on the ramp, practicing bows, smiling and giving the impression of a certain unreality. The older harlot,* JEANNETTE, *sits provocatively with legs apart and (despite the 15th-century locale) is busily chewing bubblegum, snapping the bubbles as loudly as she can. Apart from everyone, and nearly immobile, stands a stern elderly man, the* BISHOP D'AUSSIGNY. CATHERINE DE VAUSSELLES *walks to and fro, nervously clenching and unclenching her hands. Everybody is avoiding everyone else, and a feeling of general wariness prevails.*

The FATHER *approaches from the back of the room as the servant of the court, carrying a fat file and ringing a small bell. He always acts kindly, deferentially, and with the slightly distracted air of old age. He smiles sheepishly, takes a look around and says to no one and to everyone:*

FATHER: Yes, yes . . . Everyone here?

[*No one has anything to say.* FATHER *opens the file.*]

FATHER: Allow me . . . Paris, Advent, 1462. The tribunal of Paris versus François Montcorbier, alias Villon. Witnesses . . .

[*At this moment a latecomer bursts in:* GUY TABARY, *an uncouth dandy with a broad smile. He cheerfully snaps his fingers.*]

TABARY: Well, well, well! This is some gathering we have here! Salutations to you all! [*To* FATHER.] I'm the Tabary guy.

[*Everyone pretends not to have heard.* FATHER *coughs uneasily.*]

FATHER: Uh, so . . . Madame Montcorbier, mother of the accused . . .
MOTHER: [*Skittishly.*] That's me.

[*Another latecomer hurries in:* RÉGNIER DE MONTIGNY. *He looks like a contemporary newsman, complete with tape recorder and flash camera. He ignores everyone and glowers overbearingly. He sits down on the nearest seat and proceeds to arrange his equipment. Everyone stares at him.*]

FATHER: [*Hesitantly.*] Excuse me, sir . . . this is a courtroom . . .
RÉGNIER: [*Without deigning to look up, he flashes a scrap of paper in his hand and snaps.*] Press!
TABARY: Why that's . . . but there's no way . . . That's Régn!

[*He comes vividly alive and tries to get* RÉGNIER'*s attention. He makes conspiratorial gestures, and he even howls like a wolf.* RÉGNIER *doesn't react at all.*]

TABARY: Régn! Régn!
FATHER: Well, of course . . . going on . . . Mademoiselle Catherine de Vausselles, the fiancée of the accused . . .
CATHERINE: [*Instantly and emphatically.*] No!
FATHER: I beg your pardon?
CATHERINE: Mademoiselle Catherine de Vausselles, yes. Fiancée of the accused, no.
PHILIPPE: [*Rises, taking a pompous, rhetorical stance.*] Within your documents there lies not

only a grave error of fact, but a very grave offense. And I venture to suggest that I know how it came to be there . . .

CATHERINE: [*Freezes him with a word.*] That's all right.

[*At this moment there blasts into the order of the day, very loudly and in the middle of a verse—like an arbitrary segment of a cassette—a song in modern arrangement, sung in contemporary style.*]

TAPE RECORDER: ". . . Where are the snows of yesteryear . . ."

[*Everybody turns around.* TABARY *is ecstatically stamping to the beat, whistling along.*]

FATHER: Sir! Please!

RÉGNIER: Yeah. [*He lowers the volume and scribbles in his notebook. The song plays on.*]

FATHER: The Reverend Father Philippe Sermoy, from the Cathedral of Nôtre Dame . . .

PHILIPPE: [*Pausing for dramatic effect.*] Here.

FATHER: Your . . . your relationship to the accused?

PHILIPPE: Victim.

FATHER: Sorry?

PHILIPPE: Victim. Treacherously murdered by the accused, May of '55.

[*A moment of silence.* CATHERINE *takes a sharp breath.* JEANNETTE *looks amused and lewdly smacks her lips at* PHILIPPE. RÉGNIER *stops the song and rewinds. The loud "monkey-talk" of the rapidly rewinding tape.*]

FATHER: His Eminence, the Rector of the University of Paris.

BISHOP: Present.

[FATHER *abruptly changes his role. As he looks at the* BISHOP *he seems to shrink and become a timid old man. Trembling, he lays aside the file.*]

FATHER: Your honor . . . pardon an old man . . . permit me to ask . . . the student Montcorbier, François Mont-cor-bier . . .

BISHOP: And you are?

FATHER: His foster-father, your honor. The accused's foster-father. Father Villon, priest from St. Benoît, should you be so kind as to . . .

[*An inhuman scream suddenly comes from the tape recorder. Everyone jumps.*]

VILLON: [*Voice from the tape recorder, shouting.*] Aaaaa! Enough! Aaaaa!

[MOTHER *stares at the tape recorder, stunned but mesmerized.* TABARY *squirms uneasily.*]

TABARY: This is unnecessary! It's too much! After all . . .

BISHOP: [*Stepping over to* RÉGNIER, *sharply.*] That's enough!

RÉGNIER: [*Standing his ground.*] Just a second.

[*The scream continues for a moment, then abruptly stops without* RÉGNIER's *help.* RÉGNIER *makes a rude face.*]

RÉGNIER: That's where he passes out.

[*The crowd murmurs.* FATHER *claps his hands for silence.*]

FATHER: Ladies and gentlemen! Ladies and gentlemen!

RÉGNIER: [*Coolly, informatively.*] Water torture. In the year 1460.

FATHER: Quiet, please! Please! Guy Tabary, companion of the accused . . .

TABARY: [*Dejectedly.*] Here.

[*The song "Where are the snows of yesteryear" again comes from the tape recorder, continuing throughout the scene.* RÉGNIER *gets up, strolls around with his camera, turning on and shutting off small floodlights, while nobody pays him the slightest attention.*]

FATHER: Margot, also known as Fat Margot, innkeeper . . .

MARGOT: Yeah.

FATHER: Jeannette, harlot.

[JEANNETTE *smacks her lips, throws back her head, and spits her bubblegum into the air. It describes a large arc and falls into her outstretched palm.*]

FATHER: Monsieur RÉGNIER de Montigny, also known as "Wolf," head of the criminal gang of which the accused was a member . . .

[RÉGNIER *turns on a floodlight and shines it into his own face. Everybody turns to look at him.* JEANNETTE *whistles in approval.* FATHER *sighs.*]

FATHER: Yes, yes . . . Go ahead, ladies and gentlemen.

[*Everyone leaves the stage. Only* ANGÈLE *and* FATHER *remain.* ANGÈLE *runs over to him.*]

ANGÈLE: And me? What about me?

FATHER: Sorry. And who are you?

ANGÈLE: I'm Angèle!

FATHER: Are you a witness?

ANGÈLE: [*Childishly.*] I'm . . . I'm his bride!

[FATHER *fumbles through the file.* RÉGNIER *aims the floodlight at* ANGÈLE. *She covers her eyes.* RÉGNIER *chuckles.*]

RÉGNIER: She never existed. Don't look for her.

FATHER: I'm sorry, Mademoiselle . . .

ANGÈLE: [*Pleading.*] But I've got to be in there somewhere!

RÉGNIER: I'm telling you, stop looking. She's a phantom. The romantic invention of Villon's biographers. Can I turn this thing off, Gramps?

ANGÈLE: [*Still childishly, playing her trump card.*] I'm his guardian angel!

[RÉGNIER *laughs.* FATHER *gives* ANGÈLE *a push and they both disappear. The song continues to play,* RÉGNIER *whistling it to himself. Then he pulls out his flash and aims it at the courtroom. Abruptly the lights go out: the sharp light plucks a new figure out of the darkness. A young man in handcuffs stands on the bench for the accused. He is looking out into the audience.* RÉGNIER *gives a short wolf-howl.* VILLON *notices him and smiles happily.* RÉGNIER *makes the secret sign and* VILLON *shakes his handcuffs in comical helplessness. Like a newsman,* RÉGNIER *quickly uses his flash to take pictures of the whole scene,* VILLON *disappearing into the darkness and then reappearing again in the bright light. The following exchanges between him and* RÉGNIER *come across as a series of flashes rather than a coherent conversation.*]

RÉGNIER: How do you feel?

VILLON: Like the sole of my own shoe!

[*He strikes a pose of clownish misery. Darkness, flash, light.*]

RÉGNIER: [*Furiously.*] Why are you here? What are you doing in Paris?

VILLON: Where else could I be! I had to come to Paris! Régn!

[*Darkness, flash, light, a new position.*]

RÉGNIER: [*With sudden compassion and concern.*] Are they going to get you, Villon?

VILLON: No . . . Yes . . . I don't know! What can I do? [*He suddenly leans as far forward as he can and whispers desperately.*] Régn! Régn! Did they really hang you?

[*Darkness. A moment of silence. Suddenly bells ring out, one after another, many bells, until the entire space is filled with their sound. Slowly the light returns and we see the Senate walk onto the stage: nine figures, wrapped in black gowns that cancel out their individuality. Slowly they take their places. Both bailiffs—* MOUSTIER *and* PICHART*—stand behind* VILLON. FATHER *stands on the side. They all look intently at* VILLON.*]

BISHOP: In the name of God!

[*The bells stop ringing. They all bow their heads for a moment, then sit down.*]

BISHOP: [*Matter-of-factly.*] We hereby open the case against François Montcorbier, also known as François Villon.

VILLON: [*Smiling and somewhat taunting, with an exaggerated nasal sound on the name* VIL-LON.] Master François Villon. [*The* BISHOP *looks at him fixedly with no other reaction.*] Your honors! Although my studies did at times resemble a galloping ride on a lathering horse, nevertheless I finally managed to reach my goal! With characteristic mercy, the great University of Paris proclaimed me a master of liberal arts. Which is why, respectfully, I sign myself Master François Villon.

[*The* BISHOP, *still staring at* VILLON, *impatiently taps the table with his knuckle.* VILLON *smiles and starts tapping out the same rhythm. The* BISHOP *jerks his hand back and nods almost imperceptibly to the bailiffs. One of them gives* VILLON's *shackles a sharp yank and* VIL-LON *collapses under the bench. Unperturbed, the* BISHOP *continues.*]

BISHOP: Is the Prosecution present?

PHILIPPE: [*Rises.*] The Prosecution is here!

BISHOP: So.

[PHILIPPE *takes his position. Carefully controlling his temper, with professional poise and polished diction, he reads.*]

PHILIPPE: The punishable act took place this year, on the day of Saint Boniface, in the small marketplace in Paris. It was long past midnight but the windows of the honorable Monsieur Ferrebouc's writing office were still lit. All at once the peaceful, Godfearing clerks were frightened by a suspicious noise. A gang of ruffians, led by the accused Villon, appeared and began hurling rocks at the clerks. These clerks, all of them monks, responded with Christian appeals.

VILLON: [*To the bailiff.*] Hey! Who ratted on the gang that night at Blois?

PICHART: Shut up!

PHILIPPE: The Bishop's secretary, the most highly respected Monsieur Marcel Ferrebouc, intervened. He stepped before the ruffians as an emissary of peace, hoping to restore order, and at that moment the accused rushed upon him with a dagger and stabbed him without mercy.

VILLON: [*Amazed.*] What? That's a lie! [*Bursts into a fit of stamping, whistling and shouting throughout the following lines.*]

PHILIPPE: Yet this attack, however condemnable, is not the first reprehensible act of the accused Villon. On the contrary, it is merely the logical culmination of a sad succession of seven serious and countless less-serious offenses.

VILLON: [*In a fury.*] This is treachery! I protest! It's a filthy lie!

PHILIPPE: It is known to the court that even as a student the accused thought nothing of robbing the safe of his own alma mater. The court is aware that for several years the accused was a member of the Wolf Pack, the worst criminal gang that has ever devastated this land with its robberies and assaults.

VILLON: The court knows nothing, you cockatoo!

PHILIPPE: The court knows that the accused did not stop even at sacrilege! He stole from the Church! He stole the most sacred statue of our Lord Jesus Christ.

VILLON: [*To the bailiffs, quickly.*] Who ratted?

MOUSTIER: Quiet!

VILLON: Who snared the wolf?

PICHART: Hold your tongue!

VILLON: [*Savagely wrestling with the shackle around his throat.*] I'll shit on your grave, baby!

[PICHART *harshly strikes* VILLON *across the fingers with a key.* VILLON *gasps and lets go.* PHILIPPE *lays down the file and stares straight ahead. When he speaks, his tone is different. He has dropped the restraint of his former testimony and now speaks more dramatically, as if in a pulpit.*]

PHILIPPE: Let us turn our gaze and peer into the depths of the past. Let us look down the steep path of Time. Here there once lived a scholar, wild as a poppy seed, a poet blessed by God, the joy of Paris. But he was not content with the gift of God. The voice of the Devil called to him from the slimy darkness, and he set off. He goes forth, rushing toward Satan. The sparks of God die out and dark eccentricities rise from the depths to take their place.

VILLON: [*Disgusted.*] Aaaaa!

PHILIPPE: Where is he heading? How deep does he try to sink? Is it blood you thirst for? Yes! [*Pointing to* VILLON.] The rabble-rouser, the marauder, the thief . . . is also a murderer!

[*Suddenly one of the female jurors rushes from her place. As she runs, she throws off her robe, revealing herself as* CATHERINE *in full historical costume. She begins to shake* VILLON *hysterically.*]

CATHERINE: Murderer? You killed him! He's dead! You hear me?

VILLON: [*Taken aback, he manages to grab her wrists.*] Catherine!

CATHERINE: You ruined it all! How am I ever supposed to live with you!

VILLON: [*Paralyzed.*] Get hold of yourself, sweetheart.

CATHERINE: Just look what's following you! Chaos! Wolves! With blood on their noses!

VILLON: Catherine! It's just a story.

CATHERINE: [*Hysterically.*] What story?

VILLON: A story! Fiction! About me. [*Quietly, mysteriously.*] Don't believe everything they tell you about me.

CATHERINE: [*Throws her arms around his neck and whispers imploringly.*] Did you kill him, François?

VILLON: [*Miserably.*] They told me he died from the filth in the hospital.

[CATHERINE *begins screaming in uncontrolled, spastic cadences. The* BISHOP *gestures to* PHILIPPE, *who approaches* CATHERINE *and gently but firmly pulls her away from* VILLON.]

CATHERINE: [*To* VILLON.] I curse you! I curse the day you were born! [*To* PHILIPPE.] Get your priestly paws off me, you piece of filth! You just want what François has! Go on and envy him! Devour yourself with envy! You're the one to blame for it all anyhow.

BISHOP: [*Drily.*] Who are you?

[CATHERINE *turns around. In an instant she has changed into a self-assured, cold woman with a slightly defiant manner. She steps into the witness box and places her hand on the Bible.*]

CATHERINE: I am Catherine de Vausselles.

BISHOP: Relationship to the accused?

CATHERINE: No.

BISHOP: Answer the question.

CATHERINE: I am answering. Between myself and the accused there is not now, there never was, there never will be any "relationship." I barely knew him. Quite frankly, it amazes me that I am here as a witness in such a common trial.

BISHOP: The court is informed that you maintained an intimate relationship between yourself and the accused.

CATHERINE: Obviously the court has not been informed of the origin of this ridiculous rumor. Could you put this on the record? So then. The accused himself spread this rumor. Why? To glorify himself! He exposed me to the ridicule of the riff-raff to soothe his wounded vanity. I suppose that in this sense there IS a relationship to the accused, but a victimizing one, and in that case I too exert my right to press charges.

BISHOP: Hmmm. What can you tell us about the accused?

CATHERINE: Your honor. Is the word "buffoon" comprehensive enough for you?

BISHOP: What do you know about the event that has just been described?

CATHERINE: About the murder? It was regrettable. Repeat, regrettable.

BISHOP: Were you present when it occurred?

CATHERINE: [*Astonished.*] Oh no!

BISHOP: Did you know the victim?

CATHERINE: [*Conversationally.*] You mean Sermoy? Slightly. He was a sort of fashionable preacher. He and Villon would go at each other like two cocks on a dunghill. He always gave me the impression of being somehow possessed. Not by the Devil, God forbid, but rather by himself.

BISHOP: Get to the point, witness.

CATHERINE: The point? There was no point.

BISHOP: I am finished. Does the defense wish to question the witness?

[*He looks around, but no one reacts. He angrily strikes his gavel.*]

BISHOP: Where is the defense? Who was assigned to defend Villon?

ANGÈLE: I!

[*Another member of the jury jumps up. From beneath the hood emerges a girlish, almost child-ish, head.* ANGÈLE *tears at her robe and runs to* VILLON. *The bailiffs laugh, and a murmur runs through the Senate.*]

ANGÈLE: I will defend him! [*To* CATHERINE, *as she runs.*] I'll defend him! I'm coming, François!

CATHERINE: [*Disdainfully.*] Who is that?

MOUSTIER: Where are you off to, kid? How old are you anyway?

ANGÈLE: [*Falls to her knees before* VILLON, *clumsily unbuttoning her robe.*] I turned sixteen yesterday. François!

[VILLON *watches her, slightly annoyed.*]

VILLON: Angèle, go home.

ANGÈLE: I know, I know. You think I don't understand anything! But I'm not afraid! [*To the Senate, challengingly.*] I'm not afraid! [*To* VILLON.] Help me with these God-awful clothes!

VILLON: Cut it out! We're not alone here! There are people!

ANGÈLE: What are they to you? What do you expect from them? Screw 'em, François!

VILLON: Not possible. Come on, come on. Cover up!

ANGÈLE: [*Passionately.*] You think they're on your side? [*Slipping into street slang.*] They ain't! They're scared o' you!

VILLON: Go home!

ANGÈLE: [*Again the street slang.*] They're scared! They're scared! [*Assuming proper speech.*] I can tell when people are frightened! [*She embraces* VILLON's *knees, whispering with the utmost urgency.*] François! They made a deal about you!

[*Another juror abruptly leaps up and strikes the table with his fist.*]

RÉGNIER: That's enough! [*With authority.*] Why are we tolerating this? What kind of a pseudo-historical masquerade is this? An omelet of emotions with a cherry on top! [*Roughly buttons up* Angèle *and pushes her away.*] Beat it! I am Villon's defense.

PHILIPPE: [*Stands up.*] Sir! Who are you?

RÉGNIER: Régnier de Montigny, sir. And you know very well who I am!

PHILIPPE: What makes you think you are qualified to defend Villon?

RÉGNIER: Thank God it's nothing that you, sir, are qualified to ask. [*To the* BISHOP.] I ask the distinguished ju . . .

[*The* BISHOP *silences him with a gesture. He looks him up and down for a long moment. In the meantime* ANGÈLE, *defeated, dawdles back to her place.* JEANNETTE *peeks out from under her cowl.*]

JEANNETTE: [*Amicably.*] You blew it, you little cow. Hmmm? [*Withdraws back under her cowl.*]

BISHOP: [*Cautiously.*] The court knows . . . Monsieur de Montigny. A former university man, if I'm not mistaken. Is that correct?

RÉGNIER: You're not mistaken, your honor.

BISHOP: Your studies came to a rather . . . abrupt end?

RÉGNIER: Again you are not mistaken. May I defend Villon?

BISHOP: Do you think that you, especially . . .

RÉGNIER: For a third time you're not mistaken, distinguished judge. [*With the professionalism of a lawyer.*] Pro primo: within the means of the procedural code I move that all heretofore recorded statements be stricken from the record. Pro secundo: by virtue of the corpus iuris ordinalis I assert my right to speak with my client.

[*The* BISHOP *nods.*]

PHILIPPE: May I ask my colleague what was the reason for the delay?

RÉGNIER: [*Defiantly.*] Of course you may. Five years before this latest judicial farce about Villon, I was hanged.

[*He walks over to* VILLON. *The bailiffs remove* VILLON's *shackles and leave. The Senate disappears in darkness and we see only* RÉGNIER *with* VILLON. VILLON *grins happily and makes the conspiratorial sign. Then he shakes out his stiff arms and with great dexterity turns somersaults as he talks, stretches and in general behaves like a puppy in a field.*]

VILLON: [*Holds out his arms, laughs.*] Régn! My wolf! Is it really you?

RÉGNIER: [*No reaction but anger.*] What are you here for?

VILLON: Where?

RÉGNIER: [*Ironically.*] In Paris! In Paris, my friend! In the world's teeth! [*Fiercely.*] Among this sewage!!

[VILLON *singing, tapping out the rhythm on the wooden courtroom benches. Sings* "The Best Tongues Wag in Paris."]

RÉGNIER: Shut up!

VILLON: [*With the exaggerated sigh of a scolded student he falls to his knees before* RÉGNIER.] Don't you know me [*Mockingly emphasizing the rolled French "R."*] RRRRRRégn? Anywhere else I wilt like wet underwear, RRRRRégn! I bloom only in the Parisian flowerpot, RRRRRégn! Anywhere else my roots rot, RRRRRégn!

RÉGNIER: You're up to your ears in rot now. Serves you right.

VILLON: I need Paris! I tried living without it, you know I did, but it didn't work.

RÉGNIER: Well, Paris has had it up to here with you! She'll take three bites and spit you into the woods!

VILLON: Oh no! Not the woods! The minute I see trees I break out in hives!

RÉGNIER: You're mad. But let's get to the point. Were you the one who stabbed that scumbag official?

VILLON: No. [*Suddenly wild.*] Régn! Who squealed on me that time in Blois?

RÉGNIER: Shit on Blois! Who threw this lawsuit at you?

VILLON: [*Seizing* RÉGNIER *by his shirt.*] Swear to me it wasn't you!

RÉGNIER: [*Roughly twisting his arm.*] Get your hands off me!

VILLON: If it was you, then I swear to God I'll go dig up your rotten corpse and saw off its legs! [*Desperately.*] Swear it, Régn!

RÉGNIER: You talk too much, and I'm in a hurry. Will anyone back up your testimony?

VILLON: [*Suddenly downcast, he sits.*] I hope so. Dogis will swear that he stabbed the old geezer.

RÉGNIER: Dogis? Which one is that?

VILLON: That one. That scorpion in jello! Ha!

[*The light locates* TABARY *in his robe. Surprised by the light,* TABARY *begins to bow, somewhat uncertainly, until the light goes off.*]

RÉGNIER: That's something, anyway. Back to work. Beat it.

[*He pushes* VILLON *off into the darkness, then returns to his seat. As he walks he removes the robe and is once again a modern newsman. He pulls out his notes.*]

VILLON: [*From the darkness.*] Régn! What's it like to die on the gallows?

RÉGNIER: [*Peers into the darkness and laughs.*] Delightful, my friend. [*Sarcastic.*] Like any old priest will tell you, the victim doesn't suffer at all. [*Fiercely.*] Your brain howls for half an hour while every bone in your body screams for mercy. [*Abruptly he turns around, holds out his hands and begins to lecture.*]

And then we're supposed to believe in something, my friends! That's how we're led around by the nose all our lives. What kind of literary fantasy engendered this version of Villon? What sort of romantic creature emerges before our eyes? Who is it? I have occupied myself with research material about François Villon for many years, and I keep running into the same two enduring phantoms. One is a kind of wax-works angel with its eyes fixed on the future: he's supposed to keep track of our moral debts—OURS! The other is simply a common rogue. This criminal, scoundrel, gangster, tumbling head-over-heels through the Middle Ages. Except . . .

[*A cough of disagreement. The light discovers* PHILIPPE, *also dressed as a modern man of science, seated in his professor's chair. His attitude is one of irony and reserve.*]

PHILIPPE: Permit me, my respected colleague. It isn't exactly leading one by the nose. To the extent that our awareness reaches, even in that narrow strip of ten or twelve years of Villon's career that has been SO touted by literary history, we have indisputable proof of seven serious transgressions . . .

RÉGNIER: [*With zeal.*] To the extent that our awareness reaches! Where does it reach? [*He mimics groping in the dark with an outstretched hand.*] How far can we reach through the mud of time? What can filter through the screen of six centuries?

PHILIPPE: Well, if you want to dispute the facts . . .

RÉGNIER: I want to dispute YOU! No civilized system of law accepts testimony from a secondhand witness! An event perceived only through what was heard is of interest to no one! And what can we possibly hear from the year FOURTEEN-HUNDRED-AND-WHATEVER?

PHILIPPE: Professor, this is an academic discussion, not a barroom dispute.

RÉGNIER: Shove it, Professor! As long as we're treating Villon like a criminal and a demon, we're completely off the mark. You know that.

PHILIPPE: A demon? Oh no. Merely a medieval highwayman of a routine sort. Every society knows these compulsive troublemakers and has the joyless task of dealing with them, all the less pleasant because, in most cases, they don't have artistic genius to mask their personal aberrations.

RÉGNIER: Personal aberrations! For Christ's sake! The entire time into which Villon was born was one enormous aberration! Villon's Paris was like a cat that howls because it feels an earthquake coming! That era was bursting at the seams!

PHILIPPE: It was no abstract era bursting at the seams that slashed open Father Sermoy's stomach. It was François Villon in person!

RÉGNIER: Villon! I'll tell you who Villon is! He is one hair standing straight up in terror on the scalp of his time! He is the counterblast of history, exploding through the narrow throat of a single individual!

PHILIPPE: [*Drily.*] Sir. If you are determined to create a "Hero of the Masses," may I suggest you pick someone who is not one-hundred percent a criminal.

RÉGNIER: Do you know what the Middle Ages are? They are no academic ground, they are a moral jungle, and the law of the jungle prevails. To pick on the details: your pitiful anecdote about that church braggart, that Sermoy or Chermoy or however he spells it, who didn't die from a stomach wound anyway but from the filth in the hospital, because the jungle was filthy, because no one ever swept and disinfected the jungle . . .

PHILIPPE: [*Insulted.*] I have no more to say. I have no more to say!

RÉGNIER: [*Passionately.*] I'm glad of that!

[*Both sit down, seething with rage. A pause.*]

PHILIPPE: There is a question from the general assembly. Go on and answer it.

RÉGNIER: [*Startled.*] What?

[*Light up on the stools, which are empty except for* JEANNETTE, ANGÈLE *and* TABARY *dressed as modern students.* JEANNETTE, *the most hippie-looking of the three, raises her hand.*]

JEANNETTE: What is the law of the jungle, Professor?

RÉGNIER: [*Taken aback by the stupidity of the question.*] What? Why surely . . .

PHILIPPE: [*Smugly.*] If I may. The strong eats the weak. Isn't that what you meant, Professor?

RÉGNIER: [*Recovering.*] That's all we need, for the weak to eat the strong. What a lot of leftovers there would be. Hmmm?

JEANNETTE: Thanks.

TABARY: Could you define medieval for us?

RÉGNIER: Gladly. The stronger eats the weaker, and between bites forces it to say "Bon appétit!"

JEANNETTE: [*Trendy.*] Cool!

RÉGNIER: [*To* ANGÈLE, *who has raised her hand.*] And you?

ANGÈLE: [*Naively, trying hard.*] I would just . . . I think that Villon was so . . . so awesome . . . that he shouldn't be judged like others . . . In a way, maybe he had the right . . .

RÉGNIER: [*Very theatrically collapses into a chair.*] Whew! Sit down, Mademoiselle, and I'll answer you. [*Jumps up.*] My answer is: No, no, no! For God's sake, understand that! The Middle Ages were like a cannibal, and the world looks a lot different from behind a cannibal's teeth than it does in a panoramic view from 600 years later! "He had the right"! Mademoiselle! Do you know about the Inquisition's idea of justice? Take that idea and torture it until it screams out a definition of justice. Then we'll talk some more!

PHILIPPE: Oh come now. That's laying it on a bit thick, isn't it?

[RÉGNIER *starts, annoyed. He dons his robe.*]

RÉGNIER: I'm going to turn this ridiculous trial inside out! Young lady! Do you have any idea of what torture is? Water torture? Well? It's when they open up your pretty little mouth like this and pour salt water into you, and they pour and pour and go on pouring and keep pouring . . .

[*A muffled cry in the dark. The light catches* VILLON'S MOTHER, *without a robe, dressed as a peasant woman. She shields her eyes, holding up her arms to protect herself from the bright light.*]

PHILIPPE: [*Jumps up.*] That's enough!

RÉGNIER: Enough? Enough to quench your thirst, certainly. But no, it's not enough. You're lying there strapped down . . .

PHILIPPE: [*Grabs* RÉGNIER *by the shoulder.*] Control yourself!

MOTHER: François? What's wrong with François? Sir, I am his mother . . .

RÉGNIER: [*With emotion.*] And it's pouring out of your kidneys, that is if you're goddam lucky and your kidneys are still working, going full throttle: whirr! whirr! whirr!

ANGÈLE: [*Plugging her ears, imploringly.*] Enough, please, enough!

PHILIPPE: Enough!

MOTHER: Where is the Bishop?

RÉGNIER: They tortured Villon with water for four straight days! Four days! Are you still interested in the concept of justice?

BISHOP: [*Very loud.*] Enough!

[*The turmoil subsides. The light floods a different part of the stage.* VILLON *is lying on a plank bed, face down, paralyzed. A pitcher stands by the bed. Above the pitcher stand both bailiffs. The* BISHOP *slowly walks to them and gazes intently at the prone* VILLON.]

BISHOP: Did he talk?

PICHART: No.

BISHOP: Nothing at all?

MOUSTIER: [*Snickers.*] Just curses.

BISHOP: Hmm. Go away. Go.

[*Dismisses the bailiffs with a gesture. He stares searchingly at* VILLON, *then is about to leave. Suddenly* MOTHER *throws herself at his feet and seizes his hand.*]

MOTHER: Your honor! In the name of God! Is my son a criminal?

BISHOP: [*Pulling loose, grudgingly.*] What is crime? What is a criminal? Who knows?

[*The* BISHOP *leaves. The* CHORUS *launches into a wild song.* MARGOT *enters, carrying a table, begins to set it, shakes the paralyzed* VILLON. *Her remarks mingle with the singing of the* CHORUS.]

MARGOT: [*Over the music.*] Move it, you pig. I've gotta set the table!

[*She shakes* VILLON, *who moans drunkenly.* MARGOT *slaps his face, pulls his hair, her actions gradually turning into gruff embraces.*]

MARGOT: You're drunk as a monk again.

[*She yanks* VILLON *into a sitting position by his hair.* VILLON *jerks away, seizes his head in his hands and painfully shakes it.*]

VILLON: Ow! I've got mice in my head!

MARGOT: [*Embracing* VILLON, *who responds agreeably.*] You are a pig, aren't you?

[*An exhilarated group of Parisian young people bursts onto the scene:* RÉGNIER, TABARY, JEANNETTE, ANGÈLE, PICHART. *As a trophy from one of their successful raids, they triumphantly carry a signboard of a butcher's shop. Dissonant song, laughter, arbitrary exclamations.* VILLON *pushes* MARGOT *away, sits up, becomes alert.*]

VILLON: Is that Régn?

MARGOT: Aren't you a little pig!

VILLON: Shut up a minute! [*Calls out.*] RRrrrégn!

MARGOT: [*Insulted, gets up.*] Get up, varmint! Move! Feet off the table!

[*The excited young people crowd to* VILLON. PICHART *sits off to the side, snaps his fingers at* MARGOT, *who brings him wine, after which he sits drinking in silence and warily listening. The others are shouting at each other, the remarks coming all at once.*]

TABARY: [*Thrilled.*] Franky is here! Franky, get up! Your buddy's here! Guy Tabary!

JEANNETTE: [*Excited.*] Franky! Everybody in Paris is at each other's throats! It's a fantastic bloodbath!

MARGOT: [*Harshly knocking* VILLON *off the table.*] Off!

TABARY: [*Angry.*] Watch it, woman! This is the Maestro! He's our genius!

[RÉGNIER *pushes aside the group, grabs* VILLON *and yanks him to his feet.*]

RÉGNIER: Move it, genius!

VILLON: Régn!

TABARY: [*Slapping out a rhythm on the signboard as if he were playing a tabla.*] Let's have a pitcher here! Fast!

MARGOT: When pigs whistle. Who's paying?

TABARY: Right here! Guy Tabary! Guy Tabary does anything for his friends!

VILLON: What's up?

TABARY: A job, buddy. No shit, a real job.

JEANNETTE: [*Simultaneously with above.*] The cops are pissed, really pissed. The students ripped off the butcher shop.

RÉGNIER: [*Leaps onto the table, throws open his arms, elated.*] Chaos! Magnificent, sublime chaos! Another chunk of Paris in shambles! Gloria! One blessed day it will all blow up in smithereens and the only thing left will be a nasty stink!

[VILLON *leaps onto the next table. He strums his lute and, like* RÉGNIER, *shouts in high spirits. The entire dispute that follows is in the spirit of a high-spirited confrontation, not a philosophical discussion. Both men are enjoying themselves mightily, and their argument is accompanied by much laughter.*]

VILLON: I protest! I have Paris under my thumb, my MERCIFUL thumb! Paris is the ear of the world! Where else would I find an ear?

MARGOT: [*Fuming.*] I'm going to throw out every last one of you. You'll end up bringing the cops in here!

RÉGNIER: The only word you have to whisper into this brazen ear is the word [*Shouts it out.*] NO!

TABARY: [*Drunkenly embraces* MARGOT, *his retort mingling with* RÉGNIER's *and* VILLON's *dialogue.*] Forget the cops, Margot! You know what I'd like to do to the cops!

JEANNETTE: And with a full bladder!

TABARY: [*Displaying a full wine glass.*] Tabary always has a full bladder!

VILLON: I protest! I'm not going to settle for just one word! I won't stop until I've used every word in the French language!

TABARY: I'm a student! I have academic immunity! No cop is allowed to lay a finger on me.

MARGOT: Get your head out of your ass, you idiot. When they catch you they'll make mincemeat out of all of you. And you'll have it coming!

RÉGNIER: The world is rotting! Let it rot! Villon! Join me! I declare a full-scale attack on the world. You and I together will give it direction!

VILLON: Am I allowed all the words I want? I demand freedom!

RÉGNIER: Freedom doesn't exist! Freedom is only necessity in disguise! Our battle cry should be a deafening "NO!"

[VILLON *and* RÉGNIER *laugh.* TABARY, *very drunk, staggers over.*]

TABARY: Sure, Régn. You can count on me. Always. I'm a devil. A devil of a guy.

RÉGNIER: [*Jumps off the table, drinks. Kindly.*] You're no devil. You're God's doormat.

TABARY: [*Offended.*] So what's wrong with that? We all want to get to Heaven. [*To* VILLON.] You care about going to Heaven, don't you?

VILLON: [*Laughing, strumming along.*] Paris is good enough for me. "Why Paris, Paris is number one . . ."

TABARY: [*Badgering.*] You don't want to go to Heaven?

VILLON: A cat's heaven is exactly the same as a mouse's hell. It depends who's the cat and who's the mouse.

RÉGNIER: [*Laughing, poking* TABARY.] Which one are you, Tabary?

TABARY: Both.

[VILLON *strums.*]

MARGOT: [*Whacking* VILLON *across the back of his calves with a ladle.*] Get down, pig!

VILLON: [*Laughing.*] Ow! [*Blows her a kiss.*] Don't interfere, you sow! I was just coming up with a rhyme for you!

JEANNETTE: Do you know there are already thirty dead students? That's something, huh?

TABARY: [*Shouts.*] Quiet! Quiet! The Maestro is going to sing!

[*Everyone falls momentarily silent.* JENNETTE *swings herself onto the table and sits, legs folded, at* VILLON'S *feet.* VILLON *beams happily. He begins to sing Song 1 in a clear, sure voice.*]

TABARY: [*Ecstatic.*] Jesus! That's great! Straight out of hell!

[VILLON *continues to sing Song 1.* TABARY *flamboyantly kisses* VILLON'S *shoe. Everyone laughs. By the end of the first verse, the* CHROUS *has begun to join in with various lutes, later singing the words.* MARGOT *keeps time by furiously hitting the backs of* VILLON'S *legs with her ladle.*]

MARGOT: Slop face! Get out!

[*Loud noise from outside: banging, clatter of hooves, horses neighing, shouting. Everyone falls instantly silent.* ANGÈLE *runs to see what's going on, immediately returns.*]

ANGÈLE: François! Run! Police!

[*Everyone scatters, knocking the table over. Chaos ensues and increasing noise comes from outside.*]

RÉGNIER: The lights!

[*Someone douses the lights. Darkness. Horses neighing.*]

MARGOT: God! For them to bust you all like this!

[*A high-pitched, metallic, vibrating tone sounds. A bright light appears in the darkness and shines on the fleeing* VILLON.]

VILLON: Idiot! Turn that off!

[*The fighting noise stops, and only the metallic tone—as of a tuning fork vastly amplified—continues.* VILLON *shields his eyes from the glare of an approaching light. He starts to move out of the way, but* MOUSTIER *grabs him by the shoulders and forces him to sit.*]

PICHART: Which interrogation is this?

MOUSTIER: The ninth.

[*Part of the stage becomes dimly lit.* PICHART *is seen tying* VILLON *to a chair, aiming the floodlight directly into his eyes. Interrogation scene.* MOUSTIER *holds a kind of large metal tuning fork. He has just struck it and listens maliciously to its vibrating tone.*]

VILLON: Get that light away!

PICHART: I just want to look at you. Hmmm . . . Impressive little scar there . . . where'd that come from?

VILLON: I've told you.

PICHART: No you didn't.

VILLON: I did.

[MOUSTIER *steps over and sets the fork vibrating directly into* VILLON'S *ear.*]

PICHART: Let him be. He'll tell us. [*Soothingly.*] I like listening to him. He has a voice like a bell. Must be quite a little singer, mustn't you? [*Abruptly shouting.*] Talk, scum bag!

VILLON: [*Meekly.*] Philippe Sermoy slashed my lip with his dagger.

PICHART: When? Where? How? Why?

VILLON: When: June fifth. Where: in front of the church of St. Boniface. How? Like this!

[VILLON *suddenly shouts and jumps up, chair and all, attacking* PICHART *karate-style. The bailiff falls.*] LIKE THAT! Like a bombshell! Like a bandit! Like a blow of fate!

MOUSTIER: [*Shouting.*] Guards! Guards! You bastard!

[*They knock* VILLON *down, along with his chair. The* BISHOP *emerges from the darkness and watches. After a moment he motions them to pick up* VILLON, *who spits at the bailiffs. The*

BISHOP *sends them away, then pulls up a chair facing* VILLON. VILLON *is defiant, the* BISHOP *polite, making no effort to sweet-talk him.*]

BISHOP: Does the light bother you?

VILLON: No.

BISHOP: [*Gets up, turns the lamp away, sits back down.*] Better?

VILLON: Umm.

BISHOP: [*After a pause, pensively.*] You know, there is a certain order here. An order of things. God's order.

VILLON: Umm.

BISHOP: It is necessary to protect it. Disorder is a cauldron of both good and evil, and only the evil serves to thicken the soup.

[VILLON *is silent. the* BISHOP *suddenly shakes his head, breaking the mood. Now in a lighter tone, he says.*]

You were a student, weren't you?

VILLON: Umm.

BISHOP: Students! The black sheep of Paris. Do you like Paris, Villon?

VILLON: [*Cautiously.*] Why?

BISHOP: I've heard a lot about you. I even had two or three of your ballads copied. You are a gifted young man, Villon.

VILLON: Umm.

BISHOP: Would you like to know which ballads I selected?

VILLON: [*Pause, curious in spite of himself.*] Well?

BISHOP: [*Also smiles, but unexpectedly waves aside the question. Amicably.*] Listen here. Did you know Sermoy?

VILLON: Sermoy? The biggest fool in Paris!

BISHOP: [*Gently.*] We are talking about a servant of God, Villon.

VILLON: [*Clownishly.*] An eloquent fool, to be sure. The most eloquent fool in Paris.

BISHOP: And, uh . . . you had a quarrel?

VILLON: A quarrel! Thousands of quarrels. He kept one hand on the pulpit while the other hand was fondling the saints. And all the time he was telling lies about me! [*Suddenly intense.*] He threatened to kill me!

BISHOP: Well, it turned out quite the opposite, did it not?

VILLON: What was I supposed to do? What would YOU do if someone attacked you from behind?

BISHOP: From behind? Was it from behind?

VILLON: [*Dejected.*] Forget it.

BISHOP: And was there . . . any kind of . . . reason?

[VILLON: *is silent. The* BISHOP *gets up, turns on a lamp high above his head and smiles.*]

BISHOP: Full moon!

[*He signals to the bailiffs who silently remove* VILLON's *shackles and disappear.* VILLON *covers his face with his hands. After a while he removes his hands and softly asks.*]

VILLON: Is she here?

[*But the* BISHOP *is no longer present.* VILLON *gets up and looks restlessly around.*]

Catherine! Catherine! Are you here?

[CATHERINE *runs in from the dark. She has changed since the opening scene: now she is young, girlish, in love, slightly feverish.*]

CATHERINE: It's enough that you remembered me! [*Tosses him a lute.*] It is yours, isn't it?

[VILLON *catches the lute. Suddenly he laughs. Won over by* CATHERINE's *different tone, he is suddenly youthful, happy, enchanted.*]

VILLON: May the earth open and swallow me! Catherine! Is it really you?

CATHERINE: [*Plucks at his rags with mock squeamishness.*] Some scholar! You dress like a tramp!

VILLON: [*Laughs.*] Oh, pardon me! [*He pulls a student's cape off a lamp, puts it on, strumming.*] "Why Paris, Paris is number one . . ."

CATHERINE: And what is it you've done this time?

VILLON: [*Abruptly trying to change the subject.*] It's a full moon! What a heavenly body! A sign from above!

CATHERINE: [*Yanking his hair.*] I'm asking a question!

VILLON: Ah, but the lady knows everything! Did the wind whisper the truth?

CATHERINE: You're all over Paris!

VILLON: "Why Paris, Paris is number one . . ."

CATHERINE: [*Impatiently.*] So are you going to tell me?

VILLON: Every day a black cloud of gossip floats up from Paris, bangs on the gates of Heaven and howls like a hurricane: Villooooon! Villooooon!

[CATHERINE *lets go of his hair, nervously shuts and opens her palms.* VILLON *notices the action. He stops strumming and seizes her wrists. The action guiltily stops.*]

VILLON: What are you doing?

CATHERINE: [*Trying to pull her hands away.*] Nothing.

VILLON: I've noticed it a lot. Pulling your claws in and out. Like a cat when it's scared.

[*He places her palms to his neck.* CATHERINE *sighs. Suddenly she is different, again unco-quettish and real.*]

CATHERINE: I'm impatient.

VILLON: [*Softly, kindly.*] Impatient for what?

CATHERINE: I don't know. For nothing. I'm restless . . . like Purgatory. Life drags on so, just creeps along . . . everyone babbles. Do you ever get bored, Villon?

[VILLON *shakes his head.*]

CATHERINE: I do. All the time. I am so bored I sometimes just sit and count my toes.

VILLON: What do you actually do . . . all day and all night, Cathy?

CATHERINE: [*Bitterly.*] I sleep. I sleep like a fugitive. Whenever I can. I lie down, to bury myself in the sand like an ostrich. I dream. I dream I'm a student and as crazy and no-torious as Villon. No! I'm even more notorious than that!

[VILLON *grins, pleased. Even* CATHERINE *smiles slightly.*]

CATHERINE: What else . . . I try to see how long I can hold my breath, until I almost faint. I'm sitting at a banquet and ever so quietly I'm suffocating. And to this day I bite my nails. Really. Look!

[VILLON *examines her hands, kisses her palms.*]

CATHERINE: I live in dread that one day I'll just chew myself up—my nails, then my fin-gers, then my hands—like a fox in a trap.

[VILLON *quietly starts to laugh. He smiles ardently at* CATHERINE *and slowly draws her to-ward him.*]

CATHERINE: What should I do, Villon?

[PHILIPPE, *dressed as a priest, suddenly steps from the darkness, a breviary in his hand.*]

PHILIPPE: [*Admonishingly.*] Mademoiselle de Vausselles?

CATHERINE: [*Pulls away, shielding her eyes against the floodlight.*] Who's there?

PHILIPPE: What brings you out alone at such an inopportune hour?

CATHERINE: [*Challengingly.*] Am I alone?

VILLON: [*Angry, provokingly.*] Ah, the mouth of God among us! God in His generosity sticks out His holy tongue at us. Fire away, sir mouthpiece!

PHILIPPE: [*Ignoring him.*] Does her ladyship your mother know where you are at this hour? I will accompany you home, Mademoiselle de Vausselles!

VILLON: You are pushing, my friend. Beat it!

PHILIPPE: Did someone give you permission to be out?

CATHERINE: [*Still sprightly, but growing nervous.*] You see, Father Sermoy, I sleepwalk. I am powerless against the full moon. [*Suddenly wails wildly.*] Tooootally powerless!

[*Holding her arms straight in front of her,* CATHERINE *begins behaving like a sleepwalker.* PHILIPPE *tries to grab her.*]

PHILIPPE: Mademoiselle de Vausselles!

VILLON: [*Pushes him away, gruffly.*] Move off, move off, Pater!

PHILIPPE: I haven't addressed you, Villon!

VILLON: You are superfluous. Unnecessary. Not wanted.

PHILIPPE: Mademoiselle de Vausselles!

[VILLON *seizes a long, flexible stick and casually knocks the breviary out of* PHILIPPE's *hand.*]

VILLON: Don't drop that breviary!

PHILIPPE: Don't provoke me, Villon!

VILLON: [*Poking him with the stick.*] Here kitty kitty kitty kitty . . .

[PHILIPPE *tries to seize the stick, but it breaks in half.* VILLON *immediately assumes an "en garde" fencing position and begins to wave the stick at* PHILIPPE *like a sword. The* CHORUS *appears on the gallery. They back the rhythm of the evolving fight with whistling.*]

PHILIPPE: Remember that I am a servant of God!

VILLON: Ohh! "And they have their ways of striking back!"

PHILIPPE: You don't want to regret this.

VILLON: [*Half singing, he invents a mocking tune.*] "But one must honor whatever is honored by the church of God." [*As if calling fowl.*] Here chick, there chick, everywhere chick chick! Come on, goosey goosey gander . . .

PHILIPPE: Don't try my patience!

VILLON: ". . . and so being their servant in everything I say or do, I agree to honor them with all my heart and obey without argument."

CHORUS: [*Picking up the song.*] "They have their ways of striking back."

PHILIPPE: Stop it!

VILLON: You jealous old ham!

PHILIPPE: [*Helpless with rage.*] I'll kill you!

[*They fight.*]

[*Chorus continues song.*]

[*During the brawl the Senate body comes in and follows the action intently.* CATHERINE *sleepwalks among them, occasionally bumping into someone, then goes on.* VILLON *soon overpowers* PHILIPPE, *forces him to the floor and kneels on top of him so that* PHILIPPE *is immobilized.*]

VILLON: [*To* CATHERINE, *cheerfully, victoriously, boyishly.*] Catherine! What should I do with him? He's ours!

CATHERINE: [*In a fit of reckless giggles.*] Finish him off, Villon! Finish him off and let's run away from Paris together!

PHILIPPE: [*Prone, choking.*] Villon, stop in time!

[VILLON *lets him go. He is laughing while* PHILIPPE *is getting up.*]

VILLON: Go back to your preaching! And let's hear a blessing! Say "God be with you!"

[PHILIPPE, *without turning around, climbs onto the highest stool, the "pulpit." He bows his head and gives the blessing.*]

PHILIPPE: [*Exhaustedly.*] God be with you!

[*Everyone except* CATHERINE *and* VILLON *kneel. A church bell rings.* FATHER *swings a censer.*]

ALL: And also with you.

CATHERINE: [*Sleepwalking, bumps into* VILLON, *feels his face, then opens her eyes. In a fit of laughter.*] I didn't see a thing! I didn't see a thing! Where is he?

[*She again bursts into laughter and falls to her knees before everyone. Her laughter turns into spasmodic, uncontrollable sobbing.* PHILIPPE *stands in the pulpit, his face hidden by his hands. Then he slowly uncovers his face. He begins to preach and suddenly, stronger than ever before, his fanatical but coldly professional character is revealed.*]

PHILIPPE: Weeping! Weeping! I hear weeping. Paris echoes with weeping.

[*A long pause.* CATHERINE *raises her head and stops crying.*]

PHILIPPE: Matthew, chapter 18. "Woe unto the world because of offenses! For it must needs be that offenses come; but woe to that man by whom the offence cometh!" [*Pause.*] Woe! Woe to whom? Through whom—like through a gate of hell, with voraciously gaping jaws dripping protruding intestines, does weeping enter our homes?

[*He buries his head in his hands.* VILLON *is the last to kneel with the others. Among those kneeling is* TABARY, *who gives* VILLON *a cheerful nod. Conspiratorially he points to a string on a lute.* VILLON *smiles.*]

PHILIPPE: Brothers and sisters! The bells of Paris are mute with terror! Blood soaks the pavements. How much longer am I to remain silent about the bloody games of the students? Is not their arrogance deadly? Students, the black sheep of Paris! But are they not in fact wolves dressed as sheep? Thus asks our Lord. [*Pause.*] By not putting a stop to evil, we are opening the doors to Satan. If we fail to punish those who are guilty, the hurricane will sweep away through those who are innocent!

[TABARY *slides his finger down the string. The string wails like the wind. Someone cries out in fright, someone else laughs. A murmur.*]

PHILIPPE: [*Raising his voice.*] And soon the hurricane will be raging in us as well! The winds of impurity will roar through our souls!

[TABARY *and* VILLON *are handling the sound effects. Finally* TABARY *roars like a "wind of impurity." Scandal.*]

PHILIPPE: Who was that?

[*From outside, sounds of horses, blows and cries are heard.* JEANNETTE *runs in.*]

JEANNETTE: Help! They're slaughtering the students!

[*Chaos. Some people run out, others remain kneeling. Shouts. The noise from outside grows louder.*]

PHILIPPE: [*Shouting over them.*] Brothers and sisters! Remain calm! Sing! Sing!

[*A church hymn begins. Some gaze into the distance.* JEANNETTE *climbs onto the judges' stools and, standing up, surveys the action, whistling on her fingers.* CATHERINE *joins the group with whom* VILLON *is standing and asks formally.*]

CATHERINE: So what is happening now, gentlemen?

VILLON: At your service, Mademoiselle de Vausselles. Two sergeants killed a student.

JEANNETTE: [*Shouting from above.*] Wrong! Two students killed a sergeant!

VILLON [*Laughs.*] Much better!

MOUSTIER: Strap 'em to a horse face down and drive 'em out of Paris!

[*The group dissolves. Only* VILLON *and* RÉGNIER *are left.* PHILIPPE, *wearing a grave expression, slowly comes down from the pulpit and approaches the two.*]

PHILIPPE: Monsieur Villon.

VILLON: [*Roguishly.*] Here!

PHILIPPE: A few words.

RÉGNIER: [*Settles onto the floor, uncorks a bottle. Amiably.*] Mind if I listen?

PHILIPPE: I would prefer to speak with you alone, sir.

VILLON: [*Clownishly.*] Régn here is my attorney. I don't know how to converse with a professional person. Ballads are one thing. But when it comes to straight talk, I can't keep myself straight. Rrrrégn!

[RÉGNIER *tosses him the bottle.* VILLON *sits down, drinks.* PHILIPPE *stands stiffly between the two. But now he is neither ridiculous nor preacher-like; he is, in fact, unusually real.*]

PHILIPPE: Villon, as enemies, we are the laughing stock of all Paris.

VILLON: Régn! [*Tosses him the bottle.*]

PHILIPPE: How far do you want this to go, Villon?

RÉGNIER: [*Cheerfully.*] The defense advises: no comment.

PHILIPPE: I'm giving you a friendly warning, Villon. God's patience is bottomless, but when one reaches the bottom, one disappears beneath it.

VILLON: [*Somewhat drunk.*] You talk like scripture, Father. It's a good thing you don't rhyme: Paris wouldn't want me anymore.

PHILIPPE: [*Gravely.*] Never joke about a gift from God. I may not understand you, but this much I do know: that you bear the weight of God's talent. And one day God will call on you to settle the account.

VILLON: Let me tell you how it is, Father. Paris is too small for you and me. We're two arms in the same sleeve. And I'm the arm with the biceps. [*He gives him the universal "up yours" gesture.*]

PHILIPPE: Why can't you understand that I want to save you from yourself? Villon! One cold night in the seminary, the Tempter appeared to me. And he mocked everything, just as you do.

VILLON: I've dreamed about you too, Father. You were hanging from a cloud by one foot and peeping into bedroom windows.

PHILIPPE: Monsieur de Montigny! Do you agree with this childish outburst?

RÉGNIER: [*In mock amazement.*] Me? I never agree! That's my mission!

PHILIPPE: [*Looks at them both for a while, then shrugs in defeat.*] I shall pray for you, Villon.

[PHILIPPE *leaves. As he goes,* VILLON *throws* RÉGNIER *the bottle which, by sheer bad luck, strikes* PHILIPPE's *head.* PHILIPPE *whirls around. At once he changes into a ravenous, aggressive prosecutor. The light reveals the Senate in full attendance.* VILLON *yawns and starts dropping off to sleep.*]

PHILIPPE: [*Very aggressive.*] I object!

RÉGNIER: [*Quickly jumping up, donning his robe. Just as sharply.*] One moment!

PHILIPPE: I refuse to deal with a defense lawyer who considers disagreeing to be his mission in life! I refuse to deal with an individual who has made hate his profession! I do not recognize a defender of the law who does not recognize the law!

RÉGNIER: [*Already in his robe.*] Disagreement with what? Hatred toward what? And the law? Whose law?

PHILIPPE: Stop quoting!

RÉGNIER: Do you really believe that Villon hates? That he is rebellious? Bull! He is a young billy-goat who's not even aware of what he does! But within him, deep within him, is that secret crevice through which blows the wind of the times . . .

PHILIPPE: The wind of the times? This drunken masquerade? This looting of shops? These brawls with policemen?

RÉGNIER: Open your eyes! You're up to your ankles in law and up to your neck in blood!

BISHOP: [*Tapping his gavel, drily.*] Monsieur defense.

RÉGNIER: Yes?

BISHOP: [*Unperturbed.*] Would you like to base the defense of your client on an indictment of the Middle Ages? Of King Charles? Of France? Of holy justice? Of me?

RÉGNIER: No. My dispute with all those natural phenomena just named is already concluded and committed "ex post facto." But I protest against the prejudice of the prosecutor, who has become bogged down in personal spite and is trying to turn this trial into a Sunday sermon!

PHILIPPE: I'm only beginning. We will move on to other parts of the accusation.

RÉGNIER: Yes, to the murder. Before we know it, Sermoy, you'll be dead and I'll be hanged. And Villon? What will happen to him?

[VILLON *is sleeping,* ANGÈLE *sitting beside him and tickling him with a straw.* RÉGNIER *is walking around the Senate, but everyone is looking away, as if* RÉGNIER *had mentioned an unmentionable question.*]

RÉGNIER: I ask: What will you do with Villon?

BISHOP: I object to that question!

RÉGNIER: Aha!

[*A moment of silence. The sleeping* VILLON *sneezes.*]

BISHOP: Bring forth Villon!

FATHER: [*Frightened.*] I'm coming, I'm coming . . .

[*The* BISHOP, *with an imperious gesture, makes it clear to the Senate that he wishes to be alone. The members of the jury leave.* FATHER *inches over to* VILLON. *He plays two roles now: as the servant of the court, he calls out impersonally. As foster-father, he is anxious and sympathetic.*]

FATHER: Student Villon! François Villon [*Quietly to* ANGÈLE]. Go on, dear.

[ANGÈLE *becomes frightened. She jumps up, grabs her robe off the back of her chair, throws it over her arm and runs out after the others.* VILLON *sits up, drunkenly rubs his eyes.*]

VILLON: What's happening?

FATHER: [*Close up.*] Son, son . . . what will they do to you? How will it end up?

VILLON: [*Merrily, warmly.*] Father! Is that you?

FATHER: [*Calling out.*] Villon! François Villon!

VILLON: Forgive me, father, for not answering. My life has become kind of hectic . . . it's bucking and kicking . . . but it gallops like a champion!

FATHER: [*Quietly.*] I know, I know. Just hope the rector will be patient, François!

VILLON: [*Alarmed.*] The rector? Why?

FATHER: [*Calling out.*] His honor the rector of the university is expecting the student Villon!

[VILLON *gets up, and his* FATHER *dusts him off. The only one now seated on the stools is the* BISHOP, *caught up in some paperwork.* VILLON *kneels, bows his head.*]

FATHER: Your Magnificence. [*Exits.*]

BISHOP: [*Looks up, waits a moment, then unpleasantly.*] Well, up, up! I'm not interested in your back. You know why you're here. Don't you?

VILLON: [*Humbly.*] I don't dare say, your honor.

BISHOP: [*Sharply.*] Oh go ahead and dare!

[*Silence. The* BISHOP *taps his finger impatiently.* VILLON *stares at the finger. The* BISHOP *hides it. Suddenly he leans forward and roars.*]

BISHOP: Do you understand at all that you are a student at the holy university of Paris?

VILLON: [*Contritely.*] Yes.

BISHOP: And don't you realize you have gone way over the line with your vulgar tomfooleries?

VILLON: I'm as unripe as a pear in Maytime, Your Magnificence.

BISHOP: [*Shouting.*] You're a punk!!

[*The* BISHOP *gets up and paces back and forth. He talks without sympathy.*]

BISHOP: I know your type. You go against the time you were born into. But time, Villon, time is going against you!

VILLON: [*Quietly, kneeling.*] I know.

BISHOP: At eighteen you're a bird of song. At twenty-five you're a stray dog. And at thirty you're a wolf. [*Crosses the room, stops next to* VILLON *and suddenly speaks confidingly.*] But time, young man, gets less juicy year by year. Time dries up. You are walking into a desert exile, Villon. [*He sits back down to his paperwork and resumes an utterly businesslike tone.*] Is it true you are one of the perpetrators of a string of disturbing incidents, that you join in the looting of taverns and shops and provoke fights with the police?

VILLON: [*Humbly.*] His Magnificence surely knows that the Parisian police provoke fights with us.

BISHOP: [*Slams his fist on the table.*] Silence! Are you aware that these incidents already have claimed more than thirty lives?

VILLON: With deepest regret I am.

BISHOP: Are you aware that on countless occasions you have disrupted the order of the university?

VILLON: Yes.

BISHOP: [*Searchingly, curious.*] And are you aware that order is more powerful than you are?

[VILLON *raises his glance. He doesn't protest, but he is thinking. Both men look at each other for a long time. Then the* BISHOP *abruptly claps closed the folder containing his paperwork and rises.*]

BISHOP: Leave. And make sure I never hear about you again.

[*Departs, walking past the kneeling* VILLON. *He has already passed* VILLON *when he suddenly remembers something and returns. Quietly, emphatically.*]

BISHOP: Listen, Villon. I am here thirty-five years. I have seen a bunch of you. And I tell you this. Without even realizing it's your last step, you'll cross the boundary.

VILLON: And if I'm careful?

BISHOP: [*Thinks.*] Then . . . then it may happen that the boundary will grow impatient, and IT will cross YOU.

[*The* BISHOP *leaves.* VILLON, *kneeling, lays his head on the ground. After a while* CATHERINE *steals into the room in a scholar's robe, her hair concealed under a cap. She looks around without seeing* VILLON. *Still kneeling,* VILLON *suddenly pounds the ground with his fists and emits a desperate scream—venting his tension.* CATHERINE *gives a yell,* VILLON *spins around with lightning speed.*]

VILLON: [*Raging.*] Who's here?

[*He leaps after her.* CATHERINE *tries to run away, but* VILLON *catches her. A brief struggle, then he dexterously knocks her to the floor and non-erotically, boyishly, squats down across her buttocks.*]

VILLON: Who are you spying on? What are you doing here? Talk!

CATHERLINE: [*Being crushed.*] Get off me, Villon!

VILLON: [*In amazement.*] What? What's this? [*Pinches up* CATHERINE's *cap, ceremoniously removes it. In the same slow way he lifts up a long strand of hair.*] Mademoiselle de Vausselles!

[*He raises himself slightly,* CATHERINE *rolls over into a half-sitting position,* VILLON *squats down over her knees.*]

CATHERINE: Get off me! Now! I can't breathe!

VILLON: What are you doing here?

CATHERINE: You're taking advantage of the situation, Villon!

VILLON: Oh no! The situation is taking advantage of me!

CATHERINE: [*Hitting him with her fists.*] Let me go!

VILLON: This situation is pulling at me like an undertow! Catherine!

CATHERINE: Shut up! I didn't come to see you!

VILLON: But the result's the same. Thanks be to God!

CATHERINE: I want to see the university. I want to see the Paris that's not sleeping! Every fly up there on the ceiling knows a thousand times more about life than I do! [*Hisses.*] And tonight I'm going to visit a brothel!

VILLON: [*Jumps off, opens his arms.*] You've arrived! You're inside the living heart of the world! Paris . . . is Villon! The university . . . Villon! I am the heart of Paris!

FATHER: [*Offstage.*] Who's there? Are you still there, Villon?

[VILLON *and* CATHERINE *duck behind the stools.* FATHER *looks in.*]

FATHER: No one here? I'm locking up!

[*The sound of a key, then departing footsteps.* CATHERINE *gets up. Her behavior is now a mingling of anxiety and a kind of magical coquetry.*]

CATHERINE: My God! Is anybody else here?

VILLON: [*Falls to his knees, stretches his hands up to the ceiling.*] No one. Just you and me and the flies on the ceiling.

[*He opens his arms to her.* CATHERINE *backs away.*]

CATHERINE: No. Not you, Villon. You have a hoofprint on your back.

VILLON: What's that?

CATHERINE: [*Backing up, whispering.*] All Paris knows it. You signed yourself to the Devil. For the ballads. He pours rhymes into your left ear. You have his signature on your back . . . every full-moon it blisters, every new moon it bleeds again . . .

VILLON: [*Taking up the erotic mood that has now begun.*] You frighten me. I haven't seen my back for a long time. Reassure me, Catherine.

[*Swiftly he undresses himself to the waist, then turns his back to* CATHERINE. *Transfixed,* CATHERINE *studies him.*]

VILLON: Is it there?

CATHERINE: [*Hoarsely.*] There is a birthmark there. [*Points to it with her finger.*]

VILLON: Maybe the Devil's signature is somewhere else. Look a little lower.

[CATHERINE *lightly grazes his back with her finger. She slides it down his spine. Then she presses her palm against* VILLON's *back. She is silent, fascinated. A moment with no motion.*]

VILLON: [*Earnestly.*] Oh! Oh for this moment to last forever!

[CATHERINE *slowly bends her head down and kisses* VILLON's *back.* VILLON *turns around. Swiftly he embraces her, but* CATHERINE *begins to scream—not coquettishly, but out of sincere, neurotic anxiety.*]

CATHERINE: No! No!

VILLON: [*Dumbfounded.*] What is it, Catherine?

CATHERINE: Don't you dare! Let go!

[*She succeeds in freeing herself. She runs to the door and pounds on it with her fists.*]

CATHERINE: Help! Where is somebody!

VILLON: There's not a soul here. Catherine, what is it?

CATHERINE: [*Suddenly falls silent, as though coming around, quietly.*] I'm afraid.

VILLON: Of what?

CATHERINE: Of you, Villon.

VILLON: [*With sincere amazement.*] Of me? Why?

[*Carefully opens his arms and embraces her.* CATHERINE *stands still for a moment, lets herself be held, but suddenly starts screaming again, throws herself against* VILLON *and shouts.*]

CATHERINE: Help! Come here!

[*A mob of news reporters comes running in from all sides:* PICHART, MOUSTIER, JEAN-NETTE, TABARY, RÉGNIER. *They have flashbulbs, tape recorders, microphones, pads, and they are in modern dress. Except for* RÉGNIER, *who stays off to the side, they behave like the worst kind of stereotypical reporter: sensationalist, rude, noisy. For a moment,* VILLON *doesn't "register" them.*]

VILLON: There's nobody here! We're alone! Don't be afraid.

[CATHERINE *wrenches herself away, runs toward the reporters who are photographing the whole scene, shouting and shoving at each other. While she is still running she cries out.*]

CATHERINE: You're the heart of Paris? Every sleaze bar in the world has plenty of creeps like you!

MOUSTIER: [*Aiming the flashbulb at him, shouting over the din.*] Maestro! Say cheese!

VILLON: [*Disheveled, astounded, not taking them in.*] Catherine!

JEANNETTE: [*Hippie, interviewing* VILLON.] *Paris Morning!* I'm interested in the social context of your work! Why are you showing yourself off half-naked? Do you mean it as a revolt against convention?

VILLON: Catherine!

TABARY: [*Excited.*] Villon, what do you have to say about our billing you as one of the greatest poets of all time?

PHILIPPE: And a cynical cutthroat! What is your position on that dichotomy?

JEANNETTE: What was the meaning of sex for the young people of your generation?

VILLON: [*Coming around, tired, unwilling.*] What?

PICHART: [*Aiming the flashbulb, snapping his fingers.*] Here! Over here! Look over here!

JEANNETTE: Were your "happenings" designed to shock the bourgeoisie of that time?

PHILIPPE: Do you consider yourself a criminal?

JEANNETTE: [*Angrily.*] That was MY question!

PICHART: What was your punishable activity? Be specific about the individual crimes!

VILLON: All right. The unintentional killing of the priest Sermoy . . .

MOUSTIER: The punishment?

VILLON: I was pardoned.

MOUSTIER: Continue!

VILLON: Burglarizing the theological faculty in the year '58 . . .

PHILIPPE: Do you insist on the term "unintentional killing"?

VILLON: [*Looks at him.*] Absolutely.

JEANNETTE: Were your criminal actions socially motivated? Were you expressing the rebellion of the oppressed classes?

VILLON: [*With consternation.*] What's that?

JEANNETTE: Did you long for the destruction of the world into which you were born? Was annihilation your goal?

VILLON: No.

PHILIPPE: The world longs to see greatness in its artists. Do you consider yourself a man of greatness, Villon?

VILLON: [*Suddenly gruff.*] Get lost!

TABARY: Would you sing one of your ballads for us, Maestro?

VILLON: Go to hell!

TABARY: I have a little something here . . . it's actually pretty good! You'll like it, Villon!

[*Plays the tape recorder. The song—"Where are the snows of yesteryear"—comes on as in the first scene, this time as a pop song.* VILLON *covers his face. The others quiet down for a moment and listen. The song is heard even throughout the following remarks.* CATHERINE *emerges from the group.*]

CATHERINE: [*Like a reporter.*] Who was the mysterious Catherine of your ballads? Did she exist?

VILLON: [*Looks at her closely, then harshly.*] Of course. Catherine de Vausselles was the shrewdest whore in all Paris. She carried herself around like a donkey's tail and she had a black hair sticking out of her nose.

CATHERINE: [*After a moment.*] Thanks.

TABARY: Come on now, be quiet! Listen to this!

[*Everyone is quiet for a moment. The song. Suddenly* RÉGNIER, *who has remained silent until now, comes forward and speaks ironically and confidentially.*]

RÉGNIER So did they twist your arm in the end, Villon?

[*Everyone reacts as though they had just heard something bordering on bad taste.* VILLON *looks up, confused.*]

RÉGNIER: What kind of a deal did they end up making with you?

PICHART: [*The first to regain his composure.*] Light! Give me some light on that chin! Move over! There!

[JEANNETTE, TABARY, *both bailiffs are raising such a stir around* VILLON *that it is nearly impossible to see past them. They are rearranging lights, flashing cameras, shoving people and each other about.* VILLON *shields his eyes from the glare.*]

VILLON: Will you cut it out with those lights!

PHILIPPE: [*Thrusts a microphone at* VILLON.] Are you claiming Sermoy stabbed you in the back? Do you continue to claim that?

VILLON: Damn! My eyes are like fried eggs! You've burnt them to a crisp!

PHILIPPE: You still have a chance!

VILLON: [*Nervously.*] How did they twist my arm, Régn?

[*The song stops in the middle of a word. All the lights go out. While it is dark, the reporters vanish, then a single light goes on, directly opposite* VILLON. *Both bailiffs, already in their bailiff's shirts, are tying* VILLON *to a chair. The* BISHOP *steps out of the darkness. This time he is severe, without a trace of friendliness.*]

BISHOP: You still have a chance, Villon.

[MOUSTIER *twists* VILLON's *arms. From this point on everything moves along with the rhythm of the headlong, confusing trial. Questions fly, though nobody has the chance to answer them. Much clamor. The* BISHOP *sits rigidly and looks on.*]

MOUSTIER: Why did you kill Sermoy?

VILLON: He started himself . . .

PICHART: Who helped you rob the college in Navarre?

VILLON: That case is closed.

MOUSTIER: Answer the questions!

PICHART: Name your accomplices!

VILLON: Whom?

MOUSTIER: Who is your gangleader? Who is the Wolf?

PICHART: Names, names, names!

VILLON: I don't remember. I was drunk.

PICHART: We have witnesses who say you were the one who stabbed Ferrebouc!

VILLON: I've never laid eyes on him in my life!

MOUSTIER: You've never seen the Wolf?

VILLON: I've never seen Ferrebouc!

PICHART: How and why did you attack His Holiness the Bishop?

MOUSTIER: With what weapon did you attack Ferrebouc?

VILLON: I didn't attack anyone! I was asleep! I told you that!

PICHART: Are you implying that the Bishop d'Aussigny attacked you?

VILLON: [*Shouting.*] No! Sermoy attacked me!

[*Suddenly the* BISHOP, *with an imperial gesture, interrupts the hearing. The bailiffs disappear. The* BISHOP *himself turns the lamp away and loosens* VILLON's *bonds.* VILLON *slumps over, puts his head on his knees.*]

BISHOP: Unnecessary tumult. Lights . . . shouting . . . confusion . . . we can surely come to an agreement in peace, hmmm? So then. Who was the woman who witnessed the murder?

VILLON: [*Exhausted.*] There wasn't any.

BISHOP: And her name?

VILLON: No.

[*The* BISHOP *snaps his fingers. The light reveals a veiled woman. She is stiff as a puppet, anonymous, erect.*]

BISHOP: So now. Go to her.

VILLON: What should I do?

[*The* BISHOP *shrugs his shoulders. A lute is lying on the floor, and* VILLON, *at a loss for what else to do, begins to strum it softly.*]

VILLON: [*Singing quietly.*] "Where are the snows of yesteryear . . ." etc.

BISHOP: Sermoy was alone?

VILLON: Alone.

BISHOP: Continue!

[VILLON *sings.* PHILIPPE *emerges from the darkness, a dagger in his hand. He waits.*]

BISHOP: He attacked you from behind?

VILLON: [*Strumming.*] That's right.

[PHILIPPE *walks up behind* VILLON *and stabs him in the back.* VILLON *groans, falls to his knees.* PHILIPPE *disinterestedly steps away.*]

BISHOP: Does he have a scar on his back?

[*The veiled woman is* CATHERINE, *who now speaks in a high, unnatural voice.*]

CATHERINE: [*Pushes aside* VILLON's *tatters.*] He has a birthmark there.

VILLON: [*Turns around, wildly.*] BITCH!

[PHILIPPE, *provoked, suddenly changes from his passive stance into a participant in sharp, live action.*]

PHILIPPE: What? Such talk at the very gates of a cathedral? Apologize!

[CATHERINE *breaks into neurotic, uncontrollable laughter.*]

VILLON: [*Increasingly emotional.*] Catherine! [*To* PHILIPPE, *who grabs him and prevents him from running to* CATHERINE.] Out of my way, asshole!

CATHERINE: [*Gasps between her fits of laughter.*] So go ahead . . . tell me you're sorry . . . well . . .

BISHOP: [*In a loud voice, across the whole stage.*] Who witnessed the murder?

VILLON: Let me go! You slimy scumbag! You wrung-out eunuch, you squealing church rat!

PHILIPPE: In the name of God, don't provoke me!

VILLON: So defend yourself!

CATHERINE: [*Holding up both palms to her face, convulsing with laughter.*] I didn't see a thing! Not a thing!

[PHILIPPE *draws a dagger. Fight.* PHILIPPE *slashes* VILLON's *lip.* CATHERINE *stops laughing, takes her hands away from her face, throws off her veil and watches the scene as if paralyzed with fright.*]

VILLON: [*Beside himself.*] Aaaaaaaaa!

[VILLON *wrenches* PHILIPPE's *dagger away and stabs him with it.* PHILIPPE *yells and collapses.* VILLON *picks up a rock, swings it at* PHILIPPE's *cheek. Before he can strike,* CATHERINE *runs to him, slides to her knees before him, embraces his legs. In terror, quietly.*]

CATHERINE: I saw it, Villon. I saw it.

[*The bailiffs bear* PHILIPPE *away. The jury's seats slowly become illuminated, the senate body seated on them in their robes, all looking sternly at* VILLON. VILLON *stands as one who has just been awakened. He doesn't register* CATHERINE *at all.*]

CATHERINE: [*Kneeling, whispering.*] Run away! Hurry!

VILLON: [*Miserably, unnaturally, not noticing* CATHERINE.] He was asking for it, that sonovabitch. He won't be back in the pulpit for at least a week.

[*A bell tolls.*]

VILLON: What is it?

[FATHER, *the servant of the court, comes in ringing a bell like a death knell. Calls out.*]

FATHER: The session has ended! Clear the room!

VILLON: Father! What's going to happen to me?

CATHERINE: What will happen to me? François, don't leave me here alone!

FATHER: [*Next to* VILLON, *quietly, sternly, pushing him out.*] My boy! They know everything! You've got to leave Paris!

[*The jury is dispersing.*]

FATHER: Clear the court at once!

VILLON: But I can't leave Paris! Father! Why have you abandoned me?

FATHER: [*Ringing.*] There will be an intermission of five years!

[*End of act one.*]

ACT TWO

The CHORUS *begins singing before the start of Act Two.*

[*During the course of the song, the robed members of the Senate gather,* FATHER, *servant of the court, ringing a bell,* RÉGNIER *enters last, striding in quickly and giving* FATHER *a friendly nod.*]

RÉGNIER: So what's up?

FATHER: [*Stops ringing. Surprised but worried.*] Monsieur de Montigny!

RÉGNIER: What's with François?

FATHER: Oh God. [*Quietly.*] He disappeared. I haven't heard a thing from him in almost five years.

[RÉGNIER *nods, smiles and begins to leave. But* FATHER *grabs him imploringly.*]

FATHER: Forgive me, sir . . . You know about him, don't you? Is he at least alive?

[RÉGNIER *gives him a friendly grin, a pat on the back, and goes over to his place.* FATHER *recovers himself, starts ringing again with renewed intensity. The* BISHOP *enters. The Senate body rises.*]

BISHOP: In the name of God. The case of François Villon. [*Sits down, opens a file, waits. Suddenly raises his head in surprise.*] Where is the accused?

[*Everyone looks at each other.*]

TABARY: [*Uncertainly, servilely.*] The honorable Monsieur Ferrebouc eagerly awaits a verdict . . .

BISHOP: [*Interrupts him, slams down his gavel.*] The court asks again! Where is the accused?

PHILIPPE: [*Rises. Drily and calmly.*] I pronounce an authoritative assumption, namely that the accused has fled Paris in defiance of the law. Item: this occurred with the direct assistance of the defense. Item: the defense is aware of the whereabouts of his client. Item: the defense maintains secret contact with the accused. On the grounds of my statement, I request that the defense be removed from this case.

[*Sits down. Excitement in the courtroom.* RÉGNIER, *with a smile, comfortably sprawls in his chair.*]

BISHOP: Order in the court! Defense!

RÉGNIER: Here.

BISHOP: Have you anything to say?

RÉGNIER: [*Looks over his shoulder at the window. Sarcastically.*] It's raining outside. Item: it is getting dark.

BISHOP: Excuse me?

RÉGNIER: Twilight. Dusk. The hour between dog and wolf. Or do you mean I should say something about Villon? I have nothing to say.

BISHOP: Do you know of his whereabouts?

RÉGNIER: I released him from his obligations in the year A.D. 1459.

BISHOP: [*Thundering.*] Do you know?

RÉGNIER: No.

TABARY: [*After a moment, again servile and embarrassed.*] If we keep Monsieur Ferrebouc waiting, he will complain to the throne.

[*The* BISHOP *taps his knuckle impatiently.* FATHER *approaches him in agitation.*]

FATHER: I humbly beg the court's patience for a moment. I will bring the accused here.

[*The* BISHOP *abruptly claps the file shut. Before leaving, he turns.*]

BISHOP: [*Drily.*] Inform the court of all facts in time.

RÉGNIER: [*Gets up, tauntingly.*] Inform me as well.

[*He leaves.* CATHERINE *gets up, doesn't look at anyone, wordlessly goes out in the opposite direction.*]

TABARY: [*Confused.*] What's going on? Is there a recess or what?

[*Nobody answers him.* TABARY *shrugs, also leaves. The remaining people yawn, are silent, or stare out the window.* PHILIPPE *is writing something.* MOUSTIER *and* PICHART *pull out lutes, and each begins to strum a completely different tune. General discomfort. Finally* ANGÈLE, *emotionally and naively, speaks.*]

ANGÈLE: [*Very loudly.*] Wow, is it hot! Does it always take this long for a trial to get started? [*Takes off her robe, revealing the costume of a lady-in-waiting. She spreads the robe on the floor like a blanket, stands and stretches.*] Go ahead, Countess. Take your robe off too. The sun is too hot! Gentlemen! Slip into something more comfortable! We ladies give you permission!

[*One after another, all take off their robes. The bailiffs and* PHILIPPE *are dressed as young noblemen. Even* PHILIPPE *pulls out a lute and the disharmonious prelude gets louder and more dissonant.* MOTHER, *now the Duchess of Blois, anxiously and thoughtfully walks back and forth along the gallery.* JEANNETTE, *now a Lady-in-Waiting, also sheds her robe. She stretches expansively and heads over toward* ANGÈLE, *who has seated herself on the floor on her robe.*]

JEANNETTE: This is a lousy place! [*Yawns, sits down to join her.*] Every half-decent castle at least has a jousting tournament. Wouldn't you know that the Lord of this particular manor has a thing for poetry? That's what we need around here, a poetry contest. Yuch!

ANGÈLE: [*Fascinated.*] Who do you think will win?

JEANNETTE: [*Points to* PHILIPPE.] That one. The one that looks like a sick fish. [*Removes her shoe, discontentedly wiggling her toes.*] Shit, I'm going to junk these shoes. [*Back to the poetry contest.*] He always wins. All you have to do is say BAM! to him and he's off on a roll. Bam Slam a-la-ka-zam! Instant diarrhea. [*Hitting the shoe against the ground.*] God! Pointed toes! They're impossible!

ANGÈLE: [*Pointing.*] Are they all poets?

JEANNETTE: Yeah. So what're we waiting for? Where's the duke?

[MOTHER/DUCHESS *on the gallery is scrutinizing herself carefully. She runs her hand over her belly.* ANGÈLE *notices her. Nudges* JEANNETTE.]

ANGÈLE: Look! The Duchess!

JEANNETTE: [*Coming alive.*] Hey wow! Blow my mind! Do you see what I see?

ANGÈLE: See what?

JEANNETTE: Well, I'll be . . . She looks like she got knocked up!

ANGÈLE: [*Moved.*] That's wonderful!

JEANNETTE: [*A gossip in full glory.*] Oh my God! You can't turn your back on anybody! Wonder who she's been screwing?

ANGÈLE: [*Earnestly.*] Well, the Duke, of course!

JEANNETTE: Ha! All he can spout these days is poetry!

[FATHER/DUKE *appears on the gallery. He kisses* MOTHER's *hand, first the back of it ceremoniously, then the palm.* ANGÈLE *melting,* JEANNETTE *snickering.*]

JEANNETTE: Maybe they BOTH go for poets!

MOTHER: Let's begin, dear. The gentlemen are waiting.

FATHER: Yes. Of course. I'll just get my robe.

MOTHER: What theme did you choose this year?

FATHER: [*Takes her finger, presses it to his lips, smiles.*] Shhh!

[*Fanfare. The ladies jump up, scrambling to their places.* JEANNETTE *can't get her shoe on.*]

JEANNETTE: Fucking shoe . . .

[*The poets rise, holding their lutes to their chests, then drop to one knee. The ladies drop curtsies as they scramble. The* DUCHESS *enters, the* DUKE *lags behind. Suddenly* VILLON *appears on the gallery: he's in tatters, coarser, more scarred, aged. He no longer comes across as a handsome rake but instead seems almost vulgar. He gives a quiet hiss at* FATHER, *motioning him to come over.*]

FATHER: [*Surprised but polite.*] Sir? Are you calling me?

VILLON: Just for a moment.

FATHER: Please?

VILLON: Where can I find the entrance to this castle?

FATHER: [*Taken aback but still friendly.*] Might I know, sir, who you are?

VILLON: [*Grimaces.*] A poet. Does that lord of yours turn his dogs loose on uninvited guests?

FATHER: [*Hesitantly.*] If you're a poet . . . the doors of this house have always been open to poetry . . .

[VILLON *asks no further but jumps over the bench. Meanwhile,* PHILIPPE, *kneeling, has already begun singing before the* DUCHESS.]

PHILIPPE:

Lady, before your gracious gaze,
A row of poets homage pays . . .
And now allow your hand to sway . . .
Permit us our respects to pay . . .

VILLON: [*Whispering to* FATHER *over the song.*] So where's that lord of yours? Hm?
FATHER: [*Smiling, not taking offense.*] Shhh.

[*Leaves* VILLON *standing there, steps up to his elevated place. Bowing erupts all around.*]

FATHER: Gentlemen, I will not exhaust your patience with a long speech. I humbly give thanks to Poetry, which has been bringing you here for so many blessed years. The theme of this year's poetry contest is: "I die of thirst beside the fountain." I will be expecting your compositions after sundown. Meanwhile, I wish you all a happy and free spirit. Gentlemen.

[*Commotion. The poets pull out their pads, scribble away. Incongruous strumming.*]

JEANNETTE: [*Nudges* ANGÈLE, *points to* VILLON.] Jesus! Who's that bag of rags?
ANGÈLE: [*Motionless, hypnotized by the sight of him.*] Poor soul! He's frightened!
JEANNETTE: [*Tapping her forehead.*] Like I'm sure. Of WHAT?
ANGÈLE: I don't know. But I can tell when people are frightened.

[VILLON *turns toward her voice. He looks intently at* ANGÈLE *but suddenly turns away, moves to center stage and shouts.*]

VILLON: [*Belligerently.*] Which one of you gentlemen will lend me a lute?
FATHER: [*Calming the annoyed bystanders.*] Do you mean you would like to sight-read, Monsieur . . . Monsieur?
VILLON: Sight-read, my ass! Gentlemen, that lute!

[*No one moves. Finally a member of the* CHORUS *whistles and tosses* VILLON *a lute.* VILLON *laughs, cockily plucks a string. Everything becomes hushed.* VILLON *waits, then starts his song. After a few moments the* CHORUS *joins in, merging into a recorded version, and the singing evolves into a multivoiced chorale. This musical number should sound somewhat grand.*]

[*A moment of total silence.* ANGÈLE *tosses* VILLON *a rose.* VILLON *sticks it behind his ear, grins.* FATHER *gets up.*]

FATHER: My beloved Poetry has visited our home today.
ANGÈLE: Well, isn't he fabulous?

[*The* DUCHESS *suddenly sways slightly and begins to fall.* FATHER *just manages to catch her.*]

FATHER: Excuse us. Her Majesty is exhausted by the heat. I will expect you in the great hall after sundown. You are my guests, gentlemen. [*Ceremoniously bows to* VILLON.] You have brought light into this old heart, sir. I will be expecting you.

[VILLON *throws the lute back to the* CHORUS. *He shuts his eyes ecstatically. The* CHORUS *strums quietly. The ladies lead away the* DUCHESS. FATHER *begins to leave.*]

MOUSTIER: [*Suspiciously, spylike.*] Who is that?
PICHART: [*Same.*] Haven't we seen him someplace?
MOUSTIER: He's all scarred up somehow.
PHILIPPE: Considering that we were given the theme, that the ballad form is inherited, that certain rhymes in turn demand only certain other rhymes . . . after all, there's no new thing under the sun.
FATHER: [*Overhears him, turns around, smiles. Conciliatingly.*] It might not be new for the sun, but it is for me. Good day!

[*All disperse.* VILLON *remains alone. He stretches in delight, collapses onto* ANGÈLE's *robe that has been left behind. He whistles along to the quiet strumming of the* CHORUS. *Suddenly a long howl is heard. The song stops at once.* VILLON *sits up uneasily. The howl is repeated.* VILLON *howls back, looking upset. Dusk is falling. From the increasing gloom emerge* TABARY *and* RÉGNIER, *dressed as medieval highwaymen. They raise their hands in the familiar gesture.* TABARY *joyfully runs toward* VILLON.]

TABARY: Franky! My man!

RÉGNIER: [*Maliciously, harshly.*] Get up!

VILLON: [*Gets up immediately, but unsurely.*] Wolf! How did you get here, Régn?

RÉGNIER: [*Unfriendly.*] What are you doing here?

TABARY: Ho, ho! Frank's sitting pretty! Franky's at court!

RÉGNIER: I'm asking a question!

VILLON: [*Rebelliously.*] I'm still free to walk where I please, am I not?

RÉGNIER: [*Jumps at him, knocks him down, explodes.*] You're not free to do anything! You are totally bound up by your allegiance to me!

VILLON: [*Getting up, just as passionately.*] Rrrrégn! I can't! I can't spend my life buried like a louse!

RÉGNIER: [*Draws a dagger and holds it to* VILLON's *scar.*] The warrant for your arrest is written on your lip. And if you don't know it, I'll make you a copy, friend!

VILLON: Rrrrrégn! Let me go! I'm heading for Paris at the first sign of frost!

RÉGNIER: [*Gestures with his dagger.*] Feet first! That's the only way you'll go!

[*The sound of medieval dance music. Dimly lit couples are seen dancing along the gallery.* ANGÈLE *runs onto the gallery and longingly looks down. Only* TABARY *notices her.*]

TABARY: Hey! Quail! Quail *du jour!*

[ANGÈLE *tries to attract* VILLON's *attention.* TABARY *blows kisses to her, making slightly lewd gestures, and is totally unaware of the bitter quarrel taking place between* VILLON *and* RÉGNIER.]

VILLON: Régn! I've got to go to Paris! I've got to! And I'm going to get there!

RÉGNIER: [*Shakes his head. A shade more friendly.*] Twilight. The hour between dog and wolf. Dogs drag themselves home and the wolves head out. The wolf hunts, the dog pisses against the inside of a locked door. [*Shaking* VILLON, *urgently.*] Don't die like a dog, Villon!

VILLON: [*Pounding his head with his fists.*] Everywhere else I go mad! I feel like I've been robbed. I'm hollow as a log!

RÉGNIER: Catherine has taken to young boys. She's not too picky. Her scratches and teethmarks are all over Paris.

VILLON: [*Desperately.*] What do I care! Régn! I'm rotting here from my feet up!

[ANGÈLE *dances over, whirling around by herself, but only* TABARY *sees her. He wiggles his tongue at her, but* ANGÈLE *doesn't notice him. She has eyes only for* VILLON, *who in turn doesn't notice her.* RÉGNIER *gets up. There is no trace of friendliness left: again he's the Wolf.*]

RÉGNIER: So listen here. Your successful career at court ends tonight. [*He pulls out a key and dangles it meaningfully.*] The chapel at Blois has one utterly superfluous figurine of the Infant Jesus.

VILLON: [*Staring in horror at the key, shaking his head.*] No way. I'm not in on this one.

RÉGNIER: [*Striking* VILLON *in the face with the key.*] This is NOT a theme for poetic flourishes! It's an order! Get going!

VILLON: Wolf! Rrrégn! I can't risk it! If I'm not back home by winter, then these bare woods will devour me!

[ANGÈLE *dances away in disappointment.* TABARY *returns to the twosome.*]

TABARY: [*Animatedly.*] What's your problem? It's kid stuff! A small-fry venture!

[*In the twilight the* DUCHESS *has walked over to the cross. She kneels, prays.* VILLON *watches her.*]

You'll just unlock the door, get everything ready . . . and little Guy Tabary here will be there in person! Sooo quietly, like a snake sliding over moss, he'll take the Infant Jesus . . .

RÉGNIER: Shut up! [*To* VILLON.] You'll be out of that chapel by midnight.

VILLON: [*Wildly rebellious.*] Rrrégn! You think you're so fantastic! Have you been deafened by your resounding NO?

RÉGNIER: [*Stiffens.*] What?

[*Both fall silent, measuring each other with their eyes.*]

TABARY: [*Uncomprehending.*] It's kid stuff! Seriously!

[*In the increasing dark the* DUCHESS *has risen and now stands, shading her eyes, trying to peer into the gloom.*]

DUCHESS: [*Uneasily.*] Is someone there? Who's talking over there?

[TABARY *instantly hits the ground.* RÉGNIER *seizes* VILLON *by the neck of his shirt and for a moment stares at him closely. Then he hands him the key.*]

RÉGNIER: It's an order. And then . . . you're free. Start for Paris.

VILLON: Régn . . .

MOTHER: Sir! Is that you?

[RÉGNIER *disappears.* VILLON *walks straight toward the approaching* MOTHER. *He continues to hold the key in his hand. He falls onto one knee.* MOTHER *looks him over shortsightedly.*]

VILLON: Madame.

MOTHER: [*Unsurely, gently.*] Sir . . . sir . . . how old are you?

VILLON: Twenty-eight, Madame.

MOTHER: Twenty-eight . . . [*Becomes confused, not knowing what to say.* VILLON *gently places the key in her décolleté, smiles at her.* FATHER *approaches, carrying a shawl.*]

FATHER: Marie! Put on a shawl, you'll catch cold . . . Aahh! Monsieur . . . monsieur . . .

VILLON: You could say Montcorbier. Why not?

FATHER: Why weren't you at the banquet, Monsieur Montcorbier?

VILLON: I was howling with wolves, Your Grace.

FATHER: Sorry?

VILLON: I was howling at the moon.

FATHER: Hmmm . . . as you wish. [*With a gesture he invites everyone to be seated, but in the background the dance continues. Suddenly raises his eyes alertly.*] Will you stay here with us, Monsieur Montcorbier?

VILLON: [*Verging on rudeness.*] How do I know?

FATHER: And who else would know?

VILLON: The world's full of riddles.

FATHER: You would be welcome here.

VILLON: Give the devil your hand and he'll take your arm.

FATHER: I beg your pardon?

VILLON: [*Insincere smile.*] Nothing. You know, Your Grace, I'm a man who bites a coin before he puts it in his pocket.

FATHER: Would you like some time to make up your mind?

VILLON: I'm stingy with my time. I hoard it like a peasant hoards cups of coins. I have a cup for sleeping, a cup for playing, a cup for things not so good. I don't have a cup for making up my mind.

FATHER: [*Gently.*] Forgive my question, sir, but are you in some kind of trouble?

VILLON: [*Laughs in surprise, then unpleasantly.*] Your Grace! When you look at me, you see nothing that is mine. This shirt came from a dead tramp in your woods. The shoes from a live one. [*Leans close and provocatively says straight into his face.*] And in my hair I have a stolen louse!

[*Laughter erupts from the dancers. Out of the darkness a howl is heard.* FATHER *examines* VILLON *for a long time. When he next speaks, it is very softly and politely.*]

FATHER: Forgive an old man for saying his mind. But I have been on this earth for a long time, and many a poet has passed through this court. But sir, your mother had God's finger pointing at her womb.

VILLON: Hmmm.

FATHER: Believe me. God never pointed at me. He only motioned my way [FATHER *motions with his finger.*] and said, "I am placing them under your care. Towards that care I will lend you . . . well, how much do you think you'll need? A thousand francs? Ten thousand francs? And I'll lend you a castle for them."

[*Instead of looking at* FATHER, VILLON *makes an unpleasant face into the audience.*]

FATHER: I too once wrote poems . . . they were flawless. At least as far as I can remember. I haven't read any of them for a long time. They were rounded out . . . smooth . . . like eggs. But hard-boiled eggs. I would sit over a ballad for weeks, only to finally realize I was trying to hatch a hard-boiled egg. My tongue is tied. For ten years I implored God on my knees to loosen the knot, but He only pulled it tighter.

MOTHER: [*Places her hand over his. Beseechingly.*] My husband . . .

VILLON: [*Impudently.*] So?

FATHER: So . . . I am offering refuge, young man. Security. If you want it, that is.

VILLON: Hmmm. Why? And at what price?

FATHER: [*Shakes his head.*] There is no price. You may do as you like here. God has lent me a franc a day for you. Our woods here are lovely.

VILLON: [*Whistles softly to himself for a while, rocking in his chair.*] You're not exactly cautious, are you? Caution. The mother of wisdom.

FATHER: [*Smiles.*] Where I came from they used to say "Desire is the father of thought."

VILLON: Caution and Desire. What a happy couple! What do you think the pair of them would produce? Ahh! Probably just another hard-boiled egg.

[*A howl from the darkness.* MOTHER *grows uneasy.*]

MOTHER: Wolves . . .

FATHER: The only thing of any value in this miserable world is song. If one can sing—and you can, my boy—fear nothing and sing out, sing out. Desire nothing more. Generation after generation will carry the words from your lips like the wind . . .

[MOTHER *places her hand on his shoulder.* FATHER's *excitement is interrupted, extinguished.*]

FATHER: Yes, yes. Come along, it's raw out. The hour between dog and wolf. [*Gets up.*] Well . . . good night.

[VILLON *kneels ceremoniously.* FATHER, *stooped and looking oddly defeated, departs.* MOTHER *stops, hesitantly places her palm on* VILLON's *hair.* VILLON *bows his head.* MOTHER *leaves.* VILLON *falls to the floor and begins pulling himself across the entire stage towards the cross. Up on the gallery* FATHER *is stopped by* PHILIPPE—*ceremonious show of homage.*]

PHILIPPE: Your Majesty!

FATHER: Yes?

[PHILIPPE *leans over, whispers something to him.* VILLON *creeps along.* FATHER *hears* PHILIPPE *out and then very distinctly, in emphatic disagreement, answers.*]

FATHER: Sir! I am afraid you have delivered this news to the wrong place!

[FATHER *departs.* PHILIPPE *stands for a while, then turns to the highest court stool. The light reveals the* BISHOP *seated, deeply absorbed in reading the Bible. In his bishop's garb he carries himself more severely, is somehow more medieval. The bailiff calls out.*]

MOUSTIER: The Vicomte de Montcourt most humbly begs the ear of his Holiness the Bishop d'Aussigny!

BISHOP: [*Putting aside the Bible.*] Speak my son.

PHILIPPE: [*Falls to his knees, devoutly.*] Your Holiness. The Bible asks: Am I my brother's keeper? Therefore may I, the smallest of the small, be the moral guardian at court?

BISHOP: [*Impatiently.*] Speak!

[VILLON *has reached the cross. Silently he begins trying to rip the figure of the crucified One from the cross.*]

PHILIPPE: [*Humbly.*] As your Holiness surely knows, the castle of Blois is open to guests. The blessedly trusting nature of the Duke Charles, our venerable lord . . .

BISHOP: [*Sharply strikes the table with the Bible.*] Time, my son, is a gift from God. Get to the point, or get out!

[PHILIPPE *gets up, snaps his fingers. The bailiff hands him his robe. In a flash* PHILIPPE *turns into the Prosecutor. There is no trace of humility. The light illuminates the entire array of court stools filled by members of the jury in their robes.*]

PHILIPPE: [*Aggressively.*] To the point! I accuse! I accuse François Villon of abusing the gift of his own soul! I accuse him of committing actions which contradict and betray the nobility of his own words! I accuse him of hiding his treachery behind the mask of Art!

[*The* BISHOP *has risen, taken his staff and is pointing to where* VILLON *is struggling with the cross.*]

PHILIPPE: I accuse and I warn. I warn you of a voice that trembles in fear of justice. I warn you of a poem whose pages are stuck together with blood!

[*Looks intently at* VILLON, *at whose back the* BISHOP *is already standing. In a different tone, suddenly more human, as it were, calls out in anguish.*]

PHILIPPE: I warn you, François!

[*The* BISHOP *walks all the way to* VILLON. *He goes by himself. He talks calmly, coolly, and with the utmost certainty. He is utterly convinced of his authority.*]

BISHOP: What are you looking for here?

[VILLON *whirls around. In front of him, like a heavy shield, he holds the cross.*]

VILLON: Get away!

BISHOP: Who are you?

VILLON: Watch out! I have a knife!

BISHOP: [*Shakes his head.*] No. I'm the Bishop. Against the Bishop you shall raise neither your hand nor your knife.

VILLON: Let me pass. I will go peacefully. Step aside.

BISHOP: Do you have a nickname, Villon?

VILLON: If you don't step aside I will kill you!

BISHOP: [*Smiles, coldly and calmly.*] I am the Holy Church. You will not touch me even with your finger.

[*Holds out his staff, pointing the point toward* VILLON, *and steps closer.* VILLON *cries out and hurls the heavy cross at him. The* BISHOP *barely dodges it.* VILLON *wrenches away his staff and with its point pins him to the wall by the back of his neck. The* BISHOP *gurgles. In the Senate,* ANGÈLE *starts screaming.* JEANNETTE *swings herself up to the judge's stool, her hood slips off, and with disheveled hair and in great excitement she begins whistling on her fingers.*]

VILLON: You're not going to get me! Nobody's going to get me!

BISHOP: [*Gurgling.*] Guards!

[*Bright lights go on, turmoil sets in. Both bailiffs run at* VILLON. JEANNETTE *is whistling, the bailiffs are shouting. They manage to set up the plank bed and after a brief struggle subdue* VILLON *and strap him onto it.*]

MOUSTIER: You crook!

PICHART: We've got you now!

MOUSTIER: Say your last Amen, you scum!

[BISHOP, *coughing, gurgling, feeling his throat.* MOUSTIER *lights a piece of kindling wood.*]

MOUSTIER: Does your Holiness agree to torture?

BISHOP: [*Absently, in a damaged voice.*] The Holy Church passes judgment but does not punish. Worldly power punishes. [*Suddenly turns to the Senate and with a powerful voice, for the first time wild with rage, shouts.*] Clear the court! Now! Clear the court!

[*Everyone hurriedly leaves. Only* VILLON *and the two bailiffs stay behind.* MOUSTIER *brings the burning piece of wood close to* VILLON's *face.*]

MOUSTIER: Smell good? Have a sniff! So the names! The names! Start singing, songbird!

PICHART: Who are the other upstarts?

[VILLON *screams.*]

MOUSTIER: Who's your leader?

PICHART: Who's the wolf? Who's the capo? Come on!

MOUSTIER: [*Rhythmically prodding* VILLON *in the ribs with the piece of wood.*] Ca-po! Ca-po! Ca-po! Who's coaching you? Sing out!

VILLON: Shit on you! [*Screams.*] Stop! Aaaahhh . . .

MOUSTIER: Keep on screaming, baby! It's good practice for your voice!

PICHART: Let's hear it! Who's the Wolf?

[VILLON *screams. Suddenly another cry adds itself to his. The* MOTHER/DUCHESS *staggers in, unmistakably in her ninth month. She leans against the wall. Clutches her abdomen. Groans.*]

MOTHER: It hurts! Hurts!

MOUSTIER: It hurts? Hurts?

VILLON: I curse you! May you shit blood! Drown in maggots! Die!

[*In midcry,* VILLON's *head lolls to one side.*]

MOTHER: [*Screaming.*] Help! Somebody help! Where is someone!

PICHART: [*Slapping* VILLON.] Is he dead?

MOUSTIER: [*Pressing his ear to* VILLON's *chest.*] No. This one's tough.

PICHART: [*Sits down, rubs his knuckles.*] Pig shit. Deserves three times as much. That Wolf Pack of theirs has already robbed half the country. They've gone wild.

MOTHER: God! Can't anyone hear me?

[*The bailiffs are resting. One has fallen asleep, the other is sitting, eating.* ANGÈLE, *got up as an angel, runs in, barefoot and in a nightgown. She's still half-asleep, frightened, confused.*]

ANGÈLE: Forgive me, Madame. I was asleep. Oh my God! Is it time already! I'll get a doctor!

[*The* BISHOP *enters in a white coat. Behind, dressed the same way, come* RÉGNIER, CATHERINE, *and* TABARY. *They look like a doctor and orderlies doing their rounds.*]

BISHOP: [*Authoritatively.*] Nurse! Where are you?

ANGÈLE: [*Runs to him in confusion.*] I'm here!

BISHOP: [*Feels the pulse of the unconscious* VILLON. *To* ANGÈLE.] Take off the bandage. [*To* MOUSTIER.] In coma?

MOUSTIER: [*His mouth full.*] Uh-huh.

BISHOP: Did he talk?

MOUSTIER: He cursed a lot.

[ANGÈLE *hurriedly, clumsily unbinds* VILLON. RÉGNIER *and* PHILIPPE *look on with deep interest.* CATHERINE, *totally uninterested, is looking elsewhere.*]

BISHOP: [*Lecturing impersonally.*] A male, twenty-eight years of age. A compulsive troublemaker, habitually unemployed, repeatedly punished. Vague amnesia, father unknown, lived a childhood of poverty. Superior intellect. Exceptionally self-promoting. Simultaneously a mitigating coma with magical qualities. Clinical portrait is of a psychopathic personality with criminal traits. Any questions?

VILLON: [*Groans, opens his eyes.*] An angel! Here's an angel! Angèle? Is that you?

ANGÉLE: [*In fright.*] Shhhh!

PHILIPPE: How should I say it . . . a feeling for society . . . is there any trace of that here . . .

BISHOP: An unusual question. What is actually meant by that?

PHILIPPE: Well, say . . . a reverberation of social existence—

BISHOP: A reverberation of an utterly extraordinary degree. Behavior, unfortunately, unacceptable.

PHILIPPE: Is there any possibility for reintegration into society?

BISHOP: Of course.

RÉGNIER: Will society welcome such a reintegration?

BISHOP: [*Looking at him for a moment. Then emphatically and drily.*] No.

PHILIPPE: [*In sincere consternation.*] But . . . that's no question for a doctor.

BISHOP: It isn't. Nurse, injection!

[*The* BISHOP *leaves. The doctors seat themselves on the stools.* ANGÈLE *finally succeeds in untying* VILLON, *who collapses into her arms with a groan.* ANGÉLE *gives a cry.*]

RÉGNIER: [*Ironically.*] Behold the man!

PHILIPPE: [*Up to now sincerely taken aback, not soliloquizing.*] That question of yours, why it's . . . I mean, is Man supposed to live his life alone?

RÉGNIER: [*Without interest or sympathy.*] Who knows.

PHILIPPE: Well. We all must adapt ourselves to the time and the society in which we live!

RÉGNIER: [*Snorts.*] Yeah. We'll give him back to society, society will take three bites of him [*Grimaces.*] and then it will spit him out again, along with the plastic bag that we sent him in. It's too bad. He's not fit for civilization, but rather for a wild forest . . .

CATHERINE: [*Turning around for the first time. Haughtily, coolly.*] Wild forest? Come on now!

VILLON: [*To* ANGÈLE, *dazedly.*] Where am I?

ANGÉLE: [*Whispers, mysteriously, angelic.*] In heaven! In the court of God, François!

CATHERINE: He'll come crawling back to you from the wild forest on all fours. Such a show-copath. He needs an audience.

PHILIPPE: Show-copath! What a word! Is it a literary term?

CATHERINE: [*Laughing at him.*] No. An off-the-top-of-my-head term. In other words, a clown.

VILLON: [*Points to them.*] Is that the jury? Where is God?

ANGÉLE: [*Whispering.*] He's not here. Shhh!

PHILIPPE: [*To* CATHERINE.] You know him? That one over there?

CATHERINE: Me? No. This is the first time I've ever seen him.

RÉGNIER: But he fascinates you, doesn't he?

[CATHERINE *and* RÉGNIER *eye one another, taking each other's measure and finding they dislike what they see.*]

CATHERINE: [*Turning to him.*] You would be amazed to know how rarely anything fascinates me.

[CATHERINE *pulls out a cigarette.* PHILIPPE *offers her a light, but she lights it herself. She turns away again, rocking in her chair.* RÉGNIER *whistles "Where are the snows of yesteryear" to himself.*]

VILLON: [*Points to* MOTHER.] Is that the Virgin Mary? The one with the big stomach?

ANGÈLE: Shh, François, shhh . . .

VILLON: So when is the trial going to start? Will they let me go in? Will somebody lend me a lute? Let's go! Gentlemen!

[FATHER *appears on the gallery. He comes dressed as the servant of the court, carrying some documents under his arm. He tries to pass through as unnoticeably as possible, but* VILLON *spots him and immediately sits up.*]

VILLON: Why that's Father! Father Villon! Hey girl, that's my foster-father! Hey! [*To* ANGÈLE.] Well, what are you looking at! Grab him! Father Villon!

FATHER: [*Goes to him, perplexed.*] François!

VILLON: [*Grabs onto his sleeve, rattling away ever more feverishly, slightly nonsensically, sometimes aggressively.*] What brings you here? [*Conspiratorially, with laughter.*] Do you know I'm in heaven? Except God . . . pouf! . . . he's flown the coop! [*Grimaces.*] Ah, old man, pretty amazing . . . What a way to end, huh? [*Recites.*] "I'm wheezing like an old geezer, God. And I'm still a young rooster, God!" Ah well, forget it. This is my guardian angel, have a look at her. Hasn't said much for herself so far, has she? [*Laughter.*] I'm falling headfirst, daddy-boy . . . Did you know they've been torturing me? [*Cries out.*] Torturing me! Where are you, God? [*Instant change to muttering.*] And what are you doing here, Father? It's not like you don't deserve to go to Heaven, but don't tell me you've bit your boots already . . .

FATHER: [*Interrupts him, apologetically, calmly.*] François, I am God.

[ANGÈLE *falls to her knees in fright.* VILLON *becomes instantly alert.*]

VILLON: [*Questioningly, not accusingly.*] And why do you allow it?

FATHER: [*Smiles.*] François, I don't make any decisions.

VILLON: How come?

FATHER: I'm not the only one here. The smallest angel [*points to* ANGÈLE] has more power than I have.

VILLON: Why?

FATHER: When someone is supposed to do something, they must be allowed to make mistakes. I cannot be all-powerful AND all-knowing, François.

VILLON: But you created it!

FATHER: [*Cheerfully and comfortingly.*] There is an opening in an hourglass, narrow like this. [*Makes a measuring gesture.*] All of the past pours into it like sand . . . and whatever falls through is claimed by the future. And you are stuck in the present, that tiny groove, like a dried up plum. And now: try to create! [*Winks at* VILLON, *almost jokingly.*] It really does get pretty cramped in there, François.

[FATHER *gives* VILLON *a friendly pat on the back and shuffles elsewhere.* VILLON *cries out.*]

VILLON: But I'm suffering! My muscles are popping! They're pouring a dozen jugs of salt water down me! My kidneys are bursting!

[MOTHER *gasps.* ANGÈLE *and* JEANNETTE *run to her,* FAT MARGOT *appears as the midwife.*]

MARGOT: Water! Quick! Lots of water! [*Slapping* MOTHER'*s cheeks.*] Hang on, honey!

[*The ladies-in-waiting mill around the quietly moaning* MOTHER. *Another moaning is added to hers: the bailiffs drag in a mangled* TABARY, *pulling him along the floor, kicking him as they go.*]

MOUSTIER: So they clipped your wings, you little vulture! Let's see you fly now! Try singing!

TABARY: Help! Ahhh!

MARGOT: [*To* MOTHER.] Shhh, shhh, shhh . . .

PICHART: Names! Ready?

MOUSTIER: Open your little beak and sing! [*Sweetly.*] Or else uncle here will cut out your tongue and it'll be too late . . . [*Kicks him, shouts.*] Scum! Talk!

MOTHER: Nobody can stand this!

MARGOT: Sure they can, honey. Just bite down and hang on.

PICHART: I'll count to three. One . . .

TABARY: No knife! No knife! I'll talk!

PICHART: Two . . .

TABARY: Régnier de Montigny . . .

MOUSTIER: See how easy it is when you cooperate? Just one more little song for granny! Who's the other double-crosser?

TABARY: I don't know! On my mother's grave, I don't know!

[PICHART *works the point of his shoe into* TABARY's *stomach.* TABARY *and* MOTHER *cry out.*]

MARGOT: Just don't give in to it! You can do it!

TABARY: Villon! François Villon!

[*The bailiffs instantly release the half-dead* TABARY *and kick him away.*]

MOUSTIER: [*Shouting.*] Villon! François Villon!

[RÉGNIER *gets up, takes off his white coat. Underneath, he wears a torn shirt. Slowly he makes his way up to the gallery.*]

PHILIPPE: [*Calling after him.*] Where to?

RÉGNIER: [*Turns around, makes a face.*] This is my big moment. To the gallows.

[*In the meantime the bailiffs are dragging a struggling* VILLON *back to the plank bed.*]

VILLON: No! Not the water! No!

MOTHER: [*Clutching her belly, running to center stage.*] At least save the child!

JEANNETTE: [*Shouting at the top of her lungs.*] Her Majesty is giving birth! Everybody away!

[*She tears at the curtain to hide the event from unauthorized eyes. The singing* CHORUS *lurches before the curtain.*]

CHORUS: SONG

"Who's there?
It's I.
I who?
I, your heart" (*etc.*).

[FATHER *steps before the curtain, as the servant of the court, and at once everyone falls silent.* FATHER *ceremoniously strikes a staff against the ground and majestically reads from a scroll.*]

FATHER: In the name of the King. In honor of their first-born daughter, the noble princess Marie, His Highest Majesty the Duke Charles d'Orléans and his spouse, Her Majesty Marie de Cléves, hereby pronounce amnesty for all prisoners regardless of their crimes.

[*The* CHORUS *scatters. The curtain goes up.* VILLON *is seated on the plank bed, looking absentminded. The bailiffs are prodding him.*]

MOUSTIER: [*Jovial.*] Well, go on, go on! The Devil stands by his own. You're free.

[VILLON *gets up in a daze.* FATHER *goes over to him, holding out his arms. The bailiffs stretch, yawn, leave disinterestedly.* VILLON *staggers slightly,* FATHER *barely catches him.*]

FATHER: [*Now like a foster-father, shaken-up, like an old man.*] Oh François, François . . . that was some luck. Lean on me, boy. The Mother of God herself holds her hand over you! But now, son, you've got to stay out of trouble!

[*The Senate is entering, taking their seats on the stools.* FATHER *leads* VILLON, *who still doesn't look entirely with it.*]

FATHER: [*Babbling.*] Paris has become strict now, son, yes indeed. It's gotten so tough here. Paris is nasty. She has no patience. I don't know why, she was never as impatient as she is now. She's scared, scared . . . but her memory is long, boy, yes indeed, here everyone knows everything about everybody!

VILLON: [*Absently.*] What's that gallows there?

FATHER: You can't provoke them, son. Above all, don't make noise. These days you're best off if you stay in the back . . . There's a lot of hanging now, son.

VILLON: [*Not listening.*] Who's that hanging?

FATHER: Oh . . . I think you knew him too. What was his name . . . Monti? Montigny?

VILLON: [*Stopping.*] Is that Régn?

FATHER: Yes, yes . . . Montigny . . . now I remember . . .

[VILLON *starts swaying slightly with an ever-increasing momentum until he collapses onto the floor before the judge's stool, right at the feet of* CATHERINE *in a robe.* FATHER *steps before the* BISHOP, *in the tone of the servant of the court.*]

FATHER: Great Judge, the accused Villon is here.

BISHOP: [*Sends him into the witness box.*] Are you Father Villon, priest at St. Benoît, foster-father of the accused François?

FATHER: [*His hand on the Bible.*] Yes, I am.

BISHOP: When he returned to Paris, did you take him in?

FATHER: [*Frightened, now an ordinary elderly person before a court.*] I . . . your honor, François has changed, he's changed a great deal . . . life has taught him a lesson.

BISHOP: Answer the questions! How does the accused earn a living?

FATHER: Honestly, completely honestly. He is my scribe. I pay him myself.

BISHOP: Do you know that your ward to this day owes the royal treasury for the robbery at the college in Navarre, and that is . . . that is . . . [*Searching among his papers.*]

FATHER: [*Taking advantage of the pause, starts babbling again.*] Poverty has taught him, your honor . . . why, he dragged himself home like a beaten dog. He has outgrown those green years now, he is not a child anymore. Now he's up to nothing but good. He keeps to himself, and we live a nice quiet life . . . One used to see him all over the place. I would say to him, François [*Laughing the rattling laugh of an old man.*] God sure made you different!

PHILIPPE: [*Interrupts.*] And what does he actually want in Paris?

FATHER: [*Taken aback.*] And what should he want? Why, this is his home, isn't it?

[VILLON *comes to, looks up toward* CATHERINE. *From here proceeds a double-dialogue:* VILLON *and* CATHERINE, FATHER *and the* COURT.]

VILLON: Catherine! Is that you?

[CATHERINE *turns away.*]

BISHOP: Are you solvent? Are you willing to pay Villon's debt?

FATHER: That would be how much?

VILLON: Catherine! I'm back in Paris!

CATHERINE: [*Vexed.*] Shhh!

PHILIPPE: One moment!

[*He leans over to the* BISHOP, *whispers something to him. From this moment on, they stop listening and sit leaning toward each other, discussing something.*]

FATHER: I'll see to him! I will watch over him as I would my own salvation! Just don't lose your patience with him, gentlemen!

VILLON: In Paris forever! Amen. Catherine!

CATHERINE: Stop interrupting!

VILLON: Are you still living, Catherine? They told me that you were still living. How?

CATHERINE: Do be quiet!

FATHER: Patience is a heavenly virtue, Saint Thomas says . . . the armor of angels . . .

VILLON: Look at me!

CATHERINE: [*Really looks at him for the first time, even leans over to get a better look. With hostility.*] What do you want here?

VILLON: I can't exist anywhere else.

CATHERINE: YOU can't exist anywhere, Villon!

FATHER: And faith, faith is a virtue of God! [*Moved.*] Have faith in him!

VILLON: Everywhere else I begin to rot. For five years I was devil knows where, Catherine. I turned my back on Paris . . . Actually, she turned her back on me. Did you know she's got a birthmark on her back?

CATHERINE: [*Bangs her fist on the stool.*] Be quiet!

FATHER: He's learned his lesson, you won't even know he's here . . .

VILLON: I'm not a wolf. I'm a dog who heads home at the first sign of dusk . . . Where is your look of a lost skylark, Catherine? Now you look like a rabid bat in the middle of the night. Do you still bite your nails? Let's see your hand!

CATHERINE: [*Coldly.*] I've practically consumed myself. What's left, Paris is finishing off.

VILLON: Catherine. I'm here. No one will ever get me away again.

CATHERINE: [*Bends down to him, nastily and aloud.*] If you think Paris will tolerate you, you are very much mistaken. In Paris they want you the way they want lice.

[VILLON *gets up. He crosses to the middle of the stage. Then clownishly holds out both arms and gives a wild, inarticulate cry.*]

BISHOP: [*Pounding his gavel.*] Silence in the court! Silence!

[VILLON *sits alone at the edge of the stage, hunched over, head on knees.* PHILIPPE *continues whispering to the* BISHOP. *The bailiffs give each other a questioning glance and stand up.*]

PICHART: [*To the* BISHOP.] Now?

BISHOP: Just a moment.

[RÉGNIER *sprawls out, whistling to himself. After a moment the* BISHOP *wordlessly points to several members of the Senate: at* TABARY, JEANNETTE, MARGOT *and both bailiffs. All take off their robes.* MARGOT *and* JEANNETTE *are dressed as in Act One,* JEANNETTE *is pregnant, the other three are wearing medieval bourgeois costumes.*]

ANGÈLE: [*Anxiously.*] Where are they going?

[PHILIPPE *looks questioningly at the* BISHOP.]

BISHOP: [*Shakes his head almost imperceptibly.*] Not her. [*Aloud to all.*] Clear the court. Be off!

ANGÈLE: What is it? What's going on? [*To* PHILIPPE *who is vehemently pushing her after the others.*] Let me be!

BISHOP: [*To* FATHER, *who is still humbly standing in the witness box.*] Given the new and unexpected circumstances, the court will pronounce its decision later.

FATHER: [*Fearfully.*] What's that? Given what circumstances? [*Looking around, shading his eyes.*] Where is that boy? François!

[PHILIPPE *manages to push even* FATHER *out. Meanwhile,* MARGOT *and* JEANNETTE *are arranging a tavern scene. The Senate is gone, and only the hunched-over* VILLON *remains.* MOUSTIER *happily slaps him on the back.*]

MOUSTIER: Why the long face, buddy?

VILLON: [*With a start.*] What?

MOUSTIER: All your birdies flown away? Somebody step on your cookie?

VILLON: Get lost. I'm in no mood.

PICHART: [*With drunken bawdiness, but not entirely natural—both men have the unmistakable air of spies.*] Cut the talk, guys! We're off to Margot's.

JEANNETTE: [*Runs to* VILLON, *throws herself around his neck.*] Oh no! I'm going to faint! It's François! Water! Water!

VILLON: [*Rather indifferently, but friendly, to* JEANNETTE.] Yep. It's me again.

JEANNETTE: Margot! It can't be for real! Franky, you old pirate! Come on!

MOUSTIER: [*Bawdily, falsely, as in a song.*] Gimme a little kiss, would ya, huh? [*Shouting to* MARGOT.] Hey there! Let's have a jug! [*Pushes* VILLON *to the table, snaps his fingers for a jug.*]

MARGOT: Well, who do we have here! Stop licking him, Jeannie! You'll catch something.

PICHART: [*To* VILLON.] I'm Pichart. You can call me Peachie.

MOUSTIER: I'm Houtin. You can call me Houtin.

[VILLON *takes a seat more or less passively. Suddenly notices* TABARY. *Suspiciously.*]

VILLON: You there! Which one are you?

TABARY: [*Uneasily.*] Dogis. At your service. My name is Dogis, I'm a clerk.

VILLON: Don't we know each other?

TABARY: Up to now, I haven't had the honor.

[VILLON *looking.* TABARY *turns his eyes away. The bailiffs nudge each other.*]

MOUSTIER: So what about a song? I hear you've got a voice. A lute! Let's go!

[MARGOT *hands* VILLON *a lute.*]

VILLON: [*Softly.*] How's it going?

MARGOT: [*Hard.*] It's going. So what?

MOUSTIER: All right, songbird, on with it!

JEANNETTE: Franky! Please! Just not another one against the king! And no provocations in general. Okay?

VILLON: [*Absently.*] What's that?

JEANNETTE: You heard me. I want peace and quiet for my kid.

MARGOT: Whoa! Whoa! Just because you got yourself knocked up . . . !

JEANNETTE: [*As fiery as ever.*] And what if I did? There's some point to that. But what's the good of making another noise about the king? It's as pointless as tickling a fly's ass. Well, go on, tell us yourself! Is it or isn't it?

MOUSTIER: [*Laughs, slaps her on the rump.*] 'Atta girl!

[VILLON *begins to sing. Not looking at anyone, strumming and whistling. Then he begins to play, but without energy. The* CHORUS, *taken aback by his unsureness, hesitantly tries to accompany him.*]

VILLON:

[*Suddenly with bizarre aggression. Continuation of song.*]

[*No one is listening closely.* PICHART *is fondling* MARGOT, MOUSTIER *is drinking and yawning,* TABARY *is staring at the table throughout the entire song.* VILLON *suddenly seems to wilt, leaves off singing halfway through a verse.* MOUSTIER, *on the other hand, springs to life.*]

MOUSTIER: All right. Time for us to go again. Jump up, minstrel!

[PICHART *and* MOUSTIER *get up, begin to leave, yawning.*]

PICHART: Hey, they've still got their lights on across the street!

MOUSTIER: Who has?

PICHART: Old Ferrebouc's clerks.

MOUSTIER: The ones with the hoods? Those praying fools? [*Folds his hands and hunches over, beginning to spin around, mimicking the shuffling walk and mumbling praying of monks.*] Ahh ta ta ta ta . . . Ahh ta ta ta ta . . .

[VILLON *absently stares elsewhere, oblivious to the action behind him.* ANGÈLE *comes running down from the gallery in a courtesan's dress.*]

ANGÈLE: François! You've come back, François!

VILLON: [*Not caring particularly, always slightly out of it.*] Ah, Angèle . . . So, have you been keeping an eye on Paris for me?

ANGÈLE: Paris is just awful now. Awful. Be careful of yourself, François.

VILLON: Once I had a dream about you . . . you looked like an angel. [*Laughs.*] I should've married you and stayed put. Go on, little girl. Go on.

[ANGÈLE *is not happy to leave. She keeps turning back to look at* VILLON, *who sits down alone at the edge of the stage, hunches over and seems to be asleep.*]

PICHART: [*Yawning.*] Ahh, taste that air! Nothing beats Paris at night!

MOUSTIER: Ahh ta ta ta ta . . . Ahh ta ta ta ta . . .

PICHART: [*Picks up a rock and weighs it in his hand with satisfaction.*] So what do you say? You think I can hit it? When I was a kid I could hit a sparrow dead in the eye!

[*Takes aim for a long time. Then he makes the throw. The loud shatter of broken glass is heard. At this cue the stage grows dark, we hear noise, clashes, cries, blows, but all we see is the supposedly sleeping* VILLON. *With whistling and shouting the* CHORUS *bursts onto the front, illuminated portion of the stage. It sings the refrain of the preceding text, but where previously the number was indistinct, rather nostalgic, it is now a song of wild protest.*]

[*A cry sounds in the darkness.*]

PICHART: Look out! He's got a dagger!

RÉGNIER: Enough!

[CHORUS *immediately falls silent. The lights go on. We see* TABARY *standing in the middle of the stage with a dagger in his hand. Slowly and in surprise he lets it fall to the ground. Otherwise the entire Senate is seated in their seats.*]

RÉGNIER: [*Shouting.*] OBJECTION!! It's a set-up! Villon! Wake up!

PICHART: [*Shaking the sleeping* VILLON.] Come on! Wake up!

MOUSTIER: [*Happily.*] So songbird! You're all sung out!

RÉGNIER: Bastards! Shame! Farce! Villon!

VILLON: [*To* MOUSTIER, *awakened.*] Beat it! I'm sleeping!

MOUSTIER: Just about anybody could say that! Shouldn't do such things, boy! Poking Monsieur Ferrebouc the scribe! And on top of that, in a state of intoxication? And on top of that, into his stomach!

[PICHART *whispers something to him.*]

MOUSTIER: Where? His leg too?

VILLON: Get lost!

[PICHART *grabs* VILLON *and stands him up. The bailiffs shackle him and drag him, resisting, before the Senate.*]

RÉGNIER: [*To the* BISHOP *in the meantime.*] I demand that the witnesses be taken into immediate custody. I demand that proof be submitted.

MOUSTIER: [*Victoriously, to the* BISHOP.] Here he is!

RÉGNIER: In the name of my client I protest . . .

BISHOP: [*Shouts.*] Silence! [*More calmly.*] Prosecution.

PHILIPPE: [*Rises, perfunctorily reads.*] Yesterday, on St. Boniface, a band of hoodlums attacked the peaceful, God-fearing industrious scribes. The bishop's scribe, Monsieur Ferrebouc, in an attempt to discover the cause of the unrest, stepped out into the street. The accused Villon, leader of the band of ruffians, went at him with his dagger and stabbed him mercilessly.

RÉGNIER: Liars! Bastards!

BISHOP: Defense, silence. You will be questioned later.

RÉGNIER: Questioned? I do the questioning! Who's responsible for this disgraceful charade?

PHILIPPE: [*Reads.*] And because this is not the first time that the court has encountered the accused . . .

RÉGNIER: Answer me! Who identified Villon?

[PHILIPPE *leans over to the* BISHOP, *questioningly whispers to him. Then, with dignity.*]

PHILIPPE: The prosecution will shortly call the witnesses.

RÉGNIER: Witnesses? Whose witnesses? Where did you come up with witnesses? Who are they?

BISHOP: [*He has had enough and jumps up in a rage.*] Enough, or I'll break off the trial! The prosecution has the floor!

PHILIPPE: I summon the honorable Monsieur Houtin de Moustier!

[MOUSTIER *comes forward, takes up the witness position and, with his hand on the Bible, mumbles through his oath. Meantime,* RÉGNIER *whistles on his fingers.*]

RÉGNIER: Villon! What're you waiting for? Defend yourself!

VILLON: [*Resignedly.*] They've got me, Régn.

PHILIPPE: [*To* MOUSTIER.] Are you a direct witness to the incident?

MOUSTIER: I am.

PHILIPPE: Would you recognize the assailant?

MOUSTIER: Certainly. [*Points to* VILLON.] That's him.

RÉGNIER: Don't tell me you're giving up? Damn you! Shout!

VILLON: You haven't been around for a long time. You don't know what they're like anymore, Régn.

RÉGNIER: [*Enraged.*] Shut up! [*To* MOUSTIER.] Defense. Where was the light?

MOUSTIER: What? What do you mean "where"?

RÉGNIER: I am asking you clearly. WHERE . . . WAS . . . THE . . . LIGHT?

[PICHART *stuffs himself into the witness box, places his hand on the Bible and begins mumbling. He is obviously acting as a distraction.*]

PICHART: I, Rogier Pichart, do solemnly swear, that . . .

MOUSTIER: Well . . . the moon, right?

RÉGNIER: A lie! Yesterday was the new moon!

PHILIPPE: The light from the clerk's house was bright enough . . .

RÉGNIER: Again a lie! The first stone they threw broke the lamp. The oil stain [*Points to the floor.*] is still visible on the pavement!

PICHART: [*Talking above them, mumbling.*] . . . and so help me God!

VILLON: [*Whistling, shouting across the whole stage.*] It's no use, Régn!

RÉGNIER: [*Furiously.*] No use, maybe, but necessary! I summon the witness Dogis!

[*A murmur passes through the jury. In the Senate, slightly hesitant and clownish as usual,* TABARY *stands up.*]

TABARY: Me? Why me? I am the king's clerk!

RÉGNIER: [*Harshly.*] Come on, get out of that robe! Action! Action! That's it!

[*He personally takes hold of* TABARY's *shoulder to push him out and remove his robe.* TABARY *is dressed as in the scene at* MARGOT's. *He is uneasily looking over the jury, but* RÉGNIER *shoves him into the witness box and* TABARY *mumbles over the Bible.*]

VILLON: Rrrrégn! Do you know who dropped the noose around your neck?

RÉGNIER: [*Gestures leave-me-alone. To* TABARY.] Did you witness the accident?

[TABARY *hesitantly looks around. The* BISHOP *nods almost imperceptibly.* TABARY *brightens somewhat and during the following exchange begins to present himself in an obnoxiously cocky fashion.*]

TABARY: That's so.

RÉGNIER: [*Aggressively, quickly, Perry Mason–like.*] Did you see the assailant?

TABARY: Certainly.

RÉGNIER: From what angle?

TABARY: [*Points.*] From there.

RÉGNIER: So you didn't see his face!

TABARY: [*Laughs: you won't confuse me!*] Oh yeah! Quite clearly! I was standing immediately opposite him! It was this gentleman!

RÉGNIER: Did he have a dagger?

TABARY: Yes.

RÉGNIER: His own?

TABARY: How should I know?

RÉGNIER: What did Ferrebouc say immediately after being wounded?

TABARY: [*Making a production of himself.*] What would YOU say if somebody stabbed you in the leg?

RÉGNIER: What did he say?

TABARY: [*Mocking the examination.*] Nothing! His eyes were popping out!

RÉGNIER: A lot?

TABARY: What kind of a question is that!

RÉGNIER: How? [*Bulging his eyes.*] Like this? Or more?

TABARY: [*Gestures: look at this fool.*] You do that very well, sir! Yes, as far as I can recall, it was just like that!

RÉGNIER: [*Bulging his eyes more and more, then with horrendously bulging eyes he slowly approaches* TABARY.] Like this? Precisely? Are you certain?

TABARY: [*Growing uneasy.*] Excuse me, sir . . .

VILLON: Régn!

RÉGNIER: [*Suddenly jumps at* TABARY, *grabs him under the neck.*] And from what angle did you see this? Were you standing right opposite the assailant?

[*At this signal a racket erupts in the courtroom. Both bailiffs are pounding the floor with sticks, ringing, shouting, artificially creating chaos.*]

PICHART & MOUSTIER: The witnesses are asked to leave the court!

RÉGNIER: [*Holding on to* TABARY.] Do you want blood on your conscience?

PICHART & MOUSTIER: All other persons will leave the vicinity of the court! Otherwise we will clear the room!

TABARY: [*Breaks down.*] I confess.

[*Everyone falls silent with expectation.*]

TABARY: I, Rogier Dogis, born and presently residing in Paris.

PHILIPPE: The court is incapable of making a ruling. [*Points to* TABARY's *seat.*] A juror is missing.

TABARY: This year, on the day of St. Boniface, I . . .

PICHART: [*Takes him by the shoulder.*] That goes for you too, Dogis!

RÉGNIER: Dogis, talk! For the record!

TABARY: . . . was invited by two members of the king's guard . . .

MOUSTIER: [*Hands* TABARY *his robe, begins dressing him in it himself.*] There we go, now! We'll talk about this some other time. Right now, it's time for you to go!

RÉGNIER: Dogis!

TABARY: [*While both bailiffs are stuffing him into his robe and trying to stop him from talking, over the din.*] I was the one who stabbed Ferrebouc!

RÉGNIER: Did everyone hear that? Hear that?

TABARY: [*A desperate cry.*] Villon!

[*The bailiffs finish buttoning him up. Once he's in the robe, he changes immediately, adopting a starched, impersonal expression. He pushes the bailiffs away and puts on his hood by himself.*]

RÉGNIER: [*Shouting.*] Talk, Dogis!

MOUSTIER: [*Victoriously.*] The witness Dogis has departed, sir. [*Affectionately patting* TABARY.] There.

FATHER: [*Ringing a bell.*] To your places, gentlemen!

[*Full light. The entire jury, except for* RÉGNIER, *stands up.*]

BISHOP: Paris, Advent, 1462. By law and in the name of God, François, called Villon, is sentenced to death by hanging. The law will be carried unto justice after the Christmas holidays. With this I pronounce the case closed. Take Villon away.

VILLON: [*More surprised than frightened.*] What was that . . . Régn?

[*The bailiffs are pushing him out, the jury is dispersing, the bailiffs are urging them to move faster.* VILLON *is looking back inquisitively.*]

VILLON: Régn? Régn?

[*Empty stage except for* RÉGNIER *alone. He sits immobile for a moment. Then he gets up, picks up his papers and hurls them at the wall. The papers scatter.* RÉGNIER *sits down on the floor, bows his head. The* BISHOP *walks in, watches him thoughtfully. After a while he says calmly.*]

BISHOP: Counsellor.

RÉGNIER: [*Defiantly ignores him, rhythmically tapping his palm on the floor and half-singing.*]

SONG: "Quatrain (Epitaph)"

"I am Francois which is my cross
Born in Paris near Pontoise
From a fathom of rope my neck
Will learn the weight of my ass.

BISHOP: Calm yourself.

RÉGNIER: [*Continues song.*]

BISHOP: Mistake.

RÉGNIER: [*Continues song.*]

BISHOP: No. [*Picks up a bell, pensively toys with it.*] Your client will be granted pardon, Counsellor.

RÉGNIER: [*Looks up with disbelief. After a moment, alertly.*] How come?

BISHOP: [*Slight smile.*] I wouldn't like to go into the details.

RÉGNIER: So then what was the point of this court comedy?

[*The* BISHOP *hands him the bell and goes over to sit down in his seat. He is now neither evil nor stupid. He is in his own way convincing. Both talk to each other with unusual calm, in turn, without unnecessary fuss.*]

BISHOP: Sir, your distress is misdirected. Villon will not die.

RÉGNIER: So all that uproar . . . what was the purpose?

BISHOP: The court will shortly reconvene and pronounce an amended sentence.

RÉGNIER: Will they pardon Villon?

BISHOP: Of course.

RÉGNIER: Free him?

BISHOP: Of course.

RÉGNIER: Will he be able to leave prison?

BISHOP: Of course.

RÉGNIER: All right. [*Turns around, wants to leave.*] Reconvene the court.

BISHOP: Of course. The sentence is: banishment from Paris.

[RÉGNIER *turns in a flash. Stares at the* BISHOP *as if struck by lightning. He slowly removes his cap, throws it on the floor. Then his robe. He appears in modern dress.*]

RÉGNIER: [*Flabbergasted.*] No.

BISHOP: Oh yes.

RÉGNIER: He's thirty-three. You can't bury him alive.

BISHOP: We aren't burying him.

RÉGNIER: If he loses Paris, he will never write again as long as he lives. He will be extinguished.

BISHOP: We are here and now. It is the first Friday of Advent 1462. I am with God's grace the judge of Paris.

RÉGNIER: [*For the first time emotionally.*] Here? Now? Pray that your tongue doesn't fall out, judge of Paris! [*Like a town crier.*] I am with God's grace the eye of history! I am with God's grace the ear of the future! You know, should you banish this man, you will destroy one of the greatest poets of all time!

BISHOP: [*Softly, emphatically, knowingly.*] I don't know about that. I don't know it. I am not the eye of the future. I am the hand of the present, esteemed sir.

RÉGNIER: [*Calm again.*] Well, then, I am telling you, esteemed sir. Do you know what it is to skid? Ah, no you don't, you are not the eye of the future. January 9, 1463, Villon is leaving Paris and just a few steps beyond its border he trips. [*Taps his temple.*] Here: a skid. His words fly out of his hands. With a loud clatter, his talent slips out from under his feet. Never again will he compose a single verse. He will live on for decades more, but he won't write even one phrase. That's what I call capital punishment!

BISHOP: But we are here, and this is now. And I cannot accept this argument.

[RÉGNIER *throws up his hands helplessly. Paces back and forth. Then stops.*]

RÉGNIER: Imagine that you are a crow, dear Judge-By-God's-Grace. Here and now, a crow. You are flying over France. It is night. The deathly stillness of a forest. It is desolate, snowdrifts. And then you find yourself above Paris. And suddenly: Shshshsh! A flaming blast of sound. A steaming murmur. The hiss of voices rising toward heaven. Bells. Someone is whistling. Chairs are scraping floors. Thoughts grinding—GRRRR GRRRR GRRRR!! Paris! The sound of Paris!

BISHOP: And so?

RÉGNIER: Villon drinks in that sound! It's an addiction!! And through him—only through him—can that Babel of towering cacophony be transmuted into song!

BISHOP: My client is not song. My client is order.

RÉGNIER: Order? Order? [*Shakes his head.*] There is no order! There is only the red-hot thread of Time connecting the past with the future. It passes through one in a million. It passes through Villon. NOT through us.

BISHOP: [*Calmly, pensively.*] You talk about time as if you had swallowed it. Maybe you have. I don't know. But for me, time is not a thread. For me, time is the valley before the Last Judgment, and I keep order in this valley.

RÉGNIER: [*Emphatically.*] I request total and unconditional freedom for Villon!

BISHOP: [*Laughs slightly, says peacefully.*] Freedom? There is no freedom. I thought you knew this. Freedom is merely necessity in disguise, and our task is to serve this necessity.

RÉGNIER: [*Looks at him for a while, then gives a slight laugh.*] I protest. Necessity serves itself. If anything needs our help, it's freedom.

BISHOP: [*Laughs openly, amicably.*] Monsieur de Montigny. If you were not already hanging somewhere near Blois, I would even banish YOU. [*Loudly.*] I convene the court!

[*The jury approaches.* FATHER *brings in* VILLON. *All take their places. The* BISHOP *rises.*]

BISHOP: Hear the sentence!

[*The massive sound of the Paris bells covers the words. As they ring, the Senate disperses. Left on the stage are only* RÉGNIER, *who sits down on the floor by himself, exhausted,* VILLON, *and* FATHER, *who starts tidying up. He shuffles obliviously around, picking up papers, pushing in chairs. The bells stop.*]

VILLON: Did we lose, Régn?

RÉGNIER: Yes.

VILLON: Will I live?

RÉGNIER: Yes.

VILLON: Will I come back?

RÉGNIER: No.

FATHER: [*To* VILLON.] The trial is over. We have to go now, young fellow!

VILLON: The trial is over?

RÉGNIER: No.

VILLON: No?

RÉGNIER: We will appeal!

> [*Abruptly rises, picks up the robe and goes to his seat.*]

RÉGNIER: [*Blazing.*] We will appeal the case!

FATHER: [*Begins shutting off the lights, to* VILLON.] Go on, son, go on . . .

RÉGNIER: I demand that the case of François Villon be reopened!

FATHER: [*Gives* VILLON *a push.*] Come on boy! It's time. Let's go.

VILLON: I have to go, Régn!

> [VILLON *is leaving. On the border between light and dark, he still turns around, raises his hand in the familiar gesture.*]

VILLON: Rrrrrégn!

> [*In the gallery the* CHORUS *starts to play its lutes. After a while the tape-recorder joins in. Their song and the recordings cover each other, it is not a single song but an overpowering, strengthening disjoined flow. Excerpts from* VILLON's *ballads, fragments of his texts, merge together, the noise level begins to drown* RÉGNIER's *talk. The last thing we can understand is.*]

RÉGNIER: [*Shouting over the voices.*] Here and now. Prague, March 23, 1979! I summon the jury!

> [*The singing overpowers him. As it does, it comes together into a single massive river of voices filling the entire theater.* FATHER, *now living outside these events, is obliviously turning off the lights, one after the other. The stage sinks into darkness. Finally even the last lamp goes out above* RÉGNIER's *head. For a while longer, one hears the the singing coming from the darkness.*]

[*The End.*]

Elfriede Jelinek (b. 1946)

Elfriede Jelinek's highly visible and very prolific career as a novelist, playwright, poet, radio, TV- and screenwriter, and political essayist has strong roots in her dislike of the surrounding mainstream Austrian culture. During the Second World War Austria was of course joined with Germany. In 1955 the country had to accept a cautious neutrality to regain its independence. This history and the country's uneasy position between East and West contributed to a literary and cultural milieu that was intensely conservative. In the sixties an artistic avant-garde emerged antagonistic to this climate. Jelinek became a principal figure in that group, specifically associated with the Graz Writers' Association (Grazer Gruppe).

Although Jelinek's art has generally inclined toward the avant-garde, with a marked appreciation of the powers and flexibility of language as a cultural tool, her impulse has been consistently political. It has always included a mixture of Marxism and feminism, though of shifting proportions. Her analysis of the sociopolitics of Austria in particular and of Western capitalism in general concludes that for feminism to succeed society must change its economic structure. Her first play, *What Happened After Nora Left Her Husband* (*Was geschah, nachdem Nora ihren Mann verlassen hatte oder Stützen der Gesellschaften*, 1980), follows Ibsen's disavowing protagonist into the inhospitable world of industrial capitalism.

Since the eighties, Jelinek has been a visible and provocative writer and has been frequently interviewed. Because the immediate focus of her criticism is often on her own country, she has had difficulty getting performed and recognized in Austria. Many of her plays, including *Clara S.* (*Clara S., Eine musikalische Tragödie*, 1981), *Burgheater* (which attacked Vienna's revered theater and its actor-family— the Hörbigers, 1982), and *Illness, or: Modern Women* (*Krankheit oder Moderne Frauen*, 1984), premiered in Germany.

Her novel *Desire* (*Lust*, 1989), an uncompromisingly analytical reworking from a female perspective of a pornographic story, became a best-seller. Since its publication Jelinek has been more positively recognized in Austria, with a secure and growing international reputation. She is the best-known feminist currently writing in German, with a number of literary awards and prizes to her credit.

As a critic of society, Jelinek's depictions are, she acknowledges, pessimistic, with few, if any, appealing, positive characters. She never portrays motherhood favorably, does not think a woman can satisfactorily be fullfilled within a heterosexual relationship and live an independent life as an artist. Originally, her emphasis was first on Marxism and social justice (wary as she is of the fascist undercurrents

Elfriede Jelinek, ca. 1998. (Photographer: Isolde Ohlbaum.)

still apparent in Austria) and then on feminism. This priority has been altering, though she remains pervasively political and socialist, believing that gender oppressions cross all classes. This shift can be seen in going from *Nora,* with its economic criticism of society, to *Clara S.,* which is more immediately feminist. Subsequent plays, like *Illness,* increasingly question the possibility of communication between men and women. She finds a poststructualist approach, with its possibilities for political expression, more congenial than she does the essentialist biases of the French *écriture feminine* or the Austrian *Frauenliteratur,* which stress inherent, intractable differences between the sexes.

Jelinek is a severe critic of popular culture, who claims to delight in *Dallas* and *Dynasty,* a Marxist who is impatient with myths about the nobility of work. She is a trained musician and tends to reify her characters into speech patterns or voices. Her cold, analytic gaze is often criticized for its lack of emotion. She does not see herself as part of the majority tradition of conservative Austrian literature and culture, but more in line with German realist and Eastern European Jewish literary currents.

Clara S. is a harsh critique of the barriers women artists face in a man's world. The historical figure of Clara Schumann (1819–96), wife of the composer Robert (1810–56), is a powerful vehicle for Jelinek's purposes. The infamous example of the celebrated pianist and composer, Clara Wieck, who became Frau Schumann, with her eight pregnancies and mentally unstable husband, transferred onto the stage the impossible conflict between woman as talented artist and woman as self-denying, nurturing factotum. The style is postmodernist and the structure crosses historical periods; together they embrace the poet Gabriele D'Annunzio and extend the tentacles of society's trap (so vividly realized with Logier's training contraption) to include the inadequate and debasing heterosexuality available to women. D'Annunzio, identified with fascism and Mussolini, is equally at home in the nineteenth-century patriarchy of Clara's father and husband as he would be in the contemporary society Jelinek satirizes. The strikingly divided set, an elegantly furnished room overhung with stalactites, announces the discordant, but universally pertinent drama of Clara's oppression.

Clara S(chumann) is further interesting as a recently revisited historical figure. Lauded as an incarnation of dutiful, self-effacing domesticity in Mussolini's Italy, she more currently exemplifies a neglected and stifled woman artist. In the midst of all of the references to illness and the conflicting demands of her husband and her pursuer, Clara frets, "artists' wives always pay. If she's an artist in her own right her limbs rot away one by one as her husband goes on producing art." This artistic *Totentanz* ends with the death of Robert and then of Clara—in a posture that is not, we are alerted, to suggest a Pièta.

SELECTED BIBLIOGRAPHY IN ENGLISH

Fiddler, Allyson. *Rewriting Reality: an Introduction to Elfriede Jelinek.* Oxford: Berg Publishers, 1994.

Gannon, Caitlin. "Clara S. and Her 'Men-tors': The Annihilation of the Female Artist." *New German Review* 10 (1994), 149–56.

Honegger, Gita. "This German Language: An Interview with Elfriede Jelinek." *Theater* 25 (1994), 14–22.

Lamb-Faffelberger, Margarete. "Austria's Feminist Avant-Garde: Valie Export's and Elfriede Jelinek's Aesthetic Innovations." *Out From the Shadows: Essays on Contemporary Austrian Women Writers.* Ed. M. Lamb-Faffelberger. Riverside, Calif.: Ariadne, 1997. Pp. 229–41.

———. "In the Eyes of the Press: Provocation—Production—Prominence. A Critical Documentation of Elfriede Jelinek's Reception." *Elfriede Jelinek: Framed By Language.* Eds. Jorum Johns and Katherine Arens. Riverside, Calif.: Ariadne, 1994. Pp. 287–301.

Sieg, Katrin. *Exiles, Eccentrics, Activists: Women in Contemporary German Theater.* Ann Arbor: University of Michigan Press, 1994.

CLARA S.

A Musical Tragedy

Elfriede Jelinek

Translated by Anthony Vivis

CHARACTERS

CLARA S

ROBERT S

MARIE

GABRIELE D'ANNUNZIO   known as THE COMMANDANTE

LUISA BACCARA

AELIS MAZOYER

DONNA MARIA DI GALLESE, PRINCESS OF MONTENEVOSO

CARLOTTA BARRA

TWO PSYCHIATRIC NURSES ("MINDERS")

There are also several WOMAN-SERVANTS *and a young local* PROSTITUTE.

The action takes place in the Vittoriale near Gardone, D'ANNUNZIO's *villa.*
    The time is late Autumn, 1929.
    As far as the atmosphere and costumes are concerned, it is perhaps best to follow the style of Tamara de Lempicka's paintings.

PART 1

A luxuriously appointed room, which somehow rather resembles a cave with stalactites. Stalactite-like protruberances hang down from the ceiling and are covered with what looks like mossy velvet. The whole decoration is overwhelmingly ornate—and utterly tasteless. In the background, a concert grand. On it young MARIE *is loudly and stridently practicing scales and trills by Czerny; she is strapped into a kind of training frame—this frame, the so-called Logier'sche Gestell, dates from the 19th century and has already ruined one of Robert Schumann's fingers—which is supposed to teach pupils the correct way to hold their bodies while playing. We hear a metronome ticking. After a few moments* CLARA *runs across the stage in considerable distress, wringing her hands. She is hotly pursued by the plumpish, sensual figure of* LUISA BACCARA, *who is screeching with delight, and who comes into view a little while after* CLARA.

LUISA *is rather commonly Italian, whereas* CLARA *is like a German roe-deer on the run.* LUISA *catches up with* CLARA, *and puts her arms around her. Panting anxiously,* CLARA *lets herself be embraced. Mannered, exaggerated gestures.*

LUISA: Right, caught you at last, Cara!
CLARA: Clara, not Cara! [*Panting.*] My insides are fighting a losing battle against my outside. Of course, any woman of spirit won't even notice anything external. Any minute now my heart's going to gush out and spill all over the floor.
LUISA: Don't talk rubbish! Of course it won't!
CLARA: Women virtuosos build up a reputation abroad which they then try to market at home. When I say home, of course, I mean Germany, my home. Soon the whole world will feel like home.
LUISA: [*Kissing her.*] If you ask me, this aversion of yours to any physical contact is beginning to get to you. Any minute I'm afraid you're going to tear in my hands like a sheet of paper. I can sense it. Once a German spirit gets a taste for it, it'll start to rip up all the bodies that have the temerity to show their faces. But be that as it may! I was just about to tell you something about my artistic development, I—
CLARA: [*Interrupting her.*] I'd rather you didn't—
LUISA: You never let me finish because you think you're an artist and I'm not. Well, this time you will listen!

[*She gets a firm grip on* CLARA, *who tries to wrench herself free, but* LUISA *is stronger.*]

LUISA: Listen to me, I said. I've always tried really hard to be awkward, someone who's valued for being different. Lately, though, I've decided not to kick against the pricks.
CLARA: Talk, talk, talk, that's all you can do . . . A German, on the other hand, can act or think without saying a word!
LUISA: Did something kill off all your sensuality? An accident of some kind? I do hope not!
CLARA: [*Closing the neckline of her dress with exaggerated modesty.*] My father, that great, highly respected teacher, and later on my husband, Robert, that bastard.

[LUISA *giggles in an exaggerated and teasing way.*]

CLARA: [*Forcefully.*] Stop laughing!
LUISA: [*As she kisses the reluctant* CLARA *once again.*] How can you call him a bastard today when only yesterday you said he was a divine genius? Love! Follow my example! I'm happy to give a male composer anything he wants to take from me. Without any compunction whatever. None whatsoever, my darling Clara! [*She starts giggling again.*]
CLARA: To me your giggling sounds triumphant, contrived.

[LUISA *giggles even more loudly, and kisses* CLARA's *throat.*]

CLARA: Get away from me! [*She pushes* LUISA *away.*] My father dinned the male idea of genius into me, but my husband snatched it back because he wanted it all for himself. Our own head is where the censor sits.
LUISA: So why write compositions yourself? So many compositions already exist—I mean, you could spend your whole life rolling about in them like a pig scratching for truffles!

[LUISA *pulls away* CLARA's *hand, which is still woodenly trying to hold her dress together, and*

406   *Elfriede Jelinek*

starts touching her. CLARA *jumps up in horror and rushes away, half-demented. Giggling delightedly,* LUISA *sets off in pursuit. The child goes on practicing stridently.*]

LUISA: Women are soft and usually yielding, whereas men are hard and always thrusting forward, no matter where it ends. In composing a piece of music, for instance. More's invested in men than women, so they can produce more when the need arises. It's all a matter of supply and demand, my treasure.

CLARA: [*Breathlessly throwing herself into a vulgarly tapestried armchair.*] That bastard Robert fantasizes the whole time about going crazy. On the way to Eudenich he behaved himself as far as Cologne, but after that he kept trying to jump out of the carriage. All through the Rhineland he was forever wrenching open the door and trying to throw himself out—he had to be forcibly restrained.

LUISA: How awful! Cara! Bella Tedesca!

CLARA: [*Rhapsodic, almost in tears.*] Inside this head of mine, he says, everything flows together and gets compacted by some mysterious machinery. Which explains why he's so terrified of losing his head! Because he knows his genius lives in it as snug as a worm in an apple. Every now and then the worm pops its head out, then, shocked by the world, pulls back inside the head, and goes on munching away in there, feeding off the brain.

[*The* COMMANDANTE, *an elderly man, shambles in.* CLARA *throws herself into his arms.*]

CLARA: My friend, my fellow art-lover!

COMMANDANTE: Now, now, steady on. [*He fondles her.*]

CLARA: No, no! Let me kneel before you! [*She is about to kneel down but he won't let her.*] Well, if you won't let me go down on my knees to you, at least let me admire your very noble bearing! I know you can never understand my husband Robert's genius—fine—but you can pay due respect to his great gifts by generously financing his latest creation— a really up-to-the-minute composition—after all, your bearing's what makes you look so fit.

COMMANDANTE: Before you start admiring my physique, my dear, I suggest you let me enjoy your body!

[*He tries to grope her, but she breaks free.*]

CLARA: The state's paid you money for works of art, so by rights you ought to pass it on! Power's never had any feeling for art. All it does know is that somebody's got to pay for it.

COMMANDANTE: The Duce has shown his gratitude for my art. Go and find another patron! But first come here a minute! [*He drags her towards him.*]

CLARA: No! [*She wrenches herself free.*] I'd rather kneel, thank you! Let me go, you . . . you . . . obtuse Italian!

COMMANDANTE: Oh, right, Italian am I now! I'll have you know I've flown over Vienna in an airplane. And, what's more, I took a capsule of deadly poison with me, just in case anything went wrong in the air. My male lust for conquest was telling me: fly! My male death-wish was telling me: die! Art was telling me: write! My lust for conquest won. Through heavy, gelatinous air I shot forward irresistibly, scattering leaflets right and left. The greater you are, the sillier you behave.

CLARA: [*Resisting him.*] Wouldn't today be the ideal time to take your poison? [*Pushing him away.*] Leave me alone! I'm the embodiment of art and motherhood. A symbiotic combination. You ought to shrink back from it in horror—as if you were faced with your own innards, which—thank God—you never have to see. Motherhood thrives on art and vice versa.

COMMANDANTE: Well, my dear, which is it to be: Shall I finance a symphony from your cheese-brained original genius, or shall I take poison? You decide.

CLARA: First, give genius a helping hand, then commit suicide—nice and quietly. You'll live on in my Robert. And Robert's name will live forever: so everybody's happy!

[*The* COMMANDANTE *again puts his arms around* CLARA, *attacking her; offended—and neglected—*LUISA *has withdrawn, and she starts halfheartedly reading a book.*]

CLARA: Even if you can't show proper respect for my motherhood, at least have some for the artist in me. Keep your distance!

COMMANDANTE: I don't care a damn whether you give yourself to me as a mother or an artist. And anyway, apart from my creative work, it's my priceless armchairs I live for—covered with original Renaissance chasubles. I also own thousands of other antiques, so we can be sure of a rich inheritance. I own odes, sculptures, sonnets and statuettes. Lots of them created by masters more famous than your Robert will ever be.

CLARA: Monster! Philistine!

COMMANDANTE: I can talk poetically any time I choose. Now, for instance—I'll talk poetically right now. [*He grabs hold of* CLARA, *who resists his advances.*] Listen to me, will you! What I desire in you, in this knowing yet desperate woman, is the individual who has given her eternally subjugated feminine nature the slip and who is destined to surrender to the sudden spasms of her sexuality; who has succeeded in quenching—in nights of unbridled lust—the fever which the lights of the concert-hall first kindled in her; I adore and desire the passionate pianist who can move from the crowd's delirium to the power of a man, that Dionysian creature who crowns the mysterious act of worship with an orgy of life!

CLARA: If that's anything to go by, you'll never even catch my Robert up, let alone overtake him!

COMMANDANTE: As you'll have noticed, I had no problem switching from normal language to the language of poetry.

CLARA: The truly German composer I married has always had to overcome colossal artistic obstacles to build that cathedral of notes. On the other hand, that's why his work will endure, whilst yours will soon be forgotten. And most of all because as a person and a man you're a total flop.

COMMANDANTE: For decades now my manhood's never flopped! And as a person I'm demonic. And I'll show you what I mean by demonic, so just listen: As I devour you with greedy looks, your flesh flinches away, greedily warding off the shame you'd find so painful. My desire cuts into you like a deadly wound, because you know how much bitter lust lies behind my sudden desire. Am I right?!

CLARA: You animal! I so want the clear, pure transparency of Robert's Sonata in F-sharp Minor.

COMMANDANTE: If you must know, I think you're utterly depraved and corrupt, highly experienced in all the arts of love and lust—in a word, an insatiable temptress. You make a German mountain torrent look like a trickle. Trout would drown in your fierce currents.

CLARA: My artist's body, which even used to compose all by itself when it had time, is immune to your advances.

COMMANDANTE: Yours is not the only artist's body in this house. Right now, for instance, a ballet-dancer's body is spinning this way.

[CARLOTTA BARRA *comes in, wearing a track suit, and does bar-exercises at a rail in the background, without taking any notice of the others.*]

COMMANDANTE: I'll tell you one thing I can't abide: the body of your husband, that German composer.

CLARA: Because he's got genius, that's why. His genius means he always goes to extremes—which is often painful for other people. Sometimes he goes that bit too far, straight into the arms of madness. Robert knows no bounds. In his desires or his demands.

COMMANDANTE: I know exactly what you mean! I'm a genius, too, so I follow you perfectly.

CLARA: Oh no you're not! Oh no you're not!

COMMANDANTE: Oh yes I am! Oh yes I am!

CLARA: All you know is women's bodies, not the inner mysteries of art. Artists are priests, dedicated exclusively to creating art—they're deaf to everything else. You can't claim anything of the kind.

COMMANDANTE: Oh yes I can. I know all about extremes, from personal experience. Take my desires, for instance, they're pathologically extreme. One kind of desire encompasses the life of the defeated masses and the ecstasy of the unknown lovers my various mistresses have taken. The other kind of desire embraces my vision of orgiastic congress. Well, now what do you say?

CLARA: My Robert is living proof that an artist can exist apart from the world. You're living proof that a dilettante can never be a true artist! I'm not denying some important artists flirt with unhealthy extremes, like the virtuoso-composer Liszt, or that shit Meyerbeer, but you're not in their class! If Robert is a mountain lake or torrent, you, Gabriele, are just a sewer! Your money stinks!

COMMANDANTE: I am not a sewer! I'm a highly successful combination of cruelty, resentment, jealously, poetry and pride.

CLARA: Philistine!

COMMANDANTE: [*Offended.*] To be frank, I wonder how you can bear to stay here if I'm such a sewer. Can a woman like you open her legs to a sewer of a man?

CLARA: My dear Commandante, there is absolutely no question of me opening my legs. I'm appealing to your powers of patronage, not your senses.

COMMANDANTE: What exactly would I be paying for, Clara, my dear? For weeks now your Robert's been sitting on an egg that hasn't even hatched yet. All he can manage is the sullen genius look. I, on the other hand, am Ariel, the spirit of the air. Shall I ask Aélis to help you pack? Then Charles will drive you to the station. Would you like me to book you your usual room at the Palace, my treasure?

CLARA: [*Horrified.*] Oh God, no! Please don't leave a woman when she's so full of longing!

COMMANDANTE: [*Knowingly.*] Right!

CLARA: [*Making a huge effort, she goes over to him, and gives him childlike kisses on his cheeks.*] Do let me stay here, please, Gabriele, so I can sit at your feet!

COMMANDANTE: [*Groping her.*] It's real agony to me that I've never possessed you after an enormous triumph on the keyboard, still warm from the public's excited breath, drenched in sweat, panting and pale. After the Hammerklaviersonate, for example. Or after that sweat-inducing Tchaikovsky concerto. In either case one looks a fright.

CLARA: [*In desperation.*] Ariel! [*Like a small girl, she jumps up to his neck, and tries to put her arms around him.*] You poet prince from Italy! [*Weeps.*] You . . . [*Sobbing.*] priest of your art! . . .

COMMANDANTE: [*In a tired, routine manner.*] I can see you spread out as if lit by a flash of lightning. Within you all the power to have silenced the howling public. Now you're weary and you're aching with desire to be possessed and penetrated. Come on, then, let's do it right now! Afterwards I'll explain what makes a fearless conqueror different from an equally fearless artist. That is: nothing of substance.

[*He is about to lead* CLARA *out.* CARLOTTA, *who notices this, rushes downstage to him, jealous because she is being ignored as an artist. She makes very graceful hand movements—fluttering gestures—in front of his face. The* COMMANDANTE *tries to touch her breasts, but she gracefully eludes him, and whirls away.*]

CARLOTTA: [*As she whirls off.*] Unlike most people, we dancers are downy feathers in the wind. Light and air can pass through our bodies. Nothing holds us fast to the ground. Sometimes we're not so much light and air as ecstatic priestesses of our art. [*Whirling away.*] Like just now. People go in search of us like a pilgrim seeking out a distant altarpiece!

[*In the doorway she bumps into* LUISA, *who is on her way back in, nibbling biscuits.*]

LUISA: [*Quietly to* CARLOTTA.] In the end, love, if you go on steadfastly turning him down, you'll find yourself with no booking at the Paris Opera.

CARLOTTA: [*Quietly.*] That German cow has been laying it on a bit thick. Just now she was saying she's a priestess. That's my line. You specifically said I could try my luck with the nun number, and now that German woman's trying it on, without checking with me first. I don't care what the fuck she calls herself—a bird, if she likes—a phoenix, for all I care—or a little roe deer.

LUISA: Calm down, Cara. The best thing to do is let him screw you.

CARLOTTA: Never! I shall captivate him with my art.

LUISA: [*Skeptical.*] Suit yourself. After all, you were here first. By all means try the priestess line. I'll have a word with the German woman. Get her to stick to being a roe deer from now on, then maybe this Robert of hers will make a plausible white stag.

[*The two women giggle.* CLARA *and the* COMMANDANTE, *who have both been worried about* MARIE *in the frame, now listen attentively.*]

CARLOTTA: [*Quickly, to* LUISA.] Talk to him today, while you're submitting to him. You'll get your 30 percent cut.

LUISA: 40 percent!

CARLOTTA: Okay, then, 40. What one does for art!

LUISA: [*Offended.*] I'm an artist, too. I practice exactly the same art as you do, only I'm more experienced and in a different field: the piano. Let's not quarrel about it: 30 percent.

[CARLOTTA *whirls out of the door.*]

LUISA: The biter bit! While I'm submitting to him I never stop talking about the concert evenings I'm going to give in the States. It's all arranged for Spring. The Commandante's signed the contract and paid a deposit. Only 120 more submissions to go! At most!

[*At this moment the* COMMANDANTE *collapses, wheezing, at the piano.* LUISA *rushes to help him, rings the servants' bell furiously.* CLARA—*playing mother—corrects her daughter's posture at the piano.*]

COMMANDANTE: [*Wheezing.*] Beauty obsesses me: trees, flowers, dogs, and, of course, women! I couldn't stand it if the woman I happened to be with wasn't beautiful. And I'd find it even more intolerable if some other woman who wasn't mine was even more beautiful! [*He almost chokes.*]

[AELIS *rushes in; she and* LUISA *make the* COMMANDANTE *comfortable on a pile of satin cushions, feel his pulse, rub his temples, etc. While they are doing all this, the* COMMANDANTE *gropes both women, sliding his hand under their clothes, etc.* MARIE *misplays some triads;* CLARA *corrects her.*]

COMMANDANTE: [*Still wheezing.*] I've had plenty of practice, living with beautiful women. Something happens when you look into a lovely human being's eyes: You see an open, honest face. But what is beauty, anyway? A goat on top of a mountain is beautiful, so's the much maligned sunset. What matters more than beauty is . . . [*He is now wheezing so heavily that he has to take a sip of water.*] being loved, to seem beautiful to a man! [*He coughs, half choking, so that some of the water trickles back out of his mouth.* MARIE *is now playing wrong notes again.*]

COMMANDANTE: [*With a great effort.*] Take the poor child out of that frame!

[AELIS *hands him a bottle of smelling salts, which he sniffs.*]

CLARA: [*At the piano.*] In your condition you can't possibly appreciate my daughter's colossal talent!

COMMANDANTE: Out of that frame!

CLARA: Still not over it yet? Animal! Monster! You ruthless male tyrant, you!

COMMANDANTE: I'll make sure your husband gets locked up in a loony bin until the situation is clarified. Then I'll make doubly sure his now defenseless wife convulses in one final spasm of submission to a violent embrace before finding release in deep, dreamless slumber. [*He recovers noticeably.*]

CLARA: You inhuman tyrant! Long before any of that, Robert will have composed his greatest work, a symphony. Here in this house. And as a result your house will go down in musical history.

COMMANDANTE: No need. My presence has already guaranteed it a place in literary history. I'm a member of the Olympus of Italian poets. Gabriele d'Annunzio.

CLARA: My husband will be much more immortal than you are, Commandante!

COMMANDANTE: No. I'll be more immortal. Beg me not to be cruel! [*Wheezing horribly, he almost dies.*]

CLARA: Don't be cruel, I beg you.

COMMANDANTE: Now beg me not to hurt you! Because, you see, there are moments when I forget myself and think I'm a wild animal—a lion, perhaps, or a bear.

CLARA: [*Holding her daughter close.*] No, I won't! Once he threw his precious wedding-ring into the Rhine. From now on I want to devote my life to Robert.

COMMANDANTE: Don't worry, I've decided after due reflection I won't do you any harm. [*He again breaks down completely.*]

CLARA: [*Pressing her child close to her, stepping out of her role.*] At first they said my Robert worried for ages about losing his reason. In fact, of course, this was putting the cart before the horse. What he was really worried about losing was his cock. When the censor's no longer in control, suppression doesn't really work. We've all got our problems.

COMMANDANTE: [*Perking up.*] Would madame like to see how well endowed I am? [*He is about to undo his trousers.* CLARA *immediately backs away.* AELIS *restrains and caresses him, at the same time poking her head out and peering into the corridor.*]

AELIS: Commandante, Carlotta Barra is still standing out there, working up a hand gesture that's supposed to look graceful. You're expected to look at her and get her a booking at the Paris Opera, otherwise she'll have a breakdown.

COMMANDANTE: [*Coughing.*] Is she anyone I've known?

CLARA: You really mortify me when you talk like that, Commandante!

COMMANDANTE: My justly infamous Leda Room awaits you. Still awaits you. What's more, my petit prince is also at your service. You know who that is. If not, read the relevant literature! Shall I show you the state you've reduced him to by constantly saying no?

[*He reaches for his penis,* CLARA *again hides her face; hysterically.*]

CLARA: No, don't! Please don't!

COMMANDANTE: And in my generosity I've even ordered a trough of German fodder, specially for you. Sauerkraut mostly. If you don't do for me, this food definitely will. And I can also offer you a pinch of my White Lady. [*He taps his box of cocaine.*]

CLARA: No! I'll never let some devilish drug cloud the limpid clarity of my German mind.

COMMANDANTE: I see—so that's what an artist's intensity in life really amounts to? They tell me you can't separate art from life because they mirror one another exactly.

CLARA: I owe my intensity as a German pianist solely to violent dissonance in childhood!

COMMANDANTE: An artist is often shaped by the suffering that stalks him. Take me, I'm a great writer, and from my darkest depths a savage instinct often escapes, which I just can't tame. From the same depths—but not very often—feelings of human compassion also emerge. But they're not nearly as powerful as the savage streak. I'm more Satanic than your Robert.

CLARA: No, my Robert's more Satanic than you. Initially, my father cast a shadow over my life, now the shadow is a problem with my partner. Ordinary people flee these complications like the plague, but artists obsessively seek them out, so they can reflect them in their work. They're known as a work's depth. In work by women it all gets weakened. After childbirth, depth disappears.

[*She stares pensively into the distance, having let go of her child, who tears herself away, runs to the* COMMANDANTE *and snuggles up to him. The* COMMANDANTE *wheezes and lets* AELIS *pour him some medicine.* AELIS *signals to the child to press up against the* COMMANDANTE, *and shows her how. The* COMMANDANTE *rubs himself up against* MARIE, *breathing heavily.* LUISA, *who has stood apart the whole time, spooning caviar, observes all this jealously, and bites a hibiscus petal.*]

AELIS: Luisa Baccara is so upset she's biting a flower-blossom!

LUISA: [*Tries to reach the* COMMANDANTE, *but* AELIS *stops her.*] Commandante, the rank passions of pitch-black night are thrusting us forward and tossing us on top of one another!

AELIS: But it's midday.

[*The* COMMANDANTE, *still with the little girl, groans.* CLARA, *her mother, stands by the window and—as enigmatic as Mignon—stares into the distance, gesturing vaguely. She does not notice what her daughter is up to.*]

CLARA: Oh Germany, Germany, it's such a long way from here back to you, my fatherland. Cue for an anecdote or two about my varied life.

LUISA: [*With malicious jealousy.*] You still have time to leave the room before a German destiny is splattered all over the floor! German artistic destinies are particularly heavy going.

[*The* COMMANDANTE *signals to the faithful* AELIS *to distract* CLARA's *attention away from her daughter, with whom he is smooching.* AELIS *understands at once, and crosses to the window, where, in half-feigned, half-genuine solidarity, she puts her hand on* CLARA's *shoulder, pressing softly against her.*]

CLARA: [*Unhappy, almost weeping, over-the-top.*] This ghastly foreign country is more than my nature can cope with! Nature! The night seems about to give birth to miracles. Eternal forces are creating a balance between the earth and the stars.

[AELIS *taps her consolingly but lightly on her back; even so, she looks past her in* LUISA's *direction, and theatrically rolls her eyes, to indicate that* CLARA *is getting on her nerves.* LUISA *returns the gesture with interest.*]

CLARA: Ah, nature! Men have two great fears: nature and women. But even greater is their fear of their own bodies.

[*A shrill giggle from the* COMMANDANTE, *who is pressing himself against the child, rubbing up against her vigorously.* CLARA *takes no notice of him.*]

CLARA: [*While, behind her back,* AELIS *shrugs her shoulders and pulls a "telling" face at* LUISA.] These landscapes of terror in extinct male heads! All that men can see in nature is darkness, which they proceed to depict in their art! It's the old middle class dream of the head as the seat of genius. [*She now speaks with real emotion.*] An empty delusion of grandeur! A house of dark passages. And they drag that leaden head-weight through them, the whole time. They're constantly searching for something which hasn't yet been written, composed, spoken. Or-ig-in-al-ity! [*Feeling nauseous, she chokes.* AELIS *ab-*

sentmindedly strokes her head.] As if that weren't bad enough, they have this obsessive need to go on talking . . . talking . . . talking about it . . . this constant compulsion for extreme uniqueness . . . sets all this energy free, you see, so the art-machine goes on churning out art, on and on . . .

AELIS: Calm yourself, darling! It's got to happen sooner or later. You know what he's like. And anyway . . . [*Whispering.*] . . . he's hardly capable of anything any more. We've been keeping up appearances for him for weeks . . . there are certain . . . tricks . . .

CLARA: [*Shouting.*] Tricks!

AELIS: Do stop shouting!

CLARA: [*Bitterly.*] Tricks.

AELIS: Well, you know. Or however you want to describe it. Pop up to my room after tea and I'll be happy to show you how one . . .

CLARA: [*Has not been listening, and now interrupts her brusquely.*] Women pay the price for men's fantasies of self-fulfilment. [*Exhausted.*] Artists' wives pay particularly dearly. If she's an artist in her own right, her limbs rot away on her living body while her husband goes on producing art.

AELIS: Just listen to me for a moment, will you! I'm trying to help you! She needs the money.

CLARA: Artist husband and artist wife: You can't split the blood of one from the blood of the other. They both overlap and you can't wrench them apart. Either they stride together towards the same sunrise or they stumble into a ditch over each other's legs. But by then the woman's usually a shrivelled-up root, whilst the man's still full of sap.

MARIE: [*To the* COMMANDANTE, *who caresses and calms her, moaning.*] I want a glass of raspberry juice! And an ice-cream with loads of . . . slices of melon all over . . . like yesterday for supper!

[*The* COMMANDANTE *murmurs something to her,* CLARA *ignores them both.*]

AELIS: [*To* CLARA, *not without sympathy but with slight amusement.*] Lie down a bit, my love! Have a rest!

CLARA: No! I've got to finish what I was saying, Mademoiselle Mazoyer! I've got to show I'm different from those two piano-machines, Liszt and Thalberg.

AELIS: But you're tired, Frau Schumann.

CLARA: First I'll tell you all about my father, who made me what I am . . .

[*Shouts from various corners of the room:* "Oh, my God! Oh, no! Not her Daddy! Not again! Please!" *etc.* CLARA *takes no notice.*]

CLARA: [*Rhapsodically.*] My father was a piano-exporter. Everywhere you looked—dead instruments of art. You could hardly pick your way through them all. And as if they weren't bad enough, there were all these oafs who kept fiddling with them! Provincial pianists with delusions of grandeur! Then, once in a while, the odd early developer, as we call them in the trade. But very rarely. I tell you, Aélis, genius will strangle at birth any creativity that's in your own mind! I was surrounded—all day every day—by Chopin études, bravura numbers by Liszt, and pieces by that vastly overrated Mozart. I didn't learn to talk till I was five. But my hearing was razor-sharp. My father used to write my diary for me whilst piano-thumpers of all ages would reach under my little skirt. I couldn't say a word! And all round me lay the country which never stops vomiting forth German artists—after all it is German.

AELIS: [*Consoling her.*] Oh dear, it can't have been that bad, surely.

CLARA: Oh yes it was! Even worse! Like any artist worth their salt, I have to insist my destiny was exceptionally tough and my childhood even harder.

AELIS: You poor love!

COMMANDANTE: [*From the background, laboriously, caressing the child.*] This impermeable, unfeeling flesh, in which human beings are so solidly imprisoned. It's so hard to pierce through it! But by now I can see your soul—there it is, look! It reveals itself to me as powerfully as a piece of music! An inexpressibly delicate yet overwhelming ability to feel. I sense it loves me, not just my body.

CLARA: All that emerged of me externally was my delicate mechanical ability to depress piano-keys—in the right order. Anybody who practices can do it. Anybody who practices a lot can do it really well.

[*At this moment the* PRINCESS OF MONTENEVOSO, *the* COMMANDANTE's *wife, trails in, and looks the group over contemptuously.*]

PRINCESS: I gather you have yet again tarnished my wifely honor while I'm staying under your roof.

[*The* COMMANDANTE *jumps up and kisses her hand reverentially, pushing* MARIE *aside.*]

PRINCESS: By attracting a never-ending stream of female artists here, even though I've begged you several times not to . . . despite my beseeching you time after time you . . . [*He gives her a black look, whereupon she loses her thread and stops talking.*]

COMMANDANTE: Maria, as you very well know, I need these creatures about me. Only they, these women artists, as you contemptuously choose to call them, offer me the background against which my poetic blood can start to course, if you follow? In their chaste fragility they create the delicacy of flowers whilst I supply the hard strength of marble and the energy of lightning, as well as all the shadow and all the light. Are you with me, Maria?

PRINCESS: Oh yes, my love!

COMMANDANTE. Off you go, then, there's a good Maria!

PRINCESS: Gabriel! Ariel!

COMMANDANTE: Out! [*The* PRINCESS *trails out.*]

PRINCESS: [*As she walks away.*] Needless to say, I couldn't bear my children to be present. I'll write you a long letter from Monte and explain things in a little more detail.

[CLARA *turns round at the exact moment the* COMMANDANTE *is once again focusing his attention on little* MARIE. *She notices what is going on, and tears herself free from* AELIS, *who tries to hold her back so as not to spoil the* COMMANDANTE's *pleasure.* CLARA *rushes towards the* COMMANDANTE, *wrenches her daughter away, and drags her off with her in an onrush of romantic exuberance.*]

CLARA: [*Extremely agitated.*] Je vous supplie, si ce n'est pas de "l'aveugle rancune," expliquons-nous, parlons! Pourquoi ridiculariser les moments qui étaient beaux et spontanés? Je vous parle au nom du "clairvoyant amour"! (I beg you, if this isn't just "blind spite," let's explain ourselves, let's talk this through! Why make these moments ridiculous when they were so lovely, so spontaneous? I appeal to you in the name of our "clear-sighted love"!)

[*For her part, however,* MARIE *wants to go on, she tries to break free from her mother's hand, as the* COMMANDANTE *gropes for her.*]

MARIE: [*Hesitantly, and childlike.*] Surely you've realized . . . mother darling . . . that although . . . at this relatively young age . . . I can walk really well . . . as far as speaking goes . . . I'm not yet quite . . . er . . . there. But my hearing . . . like yours when you were small . . . has developed . . . very far indeed. But more for . . . musical notes . . . than language . . . Which I'm learning to speak . . . something you've . . . never bothered to teach me . . . as you've always been so anxious . . . to make . . . me a pianist of genius . . . so by now I'm nothing but . . . a pair of hands . . . with a body hanging from them.

[*She tries to get back to the* COMMANDANTE, *but* CLARA *drags her away in a tight embrace. Standing on tip-toe, the girl peers over her mother's shoulder at the* COMMANDANTE, *around whom* AELIS *and* LUISA BACCARA *are fluttering.*]

CLARA: [*Whispering into* MARIE's *ear, commandingly.*] You're staying right where you are! One of the very few creatures I've given birth to who wasn't a total write-off! Practically every one a dead-loss! Eight pregnancies, and most of them a waste of time. Shame I made the effort. One just dies on me, after hardly a year: gland trouble! Mostly sons, you notice! Defective stock! Ludwig was loony like his dad, and I didn't even have the comfort of relatives visiting the asylum. Ferdinand: drugs, and downhill all the way. Felix: TB, Julie: TB. You're the pitiful leftovers, Marie my darling.

MARIE: Let me out, Mummy! Let me go! [*She tries to escape.*]

CLARA: Needless to say, during my all-too-frequent bouts of breeding, which made my belly swell up like a pumpkin, I couldn't appear anywhere. You can't imagine how much money and intellectual companionship I lost in the process! I would have been pushing my luck with music-lovers' tolerance. And on top of everything else, I had to put up with the inspired father's constant complaining about our little brood. On trips, he'd always be griping and groaning because nobody knew him, while everybody knew me. He made me feel my presence was a personal affront to him, so I had to sit around in hotels and guest-houses with an appropriately absent expression on my face.

MARIE: Don't talk about him . . . like that . . . my darling daddy!

CLARA: In the end your father's insanity . . . turned out to be . . . incurable. My incessant pregnancies . . . that excess of nature, which a sensitive person just can't stand . . . that clenched fist of womanhood . . . any kind of progress just crumbles before it . . . The artist in you keeps feeling sick when she sees that swollen belly . . . Now he keeps saying he feels drawn to Lake Garda, somewhere to drown, he says. He wants to disappear into the great outdoors. He tried it once before in the river Rhine. But what scares him most is something disappearing from me, out of whom all the products of his cock kept crawling for years on end. Repulsive little white larvae, including you, my darling Marie.

[*She belabors her lightly about the head.* MARIE *finally breaks free and rushes squealing and grinning stupidly back to the* COMMANDANTE. *She jumps on him, and he strokes her lecherously.*]

CLARA: [*Watching her go, with a pained expression.*] The first law of art is: technique as a means to an end. If technique becomes an end in itself, art just goes by the board!

[*The* COMMANDANTE *is busy with* MARIE *again.*]

MARIE: [*Flatteringly to the* COMMANDANTE.] Later on, please may I . . . go and look at the airplane . . . please say I may, please . . . [*She hops about on his lap teasingly.*]

COMMANDANTE: Of course, my child, of course you may. [*Uninterested and speaking casually, almost incidentally.*] As it takes firmer shape, your mouth is acquiring a hardish outline in your pallid face, as if tormented by insatiable thirst, created only to draw things into it, to swallow them, hold them fast.

MARIE: The . . . lovely . . . airplane!

[*Meanwhile in the background* LUISA BACCARA *and the* WOMAN-SERVANTS *have laid the table for tea—with yellow roses, etc. Now* LUISA *practices finger-movements silently on the tablecloth, exchanging jealous-soloist looks with* CLARA.]

LUISA: [*To* CLARA.] I'm the epitome of Venetian woman soloists, whereas you're the honest but unimaginative representative of the German piano-playing sisterhood. I'm sluttish, generous, all over the place with my tempi, but with a good physique and highly adorable. Simple, solid and blessed with a dark complexion.

[CLARA *stares at her briefly, uncomprehendingly, then she again makes for the* COMMANDANTE, *who is now exchanging kisses with* MARIE, *and tells him what's what with a desperation which belies her actual words—while the* COMMANDANTE's *bombast is more or less incidental.*]

CLARA: Her ear! Her ear! My little Marie's ear can distinguish a great deal other people just don't notice! Slowly but surely I'm training her to be a specialist, just like my father trained me so magnificently all those years ago. She can already go straight for all the upper and lower dominant chords, and she can modulate them when, where and why she wants!

[*Now that* CLARA *is beginning to get on his nerves, the* COMMANDANTE *signals to the faithful* AELIS, *behind* CLARA's *back, that she should get rid of her.* AELIS *takes hold of* CLARA's *arm and tries to lead her away—though affectionately! Needless to say,* CLARA *resists!*]

CLARA: [*Overwrought.*] It's the sexual side that finishes us all off. Even you, Ariel! It's a disease that kills us by natural means. It ruins even the deepest of intimacies between a man and a woman. My father and Robert both said so. As a person I was very soon deadened by being sanctified, being turned into an ideal. Into a passive presence, that was so distant it was no longer dangerous. The upshot is I've spent all my life not living. But to make absolutely sure I was dead, Robert killed me completely with his genius.

AELIS: Do calm down, please! You simply can't behave like this here. Kindly remember you're a guest! In this house one's used to hearing cries of lust, something very akin to death, I admit. As close as genius is to insanity.

LUISA: And as if that wasn't bad enough, she plays the presto movement of the "Moonlight Sonata" much too slowly. Like all Germans. [*She bites into a peach, until the juice runs out.*] I wish I'd been a singer. People are much more taken with a woman who produces notes only from her body, without the help of instruments.

AELIS: [*Affectionately.*] You shouldn't eat so much, my darling!

LUISA: But sad to say, this generously built body houses nothing more than an average voice. [*She goes on eating.*]

CLARA: [*Exultant.*] I was never allowed to compose on my own. Even though I wanted to very much indeed. He got me to believe I couldn't possibly want to compose in his shadow. A genius wants to journey into the realms of the abstract unencumbered by his wife. A wife is just so much bone-meal.

[*She pulls away from* AELIS, *who is trying to calm her down, and rushes towards the* COMMANDANTE *and her daughter.* AELIS *tries to hold her back.* CLARA *hurls herself on the smooching couple—the* COMMANDANTE *and* MARIE. *They fight back.*]

CLARA: [*Rhapsodically.*] But she easily gets wilful, does my little Marie! And then there's no holding her. Artists always ought to be modest, so my Robert says. Because they've got a gift other people haven't got, the gift of being gifted, so Robert says. She's even giving [*Conspiratorially.*] small concerts already, and I've even noticed lots of little attempts at her own compositions! Me, her mother!

[*Once again the* COMMANDANTE *wheezes asthmatically, involuntarily letting go of little* MARIE, *who presses childlike kisses on his eyes, and snuggles up to him.* AELIS *leaves* CLARA *and rushes for the* COMMANDANTE, *tests his pupil-reactions, picks up a nearby syringe and routinely injects him. The* COMMANDANTE *soon calms down. Lies still.* CLARA *seizes her opportunity to get her daughter back. She picks up the girl, who kicks her legs in protest, and quickly carries her out.*]

[*Meanwhile,* LUISA *spends the whole time jealously and greedily stuffing herself with sweets, occasionally remembering to dart meaningful sidelong glances at* AELIS. *Outside we can hear a whining child's voice—*MARIE—"But I want to see the airplane, you promised!" *Servants' whispering voices calm her down.* CLARA *comes back in. She kneels down beside the* COMMANDANTE, *feels his pulse, murmurs imploringly.*]

CLARA: Before you finally bow out, Commandante, please, please finance my husband, even if it's only for a year. I beg you! And my daughter needs subsidizing, too, as you've seen, I'm sure. Her little compositions are usually fine rhythmically, only the base-line is not quite what it might be. At least she can detect the major third as one of the harmonics of the keynote! Not bad, eh? [*As if it were a matter of life and death.*] Yes, I am trying to scotch the rumor that my little Marie grew up too soon because of too much practicing. On the contrary: it's helped her express her feelings! And that takes a sizeable financial investment!

COMMANDANTE: How does any land achieve fame? Through its famous sons, of course!

CLARA: Sons! Sons! Let me tell you, Gabriele, my sons were even more useless than my daughters, apart from Marie, of course. And naturally, they all wanted to compose, all the little lads. Sadly, though, they failed. Even more miserably than me. Their father's shadow hung over each one of them like the sword of Damocles. They were riddled with his genius like a cancer: they were just a collection of mortal illnesses, my sons.

[AELIS *leads in a* village PROSTITUTE, *helps her undress, and signals to* CLARA *to go to the piano and play something—but she proudly refuses. While the* PROSTITUTE *settles down with the half-senile poet.*]

COMMANDANTE: I represent a colossal financial power—and an even greater intellectual one. What's more, my prestige is very high with the new people in charge—in fact, it couldn't be higher.

[*The* PROSTITUTE *kisses him. Seeing that her chance to shine has finally come,* LUISA *triumphantly takes her place at the piano and gaily plays a Rossini overture, "La Gazza Ladra" perhaps, and keeps looking round to make sure she is being noticed enough.*]

CLARA: [*Contemptuously.*] Sloppy fingering. Wrist-action much too loose. Shoddy technique and interpretation. Not to mention the choice of program.

COMMANDANTE: [*Gasping for air. To the* village PROSTITUTE *who cannot understand a word.*] Talk! Answer! Tell me you can't experience another dawn without me, just as I can't without you! Say something!

[AELIS *signals to the* PROSTITUTE *to say yes, which she does.*]

COMMANDANTE: Maybe now's the time to make you one of those really important sons I've just been talking about. Maybe now's the time!

CLARA: Being a son means becoming like your father, in other words, ensuring your own death. Just look at my three sons! A series of deadly diseases. Petrified limbs, tiny, gravelly brains, eyes like quartz crystals, shrivelled-up heads. Inadequacy of the worst possible kind.

COMMANDANTE: And later on I could father another son! Then a third! And even a fourth!

CLARA: From the very start my most insane son wanted to do nothing but compose. He tried to play every instrument he clapped eyes on. Harps, cellos, double-basses, tubas, drums—he had to be pried away from them all. He'd glue himself to them like a snail clamped on to a stone. His great mistake was to believe genius is just going beyond what's already there. In fact, of course, genius should never try to improve on anything. It'll only fill perfectly good linen sheets with more stillborn babies. There's nothing new under the sun. Only women have no place—and never will.

COMMANDANTE: [*Perking up a lot.*] So, we live to fight another day! What was in that syringe this time, Aélis? Amazing!

[LUISA *plays the Overture to "William Tell."*]

CLARA: [*Hysterically.*] My God, everything already exists! There's no point in anyone proving they first thought something up. Yet it doesn't stop these note-merchants spewing out endless cycles of words and notes—the more they churn out, the more meaningless it all becomes. Bursting bubbles of words and sounds!

COMMANDANTE: [*Jubilant.*] Oh, yes. Yes, please! Right now!

CLARA: [*Turning towards him as if in a dream, even though he takes no notice of her.*] Tout passe, tout casse . . . et cette fougue douloureuse, si aigre, ces derniers jours, passera peut-être, comme tout passe . . . (Everything passes, everything breaks . . . and this painful passion, so bitter, these last few days, will probably pass, like everything else passes . . .)

[*The door opens, little* MARIE *shouts defiantly, stamping her foot.*]

MARIE: When can I go and see the lovely airplane like you promised? I want to see it now!

[AELIS *and one of the* WOMAN-SERVANTS *lead little* MARIE *out again, calming her down and making promises in subdued voices. Two other* WOMAN-SERVANTS *stand around the* COMMANDANTE *and the village* PROSTITUTE *and applaud. This applause is a magic sound which the two pianists recognize as if with a Pavlovian reflex, reacting accordingly.* LUISA *half-rises from her piano-stool inquisitively, bows, then curtseys. At that moment,* CLARA *maliciously pulls the stool away and sits down on it herself. She immediately begins playing Schumann's "Carnaval" or "Kreisleriana"—something German, anyway. She takes no notice of* LUISA, *who falls heavily onto the floor. Offended,* LUISA *crosses to the little table and eats something else, pouring herself champagne, etc.*]

CLARA: [*Elegiacally, playing the piano.*] Wherever we go, the public comes too, always pestering us, never leaving us alone with one another. We belong to the whole world and the world belongs to whoever grabs hold of it. Male geniuses come first, closely followed by child prodigies—of which there are even fewer examples. I should know, I was one. My father sent me out into the soloists' wilderness. Everywhere you go, pianistic pitfalls! Faced with that crushing isolation, all I could do was develop my piano-playing range and expertise further and further all on my own.

[*She breaks off discordantly and buries her face in her hands. Quickly reconciled,* LUISA *offers her a slice of melon.*]

CLARA: I soon started making artistic fame my principal aim in life. The world became my oyster. Usually, women just disappear without trace. Once I was even compared to an elfin child!

[CARLOTTA *whirls in on cue. She makes balletic movements, waving her arms.*]

CARLOTTA: So, you're talking about art, I hear. I'm very artistic, and I'd like to say my piece on the subject.

LUISA: My marvellous piano-playing's given pleasure to thousands, and people not lucky enough to hear me in the flesh were able to listen to me on the wireless.

CARLOTTA: I express art solely by means of my body—I'm able to bend—or twist—every millimeter of my anatomy in the most unlikely of ways. I'm what you might call art personified. Let me show you what I mean! [*She dances.*]

LUISA: Loads of people who listened to me on the wireless wrote me fan-letters.

CARLOTTA: I used to get loads more fan-letters than you! From millions of balletomanes. Sometimes I'd have a part written specially for me to dance.

LUISA: I've had trillions of piano-pieces dedicated to me! Composed for me personally. Sometimes, a piano fan's only had to catch sight of me to go completely barking mad. The minute a piano-buff's clapped eyes on me, he'd go berserk—"Luisa, Luisa, Luisa!" he'd start screaming.

CARLOTTA: Whenever I appeared, the balletomanes would all shout "Carlotta! Carlotta! Carlotta!"

CLARA: [*Who has not been listening.*] Luisa . . . listen, please . . . it's a dark, heavy weight to drag around—when your husband, who's also an artist, goes insane. Do you understand? Yet it's the Commandante, with his extraordinary ability to treat insanity as genius, we've come here to see. [*Alarmed, she stops talking.*]

COMMANDANTE: Yet another woman screaming for me. This woman here, unless I'm mistaken.

[COMMANDANTE *crawls towards* CLARA. *Clinging to her, he pulls her down to him by the legs. She can't stay upright, so topples over the* COMMANDANTE.]

AELIS: [*Commenting.*] Oh, yes. Nobody can resist him. And nobody ever has.

LUISA: [*Giggling.*] He's totally insatiable. His physical greed can only be compared to your Goethe's!

CARLOTTA: [*Performing ballet and giggling.*] Una volta—per eccitarmi!—mi disse che Goethe, quando non aveva donne a portata di mano, invece di perdere tempo a cercarne una, si faceva una sega sotto la scrivania, così poteva riprendere subito a lavorare. (He once told me—in order to excite me!—how Goethe, when he had no woman handy, rather than waste time looking for one, would jerk himself off under his desk so as to be able to get back to work immediately.)

CLARA: Our prince of poets! [*She struggles with the* COMMANDANTE.]

COMMANDANTE: [*Gasping.*] And I'm just as good a prince of poets as him. Look at me, my love, my darling, with the eyes of an adoring woman. Go on, look! Go on! Look at me as lustfully and imperiously as possible. As if you were sure you had the love-potion that would bind me to you for ever.

CLARA: [*Pushes him away and scrambles to her feet.*] Huh! So you claim to be a prince of poets, do you? Ariel. Gabriele d'Annunzio! Whereas we women are confined to soundproof, lifeless holes in the ground.

COMMANDANTE: Say something to me! Say YES to me!

CLARA: [*Scornfully.*] And we're often cast in the role of the passive, distant saint. As I've already said, I'm more the elfin child type. Sometimes just called angel-child for short. Someone who sits on their stool and thinks about songs. Then touches black and white, weaving magic left and right, creating figures tame and wild, Erlking old and Mignon mild, and a valiant knight in armor bright, and a kneeling nun, her veneration done. All the people who listened to me playing clapped as if they had a singer trapped, but the angel spread its wings and fled. Did you get that bit about the nun, Luisa, my treasure?

LUISA: The bit about the singer meant more to me. Personally I've earned more applause than la Patti, la Melba and la Malibran put together.

COMMANDANTE: [*Coughing.*] Maybe it's more accurate to say a woman is nothingness. Yes, nothingness! The harder you try, the less you can touch her. You'd do better to stare for hours at a naked flame than try to understand a woman. The truth is, you see, women have insatiable needs which no man can ever satisfy. The upshot? Blind terror! And as a result men turn women into something disgusting, even putrescent, so they won't want to go near them.

[COMMANDANTE *vomits noisily into a bowl, which* AELIS *has quickly fetched and held out for him.*]

COMMANDANTE: You see, even thinking about it makes me vomit. From sheer disgust. Sometimes women are like a grave, but much more often, a kind of butcher or cook. [*He again chokes.*]

LUISA: [*Rushing to him.*] Commandante, my love! Gabriel! Ariel! Ariosto!

CLARA: [*Disgusted.*] My father, the piano-salesman, to whom I keep coming back, once said in company that an inquisitive snowflake had settled on his arm, and lo and behold!— that snowflake was me! But no man who can say anything as unappetizing as that remark about the butcher deserves to hear about snowflakes. [*She goes back to playing "Carnaval."*]

COMMANDANTE: Oh, exalted moment that can never return! Before your soul is even aware of it, your hands reach out. They enjoy the flesh they have drawn towards them.

CLARA: Listen to me, Gabriel, I'm saying it only to you. In confidence! Since his outbreak of insanity my husband Robert has spoken more than ever about his extraordinary products. The only trouble is he's not producing anything any more! Like him, I think his insanity is the reason he can't create any delicate patterns of notes any longer.

[LUISA *feeds the* COMMANDANTE *tenderly and teasingly, cooing childishly at him, as if he were a babe-in-arms, tickling him and asking things like "Well, now, what's he up to, then?" . . . etc. Nauseated,* CLARA *plays Schumann.*]

COMMANDANTE: [*To the pleasantly surprised* LUISA.] Louise, ma chère! Je reçois votre lettre qui me déchire trop doucement. Le malentendu se prolonge. Je vous attendais tandis que vous m'attendiez. Venez! (Luisa, my treasure! I got your letter, which tore me into pieces very gently. The misunderstanding goes on. I was waiting for you while you were waiting for me. Come on now!)

[*Groaning, and supported by* LUISA, *he scrambles to his feet. She goes on supporting him and leads him out, darting looks of triumph at* CLARA *and* AELIS *as well as* CARLOTTA, *who is practicing.*]

COMMANDANTE: [*From outside.*] J'attends, j'espère! Je veux! (I'm waiting, I'm hoping! I want!)

AELIS: [*To* CLARA, *drily.*] The American tour does seem to be on! [*To the* WOMAN-SERVANT.] Tidy up this mess, please!

CLARA: [*Disheartened.*] Aélis, you've got to help me!

AELIS: I have?

CLARA: If I'm thrown out of here I can't possibly pay for me, Robert, the child and the nurses to stay one night in a cheap pensione. Even out of season!

AELIS: [*Showing sympathy and solidarity.*] You mean it's been so long since you had any income, my love?

CLARA: What do you think that quality of mental home costs? In the end I had to remove him. The Commandante is our last hope. [*Eagerly.*] Do you think he heard me talk about the snowflake just now? Should I tell him I'm at the crossroads between childhood and girlhood?

AELIS: Don't exaggerate!

CLARA: I'm not, honestly. Going on about having no body doesn't cut much ice with him. Maybe I should say a woman is a silent but rotting hole?

AELIS: Don't say any such thing. That's the kind of image that made him sick just now. You really shouldn't go in for such unappetising metaphors. Typically German, is it?

CLARA: Germans are much fonder of their excrement than any other nation. You only have to look at a typically German toilet! I need the money!

AELIS: [*Sympathetically.*] Potrei consigliarti di trovare il modo per soddisfarlo nelle nudità, perché è un tipo particolarmente curioso delle caratteristiche fisiche. Ma, adesso mi dirai quanto tu sia timida in sua presenza e mi dirai che non appena smetti di suonare il piano diventi quasi brutta, come un palo. (I could advise you to find a way to please him in the nude, because he is especially curious about your physical characteristics. But I'm sure you will tell me now how timid you are in his presence and say that as soon as you stop your piano playing you become almost ugly, like a post.)

[*In desperation,* CLARA *strikes her head with her fist.*]

AELIS: Look around you! Do you honestly think a man with taste like this could fall for anyone claiming to be artistic?

[*She points to the architectural monstrosities all around.*]

CLARA: I still believe the longer I resist him—something he isn't used to—the more I'll mean to him.

AELIS: Maybe, maybe not. The day before yesterday he suggested the two of us should fuck outside your door one night, groaning loudly or possibly even shouting, so as to arouse your jealousy, and at the same time make you scared you didn't mean anything to him.

CLARA: Shall I pretend to go away?

AELIS: It might work, it might not.

CLARA: Right then, later on when we eat, I'll make sure I . . . [*Sobbing.*] . . . talk about the ghastly torture of artistic production while longing for the product itself. I shall [*Weeping.*] talk about the pressure from my father and husband, always eating me alive. Never free of money, that corpses' shit.

AELIS: [*Sympathetically.*] . . . which you need very urgently at the moment, my dear Clara.

[*Shrugging her shoulders, and breaking off a few withered blossoms from a pot-plant, she goes out. Now that she doesn't have to pull herself together any more,* CLARA *collapses over the piano, giving her desperation free rein as she plays a few bars of Schumann.*]

CLARA: [*Serious, but not hysterical.*] For so long they've kept on telling Robert all his melodious ideas emerge from his own head that it's just shattered under the strain. Loving the abstract is a terrible thing! And music's totally abstract. Anything that comes out of a body—a child, for instance—disgusts men. But at the same time they're forever getting women to reproduce, to stop them creating art. They don't want to see any kind of competition develop. [*She plays.*] A man's body can only produce a fatal ulcer now and again or a suppurating tumor you can stick a knife into. These head-merchants! They try to destroy their bodies. So they end up with terrible inhibitions which lead straight to lethal diseases of the head! First, they deny the body by making women responsible for it, then their creative head shatters into fragments.

PART 2

The dining-room. Which is just as cluttered as the drawing-room. From the ceiling hangs either an enormous model of a whole airplane or an airplane-part—but in the latter case, natural size. A large, elaborately covered table, with all manner of luxuries and flowers on it. The same characters are sitting around the table higgledy-piggledy, constantly changing places, eating with very little appetite, tossing bones on to the floor, etc.—This all needs choreographing!

The COMMANDANTE, *who was wearing a brocade dressing-gown in Part 1, is now wearing a fascist uniform with shiny riding-boots, and holding a riding-whip. At a side-table sit the mentally disturbed composer,* ROBERT SCHUMANN, *with two* PSYCHIATRIC NURSES, *who must appear very simple, and who look after him—but harshly. They are "minders," with shaven heads, and white coats.* CLARA *again jumps to her feet and rushes to the window, gracefully leans out, and shields her eyes with her hands.*

CLARA: [*Effusively.*] My arms are completely bare and very well shaped. It's not hard to see I was once a flower among women. Until the frost made me lose my bloom—the same insanity that makes some artists blossom.

ROBERT: [*Also effusively, but in short bursts.*] How magnificently I suffer! I'm so wonderfully wounded! [*He giggles.*] My hearing's impaired. Angels flutter down! And save me all the trouble of composing symphonies. With all that that implies. I'm so lucky! I keep getting these peculiar hallucinations. My angels are sometimes relieved by devils. I'm sick in the head, you see—it's lovely. It takes up my whole existence, so I myself have no further responsibility for it. Today, for the third time of asking, I'll throw our wedding ring into Lake Garda. This time, I hope, nobody'll bring it back. That ring proved to be surplus to requirements—the wife overtook the husband, you see, even though she lost her footing in the process. [*He giggles.*] Oh Christ, my head doesn't half ache! [*A* NURSE *force-feeds him.*]

COMMANDANTE: [*Biting* LUISA *in the neck.*] For me the best symphony consists of engine noise. And sometimes, in countries not so mamma-mollycoddled as this Italy of ours, a man will say: "When a man's got to get away, away he's got to get." However much his wife and child may cling to him and say: "Stay here, don't go," he'll push them aside, build up his flying hours, climb aboard his flying-machine and take off. That's what Charles Lindbergh did, when he crossed the Atlantic. He just knew: I've got to cross this water right now and can't stop till I'm over!

ROBERT: [*Suddenly giggles loudly. A* NURSE *raps his knuckles with a spoon as he tries to empty the whole saltcellar over his food.*] When I'm really excited I start mixing up ideals with life, achievement with hope! Though in any comparison my darling Clara is always the loser. Especially when I compare something commonplace to an ideal of some kind.

[CLARA *rushes towards him, buries her head in his lap. The* NURSES *push her away like a piece of wood, as she is interrupting their force-feeding.*]

CLARA: [*Still as effusive as before.*] My dearest darling! My melody magician! Think positive, and you'll soon get well again! These encounters with your brain-tumor spoil your enjoyment in life. Why not pass the time with a spot of composition?

[ROBERT *giggles like a child.*]

ROBERT: Choirs of angels! Suddenly turning into choirs of demons! Then a flood of exquisite harmonies!

CLARA: [*To the* COMMANDANTE.] You hear that, Gabriele, he's still composing! He's his old self again—an artist like you. In no time at all the new symphony will be published.

COMMANDANTE: Men are always striving for conquest! Over alien territory, say, as far away as possible—or else over a woman or an air-corridor. The misled masses applaud him. Like women, crowds focus on the physical. Which means you can possess them at will. Only yesterday I saw an enormous mass of young bodies in sports clothes. White torsos in black PT shorts. Very fetching. And most tasteful. They were swinging clubs. Magnificent!

LUISA: [*To* AELIS, *who is supervising the table.*] Have you read that book he wrote? They do a lot of prancing about and some juice runs down their legs, because they're moving so jerkily. Mostly pomegranate juice. Which stains their splendid costumes. Then one of the bodies vibrates as if on fire, and somebody or other sinks in a river, which is either boiling or freezing—I forget which. And after all that's been going on for ten pages, the woman says: I'm going off with the others now. I'll meet you by the railings of the Gradenigo Garden, or near one or other cypress-tree—which one we still haven't decided. [*She giggles.*]

[AELIS *pretends to threaten* LUISA, *and serves her with extra food. Whenever the* COMMANDANTE *looks her way,* CARLOTTA *makes graceful arm and leg movements—only he doesn't take much notice of her.*]

ROBERT: Genius has lighted on the pistons of my art-engine like a heavyweight phantom. Abracadabra—a note emerges! Listen! [*Trembling, he sings a note.*] Did you hear that?

CLARA: [*Ecstatic.*] Yes, I did, my darling, there you are, you see! You've started. As you mean to go on!

COMMANDANTE: I can't hear a thing.

[*The women parody* CLARA, *drawing each other's attention to sounds that no one can hear, laughing soundlessly, pressing their hands on each other's mouths, shaking with silent mirth.*]

ROBERT: Sorry, got a slight production problem here. Brilliant idea got stuck in my head-tumour, see, and we'll have to wait for it to swell and burst. Christ, my head hurts! [*He puts a hand on his head.*] Tell you what: I'll try screaming. [*He does so.*]

COMMANDANTE: [*Is obviously losing patience. He takes an orange from the fruit-basket. To young* MARIE.] If you can find the orange and eat it all up where you find it without touching it with your hands, I'll give you one of those pieces of jewelry for which Roman society is justly famous worldwide.

[*With a whoop of joy* MARIE *jumps up. Concealed by the tablecloth, the* COMMANDANTE *hides the orange somewhere about his person. Immediately,* MARIE *crawls under the table and starts fumbling around furiously.* CLARA *doesn't notice.*]

PRINCESS: [*Who never says anything, but remains elegantly distanced.*] All this you can calmly do with your wife looking on, Gabriele, even if your son isn't with us—too busy with his recent drug addiction, no doubt. Desist. Please.

COMMANDANTE: But I want to go on doing this! So I will!

[CARLOTTA *makes ludicrously graceful movements.*]

ROBERT: [*Perking up.*] Purple wounds, shading into violet. The head can always talk itself into feeling strong. Brilliant ideas! Women can only manage speech-balloons. Loads of fetuses. Not even shadows of great deeds. A mass of physical disabilities. Repulsively natural! Here, no less than in Germany, women are a real danger. Re-pul-sive examples of natural forces at work.

CLARA: A musical idea, please, Robert, not a poetic one! Music! Creative work for piano and violin which will bring in some money! Go on, then, get on with it! Your material situation needs to improve dramatically.

ROBERT: [*Acting sensibly, as he wrests the spoon from the* NURSE's *grasp and eats by himself more or less decently.*] And by the way, none of those female music-lovers who hurled their passion-eaten bodies at me was able to captivate me for long. And anyway, their letters were riddled with stylistic and grammatical mistakes. They never came up to scratch.

CLARA: [*Tries to kiss him, but he turns away.*] Tell us about the angelic child again, Robert! The Commandante wants to hear it again!

COMMANDANTE: Absolutely not. You're quite wrong. What I most want to hear is the familiar drone of airplane engines.

[COMMANDANTE *groans as* MARIE *does something or other under the table.*]

ROBERT: My parietal bone! My fontanelle! Nature shows no mercy! Deliberately causes me frightful pains in the head. And all the time angels make sure art goes on.

COMMANDANTE: [*To* AELIS. *With a brief groan, he places the child's head somewhere else.*] In earlier times we challenged the most beautiful women in society to bite a piece of fruit. Then the bitten fruit would be auctioned to the highest bidder for—let's say—an orphanage or a maternity home. Men's mouths would roughly enlarge the tiny bite-wound in the apple. They even charged men money to drink out of beautiful women's hollowed hands. Enormous sums were offered Countess Scerni for wiping her hands in a blond beard. Once, Countess Lucoli gave me a Havana cigar—I forget how much she asked—which she'd first held in her armpit.

CLARA: [*Appalled.*] Oh! Ugh! Urghh!

[AELIS *laughs with a cooing sound.* LUISA *comes in, tries to wipe her fingers on the* COMMANDANTE, *but he knocks them away.* CARLOTTA *performs another dance.*]

CLARA: What have you done with my daughter?

COMMANDANTE: Good question, what have I done with your daughter? Now, I wonder where she's got to? Do you happen to know, Aélis?

AELIS: Sorry, no idea.

[*The other women all talk at once: "No. Where can she have got to? Where is she? Where on earth is she?" etc.*]

COMMANDANTE: [*To* CLARA.] Mi chiedo che cosa stai facendo nel tuo letto da sola, tutta da sola, con le gambe allargate! Sto aspettando i tuoi baci pieni di sentimento, di cui mi hai tanto parlato, il modo in cui ti piace essere baciata sotto le ascelle e così via. (Wonder what you are doing alone in your bed, all alone with your legs spread! I'm waiting for your soulful kisses you told me about, the way you like to be kissed under the armpits and so on.)

CLARA: This is mother animal calling: Marie, Marie! [*She shouts.* MARIE *is under the table, half smothered in clothes.*]

MARIE: Here I am, mother.

[*With a shout of fury* CLARA *dives under the table and drags her rather crumpled daughter out by the legs. We see her knickers, at which the* COMMANDANTE *is ecstatic.*]

CLARA: [*Effusively.*] Pay for . . . the symphony! Give his . . . melody the recognition it deserves!

COMMANDANTE: [*To* CLARA.] That Robert of yours is too discombobulated to create anything! And even if he did compose a piece, he'd have to flee the public like that deathly disease which has finally caught up with him. This is my dream, as the poet, Gabriele d'Annunzio. Just one copy of a work of art, dedicated to one woman only, renouncing every single benefit except love-making. The true connoisseurs of my art won't buy my books—they'll love me. The laurel's only purpose is to attract the myrtle.

CLARA: [*Desperately, while* ROBERT *chuckles happily.*] But what about fame! The world!

COMMANDANTE: You're never famous till after you're dead, as every schoolchild knows. You never enjoy it while you're alive. More's the pity.

CLARA: But our financial situation!

COMMANDANTE: Could be dramatically improved overnight if the flesh were willing.

CLARA: [*Sobbing.*] But I can't see your flesh lasting out more than a fortnight.

COMMANDANTE: Oh well, you know. Art does last longer, admittedly.

MARIE: Is that the airplane?

[MARIE *goes across to the enormous airplane fuselage and fingers it inquisitively.*]

COMMANDANTE: Leave that airplane alone. I don't want it damaged! It's not for children to fiddle with. Even women, unaware though they are, can't cope with automatism, anything that moves automatically. Only a man is capable of being a machine within the machine, in other words, racing over the water in a motorboat or climbing into the sky.

[*All the women exclaim in astonishment and delight. For inexplicable reasons,* ROBERT *is suddenly very alert. He has a moment of total clarity. He seizes the heads of his two "*MINDERS*" and bangs them together, so that they both lean back on their chairs dazed and groggy.* CARLOTTA *flails her arms about. Everyone ignores her.* LUISA *eats piggishly without talking to anyone. She then smears the* COMMANDANTE'*s face with chocolate, which looks like shit, and giggles drunkenly. The* COMMANDANTE *absentmindedly kneads* LUISA'*s body, without letting the German couple out of his sight.*]

ROBERT: [*Completely rational.*] Colonel, as you were kindly explaining the nuts and bolts of machinery, it suddenly struck me how incapable my wife Clara has always been of composing her own music. Of any artistic magic, in fact. She can't even grasp the difference between sanity and madness. I cross this boundary every day, without even thinking about it, back and forth, then back again. The mysteries of madness will always be lost to her. Insanity's an affliction that dare not speak its name. She couldn't even act decisively against her artificial impotence. No kicking against the pricks. No athletics in woods, no pointless running through parklands. Even now she doesn't realize that the most brilliant of compositions will inevitably peter out in one ridiculous phrase of single notes. [*He laughs good-naturedly, but rationally.*] The only thing her attempts at composition achieved was a gradual weakening of her sexual attractiveness for me.

[*He good-naturedly strokes the two grunting heads near him.*]

CLARA: [*Coldly.*] If anyone thinks about me it's not like a brother thinking about a sister, or a lover about his beloved, it's more like a pilgrim imagining a distant altarpiece!

[ROBERT *immediately goes crazy again. He mischievously hurls himself on the floor and bites the carpet. The two* NURSES *are rather puzzled about how to deal with him.* ROBERT *screams shrilly on the floor. The people eating at the table have jumped up in order to enjoy the spectacle. The* COMMANDANTE *entices little* MARIE *back by holding something up in the air. She jumps up high, trying to reach it; but he holds it higher and higher—out of her reach. Finally,*

AELIS seizes the girl under the armpits and lifts her up high, so that she can grab hold of the object. She looks at it with shouts of delight, and kisses the COMMANDANTE, *who whispers something into her ear.* MARIE *laughs brightly. She is kissed and caressed.* LUISA *again jumps up jealously, and tries to come between them, but* AELIS *skilfully pops a large black grape into her mouth, so that* LUISA *falls back into her chair, gasping and nearly choking.*]

ROBERT: [*Screeching.*] I am a very naughty bunny. A phrase I've just heard! Now I know what it means! [*He sings a few bars of an operetta melody.*]

LUISA: [*Having finally swallowed the grape, furiously.*] That's what I am! That's what I am, a very naughty bunny! And I've explained why.

ROBERT: [*Petulantly.*] Oh no you're not, I am!!! The first time I was pretty sure I was going mad Clara was half child, half girl. Find a wife, the doctor told me, that'll soon sort you out. I pursued Ernestine von F, my first serious fiancée, but then dropped her in favor of Clara, the virtuoso hyena. [*He giggles shrilly.*] All the time I've known her I've been sketching out new compositions—now I'm finally going to sing the opening bars of my new symphony!

[*He sings the opening bars of some well-known tearjerker of the international concert scene— the "Blue Danube," for instance—or Beethoven's "Fifth." The choice is up to the director. But obviously it must not be by Schumann.*]

LUISA: [*Unable to contain herself.*] Excuse me, maestro, but I have a feeling that particular revolutionary new modern work already exists!

[ROBERT *goes on singing more and more hymnally. Huge merriment around the table, with people falling over one another, shrieking.* CLARA *is extremely annoyed. She stamps her foot, and tugs* ROBERT's *sleeve, but to no avail.*]

ROBERT: [*Although still singing, he breaks off for a moment.*] The mechanism's been over-wound! Look!—another stray note, which I grab hold of in midair. For now it belongs only to me, though soon it'll belong to the public—a few thousand concert-goers, let's say, though it might as well be the world and his wife. [*He sings, though stopping at times, short of breath.*] Itching, scabies, putrescence, ulcers, secretions . . . the whole heap of shit! [*He sings hymnally.*] The composer wallows in it all, while a woman soloist sings the high note—like this [*He sings it.*]

CARLOTTA: Didn't anyone at all see that arm-movement I just made?

CLARA: [*Shouting.*] My wonderful Robert . . . confined to a mental home! Never!

COMMANDANTE: [*Absentmindedly, looking down at* ROBERT.] Needless to say, there are some forms of sport which keep people's feet firmly on the ground, where, if need be, they can perform exercises. But air is the best element, though only so long as a select few can, as it were, rise to the occasion.

CLARA: Sadly, Robert, I was a sacrificial victim of your genius!

[*Just as* CLARA *now becomes calmer and cooler, so the* COMMANDANTE *turns his attention away from her and towards the other women, molesting them, and giving them food.*]

[CLARA *speaks quietly to* ROBERT, *who stomps about the room, daubing the* NURSES' *faces with ice cream, and getting smacked for it.*]

CLARA: It was such a nightmare being married to you! Every time I went to the piano to compose something, the piano-seat would be already occupied—by you!

[*Provocatively,* ROBERT *sings the hit tune from just now.*]

CLARA: Playing the piano was the way I earned money—usually our only source of income! Now I'm thrown back on myself!

COMMANDANTE: [*Casually to the others.*] Il freddo e la cavalcata mi hanno fatto venire una fame da lupo, ma sopratutto una gran voglia to fuck. (The cold weather and the ride in the Mas have given me a terrible hunger but especially a great desire to chiavare.)

[*Turning his back on the audience, he exposes himself to* AELIS, MARIE *is still on his back, and from there she tries to reach the airplane, to set it in motion. To* AELIS.] Non vedi in che stato si trova il principino? Spero che questa orribile donna tedesca se ne vada presto! La gente alla stazione si è precipitata verso di me, chi urlando "Principe!" chi "Eccellenza!" e la tedesca è rimasta a bocca aperta. (*Can't you see what a state the little prince is in? I hope this horrible German woman will leave soon! All the people at the station rushed up to me, some yelling "Prince!" others "Excellency," and the German woman was dumbfounded.*)

[AELIS *applauds, which is the cue for* LUISA, *who staggers to the piano rather drunk, and unsteadily plays the hit-song which* ROBERT *has just been humming.*]

ROBERT: [*Howling.*] A tigress! Oh, my lioness! The woman I've been waiting for my whole life! A partner who's the equal of me! Bravo, bravissimo! [*He lunges at* LUSIA, *and the* NURSES *have difficulty restraining him.*] My hearing! My miraculous hearing! How limpid everything sounds! At long last I'm in intimate touch with a female spirit! Marvellous! I can hear it so clearly!

[*He half-drags the* NURSES *along with him.*]

Nobody else can hear it or understand it! My body is a mass of sensitive ears, like feelers. Tiny tactile hairs. My senses are stimulated by real art—and look, there they are! Short fine hairs! Look! Marvellous, don't you think! Do you compose freehand? My hearing pushes my ideas right into the background. How wonderful! I'm a living mountain. Mount Olympus, to be precise. I can hear loud draughts of air, stamping along like herds of machines! Hey! You there!

CLARA: [*In despair.*] If a woman's abilities develop beyond the usual norms, a monstrosity results. It's an offense against a man's rights of ownership which any female animal has to obey. A woman's mind [*Extremely upset.*] should be permanently focused on creating new dishes and disposing of household waste. [*She sinks down exhausted.*]

ROBERT: [*Jubilant.*] Oh, yes. Play that passage once again, will you, you wonderful woman!

CLARA: I wasn't even allowed to use the second piano we acquired later, in case it disturbed him while composing!

COMMANDANTE: [*Looking longingly at the slobbering* ROBERT.] What if I were to lose my mental powers, too? The mind can go into steady decline without you consciously realizing. An artist whose mind is going needn't be any more aware of his own imbecility than someone mentally ill [*Pointing to* ROBERT *like a circus ringmaster.*] is aware of his own insanity. Which is panic-inducing!

[*He cries out in passion.* AELIS *sinks down backwards, smiling. The* COMMANDANTE *makes a violent movement.* MARIE *almost falls off his back. She clings on desperately, squeaking with annoyance.*]

[ROBERT *throws himself around one of the* NURSES' *necks, and kisses him ecstatically, tenderly. The* NURSE *is utterly bewildered and defends himself, but* ROBERT *develops enormous physical strength. Having pulled himself together again, the* COMMANDANTE *hops around with* MARIE *on his back and—as in a theater—follows the drama going on between* ROBERT *and* CLARA, *which is nearing a climax.*]

ROBERT: [*Tenderly to the* NURSE, *who pushes him away.*] Darling, I work so hard composing every day, please be nice to me! All too often, my hearing works against me, and destroys everything I've created. But not today! Listen! I'm going to let you hear something I've composed.

[*Insanely loudly he sings the tearjerker from earlier, accompanied by* LUISA *on the piano. The Venetian woman laughs heartily while playing, thinking it a good joke.*]

ROBERT: Bit by bit my hearing annihilates everything I've [*He sings.*] already finished composing. Anything that's left [*Singing.*] is insanely complex and very modern! A musical fragment! [*He starts singing again, then stops after a while, exhausted. Pause. Outside the windows we hear the sound of marching boots. A squad approaches. Pause. Then, from outside, we hear the strains of the "Giovinezza." Everyone present stops talking. The* COMMANDANTE *stands to attention.*]

CLARA: [*Frantically flapping pages of newspaper.*] Let me read out my reviews—and Robert's.

COMMANDANTE: Quiet!

CLARA: [*Although "shushed," she excitedly reads from the newspapers.*] Here you are, Commandante . . . listen . . . You can read it for yourself! [*She reads out.*] "I tell you in person and I'm also about to write in my new music magazine that in your" . . . the bastard means my! . . . "piano concerto, one notices at once a young phoenix fluttering up into the air. Yearning white roses and glistening calyxes of lilies. And at the very center, the radiant face of a young girl. Boats bravely breast the waves . . . and *all that's needed is a master's hand on the tiller to make it sail successfully and swiftly*" . . .

[*At this moment* ROBERT *suddenly bursts into shrieks of laughter.* MARIE *breaks the silence by bawling out.*]

MARIE: Daddy, I'm frightened! There's so many sounds! Daddy! [*To the* COMMANDANTE.] Does the lovely airplane fly, too, uncle?

[*They immediately pacify her. Drunkenly,* LUISA *plays the tearjerker.* ROBERT *helps conduct— rhapsodically.* CLARA *is furious and jealous.*]

ROBERT: This . . . lady here [*He means* LUISA.] . . . is wonderful. She's never once given me a thrashing. She's such a good woman! She plays my ideas even before they've been fully thought-through! The original notes come shooting out of me supersonically, and she catches them in midflight. Bravo! [CLARA *responds emotionally.*] My hearing! My ears are such torture! And the pain penetrates into every cavity of my body. I can't seem to control my ears. My ears gobble up all my ideas. I'm all head. [*He giggles, and spits out spinach.*]

CLARA: [*Desperate.*] Your great F-sharp Minor Sonata is just one long cry from the heart towards me, one I'm not allowed to answer. So I respond artistically!

[*She makes for the piano to play the F-sharp Minor Sonata. But* LUISA *is already sitting there, grinning spitefully.* CLARA *drags her from the piano-stool.* LUISA *falls down and starts howling.* CLARA *sits down and plays some Schumann, which makes the composer extremely angry. He tries to hurl himself at her, but he is firmly held back by the* NURSES.]

CLARA: [*Sobbing as she plays.*] Through a series of strategically placed childbirths you kept on torpedoing my modest progress! You didn't review my Piano Concerto No. 7 in your magazine! Instead, you wrote a rave about William Sterndale Bennett! According to you—my lover!—my efforts at composition were little better than sheep bleating. You forget a good pianist is always creative, too! Creative in their own right.

[MARIE *rubs herself back and forth on the* COMMANDANTE's *neck for so long that they both fall over. The women rush over to help, shouting things like: "Are you hurt, Commandante? Commandante! For heavens' sake," etc.* CARLOTTA *waves her arms about as before. There are now heaps of people on the floor.* CLARA *plays the Schumann F-sharp Minor Sonata ecstatically.* ROBERT *goes white with fury.*]

ROBERT: Stop that racket! Get out! Get rid of that rubbish—composed by strangers for strangers! Amateurish shit! Second-rate! Derivative! Riddled with anxiety! Obsessed about impotence! That's what comes of puritanical clockwork in the head.

[*He vomits loudly on to the middle of the table. Disgusted, shocked and upset, the* COMMANDANTE *crawls over to* CLARA, *whimpering.*]

COMMANDANTE: Ma guarda il mio tormento, la mia commozione . . . Posso baciarti sotto le ascelle! Per favore? (Just look, darling, at my torment and my emotion . . . May I kiss you under the armpits! Please?)

CLARA: [*Triumphantly playing Schumann.*] Faithful to the last! Can you hear? Can you hear how exquisitely I play your F-sharp Minor Sonata!?

ROBERT: [*Having broken free, he rushes for* CLARA *once again.*] Devil's drone! Play what we heard just now! Please! Play a new piece! The one that other lady was playing!

CLARA: But what you call that new piece already exists, Robert!!!! This piece is your F-sharp Minor Sonata!

ROBERT: [*Shrilly.*] Animal! Devil! As for that ghastly racket, I can't hear any of the breadth so typical of me! Give the myrtle crown to that woman!

CLARA: [*Playing.*] But Robert . . . this is the same piece as you originally composed a while ago . . . do you want to see the notes? Here they are, Robert—the same notes! Breitkopf & Härtel, Leipzig. In black and white! Sonata in F-sharp Minor by Schumann, Robert.

ROBERT: [*Incandescent with rage.*] Vermin! Bitch! Forger! Destroyer of compositions! Slayer of spirit! Assassin of potency! [*In tears.*] Musical talent is such a heavy cross to bear. Can't you see [*Suddenly calm and desperate.*] Clara, how my ideas are constantly moving forwards? They're self-motivated! I don't have any influence over them! None whatsoever! [*He shakes* CLARA *violently; she continues playing desperately.*]

MARIE: [*From some distance away.*] Let Mummy go, Daddy! Let her out!

CLARA: [*Wearily.*] Help!

ROBERT: Stop playing!! [*He lunges at her.*] Stop it! Stop this minute, child!!

CLARA: [*Calmly.*] When you call me "child," it sounds loving, but when you think "child" of me I see red and say: you're wrong!

ROBERT: [*Choosing his words carefully, he wrenches* CLARA *away from the piano-stool.*] I want to hear my composition again, the one that beautiful lady just played with such perfect tempo and dynamics! Not that heap of sound-shit! That was probably one of your own dilettante efforts! Ugh! Urrgh!!

CLARA: Robert! Everything I've been playing was composed by you. That was your F-sharp Minor Sonata!

[ROBERT *now wrestles with* CLARA. *The others form a silent circle around them. The* NURSES *do not intervene, but stand ready to do so.*]

ROBERT: A pretty little house, not far from the city, living there with you happily and peacefully! You'd cultivate your art, of course. [*He chokes as* CLARA *begins to throttle him.*] But not so much for the public at large or for money, more for a select few individuals, especially me! And to increase our happiness! [*Breathing more heavily.*]

CLARA: [*Groaning with the effort.*] Just tell me this: Why do you avoid every opportunity to mention me in your magazine? [*She applies even more pressure.*]

ROBERT: [*Who is by now half throttled.*] The piece she just played . . . my head . . . Christ . . . Oh Christ, that hurts! . . . My head hurts . . . Women can't achieve anything artistic . . . All they can manage is the natural performance of bodily . . . because . . . women . . . are . . . pure nature.

[ROBERT *dies, throttled by* CLARA.]

CLARA: [*Straightening up, exhausted.*] Nimble, powerful, well-trained fingers are well worth having. These are well versed in the arts of knitting, embroidery and sewing.

[*She examines her fingers and does five-finger exercises to make them nimble again. The others stand around her deathly still.*]

CLARA: [*Wearily.*] The world of the male genius is a landscape of death. A graveyard. [*The curtain slowly falls.*]

EPILOGUE

The same room as in Part 1. Only this time a kind of Alpine garden (an imitation of the "Zugspitze") has been built out of blocks of stone at one of the tall windows. On the top, high up, a cross on the mountain summit. The whole thing should be as high as possible. Gentians, Alpine roses and edel-

weiss are growing on the mountain. Perhaps a clear streamlet made of plastic could be flowing over them. CLARA *is sitting at the base of the mountain, and is cradling the head of* ROBERT, *whom she strangled, in her lap. But any Catholic Pietà atmosphere should be avoided! She is wearing a "Dirndl" dress. The two* NURSES *are watching her from some distance. They are wearing knicker-bockers, white knee-length stockings and brown shirts. The other characters are lying around informally. They are wearing fashionable skiing clothes, very chic and exclusive ski-caps and pullovers. Only the* COMMANDANTE *has kept his uniform on. Nor has* AELIS *changed her clothes. Skis are leaning against the walls. Apart from that, there is a little snow on the mountain-summit! The lighting is such that it falls brightly on the summit and the summit-cross, illuminating both in a rather supernatural way. Needless to say, the whole scene looks a little vulgar!*

CLARA: [*To* ROBERT's *head.*] Your mind has always astonished me—all those innovations in the "Kreisleriana," for instance. Not to mention your miraculous F-sharp Minor Sonata, which you just denied having written. By the way, sometimes when I look at you I get this terrible panic and ask myself: did this man really become your husband?

COMMANDANTE: [*Shaking his head.*] For the first time in my life I now find myself experiencing one of those rare feminine feelings which light up the grey, changeable sky of human love like a beautiful but terrifying stroke of lightning.

[*A flash of lightning lights up the Alpine garden.*]

COMMANDANTE: But it doesn't bother me.

CLARA: I sometimes feel I wasn't able to satisfy you, even though you loved me all the same! Well, now at least I understand everything, and your music makes me very happy.

[*She kisses the head. Another flash of lightning over the Alpine garden, then a subdued rumble of thunder—still a long way off.*]

LUISA: [*To* AELIS.] My sleeper is leaving in half an hour, and there's still no sign of the police.

AELIS: Just be patient, darling! We're a bit off the beaten track out here, and there's another rally today.

CLARA: I'm feeling something quite new, and I've developed it all by myself. Anything artists experience they transmute into a work of art. And they experience everything on a deeper level than nonartists.

CARLOTTA: [*Performing ski-gymnastics.*] That gentle tapping of beaks I can hear is made by all those little birds out there, and they've never been to a concert or a theatre. Right now they're screeching softly. Poor frail creatures!

LUISA: [*Chewing.*] Loneliness is often the price you pay for fame.

CARLOTTA: All those birds I just mentioned wouldn't mind being lonely if only they were famous! [*They both giggle.*]

PRINCESS: Ladies, please, show some respect in the presence of the dead.

[*A flash of lightning.* CLARA *kisses the head. Sheet lighting in the sky, subdued thunder.*]

CLARA: [*Suddenly shouting out.*] Robert, I'll bring you some edelweiss from up there! From that steep mountain-peak. [*She gets ready to climb up the Alpine garden, dislodging some small stones.*] I want to make sure I don't frighten the game—the chamois, say, or the ibex, which is even more timid!

[*The others look baffled.* CLARA *starts climbing. A light wind has sprung up and blows through the room, so that we feel the gentle power of nature.*]

CLARA: Say something, Robert! All you did while you were alive was bury heaps of still-born babies in the sand. Maybe your death has freed your musical creativity from madness. I'm not frightened of radical females any more, and so I'm climbing this phallic symbol. And you can't stop me! [*She goes on climbing.*]

[*A flurry of wind from time to time. Doors fly open but in a restrained way.*]

CLARA: [*Battling against the mountain.*] Men depict, women are mere illustrations. I've done nothing but interpret your masterpieces on the piano. [*Panting, she reaches the edelweiss, as the wind grows stronger.*] Men spill over with potency. Women only froth within themselves. Like washing-powder, hopelessly trapped in a machine.

[*She has picked the edelweiss, and now slides down the slope in a hail of pebbles, then sticks the flower into* ROBERT'*s mouth like green twigs when a deer has been shot.*]

I'm almost ill with delight—this time over your superlative imagination! [*The wind starts roaring more strongly, making objects in the room move about.*] I go hot and cold all over. Just tell me what your mind's like, so I can copy it. Once I'm totally united with you, I won't think about composing any more! I'd be a fool, wouldn't I? [*The wind howls. She kisses* ROBERT.] You could only write the "Novelettes" because you'd touched lips like mine! I always felt a funny sort of fear showing you my compositions—I always felt ashamed, somehow. Even of my Idyll in A-flat Major. [*She suddenly pushes the corpse away, gasping.*]

COMMANDANTE: [*Nauseated, to his wife, the* PRINCESS.] Beethoven's the only composer I rate—he's superhuman, if not supernatural. Yesterday—I'll never forget it—she played us the two Sonata Fantasias Opus 27, right through. What a pianist! The "Moonlight" Sonata, the one that's dedicated to Giulietta Guicciardi, is full of hopeless resignation. But it also describes waking up after a dream that's been dreamt too long. In the other one, from the very first bars of the andante, you can hear the calm after the storm. Later, bit by bit, a new courage—almost passion—emerges right at the end, from the allegro vivace.

CARLOTTA: [*Kissing* LUISA.] Listen, Louison! Hear them? They're battering against the walls again from outside! Hear those beaks? Thousands of them! Millions! Meanwhile, piano-students are bent over their radios the whole time, the wireless is blaring out, experts never stop rabbiting on about slight differences you can't distinguish. One of them hears a nuance, the next hears the same nuance but quite differently. The third student hears something different again. It tears your head open.

[*Lightning flashes, thunder growls, the snow on the mountain is lit up. Individual withered leaves flutter through the room.* MARIE *feels frightened and flees to* CLARA. *She pushes her away so roughly that the child topples over. Bawling, she lets herself be comforted by* AELIS.]

CLARA: [*Shaking* ROBERT'*s corpse.*] Robert! Listen! You said my lovely composition shouldn't be called "Idyll." You were dead set on "Nocturne," but you also thought "Heimweh" or "Mädchens Heimweh" would be appropriate. You couldn't even let my little composition keep the title I'd chosen for it! And anyway, it was more a waltz than a nocturne. [*Apologetic.*] Forgive me, Robert, all I wanted to convey was . . . Then you changed it. Radically. I'm sure you'll forgive me saying I didn't like it so much after you'd changed it. And I hope you'll forgive me for your not liking it. [*She shakes the corpse violently. The* NURSES *come closer.*] Robert, your love makes me inexpressibly happy! [*Shaking him.*] One thing does bother me, though, sometimes—whether I'll be able to keep you fascinated. I really try to be an artist and a housewife, I really do! It's not easy.

[*Leaves whirl through the room, mist rises, in the distance we can hear yodelling, the wind roars more loudly.*]

I'd love to compose musical pieces of my own—soloists are soon forgotten! But I can't. No woman's ever managed it, so why should I? No, no! What an arrogant idea! I want to be your darling little wifey, that's all!

[*She collapses over his corpse. Something rustles in his breast pocket, which she notices. She pulls out a sheet of paper, smoothes it, reads it.*]

Oh, a last loving greeting from you! Thank you. Clara, your obedient wife. [*She drops the piece of paper heedlessly.*] But I can't set this song to music, even if you want me to. It's not laziness! No, it's just that it would need the kind of mind I haven't got.

[*She goes over to the piano and begins to play the Salon Piece, which was* ROBERT's *undoing. She plays with increasing intensity, getting faster and faster and more and more hectic. Parallel to this, the stormy atmosphere in the room also intensifies—a combination of romantic wildness, storm, thunder, flashes of lightning. After a while, things become calmer, and snow starts fluttering down on to the summit-cross—as in a glass globe you turn upside down to make snow.*]

AELIS: [*Putting down a tray and shouting above the noise.*] Mi ha detto che [*Pointing to* CLARA.] è riuscito a farle prendere un po' di cocaina e che l'effetto è stato eccellente, perché immediatamente lei è entrata in una specie di stato incosciente! Lui ne ha subito approfittato per guardarle tutto il corpo. L'ha baciata dappertutto e si è pure strofinato il suo hai-capito-che-cosa sul robusto braccio di lei, proprio come un barbiere di campagna affila il suo rasoio. (He told me [*Pointing to* CLARA.], he had succeeded in getting her to take a little cocaine and that the effect had been excellent, because right away she had entered into a kind of unconscious state! He immediately took advantage of it to look at all her body. He kissed her all over and he also rubbed his you-know-what on her stout arm, like a village barber whetting his razor.) [*Laughs out loud.*]

[*The piano-playing intensifies.* CLARA *begins to gasp.*]

CLARA: The universe of music is a landscape of death. White wastes, ice, frozen rivers, streams, lakes! Colossal sheets of Arctic wilderness, transparent to the very bottom, no trace of a predatory polar bear's paw. Nothing but geometrically organized cold. Lines of frost straight as a die. Deathly silence. You can keep all ten fingers pressed against it for hours on end, and the ice still won't show the slightest mark.

[*She moves her lips more, but she is playing so loudly that we can't make anything out. Everyone looks at her attentively. We wonder: which will come to grief first—the piano or her? Finally, after the music has reached an insane crescendo,* CLARA *sinks down from the stool. Deathly silence at this moment. All we hear is the snow falling gently on to the summit-cross. Everything is still.*]

[NURSE 1, *followed by* NURSE 2, *comes in hesitantly, picks up the piece of paper from the floor and reads it out haltingly, like someone illiterate. We notice he has wolf's jaws. While he is hesitantly reading,* NURSE 2 *takes the opportunity to kick the two corpses in the ribs or elsewhere with his mountaineering boot—slyly, so that the others do not see.*]

NURSE: Green, green the . . . jasmine bush . . . fell asleep at night . . . when the . . . sunlight . . . struck it . . . with the breath of the dawn . . . he woke up white as snow: . . . What happened to me during the night? Look, if trees could dream . . . this is how the spring would seem.

[*Snow trickles down gently without a sound. The curtain falls.*]

For the Musical Tragedy, Clara S., quotations from the following works, among others, were woven into the text:

Clara Schumann: *Tagebücher, Briefe (Diaries, Letters)*
Robert Schumann: *Briefe (Letters)*
Gabriele d'Annunzio: *the novels*
Tamara de Lempicka and Gabriele d'Annunzio: *Correspondence*
Aélis Mazoyer: *Diaries*
Ria Endres: *"Am Ende Angekommen" ("Reaching the End")*

[*The translator would like to thank Eugenia Loffredo for translating the English passages in the German text into Italian, as well as Dr. J. M. Catling (University of East Anglia, Norwich) and Professor Alan Barr (Indiana University Northwest) for their kind advice. The translations in parentheses of the French passages are mine.*]

Ludmila Petrushevskaya (b. 1938)

The early decades of this century witnessed a magnificent eruption of dramatic imagination in Russia—the censorious regimes of the czars and the Soviet Union notwithstanding. The plays of Chekhov, Maxim Gorky, Leonid Andreyev, and Vladimir Mayakovsky and the revolutionary directing of Konstantin Stanislavsky at the Moscow Art Theater edged aside the melodramas and well-made European plays of the previous century and helped initiate a remarkable era of modern national drama.

Striking by their absence were the women dramatists, and it does not seem to matter greatly whether it was under the *ancien régime* of the czars or the revolutionary, legislated egalitarianism of the Soviets. There were actresses, but published and produced female playwrights were disproportionately rare. They existed, were known, and were talented, but they remained marginal. Zinaida Gippius wrote three impressive plays before World War I: *Holy Blood* (*Sviataia krov'*, 1900), *The Red Poppy* (*Makov tsvet*, 1912), and *The Green Ring* (*Zelenoe kol'tso*, 1914)—ranging in style from lyrical and mythical to realist. All ran into censorship problems, which, combined with Gippius's emigration, led to her exclusion from the canon. Marina Tsvetaeva (1892–1941), who also left the country (from 1922 to 1939), Lidia Seifullina (1889–1954), who attempted to work within the new politics, and Ol'ga Forsch (1873–1961), who declared her strong interest in the "New Soviet Woman" and the woman question, were all minimally recognized in their time. Vera Panova, though primarily known as a novelist, was more successful in establishing for herself a place in the Soviet theater, with such plays as *The Snowstorm* (*Metelitsa*, 1945), *Farewell to the White Nights* (*Provody belykh nochei*, 1961), and *It's Been Ages!* (*Skol'ko let, skol'ko zim*, 1967).

The difficulty women have had succeeding as dramatists in Russia reflects that society's general unease with the women's movement. As some have observed—at times, laceratingly—whether czarist, Stalinist, Glasnost, or post-Soviet, any kind of *de facto* social and political equality has been extraordinarily difficult for women to realize—or even credibly to demand. Women's ideal role of patriotic motherhood was strongly promoted under Stalin, and the resistance to "Western" feminism—even among women artists—has been pervasive. In the last decade, women have been forming political, social, and artistic organizations, with the intention of examining their situation and improving it. The complaints are clear—from alcoholism and abuse to unequal workloads and male opacity. But as we enter the new

Ludmila Petrushevskaya, ca. 1997. (Photographer: Giovanna del Magro.)

millennium, these groups and this political agenda represent a decidedly minor force in Russia.

Toward the end of the 1970s a new wave of writers began to emerge—one vaguely reminiscent of Britain's "angry young men," in its focus on domestic malaise and mundane grimness. Ludmila Petrushevskaya is at the vanguard of this current generation. Although she struggled for almost a quarter of a century for publication and recognition, her stories and plays have now made Petrushevskaya the most acclaimed writer in Russia. She does not present herself as political and shies away from any label like "feminist" or women's writer, seeing herself as writing in a "male mode" and being "for children." Her portraits of domestic ills are gritty and uncompromising: alcoholism, poverty, loveless relationships, and abuse; "Nets and Traps," the title of one of her best-known works, captures her sentiment.

Much like Chekhov, to whom she is sometimes compared, her writings occupy an interesting continuum between short fiction and drama. The stories, which are told in an out-of-breath, first-person narration, could often as well be presented as monologues or short plays (much like Chekhov's "On the Harmfulness of Tobacco Chewing"). Her attention is directed, exquisitely, to tone of voice, or voices—in the case of dialogues, where the speakers charge on unresponsive to each other.

Though the reality she reveals is bleak, lurking behind and perhaps intensifying this grimness are comedy and irony. What she clearly does not have (and evidently has little sympathy with) is Chekhov's genteel graciousness. The air of autumnal frustration of his plays yields to more overt pain and disgruntlement in hers.

Petrushevskaya's concern with the world that women occupy leads her to take advantage of the notorious lack of space in Russian apartments. The literal, familiar scarcity of rooms becomes an effective metaphor for the cramped, truncated lives that people—especially women—lead and for the anything-but-quiet desperation of their lives. Petrushevskaya's disinclination, inability, or refusal to find any persuasive reason for hope, not even in that last resort of the culture, the Russian intelligentsia, has made her controversial and for some unpalatable. But in this she is no different from Beckett or Pinter—who also favor drama within a confining room.

Music Lessons (*Uroki muzyki*, written in 1973, published in 1983) was Petrushevskaya's first full-length play. The two families, the Gavrilovs and the Kozlovs, parallel each other in their similarly inhospitable and claustrophobic apartments, converging to squelch any possibility that the young Nina has of thriving. Children are a threat and an impediment; in this battle for space among the generations, they crowd you out. Marriage is debunked, as Granya wonders why have "some useless man hanging around. . . . Washing and cooking for him and all that." At base, family life involves learning how to lie. The music lessons that Nikolai never completed come to represent his general failure. The grotesque, surrealist final scene, with Nadya and Nina swinging threateningly over peoples' heads, forecloses any possibility of satisfying domesticity, child-rearing, or love.

SELECTED BIBLIOGRAPHY IN ENGLISH

Goscilo, Helena. *Dehexing Sex: Russian Womanhood During and After Glasnost.* Ann Arbor: University of Michigan Press, 1996.

——— . "Introduction." *Lives in Transit: A Collection of Recent Russian Women's Writing.* Ed. Helena Goscilo. Dana Point, Calif.: Ardis, 1995. Pp. xi–xix.

——— . "Introduction." *Glasnost: An Anthology of Russian Literature Under Gorbachev.* Eds. Helena Goscilo and Byron Lindsey. Ann Arbor, Mich.: Ardis, 1990. Pp. xv–xlv.

Kolesnikoff, Nina. "The Generic Diversity of Ljudmila Petrushevskaja's Plays." *Slavic Drama: The Question of Innovation. Proceedings.* Eds. Andrew Donskov *et al.* Ottawa: University of Ottawa, 1991. Pp. 215–25.

Laird, Sally. *Voices of Russian Literature: Interviews with Ten Contemporary Writers.* Oxford: Oxford University Press, 1999.

Smith, Melissa T. "Waiting in the Wings: Russian Women Playwrights in the Twentieth Century." *Women Writers in Russian Literature.* Eds. Toby W. Clyman and Diana Greene. Westport, Conn.: Greenwood, 1994. Pp. 189–203.

Vainer, Victoria. "An Interview with Liudmila Petrushevskaya." *Theater* 20 (1989), 61–64.

Woll, Josephine. "The Minotaur in the Maze: Remarks on Lyudmila Petrushevskaya." *World Literature Today* 67 (193), 125–30.

MUSIC LESSONS

Ludmila Petrushevskaya

Translated by Stephen Mulrine

CHARACTERS

The GAVRILOVS:

GRANYA   thirty-eight years old

NINA   her daughter, eighteen years old

VITYA   her son, a schoolboy

IVANOV   GRANYA's husband, thirty-five years old

The KOZLOVS:

FYODOR IVANOVICH (FEDYA)

TAISA PETROVNA (TAYA)

NIKOLAI   their son (KOLYA)

VASILIEVNA   the grandmother

KLAVA   TAISA's sister (KLAVDIA)

UNCLE MITYA   KLAVA's husband

NADYA   NIKOLAI's girlfriend

GIRLS IN THE STUDENT HOSTEL

ANNA STEPANOVNA   the GAVRILOVS' and KOZLOVS' neighbour

SERGEI ILYICH   her husband

ACT ONE

Scene One

The scene is a large room in the GAVRILOVS' *apartment. It is clean and tidy, although the signs of hardship are everywhere. In the corner, a television set is switched on, and the* GAVRILOV *family,* GRANYA, NINA, *and* VITYA, *are watching a programme.* GRANYA *and* VITYA *are lying on the bed.* NINA *is sitting at the table, weeping. The doorbell rings, and* VITYA *springs up to open the door.* NINA, *her eyes red with weeping, rushes to the door at the same time and stops him, calling out "Who is it?"*

WOMAN'S VOICE: Open the door, love, it's me.

[NINA *hooks up the security chain and part-opens the door. She stands looking at her a few moments before admitting their neighbour,* ANNA STEPANOVNA. ANNA STEPANOVNA *is a little old dried-up woman who works as a night concierge and is thus free during the day. She is wearing a pinafore, with her sleeves rolled up, and a profoundly sad expression.*]

ANNA STEPANOVNA: [*To no-one in particular.*] So what's happening, eh? Flat on his back, is he, the dirty pig? We should call the police right now. Use the phone-box. [*To* GRANYA.] Is she asleep?

GRANYA: I think so.

[*There is a faint smile on* GRANYA's *face. She is a tall, thin, subdued woman, with metal false teeth, wearing earrings. She speaks softly, even at moments of intense emotion.*]

ANNA STEPANOVNA: She's a little sweetheart, as good as gold, eh? My first was like that, Gena—just ate and slept, a right little dumpling. That's what everybody said, a little dumpling. But your little Galya—well, who'd have thought it? Her father—[*A cautious nod in the direction of the hall door.*]—her father's thin as a rake, skin and bone. And your people, the Gavrilovs, they're just the same. [*Then, out of the blue.*] Has he arrived yet? Is he home?

GRANYA: Yes, he's home.

ANNA STEPANOVNA: What a carry-on! [*Wringing her hands.*] And what are you going to do now? [GRANYA *shrugs.*] Well, I suppose one way of looking at it, he is the baby's father. He is her father. But then again—he won't forgive you. He's not going to forgive you, no way. Maybe he's come back to get you, eh? You think about that.

[NINA *is sobbing now.* GRANYA *absently watches television.*]

ANNA STEPANOVNA: I mean he's going to remember it was you got him put in jail. D'you think he won't remember? He will. What was it he said when they were taking him away? Granya? "I'll be back."

[GRANYA *nods in agreement, sends* NINA *into the adjoining room.* ANNA STEPANOVNA *looks around her.*]

ANNA STEPANOVNA: Well, you've got a really nice place here, you keep it nice, everything clean and tidy. Still, Nina'll soon be bringing home a good wage, Vitya's a boarder, you'll be able to buy some clothes, a few things for the house. Not all at once, of course. Three kids, it's nothing but expense. Just one thing—don't you let that man of yours hang round your neck, let him go to hell! I mean, you weren't exactly happy when he was living here, were you? Eh? Just thank your lucky stars they put him in jail for a year, and not thirty days. You should get down on your knees and thank the court—I mean, just look, a whole year he's been away and you've had your little Galya in peace, nobody's been beating the kids, or swearing at them. And you yourself—

GRANYA: He didn't swear at them.

ANNA STEPANOVNA: [*Regardless.*] And you're on your own—a great life. Come home in the evening, pamper yourself, have a nice warm bath, get into bed all nice and fresh, your own boss. And if you need a man, well, just whistle, there's plenty of them all ready and waiting. They'll give it to you in a gift!

NINA: [*Entering.*] Mama, Galya's woken up, and she's hungry. [GRANYA *exits.*]

ANNA STEPANOVNA: And she's not crying? Just lying there? Just smacking her little lips? Well, she's a darling. My first was the same. Gena would wake up and turn his head round and give a sort of little cough. But he wouldn't cry. Just this little coughing sound . . . ahah-ahah . . . like that. [*Laughs.*] And the minute he started, I'd wake up instantly. Nothing else'd waken me, shouting or whatever. And we were two families living in that room, me and little Gena, and my Sergei, my husband. And there was another woman, Marta, with her little boy—he was born same day as Gena. Me and Marta were in the same maternity hospital, in adjoining beds. Marta had no place to go— she'd been brought up in an orphanage, and she'd no husband. I took her home with me. And her little boy used to howl the place down, and I'd just sleep on. But the second my little Gena started to cough, I'd be out of bed like a shot. He just used to whimper, never cried. So that's why—it's because of that me and Sergei used to be so quiet. Sergei's still quiet, maybe even too quiet. It's all boiling up inside, but it doesn't show on the surface. Me, I can't sit still, I've got a bee in my bonnet the whole time. I've got clothes soaking and I was going to wash them. Then our Yuri went down for a newspaper and when he comes back he says Ivanov's asleep beside the radiator in the entry.

[NINA *exits.* ANNA STEPANOVNA *is shouting into the next room, but watching television at the same time.* VITYA *is also entranced, watching TV.*]

ANNA STEPANOVNA: Anyway I took Marta home, although we'd hardly room to turn round. Twelve square metres, and a stove, the three of us, plus the two of them. The neighbours started complaining, kicking up a fuss. I used to hang my nappies up in the kitchen, and nobody said a word. But when Marta started to hang hers up, they complained and took them down. So we had to dry Marta's nappies in our room. And what with the condensation and damp, the window steamed up—it was winter, of course. So anyway, we messed about like that for two months, and I took Gena out for a walk one time, and when I came back, Marta was gone. She understood, and she just left of her own accord. Certainly the neighbours had called out the police twice, because Marta hadn't a resident's permit. But I never said a single word to her, nor did Sergei. She wasn't like some people, you could spit in their eye and they'd just wipe it off and carry on regardless.

[*There is a patriotic war film on TV.* ANNA STEPANOVNA *waits for the occasional lull in the fighting, then hurriedly speaks her piece.*]

ANNA STEPANOVNA: Well, anyway, I thought he'd come back to you. Not because he'd said he would, or thinks anything about you at all. No, it's because he's got no place else to go. You mark my words—he's no good. Don't take him in—we need drunks in this block like a hole in the head. And your Nina's a young woman now, what's she going to do with somebody else's old husband? She's not going to wash and clean for him.

GRANYA: [*Appearing in the doorway.*] He's not that bad. Nina's been like a daughter to him.

ANNA STEPANOVNA: Oh, God forgive you, Granya!

GRANYA: What do you mean?

[*The baby suddenly begins to cry.*]

ANNA STEPANOVNA: I'm going. I'd better go, love.

[NINA *enters carrying a bundle of nappies.*]

ANNA STEPANOVNA: And your fiancé's back home from the army, did you know? The Kozlovs' boy Nikolai, you remember. He always used to laugh at you—that's my girl-friend just run past, he'd say. [NINA *nods.*] That's my fiancée in the fifth grade. Yes, he's come home a big grown-up fellow. Drove up in a taxi just this evening. And he had a girl with him. Maybe he picked her up at the station, or else he's brought her home with him from the army, who knows? Anyway I had to run and get the washing on. Nikolai says to me, he says, "Why don't you pop in, Stepanovna?" But I haven't got the time.

Scene Two

A large room in the KOZLOVS' *apartment. The layout is similar to that of the* GAVRILOVS', *but the furnishings, etc., are very different. True, the television set stands in the same corner, the screen turned from the audience, but there are carpets, crystal, highly-polished furniture. The table is extended, and the* KOZLOVS *are seated round it.* NIKOLAI's *mother,* TAISA PETROVNA, *his father* FYODOR IVANOVICH, NIKOLAI *himself in civilian clothes, with a moustache, and his girlfriend* NADYA TIMOFEYEVNA. *In appearance, she is the perfect image, in our modern situation, of the well-paid department store salesgirl, hairdresser, factory worker, or, as in this case, house-painter.* NADYA *is smoking, opposite her sits* NIKOLAI's *grandmother,* VASILIEVNA, *as if mesmerised, following with her eyes each puff of smoke as it rises to the ceiling,* ANNA STEPANOVNA *is also there, wearing the same house-coat, and with her sleeves still rolled up. She is sitting on the edge of her chair, with her glass raised high. She appears rather ingratiating, her face is flushed, and she is silent. Indeed, everyone at the table looks a little flushed.*

FYODOR IVANOVICH: So you'd a good time in the army, had a bit of luck, too, as you've been telling us. And we'll fix you up with a good job. Not what you were doing before. Now on you go, son, over to the piano, it's time we had a few songs. I've missed the singing while you've been away, the vocals. On you go, you can do your courting later, now it's your father calling you to your duty. What did you study six years for, eh? And if you hadn't given up you'd have finished music school, you'd have a certificate by now. Anyway, I've wasted my money, six years out of my life. All you can do is accompany your old man, and I've got to persuade you to do that, even.
NIKOLAI: Give over, Papa!
FYODOR IVANOVICH: Well, come on—ye gods, the coaxing it took when you were a child! Go on, sit down at the instrument, for God's sake!
NIKOLAI: I even tried to keep quiet about it in the army, that I could read music. Then this lieutenant comes up and says, "You've got an intellectual face, you can sing in the choir." So, I wound up in the choir. Still, it often got us out of duties, travelling away to competitions and reviews.
ANNA STEPANOVNA: Come on, Nikolai, play for us, please!
FYODOR IVANOVICH: [*About to fly into a rage.*] Well?

[NIKOLAI *shrugs and sits down at the piano, his father stands alongside. The influence of television is obvious, his father sings a gypsy romance, "As Soon As Azure Night Falls . . ." He sings tensed up and straining—not in the manner of someone singing at the dinner table, wholeheartedly—but like someone whose whole life's ambition has been to sing. Singing of this kind doesn't produce a pleasant or joyful impression—on the contrary, everyone at the table averts their eyes. Only* ANNA STEPANOVNA, *who is extravagantly pleased with everything, joins in, in a quavering treble.* TAISA PETROVNA *pays no attention to her husband and busies herself looking after her guests—she picks up their plates, takes them out to the kitchen.* TAISA PETROVNA *pushes a pastry slice at* ANNA STEPANOVNA. *The latter, jolted out of her reverie, briefly protests, then immediately launches into song again with her mouth full, rocking on her chair.* NADYA *pours herself some wine.* VASILIEVNA's *fierce staring eyes follow her every move, but* NADYA *is not in the least embarrassed, she pays no heed to anybody. The song comes* to an end, and only ANNA STEPANOVNA applauds. NIKOLAI, *his face flushed, stands behind* NADYA*'s chair leaning over her. His face practically buried in her back-combed, silvery-pink rinsed hair.* ANNA STEPANOVNA*'s eyes are burning.*]

NADYA: Listen, to hell with this crap, I want to dance.

[FYODOR IVANOVICH *is standing by the piano, ready to sing on and on, but* NIKOLAI *takes* NADYA*'s arms and leads her to the radio,* NIKOLAI *turns the volume up full—it is playing the "Adagio" from* Swan Lake. NIKOLAI *and* NADYA, *pressed tightly against each other, mark time on the spot to the music.*]

ANNA STEPANOVNA: [*Suddenly clutching at her pocket.*] Oh, what's the o'clock! Oh, I've got the washing on to soak! Oh!

FYODOR IVANOVICH: You've let the whole world slip away, that's what you've done. Your Sergei'll think you've disappeared off the face of the earth, most likely he'll be killing himself laughing.

ANNA STEPANOVNA: [*Coming to her senses, coldly.*] Sergei? My Sergei'll come for me and take me home and never say a word.

FYODOR IVANOVICH: [*Nodding sarcastically.*] No doubt, no doubt—you'll say enough words on his behalf, so he won't get a look in. [ANNA STEPANOVNA *hurries out.*] She's running out . . . there goes people power in action, the granny police!

[*The dancing at the* KOZLOVS' *continues.* NADYA *and* NIKOLAI *are now dancing to Khachaturyan's "Sabre Dance." The* FATHER *leaves the piano and sits down at the table.* MOTHER *carries in the tea-pot,* GRANDMOTHER *stares fixedly at* NADYA, *at her boots, her dress, etc.* NADYA *has a bandage on one of her fingers.*]

TAISA PETROVNA: [*Projecting over "The Sabre Dance."*] We'll have a drink of tea at least, before you go home. It's getting late, and Fyodor Ivanovich has to get up at six for work tomorrow.

NIKOLAI: [*He is already in a wild state of excitement from jumping around, and he is shouting.*] What work, Mother! Tomorrow's Sunday!

TAISA PETROVNA: Oh, I'm getting the days all mixed up. Anyway, sit down and have some tea just the same.

NIKOLAI: And you're chasing our guests out too early. Anybody else's house they'd have invited forty people, and they'd be partying till morning.

FYODOR IVANOVICH: Other people's houses are one thing, ours is another.

NIKOLAI: I mean, you only come home from the army once in your life. Isn't that right, Nadya?

NADYA: Of course.

NIKOLAI: That's it, sweetheart, you stick up for me!

[*A news broadcast on the radio.* NIKOLAI *and* NADYA *dance to the news for a little while, but eventually the jollification peters out, of its own accord, and the two young people sit down at the table.*]

NADYA: Oh, it's cake. I don't eat cake.

GRANNY: [*Putting in her oar.*] Oh yes, and what *do* you eat?

NIKOLAI: [*Pedantically.*] Grandma, you've got to respect other people's tastes.

GRANNY: [*Sotto voce.*] Respect my arse. Her taste's all in her mouth, that one.

TAISA PETROVNA: [*Kindly.*] Have some jam, Nadya. I made it myself in the summer, our own strawberries. We have a little garden plot, and the strawberries were just unbelievable!

NADYA: You have a plot? And a house? How many rooms?

TAISA PETROVNA: [*Gently.*] How many do you need?

NIKOLAI: Mama, I've just got out of the army!

TAISA PETROVNA: No, really, how many rooms do you young people need? And how many will you leave us for our old age?

NADYA: How many do we need? You've got two rooms, haven't you? Well, we'll take whichever is the smaller.

FYODOR IVANOVICH: Thanks very much, you're too kind.

NADYA: Because when the children arrive, they'll be sleeping with their grandparents, not their mother and father.

GRANNY: [*Loudly.*] Over my dead body. What damnable cheek!

NADYA: [*In a loud, distinct voice, without a trace of embarrassment.*] The furniture in here takes up too much room.

GRANNY: And the furniture's wrong as well!

[*Nobody takes any notice of her. As if spellbound, everyone turns to look at the objects* NADYA *directs her attention to.*]

NADYA: You shouldn't have so much furniture. What do you want that dresser for, that crockery exhibition? And what do you want with that coffee table? You've no books to put on it. And carpets should be deep pile, so your feet sink into them.

[NIKOLAI *is nodding mechanically, his arm round* NADYA's *shoulders.*]

FYODOR IVANOVICH: Oh, of course, we're the ignorant masses. Working class origins.

NIKOLAI: Nadya's working class too. [*Lays his head on* NADYA's *shoulder.*]

GRANNY: [*Suddenly.*] So, you get that room, where do I go? Into the kitchen?

NADYA: Of course your flat is a bit cramped for three generations.

TAISA PETROVNA: [*Placating.*] Well, it doesn't matter. We'll get by somehow. Nadya love, come and give me a hand, and we'll wash the dishes.

NADYA: No fear. You're on your own.

[FYODOR IVANOVICH *slams his fist down on the table, gets up decisively and follows his wife through to the kitchen.* GRANNY *takes herself off to her own room, carefully jamming the door shut behind her with a piece of paper.* NADYA *and* NIKOLAI *converse in whispers about something, then he rushes, dishevelled, into the kitchen.* NADYA *goes up to the piano, and plays "Chopsticks" with her thick, clumsy fingers. In the kitchen they all stand rooted to the spot, listening.*]

FYODOR IVANOVICH: Now she's wrecking the instrument. Go right ahead! Give it hell!

NIKOLAI: You see, Mama? I'm just back, just home from the army and he's started already!

TAISA PETROVNA: Fedya, Nadya wants to stay the night here with us.

NIKOLAI: I want her to!!!

FYODOR IVANOVICH: Oh yes, and is there anything else she wants?

TAISA PETROVNA: Wait, Fedya. I mean, if you think of it, we can put Mama on the couch, and the two of us can sleep on the divan.

NIKOLAI: Yes, you can crash down there for one night, surely.

FYODOR IVANOVICH: Yes, if it is just one night, but supposing she doesn't leave.

NIKOLAI: [*Cheerfully.*] So maybe I'll have to go?

FYODOR IVANOVICH: You keep quiet, Kolya, while you've still got a tongue in your head. You've said too damn much today already.

NIKOLAI: See? There he goes again.

FYODOR IVANOVICH: How can you speak like that to your father?

[*In the lounge,* NADYA *is playing "Chopsticks,"* NIKOLAI *brings a pillow, etc., out of his grandmother's room, trailing the sheets along the floor.* GRANNY *rushes after him, picking up the sheets.* TAISA PETROVNA *takes fresh linen into* GRANNY's *room. All of this takes place at high speed, to the music of "Chopsticks." Suddenly* GRANNY *is already sitting on the couch in her nightgown, staring dumbly at her bedroom door, which* NADYA *and* NIKOLAI *are jamming closed with the paper wad, from the other side.*]

Scene Three

Morning in the GAVRILOVS' *flat.* GRANYA *is carrying the baby through into the kitchen, and pauses en route beside* NINA.

GRANYA: Honestly, I'm surprised at you. For a start he's got no place else, that's why he's come here. Anyway, he'll be going soon, I couldn't just leave him sprawled out in the entry. People would talk. So he's spent the night in the bathroom, big deal. I threw some old rags down for him on the floor. [*Exits.*]

[VITYA *enters.*]

VITYA: Ivanov's sitting in the kitchen with Galka.
NINA: It's all right, he'll be leaving soon.
VITYA: He says he's staying with his daughter from now on.
NINA: Yes, well Mama won't let him stay here.
VITYA: She's telling him, "Go away, for God's sake, or it'll all just start over again." And he's saying, "No, it won't, definitely not, no way." That's what he's saying, I knew he would. She's given him a mirror to have a shave.
NINA: Well, it certainly won't make life easier for him, if he goes away looking like that.
VITYA: And she's told him to hang on, we're going to have breakfast.
NINA: And where's Galka? Bring her in here.
VITYA: He's holding onto her. She's told him to get shaved now, and give Galka back. But he keeps saying wait, wait.
NINA: Yes, he's only like that when he's sober.
VITYA: Too true.
NINA: Go and get Galka. If he's going to shave, and Mama's making breakfast, they won't know where to shove Galka anyway.

[VITYA *exits.* NINA *gazes absently out of the window.* VITYA *reenters.*]

VITYA: Mama's taken the pram through there. They've put Galka in the pram. He's shaving and watching Galka at the same time.
NINA: And what about Mama?
VITYA: Mama's making the kasha.
NINA: He'll be going soon.
VITYA: Mama says he should go to the country, to our folks. She'll give him a letter. And in the summer she'll take Galka down there, to Granny's.
NINA: Of course. He'll get work there—as something, maybe a nightwatchman.
VITYA: Yes, and he'll get blind drunk, and that'll be the end of the nightwatchman's job. They'll kick him out. Uncle Vanya at Auntie Marusya's just the same. She told Mama, your Ivanov's incorrigible, a drunken slob, same as my Ivan.
NINA: Well, it doesn't matter, he'll be leaving anyway.

Scene Four

Morning in the KOZLOVS' *apartment. The beds have been tidied away, and the table laid.* MOTHER *is wearing her Sunday best,* FATHER *an open-necked shirt,* GRANNY *in a flower-patterned dress, all seated at the table, waiting to see what transpires. The door opens and the wad of paper falls to the floor.* NADYA *emerges, without make-up, in her silver dress, and mules on her bare feet.* NIKOLAI *enters behind her, screwing up his eyes.*

NIKOLAI: Mama, give Nadya a towel, to get washed.
TAISA PETROVNA: [*Cheerfully.*] Of course, dear.

[*She takes a large towel from the cupboard.* NIKOLAI *accepts it, and the young couple go out. There is the sound of running water, then the bathroom door is closed.* MOTHER *goes back to the table, shrugs.* FATHER *settles down to his breakfast. They all watch television, a children's programme of some kind. A little boy is singing.*]

GRANNY: She's put us all in our place, that one. She's taken over. That's what's in store for us. We'll all be jammed in together, then we'll die off, give way to the kids, die the death of the righteous. You here, us there, the grandchildren in with the grandparents, and me off to the boneyard. And the carpet's not deep enough for her.

TAISA PETROVNA: Yes, well she likes everything *too* much, just as long as she can have her own way. This'll do her nicely. I mean, she's from a hostel. She's got her beady eyes on this apartment, and that's a fact. But she doesn't want our Nikolai for love nor money. It's him that's trailing after her. She's only got to snap her fingers.

GRANNY: [*An afterthought.*] She's a gold-digger.

FYODOR IVANOVICH: Isn't she just! They're not even like that in our place. Personally, I wouldn't have her kind on the payroll.

TAISA PETROVNA: She's a painter on a building site.

FYODOR IVANOVICH: Well, you get all sorts of painters. But this one gave herself away immediately.

TAISA PETROVNA: I didn't like her any better the last time, when Nikolai wasn't here, and she came to introduce herself.

FYODOR IVANOVICH: What I can't fathom is why she behaves like that? Eh? Why is she so obvious, coming straight out with it? Anybody else would have washed the dishes, and helped clear the table—they'd have held their tongue and not made an exhibition of themselves right off! For God's sakes, she was in her fiancé's *house!*

GRANNY: [*Splutters.*] Fiancé?

FYODOR IVANOVICH: No, but why is it—I mean, does she really not understand that she can't behave like that? Rubbishing us all because of the furniture!

GRANNY: And she couldn't even dream of buying a suite like that.

FYODOR IVANOVICH: And she's spent the night with a strange man, eh?

TAISA PETROVNA: That's true, we could've put up a folding bed for Kolya in the kitchen.

GRANNY: Yes, and they'll get married, then it'll be *me* on a folding bed in the kitchen!

FYODOR IVANOVICH: God, you're like a stuck record.

GRANNY: Of course I am. Kolya'll get married, and I'll have to live in the kitchen, but you and our Kolya'll have a room to yourselves, that's *very* nice. And eventually I'll go further than the kitchen, into my grave!

TAISA PETROVNA: Oh, you and your grave—you keep on about it the whole time. On the slightest pretext, you're going to your grave!

GRANNY: So where else would I go? There's no room for me here, I've outstayed my welcome. There's no room at Klavdia's either. It'll have to be the old folks' home.

TAISA PETROVNA: Klavdia has the same kind of apartment as ours, except it's in a bigger mess.

GRANNY: Don't shout at your mother.

TAISA PETROVNA: Who said a word to you?

[*A silence. The sound of running water.*]

FYODOR IVANOVICH: That Stepanovna turned up yesterday, we hadn't seen her for ages. She came to sniff out what kind of fiancée Nikolai's got himself. What did you invite her for?

TAISA PETROVNA: Me? [*Highly indignant.*] It was Nikolai invited her—if he had his way he'd invite the whole block, the whole crowd of them.

GRANNY: Well, you've done it now. They'll all want to know, all the old wives down on the benches.

FYODOR IVANOVICH: They can all just bugger off!

[*A procession passes through the room,* NADYA *at its head,* NIKOLAI *following, jamming the door shut behind them with the paper wad.*]

GRANNY: Not so much as a by your leave.

TAISA PETROVNA: [*Exaggeratedly loud.*] Who wants tea? Kolya? Kolya? Will you have tea, or instant coffee?

NIKOLAI: [*From his room.*] Mama, give it a rest!

FYODOR IVANOVICH: Don't bother them. You see? They're not pleased.

[NIKOLAI *emerges, jams the door with the paper wad as before.*]

NIKOLAI: Well, good morning.

FYODOR IVANOVICH: Good morning! We didn't get round to saying it last time.

NIKOLAI: That doesn't count. You should have closed your eyes while we slipped past. It's these damn connecting rooms. It'll be like that all the time now—"Excuse me, I hope I'm not disturbing you?" and all that.

FYODOR IVANOVICH: Why's that? Why is it going to be like that?

TAISA PETROVNA: Fedya.

FYODOR IVANOVICH: Yes, well nobody's asked *me* yet, by the way, how it's going to be in my own house. I mean, I am still actually here in my own home!

NIKOLAI: Oh yes, so what does that make me? Am I not?

FYODOR IVANOVICH: No, you're in your parents' home, all right?

NIKOLAI: God almighty—does that mean I'm just here on sufferance?

TAISA PETROVNA: Father, go into the kitchen. I've got a pie in there, check it's not burning.

FYODOR IVANOVICH: [*Furious.*] A pie! [*Exits.*]

TAISA PETROVNA: Kolya, Kolya, you really shouldn't! I mean, after all . . .

NIKOLAI: Nadya came to see me at Syzran twice. She's my wife.

TAISA PETROVNA: She came to see you twice, but your father's devoted his whole life to you. He's brought you up, fed and clothed you.

NIKOLAI: I won't speak like that to my children.

TAISA PETROVNA: You haven't got any yet. You've got to live a bit, before you raise your own.

NIKOLAI: Here we go again!

TAISA PETROVNA: Nobody's said anything to you, have they? We need to sit down and discuss all this calmly.

NIKOLAI: Yes, and meanwhile you're rubbishing her.

TAISA PETROVNA: Listen, if you want my opinion, it's like water off a duck's back with her.

[NADYA *enters.*]

NADYA: [*In her impertinent voice, expressionless.*] What's all the noise? I'll hold your coats, if you like?

NIKOLAI: It's okay, there's no problem. Sit down and have some tea.

TAISA PETROVNA: Sit down, sit down, Nadya dear, take the weight off your feet. [NADYA *sits.*] And good morning.

NADYA: Good morning.

GRANNY: Huh—that's them got the formalities over!

FYODOR IVANOVICH: [*Enters.*] Taya, you'd better take out that pie.

[TAISA PETROVNA *exits,* FYODOR IVANOVICH *sits down.*]

FYODOR IVANOVICH: Well, look who's here. Cheers!

NADYA: Cheers.

FYODOR IVANOVICH: What are we thinking of, a day like this and no wine. Kolya, get your skates on, nip down to the corner shop. We'll drink to the bride and groom.

NIKOLAI: Now you're talking, Papa. That's a great idea! Absolutely, I'll be back in a second. Nadya, don't be getting up to mischief now. [*Hurries out.*]

FYODOR IVANOVICH: There's money in my coat, in my purse! [*Pause.*] Meantime, let's have a drink of tea, okay?

NADYA: I won't have any tea. I'll wait for the wine.

FYODOR IVANOVICH: So you don't like mixing your drinks? Well, that's something at least.

GRANNY: Bloody hell!

FYODOR IVANOVICH: My wife's mother's a great woman. She'll call a spade a spade. You're still swithering, wondering whether or not to speak, and she's already jumped in, with both feet.

NADYA: That's a sign of ill-breeding.

GRANNY: Oh-ho-ho-ho! Oh, that's priceless! [*Laughs, starts to cough.*]

FYODOR IVANOVICH: Oh yes, and what kind of upbringing d'you think our grandmother had, eh? She worked in a mill, she was a weaver. Three years at school, and bye-bye, that's your lot! That's all the education she's had. And what sort of culture do you pick up on the shop floor, eh? All swearing like troopers. But of course, your building site, that's a different story. They say "How do you do" when they clock in, "Thank you" when you pass them the mortar, "Excuse me" when they stand on your foot. And in the hostel, no doubt you get lectures all the time on the cultured life. Like how to behave in somebody else's house!

NADYA: We had a lecture recently on love and friendship.

GRANNY: Yes, love and friendship behind the bush!

NADYA: No, just love and friendship. What love is, ideologically, and how to disprove it. You wouldn't happen to have a match?

FYODOR IVANOVICH: Granny and I don't smoke.

NADYA: I need to pick my teeth. I'm going into the kitchen.

[TAISA PETROVNA *enters with the pie.*]

TAISA PETROVNA: Nadya, dear, where are you going?

FYODOR IVANOVICH: She's looking for matches.

TAISA PETROVNA: [*Calls after her.*] They're by the cooker, on the little shelf.

[*They sit in silence at the table, watching television. The outside door slams.*]

FYODOR IVANOVICH: That'll be Kolya back, Kolya! [*A silence.*] Nikolai?!

TAISA PETROVNA: He's probably gone into the kitchen, to see Nadya.

FYODOR IVANOVICH: She's a real bitch, that one. She'd bite you as soon as look at you.

TAISA PETROVNA: Kolya chose her, Kolya knew what she was like.

FYODOR IVANOVICH: Kolya chose *her*? He was hand-picked, I'm telling you, and they've just strung him along.

TAISA PETROVNA: Well, so? I mean, I picked you, didn't I.

FYODOR IVANOVICH: I was the only one after you, there was nobody else to pick. I was the only one tempted.

GRANNY: Is that how you remember it? You don't remember how I wouldn't let you into the house? You'd come in and sit down, your eyes never away from the door. When's Taya coming, when's Taya coming? I had to ask you to leave with a brush in my hand! And you'd go out and stand in the entry. I sent Klavdia out to have a look, and she comes back: "He's still there, Mama, what'll we do with him?"

FYODOR IVANOVICH: Yes, you were ill-bred then, and you've remained ill-bred. Nadya was telling the truth.

GRANNY: Oh, of course, and you were so *well*-bred. The minute you moved in you showed yourself in your true colours, your foul temper. I didn't know how the hell to get rid of you!

TAISA PETROVNA: Mama! . . .

GRANNY: He raised his hand to me.

FYODOR IVANOVICH: Oh God, here she goes again!

[*The outside door slams.*]

TAISA PETROVNA: What's that?

[NIKOLAI *enters, flushed and out of breath.*]

NIKOLAI: There was a queue. At this hour in the morning, would you believe. I got a bottle of white. So where's Nadyezhda then?

TAISA PETROVNA: She's in the kitchen.

NIKOLAI: Have you chased her out? [*Exits, re-enters.*] She's gone. She's just left. [*Sits down, still in his overcoat.*]

GRANNY: And a good thing too.

FYODOR IVANOVICH: Young girls are headstrong. Don't worry about it.

TAISA PETROVNA: I wasn't here. What happened?

GRANNY: She told me I was ill-bred. I'm too ill-bred for her.

NIKOLAI: Granny, really—for Heaven's sake, Gran.

TAISA PETROVNA: Anyway, take off your coat.

NIKOLAI: I'm going out after her.

TAISA PETROVNA: You're not serious? Where will you go? Maybe she's not even in the hostel now. She could be anywhere.

NIKOLAI: Where else can she go? She doesn't have anybody here, she's practically an orphan.

TAISA PETROVNA: All right, all right. But you'll drink some tea first, and have a piece of pie, and this bottle of yours . . . do you want anything else? I'll make some sandwiches. And there's some sweets there, a few biscuits. Take your coat off, have some breakfast, and then you can go.

Scene Five

Breakfast at the GAVRILOVS'. VITYA, IVANOV *and* GRANYA *are sitting at the table. The pram is also in the room.*

GRANYA: We should have had something to celebrate your return, but there's no money. Nina gets paid on a Thursday, she gets a junior's wage, twenty-three roubles. And I don't get paid until Monday.

IVANOV: That's enough, I said! I'm off the drink.

GRANYA: You could've had a glass of something, but there's no money for it.

IVANOV: I've already told you.

GRANYA: Anyway, about your residence permit. That's only if you keep off the drink. Or else I'm not registering it. I can't register you staying here otherwise, I just can't.

IVANOV: You can't?

[*A pause.*]

GRANYA: I mean, what are you to me? They'll say: what's your relationship to the person you wish to register? Just passing?

[*A pause.*]

IVANOV: Possibly.

GRANYA: Well, you think about it.

[*A pause.*]

IVANOV: What's to think about?

GRANYA: What?

IVANOV: I'll go and enlist.

GRANYA: I'm not throwing you out.

IVANOV: Yes, well they won't register me anyway.

GRANYA: They won't register you just like that.

IVANOV: So how?

GRANYA: How, how—they'll register a husband with a wife, that's how.

IVANOV: But you and I . . .

GRANYA: You and I what?

IVANOV: [*Finally understands.*] Well, carry on . . .

GRANYA: Your neighbours have signed you off at that place, at Zelyony Road. I found that out. They took you off the register six months ago.

IVANOV: I went there as well. So why should they bother about me? It suits them better this way.

GRANYA: [*Heatedly.*] I went out there, and Mitrevna barely opened the door to me, she kept the chain on, and she says, "You needn't bother hanging around here, we've signed Ivanov off!" They've got a new tenant in there, presumably. Vitya, go and call Nina in, before she freezes.

VITYA: She won't come.

GRANYA: [*Glances quickly at* IVANOV.] What d'you mean, she won't come? Why won't she come? You just tell her to come right now! I won't tell her a second time!

VITYA: [*Goes to the door of the adjoining room.*] Mama says you've to come in. Before she comes for you herself.

[NINA *emerges sidelong, sits down.*]

GRANYA: And just stop this carry-on, or I'll give you a good hiding! Fiancée or no fiancée . . . [*To* IVANOV.] She's supposed to be engaged to the Kozlovs' Nikolai, they're on the sixth floor . . . But that won't stop me.

[IVANOV *nods. In his present state he will accept absolutely anything.* NINA *is offended.*]

GRANYA: It's all right, I was only joking. That's Kolya Kozlov—when she was still just a girl, taking our Vitya out for walks all the time, he used to say, "There she is, that's my fiancée." He used to give her sweets. Nina was small, and our Vitka was a big fat lump, just the way Galka's growing now. She could barely lift him up. They even used to call her that in the street—Kolya's fiancée. He's back from the army now, probably he's got a girlfriend of his own now. Stepanovna said he arrived back from the army in a taxi, with some girl.

[*They eat in silence. The conversation is strained.*]

GRANYA: Anyway, that's our Nina left on the shelf now. [*To* NINA.] Well? Why aren't you laughing, eh? You know, I've devoted my whole life to you. Eh?

IVANOV: They don't give a damn!

GRANYA: And you'd better keep quiet, just keep out of it.

IVANOV: Fair enough.

GRANYA: You might at least say something to your mother.

NINA: I don't object, why should I? He can have something to eat with us. His things are in the suitcase, I'll bring it. [*Fetches the case.*] They're all here. I've washed and ironed them.

IVANOV: Thanks, you shouldn't have bothered.

[*Makes to rise.*]

GRANYA: Sit down. We'll have some tea in a minute.

IVANOV: Anyway, I apologise if I've . . .

GRANYA: Go on, sit down. [*To* NINA.] Since when did you take over? Where did you learn to throw people out? Eh?

NINA: All right, he can have some tea.

IVANOV: Look, I'm sorry if that's how it is. [*Tries to stand up, but* GRANYA *makes him sit down again.*]

GRANYA: "No, he's not having any tea! No, he can't stay for tea!" What a determined little madam!

NINA: Just because we don't have room, doesn't mean anybody's throwing him out. He can stay with our Aunt Marusya at Chulkovo.

GRANYA: Aunt Marusya has three kids in that little house, and Granny and Uncle Ivan. Aunt Marusya's got enough on her plate without us. You used to go to Aunt Marusya's for the summer, and she needed you there like a hole in the head!

VITYA: We used to pick fruit there, and gather mushrooms . . . And we swam in the pond. Chulkovo's great. And there's plenty of room in the house. Auntie Marusya's out in the fields all day, and Uncle Ivan's either asleep, or at his work. They're never there. Granny's left on her own with us.

GRANYA: Well, well, so that's the radio switched on, is it? There hasn't been a squeak out of you for ages, and now suddenly it's come to life!

VITYA: Sergei, the one that's got no arms, he was always inviting us: come down and see us, he says. His brother's house is lying empty. The whole place! And it's got a stove, and a cellar. And a little shed.

NINA: You could get a job as a nightwatchman there.

GRANYA: Vitya, pour the tea.

NINA: I'll do it. [*Gets up.*] The train ticket costs eight roubles. We always used to take Vitka without a seat reservation.

IVANOV: Anyway . . . in this case . . . Thanks, all the same, thanks. I can go up North and enlist.

VITYA: Chulkovo's up North too. And Mama can bring Galka there in the summer.

IVANOV: Whatever you like. It's up to you, family business.

GRANYA: Don't listen to them, they're just kids.

IVANOV: Out of the mouths of babes . . .

GRANYA: So what do you want? D'you want the red carpet rolled out, like a cosmonaut? It's you that made this mess, you brought it on yourself, you went to jail, and now you think the children are just going to accept you?

IVANOV: It was you that put me in jail, that's the truth of it.

NINA: Mama!

IVANOV: Yes, it was you all right. But I thought, well, I've got a family, I'll be going back to my daughter, to my wife. Like a human being, I thought. A bit of humanity.

GRANYA: And so there is, there will be. Only not right away. If you behave like a man, there'll be some humanity. Like a man, and not a drunken animal. Do you understand?

IVANOV: I do. I just wish you understood me.

NINA: Mama, why are you talking to him?

GRANYA: [*To* IVANOV.] Do you think I don't understand you? Who was it had to pick you up off the radiator? And I brought you up here, regardless of what other people thought, not even my own children, nobody.

IVANOV: Yes, that's you all right. I know you.

NINA: Mama, why bother with him? Don't lower yourself.

GRANYA: You know me? You know another side of me too. And I know another side of you. I wish to God I didn't.

IVANOV: It'll be all right again, I've promised.

GRANYA: Huh, promises.

NINA: Mama, he's not staying here?

GRANYA: Don't you raise your voice to me.

NINA: He's staying here? Eh? [*Weeps.*] Oh God, what am I going to do? What can I do? Help me, somebody! . . . [*Gets up from the table, reeling.*]

Scene Six

NINA *is standing by the entry. The yard presents a familiar picture: a heap of boxes in the corner, a bench alongside the steps, windows heavily curtained.* NINA *stands quite motionless, wearing felt boots and a shawl.* NIKOLAI *comes past her from the entry, carrying a string bag containing a bottle, various parcels, boxes, packages.*

NIKOLAI: Hi there, fiancée. What grade are you in now?

NINA: None.

NIKOLAI: [*Oblivious to* NINA'*s irritated tone.*] No, that's not possible! What, have you finished school already?

NINA: Yes, I've dropped out.

NIKOLAI: [*For form's sake.*] So . . . what are you doing now?

NINA: I'm working. A trainee.

NIKOLAI: Where?

NINA: At the grocery store.

NIKOLAI: Well, you've landed on your feet, eh? And you've grown up! You've got it all now. I *was* going to treat you to some sweets, but maybe I'd better not, I don't know what you'd think. Well, I'd better run.

NINA: Best of luck. [*Turns away.*]

NIKOLAI: I'll see you again. I mean, we are neighbours! [*Exits.*]

[NINA *remains standing with her back to the audience.*]

Scene Seven

A girls' hostel. Four beds, a wardrobe with a mirror, a table in the middle of the room. The furniture is similar to that in a hotel, except that NADYA'*s dress hangs on a coathanger on the window latch. On the wall above each bed is fastened a rug or wall-mat, and on the night-tables stand make-up bottles, jars, boxes of face powder, etc.* NADYA *is sitting at the table in a dressing-gown, her legs crossed, wearing mules and chewing something.* NIKOLAI *enters, having first given a warning knock and receiving no reply.*

NIKOLAI: The door was open . . . Hello there, Nadyezhda love!

NADYA: Hi.

[*Before her on the table is a loaf of bread, sliced sausage, a bottle of milk, and a packet of sugar. There is a kettle on the floor.*]

NIKOLAI: Is that your lunch? Why didn't you have something to eat at our place?

[*He takes off his coat and places it carefully over* NADYA'*s Sunday dress, hanging on the window latch.*]

NIKOLAI: Too proud, are we? . . . I mean, you just pissed off, you might've waited. So big deal, they offended you. They've done plenty worse to me. I mean they're your folks, your parents, what can you do about them, eh? You always end up going back to them, anyway.

[NADYA *carries on chewing, all the while gazing at* NIKOLAI, *deep in thought.* NIKOLAI *produces a bottle from the string bag and stands it on the table. He moves* NADYA'*s food aside, and takes out a pie, biscuits, sandwiches, various packets and paper bags.*]

NIKOLAI: What's that junk you're eating? Here, be my guest, the pleasure's mine! Mama made up some sandwiches as well. [*Sits down contentedly.*]

[NADYA *knocks on the wall without getting up. There is a gentle scratching at the door, then a faintly embarrassed group of girls files in, in dressing-gowns, one in pyjamas, one in a winter coat and fur hat, and one wearing a muffler.*]

NADYA: Help yourselves, it's all yours. Tuck in, it's going cheap!

[NADYA *takes a paper bag and empties it out over the table. Sweets shower out in a heap. It is as if a signal has been given, and in an instant the bottle has vanished from the table, nimble fingers have torn the cardboard box-lid off the biscuits, greedy hands have plunged in to divide up the pie, and the jam is being spread.* NIKOLAI *can hardly be seen behind the backs of the young women milling round the table.* NADYA *sits apart, on her own bed. The most striking thing about the girls' violent demolition of the food* NIKOLAI *has provided is their casual ruthlessness, their mischievous waste of, and even contempt for the food. They spread jam over a newspaper, and throw biscuits at the hopper window, so that they land on* NIKOLAI'S *coat, which is instantly marked with flour.* NIKOLAI *rushes over to wipe his coat, and at that point they pour wine down his neck.* NIKOLAI *at first tries to join in their merriment, but soon becomes disillusioned and bored, then intensely irritated. Flushed with anger, he starts to protest.*]

NIKOLAI: Give over! Stop it, for God's sake, that's enough!

[*Almost beside himself with rage,* NIKOLAI *tries to pinion the girls' arms, to stop them pulling his coat down onto the floor.*]

GIRL WITH MUFFLER: Oh, he wants a fight! He's going to hit us! What a thug!

[NADYA *meanwhile sits apart, uninvolved, on her bed with her own food packages, drinking milk out of a bottle. Suddenly the doorbell rings. The* GIRL IN THE OVERCOAT, *whose fur hat has slipped to one side, exits to the hall. She shouts from there.*]

GIRL IN OVERCOAT: It's somebody looking for Semyonova.
GIRL WITH MUFFLER: She's gone home to Kashira, she'll be back tomorrow morning.

[*The* GIRL IN THE OVERCOAT *disappears, and the others follow her out of the room.* NIKOLAI, *dishevelled, his shirt soaking wet, picks his coat up off the floor and shakes it out.*]

NIKOLAI: So, is this how you treat all your guests? That's terrific. I came out here, my mother baked a pie for you. She spent last night mixing the dough. Huh—you can tell a person's character from the company they keep. Mama put sandwiches in for you as well, same as she'd do for any *decent* person. And she let you spend the night with us. You know, after this kind of . . .
NADYA: [*In her haughty, metallic voice, as if delivering a proclamation.*] Oh, forgive me, Kolya, I'm sorry I've corrupted you!
NIKOLAI: [*Gasps, astonished.*] You've done what to me?
NADYA: [*Not listening.*] I'm sorry I've corrupted you, yes. But you're not my type.

[NIKOLAI, *deeply offended, flings on his coat, which he has now dusted down, and circles the room slowly, picking his way through the litter. He rummages around in the debris. Finally, he locates his string bag under the table, shakes it out and puts it in his pocket.*]

NIKOLAI: So, that's it then? That's it? Well, I'm sorry. I'm sorry I bothered you.

[NADYA *raises her arm, switches on the radio. The rousing march "The Slav Maiden's Farewell" floods the room, and* NIKOLAI *exits in time to the march.* NADYA *picks up her coathanger from the floor, with her Sunday dress on it, dusts it off and hangs it back up at the window.*]

Scene Eight

The yard as before. NINA *is wheeling the pram back and forth by the entry.* VITYA *emerges from the entry and approaches her.*

VITYA: Nina, Mama wants you to bring Galka home.
NINA: Take her.
VITYA: Mama says you're to bring her.
NINA: I'm not coming.
VITYA: Mama says Galka'll get frozen.

NINA: Well, she can just damn well come and get her. I'm not going back home.
VITYA: [*Reproachfully.*] That's you all over. You're not nice.

[*A silence.*]

NINA: Anyway she's not frozen. I checked her little nose, and I'll try again now—[*Leans over the pram.*] See—it's warm.
VITYA: He's gone into the bathroom, to have a bath.
NINA: So?
VITYA: Mama's changing the bed.
NINA: So who cares?
VITYA: And where am I going to sleep now? [VITYA *asks more as a rhetorical question, thinking aloud, than in a practical sense.*]
NINA: My bed.
VITYA: What about you?
NINA: I'll be by the radiator, in the hall.
VITYA: And what if I tell Mama?
NINA: [*Shrugs.*] Go ahead.
VITYA: I'll tell Mama everything, you just wait! [*A pause.*] Nina, let's go home. We can stay with Galka, the three of us together. Really! They can have one room and we'll have the other. And that'll be fine. Really, truly! We can put a lock on the door, and he won't be able to get in at all.
NINA: Yes, and he'll take a stick, same as he did last time, and batter the door down.
VITYA: Well, we can shut our ears.
NINA: We can't shut Galka's.
VITYA: I'll take my pistol to him. Bang! Bang! I've got a pistol that fires suckers. Phhht! A sucker right between the eyes! [NINA *laughs weakly.*] Nina, let's go home! There'll be cartoons on the TV.
NINA: I don't want your cartoons.
VITYA: Yes, you do! Come on. We'll sit down and watch whatever's on.
NINA: I'm not coming. You take Galka.
VITYA: No! Mama said you had to! [*Runs off.*]

[NINA *stands pushing the pram back and forth.* NIKOLAI *appears, empty-handed, turns towards the entry and bumps into* NINA.]

NIKOLAI: What's this, are you waiting for me? [NINA *is silent, abstractedly rocking the pram.*] Why aren't you speaking? I mean, that's your fiancé home from the army, as you might say, and you won't speak to him, no welcome of any kind? Well?

[NINA *is silent still, rocking the pram.*]

NIKOLAI: I can see you haven't been wasting any time. [*Nods towards the pram.*] Are you married?
NINA: No. [*Turns away.*]
NIKOLAI: Unmarried mother?
NINA: Look, why d'you keep pestering me? It's my mother's little girl. My sister. All right?
NIKOLAI: [*Whistles.*] Your mother's had a baby?
NINA: Yes.
NIKOLAI: But she's old.
NINA: She's thirty-eight, that's not old.
NIKOLAI: Is she married, then?
NINA: No. Well, I don't really know, she's going to, I think.
NIKOLAI: Yes, women are always going to, but the reality's another story.
NINA: No, it's him that wants to get married.
NIKOLAI: And she's not sure?

NINA: That's right. What does she want some useless man hanging round her neck for? Washing and cooking for him, and all that.

NIKOLAI: Well, that means she doesn't love him. When I get married, I won't mess about with my wife. It'll be "Right, get that bed made! One-two!" [NINA *has to laugh.*] So, have you been out here since morning?

NINA: Yes.

NIKOLAI: I see. A bit of fresh air. That's nice. Anyway, I've been invited out again today. A get-together with the lads, and so forth. I've still got to find time to buy something.

NINA: Is it Boris's you're going to?

NIKOLAI: Why do you ask?

NINA: He's supposed to have some terrific records.

NIKOLAI: No, it's not Boris's place I'm going. Anyway, I'll see you.

NINA: Cheerio.

[NIKOLAI *hurries in.* ANNA STEPANOVNA *emerges with a basin of damp washing, and her husband,* SERGEI ILYICH, *carrying a wash tub.* ANNA STEPANOVNA *stops beside the pram, takes a look inside, chirping at the baby and repeating, "Who's a little darling?"*]

ANNA STEPANOVNA: Hello, Nina dear. God knows, I could dry these at home, but they just wouldn't smell fresh. I've got used to hanging things up outside from the old place. So what are you doing out here? I can see you from the window, walking up and down the whole time. Has somebody offended you? Oh dear, this isn't good, you know, it bodes ill, you mark my words. Come on, Sergei, that's enough of a rest.

[*They hang out the washing some way off.* ANNA STEPANOVNA *then hurries up to* NINA.]

ANNA STEPANOVNA: Nina dear, while you're standing here with the baby, would you keep an eye on my washing?

Scene Nine

The KOZLOVS' *apartment. The table is laid, and there are guests—*KLAVA, TAISA PETROVNA'S *sister, and her husband,* UNCLE MITYA. NIKOLAI *enters.*

KLAVA: Oh, it's Nikolai the soldier! What a lovely man the boy's turned out!

[*The guests eat and drink.* UNCLE MITYA *eats very little, and carefully inspects every morsel, chewing it over, deep in thought, as if listening to some inner rumblings.*]

KLAVA: Some grow up, some grow down. Me and Uncle Mitya are growing down the way, isn't that so, Nikolai?

NIKOLAI: Nonsense, Auntie Klava, you're still in your prime.

KLAVA: Let me give you a big kiss, my own lovely boy!

[*They embrace.*]

FYODOR IVANOVICH: Come on, take your coat off and sit down with us. As you can see, we've got to keep the table laid. I thought the two of you would be coming back?

NIKOLAI: I've got to go out some place now.

FYODOR IVANOVICH: What place is this you're going? [*He is flushed from drinking.*] What place? You should have some respect for your own family first, for Uncle Mitya and Auntie Klava, they've come here out of the goodness of their hearts, maybe they'll be able to advise you, since you treat your own parents like dirt.

NIKOLAI: [*To his silent mother.*] Mama, let's go into the other room.

[NIKOLAI *and his mother exit.*]

KLAVA: My my, secrets and more secrets.

[TAISA PETROVNA *re-enters.*]

KLAVA: Secrets, I'm saying.

TAISA PETROVNA: [*Shrugs.*] He wanted a shirt to change into.

KLAVA: She's managed to make a real mess of his shirt. What was it, lipstick?

TAISA PETROVNA: I didn't see. He didn't show me it. He had his jacket on.

[NIKOLAI *comes out of the room, heading for the bathroom, carrying his shirt in a crumpled heap.*]

TAISA PETROVNA: Kolya, put that into the laundry bin and I'll give it a wash.

NIKOLAI: I'll do it myself, it's okay.

KLAVA: You see what good care he takes of his mother?

[NIKOLAI *exits. A pause.* UNCLE MITYA *shakes his head censoriously. He is annoyed at* KLAVA.]

KLAVA: Well, why not? It's true, he looks after his mother, he should look after her, she's the only mother he's got.

[UNCLE MITYA *shakes his head again.*]

UNCLE MITYA: She's getting carried away, her jaw never stops.

KLAVA: What did I say?

FYODOR IVANOVICH: Let him do it, let him wash it himself. At least he's still got some shame.

KLAVA: All the same, it's a pity for the lad. I mean, you've had your day. But it's a pity for the boy, just starting out in life and getting mixed up with a trollop. You'll get by, it's no big deal, you let them have that room, and you sleep with Granny. You're not young things, you won't blush. Your mother's your mother, you used to live in the same room with her. I mean how did Mitya and I live? Mitya and I, and his mother and Granny Varya, all at the same time—plus Mitya's brother, and his brother's wife. Yes, and then we had Kostya. And all in one twenty-metre room.

FYODOR IVANOVICH: And fought like cats and dogs.

KLAVA: What do you mean? All right, there were fights at times, but Granny Varya always calmed things down. She was some woman, Granny Varya. Eh, Mitya?

UNCLE MITYA: Granny Varya's a wonderful person, not like you.

KLAVA: Huh, look who's talking!

UNCLE MITYA: What d'you want to get involved in other people's lives for?

KLAVA: Well, why do you think they've invited us?

UNCLE MITYA: I don't know why they invited us, but I know why you wanted to come.

KLAVA: Oh, don't talk rubbish!

UNCLE MITYA: Why do you always have to poke your nose into other people's business? You're always the first, in nosying around.

KLAVA: You're in an absolute foul mood because of that chess tournament of yours. You didn't qualify, and now you're taking it out on me. King pawn two! Knight three!

GRANNY: Oh shut up, Klavdia! Nothing suits you. Mitya used to drink, and you couldn't be doing with that. He's got an ulcer, and you gave him a hard time again. Now he plays chess, and you're still not happy. D'you remember how you complained when Mitya was sick, and going on about his illnesses all the time? Eh? You used to say he'd be better drinking like other people, instead of smelling like a chemist's shop!

UNCLE MITYA: Oh, that's great. Now they've turned on me.

[NIKOLAI *enters.*]

KLAVA: Sit down, sit down beside us, have a seat by the old folks. Take your time. You just wait till you get married, then you'll realise you were running for nothing!

FYODOR IVANOVICH: Sit down, sit with us a while.

NIKOLAI: Papa, I've got to go. Well, okay, I'll have a bite to eat. What the hell, I'm hungry, comrades.

TAISA PETROVNA: Obviously they didn't feed you right at that place. And I made a whole pile of sandwiches.

KLAVA: It's not a matter of what they fed him, but of what gives him an appetite. Isn't that right, Kolya? Let's have a drink.

UNCLE MITYA: Go ahead and eat, don't listen to them. And don't drink. I'm not drinking either, just eating, so you and me'll make two. Let's have some tea.

KLAVA: You'd be better off having a drink with me, Kolya.

[*They drink.*]

KLAVA: So. We've heard all about her, we've been hearing about your girlfriend.

NIKOLAI: What have you been hearing?

KLAVA: That she's a smart girl, game for anything, independent, that she works hard on a building site. She's what, casual labourer?

NIKOLAI: That's right.

FYODOR IVANOVICH: She's a painter.

KLAVA: Well, so what if she is just a labourer? That's all the same to you, Kolya, isn't it? You don't choose a wife for her education, or her certificates, right? So what if she can't even read! All you need is a nice lively girl, one that'll run after you, and dye her hair, and pluck her eyebrows and so on. Somebody that smokes and can take a drop of vodka, right?

NIKOLAI: Yes, well, you can take a drop yourself.

KLAVA: Who do you think you're talking to? I'm too old to be spoken to like that.

TAISA PETROVNA: Kolya, that's enough.

NIKOLAI: What are you getting so agitated about? D'you think I'm in some kind of danger? There's no danger, you can relax.

FYODOR IVANOVICH: We're not worried. In any case, we'll soon be getting carried out of here feet first.

TAISA PETROVNA: Kolya, why don't you see what's going on? How is it possible? I mean, you've been in the army, didn't the other lads talk to you?

KLAVA: All they get in the army is refresher courses in patriotism.

NIKOLAI: Exactly.

KLAVA: They teach them all to get married straight off. If you take a girl out, that's a commitment. Grab the first thing that comes along, as soon as you've got your hands on it.

TAISA PETROVNA: That's not the army, he's learned that from his father and me. He hasn't been brought up to anything else. But it's not the same thing as Fedya and me. We came together once and for all, for life. And that's a rare event. You don't find that right away.

UNCLE MITYA: So how then, by trial and error?

KLAVA: Trial and error if need be. You should understand, a man can look around nowadays, take time to think. You didn't think, you just got married. Now it's one word from me, and two from you, and that's it.

TAISA PETROVNA: I didn't want to tell you why this girl's hanging onto you, *why* she went to see you twice in Syzran, and visited me, taking a good look at what we had in the house.

NIKOLAI: Oh, of course, Mama, I'm well aware she wants our flat—our *lovely* polished furniture, the chandelier, Czechoslovakian glass, oh yes, and the carpet.

FYODOR IVANOVICH: [*Laughs.*] Well, you can joke, Kolya, but there's a grain of truth in every joke. A grain of truth, believe me.

NIKOLAI: And a grain of lies.

KLAVA: Well, my God, we'll find you a bride all right! Some good, hard-working girl that doesn't drink or smoke, with her hair in a braid . . . and younger than yourself.

NIKOLAI: Why go looking for her? She's there already, standing downstairs, waiting. She's been waiting for me since first grade at school. Doesn't smoke, drink, she's even got a pigtail, if she hasn't hacked it off.

TAISA PETROVNA: Your fiancée, do you mean?

NIKOLAI: That's her! I mean, she absolutely dotes on me. Everybody used to laugh at her, the way she ran after me. We'd go to play football, and she'd trail after me, carrying her little brother. Totally besotted, what more can you say?

KLAVA: [*Cheered.*] So bring her up here! Let's meet her!

UNCLE MITYA: Listen, it's time we were going home.

KLAVA: You go, I'll come later.

UNCLE MITYA: No, we're going!!!

KLAVA: Why, why can't you wait?

[*The doorbell rings.*]

NIKOLAI: I'll get it. It'll be for me. [*Exits.*]

FYODOR IVANOVICH: That'll be her from the hostel turning up now to spend the night. Bag and baggage on the doorstep, as they say.

KLAVA: I'll keep her in order.

UNCLE MITYA: And I'll keep you in order now. [*Makes to rise from the table.*] I'll sort you out.

KLAVA: Oh, Mama!

GRANNY: Huh, she's remembered she's got a mother.

KLAVA: We'll go now, Mitya dear.

[NIKOLAI *ushers in* ANNA STEPANOVNA.]

FYODOR IVANOVICH: [*Sarcastically.*] Ah, it's our dear invited guest!

TAISA PETROVNA: Fedya! Anna Stepanovna, sit down, have a bite to eat.

ANNA STEPANOVNA: No, no, I've no time. Taya, can you lend me a drop of salt? I've brought a glass. I'll give you it back.

GRANNY: Never give back salt or bread.

TAISA PETROVNA: Anna Stepanovna, of course I can, and I'll be obliged to you some time.

NIKOLAI: Sit down, Auntie Anna.

UNCLE MITYA: [*Pushes up a chair.*] You won't offend us, surely, by running away? What's your name?

ANNA STEPANOVNA: Anna Stepanovna.

UNCLE MITYA: [*Ushers her onto the chair.*] My dear Anna Stepanovna . . .

KLAVA: Now he's gone completely soppy.

[ANNA STEPANOVNA *reluctantly sits down.* UNCLE MITYA *pushes a plate and a glass towards her.*]

ANNA STEPANOVNA: No, thank you, I haven't time. They say an uninvited guest is worse than a Tartar.

FYODOR IVANOVICH. You might as well stay, now you've dropped in.

ANNA STEPANOVNA: I've no time, honest—I've been making rissoles, and the salt ran out. Then I remembered your gran got a packet off me, so I thought it would be easier to borrow from her.

GRANNY: When was this?

ANNA STEPANOVNA: It was last year, one Sunday evening after the grocer's was shut.

GRANNY: I did not.

ANNA STEPANOVNA: And I gave you a packet of yeast as well.

GRANNY: You certainly did not!

NIKOLAI: Granny has a terrible memory.

GRANNY: Yes, and why's that?

TAISA PETROVNA: [*Returns with the salt.*] Here you are, Stepanovna.

GRANNY: Oh, that's right!

ANNA STEPANOVNA: That's right, I did. Well, anyway, I'll have to go. [*Stands.*]

UNCLE MITYA: Sit down, sit down. [*Sits her back down.*]

[*There is a silence at the table.*]

ANNA STEPANOVNA: The Gavrilovs' girl's still standing outside.

TAISA PETROVNA: Who is?

ANNA STEPANOVNA: The Gavrilovs' girl, I said, from the first floor—she left the house this morning and she's been standing there the whole day.

FYODOR IVANOVICH: What's she doing that for?

NIKOLAI: I told you, she's waiting for me.

ANNA STEPANOVNA: Really! Ivanov's out of jail. You remember he got put in jail a year ago? And I'll tell you why—he'd come home blind drunk, and Granya didn't want to let him in, so he grabbed a lump of wood and started battering the door down. Galkin tried to drag him away, and he knocked Galkin out, concussion. Galkin wouldn't forgive him—he could've dropped the charge but he refused. Galkin used to be our locksmith, at the Housing Office. He quit not long ago.

GRANNY: I don't remember him.

ANNA STEPANOVNA: Galkin, of course you do. A lump of ice fell off the roof onto him that winter as well. They were clearing snow off the roof, and he was standing down below, to show it was a danger area. And it fell right on top of him. Knocked him out again.

GRANNY: I don't remember it.

ANNA STEPANOVNA: He brought you a toilet cistern as well, trying to sell it, and tripped on the doormat and smashed it. A toilet cistern!

GRANNY: What's he got to do with us?

ANNA STEPANOVNA: It's that Galkin I'm talking about.

GRANNY: He's back out of prison?

NIKOLAI: No, it's Ivanov that's out of prison.

ANNA STEPANOVNA: Their Nina was crying yesterday. Granya took him in, and Nina went out in the morning, and she's still standing there. That's seven hours already she's been stood there, and she won't go home. Sometimes she's standing on her own, sometimes Vitya wheels the pram out to her. I asked her what she was doing, she said she was out for a walk.

KLAVA: [*Brightly.*] She can come up here to us. Why not? Nikolai, go down and get her.

TAISA PETROVNA: Do, Kolya. On you go.

ANNA STEPANOVNA: I was a bit embarrassed to invite her to our place, she didn't want to admit she'd left home. It's Granya that's the problem, she's got no shame. Well, anyway, I'm off.

FYODOR IVANOVICH: Come again, bring us some more news. Give our regards to Sergei, why doesn't he drop in?

ANNA STEPANOVNA: He hardly ever drops in on anybody.

FYODOR IVANOVICH: He could always pop in and see me.

ANNA STEPANOVNA: That's not likely. Anyway, I'll be seeing you.

FYODOR IVANOVICH: Suit yourself.

[*They all say goodbye to* ANNA STEPANOVNA, UNCLE MITYA *even stands for the occasion.*]

Scene Ten

The yard. NINA *is standing with the pram.* ANNA STEPANOVNA *hurries past.*

ANNA STEPANOVNA: Well, are you still keeping an eye on my washing?

NINA: Of course I am.

ANNA STEPANOVNA: Hm—with all these jailbirds on the loose, a person can't live in peace. Well, I'm off, bye-bye for now, I'm making rissoles. [*Exits, and almost instantly returns.*] Oh, Nina, this is too much, I can't put up with this! I'm going to call the police! I can't have this, this is a dreadful carry-on! Oh!

NINA: What's up! What is it!

ANNA STEPANOVNA: Ivanov's in the entry, he's sitting there at the radiator. On his suitcase. Somebody should go to the phone-box, get them to come and damn well remove him! I'm going to tell Sergei, he can go and phone. Oh, this is a terrible business! [*Hurries out.*]

[NINA *wheels the pram to and fro, absently, for a few moments, then lifts the baby out and exits to the entry. After a while* IVANOV *emerges from the same place, looks around, shrugs, and stands beside the pram. Deep in thought, he takes the handle of the empty pram and begins to rock it, his face expressionless.* NINA *emerges from the entry.*]

NINA: Go home. Go on, take the pram up.

IVANOV: I haven't the right.

NINA: For God's sake, go.

IVANOV: I've just been released from detention, you know that.

NINA: Go on, take the pram, and carry it upstairs.

IVANOV: Is that any way to treat a person. One chases him out, another one chases him back. Is it? I'll just leave now and that'll be the end of it.

NINA: My God, he's like a child.

IVANOV: I don't want to, I'm not going back. So thanks for nothing, as they say, that's me finished.

NINA: I'll move out to a hostel, right? I won't bother you. You two can live however you like, without me.

IVANOV: I've no intention of bothering you, if it's me that's the trouble.

NINA: Anyway, just go.

[SERGEI ILYICH *emerges from the hallway and turns round the corner.*]

NINA: That's Uncle Sergei gone out. Honestly, you'd better get out of here quick. Sergei's gone to fetch the police. Go home.

IVANOV: Was it you that called them?

NINA: It wasn't me. [*An afterthought.*] Supposing it was me, what of it?

IVANOV: Well, if you called them, all right, we'll just wait to hear what you say. So what if I wind up in prison? [*Emotionally.*] First it's a children's home, then a hostel. You haven't a corner to call your own there either. They give you a room, that's it, and you can kiss that goodbye the same way. And now it's prison, that's my home. Eh? My God! [NINA *is crying.*] I thought, at last I had some place I could call my own. So, I got drunk, what of it? Does that mean you don't let a person in? Maybe I wasn't going to do it again. Let's say I wanted to apologise. And that was the reason I was knocking at the door. And then that Galkin appears. Trust him to poke his nose in! Shouting, don't you dare hit me, I've got a weak head! And I tell him to piss off. I told him didn't I? I did warn him?

[SERGEI ILYICH *returns and exits to the entry. He nods to* NINA *in passing.* NINA *tearfully tries to pull* IVANOV *into the entry, dragging the pram with her other hand.* IVANOV *won't let her wheel the pram, it's important that he explains himself.*]

IVANOV: I warned him, didn't I. Go away, I said, or I'll do you an injury. I'll thump you one . . .

[NIKOLAI *emerges from the hall.*]

IVANOV: I'll hit you so hard, you'll remember the name of Ivanov all right. He was told to clear off. I mean, I'm frightened of nothing. That's what I told him. Your weak head doesn't scare me.

NIKOLAI: Hey, take it easy, old man. Who are you going to thump? Maybe you want to try me, eh?

NINA: Kolya! Oh, Kolya love, leave him, let him go! [*Sobbing.*]

IVANOV: And who the hell are you?

NINA: Kolya, don't go near him, Kolya darling, please, don't touch him! Kolya! [*Flings her arms round him, restraining him.*]

IVANOV: Come on, who do you think you are?

NINA: Run, before it's too late!

IVANOV: Ivanov doesn't run. Who is this?

NINA: Kolya, I'll explain . . . I'll tell you all about it later. Please, Kolya, please, love, don't get involved with Ivanov.

NIKOLAI: I'm not scared of him.

NINA: Oh, God in Heaven, nobody's saying you're scared! I mean, he's a shrimp in comparison with you! He's old, he's weak.

IVANOV: Who's weak? Eh?

NIKOLAI: Yes, well, he's not too weak to beat up young girls.

NINA: Nobody was beating me up. Let's go, Kolya, I've got something to tell you. Come on. [*To* IVANOV.] Didn't I tell you to go home? Eh? Galka's got no pram there, there's nowhere to lay her down. Get away from here, run!

IVANOV: [*Querulous.*] Who is she to tell me to run?

NINA: Look, go away, Father, move!

[IVANOV *makes a grand exit to the hallway, with the pram under his arm, and carrying his suitcase.* NINA *releases* NIKOLAI. *She is breathing heavily. She fixes her braid at the back of her head, pulls up her shawl, with trembling hands, and smiles.*]

NINA: Now, why'd you have to get mixed up in other people's business?

NIKOLAI: It's always the same—when a bloke's beating up a woman, it's best not to interfere. The woman'll only start swearing at you as well. What were you defending him for? I'd have given him such a doing, he'd have forgotten the road home.

NINA: And who are you to do that?

NIKOLAI: Well, I had to defend you.

NINA: From him? He hadn't even touched me.

NIKOLAI: Yes, you can tell that to the birds. I mean, I heard him: 'I'll do you an injury, I'll thump you one!'

NINA: That wasn't at me.

NIKOLAI: Really? So who was it at then?

[IVANOV *emerges from the hallway without the pram, but carrying his suitcase.*]

NINA: What is it now?

IVANOV: I handed in the pram.

NINA: And what about yourself?

IVANOV: Well, she won't let me in.

NINA: Then I'll just have to go with you. [*To* NIKOLAI.] Can you wait here for two or three minutes, while I'm away?

NIKOLAI: Of course. [*Shakes his head wonderingly.*]

[NINA *and* IVANOV *go out to the entry.* SERGEI ILYICH *emerges soon after.*]

SERGEI ILYICH: Hello, Nikolai. Finished your army service now?

NIKOLAI: Hi. [*They shake hands.*] Yes, seems so.

SERGEI ILYICH: So you'll be going out to work?

NIKOLAI: Yes, looks like it.

SERGEI ILYICH: Mm. Well, I suppose so. Yes. Listen, you couldn't lend me a loaf of bread, could you? I went down to the bakery, but they're closed. Didn't make it in time. First she's no salt, next it's no bread.

NIKOLAI: I'll do that, sure.

SERGEI ILYICH: Well, could you run along and get it? Only don't say who it's for.

[NIKOLAI *exits.* NINA *reappears.*]

NINA: Hello, Uncle Seryozha.

SERGEI ILYICH: We've already met today, sort of. How are you doing?

NINA: Uncle Sergei, did you call the police?

SERGEI ILYICH: What? What police?

NINA: So where were you running off to?

SERGEI ILYICH: To the bakery. Why?

NINA: Auntie Anna told me she was going to send you to call the police.

SERGEI ILYICH: Huh, she wouldn't dare. What was this all about?

NINA: It was because of Ivanov—well, because our Ivanov was sitting in the entry.

SERGEI ILYICH: Oh I see, so we've to call the police? What, did he steal something or what? He's sitting there, so where's he going to go? He'll just sit for a while, and then he'll go. We should give him a bit of bread, and some money, and then he'll clear off. He doesn't have any other option.

[*A pause.*]

NINA: [*Carefully.*] So—has Auntie Anna sent you down to look after her washing?

SERGEI ILYICH: What's all this about sending? She sends me to the police, she sends me to the bakery, she sends me to keep an eye on her washing. I'm damned if I'll be sent anywhere!

NINA: [*Hastily.*] That's all right then, I'll look after it. I'm out for a walk anyway.

SERGEI ILYICH: What for? Go on home, go on. Standing guard, huh. Nobody's going to steal it, and she's hired somebody to stand guard!

NINA: Nobody hired me. It doesn't matter, it's okay.

SERGEI ILYICH: No, it's not. On you go home. Dammit, I'll look after the washing myself. It's my washing. On you go, there's no point in hanging about here.

[NINA *slowly goes up into the entry.* NIKOLAI *hurries out with the loaf of bread.* NINA *stops.* SERGEI ILYICH, *slightly embarrassed, takes the bread and thanks him, and without acknowledging* NINA, *goes past her into the entry.* NIKOLAI *stands at the foot of the stairs,* NINA *in the porch.*]

NIKOLAI: [*After a silence.*] Well, what is it you want? I've got to hurry to the shop, I've only half an hour.

NINA: What do I want? I don't want anything. It's just that Auntie Anna asked me to keep an eye on her washing, and I wanted you to stay for a while.

NIKOLAI: Oh, you're a crafty one, like a little mouse.

NINA: And you're thick, like an old felt boot. [*Laughs.*]

NIKOLAI: What are you laughing at?

NINA: I'm just laughing.

NIKOLAI: Well, anyway. I'll be seeing you.

[*Pause.*]

NINA: Cheerio.

[*Pause.*]

NIKOLAI: You know, you could go to our place. Mother's invited you.

NINA: [*Immediately.*] Let's go.

NIKOLAI: Well, I've got to dash out to the shop first. So wait for me.

NINA: Okay.

NIKOLAI: Right, I'll see you.

NINA: Cheerio.

[NIKOLAI *disappears round the corner.* NINA *rushes headlong into the entry.*]

Scene Eleven

The GAVRILOVS' *flat.* NINA *is rummaging in a wardrobe, while* VITYA *watches television.* IVANOV *is hiding in the kitchen.*

GRANYA: I don't want to speak to you. Not after that.

NINA: Mama, let me get changed in peace.

GRANYA: At least have your supper first. Really!

NINA: I've got ten minutes.

GRANYA: What's this all for? You're not going anywhere. It's late.

NINA: Mama, let me wear your blouse. The sparkling one.

GRANYA: Where do you think you're going? Who gave you permission?

NINA: Mama! Please—it's just next door.

GRANYA: Going out who with?

NINA: With nobody, I'm going to Nikolai's house.

GRANYA: What's this all about?

NINA: His mother's invited me, all right?

GRANYA: What on earth for?

NINA: Well, what if I just go and get married?

GRANYA: You haven't asked anybody's permission, and you're just going like that? Who says you can?

NINA: Mama, it's best if I just go my own way, I can't live here any longer.

GRANYA: And who's stopping you? Are we going through this again?

NINA: Nobody's stopping me, nobody, but please don't you try and stop me either, Mama. Let me have your blouse.

GRANYA: Take it.

NINA: Mama, don't think badly of me, please?

GRANYA: That's all you need, nothing's happened yet, he's not even proposed, and you're rushing straight in as if you were married already.

NINA: I'm going to get changed. [*Exits to adjoining room.*]

Scene Twelve

The yard. NINA *is standing in the same jacket, but wearing a fur hat, and leather, not felt, boots. She is carrying a handbag.* NIKOLAI *appears.*

NIKOLAI: Okay, let's go. What did you get all dolled up for? Did you nip home?

NINA: What business is it of yours?

NIKOLAI: Do what you like, it's all one to me. It was Mother that invited you.

NINA: Well, then, hold your tongue.

NIKOLAI: The wit's fairly sparkling tonight.

[NINA *laughs happily. They go upstairs to the entry.*]

Scene Thirteen

The KOZLOVS' *apartment,* NINA *is out of sight, in the hall.*

TAISA PETROVNA: Come on in, Nina dear, take off your coat and come in. Make yourself at home. You must be frozen? [*A silence.*] Well, I can see you are. It's been cold today, all the same.

[NINA *enters, followed by* NIKOLAI.]

TAISA PETROVNA: Oh, what a beautiful blouse you're wearing. Did you really buy that on your salary? [NINA *shakes her head.*] Go on in to the table. I'm making tea just now for the fifteenth time. We've had one visitor after another today. That's our relations just left, which is a pity. They'd have liked to meet you. You must be hungry? [NINA *shakes her head.*] Well, it doesn't matter.

NIKOLAI: [*Sarcastically.*] She's struck dumb at our magnificent splendour. The carpet, the sideboard, the chandelier. We dazzle everybody with these things.

TAISA PETROVNA: Really, Nikolai, why are you in such a bad mood? Don't take any notice of him, Nina. He's not as nasty as he seems.

NIKOLAI: Oh, stop twittering.

TAISA PETROVNA: Sit down there alongside Fyodor Ivanovich, introduce yourself. He'll look after you. I'll go and put on the tea. This is two days in a row we've been entertaining, so the table's a bit of a mess. [*Exits.*]

NIKOLAI: That's quite true; two days' entertainment.

FYODOR IVANOVICH: So, what's your place of work, Nina?

NINA: The grocery store. [*Clears her throat.*]

NIKOLAI: [*Sarcastically.*] She's lost her voice.

FYODOR IVANOVICH: No wonder! Standing all that time in the freezing cold. How many hours were you standing out there, Nina?

NINA: I wasn't standing. I was out for a walk with my little sister.

TAISA PETROVNA: [*Returning with a plateful of pastry slices.*] Well, these pastries have certainly come in handy. When I was baking, I was thinking it'd be the same as usual, we'd eat as many as we had room for, and nobody would want to see any more of them. But here they are, they've come in handy again. We've had a lot of people. I like a lot of visitors. A house without visitors is empty.

NIKOLAI: My, my, you'd have had to chuck them out, and now you don't need to.

[TAISA PETROVNA *gestures to her, to pay no heed to* NIKOLAI.]

FYODOR IVANOVICH: That little sister of yours—are you looking after her yourself?

NINA: Why? No, with Mama.

FYODOR IVANOVICH: But it was you that brought up your brother. I remember that.

NINA: Not at all. Mama helped.

TAISA PETROVNA: Mama helped! Some people help their mother, but here it's the other way round.

FYODOR IVANOVICH: Anyway, it looks as if you've brought up two kids on your own.

GRANNY: I was the same, we were left orphans, six of us, and I was the eldest. Father just wouldn't get married. And I was fourteen years old. The house caught fire one time, and I woke up—we were on fire!

FYODOR IVANOVICH: We've heard it before.

GRANNY: You've heard it, but she hasn't. Anyway, what could I do—I got everybody up, stood them on the windowsill, and opened the hopper. "Breathe in," I said, "And don't fall out!"

FYODOR IVANOVICH: What department do you work in?

NINA: I'm a trainee in the dairy section. [*Clears her throat.*]

FYODOR IVANOVICH: Is it hard work?

NINA: It was worse on the building site. Outside all the time, my nose swelled up, I had a fever, so I left.

GRANNY: I started at fourteen, glueing boxes. I'd set them all down beside me, and we used to complete a full person's norm in a day.

FYODOR IVANOVICH: [*To* NINA.] Come on, eat up, a working girl's got to eat.

NINA: No thanks, I don't want anything.

FYODOR IVANOVICH: You don't want anything? If you've come into our house, that's it, you've got to do what you're told. I'll give you a little bit of herring. And maybe you'll take a spot of wine, eh?

TAISA PETROVNA: That's enough from you.

FYODOR IVANOVICH: Oh, come on—you'll surely have a drink? Come on, don't be shy. Young girls aren't shy nowadays, they're into everything. Have a drink, we're all at home here, and you're one of us now, Kolya's fiancée, so they tell me.

[NIKOLAI *grunts,* FYODOR IVANOVICH's *persistence has more to do with contrasting* NINA *and* NADYA, *for* NIKOLAI's *benefit.*]

FYODOR IVANOVICH: Anyway, let's have a little drop. I'll pour you some.

NINA: [*Her mouth full.*] I don't want any!

FYODOR IVANOVICH: Oh, come on, let's get past "I don't want," eh?

TAISA PETROVNA: It's all right, that's enough. It's tea she wants.

FYODOR IVANOVICH: Maybe you'll have a smoke, then? Nina, love?

[NINA *looks in wonderment at* FYODOR IVANOVICH.]

NIKOLAI: Anyway, I'm off. I wish you all a pleasant evening's entertainment.

FYODOR IVANOVICH: [*Distracted from his little game.*] What are you rushing away for? Your fiancée's here. Sit down.

NIKOLAI: Fiancée yet! That'll be right.

TAISA PETROVNA: Where are you off to? It's late.

NIKOLAI: I told you, I had to rush.

TAISA PETROVNA: Nina's just arrived, and you're leaving? Maybe you could take Nina with you?

NIKOLAI: What d'you want to drive your visitor out of the house for? You invited her, she's your guest.

TAISA PETROVNA: But she'd love to go with you. Why should she want to stay with us? Isn't that right, Nina dear? You do want to go with Kolya?

NIKOLAI: I don't think anybody's asked me yet . . .

FYODOR IVANOVICH: Young people should be with other young people.

NIKOLAI: Anyway, I'm off.

TAISA PETROVNA: That's very nice! At least be back soon.

NIKOLAI: Yes, well, maybe I won't come back alone. Still want me back soon?

[*A silence.* NIKOLAI *exits.* FYODOR IVANOVICH, *deep in thought, strikes the table with his fist a few times.*]

TAISA PETROVNA: There'll be a film on the TV now. Nina dear, you're my guest, and I'm not letting you go anywhere. The men can go out wherever they like, but we two'll just sit here and twiddle our thumbs.

FYODOR IVANOVICH: He'll bring back some other one-night stand.

TAISA PETROVNA: Where to? There's no room for her here. We've no room now. Nina dear, you'll stay with us, won't you?

[NINA *nods. They all sit round the television set.* GRANNY *lies down on the couch and instantly falls asleep.* FYODOR IVANOVICH, *sitting in the armchair, nods off.* TAISA PETROVNA *closes her eyes, and* NINA *also dozes off. Intermittent gunfire on the TV, another patriotic war film. The doorbell rings, and* TAISA PETROVNA *goes to answer it. It is* GRANYA, *standing in the doorway.* TAISA PETROVNA *goes out onto the landing, closing the door behind her.* NINA *strains to hear them, from the other side.*]

GRANYA: I'm sorry to disturb you. You've got my Nina there.

TAISA PETROVNA: Yes?

GRANYA: She's got to get up early in the morning . . . so . . .

TAISA PETROVNA: I'm sorry, we're neighbours, but I don't know your name.

GRANYA: Agrafena Osipovna.

TAISA PETROVNA: I think we need to have a little talk.

[GRANYA *is alarmed.*]

TAISA PETROVNA: I know your situation. He's out of jail . . .

GRANYA: Oh, that's no problem.

TAISA PETROVNA: I mean you have to make up your mind—it's either him or your Nina. She's a grown-up young woman, it's awkward for her. She doesn't want to stay.

GRANYA: Well, that's all right, he can just go.

TAISA PETROVNA: But why? Look, I understand. You're still a young woman, younger than me, I'm quite sure. You haven't had much of a life. Is that right?

GRANYA: Well . . .

TAISA PETROVNA: But Nina's a fine-looking girl, decent, hardworking. She'll soon get married in any case. And you'll be on your own again.

GRANYA: So?

TAISA PETROVNA: Anyway, I can take Nina in. We all like her. You understand? She'll live with us, get used to us. No one'll harm her. We won't touch her. She needs to study more, too. Get some decent qualifications, unlike now.

GRANYA: She didn't manage to get an education, of course.

TAISA PETROVNA: So you understand . . . You think about it. You'll get settled down meantime, he'll find a job, but Nina has to study. Only how are you going to get along without her? She's practically like an unpaid nanny to your little girl. I can well understand you won't manage without her.

GRANYA: There's no need to think like that.

TAISA PETROVNA: Well, I know how difficult it is with a young baby.

GRANYA: Difficult or not, I'll get by. Of course, she should have qualifications. And she's clever with her hands, too.

TAISA PETROVNA: I'll tell you what. Let's you and me make an agreement, my dear. If she's going to stay with us, she won't come back to you again. Why should she? She'll have a family here, there's no sense her battling on two fronts. Right?

GRANYA: Well . . .

TAISA PETROVNA: So I'm asking you not to bother her. Don't come for her, don't phone her up and so on.

GRANYA: Let her come back home just for today. Just today. To get something together for her.

TAISA PETROVNA: No, no, don't bother—she doesn't need a dowry.

GRANYA: Let her come home today.

TAISA PETROVNA: All right, have it your way. But if you're going to ask that right at the start, then that's it, I'm not keeping her. That's the end of it.

GRANYA: I'm not asking. I just thought . . .

TAISA PETROVNA: Well, you know what thought did—if you'll pardon the expression.

GRANYA: [*On the verge of tears.*] Taisa love, you'll look after her, won't you.

TAISA PETROVNA: What on earth are you saying that for? That makes me sick, that kind of talk.

[GRANYA *shrugs.*]

TAISA PETROVNA: Well, then, I wish you all the very best.

GRANYA: And the same to you.

TAISA PETROVNA: Only I'm asking you—don't bother her. Don't keep coming to the door.

GRANYA: I understand. So—goodbye for now.

TAISA PETROVNA: Goodbye.

[NINA *has been listening to the whole conversation reacting to every turn of events, now giv-ing little noiseless starts, now clenching her fists.* TAISA PETROVNA *comes into the room.* NINA *greets her with an exultant expression, ready to fling herself round her neck.*]

TAISA PETROVNA: This table needs clearing. [*Yawns.*] All that eating and drinking.

NINA: I'll take these out, shall I? [*Begins to clear the table.*]

ACT TWO

Scene Fourteen

The KOZLOVS' *apartment three months later.* NINA *is alone, wearing a new coat. She is standing in front of a mirror, having a look at the back and sleeves. This dumb show is interrupted by a ring at the doorbell.* NINA *goes to open it, and ushers in* GRANYA, *with baby* GALKA *in her arms.* GRANYA *kisses the dismayed* NINA *and sits down with the baby at the table . . . She looks frantic, although she continues to smile.* NINA *had managed to whip off the coat quickly, and now takes it to hang up in the wardrobe.*

GRANYA: They've bought you a new coat?

NINA: What do you want? Mama, what is it you want?

GRANYA: Go on, put it on.

[NINA *reluctantly puts the coat on.*]

GRANYA: Hm. It's too big.

NINA: So?

GRANYA: How much did they pay for it?

NINA: Mama, honestly—you've come in here . . .

GRANYA: Yes, I'm here, so what? I've got to go into hospital . . . it's just for three days . . .

[*A pause. The implication is that it's for an abortion.*]

I might be home earlier, I'll try anyway.

NINA: Oh, I see.

GRANYA: Well, you'll understand now.

[*A pause.*]

NINA: You know, I don't have any say here. I can't do anything.

GRANYA: They bought you a coat.

NINA: A coat's different. That's different altogether.

GRANYA: Let's go home.

NINA: No.

GRANYA: I'm afraid to leave Galka with him. He's already taking her out for walks, getting a little nearer to the off-sales each time. Where all that mob are.

NINA: Mama, how can I? I'm here today, but they could ask me to leave tomorrow, don't you understand?

GRANYA: Let's go home then.

NINA: You're only thinking of yourself, you don't think about me. You only need me as a babyminder. But I'm a human being.

GRANYA: But Galka's got to be fed, for a day and a half at least.

NINA: Take her with you.

GRANYA: They won't allow her in.

NINA: Well, I don't know.

GRANYA: [*Sighs.*] You know, you've become so . . .

NINA: So what?

GRANYA: Look, take her and change her nappy, do. My arms are about dropping off.

NINA: [*Takes the baby.*] My goodness, you've got so heavy! Who's my lovely little girl, eh? Are you my Galya? Are you my darling little Galka?

[*She takes* GALYA *with the bag of nappies into the next room.* GRANYA *puts some prepared baby's bottles on the table and quietly exits. The front door slams.* NINA *rushes out with the unfolded nappy, runs out to the hall, comes back in again, sees the feeding bottles, sits down at the table and starts crying. Then, still racked with sobs, she picks up the bottles, and goes into the adjoining box-room to fix the nappy. There is a noise at the outside door, and* GRANNY *enters. She listens to* NINA *weeping bitterly, sits down on the settee, sees the discarded coat, and shakes her head, hangs the coat up in the wardrobe. She sits down again, takes a nightdress out of her bag, and tries it against herself, looking in the mirror. The tearful* NINA *emerges then, cautiously, draws the door tightly shut behind her, locks it, and puts the key in her pocket.*]

NINA: That's very nice.

[GRANNY *says nothing, turns this way and that, inspecting herself in the mirror.*]

NINA: It's a good thing it has long sleeves. Keep you warm.

GRANNY: I'm too warm as it is in that kitchen.

NINA: Did you get your pension?

GRANNY: Mind your own business.

NINA: [*Silenced, briefly.*] How much?

GRANNY: What?

NINA: How much was it? [*Clears her throat.*]

GRANNY: It's my own money. Supposing it was just three roubles, it's mine.

NINA: That's good. Quite cheap.

GRANNY: Yes, well, I can't buy dear. I've got to get ready . . . for the old folks' home. I can't sleep in that damn kitchen the rest of my life. Supposing I take ill. They'll all start wiping their feet on me.

[NINA *sighs.* GRANNY *lays the nightdress down, sits deep in thought.*]

GRANNY: You think you've got everybody under your thumb here. What were you trying on Taisa's coat for?

NINA: She said she'd make me a present of it.

GRANNY: Huh—nobody ever gives me anything. They'll give me a shroud, maybe, for my grave. Unless they bury me in my old nightdress.

NINA: You shouldn't talk like that, Granny. It isn't nice.

GRANNY: You dry your own tears. It's not right, you know—you've driven an old person out of her own bed. You're crying, but I'm not. Why don't you just bugger off out of here, eh? What are you doing here anyway? You've got no shame. He's not going to marry you, he needs you like a hole in the head.

NINA: Don't you nag at me, Granny. I've enough without you. I don't need you as well.

GRANNY: [*Not in the least angry.*] Huh, now you're talking like a human being, on your own account. Well, you speak the truth, do you hear, don't put on an act for people, or make things up. And I'll tell *you* the truth. You're fed up here, right? And for why? I mean, who are you, to start with?

NINA: I'm Kolya's wife.

GRANNY: So who's taken you to the Registry Office, then?

NINA: That's only a bit of paper, that's all.

GRANNY: So why don't you have one? A scrap of paper, but you haven't got one. That's because he doesn't want you.

NINA: Why's that? He would tell me directly, surely.

GRANNY: Why should he? This suits him nicely. He wants you all right, for all kinds of things, he's not fussy. But he doesn't want you as a human being. No way.

NINA: You can't know that.

GRANNY: Because he doesn't fancy you. You're too young, whatever it takes you haven't got it, you're no good at it.

NINA: You can't know that.

GRANNY: You should've led him on, the way young girls do, the way all women do. You should've made yourself up, had your hair permed. You should have had a laugh with him, joked a bit. You shouldn't have let him see you needed him. You'd have got your feet under the table straight away. Now he's maybe got another girl.

NINA: That's not true.

GRANNY: It is true. He's just sticking with you because he's bored stiff. To tell you the truth, his parents have flung you at him. And he's a young lad, fresh out the army. He's never given it a thought.

NINA: You can't know that.

GRANNY: I can't? Oh yes I can! At first he didn't even want to know you. Then his parents put up a folding bed for him in your room. And chucked his old granny out into the kitchen, for God's sake! And you're delighted.

NINA: [*Flushed with anger.*] You don't know anything, how can you talk like that.

GRANNY: So how should I talk? You're crying, that's just water. It's me that should be crying. You can go anywhere you like—even to a hostel, or back to your mother. But where can I go? Klavdia's, that's all, and she makes so much damn noise, she doesn't even scruple to shout at her own mother. That's why I can't live with her, on account of all the shouting. She's kind enough, but her tongue goes all the time like the clappers. And now it's even noisier here . . . Oh, anyway, I suppose I'd better put away my nightdress. [*Goes to the door, tries the handle.*] What's this? What's going on?

NINA: You can't go in there.

GRANNY: What d'you mean, I can't? D'you expect me to drag this around in my teeth, is that it?

NINA: Don't go in there.

GRANNY: Give me the key, I'm telling you! You're getting above yourself.

NINA: Later.

GRANNY: Well, you just wait! [*Sits down distractedly.*]

[TAISA PETROVNA *enters.*]

TAISA PETROVNA: It's pretty cold.

[*A silence.*]

TAISA PETROVNA: Did you buy something?

[*She goes to the wardrobe, changes her clothes behind the door.*]

GRANNY: I bought . . . my shroud [*Starts crying.*]

TAISA PETROVNA: Listen, you're still . . . [*Struggling out of her dress.*] You're still going to outlive us. Now that's enough.

GRANNY: Well, you just wait, and I'll tell you . . .

[NINA *opens the door and instantly vanishes into the next room, closing the door behind her.*]

GRANNY: Did you see that? Did you see her? She won't let me into my own room, to put my clothes away. Into my own room!

TAISA PETROVNA: That's the trouble with you two . . . you've nothing to do. You're at it the whole time, squabbling from morning to night.

GRANNY: Don't you lump her along with me.

TAISA PETROVNA: Mama, I'm just in from work. Are we going to eat? Let's just wait for Fedya. Oh, my feet are killing me. So, all right, you sit on your behind all day at work, but then you've got to stand on the metro, and stand on the bus as well—you just get so *tired.*

GRANNY: And I come in, you understand, and I want to put something away in my own chest of drawers . . . my own chest of drawers.

TAISA PETROVNA: Well, we can put it in the wardrobe.

GRANNY: Why should I do that? I want to put it away in my own room. [*Crosses to the door and pounds it with her fist.*] Open up, d'you hear!

TAISA PETROVNA: That's enough, don't start hammering at the door. My head's splitting without that. We've too much stuff here anyway, more than we need.

GRANNY: So, does that mean me? Am I more than we need?

TAISA PETROVNA: Why you? Why does it always have to be you? You take everything to yourself.

GRANNY: And as for her—I told her to go home to her own house.

[TAISA PETROVNA *emerges from behind the wardrobe door, lies down on the divan, leafs through the television programmes.*]

TAISA PETROVNA: Obviously Nikolai's not keen on this arrangement. Not much, anyway. And we've done our bit, what more can you ask?

GRANNY: That's what I'm saying.

TAISA PETROVNA: [*Yawns.*] For some reason it just hasn't worked out. Kolya does nothing but sleep here. He's cut himself off.

GRANNY: He'll start drinking like that, and going out whoring, he'll keep going out. There's nothing of any interest to make him come home.

[*She says all this loud enough to be heard behind the door.*]

GRANNY: What I'd like to know is where he goes.

TAISA PETROVNA: [*Equally loud.*] Well, he's a young lad. Who knows?

GRANNY: She hasn't house-trained him, that's for sure.

TAISA PETROVNA: That's true. [*Yawns.*] Huh, hockey again. [*Now speaks normally.*] Fedya'll be home directly, he'll be a pain in the arse the whole evening.

GRANNY: [*Towards the door.*] And she's locked herself in, yet! [*Goes up to the door, pounds it with her fist.*] Open up! Open up, or it'll be the worse for you!

TAISA PETROVNA: Don't, that's enough.

GRANNY: [*Retreats.*] Well, I'd like to know just what's going on?

[*A noise at the outer door.*]

TAISA PETROVNA: That's Fedya coming in. That's him now. Mama, go and heat something up for him, my feet are about dropping off . . .

[GRANNY *exits.* FYODOR IVANOVICH *enters.*]

FYODOR IVANOVICH: Good evening. There's hockey on tonight. No sign of the young people?

[NINA *emerges, as if she has just been waiting for him.*]

NINA: [*Delightedly.*] Good evening!

FYODOR IVANOVICH: What, have you been sitting in the dark? Is Kolya asleep?

TAISA PETROVNA: He hasn't come home yet.

FYODOR IVANOVICH: So, have you been asleep then?

[NINA *shakes her head.*]

FYODOR IVANOVICH: Your face is all red.

[NINA *shrugs.*]

TAISA PETROVNA: She and Mama have been fighting again.

FYODOR IVANOVICH: [*Waves his hand dismissively.*] How many times have I told you, Nina love—you shouldn't take offence at people not right in the head . . . Really, Nina, don't take things to heart so much. I mean, I don't know how many rows I've had with my mother-in-law, I've tried to keep the peace as well. Nothing worked. So I've given up, what the hell, and just stopped paying her any attention.

TAISA PETROVNA: Fedya, how could you! I don't know how you can say that!

FYODOR IVANOVICH: Well, all right then—

TAISA PETROVNA: I mean, really . . .

FYODOR IVANOVICH: Okay, okay.

TAISA PETROVNA: I don't allow people to shout at Mama, and I never have.

FYODOR IVANOVICH: Oh, give it a rest.

TAISA PETROVNA: Now, just hold on, why do you always make me shut up? Why do you do it?

FYODOR IVANOVICH: Me?

TAISA PETROVNA: I won't have people shouting at Mama, raising their voices to her. Nobody, do you hear? Nobody's to be rude to my mother, she's had a lot to put up with in her life, you know! And now she's still got to cry?

NINA: I didn't . . .

TAISA PETROVNA: It's bad enough my mother has to live in the kitchen, to spend her last days there. My heart bleeds for her, but Fyodor Ivanovich and I are saying nothing, we're not saying a word, because what can we do, after all? You've got to give way to the young people. And we're giving way. But the young ones owe us something, too. Even if it's only not to show their bad character.

NINA: I didn't show anything of the kind.

TAISA PETROVNA: God almighty, I'm sick of this. Young people nowadays are so damned clever, is it really that difficult to understand that it's not easy, living together? And if people are openly rude, if they're just going to come right out with it, in this kind of situation, well then, you can't even live in your home!

NINA: But I wasn't rude . . .

FYODOR IVANOVICH: Now you shut up and listen.

TAISA PETROVNA: People don't cry for nothing. Mama didn't even cry when Papa was killed at the Front, and now she's going to cry because of you? That's too much, surely!

NINA: What was she crying about?

FYODOR IVANOVICH: Listen, listen.

TAISA PETROVNA: And in any case I'm going to tell you a thing or two . . .

[*The doorbell rings.*]

NINA: [*Rushes to open the door.*] It's Kolya!

[NINA *ushers in not* KOLYA, *but* IVANOV. *He looks agitated.*]

IVANOV: Hello, everybody. Hello, Nina.

[NINA *is stunned, nods. The others remain silent.*]

IVANOV: Nina, I want a word with you.

[NINA *and* IVANOV *move a little way apart. He whispers.*]

IVANOV: So where's my Galka, then?

NINA: [*Whispers.*] What do you mean?

IVANOV: [*Whispers.*] Granya—did she take her with her to the hospital?

NINA: [*Whispers.*] How should I know?

IVANOV: [*Out loud.*] She didn't say anything, she just went off with Galya. [*Whispers.*] She didn't leave any money . . .

NINA: She'll be back tomorrow night.

IVANOV: And what'll I do meanwhile?

[*The whole of the ensuing conversation is in whispers.*]

NINA: I don't know, I haven't anything.

IVANOV: Ask them for three roubles.

NINA: What for?

IVANOV: I haven't anything to eat.

NINA: Mama's surely left something. Try the plastic bag hanging up by the window.

IVANOV: Since when? [*Aloud.*] You couldn't let me have a three-rouble note till tomorrow night?

[NIKOLAI's *parents exchange glances.*]

FYODOR IVANOVICH: I've hardly anything on me. Hold on and I'll see.

[*Rummages in his jacket pocket, glancing at his wife.*] ·

TAISA PETROVNA: [*Not looking at* IVANOV.] We're not a savings bank, you know.

IVANOV: I will give it back.

FYODOR IVANOVICH: I think I've got something here . . . two roubles.

IVANOV: That's fine, that'll do. I mean, I'll give it back. [*Solemnly places the two roubles in his pocket.*] So, until we meet again . . . Huh, family—well, they . . . you know how they treat each other. Thank you for your kindness anyway.

FYODOR IVANOVICH: That's okay. No problem.

IVANOV: Well, I'll excuse myself in that case. [*Exits.*]

TAISA PETROVNA: Well!

NINA: What did you want to give him money for? Oh!

TAISA PETROVNA: [*Changed tone.*] You're a strange girl. We're not beasts, you know. We had to give him it.

FYODOR IVANOVICH: Today we give him, tomorrow he gives us. He'll help us out too.

TAISA PETROVNA: We're always ready to help anyone, Nina. You know that yourself. But you know what happens—you give a person your whole heart and soul, and they give you their arse to kiss. It's not a nice thing to say, but that's how it is.

NINA: But why did you give to him!

TAISA PETROVNA: We give to everybody. We don't ask anything from anybody, but they all batten on us. Because they know what we're like. Everybody hangs round our neck, literally everybody, and we have to carry them all. Why is it we've always got, and they haven't? I mean, we could be as bad as them, we could go around with the arse out of our trousers, and not give it a thought. We could have an easy life, you know, and not give a damn. But we take on the world's burdens. We're ready with two roubles, or a coat, or whatever, anything for peace.

[NINA *is about to speak.*]

FYODOR IVANOVICH: No, Nina, you listen.

TAISA PETROVNA: It's as if we were the only people in the world that had anything to give. Because nobody but us seems to bother, nobody takes thought, or saves anything. But we never throw anything out, we hold onto everything. So because of that we've got to be the fairy godmothers, and dole out to everybody, right, left and centre. But we need some peace as well. So people aren't tormenting us the whole time, but let us have our last few years in peace. We've never lived just the two of us, Fedya and I, on our own, I can tell you. There's always somebody or other.

FYODOR IVANOVICH: [*Animatedly.*] That's absolutely right. I'll vouch for that. We've always had the mother-in-law.

TAISA PETROVNA: We need to have a serious think about this, Nina. And most of all *you've* got to think. About what your position is in this family, and how you should behave.

NINA: But I didn't say anything.

TAISA PETROVNA: Anyway that's no longer the point. Time's running out. I mean, Fedya and I . . . you understand? I mean, it doesn't depend on us. After all, we can't . . . we can't marry you. [*An involuntary smile.*]

NINA: What d'you mean?

TAISA PETROVNA: Well . . . [*Smiles again.*] I mean, it's got to be Kolya. You can't force him, after all. And it's not up to us—without him, we can't . . .

NINA: Of course not.

TAISA PETROVNA: How, of course not? Does that mean Kolya has . . . ?

NINA: [*Startled.*] Kolya has what?

TAISA PETROVNA: I mean, has Kolya said anything?

NINA: I don't know . . .

TAISA PETROVNA: What's to know? Has he said anything to you?

NINA: Sort of.

TAISA PETROVNA: What did he say?

NINA: He did say something.

TAISA PETROVNA: That he'd marry you?

NINA: No. Well, he said something . . . just bits and pieces.

TAISA PETROVNA: Oh, I see, that. That doesn't count. There'll need to be a serious talk with Kolya about this matter. It's got to come out into the open. What his intentions are. You can't drag him by the hair.

FYODOR IVANOVICH: These things have to be gone into willingly.

TAISA PETROVNA: Because we're already being treated as if we were your relatives here, and Kolya seems to know nothing about it.

NINA: Oh, that's just Ivanov . . . He's like that. He was only joking.

TAISA PETROVNA: Because we'll wind up related to God knows who. I mean, Kolya's young, he's hanging around God only knows where, he's maybe making other relatives for us! [*A pause.*] Anyway, Nina, we agreed that none of your relations, while you were staying here out of Ivanov's road, would come to this door.

NINA: They won't, they won't, honestly.

TAISA PETROVNA: Somehow I find that hard to believe.

[*The sound of a baby crying is heard.* NINA *rushes headlong into the other room.*]

TAISA PETROVNA: What's that? Eh? What is it?

[TAISA PETROVNA *and* FYODOR IVANOVICH *peer cautiously into the other room, and stand dumbstruck.* GRANNY *emerges from the kitchen, and also has a look.*]

GRANNY: Well, well—there it is.

[TAISA PETROVNA *and* FYODOR IVANOVICH *return to their seats at the table.* GRANNY *remains standing by the door, as if she's determined not to let anyone close it again.*]

TAISA PETROVNA: Well . . . that's interesting.

FYODOR IVANOVICH: What the hell are we going to do now? [*Attempts a joke.*] Maybe we should adopt this one too?

TAISA PETROVNA: Yes, it's a true saying—good deeds need to be able to use their fists. Otherwise people'll sit down and eat you out of house and home.

GRANNY: [*Into the doorway.*] She's got the teat plugged up—she's got it clogged. Turn the bottle up, don't you see? Oh, you're hopeless!

[*Exits into the side room.*]

TAISA PETROVNA: You know what's going to happen now?

FYODOR IVANOVICH: Yes, yes.

TAISA PETROVNA: They'll dump her little brother on us next. We'll have a children's home here. Because that drunk's sitting up there, and the children have no place to go!

FYODOR IVANOVICH: Yes, yes.

[GRANNY *returns to her post but can't resist prompting her.*]

GRANNY: Her nappy's worked loose. Her legs are right out—and it's winter yet! I can't stand this.

[*Again she exits into the adjoining room.*]

TAISA PETROVNA: We'll need to do something.

NINA: [*Appearing at the door.*] They've taken Mama into hospital.

TAISA PETROVNA: Hospital?!

NINA: It's only for three days. Maybe less.

TAISA PETROVNA: [*Stunned.*] Well, really!

NINA: And that'll be it finished, then.

TAISA PETROVNA: Well, thank God for that at least.

NINA: It's for three days, that's all. Maybe even less.

TAISA PETROVNA: And why's this landed on us?

[*The doorbell rings.*]

NINA: It's Kolya!

[*She rushes into the hall, they all stand looking towards the door.* NINA *ushers in a young girl, pregnant, with her face muffled up.*]

TAISA PETROVNA: Nina, there must be some mistake. What did you bring her straight in here for? Who is it you're looking for? Who do you want?

[*The girl removes her headscarf. It is* NADYA.]

NINA: She said she was looking for Nikolai.

TAISA PETROVNA: Nikolai who?

NADYA: Kozlov.

TAISA PETROVNA: What for?

NADYA: On a personal matter.

[*She wipes her nose with the end of her headscarf.*]

FYODOR IVANOVICH: Which Kozlov?

NADYA: Yours, of course. [*Stuffs her headscarf into her bag.*]

FYODOR IVANOVICH: [*Recognises* NADYA.] Oh yes—and who might you be, when you're at home?

NADYA: That's of no consequence.

FYODOR IVANOVICH: I see—so that's how it is.

[GRANNY *appears in the doorway.*]

GRANNY: Oh! Long time no see. It's her! Ai-yi-yi . . .

[TAISA PETROVNA *sits down on a chair.* FYODOR IVANOVICH *slumps against the wall.*]

GRANNY: Hello!

NADYA: Cheers. [*Her manner is rather off-hand and listless.*]

TAISA PETROVNA: And you're who—forgive me, what's your name?

NADYA: Nadyezhda.

TAISA PETROVNA: How come I didn't recognise you straight away?

GRANNY: She's changed.

FYODOR IVANOVICH: She certainly has changed.

[NINA *exits to the side room. A silence. It is clear that* NADYA*'s appearance has produced such a grave and terrible impression on them all, that they feel an involuntary compassion for her, but they successfully manage to overcome this feeling.*]

TAISA PETROVNA: [*Finding the necessary tone.*] Well, just think, eh?

FYODOR IVANOVICH: Yes, you couldn't dream up a situation like this if you tried.

GRANNY: These women again . . .

TAISA PETROVNA: [*Sympathetically.*] Are you hungry?

NADYA: Yes.

TAISA PETROVNA: Take your coat off and sit down. Mama, let's have some supper in here.

[NADYA *takes her coat off in the hall, re-enters the room and sits down.* GRANNY *and* TAISA PETROVNA *lay the table, bring in the food.*]

TAISA PETROVNA: Sit in at the table, Nadya. There's bread there, and butter.

[NADYA *begins eating, while everyone watches her.*]

GRANNY: She's changed . . .

FYODOR IVANOVICH: Certainly has.

TAISA PETROVNA: What month are you in, Nadya?

NADYA: Seventh.

FYODOR IVANOVICH: You don't say! [*Checks himself.*] Yes, Nadya, if you don't mind me saying so, you look . . . well . . . you don't look right, your hair isn't right.

NADYA: I've been in hospital.

TAISA PETROVNA: Nothing serious, I hope?

NADYA: Well, it was a bit . . .

FYODOR IVANOVICH: Well, well . . . so . . . so, what are you going to do now?

NADYA: [*Shrugs.*] God knows.

FYODOR IVANOVICH: Have you registered a husband?

NADYA: A husband? Not officially.

FYODOR IVANOVICH: And you're living in the hostel?

NADYA: Yes.

FYODOR IVANOVICH: They've promised you a room?

NADYA: They've sort of promised—a while ago. Because I'm an orphan, so they said.

FYODOR IVANOVICH: So when are they going to give you it?

NADYA: In about two years from now, probably.

FYODOR IVANOVICH: Well, you should get one through your deputy. As a single parent.

NADYA: Yes, I should. I was flat on my back in hospital nearly two months.

TAISA PETROVNA: You should apply to the building site committee. The local committee women at our place make a fuss about these things.

NADYA: Yes. You wouldn't have a smoke, would you?

FYODOR IVANOVICH: I'm sorry, we don't smoke. Anyway, so who's the father?

TAISA PETROVNA: [*Interrupting.*] We don't smoke. We have a small child in the house.

NADYA: You have?

TAISA PETROVNA: That's right, we have.

NADYA: Since when?

TAISA PETROVNA: Not long since. [*Shouts.*] Nina love, come out here a second!

[NINA *appears in the doorway.*]

TAISA PETROVNA: There—this is Kolya's wife. An old flame, you could say.

FYODOR IVANOVICH: An old flame never dies out, eh?

TAISA PETROVNA: She's loved him since first grade at school, and now she's got him. Nina dear, sit down with us for a bit.

NINA: In a minute. I've just got to wash out some nappies.

[*Disappears into the bedroom and emerges with a pile of nappies, carries them through to the bathroom.*]

TAISA PETROVNA: [*To* NADYA.] So then, what brought you to see us?

NADYA: Well . . . I didn't have far to walk. I was passing by, and it occurred to me I knew some people here. I don't know anybody, apart from you.

FYODOR IVANOVICH: That's a likely story. I think you know plenty of people.

NADYA: Not those sort.

FYODOR IVANOVICH: Yes, I've heard that one before.

GRANNY: My, how you've changed—you just wouldn't believe it.

[*The baby cries.* TAISA PETROVNA *suddenly springs from her seat and rushes into the adjoining room, followed by* GRANNY. NINA *hurries in, wiping her hands en route.*]

FYODOR IVANOVICH: It's all right, it's all right, Nina love. They've gone in . . . the grannies have run in.

[NINA *exits again to carry on with the washing.*]

FYODOR IVANOVICH: They're all baby-mad, these women.

NADYA: Is it a boy or a girl?

FYODOR IVANOVICH: It's . . . er . . . what d'you call it . . . a little girl.

NADYA: What's her name?

FYODOR IVANOVICH: Er . . . we don't know yet.

NADYA: You haven't made up your minds?

FYODOR IVANOVICH: No.

NADYA: Mine's going to be a boy. Nikolai.

FYODOR IVANOVICH: [*Slyly.*] And the middle name?

NADYA: Nikolaevich, of course.

FYODOR IVANOVICH: What do you mean, Nikolaevich?

NADYA: It's Kolya's.

FYODOR IVANOVICH: Get away with you, that's nonsense! When was it you spent the night here?

NADYA: I travelled to see him at Syzran, you know.

FYODOR IVANOVICH: [*Scoffing.*] Oh come on, that goes for nothing—it could've been anybody's. Give over. Just what are you up to, for God's sake? I mean, it doesn't make any sense.

NADYA: So when did he manage to make a baby then?

FYODOR IVANOVICH: What, d'you think you're the only one that visited him in the army? Eh?

NADYA: Really? You're having me on.

FYODOR IVANOVICH: You think so? So when was it you came here with him to us, eh?

NADYA: Well, anyway—

FYODOR IVANOVICH: [*Making it up as he goes.*] We didn't want to tell Kolya about it straight away, to spoil things for him. I mean, after all, you only come out of the army once. But she lives in our block, everybody knows about it. She suffered too, you know, when Kolya brought somebody home.

NADYA: She did? Well, I suppose so. It'd be surprising if she didn't.

FYODOR IVANOVICH: Anyway, that's how things are. That's why we received you the way we did. You know yourself. You understand now?

NADYA: I just thought you were all nuts. Behaving like wild beasts. I thought, hell, what kind of family's that, I'd better off staying an orphan. And Kolya also seemed . . . Well, he wasn't his own man, he seemed weak. Not an independent person. A pain in the arse, frankly. Not my type, anyway. And that's what it was . . . Well . . .

FYODOR IVANOVICH: So why have you come to see us now?

NADYA: The other girls said he'd been in to see me. He'd looked in on the girls, but I'd asked them not to say anything to anybody.

FYODOR IVANOVICH: Well, you can drop in on us, if you want. Look in anytime. We're decent people, we'll do what we can. There's nappies there, matinée coats. We won't refuse you. We give to anybody that asks. But as for that being Kolya's, well, come on, I think you're exaggerating a bit there, wouldn't you agree?

NADYA: No, I wouldn't.

FYODOR IVANOVICH: [*Not listening.*] Still, we can always manage a little help. If a person's in trouble, and they've got no relatives, nobody they can turn to. Anyway, you just drop in, whenever.

NADYA: I'll be off now. First I've got to go somewhere.

FYODOR IVANOVICH: D'you want me to show you where it is?

NADYA: No, I remember. [*Exits.*]

[TAISA PETROVNA *and* GRANNY *are listening from the side room.* NINA *enters from the hall, disappears into the bathroom.* TAISA PETROVNA *enters.*]

TAISA PETROVNA: Well, let's have a bite of supper now, shall we?

[*The main door slams.* TAISA PETROVNA *and* FYODOR IVANOVICH *strain to hear—*NIKO-LAI *enters.*]

NIKOLAI: Who's here? Somebody's coat's hanging up.

TAISA PETROVNA: That belongs to Nina, it's Nina's. Come here, Kolya, come in. I've something to show you.

NIKOLAI: Let me get washed from work.

TAISA PETROVNA: Come on, come on. Guess who's in our bed there!

NIKOLAI: In our bed? [*Suddenly alarmed.*] Who is it?

TAISA PETROVNA: Come and see. [*Ushers* NIKOLAI *out.*]

[FYODOR IVANOVICH *jumps up, goes out into the hall, carefully closing the door behind him. The front door slams, it is* NADYA *leaving.* NIKOLAI, *and* TAISA PETROVNA *emerge from the side room.*]

NIKOLAI: What's she up to?

TAISA PETROVNA: Well, you see, Nina's mother's had to go into hospital. Not for very long. They've nobody to leave her with.

NIKOLAI: Yes, and for some reason or other, you're delighted. So where's she going to sleep?

TAISA PETROVNA: We'll put her on the folding bed.

NIKOLAI: And what about me?

TAISA PETROVNA: The same as always. With Nina.

[*A pause.*]

NIKOLAI: [*Gloomily.*] I see.

TAISA PETROVNA: Or we can fix up the armchairs. We can push the armchairs together.

NIKOLAI: What the hell did she bring her here for? That's bloody marvellous.

TAISA PETROVNA: Where have you been?

NIKOLAI: Why do you want to know?

TAISA PETROVNA: You're never at home, that's why.

NIKOLAI: So what am I supposed to do, enjoy myself here with you?

TAISA PETROVNA: And just who *have* you been enjoying yourself with? Are we allowed to know?

NIKOLAI: A few mates, that's all—we were making something. In one of the chaps' garage.

TAISA PETROVNA: Haven't you enough money?

NIKOLAI: God, you want to drag out every bit of information, everything. You keep on and on.

TAISA PETROVNA: Why can't you be like you used to be? Why d'you have to land up God knows where, when you've got your own home here.

NIKOLAI: What's this, d'you mean I'm not allowed out?

TAISA PETROVNA: Why do you have to go out all the time? You've got itchy feet. You've surely sown your wild oats now.

[FYODOR IVANOVICH *enters.*]

FYODOR IVANOVICH: Kolya, Kolya—East, West, home's best. I'm telling you that as a fact of life.

TAISA PETROVNA: What is it with you, Kolya, why are you deliberately closing your eyes to it all? Are you doing it on purpose? I just don't understand you.

FYODOR IVANOVICH: Well, Mama, it's time we married off our son.

NIKOLAI: What, has something happened?

TAISA PETROVNA: Why should anything have happened? Nothing of the sort.

FYODOR IVANOVICH: I mean, just how long can this go on?

NIKOLAI: As long as it takes, that's how long.

TAISA PETROVNA: No, don't say that, Kolya. That's never been the custom in our family, thank God. This is the first time this has happened to us, and we don't know what to do.

FYODOR IVANOVICH: But we understand. I mean, basically, we do understand. We know what it is, d'you see? I mean, a man's always going to come up against something for the first time, but there's got to be some rules.

NIKOLAI: Now hold on just a minute. You don't know the rules any longer, these rules you're talking about. People nowadays live all kinds of ways.

FYODOR IVANOVICH: Yes, people *may* do, but we do things *our* way. Maybe we're not modern! Out of the last century, eh?

TAISA PETROVNA: I mean, look at you, you're a married man, but you're carrying on like a bachelor.

NIKOLAI: That's rich. How come I'm a married man?

TAISA PETROVNA: Because when two people are living together, they're man and wife.

NIKOLAI: I can't believe what I'm hearing.

TAISA PETROVNA: Look, to get right to the point, I'm sick of this. There's nothing to discuss, I don't want to hear any more nonsense. Nina's living here, isn't she?

NIKOLAI: So, she can go.

FYODOR IVANOVICH: We'll see about that!

TAISA PETROVNA: What do you mean, she can go? How could she look people in the eye? She's had her time, she can just up and leave? Is that it? We took her into our house, then we got fed up with her, and now it's the parting of the ways?

FYODOR IVANOVICH: I won't have that.

NIKOLAI: God almighty.

FYODOR IVANOVICH: Nina, come out here.

[NINA *enters, wiping her hands.*]

TAISA PETROVNA: Sit down, Nina sweetheart.

NIKOLAI: Huh, it's Nina sweetheart next.

FYODOR IVANOVICH: The fact of the matter is, my dears, you'll just have to go and register your marriage.

TAISA PETROVNA: We want a bit of peace and quiet. And Mama can't sleep in the kitchen the rest of her life.

NIKOLAI: Well, that's fine, I'll sleep in the kitchen.

TAISA PETROVNA: No, it's too cramped here for us, with three generations.

NIKOLAI: As a certain smart young girl called Nadya said.

FYODOR IVANOVICH: Anyway, you'll have to register. That's enough. Dashing about here, there and everywhere, we've had enough of that.

TAISA PETROVNA: And see about buying a co-operative flat.

FYODOR IVANOVICH: That's a great idea. Melkonyan at our place has just been made chairman of the co-operative. Let me know, he says, if there's anything you need. Just the other day!

NIKOLAI: Look, if something's happened, you can tell me, surely. You're holding something back. I know you too well.

FYODOR IVANOVICH: It's just suddenly all boiled up. I mean, your place is here, in your own home, you ought to know that. You've done enough running around the hostels.

NIKOLAI: Not yet, I haven't.

FYODOR IVANOVICH: Well, I'm telling you that's it, finished, enough. Nina, you don't have any objection, do you?

NIKOLAI: Oh, she'll vote "yes" with both hands!

FYODOR IVANOVICH: Why do you have to act like this?

TAISA PETROVNA: You shouldn't hurt people's pride.

NIKOLAI: Well, that's rich. Pride! That's hardly the word here. Nadya's proud. *That's* pride.

FYODOR IVANOVICH: Huh, a lot you know.

TAISA PETROVNA: [*Interrupting.*] Anyway, you can go and apply at the Registry Office to-morrow.

NIKOLAI: Really?

FYODOR IVANOVICH: Yes, once you're registered as a family, then you can get your name down . . . for a car, for a Zhiguli.

TAISA PETROVNA: We'll need to buy Kolya a new imported suit then.

NIKOLAI: Is that a fact?

TAISA PETROVNA: And I've got some dress material, white. Now, hasn't that come in handy!

FYODOR IVANOVICH: We'll get you your own place, you'll be set up then, and we'll be fine here.

TAISA PETROVNA: Only there's to be no funny business tomorrow. You can ask for time off work. And it's maybe better if I call in for you, along with Nina.

NIKOLAI: Oh yes? And maybe I've got other plans.

FYODOR IVANOVICH: Whether you've got other plans, or another girlfriend, we don't know and don't want to know. That can stay shrouded in mystery, nobody's going to say another word about it. And it's no longer your concern.

NIKOLAI: My concern's my business, and mine only. Nobody else's.

FYODOR IVANOVICH: You'd better believe it.

TAISA PETROVNA: And that's exactly why you'll walk right into a trap.

NIKOLAI: What trap? I can take care of myself. Why can't you understand that?

FYODOR IVANOVICH: We understand perfectly well. But you're marrying Nina.

NIKOLAI: [*Genuinely.*] Why?

TAISA PETROVNA: Kolya, when you grow up you'll realise eventually how much we do understand. But it's got to be Nina, and only Nina, nobody else.

NIKOLAI: Nina, do you want to marry me that much?

[NINA *is silent.*]

NIKOLAI: I mean, I'll tell you the honest truth, I don't want to marry you. So how can you possibly go ahead after that?

NINA: That's up to you, Kolya.

TAISA PETROVNA: [*Outraged.*] What, you think the girl's in your power? You can treat her any old how?

NIKOLAI: Look, what's all this about? I don't understand why you're all pretending, when it's really quite simple. My God, you're something else. Nina knows all this, I've told her repeatedly. She's said herself that she knows, but this arrangement still suits her.

TAISA PETROVNA: Because she loves you!

NIKOLAI: Not quite, not quite, hold on a minute. It's Nina's own family she can't be doing with, that's why she was so willing to come here.

TAISA PETROVNA: But she's living with you!

NIKOLAI: Yes, she is. That's because she has to, she needs to. But I warned her, isn't that the truth, Nina? It's not very nice for her, to come out with it here in front of you, but it needs to be said, I think. Two people, a young man and a young woman, can live to-gether quite happily, if that's how they want it, if they're normal, healthy adults. That doesn't mean there's any feeling behind it. It's not unusual, a lot of people live like that. Their whole life even. A man needs to live with somebody, to satisfy his animal nature. You can't fight the battle on your own, as they say.

FYODOR IVANOVICH: What rubbish you talk, that's ridiculous!

TAISA PETROVNA: He's just picked that up from somewhere or other.

NIKOLAI: Raising a family isn't a chance business, it's something you have to think about. I've no intention of marrying Nina, I told her that right at the start, and she accepted it.

FYODOR IVANOVICH: Yes, well that's as may be, but we know you better than that, we know what's been going on, and who's been stirring up trouble. We know the score, Kolya. You think we don't know anything, but we do.

TAISA PETROVNA: It would suit you better to listen to what your father's saying, before it gets any worse.

NIKOLAI: Okay, but I'll go and get washed, my hands are all sticky.

FYODOR IVANOVICH: All right, if you must.

NIKOLAI: My hands are sticky.

TAISA PETROVNA: You see, Nina? Since childhood Kolya's been trained to wash his hands, that's how you should bring up your own children.

[NINA *nods, mechanically.*]

TAISA PETROVNA: And don't you worry. That's it now, you're on the right track. Did you think it was going to be so easy to get a man married off? You have to get up to all sorts of tricks. Even given them love potions to drink, all that sort of foolishness.

[*Whispers in* NINA*'s ear, laughs and spits.* NINA *nods.*]

FYODOR IVANOVICH: Is that the Solovievs you're talking about?

TAISA PETROVNA: Yes. Even saying this makes me sick, but they all do it.

[*Looks over at her husband.*]

TAISA PETROVNA: Still, when a man marries, that's him finished. On a leash. He gets used to one place, doesn't like losing it, it's too much effort. He'll stay where he's put, only you've got to meet him halfway, so he has some freedom. You can let him out, it's no big deal, he's not soap, he's not going to melt away. He'll drink beer in the pub, he'll play dominoes there, and whatever else. He'll watch football on the TV And you'll give him a baby. And that's it.

[NINA *nods.*]

TAISA PETROVNA: The main thing is that he should feel he's the boss.

FYODOR IVANOVICH: And he will be the boss. He's lucky to get you, Nina, don't put your-self down.

[NIKOLAI *enters. They all sit at table.* GRANNY *brings out the baby.*]

NIKOLAI: What have you brought her in for?

GRANNY: Let her have a look at people for a bit.

NIKOLAI: What's she going to see there? Upside down.

NINA: She sees everything. Anyway, it's time for her sleep, her little eyes are starting to close.

TAISA PETROVNA: We'll push the armchairs together for her at night. After Fedya's watched the TV, he likes to watch from the armchair. Lay her on the bed meantime.

NIKOLAI: I really don't like babies, I can't stand them. I get sick at the sight of them.

GRANNY: Put pillows round her in there, so she doesn't roll off.

[NINA *exits with* GALKA.]

FYODOR IVANOVICH: You get sick at the sight of other people's kids. But you can't see enough of your own. When you were a little boy, we went to see the city lights, and the fireworks. The cannons made so much noise, you were clinging onto my knees like grim death. You were shaking all over, cowering down, tears in your little eyes. It was so funny.

NIKOLAI: So why did you take me there, if I was frightened?

FYODOR IVANOVICH: Because I was going to root the fear out of you. I took you right underneath the cannon.

NIKOLAI: You wanted to make a man out of me? Totally fearless?

FYODOR IVANOVICH: You could say that.

NIKOLAI: That's all bullshit, as a certain girl used to say.

FYODOR IVANOVICH: You wait until Nina's had your son, we'll see what kind of father you turn out.

NIKOLAI: So what the hell, I won't make a good teacher. What can I teach anyway?

FYODOR IVANOVICH: Well, everyone sees where they've failed in their own lives, and they want their son to make up for it.

NIKOLAI: Make up for what?

FYODOR IVANOVICH: Well—everything. So that he'll forge ahead, develop his talents, if he has any talents. In music, for example. So he won't spend his life telling lies.

NIKOLAI: You used to beat me with a belt for telling lies.

FYODOR IVANOVICH: So I did.

NIKOLAI: And because of that I began to lie so well that you never suspected. And I know damn well when other people are lying. You two lie all the time, for example.

TAISA PETROVNA: And what do we lie about, I'd like to know, go on, tell us!

NIKOLAI: Everything.

FYODOR IVANOVICH: I can't believe my ears, I'm speechless.

NIKOLAI: Don't pretend you don't.

TAISA PETROVNA: You just remember what sort of mess we got you out of.

NIKOLAI: What you got me out of? Away from Nadya, do you mean? Is that it?

TAISA PETROVNA: What's Nadya got to do with it? We've saved you from messing up your life, you just think.

NIKOLAI: There was nothing to save me from. That's almost funny.

FYODOR IVANOVICH: I mean, basically, you're still a nobody. You see nothing and know nothing, like a blind man.

NIKOLAI: You don't say.

TAISA PETROVNA: Without us you'd fall flat on your face.

NIKOLAI: Yes, well that's where you're mistaken. I'm not going down the tubes anywhere or anytime. Nobody's going to have me for breakfast, so get that straight. I'll stand on my own two feet. I'll do my own thing.

FYODOR IVANOVICH: Yes, rubbish—that's your thing. Rottenness. That's what destroys a man. Drunkenness and all that carry-on. And that's just where you're headed.

NIKOLAI: Well, that's where you're severely mistaken. I know what I'm doing, and I'm not giving it up. I'll hang onto it with both hands.

FYODOR IVANOVICH: Yes, and what do you want to hang onto that one for? She's nothing but an unstable mess! She'll blame God only knows what on you, and you're happy.

NIKOLAI: I don't know what you're talking about.

[*The doorbell rings. They all fall silent.* FYODOR IVANOVICH *goes to open it and ushers in* ANNA STEPANOVNA.]

FYODOR IVANOVICH: [*Brightly.*] Well, it's our dear visitor dropped in to say hello again— look who's here. So what's new? Sit down, Stepanovna.

ANNA STEPANOVNA: I've only popped in for a second. Is Nina here?

FYODOR IVANOVICH: Nina!

[NINA *enters.*]

ANNA STEPANOVNA: Well, my God almighty, you should see what's going on downstairs. On the first floor!

FYODOR IVANOVICH: You see, I was right. She's brought some news again.

ANNA STEPANOVNA: Nina dear, Ivanov's got the whole flat full of people, he's brought them all in from the off-sales. There's two dockers there, and the old man from the first landing. That's as much as I saw. They've got the door wide open. They're watching hockey on TV, would you believe, and drinking and God knows what all. Granya's in hospital, of course, she came to see me this morning with Galka. By the way, where is Galka?

TAISA PETROVNA: She's here with us, and where are we going to put a baby?

ANNA STEPANOVNA: Well, that's right, I mean, Granya wanted to leave her with me. But why should I take her, when the house is full of her own folk? Isn't that right? I says to her, Granya, make use of your own people, let them do their bit for you. It's better when people help their own. It strengthens good relations—peace and friendship, you know? All the same, God knows, your own folk aren't your own these days, there's very few on good terms with their kin. They all want their own space, and that's not right. My Lyubochka and her husband, Volodya, are clearing off from us as well, they've built a co-operative flat. My son-in-law Volodya's a good lad, but that's because he's mean. We'll still come to you for meals, Mama, he says. They're putting by one hundred roubles a month each, saving up for a set of furniture. These days an unfurnished flat counts for nothing. Well, anyway, Nina, what are we going to do? How are we going to get rid of them?

NINA: Get rid of them? Why should I get rid of them? They're his guests. They came to see him. He is in his house, after all. Why should I get rid of them? I can't do that.

ANNA STEPANOVNA: That's all well and good, Nina dear, but these people are like children. He'll let them have something, and he'll take it back, and he won't even notice. Before he can blink, they'll be carrying out the furniture. Those kind of people have got just about enough brains to lift the first thing that comes to hand and sell it. That old man from the first landing, old Senya, sold his old dear's milk churn not long ago, for a rouble. I mean, they don't give a damn that it's somebody else's house. All you'll need to do is take them by the hand and bingo! They can just about make it round the corner to the off-licence, for a drink.

TAISA PETROVNA: Nina dear, you'd better go just the same and straighten things out. Kolya, go with her, make sure there's no carry-on.

NIKOLAI: Let her go herself, she can manage. Besides, what's somebody else's place got to do with me, who am I to them? No, when she needs to, Nina's not frightened to go anywhere, she's not shy.

FYODOR IVANOVICH: Count me out, is that it?

NIKOLAI: Yes, count me out. That's all you can remember about Nadya, that's imprinted on your mind. But she had a poisoned finger then, she couldn't wash the dishes.

TAISA PETROVNA: Anyway, Nina love, I think you and Anna Stepanovna can do what's necessary. Somebody's got to do it. On you go, on you go.

ANNA STEPANOVNA: Yes, it'll take two minutes to show the whole lot of them the door, and that's it. Let's be going.

NINA: In a minute, Auntie Anya.

[*Exits to the adjoining room, they are silent.* FYODOR IVANOVICH *switches on the TV.* NINA *quickly emerges with the baby, and the string bag with its feeding bottles.*]

NINA: Let's go, Auntie Anya. I've just got to fling on my jacket.

GRANNY: Where've you taken Galya? Where are you taking her? Can't I sit with her a while?

NINA: That's about the lot, I think. I don't think I've forgotten anything. I've left the clothes you gave me there. You can chuck out whatever you want. So—cheerio, I'm off. And you, Kolya, you should go to a hostel.

TAISA PETROVNA: What's all this, Nina? We're not letting you go anywhere.

FYODOR IVANOVICH: And he's not going to any hostel.

NINA: You should go, Kolya. You'll find it interesting.

NIKOLAI: Don't you worry.

NINA: Anyway, cheerio, I'll be seeing you.

FYODOR IVANOVICH: Look, you just throw those people out, and then come back, d'you hear? Don't pay any attention to him, he's off his head.

[NINA *and* ANNA STEPANOVNA *exit.*]

TAISA PETROVNA: Well, Kolya, you've done it now. God only knows what you'll do next. You did it, it was you that drove her out, nobody else. Have you no conscience? Or what have you got in place of a conscience, eh? How is Nina going to show her face in the street now?

NIKOLAI: Same as always. Anyway, whose business is it?

FYODOR IVANOVICH: It'll be Stepanovna's business, if nobody else's.

GRANNY: They'll be giving us all our blessings on the benches, you won't be able to go out.

NIKOLAI: So what's all the shame? I don't understand this. We lived together a while, and then split up, so what? I mean, you lived with somebody in your block. When you were younger.

TAISA PETROVNA: What!!!

NIKOLAI: I know you did, for a fact. Anyway, you had somebody before father. It's no big deal.

FYODOR IVANOVICH: You . . . snivelling creep!

NIKOLAI: Yes, and don't start a row. This isn't the time to discuss these things. Besides, it's no secret.

FYODOR IVANOVICH: And just who told you this filth?

NIKOLAI: Somebody told me, that's all.

TAISA PETROVNA: Klavdia, most likely.

NIKOLAI: Well, so you lived with him, so what? It doesn't matter.

FYODOR IVANOVICH: Go ahead, that's right, bad mouth your own mother.

NIKOLAI: No, I respect that. I really do. But you should have some respect as well. I did my thing, you did yours.

FYODOR IVANOVICH: Don't you dare compare yourself with us! My God, what a bloody cheek!

NIKOLAI: Yes, well, I'm a human being, same as you.

FYODOR IVANOVICH: That's just the point, you're not the same. You've no shame, but we have. Your parents have run themselves ragged for you their whole lives, and you're just going to dump God knows what kind of wife on them, with God knows whose child. Is that what you want, is that what you're bringing down on us?

TAISA PETROVNA: [*Gently.*] You've just no idea about loyalty, Kolya son. I'm sorry, but as a man, you're nothing. That's almost three months now you've been living with Nina, and you've sent her packing. And what was that other one? You think that was true love? That was just a moment's passion. Made-up eyes, dyed curls, and that was it. But if you'd seen her without her eyes made-up, you'd have run a mile. And after the wedding you'll see precious little of that make-up. You'll see her bare face, the one God gave her.

FYODOR IVANOVICH: Besides which you've still got to find out whose the child is. You can't tell for seven years, so the peasants say, then you've just got to look and you can tell whether it's yours or not. And you're already making plans. It only takes a minute's work to make babies, you know. So what are you so bothered about?

TAISA PETROVNA: That's not love, Kolya, it's blind passion. It soon fades. You'll rub your eyes one minute, and there it is—just pure ignorance, no sort of culture. Just made-up eyes.

GRANNY: He should have seen her. She looked horrible enough without eye make-up. They were black enough without it.

TAISA PETROVNA: Anyway I'm sure he's already seen her. Have you seen that Nadya of yours, how she's looking these days?

NIKOLAI: No, I haven't.

GRANNY: Oh, she looks terrible. Her big eyes sunk right in, her lips black . . . she can scarcely put one foot in front of another.

TAISA PETROVNA: Well, she doesn't look quite *that* bad. All women feel a bit like that . . . There's nothing especially remarkable about it.

NIKOLAI: That's because she poisoned herself!

GRANNY: Poisoned herself!

NIKOLAI: Her flatmate at the hostel told me. I did go there, you know.

TAISA PETROVNA: Well, that's it. That means the baby'll be born a freak. That's the end.

NIKOLAI: They even had to send her to the hospital.

TAISA PETROVNA: And you know what that means. No arms, or two heads!

NIKOLAI: Well. So what?

TAISA PETROVNA: Oh, so you don't care what kind of child you have? You're so hard, you're like a stone.

FYODOR IVANOVICH: Kolya, you're taking on a whole mess of trouble for yourself, and you'll be stuck with it your whole life.

NIKOLAI: What are you all shouting for? I'm standing here looking at you, and thinking, what are they shouting about? I just don't feel like arguing with you. I mean, you're really weird!

TAISA PETROVNA: So it's all settled for you, is it?

NIKOLAI: As it happens, yes.

TAISA PETROVNA: Are you going to be bringing her back here again?

NIKOLAI: [*Amused.*] Why should I do that?

FYODOR IVANOVICH: So what are you going to do then? Find a corner to rent some place? Well, let me tell you, if that's the case, I'm not your father any longer, I don't want to know you.

NIKOLAI: Does that mean you're not going to help? Oh, this is too much! [*Starts laughing.*]

FYODOR IVANOVICH: What are you laughing at? Do you want the belt?

NIKOLAI: [*Laughing.*] This is really too much. The belt belongs in the past, Papa.

FYODOR IVANOVICH: We'll see about that.

[*Tries to take the belt out of his trousers, but his hands won't obey him.*]

TAISA PETROVNA: [*Shouting.*] Making a fool of your father, who's brought you up, who's devoted his whole life to you, who helped you with your music lessons!!!

FYODOR IVANOVICH: [*Still struggling with his belt.*] I'll show him, I'll give him music! I'll show him right this minute!

[*Whips out his belt and starts to beat* NIKOLAI. GRANNY *rushes between them.* NIKOLAI *falls down helpless with laughter.*]

GRANNY: Don't touch him! He's your only son—your only son! Leave him alone, I'm telling you, you rotten bugger!

[*She is shielding him with her body.* FATHER *throws the belt into a corner, stands breathing heavily.* TAISA PETROVNA *sits, stunned,* FYODOR IVANOVICH *walks up and down, from corner to corner,* GRANNY *sits* NIKOLAI *on a chair, stands over him.*]

FYODOR IVANOVICH: You think we've had an easy life, eh? You think there's never been any differences between me and your mother, eh? We've had the lot. I'm a normal man too, you know. I've got some life in me as well, some feelings, but there comes a time when you've got to call a halt, take stock of your life, and just switch off.

TAISA PETROVNA: Your father's not made out of wood either. He's made his mistakes. But he put them all behind him for your sake, for your sake alone. And he came back to me.

GRANNY: Yes, they got together again. God knows what for.

FYODOR IVANOVICH: I can't count the number of times I changed my mind at that time. But I decided, no. Absolutely not. I have a son growing up.

NIKOLAI: Yes, I know about that, Mama even went to your boss at work about you.

FYODOR IVANOVICH: All right, if you know that much, you can maybe appreciate it then. You're a grown man now, you can understand that nothing'll hold a man back, no boss, no parents, nothing. Same as yourself. But a man will listen to his conscience. You're doing your own thing, I can accept that. But we're Kozlovs, do you understand? Everything we do, we do for the family, for our own. Beating our brains in, your mother and me, and it's all for you. Who else would we do it for? We don't need it ourselves.

NIKOLAI: Fine. Now I want to say something. I just want to bring a little light to bear on this matter. [*Pause.*] In fact, I share your point of view totally. I'm in complete agreement with you.

[*A pause.*]

TAISA PETROVNA: Well, that's fine. Bravo!

FYODOR IVANOVICH: What are you saying?

NIKOLAI: I'd nothing like that in mind at all, not remotely. But it was you, making my mind up *for* me, assuming that was what I was going to do. I'm not getting married at all, and that's that.

FYODOR IVANOVICH: How d'you mean?

NIKOLAI: Well, I would have gone after Nadya, but when her girlfriends there told me what the score was, I bailed out straightaway. Poisoned herself—I mean, that's heavy. That could stir up all kinds of trouble, that could mean a term in prison. You're better not to get mixed up in that kind of business. A suicide attempt, that's how it's described. She's something else, her, and so proud.

TAISA PETROVNA: Yes, well, she's not that extraordinary, not really. If you want to know the truth, I'll tell you. She came here to us, to wait for you.

NIKOLAI: So what did you do?

TAISA PETROVNA: We showed her out, after doing the decent thing.

NIKOLAI: You did the right thing then.

[*A pause. They have all come round now.* GRANNY *sits down. Order is restored.*]

FYODOR IVANOVICH: Anyway, why don't you get married to Nina?

[NIKOLAI *shrugs.*]

TAISA PETROVNA: He's said, it's too soon for him.

FYODOR IVANOVICH: [*Slowly.*] Well, I'm really surprised at you. I never expected it.

NIKOLAI: Never expected what?

FYODOR IVANOVICH: This. I mean, there we were fighting, and you're just watching and thinking, well, okay, let them get upset for a bit, and I'll just enjoy it. That's so funny— there they are beating their heads against the wall.

NIKOLAI: Well, you wouldn't let me get a word in.

FYODOR IVANOVICH: You managed to get your oar in when you wanted to.

TAISA PETROVNA: Actually, it wasn't very nice. You could have spared a thought for us. I mean we were only thinking of you.

FYODOR IVANOVICH: You're still young, Kolya, and look at the mess you've created already. You've almost driven two young women into an early grave.

NIKOLAI: Here we go again.

FYODOR IVANOVICH: I mean, did I bring you up like that?

NIKOLAI: Like a stuck record.

FYODOR IVANOVICH: [*Quieter.*] The word "conscience" means nothing to you.

NIKOLAI: Let's watch the hockey.

[*They sit watching TV.*]

FYODOR IVANOVICH: Mama, bring me a glass of water, to take my pill.

[*He is clutching his head.* TAISA PETROVNA *goes out of the room, steps into the hall, and immediately returns closing the door behind her.*]

TAISA PETROVNA: Nina's standing out there. In the hall. With Galka in her arms.

[*The whole of the following scene is experienced by the* KOZLOVS *like a bad dream. They fall silent.* GRANNY *stands up.*]

GRANNY: [*Exits to the side room.*] I've had enough of this.

NIKOLAI: I told you—this pride thing, it's all rubbish. She's out to get me.

FYODOR IVANOVICH: Somebody loves you at least.

NIKOLAI: Lots of people love me.

[GRANNY *crosses the room, carrying a bundle.*]

GRANNY: I'll be seeing you. I'm off to Klavdia's.

TAISA PETROVNA: Mama, you can see what's going on. I'll take you back when everything's settled.

GRANNY: Huh, I'm nothing to you—a trunk full of bedbugs. You won't take me back.

TAISA PETROVNA: Don't get angry. I'll come for you.

GRANNY: Yes, meanwhile, I'll be seeing you. [*Exits.*]

[*Above the darkened stage a swing is illuminated.* NINA *begins to swing backwards and forwards on it, slowly and sadly, the baby in her arms.*]

FYODOR IVANOVICH: For God's sake, get me some water.

TAISA PETROVNA: I can't. I can't move.

FYODOR IVANOVICH: You get it, Kolya.

NIKOLAI: Papa, it's the third period.

[FYODOR IVANOVICH *goes out into the hall and immediately returns.*]

FYODOR IVANOVICH: That isn't Nina, that's Nadya standing there with a baby. You get every damn thing mixed up. [*Sits down, clutching his head.*]

TAISA PETROVNA: Granny must've let her in, surely? Why's the baby there?

[*The door slowly opens, and a muffled figure enters holding a baby.*]

NADYA: I've come to stay here with you. It's nice here, you've got two rooms. Furniture.

NIKOLAI: Have you really had a baby? It's got nothing to do with me, nothing at all. I can prove it, I can count up.

NADYA: I've come to live with you. My baby's been born without a head, I can't feed him.

TAISA PETROVNA: That's because you took poison.

[NADYA *slowly and sadly also mounts the swing, where* NINA *is already sitting.*]

TAISA PETROVNA: Don't pay any attention to them. If you don't pay them any attention they'll go away. [*Animatedly.*] Will the hockey be over soon? I want to go to bed.

NIKOLAI: It's finished. [*Gets up, and stretches, but is forced to crouch down as* NADYA *swings over his head.*]

[TAISA PETROVNA *stands up and walks with her knees bent, while the swing spins out of control around her. The swing comes down lower.* FYODOR IVANOVICH *gets down on all fours and crawls into the kitchen.*]

[NIKOLAI *sinks his head deeper into the armchair and freezes into an almost horizontal position, drawing his legs up, ready to repel the flying swing.*]

[*The curtain falls.*]

Bjørg Vik (b. 1935)

The struggle to loosen Norway's rigid traditional society had its roots in the second half of the twentieth century, played out in part in the nation's theaters. We need only recall the stern dramas of Ibsen, his own discontent with Norway, his self-exile, and the response to the infamous door-slam announcing the departure of Nora to realize how different things were only a little more than a century ago. Ibsen's protest, of course, reflects an important and effective spirit that was emerging. The early wave of the women's movement had succeeded in winning the vote as early as 1913. The founding of the social welfare state and the coming to power of the labor government, which occurred in the years between the world wars, were further evidence of strong progressive forces. In the sixties feminism gained momentum and contributed notably to the forging of Norway into a socially advanced, modern, liberal society.

Since the end of the last century women writers have made themselves an increasingly visible and numerically significant force in Norway. In the 1960s, they began to achieve international recognition. Bjørg Vik has been an important early part of that wave of writers anxious to assert their views and determined to present the case for what they called the new feminism. She was a member of the original editorial board of the Norwegian feminist periodical *Sirene*. Through the seventies, she remained at the forefront of the movement to achieve equality and recognition for women—through her writings and speaking.

From a nonacademic, lower-middle-class Oslo family, Vik began as a journalist and short story writer, taking many of her themes from the families, patterns, and relationships she saw at hand. Initially most comfortable with short fiction, in 1963 she published her first collection, *Sunday Afternoon (Søndag ettermiddag)*. She was particularly skillful at conveying the helplessness people felt in their lives, their recurring problems and discontent, and the dearth of satisfactory resolutions. In this and her next, highly successful volume of stories, *An Aquarium of Women (Kvinneakvariet, 1972)*, Vik is not only articulate and vocal as a feminist, but she shows herself to be strikingly comfortable exploring sex and lust as subjects, more comfortable, perhaps, than many in her contemporary reading public were ready to appreciate.

Two years later, Vik became the first Norwegian woman since the turn of the century to succeed as a dramatist, with *Two Acts for Five Women (To akter for fem kvinner, 1974)*. Traditionally and naturalistically styled, this discussion play presents five women talking about, exploring, and groping with the diverse situations

Bjørg Vik, no date. (Photographer: Roger Neumann.)

of their lives. It has remained a staple in Norwegian theaters; it also probably represents Vik at her most didactically political. Subsequently, her feminist concerns and orientation tended to become more suffused in the careful presentations of characters and situations. In *Daughters* (*Døtre*, 1979), she concentrates on the mundane lives and dealings of three generations of women sharing the same frustrating, familial surroundings.

In *The Trip to Venice* (*Reisen til Venezia: en vemodig komedie*, 1992), her most accomplished stage play, Vik offers time travel with a twist. Set in the apartment of the elderly Tellmanns, the eccentricities, poignant worries, and the humor of aging are deftly woven together. The pervasive cats suggest the almost clichéd zaniness of old age; they also suggest, as the plumber makes clear, its very real shittiness. Just as we appreciate the present reality of the cats and the underlying difficulties with money, we accept Oscar and Edith's ludic form of travel. They start the day by visiting with Ibsen's Peer Gynt, through Oscar's declamation, and then it is off, imaginatively, to Venice. Memory, which is getting to be so fragile and tenuous (realism is a hallmark of Vik's) fuels this excursion. It also reminds Edith of her three miscarriages and of the week-old child she lost forty years prior. In her nuanced depiction of the couple, Vik is not shy about recognizing the strong geriatric interest in sex—whether it be Edith's reading from *Lady Chatterley's Lover* or Oscar's joke about the old man who was so keen on girls but couldn't remember why—which join the subjects of sex, memory, and aging.

Life as a trip or journey is a metaphor that Vik builds into her gray comedy. But if the young maid Vivian finds their make-believe "a comfortable way of travelling," Oscar's larger view is more sobering. As old as he is and and as much as he's thought about death, he's still not adjusted to the idea; he's "got used to being alive." Sharing some of the comic pathos of Chekov, the exuberant absurdity of Ionesco, and even a touch of the implicit desolation of Pinter, Vik creates an engaging and observant drama—distinctively her own—of the sad comedy of later life.

SELECTED BIBLIOGRAPHY IN ENGLISH

Garton, Janet. *Norwegian Women's Writing: 1850–1990*. London: Athlone, 1993.
Garton, Janet, and Henning Sehmsdorf, eds. *New Norwegian Plays*. Norwich, England: Norvik, 1989.
Naess, Harold S., ed. *A History of Norwegian Literature*. Lincoln: University of Nebraska Press, 1993.

THE TRIP TO VENICE

Bjørg Vik

Translated by Janet Garton

CHARACTERS

EDITH TELLMANN

OSCAR TELLMANN

CHRISTOPHER KARLSEN   a plumber

VIVIAN SUNDE   a home help

VARIOUS CATS   (more or less visible)

In the Tellmanns' somewhat shabby and untidy sitting room, a warm and welcoming room, still with an atmosphere of culture.

> [OSCAR *sneezes a couple of times.*]

EDITH: [*At the piano, leafing through music, looking for the right glasses.*] Have you got a cold?

OSCAR: I think it's the dust.

EDITH: Oh dear, yes. She stopped coming, that last one, didn't she?

OSCAR: The wind from the north.

EDITH: [*Playing the piano a little as they chat.*] Yes, that's what you called her. [*Imitates a Northern accent.*] "That's that. I can tek na' more o' this."

OSCAR: So there'll be no-one coming to clean for us now, then? [*He swats at flies with a rolled-up newspaper.*]

EDITH: "It's not that I've owt again cats, but I can tek na' more. It's drivin' me potty." What are you waving at?

OSCAR: Flies.

EDITH: There aren't any flies here.

OSCAR: Yes there are. [*Swats one.*]

EDITH: And even if there are one or two—which I don't believe—you can't possibly see them.

OSCAR: I can hear them!

> [OSCAR *seizes the victim triumphantly and waves it in the air, while* EDITH *watches without much interest.*]

EDITH: She was going to tell them at the home help center. We'll get another one.

OSCAR: All these different women. Interfering women with brooms and dusters who move our glasses and books and everything. How many have we had, do you think?

EDITH: [*Shrugs her shoulders.*] We get to know lots of people like that.

[OSCAR *shuffles around with his newspaper, listening intently, hunting for flies.*]

EDITH: "Two nice old folks like you and Mr. Tellmann, up to your ears in this great pile o' cats, I can't mek it out . . ." Why do they make such a fuss about it, all of them?

OSCAR: There . . . there it is. *Got* you!

EDITH: There are no flies here. "Catshit and hairs and dust everywhere. And a grand old lady like you, Mrs. Tellmann. I can't mek it out!"

OSCAR: I can't see them any longer. And you've stopped hearing them.

EDITH: What's that?

OSCAR: But I catch them anyway.

EDITH: Do you know who you remind me of just now, Oscar? Don Quixote. You're just like Don Quixote. Oh, I know what we'll do. [*Walks away from the piano.*]

OSCAR: Do some dusting?

EDITH: [*Looking through the chaotic bookshelf.*] We'll read Cervantes!

OSCAR: We've read that before.

EDITH: So what? When you get old you've forgotten most things. And then you can read all the good books again. That's what's so great about it. But where has it got to? It was you who taught me to like Cervantes as well. Have we lent it to someone? All the things you've taught me, Oscar. Everything from spelling to table manners. Geography. History.

OSCAR: That was my special field. Now you're sitting here with a moth-eaten lion—who goes hunting for flies in slippers.

EDITH: [*Takes no notice.*] But here's . . . would you believe it, it's Dostoevsky! You know how I was looking for him recently. *The Idiot.* That's the one. Shall I read some of the sections we liked so much? The diamond earrings, do you remember them?

OSCAR: Diamond earrings? Yes. Oh yes.

[*Every now and then there is a plopping sound from the kitchen, as well as meowing from the cats, at least one cat should come in to the sitting room from time to time.*]

EDITH: [*Turning the pages eagerly.*] Listen. Listen to this, Oscar. "He had the greatest respect for his wife, indeed at times he was so frightened of her that he even loved her." Isn't that marvellous?

OSCAR: That he even loved her . . . [*Chuckles.*]

EDITH: The story about the earrings was near the beginning, when they're sitting on the train to Petersburg. What was he called now . . . Rogozhin, that's right. It's Rogozhin talking about his hopeless love for Nastasya Filippovna. And his father was that old miser, stinking rich. Do you remember, Oscar?

OSCAR: Nastasya Filippovna. Great.

EDITH: [*Reading from* The Idiot.] It's when Rogozhin has seen Nastasya Filippovna at the Bolshoi, she was sitting in her box on the balcony. And he can't sleep all night. "The next morning the old man—that's his father—came in with two five percent bonds, each for five thousand roubles. 'Go and sell these bonds,' he says. 'Then you are to pay seven thousand five hundred at Andreyev's office, and the rest you must bring me without stopping anywhere on the way, and I'll be sitting here waiting for you.' I sold the bonds and took the money, but I didn't go to Andreyev's office; without hesitating I went straight to the English jeweller's and bought a pair of earrings, each with a diamond as big as a hazelnut. I was four hundred roubles short, but I gave them my name, which was a good enough guarantee. Then I went to Zalyozhev with the earrings and explained everything to him, and said: 'Come, let us go to Nastasya Filippovna.' So we did . . ." Marvellous, isn't it? Isn't it marvellous?

[OSCAR *nods sadly.*]

EDITH: What is it? What is it now, my love?

OSCAR: You never got any diamonds.

EDITH: What would I do with them? You know how I love brass and beads and chunky glass.

OSCAR: And I only had . . .

BOTH: . . . a humble lecturer's salary.

EDITH: We've never been short of anything. Of earthly goods.

OSCAR: I used to love drawing maps on the blackboard. The chalk sketched out contours, frontiers. Europe was most fun. When I got to the Italian boot, the whole class would sigh. I really had a flair for it.

EDITH: You were very gifted.

OSCAR: Maps were something I knew about. I could draw them blindfold.

EDITH: You should have been a professor. I'm sure you could have been a professor of geography. Or history.

OSCAR: When we had written tests on rainy days, I used to like that. The silence in the classroom, the dry scratching noise of pencils and pen nibs. The bent necks, the young, concentrated faces.

EDITH: Did you—did you sometimes used to think of *him* then?

OSCAR: [*Doesn't answer at once, thinks about it.*] Perhaps.

EDITH: Perhaps—. What do you mean, perhaps?

OSCAR: Nothing, my love. I didn't think about him as much as . . . as you did. Perhaps . . .

EDITH: Oh . . . ? What did you think of?

[OSCAR *silent, looking towards the kitchen.*]

EDITH: What did you think of, then?

OSCAR: Good lord, how dishevelled Mozart looks. He's getting long in the tooth, him as well. What did I think of? It's so long ago. His hands. His tiny, tiny hands. And I could see that he would have long, fine fingers. Violinist's fingers, I thought. [*To the cat.*] Your coat's all lank, poor thing. Ragged.

EDITH: Mozart's one of our old lads.

OSCAR: [*Runs his hands through what's left of his own hair.*] Oh well, it comes to all of us in the end. Lank . . . in more than one way. But there's still something left of the virile tomcat. Something about the back of the neck.

EDITH: [*Stroking lovingly over his hair and neck.*] Indeed there is. But we're off on our travels today, you know. You haven't forgotten?

OSCAR: I don't know . . .

EDITH: I've put out your clothes.

OSCAR: I don't know if I've got the energy. These miserable legs of mine. They ache so.

EDITH: Of course you've got the energy! You'll feel so cheerful and strong, as soon as we're on the way. Perhaps there'll be a little surprise too.

OSCAR: Really?

EDITH: I've been so looking forward to this trip.

OSCAR: I feel so tired, Edith. So godforsaken tired and past it.

EDITH: You shouldn't take God's name lightly, Oscar.

OSCAR: I'm not doing, by God.

EDITH: Just you listen to a wise old woman. You can *see* . . .

OSCAR: Not all that well, I can't.

EDITH: You can *hear.*

OSCAR: I've finally got to the age when I hear what I *want* to hear. Often I think that I've heard more than enough already.

EDITH: You can *talk.*

OSCAR: A bit of old man's gossip.

EDITH: You can *walk*.

OSCAR: Shuffle, you mean.

EDITH: You can eat and drink.

OSCAR: Thank God. Have you heard about the old man who was so keen on girls? The only problem was that he could no longer remember *why*—. Ha ha.

EDITH: Count your blessings. It was *you* who taught me that. Here are your clothes then. I think it's time . . .

OSCAR: Just a minute. There's something . . . I'm trying to get hold of. It's been kind of . . . knocking around up here all day. I knew it so well once . . .

EDITH: What do you think the weather'll be like?

OSCAR: "And if today were the last time I saw . . ." And then it's gone, I can't remember a word more. It's a beautiful poem. "And if today were the last time I saw . . ."

EDITH: It's lovely up there even when it's raining.

OSCAR: "If my heart were to beat no more . . ." But there's something in between . . . if I could just work it out.

EDITH: The clouds hanging over the mountain tops. Just like caps. Do you remember the sound of the rain in the newly sprung birch leaves? Raindrops on small soft dwarf birch leaves. Our Lord's finest little prelude.

[*Loud meowing from the next room or by the door.*]

EDITH: I think someone wants to go out? [*Opens a door to the corridor, lets the cats out.*] There you are, out you go then, my little tearaways . . .

OSCAR: We must ring the vet soon.

[EDITH *not listening to him, sorts out the travel gear.*]

OSCAR: I trip over cats here like other people trip over slippers or doorsills.

EDITH: I've packed the picnic.

OSCAR: When I let them out or in in the evening, I can make out some I don't know at all. Cats I've never seen before! There's always one on the sofa in the evening, a big black shaggy one. Which one's that?

EDITH: Oh, that one. It's only the old tom of fru Ludvigsen's. He doesn't like being out at night any more.

OSCAR: Oh, I see.

EDITH: He just sleeps here. Then he wanders off again.

OSCAR: We'll have to get those young chaps castrated.

EDITH: There's no rush.

OSCAR: Do you think I can't see anything at all? I can see very well what they get up to. In here and outside. Where's my pipe? Strange how everything moves around the place . . . the whole time.

EDITH: Look in your pocket. They're our children, these cats.

[OSCAR *is amazed to find his pipe in his pocket.*]

EDITH: God gave us many four-legged little ones.

OSCAR: [*Turns over some papers and bills by chance.*] What are these? Bills? Unpaid, I expect? They look rather unpaid.

EDITH: [*Snatches up the bills discreetly and puts them out of the way.*] You know I look after that kind of thing.

OSCAR: My little bookkeeper. I don't understand how you manage it. Making ends meet.

EDITH: [*Putting out walking gear: anorak, plus-fours, ski hat, rucksacks.*] Shall we get ready?

OSCAR: Is *that* where we're going?

EDITH: Yes, you knew it was!

OSCAR: I don't think I did.

EDITH: Today we're going to the mountains. Rondane.

OSCAR: Well, why not? It's bound to be nice weather.

EDITH: Here you are, look, your plus-fours. Shall I help you?

OSCAR: No thanks, I can manage to put on my own trousers still . . .

EDITH: Some fresh mountain air, and then all this dizziness will be blown away!

[OSCAR *fumbles with his trousers, she puts out his ski boots, a nearly empty rucksack, his stick.*]

OSCAR: We've had many fine mountain hikes. My word, how we walked, for hours and hours.

EDITH: [*Hangs up a brightly coloured tourist poster with mountains etc.*] And now we're off on a hike again.

OSCAR: Those pictures, my love. Won't they be ready soon? The ones you sent to be cleaned or whatever it was?

EDITH: I've just forgotten to pick them up. Can you manage the boots? [*Places three or four chairs in a row in the middle of the floor, the normal preparation for a train journey.*]

OSCAR: It was as if you never got tired up there in the mountains. And then we were young.

EDITH: [*Looks at the train compartment, puts extra cushions in a couple of the chairs.*] First class as usual. I'll always travel first class . . .

OSCAR: Young and strong, we were. It's as if this is the punishment, punishment for a long life.

EDITH: Punishment? Rubbish, my love. The way of all flesh, that's what it is.

OSCAR: Perhaps you'll help me with these laces? They've got so small. Almost invisible. They didn't used to be like that, surely?

EDITH: [*Helps him with his boots and the rest of his clothes.*] How good you look in your mountain gear, Oscar. Those trousers really suit you. But you must come now. The train is leaving! [*Music, she puts on a record or plays the piano, something which evokes an atmosphere of mountains and nature.*]

OSCAR: But my glasses? Where are my hiking glasses? [*Shuffles round looking.*]

EDITH: Perhaps you've got them on you?

[OSCAR *finds his glasses, either on his head or in a pocket. They take their places on the chairs, she sits in front and he behind with his stick, she pulls a train whistle out of her pocket and blows loudly, they mime a short train journey, look out of the window, enjoy the view, she shows the tickets, flirts with an invisible conductor etc.*]

EDITH: [*Gets up and picks up her rucksack.*] What a lovely trip!

OSCAR: Good to get out of the train. It always was.

EDITH: The conductor was very obliging. They always are, don't you think? There was something about his eyes. A kind of dark area around them.

OSCAR: You and these conductors of yours. Look around! All the mountaintops . . . the eternal snow . . . full many a glorious morning have I seen flatter the mountaintops with sovereign eye . . .

[*A plopping noise of water from the kitchen.*]

EDITH: Can you hear the stream?

[*Cat cries, meowing.*]

OSCAR: What was that? A lynx? An eagle? An eagle taking a hare.

EDITH: Definitely. And here are reindeer tracks. A large herd. [*Stumbles over slippers and socks.*]

OSCAR: Are we going far today?

EDITH: We have to go to the top if we're going to see the view.

[*They trudge around the room,* EDITH *opens the window and climbs up on a chair.*]

EDITH: Just breathe that wonderful mountain air! What a view!

OSCAR: [*Looking out of the window.*] Wonderful!

EDITH: Now don't overdo it. Remember the thin air. Can you see the cloudberries? Those honey-yellow cloudberry patches?

OSCAR: We can pick some on the way home. I think I'll just stop to catch my breath.

EDITH: Yes, why don't you. I'll go on a bit.

[EDITH *tramps steadily onwards, singing a lively walking song, while* OSCAR *finds a stool.*]

OSCAR: I'll just sit down—on this tree stump.

EDITH: Ho ho!

OSCAR: Ho ho.

EDITH: Did you hear the echo? Ho ho!

[*Meowing from the corridor.*]

OSCAR: You're frightening the wild animals. Be careful you don't get blisters.

EDITH: [*Peering out of the window.*] From here I can see the whole of Jotunheimen and half the kingdom!

OSCAR: My oh my. And the prince?

EDITH: Peak after peak. Vista after vista.

[*The plopping sound from the kitchen.*]

OSCAR: And the stream runs into the meadow . . .

EDITH: The prince? Ah, the prince . . . [*She sits down, unpacks the rucksack, the sandwiches, flask, cups, a cloth, a flag etc. The plopping sound from the kitchen can be heard intermittently.*]

EDITH: What a lovely place you have found today. And that stream makes such a friendly sound. And now . . . now it's time for a little picnic! [*She arranges the meal on the floor, looks for more in the rucksack, and pulls out a hip flask.*] There you are!

[EDITH *pours some into the cap and offers it to* OSCAR.]

OSCAR: Well, what have we here? [*He sniffs at the little container, then drinks with shaking hands.*] Real cognac . . . [*Breathes a sigh of contentment and gives her the cap.*] God must have been in a good mood when he created you, Edith.

EDITH: [*Pours some out and has a drink herself.*] Cheers, my beloved travelling companion!

OSCAR: Where in all the world did you get that?

EDITH: *You* got it. You got it for your eightieth birthday from Victor. You haven't forgotten? When you were eighty . . .

OSCAR: Victor . . . He's dead and gone too.

EDITH: I thought we ought to taste it.

OSCAR: He was lucky. It was a peaceful end.

[EDITH *passes* OSCAR *the cap again.*]

OSCAR: Did he really buy that for me? Victor?

EDITH: Had you forgotten?

OSCAR: But I can't really believe that Victor bought me such a fine cognac. He was normally so . . . careful with money.

EDITH: Careful? The man was abnormally tight-fisted.

OSCAR: Thank you anyway, Victor. Cheers. We'll be meeting soon.

EDITH: Don't you remember how he plagued his poor wife? She never had any money for anything. She had to switch off all the lights in the flat in order to be allowed to iron a blouse or two.

OSCAR: He must have had an attack of frivolity. Or megalomania. Good thing I was on the receiving end. He he.

EDITH: [*Takes out the sandwiches.*] And now the mountaineers have earned some sandwiches. There's hot coffee in the flask. That flask . . . [*Becoming thoughtful.*] And I must admit that I was kind of hoping . . .

OSCAR: I know! My party piece.

EDITH: Will you do it?

[OSCAR *empties his cup, then stands up and delivers a dramatic recitation of the ride on the buck's back from* Peer Gynt. *In the middle* CHRISTOPHER *the plumber arrives, and stands listening in amazement. He makes a couple of remarks when* OSCAR *takes a breath now and then.*]

OSCAR:

> Have you seen or
> been on Gjendin ridge before?
> Two miles long, perhaps, or more,
> stretching like a scythe's sharp blade.
> Down past glacier, slope and slide
> you could see where grey screes made
> mirrors of the tarns that cower
> black and heavy, some thirteen or
> fourteen hundred metres lower.
>   Along the ridge we raced together,
> slicing through the wind and weather.
>   What a colt to ride—amazing!
> As we started on our run
> it was just like suns were blazing.
> Eagles, brown-backed every one,
> hung in space between us there

[CHRISTOPHER *enters.*]

OSCAR: [*Continues, carried away by his own eloquence.*]

> and the way-down stretch of water,
> specks of dust upon the air.
>   Ice-floes grind at every quarter
> of the shore-line, but no rumbling;

CHRISTOPHER: Blimey, what a lot of cats you've got here!

OSCAR:

> only wisps of vapour whirled
> like they were dancing—sang and swirled,
> set the eye and ear a-fumbling.

EDITH: O, God help us!

OSCAR:

> Like a shot,
> in a desperate, headlong spot.

CHRISTOPHER: Have I come to the wrong place?

OSCAR:

> a cock-ptarmigan arose,
> cackling, flapping, wild with shock,
> from its hidden perching-rock
> underneath our very nose.

CHRISTOPHER: The door was open.

OSCAR:

> Then the buck half-twisted round
> rocketed right off the ground,
> out in empty space we find us.

CHRISTOPHER: Mr. and Mrs. Tellmann?

OSCAR:

> The mountain wall was black behind us,
> under us a gaping pit.

CHRISTOPHER: [*Sniffing the heavy stench of cats, mutters to himself.*] Bloody hell!

EDITH: Sorry, what did you say?

CHRISTOPHER: Wasn't it here you needed a plumber? Tellmann, number 12?

EDITH: Plumber?

CHRISTOPHER: Karlsen Plumbing. Plumb crazy! Ha ha.

EDITH: I'd quite forgotten. We're just setting off, you see, Mr. . . . Mr.?

CHRISTOPHER: Karlsen.

EDITH: We're going on a trip to Rondane.

CHRISTOPHER: Oh. Oh yes, I can see that. I can come back next week. I've got another job further down the street, at Steffensen's.

EDITH: No, no, it's quite all right. Just help yourself to what you need, Mr. Karlsen.

OSCAR: [*Embarking on* Peer Gynt *again.*]

> First a band of mist we shattered
> then a flock of gulls we scattered
> every whichway sent them streaking
> rousing echoes with their shrieking.

CHRISTOPHER: I can easily do the other job first. No problem.

OSCAR:

> Down we go. No time to ponder.

CHRISTOPHER: Yes, I expect you're in a hurry to be off.

OSCAR:

> But there's something gleams down yonder

EDITH: Oh no, there's no hurry.

OSCAR:

> whiteish, reindeer-like a bit.
> Ma, it was our own reflection
> in the fell-tarn's still complexion—
> up towards the surface scurrying
> in the self-same wild career
> as we down and down were hurrying.

EDITH: To tell you the truth, we've already arrived.

CHRISTOPHER: Arrived? Where . . . where are you?

EDITH: Don't worry about it. We travel in our own way, Oscar and I. Just carry on with your job. I think there must be a blockage somewhere? It makes such a lovely plopping sound. We poured something into it. But it just goes on plopping, plip plop. The kitchen's out there.

[EDITH *points, winks at* OSCAR *and unpacks the sandwiches, while the puzzled plumber picks up his tools, shaking his head, and begins work in the kitchen, muttering to himself.*]

EDITH: [*In a low voice.*] What a nice young man. Friendly.

OSCAR: Was he? I thought he was . . . quite ordinary,

EDITH: Go on, darling. The party piece. You hadn't finished.

OSCAR: What was so special about him then?

EDITH: Didn't you hear it?

OSCAR: What?

EDITH: His voice. That attractive voice. Do go on!

OSCAR: Where had I got to?

EDITH: In the self-same wild career as we down and down were hurrying.

[OSCAR *is ready to continue the performance at once, now clearly inspired by having a further listener.*]

OSCAR:

Buck from over, buck from under
clashed as one, from far asunder
and the foam about us crashed.
Well, we lay there and we splashed . . .

CHRISTOPHER: [*Coming in.*] Yes, it's splashing about all over the place. I'll have to go out to the car for the wrench. And the plunger. [*Goes out quickly.*]

OSCAR: I think I've lost the thread.

EDITH: You know it so well. Mr Swot the teacher.

OSCAR: [*Muttering.*]

Buck from over, buck from under
clashed as one, from far asunder
and the foam about us crashed.
Well, we lay there and we splashed . . .

EDITH: Then we made . . .

OSCAR: What's that?

EDITH: Then we made!

OSCAR: Of course.

Then we made the north side, mother,
managing one way or another;
off the buck swam, me behind him;—
I came home—

EDITH: But what about—?

CHRISTOPHER: [*Comes in again, in a hurry.*] Yes, I found it. The wrench. Everything in its place. I took the pump wrench too. You never know.

OSCAR:

Oh, he'll still be there, no doubt.
You can have him . . .

CHRISTOPHER: Yes, we'll soon have it now. All straight. I've got the wrench.

OSCAR: You can have him if you find him!

[EDITH *applauds enthusiastically.*]

CHRISTOPHER: [*Amazed.*] Blimey!

EDITH: That's just what I've always said. That man ought to be an actor! Isn't that right?

CHRISTOPHER: Could well be.

EDITH: He's so clever, that man is. And the things he *remembers*.

CHRISTOPHER: [*Walking towards the kitchen.*] I'd better be getting on.

EDITH: Perhaps it's making a plopping noise like that over at Steffensen's too? What fun. You can hear that it's a mountain stream, can't you? It almost seems a shame to repair it.

OSCAR: What did you say? I was thinking of something else.

EDITH: I like that noise. The plopping.

OSCAR: The floor out there has got very wet.

EDITH: Now you must eat, my dear. Smoked sausage, flatbread and cream. Real mountaineers' fare. And lovely hot coffee. What is it?

OSCAR: There's something about evening sun . . . It's this poem, I can't relax until I remember it. Evening sun . . . it rhymes with let it be done . . .

EDITH: It sounds like a sad poem.

OSCAR: And if today were the last time I saw . . . It's Hamsun. You can hear it, can't you?

CHRISTOPHER: [*In the doorway.*] I'm trying to clear it. Loosening the clamp on the U-bend, and then using the plunger. It should be OK. But is it possible to get rid of some of these animals? I keep falling over them. Standing on them.

EDITH: Oh . . . I'll help you.

[*She chats to the cats in the corridor, while* OSCAR *sits muttering, trying to remember the poem.*]

EDITH: Come on then . . . out you go, children . . . Mozart, old chap, out you go again now, there's a good boy. This man's going to mend things for us. Missi, my sweet, out you come. Petrus, pass . . . oh no, not under the bench, Petrus. You little rascal. Yes, yes, I know that you're in a bad mood today, Miss Pettersen isn't always as friendly as she might be. That's just the way things are. That's life. Oh no, what *have* you done there, Pickle? Shame on you.

[CHRISTOPHER *looks around the room while* EDITH *is sorting out the cats.*]

CHRISTOPHER: It's a neat place you've got here.

OSCAR: What?

CHRISTOPHER: I just said this is a neat place. Cosy. Gosh, what a lot of books. And a piano.

OSCAR: We've got a lot of nice things. Fine old things. At least, we *had* . . .

CHRISTOPHER: I like old things. It's modern now as well, anything old.

OSCAR: The finest thing of all—oh no, it's not here right now. An ancient rose-painted chest. It's . . . it's being restored. And some of the paintings are being cleaned.

CHRISTOPHER: I collect old tools. All sorts of things, axes, sledgehammers, old ice-saws. Anvils. My wife isn't very keen.

OSCAR: Isn't she?

EDITH: [*Enters.*] Poor little Pickle. He had a little accident out there.

CHRISTOPHER: [*Going out again.*] Yes, it did smell a bit suspicious out there. But a plumber has to stick his nose into all kinds of things.

OSCAR: I was telling the plumber about our old chest. The one that's being . . . restored?

EDITH: [*Not listening.*] I just hope Pickle isn't sick. He's been looking a bit under the weather recently, don't you think?

OSCAR: It's been gone quite a while now, hasn't it? [*Drinks coffee, spills a little.*] The cognac was better. I don't suppose there's a little drop . . .

EDITH: Of course. [*Pours some into the cup.*]

OSCAR: What about you?

EDITH: I'll wait a little. Perhaps there'll be some more surprises? Who knows?

OSCAR: But that chest . . .

EDITH: Have you remembered it now? That poem? The sad one.

OSCAR: It's not sad, Edith. It's beautiful. Just wait . . . Just wait until it falls into place . . . in my old head. [*Drinks cognac and mutters the poem to himself.*]

CHRISTOPHER: [*In the doorway.*] They are pretty old, yes. Old and rusty. I really ought to change the joint and parts of the pipe.

EDITH: Ought you to, Karlsen?

CHRISTOPHER: You could do with new PVC sections for the waste pipe as well. I've fixed the outlet for the moment. I'd better pop back to the stores and pick up a few parts.

EDITH: I suppose it'll cost quite a bit?

CHRISTOPHER: Could be. I'll pop back a bit later, OK?

OSCAR: Just pop in and out as you like, my good man. We'll be here!

CHRISTOPHER: It certainly looks like it. But . . . they'll all come running back in again, all those animals, when I go out?

EDITH: Don't worry about that. They do what they want, those cats. That's what's so lovely about them.

CHRISTOPHER: So I'll just let the whole gang in again, shall I?

EDITH: That's right.

[CHRISTOPHER *goes out shaking his head, loud meowing can be heard as he lets himself out, muttering.*]

EDITH: What a nice young man.

OSCAR: Most obliging. He liked old sledgehammers.

EDITH: Did he?

OSCAR: Sledgehammers and axes and that kind of thing.

EDITH: Sledgehammers and axes . . . how strange.

OSCAR: [*Sitting staring at the piece of flatbread he is chewing.*] Edith! Look! A country in Europe. You can have three guesses.

EDITH: [*Looking closely at the flatbread.*] England.

OSCAR: No, no, you can see that's not right. Look closely.

EDITH: Belgium.

OSCAR: That's better. But look at that little point. That stretches out into the sea.

EDITH: France.

OSCAR: [*Enthusiastically.*] That's right! You recognized it from Brittany, didn't you?

EDITH: Of course.

OSCAR: And where is Paris?

EDITH: There.

OSCAR: No, no, you're right up in Normandy. There. There's Paris, my love.

EDITH: Yes, of course. [*She nibbles pieces out of her flatbread eagerly, looking at it in between.*]

OSCAR: No, it's no good doing that, Edith. You can't sit and nibble it to make Italy. That's what you were trying to do, wasn't it? It just has to happen, completely by chance. That's the secret.

[*Both sit and study their pieces of flatbread surreptitiously, without finding anything else.*]

EDITH: I don't think he really knew what was going on with our mountain walk.

OSCAR: It does taste good. I suppose he's going to need paying?

[EDITH *shrugs her shoulders.*]

OSCAR: Expensive people, plumbers.

EDITH: We've always been comfortably off. Don't think of money now.

OSCAR: All right. Many thanks, Madame accountant.

EDITH: Don't mention it, Mr. schoolmaster. Besides, maths was never your subject.

OSCAR: It wasn't yours either, if I remember correctly?

EDITH: I have what you might call a more . . . practical attitude to life.

OSCAR: Did you say practical? I think I would be inclined to say that you have a more . . . imaginative attitude to life. [*Puts on his glasses and points.*] Look! Can you see that fly on your flatbread?

EDITH: There are no flies here.

OSCAR: A European capital. Quick, before it goes.

EDITH: So there is. I almost ate it.

OSCAR: Sofia!

EDITH: What? Have you given them all names?

OSCAR: The capital of Bulgaria. That's just where it is. If that man's going to put in some new pipes, it'll cost several hundred kroner. That's for sure.

EDITH: We've always been comfortably off.

OSCAR: Yes, so you tell me. But in fact . . . in fact we only have my pension to live on?

EDITH: Have you had enough? Then we'll clear up. And now Mr. Swot must promise me not to fill his clever head with money worries. Wasn't that a lovely walk in the mountains? [*Hums a little walking tune.*]

[OSCAR *is about to lie on the sofa.*]

EDITH: No, no, not there, my love. That's Mozart's place. *He* lies here and *you* lie there. [*Leads him gently over to the divan.*] There you are. This is your place.

OSCAR: You've kept a lot of things from me, Edith.

EDITH: Now you must lie down a little. There you go. [*Helps him to take off his anorak and boots, covers him with a rug.*] Now you must rest, Oscar. And afterwards perhaps we'll . . . [*Goes out to the kitchen with the rucksack, chats to the cats.*]

OSCAR: [*Mutters to himself tiredly.*] All the paintings and those old things . . . Oh well. And the first editions of the classics. When will I see them again? We can't just . . .

[EDITH *busy doing things in the kitchen, comes in again after a while and sits down at the piano.* OSCAR *dozes, while* EDITH *plays a nocturne. Gradually the music changes from her playing to taped piano music, it is* EDITH*'s advanced pianoforte exercises from long ago.*]

[OSCAR *wakes up, listens, half sits up, the music forms a transition to the monologues.*]

OSCAR: She sat there practising on the landlady's piano, in the cold dining room. Sometimes I could see that she had been crying. I lent her a sweater. I filled a flask with hot chocolate and put it on the piano before I went to the university. You played and played . . . you could have gone a long way.

[*The music suddenly ceases, spotlight on* EDITH *who puts her hands on her heart.*]

EDITH: One week. One brief week was all he was given. Seven days and seven nights we were allowed to keep him. And then . . . Again and again I would wake up in the middle of the night and hear the midwife's voice, it left an echo in my head, a cold echo, Mrs. Tellmann, can you hear me? Your little boy . . . we couldn't save his life. Your little boy is dead . . .

[*The music on the tape can be heard again.*]

OSCAR: I could hear her playing right through into my room. When she wasn't at the conservatory, she just sat and practised. And froze. For hours she sat and practised. She had to play it out of her system, play herself through it. I tiptoed into the sitting room, sat quietly in a corner and listened to her. Looked at her. It was a long time before *she* saw me . . .

[*The music disappears again suddenly.*]

EDITH: It'll work out better next time, the doctors said. But it didn't. Three times I lost it too early.

[*The music returns.*]

OSCAR: She was just thinking about that bastard, that miserable cellist. As if playing a cello was as wonderful as all that. For a while I even thought of learning it myself. Playing the cello. So that she would notice me . . . And *him*, he promised her everything, got what he wanted and betrayed her. For someone else. Ah well.

[*The music vanishes.*]

EDITH: Just little Alexander saw the light of day. What was it that was wrong with me? Was I a barren garden that wouldn't bear any fruit, from *him* . . .

[*The music returns.*]

OSCAR: It always makes me sad to hear a cello.

[*The music vanishes.*]

EDITH: Now and again I have . . . hated this body. This frozen earth, this barren garden . . .

[*The music returns.*]

OSCAR: You never became what you struggled to be, Edith. You gave up, so that I . . . Oh well, it's too late for all that. You got what you wanted. I think—. You were always the one who decided. [*He lies down on the divan again, then sits up again straight away, thoughtful.*] Weren't you?

[OSCAR *lies down again, the light changes to what it was before the monologues.* EDITH *begins to play again, the other music dies away, the light fades.*]

[*Pause.*]

[OSCAR *has settled himself in the comfortable armchair, perhaps with a cat on his knee, while the other cats can be heard at regular intervals.* EDITH *is leafing through* Lady Chatterley's Lover, *and finds the place where they last stopped reading aloud.*]

EDITH: Are you ready, my dear? This is where we stopped yesterday. "He could get up if he liked, and stand there, above her, buttoning down those absurd corduroy breeches, straight in front of her. After all, Michaelis had had the decency to turn away. This man was so assured in himself, he didn't know what a clown other people found him, a half-bred fellow. [*Reads with real feeling.*] Yet, as he was drawing away, to rise silently and leave her, she clung to him in terror. 'Don't! Don't go! Don't leave me! Don't be cross with me! Hold me! Hold me fast!' she whispered in blind frenzy, not even knowing what she said, and clinging to him with uncanny force. It was from herself she wanted to be saved, from her own inward anger and resistance. Yet how powerful was that inward resistance that possessed her!"

[*In the middle of the reading the new home help makes her entrance, an energetic young woman who holds herself suspiciously straight.*]

VIVIAN: Excuse me. I'm really very late. Had such trouble finding the way. It's Tellmann, isn't it?

OSCAR: And who are you?

VIVIAN: The new home help. At your service!

EDITH: Good heavens, I'd quite forgotten. So you're the new lady?

VIVIAN: Vivian Sunde.

OSCAR: [*Gets up and bows gallantly.*] Tellmann, Oscar Tellmann. And this is my wife, Edith.

EDITH: How do you do, my dear. Yes, it is Thursday today, isn't it?

VIVIAN: I think so. But I'm not at all sure. There are some cats here, they said. The one before me was allergic to them? What rubbish. I love cats, I do. Perhaps I'd better get started then? The usual thing, is it? [*Looks around a bit, runs her finger over the layer of dust on the bookshelf, etc.*]

EDITH: You'll find the cloths in the kitchen and . . .

VIVIAN: That's OK. Just relax. I'm used to this job. I'll find what I need. [*In the kitchen, chats to the cats, opens and closes cupboards, etc.*]

OSCAR: [*In a low voice.*] What's wrong with that woman?

EDITH: I'm blessed if I know.

[EDITH *and* OSCAR *try to continue with the reading, at the same time as they follow what* VIVIAN *is doing and gradually become more preoccupied with her than with* Lady Chatterley.]

EDITH: [*Reading, a little absent-mindedly.*] Let's see . . . where had we got to now . . . "He took her in his arms again and drew her to him, and suddenly she became small in his arms, small and nestling. [VIVIAN *enters.*] It was gone, the resistance was gone, and she began to melt in a marvellous peace."

[VIVIAN *starts tidying up and dusting in the room, waters the plants, working with energetic but not quite coordinated movements. It gradually becomes apparent that she is far from sober, but nonetheless determined to do a respectable job. While she works she picks up a sentence or two from the reading, and reacts with surprise, thoughtful seriousness and appreciative nods.*]

VIVIAN: Don't worry, I'll not disturb you. Whoops, that was a near thing! [*She almost knocks over a vase, but saves it.*]

EDITH: [*Reading.*] "And as she melted small and wonderful in his arms, she became infinitely desirable to him, all his blood-vessels seemed to scald with intense yet tender desire, for her, for her softness, for the penetrating beauty of her in his arms, passing into his blood."

VIVIAN: [*Almost has an accident again, this time with a little plaster cast of Beethoven.*] God almighty, I'm having some close shaves today. That's worth a bob or two, I should think.

EDITH: Beethoven.

VIVIAN: Yes, I thought there was something familiar about him.

EDITH: You don't need to dust *everything*. We're not so fussy as all that.

[EDITH *and* OSCAR *follow* VIVIAN's *excursions around the room with increasing concern.*]

OSCAR: Are you going to read some more?

EDITH: Perhaps we're disturbing you? I don't want to distract you from your work . . .

VIVIAN: Distract me? No way. It's really . . . really interesting. Just carry on.

EDITH: [*Carries on reading.*] "And softly, with that marvellous swoon-like caress of his hand in pure soft desire, softly he stroked the silky slope of her loins, down, down between her soft warm buttocks, coming nearer and nearer to the very quick of her."

[OSCAR *clears his throat.*]

EDITH: We . . . we'd perhaps better stop there.

VIVIAN: [*Spontaneously.*] Oh no, don't do that! It was so exciting. So . . . so lovely?

EDITH: [*Reads a couple more lines, rather hesitantly, looks across at* OSCAR.] "And she felt him like a flame of desire, yet tender, and she felt herself melting in the flame. She let herself go. She felt his penis risen against her with silent amazing force and assertion and she let herself go to him." [*She closes the book with a decisive bang.*] No, that's enough now. Enough Lady Chatterley.

VIVIAN: Oh, is that what the woman's called? Lady . . .

EDITH: Chatterley. English.

VIVIAN: I see. [*Still cleaning the room.*] Yes, well, those English ladies were no better than they ought to be, some of them. I've seen them, I have. On board.

EDITH: On board?

VIVIAN: Yes, sir! On the voyage of life, so to speak.

EDITH: The voyage of life . . . What does that mean?

VIVIAN: It's a long story. *Many* stories. [*At that moment* VIVIAN *trips over the carpet or a table leg, she falls forward, but saves herself at the last moment.*] Oh my giddy aunt, I nearly did it that time! That's what happens when you've been on a trip. [*Shakes her head in exasperation.*]

EDITH: On a trip, you said. We often go on trips too.

VIVIAN: Yes? But not boat trips, I hope. That's where I've been.

EDITH: Why don't you sit down and . . . take the weight off your feet. You look worn out, poor thing.

VIVIAN: Can I smoke?

OSCAR: Of course. As much as you like.

VIVIAN: [*Sits down, finds cigarettes and a lighter in her bag, lights a cigarette.*] It's great to read books. I used to read too. I liked it. Should have read much more.

OSCAR: Was it good on the water? It's a long time since we've done that.

VIVIAN: Good? There was quite a swell, if you understand what I mean. Ugh. And then that stupid man . . . that idiot . . . I mean, . . . I'm talking about my bloke. Perhaps I shouldn't talk like that about him, but there you go. Men and boats, I say. Best to keep away from them. Well away.

OSCAR: [*Interested.*] You think so?

VIVIAN: Ropes and anchors and islands and rocks. Nothing but trouble. And suddenly . . . suddenly: *clouds* of smoke from the engine and a lot of nasty little bangs . . . [*She imitates the bangs.*]

EDITH: Oh dear.

VIVIAN: His mate was with us as well. So off they go quarrelling like a couple of kids. The sparking plug, one of them says. Must be that, mustn't it? I'm sure it's the sparking plug. No, it's not that, says the other. It's the carburettor. Dust in the carburettor.

OSCAR: Dust in the carburettor, yes. I've heard of that.

VIVIAN: So there they are head first in the engine box rummaging away and swearing at each other. And there I am, just sitting there as still as a mouse! I just asked, as timid as you like, if they'd remembered to turn the petrol on? They didn't half lay into me, the pair of them. Super boat trip, wasn't it?

OSCAR: Well, it's obvious you have to turn the petrol on.

VIVIAN: It's the battery, says one of them. There's no life in the battery. Then it's the magneto, says the other. Magneto my arse, says I. So there we are drifting. Do we ask someone for help? Not likely. The lads are going to fix this. So . . . well, I just had a little sip, just to pass the time, while the lads were messing about with the engine. And then I get torn off a strip for that too! Well, it was perhaps one too many. But only a little one . . . It's not all that easy. [*Stubs out the cigarette.*] Now I'll do the kitchen and the hall. That's all I'll have time for today. [*Goes out.*]

EDITH: You can do the rest next time. [*In a low voice.*] What do you think's wrong with that woman?

OSCAR: I'm not sure. She'd been on a boat trip.

EDITH: [*Looks round nervously to see what has been damaged.*] I think everything's OK. But still.

OSCAR: Do you think . . . do you think she'll come . . . often?

EDITH: [*Thinks about it, then nods, a little worried at the thought.*] Once a week, I think. Every Thursday.

OSCAR: Good lord . . . Do you think . . . , do you think the woman was drunk?

EDITH: I don't think. I'm quite certain. I haven't seen anyone so tipsy since . . . since Maria's seventieth birthday. Or was it her eightieth?

OSCAR: The years pass so quickly.

EDITH: Do you remember, do you remember that we sang for her? [*Sings.*] "I've just met a girl called Maria . . ." Ladies and gentlemen, I feel so moved, she said. I feel so moved that I must stand up . . . And she was such an elegant old lady with her silk blouse and pearl earrings. And rolling drunk.

OSCAR: Maria, yes.

EDITH: And she always had that lovely plait around her head. Like a diadem.

OSCAR: She was a sweet little thing.

EDITH: She really had a skinful on her birthday. Was it real, do you think? I've always wondered whether it was real.

OSCAR: Now she's gone as well . . .

EDITH: Do you think the plait was real?

OSCAR: And the rest is silence . . . What happens to them, all of them? All our dead friends . . . relations, neighbors, people we met . . .

EDITH: It might have been a false plait.

OSCAR: Sailing round in eternity . . .

EDITH: Probably nun's hair. Nun's hair is the finest you can make wigs of. But Maria! With nun's hair! That little butterfly . . . Hush! What's going on now?

[*The sound of smashing plates from the kitchen.*]

OSCAR: I think she broke something. One of the cats' saucers perhaps?

EDITH: It sounds more as if she was stamping on them. Or throwing them at the wall?

OSCAR: It look as if things are going to be quite lively here with that woman in the house. She's attractive as well.

EDITH: Oh? What do you mean?

OSCAR: What do I mean? What do you mean, what do I mean?

EDITH: And what do *you* mean with "attractive as well"?

OSCAR: Just what I said. Attractive and chic.

EDITH: Attractive and chic. Just think. Chic as well.

OSCAR: Stop it, Edith. Don't be childish.

EDITH: She's more your type perhaps? Perhaps that's what you mean? An attractive and chic swingalong girl.

OSCAR: Not so loud. She might hear you.

EDITH: If she hears *you*, she'll really fancy herself.

OSCAR: You don't think that she's bothered about an old chap like me. You really are sweet, Edith.

EDITH: I don't like you looking at other women. [*She is looking for something in the cupboard.*]

OSCAR: I know, my love. But I can't see so much any more, you know.

EDITH: I don't like it. [*She finds a couple of bottles of chianti and puts them out on the sideboard.*]

VIVIAN: [*Enters, notices the wine bottles at once but pretends that she doesn't see them.*] Jesus Christ, my poor head. I've had a bit of an accident, I'm afraid. A couple of saucers went west. And a glass. Sorry. I'll buy some more.

EDITH: Oh, don't worry about it, my dear. Breaking a glass brings good luck.

VIVIAN: I think I've had too much sea air today. It must be the sea air.

OSCAR: I'm sure it was.

VIVIAN: Next time it'll all be in apple-pie order. Ship shape. Not a single bit of cat shit left, I promise!

EDITH: Thank you very much.

VIVIAN: You do have it nice here, don't you?

EDITH: Well, this worked out . . . all right, didn't it?

VIVIAN: It all works out, you know. It all works out. Always look on the bright side! Cheerio.

OSCAR: [*Jumping up.*] Cheerio! Let me help you with your jacket!

[OSCAR *helps* VIVIAN, *half-clumsily, half-gallantly,* VIVIAN *laughs a little, gets the jacket on in the end.*]

VIVIAN: I'll be here on Thursday again, then. Cheerio. [*Waves and goes.*]

EDITH: What's got into you?

OSCAR: [*Groans and staggers over to the sofa.*] God, these miserable knees of mine.

EDITH: Well, you will strut around to impress the ladies.

OSCAR: Nothing left but chalk and dust. Next stage—ashes. [*By the sofa.*] I'd better lie down a bit, I think.

EDITH: Chic, you say . . . [*Attending to the cats, then doing something in the kitchen.*] [*To* OSCAR.] Well? Are you lying there thinking about death again now?

OSCAR: Yes.

EDITH: Well, stop it.

OSCAR: Isn't it strange, Edith? When you're as old as I am and have thought so much about death, you'd think you got a bit used to the thought! But the truth is that I've got so used to being *alive* . . .

[*While* OSCAR *lies there, he finds some papers on the table beside the sofa and looks through them. There are a number of unpaid bills which he studies with interest.* EDITH *chats partly to the cats, partly to him.*]

EDITH: You ought to stop it. Nothing good'll come of it. Do you think the cats worry about death? [*Puts her head round the door.*] What are you messing about with now?

OSCAR: Nothing.

EDITH: There'll be a little surprise soon. From my little kitchen.

OSCAR: You think I don't understand anything, don't you?

EDITH: What do you mean?

OSCAR: The first editions which disappeared. The pictures. No, no, don't play games any more. I understand. That you had to.

EDITH: [*Silent for a moment.*] How . . . how long have you . . .

OSCAR: You were hoping I would forget the books and the pictures. And the chest.

EDITH: Are you . . . cross with me?

OSCAR: We can't take it with us anyway.

EDITH: [*Has sat down, taken aback, puts her hand on her heart.*] I just wanted to spare you. You were so fond of those pictures.

OSCAR: It was fun for a while. To pretend that I knew nothing. And what have you thought of doing with . . . with all these? [*Waves the bills.*]

EDITH: Oh, I'll think of something. Perhaps I could take some pupils again?

OSCAR: [*Looking around.*] The candelabra?

EDITH: Perhaps.

[OSCAR *nods, resigned.*]

EDITH: [*Changes the mood abruptly, claps her hands.*] Do you know where we're going today?

OSCAR: I didn't think we were going anywhere. We've already been on a trip today.

EDITH: We're going a long way. And you're coming too, my sweet . . .

[EDITH *quickly throws a cloth on the table and brings in a tray with glasses and a bottle of chianti, bottles of oil and vinegar etc., dresses herself and* OSCAR *in straw hats and neckerchiefs. Piano or record music.*]

OSCAR: But why . . . why are we doing so much travelling today of all days?

EDITH: [*Interrupting him.*] You know that very well. If you think about it.

OSCAR: Do I?

EDITH: We're off to a place where we loved to be. A place that smelt of cats and garlic and cooking oil and sewers and wet walls. And all the alleys were swarming with people, and we drank wine in the middle of the day and you bought me necklaces of glass beads . . .

OSCAR: What are you telling me . . .

EDITH: Venice! To Venice!

OSCAR: Are we really going there?

EDITH: Do you recognize that smell? I'm cooking onions in olive oil. Very Italian.

OSCAR: Where shall we live?

EDITH: You know that!

OSCAR: At the Lido? That beautiful hotel. What was it called now . . .

EDITH: Hotel des Bains.

OSCAR: Hotel des Bains.

EDITH: A large old double room overlooking the beach and the sea. If you don't feel like going to the beach, we'll go down into the lovely garden and sit in wicker chairs and listen to the grasshoppers.

OSCAR: Wonderful. [*Pours out wine.*]

EDITH: And whilst we're waiting for . . . the waiter . . . we'll look around a bit.

[EDITH *has fetched out an album with photos from their Italian journeys, and they leaf through it eagerly, pointing.*]

EDITH: There you are, Oscar. In front of the Doge's Palace. My word, you do look handsome. And the church of St. Mark.

OSCAR: Basilica di San Marco. Built around the year 800, strong Byzantine influence in the architecture.

EDITH: You remember everything, don't you? Mr. Swot. Do you remember the concerts in the church?

OSCAR: The Rialto bridge. There you are, wearing a straw hat and with flowers, your arms full of flowers. You're so pretty, Edith.

EDITH: [*Looks closer at the picture.*] That . . . that isn't me. Who is that woman? Surely you can see that it's not me?

OSCAR: Isn't it? Who can it be then?

EDITH: I remember. That Swedish woman who was living at the same hotel. Ulla-Gulla something or other. She even boasted about being an aristocrat.

OSCAR: Ulla Birgitta she was called.

EDITH: So you remember that?

OSCAR: As it happens.

EDITH: Why did you take a picture of *her* then, on the Rialto bridge?

OSCAR: I really can't remember that after all these years. Perhaps *you* took it?

EDITH: Me?

OSCAR: Let's go on. Cheers, by the way.

[*Next picture, a familiar-looking tower, a powerful and phallic picture.*]

EDITH: But that tower there . . .

OSCAR: Ai ai. Now if I'd had one like that . . .

EDITH: That tower isn't from Venice. It's Pisa. You're saying some very strange things today!

OSCAR: Am I? Do you know, I think I may have a touch of satyriasis. A fun illness—that'll make a change!

EDITH: It's that home help. Your head's been turned by that . . . that chic lady parading around.

[EDITH *goes out to the kitchen to get the food, while* OSCAR *silently turns the album pages back, a little guiltily, until he finds the picture of the Swedish woman, smiles.*]

OSCAR: Ulla Birgitta . . . little countess . . .

[OSCAR *enjoys his happy memories, drinks to her, then pulls himself together, a little shame-faced, as* EDITH *comes back.*]

[EDITH *serves a simple spaghetti dish, salad, cheese, fruit, while she is a waiter and a customer at the same time, and conversing in Italian.*]

EDITH: Cameriere, mi dia la lista per favore! Che cosa può raccomandare? E la specialita della casa . . . un antipasto misto e una pastasciutta.

OSCAR: E come secondo?

EDITH: Frutto e formaggio.

OSCAR: Ah, Gorgonzola!

EDITH: Mi dispiace. Nix Gorgonzola. Jarlsberg.

OSCAR: Va bene. [*Pouring wine.*] Scusi: Attenzione. Il vino rosso . . . buono . . . molto buono . . .
Do you remember in Germany . . . What a great time we had. That wonderful nudist beach. We went there several years running. What was it called now?

EDITH: Yes, what was it called?

OSCAR: Oh yes, those were the days. All those attractive people. [*Lost in happy memories.*] Wilhelmsruhe! Strandbad Wilhelmsruhe! That was it.

EDITH: Wilhelmsruhe. That's right.

OSCAR: I've never felt so free and happy. You liked it as well, didn't you?

EDITH: [*Nods, smiling.*] But we're in Venice now.

[OSCAR *and* EDITH *eat and drink, turning every now and then to the invisible waiter.*]

OSCAR: Delicato.

EDITH: Per una notte. Per una ristorante.

OSCAR: Per una signora.

EDITH: Per un signor. Siete contenti?

OSCAR: Scusi, da dove viene?

EDITH: Vengo dalla Norvegia.

OSCAR: Norvegia? Ah, bella bella Norvegia!

[CHRISTOPHER *has let himself into the hall, comes in stumbling and muttering in the midst of the lively meal with* EDITH *and* OSCAR *talking and gesticulating eagerly, both dressed up in straw hats and neckerchiefs.*]

CHRISTOPHER: Bloody hell . . . they make you dizzy, all these cats . . . keep shooting out of nowhere. They hiss at you as well. Oh . . . am I interrupting something?

OSCAR: [*In great spirits, raises his glass.*] Buon giorno, signor! Buon giorno!

CHRISTOPHER: Hi.

EDITH: Buon giorno.

OSCAR: Buon giorno, il Plumbo! Ha, ha, not bad, what?

CHRISTOPHER: I've picked up that PVC piping.

EDITH: Wouldn't you like to have a little taste? It's good. Antipasto misto. Pastasciutta.

CHRISTOPHER: I'm expected home for dinner. Thank you.

OSCAR: Il Plumbo non appetito? Come va?

CHRISTOPHER: You know . . . really you need a completely new system.

EDITH: Do sit down for a minute. [*Persuades him to sit down.*]

CHRISTOPHER: You're off on your travels again, are you? It's just like Mallorca, this is.

OSCAR: Mallorca? No, no Mallorca. Venezia.

EDITH: Actually . . . actually we're sitting in a little restaurant on the Lido in Venice and looking towards the town. You can sit out on the pavement. And there are lots of thin cats. And . . .

CHRISTOPHER: Yes, I can see the cats!

EDITH: And *stunning* waiters. [*She winks at an invisible waiter.*]

CHRISTOPHER: Are there?

EDITH: A bit small. But very attractive. And so polite. Signora, they say. Per favore, signora. Scusi, signora. Oh yes, they have style, the people here. That I must say.

CHRISTOPHER: Well, you two are having a fine time. [*Starts to eat absentmindedly.*] I like sitting at home in the garden grilling some nice thick cutlets. It's just like being on holiday.

EDITH: There, you see! [*She has poured him some wine.*]

OSCAR: Salute, signor.

CHRISTOPHER: Salute. Cheers.

OSCAR: Va bene. Arrivederci.

CHRISTOPHER: Arrivederci. Good Lord, what am I doing? I wasn't going to have anything. I get all confused in this house.

EDITH: Can I call you by your first name?

CHRISTOPHER: Yes, of course. I'm called Christopher. This is a good wine.

EDITH: I'm so glad you called here today. This is a very special day, you understand.

OSCAR: Uno giorno speciale.

EDITH: You have such a fine voice, Christopher. I noticed it at once.

OSCAR: Signora . . . musicale . . . signora pianissimo pedaogoga . . . signora romantica . . . molto romantica . . . D'you know, I really think I'm getting a bit merry!

EDITH: It's the change of climate.

OSCAR: Perhaps it's the sea air?

EDITH: Just think, here we are sitting together with a handsome young man. It's just as if . . . as if you've dropped from heaven.

CHRISTOPHER: Really?

EDITH: Now you must taste this little dish of spaghetti.

OSCAR: Una pastasciutta . . . buono . . . molto buono. Delicato.

[EDITH *serving* CHRISTOPHER *in a friendly, almost tender fashion, offers him a straw hat, which he puts on a little hesitantly.*]

OSCAR: Have you heard about the old man?

EDITH: Oh, Oscar!

OSCAR: Have you heard about the old man who was so keen on . . . girls? It was just that he could no longer remember *why* . . . He he he.

[EDITH *has sat down at the piano, plays music to create the mood,* OSCAR *and* CHRISTOPHER *drink a toast.*]

EDITH: They are so beautiful . . . evenings by the sea. The light, that soft light, the scent of the sea and ancient stone houses . . . the smell of cats and garlic fried in oil . . .

CHRISTOPHER: [*Sniffing.*] I can smell it. I can actually smell it!

EDITH: There you are. It's not difficult at all.

CHRISTOPHER: You just have to . . . to let your imagination run away with you!

EDITH: That's right!

CHRISTOPHER: Lovely country, Italy. Good food, good wine. I've never been there, but I don't suppose that matters?

EDITH: It doesn't matter in the slightest. And now, right now, that's where we are . . . in beautiful old Venice. All the canals and the bridges . . . shutters on the windows . . . the markets. The narrow alleyways, all the stalls with glass beads, the churches . . .

CHRISTOPHER: St. Mark's Square!

EDITH: Of course.

CHRISTOPHER: The gondolas!

EDITH: The gondolas . . . fancy me forgetting the gondolas!

CHRISTOPHER: The square with all the doves. I can see it before my eyes. Quite clearly.

EDITH: It's just rained, can't you see? There's a fine reflection across the whole square . . . the old houses and the church mirrored in the water . . .

CHRISTOPHER: And there are some . . . some gorgeous girls here. Little and dark, just like I like them.

EDITH: And gorgeous waiters. A bit small, very handsome. And very polite.

OSCAR: You and your waiters. And the train conductors.

CHRISTOPHER: Tanya, that's my wife, Tanya sometimes looks a little Italian. Specially in the summer.

EDITH: Signora, they say. Isn't that splendid?

CHRISTOPHER: [*Hesitantly.*] Signora . . .

EDITH: A bit more fire. *Signora. Prego, signora.* That means you're welcome, madam.

CHRISTOPHER: Prego, signora.

EDITH: Scusi, signor.

CHRISTOPHER: Scusi, signora.

OSCAR: Salute, signora. Bravo. Bravissimo.

CHRISTOPHER: Salute! Bravo!

[*While the three of them are drinking and laughing,* VIVIAN *suddenly returns.*]

VIVIAN: Excuse me. The door was open.

OSCAR: [*Getting up.*] What a surprise!

VIVIAN: You've not seen my handbag by any chance? I think I must have left it . . . in the kitchen? Hello puss, are you there again? [*Glances longingly at the table and the glasses, and finds her bag.*]

OSCAR: Come in, come in! Per favore.

VIVIAN: Thank goodness. I found it. Not that there's all that much in it. Gosh, you look as if you're having a party!

OSCAR: [*Politely offering her a chair.*] Please sit down. Now we've really got company!

EDITH: [*Brings over a glass, plate etc.*] I'm glad you came back.

VIVIAN: But are you sure this is all right? I'm not one to stand on ceremony, but . . .
CHRISTOPHER: [*Stands up and bows.*] Karlsen. Karlsen Plumbing. Plumb crazy. Christopher, my name is.
VIVIAN: I'm Vivian.
CHRISTOPHER: We're in . . . in Italy, you see. Venice.
VIVIAN: It's not difficult to see that.
OSCAR: We do like going on trips, you see.
VIVIAN: It's certainly a comfortable way of travelling. I didn't mean to come back and disturb you any more today. I'm sure I've disturbed you enough. But it's just this bag . . . [*Searches around in it, looking for something.*] There it is. [*Relieved.*]
OSCAR: Have a drink with us and enjoy the view. The sea, the beach, the cypresses, the olive trees . . .

[EDITH *fetches the other bottle of wine,* CHRISTOPHER *pulls the cork out, plays the part of gallant waiter as he pours wine for them all.*]

CHRISTOPHER: Prego, signora. Prego, signor. Prego, prego!

[*All drink a toast.*]

CHRISTOPHER: I liked St. Mark's Square best. With all the doves. And the reflection of all the old buildings . . . after it had rained in the square. You described it so well . . .
EDITH: [*Gently stroking his hand or his hair.*] Just think, you've finally come . . . You've grown so big, Alexander. A grown man.
CHRISTOPHER: Christopher.
EDITH: I'll call you Alexander. Just for a while? It's so good to have you here—. I like so much to hear you talk. Your beautiful voice.
CHRISTOPHER: [*Clears his throat, sits up, takes another mouthful of wine, stands up and launches into a melodious song, e.g. "Drink to Me Only." He sings well, and the others listen in surprise.*]

Drink to me only with thine eyes
and I will pledge with mine.
Or leave a kiss but in the cup
and I'll not look for wine.

The thirst that from the soul doth rise
doth ask a drink divine
But might I of Jove's nectar sup
I would not change for thine.

[*All applaud enthusiastically as he sits down again, a little embarrassed.*]

EDITH: Wonderful.
OSCAR: Bravo, bravissimo!
VIVIAN: Brilliant. Are you in a choir?
CHRISTOPHER: Yes. Tenor in a mixed-voice choir. That's where I met my wife. She's a contralto in the choir. Well, it's not a professional group, but it's fun. We sing a cappella.
EDITH: Just so. To think that you sing as well—. I could hear it from your voice, actually.
CHRISTOPHER: It's the breathing that's important. To breathe properly. A choir shouldn't sound like a pair of bellows. The breathing's got to be silent.
VIVIAN: It's so cosy here. [*To* OSCAR.] You two do have a good time here together.
OSCAR: Well, we are lucky right now—that you came back again to see us, my dear. I can call you that, can't I? [*Winks and drinks to her.*]
CHRISTOPHER: [*Getting up.*] Excuse me, but I've got to fix these pipes. While I can still see one end of the wrench from the other . . .
EDITH: Oh, there's no hurry!

CHRISTOPHER: She'll be expecting me. Thank you very much. That was lovely. [*Goes out to the kitchen.*]

VIVIAN: That's all right, ducks—if I can be so free.

OSCAR: Of course you can—or call me Oscar.

VIVIAN: That's a bit familiar, isn't it?

OSCAR: Do you think so? Little signorina Miriam?

VIVIAN: Vivian. Actually I'm a signora really. I was married—once.

OSCAR: You've been in Italy too, haven't you?

VIVIAN: Sure have. I've been halfway round the world.

OSCAR: Really?

VIVIAN: I signed up for years, I did.

OSCAR: Signed up?

VIVIAN: Merchant navy. Sailed with my husband. He was a machinist. And I was a stewardess.

OSCAR: How interesting!

VIVIAN: It was a hard life. But it was fun too. And we made good money. Oh well, those times are gone. And so is *he* too . . .

OSCAR: How sad.

VIVIAN: Yes.

[OSCAR *pours out more wine for her.*]

EDITH: You must taste this cheese. It should have been real Gorgonzola, but it's only Jarlsberg.

VIVIAN: The wine is lovely. It's been quite a day. Poof . . .

EDITH: We got the impression that you . . . that you really put your back into things.

VIVIAN: I wasn't quite on form today. But I'm not afraid of hard work. When I was at sea, lord, you should have seen my station! It shone! No balls of fluff under the bunks there, there weren't. On some of the boats we exchanged stations. One week on one, the next on the next, you see?

EDITH: Stations?

VIVIAN: That means so many cabins and so many toilets, you see. And when we did that, the other girls left all the muck for Vivian, because *she* made it all shiny again! They knew that, the lazy bitches. So I put my foot down. It's OK, captain, I said, I'll do my station, but I'm not going to swop round. So that's what we did.

OSCAR: It's such fun to hear you talk about it.

VIVIAN: I've got a lot of strange stories, I have. I could keep going for a thousand and one nights. Easy.

OSCAR: I believe you! I'm quite sure you could.

EDITH: Oscar—.

OSCAR: By the way, have you heard of the old man who was so keen on . . .

EDITH: [*Warning.*] Mr. Tellmann!

OSCAR: [*Chuckles to himself.*] It's touching. After all these years . . . [*To* VIVIAN, *in a low voice.*] My wife is jealous!

VIVIAN: I can well understand that. I'll be like that too. Definitely.

EDITH: My husband has always had a weakness for young ladies. I used to have pupils . . . [*Nods at the piano.*] He used to love listening to them. Looking at them too.

OSCAR: But my love. It was only because—

EDITH: Because they reminded you of me? I know you.

OSCAR: What do you mean by that? I know you?

EDITH: Do you remember . . . do you remember for example our little Goldilocks? The one with plaits the color of honey? You couldn't take your eyes off her.

OSCAR: Now I don't want to hear any more of this rubbish! You're the only one. You know that.

EDITH: Do I know it? How can I—

OSCAR: Of course you know it! And you've always known it. Since the first time I set eyes on you!

VIVIAN: How sweet you are. [*She suddenly starts crying.*] That's the way . . . just the way . . . we could perhaps have been too. Me and my husband. But we'll never get the chance. He was ill. And then he died. And now . . . now everything's just a mess . . .

OSCAR: Don't cry, my dear.

EDITH: No, don't cry. We were having such a nice time together. Is it our fault you feel so bad?

VIVIAN: [*Pulls herself together.*] No, no, it's not you . . . Always look on the bright side! [*Finds a hankie in her bag, blows her nose, takes a couple of photos out of her bag and shows them to* OSCAR.] That's him. Good-looking chap, wasn't he?

[OSCAR *looks around for his glasses.*]

EDITH: You're wearing them, my love.

OSCAR: So I am. Your husband, was he? A stylish fellow. Masculine. Virile.

[EDITH *clears her throat.*]

VIVIAN: We had great times together, so help me—. [*Shakes her head, smiles distantly.*] But we never had any children.

EDITH: [*Looking at the pictures.*] We didn't either. None that lived.

VIVIAN: [*To* EDITH.] How beautiful you are. You have such lovely wrinkles. You . . . you're like silk. You know, that thin fine silk which creases easily. We always used to buy some silk like that when we sailed to the Far East.

EDITH: What a lovely thing to say.

OSCAR: Like silk, yes—.

EDITH: But what are you then, Vivian, if I'm like silk?

VIVIAN: Me? I'm more like acrylic and nylon, I suppose. No, I know—PVC.

EDITH: PV what?

VIVIAN: PVC. It's what they make macs of, you know. Tough stuff. Takes a lot of battering.

EDITH: [*Nods thoughtfully.*] How did you know that? About the macs?

VIVIAN: Because I've sewn them. At a factory.

CHRISTOPHER: [*Enters.*] That's done, then. [*Makes notes on his job schedule.*]

VIVIAN: Well, I must get going. This was really nice.

CHRISTOPHER: [*Muttering as he writes.*] Change the joint, clean the passage, change pipes . . . Driving . . . [*Looks at his watch.*] . . . labor time . . . VAT . . .

VIVIAN: You must forgive me if I've been a bit . . . strange. Now and then . . . now and then I have these kind of black days . . . Always look on the bright side, Vivian, I tell myself. It's not always that easy.

EDITH: We know.

VIVIAN: [*Winks at* EDITH.] Take care of that husband of yours. He's a bit of a rascal, you know! [*Winks at* OSCAR *as well on the way out.*] I'll be here on Thursday again, then. I'm looking forward to it already! Hello puss, is that you again . . . [*Goes out.*]

[OSCAR *follows the plumber's calculations rather uneasily, makes worried signs and grimaces at* EDITH, *all the unpaid bills and where are they going to find the money, he drums nervously on the table.*]

EDITH: [*To* CHRISTOPHER.] What a pity that you have to go.

CHRISTOPHER: I may be back soon, you know! It's not at all certain that this will last, the way it's patched together. Really ought to have a whole new system.

EDITH: Perhaps you'll come and join us on a journey again. We're always setting off for somewhere, Oscar and I.

CHRISTOPHER: Perhaps I will! [*Smiles, thinks for a minute, and then slowly tears the bill in two.*]

OSCAR: [*Waving his glass.*] Il conto! Cameriere, il conto!

CHRISTOPHER: Nix. There'll be no account for this. This was so . . . so enjoyable! The most enjoyable job I've had for a long time.

OSCAR: [*Takes off his hat and bows.*] Grazie, signor.

CHRISTOPHER: Prego, signor! The pleasure was all mine. [*To* EDITH.] Many thanks.

EDITH: [*Taking his hand.*] You don't know how happy you have made me. Perhaps we shall see you again one day?

CHRISTOPHER: That's not impossible.

EDITH: Are you going home to your little dark wife again now?

CHRISTOPHER: Yes, she'll be waiting for me now.

EDITH: You make sure you keep going to that choir!

CHRISTOPHER: Of course. Look after yourselves, both of you. [*Goes out.*]

> [EDITH *and* OSCAR *alone at the table, nibble at the food, take a sip of wine,* EDITH *stops eating and becomes distant and thoughtful, takes off her hat.*]

OSCAR: What is it? Is something wrong?

EDITH: I thought . . . you had remembered.

OSCAR: Remembered? Remembered what?

EDITH: What day it is. The twenty-fifth of August.

> [OSCAR *catches his breath.*]

EDITH: Today . . . today would have been his fortieth birthday.

OSCAR: Fortieth . . . is it possible?

EDITH: We would have had a fine, grown-up forty-year-old son.

OSCAR: Just think—.

EDITH: He would probably have had a wife and children. So we would have had grandchildren too. Who came and gave you lovely sticky kisses on the cheek and asked if you'd got any sweeties in the cupboard.

OSCAR: Well, it wasn't to be. No doubt there was a meaning to it.

EDITH: Sometimes I've thought that perhaps . . . perhaps he would have become a criminal? Or a drug addict? Who knows? And perhaps it was best that he left us again . . .

OSCAR: Perhaps it was.

EDITH: But I don't believe it. I think he would have become an artist.

OSCAR: Like his mother.

EDITH: Me?

OSCAR: Edith my love, you are a master of the art of living.

EDITH: Seven days he was with us. Alexander.

OSCAR: Little Alexander's death was his own. The sorrow is ours. A life is a life, short or long.

EDITH: Seven days and seven nights I was with him. And we didn't have any more after that.

OSCAR: We had a lot of other things.

> [EDITH *nods silently.*]

OSCAR: Do you want to hear Hamsun? I've remembered it now.

EDITH: Yes please.

OSCAR: [*Takes off his straw hat, declaims from memory.*]

> And if today were the last time I saw
> people, the earth and the evening sun
> if my heart were to beat no more
> is this farewell, then let it be done—
> with death a new life is begun.

EDITH: Thank you.

[*Meowing and noise from the kitchen.*]

EDITH: I'd better give them some food. [*Gets up and goes towards the kitchen.*] We've trav-
    elled so much today. I'd almost forgotten them, poor things. [*Stops.*] I know!

OSCAR: What?

EDITH: Now I know where we'll go next time, Oscar!

OSCAR: Yes?

EDITH: To Germany.

OSCAR: To Germany? Ah . . . you mean that wonderful nudist beach . . .

EDITH: That's right! Strandbad Wilhelmsruhe . . .

OSCAR: Of course! I'm looking forward to that . . . I'm really looking forward to
    that . . . You and I at Strandbad Wilhelmsruhe . . .

[*Lights fade, curtain.*]

The excerpts from Peer Gynt *are borrowed—with his kind permission—from John Northam's
translation.*

Kristina Lugn (b. 1948)

Until about 1870, the Swedish theater was undistinguished, relying upon imports—usually melodramas and spectacles—from other countries. Then, impelled with the appearance of Strindberg and such Scandinavian contemporaries as Ibsen, Georg Brandes, and Bjørnstjerne Bjørnson, the slow and rocky "Modern Breakthrough" began. Though he is the undisputable if difficult star in their theatrical firmament, the Swedish response to Strindberg was initially unfavorable. The established theater did not take quickly to either his early naturalistic or his later surrealist, avant-garde plays. The experimental spirit in Sweden lagged behind that of France, Germany, and even Russia in the early decades of this century. Not until 1919, when Olaf Molander became director of Dramaten (the Royal National Theater) was Strindberg appreciated as a major force in modern drama.

Although there were individual instances of notable women writers earlier, the substantial body of literature by women in Sweden also dates from the 1870s and 1880s, when Sweden's first generation of professional women authors appeared, figures like Victoria Benedictsson and Anne Charlotte Leffler, followed immediately by Selma Lagerlöf. Most, like Lagerlöf, wrote fiction or essays—often decrying the constrained lives women led, arguing for change: the vote (which came in 1921), a more humane sexual code, and greater freedom. Still, as in the instance of Leffler, whose plays, *The Actress (Skådespelerskan,* 1873) and *True Women (Sanna qvinnor,* 1883), were for a time more popular than Strindberg's subsequently recognized masterpieces, their contribution to late nineteenth-century Swedish drama was substantial.

The periods before and certainly during the Second World War were difficult and restrictive. After the lifting of the censorship and the securing of the social welfare state, the performing of native drama was still a minority occurrence, even with the plays of Strindberg being succeeded by those of Hjalmar Bergman and Pär Lagerkvist. By the 1960s and '70s, however, state support for the arts led to a democratization and flowering of the drama. Contemporary social, political, and domestic problems and issues of social reform became prominent onstage, along with the psychological, O'Neill-influenced dramas of Lars Norén.

It also coincided with the resurgence of a strong feminist movement and the appearance of a number of very accomplished women dramatists. Kristina Lugn, Agneta Pleijel, Margareta Garpe, and Suzanne Osten are artists who have helped earn international recognition for current Swedish drama. As a group—occasionally as if reacting against the figure of Strindberg—they tend to focus on family sit-

Kristina Lugn, ca. 1999. (Courtesy of Nordiska Strakosch Teaterförlaget.)

uations (often between mothers and daughters) from a perspective sympathetic to women, in a fairly plain, earthy, or even "kitchen sink" style. One such play, Garpe's *For Julia* (*Till Julia*, 1987), clearly takes its departure from Strindberg's *Miss Julie*.

Lugn, now a staff playwright for Dramaten and artistic director at Stockholm's Brunnsgatan Eyra theater, is a prominent figure in contemporary Swedish literature, winning—most recently—the 1999 Selma Lagerlöf Foundation literary prize. She is known equally as a poet and as a dramatist, and she frequently performs—both in poetry readings and onstage. She writes in a subjective and often simple style, focusing her leftist and feminist perspectives on the ironies and discontents latent in the gender roles we assume and the families we construct. She finds both the roles and constructs imprisoning. Ordinary, banal circumstances and the relationships within families are enveloped in frustration and even hopelessness. Behind the ordinary and the mundane is a world as absurd as those of Ionesco or Beckett—though sharing little of their overtly metaphysical suggestiveness.

The title of Lugn's first successful volume of poetry, *To My Husband, if He Could Read* (*Till min man, om han kunde lasa*, 1976), conveys her tone and poetic persona. In *The Old Girls at Lake Garda* (*Idlaflickorna*, 1983), two runaway mothers meet at the Italian lake on holiday from their husbands and inevitably discuss the stress and tedium of their family and sex lives. In *Hour of the Dog* (*Det vackra blir liksom över*, 1989), three female voices poetically bewail the emptiness and unhappiness of family life. *Roger and Ruth* (1997) portrays a divorce by parodying a marriage ceremony.

Between its two protagonists, Blossom and Baby (Googy), *Aunt Blossom* (*Tant Blomma*, 1993) succeeds in questioning the nuclear family as we know and evidently do not love it, childrearing, and the difficult, conflictual choices foisted upon women—especially mothers. Blossom begins by singing, "I want to be free." By the end of the play, after fruitlessly waiting for Baby's mother, she changes her tune, now singing, "I was a blossom. I became an aunt . . . am I a joke?" Baby lyrically envisions moms stuck "between an eighteen-wheeler and an ambulance." The play insistently wonders about being a mother (escaped), being a child (expecting to be mothered), and being a replacement mother ("aunt"). It even tauntingly confuses genders, suggesting their arbitrariness: Baby's Teddy "was his daddy's very youngest daughter" and at one point Blossom moves in imitation of a transvestite ("vogues"). Are these tensions—Baby's demands for attention and Blossom's chafing to be free—reconcilable? Are existing social structures viable? The failure of Baby's mother to appear, stuck in life's traffic as she presumably is, and Blossom's thumping defenestration do not suggest hope. The splatter of references to American popular culture, from *Casablanca* and Marlon Brando to the Statue of Liberty, sardonically extends the criticism internationally.

SELECTED BIBLIOGRAPHY IN ENGLISH

Algulin, Ingemar. *A History of Swedish Literature.* Trans., John Weinstock. Uddevalla, Sweden: The Swedish Institute, 1989.

Anderman, Gunilla M., ed. "Introduction." *New Swedish Plays.* Norwich, England: Norvik Press, 1992. Pp 9–32.

Warme, Lars G., ed. *A History of Swedish Literature.* Lincoln: University of Nebraska Press, 1996.

AUNT BLOSSOM

Kristina Lugn

Translated by Verne Moberg

CHARACTERS

AUNT BLOSSOM

BABY

THE BUILDING SUPERINTENDENT

[*All the other children have gone.* BABY *is alone in playpen.*]

AUNT BLOSSOM: [*Enters and checks out the audience—in the background pop dance music.*] We're so well off, we really are. [*Sings to music. Stops singing.*] "No one knows why I travel, or where my travels will take me on the flight from memory and a ring. But wherever my destination might be, I always want to be free. I can live on everything and nothing . . ." I have to pick up a little here . . . [*In the manner of a TV personality.*] Hi there, all you daycare kids, from your own Aunt Blossom. Wave to Pernilla and Oliver—you too! [*Takes* BABY's *hand and waves it.*] Why, there's Sabina and her mama. They're going to go home now. Sabina's mama is very, very nice, I think. Oh, well what do I see, this isn't supposed to go there, it's supposed to go here, and this is supposed to be here. Why don't you wave?

[*Elevator sounds. Steps in the stairwell. Door closes.*]

AUNT BLOSSOM: It's probably your mama coming now. No, hoh. I have a little picking up to do.

BABY: When I get big I'm not going to have any daycare kids or potted plants.

AUNT BLOSSOM: Do you have to go potty?

BABY: Huh?

AUNT BLOSSOM: Do you have to go potty?

BABY: Do you have to go potty? No. Do you have to go potty?

[*Sounds from elevator, stairs, door.*]

AUNT BLOSSOM: It must be her now finally. It wasn't her. She probably got stuck in some traffic someplace or in the health food store. Typical. I'm going out this evening.

BABY: Now all the traffic jams are full of mamas. Who got stuck there and can't pick up their kids. No matter how bad they want to. Because they're stuck. Between an eighteen-wheeler and an ambulance. I think the police should come and liberate the mamas so they can take care of their kids for once. Who they truly are responsible for. You might wonder why people put up with being babies when there isn't anybody to pick them up from Aunt Blossom. Why doesn't Sabina's mama ever get stuck in a traffic jam? It's probably because Sabina is so timid, of course. She could never get along without her mama. I'd like some French fries. If Mama doesn't come soon and tell me I have to be nice, then I'll probably get nasty, though actually I'm really kind.

AUNT BLOSSOM: Yes, you are! My little sugar piggy.

SONG

BABY:

You, little mama, looking fine
through the door to a dream of mine
I wanted to be so wonderful
so you wouldn't have to leave anymore.

AUNT BLOSSOM:

You have a mama looking in
through the doorway to my porch
She's so pretty and nonchalant
She's a mommy; I'm an aunt.

BABY:

A little mama can go astray
a life can end horribly one short day
A bus might come and run her down
A little mama with eyes of brown.

AUNT BLOSSOM: [*From rear of stage center, over* BABY's *shoulders.*]

You little butterball, whining all the time
I'm telling you now this one last time
I'm just so tired of being kind
When Mama comes back she'll get a whack.

BABY:

Oh my, Aunt Blossom, now you were dumb
Shame on you, go to your room,
I want to run off on a field of dreams
Out through the wooden bars of my bed . . .

[BABY *cries.*]

AUNT BLOSSOM: WELL SO WHAT IS IT NOW? What's the matter, little friend, do you have to go potty? How goes it, little fella? Do you have a temperature?

BABY: I really am kind! I actually am! Verily I say unto you. Baby is kind.

AUNT BLOSSOM: Why, of course you are. You're just a little precocious. And unusual, so to speak. You are. But mean, no, you're not. I don't think one can say so. Well, I'll just go call Ruthie. You know we're going out this evening and maybe there will be a rendezvous. Do you have to go potty?

BABY: Sometimes I get an urge to start kicking, Aunt Blossom. Mama probably put these rompers on me so I would be able to kick, Aunt Blossom. Sometimes I can only obey Mama. Only her. The best thing would probably be for her to come here now and command me not to disobey you and your fuckin' geraniums. [*Throws a geranium.*]

AUNT BLOSSOM: It's important for children to have an outlet for their feelings. But now that doesn't mean that you can act any way you please. You're not allowed to fight, for example. With other people. Or their home furnishings. When something bad happens to happen to you, you should try to make yourself think of something interesting. If it weren't so damned messy . . . No, you know what—I think we should sing our pretty, crazy little song instead. You know that song that makes us all so happy although we really are very, very irritated. On with your hat and here's your cane.

SONG

AUNT BLOSSOM:

> Every time life seems in vain
> we take out Aunt Blossom's cane
> Then we put on our hat!
> reminding me that—I really love these brats!

BABY:

> At Aunt Blossom's I'll find a way
> to be happy every day
> She isn't pretty at all but
> she seems to have a ball!

BOTH:

> Being a kid is kind of funny
> your disposition's glad and sunny
> Why should little kids ever mind?
> we are kind!

BOTH:

> At Aunt Blossom's everything's free!
> What good luck that I am me!
> I'm so happy today!
> Now just raise Aunt Blossom's pay!

BOTH:

> At Aunt Blossom's I'll find a way
> to be happy every day
> She isn't pretty at all but
> she seems to have a ball!

BOTH:

> At Aunt Blossom's everything's free!
> What good luck that I am me!
> I'm so happy today!
> Now just raise Aunt Blossom's pay!

AUNT BLOSSOM: Well, that cheered us up a bit, now, didn't it? The mood has lightened significantly, I think. Actually, I'm really off work now. This is my free time.

BABY: Aunt Blossom!

AUNT BLOSSOM: [*Sitting.*] Yes. What is it, little friend?

BABY: As soon as you don't get paid for it, you won't like me any more?

AUNT BLOSSOM: Of course I will. I like all children. And grandchildren. I'm one of those few people who really understand how important it is for children to have contact with grown-ups. Those skinheads, for example.

They've never had any adults who've taught them to find an outlet for their feelings. In a creative way. In their rompers. You don't want to become one of those skin-heads, do you? Or be in an immigrant gang? You don't want to do that, do you?

BABY: I didn't eat up Victor's candy from Saturday.

AUNT BLOSSOM: Are you sure? [*Stands, mimics* Casablanca.] Is that really true? You aren't kidding me now, are you?

BABY: I never ever did eat up Victor's Saturday candy.

AUNT BLOSSOM: Can you swear to that? [*Picks up geranium.*] Can you swear on this geranium—which you've mistreated terribly—that you never ate up Victor's Saturday candy?

BABY: [*Mimics Richard Nixon.*] I swear on the head of this geranium that I never did eat up Victor's Saturday candy. And that Mama will come soon.

AUNT BLOSSOM: I'm going out to a restaurant this evening. I'm going out dancing. With a man. Do you have to go potty? [*Replaces geranium.*] Sweet Lord, I really hope your mama will come soon. I'd thought of taking a nice, long bath. And maybe of going so far as to put on a facial mask. It's important. It's important for a person to take time to look after themselves a little bit too. Otherwise they just get bitter.

BABY: My mama said that you don't have a man.

AUNT BLOSSOM: Your mama does not know everything.

AUNT BLOSSOM'S SONG

Soon I'll be a bride
in the church of my childhood.
The love song I'll sing
will be sung to you.
I don't want to die
like a nasty old maid
I want to be pretty
and happy today!

My mind is awhirl, like a five-speed blender!
My body's a stick-proof casserole!
I'm like a pony wandering around
—as if I were drunk!
I don't know left from right, my friend
that's love!
I'm like a person possessed!
I'm like a girl again!

Now I'll be a bride
in the church of my childhood [BABY *clasps hands in prayer.*]
I'll break out into
a love song to you!
I will never more
be ugly and lonely
May I never die!

[BABY *cries.*]

AUNT BLOSSOM: That wasn't anything to cry over, was it? I'm going to tell you a story. No. This is true. Come on. Let's go sit down here in this comfy Cozy Corner.

BABY: That's no comfy Cozy Corner. That's a stinky Cozy Corner. Things are cozy at home at my place, though we don't have a Cozy Corner. I have an electric train almost. And hamburgers for dinner. My mama is an intellectual, she says. When Papa comes home.

Then I'll be a slalom skier, when I get big. The President and First Lady will be there for show. On TV. [*Slaloms.*]

AUNT BLOSSOM: I have time to tell you a story. But then I really must . . . Come on. Come. We'll go and sit down here in the Cozy Corner.

BABY: [*Continues to slalom.*] I think I'd rather watch TV. The people on TV know me.

AUNT BLOSSOM: The people on TV know him. [*Takes away* BABY's *imaginary ski poles.*] You'll get to watch TV later. But just now it's important for your creativity to sit and listen to somebody telling about how things were when I was little. Once upon a time I was little. At that time I was my father's youngest and very dearest daughter. I had long, long, golden blond hair and I loved flowers. That's why they gave me the name Aunt Blossom, you see. Well. One day I was out walking in the woods together with my horse. A white charger. It was sunny and green wherever I looked, and on the spring-green field the dandelions shone like medals. The little princess—me, in other words—was out walking in the forests, and the cows were out in the spring pasture. The very dearest cow was adorned with flowers. I . . .

BABY: Adorned with flowers! Maybe there's an angry cow standing behind the yucca palm! [*Fixated upon imaginary cow.*]

AUNT BLOSSOM: It's nice you have a lively imagination. [BABY *begins to moo.*] Really very nice. But let's see if you can concentrate on the story now.

[*Concentration broken by* AUNT BLOSSOM, BABY *begins to cry.*]

AUNT BLOSSOM: Since I'm taking the time to tell it to you. I-I-I-I am here, you know, I am here. [*Crosses right, behind yucca.*] I promise to check that there aren't any cows standing behind the yucca palm. I . . .

[*Sound from stairway.*]

AUNT BLOSSOM: Thank God, she's finally coming now!

[*Both listen with extreme care, staring intently offstage right.*]

AUNT BLOSSOM: [*Continues.*] No. It wasn't her. What can have happened? Well, now it's just a matter of establishing the facts. Something must have happened! You're going to get a cookie while you wait. Yes, yes, I know it's not good to have sweets, like cookies and such—before dinner like this. But now I feel a little sorry for you. I must say that she could have phoned at least. When she knows I'm going out this evening besides. I'm a working woman too. It's as if people couldn't get it into their heads that it actually is a profession to be a daycare worker. [*Vogues, downstage right.*] I'm not afraid to say so, I think it shows no respect. I'm in the middle of my career too. It's woman's eternal dilemma.

BABY: [*Mimics Marlon Brando as Stanley Kowalski.*] You can't be a day mama. You can't be a mama just during the day. If you're a mama, then you're a mama for good. My mama is a little sloppy, she is. That's part of her charm. I want to tell you, Aunt Blossom, that my mama is prepared to do absolutely anything for me. She lies awake at night crying sometimes because she can't think of any way to save me from environmental destruction. But deep down she knows she'll manage. Everybody knows that.

AUNT BLOSSOM: Behind Aunt Blossom's tulle curtain at night. Shines the black water of death.

BABY: Hungh?

AUNT BLOSSOM: Hungh? Oh, it was just me talking to myself. It's a bad habit you get when you're very, very alone. In my little little world of flowers . . .

BABY: Aunt Blossom . . .

AUNT BLOSSOM: Yess!

BABY: Should we take pity on you?

AUNT BLOSSOM: [*Crosses left.*] No! No! You certainly shouldn't pity me! Why, there are plenty of people who care about me. And I have my flowers, yes I have. Why, I have my beautiful, dear potted plants!

BABY: Mama says it's a pity about you.

AUNT BLOSSOM: [*Sits.*] That little, little princess who was me, that is, was out riding on my stallion Silver Star. And suddenly I came to a meadow that was bordered by rose bushes, thousands and thousands of rose bushes! But oh how dry the rose petals looked. They probably hadn't got anything to drink ever since Uncle Louie was little! I . . .

BABY: [*Mimics Joel McCrea.*] Louie! Who's that? Louie! It sounds shady, if you ask me. Who is Uncle Louie! Is it that guy standing over there?

AUNT BLOSSOM: [*Hand on playpen.*] Uncle Louie is no yucca palm. Uncle Louie was the first and only great love of my life. A prince.

BABY: Is he dead now?

AUNT BLOSSOM: No. He's in Hackensack. Together with somebody named Tess. Listen. I really have to go now. To that little room, you know. I'm going to that little kids' room, you know, to that secret room. Where you'd rather be alone, you know. Wait here a little while. [*Exits right.*]

BABY: [*To teddy bear.*] If we just stand here and wave and wave, then Mama will probably come soon and wave back at us. Now you don't need to be afraid, don't be afraid. Mama is coming any second now. And then she'll sing a song to comfort me . . . [*Sings.*] "Come, and I'll Whisper Something Nice in Your Ear." [*Speaks.*] I've seen on TV that there are people who work at being beautiful and standing onstage . . . I'd like to do that. And then there'd be lights, spotlights like this . . . [*Tosses teddy bear over shoulder and vaults over front rail of playpen.*]

SONG

Should little boys live
in Aunt Blossom's world?
I'm shut in here and now
I wanna leave, want to leave!
Aunt Blossom's land
where flowerpots bloom
but wild plants wither and fade
want to go away!
For all the loneliness in my crib
is not my own
it's just passing gloom,
I see a golden room!
The music will play!
Here's looking at me!
I get so happy when I
do as I please!
I'll give you all I'm worth!
I am the salt of this old earth!
I am myself! Myself!
I'm me!

I'm a child who doesn't at all
wanna be cute
I'm a big strapping lunk!
They call me Superhunk!
I'll dance off my soles
so they're scared to death
My playpen is mine!
Now I'm staying here!
It's so lovely to get
some peace and quiet!

I'm gonna play it cool.
I will be no man's fool!
I'm myself! Myself, I'm me . . .

[*Sound in the stairway.*]

BABY: Finally! Mama!

BUILDING SUPERINTENDENT: [*Enters right.*] That was the first time anybody ever called me Mama! [BABY *afraid.*] My Lord, how you're pouting. Get a hold on yourself, boy! Are you ticklish? Koochi-koo! What do you youngsters do for fun? Eh? Shall I come in a while and play Horsey with you?

[BABY *rejects all his suggestions.*]

BUILDING SUPERINTENDENT: No, no. If it's not welcome, I won't press it. I'll sit down here and tuck in a plug of snuff.

BABY: Who are you? What are you doing here?

BUILDING SUPERINTENDENT: I'm a building superintendent, can't you see. Why, I've got overalls on. I have to turn off the circuit breaker. Cause I'm going to fix something on the elevator! A body doesn't want to get grilled just because an old woman got stuck in the elevator.

BABY: Did Mama get stuck in the elevator now too?! [*Blackout.*] Help! I disappeared! Imagine if I turned invisible! Then Mama would never find me! If I turned invisible!

BUILDING SUPERINTENDENT: [*Shines flashlight on* BABY.] I see you plain and clear! You're shining like a full moon!

BABY: Mama!

BUILDING SUPERINTENDENT: Stop calling me Mama!

BABY: I want you to come now, Mama! And settle this whole thing! Mama! Mama! [*Hyperventilating.*]

BUILDING SUPERINTENDENT: Your mama will come soon, okay. Calm down, kid.

[BABY *puts thumb in mouth. Continues to hyperventilate. Slows down.*]

BUILDING SUPERINTENDENT: Listen. I'm going to tell you something. Just between you and me. Women can be a BIG pain. They can come up with the damnedest things. But they never let go of their children. The fact is clear as day. Once they got a youngster, they never give it up. I tell you, my mother, she phones me every day and asks, "Arnie"—[*Shakes hands with* BABY.] yeh, my name is Arnie—"did you eat right." And me, I'll soon be fifty if a day! I don't get it, why don't you get it? The dark isn't dangerous. I think Aunt Blossom's interior decorating looks much better in this light.

BABY: There's something in what you say.

BUILDING SUPERINTENDENT: Now I have to fix the elevator. Otherwise the old woman standing in it will get "absolutely hysterical" [*Imitating a hysterical dowager.*] I know. I'll light a wax candle. I'll light two candles. I'll light all the candles! Goddamned Christmas Eve! Nice, huh?

BABY: Nice. Awful. But nice. Awfully nice. Now anyway I see that I exist. But those sounds. That dragging! That shuffling! It's probably Aunt Blossom dragging her feet in the twilight. But she sounds so different somehow. Everything is scary in here. This is Aunt Blossom's scary apartment.

THE TOOL-BELT TANGO

[BUILDING SUPERINTENDENT *dances.* BABY *sings.*]

Fear fills the air in
this apartment
Where now there sneaks
a murderer at large

[BUILDING SUPERINTENDENT *throws shadow of hammer against wall with flashlight.*]

He has a horrifying hammer
that he'll use to knock off
little Googy
trembling in fright

Then he'll do something else
and put on a glove

[BUILDING SUPERINTENDENT *puts on grotesque glove.*]

and sneak around me
to try to choke me
He is so awful
and horrid is he
so dangerous he is then believe me
He measures off my coffin now
and then he saws me right in two

[BUILDING SUPERINTENDENT *wafts saw in the air.*]

and makes little stuffed cabbage rolls
and meatballs of me
so farewell, Little Googy, farewell
So long to you, bye-bye.

BABY: [*Speaks, mimicking Marlene Dietrich.*] Childhood is the most important time in a person's life. That's why they shut babies up in this kind of playpen. So they won't take off and run away from their whole childhood.

BABY: [*Sings.*]

Fear fills the air in
this apartment
Where now there sneaks
a murderer at large
He has a horrifying hammer
that he'll use to knock off
little Googy
trembling in fright.

[BUILDING SUPERINTENDENT *exits right. Lights up.*]

BABY: [*Speaks.*] I'd like to go to sea. I'd like to sail the seven seas. Carnival Line. At home at my place I have a bathtub. It's not as big as the sea, of course. But I fit in it. I have a rubber ducky too. Tax-free liquor. Say, there, Teddy. You want me to tell you a story, Teddy? Once upon a time there was a little boy. He was his daddy's very youngest and very dearest daughter. And the wind played through the locks of her hair, and she was out walking with her horse. Mama says that Aunt Blossom is dumb in the head. Uneducated. It's strange, my mama leaving me with a stupid, uneducated person. Actually I'm gonna go phone Mama. Hello! Mama! Hi there, little lady! This is Aunt Blossom's daycare kid calling you! Actually, I've begun wondering how things are going with you, Mama? Hasn't Daddy sent any money? Oh, say, there was one thing I thought I'd take up with you. For discussion. It's about childhood. You know, you often say that Aunt Blossom is stupid and uneducated and a failure and so on. And now when I stand here figuring things out a bit for myself in my own little world of blasted geraniums, I came to think of it. How did you dare? How did you dare leave me here? Why, I'm the most precious thing you've got! If I were the most precious thing I had, then I wouldn't turn me over to a person like that. I really wouldn't. Especially not now, when I'm so little. You didn't get mad at me, did you? Why, that was just pretend! Why, that was just a play telephone. Now I'm going to tell a story. Once upon a time there were some chil-

dren who found a golden egg that the sun had laid which actually was a damned orange although those idiots didn't realize it and then there came a weird building superintendent and an absolutely daft-but-pleasant daycare mama whose name was
Aunt Blossom, which is an exceptionally silly name for an adult, single, professional,
women's movement.

AUNT BLOSSOM: [*Enters from right with cocktail shaker.*] Oh, how happy I'm going to be! This
is going to be the most wonderful evening in my life, I feel it!

SONG

BABY:

Oh, little mama, wherever you may be
here is a boy who's in love with you.
His name is Googy—you remember me, don't you?
I am a gift from God to you.

Oh, oh, Aunt Blossom, don't give up!
Be like a beacon for your professional group!
When sorrow freezes your soul into ice
then remember Mama's little piggy's nice.

I know, Aunt Blossom, your life is rough.
Being a mama is also tough.
Being a daddy isn't easy.
Being a child can make you queasy.

AUNT BLOSSOM:

I was a blossom. I became an aunt.
I started wondering, do I look gaunt?
Am I happy, though always broke?
Oh, dear daycare child—am I a joke?

BOTH:

We must hope that all goes well—
that the story ends as stories shall.
We probably don't think that this will be.
But let's hope like the devil anyway!

BABY: [*Speaks.*] But Aunt Blossom! Why do you have such big eyes?
AUNT BLOSSOM: [*Mimics the Big Bad Wolf, having put cucumber slices over eyes.*] These are not
eyes. They're fresh cucumber slices. When you work as hard as I do, it's easy to get eye-
bags. I put on a facial mask. [BABY *and* AUNT BLOSSOM *each eat one slice.*] Now I'll really be myself! Oh! There it goes. My whole body is tingling! I'm literally seething with
life! I think I'll have myself a little drink! [*Sounds in the stairway.*] That's probably Ruthie
coming now. She was going to be here at six, she said. So we'll have time to have a drink
before we go. So we'll get in the mood. Nope, it wasn't her. But well, it's only five after.
Heck! Yippy aaiii yeeee, yippy aaii yaayyyy! I think I'll have a drink anyway; while I
wait. I've got to take it easy! So I'll be relaxed later, when I'm going to dance. I'm going
to dance! Dance!
BABY: [*No sound.*] I thought I heard a sound in the stairwell. It must be Mama.
AUNT BLOSSOM: It must be Ruth. [*Pause.*] Yes, yes, I realize you're wondering how things
will go with you if your mama doesn't come by the time I have to take off. But that's no
problem. No-hoh. I've thought of that too, believe me! I'll leave the outer door un-
locked—simple. Then she can come and pick you up whenever she pleases. Your

mama. You don't just happen to have a can of Town 'n' Country stew. You can look in the pantry while you wait. How will things go for Dick and Jane, etc. Even you must understand that I absolutely cannot miss this chance to be happy. Why, it's so seldom that Ruth's husband is out of town. [*Sits and poses like Statue of Liberty with drink in left hand like torch.*] And I don't like to go to those kind of places by myself. We women have to have our girlfriends with when we're going out to entertain ourselves. That's about as far as we've got in our liberation struggle.

BABY: Poor women! Poor women who always have to have girlfriends! Oy, oy, oy! But then Mama—suppose the building superintendent hasn't got her out of the elevator! And she's standing there all alone! Without girlfriends! Why, she doesn't even have me! Aunt Blossom, I don't want you to go and leave me alone.

AUNT BLOSSOM: But why doesn't Ruth come? She hasn't missed the bus, has she? Or did she get stuck someplace too? Heck! It's clear she hasn't. She's probably just got hung up on some little thing. Maybe her husband has come home! No, no, I mustn't think that way! Say. I happened to think of one thing. When I was in there going . . . Then I came to think of that problem, that I'm so insignificant. I've practically taken for granted that it will always be that way. I've been seeing myself as a zero. I have such terribly poor self-esteem. BUT! [*Stands.*] But if I meet someone who looks at me with. Yes. With love. Then I'll become beautiful. You understand? I know that there is a man. At a dance restaurant. He's waiting for me there. As soon as I hover into his field of vision I will become beautiful!

[*Sound of egg timer.*]

AUNT BLOSSOM: THE SPONGE CAKE!

[AUNT BLOSSOM *rushes offstage left. Explosion and smoke.* AUNT BLOSSOM *reenters left with pan of cinders.*]

AUNT BLOSSOM: Here Googy . . . But why doesn't she come then! I don't understand why people can't be on time. It's so inconsiderate that I have to give this geranium a kick. So there. Very nice. Now I've got my anger out.

BABY: Actually I think I have to go now. [*Crosses legs.*]

AUNT BLOSSOM: [*Ignoring* BABY.] You're going to get a jar of pickled pigs' feet. Ugly people are ugly because nobody loves them. These playpens are really good to have when you don't have time to keep track of children. You can feel completely secure. You're going no place.

[*Telephone rings.*]

BABY: [*Eagerly, urgently.*] It's probably Mama calling to say that she's coming now.

AUNT BLOSSOM: [*Continuing to ignore* BABY.] . . . Ruth. Oh really. Yeh, yeh . . . No. No, I didn't at all. On the contrary, you see, I'd just thought of phoning you. Well, I actually had a bit of a guilty conscience for not having been in touch earlier . . . but people have been calling all day and I've been busy here . . . but anyway, you realize that I don't have time to meet you this evening . . . Since, some—well, some things have turned up . . . yes, you should only know! No, I can't tell you about it just now . . . I'm not alone, if you get what I mean. But we can get in touch sometime, Ruthie . . .

BABY: [*Unable to wait any longer.*] Beyond Aunt Blossom's tulle curtain at night. Shines the black water of death.

AUNT BLOSSOM: That's good, Ruthie. Thanks and bye. Mud in your eye! I feel pretty, oh so pretty, I feel pretty and witty and bright [*Weeping.*] and I pity every girl who isn't me tonight—[*Mimicking Bette Davis.*] Aren't you going to ask for your mama now? I haven't heard anything about your mama in a very long time now! Do you hear what I'm saying? You've forgotten to nag about your mother for several minutes now! What's the matter with you? Are the pickled pigs' feet gone? [*Crosses upstage right.*]

BABY: [*Sweetly, sincerely.*] If Mama comes now, I'm going to tell her that we can just as well ask Aunt Blossom if she wants to go home with us tonight and watch the new "Love Boat."

AUNT BLOSSOM: Why is it always me taking responsibility for everything? That's so typical! Just because I'm not in a couple, people take for granted that I'll have time to do cleaning the whole time! [*Crosses downstage right.*] And water flowers! If this were a TV series. Then everybody would wonder how things would go for me in the next segment . . . But let me tell you that there will be no more segments in this series. And no reruns either. And no reruns either. It's over. End of story. Hugs and kisses. [*Crosses downstage left.*]

BABY: Hugs and kisses, Aunt Blossom.

AUNT BLOSSOM: I'll never get to join Butch Cassidy and the Sundance Kid. But I am actually quite an ordinary person. With other needs than geraniums. I am nice! I am extremely nice!

BABY: You're extremely nice, Aunt Blossom. Verily, I say unto you. Aunt Blossom is extremely nice.

AUNT BLOSSOM: I know very well that nobody loves me. Never ever will there be a man sitting at a dance restaurant. [*Moves far upstage left and puts down drink.*] And waiting to be happy together with just me. That I know very well. I will never have any other family than this storybook. [*Closes book.*] Of Aunt Blossom.

BABY: Mama really is a real pig, not coming to pick me up when she said she would. It's wrong both to me and you, Dearie. I think that we should teach her a lesson.

AUNT BLOSSOM: If one admits that one knows certain things, one can't bear it. Do you have to go potty?

BABY: I'll keep you company as night arrives and Mama doesn't come.

AUNT BLOSSOM: At least that's clear, little friend, she'll come. Why, she loves you.

[AUNT BLOSSOM *jumps out through the window, screams.*]

[*Offstage a watermelon drops with a thump, splattering.*]

BABY: It'll all work out . . .

[*The End.*]

Astrid Saalbach (b. 1955)

A curious rhetorical jousting punctuates discussions of Danish theater history. While some liken Denmark's unexceptional, older drama to the country's flat and gently rolling topography, wistfully looking across to the Norwegian mountains and fjords, others stress the important contributions of dramatists like Kaj Munk (1898–1944) and Kjeld Abell (1901–61)—the most important post–World War II dramatist writing in Scandinavia. If Denmark lacked such artistic peaks as Ibsen and Strindberg, it did in the eighteenth century contribute the wonderful comedies of Ludvig Holberg and establish the first national theater in Scandinavia, the Royal Theater (1748).

Since the Theaters Act of 1963, the Danish theater has been generously subsidized, and the number of playhouses per population is extraordinary. Danish theater has been flourishing—including the very successful genre of radio plays. It became more international—interacting with other dramas (Scandinavian, British, and American), and it became more Danish, with a burgeoning of native playwrights and productions. As was the case in much of Europe and the United States, the drama turned political in the seventies and then, in the eighties, reflected skepticism that it could effect social change.

When Georg Brandes (1842–1927) wrote his influential social commentaries, he not only urged Denmark and its neighbors to enter modernity—as he saw it—giving definition and immediacy to the notion of "the Modern Breakthrough," but he specifically attacked the rigidity of marriage and the family and how these church-fostered institutions curtailed the freedom of both women and men. In 1869, the same year that John Stuart Mill's *On the Subjection of Women* appeared in England, he published a Danish translation. Though it is paradoxical that his own *Men of the Modern Breakthrough* (1883) in fact considers only men, Brandes did help make Denmark more receptive to such women writers as Emma Gad (1852–1921) and Erna Juel-Hansen (1845–1922). By the 1970s this influence had joined with the impetus of the general European women's movement and interjected its specific political element into the theater. This is evident in the plays of Ulla Ryum and Inger Christensen.

Astrid Saalbach is among the current generation of accomplished and diverse dramatists now receiving recognition at home and abroad; others include Line Knutzon, Jess Ørnsbro, Stig Dalager, Suzanne Brøgger, and Erling Jepsen. Saalbach trained as an actress, but turned to writing, making her debut in 1981, with a very successful radio play, *Tracks in the Sand (Spor i sandet)*. She became resident drama-

Astrid Saalbach, ca. 1997. (Photographer: Rigmor Mydtskov.)

tist at the Århus Theater and has received several awards, including, in 1994, the Dramatist of the Year from the Danish Dramatists' Union. She has also written a collection of short stories and two novels.

In Saalbach's plays, the outlook is generally pessimistic. Present family patterns do not work; a more female-centered world, as she envisions it, is perhaps even worse. *Morning and Evening* (*Morgen og aften*, 1993) is the first part of a trilogy she wrote that variously looks at humanity's prospects, given the present social arrangements and psychological dispositions. The subsequent plays, *The Buried Child* (*Det velsignede barn*, 1996) and *Ashes to Ashes, Dust to Dust* (*Aske til Aske—Støv til Støv*, 1998) are perhaps even starker in their pessimism. Each play is in a different style, but they are equally—or increasingly—confounded by the human condition.

Morning and Evening appears at first structurally baffling. Divided into two acts, with four intermezzo vignettes separating them, the parts don't obviously cohere. The twenty-three roles are to be played by eight actors, with the triplings carefully specified. This is not done simply to keep it economical in the tradition of chamber theater, but to convey the multiplicities within characters. The genuinely ill Lotte contains the *malade imaginaire* Julie, just as Cecilie, who paints and would masochistically take Jonas in, physically echoes Helene, who abides and would even marry the misanthropic Torben.

What makes the play effective is how the isolated parts do contribute to a coherent dramatic whole. More than seeing the characters and actions as slices of life that in some general way comprise a totality, the images become motifs that reverberate and achieve the darkness and disconnection of the final curtain. The title obviously suggests a metaphor for the day that is our life, with its brief sallies, hopes, frustrations, and enigmatic conclusion. The ill-fitting clothing that recurs, the food that Lotte can't tolerate and that Johanne can't stop gobbling, the illnesses—real and presumably fatal, as in the case of Lotte, or fabricated and theatrical, as with Julie—all stress the figures' tenuous relationships to an inhospitable world. Anders at the beginning and Morten in grand style in the Evening may offer delicacies and gourmet feasts, but the lovely garden of Cecilie's painting, which is realized in Act II, remains an alien, elusive paradise. Minna may reconsider and decide to attend to her family, but in a final scene that recalls Ulla Ryum's apocalyptic radio play, *And the Birds Are Singing Again* (*Og fuglene synger igen*, 1980), the darkness and wind descend, as the birds anomalously sing late into the night.

SELECTED BIBLIOGRAPHY IN ENGLISH

Andersen, Hans Christian, ed. "Introduction." *New Danish Plays*. Norwich, England: Norvik Press, 1996. Pp. 7–28.

Bredsdorff, Elias, ed. "Introduction." *Contemporary Danish Plays: An Anthology.* Copenhagen: Gyldendal, 1955. Pp. 7–16.

Jensen, Astrid. "Women Dramatists in Denmark at the Beginning of the 20th Century." *20th Century Drama in Scandinavia.* Proceedings of the 12th Study Conference of the International Association for Scandinavian Studies, 1978. Eds. John Wrede et al. Helsinki: University of Helsinki, 1979. Pp. 137–45.

Kvam, Kela. "From Theatre of Words to Theatre of Images: Danish Theatre in the 1980s and 1990s." *Scandinavaca* 31 (1992), 155–65.

Marker, Frederick J., and Lise Lone-Marker. *A History of Scandinavian Theatre.* Cambridge: Cambridge University Press, 1996.

Rossel, Sven H. *A History of Danish Literature.* Lincoln: University of Nebraska Press, 1992.

MORNING AND EVENING
Astrid Saalbach

Translated by Malene S. Madsen

CHARACTERS

LOTTE   also plays "SHE" and JULIE aged 25

ANDERS   also plays "HE," man "A" and MORTEN aged 30

CECILIE   also plays woman "B" and JOHANNE aged 35

JONAS   also plays man "B" and TORBEN aged 43

BEATE   also plays MRS. BRANDT and MINNA aged 65

TOVE   also plays woman "A" and HELENE aged 43

PALLE   also plays the ESTATE AGENT and MIKKEL aged 22

ANNA   aged about 5

ACTION

Morning, Scene I Lotte and Anders

Morning, Scene II At Cecilie's flat

Morning, Scene III Somewhere in a church

The Beggar, Part 1

Shooting Star

Buying and Selling

The Beggar, Part 2

Evening, Scene I A large, old garden close to town

Evening, Scene II Later, same place, same evening

Evening, Scene III Later still, same place, same evening

MORNING

Scene I

LOTTE *and* ANDERS *are getting dressed.* LOTTE *in a simple, white dress which is a little too big.* ANDERS *in a suit and tie with a white shirt. There is a couch and a full-size mirror.* LOTTE's *white shoes and* ANDERS' *dark ones are standing next to the mirror.*

LOTTE: . . . Do you like my dress?

ANDERS: Your dress? . . . It's nice. Simple.

LOTTE: You shouldn't really have seen it before we got to the church.

ANDERS: Why not?

LOTTE: It's tradition.

ANDERS: I bet nobody takes any notice, though.

LOTTE: Yes, they do—everyone does! You're supposed to respect the old traditions, didn't you know that? The bride is supposed to put a penny in her shoe for luck and wear orange blossom in her hair, even if she isn't a virgin. Some people put a horseshoe over the door where the newlyweds live, or throw rice at them when they leave the church. The older and weirder the tradition, the better. The best thing is when you can come up with something everyone else has forgotten.

ANDERS: You have to be careful when something becomes trendy—it can get a bit much.

LOTTE: [*Stands in front of the mirror.*] It was a better fit when I bought it.

ANDERS: It fits beautifully. It's perfect!

LOTTE: You can see I've lost weight, though.

ANDERS: You'll have to eat more, even if you have to force it down. I'll go and make you a sandwich.

LOTTE: No, don't.

ANDERS: What about some toast, then?

LOTTE: No thanks.

ANDERS: Some yogurt? Or a small omelette? It wouldn't take long to make.

LOTTE: Stop it—

ANDERS: Would you rather have something to drink? Some milk? Or some fresh orange juice?

LOTTE: Stop it! I'd love to eat all the snacks you make me, and all those expensive delicacies. But I can't! And every time I try, I just make myself even more ill. It's a waste, can't you understand that? I feel fine right now, and I'd rather not spoil that.

ANDERS: I'm sorry. I think I've become obsessed, all I can think about is how to make you eat something. Even when I'm at work. Yesterday I caused a short circuit when I was installing something, because I was trying to remember the name of a fruit I'd heard of which is supposed to be really healthy and easy to digest.

LOTTE: [*Laughs.*] You're mad! You could have been electrocuted!

ANDERS: It's like in one of those fairy tales where you have to solve an impossible riddle to win the hand of the princess. I fantasize about you sitting at a table with lots of food and a white tablecloth and everything, and just stuffing your face. Plateful after plateful . . .

LOTTE: I will do. In a couple of months, when I've had the last treatment and I'm fine again.

ANDERS: Then you'll eat. Till you're big and fat and round!

LOTTE: I can't really see it—

ANDERS: [*Struts about a bit.*] What do you think? Does it suit me?

LOTTE: You look like a lawyer, or a stockbroker maybe. Someone who makes lots of money.

ANDERS: Do you wish I did?

LOTTE: [*Shrugs.*] I don't know. Aren't you going to do up your tie?

ANDERS: [*Hesitates.*] Yeah . . .

LOTTE: [*Giggles.*] Don't you know how to do it?

ANDERS: Yes, of course I do. [*Tries to tie it.*] It's something like over, and over and through here . . . [*The knot comes undone.*]

LOTTE: Let me . . .

ANDERS: [*Pulls her close, caresses her.*] At least there's a bit of meat on you—

LOTTE: [*Tries to knot the tie.*] . . . Can you smell it?

ANDERS: Smell what?

LOTTE: That smell—I can't get rid of it, no matter how many times I take a bath. A sort of rank smell.

ANDERS: It's just your imagination.

LOTTE: Do you think so?

ANDERS: [*Pulls her closer.*] Let me have a sniff. Let me smell you up close . . .

LOTTE: It tickles!

ANDERS: Hmm—you smell of grass. Like freshly mown hay—like summer . . .

LOTTE: [*Still trying to tie the tie.*] Maybe it's the other way round. Over, and over . . .

ANDERS: [*Spins her round.*] And over, and over, and over!

LOTTE: Anders, don't! Stop it!

[*They collapse on the couch. He caresses her.*]

ANDERS: Your skin's so white and pretty. You can see the blood vessels through it. You can see the blood pulsing, just underneath it . . . It's blue! Very elegant . . . Let me just check. Maybe there is a funny smell . . . [*Kisses her.*] I think it's coming from here . . . [*Kisses her again.*] Or is it from here? . . . What's the matter? Is something hurting?

LOTTE: No.

ANDERS: Yes, it is. I can see it in your eyes, the pupils look like tiny black dots.

LOTTE: It's just the light, it's really bright today. No, don't get up!

ANDERS: [*Stands up, walks over to the window.*] . . . The roofs are all shiny, it must have rained last night.

LOTTE: That must have been what I heard then, I thought I was just dreaming.

ANDERS: Do you want me to fetch your pills?

[LOTTE *shakes her head.*]

ANDERS: I don't feel too good, either.

LOTTE: . . . Sorry?

ANDERS: I'm a bit cold, and my head hurts. So does my throat, actually. I hope I'm not getting 'flu.

LOTTE: [*Snorts.*]—'flu!

ANDERS: [*Surprised.*] What?

LOTTE: Oh, nothing . . .

ANDERS: Mum always used to make us some chicken soup when we were ill. She'd take time out to sit and talk to us or read to us. It was really nice. Why don't you go and stay with my parents for a couple of weeks? The air would do you good, and mum would love to look after you—and you wouldn't be able to resist her cooking! You could go for walks in the woods and sit in the deck chair on the front patio and look out over the fields! Go on, Lotte!

LOTTE: I don't want to go anywhere. I don't want to miss any more at the academy than I already have.

ANDERS: What does it matter whether you finish six months earlier or later?

LOTTE: I'm already the oldest one there. Besides, singing is good for you. Vera Holm says it might even make you better. She wants to give me extra lessons.

ANDERS: Vera Holm—does she know?

LOTTE: I had to tell her, she couldn't understand why I was ill so often. Or why my voice wasn't developing the way she expected. Haven't you told anyone? Anyone at all?

ANDERS: You asked me not to.

LOTTE: I know, but you might have done.

ANDERS: You look almost disappointed!

LOTTE: No, no—But I would have understood if you'd told someone. In confidence.

ANDERS: Sometimes I really can't figure you out.

LOTTE: I wouldn't worry about it, nor can I.

ANDERS: Bloody illness.

LOTTE: Don't say that. It's given me a lot.

ANDERS: Given you what?

LOTTE: It's as if everything's come closer. I can see and hear everything in a different way, much more clearly . . . No, I can't explain it. I always used to be in such a hurry. Time flew by and I still didn't think it was going fast enough.

ANDERS: That's what it's always like. That's life!

LOTTE: Is it? . . . Anders? . . .

ANDERS: It's getting late, we'll have to make a move.

LOTTE: [*Stands up, looks in the mirror.*] I look awful . . .

ANDERS: You look the same as you always do.

LOTTE: I'm not blind. [*Takes out a makeup pouch.*]

ANDERS: No, don't! It suits you, being pale. It makes you look mysterious and ethereal!

LOTTE: I thought you preferred girls with a bit of colour.

ANDERS: Are you sure there's nothing you want before we go? Half a banana? Some warm milk with honey? An almond? There's something in almonds, but I can't remember what.

LOTTE: Go on then, give me an almond—in honour of the occasion.

ANDERS: Do you want me to blanch it? Or do you want it as it is?

LOTTE: Just as it is!

ANDERS: [*Leaves; comes back holding a plate with an almond on it; he has a white cloth draped over one arm.*] Dinner is served!

LOTTE: You don't have to watch me.

ANDERS: [*Walks over to the window.*] Look at that sky! Not a cloud in sight. It must be a sign, don't you think? So much for putting pennies in your shoes or horseshoes over the door.—Is the almond OK? You told the minister as well.

LOTTE: I don't know why. She was really nice and warmhearted, like you could tell her anything.

ANDERS: I thought she was a bit overwhelming.

LOTTE: How do you mean?

ANDERS: The way she held your hands and stroked your hair, like you were a little girl. It was a bit much. Just like the way she hugged and kissed you when we were leaving, as if you'd known each other for ages!

LOTTE: You're so cynical! How long do you have to know someone before you can touch them? A year? Three weeks? A day? A night?

ANDERS: It's something people like her do. It's a role they play. Like they keep mentioning your name. "How many years have you been at the academy of music, Lotte?" "So you're an electrician, Anders, that must be an exciting job!" It doesn't mean anything. They've forgotten all about you as soon as you walk out the door.

LOTTE: That's not true!

ANDERS: You're so naive.

LOTTE: Don't let's fight. Not today!

ANDERS: No—today we're going to be happy from morning till night.

LOTTE: Everything should be peaceful.

ANDERS: It will be, I promise.

LOTTE: I'm nervous.

ANDERS: So am I. [*Looks down at one of his hands.*] My hands are shaking—how ridiculous—

LOTTE: [*Puts on her coat.*] What are you going to do about your tie?

ANDERS: [*Once again attempts to tie it, but has to give up.*] Are you going to say no, if I don't tie it?

LOTTE: [*Laughs.*] Oh, I don't know . . .

ANDERS: What am I going to do?! I'll have to ask someone on the street. Lots of people wear ties nowadays.

LOTTE: [*Laughs.*] Don't make me laugh, it'll start to hurt again!

ANDERS: I could just tie it in a bow. Or ask the minister! She was quite masculine!

LOTTE: I'd rather you asked someone on the street. Come on, let's go. I don't want to be late.

ANDERS: There's only the two of us, anyway.

LOTTE: I know, but still.

ANDERS: Hang on! I've got something for you . . . [*Leaves; returns carrying a bouquet of white and purple lilac.*] For you!

LOTTE: Lilac! What a lovely smell! But I told you, I didn't want any flowers!

ANDERS: You have to have flowers. It's tradition.

MORNING

Scene II

At CECILIE's *flat.*

An easel with a canvas, a small table with a palette, a few tubes of paint and some brushes on it. A couch covered by a blanket. Leaning against the walls are several paintings turned inwards. CE-CILIE *is wearing a kimono. She is bare-legged.* JONAS *is wearing a cotton raincoat over a pair of trousers and a creased shirt. He's brought a red sports bag, packed to the brim.*

CECILIE: [*From outside.*] Jonas? I nearly didn't recognize you! Come on in . . .

[JONAS *and* CECILIE *enter.*]

JONAS: I hope I didn't wake you.

CECILIE: I've been up for ages. I always get up early, just to keep to some kind of routine. [*Looks at the bag.*] Are you going somewhere?

JONAS: No, it's just some clothes . . .

CECILIE: It must be fate. I was hoping somebody would come by. And then you rang the bell!

JONAS: What are all these pictures? [*Looks around him.*] Who's the artist?

CECILIE: Me.

JONAS: You?

CECILIE: I've got nothing else to do. And I've always liked painting and drawing. Don't you remember? I tried to paint your portrait, back then, but it didn't turn out very well. It's supposed to be difficult to paint someone you love.

JONAS: Aren't you teaching?

CECILIE: No, I haven't done for quite some time. There's no demand for school teachers any more, the number of kids keeps falling.

JONAS: [*Surprised.*] Does it?

CECILIE: [*Suddenly not so sure.*] Doesn't it?

JONAS: [*Studies the picture on the easel.*] That garden looks really familiar—

CECILIE: It's just something I made up.

JONAS: The way the trees are spaced out, letting the branches grow unhindered. The blue flowers climbing up the wall—

CECILIE: It's a clematis.

JONAS: The roses—and the little bush with all the butterflies on it.

CECILIE: That shadow was actually supposed to be a house, but I couldn't figure out how to do it. You have to imagine it's just outside the picture.

JONAS: I've been there. I'm sure I've been in that garden.

CECILIE: But it doesn't even exist!

[JONAS *sits down on the couch.*]

CECILIE: What's wrong with your eyes?

JONAS: Nothing, it's just the light. [*Cries.*]

CECILIE: Jonas—what's happened?

JONAS: Nina and I have split up. It's over a month ago, but it just gets worse and worse.

CECILIE: A month is no time at all.

JONAS: It's worse in the mornings. Especially when the weather's like today. Everyone's so happy. There was a young couple waiting for the bus, completely entwined. The world could have stopped, and they'd never have noticed. She was carrying a bunch of flowers—

CECILIE: I'm glad you came. It's been so long! I thought you'd forgotten me.

JONAS: I suddenly felt like there were children everywhere. Everyone was pushing a pushchair, or had an empty child seat on their bike, like they'd just dropped their kid off somewhere.

CECILIE: You and Nina have two kids, don't you?

JONAS: Cecilie and Amalie.

CECILIE: [*Beaming.*] Cecilie? Is she really called Cecilie?

JONAS: It was Nina's mother's name.

CECILIE: Oh.

JONAS: They can't understand why I don't live with Nina and them any more. We've tried to explain it to them, but they still don't seem to grasp it, or maybe they don't want to. When I go home to fetch something they act strangely. Especially Cecilie.

CECILIE: She's what, four or five now?

JONAS: Eight.

CECILIE: Already.

JONAS: She's mad at me. She won't talk to me, and she hardly says hello. Nina has to make her. It's easier with Amalie, except that she's started to talk like a baby again, and she's gone back to sucking her thumb. The kindergarten says that she won't play with the other children, she just wants to sit with one of the adults . . . [*Cries.*] I can't seem to stop! The worst thing is I can't even stop when I go and see the kids. And when I start, Nina does as well, and then Amalie starts crying too. The only one who doesn't cry is Cecilie. She just hops up and down on the couch and laughs. Her eyes look so cold you wouldn't believe she was just a kid.

CECILIE: . . . Do you want me to take your coat?

JONAS: [*Shakes his head.*] I'll go in a minute.

CECILIE: You're going to work?

JONAS: No, I haven't been for weeks. I handed in my notice.

CECILIE: Handed in your notice?!

JONAS: The company won a big order. A new conference centre, with a casino and a stage and everything. Everyone was really chuffed. We sketched and assessed for days. But I couldn't concentrate. My work just got worse and worse. Suddenly it was all so trivial—as if the world needed a new conference centre!

CECILIE: But you're so talented. You'll easily find another job.

JONAS: I don't want another job.

CECILIE: What are you going to do, then?

JONAS: [*Shrugs.*] Nothing.

CECILIE: If you don't want to do anything, then stay. I'm not doing anything either. I'll give myself a day off. Please stay? It's been so long.

JONAS: [*Strokes* CECILIE's *hair.*] . . . Your hair's falling out.

CECILIE: I know.

JONAS: You're looking quite thin. Aren't you eating properly?

CECILIE: I keep forgetting. When I'm painting I don't notice a thing, not even the time. Suddenly the day's over and it's evening, and I haven't even noticed.

JONAS: Did you paint all of them?

CECILIE: Yes.

[JONAS *turns over one of the pictures and studies it.*]

CECILIE: That's one of the first ones I did.

JONAS: What's it supposed to be?

CECILIE: Ghandi's murder. Not the son's, the mother's.

JONAS: It's, er . . . good.

CECILIE: You can have it, if you like.

JONAS: Thanks, but I've got nowhere to hang it.

CECILIE: Where are you staying?

JONAS: With friends. One night here, one night there. That's why I've got this with me. [*Nudges the bag with one foot.*]

CECILIE: You can stay here if you like. You can take the bed and I'll have the couch.

JONAS: It's nice of you, but it wouldn't work. There's hardly room for one person, let alone two. Besides, the fumes give me a headache.

CECILIE: Is it that bad? I can't smell it any more.

JONAS: Those kinds of fumes are dangerous.

CECILIE: I know. [*Laughs.*] Sometimes I feel quite drunk! We got on well, when we lived together. I've never been happier with anyone else.

JONAS: I used to hit you!

CECILIE: Only right at the end. Once.

JONAS: I hit you lots of times. Once you got a bloody nose—another time, you got a black eye and had to take a week's sick leave from the school.

CECILIE: [*Genuinely surprised.*] I don't even remember . . .

JONAS: How can you forget something like that? I was always completely out of it when it happened. And then you had to console me. But I kept doing it, again and again and again—

CECILIE: Have you ever hit Nina?

JONAS: She's not the type you hit. But she says she's been scared of me. So have the kids . . . What kind of a person am I? I ruin everything. Everything! I can't help it.

CECILIE: That's not true! You're the finest person I know.

JONAS: You don't know me. I'm rotten inside. Rotten to the core. Cecilie, I'm scared! I'm so scared—!

CECILIE: [*Puts her arms around him.*] You'll get over it. In a while, you won't understand why you were so unhappy. You might not even remember why. Don't be scared—you'll find someone else.

JONAS: No—it's too late. I'm too old. I can't start over again one more time. Anyway, it doesn't matter—the worst thing is the children. You can't imagine . . .

CECILIE: Yes, I can.

JONAS: No, you can't. You have to have kids to understand. Aren't you going to have any children?

CECILIE: Children? I wouldn't mind.

JONAS: Then why don't you?

CECILIE: Who with?

JONAS: Anyone. It doesn't matter, you only end up getting divorced anyway. But you'd better hurry, you're not that young any more.

CECILIE: Don't you think I know?

JONAS: [*Picks a few hairs off his coat and trouser legs; surprised.*] They're everywhere!

CECILIE: Oh, I've just cleaned . . .

JONAS: You'll go bald if you carry on like this.

CECILIE: I just moult, like animals do. They change their coat in the spring.

JONAS: Cecilie—it's not spring!

CECILIE: Isn't it? [*Laughs.*] No, it isn't, is it . . .

JONAS: Don't you ever leave this room? When did you last go out?

CECILIE: Yesterday. Or maybe the day before. I had to get a new tube of green, that's the colour I use the most.

JONAS: How can you live like this? All alone—not having to do anything other than what you choose. Always in the same little room. I'd go round the bend.

CECILIE: Why do people always ask that? As if it's any of their business?!

JONAS: I didn't mean to hurt you.

CECILIE: What, then? Why else would you ask? I'm fine. I paint. Maybe one day I'll be good at it. That's my biggest wish.

JONAS: Then I'm sure it'll come true.

CECILIE: You think so? Do you really think so?

JONAS: Well, why not?

CECILIE: Lots of people have dreams like that. But I'd give anything. Anything! I don't care if I never have children, or get married. I don't mind having to live here for the rest of my life—as long as I become a good painter, one who gets pictures exhibited, or even sold.

[JONAS *rises.*]

CECILIE: Are you going? You've only just got here.

JONAS: I'm so tired.

CECILIE: Lie down on the bed and sleep. I promise to be quiet.

JONAS: I can't bear the fumes. They make my eyes water . . .

CECILIE: Then let's go for a walk?

JONAS: It's not a good idea. There's something I've got to sort out—

CECILIE: . . . What?

JONAS: It's personal. Lots of stuff. The bank, and that kind of thing, to let them know I've moved. [*Picks up his bag. Stops on his way past the easel.*] I'm sure you'll become a good painter. You already are. That garden . . . If only I was there . . .

CECILIE: How do you mean?

JONAS: The peace—complete harmony. I'd love to lie on the grass under one of the big trees and sleep. Just sleep . . .

CECILIE: You're acting so strange. Don't leave—

JONAS: Let me go.

CECILIE: Couldn't you leave your bag here . . . ?

JONAS: My bag? Why should I?

CECILIE: Then you wouldn't have to carry it around. And you can always come and get it when you need something. I'll be home.

JONAS: Thanks—but I'm used to having it with me. Goodbye Cecilie.

CECILIE: 'Bye Jonas.

[JONAS *leaves.*]

MORNING

Scene III

A small room in a church. Remains of vaulted ceilings and arched windows. Possibly a pillar. Sparingly furnished; a flimsy table covered by a waxed tablecloth on which stand three coffee cups and a bowl of biscuits. Chairs and a small mirror. BEATE *enters, wearing her cassock.* TOVE *follows quickly, wearing dark, bleak clothes. Church bells can be heard.*

TOVE: [*Helps* BEATE *to take off her cassock and hangs it up.*] . . . Didn't they look happy!

BEATE: So much in love!

TOVE: They couldn't take their eyes off each other. She tripped and almost fell over on the steps outside because she wasn't looking where she was going! But he caught her and took her in his arms!

BEATE: —She got dizzy . . .

TOVE: I think she was overcome by happiness and by the light! Just how a wedding should be. Really simple—just the couple, the vicar and a witness. What else do you need?

BEATE: I must admit I quite like the big weddings too—like the one we had last week when the bride arrived in a carriage.

TOVE: The horses got spooked every time the bus drove past. Palle really wanted to go and pat them, but I wouldn't let him. It would only have made them even more frightened.

BEATE: The bride wore a wedding dress with a train which was carried by little girls who were all dressed in white and had flowers in their hair, just like the bride. Someone sang a solo and they played the Wedding March. They had a guard of honour and everyone threw rice at the couple!

TOVE: It won't do any good, though.

BEATE: How do you mean?

TOVE: . . . It still won't last.

BEATE: Why on earth shouldn't it last?

TOVE: You could tell—by the dress. There were too many ribbons and bows. It was too frilly . . .

BEATE: —And then it won't last?

TOVE: No . . .

BEATE: [*Laughs.*] You mean you've actually worked out a method to tell if it will work or not?

TOVE: No, it's not really a method, it's more like a feeling.

BEATE: Oh, Tove. You're so scared of anything that's happy and festive! Anything that's out of the ordinary.

TOVE: My dress had ribbons and bows and a small train. My mum spent all her savings on it. And how long did the marriage last? Not even a year.

BEATE: —So tell me what's going to happen to the young couple I just married.

TOVE: They'll be happy, anyone could see that. They'll probably have children soon, too. Maybe that's why she felt faint, she's pregnant. First a girl and then a boy. Healthy, normal kids . . .

PALLE: [*Enters.*] ". . . to have and to hold, in sickness and in health, for better or worse, [*Insistently.*]—until death us do part!"

BEATE: You're quite right Palle, I didn't say that.

PALLE: You have to say that! "Until death us do part." You can't miss it out.

BEATE: They asked me not to say it.

TOVE: See! You can't leave a single word out without Palle noticing. He knows all the services off by heart. And people say he's simple!

PALLE: ". . . to love and to honour, for better or worse, in sickness and in health, until death us do part."

BEATE: All right Palle, we heard you.

PALLE: "For better or worse, in sickness and in health, until death—"

TOVE: That's enough. Didn't you hear what Beate said?

[PALLE *goes over to a corner of the room. He sinks down and begins to rock backwards and forwards.*]

TOVE: She was so lovely, the bride. She looked exquisite and delicate—just the way I wanted to look when I was young. I starved myself to get as thin as that, but it didn't work. I still looked like a healthy country girl.

BEATE: And just you be glad!

TOVE: And she could sing, too! It's amazing that one person can be so lucky.

BEATE: What's Palle doing?

TOVE: Oh, he's just started that . . . Palle? Sit still, it's really annoying. Do you hear?

[PALLE *continues to rock back and forth, without seeing or hearing anything.*]

TOVE: Couldn't you try? You could make him stop, you can make him do anything.

BEATE: He'll stop when he gets tired.

TOVE: He can sit like that for any length of time.

BEATE: [*Approaches* PALLE *and puts her arm round him.*] Palle? Palle, listen to me . . . Why does he always wear that blue jumper? It's too small.

TOVE: The water was too hot when I washed it.

BEATE: Hasn't he got any others?

TOVE: Yes, lots, but he'll only wear that one since you gave it to him.

BEATE: Did I?

TOVE: Have you forgotten? It wasn't long after we started coming to church. You invited us home for a cup of tea—you were so kind. And you'd bought the jumper for Palle.

BEATE: Oh yes, I think I remember—

TOVE: If it was up to him, he'd wear it to bed.

BEATE: [*Strokes* PALLE'S *hair.*] What's the matter with you Palle? Why are you doing this? Tell Beate . . . Calm down now, don't bunch up your fists. Look at me—that's right . . . There you go. Steady, steady . . . Calm down . . .

TOVE: I told you!

PALLE: [*Sinks down in front of* BEATE *and buries his head in her lap.*] I want to get married.

TOVE: That's all we need.

PALLE: I want to get married!

TOVE: Get up, you're drooling all over Beate's skirt. Come on, get up. [*Hoists him up.*] Now go to the toilet.

PALLE: [*Surprised.*] Why?

TOVE: Because you need a wee.

PALLE: No, I don't!

TOVE: Yes, you do. I can tell by your trousers.

PALLE: [*Looks down.*] All right . . . [*Exits.*]

TOVE: It's the wedding that's upset him. It's hard to see others being so happy when you're not.

BEATE: Palle isn't unhappy. He just lives in his own little world, like a child who sits and dreams about being somewhere else! [*Looks at herself in the mirror.*]

TOVE: Do you want some coffee?

BEATE: I haven't got time. I have to go and see the three refugees in the crypt. There's a journalist coming, I'm trying to get the press interested.

TOVE: Just a quick cup? I've even bought some biscuits, your favourites.

BEATE: I'm sorry. Save me a couple.

TOVE: You never have the time any more. It's not like it was in the beginning. You always had time for us, and you came and talked to us when we came to church—

BEATE: You sat there like two frightened animals that no-one had talked to for years.

TOVE: You always used to hold my hands. You were the one who told us to come round for coffee after the service and wanted us to sit next to you, even if everyone else had to move. And now you don't even see us any more, it's as if we don't exist.

BEATE: What are you talking about?

TOVE: Others have come who are more interesting. The three refugees and the young widow who's always running round after you.

BEATE: The three refugees are in trouble, and I'm all they've got. They could be arrested and deported at any time. And the young widow's so depressed she's likely to do almost anything.

TOVE: She's the one you invite home, nowadays. You hold *her* hand, and buy *her* clothes.

BEATE: Didn't I make sure you got a job in the church which lets you bring Palle with you?

TOVE: Yeah—

BEATE: Didn't I find you a decent place to live?

TOVE: Yes, yes! And I'm really grateful, it's not that!

BEATE: [*Takes* TOVE's *hands.*] There are lots of people who need me. I'd really like to help them all, but there's only one of me. There's going to be times when we don't see much of each other. That's just the way it is. It's like a marriage, the honeymoon doesn't last forever.

TOVE: I know . . .

[PALLE *enters.*]

BEATE: Palle, can you do me a favour? Could you get your broom and sweep the steps. They're covered in dirt and dust.

PALLE: I've already done the sweeping!

BEATE: Yes, but it already needs doing again. The wind is blowing dust everywhere.

TOVE: Do as Beate says.

[PALLE *exits.*]

TOVE: I wonder what the young couple are doing right now? Where do you think they are?

BEATE: I don't know.

TOVE: The weather's nice—maybe they've gone to a café to have lunch, just the two of them.

BEATE: Maybe.

TOVE: The waiter will probably be extra nice to them, when he finds out they've just got married. I wish I could look into the future.

BEATE: Why?

TOVE: To see if something horrible will happen to them one day.

BEATE: Why should it?!

TOVE: To balance out all that happiness.

BEATE: Envy isn't a very noble sentiment.

TOVE: Why do some people get everything and some people nothing? Why is everything always so unfair?

BEATE: I wouldn't worry, their happiness has already been shattered.

TOVE: . . . How do you mean?

BEATE: She's very seriously ill.

TOVE: Oh, no. Oh, my God, no . . . !

BEATE: There's your justice.

TOVE: Seriously ill—but it's not incurable, is it?

BEATE: They don't know.

TOVE: Surely there must be something the doctors can do! There's so much they can do nowadays.

BEATE: Yes, but they can't cure everything.

TOVE: That's awful. Such a young girl . . . how can you be so calm about it all?

BEATE: I see so much—

TOVE: Why didn't you tell me? Why did you let me talk about their future?

BEATE: That kind of information is confidential. I shouldn't really have told you.

TOVE: Isn't there something we can do? Help her in some way? I'd do anything! Give anything, if she needs blood, or a kidney. I'd even give her my heart—

BEATE: They're doing everything they can. The rest is in God's hands.

TOVE: So that's why they asked you to leave out the bit about 'until death us do part'. And that's why she suddenly got pale and nearly fainted. Not because she was happy . . .

BEATE: No.

TOVE: I'll pray for her, every day. Every hour, every day!

BEATE: Calm down.

TOVE: Why did I say it?! I didn't mean it that way!

BEATE: If only you could learn to be grateful for what you've got—

TOVE: I don't deserve to live.

BEATE: —Learn to appreciate the little things in life. Just enjoy life the way it is!

TOVE: I can't. I just can't.

BEATE: Well try, for my sake. I'm going to go and see our friends in the crypt. If the journalist should happen to come in here, will you show her the way? [*Exits.*]

TOVE: Yes, of course. You're so kind . . . [*Gathers up the cups and puts the biscuits back in the bag.*]

The Beggar, Part 1

A street.

Two women, A and B. A walks quickly down the street, on her way to work. She is elegantly dressed, handbag over one shoulder and an attaché case under the other arm. B is slumped against a wall. She is averagely dressed, with a childish streak, otherwise very normal and unremarkable. B stops A.

B: [*Reaches out one hand.*] Can you spare a couple of quid?

A: [*Somewhat surprised.*] I beg your pardon?

B: [*Hand still out.*] Can you spare a couple of quid. I've lost my purse and I need money for the bus. My two kids are on their own, they're probably wondering where I am—

A: [*Takes out a ten pound note from her purse.*] You can have this—

B: [*Quickly reaches for the note, but doesn't manage to get hold of it.*] Ten quid!

A: If you bless me.

B: Eh? If I what?

A: Wish me luck. You don't get something for nothing.

B: I've wished myself luck lots of time, it ain't done me no good.

A: It's different if you wish it for someone else.

B: All right, if you think I can do it. If you really think it'll work—

A: I'm sure it will. I don't know why. Maybe because you don't really look like one of them.

B: Give us the money, then.

[*A gives B the ten pounds and leaves.*]

B: [*Shouts after A.*] When do you want me to start?

A: —Right away! [*Continues walking.*]

B: [*Looks at the note.*] Ten quid,—quite cheap really . . .

SHOOTING STAR

Two men, A *and* B. A *is standing by a window.*

B: What are you looking at?

A: I saw a shooting star . . .

B: Better make a wish, then!

A: Yeah, I know, but I can't think of anything.

B: Haven't you got any wishes at all?

A: Well, you can't just wish for anything, can you. It has to be something suitable, something really special—

B: I know what I'd wish for.

A: You didn't see it, though. It really surprised me, actually—I was just looking at the star, and then it fell! You really ought to know these things in advance, so you can prepare yourself.

B: It must be a sign that you're happy as it is—if you haven't got any unfulfilled wishes.

A: I've got thousands of wishes! I just can't decide which one to go for.

B: Then wish for total happiness!

A: You can't, that's too general. What would you wish for?

B: A steady job. Somewhere else to live. Money!

A: That's boring. I can't make myself wish for something like that. I mean, money—

B: Then think of something else. It'll be too late soon. You have to make the wish straight away if you want it to come true.

A: [*Moves away from the window.*] . . . I give up. I can't think of anything that means something to me. The more I think about it, the less I can come up with. I once had goals—things I really wanted to do. But I don't any more. Life has lost its meaning. I'm just drifting along from one day to the next. It's awful! I wish . . . I wish I'd never seen that shooting star!

Buying and Selling

An ESTATE AGENT, *a young man wearing a coat with a briefcase under one arm;* MRS. BRANDT, *an elderly woman; a young, somewhat badly dressed couple, she is pregnant.*

ESTATE AGENT: [*Leads the way, showing off the house.*] . . . yet another room.

[MRS. BRANDT *mumbles something.*]

SHE: What did she say?

HE: Nothing, she's just senile. Don't worry about her.

SHE: Just think, she lives here all alone—

HE: It's a waste, it shouldn't be allowed.

MRS. BRANDT: . . . The worst thing is all the voices, Victor's, and the children's. Whenever I sit down and shut my eyes, they're there, just like in the old days. Victor's voice right behind me, as if he's bent down to whisper in my ear, the children's voices further away, in their rooms, or in the corridor where they used to chase each other. So I have to get up, and walk from room to room and look—but there's never anyone there. Noone, and still . . .

ESTATE AGENT: You can safely leave the tour to me, Mrs. Brandt, you don't need to come with us. [*Continues.*]—The box room, and the pantry which could be knocked through to the kitchen . . .

SHE: [*Quietly.*] I don't like this, anyone can see we don't have the money.

HE: Maybe they'll just think we don't spend it on clothes.

ESTATE AGENT: [*Glances at his watch; continues.*]—And here's the dining room. Have a look at the stucco ceiling, the panels and the beautiful French doors.

SHE: [*Giggles.*] It's bigger than the whole of our flat!

HE: Shhhh . . .

ESTATE AGENT: I presume you're actually interested—?

HE: Of course! It's precisely the kind of flat we had in mind.

[SHE *giggles.*]

ESTATE AGENT: Here's the new proposal with the changes to the loan. [*Quietly, so that* MRS. BRANDT *can't hear.*] We can talk about the down-payment,—

SHE: Look at the chandelier!

HE: I wonder if it comes with the house?

SHE: [*Giggles.*] You must be joking!

ESTATE AGENT: I think I can safely say that it does. Mrs. Brandt won't have room for it in her new home.

HE: Just think of the dinner parties you could hold here!

MRS. BRANDT: Watercress soup, duck à l'orange, Black Forest gâteau! On the blue and white dishes with the gold rim. Mrs. Hansen served the meal, helped by her daughter when there were many of us. The chandelier was lit—everyone talking and laughing, glasses clinking. Those beautiful, hand-cut glasses . . .

SHE: I would be so happy, if I lived here.

HE: I thought you were happy.

SHE: I am, I just mean even happier. Completely happy!

HE: So would I . . .

MRS. BRANDT: I can still hear them,—all those voices . . . Like a wave! An ocean which rises and falls, rises and falls . . .

SHE: Our own flat is going to look darker and even smaller after this. This isn't funny any longer, I don't want to see any more.

ESTATE AGENT: [*Glances at his watch; walks on.*] . . . The study. There's a door on to the balcony in here . . .

[*The young couple and* MRS. BRANDT *follow him into the next room, off stage.*]

The Beggar, Part 2

Same location as in Part 1.

A *and* B, *dressed as in Part 1.*

B *is waiting. She's shivering and coughing, and generally looking quite ill. A comes walking down the street. She's humming and looks like someone who's had a really good day. B walks up to her.*

A: [*Surprised and sarcastic.*] I thought you were in a hurry to get back to your children?

B: [*Takes out the ten pound note.*] Here—I don't want it after all.

A: Why on earth not?

B: I've felt really odd since you gave it to me. My heart's been racing and it hurts everywhere. I feel dizzy and I keep getting hot and cold.

A: [*Takes a step back.*] I hope it's not catching . . .

B: [*Tries to put the money in* A's *hand.*] Here—take it . . .

A: Absolutely not. Use it to get a cab home. You probably caught something standing here all day.

B: I was waiting for you.

A: [*Laughs.*] I've had a fantastic day! Everything's gone right. And I've been promoted, ahead of everyone else! I feel all giddy, almost as if I were drunk!

B: It's like something's happened to me. I don't know what—I feel like I'm gonna die. Take the tenner back—please!

A: Absolutely not, the money's yours. You've well and truly earned it. Anyway, I have to go, I've got to do the shopping so we can celebrate my new job tonight! [*Leaves.*]
B: [*Shouts after her.*] . . . Don't go! Wait! I'm scared . . . !

[*Interval.*]

EVENING

Scene I

A large, old garden, somewhere in town. In the background is an old wall covered in blue clematis. There's a faint hum of traffic and the sound of a train in the distance. The late sunshine falls through the leaves, leaving a pattern on the table centre stage. The table is covered with a white tablecloth and surrounded by seven different chairs. MORTEN, *wearing an apron over a roll-neck sweater and a pair of jeans, is laying the table.* JOHANNE *appears. She is heavily pregnant and is wearing a large, loose dress. She shudders a little and yawns.*

MORTEN: Oh, you've woken up? [*Distributes the plates.*] I'll give Torben the yellow one with the pheasant and Julie the one with the flowers . . .
JOHANNE: [*Takes a few olives from a small bowl on the table.*] I want the blue and white one with the gold rim.
MORTEN: OK, you have the blue and white one with the gold rim. Mikkel can have the green one with the crack, he won't notice anyway. Helene can have the white one with the scallop pattern, and I'll take the old red one with the landscape. [*Looks at the plates.*] It's almost disappeared completely. You nearly can't see the sheep, and the shepherd's fading too.
JOHANNE: [*Takes another olive.*] What are we having?
MORTEN: Avocado soup with crab meat, followed by leg of lamb with sweetbreads and mustard, then cheese, and we're finishing off with passion fruit sorbet and blackberries.
JOHANNE: I thought it was just going to be an ordinary dinner, like we used to make!
MORTEN: I felt like making an effort. I wanted to surprise everyone with a really special dinner on a normal day.
JOHANNE: [*Shudders and yawns again.*] . . . How long did I sleep for?
MORTEN: A couple of hours.
JOHANNE: I only wanted to take a quick nap. Why didn't you wake me? I was supposed to finish a dress, I still have to put on the collar and the train. She's coming to try it on tomorrow.
MORTEN: I called you a couple of times, but you were fast asleep.
JOHANNE: You really shouldn't sleep during the day. It messes everything up. God, I feel sick—[*Eats yet another olive.*]
MORTEN: Leave some for the guests.
JOHANNE: Where's Anna?
MORTEN: Down by the bushes. She's building a cave for her and Marie.
JOHANNE: We don't even know if they're bringing Marie.
MORTEN: Let's pray they don't. I hope she's at her mother's this week.
JOHANNE: Anna'll be disappointed.
MORTEN: Marie just orders her around all the time.
JOHANNE: Oh, Anna quite likes it, it means she doesn't have to take the initiative.
MORTEN: I don't like seeing my kid humiliated like that. And what are we supposed to do if she takes money out of Anna's piggy bank again? Or takes some of her toys home with her? I wouldn't mind, but she always takes the expensive stuff—
JOHANNE: It was Anna that gave her the cooker.

MORTEN: That's just something she said to cover for Marie. Anna's so loyal, she's so inno-cent compared with Marie. Have you noticed the way she nearly closes her eyes and looks away when you're talking to her? It's impossible to look her in the eye.

JOHANNE: We ought to talk to Torben and Helene about it. Maybe Marie's having prob-lems.

MORTEN: I know we should, but we aren't going to.

JOHANNE: We'll have to set a place for her so it looks as if she's welcome.

MORTEN: [*Puts a plate on the table.*] She can have the ugly one with the zigzag pattern.

JOHANNE: [*Sits down and puts a hand on her stomach.*] It's really kicking—

MORTEN: [*Looks at the table.*] There's a knife missing.

JOHANNE: Much more than Anna used to—it feels like it's panicking.

MORTEN: Probably running out of space. [*Glances at his watch.*] I have to turn the meat! [*Walks up towards the house, humming to himself.*]

[JOHANNE *eats olives, one after another. Then she leans back and shuts her eyes. A ray of sun-light falls across her face.* MINNA, *an older, well-dressed woman appears. She carries a thick briefcase under one arm and jangles a set of car keys from one finger. She stops and looks at* JOHANNE.]

MINNA: Johanne . . . ?

JOHANNE: Mum—you're home.

MINNA: Isn't it lovely. The garden's so beautiful at this time of the year. You ought to sit here all day and look at the roses and the leaves changing colour, and the sky . . .

JOHANNE: You look tired.

MINNA: I am. It's been one meeting after another, ever since this morning. I didn't even have time for lunch. Everyone's pulling and tugging at me to make me do something for them. They completely besiege me! I don't know who they think I am—God? [*Stud-ies the table.*] That looks nice.

JOHANNE: Won't you join us? There aren't many coming, and Morten's cooked a beautiful meal.

MINNA: Thanks, but I just need time on my own. I have to prepare my speech for the hear-ing tomorrow, about the civil war in Czechoslovakia.

JOHANNE: Is there a war in Czechoslovakia?

MINNA: Didn't you know? Don't you keep up with anything?

JOHANNE: Yes. Well—no, I probably don't, actually.

MINNA: You really should. You could at least read the paper or watch some TV. You just sit there sewing one wedding dress after another while the world falls apart.

JOHANNE: That's my job.

MINNA: My secretary told me there was a picture of one of your dresses on the front page of one of the big magazines. Why didn't you tell me?

JOHANNE: I did. The magazine's been on your desk for days.

MINNA: Has it? I'm afraid I haven't seen it. Oh, I have a headache, I'm getting too old for this. I was sitting in a meeting today, and suddenly I could hear my own voice like it was someone else's. The words just came by themselves. I felt like shutting up and never saying another word.

JOHANNE: You need a break. When did you last take a day off? Or even an evening?

MINNA: I can't remember.

JOHANNE: Then take tonight off! Come and eat with us. You've got to eat anyway, haven't you? And you don't have to stay long.

MINNA: I really can't. I've got to prepare myself for the hearing; it's being broadcast live. [*Sits down.*] Is it kicking? [*Puts a hand on* JOHANNE's *stomach.*] I haven't been a very good mother . . .

JOHANNE: [*Surprised.*] Yes, you have!

MINNA: I'm always busy. So was your dad, when he was alive. We wanted to save the whole world, but we still neglected our own child.

JOHANNE: I was OK. I had the whole house, and the garden,—

MINNA: You were always left with a baby-sitter, or on your own when you got older. You were alone so much you invented people to talk to.

JOHANNE: I learned to look after myself, there's nothing wrong with that.

MINNA: Once I came home,—it was late in the afternoon, like now, and you were sitting out here waiting, with some of the people from your class. It was your birthday and we'd invited them, but I had forgotten and there was nothing in the house. I didn't even feel very guilty. I thought you had so much, compared to children elsewhere.

JOHANNE: You always brought me presents when you had been travelling. Once I got a doll that was as big as me.

MINNA: We never bought you anything. Without really meaning to, I think we wanted to punish you, somehow . . .

JOHANNE: And once I got three small wooden elephants decorated with mother of pearl.

MINNA: It must be something you dreamed.

JOHANNE: I don't get it. It's as if you're talking about someone else.

MINNA: You've just shut it out. It's normal. [*Stands up.*] I'll go and take a nap before I get on with my work. [*Strokes* JOHANNE's *hair.*] Your hair is falling out—

JOHANNE: Yes, I know.

MINNA: [*Takes a handful of* JOHANNE's *loose hair and lets it blow away in the wind.*] There you go, birdies, something for your nests! [*Picks up her bag and enters the house.*]

[JOHANNE *eats a few more olives.* MORTEN *comes out into the garden, wearing an oven-glove on one hand.*]

MORTEN: [*Looks into the bowl.*] It's empty! You've eaten them all!

JOHANNE: There are two left.

MORTEN: You said you were feeling sick.

JOHANNE: I am! That's why I have to keep eating all the time.

MORTEN: Hmm . . . [*Looks around for* MINNA.] Is your mum back? [*Eagerly.*] Do you think she might want to join us? She's never met any of our friends.

JOHANNE: She hasn't got time. She's got to prepare a speech for a hearing tomorrow about the civil war in Czechoslovakia.

MORTEN: Is there a civil war going on there?

JOHANNE: Didn't you know? Don't you keep up with anything? Don't you read a paper? Or watch TV?

MORTEN: Eh? Yes! Well—maybe it's been a while. Here's Torben and Helene. I can't see Marie,—maybe we'll be lucky . . .

[TORBEN *and* HELENE *appear.* MORTEN *and* JOHANNE *walk towards them. They embrace and say hello.*]

MORTEN: . . . Where's Marie?

JOHANNE: Haven't you brought Marie along?

TORBEN: I didn't know if we were supposed to bring her.

JOHANNE: She's always welcome, you know that.

MORTEN: We've set a place for her.

JOHANNE: Anna had been looking forward to it.

HELENE: See, I told you we should have brought Marie. [*Spots the table.*] Oh, doesn't it look beautiful!

TORBEN: Are we celebrating something?

HELENE: Hang on! Quiet everyone! I've seen all this before; the table laid out outside with a white tablecloth and everything, exactly like this. The rest of the food was on the table

but there was no-one there, and all the chairs had been knocked over like something
    had happened—

JOHANNE: What?

HELENE: I don't know. Nothing moved,—except for the tablecloth blowing in the wind—

JOHANNE: It sounds really eerie, you're making my skin crawl . . .

MORTEN: It sounds like something out of a film.

HELENE: No, it's not from a film, it's something real. If only I could remember—

TORBEN: Think of something else, then it'll come back to you.

ANNA: [*Appears.*] . . . Where's Marie?

JOHANNE: Marie—she's not here.

TORBEN: Our neighbour is looking after her.

[ANNA *runs off.*]

JOHANNE: Anna? Don't worry, Marie'll come next time. We promise! Anna, wait . . . !
    [*Follows her.*]

MORTEN: . . . Have an olive!—I wonder what's happened to Mikkel? He's bringing his
    new girlfriend. Julie, I think her name is. They're very much in love.

TORBEN: That must be wonderful. I've almost forgotten what it feels like. Maybe I've never
    actually felt like that, at all.

HELENE: I read about Mikkel's new exhibition. They made him sound like the new Van
    Gogh.

TORBEN: Personally, I think Mikkel's pictures could have been painted by a child or a chim-
    panzee.

HELENE: You don't know the first thing about art.

MORTEN: That's precisely what's so good about his pictures. Their primitive, unschooled
    quality. They have this sense of naivety, this primordial force!

HELENE: An eternal light!

MORTEN: Mikkel has kept in touch with the child within himself. With his animal instincts.

HELENE: All the pictures were sold an hour after the opening.

MORTEN: [*Looks at his watch.*] I have to go and check on the food. [*Exits.*]

HELENE: . . . Why don't we live here? It must be fantastic to have a garden like this in
    the middle of town.

TORBEN: Would you want to move back to your parents and have your mother living up-
    stairs?

HELENE: If my parents had lived in a house like this, and my mother was anything like Jo-
    hanne's.

TORBEN: The place is old and rotten—and so's Johanne's mother.

HELENE: She fights for those who are less fortunate even though it's not the thing to do
    nowadays. She dares show her feelings unlike most of the other politicians—especially
    the men. Can you remember how she cried on live television when she came back from
    some war zone recently?

TORBEN: Go and ask if you can kiss her arse, she'd love that!

HELENE: Why do you say things like that? Why are you always impossible to talk to?

TORBEN: You're too old to fall in love with people just because they're famous.

HELENE: You're only saying that because you find it impossible to admire anyone or any-
    thing. You're always negative and mean. You even run down your friends behind their
    backs!

TORBEN: I criticize them.

HELENE: You run them down, you slander them!

TORBEN: There's no need to shout.

[ANNA *appears, unnoticed.*]

HELENE: You hate everyone because that's all you can do. Because you think it'll help you escape the self-hatred you're wallowing in!

TORBEN: Shut up.

HELENE: You're warped! You're sick!

TORBEN: [*Hisses.*] Not so loud!

HELENE: You don't deserve to be loved by anyone! You don't deserve any friends! Why can't you just die?!

TORBEN: [*Puts a hand over her mouth.*] That's enough!

HELENE: Let go, you bastard!

TORBEN: [*Spots* ANNA; *lets* HELENE *go.*] Hi Anna . . .

HELENE: Hello Anna . . .

ANNA: Hi! [*Picks up a ball and disappears again.*]

HELENE: [*Quietly.*] I hate you . . .

TORBEN: I hate you too.

[MIKKEL *and* JULIE *appear, arm in arm. They're talking and laughing.* MIKKEL's *suit is elegant, but slightly too large.* JULIE *is dressed in a short, tight skirt, a large sweater and dark glasses. She's carrying a bouquet of blue and white lilacs.*]

TORBEN: Here come the young lovebirds!

[JOHANNE *comes out of the house carrying a basket full of bread, followed by* MORTEN *with a couple of wine bottles.*]

MIKKEL: May I introduce Julie! Julie, this is Johanne, Helene, Torben and Morten!

[JULIE *hands the bouquet to Johanne.*]

JOHANNE: Lilacs! Oh, what a beautiful smell! It's enough to make you dizzy . . .

JULIE: I'm sorry we're late, but the trains were delayed.

MIKKEL: Someone had been run over.

JULIE: We sat and waited for twenty minutes while they cleared the track.

MIKKEL: Luckily we couldn't see anything. Just a red sports bag lying between the tracks. It was full of clothes—

JOHANNE: Imagine taking your own life like that.

MORTEN: I don't understand it.

HELENE: Surely you can always find something worth living for.

TORBEN: That's what you think.

JULIE: I'd never do it like that, though.

MORTEN: Nor would I. You could just end up crippled for life.

TORBEN: Don't even talk about it!

HELENE: I'd take pills.

JULIE: So would I.

MIKKEL: I'd never do it. Never—!

TORBEN: [*Looks at* MIKKEL.]—You're looking very posh, Mikkel!

MIKKEL: [*Pleased.*] You think so?

MORTEN: Your own mother wouldn't recognize you!

MIKKEL: This is how artists dress abroad. I don't even think they've got paint under their fingernails.

MORTEN: [*Takes hold of* MIKKEL's *tie and pulls.*] Elastic! That's cheating.

TORBEN: Aren't the trousers a little too long? Don't they trip you up?

MIKKEL: Yes—the jacket's a bit too big as well; I have to roll the sleeves up, but they told me that's how it's supposed to be nowadays.

JULIE: [*Giggles.*] They just didn't have his size.

MIKKEL: Where's Anna? We've got something for her.

[MORTEN *calls* ANNA *who appears with her ball.* MIKKEL *hands her a bag of sweets and chats to her.*]

HELENE: [*To* JULIE.] Don't you remember me?

JULIE: [*Looks closely at* HELENE.] . . . I'm not very good with faces.

HELENE: I recognized you right away. You wrote poetry, I seem to remember.

JULIE: I still do. I've just finished an anthology. It's called "The Colours of Darkness" and it'll be out this spring.

[MINNA *appears; she has changed into more relaxed, younger-looking clothes.*]

MINNA: Is the invitation still open?

JOHANNE: Of course it is!

MINNA: It's such a wonderful evening. I could hear you all talking and I suddenly felt like joining you.

[*Says hello to* MIKKEL, JULIE, TORBEN *and* HELENE, *shaking hands with each in turn.*]

TORBEN: [*To* HELENE.] You're blushing.

HELENE: Shut up.

MORTEN: Sit down everyone. Dinner is served!

[*They all sit at the table.* MORTEN *disappears into the house and reappears a moment later wearing a white cloth over one arm and carrying the first two bowls of soup which he proceeds to serve with a flourish.*]

MORTEN: Avocado soup with crab meat and a pinch of white wine!

[*Delight and admiration from all.*]

EVENING

Scene II

Later the same evening. One by one, the guests finish their main course. JOHANNE *is still eating.* ANNA *is sitting on her lap, sucking her thumb.*

MINNA: That was wonderful!

JULIE: Divine! Absolutely divine!

TORBEN: I've never tasted anything like it!

HELENE: [*Laughs.*] Yes, it really was quite sublime!

JOHANNE: [*Eating awkwardly because of* ANNA.] Anna—why can't you sit on your own chair?

MORTEN: What about the meat? Was it tender enough?

MINNA: Perfect!

JULIE: It melted on the tongue!

HELENE: And it was exactly the right colour!

TORBEN: The taste made me think of grassy slopes and green meadows . . .

JOHANNE: At least take your thumb out of your mouth, you're not a baby any more.

MINNA: I didn't realize you were such a culinary expert, Torben. I think you'll have to be a chef in your next life.

MORTEN: Helene—you're hardly touched the vegetables . . .

HELENE: I'm allergic to root vegetables.

TORBEN: She's allergic to just about everything. Even me. If I so much as touch her she breaks out in a rash.

JULIE: I'm allergic to citrus fruits. And nuts. My tongue swells up and I get this rash—

JOHANNE: I'm sure Anna's allergic to something, too. Anna, show us your arm . . .

[ANNA *pulls up her sleeve and shows them one arm.*]

JULIE: My God, that looks terrible.

MORTEN: It's got worse, we'll have to take her to the doctor.

HELENE: Does it itch?

JOHANNE: Only at night. She scratches herself so much she bleeds.

MORTEN: How was the gravy? Could you taste the sweetbreads?

JULIE: The gravy was wonderful!

MIKKEL: Full of juices!

MINNA: Worthy of a master chef!

MORTEN: [*Spots something in the gravy; grimaces as he removes a hair.*] Johanne! Look! Look what was in here!

JOHANNE: [*Guiltily.*] . . . Is it one of mine?

MORTEN: Where else would it have come from? They're everywhere! You really ought to wear a hairnet. I hope everyone had finished?

[*All nod, looking very full.*]

JOHANNE: [*Pleading.*] There just isn't room for both of us, Anna, you're too big. I can't breathe—!

JULIE: [*Reaches out.*] Do you want to sit with me?

[ANNA *shakes her head and snuggles up to* JOHANNE.]

MINNA: Come sit with Grandma, you'd like that, wouldn't you—? [*Stands and is about to lift* ANNA *up.*] Come on, Anna dear . . .

ANNA: [*Clutches* JOHANNE.] No, no!

JOHANNE: What's the matter with you? What are you afraid of?!

MORTEN: [*Rebukingly.*] If Anna is scared she should be allowed to show it.

MINNA: It's no wonder; I'm never home. I remember when Anna was little, she used to scream when I wanted to pick her up from her playpen. That's the price for living the life I do. You become a stranger even to your own family. Maybe even to yourself. [*Empties her glass.*]

MORTEN: More wine? [*Pours wine into* MINNA's *glass and then into the other glasses. Misses out* JOHANNE's.] You've had enough.

JULIE: Poor Johanne—it's no fun being the only one who's sober.

MIKKEL: [*Raises his glass.*] Let's have a toast to Morten!

[*They drink and toast.*]

MORTEN: Something really funny happened today. I had just been to a lecture about "Eckersberg and his contemporaries, seen through deconstructivist eyes." I was on my way home wondering what we were going to have for dinner, and then someone stopped me and asked if I could spare a few quid—

MINNA: You shouldn't give them anything.

HELENE: It just covers up the social problem.

MORTEN: I wouldn't normally, but then I realized it was Frederik, a guy I went to school with when we both lived out in the country.

JULIE: Did he recognize you?

MORTEN: I think so, but he didn't say anything.

TORBEN: So what happened? Did you give him anything?

MORTEN: I gave him what he asked for. And then I regretted that I hadn't given him any more. He was barefoot, and he was missing a couple of teeth. He looked like he hadn't had a wash for years. I don't get it. He was one of those who always did his homework and he always got good grades.

MIKKEL: People change.

MORTEN: That much?

MIKKEL: Some change a lot, some don't. But we all change. The world changes so quickly you hardly notice! It's this way one day, and different the next. People are one way one day, and they've changed the next. You even change from morning to evening—

TORBEN: I don't! I'm always the same, that's *my* bloody problem.

[*A telephone rings inside the house.*]

MINNA: [*Stands up.*]—I think that's for me. Excuse me . . . [*Enters the house.*]

MIKKEL: I don't know if it's the wine, or the food, or the wonderful company, but I feel quite clearheaded! I feel like I understand everything! The deeper meaning of it all!

TORBEN: [*Pours wine into his glass.*] It's the wine.

HELENE: I know what you mean, I feel like laughing all the time—!

JOHANNE: [*Startled.*] Ouch, Anna! Watch your elbow! If you can't sit still, you'll have to get down. Go sit on your own chair.

[ANNA *hops down from* JOHANNE'*s lap and runs off, crying angrily.*]

JOHANNE: Anna? Where are you going? Stay here . . . Anna?

MORTEN: She'll be OK. [*Gets up and begins to clear away the plates; to the others who are trying to help.*] Don't worry, I'll do it, just stay here—

JULIE: [*Stands up.*] Where's your loo?

[*The gathering round the table breaks up.* MORTEN *clears the table and gets ready to serve the next course.* MIKKEL *helps him.* JULIE *goes to the toilet.*]

HELENE: . . . I saw Isabella yesterday. I nearly didn't recognize her, she's got so thin. Her skin looks all yellow.

JOHANNE: It's spread to her liver.

HELENE: Oh no—!

JOHANNE: They say she still has a small chance.

TORBEN: —Is Isabella ill?

HELENE: I've told you.

JOHANNE: She noticed a lump the day after the party we had a few months ago, it was no bigger than a pea.

HELENE: It's getting to the stage where you hardly dare touch yourself. She was sitting right there, in that chair.

TORBEN: [*Ill at ease.*] Here? In this chair? [*He gets up.*]

JOHANNE: She was in such a good mood. Just imagine if she'd known—just imagine if we knew . . .

HELENE: One of my colleagues, a young guy, has just had it diagnosed in his testicles . . .

TORBEN: Stop it! I can't bear to listen to it. Why do women always talk about illness? I think you actually enjoy it. I think it gives you some form of perverse satisfaction!

JOHANNE: What a thing to say!!

HELENE: You're scared!

TORBEN: Of course I'm scared! Who wouldn't be when you lot start telling stories?!

MORTEN: [*Appears with a basket of bread and a pot of butter.*] Talking about other people's problems always makes you feel better. It makes all your own troubles look insignificant. You end up feeling quite lucky! [*Disappears into the house again.*]

HELENE: What are we allowed to talk about, then? The weather?

JOHANNE: Those who are healthy?

HELENE: Anyone who's successful?

[*The sound of crockery smashing. Silence.*]

JOHANNE: [*Sighs.*] It's the same story, every time Mikkel lends a hand.

TORBEN: You'd think he was an idiot! I'll go see how much he dropped, then you can carry on with your favourite subject! [*Exits.*]

MINNA: [*Reappears.*] It sounded worse than it was; he only dropped a single plate. [*Sighs deeply.*] I can't remember when I last spent an evening in the garden—listen to the train, there's something really soothing about that sound. When I can't sleep, I lie awake and listen to the trains going past and try to imagine where they're going . . .

HELENE: I wouldn't be able to sleep a wink if I had the kind of responsibility you do.

MINNA: As long as you know that what you're doing will actually help someone—that there really is a point to all the meetings and the discussions and the debates and the hearings. I'm beginning to doubt it more and more. I had to admit long ago that I can't save the world. I just wonder if I've ever helped *anyone*?

HELENE: It was brilliant, what you said on the telly the other night. Nobody else dares say anything like that!

MINNA: On the television . . . What did I say?

HELENE: "We live in a dream where everything is peaceful. But the alarm bells have begun to ring, and by the time we wake up to the real world with all its poverty and horror, we'll regret having wasted our time sleeping!"

MINNA: [*Surprised.*] Did I say that?

HELENE: "The heat of the bed will be replaced by wind and icy temperatures, and we'll no longer be able to return to our cosy nest!"

MINNA: [*Surprised.*] That doesn't sound like me at all . . .

HELENE: [*Laughs.*] The journalist looked quite shocked, it was great. I could have kissed the screen!

TORBEN: [*Walks up to them.*] What are you talking about? New illnesses? Death and destruction?

HELENE: None of your business.

MINNA: I'm not going to stand at the next election.

JOHANNE: Why not?

MINNA: I want to devote myself to my family.

JOHANNE: You mean . . . us?

MINNA: Who else? I wasn't there when Anna was born. This time, I want to be there to help you.

JOHANNE: You don't have to, we can manage by ourselves! Don't worry about it!

MINNA: That's what you're saying now—but just wait! You'll need me. I'll do the garden and look after you all. I want to know what it's like to live a normal life. Come on, let's take a walk around!

JOHANNE: [*Puts a hand on her stomach.*]—It's kicking so hard I'm running out of breath . . . It almost hurts . . . [*Sits down.*] You go, I'll sit here. [*Takes a piece of bread, butters it and eats it. She automatically takes another piece of bread, and then another, repeating her actions.*]

MINNA: [*To* HELENE *and* JULIE *who have joined them.*]—Look at the roses, they look like they're on fire! The whole garden looks enchanted tonight. The trees and the blue clematis—even the weeds. We'll have to thin out the bushes, they're spreading everywhere. [*Takes a deep breath.*] Oh, what a wonderful smell! It's much stronger and more perfumed than during the daytime. [*Moves on, stops again.*] Anna and I sowed carrots here in the spring, when I had an hour to spare. But I don't know if they're going to come up or if they've rotted—

[JULIE *stumbles and falls.*]

HELENE: How about taking your glasses off? The sun's gone down now.

JULIE: My eyes can't take the light. Even if it's just for a moment, they start aching.

HELENE: [*Guiltily.*] I'm sorry . . .

JULIE: It's hereditary. My dad had it too. He went blind and they've told me I ought to be prepared for the same thing to happen.

HELENE: Blind . . . ?

MINNA: Can't they do something?!

JULIE: The doctors are doing what they can, but I'm getting worse and worse. When we meet someone we know, I can't recognize them until I've heard their voice.

MINNA: [*Strokes* JULIE's *hair gently.*] Such a young girl—

JULIE: I've got used to the idea. I've started learning braille so I can carry on writing poetry.

MINNA: Maybe the doctors abroad can do something—I'm seeing the Minister of Health tomorrow, I'll ask her if something can't be done. [*Puts her arm round* JULIE *and guides her gently.*] Watch out . . . Here's a step . . . That's it . . . And there's a few branches . . .

[HELENE *stops and watches* MINNA *and* JULIE *as they carry on, deep in conversation.* MIKKEL, *now wearing a sticking plaster on two of his fingers comes over, followed a moment later by* TORBEN.]

MIKKEL: [*Watches* MINNA *and* JULIE.] Look at them . . . You'd think they'd known each other all their lives! That's Julie, though, everyone loves her.

HELENE: Julie says she's going blind.

MIKKEL: Has she told you? She didn't want anyone to know. She doesn't want to be pitied. Julie says it's only when you're about to lose your sight that you discover all the beauty in the world. There's beauty everywhere, in everything, even in small, trivial things! I've started painting in a whole new way after meeting Julie, with her knowledge that one day it'll all just be darkness.

TORBEN: Why is it only when you're about to lose something that you learn to appreciate it? Why is the world so unfair? I'd love to be able to appreciate beauty.

MIKKEL: Drink a bit more—it'll come!

[TORBEN *strolls around the garden with his glass trying to discover beauty.* HELENE *helps* MORTEN *who is arranging the cheese. The phone rings.*]

MINNA: [*Sighs.*] Not again. Mikkel? Come and look after Julie. She can't walk round by herself, there are too many things lying around for her to trip over. [MIKKEL *takes* JULIE's *arm.* MINNA *enters the house.*]

MIKKEL: You told them about your eyes.

JULIE: Was it wrong of me? Shouldn't I have done?

MIKKEL: Of course you should. You should do what you feel is best.

MORTEN: [*To* JOHANNE.] Are you ever going to stop?!

JOHANNE: I can't.

MORTEN: Where's Anna?

JOHANNE: I thought she was in the house with you.

MORTEN: I thought she was out here! Anna? Anna . . . ? Where are you?

[*Everyone, except for* MINNA, *and* TORBEN *who has disappeared, begins to look for* ANNA.]

JOHANNE: Anna—come on out! It's not funny . . . !

MORTEN: You can stay up as long as you want!

MIKKEL: Do you want to see a magic trick? I've got one you haven't seen yet—!

JOHANNE: You can come and sit on my lap—as long as you come out. Anna—where are you?—Anna!

TORBEN: [*Appears holding* ANNA *by the hand.*] She's here, she's built a cave. You can't see it from the outside, but she let me come in. It's completely dark and covered in grass to make it soft. We're not going to tell them where it is, are we Anna?

MIKKEL: Do you want to see a trick?

[MIKKEL *shows* ANNA *a trick.*]

[ANNA *pulls up one sleeve and shows* MIKKEL *her rash.*]

MIKKEL: Let me see—[*Holds* ANNA'*s arm and examines the rash.*] It looks like an angel.

ANNA: An angel?

MIKKEL: Can't you see it? She's bowed her head and her wings are stretched out—

[ANNA *pulls her arm back.*]

MINNA: [*Comes out from the house.*] It looks like no-one is capable of making a decision without asking me first.

MORTEN: Come and have some cheese! Beautiful French cheese and a bit of bread that Johanne has left us. Come on!

[*They all sit back down at the table,* ANNA *on* JOHANNE'*s lap.*]

TORBEN: [*Tips his chair back.*] Look at the stars!—Am I seeing double or are there a lot more than usual?

MIKKEL: No, you're right, there's loads more than normal. And they're much brighter! Like an electric light bulb just before it pops.

HELENE: It's odd . . .

TORBEN: [*Tips his chair dangerously far back.*] I think I'm going to start studying astronomy. The stars and the planets—

MIKKEL: [*To* JULIE.] Are we going to tell them? Isn't this the right moment?

JULIE: Mikkel and I are getting married.

TORBEN: [*His chair falls over and he remains on the ground.*] Married!

HELENE: [*Delighted.*] You're getting married!

MIKKEL: You'll all be invited of course, we'll send you a written invitation. Morten is going to be a witness.

JULIE: Johanne's going to make my dress!

JOHANNE: I can't—I mean, when am I going to do it? I can hardly reach the machine and when the baby's born . . .

MINNA: I'll look after the little one while you sew, it won't be a problem.

JULIE: I know exactly how I want it—tight at the waist with big sleeves and loads of lace and layers and ribbons. And maybe a small train.

MIKKEL: Julie's going to arrive at the church in a carriage!

JULIE: And we're going to have a huge party afterwards!

MINNA: This calls for a celebration! Morten, give me a hand!

[MINNA *and* MORTEN *exit.*]

HELENE: I want to get married, too.

TORBEN: Why? We've lived together for eight years now, without being married.

HELENE: I can't think of anything more splendid than walking down the aisle as the organ plays! To stand there, in front of the altar and say yes—!

JOHANNE: Provided you're sure. As long as you know it's the right person you're saying yes to.

TORBEN: Well, nothing personal, but I never want to get married. To anyone!

[MINNA *and* MORTEN *reappear with their arms full of champagne bottles.*]

MINNA: I was given them by the French Embassy once, as a thank you for something or other. It's time they were drunk!

[*They pop the corks, fill their glasses and make a toast. A moment's silence. The phone rings.* MINNA *ignores it.*]

JOHANNE: Aren't you going to get that?

ANNA: Can I? Can I get it?!

MINNA: Let it ring. I don't want to be disturbed any more.

[*They toast again. The phone stops ringing. A chorus of wildly chattering birds replaces the sound of the phone.*]

HELENE: [*Listens.*] Listen . . . Quiet, listen to that!

[*One by one, they raise their heads and listen.*]

TORBEN: [*Looks at his watch.*] That can't be right . . .

MIKKEL: Why are they singing now?

JULIE: [*Laughs.*] It's quite scary!

MINNA: [*Raises her glass.*] Cheers! Let's have another toast! To the new baby! To Anna! To all of us!

[*They toast again as the birds continue singing loudly.*]

EVENING

Scene III

Very late evening.

The table is full of empty bottles. MINNA, HELENE, JULIE, MORTEN *and* TORBEN *are looking at* JOHANNE *who is eating the rest of the dessert right out of the bowl.* MIKKEL *is wandering around the garden. The sound of a bird singing can be heard.*

MIKKEL: —Where are you? [*Bends over and picks up a stone.*] I'll find you, you stubborn git . . .

JULIE: Leave it alone! You've frightened away all the others now.

HELENE: Why can't you just leave it?

MIKKEL: Because it's wrong. Completely wrong, can't you understand that?

JULIE: You're acting like an animal.

HELENE: Surely they can decide when they want to sing?

MIKKEL: No they can't. There has to be some kind of order—a certain system if you like . . . [*Takes aim, throws the stone; followed by the sound of a bird taking flight and fluttering away.*] Now, could we please have some peace and quiet.

[*Rejoins the others.* JOHANNE *is still eating. She picks something out of her mouth.*]

MORTEN: . . . What was it?

JOHANNE: A hair—[*Continues eating regardless.*]

MORTEN: Yuk!

TORBEN: That's disgusting!

JULIE: I want to be sick!

HELENE: [*Laughs.*] Johanne's eaten enough for four tonight!

MORTEN: For ten, more like. That's all she does all day—eats and eats and eats!

MINNA: Where does she put it?! If I ate even half as much—!

MORTEN: I wonder what you've actually got in there!

HELENE: [*Puts a hand on* JOHANNE's *stomach.*] It's moving—

MIKKEL: Let me have a go!

JULIE: And me!

TORBEN: Me too!

[*They all move closer to* JOHANNE *and put their hands on her stomach.*]

MIKKEL: It's a monster with two heads and six eyes!

JULIE: And a hundred mouths! And a thousand arms!

TORBEN: Quiet! It's trying to tell us something . . . "Knock—knock—knock!" Did you feel that? There it is again!

MIKKEL: Knock, knock, knock . . . knock, knock, knock! It's an SOS!

JULIE: Let me feel!

HELENE: And me!

TORBEN: Me too!

MORTEN: And me!

JOHANNE: Not so hard! You'll harm the child! Get your hands off me, have you all gone mad?

HELENE: Sorry . . .

[*Silence. They all sit down again.*]

TORBEN: I was going to say something, but I can't remember what it was—everything's spinning round . . .

HELENE: You're drunk.

TORBEN: So are you.

HELENE: Not as drunk as you.

MORTEN: It's odd, but I can't even get drunk tonight. Not really.

TORBEN: Just keep drinking, it'll come! Don't give up! Suddenly you'll hear bells ringing and then you're in paradise! [*Flings his arms out. Surprised.*]—Where have all the stars gone? Look—there isn't a single one left! They've all gone!

JULIE: The moon's disappeared as well—!

TORBEN: [*Yells towards the sky.*] What's going on? Why have you turned the light out?!

MIKKEL: [*Stares at the sky.*] There's nothing there—just darkness . . .

TORBEN: Put the stars back on!

JULIE: And the moon! Put the moon back on, too!

TORBEN: We want light—do you hear me? What's it gonna be? Do you want me to get mad? Want me to spit at you? Or should I throw a stone at you as well? [*Takes a stone and chucks it up in the air.*] Come on then, you old idiot! We want light! Lots of stars and moons like before!

MORTEN: [*Hushes* TORBEN.] You'll wake Anna.

TORBEN: [*Yells.*] Can't you find the switch? Look how dark and empty it all looks. It's not fair.—He's not listening.

MORTEN: Maybe he just doesn't care.

MIKKEL: I'd love to paint a picture of the garden in this light—

TORBEN: You mean darkness?

MINNA: Yes, paint a picture of the garden! I'd like that.

TORBEN: You wouldn't recognize it. It'd probably look as much like a pig's intestines as it would this garden. Tell me, Mikkel, are you going to paint with your fingers or your toes?

[MIKKEL *laughs loudly.*]

JULIE: I want to go home.

MINNA: Why? Aren't we having fun? It's such a special evening, let's enjoy it together for just a while longer. Johanne, go and get some candles, we nearly can't see each other any more. I'll go down to the cellar and get some more bottles. Who's going to come with me?

[TORBEN, MORTEN *and* MIKKEL *all stand up.*]

TORBEN: Mikkel can hold the doors, just don't let him carry anything.

[*They exit.*]

HELENE: Your hair was different before.

JULIE: Sorry? Yes . . .

HELENE: Completely different.

JULIE: Mmm.

HELENE: You could have sent us a card, when you disappeared. Or rang and told us where you were and if you were OK. Do you hear me? I was so worried.

JULIE: I'm sorry—

HELENE: No-one knew where you had gone or why? Just that you had suddenly left college.

JULIE: I wanted to spend all my time on my poetry.

HELENE: A while after you left, I talked to one of the other teachers about you—Ingrid, remember her?

JULIE: No. Yes—

HELENE: I told her I was worried—about your heart condition and the operations you'd had and those terrible attacks I'd seen you have—

JULIE: You promised not to tell anyone!

HELENE: Ingrid knew anyway. You had told her all about your illness too, but she hadn't wanted to talk to anyone about it since she had promised you she wouldn't. We decided to ring the hospital and ask if they knew where you were, but they told us you had never been a patient there.

JULIE: They probably got rid of my records when I moved.

HELENE: I talked to a doctor who said that no-one would have been able to move about the way you did, if they had that disease.

JULIE: But I nearly *couldn't* move, that's why it was so painful.

HELENE: [*Laughs.*] We'd been so worried, and felt so sorry for you!

JULIE: I *was* ill, though, I really was. Anyway, I don't want to talk about it.

HELENE: Show me the scar you said you got after that big operation.

[JULIE *remains motionless.*]

HELENE: You made such fools of us. First, we were furious, and then we were so relieved that you were OK that we went out and celebrated!

JULIE: I didn't make fools of you!

HELENE: What would you call it then? You made fools of us, just like you're making a fool of Mikkel.

JULIE: What do you mean?

HELENE: There's nothing wrong with your eyes.

JULIE: How do you know? I don't see very well. When the light's very bright I nearly can't see anything! Sometimes I get horrible pains . . . [*Puts her face in her hands.*] It's starting again . . . It hurts! It's like someone sticking knives in my eyes . . . ! [*Rocks back and forth like an automaton, still with her face in her hands.*]

[MINNA *and her assistants return with more bottles.*]

MIKKEL: [*Rushes over to* JULIE.] Julie—what's happened? What's wrong?

JULIE: Nothing . . . Ow! What are you doing? [*Pushes* MIKKEL *away.*]

MIKKEL: Sorry . . . I'm always so clumsy. I only wanted to rub your temples, it helped last time you were in pain, remember? Isn't there something I can do? Julie, say something . . .

JULIE: [*Rocks back and forth with her face in her hands.*] Leave me alone. Go away. Everyone . . . [*Moans quietly.*] My eyes—oh, my eyes . . .

MINNA: [*Goes over to* JULIE *and puts an arm round her.*] There, there—take your hands away and look at me. There, that's a good girl . . .

JULIE: It hurts! It just hurts so much . . . !

MINNA: [*Strokes her hair.*] Poor, little girl . . . [*Puts a glass of wine to* JULIE's *lips.*] Come along, drink a little of this, it'll do you good . . . A bit more, it'll calm you down . . .

[JULIE *sinks down in front of* MINNA *and buries her face in her lap.* MINNA *strokes her hair.* MIKKEL *stands nearby, watching. He takes his glass, fills it and drinks it down in one gulp.*]

TORBEN: [*To* HELENE.] What were you talking about?

HELENE: Nothing much.

TORBEN: You're beautiful—

HELENE: That's the first time you've ever said that!

TORBEN: I couldn't see it before. [*Wants to kiss* HELENE *but she avoids him.*] What's the matter? Can't I kiss you?

HELENE: No.

TORBEN: But I want to. I want to kiss you.

[TORBEN *chases* HELENE. *He catches her and kisses her and they fall to the ground. She gets up, but* TORBEN *stays on the ground.*]

TORBEN: Mmm . . . It smells of earth.

HELENE: Get up.

TORBEN: No, I like it down here. I could stay here forever . . .

HELENE: [*To* MIKKEL *who is peeing behind a bush.*] You pig! What do you think the loo is for?

MIKKEL: I had to go now.

HELENE: Look at your trousers—

MIKKEL: You're not my mother!

HELENE: I could have been.

MIKKEL: Could you? I doubt it, you're quite pretty.

HELENE: Do you want to paint me?

MIKKEL: If you'll let me.

HELENE: Only if it actually looks like me.

MIKKEL: I'll do my best.

HELENE: I'm thirsty. Come on, let's go get another drink!

[HELENE *and* MIKKEL *return to the table where* MORTEN *is uncorking bottles.* JOHANNE *appears with a candle.*]

JOHANNE: [*Lights the candle.*] I could only find this one—

HELENE: Let's have some fun! I want to dance! Music!

[JOHANNE *hushes them.*]

MORTEN: What's the matter.

JOHANNE: Was that Anna calling?

MORTEN: I didn't hear anything.

JOHANNE: You never do.

[*Silence.* MINNA *and* JULIE *have joined the others. All listen.*]

MIKKEL: . . . Isn't it quiet?

MORTEN: It's almost unnatural. I mean, right here, in the middle of town. There's normally cars going by—

MINNA: Or a train. [*Looks at her watch.*] The freight trains normally come past about now.

HELENE: There must be something wrong—

MORTEN: Something's happened. Something major!

JULIE: Like what?

MORTEN: I don't know.

MIKKEL: We're the last people on Earth! We can do what we want! Everything belongs to us now!

[ANNA *appears, wearing her pyjamas. She is barefoot.*]

JOHANNE: Anna . . .

MINNA: Did we wake you?

JOHANNE: [*Reaches for* ANNA *who pulls away.*] What's the matter? Can't you see it's me?

MORTEN: She's not awake. Anna—come over here.

[ANNA *runs over to* MIKKEL *and whispers something to him.*]

MIKKEL: Aa, that tickles! What did you say?

[ANNA *runs over to* MINNA *and whispers something to her.*]

MINNA: I didn't hear—wait. Wait a minute, child!

[ANNA *runs to* MORTEN; *whispers.*]

MORTEN: What? Why can't you just say it out loud. You know I hate all this whispering nonsense!

[ANNA *runs over to* JOHANNE; *whispers.*]

JOHANNE: [*Listens.*] She's afraid—what? Speak up so I can hear you! The angel . . . ? What angel? What are you talking about? [*Pulls* ANNA *on to her lap.*] What's the matter with you, you're shaking—

JULIE: I want to go home.

MINNA: No—not now! We have to stay together, do you hear? No-one should leave. Does anyone want something to drink? Julie? [*Pours more wine into* JULIE'S *glass.*]

JULIE: I'm cold . . .

MINNA: Do you want a rug for your legs?

JULIE: No. No, thank you.

HELENE: [*Goes over to* TORBEN *who has fallen asleep on the grass.*] Torben? The grass is all wet, you'll make yourself ill.

TORBEN: —What's it to you?

HELENE: I care.

TORBEN: [*Stands up; walks over to the table and sits down.*] You look like someone who's been travelling for a long time.

MINNA: That's the way it feels, all of a sudden.

JOHANNE: [*Soothingly, to* ANNA.] There's nothing to be afraid of. We're all here. Dad and mum, granny, Torben and Julie—

JULIE: I was scared of the dark, when I was a child. Sometimes I still am.

JOHANNE: [*To* ANNA.] Tomorrow, you won't even remember why you were afraid. You'll probably just think it was funny!

MINNA: Yes—let's talk about tomorrow! Let's all say what we're going to do tomorrow. Torben, you start . . .

[*Silence.*]

TORBEN: I don't know . . . It's this silence . . .

MORTEN: If you could only hear a car, or something. It's ridiculous, but my dearest wish right now is just to hear a car drive by . . .

MINNA: And mine.

JOHANNE: Or a train. A freight train, with hundreds of carriages . . .

MIKKEL: Anything.

JULIE: [*Stands up.*] I want to go home.

MINNA: You can, in just a while.

JULIE: I want to go home now, even if I have to walk all the way. I want to go home and go to sleep so I can wake up tomorrow and know that this was just a dream—

MINNA: Sit down. [JULIE *sits down.*]

[*Silence. A puff of wind stirs the tablecloth.* ANNA *grasps* JOHANNE *tightly.*]

JOHANNE: Ow, Anna! You scratched me! [*Puts a hand to her face.*] Look, it's bleeding . . . ! What's the matter with you? It's only the wind—can't you see that? It's just the wind making the tablecloth move . . .

[*All sit motionless. Another puff of wind blows out the candle. Darkness.*]

Hrafnhildur Hagalín Gudmundsdóttir (b. 1965)

Icelandic literature usually calls to mind the Eddas and the Skaldic poetry and sagas—composed between the ninth and the thirteenth centuries. In the twentieth century, however, this island nation of nearly 300,000 inhabitants has once again been contributing healthily to world literature, both with the remarkable novels of Nobel Laureate Haldór Laxness (1902–98) and with an impressive achievement in drama. But discarding a wariness of the world beyond its shores and an inclination toward insularity did not come quickly and easily to Iceland, and probably did not come substantially until after World War II.

There is discernible an underlying, historical tension felt by Icelanders toward the outside world. It probably dates from the earliest settlements in the Viking Age, to be reinforced during their subsequent rule by Denmark. That even Britain and the United States were brief, wartime occupiers before the country gained its independence in 1944 did not help. Once manifested as a feeling of oppression, impoverishment, and isolation, this wariness more recently expresses itself as a critical view of the modern trend toward urbanization and toward the commercial and material values that ostensibly accompany it. Iceland very hesitantly joined NATO in 1949 and has often pointedly disagreed with American/Western policies—most vociferously, during the Vietnam War. The island seems pulled between its old, revered folk and rural culture and literature and the lure of contemporary Europe and America.

The poetry and prose, along with the drama—which did not really appear until the 1790s with the comedies of Sigurður Pétursson—have generally championed traditional ways, lauding Nature and "country" values as the real, enduring ones. Foreign influences, whether they be the Danish king, multinational corporations, or the presence of the American military, have been the targets of satire and derision in Icelandic literature.

With the beginning of modern European drama, in the second half of the last century, theater became the most popular form of entertainment in the country—and has remained so. Iceland, in proportion, can probably boast the most devoted theater audience anywhere, with the number of annual ticket sales exceeding the population. In 1897, the Reykjavik Theater Company (RTC) was established, followed a half century later by the National Theater (1950). Both thrive today, along with a number of fringe and rural companies.

Although there were occasional important earlier contributions to the national repertoire, such as David Stéfansson's *The Golden Gate* (*Gullna hlidid*, 1941) and Sig-

Hrafnhildur Hagalín Gudmundsdóttir, ca. 1990 (Photographer: S. Þór.)

urdur Nordal's *Ascent* (*Uppstigning*, 1945), it was not until the 1960s that Icelandic playwrights have constituted a significant and even predominant presence on their stages. Jökull Jakobsson's *Hard-a-Port* (*Hartibak*, 1962), Gudmundur Steinsson's sharp satires on modern life—*Matthew* (*Lúkas*, 1975), *Viva España* (*Sólarford*, 1978), and the record-breaking *A Brief Respite* (*Stundarfridur*, 1978)—and Kjartan Ragnarsson's *A Day of Hope* (*Dagur vonar*, 1987) are among the important modern Icelandic plays.

Theater is popularly supported and respected in Iceland. There is a tradition of esteemed theatrical families and even a tradition of women directors, including Vigdís Finnbogadóttir, who left her position as director of the RTC (1973–79) to become president of the republic in 1980. Hrafnhildur Hagalín Gudmundsdóttir hails from one of the country's leading theater families. Both of her parents, Gudmundur Pálsson and Sigrídur Hagalín, have been leading actors on its stages, and her father was the financial director of the RTC and a crucial figure in its successful campaign to build the new City Theater. She herself has been on and near the stage since childhood.

Hagalín clearly sees herself as an international writer, aiming for a wide audience. Her first play, *I Am the Maestro (Ég er meistarinn)*, premiered in 1990, won the Icelandic Critics' Award in 1991, and the Nordic Drama Prize in 1992. It was a brilliant debut and was quickly translated into a number of languages and staged abroad. The chamber-theater cast of two classical guitarists and their maestro incorporates the playwright's own extensive training as a guitarist as well as her confident familiarity with theatrical techniques, tones, and tensions.

Easy Now, Electra (Hœgan, Elektra), her second play, opened to rave reviews at the National Theater in February 2000, as part of that theater's fiftieth anniversary festival. It extends this confidence to the realm of experimental and multimedia theater. If *Maestro* was received as autobiographical because of its pervasive inclusion of (guitar) music, *Electra* similarly incorporates life in the theater, as part of a theatrical family, so familiar to Hagalín.

The play alternates between a video projection on-screen of a past, discontinued rehearsal with the action onstage between an older and a younger actress who are mother and daughter. It weaves in a contemporary reworking of the story of Electra and Clytemnestra, all the while probing the relationship between acting (theater) and living. Gradually, the action on-screen, which is paradoxically declared to be experimental and improvisational (paradoxical because it is fixed on tape), converges with the seemingly spontaneous drama going on between the mother and daughter. The man they await, be he father, brother, or lover, provokes a discussion of sexual ambiguity, of transvestitism, effeminacy, and role playing (the daughter as a man on screen recalls loving a girl with a beard; Electra always wanted to be a boy).

Though the action is linear insofar as the screen and stage businesses converge, the style is recursive, circling back on the same ideas and expressions. The pain of thinking, the difficulty of being fixed within a family and a gender, lead—through an ocean of Pinter-like modulations and pauses—to a blackout as complete as that at the end of O'Neill's *Long Day's Journey Into Night.* The two women, accompanied by the essentially silent Stage Manager, may wonder "how it might have been after the show, had the show been different," but the reality is that the younger actress feels locked within the four walls, and the embrace at the end is without solace. This modern Electra is no matricide.

SELECTED BIBLIOGRAPHY IN ENGLISH

Banham, Martin. *The Cambridge Guide to Theatre.* Cambridge: Cambridge University Press, 1995. Pp. 511–13.

Ibsen, Arni. "Iceland." *The World Encyclopedia of Contemporary Theatre,* vol. 1. Ed. Don Rubin. London: Routledge, 1994. Pp. 451–66.

Marker, Frederick J., and Lise-Lone Marker. *A History of Scandinavian Theatre.* Cambridge: Cambridge University Press, 1996.

Rossel, Sven H. *A History of Scandinavian Literature: 1870–1980,* vol. 4. Trans. Anne C. Ulmer. Minneapolis: University of Minnesota Press, 1982.

EASY NOW, ELECTRA
Hrafnhildur Hagalín Gudmundsdóttir

Translated by Brian FitzGibbon

CHARACTERS

YOUNG ACTRESS

OLDER ACTRESS   her mother

STAGE MANAGER

Three chairs. A large projection screen at the back of the stage. As the performance progresses, the stage gradually darkens, in a slow, continuous and barely perceptible light change. The OLDER AC-TRESS *and the* YOUNG ACTRESS *enter. The* OLDER ACTRESS *sits on a chair. The* YOUNG AC-TRESS *walks to the edge of the stage and stares into space.*

Silence.

The following image is projected on the screen: the OLDER ACTRESS *enters the acting area. She looks younger than she does onstage. She walks to the edge of the stage and directly addresses the audience.*

OLDER ACTRESS: [*On-screen.*] Ladies and gentlemen, first of all, allow me to say how delighted I am to see so many people gathered here tonight to share in this moment of experimental theater with us. Very briefly, I'd just like to point out that my . . . daughter and I . . . have been practicing the so-called art of improvisation for some considerable time now. As most of you doubtless already know, the nature of improvisation is such that the drama or piece of music can only come into being during the actual moment of performance. When actors improvise, therefore, they don't follow the script of a given author, but rather create the work themselves as they perform it. This is a truly exciting challenge for the actor and requires a lot of training. We now feel the moment is ripe for us to test our mettle before an audience and I hope that this—our debut—will be an interesting experience for you all . . .

[*Pause.*]

OLDER ACTRESS: But before we proceed any further, allow me to introduce you to the man who will be assisting us with the lighting and sound effects throughout the improvisation. Please give him a warm hand . . . Stage Manager, if you please . . .

[*ON THE SCREEN: the* STAGE MANAGER *walks on stage and bows. He sits on the side. ON STAGE: the* STAGE MANAGER *enters and sits on the side. The projection continues.*]

OLDER ACTRESS: [*On-Screen.*] Perhaps the stage manager would care to give the audience a brief demonstration? . . .

[*ON THE SCREEN: the* STAGE MANAGER *gives a brief demonstration of the lights and sound effects. The* OLDER ACTRESS *applauds.*]

[*Silence.*]

OLDER ACTRESS: Ladies and gentlemen—Nothing is predetermined in the performance you're about to witness. This is no set piece skillfully woven together by some nimble author—what we're talking about here is the art of the moment, where everything is possible and anything can happen. I'll take up no more of your time and simply end by saying: enjoy the show.

[*The screen goes blank.*]

[*Long silence.*]

OLDER ACTRESS: [*Onstage.*] The lilies should be in blossom by now, if this is spring . . . [*Dreamily.*] Spring, autumn, winter, summer . . . I used to tend to the lilies every day, spoke to them, took deep breaths and filled my lungs with their fragrance . . . I haven't seen a lily for years . . . And what use would lilies be to us here? . . . Here in this place . . . [*Looks around.*] But I can conjure up a picture of them in my mind and that's good enough for me. All I have to do is close my eyes and waves of lilies come flocking to me, acres of them, I just lie down, vanish into an ocean of flowers and drift into sleep . . .

[*She closes her eyes. Pause. Then she glances at her daughter out of the corner of her eye.*]

OLDER ACTRESS: Oh, don't just stand there like that . . . I'm tired of looking at you standing there in that place. Couldn't you at least move somewhere else? For God's sake. Go on, move!

[*The* YOUNG ACTRESS *takes a step to the side and continues to stare into space.*]

OLDER ACTRESS: Oh, sweetheart, come on over here and sit down beside me, and we'll try to turn this into a happy day . . . and enjoy life . . . That's what we're here for . . . We who have everything, and lack absolutely nothing, the luckiest people in the world . . . Go on, I know you'll do it for me if I ask you nicely. Come on over here and sit down beside me . . .

[*The* YOUNG ACTRESS *takes another side-step.*]

OLDER ACTRESS: [*With a hint of cruelty.*] Perhaps you're waiting for me to pack my bags and leave? For me to give up and get out of here? . . . Is that what you're waiting for?

[*The* YOUNG ACTRESS *slowly turns towards her, walks to her, and sits down.*]

OLDER ACTRESS: That's more like it. Give me your hand . . .

[*The* YOUNG ACTRESS *offers her hand. The* OLDER ACTRESS *kisses it. The* YOUNG ACTRESS *takes out a cigarette and smokes.*]

OLDER ACTRESS: That's it. Good girl. [*Sighs with relief.*]

[*Silence.*]

OLDER ACTRESS: What are you thinking?
YOUNG ACTRESS: Nothing.
OLDER ACTRESS: Good. That's how it should be. We don't think. Here in this place.

[*Pause.*]

OLDER ACTRESS: Why are you so sad?

YOUNG ACTRESS: I'm not sad.

OLDER ACTRESS: Yes, you are. You're always so sad. As if you were carrying the weight of the entire world on your shoulders. Just relax and try to enjoy life. You're young. You're healthy. You're not paralyzed. You've got nothing to be morose about. There now, let me see. That's it. That's better. [*Pause.*] There's so much to rejoice about, you see. These beautiful surroundings, for example. You have to admit—they are beautiful. Everything out of our own heads. Everything just the way we want it to be. We can glide across the floor, from wall to wall, from room to room . . . We can open windows, draw the curtains, open again, take deep breaths and inhale that special fragrance that follows us around . . . All of this is our world, our little universe . . . What is it? Why are you never satisfied?

YOUNG ACTRESS: I am satisfied.

OLDER ACTRESS: Good. (It's what your father would have wanted. To see you happy.)

[*Pause.*]

OLDER ACTRESS: [*Walks over to a mirror, and studies her reflection.*] What do you think of my dress?

YOUNG ACTRESS: [*Without looking at her.*] Beautiful.

OLDER ACTRESS: Might need to take it in a bit at the back. I've lost weight. What do you think? Don't you think it could do with some tightening around the waist?

YOUNG ACTRESS: Maybe.

OLDER ACTRESS: Come over here for a second and give me a hand.

[*The* YOUNG ACTRESS *goes to her.*]

OLDER ACTRESS: Here, hold onto this. There.

[*The* YOUNG ACTRESS *does as she is told.*]

OLDER ACTRESS: No, here. Yes, like that. Yes, that's just about right. What do you think?

YOUNG ACTRESS: [*Looks the other way, and avoids looking in the mirror.*] Yes, that's just about right.

OLDER ACTRESS: You're not looking at me.

YOUNG ACTRESS: I saw you.

OLDER ACTRESS: Look at me.

YOUNG ACTRESS: I can see you, I said.

OLDER ACTRESS: How can you see me if you're looking the other way? You're not a bird, are you?!

[*The* YOUNG ACTRESS *slowly turns and looks at her in the mirror.*]

OLDER ACTRESS: Well?

YOUNG ACTRESS: Yes. It looks better that way.

OLDER ACTRESS: Then I'll take it in.

[*Their eyes meet in the mirror.*]

OLDER ACTRESS: Why is it you never think about yourself, darling?

YOUNG ACTRESS: [*Moving away from her.*] I've got other things to think about.

OLDER ACTRESS: Why is it you never think about smartening yourself up a bit?

YOUNG ACTRESS: I've got other things to think about.

OLDER ACTRESS: You shouldn't be thinking at all. You know perfectly well that thoughts are nothing but a recipe for wrinkles and an ugly complexion. Look at me, I avoid thoughts like the plague . . . And do you know why? Because each new thought carves a fresh little sinew for itself and, before you know what's happening, they multiply and merge, and spread until they've burrowed themselves under your skin, and deformed your face, your body . . .

We've got to be on the lookout, we've got to look after ourselves, sweetheart. There now. Let me brush your hair a little . . .

[*The* YOUNG ACTRESS *retreats from her.*]

OLDER ACTRESS: Oh, I see. I'm tired of running around after you. Sick and tired. I did it when you were a little child, but now I've had enough . . . You've never been willing to do yourself up. Never, not for one moment. Always been like a . . . She's such a tomboy, your father used to say . . . tomboy . . . [*Laughs.*] . . . that's what he said . . . Don't know where you get it from. Not from me. [*Nonchalantly.*] Have it the way you want it. As you wish . . .

[*Pause.*]

OLDER ACTRESS: The stage was the only place that could ever transform you. Made you inches taller. Made you hold your head up high. Then you were elegant . . .

[*The memory is paralyzing to them both and weighs upon them like a cloud of lead. The* YOUNG ACTRESS *stands as if she had just heard something, and listens.*]

OLDER ACTRESS: [*Watches her, slightly apprehensive.*] Now, dear. Wouldn't you like to go and lie down now?

[*The* YOUNG ACTRESS *listens.*]

OLDER ACTRESS: [*To her, slowly, in a half whisper.*] Darling, you know there's no-one there . . . No-one. We're not expecting anyone. No-one comes here. You know that. You've often said so yourself . . . You know that! [*Looking away, louder, as if she were trying to attract her attention.*] Aren't you hungry, darling! Wouldn't you like a snack? See if there's anything in the cupboard . . . In the fridge, in the drawers, on the windowsill, there must be something there. Somewhere . . .

YOUNG ACTRESS: [*Mimicking her in a low voice.*] There must be something there. Somewhere. There must be something there. Somewhere. Somewhere there must be something.

[*The screen lights up again, and the following scene is projected.*]

[*The* YOUNG ACTRESS *enters, playing the role of a young man in male clothes and wearing a hat. She could be wearing a mask. The* OLDER ACTRESS *plays the role of a young girl. She puts her hand out and waves.*]

YOUNG ACTRESS: [*In the role of the man.*] Which way are you heading, young lady?
OLDER ACTRESS: [*In the role of the girl.*] That all depends.
YOUNG ACTRESS: We might be heading the same way.
OLDER ACTRESS: We might.

[*Pause.*]

YOUNG ACTRESS: What's a girl like you doing out in weather like this [*Eyeing her up.*] Dressed like that?
OLDER ACTRESS: Oh just . . .
YOUNG ACTRESS: Bare-legged in weather like this.
OLDER ACTRESS: It wasn't this cold when I came out.
YOUNG ACTRESS: [*Looking straight ahead.*] It suddenly chilled, something she hadn't planned for, something she couldn't have foreseen, something she couldn't possibly have anticipated—otherwise she would obviously have dressed differently. Better than . . . [*Looks at her.*] . . . that.
OLDER ACTRESS: Obviously.

[*Silence.*]

OLDER ACTRESS: [*Pointing.*] Is that your car?

YOUNG ACTRESS: What if it is?

[*Pause.*]

[*The* YOUNG ACTRESS *opens the door of an imaginary car, and offers her a seat. The* OLDER ACTRESS *sits in the car. The* YOUNG ACTRESS *slams the door closed. The* STAGE MANAGER *produces an appropriate sound effect. The* YOUNG ACTRESS *lights a cigarette.*]

YOUNG ACTRESS: And where did you say we were going?
OLDER ACTRESS: I didn't say anything about that.
YOUNG ACTRESS: Ready? Off we go then.

[*The projection stops.*]

OLDER ACTRESS: [*Onstage.*] What are you thinking about?
YOUNG ACTRESS: Nothing.
OLDER ACTRESS: That's how it should be. We don't think. Here in this place. Here we can enjoy the stillness. The silence. Isn't it extraordinary? Not a single sound. [*Listens.*] Can't even hear a bird. Such peace.

[*Pause.*]

OLDER ACTRESS: Are you happy?
YOUNG ACTRESS: Yes. If you're happy.
OLDER ACTRESS: I'm happy.
YOUNG ACTRESS: Then I'm happy.
OLDER ACTRESS: Then I'm happy.
YOUNG ACTRESS: Then I'm happy.

[*Pause.*]

OLDER ACTRESS: How slowly time seems to pass here. Sluggishly slithering along . . . Like a gooey lump of . . . dough. Perhaps we ought to bake something . . . [*Sniggers.*] What am I blabbering about? . . . Are you bored?
YOUNG ACTRESS: No.
OLDER ACTRESS: Maybe we shouldn't have let all our books go. There are times when I think it would be so good to just grab a book. Like now for example. I could have walked over to the bookshelves, closed my eyes, turned, and said: that one. Just like we used to, remember?
YOUNG ACTRESS: I don't miss them.
OLDER ACTRESS: You don't?
YOUNG ACTRESS: A decision was taken. It can't be changed.
OLDER ACTRESS: No. That's true. But you were fond of reading. Sometimes you'd lock yourself in. For hours on end.
YOUNG ACTRESS: That was a long time ago.
OLDER ACTRESS: Yes. We couldn't . . . take them with us . . . not here . . . to this place . . . They wouldn't have . . . fitted here . . . They wouldn't have . . .
YOUNG ACTRESS: . . . fitted here . . .
OLDER ACTRESS: No. [*She watches the* YOUNG ACTRESS.]

[*The* YOUNG ACTRESS *exits and returns again.*]

OLDER ACTRESS: Maybe we could have hung onto the detective novels . . . Agatha Christie, Georges Simenon . . . You were so fond of those . . .
YOUNG ACTRESS: [*Mechanically, flatly.*] They would only have diverted our attention from what is. Numbed our sense of the present. Reality doesn't need a face lift. Reality is . . . whole. One.
OLDER ACTRESS: Quite . . . [*Probingly.*] Why are you looking at me like that?
YOUNG ACTRESS: I'm not looking at you.
OLDER ACTRESS: Why are you looking at me like that?
YOUNG ACTRESS: I'm not looking at you.

OLDER ACTRESS: You . . .

YOUNG ACTRESS: [*Slightly ambiguous.*] . . . accuse you? How could I accuse you? How could anybody accuse you? You who are so beautiful . . . You who are so kind . . .

[*Pause.*]

YOUNG ACTRESS: Let's have a rest. Let's stop talking and have a rest.

[*Silence.*]

OLDER ACTRESS: If there had been a garden here, we could have been pottering about in it right now, planting flowers, raking the grass, watering, scattering seeds . . . We'd be growing flowers of every single shade and color, every shape and size, but only flowers with beautiful and peculiar names like Russian Dwarfs, Floating Hearts . . . Pyramidal Bugles, Chinese Lanterns [*Slowly at first, and then accelerating in a crescendo, which peters out towards the end.*] Burning Bushes, Golden Tufts, Policeman's Helmet's, Mournful Widows, Spring Snowflakes, Gallant Soldiers, Brass Buttons, Pink Everlasting, Whitebeams, Bermuda Buttercups, Foxgloves, Wolf Milk, Touch-me-nots, Eyebrights, Columbines, Butterfly Orchids, Shooting Stars, Crowns of Thorns, Lady's Slippers, Bishop's Hats, Bluebells, Gay Feathers, Hedgehog Brooms . . . Parrot Tulips . . . Love-in-a-mist. [*Brief silence.*] We could have watched them grow and thrive from day to day, and thought about them. They would have been our sense of time, our little clocks. Have they grown, are they any taller? Are they in blossom today, are they showing their best? Or are they starting to wilt, to shed their leaves, are their heads beginning to droop? . . . Let's pull the door back a bit, darling, and prepare for winter . . .

[*Pause.*]

YOUNG ACTRESS: [*Absently.*] There's no garden here.

OLDER ACTRESS: No.

[*Pause.*]

YOUNG ACTRESS: I'm going to try to get some sleep.

OLDER ACTRESS: No, don't go. I'm not feeling too good. Don't leave me. Don't go . . .

[*Pause.*]

OLDER ACTRESS: You didn't need much sleep when you were a child, but nothing on earth could wake you up whenever you did sleep.

YOUNG ACTRESS: How would you know? You never tried to wake me up. You were relieved when I was asleep.

OLDER ACTRESS: I was happy to see you rest . . . As mothers are. Happy to see their children rest. Mothers. To see their children rest. [*As if she were striving to remind herself, but the words sound odd to her as she speaks them.*] And I am your mother . . . You sleep so much now. You always have to lie down. One would think . . . Yes, it's just not natural for a youngster like you, to have to go and lie down like that all the time. Perhaps you ought to let someone take a look at you, sweetheart. We don't want you to be sick now, do we? We don't want some obscure growth to start festering and spreading inside you when it might so easily be prevented. Wouldn't you like me to call a doctor for you?

[*The* YOUNG ACTRESS *gives off a faint laugh.*]

OLDER ACTRESS: [*Embarrassed, then shrugs it off.*] What could possibly be wrong with you? There's nothing wrong with us. We're as fit as fiddles. We lead healthy lives, eat wholesome food. We do everything we're supposed to do to . . . You should drink more coffee, darling. Keeps you going.

[*Pause.*]

YOUNG ACTRESS: It's fifteen steps from this wall to that one. It takes me ten seconds to walk that length, and that's at a snail's pace. If I were to keep on walking all day, from morning till night, I'd be able to cover the distance between those two walls about two-thousand-five-hundred-and-twenty times. Amazing, isn't it?

OLDER ACTRESS: I get bored when you're asleep.

[*Pause.*]

YOUNG ACTRESS: I'll try to stay more awake then.

[*Silence.*]

OLDER ACTRESS: [*Looks towards the* STAGE MANAGER, *and eyes him up.*] What do you think of him?

[*Pause.*]

OLDER ACTRESS: What do you think of him?

[*The* YOUNG ACTRESS *stands up.*]

OLDER ACTRESS: Now now. For God's sake! He is here. I can't help seeing him because he's here. I can't help seeing what's right in front of my eyes.

YOUNG ACTRESS: I don't see him!

OLDER ACTRESS: No . . . You can't see what's here. You can't see that. You just see something else. Something that's nowhere else but in your head. But I see him. [*Walks over to him, in an almost festive mood.*] Welcome, young man. That's my daughter. Don't pay any attention to her. She's always hearing things . . . Just pretend you don't notice. And above all, please make yourself feel at home. Or something to that effect . . . [*Walks to the* YOUNG ACTRESS.] There now . . . There now, sweetheart. Shouldn't we try to make this a happy day for us? Think of something nice. Something really special . . .

YOUNG ACTRESS: I'm expecting a visit.

OLDER ACTRESS: [*Frightened.*] Don't be silly. Go and lie down now. Who knows, perhaps it's for the best. Off you go now, sweetheart. Off you go! . . .

[*The projection continues on the screen.*]

YOUNG ACTRESS: Have we met before?

OLDER ACTRESS: I don't think so.

YOUNG ACTRESS: Your face suddenly looks familiar. Like I've seen you somewhere before.

OLDER ACTRESS: Not that I remember.

YOUNG ACTRESS: Perhaps you appeared to me in a dream. A long time ago. Is that what you are? A fantasy?

OLDER ACTRESS: [*Laughs.*]

YOUNG ACTRESS: How old are you?

OLDER ACTRESS: Guess.

YOUNG ACTRESS: [*Looks at her.*] I'm not too good at working out women's ages. Besides, makes no difference.

OLDER ACTRESS: It doesn't?

YOUNG ACTRESS: A woman is always a woman. Isn't she?

[*Pause.*]

OLDER ACTRESS: But what if I were underage?

YOUNG ACTRESS: [*Looks at her, measures her up, then looks ahead.*] I think I'll take my chances.

[*The projection stops.*]

OLDER ACTRESS: [*Onstage.*] Now now, darling . . . Come on over here . . . Shall I sing for you?

[*Pause.*]

OLDER ACTRESS: Just think of the stillness . . . the stillness here . . . It's not the way it used to be . . . Remember that dreadful racket? . . . how hectic life could be sometimes? . . . But here we found silence. Here, in this place . . . You can almost feel it hovering in the air, can you feel it?

[*Pause.*]

OLDER ACTRESS: You spoke about it too sometimes . . . the silence . . . I wish we could find some place where we wouldn't hear a sound, you said . . .

YOUNG ACTRESS: [*Loud and abrupt, to the* STAGE MANAGER.] What day could it be today? What month, what year?! What day is it today, young man?

[*The* STAGE MANAGER *shows no reaction.*]

YOUNG ACTRESS: [*To her mother.*] He seems to be deaf.

OLDER ACTRESS: Good God, is he really? Hello.

YOUNG ACTRESS: Hello.

OLDER ACTRESS: Hello.

YOUNG ACTRESS: Hello!

[*Pause.*]

OLDER ACTRESS: What are you thinking about?

YOUNG ACTRESS: Nothing.

OLDER ACTRESS: Good. [*To the* STAGE MANAGER, *looking at her daughter.*] Look at my daughter. She's recently stopped thinking, she used to think here a little bit, but she's given that up now, fortunately . . . Or so she says anyway . . . Hang on, let's just check . . . [*Walks over to the* YOUNG ACTRESS.] What are you thinking about?

YOUNG ACTRESS: Nothing.

OLDER ACTRESS: [*Laughs coarsely. To the* STAGE MANAGER.] See, what did I tell you?

[*Pause.*]

OLDER ACTRESS: [*To the* STAGE MANAGER, *continuing.*] Will you dance with me? No. I knew a man once who never wanted to dance with me. Which was a bit of a drag because I loved dancing. And if I danced with other men, he got jealous. Strictly forbade it. And what am I supposed to do then? I asked. And what am I supposed to do then? He pulled me to the side. This was at a ball. It was spring. I looked up at the dark sky as he spoke to me. Dance in your mind, he said. Dance in your mind. And walked away. And I watched him. So what did I do? Isn't that what you're going to ask? What I did? [*Walks to her daughter.*] I tried to do it. For years. To dance in my mind . . . But who can do that? . . .

YOUNG ACTRESS: [*As if to herself.*] While I was waiting for the show, I felt like a . . . compere at a transvestite's club . . . I suddenly sensed a presence in my dressing room . . . I put my liner down and looked up, I looked in the mirror, very cautiously, through my own reflection, as if I could see through my own reflection . . . I could practically see the whole dressing room in that mirror . . . I looked around, slowly and calmly, until I suddenly caught him in my eye. He's standing there right beside me, now I can see him, now I can see him very clearly. So there you are, I say, I've been expecting you. I'm the new performer, he says. I know that, says I. How do you do? I'm the compere around here, and this, as you might have gathered, is the dressing room. I'm sorry, but this is the only room we've got, so I'm afraid you'll have to put up with sharing it with me. I hope that's okay. I presume you've been on stage before, I take it you know the ropes . . . Never sung, acted, or performed in drag in any shape or form? Well, what the hell are you doing here then? Who is it that sent you here? We only work with experienced pros . . . He doesn't answer. He just stands there with his eyes glued to the floor. So helpless and peculiar, and I just know he doesn't fit in . . . There's no way this kid will ever fit in . . . And it's only then that I stand up and am about to walk to him. I turn around . . . But there's no-one there . . .

OLDER ACTRESS: [*Cruel and merciless, but contained.*] No more than there is now. There is no-one here, apart from us and him . . . Just get it into your skull . . . No-one comes here. No-one has any business coming here! When was this actually?

YOUNG ACTRESS: It was before the show.

OLDER ACTRESS: Yes, before the show.

YOUNG ACTRESS: It's after the show now.

OLDER ACTRESS: I know.

YOUNG ACTRESS: It's long after the show now.

OLDER ACTRESS: You don't have to remind me. I know!

OLDER ACTRESS: [*To the* STAGE MANAGER, *in a light singing voice.*] Would you mind closing that window. There's such a draft. Might catch a chill. And we can't allow that to happen, nothing more catastrophic for a woman in my profession . . .

[*Pause.*]

OLDER ACTRESS: I'd also be infinitely grateful to you, young man, if you'd be kind enough to retrieve my fur coat for me, it should be there somewhere . . . or there, if you'd be so kind . . .

YOUNG ACTRESS: [*Rising to the bait.*] You're not afraid of catching a cold, mother.

OLDER ACTRESS: Nothing worse than an actress with a frog in her throat. Frog in her throat. Ha ha.

YOUNG ACTRESS: But you've given up acting now, my dear.

OLDER ACTRESS: So what?

YOUNG ACTRESS: We've given up all that acting rigmarole now. We can catch colds now and get sick like other people do. Now we can do everything like normal people. Now we can even die like other people.

OLDER ACTRESS: Nonsense! I'll never stop acting. We never stop, my dear.

YOUNG ACTRESS: What's this I hear? But we decided that after the show . . . Have you forgotten? You said that once the show was over, we'd never act again . . . We'll never tread the boards of a theatre again, you said . . .

OLDER ACTRESS: Did I say that? But that was ages ago, darling . . . No-one says that a decision has to be so final that it can't be . . . reconsidered. Who knows, if one were to be approached with the right touch of diplomacy and tact, one might even be swayed . . . [*Abruptly.*] I've changed my mind. I want us to rehearse another show. Immediately, today!

YOUNG ACTRESS: Immediately, today!

OLDER ACTRESS: The best thing to do is to repeat it and try to do it better. Otherwise we'll always be dissatisfied. Otherwise we'll always be frustrated.

YOUNG ACTRESS: [*Sarcastic.*] After all these years . . . We're out of practice, we can't do it anymore. We've forgotten it all.

OLDER ACTRESS: Nonsense, it'll all come flooding back. You'll see as soon as we start, you'll see how fast it all slides back into place just as soon as we've started again . . . We'll do all the old exercises . . . Remember how good we got? We could do anything! We could do anything!

YOUNG ACTRESS: We could do anything . . .

OLDER ACTRESS: We could do anything!

YOUNG ACTRESS: Except for one thing . . .

OLDER ACTRESS: What are you talking about?

YOUNG ACTRESS: We couldn't . . . act anymore . . .

OLDER ACTRESS: Nonsense . . . We were marvelous!

YOUNG ACTRESS: [*Looks at the* STAGE MANAGER, *and half-whispers to challenge her.*] Are you trying to tell me you're willing to risk it all again?

OLDER ACTRESS: [*Getting worked up, manic.*] What risk? What risk? There is no risk. We just carry on. Like we always did. Like we always did in those days . . .

YOUNG ACTRESS: That's not possible, we could never do that . . . You know that . . .

OLDER ACTRESS: [*Raising her voice.*] Why not? Why not?!

YOUNG ACTRESS: You know why . . . You know perfectly well!

OLDER ACTRESS: [*Getting worked up.*] No, I don't know . . . I don't . . .

[*The* STAGE MANAGER *looks up and watches them. The* YOUNG ACTRESS *notices.*]

YOUNG ACTRESS: [*Switches mood, takes her aside.*] Easy there. Let's not wake up any of the old ghosts, mother. Easy there, that's it . . .

OLDER ACTRESS: What are you on about? Where are you trying to take this?

YOUNG ACTRESS: There now, there . . . Relax . . . That's it . . . That's it . . . You know that when we were onstage we couldn't hide ourselves behind the mask of reality. Remember? Don't you remember? The stage is cold and bare . . . We walk out front, and a cruel light blinds us from above . . . No escaping . . . No refuge. Don't you remember? Remember? No curtains to draw over our faces . . .

OLDER ACTRESS: I don't know what you're talking about. Draw over what? As if I'd committed a crime. I haven't committed any crime, as far as I know . . . I haven't done the slightest thing wrong that I know of . . .

YOUNG ACTRESS: Shhh . . . Let's not get excited. We don't want to bring it all back up again. Let's forget it.

OLDER ACTRESS: Forget what? I don't remember anything. How on earth am I supposed to forget something I can't remember?

YOUNG ACTRESS: No. We don't remember anything. We don't remember anything. Come on . . . That's it . . . Who's the most beautiful . . . Who's the most beautiful?

[*The* OLDER ACTRESS *calms down. The tension is broken by laughter. The* STAGE MANAGER *stops watching them.*]

[*Silence.*]

OLDER ACTRESS: What was he like . . . This? . . .

YOUNG ACTRESS: Shouldn't we talk about something else?

OLDER ACTRESS: Just tell me . . . I'll listen . . . I'll be very quiet . . .

[*Pause.*]

YOUNG ACTRESS: [*Thinks, remembers, the memory takes over.*] He was . . . beautiful . . . Effeminate.

OLDER ACTRESS: Oooh . . . I can't bear effeminate men. Men should be made of iron and steel. You should be able to bite them and feel the vibrations buzzing in your fillings.

YOUNG ACTRESS: He was like me.

OLDER ACTRESS: You?! What do you mean?

YOUNG ACTRESS: Same hair. Same hands. Same size of shoes.

OLDER ACTRESS: You're not going to tell me you lent him your shoes?

YOUNG ACTRESS: No . . . He wore high heels.

OLDER ACTRESS: You don't say.

YOUNG ACTRESS: And a very tight dress.

OLDER ACTRESS: You did say a *man*?

YOUNG ACTRESS: Such a stunning dress!

OLDER ACTRESS: [*The dress is starting to interest her.*] Really, in what way?

YOUNG ACTRESS: Quite long . . . Pearls all over. Fringed at the bottom . . . And whenever he moved, the dress glittered as if it were made of pure gold.

OLDER ACTRESS: [*Forgetting herself, intrigued.*] Did it have patterns?

YOUNG ACTRESS: Yes. Delicate roses. Faint but visible. A fine stem around the waist . . .

OLDER ACTRESS: [*Enthralled.*] Oh, how lovely . . . Lovely . . . I could have had a dress like that when I was young . . . When I was young and pretty . . . Slim waist, delicate feet . . . slim slim waist, delicate delicate feet . . . What kind of waist did he have . . . the man?

YOUNG ACTRESS: He looked absolutely ravishing in that dress. He bought it in Spain.

OLDER ACTRESS: Was it a flamenco dress?

YOUNG ACTRESS: No!

OLDER ACTRESS: A grotesque caricature. Men in women's clothes are nothing but grotesque caricatures of women!

YOUNG ACTRESS: Drink your tea!

OLDER ACTRESS: What tea?

YOUNG ACTRESS: Drink your tea!

OLDER ACTRESS: What tea? You haven't given me any tea! What tea?!

[*The* STAGE MANAGER *looks up. They look at him, and calm down.*]

[*Pause.*]

OLDER ACTRESS: And did he stay long?

YOUNG ACTRESS: Let's talk about something else!

OLDER ACTRESS: Well I never [*But can't stop thinking about it.*] . . . So when did this happen exactly?

YOUNG ACTRESS: It was before the show.

OLDER ACTRESS: Right . . . Before the show . . .

YOUNG ACTRESS: It's after the show now.

OLDER ACTRESS: I know.

YOUNG ACTRESS: It's long after the show now.

OLDER ACTRESS: You don't have to remind me! I know!

[*Pause.*]

YOUNG ACTRESS: [*Walks over to the* STAGE MANAGER, *and addresses him.*] Sometimes I wonder how it might have been after the show, had the show been different.

OLDER ACTRESS: Come again?

YOUNG ACTRESS: She says she doesn't think. So she says. But it's not true. She thinks about it sometimes too.

OLDER ACTRESS: About what?

YOUNG ACTRESS: How it might have been after the show, had the show been different.

OLDER ACTRESS: I don't know what you're on about.

YOUNG ACTRESS: [*To the* OLDER ACTRESS.] I can see it sometimes. When you don't know I'm watching you. I can see you thinking about it: what—what if . . . What if we'd finished the show?

OLDER ACTRESS: If you'd been up to it, is that what you mean?

YOUNG ACTRESS: Just somehow different. If we'd managed to finish the show.

OLDER ACTRESS: It's very simple. I'd be six feet under!

YOUNG ACTRESS: Not necessarily . . .

OLDER ACTRESS: You bet I'd be. I knew what you were up to. [*Laughs.*]

[*Pause.*]

YOUNG ACTRESS: [*Walks to the edge of the stage, quietly, to herself.*] All I know is that we're here. Locked up. Locked windows. Locked doors. Here, between these four walls. And we can't get out.

[*Pause.*]

OLDER ACTRESS: [*Very lightly, in a singing tone.*] But we have each other. That's what matters. I have you and you have me. All we need is love! Tra la la bamm bamm baramm-bammbamm.

[*Pause.*]

YOUNG ACTRESS: [*Slowly and quietly, to herself.*] If only I'd kept my foot on the pedal and let it fly . . . If I'd just held onto that wheel and shot into the darkness, freedom for just a moment . . . and then fallen again . . .

OLDER ACTRESS: Don't talk like that. We're here. We're together. We're happy. You never meant to . . . Don't you think I know? You could never have done something like that. I know you. You're a good girl. You're a good girl.

YOUNG ACTRESS: [*Turning to face her mother, quietly, through clenched teeth.*] Girl. Girl! What are you talking about?! I—am—not—a girl!!

OLDER ACTRESS: Nonsense! Enough of that nonsense now! Course you're a girl. You're my girl . . . I ought to know. I brought you up. Squeezed you out of my very own womb. I'm your mother. Come on . . . Enough of that nonsense and come over here . . .

[*The* YOUNG ACTRESS *stares at her for a moment.*]

[*The projection starts again.*]

YOUNG ACTRESS: So tell me about yourself. Do you like music? What would you like to hear?

OLDER ACTRESS: What would you like to know?

YOUNG ACTRESS: What would you like to tell me?

OLDER ACTRESS: Oh, so you're a gentleman?

[*The* YOUNG ACTRESS *switches on a radio. Music comes on.*]

[*Pause.*]

OLDER ACTRESS: I'm not used to men treating me with such gallantry.

YOUNG ACTRESS: A girl like you?

OLDER ACTRESS: A girl like me.

YOUNG ACTRESS: A girl like you?

OLDER ACTRESS: A girl like me.

YOUNG ACTRESS: A girl like you?

OLDER ACTRESS: A girl like me, yes. No, I'm just not used to it.

YOUNG ACTRESS: [*The music fades, she gives the radio a bang, music again.*] I don't believe you.

OLDER ACTRESS: C'est la vie.

YOUNG ACTRESS: You know I'll be gallant with you.

OLDER ACTRESS: Thank you.

YOUNG ACTRESS: I'll treat you like a queen . . .

OLDER ACTRESS: Oh, so you're a romantic too then, are you? I feel so safe with you. You're so big and strong. I feel I could close my eyes and fall asleep while you take me to the edge of the world.

YOUNG ACTRESS: I'll take you anywhere you want.

OLDER ACTRESS: All the way to the edge of the world?

YOUNG ACTRESS: Whatever tickles your fancy.

OLDER ACTRESS: What's it like? . . . the edge of the world? Tell me about it.

[*Pause.*]

YOUNG ACTRESS: Well, there's kangaroos . . . penguins . . .

OLDER ACTRESS: Ha ha.

YOUNG ACTRESS: Sorry. I've never been there.

OLDER ACTRESS: Tell me about it.

YOUNG ACTRESS: [*Snappily.*] I just told you, I've never been there!

OLDER ACTRESS: Oh, okay . . .

[*The projection stops.*]

OLDER ACTRESS: [*Onstage: approaching her as if she were an untamed beast.*] Easy now, easy.

Let's try to calm down now, darling. We're safe here. We've nothing to fear. There. Don't be afraid. Don't be afraid. We should never have put on that show. It's good we stopped. Art did nothing but tear us apart. It was if as something happened between us every time we walked onstage. It separated us somehow, made us separate . . . When those house lights went down and those spotlights hit us, I felt so scared and alone. Scared to be isolated under that cone of light, enclosing me. Imagining that one fine day it would refuse to release me. That I would have to remain its prisoner for the rest of my days, trapped under that glaring light.

[*Pause.*]

OLDER ACTRESS: No, we're better off in reality. Right in the heart of things, totally submerged in them. As we are now. We're out of danger now. Here we can follow our reality without having to make it up ourselves. Now we can just be. Now we can just be.

YOUNG ACTRESS: [*Brief silence, then quietly.*] Yes. [*She rests her head on her mother's lap.*]

OLDER ACTRESS: And we have each other. I have you, you have me, I have you, you have me . . . Listen . . . Can't you hear how wonderful that silence is?

[*Silence.*]

[*They listen to the silence.*]

YOUNG ACTRESS: [*Quietly, slowly, ambiguous.*] You've given up the idea of having another show then?

OLDER ACTRESS: Yes, absolutely.

YOUNG ACTRESS: What if I wanted it?

OLDER ACTRESS: [*Apprehensive.*] What?

YOUNG ACTRESS: [*Breaking away from her.*] What if I wanted us to walk on again? And to stand under that light again?

OLDER ACTRESS: But it's too late now, darling . . . It was such a long time ago . . . We're out of touch. We wouldn't know how to move on a stage anymore, look [*She stands and moves around the stage with stiff doll-like movements.*]

YOUNG ACTRESS: We could rehearse again, just like you said . . . We could whip ourselves into shape and be better than we ever were!

OLDER ACTRESS: No . . .

YOUNG ACTRESS: We could start the whole thing from scratch again and try to do it differently.

OLDER ACTRESS: How? How?!

YOUNG ACTRESS: We could try not to interfere. Try to keep our distance from the characters we're playing and everything would be fine.

OLDER ACTRESS: That's not possible!

YOUNG ACTRESS: Nonsense!

OLDER ACTRESS: We tried it so many times. First with characters written by other authors and then we tried to build our own, but the result was always the same. Don't you understand, you can't just step out of the character you're playing, it's not possible! We've already proven that!

YOUNG ACTRESS: Let's try again. Give it another chance!

OLDER ACTRESS: No, I said no. No. You can do whatever you want. But I'm staying right here. I'm staying right here in my reality. In my silence.

[*Silence.*]

YOUNG ACTRESS: [*Whispers, gloomily.*] This? You call this reality?

OLDER ACTRESS: Well, what would you call it?

YOUNG ACTRESS: You'd have to invent a new word for it. I'll leave it up to you. Just try to find a word that can describe this . . . situation. As long as it's synonymous with . . .

OLDER ACTRESS: . . . What on earth are you on about? . . . Me, invent a word . . . I've never heard such utter . . . I'm not here to invent words, I've no interest in words. I've no interest in anything but . . . [*Frightened.*] . . . staying here. With you. Don't go away from me. Don't leave me here on my own. You can't do that. Do you hear me?!

YOUNG ACTRESS: [*Coldly.*] And if I did?

OLDER ACTRESS: You can't do this to me. You can't do this to me!

YOUNG ACTRESS: And if I did?

OLDER ACTRESS: You can't do this to me! You can't do this to me!

[*Pause.*]

YOUNG ACTRESS: [*Gives up, looks at her, then quietly.*] Of course not.

OLDER ACTRESS: [*Relieved.*] Of course not. Of course not. You're a good girl.

[*Pause.*]

OLDER ACTRESS: [*Light as a feather.*] Aren't you hungry? Wouldn't you like a bite to eat? There must be something there. In the cupboard. On the windowsill. In the drawers. There must be something there. Somewhere . . . Nothing worse for a mother than to have to see her child go without food. Nothing worse for a mother than to have to see her child go without food. See if there's something in the cupboard, sweetheart . . .

[*The projection continues on-screen.*]

OLDER ACTRESS: Aren't you going to ask me my name?

YOUNG ACTRESS: No.

OLDER ACTRESS: Ha, that's a good one!

YOUNG ACTRESS: Names only confuse people. Create a false impression of the people concealed behind the names.

OLDER ACTRESS: [*Stares at him.*] Concealed behind the names? . . . That's a bit too high-falutin for me . . . [*Reflects a moment, then.*] And what lies concealed behind your name, if you don't mind me asking?

YOUNG ACTRESS: That . . . will come to light.

STAGE MANAGER: [*Beams them with the headlights of the oncoming traffic.*]

OLDER ACTRESS: He was in a hurry. Don't you think you ought to slow down?

YOUNG ACTRESS: You're not nervous, are you?

OLDER ACTRESS: Not exactly, no.

YOUNG ACTRESS: You're not frightened of me?

OLDER ACTRESS: What should I be frightened of?

YOUNG ACTRESS: Have a cigarette. Unwind.

[*Pause.*]

YOUNG ACTRESS: Know what I think? I think this innocence of yours is just a mask. Something you slip on to cover up something else.

OLDER ACTRESS: Something else?

YOUNG ACTRESS: And more.

OLDER ACTRESS: I don't quite follow.

YOUNG ACTRESS: I've got the feeling there's more to you than meets the eye.

OLDER ACTRESS: You've got the feeling? Since when do men have feelings!

YOUNG ACTRESS: And yet you climb into the car of a total stranger with no feelings? There's something daring about you, isn't there? Something recklessly daring. Girls like you like to take risks. Girls like you long for adventure. I like that. You're my kind of girl! Cheers!

OLDER ACTRESS: [*Cautiously.*] Cheers.

STAGE MANAGER: [*Sound of glasses clinking.*]

[*Pause.*]

OLDER ACTRESS: [*Apprehensively.*] Isn't it time to stop now? I'm beginning to feel a bit queasy.

YOUNG ACTRESS: Open the window.

OLDER ACTRESS: It's open.

YOUNG ACTRESS: Close the window.

OLDER ACTRESS: It's . . . open.

YOUNG ACTRESS: Close it then.

OLDER ACTRESS: It's just that I'll need to . . . you know. Fairly soon.

YOUNG ACTRESS: Don't worry.

OLDER ACTRESS: Where are you going?

YOUNG ACTRESS: That . . . will come to light.

[*The* STAGE MANAGER *beams them with the headlights of the oncoming traffic.*]

OLDER ACTRESS: All that traffic . . . We will be stopping soon, won't we?

YOUNG ACTRESS: Soon.

OLDER ACTRESS: Do you mind if I open the window?

YOUNG ACTRESS: It's open.

[*The* OLDER ACTRESS *sticks her elbow out, deeply inhales.*]

[*The projection halts.*]

[*The* STAGE MANAGER *stands up, and stretches. The* OLDER ACTRESS *watches him.*]

OLDER ACTRESS: Well, you must be able to see him now?

YOUNG ACTRESS: Who?

OLDER ACTRESS: I see . . .

YOUNG ACTRESS: What do you mean?

OLDER ACTRESS: So tell me what you think of him. What do you think of him? Do you think he's handsome?

[*The* YOUNG ACTRESS *stands.*]

OLDER ACTRESS: Now now, he is here. I can't help seeing him if he's here. He is actually here. I can't avoid seeing him.

YOUNG ACTRESS: I don't see him!

OLDER ACTRESS: No, you don't see what's *here* . . . You don't see *that* . . . But I see him. And he looks pretty dishy to me. You can't stop me from seeing what's right in front of my eyes. You can't! [*Waves to the* STAGE MANAGER.] Yoo-hoo.

YOUNG ACTRESS: [*Fast and passionate.*] There he is. In the corner. Now I see him. Now I see him again. Now I see him perfectly clearly. So there you are then. I lost sight of you for a while . . . When am I on?, he says . . . Soon, I say, soon I'll introduce you and then you're on. Tell me something about yourself, I say. What do you want to know? he says. Where do you live? In the neighborhood, he says. Live alone?, I ask. No. With my dad, he says. He stammers a bit, well not exactly stammers, but takes a long time to find the words, as if he were always thinking it over . . . With my dad, he says . . . And your mum? She . . . died. Years ago, when I was . . . small . . . Oh . . . And what does your dad do? He looks at me, then down at the floor . . . He's . . . in bed, he says. I meant what's his occupation? . . . Yeah, he's bedridden, he says, he's got an illness. I see . . . What kind of illness? A mental illness. Sorry to hear that, I say. No need to be, he says. Has he been like that for long? Yeah, long . . . very long. And you've been taking care of everything since he . . . How do you know that? he asks. There was no-one else around to help you, right? He shakes his head. No granddads or grannies. [*Shakes her head.*] No uncles or aunts? [*Shakes her head.*] No relatives? He looks up. Sort of, he says. What do you mean sort of? [*Short silence.*] I'll tell you later, he says.

OLDER ACTRESS: [*Flirtatiously.*] How old are you, dear? You're not old . . . but you weren't born yesterday either, I mean, so you must know . . . My daughter doesn't want me to talk to you. She gets . . . You know . . . She's been like that ever since her father . . . Since he . . . My husband. My husband . . . [*Laughs.*] . . . if one can call him that . . . He wasn't very . . . You understand . . . [*Quickly glancing at the* YOUNG ACTRESS.] We carried on for a long time after that, my daughter and I, but it wasn't the same . . . so we decided to stop and we've never looked back . . . it was all such a mess, you see . . . Why are you staring at me like that? As if you were thinking . . . as if you suspected something . . . What's on your mind? . . . Surely you don't think that I . . . Oh, why am I wasting my breath on a kid like you? . . . I'll call you if I need something . . . [*Goes to the* YOUNG ACTRESS.]

[*Pause.*]

YOUNG ACTRESS: Sometimes it's as if one were experiencing something that no other person has ever experienced before. As if one were following a path that's never been taken before . . .

OLDER ACTRESS: I don't know what you're on about. This is our path. And it's wonderful. This is our wonderful path and it's unique.

YOUNG ACTRESS: Perhaps we're not what we are . . .

OLDER ACTRESS: [*Indignant.*] I've never heard such utter drivel in all my life. Not what we are! Well, I don't know about you, but if there's one thing I can be sure about it's that I'm me. Enough brooding now. You're wearing me out. Leave me in peace. I'm getting old. I need some rest. If you insist on thinking could you please do it in silence over there in the corner.

[*Pause.*]

OLDER ACTRESS: [*Looks suspiciously at the* YOUNG ACTRESS.] So who would you be then, if you don't mind me asking, if you weren't you?

YOUNG ACTRESS: I don't know. Another woman. Another man.

OLDER ACTRESS: Trust you to want to be another woman, trust you . . . [*Looks at her.*] Isn't it incredible how daughters can resemble their fathers without being men themselves . . . [*Starts to laugh to herself.*]

YOUNG ACTRESS: [*Standing, terrified.*] I warned you about . . .

OLDER ACTRESS: I didn't say anything. I didn't say anything. I only said it was incredible . . .

YOUNG ACTRESS: I've already warned you about . . .

[*The* STAGE MANAGER *looks up.*]

OLDER ACTRESS: I didn't say anything . . . I didn't say anything! Good God! Whenever you get all het up like this . . . It's as if you were about to . . . Just stop blabbing! It's all this ruminating that does it. Just stop it. Stop it now!

[*The* YOUNG ACTRESS *looks at the* STAGE MANAGER, *and calms down.*]

[*Pause.*]

OLDER ACTRESS: Shouldn't we just try to keep the peace and enjoy life . . . I'm so tired . . . Say something nice. Something good to hear. Something light and funny so that I can laugh and relax. That's so important. So vitally important to bring some lightness and satisfaction into our lives. And relax . . . Like this . . . [*She leans back and takes a deep breath.*]

[*Pause.*]

[*The projection continues on-screen.*]

OLDER ACTRESS: Things didn't quite work out for me the last time, you see. I still haven't fully recovered yet.

YOUNG ACTRESS: Sorry to hear that.

OLDER ACTRESS: He was awful . . . You know . . . No, I don't want to bring it all back up again . . . And you? Are you? . . .

YOUNG ACTRESS: No. That was a long time ago.

OLDER ACTRESS: What was she . . . like?

YOUNG ACTRESS: She was beautiful. She was stunning.

OLDER ACTRESS: Really?

YOUNG ACTRESS: But not as beautiful as you.

OLDER ACTRESS: Well, there's no need to . . .

YOUNG ACTRESS: She wasn't nearly as beautiful as you. She had one flaw.

OLDER ACTRESS: Oh?

YOUNG ACTRESS: She had a beard.

OLDER ACTRESS: [*Fighting back the laughter.*] Good heavens. Poor girl. Are you sure that . . .

YOUNG ACTRESS: What?

OLDER ACTRESS: I'm just thinking out loud here. It is rather unusual. A woman with a beard.

YOUNG ACTRESS: It happens.

OLDER ACTRESS: Does it really?

YOUNG ACTRESS: In this case it did.

OLDER ACTRESS: Incredible. And didn't you ask her to shave it off?

YOUNG ACTRESS: You can't say that to a girl you love.

[*Pause.*]

OLDER ACTRESS: [*Insecure.*] So you did love her?

YOUNG ACTRESS: All water under the bridge. Didn't last long.

OLDER ACTRESS: Because of the . . . beard?

YOUNG ACTRESS: Among other things, yes.

OLDER ACTRESS: I don't have a beard.

YOUNG ACTRESS: No.

OLDER ACTRESS: How do you find me?

YOUNG ACTRESS: Difficult to say, you're sitting so close . . .

OLDER ACTRESS: Shouldn't we stop and stretch our legs? Get some fresh air?

YOUNG ACTRESS: Afraid not. The tank.

OLDER ACTRESS: The tank?

YOUNG ACTRESS: It could start leaking.

OLDER ACTRESS: What tank?

YOUNG ACTRESS: The petrol tank.

OLDER ACTRESS: Why?

YOUNG ACTRESS: That's the way it's made.

OLDER ACTRESS: What kind of a tank do you call that?

YOUNG ACTRESS: Practically all tanks are like that.

OLDER ACTRESS: What, they leak if you stop?

YOUNG ACTRESS: Exactly.

OLDER ACTRESS: That's strange. I've never heard of tanks like that before.

YOUNG ACTRESS: Well, you have now

OLDER ACTRESS: And who mends it then—if it leaks—if you don't mind me asking? A mechanic, I presume.

YOUNG ACTRESS: Difficult to say. I'd rather not think about it. Would you like to think about it? Would you like to think about it?!

[*Pause.*]

OLDER ACTRESS: [*Panic-stricken.*] I don't know . . .

[*Silence.*]

[*The projection halts.*]

YOUNG ACTRESS: [*Onstage: looks at the* OLDER ACTRESS, *walks over to her, almost tenderly.*] You look well today.

OLDER ACTRESS: I do?

YOUNG ACTRESS: Yes. I think you look better today than you did yesterday.

OLDER ACTRESS: Better?

YOUNG ACTRESS: Yes. Even better that is. You looked well yesterday. But you look even better today. And tomorrow I'm sure you'll look even better than yesterday and today.

OLDER ACTRESS: Do you really think so?

YOUNG ACTRESS: A woman of your age. Unbelievable. You're not a bad piece of crumpet.

OLDER ACTRESS: Crumpet? You do choose the oddest of words sometimes.

YOUNG ACTRESS: You look pretty astounding for a woman of your age.

OLDER ACTRESS: Yes, well I do take care of myself, you know. Makes all the difference. I always remember to put on my creams and body lotions everyday . . .

YOUNG ACTRESS: You?

OLDER ACTRESS: If you put on your creams and body lotions everyday, you're bound to get results. Makes all the difference, to take care of oneself. I do sometimes wish you'd think a little bit more about yourself.

YOUNG ACTRESS: I've got other things to think about.

OLDER ACTRESS: You shouldn't be thinking at all. You know perfectly well that thoughts are nothing but a recipe for wrinkles and an ugly complexion. If only you'd think a little bit less, you might enjoy it here a little bit more. Those eternal thoughts . . . Look at me, I avoid thoughts like the plague . . .

[*Pause.*]

YOUNG ACTRESS: [*Looks at her, flatly.*] I'm happy if you're happy.

OLDER ACTRESS: I'm happy.

YOUNG ACTRESS: Then I'm happy.

OLDER ACTRESS: Then I'm happy.

YOUNG ACTRESS: Then I'm happy.

[*Silence.*]

OLDER ACTRESS: We'd rehearsed well for that show. We rehearsed for months on end, remember? We were well prepared. I was so supple I could have been an acrobat in a Chinese circus, you know, the ones that twist and contort their bodies with glasses balanced on the soles of their feet while they somersault around the ring in circles . . . You'd become strong, your body perfectly trained, you could easily have carried me around the stage in those arms of yours, with the glasses on my feet . . . It was all going so perfectly well until . . .

YOUNG ACTRESS: Until you walked out!

OLDER ACTRESS: Until you started that stupid car game!

YOUNG ACTRESS: Yes . . . I've always liked cars . . .

OLDER ACTRESS: You can say that again. You knew all their names since you were a little girl, kept on pointing at them, making all those silly engine sounds. Sometimes I actually had to remind myself that you weren't a boy.

YOUNG ACTRESS: You never remembered. You still don't remember.

OLDER ACTRESS: What a load of gobbledegook!

YOUNG ACTRESS: I wanted to be a boy.

OLDER ACTRESS: I know that. Don't you think I know? I know you. I'm your mother.

YOUNG ACTRESS: I wanted to be a boy so I wouldn't be like you.

OLDER ACTRESS: You were never like me. You've never been like me . . . You've always been . . . [*Contains herself, in a singing voice.*] People come in all shapes and sizes, takes all sorts . . .

YOUNG ACTRESS: And it suited you just fine . . .

OLDER ACTRESS: What did?

YOUNG ACTRESS: [*Insincerely.*] To have a little boy to dote over.

OLDER ACTRESS: No, I never had a boy. I wouldn't have minded one but then you came along. Which was a great blessing.

YOUNG ACTRESS: It suited you fine. You were lonely. You needed a strong hand to guide you. I gave you mine.

OLDER ACTRESS: Yes, we've helped each other along over the years, that's true. I've guided you and you've guided me. We're so lucky to have each other. Some people have no-one. Others too many. Imagine: those who have too many probably look at the swarm of hands being offered all around them, and don't know which one to choose . . . No, we're lucky we neither have too many nor too few.

YOUNG ACTRESS: [*Looks at her.*] It's just the two of us.

OLDER ACTRESS: Precisely.

[*Pause.*]

YOUNG ACTRESS: Do you think we would have carried on acting if the show hadn't ended that way?

OLDER ACTRESS: No, I don't think so. We'd given up long before that anyway. Or were going to at any rate. We were going to go on a holiday, remember? To Bombay or Burma.

YOUNG ACTRESS: Yes. We would have been better off doing that.

OLDER ACTRESS: Yes, we could have rested that way, recharged.

YOUNG ACTRESS: And then what?

OLDER ACTRESS: I don't know . . . What do I know?

YOUNG ACTRESS: Nothing.

OLDER ACTRESS: No, that's true.

[*Pause.*]

OLDER ACTRESS: Bombay . . . Imagine . . . Maybe we could have settled in Bombay. No-one would have known us there, we could have done anything we wanted, had a new life, sunbathed on the beach, danced all night long . . .

YOUNG ACTRESS: Is there a beach in Bombay?

OLDER ACTRESS: There must be, surely . . .

YOUNG ACTRESS: We should have gone to Burma instead. That's the place . . .

OLDER ACTRESS: Really?

YOUNG ACTRESS: All the best people go there. All the stars. We would have fitted in quite nicely there.

OLDER ACTRESS: I would have reserved a hotel room with a balcony overlooking the canal . . .

YOUNG ACTRESS: No, now you're thinking of Venice . . .

OLDER ACTRESS: I would have insisted on a suite overlooking the canal, and I would have been on the balcony every morning at the crack of dawn, long before the others woke up . . . painting watercolors . . . of the canals . . .

YOUNG ACTRESS: Watercolors?

OLDER ACTRESS: Yes, well I would have gone on a watercoloring course first, and I would have used every single moment to mix my colors and paint . . . And every time I'd have finished a picture, I'd have torn it to shreds and scattered it over the canal . . .

YOUNG ACTRESS: I didn't know you were interested in art.

OLDER ACTRESS: I would have been if we'd gone to Bombay.

YOUNG ACTRESS: Since when have you ever shown even the slightest interest in art?

OLDER ACTRESS: I would have been if we'd gone to Bombay!

YOUNG ACTRESS: Since when have you ever shown even the slightest interest in anything other than theater?

OLDER ACTRESS: I would have shown some if we'd gone to Bombay!

YOUNG ACTRESS: And why on earth would you want to rip up your paintings as soon as you'd finished painting them? . . . Surely it would have been more sensible if you'd put them up on the street and tried to sell them? . . .

OLDER ACTRESS: No. My art has never been for sale. I've never stooped to market demands.

YOUNG ACTRESS: And now you don't do anything. Art or anything else for that matter. Now you do absolutely nothing.

OLDER ACTRESS: And neither do you!

YOUNG ACTRESS: No, neither do I. Sweet damn all is what we do!

[*They stare at each other.*]

[*Pause.*]

OLDER ACTRESS: Maybe I could have given you the paintings.

YOUNG ACTRESS: And what was I supposed to do with them?

OLDER ACTRESS: Don't be so ungrateful! You could have stored them away with your belongings or hung them up on the walls. You would have done something with them . . .

YOUNG ACTRESS: My belongings? What belongings? I've never had any belongings . . . We've had common belongings, but I've never had any belongings. So it would have been absurd to give me the paintings because it would have been exactly like giving them to yourself. So do whatever the hell you want with them. I don't care, nail them to the walls, hang them on the ceiling, stuff them in the drawers or store them with your belongings, just leave me in peace!

OLDER ACTRESS: You can be so harsh. After all I've done for you . . .

YOUNG ACTRESS: [*Yelling.*] I don't want to see any watercolors!

[*The* OLDER ACTRESS *bursts into tears.*]

[*Pause.*]

YOUNG ACTRESS: Oh, now now . . . Now now . . . Come here . . . I didn't mean to hurt you . . . There now, no more crying, all right? Who's the most beautiful? Look, I'll take the paintings, see? . . . Wow, nice picture, did you paint this?

OLDER ACTRESS: [*Smiles through her tears, as timid as a child.*] Yes.

YOUNG ACTRESS: I'll hang it up over here, see? [*She hangs up the imaginary painting.*]

[*They study the painting and laugh.*]

OLDER ACTRESS: [*Happy.*] It's of us.

[*Pause.*]

YOUNG ACTRESS: What?

OLDER ACTRESS: [*More serious.*] The painting, it's of us.

[*They pause a moment to study the painting again.*]

[*The projection continues on the screen.*]

OLDER ACTRESS: This is all so . . .

YOUNG ACTRESS: So?

OLDER ACTRESS: So . . .

YOUNG ACTRESS: So what?

OLDER ACTRESS: All of this is somehow so . . . I don't know who you are. That's what it is. I can't quite figure out who you are.

YOUNG ACTRESS: I don't know who you are.

OLDER ACTRESS: I said aren't you going to ask me my name, you said no, then . . . I can't remember what you said then.

YOUNG ACTRESS: It all falls into place.

OLDER ACTRESS: I'd been standing there a long time. I wasn't waiting for anything in particular. I didn't know what to do with myself. Then I saw you. I don't normally stand on street corners like that, you know—I wouldn't like you to think . . . I'm not that kind of . . .

YOUNG ACTRESS: That kind of what?

OLDER ACTRESS: You know what I mean. No way. Not me. You might think so, just because of the way I'm dressed, but, no sir, not me. You've got to believe me.

   [*Pause.*]

OLDER ACTRESS: I was just standing there, I mean, just the way I am now . . . Then I saw you. I stopped and waved. Which way are you heading, young lady? you said . . .

YOUNG ACTRESS: Then it started to rain.

OLDER ACTRESS: That was later.

YOUNG ACTRESS: It is now.

OLDER ACTRESS: Is it?

   [*They prick up their ears and listen to the sound of the rain.*]

OLDER ACTRESS: And I thought to myself, should I . . . You know, should I? . . . And I suddenly decided to take a chance. You had that effect on me, you see . . .

   [*Silence.*]

OLDER ACTRESS: And you?

YOUNG ACTRESS: Hum?

OLDER ACTRESS: Why did you? . . .

YOUNG ACTRESS: What?

OLDER ACTRESS: Why . . . I mean why did you? . . .

YOUNG ACTRESS: It . . .

OLDER ACTRESS: Yes . . .

YOUNG ACTRESS: It . . .

OLDER ACTRESS: Yes . . .

YOUNG ACTRESS: It . . .

OLDER ACTRESS: Yes . . .

YOUNG ACTRESS: It . . .

OLDER ACTRESS: Yes, say it, say it, say it, oh, say it . . .

   [*The rain stops.*]

YOUNG ACTRESS: [*Can't say it.*]

   [*Pause.*]

OLDER ACTRESS: [*Bursts into tears.*] Oh, my God . . . My God . . . My mascara . . .

   [*The projection stops.*]

OLDER ACTRESS: [*Onstage.*] I'm glad we didn't go to Burma. I feel good here. We feel good here. Here we're safe.

YOUNG ACTRESS: Yes.

OLDER ACTRESS: Here we're happy.

YOUNG ACTRESS: Yes.

OLDER ACTRESS: Here we're . . .

   [*Pause.*]

OLDER ACTRESS: Here we are.

YOUNG ACTRESS: [*Hears something, listens, quietly.*] Did you hear that? . . .

OLDER ACTRESS: When we were acting it was as if we somehow turned into "us." A little bit too much I mean . . . Now we're more comfortably us, just the right balance, don't you think?

YOUNG ACTRESS: [*Elsewhere.*] Yes.

OLDER ACTRESS: Every time we walked onstage, it was as if we were somehow overwhelmed by ourselves, crushed under the weight of our own shadows. It was dreadful. Thank God we stopped. Thank God!

YOUNG ACTRESS: Thank God.

OLDER ACTRESS: Thank God!

YOUNG ACTRESS: Thank God!

OLDER ACTRESS: [*Looks at her, surprised.*] Since when do you believe in God?

YOUNG ACTRESS: I don't believe in God.

OLDER ACTRESS: Good God no, I was just startled, that's all. For a moment there you sounded so deadly serious. [*Laughs.*] No, what would we do with a god? It's only miserable loners that need a holy spirit to cling to, wretched souls with nothing else to hang onto when night falls and they're surrounded by darkness . . . [*To the audience.*] Wretches, poor miserable little wretches . . . Miserable lonely souls who can't even cross the street without God holding one hand and the Holy Spirit holding the other . . . [*Mockingly sings.*] Oh lead me, dear Lord, through this vale of tears . . . I'm alone when I'm without you, but never alone when I'm with you, Hosanna hey! [*Laughs.*] Poor miserable souls, what a plight. I can't think of them without tears coming to my eyes . . . well, one eye at least, because the other smiles when it remembers I have you, my darling daughter. Come over here and kiss me . . . [*Opens her arms and closes her eyes.*]

YOUNG ACTRESS: [*Quietly, as if to herself, quite fast.*] What woman is this? What woman? How did you know there was a woman? I figured it out. There is a woman behind this, isn't there? Yes, he says. There's a very special woman, he says. Oh yeah? She's an actress. Is that so? What's her name? What's her name? Hang on a second, he says, hang on . . . And suddenly it all came pouring out like a torrent, and he spouted it out like some floodgate had been opened . . . He said: he just suddenly changed . . . Dad . . . all of a sudden . . . I came home one day and saw it and asked him how he was and he said well and I said it was like something had happened or something and he said yes something happened all right I met a woman he said where I asked on TV he said and her name is Ginger Rogers. Then he described the whole film to me, from beginning to end. And he described her as well, the actress, he said she was blond and beautiful and happy and good and that he wanted to get more acquainted with her . . . Get more acquainted I said how are you going to do that and then he said that he was going to get another movie with her and if I could track one down for him and I said I'd try and I managed to find another movie for him and when he was finished watching it he wanted another one and then another one and then he refused to return the tapes and said he wanted to own them all and I had to negotiate with the guy in the video store to see if I could buy them from him and I told him about Dad and he was sympathetic and offered to order the others for me and he did that it took a while but in the end he got all seventy-three of them. Seventy-three movies with Ginger Rogers. Seventy-three movies Ginger Rogers acted in. He watched them all in a row. First one then the next and the next and when he'd worked his way through the whole collection he started all over again. A movie a night. Night after night. One movie a night with Ginger Rogers. And he was happy . . . in love . . . a young man again . . . That's how . . . that's how she came into our home . . . [*Pause. Switches tone.*] And then, after a while . . . something happened, I said. Didn't it? After a while, it wouldn't do anymore, am I right? It wasn't enough for him just to see her in the movies anymore, was it? He wanted more, he wanted more than that, didn't he? Didn't he? Tell me. Isn't that why you came here to this place? That's why you're going on here in that hideous outfit, isn't it?! That's why you're a transvestite! Isn't it?! He retreated. Afraid. As if I'd wounded him. I don't know what you're on about, he said. I don't know what you're talking about, he said. I don't know what you're talking about actually! he said.

[*The stage slowly darkens.*]

OLDER ACTRESS: [*Slyly.*] Tell me, this man . . . Did you ever meet him after that?

YOUNG ACTRESS: You know he's just a fantasy.

OLDER ACTRESS: Yes, but did you meet him, in your mind I mean, after that . . .

YOUNG ACTRESS: What if I did?

OLDER ACTRESS: You're out of your mind! Where is he? Tell me!

[*Pause.*]

YOUNG ACTRESS: I haven't thought about him. Not for a single moment since that moment before the show. Not until now.

OLDER ACTRESS: How weird. The things you fantasize about. The job of an actor is to play different characters, not to be seeing apparitions like that. Anyone would think you were a medium.

YOUNG ACTRESS: We did more than play our characters the last time, Mother. Or have you forgotten everything we did before the show? Have you forgotten the show?

OLDER ACTRESS: God, no. And thanks to you it'll be a good while before I do.

[*Pause.*]

OLDER ACTRESS: I just can't bear the thought of sitting here beside you while you're musing on some men downtown.

YOUNG ACTRESS: Don't worry, Mother. I think of nothing, imagine nothing, fantasize about nothing that you don't already know or have a part in. I think of nothing. I don't think anymore.

OLDER ACTRESS: You must understand . . . I'm not . . . You do understand that, don't you? . . . We can't just sit here side by side, unless certain rules apply . . .

YOUNG ACTRESS: Of course. Of course I understand. Now we'll shut up. Now we'll shut up. Until it's over . . .

[*Pause.*]

[*The stage darkens.*]

OLDER ACTRESS: [*Smiles.*] Until it's over . . . How much longer have we got? [*Thinks to herself, laughs.*] See, you've contaminated me with those strange thoughts of yours . . . How much longer . . . I've got the feeling we'll be eternal. Don't you think so? I feel I'm getting younger. Well, look at me. This isn't the body of an old lady. This isn't the face of an old lady! With every minute that passes, every second, it's as if the cells of my body were regenerating themselves and growing younger . . . I can feel them doing somersaults all over my body and it's a wonderful feeling. And it's all thanks to you, my dear daughter, because it's the magic of our love that's reversed the ageing process that seems to affect other women of my age . . . Maybe you could lend me some of your youth in exchange for some of my maturity and wisdom . . . which has undeniably . . . [*Meets her daughter's hateful eyes and is momentarily thrown.*] . . . grown over the years and I couldn't cope on my own . . . [*Laughs awkwardly.*] That's how we complement each other you and I, give and take . . . give and take.

[*The words fade. Pause.*]

OLDER ACTRESS: Why are you looking at me like that?

YOUNG ACTRESS: He was also quite young.

OLDER ACTRESS: Who?

YOUNG ACTRESS: The transvestite's father.

OLDER ACTRESS: You're not starting that again!

YOUNG ACTRESS: He told me before the show. But as for the transvestite himself, he looked old. Dead old.

OLDER ACTRESS: But I thought you said he was young.

YOUNG ACTRESS: But he looked old.

OLDER ACTRESS: Yes well, it isn't everyone that gets to look young in their old age. Some people insist on carrying the burdens of the entire world on their shoulders, others carry the bare minimum.

YOUNG ACTRESS: Or even less than that.

OLDER ACTRESS: Yes, or even less, and they don't wear out as fast as the others do . . . Well, it makes sense, doesn't it? I'm only asking. What's the point in breaking one's back and burdening one's self with the cares of the world when no-one, not a single soul, can do the slightest thing about them? I don't want a broken back. I don't want to be old. All I want is to gently tiptoe my way down the back paths of life, and to be able to unload the burdens of existence at regular intervals. [*Smiles.*]

[*The* YOUNG ACTRESS *stares at her.*]

OLDER ACTRESS: And I'd do the same if I were you, my love. Sometimes I think you just accumulate too many thingamajigs along the way, that's what weighs you down . . . You can't travel through life picking up every single thingamajig you come across. Surely you understand that . . .

YOUNG ACTRESS: [*Full of hatred.*] What thingamajigs are you talking about?

OLDER ACTRESS: Figuratively speaking . . . You know what I mean . . . every single piece of junk you come across . . .

YOUNG ACTRESS: What?

OLDER ACTRESS: Sorrow and grief, memories . . . You can't carry all that around with you, darling, it's just not possible . . .

YOUNG ACTRESS: It's just not possible to carry any less than one does either.

OLDER ACTRESS: [*Desperately trying to save herself.*] What do you mean? Haven't the spiritual masters always preached that one should travel through life as lightly as possible, nothing more than a little suitcase, nothing more than a little handbag, some monks come and go as they are, without anything, and nothing but sackcloth to cover them. Some of them don't even have a wallet . . .

YOUNG ACTRESS: No more than you have . . .

OLDER ACTRESS: Yes, I won't deny it, I do try to travel as lightly as possible . . .

[*The* YOUNG ACTRESS *silently stands up and slowly walks towards her mother. The* OLDER ACTRESS *looks at her in fear. The* YOUNG ACTRESS *stops behind her, cautiously raises her hands, and gently plants them on her shoulders, close to her throat. It looks as if she is about to tighten her grip and perhaps she does, or so we should feel at least. The* OLDER ACTRESS *sits, paralyzed with fear. But the* YOUNG ACTRESS *suddenly comes to her senses, the tension is released from her hands and body, and she suddenly looks exhausted.*]

[*Pause.*]

YOUNG ACTRESS: [*Defeated, quiet, lifeless.*] Enjoy it. Enjoy being lightly dressed.

OLDER ACTRESS: [*Sighs with relief and forces a laugh.*] Well I might be lightly dressed, but I'm not wearing sackcloth yet . . . I'm more of a dress person myself . . . All kinds of dresses, yellow, red, green, blue . . . with wide skirts and tight ones [*She swings around and almost falls. The* YOUNG ACTRESS *leaps up to grab her.*] Goodness gracious! [*Laughs.*] I almost fell.

[*They look each other in the eye.*]

[*The projection continues.*]

OLDER ACTRESS: There's something quite special about you, isn't there? I mean there aren't many like you around . . . Or I've certainly never met anyone . . . quite like you . . . But now of course I'm happy that I have, you see, although . . .

[*Pause.*]

OLDER ACTRESS: Hey, how about another one and turn up that racket of yours, and let's have some fun, ha! So what else have you got to say for yourself? Aren't you going to say anything? Are you just going to carry on with that mysterious air of yours, hidden behind that mask? Why else would you be wearing that mask? Makes it all the more enticing of course. You know how to go about it, don't you? How to charm a lady, you know all about that. You're like a black knight in armor that comes riding over the hill, your face hidden behind iron and steel, see nothing, nothing but your eyes, your sharp and bewitching eyes, and they look at me, and I get butterflies in my stomach . . . Then it's only much later that he removes his helmet and reveals his real face, you're familiar with all this, aren't you?

[*Pause.*]

OLDER ACTRESS: I'm just an ordinary girl, you know, quite ordinary. Everything's so ordinary. Ordinary this, ordinary that, ordinary everything and ordinary nothing . . . But I do have one thing that's out of the ordinary. I have looks. Well I'm not exactly unattractive, which is what gets me into these little adventures every now and then, such as this one here with you. And it's ever so exciting. I close my eyes and just imagine. I can imagine all sorts of things, and sometimes the fantasy becomes reality. The young knight I create in my mind can suddenly burst into life and charge towards me just as I'd imagined him . . . [*Looks at her daughter.*] Or almost as I'd imagined him.

[*The projection stops.*]

[*The* YOUNG ACTRESS *slowly helps the* OLDER ACTRESS *up.*]

[*Silence.*]

OLDER ACTRESS: [*Onstage.*] So then.

[*Pause.*]

OLDER ACTRESS: Oh, why are you always so sad?

YOUNG ACTRESS: I'm not sad.

OLDER ACTRESS: Yes you are. You're always sad. And that saddens me. There's nothing more heartbreaking for a mother than to see her daughter's not well.

YOUNG ACTRESS: I'm well.

OLDER ACTRESS: I don't want to see you looking sad. Let's smile then and look on the bright side and try to have fun!

[*The stage darkens.*]

OLDER ACTRESS: [*Looks around.*] Strange . . . It feels darker in here now . . . As if the sun had faded for a moment. But how could that be? The movements of the heavenly bodies have no influence here . . . You don't suppose another bulb has blown? See if there are any spare bulbs in the cupboard . . . Turn on the lights! You know I always want it to be bright around me! Bright and beautiful! Perhaps those bulbs are losing their sight . . . And bulbs with poor eyesight aren't much good to anyone when it comes to lighting, no-more than a half-moon is . . . Oh how often I've wished we didn't have to put up with this constant transience. If only the moon would stay put and shine on us all the time . . . Why on earth can't the moon just stay put where it is for a change? Tell me, why?

YOUNG ACTRESS: What a question!

OLDER ACTRESS: If the moon were still, I'd be totally happy. I'd be outside every day bathing in the moonlight . . .

YOUNG ACTRESS: But you know we've got nothing to fear, Mother . . . Nothing can disturb us here . . . Not even the heavenly bodies can effect us here, in this place, we're secure, immovable, we've cast our anchor, and nothing can blow us away . . .

OLDER ACTRESS: How nicely put . . . Oh, say something else, talk to me, I'll close my eyes and listen to you talking . . . Talk now, go on, talk to me . . .

[*Silence.*]

YOUNG ACTRESS: [*Quietly and slowly at first, but then louder and accelerating in a crescendo.*] I hope you get to like it here, I said. I hope you get to like it more than I do. I hope you really get to like it here.

OLDER ACTRESS: Don't start that one again . . . Do it for my sake, darling, do it for my sake and go and lie down, give yourself a little break, try to sleep a bit, do you hear me . . . do you hear me?!

YOUNG ACTRESS: I hope *I* get to like it here. I hope I get to like it here more than I do. I hope I get to . . .

OLDER ACTRESS: Stop it now, darling. Stop it now! Stop it!

YOUNG ACTRESS: I hope you're not what you seem. I hope I'm not what I seem. I hope I'm not who I am. I said. I hope no-one is who they are. I hope no-one is who they think they are. I hope everyone isn't what they think they ought to be. I hope that everyone thinks that everyone ought to be what some think not everyone ought to be and, above all, what some think no-one should ever be at any time under any circumstances!

[*The* OLDER ACTRESS *looks at her, petrified.*]

YOUNG ACTRESS: Welcome, gentlemen to the transvestite's club, the first of its kind in this wretched town of ours, the first of its kind in this miserable country of ours, the first and only club ever to dare what others have never dared, what others would never allow themselves to dare, or even dream to dare . . . Gentlemen, loosen your ties. Gentlemen, surrender to pleasure. Gentlemen . . . Feel the fatigue of this busy day flowing out of your body and give yourselves a treat. Allow your minds to wander into undiscovered territories, imagine what you've never dared to imagine and witness what you'd never have dreamt of seeing. Watch, glide, fly into the land of exotic fruit, the forbidden fruit, the sensuous fruit: Look, there are the apples, look, there are the pineapples, there are the lemons and kiwis and grapefruits and eggplant and mangoes and berries, all sorts of berries, red currants and blueberries and brambleberries and raspberries and gooseberries and unripe berries and crowberries! There are the bananas and melons and coconuts . . . Don't you want a bite, don't you want a nibble, don't you want a taste, don't you want to swallow? . . . Come on, relax, and allow yourselves to do what you would never dare do anywhere, anywhere, anywhere else but here—Ladies and gentlemen, this is the moment you've all been waiting for, tonight's the night, this is the night we've all come here to remember, the night no-one will ever forget . . . Ladies and gentlemen . . . Allow me to introduce to you . . . Ladies and gentlemen . . . Allow me to introduce to you . . . [*She suddenly stops and stares ahead.*]

OLDER ACTRESS: [*Laughs, viciously sarcastic and exaggerated.*] Poor thing . . . Poor thing, day in and day out, waiting for a man who doesn't even exist! A transvestite. A transvestite! My brother, she says. Now that's a good one. That's the best one I've ever heard! [*Shrieks with laughter.*]

YOUNG ACTRESS: [*Calmly, weary but tries to defend herself.*] Perhaps it's someone else. Someone you know even better. Someone you claimed to know. Perhaps it's . . . my father . . . Perhaps it's the man you . . . Perhaps it's the man you . . .

OLDER ACTRESS: [*Terrified.*] No. Don't say anything. Say no more.

YOUNG ACTRESS: What are you afraid of?

OLDER ACTRESS: I don't know what you're getting at. I don't know what you're getting at.

As if I'd committed a crime. I haven't committed any crime, as far as I know . . . I haven't done the slightest thing wrong that I know of . . . Why are you looking at me like that?

YOUNG ACTRESS: I'm not looking at you.

OLDER ACTRESS: Why are you looking at me like that? . . . I'll be good. Don't say anything. Say nothing. Spare me, my darling daughter. For my sake . . . I'm getting old . . . I'm getting small and old and defenseless . . . Spare me . . . Spare me . . .

[*The* YOUNG ACTRESS *walks over to her, embraces her, and leads her forward. They quietly stare ahead with expressionless faces.*]

OLDER ACTRESS: Run along now, dear, and get my evening dress for me, I feel like dressing up . . . Run along, dear, and get it for me . . .

[*Pause.*]

[*The* YOUNG ACTRESS *ponders a moment, slowly walks to the* OLDER ACTRESS *and positions herself behind her. She unzips the zip on her mother's dress and examines her shoulders.*]

[*The projection continues on-screen.*]

OLDER ACTRESS: Do you ever do that?

YOUNG ACTRESS: What?

OLDER ACTRESS: Fantasize about things?

[*Pause.*]

YOUNG ACTRESS: No.

OLDER ACTRESS: I don't believe you . . . Everyone fantasizes about something, at some stage . . . I can't believe that you've never conjured up a young princess for yourself . . . with fluttering hair . . . [*Moves closer to her.*]

[*The projection halts.*]

YOUNG ACTRESS: [*Onstage: looks at her mother's shoulders.*] Your skin is still just as white . . .

OLDER ACTRESS: [*Cheerfully.*] How old would you say those shoulders are, give it a guess?

YOUNG ACTRESS: [*Thinks a moment.*] Forty at the most.

OLDER ACTRESS: Forty?!

YOUNG ACTRESS: Thirty.

OLDER ACTRESS: That's more like it. And this throat?

YOUNG ACTRESS: Well, at a guess, thirty-one . . .

OLDER ACTRESS: And these breasts? Someone told me once that my breasts would always look twenty years younger than my age . . . which was rather sweet really . . . And not so far from the truth . . . But I also take good care of myself. Put on my creams and body lotions every day.

YOUNG ACTRESS: You?

OLDER ACTRESS: You put the creams and body lotions on me every day—I remember so clearly the moment they stopped ageing, I was very young . . . They just stopped and they've been the same ever since . . . And my legs . . .

YOUNG ACTRESS: You could run a marathon with legs like that . . .

OLDER ACTRESS: [*Looks at her legs.*] Yes, I suppose you're right. [*Stands up, runs a few steps, and laughs.*]

[*Silence.*]

OLDER ACTRESS: [*Insidiously.*] So tell me then . . . Did he go on . . . the transvestite?

[*Pause.*]

YOUNG ACTRESS: No.

OLDER ACTRESS: Why not?

YOUNG ACTRESS: Because I sent him away. I took him away and found him a hiding place, don't stay here, I said, have a rest and come along later when you've regained your strength and come looking for me.

OLDER ACTRESS: [*Sarcastically.*] And he hasn't been seen since . . .

YOUNG ACTRESS: He's coming. Wait, he said. Wait for me. Wait. Electra.

OLDER ACTRESS: Stop it now! Stop it! Once and for all!

YOUNG ACTRESS: Listen . . .

[*The projection continues.*]

OLDER ACTRESS: [*On-screen.*] Everyone fantasizes about something, at some stage . . . I can't believe that you've never conjured up a young princess for yourself . . . with fluttering hair . . . [*Moves closer to her.*]

YOUNG ACTRESS: [*On-screen. Signals the* STAGE MANAGER *to accelerate the car.*]

YOUNG ACTRESS: [*Onstage.*] I can hear him . . . now . . .

OLDER ACTRESS: [*On-screen.*] Don't you picture her, rosy cheeked and lightly dressed, and you wait for her, bursting with impatience, full of expectation, and you watch her as she slowly and carefully moves towards you, and as she draws nearer she slows down, and her silk dress flutters in the wind . . . [*Realizes how fast they're traveling.*] What are you doing?

[*The* YOUNG ACTRESS *on-screen: Accelerates even more. The lights flash by.*]

YOUNG ACTRESS: [*Onstage.*] I've been thinking of you ever since you sent me away, he says, and prepared my return and now I've returned . . .

OLDER ACTRESS: [*Onstage.*] And then what?!

OLDER ACTRESS: [*On-screen, terrified.*] Drive slower, I . . . Why are you . . . ? What are you doing? . . . I don't understand . . . We're in no hurry . . .

[*The* YOUNG ACTRESS *on-screen: accelerates.*]

YOUNG ACTRESS: [*Onstage.*] It's unbearably painful to see you dressed like this, he says . . . I barely recognized you when I came in . . . You've changed so much . . .

OLDER ACTRESS: [*Onstage.*] Stop it now!

OLDER ACTRESS: [*On-screen.*] I want to stop now. I'm tired. I've got to go to the bathroom. Immediately.

YOUNG ACTRESS: [*On-screen.*] Later.

OLDER ACTRESS: [*On-screen.*] Now.

YOUNG ACTRESS: [*On-screen.*] Later.

OLDER ACTRESS: [*On-screen.*] Immediately. I insist. I've got to get out! What are you doing? Who are you?

YOUNG ACTRESS: [*Onstage.*] You're so withered and old that I thought: is it really her? Could that possibly be her—my sister? And then I said I wouldn't have recognized you either . . . Is it really you? Look at this lock of hair, he said and handed it to me, I put it on my father's grave thinking you would find it there and know to expect me, but when I went back there a short while ago I saw the lock hadn't moved. Yes, I said. I'm sorry, I said, I haven't visited my father's grave for years, not since . . . I haven't visited my father's grave for years . . .

OLDER ACTRESS: [*Onstage.*] Stop it now, stop, I say!

[*A beep is heard on screen.*]

OLDER ACTRESS: [*On-screen, feebly.*] Help.

YOUNG ACTRESS: [*On-screen.*] Relax.

OLDER ACTRESS: [*On-screen.*] Help!

YOUNG ACTRESS: [*On-screen.*] Relax I said.

OLDER ACTRESS: [*On-screen.*] Who are you? Where are you taking me? Stop, I said! Stop!

YOUNG ACTRESS: [*Onstage.*] But now that I compare your hair to mine, there are no more doubts in my mind—it's you, my brother.

YOUNG ACTRESS: [*On-screen, accelerates even more.*]

OLDER ACTRESS: [*On-screen.*] Stop . . . stop!

YOUNG ACTRESS: [*Onstage.*] So you've finally come to take me away from this place . . .

OLDER ACTRESS: [*Onstage.*] What nonsense is this? Stop all this drivel now and get a hold on yourself!

YOUNG ACTRESS: [*On-screen, grabs her.*] You better calm down now, is that clear? You better be good. Like a doll in a shiny new box. She smiles and she's good. She blinks and she's good. And she doesn't open her mouth unless she's spoken to. Is that understood?!

[*The* OLDER ACTRESS *on-screen: nods.*]

YOUNG ACTRESS: [*On-screen.*] Fully understood?

[*The* OLDER ACTRESS *on-screen: nods.*]

YOUNG ACTRESS: Good. Now you can smile.

[*The* OLDER ACTRESS *smiles.*]

YOUNG ACTRESS: Yeah, like that. A little more.

[*The* OLDER ACTRESS *smiles a little more.*]

YOUNG ACTRESS: Excellent. Look out now and enjoy the view.

OLDER ACTRESS: [*Petrified.*] It's dark.

YOUNG ACTRESS: Rubbish!

OLDER ACTRESS: It's pitch dark.

YOUNG ACTRESS: Your eyes are closed.

OLDER ACTRESS: No, they're open. Wide open and I see nothing. Let's stop. Please, I beg you. Do it for me . . . For me . . .

YOUNG ACTRESS: [*Onstage: the tension inside her has risen to its climax.*] No, come here, brother, come over here to me . . . Don't go away . . . [*She charges towards her mother.*]

YOUNG ACTRESS: [*On-screen: As the car reaches its maximum speed, she makes a decision and suddenly breaks. The wheels and breaks squeak as she skids to a halt.*]

[ONSTAGE: *the* STAGE MANAGER *springs up, grabs the* YOUNG ACTRESS *and blocks her before she reaches her mother, she struggles desperately in his arms and then hugs him in despair. He locks her in an embrace for a moment.*]

OLDER ACTRESS: [*On-screen.*] You were going to? . . . [*Stepping out of character.*] Good God . . . Were you going to . . . This time you've gone too far . . . Do you hear me?! You've gone too far! [*She stands up in despair and storms off.*]

[*Pause.*]

[*The* STAGE MANAGER *On-screen: turns off all the sound effects.*]

YOUNG ACTRESS: [*On-screen: If she's been wearing a mask, she takes it off now. She stands up, looks at the* STAGE MANAGER, *and then makes a decision.*] Ladies and gentlemen, I would like to apologize, but due to circumstances beyond our control, we are unable to continue with this evening's performance . . . [*Exits.*]

[*The* STAGE MANAGER *on-screen: turns the lights off and exits.*]

[*The projection ends.*]

[*Pause.*]

[ONSTAGE: *the* STAGE MANAGER *releases the* YOUNG ACTRESS *who freezes.*]

[*Silence.*]

[*The stage is very dark now, we can just about make out the actresses as the scene continues and the stage gradually sinks into total darkness.*]

OLDER ACTRESS: [*Heaves a sigh of relief.*] Well then. Why don't we sit down here and relax . . . Let's try to unwind, darling . . . Why are you standing there? Come over here to me and sit down beside me . . . Did you hear what I said? Come over here, I said!

[*The* YOUNG ACTRESS *doesn't move.*]

OLDER ACTRESS: What is it? Why are you standing there like a dummy? Answer me!

[*The* YOUNG ACTRESS *stiffly turns towards her.*]

OLDER ACTRESS: That's more like it, come on over here to me . . . Come on . . . No need to be afraid, one step at a time, then another, come on . . .

[*The* YOUNG ACTRESS *becomes like a child taking its first steps.*]

OLDER ACTRESS: That's it . . . Come on . . .

[*The* YOUNG ACTRESS *takes one step towards her mother.*]

OLDER ACTRESS: Bravo! That's it, yes. Good girl.

[*The* YOUNG ACTRESS *takes another step.*]

OLDER ACTRESS: [*Applauding even more.*] Bravo!

[*The* YOUNG ACTRESS *takes several steps. The* OLDER ACTRESS *applauds frantically. The* YOUNG ACTRESS *staggers towards her mother and falls into her arms.*]

OLDER ACTRESS: Yes, that's it, that's it.

[*The* OLDER ACTRESS *leads her to her seat, sits down herself, and offers her a cigarette. They stare into space, as in the opening of the play, and smoke.*]

[*The* OLDER ACTRESS *speaks her lines as the stage falls into total darkness.*]

OLDER ACTRESS: Reality. The present. Reality and the present fill our lives, don't you find? Nothing can disturb our experience of the here and now. Neither past nor future, neither future nor past. Here we're exactly where life wants us to be. Without our intervention, without any fabrications. This is where we are, that's all . . . Here we're . . . together. Give me your hand now, darling . . . Give me your hand . . . Give me your hand . . . Where are you? . . . Where are you? . . . Where are you?

[*Silence, total darkness.*]

OLDER ACTRESS: [*Stepping out of character, calls out in the dark.*] Lights!

[*The* STAGE MANAGER *raises the lights again.*]

[*The actresses stand up and are themselves again.*]

OLDER ACTRESS: Well.
YOUNG ACTRESS: Well what?
OLDER ACTRESS: We'll stop here.
YOUNG ACTRESS: About time . . .
OLDER ACTRESS: [*To the* STAGE MANAGER.] Thank you for your help.

[*The* STAGE MANAGER *bows.*]

OLDER ACTRESS: Will you turn the lights off for us?
STAGE MANAGER: Will do . . . [*Exits.*]

[*Pause.*]

YOUNG ACTRESS: Well then . . . What did you think?

[*The* OLDER ACTRESS *sighs, gives off a faint laugh, and shrugs her shoulders. They embrace.*]

YOUNG ACTRESS: Are you coming with me?

[*The* OLDER ACTRESS *nods.*]

[*Silence.*]

YOUNG ACTRESS: [*About to exit but halting a moment, playfully.*] Tell me something, mum . . .

OLDER ACTRESS: Yes.

YOUNG ACTRESS: [*Whimsically.*] If I were a man and I were to walk up to you and propose to you, just like that . . . What would you say?

OLDER ACTRESS: [*Laughs, ponders a moment.*] What do you think?

[*They laugh and are about to exit.*]

[*The* OLDER ACTRESS *halts a moment and then slowly leads the* YOUNG ACTRESS *down to the edge of the stage. They look out. Pause.*]

OLDER ACTRESS: Theater . . .

[*Pause.*]

YOUNG ACTRESS: Theater.

[*Silence.*]

OLDER ACTRESS: Thank you for the evening.

[*They exit.*]

[*Blackout.*]